UDDHAVA GĪTĀ EXPLAINED

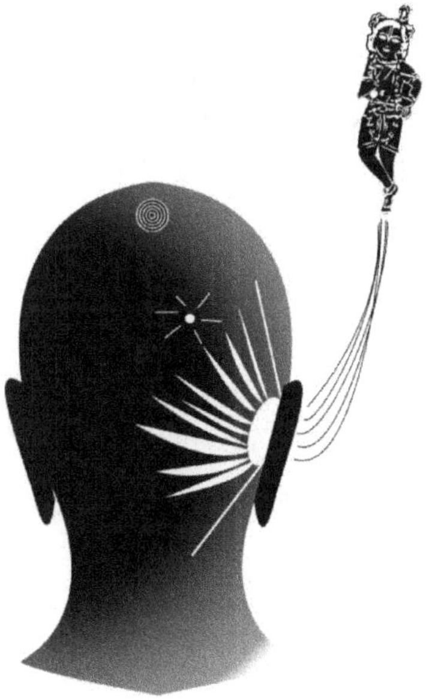

śrī-bhagavān uvāca
yogās trayo mayā proktā nṝṇāṁ śreyo-vidhitsayā
jñānaṁ karma ca bhaktiś ca nopāyo 'nyo 'sti kutracit

Desiring to give perfection of the human being, three applications of yoga discipline were taught by me, namely the application to thinking experience, the application to physical experience and the application to emotions. Besides these, there is no other method whatsoever. (15.6)

Michael Beloved / Madhvācārya dās

Uddhava Gītā Explained

The Sanskrit text was adapted from the English transliteration of *Śrīmad Bhāgavatam*, Canto 11, Chapters 6-29, which was created from GRETIL - Göttingen Register of Electronic Texts in Indian Languages, *Bhāgavata Purāṇa*, Skandha_11; download from Gaudiya Grantha Mandira - UTF-8 encoding.
Edited into present Sanskrit format using Itranslator reverse process, and ascribed with Uddhava Gītā numbers--- four/six lined format--- by Michael Beloved 2008

Preliminary Scanning:

- Bernard Adjodha

Format assistant:

- Marcia K. Beloved

1st. Cover Design Layout :

- Sir Paul Castagna

This Cover Design Layout :

- Author

Cover Feature Art+
Śrī Śrī Krishna-Balarām Art +
Śrī Śrī Krishna-Arjuna Art:
Śrī Śrī Krishna-Uddhava Art:

- Terri Stokes

2nd Edition for new cover -- 2010

Correspondence
Michael Beloved
3703 Foster Ave
Brooklyn NY 11203
USA

Email
axisnexus @gmail.com

ISBN

978-0-9819332-1-4

LCCN

2008911848

Scheme of Pronunciation

Consonants

Gutturals:	क	ख	ग	घ	ङ	
	ka	kha	ga	gha	ṅa	
Palatals:	च	छ	ज	झ	ञ	
	ca	cha	ja	jha	ña	
Cerebrals:	ट	ठ	ड	ढ	ण	
	ṭa	ṭha	ḍa	ḍha	ṇa	
Dentals:	त	थ	द	ध	न	
	ta	tha	da	dha	na	
Labials:		प	फ	ब	भ	म
		pa	pha	ba	bha	ma

Semivowels:

य	र	ल	व
ya	ra	la	va

Numbers:

०	१	२	३	४	५	६	७	८	९
0	1	2	3	4	5	6	7	8	9

Sibilants:	श	ष	स
	śa	ṣa	sa

Aspirate:	ह
	ha

Vowels:

अ	आ	इ	ई	उ	ऊ	ऋ	ॠ
a	ā	i	ī	u	ū	ṛ	ṝ
ए	औ	ओ	औ	ळ	ॡ	<	:
e	ai	o	au	lṛ	lṝ	ṁ	ḥ

Apostrophe ऽ

Table of Contents

Scheme of Pronunciation 3
Table of Contents 4
Introduction 7
CHAPTER 1 Uddhava Approaches Lord Krishna*** 9
CHAPTER 2 The Teacher of the Self*** 47
CHAPTER 3 The Blessed Lord Vishnu Is Pleased*** 97
CHAPTER 4 The Valuable Human Form*** 128
CHAPTER 5 States of Existence*** 150
.... 150
CHAPTER 6 Devotion Offered by Yoga Expertise*** 170
CHAPTER 7 Association of the Reality-Perceptive Persons*** 198
CHAPTER 8 Śrī Krishna's Swan Form*** 217
.... 217
CHAPTER 9 Spirited Devotion*** 248
.... 248
CHAPTER 10 Mystic Skills*** 279
CHAPTER 11 The Self of All Creatures*** 309
CHAPTER 12 Righteous Lifestyle*** 335
CHAPTER 13 Becoming a Devotee*** 377
CHAPTER 14 The Chief Cause of Devotion*** 410
CHAPTER 15 Three Applications of Yoga Discipline*** 438
CHAPTER 16 Vedic Incentives*** 462
.... 462

CHAPTER 17 The Contributing Factors***..485

....485

CHAPTER 18 The Supreme Lord Releases the Avanti Brahmin***..515

CHAPTER 19 Sāṇkhya Theory of Creation***....................................547

CHAPTER 20 The Unmixed Mundane Energies***............................565

CHAPTER 21 Purūravā, That Brillant Person***................................586

CHAPTER 22 Kriyā Yoga: Application of Yoga to Mystic Activity***
....606

CHAPTER 23 This Yoga Process***..638

CHAPTER 24 Go Uddhava***..667

Indexed Names of Uddhava...699

Indexed Names of Krishna...699

Index to Translation..701

LIST OF TEACHERS..739

About the Author..739

Publications..740

English Series..740

Meditation Series...742

Explained Series...743

Commentaries...744

Specialty..746

Online Resources...748

How to use this book:

Make a casual reading initially.

Make a second reading while pausing and considering verses of interest.

Make a third reading while observing the main themes in the discourse.

Finally, make an indepth study of the entire text.

A note on the diacritical marks and pronounciation:

Names like Krishna and Arjuna are accepted in common English usage. Their English spellings occur in the translation without diacritical marks.

***Here are some hints** on how to use the diacritical marks for near-exact pronunciation:*

*Letters with a **dot** under them, should be pronounced while the tongue touches and is released curling slightly at the top of palate.*

*The s sound for **ś** carries an h with it and is said as the **sh** sound in **she**.*

*The s sound for **ṣ** carries an h with it and is said as the **sh** sound in **shun**.*

*The h sound for **ḥ** carries an echoing sound of the vowel before it, such that **oḥ** is actually **oho** and **aḥ** is actually **aha**.*

*In many Sanskrit words the **y** sound is said as an **i** sound, especially when the y sound preceeds an a. For instance, prāṇāyāma should be praa-**nai**-aa-muh, rather than praa-naa-**yaa**-muh.*

*The **a** sound is more like **uh** in English, while the **ā** sound is like the a sound in **far**.*

*The **ṛ** sound is like the **ri** sound in **ridge**.*

*The **ph** sound is never reduced to an f sound as in English. The **p sound** is maintained.*

*Whenever **h** occurs after a consonant, its integrity is maintained as an air forced sound.*

*If the h sound occurs after a vowel and a consonant, one should let the consonant remain with the vowel which preceeds it and allow the h sound to carry with the vowel after it, such that Duryodhana is pronounced with the d consonant allied to the o before it and the h sound manages the a after it. Say Dur-**yod-ha**-na or Dur-**yod-han**. Do not say Dur-yo-**dha**-na. Separate the d and h sounds to make them distinct. In words where you have no choice and must combine the d and h sound, as in the word dharma. Make sure that the **h sound** is heard as an **air sound pushed out from the throat**. Dharma should never be mistaken for darma. But adharma should be **ad-har-**ma.*

*The **c** sound is **ch,** and the **ch** sound is **ch-h**.*

Introduction

This translation and commentary, using the original Sanskrit from the Śrīmad Bhāgavatam Canto 11 chapters 6 through 29, is a deep-read indepth study of the instructions given to Uddhava who questioned Śrī Krishna about the perplexities of material existence. Many readers of the Bhagavad Gītā wondered if that discourse was the complete idea of Śrī Krishna. After a fair reading of these instructions to Uddhava, anyone would conclude that the instructions to Arjuna were only part of the course. This is verified in the Bhagavad Gītā itself where Śrī Krishna said that initially He taught two yogas and then He said He would teach Arjuna the karma yoga path, leaving aside and discouraging Arjuna from the jñāna yoga approach.

Interestingly, in the teaching to Uddhava, Krishna stated that He taught three yogas, namely karma yoga, jñāna yoga and bhakti yoga. In the discussion with Arjuna He admited teachng only the first two of these three, with stress on karma Yoga which was recommended for Arjuna. The complete teachings of Śrī Krishna are given in the Uddhava Gītā.

Incidentally, the title, Uddhava Gītā, was not assigned in the original text which is part of the Śrīmad Bhāgavatam, just as the title Bhagavad Gītā was not listed in the Mahābhārata from which it was extracted. Uddhava Gītā may be called the Completed Bhagavad Gītā or Bhagavad Gītā Purṇā. All unanswered questions which Śrī Krishna either avoided or answered partially are fully dealt with in the Uddhava Gītā. For that matter instead of advocating karma yoga which is detachment with worldly life, Śrī Krishna insisted on jñāna yoga, which is detachment and full abandonment of worldly life.

Karma yoga means that a person leaves aside the result of his or her activities, both the good and bad reactions, while jñāna yoga means that a person refuses both the results ***and the opportunities*** *for activity. And that was the path which Krishna recommended to Uddhava.*

Be enlightened! Read on!

Abbreviations:

B.G. Bhagavad Gītā
U.G. Uddhava Gītā

Regarding the exhaustive Indexes:

All entries ***except*** *those for the Commentary give reference to verse numbers. The last Index which is to the Commentary is the only one which refers to page numbers.*

CHAPTER 1*

Uddhava Approaches Lord Krishna**

Terri Stokes-Pineda Art

vivikta upasaṅgamya jagatām īśvareśvaram
praṇamya śirisā pādau prāñjalis tam abhaṣata

...(Uddhava) approached the Lord of lords of the worlds in a secluded place, bowing down, with his head at the Lord's feet with palms pressed together, Uddhava spoke. (Uddhava Gītā 1.41)

* Śrīmad Bhagavatam Canto 11, Chapter 6
** Translator's selected chapter title.

श्री-शुक उवाच
अथ ब्रह्मात्म-जैःदेवैः
प्रजेशैर् आवृतो ऽभ्यगात् ।
भवश् च भूत-भव्येशो
ययौ भूत-गणैर् वृतः ॥१.१॥

śrī-śuka uvāca
atha brahmātma-jaiḥ.devaiḥ
prajeśair āvṛto 'bhyagāt
bhavaś ca bhūta-bhavyeśo
yayau bhūta-gaṇair vṛtaḥ (1.1)

śrī-śukah - the illustrious Shuka; uvāca - said; atha — then; brahmātmajaiḥ = Brahmā –Brahmā + ātmajaiḥ - with sons; devaih— by the supernatural rulers; prajeśair = prajeśaiḥ = praja – procreators + īśaiḥ – by the primal progenitors; āvṛto = āvṛtaḥ - surrounded; `bhyagāt = abhyagāt - went; bhavaś = bhavaḥ - Śiva; ca - and; bhūta – bhavyeśo = bhuta - things manifested + bhavya – things to be manifested + īśo (īśaḥ) - Lord; yayau - went; bhūtagaṇair = bhūta – elemental creatures + gaṇair (gaṇaiḥ) - by the host of ; vṛtaḥ - surrounded.

Translation

The illustrious Shuka said: Then Brahmā went, being surrounded by his sons, the supernatural rulers and the primal progenitors. And Shiva, the Lord of things manifested and things to be manifested, went, being surrounded by a host of elemental creatures. (1.1)

Commentary:

This is a discourse given by Shuka the son of *Śrīla Vyāsadeva*. This was given to King *Parīkṣit*, the grandson of Arjuna. The same Lord Krishna who lectured to Arjuna, lectured to Uddhava, giving a more complete discourse. While the *Bhagavad Gītā* was targeted to a man who was a social administrator and law man of human society, this discourse to Uddhava was targeted to a man who during his life was coversant in social affairs but who at the time of this lecture displayed an intense interest in going to spiritual territories in the world hereafter.

According to the Vedic literature, the *Brahmā* mentioned in this verse is a person who has extensive supernatural power. He is supposed to have created the planets and creature prototypes. Shiva, who is listed as the Lord of things manifest and things to be manifested, is attributed as a primeval being with an eternal relationship to *Brahmā* and to *Brahmā*'s father who is called *Kṣīrodakaśāyī* Vishnu. *Kṣīrodakaśāyī* Vishnu is said to be the real Lord of the universe.

A question arises immediately as to who is the Supreme God. Is It *Brahmā*? Is it Shiva? Is it *Kṣīrodakaśāyī* Vishnu?

Besides these three, there are the sons of *Brahmā*, who are attributed with supernatural power and super wisdom. There are also other supernatural rulers, who are *Brahmā*'s grandsons and great grandsons. Some of the sons of *Brahmā*, like *Manu* and *Dakṣa* are Primal Progenitors, who begin the sexual course of biological creature expansion. This discourse began when all these, except for the *Kṣīrodakaśāyī* Vishnu went to see Lord Krishna at *Dvārakā* City. This *Dvārakā* was a city in India. Its ruins are still existing. The question is: If these super-natural people exist, how could they visit Lord Krishna, who was a physical being, a person whose body was supposedly burned in a cremation arranged by Arjun?

इन्द्रो मरुद्भिर् भगवान्
आदित्या वसवो ऽश्विनौ ।
ऋभवो ऽङ्गिरसो रुद्रा
विश्वे साध्याश् च देवताः ॥१.२॥

indro marudbhir bhagavān
ādityā vasavo 'śvinau
ṛbhavo 'ṅgiraso rudrā
viśve sādhyāś ca devatāḥ (1.2)

indro = indraḥ — Indra; marudhbir = marudbhiḥ — with Marut storm creatures; bhagavān — Lord, Mystic Supervisor; ādityā = ādityāḥ — sons of Aditi; vasavo = vasavaḥ — Vasu; `svinau = aśvinau — two Aśvins; rbhavo = ṛbhavaḥ — Ribhus; `ngiraso = aṅgirasaḥ — descendants of Aṅgirā; rudrā = rudrāḥ — Rudras; viśve – Viśvedevatas; sādhyās — Sādhyas; ca — and; devatāḥ — supernatural rulers.

Translation

There was the mystic supervisor Indra with the Marut storm creators, the sons of Aditi, the Vasus, the two Asvinis, the Ribhus, the descendants of Angiras, the Rudras, the Visvadevas, the Sadhyas, and other supernatural rulers, (1.2)

Commentary:

Shuka addressed Indra, the chief rain producer as *Bhagavān* or Lord. Usually this term is reserved for either *Brahmā*, Vishnu, or Shiva; Since so many of these supernatural rulers are addressed as Lord or God, a question arises continually as to who is the Supreme God. *Śrīmad Bhāgavatam* gave the answer as Lord Krishna, who is described as the Source of the parallel or and serially-existing Vishnus. Some other Vedic literatures do not agree with this proposal. For instance, the Shiva *Purāṇa* lauds Shiva as that Supreme Personality. The *Devī Purāṇa* lauds Goddess *Durgā*.

In a careful revision of the Sanskrit terms of the previous verse and this one, we find however that the term *Bhagavān* is not being used whimsically nor to indicate that Indra is a Supreme God but rather to indicate that he is supreme among a set of supernatural personalities. They are listed immediately after his name. In order to complete their duties under his supervision, or with his coordination, they regard him as their manager or lord. This is why he is called *Bhagavān* by Shuka, a person who stressed over and over in the *Śrīmad Bhāgavatam* that Lord Krishna is the Ultimate Authority.

All the major personalities or players in the drama of Vedic religion, all persons who might be considered as being candidates for the God position, are met and dealt with by Lord Krishna in His pastime history as it is narrated by Shuka. They are all defeated, subdued, intimidated, enlightened, or appreciated by Lord Krishna. Thus Shuka the speaker of the text, who was a believer and mystic experiencer of what he perceived to be the glories of Krishna, could not have meant that Indra *Bhagavān* means Supreme Lord Indra. It merely means mystic supervisor Indra.

The term *marudbhih* means, with the *Maruts*. These are listed since they are the cousins of Indra and act as his assistants in weather manipulation. As the story goes, once Indra's aunt, *Diti*, wanted a son who would ruin Indra. Being aware of her motives and being defensive, Indra, with his super-natural power, entered her womb and began to cut up the fetus. He cut it into 49 parts. Each part assumed a new fetus configuration as a separate embryo. Understanding that Indra was determined to murder their embryos, the 49 entities who were themselves supernatural people, appealed to Indra to desist. They pleaded, stating that they were his cousins and that their mission was to serve him.

If we are to accept this story at face value, it would mean that these forty-nine entities were forming embryos in some supernatural dimension. Indra objected to their manifestation because he considered them to be rivals. When he got their pledge of allegiance, he accepted them.

The *Ādityās* are supernatural. They are supposed to be primal rulers of various universal phenomena. There is some contention as to their identity because the earlier Vedic literate does not agree entirely with the definition given by later writings like the *Purāṇas*. However it is foolish to apply previous definitions here. Here we should use the definition of Shuka. He is the narrator. Elsewhere in the *Śrīmad Bhāgavatam* he said:

athātaḥ śrūyatāṁ vaṁśo yo 'diter anupūrvaśah yatra nārāyaṇo devaḥ svāṁśenāvātarad vibhuḥ
vivasvān aryamā pūṣā tvaṣṭātha savitā bhagaḥ dhātā vidhātā varuṇo mitraḥ śatru urukramaḥ

Now let it be heard: The family listing which proceeded from Aditi, in which the All-powerful God Nārāyaṇa came into visible manifestation through His personal partner, is: Vivasvān, Aryamā, Pūṣā, Tvaṣṭa, Savitā, Bhaga, Dhātā, Vidhātā, Varuṇa, Mitra, Śatru and Urukrama. (Śrīmad Bhagatam 6.6.38-39)

In that listing the last name, Urukrama, is of the personal partner of Lord *Nārāyaṇa*. *Urukrama* is rated as the incarnation of Godhead among the sons of *Aditi*. The others are powerful supernatural beings. *Urukrama's* elder, *Śatru*, is the same Indra, who Shuka rated as

Bhagavān. Indra is attended by other supernatural people and by various angelic beings who are listed in this verse and in the following verse.

Some of these attendants of Indra, those like his younger brother, the personal partner of the Lord, as well as the Rudras, who are cosmic destroyers, are existentially more powerful than Indra. However on occasion, they act as attendants to Indra.

गन्धर्वाप्सरसो नागाः
सिद्ध-चारण-गुह्यकाः ।
ऋषयः पितरश् चैव
स-विद्याधर-किन्नराः ॥ १.३ ॥

gandharvāpsaraso nāgāḥ
siddha-cāraṇa-guhyakāḥ
ṛṣayaḥ pitaraś caiva
sa-vidyādhara-kinnarāḥ (1.3)

gandharvāpsaraso = gandharvạ — celestial musicians + apsaraso (apsarasaḥ) – female angelic dancers; nāgāh— sentient celestial snakes; siddha-cārana-guhyakāḥ = siddha – perfected yogis + cārana – angelic singers + guhyakāḥ – angelic guards; ṛṣayaḥ— the yogi sage; pitaraś = pitaraḥ— piously departed forefathers; caiva = ca — also + eva — indeed; sa-vidyādhara-kinnarāḥ= sa – with + vidyādhara – skilled angelic beings + Kinnarāḥ – horse faced angelic beings.

Translation

...the celestial musicians, female angelic dancers, celestial serpents, perfected yogis, angelic singers, angelic guards, yogi sages, the piously-departed forefathers along with the skilled angelic beings and the horse-faced ones. (1.3)

Commentary:

The *siddha* perfected yogis who followed Indra in that procession are perfected yogis who have not gone on to regions higher than the Swarga heavenly planes of Indra. Since they live on a subtle planet somewhere within Indra's jurisdiction, they render him social allegiance.

These perfect yogis are greater than Indra but still since they rely on social facilities, which he maintains, they are related to him socially as dependents. They do not interfere with his sovereignty. The yogi sages however, get respects from Indra just as if they were elders and so do the pious departed forefathers who have a superior status.

Some of the pious departed forefathers are awarded a superior status but some must bow to Indra as juniors. Some of the skilled angelic beings, the *Vidyādharas*, are superior to Indra. Still they offer him respects as a matter of course.

द्वारकाम् उपसञ्जग्मुः
सर्वे कृष्ण-दिदृक्षवः ।
वपुषा येन भगवान्
नर-लोक-मनोरमः ।
यशो वितेने लोकेषु
सर्व-लोक-मलापहम् ॥ १.४ ॥

dvārakām upasañjagmuḥ
sarve kṛṣṇa-didṛkṣavaḥ
vapuṣā yena bhagavān
nara-loka-manoramaḥ
yaśo vitene lokeṣu
sarva-loka-malāpaham (1.4)

dvārakām — Dvārakā; upasañjagmuḥ — travelled together; sarve — all; kṛṣṇa-didṛkṣavaḥ = kṛṣṇa — Krishna + didṛkṣavaḥ - eager to see; vapuṣā — the beautiful body; yena — by which; bhagavān — the Blessed Lord; nara-loka-manoramaḥ = naraloka — society of human beings + manoramaḥ — delight of the mind; yaśo = yaśaḥ — fame; vitene — spread; lokeṣu — through the world; sarva-loka-malāpaham = sarva-loka — all worlds, everywhere + mala — impurities + apaham — removes.

Translation

They all came to Dvārakā, being eager to see Krishna, the delight of human society, Whose beautiful body caused His fame to spread through the world, removing impurities everywhere. (1.4)

Commentary:

The supernatural beings mentioned in the preceding verses, made a trek to *Dvārakā*, a fabulous city of its time. They made their trek in supernatural bodies. Most persons using physical forms saw Krishna physically.

The supernatural people saw His supernatural body which was manifested in their dimension of vision. They saw a more attractive body than the physical one. Some contend that Krishna's body is the same as Krishna's personality, and that He did not have physical or subtle forms but that contention does not stand. The body seen by the *deva* supernatural people and their angelic attendants, was a supernatural body which existed in their dimension.

At the same time however, just as the great sages on earth, saw Krishna physical, subtle and spiritual forms simultaneously, so persons like *Brahmā*, Shiva and the *siddhas* saw Krishna's supernatural and spiritual forms simultaneously. Ordinary supernatural people only saw His supernatural body. The supernatural bodies are not spiritual bodies but they are not gross material forms either.

The physical body Lord Krishna manifested was very attractive to see. As stated it was the delight of human society *(nara-loka-manoramah)*. It was a form that was seen by the physical eyes of the human beings *(nara-loka)*. It delighted *(manoramah)* their minds, and caused Lord Krishna to become famous for all time.

According to Shuka however, the form itself and the resulting fame, caused impurities to be removed from all beings in all the worlds which were affected by Lord Krishna's advent.

It is not just this planet which was affected but rather all other locations or dimensions which were related to this place. By the same token, it is a belief only to think that everything everywhere was absolutely purified or that all the world was completely purified. Some of the locations and some of the people were purified, all depending on the amount of contact. According to the degree of contact, there was a proportionate quantity of purification.

The mere idea that the supernatural people travelled to *Dvārakā* as a large supernatural caravan, indicated that even in the supernatural world, there is privacy. Even there one person can remain hidden or isolated from another, otherwise the supernatural people would not have had to move their celestial forms. There are many narrations in the *Purāṇas* explaining that to see a certain supernatural ruler, a particular mystic travelled and made special petition to perceive a certain deity or supernatural person.

तस्यां विभ्राजमानायां
समृद्धायां महर्द्धिभिः ।
व्यचक्षतावितृप्ताक्षाः
कृष्णम् अद्भुत-दर्शनम् ॥ १.५ ॥

tasyāṁ vibhrājamānāyāṁ
samṛddhāyāṁ maharddhibhiḥ
vyacakṣatāvitṛptākṣāḥ
kṛṣṇam adbhuta-darśanam (1.5)

tasyāṁ — in that; vibhrājamānāyāṁ — glittering; samṛddhāyām — very opulent; mahārddhibhiḥ = maha – great + rddhibhiḥ - with riches; vyacakṣatāvitrptāksāḥ = vyacakṣata - they saw + avitṛpta — unsatiated; kṛṣṇam — Krishna; adbhuta-darśanam = adbhuta – spectacular + darśanam – sight.

Translation

In that glittering city, which was very opulent with great riches, they saw with unsatiated eyes, Krishna, who was spectacular to see. (1.5)

Commentary:

Adbhuta-darśana means someone or something which is super incredible, something that is spectacular to see. Generally speaking the supernatural people have the most beautiful forms. A human being also has a supernatural form but it is crudely manifested. Some of us have ugly supernatural forms. Some have vague or blurred ones.

The extremities of these forms are seen by earthly mystics as auras or as a light spreading some inches away from the subtle form. Rarely is a human being able to produce a supernatural form which attracts the supernatural people. The supernatural people were eager to see Krishna. They hurried on that supernatural trek. Somehow there was an opening in time. They took the opportunity to peer at Lord Krishna.

स्वर्गोद्यानोपगैर् माल्यैश्
छादयन्तो युदूत्तमम् ।
गीर्भिश् चित्र-पदार्थाभिस्
तुष्टुवुर् जगद्-ईश्वरम् ॥ १.६ ॥

svargodyānopagair mālyaiś
chādayanto yudūttamam
gīrbhiś citra-padārthābhis
tuṣṭuvur jagad-īśvaram (1.6)

svargodyānopagair = svarga – heavenly planets + udyāna – gardens + upagair (upagaiḥ) - obtained; mālyaiś = mālyaiḥ — with garlands of flowers; chādayanto = chādayantaḥ — covering; yudūttamam = yadu – Yadhus + uttamam — best of ; gīrbhiś = gīrbhiḥ — with sentences; citra-padārthābhis = citra — beautiful + pada – words + arthābhis (arthābhiḥ) — with sentiments; tuṣṭuvur = tuṣṭuvuḥ — they praised; jagat-īśvaram = jagad (jagat) – universe + īśvaram – Lord.

Translation

Covering the best of the Yadus with garlands of flowers obtained from the gardens of the heavenly planets, they praised the Lord of the universe with sentences consisting of beautiful words and sentiments. (1.6)

Commentary:

Flower garlands obtained from heavenly planets *(svargodyānopagair)* cannot cover a physical body because such materials are too subtle to adhere to and be borne by a physical form. This does not mean that a person using an earthly form may never see such garlands. Supernatural objects can be seen by people who have the psychic ability to see into subtle dimensions. If someone from the supernatural world garlands you, capable mystics may see the garland, but not others.

A capable mystic, if he has the capacity, can see both a physical form and a supernatural one simultaneously. Only one or two mystics are capable of it. Some can do it periodically. Only a rare few can do it consistently. Usually, if a human mystic focuses on the physical side, he loses the subtle focus. If he sees in the subtle side, the physical focus is dimmed. That is the general law of nature.

It is the same with the language of celestial people. Their sentences consisting of beautiful words and sentiments, were not heard by people who did not have an active supernatural ear.

There are many mystics. This writer is one of them, but it does not mean that I am seeing or hearing supernaturally at all times. Unless I focus supernaturally and unless that focus is effectively applied at the time of perception, I would not perceive the supernatural clearly. It would be vague. It is not just a matter of being in divine association as some contend. One may be very near to a divine being and still be supernaturally blind. It is more reliant on personal spiritual discipline and directly upon the withdrawal of one's attention from gross manifestation.

In this translation and commentary, in keeping with the mood of the *Bhagavad Gītā* translation which was already published, I will clear away missionary intentions, hocus pocus, and fraudulent intentions pertaining to Lord Krishna. This translation is not targeted to making converts or to fitting into a set scheme of what God can do or must do to be God. It is either that Krishna is the Supreme Person or He is not. We do not care if He used bodies which were different from His spiritual self but which were special forms, designed to relate to beings in particular dimensions.

श्री-देवा ऊचुः
नताः स्म ते नाथ पदारविन्दं
बुद्धीन्द्रिय-प्राण-मनो-वचोभिः ।
यच् चिन्त्यते ऽन्तर् हृदि भाव-युक्तैर्
मुमुक्षुभिः कर्म-मयोरु-पाशात् ॥ १.७॥

śrī-devā ūcuḥ
natāḥ sma te nātha padāravindaṁ
buddhīndriya-prāṇa-mano-vacobhiḥ
yac cintyate 'ntar hṛdi bhāva-yuktair
mumukṣubhiḥ karma-mayoru-pāśāt (1.7)

śrī – the glorified; devāh – supernatural rulers; ūcuḥ — said; natāh sma — we bow; te — to you; nātha — O Lord; padāravindaṃ — to Your lotus feet; buddhīndriya-prāna-mano-vacobhiḥ = buddhi — intellect + indriya — senses + prāna — vital energy + mano (manaḥ) — mind + vacobhiḥ — with speech; yac (yat) — which; cintyate — are meditated upon; `ntar antar (antah) – withiṇ; hṛdi — in the core of being; bhāva-yuktaiḥ — by those who are fixed in yoga practice; mumukṣubhiḥ — by those who strive for liberation; karma-mayoru-pāśāt = karma – cultural activities + maya — complications + uru-pāśāt — from strong meshes.

Translation

The glorified supernatural rulers said: O Lord, with our intellect, senses, vital energy, mind and speech, we bow to Your lotus feet, which are meditated upon within the core of being, by those who are fixed in yoga practice, who strive for liberation from the strong meshes of the complications of cultural activities. (1.7)

Commentary:

The combination of intellect, senses, vital energy, mind and speech is called the psyche in English language. In the language of the *Bhagavad Gītā*, this is called the environment *(kṣetra)* and the personal material energy *(prakṛtyā svayā)*. Here are a few verses:

kāmaistaistairhṛtajñānāḥ prapadyante'nyadevatāḥ
taṁ taṁ niyamamāsthāya ***prakṛtyā*** *niyatāḥ* ***svayā***

Persons whose experience was overshadowed by contrary desires, plead with other supernatural rulers, following this or that religious procedure, being restricted by their own material nature. (B.G. 7.20)

śrībhagavānuvāca
idaṁ śarīraṁ kaunteya ***kṣetramityabhidhīyate***
etadyo vetti taṁ prāhuḥ kṣetrajña iti tadvidaḥ

The Blessed Lord said: This, the earthly body, O son of Kuntī, is called the living space. Those who are knowledgeable of this, declare the person who understands this to be the experiencer of the living space. (B.G. 13.2)

These equipments; the intellect, senses, vital energy, mind and speech are developed from the mind and vital energy. From mindal energy, the intellect is produced and from the intellect the sense organs are produced. The sense organs become operative only when they are flushed, enthused, or electrified by vital energy. This vital energy is known as *prāṇa* in Sanskrit. Both *prāṇa* and mindal energy are types of mindal energy and both are derived from conscious energy called *citta*.

Sometimes it is said that only the spirit is conscious and the other aspects of reality which are below the spirit are not conscious, but this actually means that only the spirit may be objectively conscious. The other energies can only be subjectively aware. *Citta* or raw subtle material energy is quite conscious but only subjectively.

The psyche which consists of what the glorified supernatural rulers listed as intellect, senses, vital energy, mind and speech, is the skeleton of the subtle body. Beyond the subtle body is the causal form which is a very subtle cove consisting of *citta* energy, a causal state of superfine potency. Speech emanates from both the causal cove and the subtle body. It is listed since it is a special means of expression. It includes all types of gross, subtle or super subtle expressions. Using these psychic equipments, supernatural rulers bowed to Lord Krishna's lotus feet.

Unless one is fixed in yoga practice, he cannot deliberately reach the core of being or the causal body. One cannot go inward to such a degree unless he concentrates himself and his energies and redirects it all to the merging point of the gross and subtle psyche. Unless we reduce involvements or the complications of cultural activities and simultaneously take steps to retract the psyche which is the subtle body, we cannot focus on the causal cove.

The supernatural rulers admitted that even they are unable to retract their attention completely. They admire the sincere yogis who are fixed in yoga practice.

त्वं मायया त्रि-गुणयात्मनि दुर्विभाव्यं
व्यक्तं सृजस्य् अवसि लुम्पसि तद्-गुण-स्थः ।
नैतैर् भवान् अजित कर्मभिर् अज्यते वै
यत् स्वे सुखे ऽव्यवहिते ऽभिरतो ऽनवद्यः ॥ १.८ ॥

tvaṁ māyayā tri-guṇayātmani durvibhāvyaṁ
vyaktaṁ sṛjasy avasi lumpasi tad-guṇa-sthaḥ
naitair bhavān ajita karmabhir ajyate vai
yat sve sukhe 'vyavahite 'bhirato 'navadyaḥ
(1.8)

tvam — you; māyayā — by the mundane potency; tri-gunayātmani = tri-gunayā — consisting of the three influences of material + ātmani — in your spiritual influnces; durvibhāvyam — that which is difficult to conceive of, the inconceivable; vyaktam — the manifest universe; sṛjasy = sṛjasi — you create; avasi — you maintain; lumpasi — you destroy; tad-guna-sthah = tad (tat) — that + guna — mundane influences + sthaḥ — situated; naitair = na — not + etair (etaiḥ) — by these; bhavān — you; ajita —unconquerable one; karmabhir = karmabhiḥ — with activities; ajyate — are affected; vai — at all; yat — because; sve — in your own; sukhe — in happiness; 'vyavahite = avyavahite — in what is not separate, in what is continuous; 'bhirato = abhirataḥ — being absorbed in; 'navadyaḥ = anavadyaḥ — flawless.

Translation

O you, the unconquerable One, within Your own spiritual influence, through Your mundane potency, consisting of the three influences of material nature, You create, maintain and destroy the inconceivable but manifested universe. Though You are situated in that mundane energy, You are not affected by these activities, for You are flawless and are absorbed in continuous happiness. (1.8)

Commentary:

The contradiction of God being all spiritual and God being involved with mundane power was reconciled in this second verse of the address of the supernaturals. Some think that since God is all spiritual, He cannot or should not take on a material body. Others say that God should not or cannot be involved in a mundane universe. Some say that Krishna has no material body and to support their idea, they say that His body which was seen by ordinary human beings was a spiritual form.

More views are still coming one after another. Everyone has his own idea regarding why God would or would not take a material body. Some are careful not to cause any confusion about God's divinity. They want to protect God from criticism and ridicule.

Here however God's involvement with the mundane energy is clearly admitted. The Sanskrit word is *tri-gunayātmani*. This states that God operates his personal spiritual influence, the *ātmani*, through the three influences of material nature *(tri-gunayā)*. We will get details from Krishna Himself. Unless the opinion of the supernatural people is substantiated by Him, it could be subjected to some critique.

The supernaturals declared that Krishna is not affected by the investment of personal power into the mundane energy. They claim that He is flawless and is continually absorbed in spiritual happiness. His spiritual status is so powerful, so reinforced, that it is not foreshadowed by involvement.

शुद्धिर् नृणां न तु तथेड्य दुराशयानां
विद्या-श्रुताध्ययन-दान-तपः-क्रियाभिः ।
सत्त्वात्मनाम् ऋषभ ते यशसि प्रवृद्ध-
सच्-छ्रद्धया श्रवण-सम्भृतया यथा स्यात् ॥ १.९ ॥

śuddhir nṛṇāṁ na tu tatheḍya durāśayānāṁ
vidyā-śrutādhyayana-dāna-tapaḥ-kriyābhiḥ
sattvātmanām ṛṣabha te yaśasi pravṛddha-
sac-chraddhayā śravaṇa-sambhṛtayā yathā syāt (1.9)

śuddhir (śuddhiḥ) — purity; nrnām — of persons; na — not; tu — but; tathedya = tathā - as + īdya — O worshipable one; durāśayānāṁ — of those whose exploitive desires are difficult to fulfill (as – verb root = to enjoy, to fulfill, to complete, to desire, to master); dur (dus) – difficult, hard to accomplish); vidyā-śrutādhyayana-dāna-tapaḥ-kriyābhiḥ = vidyā — technique + śruta — Vedic study + adhyayana — meditation + dāna — charity + tapaḥ — austerity + kriyābhiḥ — and with mystic ritual ceremonies; sattvātmanām — of those whose selves are realistic; ṛṣabha — O greatest of all; te — your; yaśasi — in your glories; pravṛddha-sac-chraddhayā = pravṛddha — a hightened regard + sac (sat) — reality + chraddhayā (śraddhayā) — by confidence; śravaṇa-sambhṛtayā = śravana — hearing + sambhṛtayā – by clear disposition of mind; yathā — as; syāt — there is.

Translation

O worshippable One, O greatest of all, technique, Vedic study, charity, austerity and mystic ritual ceremony, do not confer such purity on those whose exploitive desires are difficult to fulfill, as it does on people who have clear disposition of mind, which is acquired by a heightened regard for Your glories which are reinforced by hearing of them. (1.9)

Commentary:

The key feature in this verse is clear disposition of mind by the particular means of a heightened regard for Krishna's glories, which are reinforced by hearing of them from Krishna Himself or from someone who is thoroughly consistent with Krishna's views as related to Arjuna in *Bhagavad Gītā* or Uddhava in this discourse.

This is not an argument about whether a person is a devotee of Krishna or not. This concerns devotees only. Among the devotees, we have those who have exploitive desires which are difficult to fulfill. We also have those who are in a stage of easy living with a very simple not-elaborate life style. Those devotees who have the simple life style and who have clear disposition of mind by virtue of having a heightened regard for the glories of the Lord, and who heard of Him from the proper sources as described further in this discourse to Uddhava, as well as by what was told to Arjuna, do acquire an especially high degree of purity.

The mystic techniques, Vedic study, charity, austerity, and mystic ritual ceremony, assist those clear minded devotees considerably, but it hardly does anything for the others. And yet, many religious authorities assure the public that these factors will give them full results.

स्यान् नस् तवाङ्घ्रिर् अशुभाशय-धूमकेतुः
क्षेमाय यो मुनिभिर् आर्द्र-हृदोह्यमानः ।
यः सात्वतैः सम-विभूतय आत्मवद्भिर्
व्यूहे ऽर्चितः सवनशः स्वर्-अतिक्रमाय
॥ १.१० ॥

syān nas tavāṅghrir aśubhāśaya-dhūmaketuḥ
kṣemāya yo munibhir ārdra-hṛdohyamānaḥ
yaḥ sātvataiḥ sama-vibhūtaya ātmavadbhir
vyūhe 'rcitaḥ savanaśaḥ svar-atikramāya (1.10)

syān(syāt) — may they be; nas = naḥ — for us; tavānghrir = tava — your + anghrir(anghriḥ) — lotus feet; aśubhāśaya-dhūmaketuḥ = aśubha – impure + āśaya — psychology + dhūmaketuḥ — a fire for consumption; ksemāya — for welfare; yo = yaḥ — which; munibhir = munibhiḥ — by the yogi philosophers; ārdra-hṛdohyamānah = ārdra – tender + hṛdā — hearts + uhyamānaḥ — carried; yah — which; sātvataiḥ — by devotees of the Sātvata family; sama-vibhūtaya — for attaining glories like Lord Krishna's; ātmavadbhir = ātmavadbhiḥ — by those who are self-controlled; vyūhe — in the many forms; 'rcitaḥ = arcitaḥ – worshipped; savanaśah — thrice per day; morning, noon, evening; svar-atikramāya = svaḥ- material heavenly planets + atikramāya — crossing beyond.

Translation

May your lotus feet be the fire to consume our impure psychology; those feet which yogi philosophers for their welfare, carry with tender hearts and which in Your many forms are worshipped in the morning, at noon and in the evening, by self-controlled devotees of the Sātvata family for crossing beyond the material heavenly planets, to attain glories like Yours, (1.10)

Commentary:

For all mystics who aspire to transcend the scope of material existence, the heavenly planets are a serious impediment. From our perspective these heavenly planets are a paradise. They consist of a mixture of various subtle energies. They are not pure spiritual existence. Sometimes people assume that when the body of a mystic dies, he will definitely go to a purely spiritual place but that is an assumption only. There are a wide range of paradises between this gross existence and the spiritual places. A mystic could be forestalled in any of these subtle locales. After staying there for sometime, and after having his attention dissipated, he again returns to this earthly location or to some other similar gross existence. Thus his plan to reach an exclusively spiritual existence, is foiled.

Just the other day, a mystic lady of some achievement, explained to me her plan to merge into the purely spiritual plane which is the first level of spiritual existence beyond these material worlds, but I tried to explain, that for her that was a fantasy. It requires much more than will power. One's material existence has to be purified, inch by inch, bit by bit, before the time of death or one will, more than likely, take another gross body. One might stay in the subtle world for a while and one might mistake those mundane paradises for the kingdom of God or for a spiritual zone, but still one will again come out after sometime, as the son or daughter of this or that man and woman, or as the offspring of some other species. It happens repeatedly.

Almost every human being wants to go to a better place after death, but such desires are pure fantasy. The plain truth is explained in the *Bhagavad Gītā*. It has to do with the texture of one's psyche at the time of death. Here is the statement:

yaṁ yaṁ vāpi smaranbhāvaṁ tyajatyante kalevaram
taṁ tamevaiti kaunteya sadā tadbhāvabhāvitaḥ

Moreover, whatever texture of existence is recalled when a person abandons his body in the end, to that same type of life, he is projected, O son of Kuntī, always being transformed into that status of life. (B.G. 8.6)

Ātmavadhih indicates control of the *ātma*, of the spirit. That is not possible unless the psychic equipments are completely curbed from their impulsive mundane activities. Some salvationists believe and teach that it concerns the spirit only and not his equipments. But this is a belief only.

If the *ātma* cannot purify and control the psychic equipments, he cannot control himself either. His spirit is a much more subtle and more subjective object. The theory that it is just a matter of controlling the spirit without respect to the psychic equipment is a farce. First you control the psychic equipments, and then you make the effort to realize the *ātma*. You practice to curb it from reliance on the faulty psychic equipments.

In any case, even if someone could prove that we could bypass the subtle equipments and control the *ātma*, there is still the question of how to purify the *ātma*. I direct readers to the *Bhagavad Gītā*, where *Śrī* Krishna stated:

tatraikāgraṁ manaḥ kṛtvā yatacittendriyakriyaḥ
upaviśyāsane yuñjyād yogamātmaviśuddhaye (6.12)

...being there, seated in a posture, having the mind focused, the person who controls his thinking and sensual energy, should practise the yoga discipline for self-purification. **(B.G. 6.12)**

Some Vaishnava commentators have given *Vyūha* as the four expansions of Lord Krishna, namely as *Vāsudeva*, *Sañkarṣaṇa*, *Pradyumna* and *Aniruddha*. However that meaning of *Vyūha* as being Lords *Vāsudeva*, *Sañkarṣaṇa*, *Pradyumna*, and *Aniruddha*, was established later on, especially by Lord Chaitanya and by the writings of *Jīva Gosvāmī*. I bring to my readers' attention that *vyūha* is a Sanskrit word which is derived from the root verbs forms of *vy*, *uh*, and *vyuh*. These terms mean to push, move, part, divide, distribute, arrange, place in order. It means a host, an assemblage, a multitude, and a military formation. Thus it actually indicates in this verse the Axis of Personalities who are expanded from Lord Krishna. In Krishna's history, we see that these personalities were led by the chief ones who were Krishna Himself as *Vāsudeva*, the son of *Vasudeva*, and *Balarāma* who is known also as *Sañkarṣaṇa*, Krishna's son *Pradyumna*, and His grandson *Aniruddha*.

Thus the conceptual basis laid down by Lord Chaitanya and the Goswamis of *Vṛndāvan*, is substantiated in the life of Lord Krishna, however in its own time and place, such a conceptual basis is not given in the *Śrīmad Bhāgavatam*. This is why I will not force that development into this translation.

There is much mention in this verse and through the *Śrīmad Bhāgavatam*, about the lotus feet of the divinities. This is actually a literal meaning and it is also a figurative one. To understand this, one has to read through the *Śrīmad Bhāgavatam* to see the circumstances under which bowing to the lotus feet is mentioned. There are many examples of great sages who saw a divinity visually, either in the gross world, in the supernatural world, or after crossing into spiritual territory. In such circumstances there was an actual bowing to the lotus feet, there is also reference to the symbolic bowing which means a surrendering to the wishes of a divinity.

Aśudhāśaya means the impure mentality or more accurately the impure psychology which is the combination of the spirit and his psychic equipments. These supernatural people are devotee associates of Lord Krishna. Still, they cry about their impure psychology. It means therefore, that the crux of the matter in the relationship with the Supreme Lord, is the degree of purity of the personal being. Uddhava asked many questions regarding this. We have ample opportunity to hear Lord Krishna's view on the matter.

यस् चिन्त्यते प्रयत-पाणिभिर् अध्वराग्नौ
त्रय्या निरुक्त-विधिनेश हविर् गृहीत्वा ।
अध्यात्म-योग उत योगिभिर् आत्म-मायां
जिज्ञासुभिः परम-भागवतैः परीष्टः ॥१.११॥

yas cintyate prayata-pāṇibhir adhvarāgnau
trayyā nirukta-vidhineśa havir gṛhītvā
adhyātma-yoga uta yogibhir ātma-māyāṁ
jijñāsubhiḥ parama-bhāgavataiḥ parīṣṭaḥ (1.11)

yas = yaḥ — which; cintyate — are meditated upon; prayata-pāṇibhiḥ — by those with folded palms; adhvarāgnau — in the sacrificial fire; trayyā — of the Rig, Yajur and Sāma Vedas; nirukta-vidhinesa = nirukta — enjoined + vidhinā — by the prescribed manner + īśa — O Lord; havir = haviḥ — ghee for offering; gṛhītvā — taking; adhyātma-yoga — in the yoga for realization of the Supreme Soul; uta — also; yogibhir = yogibhiḥ — by the yogis; ātma-māyām — your bewildering supernatural power; jijñāsubhih — by those who are inquisitive; parama bhāgavataiḥ = parama – highest + bhāgavataiḥ — by the devotees; parīṣṭaḥ — worshipped idealy.

Translation

Your feet, which O Lord, are meditated on in the prescribed manner, in the sacrificial fire, in accordance with the three Vedas, by those who take oblations with folded hands, and by yogis who are inquisitive about Your bewildering supernatural power, through the practice of yoga for realization of the Supreme Soul, and which are ideally worshipped by the highest devotees. (1.11)

Commentary:

Ātma yoga which is not mentioned in this verse but which is mentioned in the previous one, by the term *aśubhāśaya*, is defined in the *Gītā* clearly. Beyond this *ātma* yoga, is *adhyātma*-yoga which is the higher science. In *ātma* yoga one tries to get his spirit and his personal energies in clarity. But in *adhyātma* yoga, the effort is to bring the spirit and its psychic equipments in harmony with the existence of the Supreme Spirit.

After we achieve *ātma* yoga, then if we are inspired to go further, we might achieve *adhyātma yoga*. Some, by their very nature, stop at *ātma* yoga and feel that their spirituality is totally discovered there. Some go further. Besides these two types of spiritualists, there are some who follow teachers who say that *ātma* yoga can be completed by taking to the high road-of *adhyātma* yoga. It is not a point of contention. Whatever you do is based on tendency. But success is based on sincerity and steadiness of practice.

Ātma means the spirit's own creative power but in this verse, *adhyātma* applies to the Supreme Spirit's, to Krishna's creative power. For the limited spirits, personal creative power is a big problem and a bigger distraction is God's creative power. For God, it poses no problem. We will understand why as we read what Lord Krishna explained to Uddhava.

I used to think that the *Bhagavad Gītā* instruction to Arjuna was a profound and monumental discourse. I used to be fascinated with it. But whatever glorious experience I had in the *Bhagavad Gītā* was foreshadowed when I took a serious look at this discourse between Lord Krishna and Uddhava. *Bhagavad Gītā* still amazes me but now it is not so fantastic. I have got some foot hold in this instruction to Uddhava. By the grace of *Śrī* Krishna, I am stepping away from Arjuna and his emotional problems.

This verse has many in-depth concepts of the supernatural rulers. In the final analysis they speak of the lotus feet of the Lord and not symbolically but actually. They discuss His super-natural lotus feet which were before them visually.

पर्युष्टया तव विभो वन-मालयेयं
सस्पार्धिनी भगवती प्रतिपत्नी-वच् छ्रीः ।
यः सु-प्रणीतम् अमुयार्हणम् आददन् नो
भूयात् सदाङ्घ्रिर् अशुभाशय-धूमकेतुः ॥ १.१२ ॥

paryuṣṭayā tava vibho vana-mālayeyaṁ
saṁspārdhinī bhagavatī pratipatnī-vac chrīḥ
yaḥ su-praṇītam amuyārhaṇam ādadan no
bhūyāt sadāṅghrir aśubhāśaya-dhūmaketuḥ
(1.12)

paryuṣṭayā — withered; tava — your; vibho — Almighty Lord; vana-mālayeyam = vana – forest + mālayā — by the flower garland + iyam — she; saṁspārdhinī — is jealous; bhagavatī — the Supreme Goddess; pratipatnī-vac-chrīh = pratipatnī – co-wife + vac (vat) — like + chrīḥ = śrīḥ — Laksmideva, the goddess of fortune; yaḥ — which; su-praṇītam — properly done; amuyārhanam = amuyā — by this + ; arhanam — the offering; ādadan — offering; no = naḥ — our; bhūyāt — may they be; sadānghrir = sadā — always + anghrir (anghriḥ) — lotus feet; aśubhāśaya-dhūmaketuḥ = aśubhāśaya — of our impure psychology + dhūmaketuḥ — a fire for consumption.

Translation

O Almighty Lord, just as a co-wife, the Supreme Goddess Lakṣmi is jealous of Your garland of forest flowers, though they are withered. You accept the worship done by the garland which was properly offered. May Your Feet always be the fire to consume our impure psychology. (1.12)

Commentary:

By using the term *pratipatnī*, the supernatural people specifically identified *bhagavatī*, or the supreme goddess *Śrī* who is also known as *Lakṣmī*. Others such as goddess *Durgā* and goddess *Sarasvatī*, as well as goddess *Gāyatrī* and even goddess *Kālī* are also addressed as *Bhagavatī*. As we realized previously, even Indra who is merely a minor supernatural in charge of planetary weather control, is addressed as *Bhagavān* (Lord).

These titles do not in any way indicate that there is no Supreme Person but rather, sentiments of respect are offered to various powerful entities.

In this verse, the Supernatural people wanted to praise the garland of forest flowers which adorned the neck and chest of Lord Krishna. They became aware of the wife of the Lord and so they toned down the acclaim of the garland. They showed us a competitive aspect between the devotional aspirations of the Lord's wife and those of His garland.

I have used the word psychology as the English equivalent of the Sanskrit word *āśaya*. Sanskrit dictionaries gave these terms: bed chamber, resting place, asylum, place of residence, abode, seat, retreat, reservoir, seat of feelings, and heart. These meanings point towards the causal body, which is the ultimate seat of mental and emotional feelings of the living being. I used the word psychology because of the definitions indicated in verse seven, where the psychic equipments are listed as *buddhi* (intellect organ), *indriya* (sense organs), *prāṇa* (vital energy or sensual energy), *manah* (mindal space), and *vacobhih* (speech).

In the same verse seven, the same causal body is indicated by the terms *'ntar hṛdi (antar hṛdi*, which means within the core of being. The term *hṛdi* means in the causal body. In this application it has little to do with the physical heart but it includes the heart-lung functions of the physical form.

The supernaturals mentioned their impure psychology (*asubhāśaya*). This impurity keeps them at a distance from Lord Krishna. On the other hand, they recognize that due to *subhāśaya* or a pure psychology, the Lord's wife stands very, very near to Him and the Lord's garland hugs His body directly. This is a clear hint for all devotees who want to get close to Lord Krishna. The devotees with impure psychology, impure mentality and impure sensual energy are indicated in verse nine by the term *durāśayanam*. They have exploitive desires which are difficult to fulfill. We must remember these meanings since this is the crux of the issue in this discourse to Uddhava.

केतुस् त्रि-विक्रम-युतस् त्रि-पतत्-पताको
यस् ते भयाभय-करो ऽसुर-देव-चम्वोः ।
स्वर्गाय साधुषु खलेष्व् इतराय भूमन्
पदः पुनातु भगवन् भजताम् अघं नः ॥ १.१३ ॥

ketus tri-vikrama-yutas tri-patat-patāko
yas te bhayābhaya-karo 'sura-deva-camvoḥ
svargāya sādhuṣu khaleṣv itarāya bhūman
padaḥ punātu bhagavān bhajatām aghaṁ naḥ
(1.13)

ketuḥ —flagpole; tri-vikrama-yutas = tri – three + vikrama — steps + yataḥ — adorned by; tri-patat-patāko = tri-patat - falling into three sectors of the universe + patāko (patākaḥ) — flag; yas (yaḥ) — which; te — your; bhayābhaya-karo = bhaya - fear + abhaya – fearlessness + karo (karaḥ)— causing; 'sura-deva-camvoḥ= 'sura (asura) – supernatural rebels + deva — approved supernatural rulers + camvoḥ — to the armies; svargāya — for the heavenly planets; sādhuṣu — among saintly people; khaleṣv = khaleṣu — among the wicked people; itarāya to the opposite effect; bhūman — O Almighty God; pādaḥ — foot; punātu — may they rectify; bhagavān — O Blessed Lord; bhajatām — those who render worship; aghaṁ — sins; naḥ — of us.

Translation

O Almighty God, Blessed Lord, for us who render You service, may Your feet rectify our faults; those feet which with three steps became Your flagpole, with the Ganges River falling in the three sectors of the universe as the flag and which caused fear and fearlessness to the armies of the supernatural rebels and approved supernatural rulers respectively. Your feet are conducive to the heavenly planets for the saintly people but they give the opposite result to the wicked persons. (1.13)

Commentary:

Some Puranic history is required to understand this verse. This is a glorification for the incarnation of Godhead, Lord *Vāmanadeva*, who is one of the *Ādityās* mentioned in verse two.

The youngest of the sons of *Aditi* became known as *Urukram* or *Trivikrama*. He is respected as having conquered *Bali*, a crown prince who used mystic power to scare Indra and his supernatural assistants away from their heavenly paradises.

When he approached King *Bali*, Lord *Vāmanadeva*, who had a short body, begged for three steps of land. When the king agreed, the Lord strided universally. This action caused fear to the supernatural rebels and fearlessness to the approved supernatural rulers, only because the rebels desire to break the restrictions placed on them by the Supreme Lord and to upset the balance of power in material nature. Since the rebels are inclined to snatching power when it is not really due to them, they are possessed by the fear element which abounds in the material creation and which is sometimes used by the Supreme Lord to bring them in line.

Bali and his cohorts got the opposite result which was a passage to the hellish planets, but in their case it was a blessing since Lord *Vāmanadeva* took a liking to *Bali* because of *Bali's* repentance. The Lord decided to stay with *Bali* as a companion.

Generally speaking however, the system of elevation to heavenly planets and degradation to lower ones or lower species of life, is an incentive for the living beings to be cooperative with the evolutionary thrust which comes from material nature. Since the Supreme Lord is the ultimate supervisor, He gets involved in the movement of our mentality from one level to another. More of this was explained by Lord Krishna.

नस्य् ओत-गाव इव यस्य वशे भवन्ति
ब्रह्मादयस् तनु-भृतो मिथुर् अर्द्यमानाः ।
कालस्य ते प्रकृति-पूरुषयोः परस्य
शं नस् तनोतु चरणः पुरुषोत्तमस्य ॥ १.१४॥

nasy ota-gāva iva yasya vaśe bhavanti
brahmādayas tanu-bhṛto mithur ardyamānāḥ
kālasya te prakṛti-pūruṣayoḥ parasya
śaṁ nas tanotu caraṇaḥ puruṣottamasya (1.14)

nasy = nasi — through the nose; ota-gava = ota — pass through + gāvaḥ — oxen; iva — as if, like; yasya — of whose; vaśe — in control; bhavanti — they exist; brahmadayas = Brahm + ādayas(ādayaḥ) - and other supernatural rulers; tanu-bhṛto = tanu-bhṛtaḥ — body-supported souls; mithur = mithuḥ — among each other; ardyamānāḥ — fighting; kālasya — of time; te — of you; prakṛti-pūruṣayoḥ = prakṛti - material nature + pūruṣayoḥ - of the exploiter; parasya — of one who is superior; śam — welfare; nas = naḥ — for us; tanotu — may they contribute; caraṇaḥ — lotus feet; puruṣottamasya — of the Supreme Person.

Translation

May your feet contribute to our welfare! You are the Supreme Person. You are Time in Whose control are Creator Brahmā and the other supernatural rulers, who are body-supported spirits and who fight among each other like bulls with strings passing through their noses. You are superior and are the exploiter of material nature. (1.14)

Commentary:

In this verse, a distinction is made between the body-supported souls and those who do not rely on and are not in need of assistance from a *tanu* or material body. It is not merely a gross body but a subtle and causal body as well. So long as we are reliant on causal and subtle bodies to assist us in perceiving reality and in sorting out distinctions of existence, we are in the category of being *tanu-bhṛtah* or body-supported/body-subsidized. Sanskrit dictionaries give the root-term *bhṛ* as meaning to fill, pervade, bear, support, uphold, bear up, and subsidize.

A causal and subtle body usually indicates the need for and the development of, a gross form. However most of the supernatural people are above the need for gross bodies but they definitely need subtle mundane forms. On the other hand, we may contest the distinction made for the Supreme Person *(puruṣottamah)*. Why should He be regarded as being any different? If He also takes on causal, subtle and gross forms, then what is the difference in His reliance? Is He not also in the category of being a body-subsidized being? Later in this discourse, Uddhava will ask a related question of Lord Krishna.

From one view, it is said that the Supreme Person is the exploiter of material nature, *prakṛti-puruṣah*. What then, is the difference between Him and His little partners, the limited spirits? They also are trying to exploit the material nature *(prakṛti)*. In the *Bhagavad Gītā*, Lord Krishna spoke of a relationship between Himself and the limited beings, whom he termed affectionately as His partners. Here is the statement:

mamaivāṁśo jīvaloke jīvabhūtaḥ sanātanaḥ
manaḥṣaṣṭhānīndriyāṇi prakṛtisthāni karṣati

My partner is in this world of individualized conditioned beings. He is an eternal individual soul but he draws to himself the mundane senses of which the mind is the sixth detection device. (B.G. 15.7)

The difference between the Supreme Person and the limited spirits is hinted at in this verse, as being, one of jurisdictional control and jurisdictional confinement. The Supreme Person is addressed as the Time producer. The limited beings are suggested as being those who are time-regulated. In the confusion about identity, they fight each other like bulls with restraining loops passing through their noses. Basically, we fight over jurisdiction in terms of grabbing up opportunities for exploitation. In this one verse a summary statement of our material existence is described.

अस्यासि हेतुर् उदय-स्थिति-सयमानाम्
अव्यक्त-जीव-महताम् अपि कालम् आहुः ।
सो ऽयं त्रि-णाभिर् अखिलापचये प्रवृत्तः
कालो गभीर-रय उत्तम-पूरुषस् त्वम् ॥ १.१५ ॥

asyāsi hetur udaya-sthiti-saṁyamānām
avyakta-jīva-mahatām api kālam āhuḥ
so 'yaṁ tri-ṇābhir akhilāpacaye pravṛttaḥ
kālo gabhīra-raya uttama-pūruṣas tvam (1.15)

asyasi = asya — of this + asi — you are; hetur = hetuḥ — cause; udaya-sthiti-saṁyamānām = udaya — of the creation + sthiti — continuation + saṁyamānām — annihilation; avyakta-jīva-mahatām = avyakta — of the unmanifest energy + jīva — the individual soul + mahatām — of the reservoir of manifestable mundane potency; api — also; kālam — time factor; āhuḥ — The Vedas personified say; so = sah - he; 'yam = ayam — this; tri-nābhir = tri-nābhiḥ — three partitions; akhilāpacaye = akhila — of everything + apacaye — causing reduction; pravṛttaḥ — engaged; kālo = kālah — time factor; gabhīra-raya = gabhīra — imperceptible + raya — movement; uttama-pūruṣas — Supreme Person; tvam — you.

Translation

You are the cause of creation, continuation and annihilation of this manifestation. The Vedas personified say that You are the ruler of the Unmanifested Energy, of the individual souls and of the reservoir of manifestible mundane potency. You are time with its three partitions, which causes the reduction of everything. You are the Supreme Person. (1.15)

Commentary:

Besides the Vedas personified, there are others who give an opposing view. They contend that an individual person, even the Supreme Person, the Ishvara, could not be the source *(hetuh)* of the unmanifest energy, the individual souls and the reservoir of the manifestable mundane potencies. The Vedas Personified has their theistic opinion but they are not the only authorities in the material world. Other philosophers explain the creation in other ways, thus establishing and justifying other beliefs.

As theists, Krishna's supernatural visitors, accept the concept of a Supreme Person who is the cause of this creation. Their view relates to their own functions as regulators of the creation. A boy who builds a sand castle can understand how his father built a stone castle out of mortar and bricks. But another boy might feel that neither the boy nor his father are real creators since neither the sand nor limestone was created by either of them. Thus some philosophers accept these praises for Lord Krishna, as polite wording only. They see this glorification as a flattery given to a supposed Supreme Being.

त्वत्तः पुमान् समधिगम्य ययास्य वीर्यं
धत्ते महान्तम् इव गर्भम् अमोघ-वीर्यः ।
सो ऽय तयानुगत आत्मन आण्ड-कोशं
हैमं ससर्ज बहिर् आवरणैर् उपेतम् ॥ १.१६ ॥

tvattaḥ pumān samadhigamya yayāsya vīryaṁ
dhatte mahāntam iva garbham amogha-vīryaḥ
so 'yaṁ tayānugata ātmana āṇḍa-kośaṁ
haimaṁ sasarja bahir āvaraṇair upetam (1.16)

tvattah — you; pumān — the primal male being; samadhigamya — deriving; yasyasya = yaya — with, in conjunction with + asya — of this; vīryam — potency, masculine sexual power; dhatte — impregnates; mahāntam — sum-total manifestible mundane potency; iva - like; garbham — feotus; amogha-vīryaḥ = amogha - inexhaustible + vīryaḥ - creative powers; so = sah - that; 'yam = ayam - this; tayānugata = taya — with it + anugata (anugataḥ) — reinforced; ātmana — from within itself; aṇḍa-kośam = aṇḍa — developed in an egg, egg-shaped + kośaṁ - container; haimaṁ — golden; sasarja — produced; bahir = bahiḥ — outer; āvaraṇair = āvaranaiḥ — with coverings; upetam — endowed with, has.

Translation

Deriving male sexual power from You, the primal male being, who has inexhaustible creative power, in conjunction with the mundane energy, impregnates the sum total manifestible mundane potency, which is like a feotus. This sumtotal mundane power, which is reinforced by the mundane energy, developed from within itself, the golden egg-shaped container, which has outer coverings. (1.16)

Commentary:

The primal male being is known as the *Pumān*. He is described elsewhere in the *Śrīmad Bhāgavatam*. The supernatural rulers accredit Lord Krishna as being the eternal source of the masculine power *(vīryam)*, which that *Pumān* or *Mahāviṣṇu* continually produces and which is inexhaustible *(amogha)*. For the time being, we may accept this at face value, for recently we have neither seen such a primal male being, nor Lord Krishna.

The golden egg-shaped container is this universe. According to the *Śrīmad Bhāgavatam*, this universe is an enclosure. Some Vaishnavas believe that Lord Krishna is the source of Lord *Mahāviṣṇu* , who is known also as Lord *Nārāyaṇa*. This belief is based on this statement of the supernatural rulers. Thus there is a solid foundation for the beliefs of those Vaishnavas who accredit their Lord Krishna as being higher than Lord Vishnu.

In the *Bhagavad Gītā*, in the revelation of the Universal Form and the four-arm divine *Nārāyaṇa* form, Lord Krishna stood out as the source of the inexhaustible powers of the *Pumān*, the *Mahāviṣṇu* .

In the *Bhagavad Gītā*, Arjuna asked Lord Krishna to see the four-armed form. Krishna complied with that request, thus destroying all arguments as to whether He was the *Nārāyaṇa* or God of this world.

In the *Bhagavad Gītā* when Arjuna got the revelation, Lord Krishna was identical to Lord *Nārāyaṇa*. It does not give us the idea that Lord Krishna is the source of Lord *Nārāyaṇa*. Here we get another piece of information. So if on one hand, He is the source of *Nārāyaṇa*, what are we to conclude? It appears therefore, that the discourse to Uddhava is moved into high gear.

तत् तस्थूषश् च जगतश् च भवान् अधीशो
यन् माययोत्थ-गुण-विक्रिययोपनीतान् ।
अर्थाञ् जुषन्न् अपि हृषीक-पते न लिप्तो
ये ऽन्ये स्वतः परिहृताद् अपि बिभ्यति स्म ॥ १.१७॥

tat tasthūṣaś ca jagataś ca bhavān adhīśo
yan māyayottha-guṇa-vikriyayopanītān
arthāñ juṣann api hṛṣīka-pate na lipto
ye 'nye svataḥ parihṛtād api bibhyati sma (1.17)

tat — therefore; tasthūṣaś = tasthūṣaḥ — of the immovable things; ca — and; jagataś = jagataḥ — of the mobile objects; ca — and; bhavān — you; adhīśo = adhīśaḥ — Supreme Lord; yan = yat — because; māyayottha-guṇa-vikriyayopanītān = māyayā — by the mundane potency + uttha — created by + guṇa — mundane influence + vikriyayā — by the activity of the sense organs + upanītān — brought near, presented; arthān — attractive objects; juṣann = juṣan — enjoying; api — although; hṛṣīka-pate — master of the senses; na - not; lipto = liptaḥ — affected; ye — those; 'nye = anye — other; svataḥ — of themselves; parihṛtād = parihṛtāt — from the absence of; api — even; bibhyati — they fear; sma — indeed.

Translation

Therefore You are the Supreme Lord of the movable and immovable objects, for you, O master of the senses, are unaffected by the attractive objects, even though enjoying them as they are presented by the activity of the sense organs which were created by the mundane potency, and of which indeed, others fear, even when the sense objects are absent. (1.17)

Commentary:

A distinction is made between Lord Krishna and the supernatural rulers who offer their realizations, as well as between Lord Krishna and ourselves who are under the jurisdiction of the supernatural people. If the supernatural people rated Lord Krishna as stated in these prayers, then we can just understand our petty position. Though eternal, we do not have such a solid standing in the conscious existence. We are reliant on these supernatural rulers to a degree, at least in terms of our present existential consciousness. But we hear that Lord Krishna is not affected *(lipto)* like others, not even like the great sages and accomplished yogins, since on occasion they too fear the sense objects even when they are not present.

There are many sages who speak of liberation and immunity from bewilderment, but the plain truth is that most of them are fearful even when the bewildering potency is not even present. It is due to a natural susceptibility to its influence.

The term *lipto (liptah)* is derived from a Sanskrit root word, limp, which means to anoint, smear, besmear, cover, stain, pollute, defile, or contaminate. This is exactly the position. There is a related verse in the *Bhagavad Gītā*, where Lord Krishna explained that He is beyond those beings who are influenced or affected and He is also beyond those other beings who are not influenced or affected.

yasmātkṣaramatīto'ham akṣarādapi cottamaḥ
ato'smi loke vede ca prathitaḥ puruṣottamaḥ

***Since I am beyond the affected spirits and I am even higher than the unaffected ones, I am known in the world and in the Vedas as the Supreme Person.* (B.G. 15.18)**

Some commentators may not agree with my English meaning of the word, *akṣara*. But I direct readers to the Sanskrit meaning as follows:

Root word: *kṣar*

Meanings: to flow, to glide, to waste away, to perish, to become useless, to have no effect, to slip from, to be deprived of.

Those who want to establish that every spirit is absolute *(kevalam)* and who want to accredit the spirits as being capable of merging with the absolute *(advaita)*, cannot afford to regard the word *kṣara* as meaning affected. They warp the *Bhagavad Gītā* accordingly. In any case, it is not an argument. Uddhava will challenge Lord Krishna on this issue. We will read Krishna's reply.

स्मायावलोक-लव-दर्शित-भाव-हारि-
भ्रू-मण्डल-प्रहित-सौरत-मन्त्र-शौण्डैः ।
पत्न्यस् तु षोडश-सहस्रम् अनङ्ग-बाणैर्
यस्येन्द्रिय विमथितु करणैर् न विभ्व्यः ॥१.१८॥

smāyāvaloka-lava-darśita-bhāva-hāri-
bhrū-maṇḍala-prahita-saurata-mantra-śauṇḍaiḥ
patnyas tu ṣoḍaśa-sahasram anaṅga-bāṇair
yasyendriyaṁ vimathituṁ karaṇair na vibhvyaḥ
(1.18)

smāyāvaloka = smāya — smiling; avaloka — of a glance; lava — by small amounts, gradually; darśita — displaying; bhāva — feelings; hāri — alluring; bhrū - eyebrows; mandala — arch; prahita — launched; saurata — of romance; mantra — message; śauṇḍaiḥ — by rudeness, by pride; patnyas = patnyah — wives; tu — but; ṣodaśa-sahasram = ṣodaśa — sixteen + sahasram - thousand; anaṅga-bānair = anaṅga — romantic love + bānair (bānaiḥ) — by shafts; yasyendriyaṁ = yasya — whose + indriyam — senses; vimathitum — to sexually arouse; karaṇair = karaṇaih — with flirtive actions; na - not; vibhvyaḥ — they are able.

Translation

O You, whose senses, sixteen thousand wives were unable to sexually arouse, with their love shafts and allurements; their smiling glances which gradually displayed their feelings, which rendered enchanting their arched eyebrows, from which romantic messages were launched; (1.18)

Commentary:

The superiority of Krishna's senses *(indriyam)* is clearly described in this verse. Some feel that Lord Krishna was promiscuous, that he was sexually-motivated. This statement by the supernatural people contradicts that view. One important realization is this: The supernatural people reviewed the subtle body used by Lord Krishna because that body was manifested to them. And even on that level, Lord Krishna exhibited the sexual resistance which the supernaturals acclaimed here. In the discourse with Uddhava, we will get a more in-depth understanding of the difference between the senses of the Lord Krishna and that of others.

विभ्व्यस् तवामृत-कथोद-वहास् त्रि-लोक्याः
पादावने-ज-सरितः शमलानि हन्तुम् ।
आनुश्रवं श्रुतिभिर् अङ्घ्रि-जम् अङ्ग-सङ्गैस्
तीर्थ-द्वय शुचि-षदस् त उपस्पृशन्ति ॥१.१९॥

vibhvyas tavāmṛta-kathoda-vahās tri-lokyāḥ
pādāvane-ja-saritaḥ śamalāni hantum
ānuśravaṁ śrutibhir aṅghri-jam aṅga-saṅgais
tīrtha-dvayaṁ śuci-ṣadas ta upaspṛśanti
(1.19)

vibhvyas = vibhvyaḥ — are able; tavāmṛta-kathoda-vahās = tava — your + amṛta — immortality + kathoda — pastime stories + uda-vahās (uda-vahāḥ) — the water bearing rivers; tri-lokyāh — the three worlds; pādāvane-ja-saritaḥ = pādāvane — in the washing of your feet + ja — produced from + saritaḥ — rivers; śamalāni — sins; hantum — to destroy; ānuśravam — hearing from spiritual masters; śrutibhir = śrutibhiḥ — with ears; anghri-jam — produced from your lotus feet; aṅga-saṅgais = aṅga-saṅgaiḥ — by bodily contact; tīrtha-dvayaṁ = tīrtha — sanctified places + dvayāṁ - two; śuci-ṣadah — one striving for purification; ta = te — your; upaspṛśanti — they touch.

Translation

The water-bearing rivers of your pastime stories, that give immortality, as well as those which were produced from the washing of your feet, are able to destroy the flaws of the three worlds. Those who strive for purification, touch both flows of water; one through their ears and the other coming from your feet by bodily contact. (1.19)

Commentary:

Two types of streams are mentioned. The first is the narrations given by persons like Shuka, the son of *Vyāsa*. The second is the subtle rivers which sprung from the lotus feet of Lord Krishna and from the lotus feet of any parallel divinities or their empowered agents. In either case both types are capable of destroying the sins of the worlds. It is a matter of taking advantage of these sin-removing facilities.

श्री-बादरायणिर् उवाच
इत्य् अभिष्टूय विबुधैः
सेशः शत-धृतिर् हरिम् ।
अभ्यभाषत गोविन्दं
प्रणम्याम्बरम् आश्रितः ॥ १.२० ॥

śrī-bādarāyaṇir uvāca
ity abhiṣṭūya vibudhaiḥ
seśaḥ śata-dhṛtir harim
abhyabhāṣata govindaṁ
praṇamyāmbaram āśritaḥ (1.20)

śrī - the illustrious; bādarāyaṇir = bādarāyaṇiḥ - the son of Badarāyaṇa; uvāca — said; ity = iti — thus; abhiṣṭūya — praising, offering glorification; vibudhaiḥ — with the supernatural rulers; seśaḥ = sa - with + īśaḥ — Lord Shiva; śata-dhṛtir — the person with a record of a hundred sacrifices; harim — Hari; abhyabhāṣata — spoke; govindaṁ — to Govinda Krishna; praṇamyāmbaram = praṇamya — offering obeisances + ambaram — in the sky; āśritaḥ — being situated.

Translation

The illustrious son of Badarāyaṇa said: Thus offering glorification, Indra, the person with a record of a hundred sacrifices, along with the supernatural rulers and Lord Shiva, offered obeisances. Being situated in the sky they spoke to Hari Govinda. (1.20)

Commentary:

Badarāyaṇa is the son of *Parāśar* Muni. This person became known as *Śrīla Vyāsadeva*, the complier of the *Purāṇas*. Some say however that there in more than one *Vyāsadeva* and that some others who took the task of writing or editing *Purāṇas*, passed under the same name. The original *Vyāsa*, the son of *Parāśar* Muni became known as *Vyāsa* or the dividing complier, because he divided the one Veda into four, as Rig, *Sāma*, Yajur, and Atharva. His son was called Shuka. This Shuka told this story of *Śrīmad Bhāgavatam* to King *Parīkṣit*, a grandson of Arjuna.

This same *Vyāsa*, the son of *Parāśar* was the grandfather of Arjuna. However, Arjuna became known as the grandson of Vichitravirya, because Vichitravirya's wife was impregnated by *Vyāsa*, who was Vichatravirya's step brother on his mother's side.

Vyāsa is also known as *Dvaipāyaṇa* because he was born on an island. He was also known as Krishna because of his blackish complexion and because he is rated as a special agent of Krishna.

The term *Vyāsa* however, is used to signify any of the authoritative compilers of Vedic scriptures. These writers are usually rated as divine beings, incarnations of Godhead.

There is more than one person addressed as the performer of one hundred sacrifices. Usually this refers to the Indra supernatural ruler, who controls weather on earthly planets.

Shiva, another supernatural, is extraordinary. He is existentially outside of the jurisdiction of *Brahmā*. He is mentioned separately as *īśah (seśah = sa + īśah).* All of them glorified *Hari* Govinda, Lord Krishna.

The supernatural people were situated in the sky. Their bodies were floating. They did not using physical forms. They could not be seen by persons whose psychic senses were grossly-focused.

श्री-ब्रह्मोवाच
भूमेर् भारावताराय
पुरा विज्ञापितः प्रभो ।
त्वम् अस्माभिर् अशेषात्मन्
तत् तथैवोपपादितम् ॥ १.२१ ॥

śrī-brahmovāca
bhūmer bhārāvatārāya
purā vijñāpitaḥ prabho
tvam asmabhir aśeṣātman
tat tathaivopapāditam (1.21)

śrī - the accomplied; brahmovaca = brahma - Procreator Brahmā + uvāca - said; bhumer = bhumeḥ — of the earth; bhārāvatārāya = bhāra — the burden + avatārāya — for reducing; purā — previously; vijñāpitaḥ — were petitioned; prabho — O Lord; tvam — you; asmabhir = asmābhiḥ — by us; aśesātman = aśesa - without remainer, complete + ātman — soul, Personality; tat = tad - that; tathaivopapāditam = tatha eva — exactly so + upapāditam — was accomplished.

Translation

The accomplished Procreator Brahmā said: O Lord, previously You were petitioned by us to reduce the burden of the earth. O Complete Spirit, that was accomplished. (1.21)

Commentary:

Some translators give *aśesātman* as the Soul of all. I gave complete spirit. *Aśesa* means without remainder, or complete. Lord Hari Govinda, Krishna did exactly as He was petitioned to do by the supernatural rulers.

In a sense these supernatural rulers are rude in approaching Lord Krishna. Their motive is to request His departure. Since the advent of Lord Krishna, their jurisdictional control was hampered. He superseded their authority. Besides the glorifications and praising overtones in their address to Govinda, they intended to say this: "Depart immediately. Your service is no longer needed. Thank you very much. Goodbye! If we need more assistance we will call as before. But You eclipsed us. That is undesirable. We do appreciate Your efficient disposal of those who superseded our authority."

धर्मश् च स्थापितः सत्सु
सत्य-सन्धेषु वै त्वया ।
कीर्तिश् च दिक्षु विक्षिप्ता
सर्व-लोक-मलापहा ॥ १.२२ ॥

dharmaś ca sthāpitaḥ satsu
satya-sandheṣu vai tvayā
kīrtiś ca dikṣu vikṣiptā
sarva-loka-malāpahā (1.22)

dharmaś = dharmaḥ — religious principles; ca — and; sthāpitaḥ — places; satsu — in the virtuous people; satya-sandhesu — and those who are harmonious with the reality; vai — indeed; tvayā — by you; kīrtiś = kīrtiḥ — glory; ca — and; dikṣu — in every direction; vikṣiptā — was spread; sarva-loka-malāpahā = sarva - all + loka — worlds + mala — impurity + apahā — removes.

Translation

You placed religious principles in care of the virtuous people who are harmonious with reality, and you spread in every direction, Your glories, which removed the impurities of all worlds. (1.22)

Commentary:

Lord Shiva and the *siddha* yogis were there with the supernatural people but in every mention, Shuka sets Shiva apart to distinguish him from the others. From the very onset of the creation, Shiva had no political interest. He is not threatened by the assumption of sovereign power by Lord Krishna. However *Brahmā* too is not really threatened either. Lord Krishna took residence on earth and focused His reforming energy on the earthly plane. *Brahmā* lives far away existentially in his *Satyaloka* place. However, the Indra demigod was concerned that Krishna had not departed. He complained to *Brahmā*.

Brahmā is remote from our earthly situation but Indra is very near. If Indra is worried, that insecurity affects *Brahmā*'s peace of mind, *Brahmā* must speak to explain that Krishna's departure is desired. For the most part this visit by the supernatural people is a piece of diplomacy. They wanted Lord Krishna to pack up and leave.

I said above that the *siddhas* are not interested in political jurisdiction. This is a general statement. Some of the *siddhas* are. These politically-oriented *siddhas* usually amass large followings on one planet or another. They establish themselves as benevolent kings or as yogic rulers *(rājarṣis)*. After becoming rulers, they relax the austerities. They too were not in favor of Lord Krishna remaining in their provinces.

Some of them are devotees of Krishna. They come down to this planet from time to time and try to set up a system of worship of themselves as leading devotees. So long as Krishna is only present as an Idol in their temples they are quite satisfied because in that situation, they remain as the head of their operations. They do not want an actual physical Krishna as Krishna was physically present in the time of Arjuna. Such a physical presence would eclipse or supersede their importance.

Except for God, every limited being is in a sense envious of some other person. Our position is pathetic. We are such petty people. Productive religious principles can only be tended by persons who are harmonious with reality but religious values and superstitions can be maintained by any others who might choose to do so. In the *Bhagavad Gītā*, Lord Krishna listed *dharma* as His own work. He claimed that anyone who assisted in maintaining *dharma* or genuine morality as He described it, does His work. He encouraged Arjuna to do this, and incited Arjuna to be His agent in the battle of *Kurukṣetra*.

According to Lord Krishna many other ancient kings like the solar deity *Vivasvan* and rulers like *Ikṣvāku, Manu* and *Janak* specialized in establishing genuine religious principles. They did this, functioning as benevolent, stern rulers. Arjuna was advised to follow their example in practicing *karma* yoga, the application of yoga to performance of cultural activities *(karma)*.

The *kirtih* or glory of Lord Krishna and the resulting popularity, was spread by Krishna Himself as well as by sages like *Śrīla Vyāsadeva, Nārada, Asita Devala* and by others like Shuka who narrated this story to King *Parikṣit*. In modern times many, many great sages, advanced or empowered devotees of Krishna contributed to the spreading action of His stories.

अवतीर्य यदोर् वंशे
बिभ्रद् रूपम् अनुत्तमम् ।
कर्माण्य् उद्दाम-वृत्तानि
हिताय जगतो ऽकृथाः ॥१.२३॥

avatīrya yador vaṁśe
bibhrad rūpam anuttamam
karmāṇy uddāma-vṛttāni
hitāya jagato 'kṛthāḥ (1.23)

avatīrya — having incarnated; yador = yadoḥ — of Yadu; vaṁśe — into the family line; bibhrad = bibhrat — assuming; rūpam — form; anuttamam — matchless; karmāny = karmāni — actions; uddāma-vṛttāni = uddāma - superhuman + vṛttāni — deeds; hitāya — for the benefit; jagato = jagataḥ — of the world; 'kṛthāḥ = akṛthāh — you performed.

Translation

Having incarnated in the Yadu's family, and assuming a matchless form, You performed superhuman deeds for the benefit of the world. (1.23)

Commentary:

Lord Krishna incarnates or descends into the mundane dimension *(avatīrya)*, manifesting matchless mundane forms. With these forms He performs superhuman deeds for the benefit of the world. Some say however that He never took a mundane form. They claim that all His forms were pure spirit only.

To reconcile both views, that of a material form of Lord Krishna and that of His not having any mundane body, I explain the following: Despite the manifestation of mundane forms of Lord Krishna or by any of His parallel divinities, they all remain stationed in spiritual forms, while directing such mundane bodies. In that sense, they do not descend. On the other hand, since this world must be maintained by a fractional burst of their energy, they do in fact descend without jeopardizing their divine status. Lord Krishna explained to Arjuna that even though both Krishna and Arjuna took on many material bodies over millions of years, Lord Krishna does not lose touch nor forget His divine status. His spiritual perspective remained intact. Arjuna however was affected:

śrībhagavānuvāca
bahūni me vyatītāni janmāni tava cārjuna
tānyahaṁ veda sarvāṇi na tvaṁ vettha paraṁtapa
ajo'pi sannavyayātmā bhūtānāmīśvaro'pi san
prakṛtiṁ svāmadhiṣṭhāya saṁbhavāmyātmamāyayā

The Blessed Lord said: Many of My births transpired, and yours, Arjuna. I recall them all. You do not remember, O scorcher of the enemies.

Even though I am birthless and My person is imperishable, and even though I am the Lord of the creatures, by controlling My material energies, I become visible by My supernatural power. (B.G. 4.5-6)

Lord Krishna becomes visible through a material body or through the action of His agent or through His parallel or alternate divine personalities who assume mundane bodies. In some cases He acts supernaturally through impersonal powers of material nature.

यानि ते चरितानीश
मनुष्याः साधवः कलौ ।
श्रृण्वन्तः कीर्तयन्तश् च
तरिष्यन्त्य् अञ्जसा तमः ॥१.२४॥

yāni te caritānīśa
manuṣyāḥ sādhavaḥ kalau
śṛṇvantaḥ kīrtayantaś ca
tariṣyanty añjasā tamaḥ (1.24)

yāni — which ever, any; te — your; caritānīśa = caritāni — pastimes + īśa — O Lord; manuṣyāh — humans beings; sādhavaḥ — saintly beings; kalau — in the era of religious deterioration; śṛṇvantah — hearing; kīrtayantaś = kīrtayantaḥ — reciting; ca — and; tariṣyanty = tariṣyanti — they will cross over; añjasā — easily; tamaḥ — the depressive influence of material nature.

Translation

Hearing and reciting any of Your pastimes, O Lord, the saintly persons will easily cross over the depressive influence in the era of religious deterioration. (1.24)

Commentary:

This verse and others are easily exploited by modern preachers who encourage followers to take a mediocre path of devotion. Some preachers know that these verses only apply to devotees with a log of austerities, but some others, honestly believe that these statements can be applied to modern devotees who lack the disciplines. The misunderstanding arises because some preachers are out of touch with the *Bhagavad Gītā* in its own historic framework. They try to transplant it into the modern setting and waiver its difficult recommendations.

Generally these preachers focus on the terms *śṛṇvantah* and *kīrtayantah*, which mean hearing and reciting or hearing and chanting. But they ignore the word *sādhavah*. They also push aside a relevant previous verse:

śuddhir nṛṇāṁ na tu tatheḍya durāśayānāṁ
vidyā-śrutādhyayana-dāna-tapaḥ-kriyābhiḥ
sattvātmanām ṛṣabha te yaśasi pravṛddha-
sac-chraddhayā śravaṇa-sambhṛtayā yathā syāt

O worshippable One, O greatest of all, technique, Vedic study, charity, austerity and mystic ritual ceremony, do not confer such purity on those whose exploitive desires are difficult to fulfill, as it does on people who have clear disposition of mind, which is acquired by a heightened regard for Your glories which are reinforced by hearing of them. (U.G. 1.9)

Even though they do not have the credit of a *sādhavah* who lived in the time when this verse was spoken by *Brahmā*, some modern preachers rate themselves and their followers as *sādhavah*.

यदु-वशे ऽवतीर्णस्य
भवतः पुरुषोत्तम ।
शरच्-छत व्यतीयाय
पञ्च-विशाधिक प्रभो ॥१.२५॥

yadu-vaṁśe 'vatīrṇasya
bhavataḥ puruṣottama
śarac-chataṁ vyatīyāya
pañca-viṁśādhikaṁ prabho (1.25)

yadu-vaṁśe — in the family of the Yadus; 'vatīrṇasya = avatīrṇasya — of the incarnation; bhavataḥ — of you; purusottama — O Supreme Person; śarac-chataṁ = sarac (śarat) – autumn + chataṁ (śataṁ) — one hundred; vyatīyāya — passed; pañca-viṁśādhikam = pañca-viṁśa — twenty-five + adhikam — more, plus; prabho — O Lord.

Translation

O Lord, O supreme Person, a hundred and twenty five autumns passed since the time of your incarnation in the family of the Yadus. (1.25)

Commentary:

As if required, *Brahmā* tactfully reminds Lord Krishna, that it is time for the Lord to move on. Krishna's services are no longer required. The supernatural rulers who work under the direction of *Brahmā*, felt that their functions were affected by the prolonged stay of Lord Krishna. They want Him to terminate the visit.

नाधुना ते ऽखिलाधार
देव-कार्यावशेषितम् ।
कुलं च विप्र-शापेन
नष्ट-प्रायम् अभूद् इदम् ॥ १.२६ ॥

nādhunā te 'khilādhāra
deva-kāryāvaśeṣitam
kulaṁ ca vipra-śāpena
naṣṭa-prāyam abhūd idam (1.26)

nādhunā = na – no + adhunā — now; te — for you; 'khilādhāra = akhiladhara = akhila — whole universe + ādhāra - support; deva-kāryāvaśesitam = deva – supernatural ruler + kārya — work + avaśeṣitam — remaining portion; kulam — dynasty; ca — and; vipra-śāpena = vipra - learned Brahmins + śāpena – by the curse; naṣṭa-prāyam = naṣṭa – destroyed + prāyam – for the most part, almost; abhūd = abhūt — was, become; idam — this

Translation

O You, support of the whole world, now You have no more work to do for the super-natural rulers, and this family also is destroyed for the most part by the curse of the learned brahmins. (1.26)

Commentary:

Despite the glorification, the purpose of this visit is to lodge a complaint to Lord Krishna about His delay in leaving the planet. The supernatural people do not want Him to stay a second longer.

ततः स्व-धाम परमं
विशस्व यदि मन्यसे ।
स-लोकाल् लोक-पालान् नः
पाहि वैकुण्ठ-किङ्करान् ॥ १.२७ ॥

tataḥ sva-dhāma paramaṁ
viśasva yadi manyase
sa-lokāl loka-pālān naḥ
pāhi vaikuṇṭha-kiṅkarān (1.27)

tataḥ — therefore; sva-dhāma — your own place; paramaṁ — supreme; viśasva — go; yadi — if; manyase you think it appropriate; sa-lokāl = sa-lokān — with the universal population; loka-pālān — the lords of these people; naḥ — us; pāhi — protect; vaikuṇṭha-kiṅkarān = vaikuṇṭha - Vaikuṇṭha + kiṅkarān — servants.

Translation

Therefore if you think it appropriate, go to Your own supreme place, and protect us, who are the lords of these peoples, together with the universal population, for we are the servants of the Vaikuṇṭha Paradise. (1.27)

Commentary:

In studying this verse carefully and digesting the various parts of it, we find some contradictions. First, *Brahmā* asked that the Lord should relocate to His supreme place. The word supreme is there in Sanskrit as *paramam*. The word for place is there as *dhāma*. That is the first request. "O Lord Krishna, please vanish from here. You have a place, the supreme location. Go there, promptly." This is in a sense a very rude and presumptuous request.

The second request is for protection: Protect (*pāhi*) us *(nah)*. But while saying this, *Brahmā* identifies the supernatural rulers as lords of people *(loka-pālān)*. This is a piece of diplomacy. To finalize the contradiction, *Brahmā* identifies the supernatural rulers as being servants of *Vaikuṇṭha* which is the name of Lord Krishna's supreme abode.

In effect, this means that the supernatural people recognize themselves as servants of Lord Krishna, but servants who serve in the material world in a place other than the supreme place of Krishna. They feel however that so long as Krishna served here as He did at the time of His advent, their serving functions would be superseded. Thus it was necessary for Krishna to depart. In addition, they asked Him to depart and to bless them. Even though He would not be physically present, Lord Krishna would also be required to extract Himself from the supernatural world.

श्री-भगवान् उवाच
अवधारितम् एतन् मे
यद् आत्थ विबुधेश्वर ।
कृत वः कार्यम् अखिलं
भूमेर् भारो ऽवतारितः ॥१.२८॥

śrī-bhagavān uvāca
avadhāritam etan me
yad āttha vibudheśvara
kṛtaṁ vaḥ kāryam akhilaṁ
bhūmer bhāro 'vatāritaḥ (1.28)

śrī bhagavān — the Blessed Lord; uvāca – said; avadhāritam — was considered; etan = etad — this; me — by me; yad = yat — that which; āttha — you propose; vibudheśvara = vibudha – supernatural rulers + īśvara — master; krtaṁ — is completed; vah — your; kāryam — assignment; akhilam — entire; bhumer = bhūmeḥ — of the earth; bhāro = bhāraḥ — burden; 'vatāritaḥ = avatāritaḥ — removed.

Translation

The Blessed Lord said: This idea, You proposed was considered by Me, O master of the supernatural rulers. Your entire assignment was completed. The burden of the earth was removed. (1.28)

Commentary:

Brahmā is addressed very respectfully by Lord Krishna. The address *Vibudheśwara*, master of the supernatural rulers, is a title that may be used for Lord Vishnu, Lord Shiva, or Lord *Brahmā*. Some used it to address a much lesser authority, the controller Indra. By addressing *Brahmā* in this way, Lord Krishna indirectly instructed all others to respect *Brahmā*.

Krishna goes a step further to report that the assignment given to Him by *Brahmā* is completed. Such great humility is sincerely displayed here by Lord Krishna.

तद् इदं यादव-कुल
वीर्य-शौर्य-श्रियोद्धतम् ।
लोक जिघृक्षद् रुद्धं मे
वेलयेव महार्णवः ॥१.२९॥

tad idaṁ yādava-kulaṁ
vīrya-śaurya-śriyoddhatam
lokaṁ jighṛkṣad ruddhaṁ me
velayeva mahārṇavaḥ (1.29)

tad idam = tat idam — this this, this particularly; yādava-kulaṁ = yādava- Yādava + kulaṁ — family; vīrya-śaurya-śriyoddhatam = vīrya — strength + śaurya — prowess + śriyā — opulence + uddhatam — haughty; lokaṁ — world; jighṛkṣad — threatening to overrun; ruddhaṁ — stopped; me — by me; velayeva = velayā — by the shore + iva — just as; mahārṇavaḥ — great ocean.

Translation

This particular Yadu family, being haughty with the opulences brought on by strength and prowess, threatens to overrun the world and is stopped by Me just as the ocean is by its shore. (1.29)

Commentary:

The particular family members of Lord Krishna who were reinforced by their strength and prowess, were not ordinary living entities and still they had to be constrained by Lord Krishna since they became haughty *(uddhatam)* by natural power *(vīrya)*. They were comparable to the ocean and so Lord Krishna acting as a shore line, kept them under control. The Lord had no intention of allowing any of them to transmigrate freely in the earthly realms.

This statement of the Lord shows clearly His keen sense of responsibility. It tells us that He personally supervises His associates. *Brahmā* and some other supernatural people were worried about the possibility that some of the powerful associates of the Lord, might stay on, transmigrating in the earthly domain. This would be a problem for the supernatural rulers since they would be unable to supervise and manage such powerful beings who were in fact more powerful than themselves or on par in terms of spiritual power. Here Lord Krishna assured that whosoever He brought into their realm, He would take with Him and whosoever was from their jurisdiction but who became boosted in His association, would soon be disempowered by Him. In that way the whole liability of Lord Krishna's presence would be neatly accommodated and the supernatural people would be logged with no extra chores in terms of management of people and resources.

The first concern indicated was the supernatural rulers worry about Lord Krishna remaining in the earthly domain for a longer period than they considered to be necessary or desirable. The second concern is the possibility that some of the other spirits who were associated with Lord Krishna and who came into this universe with Him, might stay here as stray entities who would effectively resist the influence of Brahmā's associates.

Brahmā was concerned that perhaps some of the entities who were in the jurisdiction of the supernaturals, and who joined Lord Krishna to help in His mission or to satisfy their strong attraction to Him, might remain in a condition of boosted power and would slight the supernaturals. Lord Krishna, at this point in the meeting with the supernatural people, assured their leader, Cosmic Creator *Brahmā*, that all the liabilities involved in His stay in their zone would be responsibly resolved by Him.

यद्य् असहृत्य दृप्तानां
यदूनां विपुल कुलम् ।
गन्तास्म्य् अनेन लोको ऽयम्
उद्वेलेन विनङ्क्ष्यति ॥ १.३० ॥

yady asaṁhṛtya dṛptānāṁ
yadūnāṁ vipulaṁ kulam
gantāsmy anena loko 'yaṁ
udvelena vinaṅkṣyati (1.30)

yady = yadi — if; asaṁhṛtya — without destroying; drptānām — of the proud; yadūnām — of the Yadus; vipulam — extensive; kulam — family; gantāsmy = gantāsmi — I leave; anena — for this; loko = lokaḥ — the world; 'yam = ayam — this; udvelena — by the overstepping of boundaries; vinaṅkṣyati — will be destroyed.

Translation

If I leave without destroying this extensive family of the proud Yadus, this world will be destroyed by their over-stepping of boundaries. (1.30)

Commentary:

The power of the associates of the Lord would cause some management problems for the supernatural rulers. Therefore Lord Krishna assured them, that He was aware of the possibility. He had no intention of leaving His associates behind or of supporting anyone who would stay on to challenge the supernaturals. *Brahmā* was told in so many words, that Krishna was aware of the liabilities. His advent would be concluded responsibly.

इदानीं नाश आरब्धः
कुलस्य द्विज-शाप-जः ।
यास्यामि भवनं ब्रह्मन्
एतद्-अन्ते तवानघ ॥ १.३१ ॥

idānīṁ nāśa ārabdhaḥ
kulasya dvija-śāpa-jaḥ
yāsyāmi bhavanaṁ brahmann
etad-ante tavānagha (1.31)

idānīm — now; nāśaḥ — the destruction; ārabdhah — begun; kulasya — of the family; dvija-śāpa-jaḥ - due to the curse of the brahmins; yāsyāmi — I will visit; bhavanam — the residence; brahmann — O *Brahmā*; etat-ante = etad (etat) — this + ante – at the end; tavanagha = tava — your; anagha — O sinless one.

Translation

O Brahmā, now the destruction of the family began, by due cause of the brahmins curse. At the end of this, I will visit your residence, O sinless one. (1.31)

Commentary:

The destruction of the family of Lord Krishna is a social occurrence in the material sense only. The bodies of certain family members would be destroyed, and existentially on the supernatural level, some of their rights to remain in this realm would be cancelled. Thus by supernatural force, their spirits would have to move on to other places as planned by Lord Krishna.

The Lord addressed another issue, that of visiting the subtle dimension where *Brahmā* lived. Even though *Brahmā* did not bring up the issue in the presence of the other super-natural people, even though he addressed more serious concerns such as the possibility of the Krishna's powerful associates staying on to create disruption and rivalries, *Brahmā* wanted to host Lord Krishna. Thus the Lord assured *Brahmā* that he would do so.

In a previous verse *Brahmā* appealed to Lord Krishna for protection *(pāhi)*. Lord Krishna responded in an affectionate way by addressing *Brahmā* a sinless devotee *(anagha)*.

श्री-शुक उवाच
इत्य् उक्तो लोक-नाथेन
स्वयम्-भूः प्रणिपत्य तम् ।
सह देव-गणैर् देवः
स्व-धाम समपद्यत ॥ १.३२ ॥

śrī-śuka uvāca
ity ukto loka-nāthena
svayam-bhūḥ praṇipatya tam
saha deva-gaṇair devaḥ
sva-dhāma samapadyata (1.32)

śrī-śuka = the illustrious Shuka; uvāca — said; ity = iti — thus; ukto = uktaḥ — being addressed; loka-nāthena — by the Lord of the world; svayam-bhūḥ — the self-born, Procreator Brahmā; praṇipatya — falling to offer respects; tam — to Him; saha — along with; deva-gaṇair = deva – controllers + ganair (gaṇaiḥ) – with the groups; devaḥ — the chief supernatural ruler; sva-dhāma — to his place; samapadyata — returned.

Translation

The illustrious Shuka said: Being thus addressed by the Lord of the world, The self-born person, procreator Brahmā, fell down to offer respects. Then the chief supernatural ruler, that Brahmā, returned to his place along with groups of other controllers. (1.32)

Commentary:

Brahmā is not really a *svayam-bhūh* or a person who is self *(svayam)* created or produced *(bhuh)*. Still, he became famous as *svayam bhūh* because initially the great sages, the senior entitles in the creation, could not determine his origin. They could not locate any obvious parent of *Brahmā*. They assumed that He existed without a source or producer. However later on they questioned him and *Brahmā* explained that he was produced by another person called Vishnu or *Nārāyaṇa*. This was explained by Shuka in the *Śrīmad Bhāgavatam*.

After offering respects to Lord Krishna, *Brahmā* and the other supernatural people returned to their respective domains in the subtle world.

अथ तस्यां महोत्पातान्
द्वारवत्यां समुत्थितान् ।
विलोक्य भगवान् आह
यदु-वृद्धान् समागतान् ॥ १.३३ ॥

atha tasyāṁ mahotpātān
dvāravatyāṁ samutthitān
vilokya bhagavān āha
yadu-vṛddhān samāgatān (1.33)

atha — then; tasyām — in that; mahotpātān — great calamities; dvāravatyām — in Dvārakā; samutthitān — overtaking; vilokya — observing; bhagavān — the Blessed Lord; āha — spoke; yadu-vṛddhān — to the elder of the Yadus; samāgatān — assembled.

Translation

Then observing great calamities overtaking Dvārakā City, the Blessed Lord spoke to the assembled elders of the Yadus. (1.33)

Commentary:

The destruction of the city of *Dvārakā* is not unfortunate. It is fortunate. It shows clearly the responsible capacity of the Supreme Being. It might appear to be unfortunate, if we consider it from the body-survival viewpoint.

It appears that material nature herself, felt a bit uncomfortable. The earth herself was a bit concerned about the possibility of the powerful associates of Lord Krishna staying here. Certain reactions were triggered. Some movement of the area of *Dvārakā* manifested as earthquakes.

श्री-भगवान् उवाच
एते वै सु-महोत्पाता
व्युत्तिष्ठन्तीह सर्वतः ।
शापश् च नः कुलस्यासीद्
ब्राह्मणेभ्यो दुरत्ययः ॥ १.३४ ॥

śrī-bhagavān uvāca
ete vai su-mahotpātā
vyuttiṣṭhantīha sarvataḥ
śāpaś ca naḥ kulasyāsīd
brāhmaṇebhyo duratyayaḥ (1.34)

śrī-bhagavān – the Blessed Lord; uvāca — said; ete — these; vai — indeed; su-mahotpātā = su + mahā + uppātāḥ— a very great calamities; vyuttiṣṭhantiha = vyuttisthanti – occur + iha — in this place; sarvatah — everywhere; śāpaś = śāpaḥ — curse; ca — and; nah — our; kulasyāsīd = kulasya — of the family + āsīd (āsīt) — was; brāhmaṇebhyo = brāhmaṇebhyaḥ— by the Brahmis; duratyayaḥ— near impossible to counteract.

Translation

The Blessed Lord said, Indeed these great calamities occur everywhere in this place. The curse of our family which was issued by the brahmins is near impossible to counteract. (1.34)

Commentary:

Here Lord Krishna tells His social elders, that the curse issued on the family by some powerful sages, took effect. These social elders are spirits who used bodies which were older than Lord Krishna's physical form. As a matter of formality, The Lord respected and served the bodies of these spirits who took forms in the Yadu family. He brings to their attention that the catastrophes can not be counteracted. Some say however that Lord Krishna could have nullified the curse, but the term *duratyayah* means very difficult to counteract.

The right of the Supreme Being is the right of clarity to see exactly what can and cannot be done. Some feel however that the Supreme Being is a whimsical agent who can act haphazardly to show supreme power or to override all other realities.

The Supreme Being comprehends the various laws of nature which apply in each spiritual, supernatural or mundane dimension. As such, He does not get trapped in whimsical demonstrations of power just to counteract or waiver circumstances. That is not His primary concern. He is more concerned to honor and facilitate laws.

The word *duratyayah* also means that which is difficult *(dur)* to counteract, or that which, if counteracted would produce another reaction in another undesirable way. Even for the Supreme Being there is no point in digging a hole to fill another one, since by doing so He would only have created another problem.

Lord Krishna impressed upon the elders that He would not attempt to stop the curse. These elders were in the habit of engaging either Krishna, or His brother, *Balarāma*, in their service, but at this point Krishna stopped this. He directly told them: "This particular problem will not be adjusted by Me. We must accept it."

न वस्तव्यम् इहास्माभिर्
जिजीविषुभिर् आर्यकाः ।
प्रभासं सु-महत्-पुण्यं
यास्यामो ऽद्यैव मा चिरम् ॥ १.३५॥

na vastavyam ihāsmābhir
jijīviṣubhir āryakāḥ
Prabhāsaṁ su-mahat-puṇyaṁ
yāsyāmo 'dyaiva mā ciram (1.35)

na – not; vastavyam — should live; ihāsmābhir = iha — here + āsmābhir (asmābhiḥ)— we; jijīviṣubhir = jijīviṣubhiḥ — desire to survive; āryakāḥ— O respectful elders; Prabhāsam — to Prabhāsa; su-mahat-puṇyaṁ = su-mahat — very much, exceedingly + puṇyaṁ — holy; yāsyāmo = yāsyāmaḥ — we should go; 'dyaiva = 'dya (adya) — now + eva — even; mā ciram — no delay.

Translation

O respectful elders, we should not live here if we desire to survive. We should go immediately to the exceedingly holy Prabhāsa. Let there be no delay. (1.35)

Commentary:

To satisfy the tradition of the time, Lord Krishna recommended that the male family members go on pilgrimage to a holy place named *Prabhāsa*. This was not to avert the disaster nor to stop the reaction. It was to fulfill the curse. It might seem that Lord Krishna prescribed an action that would nullify some of the reaction but as history would have it, this action only asserted the power of the curse. So in this case, the Supreme Being accepted the reaction.

The desire to survive *(jijīviṣubhir)* is mentioned but the question is: To survive for how long? Even if they go to *Prabhāsa* to avoid the natural disasters which would destroy *Dvārakā*, still how much longer would they live? A personal conflict with destiny cannot be averted, merely by relocating to another place, or by visiting a shrine.

Once a man who lived in South America was assured by a seer that he would be killed by a horse. Thinking that the seer meant an animal, the man relocated to England. And there a jackstay plank, which is called a horse by British construction workers, fell on his head and killed his body. He relocated but it did not avert destiny. The Yadu People are merely going to get closer to their destiny by going to *Prabhāsa* and Lord Krishna knew it. Since the tendency was to follow tradition in terms of atoning for and possibly nullifying a curse, the Blessed Lord did not object to their plans.

यत्र स्नात्वा दक्ष-शापाद्
गृहीतो यक्ष्मणोदु-राट् ।
विमुक्तः किल्बिषात् सद्यो
भेजे भूयः कलोदयम् ॥ १.३६॥

yatra snātvā dakṣa-śāpād
gṛhīto yakṣmaṇodu-rāṭ
vimuktaḥ kilbiṣāt sadyo
bheje bhūyaḥ kalodayam (1.36)

yatra — where; snātvā — bathing; dakṣa-śāpād = Dakṣa-śāpāt — due to the curse of Procreator Dakṣa; gṛhīto = gṛhītaḥ— afflicted; yakṣmaṇoḍu-rāṭ = yakṣmaṅa — lung disease + udu-rāt— the king of stars, Chandra Moon Ruler; vimuktaḥ— freed; kilbiṣāt — from sinful reaction; sadyo = sadyaḥ— instantly; bheje — he assumed; bhūyaḥ — again; kalodayam = kala — phases + udayam — occurence.

Translation

At the shrine where after taking bath, Chandra, the moon ruler, king of stars, who was afflicted with the consumptive lung disease due to Procreator's Dakṣa curse, was instantly freed from the sinful reaction and again experienced the occurrence of his phase. (1.36)

Commentary:

Even though this suggestion was made by Lord Krishna, he did not mean that the curse would be averted on the physical plane, but rather he meant that the curse should be reconciled by a pious activity and by a mood of repentance for the insult the Yadu boys committed on the brahmins.

The curse was issued because the powerful children of the Yadu family did not feel that they had to respect others. Lord Krishna did not agree with their view. After all, even though, their relative was the Supreme Being and though parallel Godhead personalities like Lord *Balarāma* were in their association, still they had no right to tease the sages.

The elder Yadus, by the instruction of Lord Krishna, would be freed from any direct or indirect participation in offending the great sages who *Sāmba* teased. Thus by that repentance at *Prabhāsa*, they would be freed from any implication, just as Chandra the moon ruler, King of stars, was freed from the curse issued against him by Procreator *Dakṣa*.

वय च तस्मिन्न् आप्लुत्य
तर्पयित्वा पितॄन् सुरान् ।
भोजयित्वोषिजो विप्रान्
नाना-गुणवतान्धसा ॥ १.३७॥

vayaṁ ca tasminn āplutya
tarpayitvā pitṝn surān
bhojayitvoṣijo viprān
nānā-guṇavatāndhasā (1.37)

vayaṁ — we; ca — and; tasminn = tasmin — at that place; āplutya — bathing; tarpayitvā — offering libations of water; pitṝn — departed ancestors; surān — supernatural rulers; bhojayitvosijo = bhojayitvā — feeding + uṣijo (uṣijaḥ) — gifted; viprān — the brahmins; nānā-guṇavatāndhasā = nānā — various + guṇa-vatā — having tastes, tasting + andhasā — with food.

Translation

And we, after bathing at that place, offering libations of water to the departed ancestors and the supernatural rulers, feeding the gifted brahmins, with tasty food, (1.37)

Commentary:

The suggestion is that despite the curse of the brahmins, there are dissatisfactions felt by the departed ancestors.

Many of those departed souls got new bodies but many did not. Those who did not were frustrated in the desire for rebirth. They were still hopeful of getting bodies in the Yadu family line. In addition some other brahmins who were not involved in the curse, wanted to associate with the Yadus and wanted to benefit from their political administration.

तेषु दानानि पात्रेषु
श्रद्धयोप्त्वा महान्ति वै ।
वृजिनानि तरिष्यामो
दानैर् नौभिर् इवार्णवम् ॥ १.३८॥

teṣu dānāni pātreṣu
śraddhayoptvā mahānti vai
vṛjināni tariṣyāmo
dānair naubhir ivārṇavam (1.38)

teṣu — in them; dānāni — gifts; pātreṣu — for those worthy persons; śraddhayoptvā = śraddhayā — faithful + uptvā — offering; mahānti — great; vai — indeed; vṛjināni — the sins; tariṣyāmo = tariṣyāmah— we will compensate; dānair = dānaih — by charity; naubhir = naubhiḥ— with boats; ivārṇavam = iva — just as + arṇavam — the ocean.

Translation

...faithfully offering gifts to those worthy persons, will by the charity, compensate the sins, just as crossing the ocean with boats. (1.38)

Commentary:

As in crossing the ocean, one requires a boat, and as even when using boats one should be cautious because of the possibility of mishaps, so when living in the material world, everyone should be careful with fit or worthy people. If one offends, disrespects, or slights worthy people, one gets an undesirable reaction.

This applies to both the limited beings and the Supreme Being as well. Even the Supreme Being is careful in dealing with worthy persons. Even He cannot slight such people without having to compensate for it. The primary meaning of *pātra (pātram)* is container. But as applied to personalities, the word means those persons who act as containers or those persons who are fit to receive something. Just as a clean cup is fit for milk and a bag is fit to receive items, so a worthy person is fit to receive particular services.

Some Yadu boys slighted some sages instead of serving them, thus an offense was committed for which the whole energy, even Lord Krishna, the Supreme Being, reacted. The reaction came but still there was to be an atonement. It is this atonement only that Lord Krishna stressed. His effort may be interpreted as a means of counteraction, but it is rather, an atonement.

The Yadu children wanted to test the foresight of the great sages. This desire of theirs was offensive. With great sages, particularly great yogi sages, one is supposed to desire only one thing; their instruction for service. Otherwise one should never desire to utilize them. It is a common mistake for well-to-do people to try to use saintly or ascetic people. The well-to-do feel that even though the saintly and ascetic people are versed in religion and austerity still they are not superior because they are not expert in acquiring money. But the acquirement of money is an expression of our predatory animal instincts.

To acquire money one has to exploit the resources of material nature and to do so one must engage other human beings as servants, employees or laborers. To achieve this, one must offend the whole existence. Thus money is not a sign of superiority. It represents the animal instincts. We cannot run a society without money but the facility of capitalism furthers our animal instinct. Ultimately, it causes the expansion of the greedy nature. Under the influence of an ever-expanding greedy mentality, we choke ourselves off by mistreating higher entities.

श्री-शुक उवाच
एव भगवतादिष्टा
यादवाः कुरु-नन्दन ।
गन्तुं कृत-धियस् तीर्थ
स्यन्दनान् समयूयुजन् ॥१.३९॥

śrī-śuka uvāca
evaṁ bhagavatādiṣṭā
yādavāḥ kuru-nandana
gantuṁ kṛta-dhiyas tīrthaṁ
syandanān samayūyujan (1.39)

śrī-śuka – the illustrious Shuka; uvāca - said; evaṁ — thus; bhagavatādiṣṭā = bhagavatā — by the Blessed Lord + ādistāh — advised; yādavāḥ— the Yadavas; kuru-nandana — O pet son of the Kurus; gantum — to go; kṛta-dhiyas — having made the decision; tīrtham — holy place; syandanān — chariots; samayūyujan — they yoked their horses.

Translation

The illustrious Shuka said, O pet son of the Kurus, being thus advised by the Blessed Lord, the Yādavas, made the decision and yoked the horses to go to the holy place. (1.39)

Commentary:

In material existence there is always going to be a cutoff point, some last act, before the body dies. Thus these Yadus yoked their horses at *Dvārakā* for the last time. Whatever pastimes they enjoyed here were terminated, at least on this physical level of existence. It was over. This chapter of their lives reached a terminal point.

Death is not really related to being sick or healthy. It is a matter of time. Thus even a healthy man may one day, rise from bed, get dressed, step out of his house and drop dead. The meaning is that his subtle body has stepped out of a particular gross form for the last time. And thus from the physical perspective people regard it as death. The person lives in fact but in this world he is unable to animate his physical form.

As these Yadus taken to the terminal point by Lord Krishna, being directly supervised by Him, so we are being supervised by supernatural persons who wield mystic power. Under their authority we are conveyed to the terminal point. There is absolutely nothing we can do to prevent this. In the meantime, until we arrive there, we should try our best to take advantage of these bodies by cultivating spiritual realization.

तन् निरीक्ष्योद्धवो राजन्
श्रुत्वा भगवतोदितम् ।
दृष्ट्वारिष्टानि घोराणि
नित्यं कृष्णम् अनुव्रतः ॥ १.४० ॥

tan nirīkṣyoddhavo rājan
śrutvā bhagavatoditam
dṛṣṭvāriṣṭāni ghorāṇi
nityaṁ kṛṣṇam anuvrataḥ (1.40)

tan = tat — that; nirīkṣyoddhavo = nirīkṣya – seeing + uddhavo (uddhavaḥ) - Uddhava; rājan — O King; śrutvā — after hearing; bhagavatoditam = bhagavatā — by the Blessed Lord + uditam — was said; dṛṣṭvāriṣṭāni = dṛṣṭvā – observing + ariṣṭāni- bad omen; ghorāṇi — horrible; nityaṁ — always; kṛṣṇam — Krishna; anuvrataḥ - a devoted follower.

Translation

O King, seeing this, hearing what was said by the Blessed Lord, observing the bad omens which were horrible, Uddhava who was always devoted to Krishna, (1.40)

Commentary:

Every spirit perceives in its own way and draws its own conclusions even while observing the same conditions or circumstances. Uddhava saw what transpired, heard what Krishna told the Yadu elders and formed an opinion of what he should do. He had a feeling that the instruction given to the elders, was not for him.

Uddhava is qualified as *anuvrata*, a devoted follower. He was more deserving of the association of Lord Krishna.

विविक्त उपसङ्गम्य
जगताम् ईश्वरेश्वरम् ।
प्रणम्य शिरिसा पादौ
प्राञ्जलिस् तम् अभाषत ॥ १.४१ ॥

vivikta upasaṅgamya
jagatām īśvareśvaram
praṇamya śirisā pādau
prāñjalis tam abhāṣata (1.41)

vivikta — in a secluded; upasaṅgamya — approaching; jagatām — of the worlds; īśvareśvaram — the Lords of lords; pranamya — bowing down; śirasā — with his head; pādau — at the feet; prāñjalis = prāñjaliḥ— with palms pressed together; tam — to him; abhāṣata — spoke.

Translation

...approached the Lord of lords of the worlds in a secluded place, bowing down, with his head at the Lord's feet with palms pressed together, Uddhava spoke. (1.41)

Commentary:

Uddhava regarded the Lord with more respect that many other Yadus. He regarded Lord Krishna as the Lord of the lords of the worlds *(jagatām īśvareśvaram).* Some Yadus glorified Lord Krishna but considered Him to be their dear relative only. Uddhava had a different view.

श्री-उद्धव उवाच
देव-देवेश योगेश
पुण्य-श्रवण-कीर्तन ।
सहृत्यैतत् कुलं नूनं
लोकं सन्त्यक्ष्यते भवान् ।
विप्र-शापं समर्थो ऽपि
प्रत्यहन् न यद् ईश्वरः ॥ १.४२ ॥

śrī-uddhava uvāca
deva-deveśa yogeśa
puṇya-śravaṇa-kīrtana
saṁhṛtyaitat kulaṁ nūnaṁ
lokaṁ santyakṣyate bhavān
vipra-śāpaṁ samartho 'pi
pratyahan na yad īśvaraḥ (1.42)

śrī-uddhavah = the deserving Uddhava; uvāca — said; deva-deveśa — O God of the greatest rulers of the supernatural kings; yogeśa — O master of yoga disciplines; puṇya-śravana-kīrtana = puṇya — auspicious + śravana – hearing + kīrtana — chanting; samhṛtyaitat = samhṛtya – destroying + etat — this; kulaṁ — family; nūnaṁ — surely; lokaṁ — the world; santyakṣyate — will quit; bhavān — you; vipra-śāpaṁ — the curse of the exalted brahmins; samartho = samarthaḥ — capable; 'pi = api — although; pratyahan — counteract; na — not; yad = yat – which; īśvaraḥ — Lord.

Translation

O God of the greatest rulers of the supernatural kings, O master of the yoga disciplines, O person of whom it is auspicious to hear of and chant about, surely You will quit the world after destroying this family line, for you did not counteract the brahmin's curse, even though You were capable of doing so. (1.42)

Commentary:

Uddhava's opinion is that Lord Krishna was capable of counteracting the curse of the brahmins upon the Yadu family. How the Lord would have done so, Uddhava did not explain. Any opinion of Uddhava or of any other outstanding and reliable devotee, even that of Arjuna and even those opinions given by the supernatural people, must be carefully considered. These views may not be absolute. Personal views about Lord Krishna might relate to the time and place and to the nature and needs of the particular devotee who glorifies the Lord. It is not that Lord Krishna could not counteract the curse, but how would He have done so? This was not stated by Uddhava.

At this point also, Uddhava did not state why he felt Lord Krishna decided not to nullify the curse. Nullifying a curse can also mean taking an action which creates another reaction. That type of nullification, even if done by the Supreme Being, creates another reaction, like digging one hole to fill a depression. So long as the material energy is in a reactionary state, any action of any person, even one of the Supreme Personality, causes reactions. These actions may be regarded as fresh motivations for more actions.

The visit of the supernatural people and their concern about Lord Krishna's departure from the material world, is a case study of this. First they invited Lord *Nārāyaṇa*, the father of *Brahmā*, to come into the world to rectify a bad condition, which they could not alter. Lord Krishna came by that request. However after Krishna removed the obstacles, the supernatural people wanted Him to go away.

In addition, even though the Lord's associates assisted Him in removing the obstacles, still many of them were obstacles to be removed. The Lord took advantage of the natural violence in the material world, to get them off the planet and to transfer them into other dimensions where their existence would not interfere with the duties of supernatural rulers.

Uddhava's conclusion is that since Lord Krishna did nothing to nullify the curse, the Lord must have planned to use that unfavorable turn of events. Uddhava addressed the Lord as master of the yoga disciplines *(yogeśa)* and as the person of whom it is auspicious to hear and chant of.

These titles will be explained in more detail further on in the discourse.

नाहं तवाङ्घ्रि-कमलं
क्षणार्धम् अपि केशव ।
त्यक्तुं समुत्सहे नाथ
स्व-धाम नय माम् अपि ॥ १.४३ ॥

nāhaṁ tavāṅghri-kamalaṁ
kṣaṇārdham api keśava
tyaktuṁ samutsahe nātha
sva-dhāma naya mām api (1.43)

naham = na — not + aham — I; tavanghri-kamalam = tava — your + anghri-kamalaṁ — lotus feet; kṣaṇārdham = kṣaṇa — of a moment + ardham — half; api — even; keśava — O Person with the finest quality hair; tyaktuṁ — to give up; samutsahe — I can bear; nātha — O Lord; sva-dhāma — your territory; naya — take; mām — me; api — also.

Translation

O Person with the finest quality hair, I cannot bear to give up your lotus feet for even half of a second. Take me also, O Lord to Your territory. (1.43)

Commentary:

Uddhava assumed that Lord Krishna planned to take other Yadus, whose bodies were killed in the destruction of *Dvārakā* or whose bodies were killed at *Prabhāsa* by the force of the brahmins' curse. Sensing that he was not included in that plan to travel with Krishna after losing the material body, Uddhava made this appeal.

It is interesting that Uddhava suspected that Lord Krishna would relocate the Yadus to Krishna's private existential domain *(sva-dhāma)*. For one thing, all the Yadus whose bodies would perish would not all go to Krishna's territory. Some would remain in the material world. A devotee does not go to Krishna's territory merely because his material body is killed. Even a great devotee may not go to Krishna's territory even if his body is destroyed. Thus this assumption of Uddhava is a generalization only. Uddhava panicked. He was paranoid about His own security in reference to Lord Krishna. He did not desire to remain transmigrating in material bodies. He wanted to go wherever Krishna might go in whatever appearance Krishna might adopt so that He could be visually in touch with Lord Krishna always.

This particular sentiment of Uddhava is called the feeling of separation from the Lord. There are varying degrees of this separation. There are also varying qualities and flavors of it, according to the relation of the devotee to the Lord as well as according to the expectation which the devotee holds of the Lord.

Lord Krishna is addressed here as Keshava. This has two meanings as the killer of Keshi, a demonical horse or as a person with the finest quality hair. Some translators gave the former meaning.

This appeal of Uddhava is saturated with emotional attachment to the visual bodily presence of Lord Krishna. By bodily presence, I mean the local dimensional bodily appearance. It cannot be a sentiment relating to Lord Krishna's spiritual body in total since on the spiritual plane there is no threat of conclusion or separation. If Uddhava, was at this time, in touch with the Lord's spiritual body in total, he would not have felt this way, since Krishna's spiritual body could not be erased out of manifestation, only Lord Krishna's materially-manifest form could. Since Uddhava was at the time, focused on that materially manifested form, he was scared of its demise. He felt that he would not be able to keep track of Lord Krishna's movement in other manifested bodies or in the eternal spiritual form of the Lord. Thus in the grip of emotions, he made a desperate appeal to Lord Krishna. Obviously, Uddhava suffered terribly in anticipation of Krishna's physical absence.

तव विक्रीडितं कृष्ण	tava vikrīḍitaṁ kṛṣṇa
नृनां परम-मङ्गलम् ।	nṛnāṁ parama-maṅgalam
कर्ण-पीयूषम् आसाद्य	karṇa-pīyūṣam āsādya
त्यजन्त्य् अन्य-स्पृहां जनाः ॥ १.४४ ॥	tyajanty anya-spṛhāṁ janāḥ (1.44)

tava — your; vikrīḍitam — spiritual activities; kṛṣṇa — O Krishna; nṛṇām — for human beings; parama-mangalam = parama – highest + mangalam – good; karṇa-pīyūṣam = karṇa —ears + pīyūṣam — nectar; āsādya — having tasted; tyajanty = tyajanti — they give up; anya-spṛhām = anya — other + sprhām — desires; janāḥ — persons.

Translation

O Krishna, tasting Your sportive activities, which yield the highest good for human beings and which is like nectar to the ears, people give up their other desires. (1.44)

Commentary:

Even though there are exceptions to the rule, people have a good chance of giving up their other desires if they were to hear of the sportive activities of Lord Krishna. They may develop a liking for the Lord and may apply the advice given to Arjuna or to Uddhava.

By nature a human being is willing to aspire and work for desires. Once an idea is implanted in the mind, a human being is likely to work to achieve it. And so if he gets the idea of the association of Lord Krishna, there is a likelihood that he would want to satisfy the requests of the Supreme Lord.

Uddhava made this general statement. Similar statements by him and by other great devotees of Krishna are stressed and overstressed by some preachers. We must understand however that this is an opinion of Uddhava. And as such we have to consider the scope of his view. The reality is that for some persons, the taste of Krishna's sportive activities, is not like nectar. Some experience a bitterness in it. They cling tighter to other activities after hearing about Lord Krishna. These are realizations which contradict the view of Uddhava.

शय्यासनाटन-स्थान-	śayyāsanāṭana-sthāna-
स्नान-क्रीडाशनादिषु ।	snāna-krīḍāśanādiṣu
कथ त्वां प्रियम् आत्मानं	kathaṁ tvāṁ priyam ātmānaṁ
वयं भक्तास् त्यजेम हि ॥ १.४५ ॥	vayaṁ bhaktās tyajema hi (1.45)

śayyāsanāṭana-sthāna-snāna-krīḍāśanādiṣu = śayyā — lying down + āsana — sitting + aṭana — walking + sthāna — standing + snāna — bathing + krīḍā — sporting + āśana — eating + ādiṣu — and in other activities; katham — how; tvām — you; priyam — dear; ātmānam — of our spirits, of ourselves; vayaṁ — we; bhaktās = bhaktāḥ — devotees; tyajema — can give up; hi — indeed.

Translation

How can we, your devotees, give up your company in lying down, sitting, walking, standing, bathing, sporting, eating and in other activities shared, for You are dear and are of ourselves. (1.45)

Commentary:

The previous statement of Uddhava, is qualified in this verse by the term *bhaktās*, devotees. It is the devotees and the potential devotees, who feel that way about Lord Krishna. Others have different views and would rather not hear about Him. Certain devotees who are on par with or more advanced than Uddhava, are ever in touch with the Lord in one way or the other. Some others contact Him periodically. It varies. The degree of affinity with Lord Krishna is dependent on the status of a devotee, his affinity for the Lord, his existential status, his existential relation with Krishna and his mundane involvements.

त्वयोपभुक्त-स्रग्-गन्ध-
वासो-ऽलङ्कार-चर्चिताः ।
उच्छिष्ट-भोजिनो दासास्
तव मायां जयेम हि ॥ १.४६ ॥

tvayopabhukta-srag-gandha-
vāso-'laṅkāra-carcitāḥ
ucchiṣṭa-bhojino dāsās
tava māyāṁ jayema hi (1.46)

tvayopabhukta-srag-gandha-vāso-'lankāra-carcitāḥ = tvayā — by your + upabhukta — already used + srag (srak) — garlands + gandha — fragrances + vāso (vāsaḥ) — garments + 'lankāra (alankāra) — ornaments + carcitāḥ — adorned; ucchiṣṭa — remnants of food + bhojino (bhojinaḥ) — eating; dāsās = dāsāḥ — servants; tava — your; māyām — bewildering mundane potency; jayema — we will conquer; hi — indeed.

Translation

By being adorned in the garlands, fragrances and ornaments which were used by You and by eating the remnants of Your food, we Your servants, will indeed conquer Your bewildering mundane potency. (1.46)

Commentary:

This is another opinion of Uddhava. It is an opinion that was endorsed by other great devotees before, during and after the time of Uddhava. Thus in these modern times, some Vaishnava leaders stress such statements assuring followers that their spiritual transfer to Krishna's location was guaranteed once they accepted garlands which adorned the Deity form of Lord Krishna or once they acquired or purchased ornaments which were used for decoration of the Deity form. Some say that merely by eating the remnants of food offered to the Deity, a human being is saved immediately, just as *Nārada* Muni was when he ate the remnants of some great advanced transcendentalists whom he and his mother served.

If this opinion of Uddhava, which is confirmed by other great devotees and which is demonstrated in the life of *Nārada*, is an absolute view, then it is merely a question of time. In other words will a devotee, who used the remnants of offering to the Lord, conquer Krishna's bewildering mundane potency? In which life, will he conquer it? How long will it take for him to do so?

Another important consideration is this: What value is there in the different degrees of such offerings, in regards to who made the offering and under what condition? Unless these questions are answered perfectly, we cannot pronounce absolute statements about these verses. It is seen that many preachers who stress these verses, do so out of an artificial confidence and out of the need to influence the public to join a specific society and support it.

We should consider this: If a person like Uddhava, who lived with Lord Krishna, who saw the Lord daily, and who was a greatly advanced yogi and philosopher, if he made these assurances and if he also must ask Lord Krishna about His passage to Krishna's territories, then it tells us that Uddhava did not assume that he would be automatically transferred to Krishna's place. It means that even Uddhava must be attentive and particular in his relationship with Krishna.

वात-वसना य ऋषयः
श्रमणा ऊर्ध्व -मन्थिनः ।
ब्रह्माख्यं धाम ते यान्ति
शान्ताः सन्न्यासीनो ऽमलाः ॥ १.४७ ॥

vāta-vasanā ya ṛṣayaḥ
śramaṇā ūrdhva-manthinaḥ
brahmākhyaṁ dhāma te yānti
śāntāḥ sannyāsīno 'malāḥ (1.47)

vāta-vasanāḥ — those who survive on air; ya — who; ṛṣayaḥ — yogi sages; śramanā = śramanāḥ — ascetis; ūrdhva-manthinah — those whose semen is conserved to reach their brains; brahmākhyaṁ — known as brahman spiritual existence; dhāma — zone; te — they; yānti — go; śāntāḥ — serene; sannyāsīno = sannyāsinaḥ — those who renounced social oppurtunities; 'malāḥ = amalāh — without flaws, those whose flaws are eliminated.

Translation

Yogi sages who survived on air, who are ascetics and whose semen is conserved to reach their brains, who are serene, who renounce social opportunities and whose flaws are eliminated, go to the brahman spiritual zone. (1.47)

Commentary:

Here is another tricky and over-used statement used by some Vaishnava preachers, especially by those who do not perform yoga and who do not believe in the necessity for yoga practice. They usually segregate yogis from devotees. In the *Bhagavad Gītā*, such discrimination is not advocated and still many Vaishnava leaders indicate that if a human being is a devotee he is not a yogi and if he is a yogi he is not a devotee. Here Uddhava in his own view, for one reason or the other, imaged such a bias. To make matters worse, Uddhava was somewhat versed in yoga practice, a practice that Lord Krishna advised him to perfect, when the Lord sent him to the Badari Ashram in the Himalayan region.

It may be said that if a person tends to spiritual purification or to the purification of the subtle body and causal intentions in relating to this material world, he would have to put aside devotion to Lord Krishna, and therefore he could not function as a devotee. Such a view, however, is artificial in the final analysis but it does have some basis in fact. In the *Bhagavad Gītā*, Lord Krishna made it clear that His work *(karma),* His discipline, His Yoga, is the work done by the yogi kings like *Janak* who acted as benevolent rulers of human society.

Arjuna was inspired to do Krishna's work on the battlefield. Thus if Arjuna refused and if he shifted to yoga practice for personal purification as yogis do, then Arjuna would have neglected Lord Krishna. However this line of reasoning is incomplete. Self-purification is also Krishna's work. Krishna supervises that also. The contention that a yogi is a yogi and that he is different from a devotee, is misleading. We should analyze to see if the austerities of the yogi assist Krishna's work. One may be a yogi and be a devotee, and one may be a devotee and not be a yogi. But it is not true that all yogis are non-devotees, nor that all devotees are definitely not yogis.

Yogi sages who survive on air, are certainly not going to be helping Krishna on the battlefield as Arjun did. But that does not mean that they are not helping Lord Krishna in another area of His work *(karma)*. Those yogis whose semen is conserved to reach their brains may also qualify as devotees of Krishna. Those who renounce social opportunities and whose flaws of character are for the most part removed, may also be helping in Krishna's work. Their transfer to the brahman spiritual zone is not necessarily a denial of Krishna's association.

वय त्व् इह महा-योगिन्
भ्रमन्तः कर्म-वर्त्मसु ।
त्वद्-वार्तया तरिष्यामस्
तावकैर् दुस्तर तमः ॥१.४८॥

vayaṁ tv iha mahā-yogin
bhramantaḥ karma-vartmasu
tvad-vārtayā tariṣyāmas
tāvakair dustaraṁ tamaḥ (1.48)

vayam — we; tv = tu — but; iha — here, in this world; mahā-yogin — O great yogi; bhramantaḥ — wandering; karma-vartmasu — in the paths of cultural activities; tvad-vārtayā = tvad (tvat) — of you + vārtayā — by discussion; tariṣyāmas = tariṣyāmaḥ — will transcend; tāvakair = tāvakaiḥ — with your devotees; dustaram — difficult to penetrate; tamaḥ — depressive influence of material nature.

Translation

But O great yogi, we who are wandering in this world on the paths of cultural activities, will transcend the depressive influence of material nature, which is difficult to penetrate, by discussion about You with Your devotees, (1.48)

Commentary:

Mahāyogin means a great yogi. This means one who demonstrates practically, the benefits of yoga disciplines. But Lord Krishna is one of the great yogis. He is a very special one. There are others who are led by Lord Shiva, Lord *Brahmā*, Lord *Gaṇesh*, Lord *Karttikeya*, *Vashiṣṭha* Rishi, *Agastya* Muni, *Mataṅga* Rishi, *Śrīla Vyāsadeva*, his father *Parāśar* Muni, and Shuka who explained *Śrīmad Bhāgavatam* to King *Parīkṣit*.

Uddhava was frank when he addressed Lord Krishna as a great yogi, because Uddhava was aware of many other accomplished yogis who could free a human being by their prescriptions of yoga disciplines. But again, Lord Krishna is a special great yogi.

The specialty of Lord Krishna in being a practical, consistent and eternal great yogi is this: The Lord does not become confused even when He transmigrates. He explained this in the *Bhagavad Gītā*, by stating that His memory of past births remains intact, while for Arjuna such a prolonged and systemic recall is not possible. Categorically and existentially, Arjuna could not remember former births but Krishna could recall His own as well as Arjuna's. Krishna could view anyone else's previous births.

Even while Lord Krishna wandered from dimension to dimension on the paths of cultural activities which He termed to be His work or His yoga, He transcended the depressive influence of material nature which adversely affects the limited spirits. From place to place, Krishna pursued His own agenda, satisfying His own priorities in these material worlds but without jeopardizing His spirituality.

Uddhava claimed that merely by discussing Krishna pastimes, the devotees like Uddhava would transcend the depressive influence of material nature. However this may or may not be an absolute statement. Uddhava may have found this to be true for himself and for others who were in Krishna's direct association but is it true for every other devotee without exception? Do we actually transcend the depressive influence merely by talking about what Krishna did or by studying and trying to apply His philosophy in *Bhagavad Gītā*? The honest answer is that only in some cases is a devotee able to completely transcend the depressive mode and in other cases a devotee can do so for a short time only. This statement of Uddhava is not absolute, otherwise we would not see devotees become bogged down in material existence even after discussing the pastimes and philosophy of Lord Krishna.

रगरन्तः कीर्तयन्तस् ते
कृतानि गदितानि च ।
गत्यु-उत्स्मितेक्षण-क्ष्वेलि
यन् नृ-लोक-विडम्बनम् ॥ १.४९ ॥

smarantaḥ kīrtayantas te
kṛtāni gaditāni ca
gaty-utsmitekṣaṇa-kṣveli
yan nṛ-loka-viḍambanam (1.49)

smarantah — remembering; kīrtayantas — glorifying; te — your; kṛtāni — activities; gaditāni — words; ca — and; gaty-utsmitekṣaṇa-kṣveli = gaty (gati) — movements + utsmita — smiles + īkṣaṇa — glances + ksveli — playful pastimes; yan = yat — which; nṛ-loka-viḍambanam = nṛ-loka — world + viḍambanam — imitation.

Translation

...and by remembering and glorifying Your activities, and words, Your movements, smiles, glances and playful pastimes in imitation of the human beings. (1.49)

Commentary:

Uddhava continued to describe those activities, gestures and relationships with Lord Krishna which cause the associates to transcend the depressive influence of material nature. These devotees were in the physical presence of Lord Krishna in Dwāraka, Mathurā , Vṛndāvana, Hastinapura and other places. What was true to Uddhava is not necessarily true for all other devotees in all other times and places. First of all, some other devotees are not in the Krishna's physical, supernatural or spiritual presence in the same way and to the same degree as Uddhava. Despite these truths, this statement of Uddhava is a bright light. It is an inspiration to attain Krishna's association.

An important aspect is this: A devotee, even a great devotee like Arjuna, may get into the direct association of Lord Krishna and then for one reason or the other, be put out of it and not be able to keep himself in spiritual touch with the Lord. And for as long as he is unable to reconnect, the depressive influence might prevail over him. We heard that even in the physical presence of Lord Krishna, as great a devotee as Arjuna, lost touch with the spiritual security that is suggested by Uddhava in these verses. Such a loss should be studied by all devotees who aspire for the result of being permanently freed from the depressive influence.

In these purports, my intention is not to discourage anyone from Krishna worship but to show any realities which I may discover or be inspired to see in the discourse. I have no need to con anyone nor to give anyone a false idea, false hope, or expectation about Krishna's association. Krishna is my primal Deity but that does not mean that I am going to fantasize about Krishna or misrepresent the realities of His association.

श्री-शुक उवाच
एव विज्ञापितो राजन्
भगवान् देवकी-सुतः ।
एकान्तिन प्रियं भृत्यम्
उद्धवं समभाषत ॥ १.५० ॥

śrī-śuka uvāca
evaṁ vijñāpito rājan
bhagavān devakī-sutaḥ
ekāntinaṁ priyaṁ bhṛtyam
uddhavaṁ samabhāṣata (1.50)

śrī-śuka – the illustrious Shuka; uvāca — said; evaṁ — thus; vijñāpito = vijñāpitaḥ — petitioned; rājan — O King; bhagavān — the Blessed Lord; devakī-sutaḥ — the son of Devakī; ekāntinam — one who is totally attentive; priyaṁ — dear; bhṛtyam — servant; uddhavaṁ — Uddhava; samabhāṣata — spoke.

Translation

The Illustrious Shuka said: Being thus petitioned, O King, the Blessed Lord, the son of Devakī spoke to the dear Uddhava who was totally attentive. (1.50)

Commentary:

The illustrious Shuka, the son of *Vyāsa* who was an advanced yogi, made it clear that Lord Krishna was the physical son of *Devakī*. Despite the fact that there was a transcendental relationship of mother-son between *Devakī* and Lord Krishna, that same relationship was mirrored and shadowed in their physical relationship. That same Blessed Lord, Krishna, appeared to the human beings of His time, in a physical body.

Uddhava is glorified here by Shuka as *ekāntinam*, one who is totally attentive. Uddhava is deserving of Lord Krishna's instructions and associations because of this total focus.

This first chapter of the *Uddhava Gītā* described the visits of the supernatural rulers, as well as Lord Krishna's advisory to the Yadu elders, and Uddhava's initial approach to Him.

CHAPTER 2*

The Teacher of the Self**

Terri Stokes-Pineda Art

ātmano gurur ātmaiva puruṣasya viśeṣataḥ
yat pratyakṣānumānābhyāṁ śreyo 'sāv anuvindate

The self alone, is the teacher of the self, especially of the human being, for it learns of its well-being through direct perception and by drawing conclusions. (2.20)

* Śrīmad Bhāgavatam Canto 11, Chapter 7
** Translator's selected chapter title.

श्री-भगवान् उवाच
यद् आत्थ मां महा-भाग
तच्-चिकीर्षितम् एव मे ।
ब्रह्मा भवो लोक-पालाः
स्वर्-वासं मे ऽभिकाङ्क्षिणः ॥२.१॥

śrī-bhagavān uvāca
yad āttha māṁ mahā-bhāga
tac-cikīrṣitam eva me
brahmā bhavo loka-pālāḥ
svar-vāsaṁ me 'bhikāṅkṣiṇaḥ (2.1)

śrī-bhagavān – the Blessed Lord; uvāca — said; yad = yat — which; āttha — you said; māṁ — to me; mahā-bhāga — blessed person; tac-cikīrṣitam = tac (tat) — that + cikīrṣitam — that which was desired; eva — indeed; me — my; brahmā — Brahmā; bhavo = bhavaḥ — Shiva; loka-pālāh — the protectors of the world; svar-vāsam = svar (svah) - paradise + vāsam - residence; me — my; 'bhikānksinaḥ = abhikānksinaḥ — they desired.

Translation

The Blessed Lord said: What you said to me, O blessed one, is indeed what I intended. Brahmā, Shiva and other protectors of the world, desire the transfer to My residence in Paradise. (2.1)

Commentary:

Uddhava drew the conclusion that Lord Krishna would depart from this world. He felt this to be true because of Lord Krishna's neglect of any effort to counteract the brahmins' curse which was issued on the Yadu family. This is what Uddhava said in the last chapter:

śrī-uddhava uvāca
deva-deveśa yogeśa puṇya-śravaṇa-kīrtana
saṁhṛtyaitat kulaṁ nūnaṁ lokaṁ santyakṣyate bhavān
vipra-śāpaṁ samartho 'pi pratyahan na yad īśvaraḥ (1.42)

O God of the greatest rulers of the supernatural kings, O master of the yoga disciplines, O person of whom it is auspicious to hear of and chant about, surely You will quit the world after destroying this family line, for you did not counteract the brahmin's curse, even though You were capable of doing so. (U.G. 1.42)

Lord Krishna now affirms what Uddhava said, adding that a deeper reason was the request of the supernatural rulers for Lord Krishna's departure. The indication here is that Uddhava did not notice the arrival of the supernaturals. He was not aware of the conversation that took pace between Lord Krishna and the celestial rulers.

The terms *svar-vāsam* occur in the verse. Some commentators say that it is *Vaikuṇṭha*, and others list it as a residence in *svarga* or heaven. Vasam does mean residence; svar is given in Sanskrit dictionary as an indeclinable word meaning *svarga* or *svah*. *Svarga* means heaven or paradise. It will be obvious as we study this text that the *svar-vāsam* mentioned in this verse is Krishna's existential domain, which is known as *Vaikuṇṭha*. It is not a mundane heavenly place but rather a spiritual paradise.

If *svar-vāsam* means the mundane heaven, the demigods would not have stressed that Lord Krishna should go away, indicating that he should go beyond their jurisdiction. And the Procreator *Brahmā* would not have asked Lord Krishna about a visit to the mundane heavens in which the supernatural rulers have their own residences.

मया निष्पादितं ह्य् अत्र
देव-कार्यम् अशेषतः ।
यद्-अर्थम् अवतीर्णो ऽहम्
अंशेन ब्रह्मणार्थितः ॥२.२॥

mayā niṣpāditaṁ hy atra
deva-kāryam aśeṣataḥ
yad-artham avatīrṇo 'ham
aṁśena brahmaṇārthitaḥ (2.2)

mayā — by me; niṣpāditam — finished; hy = hi — indeed; atra — here, in this world; deva-kāryam — project of the supernatural rulers; aśeṣataḥ — completely, without remainder; yad-artham = yad (yat) — which + artham — benefit; avatīṛno = avatīrṇaḥ — incarnated; 'ham = aham — I; aṁśena

— with My partner; brahmaṇārthitaḥ = brahmaṇā — by Brahmā + arthitaḥ — requested.

Translation

Indeed, I finished the project of the supernatural rulers for which as requested by Brahmā, I incarnated in this world with My partner. (2.2)

Commentary:

Lord Krishna stuck to His point that He came on the basis of a request of *Brahmā*. He is about to leave on the same basis. His departure is not really connected to the curse which fell on the Yadus. The Lord said that He came with His partner *(amśena).* This partner is Lord *Balarāma*, Krishna's step-brother. Their physical father was Prince Vasudeva but their mothers were Rohinī and *Devakī*, two wives of Vasudeva. *Rohinī* was the mother of *Balarāma*.

The word *avatīrṇo* indicates that Lord Krishna came down to this level of existence. It is not His natural place. He descended for the particular purpose of fulfilling the request of *Brahmā*. The same *deva-kārya* is mentioned in the *Bhagavad-Gītā* or My work, My assignment, Krishna's work. Here it is listed as the project of the supernatural rulers.

कुलं वै शाप-निर्दग्धं
नङ्क्ष्यत्य् अन्योन्य-विग्रहात् ।
समुद्रः सप्तमे ह्य् एनां
पुरीं च प्लावयिष्यति ॥२.३॥

kulaṁ vai śāpa-nirdagdhaṁ
naṅkṣyaty anyonya-vigrahāt
samudraḥ saptame hy enāṁ
purīṁ ca plāvayiṣyati (2.3)

kulam — family; vai — thoroughtly; śāpa-nirdagdhaṁ = śāpa — by curse + nirdagdhaṁ — burnt; naṅkṣyaty = naṅkṣyati — will be destroyed; anyonya-vigrahāt = anyonya — mutual + vigrahāt — from fighting; samudraḥ — ocean; saptame — on the seventh day; hy = hi — indeed; enām — this; purīm — city; ca — and; plāvayiṣyati — will flood.

Translation

This family which is adversely affected by the curse, will be destroyed by mutual fighting, and the sea will flood this city on the seventh day hence. (2.3)

Commentary:

This statement indicates that the cause of the destruction of the Yadu men is their mutual hostility towards each other and not the brahmin's curse. Or rather that the brahmins curse will be instrumental in putting to task the energy of hostility that already existed between members of the family.

As the story goes, some male members of the family took rice liquor. Thereafter, they taunted each other for various grievances. Fighting began and it utilized the hostile emotions. The Lords, Krishna and *Balarāma* got involved in the conflict. Some Vaishnava teachers have told us that this all happened by the arrangement of Krishna. However the hostilities built up over years. Each person held a particular resentment for a particular incidence. These incidences were remembered during the fighting. The various clashing energies became intertwined and differences were settled by the fighting, which resulted in the deaths of their bodies. Accordingly, only Lord Krishna and Lord *Balarāma* walked away from the struggle with living material forms.

यर्ह्य् एवायं मया त्यक्तो
लोको ऽयं नष्ट-मङ्गलः ।
भविष्यत्य् अचिरात् साधो
कलिनापि निराकृतः ॥२.४॥

yarhy evāyaṁ mayā tyakto
loko 'yaṁ naṣṭa-maṅgalaḥ
bhaviṣyaty acirāt sādho
kalināpi nirākṛtaḥ (2.4)

yarhy = yarhi — when; evayam = eva — surely + ayam — this; mayā — by me; tyakto = tyaktaḥ — abandoned; loko = lokah — world; 'yam = ayam — this; naṣṭa-maṅgalaḥ = naṣṭa – lost + mangalaḥ

— good fortune; bhaviṣyaty = bhaviṣyati — it will be; acirāt — soon; sādho — saint; kalinapi = kalinā — due to Devil Kali + api — also; nirākṛtaḥ — overtaken.

Translation

When this world is abandoned by Me, it will lose its good fortune. O saint, it will soon be overtaken by the era of degradation. (2.4)

Commentary:

Even though God Himself as well as others make a claim about God's all-pervasiveness and God omnipotence, still if God is not physically present or if God does not manifest physical power His influence in this world is effectively curtailed.

न वस्तव्यं त्वयैवेह
मया त्यक्ते मही-तले ।
जनो ऽभद्र-रुचिर् भद्र
भविष्यति कलौ युगे ॥२.५॥

na vastavyaṁ tvayaiveha
mayā tyakte mahī-tale
jano 'bhadra-rucir bhadra
bhaviṣyati kalau yuge (2.5)

na — not; vastavyam — should remain; tvayaiveha = tvayā — you + eva — surely + iha — in this world; mayā — by Me; tyakte — leave aside; mahī-tale — Earth; jano = janaḥ— people; 'bhadra-rucir = abhadra-rucir = abhadra — what is inauspicious, vices + rucir (ruciḥ)— taste tendency; bhadra — good soul; bhaviṣyati — will have; kalau — in the Kali; yuge — in the era.

Translation

You should not remain here after I leave the earth. O good soul, people will have the tendency for vices in the succeeding era. (2.5)

Commentary:

Lord Krishna gave Uddhava the spiritual treatment, so that Uddhava could leave this world and achieve the desired goal of spiritual freedom from material existence. This is a warning to Uddhava not to be attached to this world and to realize that negative influences prevail here.

Devil Kali is a supernatural person who expresses a powerful degrading influence upon human society. Krishna stated that this world would soon be overtaken by Kali's influence.

The supernatural rulers wanted Lord Krishna to vanish from the world but their resumption of authority over this world would not prevent the assertion of the power of Devil Kali at least not on this planet. Kali does prevail currently. This was one reason why Lord Krishna lingered a little. He considered the situation of Kali's power.

त्वं तु सर्वं परित्यज्य
स्नेहं स्व-जन-बन्धुषु ।
मय्य् आवेश्य मनः संयक्
सम-दृग् विचरस्व गाम् ॥२.६.॥

tvaṁ tu sarvaṁ parityajya
snehaṁ sva-jana-bandhuṣu
mayy āveśya manaḥ saṁyak
sama-dṛg vicarasva gām (2.6)

tvam — you; tu — but; sarvaṁ — everything; parityajya — giving up; snehaṁ — affection; sva-jana-bandhuṣu = sva – your + jana – relatives + bandhuṣu — for friends; mayy = mayi — on me; āveśya — fixing; manaḥ — mind; samyak — completely; sama-dṛg = sama - everything as having the same existential configuration + dṛk - perceiving; vicarasva — wander; gām — over the earth.

Translation

You should give up all affection for relatives and friends, fix your mind completely on Me and while wandering over the earth, perceive everything as having the same existential configuration. (2.6)

Commentary:

Whatever concern Uddhava had for relatives was to be eliminated promptly, if he was to achieve the objective of moving on from this level and being transferred to wherever Lord Krishna would be. Uddhava's relatives and friends were devotees of Lord Krishna. Many of them were devotees of the highest order. And still Lord Krishna instructed that Uddhava gave up affection *(sneham)* for them. Why did the Lord recommended this? Some devotional authorities tell us that we should become attached to devotees of the Lord. Why is there a contradiction in this instruction?

Lord Krishna in the *Bhagavad-Gītā* discourse rejected Arjun's plan for changing his occupation. Krishna prohibited Arjun from becoming a wandering ascetic but here the Lord instructed Uddhava to do exactly that. This is a totally different instruction.

The *sama-drg (sama-dṛk)* vision was explained to Arjun in some detail in the *Bhagavad Gītā*. Here is a description:

sarvabhūtasthamātmānaṁ sarvabhūtāni cātmani
īkṣate yogayuktātmā sarvatra samadarśanaḥ
yo māṁ paśyati sarvatra sarvaṁ ca mayi paśyati
tasyāhaṁ na praṇaśyāmi sa ca me na praṇaśyati
sarvabhūtasthitaṁ yo māṁ bhajatyekatvamāsthitaḥ
sarvathā vartamāno'pi sa yogī mayi vartate
ātmaupamyena sarvatra samaṁ paśyati yo'rjuna
sukhaṁ vā yadi vā duḥkhaṁ sa yogī paramo mataḥ

With a spirit existing in every creature, and with every creature based on a spirit, a person who is proficient in yoga, perceives the same existential arrangement in all cases.

To him who sees Me in all forms and who sees all creatures in reference to Me, I am never out of range, and he is never out of My view.

Although moving in various circumstances, the yogi who is established in that harmony, who honors Me as being existentially situated in all creatures, remains in touch with Me.

He who, in reference to himself, sees the same facilities in all cases, regardless of pleasurable or painful sensations, he, O Arjuna, is considered as the highest yogi. (B.G. 6.29-32)

यद् इदं मनसा वाचा
चक्षुर्भ्यां श्रवणादिभिः ।
नश्वरं गृह्यमाण च
विद्धि माया-मनो-मयम् ॥२.७॥

yad idaṁ manasā vācā
cakṣurbhyāṁ śravaṇādibhiḥ
naśvaraṁ gṛhyamāṇaṁ ca
viddhi māyā-mano-mayam (2.7)

yad = yat — that which; idam — this manifested world; manasā — by the mind; vācā — speech; cakṣurbhyam — by vision; śravaṇādibhiḥ = sravana – sound + ādibhiḥ — by other senses; naśvaram — temporary; gṛhyamāṇam — what is perceived; ca — and; viddhi — know; māyā-mano-mayam = māyā – composition + mano – mind + mayam — formulated by.

Translation

Whatever is perceived by the mind, speech, vision, sound or by any other sense, know it, as being this manifested world, which is temporary and which is a composition conjectured by the mind. (2.7)

Commentary:

The *māyā-mano-mayam* or the composition accepted as a mundane reality which is based on the formulation of the mind and which is perceived as something distinct, is an old idea which was propagated and explained extensively even before the time of Lord Krishna. A particular rishi, named *Vasiṣṭha* Muni became famous as the advocate of that idea. In a nutshell *Vasiṣṭha* said that everything in this existence is a creation of the mind and that all such objects are insubstantial. To his view, as he explained it, everything in material existence is a mental fabrication.

There is a book by the name of the Yoga-*Vasiṣṭha* in which Rishi *Vasiṣṭha* explains this philosophy to his student *Rāma*, the son of *Daśaratha* but according to what *Śrī Vālmīki* explained in brief, in the *Rāmāyaṇa*, *Rāma* rejected the philosophy of *Vasiṣṭha*.

If I say that the world in an idea in the mind, the question arises as to whose mind I refer to. The answer to the question determines where the discussion will go.

Here we see that Lord Krishna ascribed somewhat to *Vasiṣṭha*'s philosophy, at least in reference to mundane objects which are perceived in this material world. But still the question, as to whose mind, is still not answered. At least not in this verse. Until Lord Krishna explains that, we should wait to draw conclusions.

This statement however is designed to destroy Uddhava's attachment to persons and places except the person of Lord Krishna. Uddhava was told in the previous verse to give up all affection for acquaintances and to fix his mind completely on Lord Krishna and to see the same existential configuration for everything perceived in this world.

पुंसो ऽयुक्तस्य नानार्थो
भ्रमः स गुण-दोष-भाक् ।
कर्माकर्म-विकर्मेति
गुण-दोष-धियो भिदा ॥२.८॥

puṁso 'yuktasya nānārtho
bhramaḥ sa guṇa-doṣa-bhāk
karmākarma-vikarmeti
guṇa-doṣa-dhiyo bhidā (2.8)

puṁso = puṁsaḥ — of the person; 'yuktasya = ayuktasya — of an indisciplined mind; nānārtho = nānārthaḥ = nānā — variety + arthaḥ — things; bhramaḥ — mistaken conception; sa=saḥ — that; guṇa-doṣa-bhāk = guṇa — something of value + doṣa — something faulty + bhāk — exhibiting, yeilding; karmākarma-vikarmeti = karma — cultural activities + akarma — lack of cultural activities + vikarma — forbidden activities + iti — thus; guṇa-doṣa-dhiyo = guṇa — virtue + doṣa — fault + dhiyo (dhiyaḥ) — of the person who perceives; bhidā — difference.

Translation

The mistaken conception, the variety of things, perceived by a person of indisciplined mind, yields the view of something valuable and something faulty. The differences of cultural activity, the lack of it, or forbidden acts, concern the person who thinks in terms of such virtues or faults. (2.8)

Commentary:

Lord Krishna made a categorical denial of the reality and practical aspects of this material world. This is very similar to the analytical approach Lord Krishna used on Arjuna. In the *Bhagavad-Gītā* discourse, Krishna systematically destroyed Arjuna's resistance by dismantling Arjun's arguments. Arjun became convinced. Now the same tactic is used on Uddhava.

No one can function as a constructive useful member of human society without participating in social affairs but here Lord Krishna condemns such affairs as duty-bound cultural activity. In the *Bhagavad-Gītā*, this same Lord Krishna urged Arjuna to fight and to complete social duties. He told Arjuna that duty was better than the neglect of it but here, he underscores and categorically denies. Lord Krishna wiped out the path of *karma* yoga which he recommended to Arjuna as the best path for a human being.

Some say that the *Bhagavad-Gītā* opinion of the Lord is supreme. But if it is, why does Lord Krishna give a converse view to Uddhava. Obviously, the opinions related to Arjuna and the pressures put on him by Krishna, for him to fight at *Kurukṣetra* were good for Arjuna at that time of his life. Some of those instructions were not relevant to Uddhava's life.

तस्माद् युक्तेन्द्रिय-ग्रामो
युक्त-चित्त इदम् जगत् ।
आत्मनीक्षस्व विततम्
आत्मानं मय्य् अधीश्वरे ॥२.९॥

tasmād yuktendriya-grāmo
yukta-citta idam jagat
ātmanīkṣasva vitatam
ātmānaṁ mayy adhīśvare (2.9)

tasmād = tasmāt — therefore; yuktendriya-grāmo = yukta — controlled + indriya –senses + grāmo (grāmaḥ) — group; yukta-citta = yukta — restrained + citta — mento-emotional energy; idaṁ — this; jagat — world; ātmanīkṣasva = atman — in the spiritual self + īkṣasva — you should perceive; vitatam — spread out, imaged in; ātmānam — the spiritual self; mayy = mayi — in Me; adhīśvare — in the Supreme Lord.

Translation

Therefore, controlling the group of senses, restraining the mental and emotional energy, you should perceive this world as imaged in the spiritual self and seeing the self as resting in Me, the Supreme Lord. (2.9)

Commentary:

The imaging of the world in the spiritual self and the self as resting in Lord Krishna, gives us some idea of what Lord Krishna means, by *māyā-mano-mayam* or the composition accepted as a mundane reality which is based on the formulation of the mental and emotional energy.

The question of whose mind the imagining is formulated in, is answered in this verse as being both in the mind of Krishna, the Supreme Being and in the minds of the individual limited spirits who abound in the world. We will get a more detailed explanation. However some say that *Vasiṣṭha* Rishi meant the mind of the limited spirits. Some state that even though *Vasiṣṭha* instructed *Rāma*, he gave the teaching to his other disciples as well and therefore his philosophy applies to everyone. Even today there are some spiritual teachers who tell disciples that each person is an absolute creator.

However, my readers should know that both *Rāma*, the son of *Daśaratha* and Krishna the son of *Devakī*, are Personalities of Godhead. The conceptualize of the world in the mind of *Rāma* is a much higher principle that its formulation in the mind of a limited spirit. Krishna stated that the spirits rest in Him. Elsewhere, Krishna denies that He relies on the spirits. He segregates Himself.

mayā tatamidaṁ sarvaṁ jagadavyaktamūrtinā
matsthāni sarvabhūtāni na cāhaṁ teṣvavasthitaḥ
na ca matsthāni bhūtāni paśya me yogamaiśvaram
bhūtabhṛnna ca bhūtastho mamātmā bhūtabhāvanaḥ
yathākāśasthito nityaṁ vāyuḥ sarvatrago mahān
tathā sarvāṇi bhūtāni matsthānītyupadhāraya

This world is pervaded by My invisible form. All beings survive on My energy but I am not surviving on theirs.

And the created beings are not existing on Me. Behold My psychological supremacy. While sustaining the beings and not existing on them, I Myself cause them to be.

As the powerful wind is always situated in space and is pervasive, so all beings exist under My influence. Consider this thoroughly. (B.G. 9.4-6)

We should note that a person cannot have this vision of the world unless he first controls the groups of senses and restrains the mental and emotional energy completely. He cannot have it merely by a mental concept. He should master the portions of yoga practice which have to do with *pratyāhar* for a complete mastery of the sensual energies and the mind. It is not an artificial nor rational conception of the supreme reality. It is mystic control.

ज्ञान-विज्ञान-सयुक्त
आत्म-भूतः शरीरिणाम् ।
अत्मानुभव-तुष्टात्मा
नान्तरायैर् विहन्यसे ॥२.१०॥

jñāna-vijñāna-saṁyukta
ātma-bhūtaḥ śarīriṇām
atmānubhava-tuṣṭātmā
nāntarāyair vihanyase (2.10)

jñāna-vijñāna-saṁyukta = *jñāna* — knowledge + vijnana — realization + saṁyukta — possessed with; ātma-bhūtah — the essential self; śarīrinām — of the embodied beings; ātmanubhava-tuṣṭātmā — spiritual self + anubhava – experience, realization + tuṣṭa- satisfied + ātmā — spiritual self; nāntarāyair = na — not + āntarāyair (āntarāyaiḥ) - by obstacles; vihanyase — you will be twarted.

Translation

Posessed of knowledge and realisation, with a spiritually satisfied self, with realisation of the spiritual self and experiencing yourself as being similar to the essential self of the embodied beings, you will not be twarted by obstacles. (2.10)

Commentary:

Even though I give many conceptions as we go through these instructions and explanation of Lord Krishna, still these have to be realized individually by taking up yoga practice. It is not merely a realization by mentality or by being able to follow reasonably laid-out explanations like the ones I present in this book.

I gave this information. A reader should try to follow my line of reasoning but that does not mean that the understanding derived, is complete. It is incomplete. The transmission is faulty for several reasons, mainly because my transcendental experience can only be translated in mental conceptions and words, to a limited degree. When those words hit your mind, the conversion into concepts will produce distortions.

In cases where I might transfer a transcendental experience to you individually, your mind or intellect might adjust the experience and present it in a slightly different way. These limitations of communication must be accepted. Each of us should take this into account and remain open for further clarification.

Cooking always involves the risk of poisoning but if someone is doubtful and says that we should cease all cooking who will agree with his idea? Getting sun burnt is a risk if one has a light complexion but that does not mean that one can stay out of sunshine at all times. Some risks need to be taken.

A listing of requirements are given in this verse, beginning with knowledge *(jñānam)*. That is the least requirement. Realization of that knowledge is required. That realization is mystic perception. Some feel that it is a mental understanding, but they are wrong. Mental understanding is required but it is a part of *jñāna* or knowledge. It is not mystic perception and the resulting realization *(vijñāna)*. This is why Lord Krishna added the terms *samyukta ātma-bhūtah*. In addition there must be the experience of feeling one-self on the mystic plane as being similar to the essential self of any of the other limited beings.

The importance of seeing this similarity is this: One gives up all envy and resentment towards other beings since one realizes that none of them have a particular advantage.

Anyone who has a real advantage must be the Supreme Being or someone who is His parallel or empowered divinity. Otherwise, the spirits who are on par do not have any real advantages over one another. Thus there is no need to envy nor to resent others. One should relax and move all over this creation in a congenial mood.

Seeing that all the limited beings are for the most part, existentially similar and that none have an advantage over another, one does not perceive disadvantages and so obstacles appear to be opportunities for progression and learning. One no longer feels as if the creation or the circumstances in it, are slanted to others or prejudiced to oneself.

दोष-बुद्ध्योभयातीतो
निषेधान् न निवर्तते ।
गुण-बुद्ध्या च विहितं
न करोति यथार्भकः ॥२.११॥

doṣa-buddhyobhayātīto
niṣedhān na nivartate
guṇa-buddhyā ca vihitaṁ
na karoti yathārbhakaḥ (2.11)

doṣa-buddhyobhayātīto = doṣa-buddhyā + ubhayātīto = dosa – bad effects + buddhya – on the basis of consideration; ubhayātīto = ubhaya – both + ātīto (atītaḥ) — transcended; niṣedhān = niṣedhāt — from prohibited activities; na – not; nivartate — he restrains himself; guna-buddhyā = guna – good benefit + buddhya — by reason of; ca — and; vihitam — approved actions; na – not; karoti — does; yathārbhakaḥ = yathā — is similar to + arbhakah — a child.

Translation

A person should restrain from prohibited activities but not on the basis of considering the bad effect. He perform approved actions but not by reason of the good benefits. He should be similar to a child. (2.11)

Commentary:

This is a description of a person who maintains a material existence and remains detached from it. It is a contradiction of sorts, that one may have a material body, function in it and by it and still be transcendent to it. Still it is possible by special spiritual practice.

Lord Krishna shows the motive or the functional basis of the actions of such a person whom he compared to a child *(yathārbhakah)*. Those on a lower level of advancement who act properly in this world, do so on the basis of sorting out between good and evil, in terms of what will produce a bad or a good result. Once a man sees that some action might give a bad reaction, he is inclined to restrain from doing it. In some cases, even though he sees that, still he cannot restrain, because he is impulsively pushed to complete the action.

There is another aspect; that of perceiving a long-ranged good result or a short-ranged one. For instance sugar is sweet and it is very agreeable to the mouth, but sweetness is a short-range benefit. It might carry a long-ranged disadvantage in the form of diabetes. In material nature, one should select the long-ranged advantage and overlook the short ranged ones which are merely enticements. Some of this was explained to Arjuna, when Lord Krishna described the symptoms of the modes of passion, as contrasted to that of clarity. Here are a few verses:

yattadagre viṣamiva pariṇāme'mṛtopamam
tatsukhaṁ sāttvikaṁ proktam ātmabuddhiprasādajam
viṣayendriyasaṁyogād yattadagre'mṛtopamam
pariṇāme viṣamiva tatsukhaṁ rājasaṁ smṛtam

That which initially is like poison but which changes into an experience like nectar, and which is felt through the clarity of spiritual discernment, is said to be happiness in the clarifying mode.

Thut happiness which in the beginning seems like nectar and which comes from the contact between the sense organs and attractive objects, which changes as if it were poison is recognized as an impulsion. (B.G. 18.37-38)

In some cases, a man, even though experiencing that an action gives a bad result, believes that the bad result is worth the performance of the action. This also happens. All these activities, however, are based on instinctual, subconscious or conscious decisions within the intellect and feelings of the living being.

A liberated person however functions from a different basis as described in this verse. Some other power, some other nature, some other type of motivation pushes such a person.

सर्व-भूत-सुहृच् छान्तो
ज्ञान-विज्ञान-निश्चयः ।
पश्यन् मद्-आत्मकं विश्वं
न विपद्येत वै पुनः ॥२.१२॥

sarva-bhūta-suhṛc chānto
jñāna-vijñāna-niścayaḥ
paśyan mad-ātmakaṁ viśvaṁ
na vipadyeta vai punaḥ (2.12)

sarva-bhūta-suhṛc = sarva — all + bhūta – beings + suhṛc (suhṛt) — friend; chānto = śāntah — peaceful; jñāna-vijñāna-niścayaḥ = jñāna – knowledge + vijñāna – realization + niścayaḥ — firm conviction; paśyan — perceiving; mad-ātmakaṁ = mat –my +ātmakaṁ — belonging to; viśvaṁ — universe; na – not; vipadyeta — fall into misidentity; vai — indeed; punaḥ — again.

Translation

Being the friend of all beings, having a firm conviction by knowledge and self-realization, and perceiving the universe as belonging to Me, he does not fall into misidentification. (2.12)

Commentary:

The friendship *(suhṛc)* developed with all beings is based on his vision of the comparative similarity in status between himself and others and the vision he has that none of the others in his category is at an advantageous or disadvantageous position. As far as his assessment of those who are spiritually superior, he does not envy them either. He realizes that their superiority is causeless.

We may understand this psychology by considering differing grades of mineral. Gold is mineral and so is granite but gold is preferred in certain situations. Granite though it is considered as a cheap material, has more usage in certain situations. The value of gold does not remove nor overshadow the usefulness of granite. In some applications where granite is required, gold is unsuitable. In other words in certain situations gold is useless and granite assumes all importance.

Thus there are different grades of spirits but that does not mean that one level is useless. It all depends on the various applications, exploitations and existential conditions which arise.

In the *Bhagavad-Gītā* discourse to Arjun, Lord Krishna introduced His self-importance gradually but here from the very beginning of the discourse with Uddhava, the Lord introduced Himself fully. In this verse, He states flatly that a self-realized soul perceives that the universe belongs to Lord Krishna. The word paśyan means visual. In the *Bhagavad Gītā*, Arjun visually saw Lord Krishna controlling everything when the Lord revealed the universal form *(viśvarūpa)*. It was not a mental realization or a conception. It was visual. And here the Lord said that the self realized person actually sees that the universe *(viśvam)* belongs to Krishna.

Of course if a person can actually see visually, then for sure, he would not fall into misidentification, especially if he sees such a reality continuously. For such a seer, it would be natural and easy to always know that nothing in the world belongs to anyone but Lord Krishna. However for those of us who do not have this vision or who have it periodically, we will, by necessity, fall into misidentification *(vipadyeta)*.

श्री-शुक उवाच
इत्य् आदिष्टो भगवता
महा-भागवतो नृप ।
उद्धवः प्रणिपत्याह
तत्त्व जिज्ञासुर् अच्युतम् ॥२.१३॥

śrī-śuka uvāca
ity ādiṣṭo bhagavatā
mahā-bhāgavato nṛpa
uddhavaḥ praṇipatyāha
tattvaṁ jijñāsur acyutam (2.13)

śrī-śuka – the illustrious Shuka; uvāca — said; ity = iti — thus; ādiṣṭo = ādistaḥ — instructed; bhāgavatā — by the Blessed Lord; mahā-bhāgavato = mahā – great + bhāgavato (bhāgavataḥ) — very advanced devotee; nṛpa — O King; uddhavaḥ — Uddhava; praṇipatyāha = praṇipatya — having respectfully bowed + āha — spoke; tattvaṁ — the technical information; jijñāsur = jijñāsuḥ — being desirous to know; acyutam — unto the infallible one.

Translation

The illustrious Shuka said: O King being thus instructed by the Lord, the great advanced devotee, Uddhava, being desirous to know the technical information, respectfully bowed before the infallible one and spoke. (2.13)

Commentary:

As far as the material world is concerned and in so far as we might remain here and be transcendental to this world, Lord Krishna expounded His view of the entire reality. In seven verses, 6 through 12, Lord Krishna has told Uddhava how to transcend this world and reach Krishna's divine territories.

The key point is this: If a person gets that direct vision of Krishna controlling the world, then all his misgivings about existence goes away immediately. From that vision he would need no explanations since he would be seeing the reality directly. But of course this is easier spoken of, than it is realized in fact. Even Uddhava was not satisfied at this point. Even He did not get the vision at this point. We must hear more to be inspired to strive for the realization and direct perception of these truths.

श्री-उद्धव उवाच
योगेश योग-विन्यास
योगात्मन् योग-सम्भव ।
निःश्रेयसाय मे प्रोक्तस्
त्यागः सन्न्यास-लक्षणः ॥२.१४॥

śrī-uddhava uvāca
yogeśa yoga-vinyāsa
yogātman yoga-sambhava
niḥśreyasāya me proktas
tyāgaḥ sannyāsa-lakṣaṇaḥ (2.14)

śrī-uddhava – the deserving Uddhava; uvāca — said; yogeśa — O supreme master of yoga; yogeśa = yoga + īśa – supreme master; yoga-vinyāsa = yoga – yoga + vinyāsa – treasure of yoga practice; yogātman = yoga – yoga + ātman — spirit, person; yoga-sambhava = yoga – yoga + sambhava — origin; niḥśreyasāya — for my salvation; me — of me; proktas — O you recommended; tyāgaḥ — renunciation of the results of action; sannyāsa-lakṣaṇaḥ = sannyāsa — renunciation of the explotive opportunities + lakṣaṇaḥ — objective.

Translation

The deserving Uddhava said: O Supreme Master of yoga, O treasure of yoga practice, O Yoga in person, O origin of the yoga discipline, for my salvation, you recommend the renunciation of the results of action, the objective of which is the renunciation of exploitive opportunities. (2.14)

Commentary:

In verse 6, Lord Krishna recommended the giving up of all affections *(pratiyajya sneham)* and the wandering *(vicarasva)* over the earth, with mind completely fixed on Krishna and perceiving everything as having the same existential configuration. Here Uddhava said that Lord Krishna recommended the renunciation of the results of action which is epitomized by the renunciation of all exploitive opportunities.

It may seem that Uddhava mentions a different advice that he may have received previously from Lord Krishna. However in verse 11 the description of the transcendentalist who is not motivated by positive or negative experiences but who acts like a child *(yathārbhakah)*, indicates the states of renunciation of all exploitive opportunities *(sannyāsa)*. Readers should be attentive to these details, for without such comparisons of the verses, we cannot understand the text fully.

I must alert readers, that some background of yoga practice is required for an in-depth study of this text but even if there is no such background there is no loss from a review of It. In this verse Uddhava addressed Lord Krishna by a series of terms which denote yoga practice. Krishna is addressed as a prime master of yoga *(yogeśa)*, as the treasure of yoga practice *(yogavinyāsa)*, as Yoga in person *(Yogātman)*, and as the origin of yoga disciplines *(yoga-sambhava)*.

त्यागो ऽय दुष्करो भूमन्
कामाना विषयात्मभिः ।
सुतरा त्वयि सर्वात्मन्न्
अभक्तैर् इति मे मतिः ॥२.१५॥

tyāgo 'yaṁ duṣkaro bhūman
kāmānāṁ viṣayātmabhiḥ
sutarāṁ tvayi sarvātmann
abhaktair iti me matiḥ (2.15)

tyāgo = tyag — renunciation of results; 'yam = ayam — this; duṣkaro = duṣkaraḥ — difficult to accomplish; bhūman — O infinite Lord; kāmānām — of cravings; viṣayātmabhiḥ = visaya — sense enjoyment + ātmabhiḥ — by those spirits who are absorded in; sutarām — especially; tvayi — to you; sarvātmann — O soul of all beings; abhaktair = abhaktaiḥ — by those who are not devotees; iti — thus; me — my; matiḥ — view.

Translation

O infinite Lord, for those who are absorbed in sense enjoyment and especially for those who are not devoted to you, who are the soul of all beings, this renunciation of cravings is difficult to accomplish. This is my view. (2.15)

Commentary:

Uddhava asked Lord Krishna for a personal recommendation in regards to Uddhava's desire to be transported with Krishna when Krishna left the physical body. Now Uddhava speaks on broader terms. Instead of staying on track with his own concerns, Uddhava now spreads his interest to humanity. But as we will see in the end of the discourse, Lord Krishna will again pilot Uddhava back to his liberation only.

In any case this inquiry about persons who are absorbed in sense enjoyment and who are not devoted to Lord Krishna, is of value to us. What should such people do? As Uddhava indirectly stated, they can hardly practice the renunciation of cravings.

In a round-about way, Uddhava asked Lord Krishna if the Lord did not have a keen interest in the elevation of the common people. And if Lord Krishna did have such an interest, how was that interest conveyed to the masses of humanity.

सो ऽह ममाहम् इति मूढ-मतिर् विगाढस्
त्वन्-मायया विरचितात्मनि सानुबन्धे ।
तत् त्व् अञ्जसा निगदित भवता यथाहं
ससाधयामि भगवन्न् अनुशाधि भृत्यम् ॥२.१६॥

so 'haṁ mamāham iti mūḍha-matir vigāḍhas
tvan-māyayā viracitātmani sānubandhe
tat tv añjasā nigaditaṁ bhavatā yathāhaṁ
saṁsādhayāmi bhagavānn anuśādhi bhṛtyam
(2.16)

so = saḥ — he, that person; 'haṁ = aham — I; mamaham = mama – my + aham — I; iti — thus thinking; mūḍha-matir = mudha – foolish + matir (matiḥ) — idea; vigādhas — passionately attached; tvan-māyayā = tvan (tvat) – by you + māyayā — by your bewildering potency; viracitātmani = viracita — created + ātmani — in myself; sa-anubandhe = sa — along with + anubandhe – with relatives; tat = tad — that; tv = tu — but; añjasā — properly; nigaditam — what was instructed; bhavatā — by you; yathāham = yathā — as + aham — I; saṁsādhayāmi — can faithfully execute; bhagavān — Blessed Lord; anuśādhi — teach; bhṛtyam — servant.

Translation

I am that person who thinks of "I and my". I am foolish, being personally attached to myself and the relatives, which were created by Your bewildering energy. Please properly instruct Your servant, O Blessed Lord, so that I can faithfully execute what you teach me. (2.16)

Commentary:

Uddhava identified himself with the common people but it is a superficial comparison. Uddhava is far superior to common people. At no stage was he an average human being. Therefore we need to realize his motive for this willful misrepresentation of his existential capacity. Uddhava was regarded as one of the most elevated beings in the world. He was rated as having the highest intelligence. It is said that his academic teacher was *Bṛhaspati*, the chaplain of the supernatural rulers. Thus it cannot be that he is a common human being. In addition he is a special devotee of Lord Krishna. He has access to Lord Krishna's association.

It is true however that he was thinking in terms of "I and my" *(mamāham)* but his thinking is a bit different from that of a common man. In any case Lord Krishna condemned Uddhava's possessive mentality in no uncertain terms.

Uddhava asked for a teaching but Lord Krishna, in verses 6 through 12, already gave the teaching. Obviously then, that instruction was too terse for application.

सत्यस्य ते स्व-दृश आत्मन आत्मनो ऽन्यं
वक्तारम् ईश विबुधेष्व् अपि नानुचक्षे ।
सर्वे विमोहित-धियस् तव माययेमे
ब्रह्मादयस् तनु-भृतो बहिर्-अर्थ-भावाः ॥२.१७॥

satyasya te sva-dṛśa ātmana ātmano 'nyaṁ
vaktāram īśa vibudheṣv api nānucakṣe
sarve vimohita-dhiyas tava māyayeme
brahmādayas tanu-bhṛto bahir-artha-
bhāvāḥ (2.17)

satyasya — of the reality; te — besides you; sva-dṛśa — one who is self-revealing; ātmana — of the soul; ātmano = ātmanaḥ — of the spiritual self; 'nyam = anyam — other; vaktāram — teacher; īśa — O Lord; vibudheṣv = vibudheṣu — among the supernatural rulers; api — even; nānucakṣa = na — not + anucakṣe — I see; sarve — all; vimohita-dhiyas = vimohita — mystified + dhiyas — mind; tava — your; māyayeme = māyaya — by the bewilding potency + ime — these; brahmādayas = brahma – Procreator Brahmā + adayas – and others; tanu-bhṛto = tanu-bhṛtaḥ — body-borne souls; bahir-artha-bhāvāḥ = bahir (bahiḥ) — mundane + artha — a real thing + bhāvāḥ — considering .

Translation

O Lord, even among the supernatural rulers, I see no other teacher of the soul other than you, who are self-revealing, who are of reality and of the spiritual self. Procreator Brahmā and all others led by him, are body-borne souls who are mystified by Your bewildering potency and who consider the mundane things to be a reality. (2.17)

Commentary:

Puranic history shows that of the three super controllers, Lord Vishnu is the most remote. While Lord Shiva lived physically on this planet for a very, very long time, and while Lord *Brahmā* maintains an interest here continuously, Lord Vishnu lives in a remote place and is reputed to be very reluctant to get involved in the mundane affairs.

It is said that Lord Vishnu lives on a supernatural white island. When there is a crisis which only He can solve, *Brahmā* goes near that place and calls Him. Otherwise He is not available. He is not seen by anyone. Actually each of these super controllers is remote from human beings, but in one sense each at them is very, very near.

Evidence in the Purāṇic history does attest to the fact that each of them have advised particular aspiring souls about liberation. It is not only Lord Krishna who gives advice for spiritual life.

One important statement concerns the body-borne souls *(tanu-bhṛto)*. The word *bhṛto (bhṛtah)* means supported, reinforced, borne or lifted up. Since we need material bodies in order to fulfill some of our existential needs and since without these bodies our progression and fulfillment would be forestalled, we are described as being body-supported or body-reinforced spirits. This need can be eliminated if we would become liberated from material existence but until such a time as we can attain that, we will have to remain in the category of the spirits who require mundane support.

Presently we are interwoven with material nature. This is described in a verse in the *Bhagavad Gītā*, which states:

adhaścordhvaṁ prasṛtāstasya śākhā guṇapravṛddhā viṣayapravālāḥ
adhaśca mūlānyanusaṁtatāni karmānubandhīni manuṣyaloke

Branches spread from it, upwards and downwards. It is nourished by the mundane influences and the attractive objects are its sprouts. The roots are spread below, promoting action in the world of human beings. (15.2)

So long as we are reliant on such action, we will have to take support from material nature but if we attain liberation this would be terminated and we would be free of material nature, or at least be free from an impulsive helpless reliance on that energy.

In the third Canto of *Śrīmad Bhāgavatam* Lord *Kapila* told *Devahūti*, that even after this present universe collapses, the *deva* supernatural people will come back to form another mundane creation. He advised her to become detached from and not to rely on *Brahmā* and the others.

Uddhava had some experience with the supernatural people, for he took lessons from a supernatural professor named *Bṛhaspati.* Thus Uddhava expressed a distrust of these supernatural authorities. He felt that if he associated with them he would remain in the material world as a body-reliant soul *(tanu-bhṛto).*

Lord Shiva functions as the mystic regulator of the whole scene and as the shifter of the various subtle dimensions. Lord *Brahmā* functions as the general foreman of the supernatural people and as a Procreator who takes opportunities to manifest life supernaturally on any suitable planet. Lord Vishnu, the Vishnu who coordinates with Shiva and *Brahmā* stays remote but is aware of the local situations. Uddhava preferred not to rely on them. Each of them desires to engage their devotees in some sort of duty in the material world.

तस्माद् भवन्तम् अनवद्यम् अनन्त-पारं
सर्व-ज्ञम् ईश्वरम् अकुण्ठ-विकुण्ठ-धिष्ण्यम् ।
निर्विण्ण-धीर् अहम् उ हे वृजिनाभितप्तो
नारायणं नर-सख शरण प्रपद्ये ॥२.१८॥

tasmād bhavantam anavadyam ananta-pāraṁ
sarva-jñam īśvaram akuṇṭha-vikuṇṭha-dhiṣṇyam
nirviṇṇa-dhīr aham u he vṛjinābhitapto
Nārāyaṇaṁ nara-sakhaṁ śaraṇaṁ prapadye
(2.18)

tasmād = tasmāt — therefore; bhavantam — to you; anavadyam — flawless; ananta-pāram = ananta – infinite + pāram — beyond everything; sarva-jñam — omniscient; īśvaram — lord of the world; akuṇṭha-vikuṇṭha-dhiṣṇyam = akuṇṭha — changeless + vikuṇṭha — Vaikuṇṭha Paradise + dhiṣṇyam — residence; nirviṇṇa-dhīr = nirviṇṇa — depressed + dhīr (dhīḥ) — mind; aham — I; u he — O Lord; vṛjinābhitapto = vrjina — by sins + abhitapto (abhitaptaḥ) — afflicted; Nārāyaṇam — to Nārāyaṇa; nara-sakhaṁ — the friend of the human being; śaranaṁ - release; prapady — I surrender.

Translation

Therefore, being afflicted by sins and depressed, I take shelter in You who are flawless, infinite, beyond everything, omniscient, the Lord of the world, whose residence is the changeless Vaikuṇṭha paradise, who are Nārāyaṇa, the friend of the human being. (2.18)

Commentary:

Involvement with the material energy is fatiguing to say the least. That is the nature of mundane interaction. The energy of matter, the subtle counter part of it, is called *prāṇa*, subtle life force. Isolated portions of this subtle life force becomes exhausted. Some portions of it are consumed. Even though material energy can never be created or destroyed, still portions become exhausted or changed into unsuitable forms. There is need for a constant exchange of energy. That is fatiguing.

In the *Bhagavad-Gītā*, Lord Krishna spoke of those souls who are affected *(kṣara)* and those who are not affected *(akṣara)*. Here is the verse:

dvāvimau puruṣau loke kṣaraścākṣara eva ca
kṣaraḥ sarvāṇi bhūtāni kūṭastho'kṣara ucyate

These two types of spirits are in this world, namely the affected ones and the unaffected ones. All mundane creatures are affected. The stable soul is said to be unaffected. (B.G. 15.16)

For those of us who are affected, even to the slightest degree, the involvement with material nature is fatiguing and even though as body-supported entities, we must take help from the mundane potency, it is hazardous nevertheless. Hence the need for liberation.

Lord Shiva, Lord *Brahmā* and Lord Vishnu maintain an interest in the material world. This is why they manifest supernatural mundane bodies here. Uddhava may or may not become freed from his relationship with these super-controllers. It is not just a matter of desire nor appeal to Lord Krishna for it depends on his existential standing and the force of attraction between him and a particular divinity. He cannot renounce or cut off an eternal relationship merely by disliking the duties which arise because of it.

Anyone who feels the psychological pain of material existence will develop a burning desire to get out but that does not mean that such a desire is practical. It might not be, all depending on one's eternal relationship with a particular divinity. In a very tactful way, Lord *Kapila* told *Devahūti* that if she relied on Him, He would get her out but if she relied on *Brahmā*, *Mahā*Vishnu, or Shiva, there was no hope that she would ever get out since the three of them were eternally involved in producing mundane creations, maintaining and demolishing them endlessly. They require capable assistance for the purpose. It all depends on what a particular spirit can and cannot do. It is more than desire, because we are not all-powerful. We are subordinate not only to certain higher personalities but also to certain powerful energies like the bewitching potency mentioned in the previous verse as *māyayeme*.

श्री-भगवान् उवाच
प्रायेण मनुजा लोके
लोक-तत्त्व-विचक्षणाः ।
समुद्धरन्ति ह्य् आत्मानम्
आत्मनैवाशुभाशयात् ॥ २.१९ ॥

śrī-bhagavān uvāca
prāyeṇa manujā loke
loka-tattva-vicakṣaṇāḥ
samuddharanti hy ātmānam
ātmanaivāśubhāśayāt (2.19)

śrī-bhagavān – the Blessed Lord; uvāca — said; prāyena — regularly; manujā — people; loke — in this world; loka-tattva-vicakṣaṇāḥ = loka – world + tattva — the truth + vicakṣaṇāḥ — those who really know; samuddharanti — they deliver; hy = hi — indeed; ātmānam — themselves; ātmanaivāśubhāśayāt = ātmanā — themselves + eva — indeed + aśubha – evil + āśayāt — from tendencies.

Translation

The Blessed Lord said: Indeed by their own endeavor, people who really know the truth of the world, regularly deliver themselves from evil tendencies. (2.19)

Commentary:

Uddhava made his request and gave his conclusions. However Lord Krishna will state His case and give His views, apart from what Uddhava said. Much of what Uddhava asserted was confirmed by the Lord but some of it was denied. Some of what was confirmed was substantiated from a different angle.

Lord Krishna began the reply by stating that in general, people get out of material existence by their own endeavor. This means that for purification of the *ātma*, one must use his own soul force to eliminate bad tendencies. In the *Bhagavad Gītā* this *aśubha* or impurity tendency of the spirit is indicated in a verse, where Lord Krishna stated that for purification, one must practice yoga.

tatraikāgraṁ manaḥ kṛtvā yatacittendriyakriyaḥ
upaviśyāsane yuñjyād yogamātmaviśuddhaye

...being there, seated in a posture, having the mind focused, the person who controls his thinking and sensual energy, should practise the yoga discipline for self-purification. (B.G. 6.12)

It is interesting that Lord Krishna declared that people who know the truth of the world, regularly deliver themselves. This is because it is futile to blame the controllers like *Brahmā*, Shiva, and Vishnu. The soul's susceptibility for material existence is hinged on the soul's need to be in the material world. Ultimately, the problem lies in the nature of the soul and not in the actions of the super-controllers who provide and develop the mundane environment.

The question is this: What about the spirits who do not know the truth of the world? How can they be delivered?

आत्मनो गुरुर् आत्मैव
पुरुषस्य विशेषतः ।
यत् प्रत्यक्षानुमानाभ्या
श्रेयो ऽसाव् अनुविन्दते ॥२.२०॥

ātmano gurur ātmaiva
puruṣasya viśeṣataḥ
yat pratyakṣānumānābhyāṁ
śreyo 'sāv anuvindate (2.20)

ātmano = ātmanaḥ — of the self; gurur = guruḥ — teacher; ātmaiva = ātmā — self + eva — alone; puruṣasya — of the human being; viśeṣataḥ — especially; yat = yad — which; pratyakṣānumānābhyāṁ = pratyakṣa — by direct perception + anumānābhyām – by drawing conclusions; sreyo = śreyaḥ — well-being; 'sāv = asau — it; anuvindate — ascertains, learns.

Translation

The self alone, is the teacher of the self, especially of the human being, for it learns of its well-being through direct perception and by drawing conclusions. (2.20)

Commentary:

Many spiritual masters who claim that they are devotees of Krishna deny this statement of Krishna. Those who are against yoga practice, do not like this statement. They profess that the spirit can be freed by the grace of Lord. They feel that self endeavor has little impact on liberation.

Some say that only a fool learns by experience, and that one should learn by hearing from the previous authority in discipline succession from Krishna. But the truth is this; By nature, a spirit, due to his inborn individuality, learns from various means of which hearing is just one method. Hearing is not and never was the full range of learning experience. In fact what Lord Krishna stated about direct perception *(pratyakṣa)* is the most convincing method of learning.

The drawing of conclusions *(anumānābhyām)* is also a part of the means of learning. It is due to this fact of the self being the teacher of himself, that the spirit learns so slowly in material existence, but that does not mean that the slow rate of learning can be quickened without direct perception. It cannot be in fact. To develop direct perception, the soul cultivates yoga practice to develop his psychic insight.

Uddhava pointed a finger at the super-controllers but Lord Krishna indicated that they are not the problem. The problem is the bad tendencies of the spirit itself as well as its inability to have direct perception of the truth of the world.

पुरुषत्वे च मां धीराः
साङ्ख्य-योग-विशारदाः ।
आविस्तरां प्रपश्यन्ति
सर्व-शक्त्य्-उपबृंहितम् ॥२.२१॥

puruṣatve ca māṁ dhīrāḥ
sāṅkhya -yoga-viśāradāḥ
āvistarāṁ prapaśyanti
sarva-śakty-upabṛṁhitam (2.21)

puruṣatve — among mankind; ca — and; mām — me; dhīrāḥ — those with a balanced mind;

sāṅkhya -yoga-viśāradāḥ = sāṅkhya – Sāṅkhya philosophy + yoga — yoga practices + viśāradaḥ — those who are versed; āvistarām — fully manifest; prapaśyanti — they see; sarva-śakty-upabṛṁhitam = sarva — all + śakty (śakti) — potencies + upabṛṁhitam — fully endowed with.

Translation

Among mankind, those who have a balanced mind, and are versed in the Sāṅkhya philosophy and yoga practices, see Me as fully manifest and endowed with all potencies. (2.21)

Commentary:

A balanced mind is produced by a controlled intellect and by being situated in a high quality of subtle mundane energy. We cannot leave out the subtle mundane energy, for to transcend it would mean a complete retraction from the material world in all its phases. Some spiritual masters give a pretence whereby they speak of an abrupt liberation from the mundane energy. Usually this transcendence is the transcendence of one phase or one level of mundane power.

The mundane power is gross but it is also very, very subtle. One must first learn how to transcend its grosser portions and then the undesirable phases of its subtle portion, until one has relocated deep into the clarifying mode of it. From clarity one can make an effort to exist on spiritual energy alone. It involves individual practice. It is not a group effort or an institutional achievement.

It is important to be versed in the *Sāṅkya* philosophy which is explained by Lord Krishna or alternately by His agent like *Śrī Nārada* Muni, Lord *Kapila*, or Lord Shiva. If one is not versed in this philosophy, he will get only partial assistance from his intellect. Without having the intellect as a full time ally in the battle against misconception one cannot get out of the material involvement. Besides the intellect, one has to take up yoga practice to conquer the *prāṇa*, the subtle *prakṛti*, the very, very subtle mundane energy. Even if one has the intellect as an ally, one will lose the battle if one has not understood the operations of the *prāṇa* subtle *prakṛti* energy. Thus all these aspects must be regarded.

The vision of seeing Krishna is a direct mystic perception which develops later on into a full supernatural view. Then one develops further into a view through spiritual eye-balls. This vision is not an intellectual conception or a belief mechanism which is acquired from a spiritual master.

To understand this vision we have to study what happened to Arjuna when he saw the Universal form. At first, when Lord Krishna displayed the glories of the Supreme Being, Arjuna did not perceive any wonders. Arjuna challenged Lord Krishna to prove whatever Lord Krishna had said about Himself but when the Lord showed proof Arjuna could not view it. Noticing that Arjuna was still restricted, Lord Krishna, energized Arjuna's subtle body. Then Arjuna saw what Krishna displayed. Whatever Lord Krishna showed Arjuna at that time, was being shown in a special supernatural dimension. Initially Arjuna did not see it because he was not focused on that level. Once he saw it, he became convinced of Krishna's supremacy.

Once he got used to that supernatural vision, Arjuna realized that it was an unsettling experience. He did not like it as much as he anticipated before. He asked Lord Krishna to withdraw it. It is not that Lord Krishna was to withdraw those supernatural super-personalities who were displayed but rather, Arjuna wanted to be desynchronized from the vision of it. Arjuna's existence cried out: " I do not want to see You in this way. I asked to see this form, but it is not what I really wanted. Now that I saw this, I understand that this is not what I would like to see. I am satisfied that you are God. It is fine. I will not oppose You. I no longer want proof of supremacy. I do not want to be burdened seeing You as the disciplinary Godhead. Please take away the ability for viewing this.

"Please instead, show Yourself as God without disciplinary concerns. That is what I really wish to see."

Thus after seeing those supernatural personalities, who were being supervised by God Krishna, Arjuna's subtle body was desynchronized from that vision.

Up to this day, hardly anybody understood how Lord Krishna manipulated Arjuna's existence in that way. Spiritual masters all over the world, are still baffled by how Krishna did this. Once Arjuna's subtle body was desynchronized from that super-natural vision, Lord Krishna arranged for Arjuna to see the four-handed spiritual form. These visions were real. They are not a mental concept or a belief based on what is heard. We must distinguish a real experience from what is formulated in the mind on the basis of what is heard from scripture, or from a self-realized soul. Seeing Lord Krishna as fully manifested in the material world and as being endowed with all potencies is a supernatural visual view which is very similar to the one Arjuna had when he saw through his subtle body by the manipulation of mystic powers by Lord Krishna.

एक-द्वि-त्रि-चतुस्-पादो
बहु-पादस् तथापदः ।
बह्व्यः सन्ति पुरः सृष्टास्
तासां मे पौरुषी प्रिया ॥ २.२२ ॥

eka-dvi-tri-catus-pādo
bahu-pādas tathāpadaḥ
bahvyaḥ santi puraḥ sṛṣṭās
tāsāṁ me pauruṣī priyā (2.22)

eka-dvi-tri-catuṣ-pādo = eka — one + dvi — two + tri — three + catuṣ (catuḥ) — four + pādo (pādaḥ) — legs; bahu-pādas = bahu – many + pādas — legs; tathāpadaḥ = tathā — as well as + apadah — legless; bahvyaḥ — many; santi — there are; puraḥ — constructed forms; sṛṣṭās = sṛṣṭāḥ — created; tāsām — of them; me — to me; pauruṣī — the human body; priyā — is dear, is preferred.

Translation

Many constructed forms are created; some with one, two, three, four, or many more legs, as well as those, which are legless. Of these, the human body is preferred by Me. (2.22)

Commentary:

The material body is a *purah* or constructed form, used by a spirit. The human being is not a human person, as we may childishly believe but rather, it is a habitat *(purah)* or environment *(kṣetra)* used by the spirit. And so is any other body type. In pride, some people say that once a person exists as a human being he will never take an animal form again. But this is a nonsensical idea which only reflects our pride in having the human form. It is not true that we cannot take a lower form. We certainly can. A rich man may not be able to imagine how he can survive in poverty but he certainly can.

अत्र मां मृगयन्त्य् अद्धा
युक्ता हेतुभिर् ईश्वरम् ।
गृह्यमाणैर् गुणैर् लिङ्गैर्
अग्राह्यम् अनुमानतः ॥ २.२३ ॥

atra māṁ mṛgayanty addhā
yuktā hetubhir īśvaram
gṛhyamāṇair guṇair liṅgair
agrāhyam anumānataḥ (2.23)

atra — here; mām — for me; mṛgayanty = mṛgayanti — they search for; addhā — directly; yuktāḥ — persons who are disciplined in yoga practice; hetubhir = hetubhiḥ — by conclusions; īśvaram — Lord; gṛhyamāṇair = grhyamāṇaiḥ— by subtle sense perceptions; guṇair = guṇaiḥ - by the mundane; liṇgair = liṇgaiḥ— by the characteristics; agrāhyam — beyond ordinary perception; anumānatah — by conclusions.

Translation

Here in the human form by subtle sense perceptions, by studying various characteristics and forming conclusions, persons who are disciplined in yoga practice, directly search for the Lord, who is beyond ordinary perception. (2.23)

Commentary:

The systematic search for the absolute truth is described in this verse. Lord Krishna posited the absolute as being the Lord or Supreme Being, the *Iśvaram*. Some feel that the *Iśwara* is not the absolute truth but only a person of limited supremacy who is subordinate to the Absolute truth.

Both seekers, those seek a supreme person and those who seek a supreme energy or impersonal source, must, if they are serious, use subtle sense perception, to study the various characteristics of the causal realities. For in-depth research, the seeker should be proficient in yoga practice.

अत्राप्य् उदाहरन्तीमम्
इतिहासं पुरातनम् ।
अवधूतस्य सवादं
यदोर् अमित-तेजसः ॥२.२४॥

atrāpy udāharantīmam
itihāsaṁ purātanam
avadhūtasya saṁvādaṁ
yador amita-tejasaḥ (2.24)

atrāpy = atra — here in this case + api - also; udāharantīmam = udāharanti — they cite + imam — this; itihāsam — history; purātanam — ancient; avadhūtasya — of an ascetic who totally renounced cultural activities; saṁvādam — conversation; yador = yadoḥ — of Yadu; amita-tejasaḥ — a person with matchless valor.

Translation

In this case, also, they cite an ancient history of a conversation between an ascetic who had totally renounced cultural activities, and Yadu, who had matchless valor. (2.24)

Commentary:

The ascetic was a true *sannyāsi* not a part-time one or a *tyāgi*. A true *sannyāsi* is one who renounced exploitive opportunities to such an extent that he no longer requires rationalizations for why he should participate in social history. He does not have to cite one excuse after the other and still pretend that he is renounced.

King Yadu was a *tyāgi*, an ascetic king who practiced renunciation some of the time. When he met that ascetic *(avadhūta)* he was pleased because he thought he could get some techniques from the hermit for increasing renunciation. As indicated by Uddhava in a previous verse, the *tyāgi* or part-time renunciation is epitomized by the full time abstinence from social activities.

Even though Lord Krishna discouraged Arjun from taking up full renunciation, the Lord urged Uddhava to exhibit it. Thus Krishna will cite evidence to support the cause of *sannyāsa* or a total avoidance of cultural activities. At a certain stage, participation in cultural activities is recommended but at a more advanced level it is discouraged.

अवधूत द्वियं कञ्चिच्
चरन्तम् अकुतो-भयम् ।
कविं निरीक्ष्य तरुणं
यदुः पप्रच्छ धर्म-वित् ॥२.२५॥

avadhūtaṁ dviyaṁ kañcic
carantam akuto-bhayam
kaviṁ nirīkṣya taruṇaṁ
yaduḥ papraccha dharma-vit (2.25)

avadhūtaṁ — the socially-separated ascetic; dvijam — brāhmin; kañcic = kañcit — a particular; carantam — wandering; akuto-bhayam = akutaḥ-bhayam — without fear of anything; kaviṁ — learned; nirīkṣya — seeing; taruṇaṁ — young; yaduḥ —Yadu; papraccha — questioned; dharma-vit — one versed in religious principles.

Translation

Seeing a learned and young brahmin functioning as a socially-separated ascetic, wandering about fearlessly, Yadu who was versed in religious principles questioned him. (2.25)

Commentary:

King Yadu was versed in religious principles in so far as a human being's cultural life was concerned but the king was not fearless of everything in the material world *(akutobhayam)*. Generally it is fear that causes a human being to be versed in religious principles *(dharma-vit)*, fear of backlash and rash reactions from material nature and from the human society itself. Thus King Yadu was attracted to the socially-separated ascetic *(avadhūtam)*.

Most of the ascetics who try to separate themselves from human social affairs, fail at the effort. Usually, they try for a time and then return after being pressured back into social life. But this ascetic was successful. King Yadu wanted to hear the method used by him.

श्री-यदुर् उवाच
कुतो बुद्धिर् इयं ब्रह्मन्न्
अकर्तुः सु-विशारदा ।
याम् आसाद्य भवाल् लोक
विद्वाश् चरति बाल-वत् ॥२.२६॥

śrī-yadur uvāca
kuto buddhir iyaṁ brahmann
akartuḥ su-viśāradā
yām āsādya bhavāl lokaṁ
vidvāṁś carati bāla-vat (2.26)

śrī-yadur = śrī-yaduḥ - the respected Yadu; uvāca — said; kuto = kutam — whence, how; buddhir = buddhiḥ — intellect, discernment; iyam — this; brahmann — O brahmin; akartuḥ — of a person who is exempt from cultural activities; su-viśaradā — excellent; yām — which; āsādya — have acquired; bhavāl = bhavān — you; lokaṁ — world; vidvāms — one who is educated; carati — travel; bāla-vat — like a child.

Translation

The respected Yadu said: O brahmin, who are exempt from cultural activities, how have you acquired this excellent discernment, through which you travel over the world like a child, although you are educated. (2.26)

Commentary:

King Yadu admired the mental innocence which the ascetic displayed. The ascetic reached a level of perception, whereby he could go about the world with a noncritical attitude, being free from social responsibilities for upgrading human society and still being free from the backlashes which come to people who avoid duties.

Why was material nature not attacking this particular ascetic who bypassed all social tasks and who was callous to the cultural development of human society? Although he was educated, although he had the capacity of a ruler or engineer, still he did nothing constructive. He did not endeavor for a livelihood, nor to do humanitarian work. Why was he wandering like an aimless human being?

प्रायो धर्मार्थ-कामेषु
विवित्सायां च मानवाः ।
हेतुनैव समीहन्त
आयुषो यशसः श्रियः ॥२.२७॥

prāyo dharmārtha-kāmeṣu
vivitsāyāṁ ca mānavāḥ
hetunaiva samīhanta
āyuṣo yaśasaḥ śriyaḥ (2.27)

prāyo = prāyaḥ — generally speaking; dharmārtha-kāmeṣu = dharma — virtue + artha — wealth + kāmeṣu — for enjoyment; vivitsāyām — pursuit of self realisation; ca — and; mānavāḥ — human beings; hetunaiva = hetunā — for the purpose + eva — indeed; samīhante — the extent; āyuṣo = āyuṣaḥ — long-life span; yaśasaḥ — fame; śriyaḥ — prosperity.

Translation

Generally speaking, human beings exert themselves for virtue, wealth, enjoyment, and self realisation, for the sake of a long life span, fame and prosperity. (2.27)

Commentary:

King Yadu had studied human psychology. He understood it quite well. He found that the isolationist had broken the boundaries of human sociology. The ascetic displayed no drives for acquiring a long lifespan, fame and prosperity. Most human beings act in terms of virtue, economic development, enjoyment, and philosophical consideration, for the sake of living longer, being famous and acquiring money. The ascetic was not interested in any of these things, not even in self-realization.

What exactly was he aiming for? After all, even the spirits using lower life-forms work for something objective, no matter how vague or primitive it may be. In fear of dying, people aspire for long life. To become popular they work for fame. To ward off poverty they create luxurious living conditions. How did the ascetic transcend this?

त्वं तु कल्पः कविर् दक्षः
सु-भगो ऽमृत-भाषणः ।
न कर्ता नेहसे किञ्चिज्
जडोन्मत्त-पिशाच-वत् ॥ २.२८ ॥

tvaṁ tu kalpaḥ kavir dakṣaḥ
su-bhago 'mṛta-bhāṣaṇaḥ
na kartā nehase kiñcij
jaḍonmatta-piśāca-vat (2.28)

tvam — you; tu — but; kalpaḥ — capable; kavir = kaviḥ — learned; dakṣaḥ — resourceful; su-bhago = su-bhagaḥ — good-looking; 'mṛta-bhāṣanaḥ = 'mṛta (amṛta) – sweet + bhāṣaṇaḥ — talking; na kartā — one who does not participate constructively, a loafer; nehase = na — not + ihase - you endeavor; kiñcij = kiñcit — anything; jaḍonmatta-piśāca-vat = jada — stupid + unmatta — mad + piśāca –a haunted human being + vat — like.

Translation

But you, though capable, learned, resourceful, good-looking and sweet-talking, appear as a loafer. You do not endeavor for anything, just as if you were stupid and mad like a haunted human being. (2.28)

Commentary:

Generally, a person who is capable, learned and resourceful, good-looking and sweet-talking, takes advantage of the exploitive opportunities but the socially-separated ascetic seemed to have developed a resistance even to taking any opportunities to better himself or to accept honors in human society. King Yadu would learn of the motive for the ascetic's rejection of social life.

जनेषु दह्यमानेषु
काम-लोभ-दवाग्निना ।
न तप्यसे ऽग्निना मुक्तो
गङ्गाम्भः-स्थ इव द्विपः ॥ २.२९ ॥

janeṣu dahyamāneṣu
kāma-lobha-davāgninā
na tapyase 'gninā mukto
gaṅgāmbhaḥ-stha iva dvipaḥ (2.29)

janeṣu — by the people; dahyamāneṣu — by being scorched; kāma-lobha-davāgninā = kama — lust + lobha — greed + davāgninā — in the forest fire; na –not; tapyase — you are harassed; 'gninā = agnina — in the fire; mukto = muktaḥ — freed; gaṅgāmbhaḥ = gangā – Ganges River + ambhaḥ — water + stha (sthaḥ) - standing; iva — as if; dvipaḥ — elephant.

Translation

While people are scorched by the fire of lust and greed, you, being freed, are not harassed by the fire, just as an elephant standing in the water of the Ganges River. (2.29)

Commentary:

King Yadu was perceptive. He understood that most people have no choice in the matter of activities. He realized that generally, material existence is impulsively performed with the spirits having little or no say in what they can or cannot do. But this ascetic was outside the influence of material nature, just like an elephant who stood in the water of a cool river and effectively transcended the day's heat.

The example of the elephant is appropriate. The ascetic was completely removed from material existence but he was still near to that influence. Since he was near, he could be communicated with by any soul who was eager to find the secret for a spirit's removal from human social affairs.

त्वं हि नः पृच्छतां ब्रह्मन्न्
आत्मन्य् आनन्द-कारणम् ।
ब्रूहि स्पर्श-विहीनस्य
भवतः केवलात्मनः ॥२.३०॥

tvaṁ hi naḥ pṛcchatāṁ brahmann
ātmany ānanda-kāraṇam
brūhi sparśa-vihīnasya
bhavataḥ kevalātmanaḥ (2.30)

tvam — you; hi — indeed; nah — to us; prcchatāṁ — inquiring; brahmann — O brahmin; ātmany = ātmani — in the self; ānanda-kāraṇam = ānanda — spiritual happiness + kāraṇam — the cause; brūhi — tell; sparśa-vihīnasya = sparsa – contact + vihīnasya – without the attractive objects; bhavataḥ — of you; kevalātmanah = kevala – alone + ātmanah — spiritual self.

O brahman, tell us who inquire, about the cause of the spiritual happiness which is in the spiritual self alone, even without contact with the attractive objects.

Translation

O brahmin, tell us who inquire, about the cause of spiritual happiness which is in the spiritual self alone, even without contact with the attractive objects. (2.30)

Commentary:

By asking this question, King Yadu revealed to us a great secret which is the reason for our being scorched by the impulsive fiery force of lust and greed. That secret is our quest for spiritual happiness *(ānanda).* Unfortunately we search for that unhappiness in the wrong place.

Nearly everyone in King Yadu's time and nearly everyone today, seeks this happiness and is very industrious in trying to procure it, but the socially-separated ascetic found it. He no longer engaged in any exploitive opportunities since such exploitation cannot lead to spiritual happiness, even though it gives the frustration from which we can conclude that we seek the happiness in the wrong place and by the wrong means.

Since the socially-separated ascetic was still in the material world by virtue of his having a gross material body, a subtle material form and causal mundane energy, King Yadu could understand that the ascetic had not relocated to the transcendental realms in entirety. It seemed to the king that the ascetic was enjoying the existence of his spirit only. But even so, the King wanted to know how it would be possible for a spirit to be that independent of the various grades of emotional energy.

We heard from Uddhava about the body-reliant *(tanu-bhṛt)* souls. These are souls who need a material body. But it appeared to King Yadu, that the ascetic had no such reliance, even though he did have a material form. The rarity of it!

श्री-भगवान् उवाच
यदुनैवं महा-भागो
ब्रह्मण्येन सु-मेधसा ।
पृष्टः सभाजितः प्राह
प्रश्रयावनतं द्विजः ॥२.३१॥

śrī-bhagavān uvāca
yadunaivaṁ mahā-bhāgo
brahmaṇyena su-medhasā
pṛṣṭaḥ sabhājitaḥ prāha
praśrayāvanataṁ dvijaḥ (2.31)

śrī-bhagavān – the Blessed Lord; uvāca — said; yadunaivaṁ = yadunā — by Yadu + evam — in that way; mahā-bhāgo = mahā-bhāgaḥ — blessed; brahmaṇyena — by one who is devoted to brahmins; su-medhasā — by one who is intelligent; pṛṣṭaḥ — asked; sabhājitah — honored; prāha — said; praśrayāvanataṁ = praśraya — courteous + avanatam — bowing his head + dvijah — brāhmin.

Translation

The Blessed Lord said: Being asked in that way and honored by the intelligent Yadu, who was devoted to the brahmins, the blessed brahmin spoke to the King who bowed his head courteously. (2.31)

Commentary:

Whatever the blessed Brahmin has to say to human society could not be understood nor be properly appreciated by an ordinary human being but only by someone who was near the end of his material existence, someone who was on the verge of discovering that even though there are many exploitive opportunities presented to each spirit, still, none of the spirits could find spiritual happiness by pursuing mundane activities.

King Yadu felt lucky to be conversing with the blessed brahmin. The brahmin also, greatly appreciated being petitioned by the king. The knowledge and maturity in spiritual development which was the experience of the ascetic, would be deposited with the king, thus relieving the brahmin of the responsibility for elevating human beings.

श्री-ब्राह्मण उवाच
सन्ति मे गुरवो राजन्
बहवो बुद्ध्-उपश्रिताः ।
यतो बुद्धिम् उपादाय
मुक्तो ऽटामीह तान् शृणु ॥ २.३२॥

śrī-brāhmaṇa uvāca
santi me guravo rājan
bahavo buddhy-upaśritāḥ
yato buddhim upādāya
mukto 'ṭāmīha tān śṛṇu (2.32)

śrī-brāhmana – the blessed brahmin; uvāca — said; santi — there are; me — my; guravo = guravaḥ — teachers; rājan — O King; bahavo = bahavah — many; buddhy-upaśṛitāḥ = buddhy (buddhi) — intelligence + upaśritāḥ — relying on; yato = yataḥ — from whom; buddhim — understanding; upādāya — gaining; mukto = muktaḥ — freed; 'ṭāmīha = aṭāmi — I roam about + iha — in this world; tān — them; śṛṇu — hear.

Translation

The blessed brahmin said: O King, I have many teachers, whom I rely on, through the use of my intellect. Gaining understanding from them, I roam about in this world. Hear of them. (2.32)

Commentary:

The life of the brahmin in taking lessons from more than one spiritual master *(guruvo)*, was substantiated by Lord Krishna's previous statement, when he told Uddhava:

śrī-bhagavān uvāca
prayeṇa manujā loke loka-tattva vicakṣaṇāḥ
samuddharanti hy ātmānam ātmanaivāśubhāśayāt

The Blessed Lord said: Indeed by their own endeavor, people who really know the truth of the world, regularly deliver themselves from evil tendencies. (U.G. 2.19)

If one cannot use his intelligence to draw the proper conclusions as he travels through this material existence, he cannot become freed from material bondage. A stupid person cannot become freed. It would be impossible.

A more important aspect however is humility. The ultimate form of humility was being demonstrated in the life of the wandering ascetic. He learned from anyone and from anything animate or inanimate, whenever and wherever there was something that could be comprehended for spiritual realization. He no longer felt that he was so great that he could not learn even from an insect, a reptile, or an energy.

पृथिवी वायुर् आकाशम्
आपो ऽग्निश् चन्द्रमा रविः ।
कपोतो ऽजगरः सिन्धुः
पतङ्गो मधुकृद् गजः ॥२.३३॥

pṛthivī vāyur ākāśam
āpo 'gniś candramā raviḥ
kapoto 'jagaraḥ sindhuḥ
pataṅgo madhukṛd gajaḥ (2.33)

prthivī — the earth; vāyur = vāyuḥ — the air; ākāśam — the sky; āpo = āpaḥ — the water; agnis = agniḥ — the fire; candramā = candramāḥ — the moon; raviḥ — the sun; kapoto = kapotaḥ — the pigeon; 'jagarah = ajagaraḥ — the python; sindhuḥ — the sea; pataṅgo = pataṅgaḥ — the moth; madhukṛd = madhukṛt — the honey bee; gajaḥ — the elephant.

Translation

The earth, air, sky, water, fire, the moon, the sun, the pigeon, the python, the sea, the moth, the honey bee, the elephant, (2.33)

Commentary:

If spiritual teaching pressures us from every side, why are we not learning? If even the material elements in their compacted states like clay or in their scattered states, like air, can teach us and cause us to advance spiritually, then why are we stalled in material existence? It must be our attitude towards being taught and our misconceptions about what we should comprehend, as well as our insensitivity to those teaching energies.

मधु-हा हरिणो मीनः
पिङ्गला कुररो ऽर्भकः ।
कुमारी शर-कृत् सर्प
ऊर्णनाभिः सुपेशकृत् ॥२.३४॥

madhu-hā hariṇo mīnaḥ
piṅgalā kuraro 'rbhakaḥ
kumārī śara-kṛt sarpa
ūrṇanābhiḥ supeśakṛt (2.34)

madhu-hā = madhu – honey + hā — the one who confiscates; harino = harinaḥ — the deer; mīnah — the fish; piṅgalā — Piṅgalā; kuraro = kuraraḥ — the osprey; 'rbhakaḥ = arbhakaḥ — the child; kumārī — the girl; śara-kṛt — the arrow maker; sarpa = sarpaḥ — the snake; ūrṇanābhiḥ — the spider; supeśakṛt — the wasp;

Translation

...the one who confiscated honey, the deer, the fish, Piṅgalā, the osprey, the child, the girl, the arrow-maker, the snake, the spider, the wasp, (2.34)

Commentary:

The socially-separated ascetic reached a stage where he was so humble towards material existence, that he could learn from its cruel features in the form of a callous honey-gatherer, as well as from the wasp who paralyzed other insects, securing their bodies as food for its offspring.

एते मे गुरवो राजन्
चतुर्-विंशतिर् आश्रिताः।
शिक्षा वृत्तिभिर् एतेषाम्
अन्वशिक्षम् इहात्मनः ॥२.३५॥

ete me guravo rājan
catur-viṁśatir āśritāḥ
śikṣā vṛttibhir eteṣām
anvaśikṣam ihātmanaḥ (2.35)

ete — these; me — my; guravo = guravah — teachers; rājan — O King; catur-vimśatir = catuḥ - four + vimśatiḥ — twenty; āśritāḥ — resorting to; śikṣā — instruction; vṛttibhir = vṛttibhiḥ — by the conduct; eteṣām — of these, their; anvaśikṣam — I learned; ihātmanaḥ = iha — in this existence + ātmanaḥ — the self.

Translation

...these, O King, are the twenty-four teachers whom I resorted to. From their conduct, I learned about the self in this existence. (2.35)

Commentary:

Since the selves are similar, the ascetic learned from various selves about himself. He resorted *(āśritāḥ)* to other selves for lessons because of the comparative similarity between himself and the others. All the aspects of material nature mentioned, all its configurations even the elemental ones like the earth, and air, were actually embodied. Thus all of these were displaying the potential activity of any other self.

यतो यद् अनुशिक्षामि
यथा वा नाहुषात्मज ।
तत् तथा पुरुष-व्याघ्र
निबोध कथयामि ते ॥ २.३६ ॥

yato yad anuśikṣāmi
yathā vā nāhuṣātmaja
tat tathā puruṣa-vyāghra
nibodha kathayāmi te (2.36)

yato = yataḥ — from whom; yad = yat — which; anuśikṣāmi — I learned; yathā va — as, in sequence; nāhuṣātmaja = Nahuṣa – Nāshusa + ātmaja — son of; tat — that; tathā — so; puruṣa-vyāghra = tiger among men; nibodha — listen; kathayāmi — I will tell; te — to you.

Translation

O son of Nahuṣa, tiger among men, I will tell you which lesson I learned from whom in proper sequence. (2.36)

Commentary:

As the tiger is the ruler of jungle animals, so Yadu was the ruler of men. The ascetic too, was a ruler of sensual and mental energies. In the psychic kingdom where the senses are like wild animals, the ascetic by virtue of sensual and mental control, was a ruler.

भूतैर् आक्रम्यमाणो ऽपि
धीरो दैव-वशानुगैः ।
तद् विद्वान् न चलेन् मार्गाद्
अन्वशिक्षं क्षितेर् व्रतम् ॥ २.३७ ॥

bhūtair ākramyamāṇo 'pi
dhīro daiva-vaśānugaiḥ
tad vidvān na calen mārgād
anvaśikṣaṁ kṣiter vratam (2.37)

bhūtair = bhūtaiḥ — by the creatures; ākramyamāṇo = ākramyamānah — oppressed; 'pi = api — even though; dhīro = dhīraḥ — one whose intellect (dhi) is stablised; daiva-vaśānugaiḥ = daiva — destiny + vaśānugaiḥ — by the control of, by following impulsively; tad— that; vidvān — a person who knows the facts; na – not; calen — should swerve; margād = mārgāt — from the path; anvaśikṣaṁ — I learned; kṣiter = kṣiteḥ — from the earth; vratam — regulation.

Translation

The man whose intellect is stabilised, who knows the facts, should not swerve from the path, even though he is oppressed by creatures who are controlled by destiny and who follow it impulsively. I learned of this regulation from the earth. (2.37)

Commentary:

This lesson was learned from the earth but the earth is only one of the teachers. Another ascetic in another time and place, might learn the same lessons from another aspect. The all-surrounding divine graces are pressing down on each spirit to learn all lessons which will be explained in the proper sequence to King Yadu.

This same lesson was taught to Arjuna at *Kurukṣetra* when Lord Krishna explained that all creatures are under a mundane pressure. To a degree, all of them act impulsively. Krishna told

Arjuna that repression could not be effective, since sooner or later, a man must display his tendency.

The key is this: The individual spirits are not independent. They are conditioned by the influences of material nature. In real terms, any oppression which comes upon an ascetic, comes from the all-surrounding mundane potencies. One should not be resentful of this grievous existence. The environment is actually friendly but we lose sight of the whole scope and take things personally.

शश्वत् परार्थ-सर्वेहः
परार्थैकान्त-सम्भवः ।
साधुः शिक्षेत भू-भृत्तो
नग-शिष्यः परात्मताम् ॥२.३८॥

śaśvat parārtha-sarvehaḥ
parārthaikānta-sambhavaḥ
sādhuḥ śikṣeta bhū-bhṛtto
naga-śiṣyaḥ parātmatām (2.38)

śaśvat — always; parārtha-sarvehaḥ = para — of others + artha — for the good of + sarva – all + īhaḥ —effort; parārthaikānta-sambhavaḥ = para-artha — the good of others + ekānta — only + sambhavaḥ — existence; sādhuḥ — saintly person; śikṣeta — should learn; bhū-bhṛtto = bhū-bhṛttaḥ — from the mountain; naga-śiṣyaḥ = naga – tree + śiṣyaḥ — disciple; parātmatām = para – to others, for others + ātmatām — the very self.

Translation

The saintly person should learn from the mountain how one should always dedicate one's efforts for the good of others, and one's existence should only be for the sake of others; from the tree he should learn how to live for the very self of others. (2.38)

Commentary:

The practical aspect of the extent of the humility of a saintly person is defined clearly here, to the point of endeavoring for others and total subjection of the self to the use of others. It may be contested that such an all-out servile attitude would make a saintly man a ploy or play thing of others.

However the saintly person does not become a victim of circumstances by his own conscious design but rather by the flow of destiny which imposes certain restrictions on him. He recognizes the restrictions and the source of the restrictions. If he determines that it is counter-productive to avoid, resist or ignore a circumstance, he submits himself willingly to it. As a mountain produced soil, minerals, trees, habitats, coolness, fertilization and streams, so that saintly persons produced various benefits which are utilized by human society. But as human society may not realize the benefits it gains from a mountain and as the mountain does not acclaim itself, so the advanced saint relates to human society.

As a tree bears fruits and is abused by pickers, so an advanced personality gives positive influences to others and bears the abuses they give him. Unless one reaches a state of being dedicated to the good of others, regardless of how one is treated by them, one cannot advance beyond the material world. One must be capable of seeing into the depths of the souls of others and giving them association which satisfies them deeply even though they themselves, may not appreciate the association. One who lives on the surface of his spirit, rather than deep within it, cannot appreciate saintly association. But still, an advanced person serves the deeper needs, regardless of the appreciation or insult he receives.

प्राण-वृत्त्यैव सन्तुष्येन्
मुनिर् नैवेन्द्रिय-प्रियैः ।
ज्ञानं यथा न नश्येत
नावकीर्येत वाङ्-मनः ॥२.३९॥

prāṇa-vṛttyaiva santuṣyen
munir naivendriya-priyaiḥ
jñānaṁ yathā na naśyeta
nāvakīryeta vāṅ-manaḥ (2.39)

prāṇa-vṛttyaiva = prāṇa - energizing air + vrttya — tending + eva — merely; santusyen — should be satisfied; munir = muniḥ — philosophical yogi; naivendriya-priyaiḥ = na – not + eva – indeed + indriya-priyaiḥ — with things which pleases the senses; jñānam — knowledge; yathā — so; na – not; naśyeta — be destroyed; nāvakīryeta = na—not + avakīryeta – frittered away; vāṅ-manaḥ = vāṅ (vāk) — speech + manaḥ — mind.

Translation

The philosophical yogi, should be satisified functioning just by merely tending to the energising air and not with things which are pleasing to the senses, so that knowledge is not destroyed and the speech and mind are not frittered away. (2.39)

Commentary:

The term *munir (munih)* is usually translated as philosopher but it means a yogi philosopher. In the time of Lord Krishna the philosophers were mostly yogis and the forest ascetics like the socially-separated one who spoke to Yadu, were proficient yogis. To confirm this, we must pay attention to the Sanskrit term *prāṇa-vṛttyaiva*. An ordinary philosopher who is not proficient in yoga practice and who has not mastered *prāṇāyāma* cannot be satisfied functioning merely by tending the energizing air or *prāṇa*. Therefore it is a distortion if a translator avoids mentioning that *prāṇa* is the vitalizing air.

A more important consideration is this: Most people do not practice *prāṇāyāma*. It takes time and patience to develop the proficiency of it. Therefore it is unlikely that the average person may assume its practice. Thus what should translators and preachers of *Bhāgavatam* do? Should they tell the truth about this and other similar verses which have impractical instructions for modern people. Or should they twist or manipulate the Sanskrit to suit their missionary intentions? As for the answer: Each reader should form his own opinion. Our intention in this translation, is to show what was said at the time these speeches were made.

It is indicated by the wandering ascetic who lectured King Yadu, that unless we tend specifically to the energizing air, we will tend to the unnecessary demands of the senses and our knowledge as well as senses and mind, will be fritted away. My experience in yoga practice confirms this. If a yogi does not develop his *prāṇāyāma* practice, he is forced to become more and more gross and the senses becomes more and more demanding on him. Then his understanding shifts to a more elementary level, and his speech and mind automatically adjust to support that lower plane.

The key is this: The energizing air is the manipulator of the sensual energies, to such an extent that if one uses a poor quality of air, his sensual energy becomes degraded automatically. He is then forced to seek out vices. As soon as the yogi eliminates lower energy or lower energizing air, his vision clears up. He develops a discriminatory power to direct his senses to higher realities.

It may be argued that all this can be done by other methods of concentration and by sheer will power. That is true but there is no doubt that whatever a person can achieve without *prāṇāyāma* proficiency, can be accomplished to a greater extent and with more consistency and thoroughness by *prāṇāyāma* practices.

विषयेष्व् आविशन् योगी
नाना-धर्मेषु सर्वतः ।
गुण-दोष-व्यपेतात्मा
न विषज्जेत वायु-वत् ॥ २.४० ॥

viṣayeṣv āviśan yogī
nānā-dharmeṣu sarvataḥ
guṇa-doṣa-vyapetātmā
na viṣajjeta vāyu-vat (2.40)

viṣayeṣu — amidst the attractive objects; āviśan — moving; yogī — a yogi; nānā-dharmeṣu = nānā – many types + dharmeṣu — of the values; sarvataḥ — everywhere; guṇa-doṣa-vyapetātmā = guṇa — positive aspects + doṣa — disadvantages + vyapeta – separated + ātmā — self (vyapeta - ātmā – one whose self is separated); na – no; viṣajjeta — should be attached; vāyu-vat — like the wind.

Translation

The yogi, moving everywhere amidst the attractive objects which are of many different values, should not be attached, keeping himself seperated from their positive aspects and disadvantages, just like as if he were the wind. (2.40)

Commentary:

This type of detachment, this type of neutrality towards sense objects and towards polarity in values, is developed to the highest degree through *prāṇāyāma* practice. *Prāṇāyāma* practice gives a keener detachment, which though similar, is a bit different from the detachment developed by other methods such as will power resistance, detachment by taking vows and forcing oneself to act in a certain way, and detachment by being in a society or an association in which certain rules and regulations are stressed. The point here is the basis of the detachment and the detachment itself. If it were just the detachment alone, the ascetic would not have spoke of the satisfaction of tending *prāṇa* or vitalizing energy. Detachment attained by other methods such as renunciation, a sense of shame towards certain habits, a public vow, and an agreement with others to prevent one another from proceeding with undesirable habits, is differently supported. The description in this verse applies to the type of detachment attained through *prāṇāyāma* proficiency not other-wise.

In all cases of detachment, if the basis of the detachment is removed, the person returns to old habits because he is no longer supported in the resistance. Let us take for example a vow. If I take a vow to end a bad habit, my mind will try to help me to fulfill the pledge but as soon I feel that the vow is unnecessary or that it is not a priority, I will return to the old habit. In some cases I may start with one basis for detachment and then shift to another higher or lower motive. Thus there are different types of detachment depending on the motivations.

In the case of those yogi philosophers who use *prāṇāyāma* practice as their basis, they have a solid support from getting nutrients through the energizing air. Their subtle body is directly reliant on that. If their practice is firm and consistent, they are protected from fall-down. If their practice becomes lax, they will be degraded. At a higher level of practice, one might shift to causal energy and get away from the need for even the highly energized vitalizing air which the ascetic mentioned to King Yadu.

पार्थिवेष्व् इह देहेषु
प्रविष्टस् तद्-गुणाश्रयः ।
गुणैर् न युज्यते योगी
गन्धैर् वायुर् इवात्म-दृक् ॥२.४१॥

pārthiveṣv iha deheṣu
praviṣṭas tad-guṇāśrayaḥ
guṇair na yujyate yogī
gandhair vāyur ivātma-dṛk (2.41)

pārthiveṣv = pārthiveṣu — in earthly forms; iha — in this world; deheṣu — in the bodies; praviṣṭas — having entered; tad-guṇāśrayaḥ = tad (tat) — that + guṇa – characteristic + āśrayaḥ — having taken on; gunair = gunaiḥ — with those qualities; na –not; yujyate — does become possessed; yogī — yogi; gandhair = gandhaiḥ — by odors; vāyuh — air; ivātmadṛk = iva — just as if + ātma-dṛk — one who consistently sees the spiritual self;

Translation

Even though entering earthly forms and taking on their characteristics, the yogi who consistently sees the spiritual self, is not possessed by those qualities, just as the wind is not affected by odors. (2.41)

Commentary:

The *ātma-dṛk* yogi, or the one who consistently sees the spiritual self not only of himself but of others, may enter material bodies, even lower ones in animal species and still he is not possessed by the qualities of such forms. This does not mean that those bodies will not act in a vulgar manner, but it indicates that the yogi can transcend the normal actions of such bodies. His subtle form is shielded from those tendencies which are usually acquired by any limited spirit who passes through such vulgarity.

An elevated yogi must assist others, no matter where they may be. And that entails going to the existential location of those whom he must rescue. In that mission, he must lower himself to the exact place where the helpless victims are existentially located. It might appear that such yogis become degraded when they go down to a lower state. They do however come out by the same passage through which they are lowered. They do not work on their own. They are guided by superior beings. They will not remain in an awkward position in reference to material nature.

अन्तर्हितश् च स्थिर-जङ्गमेषु
ब्रह्मात्म-भावेन समन्वयेन ।
व्याप्त्याव्यवच्छेदम् असङ्गम् आत्मनो
मुनिर् नभस्त्वं विततस्य भावयेत् ॥ २.४२ ॥

antarhitaś ca sthira-jaṅgameṣu
brahmātma-bhāvena samanvayena
vyāptyāvyavacchedam asaṅgam ātmano
munir nabhastvaṁ vitatasya bhāvayet (2.42)

antarhitaś = antarhitaḥ — present within; ca — and; sthira-jaṅgameṣu = sthira — non-moving species + jaṅgameṣu — among the moving species; brahmātma-bhāvena = brahmātma - spiritual soul + bhāvena — by the stage of realization; samanvayena — by successive contact; vyāptyāvyavacchedam = vyāptyā — pervading + avyavacchedam — non-partitioned (avyaya - unchangeable + chedam - divided, partitioned); asaṅgam — not attached, detached; ātmano = ātmanaḥ — the self; munir = muniḥ — yogi philosopher; nabhastvam — like the sky; vitatasya — of the pervasive; bhāvayet — should reflect on.

Translation

And being present within a body, the yogi philosopher by the state of realisation of the spiritual soul, should reflect on the non-partitioned, detached, and sky-like trait of the pervasive soul which can inhabit the moving and non-moving species. (2.42)

Commentary:

The individual spirit is non-partitioned *(avyavacchedan)* or absolute, but only in the sense that he cannot be cleaved. He can not be split up for any reason. Lord Krishna explained this to Arjuna in these terms:

nainaṁ chindanti śastrāṇi nainaṁ dahati pāvakaḥ
na cainaṁ kledayantyāpo na śoṣayati mārutaḥ
acchedyo'yamadāhyo'yam akledyo'śoṣya eva ca
nityaḥ sarvagataḥ sthāṇur acalo'yaṁ sanātanaḥ.

Weapons do not pierce, fire does not burn, and water does not wet, nor does the wind dry that embodied soul. (2.23)

This embodied soul cannot be pierced, cannot be burnt, cannot be moistened and cannot be dried. And indeed, this soul is eternal. It can penetrate all things. It is a permanent principle and is stable and primeval. (B.G. 2.23-24)

Some say that the living entity is absolute *(kevalam)*, but that does not mean that the living entity is God. To say that the living entity is God is to do serious damage to the meaning of the word God. No one should speak that absurdity.

The Supreme Soul is God and no one else. The others are allied to the Godhead. Lord Krishna accredit the others as being His partners (amsa):

mamaivāṁśo jīvaloke jīvabhūtaḥ sanātanaḥ
manaḥṣaṣṭhānīndriyāṇi prakṛtisthāni karṣati (15.7)

My partner is in this world of individualized conditioned beings. He is an eternal individual soul but he draws to himself the mundane senses of which the mind is the sixth detection device. (B.G. 15.7)

Some say that the individual spirit should merge into God the way a drop of water can merge into the ocean but factually a drop of water does not really merge. The individual water molecules maintain their configuration but they appear to be merged to those who cannot see the distinction between one molecule and another. Even though the spirits are so close to each other, so close that it appears there is no film or partition between them, there is a transparent partition between each of them. This partition is eternal but within the spirit itself there is no partition. This is what the socially-separated ascetic described in this verse.

Even though he does become attached from time to time, he is essentially a detached, sky-like being, just as a nomad sets up a tent nightly even though essentially he is a desert wanderer. A nomad prefers not to live in one building for life, but still he is required to live in a cornered setting from time to time. He carries a tent to created a temporary shelter which he sets up for some hours at night.

The living entity is detached but in material existence he exhibits a sense of attachment just to get by. The problem is that he forgets that the material situation is temporary, thus he may begin to think that his mundane attachment is a real necessity. Thus he becomes occupied maintaining one attached situation after another.

तेजो-ऽब्-अन्न-मयैर् भावैर्
मेघाद्यैर् वायुनेरितैः ।
न स्पृश्यते नभस् तद्वत्
काल-सृष्टैर् गुणैः पुमान् ॥२.४३॥

tejo-'b-anna-mayair bhāvair
meghādyair vāyuneritaiḥ
na spṛśyate nabhas tadvat
kāla-sṛṣṭair guṇaiḥ pumān (2.43)

tejo = tejaḥ — combustive; 'b-anna-mayair = ab-anna-mayaiḥ = ab (ap) — liquid + anna — solid + mayaiḥ — by the products of; bhāvair = bhāvaiḥ — by objects; meghādyair = megha – clouds + ādyair (ādyaiḥ) — and other types of vapor; vāyuneritaiḥ = vāyunā — by the wind + īritaiḥ — by blown about; na – no; spṛśyate — is untouched; nabhas — sky; tadvat — like that, just so; kāla-sṛṣṭair = kāla –time + sṛṣṭair (sṛṣṭaiḥ) — created by; guṇaiḥ — by the influence of material nature; pumān — a person.

Translation

As the sky is not touched by objects which are products of combustives, liquids and solids, or by clouds and other vapor, which is driven by the wind, just so a person should not be affected by things which are created by time and by the influence of material nature. (2.43)

Commentary:

As taught by the socially-separated ascetic *(avadhūta),* we must learn not to take material nature seriously. Of course, we must be practical otherwise material nature will harass us in many ways, but still we should not become too occupied trying to live in a very comfortable way.

Time and material nature *(kāla and guṇa)* may affect us but we should cope and not loose the spiritual perspective. If per chance we lose it, we should quickly re-establish it.

Just as still photographs attract us and movies keep us even more spell-bound, material nature has got some power and is reinforced by time. Even so we should transcend these aspects and eventually become immune to their influence.

Time in conjunction with material nature has caused the mundane energy to take on a shifty and evasive aspect which befools us, but we can, by retraction of our sensual interest, get our spirituality in order and view the whole scope of material existence as a distraction.

स्वच्छः प्रकृतितः स्निग्धो
माधुर्यस् तीर्थ-भूर् नृणाम् ।
मुनिः पुनात्य् अपा मित्रम्
ईक्षोपस्पर्श-कीर्तनैः ॥२.४४॥

svacchaḥ prakṛtitaḥ snigdho
mādhuryas tīrtha-bhūr nṛṇām
muniḥ punāty apāṁ mitram
īkṣopasparśa-kīrtanaiḥ (2.44)

svacchaḥ — pure; prakṛtitaḥ —natural; snigdho = snigdhaḥ — gentle; mādhuryas — sweet; tīrtha-bhūr = tīrtha-bhūḥ — place of holiness; nṛṇām — for human beings; muniḥ — yogi philosopher;

punāty = punāti — purifies; apām — of water; mitram — being similar; īkṣopasparśa-kīrtanaiḥ = īkṣā — being seen + upasparśa — being touched + kīrtanaiḥ — by being prasied.

Translation

Pure natured, gentle, sweet, and a source of holiness to human beings, the yogi philosopher, being similar to water, purifies by being seen, touched, and praised. (2.44)

Commentary:

The usefulness of the yogi philosopher is compared to the serviceability of water. As pure water serves as a source of cleanliness, so the yogi philosopher who is pure in nature and intent, natural in spiritual constitution, who is usually uninvolved with dirty emotions, serves as a psychological source of cleanliness for others who take shelter of him.

In other instances however, the yogi philosopher can be hard, sour in dealings, a source of trouble for others, seemingly unnatural and seemingly impure, just as pure water can pose a threat to those who cannot swim or who in some way are imperiled by it.

तेजस्वी तपसा दीप्तो
दुर्धर्षोदर-भाजनः ।
सर्व-भक्ष्यो ऽपि युक्तात्मा
नादत्ते मलम् अग्नि-वत् ॥ २.४५ ॥

tejasvī tapasā dīpto
durdharṣodara-bhājanaḥ
sarva-bhakṣyo 'pi yuktātmā
nādatte malam agni-vat (2.45)

tejasvī — radiant; tapasā — with austerity; dīpto = dīptaḥ — glowing; durdharṣodara-bhājanaḥ = durdharṣa — undeterred + udara – in relation to the stomach + bhājanaḥ — eating; sarva-bhakṣyo = sarva — everything + bhakṣyo (bhakṣyaḥ) — eating; 'pi = api — although; yuktātmā — one who is self disciplined by yoga practice; nādatte = na – not + ādatte — absorb; malam — contamination; agni-vat — like fire.

Translation

Radiant, glowing with austerity, undeterred, with his stomach as the only container for foodstuffs, and eating everything as destined, the person whose self is disciplined by yoga practice, being like fire, does not absorb contamination. (2.45)

Commentary:

The result of the proper austerity is a radiant glowing spirituality. This happens by conservation of sensual energies, when the yogi is able to stop his energies from being expressed randomly and from being wasted off in various sensual fulfillments. Because he reached a stage where he could afford not to take material nature seriously, he does not absorb its contamination. It does not make a big impact on his mind. It does not compel him to compete for exploitive opportunities.

क्वचिच् छन्नः क्वचित् स्पष्ट
उपास्यः श्रेय इच्छताम् ।
भुङ्क्ते सर्वत्र दातृणां
दहन् प्राग्-उत्तराशुभम् ॥ २.४६ ॥

kvacic channaḥ kvacit spaṣṭa
upāsyaḥ śreya icchatām
bhuṅkte sarvatra dātṛṇāṁ
dahan prāg-uttarāśubham (2.46)

kvacic = kvacit — sometimes; channaḥ — disguised; kvacit — sometimes; spaṣṭa = spaṣṭaḥ — revealed; upāsyaḥ — respectfully non honored; śreya — welfare; icchatām — those who desire; bhuṅkte — he utilizes; sarvatra — everywhere; dātṝnām — of donors; dahan — destroying; prāg-uttarāśubham = prāg (prāk) — past + uttara — future + aśubham — sinful reactions.

Translation

Sometimes disguised, sometimes revealed, being respectfully honored by those who desire welfare, he utilizes everything offered everywhere by donors, thus destroying past and future sinful reactions. (2.46)

Commentary:

According to the piercing depth of his vision, the ascetic realizes the various components of each action and properly assesses what should be done to reduce or eliminate any bad content which would produce hazards or any good content which would cause an addiction to pleasant results. Thus he acts in such a way, as to greatly reduce, curtail or eliminate involvements.

Each situation is regarded separately by the ascetic. Each encounter with each person is regarded freshly and he considers the mystic factors which are open to his perception. By remaining disguised, he saves himself from having to deal with too many circumstances and associations. By revealing himself he comes forward and acts in situations where his involvement would be efficient. By allowing himself to be respectfully honored he provides relief for souls who aspire but who recognize his advanced condition.

स्व-मायया सृष्टम् इदं
सद्-असल्-लक्षणं विभुः ।
प्रविष्ट ईयते तत्-तत्-
स्वरूपो ऽग्निर् इवैधसि ॥२.४७॥

sva-māyayā sṛṣṭam idaṁ
sad-asal-lakṣaṇaṁ vibhuḥ
praviṣṭa īyate tat-tat-
svarūpo 'gnir ivaidhasi (2.47)

sva-māyayā = sva – own + māyayā — by supernatural power; sṛṣṭam — manifested; idam — this; sad-asal-lakṣaṇam = sad (sat) – spiritual energy + asal (asat) — mundane energy + lakṣaṇam — characterized; vibhuḥ — the Almighty God; praviṣṭa = praviṣṭaḥ — pervading; īyate — becomes, seems to appear; tat-tat — that and that, this or that; svarūpo = svarūpaḥ — own form, particular form; 'gnir = agniḥ — fire; ivaidhasi = iva — as if just as + edhasi — in firewood.

Translation

The Almighty God having pervaded this spiritual and mundane energy, which was manifest by His supernatural power, seems to appear as this or that particular form, just as fire takes certain shapes through firewood. (2.47)

Commentary:

The *Vibhu* in this case is the Almighty God, the Supreme Personality. This cannot be the limited person or the wandering ascetic who describes this to King Yadu. The limited souls are pervasive but only to a limited degree.

The answer to the question of how it could be possible for the Supreme Being to take on a mundane form, is explained here. He does not actually take on such a form but he can have a limited body created for His usage. Through a temporary form, He can exhibit His interest in a particular dimension, just as fire takes shape in a particular place through firewood. Fire appears here and there in the creation. Similarly the Supreme God can appear in any dimension, in any form depending on the environment.

विसर्गाद्याः श्मशानान्ता
भावा देहस्य नात्मनः ।
कलानाम् इव चन्द्रस्य
कालेनाव्यक्त-वर्त्मना ॥२.४८॥

visargādyāḥ śmaśānāntā
bhāvā dehasya nātmanaḥ
kalānām iva candrasya
kālenāvyakta-vartmanā (2.48)

visargādyāḥ = visarga — birth + ādyāḥ — beginning with; śmaśānāntā = śmaśāna — death + antā (antāḥ) — ending; bhāvā = bhāvāḥ — the existential conditions; dehasya — of the body; nātmanaḥ = na — not + ātmanaḥ — of the soul; kalānām — of the phases; iva — as; candrasya — of the moon; kālenāvyakta-vartmanā = kālena — by time + avyakta — imperceptible + vartmanā —

course.

Translation

The existential conditions, beginning as birth and ending as death, pertain to the body, not the soul, just as the phases of the moon are produced by time whose course is imperceptible. (2.48)

Commentary:

The existential conditions that we have come to know as birth, continuing life, and death, are a reflection of the reality of the soul, which is the background upon which these conditions are displayed. As the phases of the moon are displayed on the basis of the moon's movement, so the various states of birth, growth, maturity, old age and death occur on the basis of the background of the soul.

Because of the gradual but certain influence of time, one hardly understands how his body changes from moment to moment. Still, the observer remains the same. But the observer experiences fluctuations in his sensuality. Thus he thinks that his energy level varies. It remains constant but since he gauges it according to how it is used, he cannot understand that he is actually detached from the varying conditions.

कालेन ह्य् ओघ-वेगेन
भूतानां प्रभवाप्ययौ ।
नित्याव् अपि न दृश्येते
आत्मनो ऽग्नेर् यथार्चिषाम् ॥ २.४९ ॥

kālena hy ogha-vegena
bhūtānāṁ prabhavāpyayau
nityāv api na dṛśyete
ātmano 'gner yathārciṣām (2.49)

kālena — by time; hy = hi — indeed; ogha-vegena = ogha — rapid + vegena — with speed; bhūtānām — of the creatures; prabhavapyayau = prabhava — birth + apyayau — and death; nityav = nityau — always; api — even; na – not; dṛśyete — seen; ātmano = ātmanaḥ — of the soul; 'gner = agneḥ — of fire; yathārciṣām = yathā — just as + arciṣām — of the flames.

Translation

Even though birth and death are always affecting the creatures through the rapid speed of time, that is not seen as an effect on the soul, just as in the case of the fire and the flames. (2.49)

Commentary:

The flames are the obvious indication of a fire but the flames flicker and flicker, constantly changing. Similarly the birth and death of various bodies are obvious indication of the spirit who uses the perishable bodies but the bodies are the temporary factor. The potential for fire though hidden, is the real constant factor. It may be said that birth and death do affect the soul since the soul's focus into this world is adjusted by the status of having or not having a material body. But a more convincing argument is this: The soul's focus does not perish with the body. The focus is a continuous fact. Even for a soul whose focus is habitually attached to material bodies, the focus remains, even when a particular body perishes. Thereafter the disembodied being again latches on to a new form, which is created on the basis of the very same focusing energy. In all cases the focusing energy remains with the spirit, despite the change of bodies.

गुणैर् गुणान् उपादत्ते
यथा-काल विमुञ्चति ।
न तेषु युज्यते योगी
गोभिर् गा इव गो-पतिः ॥ २.५० ॥

guṇair guṇān upādatte
yathā-kālaṁ vimuñcati
na teṣu yujyate yogī
gobhir gā iva go-patiḥ (2.50)

guṇair = guṇaiḥ — through the sense organs; guṇām — sense objects; upādatte — accepts; yathā-kālam = yathā – as by + kālam — time; vimuñcati — releases; na — not; teṣu — in them; yujyate —

is attached; yogī — a yogi; gobhir = gobhiḥ — by rays; gā = gāḥ — waters; iva — as if; go-patiḥ — the sun.

Translation

As the sun holds water by its rays, a yogi accepts sense objects through the sense organs and releases them at the appropiate time. He is not attached to them. (2.50)

Commentary:

Both the yogi and the non-yogi, must accept certain sense objects and must in turn, release the same at certain times. There is a force of nature, both a supernatural and natural force, which supersedes the will of both the yogi and non-yogi. The yogi releases objects willingly and in sufficient time, while the non-yogi might release an object as he or she is forced by the pressure of time, which might painfully suppress him or her until he or she releases the attractive object.

The ascetic compared the yogi to the sun. And we might compare the non-yogi to a container, both the sun and a container can hold water, but the sun releases water easily while a container releases water gradually by evaporation or by being kicked over. The yogi, by virtue of his intimate contact with spirituality, stays at a distance from anything mundane just as the sun remains afar from the earth, even though a fraction of its power is absorbed by the earth.

बुध्यते स्वे न भेदेन
व्यक्ति-स्थ इव तद्-गतः ।
लक्ष्यते स्थूल-मतिभिर्
आत्मा चावस्थितो ऽर्क-वत् ॥२.५१॥

budhyate sve na bhedena
vyakti-stha iva tad-gataḥ
lakṣyate sthūla-matibhir
ātmā cāvasthito 'rka-vat (2.51)

budhyate — is considered; sve — in itself; na — not; bhedena — split into many; vyakti-stha = vyakti — in an object + stha — situated; iva — as if; tad-gataḥ = tad (tat) – that + gatah — gone through, manifested through; lakṣyate — being identical with; sthūla-matibhir = sthūla-matibhiḥ — by the dull-witted people; ātmā — spirit; cāvasthito = ca — and + avasthito (avasthitaḥ) — situated; 'rka-vat = arka-vat — like the sun.

Translation

Like the sun, the spirit being situated in itself is not split into many, but when manifested through an object, it is considered by the dull-witted people, to be identical with that subsance. (2.51)

Commentary:

Even though each individual spirit is non-cleavable, still the spirits become confused about self identity. When a spirit is manifested through anything, its energies are to an extent reflected in, and used by the object. Thus dull-witted people *(sthūla-matibhir)* assume that the object is the spirit itself.

There is an affinity between the sub-energies and the spirit. There is a repulsion between the two as well, but since the affinity is there, it appears that the spirit becomes merged or unified. Actually the spirit remains apart as a separate reality at all times.

The dull-witted people are not necessarily non-devotees, some of them are devotees. One may be dull-witted and still believe in what Lord Krishna says. For a person can believe in something he cannot directly perceived. And if one is dull-witted, then he must necessarily consider the sub-energy to be identical with the spirit who energizes it.

Many limited spirits energize the material world but they are not doing so by choice. They are put into contact with matter by a higher power and by a greater spirit than themselves. There is a statement in the Vedic literature which means that the Supreme Spirit desired objective partners and so He put the hosts of limited spirit in touch with the material energies, through which they are objectified.

The Supreme Spirit does not become many limited individual beings but His influence is present as His power to impart objectivity to the individual spirits in this creation.

नाति-स्नेहः प्रसङ्गो वा
कर्तव्यः क्वापि केनचित् ।
कुर्वन् विन्देत सन्ताप
कपोत इव दीन-धीः ॥२.५२॥

nāti-snehaḥ prasaṅgo vā
kartavyaḥ kvāpi kenacit
kurvan vindeta santāpaṁ
kapota iva dīna-dhīḥ (2.52)

nati = na — not + ati-snehah — too much affection; prasango = prasanga — private association; va — or/nor; kartavyah — should express; kvapi = kva api — otherwise; kenacit — with anyone; kurvan — doing; vindeta — will experience; santāpam — emotional suffering; kapota = kapotaḥ — pigeon; iva — just as; dīna-dhīḥ — poor minded.

Translation

One should not express too much affection nor have private association with anyone, otherwise one will experience emotional suffering just like the poor-minded pigeon. (2.52)

Commentary:

This is actually a cutting remark made to Uddhava. It is a disciplinary recommendation made because of his attachment to certain members of the Yadu family as well as his over-all concern for their physical and supernatural and spiritual safety. In effect, Lord Krishna suggested that Uddhava tend to his own spiritual safety, disregarding the others. A similar chastisement was given to Arjuna in the *Bhagavad-Gītā* discourse:

śrībhagavānuvāca
kutastvā kaśmalamidaṁ viṣame samupasthitam
anāryajuṣṭamasvargyam akīrtikaramarjuna

The Blessed Lord said: How has this sticky emotion come to you at a crucial time? It is not suitable for a cultured man. It does not facilitate heaven in the hereafter. It causes disgrace, O Arjuna. (B.G. 2.2)

This was an instruction from the ascetic to King Yadu but Lord Krishna cited the story to instruct Uddhava in the same detachment.

Arjuna suffered from this emotional suffering *(santāpam)* because he expressed too much affection for the elders of the Kuru family. Thus he hesitated and stumbled around when it was time to treat them spiritually. He wanted to remain on the social plane for emotional dealings. Lord Krishna hammered away until Arjuna agreed with Krishna's view.

As the poor-minded pigeon had too much privacy with his companion, so any person who harbors such association suffers from emotional pain. This is a law of nature. We all experience such social activities.

Privacy with others is not for yogis. Yogis are supposed to work out their salvation in isolation as directed by superior yogis. However, it is not that easy, since freeing oneself from one's lower destiny takes a tremendous amount of consistent practice and detachment energy.

कपोतः कश्चनारण्ये
कृत-नीडो वनस्पतौ ।
कपोत्या भार्यया सार्धम्
उवास कतिचित् समाः ॥२.५३॥

kapotaḥ kaścanāraṇye
kṛta-nīḍo vanaspatau
kapotyā bhāryayā sārdham
uvāsa katicit samāḥ (2.53)

kapotaḥ — pigeon; kaścanāraṇye = kaścana — a certain + araṇye — in the forest; kṛta-nīḍo = kṛta – having built + nīdo(nīdaḥ) — nest; vanaspatau — in a tree; kapotyā — with a female pigeon; bhāryayā — with his wife; sārdham = sa-ardham — with a companion; uvāsa — he lived; katicit — for some; samāh — years.

Translation

A pigeon built his nest on a tree in a certain forest and lived there for some years, with his wife, the female pigeon. (2.53)

Commentary:

The socially-separated ascetic observed the life of a male pigeon. From that study, some lessons were derived. It is a fact however that the life story of the bird is very similar to that of male human beings. The story is directly instructive of human social relations which centered on family life. Everything in our humanity, centers on family cultivation which centers on the mutual attraction of sensual energies between the opposite sexes. Grossly speaking this centers on sexual indulgence which consists of sexual entries of the male sexual organ into a female one. From the subtle view point however, the penetration of energies, is mutual. The influences travel in both directions.

Some teachers maintain that these stories in the *Purāṇas* are merely symbolic and should not be taken literally but should be used as analogies which might relate to the struggle with our individual nature in the quest for liberation. But these teachers give a one-sided view. These stories are both historic and symbolic.

However, no one should think that these stories are fables. A story does not have to be a fable before it can assist us in the quest for elevation. We should accept these stories at face value and also take them to heart as objective lessons.

As required in material existence, we have to build a nest. It is a mandatory part of this existence. Because of the nature of the perishable bodies, we must protect them. In addition a male being usually finds for himself a female being for sharing privacy and for cooperation. Generally it is felt that a male being seeks out a female for sexual proximity but the real reason is mutual survival. The way of material nature, is such, that it is difficult to live alone. It is extremely difficult to fulfill one's desires alone. Hardly anyone knows where desires originate but each person, when he realizes a desire in his mind or emotion, feels pressured to fulfill it. Thus one spirit finds it necessary to be in a cahoots with others.

The sensual energies are polarized as positive, negative, and neutral. Every living being must bend to the rule of combination which governs the alliances of particular objects. Some beings have more masculine polarity, some feminine and others neutral. These can only combine in harmony in certain ways which are governed by laws of nature. Thus we find that usually, a male being combines in cooperation with a female. The bodies are sexually matched for social cooperation.

Generally people think that sex begins and ends with romantic flirtations and vulgar sexual entries, but these ideas are childish and primitive. Sexual exchange occurs during seemingly non-sexual services as well. For instance, usually a man is a wage earner and a woman is a homemaker. That is a sexual alliance. It is a sort of match of occupation or jobs just as a tubal male part fit into a cylindrical female part. As the socially-separated ascetic said, a pigeon built his nest on a certain tree and lived there for some years with his companion, a female bird.

The question is: Why is it that only the socially separated ascetic or a rare personality like him, may make this detailed observation? The answer is: Most human beings are too busy building shelters and consorting with spouses to make objective observations of the ways and means of social living.

Another question is this: Why was the pigeon's nest located in a certain forest? Why was it not somewhere else? Did the pigeon select that forest of his own free will? He could not have. No limited being not even a human being can have that much grasp on the scope of this existence to properly select a habitat.

It means therefore that by destiny the pigeon selected to put the nest on that tree. Ultimately, the selection resulted in frustration.

कपोतौ स्नेह-गुणित-
हृदयौ गृह-धर्मिणौ ।
दृष्टिं दृष्ट्याङ्गम् अङ्गेन
बुद्धिं बुद्ध्या बबन्धतुः ॥ २.५४ ॥

kapotau sneha-guṇita-
hṛdayau gṛha-dharmiṇau
dṛṣṭiṁ dṛṣṭyāṅgam aṅgena
buddhiṁ buddhyā babandhatuḥ (2.54)

kapotau — two pigeons; sneha-guṇita-hṛdayau = sneha — by romance + guṇita — tied + hṛdayau — their emotions; gṛha-dharmiṇau = gṛha – householder + dharmiṇau — duty bound; dṛṣtim — gaze; dṛṣṭyāṅgam = dṛṣṭyā — by intently looking + aṅgam — forms; angena — by forms, by bodily contact; buddhim — mind; buddhyā — by the intellect, mentally; babandhatuḥ — they were bound to each other.

Translation

The two pigeons with their emotions tied by romance, by intently fixing their gaze on each other's form, by close bodily contact, by mentally connecting their minds, lived as two duty-bound householders. Thus they were bound to each other's association. (2.54)

Commentary:

The close attachment experienced by the two pigeons dulled their sense of responsibility towards the Supreme Being. That caused the spiritual senior of the two, to lose the sense of purpose and to substitute the focus on his lover as the ultimate use of the attentive energies. Though tolerated by the Supreme Being, such a misuse of attention is offensive to the spiritual security of the persons concerned.

When there is a match of emotion, there arises a tendency of compatibility. This causes two spirits to feel that the mundane existence is centralized upon them. Nothing, of course, could be further from the truth. The same destiny that brought the pigeons in contact was the same energy that converted their happiness into sorrow and anguish at a future date.

The mistakes of these pigeons were threefold. First they forgot the existence of the Supreme Being. Secondly, they forgot that they were a small part in the surrounding energies and realities. And thirdly, they ignored the negative possibilities of the future. Any one who lives like this is bound to get a rude awakening sooner or later, since the all-surrounding realities do not support such a self-centered existence forever.

Of course pigeons cannot reason as well as human beings. Pigeons are prone to these errors in judgment, but human beings, despite their keener intellect, make the same blunders.

शय्यासनाटन-स्थान
वार्ता-क्रीडाशनादिकम् ।
मिथुनी-भूय विश्रब्धौ
चेरतुर् वन-राजिषु ॥ २.५५ ॥

śayyāsanāṭana-sthāna
vārtā-krīḍāśanādikam
mithunī-bhūya viśrabdhau
ceratur vana-rājiṣu (2.55)

śayyāsanātana-sthāna = śayyā — resting + āsana — sitting + aṭana — walking + sthāna — walking; vārtā-krīdāśanādikam = vārtā — chirping + krīdā — playing + aśana — eating + ādikam — and other such actions; mithunī-bhūya — being as a pair of lovers; viśrabdhau — confidently; ceratur = ceratuḥ — they acted; vana-rājiṣu = vana — forest + rājiṣu — in the groves.

Translation

In the groves of the forest, they acted as a pair of lovers, lying, sitting, walking, resting, chirping, playing, and eating confidently. (2.55)

Commentary:

The enjoyment afforded to the two pigeons was being denied to other spirits who used other bodies, but the pigeons failed to take note of the deprivations of others. Why is it that while one, two or more spirits live comfortably within their bodies, other spirits elsewhere have a miserable existence? And why is it that the parents of these pigeons were not on hand to enjoy life in the same way? Why is it that while one spirit enjoys the youth of a body, his parent might be enduring misery and inconvenience in the old age of another body?

The confidence afforded the two pigeons was merely a utility of destiny for causing the pigeons to sponsor another generation of birds, but the pigeons could not grasp their positions as servants or employees of providence. When providence struck to change that status, they were not prepared for it.

यं यं वाञ्छति सा राजन्
तर्पयन्त्य् अनुकम्पिता ।
तं तं समनयत् कामं
कृच्छ्रेणाप्य् अजितेन्द्रियः ॥२.५६॥

yaṁ yaṁ vāñchati sā rājan
tarpayanty anukampitā
taṁ taṁ samanayat kāmaṁ
kṛcchreṇāpy ajitendriyaḥ (2.56)

yam yam — what what, whatever; vāñchati — wants; sā — she; rājan — O King; tarpayanty = tarpayantī — pleasing; anukampitā — endearing; tam tam — that that; samanayat — procured; kāmam — desire; kṛcchreṇāpy = kṛcchreṇa — with difficulty + apy (api) — even; ajitendriyaḥ = ajita – not curbing + indriyaḥ — the senses.

Translation

Whatever she, the pleasing, endearing female pigeon wanted, O King, the male bird procured, even with difficulty, for he had not curbed his senses. (2.56)

Commentary:

The wandering ascetic, by keen observation, noticed that the pigeon, who was supposed to supervise himself and his companion, was instead being supervised by the female bird. The male pigeon had given over the responsibility for his family to his wife. This was a mistake on his part. It was an affront to the Supreme Being, a misuse of trust and power which was entrusted to him by providence. No one is authorized to give over authority or power to a person of lesser stature, unless that less-capable person is assigned by providence.

It is a fact however that a female usually tries to influence a male to surrender his commanding power, such that the female becomes the actual supervisor and uses the chauvinistic power of the male indirectly. Though it happens frequently, providence does not take it lightly and both partners get rash reactions as a consequence. In association with females, a male agent of providence, should constantly be on guard about being influenced to surrender his authority. Even if the female becomes irritable a man should not surrender his authority.

Even though a female is very serviceable in creating, and maintaining a household, still she is not indispensible. Nor is a male head of household. No parents of bodies are indispensible.

The indispensible factor is the Supreme Being who arranged this mundane existence. As soon as one forgets that Supreme Person, one sets a course of peril.

A responsible husband should procure most of the things required for facilitating the service of his wife, but that does not mean that whatever she, the endearing woman desires, the husband should acquire. He should use discrimination. In facilitating the legitimate services of his wife, He should not lose touch with the over all mission of a household, which is to satisfy the Supreme Being. Thus he should facilitate his wife's services only to the extent that meets the demands of the Supreme Being and not otherwise. Whatever his wife might desire outside of the bare satisfaction of the Supreme Being, should not be procured.

The socially-separated ascetic made it clear to King Yadu, that the reason for the lack of discernment in the male pigeon was the bird's failure to curb its senses. Since the bird's sensual energies were not under control, his wife's senses took control of both her discrimination and his as well. Thus they both ignored the Supreme Being and lost track of their employment as servants of evolution.

Generally speaking a man's wife is a lot closer to him than even the Supreme Being. But at the same time, the neglect of the Supreme Being invariably causes havoc in a couple's life. It is in their best interest not to neglect the Supreme Lord. If being over-powered by emotions, as women usually are, the wife does not realize this, then it is up to the husband to keep this in mind at all times and to tolerate such spiritual insensitivity of his wife. For the safety of both himself and his wife, a husband should ignore or otherwise sidestep his wife when she attempts to centralize their life's purpose on her emotionality.

कपोती प्रथम गर्भं
गृह्णन्ती काल आगते ।
अण्डानि सुषुवे नीडे
स्व-पत्युः सन्निधौ सती ॥२.५७॥

kapotī prathamaṁ garbhaṁ
gṛhṇantī kāla āgate
aṇḍāni suṣuve nīḍe
sva-patyuḥ sannidhau satī (2.57)

kapotī — female pigeon; prathamaṁ — the first; garbhaṁ — pregnancy; gṛhṇantī — experienced; kāle = kale — in time; āgate — had come, arrived; aṇḍāni — eggs; suṣuve — laid; nīde — in the nest; sva-patyuḥ = sva – her own + patyuh — of the husband; sannidhau — in the presence; satī — the faithful.

Translation

The faithful female pigeon experienced the first pregnancy. When the time arrived, she laid eggs in the nest in the presence of her husband. (2.57)

Commentary:

By the time the female pigeon experienced the first pregnancy, she was so confused about the purpose of existence, that she could not sort out between the desire of the Supreme Being and her pressing needs. She could not understand the difference between the urges of material nature and her own, nor could she see that such urges of nature should be curbed or tempered by constantly taking advice from the Supreme Being. This neglect was costly in the lives of the pigeons.

When the time arrived, she laid eggs in the presence of her husband, as if to say, "We did this. But I did this primarily, not you. You should obey me by adhering to my commands and fulfilling my needs like a dutiful servant. As I was fruitful to produce these eggs, so will I always be fruitful in the future. You should adhere to me."

In fact, the laying of the eggs was just a job, an employment. The female pigeon should not have taken it so seriously. The laying of the eggs was done by her body, with little participation from her personality. Even emotionally, the spirit using that female pigeon body, had done very little for production of the eggs. The spirits whose new bodies were developing in those eggs, had come from a previous existence, from which they lost bodies.

The assumption of the female bird that she produced those eggs was grossly inaccurate. She had not produced anything. It was all done by forces beyond her control, powers which induced her to cooperate in reproduction. The female pigeon, because she lacked subtle vision, could not understand her position. Instead of trying to figure it out she used her intellect to intimidate the male pigeon and keep him subdued. In that case however, the male pigeon was not really her stooge, because she was not a master of her own circumstance, nor was she a controller of her senses. Therefore the whole scope of the female pigeon's vision of life, was an inaccurate and dangerous fantasy.

तेषु काले व्यजायन्त
रचितावयवा हरेः ।
शक्तिभिर् दुर्विभाव्याभिः

teṣu kāle vyajāyanta
racitāvayavā hareḥ
śaktibhir durvibhāvyābhiḥ

कोमलाङ्ग-तनूरुहाः ॥२.५८॥ komalāṅga-tanūruhāḥ (2.58)

teṣu — from them; kāle — in time; vyajāyanta — were born; racitāvayavā = racita — produced + avayavā (avayavāḥ) — limbs; hareḥ — of the God Hari; śaktibhir = śaktibhiḥ — by the creative powers; durvibhāvyābhiḥ — by that which is inscrutable; komalanga-tanuruhah = komala — tender + aṅga — limb + tanūruhāḥ — feathers.

Translation

In time, young birds with tender limbs and feathers were born, being produce by the unscrutable creative powers of the God, Hari. (2.58)

Commentary:

It is a common error even of human parents to give some lip service to the inscrutable creative powers of the Supreme God and still when rearing offspring, completely ignore the Lord. For this costly mistake, the God-neglecting parents lose track of their own spiritual potential. They become absorbed in the concerns of progeny and miss the opportunity for liberation from material bondage and the resulting release into spiritual security.

Some feel that the material bodies are directly produced by the Supreme God. However we learn here that the bodies of those baby birds were indirectly created by God and directly produced by His inscrutable creative powers.

प्रजाः पुपुषतुः प्रीतौ
दम्पती पुत्र-वत्सलौ ।
शृण्वन्तौ कूजित तासा
निर्वृतौ कल-भाषितैः ॥२.५९॥

prajāḥ pupuṣatuḥ prītau
dampatī putra-vatsalau
śṛṇvantau kūjitaṁ tāsāṁ
nirvṛtau kala-bhāṣitaiḥ (2.59)

prajāḥ — offspring, baby birds; pupuṣatuḥ — nourished; prītau — both devoted; dam-patī — the pair; putra-vatsalau = putra — bird + vatsalau — both being affectionate; śṛṇvantau — both listening; kūjitam — chirping; tāsām — of them; nirvṛtau — delighted; kala-bhāṣitaiḥ = kala – sweet and primitive + bhāṣitaiḥ — by the sounds.

Translation

The happy pair, being devoted to their babies, nourished the young ones, listening to them chirp and being delighted by their sweet and primitive sounds. (2.59)

Commentary:

The parent birds, as most parents are, were miserly, being in need of some pleasure and a reward for what they did as agents of destiny. They were stealing bits and pieces of pleasure while doing their job. It is like petty theft committed by employees who work for a company. These workers are not supposed to steal from the employer but invariably they do, because they cannot control their desires and are discontent with their status and income.

Such employee theft is called pilfering. It means that an employee takes a little amount which was not noticed by the employer. For instance, if a worker steals one pound of sugar from a company which produces millions of tons annually it is hardly likely that a company official may notice the theft. But if an employee took about fifty thousand pounds of sugar, he would be detected. He would be charged with theft, and be dismissed from the job. In order to keep the job, therefore, a considerate thief who pilfers, takes a little and remains with the company without being detected.

In this living situation in material existence, there are essential two types of persons described in the *Bhagavad Gītā*. There are godly souls who are essentially saintly in character and the ungodly or wicked ones who are atheistic in their philosophical outlook. But in each case, both are thieves. It is the truth however that the godly type are petty thieves who pilfer off very little. Those parent birds who were being observed by the socially-separated ascetic, were such petty thieves.

Actually, the employer in this case, the Supreme God, did notice how they stole pleasure, but He overlooked it and allowed them to continue as good employees for they were only fooling themselves. In the end they would be intimidated by the same inscrutable creative powers which created the babies.

All this which I just explained might seem cryptic and complicated, but here is some more clarity:

The parent birds stole pleasure through their ears, eyes, nostrils, tongue, skin, vocal cord, sexual organs and through the various subtle outlets of their intellectual and emotional faculties. They pilfered much enjoyment from the job as parents. Of course, normally, parents do not consider this as thievery. The parent birds were devoted *(prītau)* to the offspring, but for the wrong reason with the wrong motive; not to serve the Supreme God but rather to procure and expand sensual fulfillments. It was just like those good employees who work dutifully for the sugar company so that they can pilfer off one or two pounds of sugar now and again and take mental pleasure knowing that the theft was unnoticed by the employer.

तासां पतत्रैः सु-स्पर्शैः
कूजितैर् मुग्ध-चेष्टितैः ।
प्रत्युद्गमैर् अदीनानां
पितरौ मुदम् आपतुः ॥२.६०॥

tāsāṁ patatraiḥ su-sparśaiḥ
kūjitair mugdha-ceṣṭitaiḥ
pratyudgamair adīnānāṁ
pitarau mudam āpatuḥ (2.60)

tāsāṁ — them; patatraih — by the wings; su-sparśaiḥ — what is soft to touch; kūjitair = kūjitaiḥ — by their chirping; mugdha-ceṣṭitaiḥ = mugdha — graceful + ceṣṭitaiḥ — by movements; pratyudgamair = pratyudgamaiḥ — by efforts to fly; adīnānām — of the happy; pitarau — both parents; mudam – cheerful; āpatuh — became.

Translation

Their cheerfulness, their wings being soft to touch, their chirping and graceful movements and their efforts to fly was the happiness of both parents. (2.60)

Commentary:

Whatever those baby forms did, the parents tried to pilfer some pleasure from it. By nature, they could not function as parents without enjoyment, just as employees of a sugar company who feel resentful, if the company officials imposed such tight security that no theft of even a grain of sugar was possible. For peace sake and to keep the material world going, the Supreme Lord slackens His hold on the creation and allows the pious entities to function culturally and carry out petty theft.

Lord Krishna told Arjuna, that the Creator *Brahmā* instructed the first human beings not to pilfer off anything but rather to act as servants and to first offer everything to the supernatural authorities. But such a stipulation is hard to follow. By nature a human being has a reward-seeking or yield-possessing mentality. The stipulation of *Brahmā* which I quote below is not adhered to by most human beings. Only one or two follow it to the letter.

sahayajñāḥ prajāḥ sṛṣṭvā purovāca prajāpatiḥ
anena prasaviṣyadhvam eṣa vo'stviṣṭakāmadhuk
devānbhāvayatānena te devā bhāvayantu vaḥ
parasparaṁ bhāvayantaḥ śreyaḥ paramavāpsyatha

iṣṭānbhogānhi vo devā dāsyante yajñabhāvitāḥ
tairdattānapradāyaibhyo yo bhuṅkte stena eva saḥ

Long ago, having created the first human beings, along with religious fulfillment and ceremonies, the Procreator Brahmā said: By this worship procedure, you may be productive. May it cause the fulfillment of your desires.

By this procedure, you may cause the supernatural rulers to flourish. They, in turn, may bless you. In favorably regarding each other, the highest well-being will be achieved.

The supernatural rulers, being manifested through prescribed austerity and religious ceremony, will, indeed, give you the most desired people and things. Whosoever does not offer those given items to them, but who enjoys these, is certainly a thief. (B.G. 3.10-12)

स्नेहानुबद्ध-हृदयाव्
अन्योन्यं विष्णु-मायया ।
विमोहितौ दीन-धियौ
शिशून् पुपुषतुः प्रजाः ॥२.६१॥

snehānubaddha-hṛdayāv
anyonyaṁ viṣṇu-māyayā
vimohitau dīna-dhiyau
śiśūn pupuṣatuḥ prajāḥ 2.61)

snehānubaddha-hrdayau = sneha — by affection + anubaddha — bound up + hṛdayāu — the two emotional sentiments; anyonyam — one to another, mutually; viṣṇu-māyayā — the bewildering energy of Vishnu; vimohitau — both entranced; dīna-dhiyau — both weak-minded, having a poor outlook on life; śiśūn — baby birds; pupuṣatuh — they reared; prajāḥ — their babies.

Translation

The two birds with their emotional sentiments, bound by mutual affection, being entranced by the bewildering energy of Vishnu, reared their offspring, while using very little insight. (2.61)

Commentary:

Some do not believe in the bewildering energy of Vishnu. Some think that it is the energy of another God. Some say it is the energy of Jehovah or Jesus Christ or Shiva or *Brahmā* or some other named Supreme God according to religious preference. Some who do not believe in God say that it is the polarized energy of the world, the lusty impetus in the creation. Some others say that it is caused by the Absolute Truth, a supreme all-pervasive impersonal energy.

These arguments are, in a sense, beside the point, The Supreme Principle, be it personal or impersonal is beyond limited minds. The parent birds, like many human beings did not develop their intellectual skills to a degree whereby they could determine whether the supreme was a person or an energy. Like most human beings, they felt their own personalities to be significant. And so they were focused on each other for mutual enjoyments.

The socially-separated ascetic could see that they were in a pitiful position because they could not see the dangers of affection. The ascetic understood that the cause of their bewilderment was the overwhelming power of the bewildering energy of God. It was not this Supreme God himself, but His energy which abounded in the creation and which comprised the emotional and intellectual senses of the parent birds. The same bewildering energy was in the body of the ascetic but his good sense was in order, so he was not mislead by it.

While it kept the birds in bewilderment, it gave the ascetic, clarity of view. Lord Krishna explained the reason for this to Arjuna:

buddherbhedaṁ dhṛteścaiva guṇatastrividhaṁ śṛṇu
procyamānamaśeṣeṇa pṛthaktvena dhanaṁjaya
pravṛttiṁ ca nivṛttiṁ ca kāryākārye bhayābhaye
bandhaṁ mokṣaṁ ca yā vetti buddhiḥ sā pārtha sāttvikī
yayā dharmamadharmaṁ ca kāryaṁ cākāryameva ca
ayathāvatprajānāti buddhiḥ sā pārtha rājasī

adharmaṁ dharmamiti yā manyate tamasāvṛtā
sarvārthāṇviparītāṁśca buddhiḥ sā pārtha tāmasī

Now, O conqueror of wealthy countries, hear of the three types of intellect and also of determination, explained thoroughly and distinctly, according to their distinctions under the influences of material nature.

That intellectual insight which discerns when to endeavor and when not to strive, what should be done and what should not be done, what is dangerous and what is safe, what brings restrictions and what gives freedom, that O son of Pṛthā, is in the clarifying mode.

That intellectual insight by which right and wrong, duty and neglect are mistakenly identified, is, O son of Pṛthā, in the impulsive mode.

That intellectual insight which is absorbed by ignorance, which considers the wrong method as the right one and perceives all values in a perverted way, is O son of Pṛthā, of the depressive mode. (B.G. 18.29-32)

एकदा जग्मतुस् तासाम्
अन्नार्थं तौ कुटुम्बिनौ ।
परितः कानने तस्मिन्न्
अर्थिनौ चेरतुश् चिरम् ॥२.६२॥

ekadā jagmatus tāsām
annārthaṁ tau kuṭumbinau
paritaḥ kānane tasminn
arthinau ceratuś ciram (2.62)

ekadā — once; jagmatus — they went; tāsām — for them; annārtham = anna — food + artham — for the sake of; tau — both of them; kuṭumbinau — two parents; paritaḥ — round about; kanane — in the forest; tasminn — that; arthinau — they searched; ceratuś = ceratuḥ — they foamed about; ciram — far off.

Translation

Once they went for the sake of food for those baby birds. Both parents roamed about and around, searching for a long time, off in the forest. (2.62)

Commentary:

Their main duty was to collect food for the young birds and to return to their nest promptly. Since they were bewildered they became distracted by many things heard,felt,seen,tasted and smelt. As such they continued the habit of pilfering off pleasure through numerous distractions. Usually, human parents are evem more bewildered than the adult birds.

दृष्ट्वा तान् लुब्धकः कश्चिद्
यदृच्छातो वने-चरः ।
जगृहे जालम् आतत्य
चरतः स्वालयान्तिके ॥२.६३॥

dṛṣṭvā tān lubdhakaḥ kaścid
yadṛcchāto vane-caraḥ
jagṛhe jālam ātatya
carataḥ svālayāntike (2.63)

dṛṣṭvā — seeing; tān — them; lubdhakaḥ — a bird catcher; kaścid = kaścit — a certain; yadrcchāto = yadrcchātaḥ — by chance; vane-caraḥ = vane — in the woods + caraḥ — rumbling about; jagṛhe — he caught; jālam — net; ātatya — spreading; carataḥ — flying about; svālayāntike = sva – their own + ālaya – nest + antike — in the area.

Translation

A certain bird catcher, who rumbled in the woods by chance, saw the adult birds flying about in the area near their nest. He caught the baby birds by spreading a net. (2.63)

Commentary:

Since the parents birds were not discreet, and since they make quite a noise in their enjoyments, and were proud of their accomplishments, they were detected by a bird catcher who rambled about in the woods looking for careless creatures. It was by chance *(yadṛcchāto)* that he came there. But this, by chance, actually meant by a plan of destiny, by supernatural arrangement. Why did he not go to another forest or even to another part of that forest? Why did he not pass, that way when the birds were quietly sitting in the nest? Obviously it was destiny that guided the cruel bird catcher. The same providence which afforded the parents birds such opportunity for family life, was the same power which sent the bird catcher.

Since the birds were distracted by the enjoyments, they could not understand that providence disapproved of the enjoying mentality. It may be said that the fault here is the cruel and greedy bird catcher but this fault is overshadowed by the stroke of destiny which inspired him to observe the birds.

कपोतश् च कपोती च
प्रजा-पोषे सदोत्सुकौ ।
गतौ पोषणम् आदाय
स्व-नीडम् उपजग्मतुः ॥२.६४॥

kapotaś ca kapotī ca
prajā-poṣe sadotsukau
gatau poṣaṇam ādāya
sva-nīḍam upajagmatuḥ (2.64)

kapotaś — the male pigeon; ca — and; kapotī — the female pigeon; ca — and; prajā-poṣe = prajā – the baby birds + poṣe — in the matter of procuring food; sadotsukau = sadā — always + utsukau — eager; gatau — the two who were gone; poṣaṇam — food; ādāya — brings; sva-nīḍam = sva - their own + nīḍam — to the nest; upajagmatuḥ — they returned.

Translation

The male and female pigeons, who were always eager for procuring food and who were gone, returned bringing food to the nest. (2.64)

Commentary:

The procurement of food *(prajā-poṣe)* is driven by the urge for sexual indulgence. Even though the pigeons were taking food-gathering trips, the actual motive was to procure more sexual contact. And the same may be applied to the bird catcher. He too was out on rounds to procure food for family but under the motive of getting more sexual opportunity.

Both the bird catcher and the parent birds were on the same course of material existence doing essentially the same thing for survival. As the bird catcher caught birds and other animals to feed a family, so the bird caught worms, insects, and other creatures to feed their offspring. In that sense, the cruel bird catcher was no more vicious than the bird parents.

कपोती स्वात्मजान् वीक्ष्य
बालकान् जाल-सम्वृतान् ।
तान् अभ्यधावत् क्रोशन्ती
क्रोशतो भृश-दुःखिता ॥२.६५॥

kapotī svātmajān vīkṣya
bālakān jāla-samvṛtān
tān abhyadhāvat krośantī
krośato bhṛśa-duḥkhitā (2.65)

kapotī — female pigeon; svātmajān — her own babies; vīkṣya — discovering; bālakān — baby birds; jāla-saṁvṛtān = jala — net + samvṛtān — caught; tān — to them; abhyadhāvat — rushed; krośantī — crying out; krośato = krośataḥ — to those who were weeping; bhṛśa-duḥkhitā = bhṛśa — much + duḥkhitā — aggrieved.

Translation

The female pigeon, discovering that her babies were caught in the net and were weeping, rushed at them, while crying out, being much aggrieved. (2.65)

Commentary:

By nature, females react more acutely in emotional situations than do males. By nature, females are more possessive than males. Thus the female pigeon, the mother of those infant birds, was the first to react to the dire predicament. Not knowing the actual origins of those baby birds, nor of the spirits for whom those bodies were developed by material nature, the mother bird, assuming that they were her offspring in total, rushed at them, while crying out and being much aggrieved but without using discrimination. Thus even though she was an adult bird, she rushed into the danger, challenging providence.

सासकृत् स्नेह-गुणिता
दीन-चित्ताज-मायया ।
स्वय चाबध्यत शिचा
बद्धान् पश्यन्त्य् अपस्मृतिः ॥२.६६॥

sāsakṛt sneha-guṇitā
dīna-cittāja-māyayā
svayaṁ cābadhyata śicā
baddhān paśyanty apasmṛtiḥ (2.66)

sāsakṛt = sā — she + asakṛt — repeatedly; sneha-guṇitā = sneha — by emotional interest + guṇitā — fettered; dīna-cittāja-māyayā = dīna – simple-minded + cittā — mind + aja — of God + māyayā — by the bewildering potency; svayam — herself; cābadhyata = ca — and + abadhyata — became caught; śicā — by the net; baddhān — the captured ones; paśyanty = paśyantī — they saw; apaṣmṛtiḥ — one who forgets herself, lost her good sense.

Translation

Even though both parent birds saw the captured birdies, that simple-minded female pigeon, being repeatedly fettered by emotional interests, through God's bewildering potency, became caught by the net, for she lost her good sense. (2.66)

Commentary:

Even though both saw the situation and did also see the bird catcher in the vicinity, they did not apply intelligence either collectively or individually. In the name of love, the male pigeon allowed his companion to go through the emotional fluttering that females are usually subjected to. Instead of thinking out the situation and deciding on a reformative course of living, he simply kept himself focused on the irrational reactions of his wife. And she, all the more for it, expanded her emotional purview more and more, to the point of stupefaction.

कपोतः स्वात्मजान् बद्धान्
आत्मनो ऽप्य् अधिकान् प्रियान् ।
भार्यां चात्म-समां दीनो
विललापाति-दुःखितः ॥२.६७॥

kapotaḥ svātmajān baddhān
ātmano 'py adhikān priyān
bhāryāṁ cātma-samāṁ dīno
vilalāpāti-duḥkhitaḥ (2.67)

kapotaḥ — the male pigeon; svātmajān — his own baby birds; baddhān — caught; ātmano = ātmanaḥ — himself; 'py = api — too; adhikān — more; priyān — dear; bhāryām — wife; cātma-samām = ca — and + ātma – himself + samām — matching; dīno = dīnaḥ — the poor fellow; vilalāpāti-duḥkhitaḥ = vilalāpa — afflicted + ati-duḥkhitaḥ — most unhappy.

Translation

The poor male pigeon, too, noting the baby birds, who were more dear to him than his own self, and also his wife, who was a match to himself, all being caught, became afflicted being most unhappy. (2.67)

Commentary:

Catching the fever of the irrational emotions *(vilalāpāti-duhkhitah)*, the male pigeon took shelter of his own emotional nature and began to feel that the baby birds were more dear to him than his own life. This was an existential farce, however, because neither those baby birds nor their bodies were really related to him as he considered. The baby birds, their personalities, were spirits who had come from a previous existence and who merely took advantage of his body's begetting power. And their bodies, were not related to him at all because they were formed from food substances which broke down in his body, and formed into his semen and was then transferred in sexual intercourse into the womb of the female pigeon.

The male pigeon, and the female one, more so, acted as if the spirits in the bodies of their offspring, were taking birth in the material world and in the bird species, for the first time. They acted as if those spirit personalities were produced by them. This is a common error in consideration, even of human parents. It is an animal's concept of true love. In such love either parent or both parents feel that children are productions from themselves. They arrange their lives on the basis of this false view.

अहो मे पश्यतापायम् अल्प-पुण्यस्य दुर्मतेः । अतृप्तस्याकृतार्थस्य गृहस् त्रै-वर्गिको हतः ॥२.६८॥	aho me paśyatāpāyam alpa-puṇyasya durmateḥ atṛptasyākṛtārthasya gṛhas trai-vargiko hataḥ (2.68)

aho — alas! What is this; me — my; paśyatāpāyam = paśyata — look + apāyam — bad luck; alpa-puṇyasya — of those whose ambition is slightly fulfilled; durmateḥ — of who miscalculated; atṛptasyākṛtārthasya = atṛptasya — of one who is dissatisfied + akṛta-arthasya — of one who has not fulfilled his purpose; gṛhas — the family life; trai-vargiko = trai – three + vargikah — objectives; hataḥ — ruined.

Translation

(That male bird thought to itself,) "What is this! Look at me! The bad luck of one whose ambition is slightly fulfilled, one who miscalculated, one who is dissatisfied, one who has not fulfilled his purposes. The family life which is the means of the three objectives, is ruined. (2.68)

Commentary:

It may be contested that the pigeon could not have said this physically since birds do not speak human language. But that is besides the point because the socially-separated ascetic was a perceptive mystic who could read the minds and speech expression of other creatures. As such we can rely on the ascetic and believe that the pigeon did consider this and did utter bird-talk which meant this.

The male pigeon thought that the whole incidence of the captured birdlings was a great misfortune. Actually he was wrong because that was his fortune. It was something brought on by providence to benefit him, to bring him into self-realization. Unfortunately he could not take advantage of the lesson. It is seen sometimes, that a human being loses a baby. Perhaps that infant was miscarried. Perhaps it was born and died in infancy. But instead of taking this as a hint for self-realization, the human parent laments, thus avoiding realization. For his part however, the observant ascetic, used that circumstance to benefit himself in further realization about the uncertainties of life.

The male pigeon felt that he miscalculated and that he did not protect the birdlings effectively. He thought that perhaps he should not have built the nest in that particular tree or that perhaps he should have settled in another forest; or that perhaps they should not have stayed so long procuring food. Or perhaps that they should not have rubbed each other's bodies in romance so often on that particular trip. His considerations were topsy-turvy. The real miscalculation is that he did not realize that he was working for the Supreme Being and that his wife was to be supervised in the venture. She was not to be given an equal say in everything since he was the supervisor who bore the main responsibility.

The male pigeon did not understand the real cause of his dissatisfaction. It was not his inability to protect the birdlings nor destiny's act to splinter his plan. It was in fact, a spiritual dissatisfaction because he failed to make use of life's opportunities for self-realization of his spiritual nature, the difference between his personality and his body; the differences between himself and his family; as well as their joint and individual relationship to the Supreme Being.

The male pigeon was right to think that the means of the three objectives was ruined but it was not ruined for the reason he considered. It was ruined because he did not pay attention to the opinions of the Supreme Being. The three objectives he considered were righteous living *(dharma),* the acquirement of commodities *(artha),* and enjoyment *(kāma).* The pigeon completely missed the fourth objective in life which is liberation from material existence *(mukti).*

अनुरूपानुकूला च
यस्य मे पति-देवता ।
शून्ये गृहे मां सन्त्यज्य
पुत्रैः स्वर् याति साधुभिः ॥२.६९॥

anurūpānukūlā ca
yasya me pati-devatā
śūnye gṛhe māṁ santyajya
putraiḥ svar yāti sādhubhiḥ (2.69)

anurūpānukūlā = anurūpā — of compatiable demeanor + anukūlā — agreeable; ca — and; yasya — of whom; me — of me; pati-devatā — who is husband, regarded as a god; śūnye — in vacancy; gṛhe — in the home; mām — me; santyajya — leaving behind; putraiḥ — with birdlings; svar — heaven; yāti — goes; sādhubhiḥ — with virtuousness.

Translation

"The one who has a compatible demeanor, who was aggreable, who regarded me as her Lord, goes to heaven with her virtuous birdlings, leaving me behind in this vacant home. (2.69)

Commentary:

The female pigeon regarded the male one as her lord superficially but the male bird thought it was a genuine regard. Her demeanor was sly and manipulative but he thought it was compatible. She did not go to heaven but he rationalized that she did. The vacancy in his life was not the vacant nest but rather his ignorance of reality and his callous neglect and complete disregard for the Supreme Personality.

A compatible wife is one who does not use her manipulative power on her husband but rather tries to assist him and encourage him in tending to the duties of the Supreme Being. Such a wife does not use her offspring as the ultimate focus but rather sees her divinely-assigned services as the objective. Some of these services include child-rearing but child care is not the aim nor absolute function of it. Child rearing, the caring of infant bodies, is limited to this world of birth and death. Therefore it cannot be an eternal divine service, since in the divine world, there is no place for it.

Nearly every religious human being feels that his or her departed spouse has gone to heaven. This is a common belief. For the most part, it is just that, a belief only. Merely because a human being is in love with someone or loves someone dearly or adores someone, does not mean that the loved one will go to heaven at the time of death. Neither do children all go to a subtle paradise if they leave their bodies untimely. The most common occurrence is this: Children come back into the world as the son or daughter of someone else. One's wife returns to this world in the same way. Heaven is not attained that easily. And besides, a person who is attached to gross mundane conditions does not aspire for heaven in fact, since his or her focus is the earthly life. Such a person merely takes his or her birth again to repeat a similar history in the new life.

सो ऽहं शून्ये गृहे दीनो
मृत-दारो मृत-प्रजः ।
जिजीविषे किम् अर्थं वा
विधुरो दुःख-जीवितः ॥२.७०॥

so 'haṁ śūnye gṛhe dīno
mṛta-dāro mṛta-prajaḥ
jijīviṣe kim arthaṁ vā
vidhuro duḥkha-jīvitaḥ (2.70)

so = sah – he; 'ham = aham — I; śūnye — in emptiness; gṛhe — in the house; dīno = dīnaḥ — wretched; mṛta-daro = mrta-dāraḥ — a man with a dead wife, a widower; mṛta-prajaḥ — one with dead children; jijīviṣe — I should desire to live; kim – what; artha — reason; vā — or; vidhuro = vidhuraḥ — afflicted; duḥkha-jīvitaḥ = duḥkha — miserable + jīvitaḥ — life.

Translation

"I am he, the wretched person, in an empty house. For what reason should

I desire to live, as a widower with dead children, being that my life is miserable and afflicted." (2.70)

Commentary:

The male pigeon was the wretched person *(dīno)* but not for the reasons cited, rather for the reasons of disregarding the association of the Supreme Being and for focusing on his wife's sensuality, for having lost his good sense in the matter of managing a family. He had allowed his motives to become mixed up with those of his wife. He could not determine right from wrong.

Merely because a man has dead children and a dead wife, is not necessarily a valid basis for his own suicide. He should first try to consult with the Supreme Being to find out if there is some other responsibility that he should fulfill in life. A male householder, though responsible for a family, should not regard the family as his ultimate objective. In that regard the male pigeon neglected to cultivate a relationship with the Supreme Being.

तांस् तथैवावृतान् शिग्भिर्
मृत्यु-ग्रस्तान् विचेष्टतः ।
स्वयं च कृपणः शिक्षु
पश्यन्न् अप्य् अबुधो ऽपतत् ॥ २.७१ ॥

tāṁs tathaivāvṛtān śigbhir
mṛtyu-grastān viceṣṭataḥ
svayaṁ ca kṛpaṇaḥ śikṣu
paśyann apy abudho 'patat (2.71)

tāms = tān — them; tathaivāvṛtān = tathā — as + eva — indeed + āvṛtān — surrounded; śigbhir = śigbhiḥ — by the net; mṛtyu-grastān = mṛtyu — the threat of death + grastān — held; viceṣṭataḥ — lost mind; svayam — himself; ca — and; kṛpanaḥ — wretched; śikṣu — in the net; paśyan — seeing; apy = api — even though; abudho = abudhah — senseless; 'patat = apatat — fell.

Translation

Even though he saw them surrounded by the net, being held by the threat of death, he lost his mind and senselessly fell into it himself. (2.71)

Commentary:

The male pigeon in the name of love of family and being obsessed with a desire to follow them all to the world hereafter, gave himself over to their misfortune. He miscalculated for there is no guarantee that a husband or father would follow his wife or children to their individual destinies in the hereafter.

A living being tries to follow his hopes and aspirations but that does not mean that he will be successful. Providence gives an individual, special preference, from time to time. In general providence is not particularly accommodating to our attachments. This act of the male pigeon of becoming entrapped was described by the socially-separated ascetic as being senseless *(abudho).* It is the way of emotions to completely disregard all good sense.

तं लब्ध्वा लुब्धकः क्रूरः
कपोतं गृह-मेधिनम् ।
कपोतकान् कपोतीं च
सिद्धार्थः प्रययौ गृहम् ॥ २.७२ ॥

taṁ labdhvā lubdhakaḥ krūraḥ
kapotaṁ gṛha-medhinam
kapotakān kapotīṁ ca
siddhārthaḥ prayayau gṛham (2.72)

tam — him; labdhvā — getting; lubdhakaḥ — the bird catcher; krūrah — cruel; kapotaṁ — the male pigeon; grha-medhinam — the dedicated family man; kapotakān — the baby pigeon; kapotīṁ — the female pigeon; ca — and; siddhārthah — one who fulfilled his purpose; prayayau — he went; gṛham — home.

Translation

The cruel hunter, getting the male pigeon, which was a dedicated bird father, along with the female pigeon and the baby birds, fulfilled his purpose and went home. (2.72)

Commentary:

The hunter was a *siddhārtha* or a person who was skilled at what he wanted to accomplish in life, while the male bird was a *asiddhārtha* or a person who did not understand what should be done to accomplish the aim. The difference was the focus of the hunter. The hunter relied more on the intellect, while the male pigeon gave in to his wife's emotions.

The irony of the comparisons is this: both the hunter and the male bird were dedicated householders, but the hunter was a little detached from his wife while the male pigeon was enamored by the femininity of his spouse. Thus the hunter was able to decisively fulfill his purpose for providing food for his family as a callous hunter. The male bird was no better for he too was a hunter of worms, insects, and vegetation but he used to go along with his wife and follow her stipulations. That was his error. Because of attachment to feminine association and because of being fascinated by feminine energies, the male pigeon lost his life, and failed to protect the very family which he was so attached to.

एव कुटुम्ब्य् अशान्तात्मा
द्वन्द्वारामः पतत्रि-वत् ।
पुष्णन् कुटुम्ब कृपणः
सानुबन्धो ऽवसीदति ॥ २.७३ ॥

evaṁ kuṭumby aśāntātmā
dvandvārāmaḥ patatri-vat
puṣṇan kuṭumbaṁ kṛpaṇaḥ
sānubandho 'vasīdati (2.73)

evam — thus; kutumby = kutumbi — a family man; aśāntātmā = aśānta — without peace, anxious + ātmā — soul; dvandvārāmaḥ = dvandva — polarity + ārāmah — delighting; patatri-vat — like that bird; puṣnam — maintaining; kutumbam — family; kṛpanaḥ — miserable person; sānubandho = sānubandhah = sa – with + anubandhaḥ - relatives; 'vasīdati = avasīdati — must suffer greatly.

Translation

Thus, a miserable human male, being anxious in his soul, delighting in polarity, maintains his family and like the male bird, suffers greatly with the relatives. (2.73)

Commentary:

All family life in the material world is miserable but the fatigue and anguish of it can be reduced by a detached mood. It was in that one area that the bird catcher had the edge over the male pigeon. Somehow the hunter learned how to be detached from his relations.

On the other hand, the male pigeon had not cultivated detachment. He was prone to attachment. He delighted in polarity of feelings in terms of happiness and distress, which are mood swings in the emotional nature.

The socially-separated ascetic instructed King Yadu, that a human being who serves as a family man, should not become attached to family members, otherwise he would suffer like the male bird. At least he should be detached like the bird catcher.

In material existence there will be some type of exploitation and some type of outwitting other creatures. It cannot be avoided. Even thought the bird catcher was involved in a cruel means of livelihood, still it must be understood that every living creature lives by some gross or sophisticated cruelty. It is the way of this existence. In the food chain one type of creature eats another. It is the way of life. Even the vegetation is involved in this cruelty. The cruelty of this life can only be reduced. It cannot be eliminated altogether.

यः प्राप्य मानुषं लोक
मुक्ति-द्वारम् अपावृतम् ।
गृहेषु खग-वत् सक्तस्
तम् आरूढ-च्युत विदुः ॥२.७४॥

yaḥ prāpya mānuṣaṁ lokaṁ
mukti-dvāram apāvṛtam
gṛheṣu khaga-vat saktas
tam ārūḍha-cyutaṁ viduḥ (2.74)

yah — who; prāpya — after attaining; mānuṣam – human; lokam — situation, birth; mukti-dvāram — door of liberation; apāvṛtam — open; gṛheṣu — in family affairs; khaga-vat — like the male bird; saktas — attach; tam — his; ārūḍha-cyutaṁ = ārūḍha — having climbed high + cyutam — fallen; viduḥ — the wise men consider.

Translation

The wise men consider that after attaining the human birth, which is an open door to liberation, anyone who is attached to family affairs like the male bird, is fallen after having climbed to a high place. (2.74)

Commentary:

As the *mukti-dvāram*, this human form of life *(manuṣam)*, should not be restricted to the three aims of life which the bird considered. These three aims of life are *dharma* or righteous life style, *artha* or economic satisfaction, and *kāma* or pleasure seeking. Besides these three there is the fourth and greatest aim of life which is *mukti* or spiritual freedom. The male bird never conceived of liberation. That was its lack of insight.

The bird catcher too like the male bird did not conceive of liberation but the hunter was closer to reaching that view by virtue of detachment *(vairāgya)*.

Even though a spirit might evolve through lower bodies and reach the human form of life, all by the grace of material nature's evolutionary thrust, still the spirit should get the hint of it and try to transmigrate in human forms until he is liberated. He should not proceed as a human being with the sentimental outlook of the lower animals. Even though a spirit is urged on and on to evolve and enter higher and higher species of life which culminate in a human birth, still it should be realized that some effort is required to remain changing human bodies. One should not allow oneself to fall back to the animal plane. For this, it is necessary to develop the one good quality of the cruel bird catcher, that of detachment.

As Lord Krishna chastised and ridiculed Arjuna about the lack of detachment and the emotional weakness, so now the Lord systematically dismantled Uddhava's family attachment. Thus the first quality which Lord Krishna invoked in Uddhava was detachment *(vairāgya)*.

CHAPTER 3*

The Blessed Lord Vishnu Is Pleased**

Terri Stokes-Pineda Art

nūnaṁ me bhagavān prīto.viṣṇuḥ kenāpi karmanā
nirvedo 'yam duraśayā yan me jātaḥ sukhāvahaḥ

Surely, due to some action or the other, the Blessed Lord Vishnu is pleased with me, since from a false expectation, this happy disgust arose in me. (3.37)

* Śrīmad Bhāgavatam Canto 11, Chapter 8

** Translator's selected chapter title.

श्री-ब्राह्मण उवाच
सुखम् ऐन्द्रियक राजन्
स्वर्गे नरक एव च ।
देहिनां यद् यथा दुःखं
तस्मान् नेच्छेत तद्-बुधः ॥३.१॥

śrī-brāhmaṇa uvāca
sukham aindriyakaṁ rājan
svarge naraka eva ca
dehināṁ yad yathā duḥkhaṁ
tasmān neccheta tad-budhaḥ (3.1)

śrī-brāhmaṇaḥ - the elevated brahmin; uvāca — said; sukham — happiness; aindriyakam — what is derrived from mundane sensual perception; rājan — King; svarge — in the angelic world; naraka = narake — in hell hereafter; eva — indeed; ca — and; dehinām — of the embodied souls; yad = yat — that; yathā — similarly; duḥkhaṁ — distress; tasmān = tasmāt — for that reason; neccheta = na — not + iccheta — should wish for; tad-budhah = tat — that + budhaḥ — a wise person.

Translation

The elevated brahmin said: O King, for the embodied souls, the happiness that is derived from mundane sense perception is experienced in the angelic world and similarly distress is experienced in hell hereafter. For that reason, the wise person should not wish for these polarized feelings. (3.1)

Commentary:

The desperation we feel which squeezes us by pressures of providence and the time factor through which we experience pleasant and unpleasant circumstances, is hereby declared to be superfluous. That was the view of the elevated brahmin. If, as the brahmin said, we will experience these aspects in the hereafter, then there is really no need for us to scramble for sense perceptions. If for instance, I am bound to be a father in many, many future lives, then there is no need to crave the status.

This reasoning of the elevated brahmin cannot be actuated in the life of a human being who is not highly evolved and who has not transcended the impulsive instincts for competition and survival. Still, it is a preview of what a human being might attain in the advanced stages. It explains to us the psychology of persons like the elevated brahmin. We must remember that King Yadu challenged the brahmin and asked for an explanation of the brahmin's complete detachment from social circumstances.

From the indications, we conclude that Lord Krishna wanted Uddhava to attain the same degree of detachment exhibited by the ascetic brahmin. Thus Lord Krishna explained this philosophy to Uddhava. The Lord did not however, encourage Arjuna on this path of detachment but rather the path of involvement in responsible duty-bound worldly affairs. Later, however, *Nārada* Muni instructed King *Yudhiṣṭhira* as well as Arjuna and the other Pandava brothers, to adopt the path of detachment.

In misleading the public, some preachers of the *Bhagavad Gītā*, even great elevated people, inform that Lord Krishna discouraged Arjuna from dry renunciation and told Arjuna to get involved but they omit that Lord Krishna encouraged Uddhava in the dry method in the end. *Nārada* seriously lectured King *Yudhiṣṭhira* in this other path thereafter. The *Bhagavad Gītā*'s instruction for Arjuna to fight as a *karma* yogi, applied to a certain stage of his life. That *karma* yoga was not an instruction for all time, otherwise Lord Krishna would not recommend the path of complete renunciation to Uddhava.

The elevated brahmin made a good point, but it is left for us to consider, when we may apply that instruction. So long as the impulsive instincts control us, we cannot take the advice. Nevertheless, we can appreciate the brahmin and understand his position. A similar brahmin was approached by King *Prahlād*. Their discourse was told to King *Yudhiṣṭhira* by *Nārada*. It is given in Canto seven of the *Śrīmad Bhāgavatam*. Some modern Vaishnava teachers scoff at such a completely detached brahmin, describing him as a selfish soul who did not have a taste for devotional service, but these teachers overlook this: The detachment of these elevated human beings is itself a form of devotional service and such service though appearing useless, is much appreciated by Lord Krishna.

The missionaries have their authorized missions as they describe. They are empowered by time, providence, and divinity, and thus a person who takes to this complete renunciation should not oppose them openly, nor harbor ill feelings towards them. Rather, one should see that they serve a purpose. They fulfill a divine mission, enunciated not so much in the discourse with Uddhava, but in the *Bhagavad Gītā* teachings to Arjuna, where Lord Krishna advocated the path of involvement, *karma* yoga. Even Lord Krishna goes so far as to explain that the ideal *karma* yoga was taught by Him to the kings of the solar dynasty, persons like *Manu* and *Ikṣvāku*. Lord Krishna identified that path as *mat karma, mat yoga*, My activity, My yoga discipline. Thus, it should not be opposed by those who take the complete non-involvement.

A sincere follower of this detachment instruction should not openly oppose one who follows the involvement path because both courses are required in the existence of human beings. Both are enunciated and recommended by the Lord for various entities at different stages. Both are supported and taught by *Nārada* and other great devotees on par with him.

ग्रास सु-मृष्टं विरसं
महान्त स्तोकम् एव वा ।
यदृच्छयैवापतितं
ग्रसेद् आजगरो ऽक्रियः ॥३.२॥

grāsaṁ su-mṛṣṭaṁ virasaṁ
mahāntaṁ stokam eva vā
yadṛcchayaivāpatitaṁ
grased ājagaro 'kriyaḥ (3.2)

grāsaṁ — food; su-mṛṣṭaṁ — very tasty; virasam — bland; mahāntam — plentiful; stokam — scanty; eva — indeed; vā — whether; yadṛcchayaivāpatitaṁ = yadṛcchayā — by chance + eva — indeed + āpatitam — required; grased — should take; ājagaro = ājagaraḥ — a python-like person; 'kriyah = akriyaḥ — without exertion.

Translation

Whether food is very tasty or bland, plentiful or scarse, a python-like person, should take what is acquired by chance, without exertion for it. (3.2)

Commentary:

Many opportunities are presented by destiny in terms of various combinations of energies which are a mixture of clarification, enthusiasm and insensitivity. These are being presented at all times in varying degrees. The example of the python is cited since after taking a meal, the reptile does not endeavor for food. The creature takes shelter in relaxation, at least until it requires another stomach full. On the other hand, human beings are habitually passionate even after fulfillment of desires.

Over all, the python body of a spirit cannot exhibit as much intelligence as the human form. Still the elevated brahmin who wandered about, cited the python, to bring to our attention one special aspect of the creature and to show that in the advanced stages one reaches a platform where one develops a lack of interest in exploitation.

The exhibition of intelligence in terms of materialism is not an advancement, although the spirit does learn something from such endeavors. And in fact, at a certain stage, if the spirit does not endeavor in the struggle for survival, his position is imperiled because his gross and subtle forms become affected by the dulling mode of material nature and through the relationship of nature, he becomes degraded even in his self conception.

If we read this verse carefully, we will understand why Lord Krishna did not advise Arjuna in the way He advised Uddhava. If Arjuna followed this prescription for living, he would not have fought the battle, which at that stage of his life was his duty. Thus the Lord urged Arjuna to fight just as the same python who might lie down for a month without endeavoring, will at the end of that time, after its food energy was exhausted, move again very swiftly to grasp another creature for a meal. Thus while the *Bhagavad Gītā* urges an aspiring yogi like Arjuna, along the path of action, this instruction to Uddhava recommended the path of *jñāna* yoga, or the application of psychic action while turning away from opportunities for physical involvement. This path was described in the *Bhagavad Gītā* as the *jñāna* yoga of *sāmkhyas* and as *sannyās* yoga also:

śrībhagavānuvāca
loke'smindvividhā niṣṭhā purā proktā mayānagha
jñānayogena sāṁkhyānāṁ karmayogena yogināṁ

The Blessed Lord said: In the physical world, a two-fold standard was previously taught by Me. O Arjuna, my good man. This was mind regulation by the yoga practice of the Sāṁkhya philosophical yogis and the action regulation by the yoga practice of the non-philosophical yogis. (B.G. 3.3)

śrībhagavānuvāca
kāmyānāṁ karmaṇāṁ nyāsaṁ saṁnyāsaṁ kavayo viduḥ
sarvakarmaphalatyāgaṁ prāhustyāgaṁ vicakṣaṇāḥ

The Blessed Lord said: The authoritative speakers know the rejection of opportunity as renunciation of actions which are prompted by craving. The clear-sighted seers declare the abandonment of the results of benefit-motivated action as the rejection of consequences. (B.G. 18.2)

Most human beings should take the path designed for Arjuna. A few human beings should follow the course, which was shown to Uddhava. After evolving for billions and billions of years, one cannot all of a sudden stop one's evolution in order to follow a path given for an elevated human being. But it is also unreasonable to expect that the advanced souls will stop their progression and go back to a general path which is not suited to their liberation needs. Thus whether food or whatever, is tasty or bland, attractive or non-attractive, an advanced human being who is reserved from all sorts of mundane emotions, should take only what is acquired by chance, without making much of an exertion to acquire things or opportunities, which are not directly presented to him by providence.

After one understands how material nature operates, one does not crave its aspects any longer. One gains indifference towards the whole range of the material, social and commercial affairs.

शयीताहानि भूरीणि
निराहारो ऽनुपक्रमः ।
यदि नोपनयेद् ग्रासो
महाहिर् इव दिष्ट-भुक् ॥३.३॥

śayītāhāni bhūrīṇi
nirāhāro 'nupakramaḥ
yadi nopanayed grāso
mahāhir iva diṣṭa-bhuk (3.3)

śayītāhāni = śayīta — should lie + ahāni — days; bhūrīṇi — many; nirāhāro = nirāhāraḥ — fasting; 'nupakramah = anupakramah — be without endeavor; yadi — if; nopanayed = na – not + upanayed (upanayet) — does not come; grāso = grāsaḥ — food; mahāhir = mahā – great + ahir (ahiḥ) — python; iva — like; diṣṭa-bhuk = diṣṭa — as destined + bhuk — eating.

Translation

He should lie many days without eating and without exertion. If food does not come, he like the great python, should remain as destined. (3.3)

Commentary:

In the material world, endeavor is regulated by the condition of the subtle passionate energy. Most people are inspired by this energy, but one may learn how to direct it with deliberation and sense control. This yogi who advised King Yadu, spoke of sense control or the controlled usage of the passionate power of material nature. There is a similarity between such a yogi and creatures like the python or sloth, or even between such yogis and dull human beings who are kept from endeavoring by a depressive emotion. However there is a vast difference between a yogi of this caliber and a dull human being.

Animals like the python or sloth, shift off to the dulling mode when they are not being driven by the passionate energy, and so does the dull human being, but this yogi shifted off to the clarifying power of material nature and to the spiritual plane which is beyond the clarifying zone. To maintain his material body and to honor the rules of material existence, an advanced yogi shifts over to passion every now and then as destined *(diṣṭa)*. By controlling eating habits by virtue of advanced yoga practice, he does not struggle for needs. Such yogis who mastered their diet are described by Lord Krishna in *Bhagavad Gītā:*

apare niyatāhārāḥ prāṇānprāṇeṣu juhvati
sarve'pyete yajñavido yajñakṣapitakalmaṣāḥ

Others who were restrained in diet, impel fresh air into the previously inhaled air. All these ascetics whose impurities were removed by austerity and religious ceremony understand the value of an act of sacrifice. (B.G. 4.30)

ओजः-सहो-बल-युतं
बिभ्रद् देहम् अकर्मकम् ।
शयानो वीत-निद्रश् च
नेहेतेन्द्रियवान् अपि ॥३.४॥

ojaḥ-saho-bala-yutaṁ
bibhrad deham akarmakam
śayāno vīta-nidraś ca
nehetendriyavān api (3.4)

ojaḥ — vigor; sahaḥ — persistence; bala — strength; yutam — endowed with; bibhrad = bibhrat — keeping; deham — body; akarmakam — without exertion; śayāno — relaxing; vīta-nidraś = vīta — without + nidras (nidraḥ) — stupor; ca — and; nehetendriyavān = na — not + īheta — should endeavor + indriya-vān — having full sensual powers; api — even though.

Translation

Keeping the body without exertion, even though it is endowed with vigor, persistence, and strength, he should relax without stupor, and should not endeavor, even though there is full sensual power. (3.4)

Commentary:

This is a description of the resulting control of advanced yoga practice. It can hardly be attained by mere will power or imaginative planning or intellectual understanding. The relaxation without stupor *(vīta-nidrah)* is the action which segregates the expert yogi from others. The reserve attitude whereby there is no endeavor even though there is full sensual power *(nehetendriyavān)* demonstrates that the yogi attained spiritual purity in terms of restricting the exchanges between the spiritual core self and the subtle equipments.

By mastership of *āsanas*, postures and *prāṇāyāma* breath nutrition methods, a limited being attains the stage where he can control his psyche in the way described. Some living beings, however, powerful mystics and gifted psychics may display these abilities even when using a physical body which was not energized by yoga austerities. But such people are in the minority. Because of the nature of their affiliation with the material energy, others cannot do it without taking up specific austerities which rid them of the controlling dominance of material nature.

मुनिः प्रसन्न-गम्भीरो
दुर्विगाह्यो दुरत्ययः ।
अनन्त-पारो ह्य् अक्षोभ्यः
स्तिमितोद इवार्णवः ॥३.५॥

muniḥ prasanna-gambhīro
durvigāhyo duratyayaḥ
ananta-pāro hy akṣobhyaḥ
stimitoda ivārṇavaḥ (3.5)

muniḥ — yogi philosopher; prasanna-gambhīro = prasanna — peaceable + gambhīro (gambhīraḥ) — profound; durvigāhyo = durvigāhyaḥ — difficult to fathom; duratyayah — unsurpassable; ananta-pāro = ananta – unlimited + pāro (pāraḥ) — unrestricted; hy — indeed; akṣobhyaḥ — one who cannot be disturbed; stimitoda = stimita — calm + udaḥ — water; ivārnavah = iva — like + arṇavah — ocean.

Translation

The yogi philosopher should be peaceable, profound, difficult to fathom, unsurpassable, unlimitedly unrestricted, not capable of being disturbed and calm like the ocean with its waters. (3.5)

Commentary:

The word *muni* has come to mean just a philosopher or at least a philosopher who is conversant with the concepts of Indian philosophy and religion. An equivalent word is *jñānī*. Formerly however to be a *muni*, one was required to have one basic qualification; expertise in yoga practice. There is a vast difference between someone who understands philosophy intellectually and one who has mastered yoga and then applied himself to philosophy.

By stating that the muni should be peaceable, profound, difficult to fathom, unsurpassable, unlimitedly unrestricted, not capable of being disturbed and like the ocean with its waters, the elevated brahmin indicated an expertise of yoga up to the stage of *samādhi*, which is complete freedom for the soul to separate itself from its psychic equipments.

Unless one is an expert yogi, it is hardly likely that one would be expert in this, because he would be too distracted. This does not hinge on religious affiliation. It depends on mastership of the subtle energy.

समृद्ध-कामो हीनो वा
नारायण-परो मुनिः ।
नोत्सर्पेत न शुष्येत
सरिद्भिर् इव सागरः ॥३.६॥

samṛddha-kāmo hīno vā
nārāyaṇa-paro muniḥ
notsarpeta na śuṣyeta
saridbhir iva sāgaraḥ (3.6)

samṛddha-kāmo = samṛddha — increase + kāmo (kāmaḥ) — enjoyable things; hīno = hīnaḥ — destitute; vā — whether; nārāyaṇa -paro = nārāyaṇa — God Nārāyaṇa + paro (paraḥ) — who is focused on; muniḥ — yogi philosopher; notsarpeta = na — neither + utsarpeta — becomes excited; na — nor; śuṣyeta — depressed; saridbhir = saridbhiḥ — by rivers; iva — like; sāgarah — the ocean.

Translation

Whether there is an increase in enjoyable things or whether he is destitute, the yogi philosopher who is focused on the God Nārāyaṇa, neither becomes excited nor depressed, just like the ocean which is not affected by rivers. (3.6)

Commentary:

Even though the ascetic was not an active preacher and had no missionary centers for preaching about the God he believed in, still he was focused on the God *Nārāyaṇa*, his chosen Deity. Thus severe asceticism or yoga need not be in opposition to devotional life. A sincere yogi can be a devotee of the God *Nārāyaṇa (Nārāyaṇa-paro).*

On the other hand, some who do not believe in the God *Nārāyaṇa* also say that they have attained a state of non-excitation. They also claim to be calm like the ocean. Perhaps they are since the spirit in detachment from material nature, would not be affected by the unpleasant or pleasant conditions of its gross or subtle body.

The gist of the brahmin's statement is that he and other yogi philosophers found their focus on God *Nārāyaṇa* to be productive in terms of giving them a total detachment from material nature.

One of the aims of yoga practice is concentration and when that concentration is focused on any object, the yogi is able to attain the closest proximity to the focused objective. It cannot be denied however that a person who is not focused on God *Nārāyaṇa* may become detached and unaffected, he may, because by his spiritual constitution as a primeval and eternal spiritual being. But all the same, the God *Nārāyaṇa* has a particular relevance. His association gives a particular type of existential coverage to a spirit.

दृष्ट्वा स्त्रियं देव-मायां
तद्-भावैर् अजितेन्द्रियः ।
प्रलोभितः पतत्य् अन्धे
तमस्य् अग्नौ पतङ्ग-वत् ॥ ३.७॥

dṛṣṭvā striyaṁ deva-māyāṁ
tad-bhāvair ajitendriyaḥ
pralobhitaḥ pataty andhe
tamasy agnau pataṅga-vat (3.7)

dṛṣṭvā — seeing; striyam —woman; deva-māyām — created by the bewildering energy of the God; tad-bhavair = tad – that + bhavair (bhāvaiḥ) — by natural features; ajitendriyaḥ — one who has not subdued his senses; pralobhitah — allured; pataty = patati — falls; andhe — into misconception; tamasy = tamasi — into darkness; agnau — in fire; pataṅga-vat — like a moth.

Translation

A person who has not subdued the senses, when seeing women, which are created by the bewildering energy of God, and being allured by the women's natural features, falls into a dark misconception just like the moth drawn into the fire. (3.7)

Commentary:

When a moth gets too close to a fire and is charred by it, the spirit using that moth form miscalculated on the basis of false interpretation by its intellect and senses. The spirit using the moth body is forced to give up that body which is ruined by the flames. It is not that the spirit is the moth body, but rather, that spirit was reliant on psychic and physical equipments for perceiving realities in this gross world. If then, the equipments are faulty, the reliant spirit, using any body, moth's or human being's, will of necessity make errors in judgment which will be revealed through undesirable and unexpected reactions.

The elevated brahmin explained to King Yadu, that most of what we perceive is being misinterpreted by our senses and intellect. On the basis of this misinterpretation, we misjudge and arrive at rash conclusions which are inconsistent with the laws of nature. Then we become entrapped by the resulting complexities.

The ascetics discussed the imperfect male psychology. This applies to females and children as well. All human beings require and carry with them a natural attraction to the adult female form. All human beings currently alive, took birth through such a form and endured the attraction to the mothering energy of an adult female.

If any human being mistakes the womanly form for a source of enjoyment, then he will of necessity fall into an illusion about the utility of the form. Thus he will commit mistakes. This occurs effortlessly. This is natural. It requires a particular effort to curb the senses and the intellect, and unless one practices the effective disciplines, he will fall into misconception and not even realize that his judgment is faulty.

योषिद्-धिरण्याभरणाम्बरादि-
द्रव्येषु माया-रचितेषु मूढः ।
प्रलोभितात्मा ह्य् उपभोग-बुद्ध्या
पतङ्ग-वन् नश्यति नष्ट-दृष्टिः ॥ ३.८॥

yoṣid-dhiraṇyābharaṇāmbarādi-
dravyeṣu māyā-raciteṣu mūḍhaḥ
pralobhitātmā hy upabhoga-buddhyā
pataṅga-van naśyati naṣṭa-dṛṣṭiḥ (3.8)

yoṣid-dhiraṇyābharaṇāmbarādi-dravyeṣu = yoṣid (yoṣit) — of women + dhiraṇya (hiraṇya) — gold + ābharana — ornaments + ambara — clothing + ādi — and the like + dravyeṣu — with mundane objects; māyā-raciteṣu = māyā — by the bewildering things + raciteṣu — with things created; mūdhaḥ — a foolish person; pralobhitātmā = pralobhita – tempted + ātmā — self, himself; hy (hi) — indeed; upabhoga-buddhyā = upabhoga — enjoyment + buddhyā — with the intellect; pataṅga-van = pataṅga — moth + van – like; naśyati — is destroyed; naṣṭa-dṛstiḥ = naṣta — is ruined + dṛṣṭiḥ — intelligence.

Translation

The foolish person, who with his intellect ruined, is tempted by the bewildering objects like woman, gold, ornaments, clothings, and other mundane objects, considering them as enjoyment, is destroyed like the moth. (3.8)

Commentary:

Since the spirit is reliant on the intellect, it is essential that the intellect be accurate in its assessments of what it perceives. But if the intellect is inaccurate, then the spirit will of necessity, be misled by false judgments. Even though the ascetic regarded the average human being as foolish *(mūdhah),* still we should not take offense, since most human beings ignore reality and endeavor impractically for bodily satisfaction and happiness. This is due to having an intellect which is imperfect, which cannot figure out its degree of error.

There needs to be a constant adjustment made by the spirit to keep the intellect in the clarifying mode of material nature and to figure the minor deviation it suffers from in that mode, but this effort may be tiring for most spirits who are transmigrating through mundane life forms. Thus in a sense, the diagnosis of the elevated brahmin about foolish people *(mūdhah)* is idealistic. It is a fact however that unless we associate with such people as this brahmin and unless we take to their advice to hear and accept the seriousness of our uncontrolled condition, we could not strive for perfection, nor affect any sort of self improvement.

These items, namely women, gold, ornaments, clothing, and other related aspects of material existence, do motivate our senses to act in a way that is detrimental to our spirituality. Gold, though just a metal has picked up for itself an attraction, because it does not tarnish easily. Since we have a tendency to want to live forever and since we are presumptuously aggravated by things which deteriorate quickly, we have a great appreciation for gold and hence we value it above the less-noble metals. In modern times however, the uniqueness of gold has decreased since researchers have figured ways of refining other durable metals like titanium and stainless steel. Still the same principle remains. We artificially place a high value on anything which resists deterioration. This indicates our strong tendency for eternity and permanence.

The brahmin listed woman *(yoṣid),* as one of the bewildering aspects, but that means more than just the female species. This term means the over-all need for mundane nutrition. It so happens that women are not to blame for it, but in the human creation, the female form is the one which provides nutrition for infants. There is no doubt about it. Since the woman's form is in such an essential position in material existence it is a threat to both male and females alike. It is not that it is a risk for just males. It is the same risk for females.

It is a fact however that usually teachers or gurus of ascetics, warn them about the attraction to females. This warning is minor in comparison to the more broad view of a woman's form as the nutritional source for both males and female infants. So long as we are desperate for nutrition, the female form will pose a threat to our stability as eternal spiritual beings. And this is the issue being raised here.

Ornaments have to do with being dissatisfied with the type of material body we receive in any given birth. When we find that a body is not to our liking or that it is not to the liking of others, whom we feel should admire it, our tendency is to try to improve its appearance by using ornaments.

The need for clothing has to do with climatic and environmental conditions such as insect harassment and adverse weather conditions. But we may also use clothing to improve the appearance of the body. All this however is to our dismay as the elevated brahmin indicated.

स्तोक स्तोकं ग्रसेद् ग्रासं
देहो वर्तेत यावता ।
गृहान् अहिंसन्न् आतिष्ठेद्
वृत्तिं माधुकरीं मुनिः ॥३.९॥

stokaṁ stokaṁ grased grāsaṁ
deho varteta yāvatā
gṛhān ahiṁsann ātiṣṭhed
vṛttiṁ mādhukarīṁ muniḥ (3.9)

stokaṁ stokaṁ —little by little, small portions; grased (graset) — should eat; grāsaṁ — food; deho = dehaḥ — the body; varteta — may operate; yāvatā — with that mind; gṛhān — householders; ahiṁsann = ahiṁsan — without bothering; ātiṣṭhet — should practice; vṛttim — habit; mādhukarīṁ — honeybee; muniḥ — yogi philosopher.

Translation

The yogi philosopher should practise the habit of a honey bee, eating small portions of food from the householders, without bothering them, for just as much as would operate the body. (3.9)

Commentary:

The principle of *stokam stokam* in regards to our needs, in reference to what we consume, should be the method of living for all aspiring ascetics. This has to do with curbing greed. Greed is the natural aspect of the sensual pursuit of the living being. Under the influence of random physical, emotional, and supernatural energies, the spirit sponsors greed which is detrimental since it causes undesirable reactions which come in the form of discomfort at some future time, soon after or long after the occurrence transpired.

The brahmin however, gave this instruction particularly to those ascetics who like to collect donations. In some modern missions we see this instruction is violated. Some spiritual masters, even those of repute, encourage disciples to take as much as possible from the general public. Many of these teachers quote this or similar verses while simultaneously indulging in the opposite feature which is to take as much as possible and to draft up programs of milking the materialistic householders. Thus the aspect of greed is ever present even in some who claim to be frugal.

The rule given by the elevated brahmin, is regulated by the aspect of how much the body requires for its basic operation *(deho varteta)*. Unless an ascetic knows exactly what his body needs for its operation in the clarifying mode of material nature, he cannot follow this rule no matter how much he may try. The sure way to know this about the body is to do *haṭha* yoga. Some disagree with this idea but their disagreement does not reduce the value of yoga, and its effectiveness on making the body very frugal. It is a fact that of all the yoga processes, *haṭha* yoga puts the material body in the frugal position. This *haṭha* yoga falls under the terms of *āsana, prāṇāyāma and pratyāhar,* in the eight part system of yoga, namely *yama, niyama, āsana, prāṇāyāma, pratyāhar, dhāraṇā, dhyāna*, and *samādhi.*

अणुभ्यश् च महद्भ्यश् च
शास्त्रेभ्यः कुशलो नरः ।
सर्वतः सारम् आदद्यात्
पुष्पेभ्य इव षट्पदः ॥३.१०॥

aṇubhyaś ca mahadbhyaś ca
śāstrebhyaḥ kuśalo naraḥ
sarvataḥ sāram ādadyāt
puṣpebhya iva ṣaṭpadaḥ (3.10)

anubhyaś = anubhyaḥ — from the insignificant creature; ca — and; mahadbhyaś = mahadbhyaḥ — from the greatest being; ca — and; śāstrebhyaḥ — from the scriptures; kuśalo = kuśalaḥ — resourceful; naraḥ — person; sarvataḥ — from all; sāram — essential lessons; ādadyāt — should take; puṣpebhya = puṣpebhyaḥ — from the flowers; iva — like; ṣaṭpadah — the six-legged creature, honeybee.

Translation

The resourceful person should take essential lessons from all, from the insignificant creature, the greatest being and from the scriptures, just as the six-legged creature takes from flowers. (3.10)

Commentary:

Honey is a blend of various nectars but in some seasons the six-legged insects take nectar from those flowers which yield a greater quantity of the sweetness. Even though a resourceful person should take essential lessons from every person, object and circumstance, still he does have one or more major teachers who are regarded as primary instructors. In some cases there is one prominent teacher, in others two or three or more. There is no hard and fast rule about this, for as the elevated brahmin advised King Yadu, it is all a matter of learning. Whosoever can teach us a valuable lesson, even if he or she used a reptile or vegetable form, is our teacher for the time being. The sum total reality is itself, the ongoing director. Unless one is resourceful and adaptable to destiny, he cannot become liberated and his spiritual advancement will of necessity, be forestalled. *Kauśalo* means skillful or resourceful.

सायन्तनं श्वस्तनं वा
न सङ्ग्‍गृह्णीत भिक्षितम् ।
पाणि-पात्रोदरामत्रो
मक्षिकेव न सङ्ग्रही ॥३.११॥

sāyantanaṁ śvastanaṁ vā
na saṅgṛhṇīta bhikṣitam
pāṇi-pātrodarāmatro
makṣikeva na saṅgrahī (3.11)

sāyantanam — for the evening; śvastanaṁ — for the next day; vā — or; na — not; sangṛhṇīta — should take; bhikṣitam — alms; pāṇi-pātrodarāmatro = pāni — with the hand; pātra — eating container + udara — belly + amatro = (amatraḥ) — a storage container; makṣikevā = makṣikā — bee + iva — like; na — not; saṅgrahī — a hoarder.

Translation

He should not take alms for the evening or for the next day. His hand or belly only, should serve as the container. He should not be a hoarder like the bee. (3.11)

Commentary:

In the aspect of sampling various nectars, the bee is to be followed but in its tendency to hoard, it is not to be admired at all. An ascetic must either have or must strive to develop a confidence in providence, such that he does not feel the necessity to hoard food and other items.

Some aspiring ascetics take a radical action, they discard their accumulated stuffs, thus declaring themselves as renunciants once and for all. Most of these radicals, are proven to be hypocrites and vow breakers. The reason is this: They are inspired by material nature to renounce. Then the same material nature inspires them to repossess what was discarded. One should not radically renounce but should steadily and definitely choke out the grasping tendency, until all of a sudden by a gradual and sure reduction, the undesirable traits go away.

Unless one has confidence in destiny, he will have to hoard because that is the nature of our situation. Thus instead of making a big act of an all-out, once-and-for-all detachment, one should work steadily with one's nature, carefully studying one's dependence on the material world. One should reduce social contacts, conclude current responsibilities, and gradually take up firm yoga austerities which help to bring one to a position, where one is not as dependent on the lower subtle energies.

सायन्तनं श्वस्तनं वा
न सङ्ग्‍गृह्णीत भिक्षुकः ।
मक्षिका इव सङ्ग्‍गृह्णन्
सह तेन विनश्यति ॥३.१२॥

sāyantanaṁ śvastanaṁ vā
na saṅgṛhṇīta bhikṣukaḥ
makṣikā iva saṅgṛhṇan
saha tena vinaśyati (3.12)

sāyantanaṁ — for the evening; śvastanaṁ — for the next day; vā — or; na — not; sangṛhṇīta — should accept; bhikṣukaḥ — a yogi beggar; makṣikā — honeybee; iva — like; sangṛhṇan — collecting; saha — with; tena — with that, what is stored; vinaśyati — is destroyed.

Translation

The yogi beggar should not collect for the evening or the next day, otherwise by collecting, if he hoards like the honey bee, he is destroyed along with the stores. (3.12)

Commentary:

This type of yogi beggar is not a householder. He is a single celibate practitioner of yoga. He has no social responsibilities. However, the same principle is applied to a householder yogi, even though it is not as extreme. If one hoards items, one develops a survival-of-the-fittest mentality and for that one is victimized by material nature.

Acquirement of an income and accumulation of goods, is sponsored by material nature, for the sake of providing for a family, a village or a nation. If one mistakes this and collects selfishly, he will be ruined, just as the honey bee is ruined by the honey collector.

Just as a honey gatherer notices the accumulated hives of the bees, so some other humans and supernatural people observe whatever a man hoards. Just as a farmer kills pigs, after allowing them to eat sumptuously to increase their body weight, so material nature through the agency of vicious creatures, deprives a hoarder of his goods. Some times we see that even religious adherents are squeezed by material nature. Even though they may believe that everything they do is for God and that their hoarded goods are kept for God, still material nature interferes causing perplexities and embarrassments.

An ascetic householder who manages a wife, children, and other relatives, should not allow them luxuries, otherwise he violates this code of frugality which was given by the elevated brahmin. Those householders who comply, set for themselves a foundation upon which they may practice total renunciation in the later years of the body. Otherwise the householder remains attached, until his dying day. He then leaves the body with the intentions of returning to this world to exploit the social privileges which he recently cultivated. Thus no matter what religion he professed or what God he worshipped, he will still remain time-bound in the mundane evolutionary cycle.

पदापि युवती भिक्षुर्
न स्पृशेद् दारवीम् अपि ।
स्पृशन् करीव बध्येत
करिण्या अङ्ग-सङ्गतः ॥३.१३॥

padāpi yuvatīṁ bhikṣur
na spṛśed dāravīm api
spṛśan karīva badhyeta
kariṇyā aṅga-saṅgataḥ (3.13)

padādi = padā — with the foot + api — even; yuvatīm — a young woman; bhikṣur = bhikṣuḥ — a yogi beggar; na — not; sprśed — should touch; dāravīm — wooden figure; api — even; spṛśan — touching; karīva = kari — elephant + iva — like; badhyeta — would be caught; kariṇyāḥ — of the she-elephant; aṅga-saṅgataḥ = aṅga – for the bodily limbs + saṅgataḥ — attachment.

Translation

The yogi beggar should not touch even the wooden figure of a young woman, not even with his foot, or he would be caught, just like the elephant, (which is captured) through its attachment for touching the limbs of the she-elephant. (3.13)

Commentary:

The reverse of this is also true, that if a female ascetic exhibits a polarized sexual demeanor in order to enjoy sexual exchanges, either with other females, or with males, she will be caught and will be implicated in responsibility of begetting in the present or in the future life.

Sexual flirtations, even the slightest type, mean inconvenience and sexual responsibility with progeny in lives to come. This is an important social law of material nature which we usually are either unaware of or overlook. There are many so called spiritual masters, pandits, ministers, and the like, sadhus, holy men, and the like. Most of them are unaware of this social law. Subsequently they go on creating a fantasy salvation for themselves and others. In that way they enjoy paradise in the mind for the time being and live in a hope of release from the frustrations and agonies of this mundane existence.

It is definite as the brahmin explained that if we indulge in sexuality then we will be caught. There is no doubt about it. There is no exception to it. Those smart preachers and religious leaders who indulge in it secretly or under the pretence of religion, will be caught.

The method of getting free from the sexual lure is explained by the word *aṇga-saṇgatah*, which means our instinctive attachment for the bodily limbs of some other person or persons. Until we can free ourselves from this natural instinct, we cannot get out of the implication of social responsibility. It is a matter of developing a resistance to sexuality.

नाधिगच्छेत् स्त्रियं प्राज्ञः
कर्हिचिन् मृत्युम् आत्मनः ।
बलाधिकैः स हन्येत
गजैर् अन्यैर् गजो यथा ॥३.१४॥

nādhigacchet striyaṁ prājñaḥ
karhicin mṛtyum ātmanaḥ
balādhikaiḥ sa hanyeta
gajair anyair gajo yathā (3.14)

nadhigacchet = na—not + adhigacchet — approach, should flirt with; striyaṁ — woman; prājñaḥ — the perceptive person; karhicin — at any time; mṛtyum — death; ātmanah — for the self; balādhikaiḥ = bala — powerful + adhikaiḥ — by others with more ability; saḥ — he; hanyeta — would be hurt; gajair = gajaiḥ — by the elephants; anyair = anyaih — by others; gajo = gajaḥ — elephant; yathā — just as.

Translation

The perceptive person should not flirt with women at any time, regarding that as the death of himself, for he may be hurt by more powerful rivals just as the elephant by others of its own kind. (3.14)

Commentary:

The term *adhigacchet*, means should go towards, *na* means not. *Gacchet* means should go but when adhi is placed before it, it means, to go with an impetus, an attraction, with a pushing or pulling urge. This sort of attraction is known as flirtation.

The elevated ascetic explained, that from flirtations come future responsibilities which divert the aspiring yogi. The responsibilities which are derived from sexual polarity cause the yogi to forego spiritual development by the demands placed on him by material nature for participation in family affairs.

In this sense, the sexual polarity is a form of self-death *(mṛtyum ātmanah)*. Apart from the liabilities which develop from a flirtation, one has to deal with the female mentality as he tries to contain or clash with her sexuality. But he must also deal with rivals who regard her as a focus of sexuality. Thus there are many perplexities. A religious leader may discover that through religious association, the sexuality which he wanted to escape from, meets him head on and causes him to flirt and become implicated with women who meet him for religious association. Future lives of responsibility may be created for any male who mixes with women in the name of religion. A cleric may be compelled to take many births and give each woman of a previous religious association many children.

न देयं नोपभोग्यं च
लुब्धैर् यद् दुःख-सञ्चितम् ।
भुङ्क्ते तद् अपि तच् चान्यो
मधु-हेवार्थविन् मधु .३.१५॥

na deyaṁ nopabhogyaṁ ca
lubdhair yad duḥkha-sañcitam
bhuṅkte tad api tac cānyo
madhu-hevārthavin madhu (3.15)

na — not; deyaṁ — what should be given away; nopabhogyaṁ = na — not + upabhogyaṁ — to be enjoyed personally; ca — and; lubdhair = lubdhaiḥ — by the greedy people; yad = yat — that; duḥkha-sañcitam = duḥkha — with trouble + sañcitam — is hoarded; bhunkte — appropiates; tad

= tat — that; api — also; tac = tat — that; cānyo = ca — and + anyo (anyaḥ) — another person; madhu-hevārthavin = madhu-hā — honey thief + iva — just as + arthavin (arthavit) — one who recognizes valuables, a thief; madhu — honey.

Translation

What greedy people hoard with trouble and would not give away, nor enjoy for themselves, that very same thing, another person who recognizes things of value, appropriates, and then again another thief takes that away just as the honey thief confiscates honey.(3.15)

Commentary:

The tendency for hoarding is so deeply rooted that even renounced monks engage in it, in a very sophisticated way that is not easily detected. Since a monk by rule of vows and by pressures from the public cannot accumulate items like the lay people, he discovers more subtle, less-obvious ways of hoarding. Thus it is important that a monk become so transformed that he is purged of the propensity for greed.

Some monks created a spiritual society and appoint disciples to do the hoarding while they pretend to be aloof. It is just like a father who runs a business concern and who turns over the more routine tasks to his able sons. In fact both he and his sons are implicated in whatever he or the sons may do. A *sannyāsi* whose disciples hoard or engage in greedy acts, is just as guilty as his followers but generally such sannyasis pass in the public as purified souls. The image-craving public, readily accepts such a *sannyāsi* as a qualified spiritualist, and the *sannyāsi* comes to believe this about himself and neglects purifying practices.

Now if these sannyasis can fall into such a hypocrisy, then we can just understand the position of ourselves since we hardly have any impetus or ambitions to motivate us to give up the hoarding and greed impulses. Material nature reminds us of our spiritually-impoverished positions by intimidating us in various ways, just as the bees are harassed by bears and human honey-thieves. Observing this, the elevated brahmin gave up the tendency for hoarding and began to consider how he could exempt himself from those activities.

सु-दुःखोपार्जितैर् वित्तैर्
आशासानां गृहाशिषः ।
मधु-हेवाग्रतो भुङ्क्ते
यतिर् वै गृह-मेधिनाम् ॥ ३.१६ ॥

su-duḥkhopārjitair vittair
āśāsānāṁ gṛhāśiṣaḥ
madhu-hevāgrato bhuṅkte
yatir vai gṛha-medhinām (3.16)

su-duḥkhopārjitair = su – great + duhkha — pain + upārjitair (upārjitaiḥ) — with all that is required; vittair = vittaiḥ — with all money; āśāsānām — of those who are eager to enjoy; gṛhāśiṣaḥ = grha — concerning householder live + āśiṣaḥ — good things; madhu-hevāgrato = madhu-ha — honey thief + iva — just like + agrato = (agrataḥ) — first; bhuṅkte — partakes; yatir = yatiḥ — a yogi ascetic; vai — indeed; gṛha-medhinam — of materialistic householders.

Translation

Just like a honey thief, the yogi ascetic is the first to partake of the enjoyable things which the materialistic householder acquired with great pains. (3.16)

Commentary:

This statement must be culturally applied since it is illegal in some societies that an ascetic to beg or request alms from others. Even though in some Eastern countries, it is allowed, in most Western countries this is not permitted and one may be arrested if one is found begging from door to door. This scriptural statement is limited to a certain time, place, and cultural setting.

On a higher level however, this statement is absolute in the sense that a yogi ascetic, *(yatiḥ)* is actually the first to acquire those enjoyable things which the materialistic householder acquires. This is because unless one is a yogi ascetic, he cannot actually enjoy anything in the material world, because he does not have the subtle perception required to really enjoy something.

Normally we think that the materialistic persons are enjoying and that the penance-performing spiritualists, are deprived. The fact is this: The spiritualists who genuinely restrict themselves from one type of life, experience more of another higher life. Thus even though on one level these ascetics are restricted, on another they get fulfillments.

ग्राम्य-गीतं न श्रृणुयाद्
यतिर् वन-चरः क्वचित् ।
शिक्षेत हरिणाद् बद्धान्
मृगयोर् गीत-मोहितात् ॥३.१७॥

grāmya-gītaṁ na śṛṇuyād
yatir vana-caraḥ kvacit
śikṣeta hariṇād baddhān
mṛgayor gīta-mohitāt (3.17)

grāmya-gītaṁ = grāmya — senuous + gītam — songs; na — not; śṛṇuyād = śṛṇuyāt — should listen; yatir = yatiḥ — a yogi ascetic; vana-caraḥ = vana — in the woods + caraḥ — roaming about; kvacit — at any time; śikṣeta — should learn; harinād = harināt — from the deer; baddhān = baddhāt — from being captured; mṛgayor = mṛgayoḥ — of the hunter; gīta-mohitāt = gīta — music + mohitāt — from bewilderment.

Translation

The yogi ascetic who roams about in the woods, should never listen to sensuous music. He should learn from the captured deer which was bewildered by the music of a hunter. (3.17)

Commentary:

Sensuous music, in fact anything sensuous is a threat to the yogi ascetic. Such things might not be dangerous for the non-yogis but they are to the yogi since they can erase his hard-earned progression. Since a yogi strives step by step, taking help from various teachers as the elevated brahmin did, the yogi cannot afford to lose progress. Still, in some cases we see that a yogi does digress when in contact with sensuous objects which bear an attraction which is more than he can resist.

This warning pertains to the sense of hearing. It is a fact that the living being is addicted to the senses. In the yoga process of *pratyāhar*, the yogi takes one sense at a time and curbs these gradually by mystic processes. These processes start with the physical postures of *Haṭha* Yoga.

One commentator, a *Swāmī* Madhavānanada, whose translation and commentary I have before me, suggested in his notation on this verse that the term *grāmya-gītam* means sensual music but he indicated that no restriction is made against devotional music. However, it all depends on what he means by devotional music and on who composes that. In modern times, we have seen sannyasis who were lured by sensual devotional music and who gave up their vows to take a female or a male sexual companion. Perhaps, *Swāmī* Madhavananda, means devotional music that is created and sung by completely purified souls and which is listened to under their direction. Any type of sensuous music is a danger because the mind has a way of perverting even the words and musical themes which are created by the great souls. The mind is so perverse that it can twist the entire purpose of this creation around and cause us to forget the creator of this world, who has in fact created this world in a way of musical composition.

I feel that if the elevated brahmin wanted to advise us to listen to any type of music, he would have stated so, because as a rule a *sannyāsi* should give up and curb all his sensual intakes, by the process of *pratyāhar*, the fifth stage of yoga practice.

Even though the deer was captured by the music of the hunter, it was neither the hunter nor the music which was really the problem but rather, the keen hearing of the deer. Thus the need is for a change of senses. Those who feel it is restraint of one wayward sense, misunderstand the yoga process. Ultimately, the restraints applied in *pratyāhar*, are done to replace, not merely to change, the present senses; to derive a new set of senses which are energized by a different type of energy.

नृत्य-वादित्र-गीतानि
जुषन् ग्राम्याणि योषिताम् ।
आसां क्रीडनको वश्य
ऋष्यशृङ्गो मृगी-सुतः ॥३.१८॥

nṛtya-vāditra gītāni
juṣan grāmyāṇi yoṣitām
āsāṁ krīḍanako vaśya
ṛṣyaśṛṅgo mṛgī-sutaḥ (3.18)

nṛtya-vāditra gītāni = nṛtya — dancing + vāditra — music + gītāni — music; juṣan — enjoying; grāmyāni — that which is sensous; yoṣitām — of women; āsāṁ — of their; krīḍanako = krīḍanakaḥ — a play thing; vasya = vasyaḥ — docile; rṣyasṛṅgo = rṣyasṛṅgaḥ — Rṣyasṛṅga; mṛgī-sutaḥ = mṛgī – female deer, doe + sutaḥ — son

Translation

Ṛṣyaśṛṅga, the son of a doe, while enjoying the sensuous misic and songs of women, became their docile plaything. (3.18)

Commentary:

In the *Rāmāyaṇa*, the story of *Ṛṣyaśṛṅga* is plainly told because of *Ṛṣyaśṛṅga's* participation in the sacrificial ceremony through which King *Daśaratha* got sons. According to that narration of *Vālmīki*, *Ṛṣyaśṛṅga* was the son of a rishi named *Vibhāndaka* and a doe. In fact it is well known that because of this, *Ṛṣyaśṛṅga* had deer-like horns growing out of his forehead. He was lured by some female musicians who were sent to capture him and bring him for the use of his good luck in bringing rain.

It is no accident that the elevated brahmin recalled the story of *Ṛṣyaśṛṅga* just after he spoke of the luring of deer by a hunter. *Ṛṣyaśṛṅga* had a body which was produced by a deer mother. His body had the strong tendency for listening to pleasing music. Through that instinct he was lured by women who were sent to take him away from his father's hermitage.

Each of us have an animal body or a body which has animalistic tendencies, both vicious and sentimental ones. We must reform the body if we want to become successful in spiritual life.

Ṛṣyaśṛṅga, by birth as the son of a rishi, was a rishi himself in the past life but since he got his body through a doe, and did not reform it, he succumbed to the tendencies of that sensually inclined form. Thus there is a necessity for us to reform and change out the lower energies in our gross and subtle bodies. It is not so much how great we were in past lives, but how much we are able to reestablish that status in the present circumstance.

जिह्वयाति-प्रमाथिन्या
जनो रस-विमोहितः ।
मृत्युम् ऋच्छत्य् असद्-बुद्धिर्
मीनस् तु बडिशैर् यथा ॥३.१९॥

jihvayāti-pramāthinyā
jano rasa-vimohitaḥ
mṛtyum ṛcchaty asad-buddhir
mīnas tu baḍiśair yathā (3.19)

jihvayāti-pramāthinyā = jihvayā — by the tongue + ati-pramāthinyā — very demanding; jano = janaḥ — a person; rasa-vimohitaḥ = rasa – flavor + vimohitaḥ – bewildered; mṛtyum — death; ṛcchaty = ṛcchati — meets; asad-buddhir = asad (asat) — unrealistic + buddhir (buddhiḥ) — intellect; asad-buddhir – a person with an unrealistic intellect; mīnas = mīnaḥ — fish; tu — but; baḍiśair = baḍiśaiḥ — by the hooks; yathā — just as.

Translation

A person with an unrealistic intellect, being bewildered by flavor, by the excessively demanding tongue, meets death just as a fish does by the hooks. (3.19)

Commentary:

Here another sense is singled out: the sense of taste. These senses exists in the subtle body as orbits of the intellect in its research of the material world. This applies to both the subtle and gross material energies which we experience as psychic and physical reality.

As stated by the elevated brahmin the intellect organ of the subtle body, the *buddhir (buddhih),* is unrealistic *(asat).* Due to its unrealistic stance, the *buddhi* misleads the *ātma,* the spirit, which uses it. It does so by giving the spirit the wrong information and by drawing incorrect conclusions. Thus symbolically, the spirit does in a sense meet with death, or is misled again and again by contributing its energies to many unrealistic schemes which seek to reverse the laws of nature but which instead are baffled and fatigued by such workings of destiny. It is just like the fish which does not consider the hook within a seemingly-tasty bait.

The material world is not put here for the spirit's enjoyment but through acceptance of a false interpretation of his intellect, the spirit makes the assumption that the world is here for his research and development, just as the fish which considers that the object hanging in the water was put there for its consumption.

इन्द्रियाणि जयन्त्य् आशु
निराहारा मनीषिणः ।
वर्जयित्वा तु रसनं
तन् निरन्नस्य वर्धते ॥३.२०॥

indriyāṇi jayanty āśu
nirāhārā manīṣiṇaḥ
varjayitvā tu rasanaṁ
tan nirannasya vardhate (3.20)

indriyāni — the senses organs; jayanty = jayanti — they conquer; āśu — easily; nirāhārā = nirāhārāḥ — those who restrict food; manīṣiṇaḥ — the wise men; varjayitvā — except for; tu — but; rasanaṁ — the tongue; tan = tat — that which; nirannasya — of one who gives up food; vardhate — become more demanding.

Translation

The wise man, who restricts food, easily conquers the sense organs, except for the tongue, which becomes more demanding to one who gives up food. (3.20)

Commentary:

Even though the senses are psychically operated in the subtle body, still their energization, is functionally based on nutrition. It is based on both gross and subtle energy. This is why yogis practise diet control and *prāṇāyāma*, which is breath nutrition control.

Those ascetics who do not practise yoga usually do not understand the necessity for it and consider it an unnecessary chore. It is a fact however that when they fast, they experience that the other senses of the body are calmed or become fatigued, de-energized, weakened, and bewildered but the sense of taste remains in good shape and induces them to eat and overeat.

From this eating and over eating, the sense of taste strengthens its allies, the other senses, and the non-yogis therefore find themselves rationalizing their failure at sense control by saying that when they die they will go to heaven or to a paradise where they will not have to deal with uncontrollable senses.

This is a good way of ignoring the problem of sense control, of not becoming disappointed, of not taking on a pessimistic or negative mood, but it contributes to a long-ranged failure and to hypocrisy and a self- righteous attitude in relating to the ordinary people who have made no religious effort. The tongue represents a higher sense organ which is the sense organ of need. Since the *ātma* is not the Supreme Being, since he is not independent or self-sufficient, he is reliant on taking energies and interacting with energies other than himself. And thus the organ of need is there as his basic desire. The only way he can use this organ in a non-harmful manner is to take what he needs from a harmless energy. His need is eternal, and he cannot get rid of it but he can better select the type of energy it absorbs.

From the physical perspective, this sense of need is a food need, a need for nutrients. This is called nutrient-craving stage. From the emotional perspective it is a need for reliant energies from superior spirits. This is called the affection-needing stage. However there are various high and low levels of this love-absorbing stage.

In any case, the more one tries to repress needs, the more there is a pressure or impulse for fulfillment. This is conquered by yoga practice.

तावज् जितेन्द्रियो न स्याद्
विजितान्येन्द्रियः पुमान् ।
न जयेद् रसनं यावज्
जितं सर्वं जिते रसे ॥३.२१॥

tāvaj jitendriyo na syād
vijitānyendriyaḥ pumān
na jayed rasanaṁ yāvaj
jitaṁ sarvaṁ jite rase (3.21)

tāvaj = tāvat — however; jitendriya = jitendriyaḥ — one whose senses are consistently controlled; na — not; syād = syāt — can be; vijitānyendriyaḥ = vijita – controller + anya – the other + indriyaḥ — sense organs; pumān — a human being; na – no; jayed = jayet — can control; rasanam — the organ of taste; yāvaj = yāvat — for when; jitaṁ — controlled; sarvaṁ — all; jite — in that which is subdued; rase — in the tongue.

Translation

However, a human being who controlled the other sense organs, cannot control all his senses consistently until he controls the organ of taste, for when the tongue is controlled, all other senses are consistently subdued. (3.21)

Commentary:

The sense of taste, power of intake, is the pivot point in a living entity's relationship with the gross or subtle material nature. Thus if he could control his access to the energy of material nature, he could very well regulate, at least to a greater extent the involvements. There seems to be a suggestion here, given by the elevated brahmin and also elsewhere in the Vedic literature, that an absolute degree of control might be attained, but practically speaking this is not possible because of a natural and perpetual relationship with material nature.

The relationship between the living entities and material nature is perpetual. Both the living entities and material nature are eternal. As such they are in perpetually interaction. In the material creation, material nature appears to take the upper hand, using the limited entities as a resource.

Lord Krishna has compared the material energy to a gigantic vegetation which feeds in part on the human being:

śrībhagavānuvāca
ūrdhvamūlamadhaḥśākham aśvatthaṁ prāhuravyayam
chandāṁsi yasya parṇāni yastaṁ veda sa vedavit
adhaścordhvaṁ prasṛtāstasya śākhā guṇapravṛddhā viṣayapravālāḥ
adhaśca mūlānyanusaṁtatāni karmānubandhīni manuṣyaloke

The Blessed Lord said: The yogi sages say that there is an imperishable Ashvattha tree which has a root going upwards and a trunk downwards, the leaves of which are the Vedic hymns. He who knows this is a knower of the Vedas.

Branches spread from it, upwards and downwards. It is nourished by the mundane influences and the attractive objects are its sprouts. The roots are spread below, promoting action in the world of human beings. (B.G. 15.1-2)

However Lord Krishna also indicated that the tree of the material nature is factually perceived as a growing vegetation if we could perceive it from a specific dimension, even though it does not appear so from our present position:

na rūpamasyeha tathopalabhyate nānto na cādirna ca saṁpratiṣṭhā
aśvatthamenaṁ suvirūḍhamūlam asaṅgaśastreṇa dṛḍhena chittvā

Its form is not perceived in this dimension, nor its end, nor beginning nor foundation. With the strong ax of non-attachment, cut down this Ashvattha tree with its well-developed roots. (15.3)

But Lord Krishna claimed that there was another special location in which the material nature is not manifested, a place where it makes no impact, no showing:

tataḥ padaṁ tatparimārgitavyaṁ yasmingatā na nivartanti bhūyaḥ
tameva cādyaṁ puruṣaṁ prapadye yataḥ pravṛttiḥ prasṛtā purāṇī
nirmānamohā jitasaṅgadoṣā adhyātmanityā vinivṛttakāmāḥ
dvaṁdvairvimuktāḥ sukhaduḥkhasaṁjñair
gacchantyamūḍhāḥ padamavyayaṁ tat
na tadbhāsayate sūryo na śaśāṅko na pāvakaḥ
yadgatvā na nivartante taddhāma paramaṁ mama

Then that place is to be sought, to which having gone, the spirits do not return to this world again. One should think: "I take shelter with that Primal Person, from Whom the creation emerged in primeval times."

Those who are devoid of pride and confusion, who have conquered the faults of attachment, who constantly stay with the Supreme Spirit, whose cravings ceased, who are freed from the dualities known as pleasure and pain, those undeluded souls go to that imperishable place.

The sun does not illuminate that place, nor the moon, nor the fire. Having gone to that location, they never return. That is My supreme residence. (B.G. 15.4-6)

It appears also from what Lord Krishna explained, that the limited spirits have to take their subtle sense organs along with them when they leave a particular body. He explained that we struggle to dominate the unruly sensuality:

mamaivāṁśo jīvaloke jīvabhūtaḥ sanātanaḥ
manaḥṣaṣṭhānīndriyāṇi prakṛtisthāni karṣati
śarīraṁ yadavāpnoti yaccāpyutkrāmatīśvaraḥ
gṛhītvaitāni saṁyāti vāyurgandhānivāśayāt

My partner is in this world of individualized conditioned beings. He is an eternal individual soul but he draws to himself the mundane senses of which the mind is the sixth detection device.

Regardless of whichever body that master acquires, or whichever one he departs from, he goes taking these senses along, just as the wind goes with the perfumes from their source. (B.G. 15.7-8)

The mastership of the sense organs is described in brief and in detail in the instructions given to Arjuna, instructions which are known as the *Bhagavad Gītā*, but Krishna also described the process of diet control which the elevated brahmin hinted at to King Yadu. This diet control is a specific discipline and those who master it are acclaimed by Lord Krishna as capable teachers of that discipline.

apare niyatāhārāḥ prāṇānprāṇeṣu juhvati
sarve'pyete yajñavido yajñakṣapitakalmaṣāḥ

Others who were restrained in diet, impel fresh air into the previously inhaled air. All these ascetics whose impurities were removed by austerity and religious ceremony understand the value of an act of sacrifice. (4.30)

tadviddhi praṇipātena paripraśnena sevayā
upadekṣyanti te jñānaṁ jñāninastattvadarśinaḥ

This you ought to know. By submitting yourself as a student, by asking questions, by serving as requested, the perceptive reality-conversant teachers will teach you the knowledge. (4.34)

As one advances he feels the need for various austerities. Thus these were explained in brief by Lord Krishna to Arjuna. The Lord validated the austerities by making the following statements:

yajñaśiṣṭāmṛtabhujo yānti brahma sanātanam
nāyaṁ loko'styayajñasya kuto'nyaḥ kurusattama
evaṁ bahuvidhā yajñā vitatā brahmaṇo mukhe
karmajānviddhi tānsarvān evaṁ jñātvā vimokṣyase)

Those who enjoy the physical and psychological results of a sacrifice, go to the primeval spiritual region. This world is not properly utilized by those who do not perform austerity or religious ceremony. How then can the other world be, O best of the Kurus?

Many types of disciplines of accomplishment were expounded in the mouth of the spiritual existence. Know them all to be produced from action. Realizing this, O Arjuna, you will be freed. (B.G. 4.31-32)

पिङ्गला नाम वेश्यासीद्
विदेह-नगरे पुरा ।
तस्या मे शिक्षित किञ्चिन्
निबोध नृप-नन्दन ॥३.२२॥

piṅgalā nāma veśyāsīd
videha-nagare purā
tasyā me śikṣitaṁ kiñcin
nibodha nṛpa-nandana (3.22)

piṅgalā – Piṅgalā; nāma — by name of; veśyāsīd = veśyā — woman who sold sexual services + āsīd = (āsīt) — there was; videha-nagare = Videha + nagare — in the city; purā — a long time ago; tasyā — from her; me — by me; śikṣitam — was learned; kiñcin — something; nibodha — learn; nrpa-nandana = nṛpa – king + nandana — dear son.

Translation

A long time ago in the city of Videha, there was a woman named Piṅgalā. She sold sexual services. I learned something from her. Hear of it, O dear son of a king. (3.22)

Commentary:

Yadu was the dear son of a king but he did not position himself to learn from any and everyone in the material creation. Thus the elevated brahmin chided him. One may be the dear son of a king and still be very naive about the movements of subtle energies. An aristocratic status does not necessarily open one's eyes to reality. In fact, since he was the son of the king, he was limited in a way, in that he could not learn lessons from those who were in dishonorable positions.

When he met the elevated brahmin, Yadu questioned about the ascetic's stupid and mad appearance. Now the brahmin answered that from the position of being stupid and mad, he had the advantage of seeing certain things. He learnt important lessons from others.

सा स्वैरिण्य् एकदा कान्तं
सङ्केत उपनेष्यती ।
अभूत् काले बहिर् द्वारे
बिभ्रती रूपम् उत्तमम् ॥३.२३॥

sā svairiṇy ekadā kāntaṁ
saṅketa upaneṣyatī
abhūt kāle bahir dvāre
bibhratī rūpam uttamam (3.23)

sā — she; svairiṇy = svairiṇī — sexual saleswoman; ekadā — one day; kāntaṁ — a lover; saṅketa — into the bedroom; upaneṣyatī — wanting to escort; abhūt — she stood; kāle — during the night; bahiḥ — outside; dvāre — in the entrance; bibhratī — holding; rūpam — her form; uttamam — very attractive.

Translation

Once, during the night, that sexual saleswoman, wanting to escort a lover into the bedroom, stood at the entrance, displaying her attractive form. (3.23)

Commentary:

Prostitution is just one of the compulsions in human existence. But it is a very important one to study since it is so forceful and degrading. For one who wants to get out of material existence, transcendence of sexuality is a necessity.

Even though *Pińgalā* was engaged in the most demeaning service, sexual service for income, still her discrimination was active but it was active in the wrong way in terms of attracting customers by assuming a sexually-appealing posture. Gradually after being frustrated repeatedly, *Pińgalā* did turn her discrimination away from the sex trade. She took to self realization.

In a way every human being is compulsively doing something that distracts him or her from self-realization. If that person can withdraw the intelligence from such things and put the discrimination to the task, great spiritual progress could be made. By the sense of observation, and the sense of discrimination, *Pińgalā* noted her condition and the status of potential customers. She wondered if there was some deeper asset in her or in anyone else. Initially that deeper asset eluded her intellect.

मार्ग आगच्छतो वीक्ष्य
पुरुषान् पुरुषर्षभ ।
तान् शुल्क-दान् वित्तवतः
कान्तान् मेने ऽर्थ-कामुकी ॥३.२४॥

mārga āgacchato vīkṣya
puruṣān puruṣarṣabha
tān śulka-dān vittavataḥ
kāntān mene 'rtha-kāmukī (3.24)

marga = marge — along the way; āgacchato = āgacchataḥ — coming; vīkṣya — seeing; puruṣān — men; puruṣarṣabha — O best of men; tān — them; śulka-dān — persons who could afford to pay; vittavataḥ = vitta – riches + vitaḥ — possessor of; kāntān — potential lovers; mene — she thought; ' rtha-kāmukī = 'rtha (artha) – money + kāmukī — a woman who is desperate.

Translation

O best of men, seeing males coming along the way, she who was desperate for money, thought of them as being rich, and of being able to afford her fee. (3.24)

Commentary:

Here in recognition of Yadu's status as a pious monarch, the elevated brahmin addressed him as best of men *(puruṣarṣabha)* in contrast to the customers of the prostitute who were the worst of men. However there is a twist of fate for some great men, in that they attain great wealth and then are drawn into sexual association with prostitutes. Even though *Pińgalā* was the lowest woman, a hooker, still she attracted high class customers because that is the nature of sexual services. It pulls down even the aristocratic gentlemen.

High class prostitutes generally do not accept idiotic customers and poor men, nor even pretensive idiots, like the elevated brahmin. Prostitutes hope for wealthy customers like the sons of politicians. As a woman desperate for money *(artha-kāmukī)*, *Pińgalā* applied herself to the task of attracting rich men. She was absorbed in flirting, fondling, and acquiring money from aristocrats *(śulka-dān vittavatah)*.

आगतेष्व् अपयातेषु
सा सङ्केतोपजीविनी ।
अप्य् अन्यो वित्तवान् को ऽपि
माम् उपैष्यति भूरि-दः ॥३.२५॥

āgateṣv apayāteṣu
sā saṅketopajīvinī
apy anyo vittavān ko 'pi
mām upaiṣyati bhūri-daḥ (3.25)

āgateṣv = āgateṣu — regarding those who came; apayāteṣu — regarding those who passed by; sā — she; saṅketopajīvinī = saṅketa – bedroom + upajīvinī — a woman who made a living by prostitution; apy = api — also; anyo = anyaḥ — some other; vittavān — a person with money; ko = kaḥ - whosoever; 'pi = api — also; mām — me; upaiṣyati — will come; bhūri-daḥ — one who will offer much money.

Translation

As they came and passed by, she who made a living by prostitution, thought that some other rich man would come and offer money. (3.25)

Commentary:

This is the procedure of hope and expectation based on prediction of the future. It is represented by the term *upaiṣyati* which is formed from the Sanskrit verb root, *iṣ*, meaning to wish, desire, or long for. *Piṅgalā* was in the habit of speculation about the future and putting her hopes into such ideation even though for the most part providence dishonored her requests.

This process however is counterproductive towards our spiritual advancement since it absorbs the discriminatory energy required for drawing the proper conclusions about our disappointments in life. From a disappointment one should draw the conclusion that one was dishonored or rejected by providence. One should learn how to be subordinate to providence so as to be realistic, but instead the discriminatory energy may be applied in creating more hopes which providence would reject.

It is not only in the business of prostitution but in every other type of mundanely-focused activity, that we commit ourselves in this foolish way and are frustrated.

एव दुराशया ध्वस्त-
निद्रा द्वार्य् अवलम्बती ।
निर्गच्छन्ती प्रविशती
निशीथं समपद्यत ॥३.२६॥

evaṁ durāśayā dhvasta-
nidrā dvāry avalambatī
nirgacchantī praviśatī
niśīthaṁ samapadyata (3.26)

evam — thus; durāśayā — with expectation; dhvasta-nidrā = dhvasta — being deprived + nidrā — sleep; dvāry = dvāri — in the doorway; avalambatī — lingered; nirgacchantī — the act of going out; praviśatī — the act of entering, coming back in; niśītham — midnight; samapadyata — manifested, came.

Translation

Thus with her sleep being deprived by that expectation, she went out and re-entered repeatedly until it was midnight. (3.26)

Commentary:

The deprivation of sleep *(dhvasta-nidrā)* causes a more speculative attitude of mind and causes more and more unrealistic considerations. Thus this is also counterproductive to the formation of the proper conclusions regarding a disappointment or frustration. Even though *Piṅgalā* was being deprived of sleep and was not gaining by it, the hope of customers kept her awake and hopeful but providence kept ignoring her requests. Every once in a while however, a man would accept her on one night or another. Sometimes she would be cheated by the man, while at other times, the customer would give her exactly what she wanted in terms of the money desired. But at other times when providence facilitated, or seemed to cooperate, the client gave her excessive pleasure and more money than expected. In this way providence used to support her periodically, and frustrate her regularly. From this *Piṅgalā* used to be fooled into thinking that even though providence frustrated, it did facilitate. Foolishly she drew a general conclusion that she could beat the odds of completely failing at her task of attracting wealthy men, offering them some sexual service and taking money in return.

तस्या वित्ताशया शुष्यद्-
वक्राया दीन-चेतसः ।
निर्वेदः परमो जज्ञे
चिन्ता-हेतुः सुखावहः ॥३.२७॥

tasyā vittāśayā śuṣyad-
vaktrāyā dīna-cetasaḥ
nirvedaḥ paramo jajñe
cintā-hetuḥ sukhāvahaḥ (3.27)

tasyāḥ — of her; vittāśayā = vita — for money + āśayā — through; śuṣyad-vaktrāyā = śuṣyad (śuṣyat) — dried up + vaktrāyā (vaktrāyāḥ) — face; dīna-cetasaḥ = dīna — depressed + cetasah — emotion; nirvedaḥ — disgust; paramo = paramaḥ — great; jajñe — arose; cintā-hetuḥ = cintā — scheme + hetuḥ — as a result of, due to; sukhāvahaḥ = sukha — happiness + āvahaḥ — caused.

Translation

Through the expectation of money, her face dried up and she became depressed. Then due to the scheme, a great disgust arose in her, that caused her to be happy. (3.27)

Commentary:

Piṅgalā became depressed *(dinā-cetasah)* because she invested energy in partially-realistic hopes, investing in a way, whereby if providence did not support her idea, her energy would be wasted. This type of investment of emotional energy causes a depression of mind and a resulting exhaustion.

Not just in the business of prostitution but in every aspect of life, this depression occurs if we plan unrealistically, thinking that providence will support our schemes. Any of us can become happy if we give up such ideas, derive disgust for our foolishness and thereby become relaxed, submissive to providence and happy in our limited positions.

Until we reach the stage of disgust *(nirvedah)* and realize that we are unrealistic and silly, we cannot get away from false hopes. They will continue to keep us captivated, while wasting the emotional energy.

तस्या निर्विण्ण-चित्ताया
गीत श्रृणु यथा मम ।
निर्वेद् आशा-पाशानां
पुरुषस्य यथा ह्य् असिः ॥३.२८॥

tasyā nirviṇṇa-cittāyā
gītaṁ śṛṇu yathā mama
nirveda āśā-pāśānāṁ
puruṣasya yathā hy asiḥ (3.28)

tasyā — of her; nirviṇṇa-cittāyā = nirviṇṇa — disgusted + cittāyā — she whose mind; gītaṁ — song; śṛnu — hear; yathā — as; mama — from me; nirveda — disgust; āśā-pāśānām = āśā — fantasies + pāśānāṁ — emotional cares; puruṣasya — of a person; yathā — just; hy = hi — indeed; asiḥ — sword.

Translation

Hear from me, as it was, how she, being disgusted, sang, for disgust is like a sword in relation to a person's emotional hopes or fantasies. (3.28)

Commentary:

Disgust is a special energy which can destroy a person's emotional hopes or fantasies.

Disgust arises from the very same emotional energy which creates the false hopes through which a person is bewildered. Since disgust is the same emotion converted, it is more effective than will power or determination. Determination works for sometime but unless disgust arises, a person usually returns to a destructive habit. In addition the disgust must be full and not partial. It must flood the whole being and not just invade merely a part of it. Then it reverses an undesirable tendency.

If a person can cause his emotional nature to be realistic, his spiritual advancement is sealed, otherwise even if he strives with determination he will never make sufficient progress.

न ह्य् अङ्गाजात-निर्वेदो
देह-बन्धं जिहासति ।
यथा विज्ञान-रहितो
मनुजो ममतां नृप ॥३.२९॥

na hy aṅgājāta-nirvedo
deha-bandhaṁ jihāsati
yathā vijñāna-rahito
manujo mamatāṁ nṛpa (3.29)

na — not; hy = hi — indeed; aṅgājāta-nirvedo = anga — O dear + ajāta — one who has not developed; nirvedo = nirvedaḥ — disgusted; deha-bandham = deha — of the body + bandham — bondage; jihāsati — desires to get rid of; yathā — as; vijñāna-rahito = vijñāna — discrimination + rahito (rahitaḥ) — being without; manujo = manujaḥ — person; mamatām — the sense of my-ness, sense of possession; nṛpa — O King.

Translation

Indeed, dear one, one does not desire to get rid of the bodily bondage, until one becomes disgusted, just as a person without discrimination, never gives up the sense of possession. (3.29)

Commentary:

The ascetic declared that until we become thoroughly disgusted we cannot get rid of bodily bondage, just as a person who has not developed a keen discrimination can never give up the sense of always trying to apply his identity to everything he encounters. This is because the sense of identity is compelling. Unless one is rooted in the converse habit of always questioning and discerning everything distinctly, one cannot be freed from it.

The elevated brahmin addressed King Yadu as *aṅga*, or dear one, because the king willingly became a submissive student. By that studentship the king relieved the brahmin of his teaching duties through the willingness to hear. Usually a king does not like to take advice from persons with low status. Here the King displayed a realistic humility and submitted himself to a person who had no mundane status but who by spiritual achievement was worthy of being the teacher of rulers.

पिङ्गलोवाच
अहो मे मोह-विततिं
पश्यताविजितात्मनः ।
या कान्ताद् असतः कामं
कामये येन बालिशा ॥ ३.३० ॥

piṅgalovāca
aho me moha-vitatiṁ
paśyatāvijitātmanaḥ
yā kāntād asataḥ kāmaṁ
kāmaye yena bāliśā (3.30)

pingalovaca = Piṅgalā-Piṅgalā + uvāca — said; aho — oh; me — my; moha-vitatim = moha – fantasy + vitatim — extent; paśyatāvijitātmanaḥ = paśyata — observe + avijita – not under control + ātmanaḥ — of the psyche; yā — who; kāntād = kāntāt — from lover-men; asataḥ — insignificant; kāmam — sexual craving; kāmaye — I desire; yena — by which; bāliśā — fool.

Translation

Piṅgalā said: "O, observe the extent of my fantasy, by which I desire the satisfaction of sexual cravings from insignificant lover-men, I am a person whose psyche is not under control, the fool that I am. (3.30)

Commentary:

There is a critical energy in every being and this power is misdirected. Instead of criticizing others, the self may do itself much favor by analyzing its own faults and taking steps to correct itself from folly. First one has to admit that one is foolish *(bāliśā)*. Instead of being a conqueror of one's psyche *(vijita)*, one usually has no control over it. Usually, one lives like an animal, chasing sensual cravings, especially the sexual fulfillments *(kāmam)*.

सन्तं समीपे रमण रति-प्रदं
वित्त-प्रदं नित्यम् इमं विहाय ।
अकाम-दं दुःख-भयाधि-शोक-
मोह-प्रदं तुच्छम् अहं भजे ऽज्ञा ॥ ३.३१ ॥

santaṁ samīpe ramaṇaṁ rati-pradaṁ
vitta-pradaṁ nityam imaṁ vihāya
akāma-daṁ duḥkha-bhayādhi-śoka-
moha-pradaṁ tuccham ahaṁ bhaje 'jñā (3.31)

santam — the substantial being; samīpe — in the vicinity, near; ramaṇam — most dear one; rati-pradam = rati — love + pradam — one who gives; vitta-pradam = vitta — wealth + pradam — one who gives; nityam — eternal; imam — this; vihāya — neglecting; akāma-dam — one who cannot satisfy desires; duḥkha-bhayādhi-śoka-moha-pradaṁ = duhkha — misery + bhaya — fear + ādhi — anguish + śoka — grief + moha — fantasy + pradam — one who can give; tuccham — small time; aham — I; bhaje — adore; 'jñā = ajñā — one who does not know.

Translation

"Neglecting the eternal substantial being, who is in the vicinity, who is the most dear lover and who can give me love, who can give me wealth, I adore a person who does not know, a small-time person, who cannot satisfy desires, and who gives misery, fear, anguish, grief and fantasy. (3.31)

Commentary:

Even though the *santam* is in the vicinity we usually cannot perceive Him. On the other hand, some feel that the *santam*, the reality, is not a person but is rather, a state of reality, a status of universal identity. But even for those people, there is neglect of the same universal reality. It is all due to wrong focus on the external realities which are thrown on our paths of destiny.

Generally speaking a husband, a wife, a child, an aunt, an uncle, a father or mother is irrelevant when compared to the eternal substantial being, the *Santam*. And as such we should not center ourselves upon the insignificant small-time persons.

Even though we share in the energy of frustration, and we also experience fulfillments, still we are not universal enough to be of much significance. Many of our actions cause misery, fear, anguish, grief, and fantasy.

अहो मयात्मा परितापितो वृथा
साङ्केत्य-वृत्त्याति-विगर्ह्य-वार्तया ।
स्त्रैणान् नराद् यार्थ-तृषो ऽनुशोच्यात्
क्रीतेन वित्तं रतिम् आत्मनेच्छती ॥ ३.३२ ॥

aho mayātmā paritāpito vṛthā
sāṅketya-vṛttyāti-vigarhya-vārtayā
straiṇān narād yārtha-tṛṣo 'nuśocyāt
krītena vittaṁ ratim ātmanecchatī (3.32)

aho — oh; mayātmā = mayā — by me + ātmā — self; paritāpito = paritāpitaḥ — afflicted; vrthā — in vain; sāṅketya-vṛttyāti-vigarhya-vārtayā = sāṅketya — privacy + vṛttyā — by the means of livelihood + ati – very, most + vigarhya — disgraceful + vārtayā — job; straiṇāt — from womanizers; narād = narāt — from men; yārtha-trso = yā — she + artha-tṛṣo (artha-tṛṣaḥ) — those who are greedy; 'nuśocyāt = anuśocyāt — from the pitiable; krītena — by which was sold; vittam — money; ratim — sexual pleasure; ātmanecchatī = ātmanā — with myself + icchatī — desiring.

Translation

"O, in vain, I afflicted myself by this most disgraceful means of livelihood, using my privacy. By the job of selling myself, I desired money and sexual pleasure from pitiable men who are greedy womanizers. (3.32)

Commentary:

We must not only become disgusted with our behavior but must also sincerely repent to ourselves about ourselves and then take steps for self-reform once and for all. Thus the energy of disappointment combined with a self dissatisfaction with our behavior, may ignite a search for self realization and bring on the power of self reformation. Merely deciding to change a bad habit is not enough. The disappointment due to frustration and the dissatisfaction with one's performance, must be added so that the emotional nature may be combined with the mental aspirations for complete conquest of lower desires.

यद् अस्थिभिर् निर्मित-वंश-वंस्य-
स्थूणं त्वचा रोम-नखैः पिनद्धम् ।
क्षरन्-नव-द्वारम् अगारम् एतद्
विण्-मूत्र-पूर्णं मद् उपैति कान्या ॥३.३३॥

yad asthibhir nirmita-vaṁśa-vaṁsya-
sthūṇaṁ tvacā roma-nakhaiḥ pinaddham
kṣaran-nava-dvāram agāram etad
viṇ-mūtra-pūrṇaṁ mad upaiti kānyā (3.33)

yad = yat — which; asthibhir = asthibhiḥ — with bones; nirmita-vaṁśa-vaṁsya-sthūṇaṁ = nirmita — made + vaṁśa — spine + vaṁśya — ribs + stūnam — bones of the limbs; tvacā — by skin; roma-nakhaiḥ = roma – hair + nakhaiḥ — by nails; pinaddham — covered; kṣaran-nava-dvāram = ksaraḥ (ksarat) — secreting + nava — nine + dvāram — opening; agāram — existential dwelling place; etad = etat — this; viṇ-mūtra-pūrṇaṁ = viṇ (vit) — stool + mūtra — urine + pūrṇam — full; mad = mat — besides myself; upaiti — would be possessed; kānyā = kā — who, which female + anyā — other female.

Translation

"Which female, besides myself, would be possessed with this existential dwelling place, which consists of bones such as the spine and which is covered by skin, hair, and nails, with nine openings for secreting and which contains stool and urine. (3.33)

Commentary:

Nearly everyone, being possessed with the existential dwelling place which consists of both the gross and subtle bodies, commits self-defeating acts which are degrading. Thus nearly every human being could learn from *Piṅgalā* how to institute self-reformation. Even if God and the saints preach to us, still we do not become reformed sufficiently until we set ourselves upon self-reflection, become disgusted with bad behavior and realize that we are disappointing ourselves and ruining the self-image.

Piṅgalā tried to sell a dear part of her existential dwelling place, the sexual access to it. Thus she disappointed herself and brought down her prestige. Focusing on sexual intercourse, she came to the conclusion that it was a great attraction to human beings and so she fell into the trade of trying to sell the participation of it.

विदेहानां पुरे ह्य् अस्मिन्न्
अहम् एकैव मूढ-धीः ।
यान्यम् इच्छन्त्य् असत्य् अस्माद्
आत्म-दात् कामम् अच्युतात् ॥३.३४॥

videhānāṁ pure hy asminn
aham ekaiva mūḍha-dhīḥ
yānyam icchanty asaty asmād
ātma-dāt kāmam acyutāt (3.34)

videhānām — of Videha; pure — in the city; hy = hi — indeed; asmin — in this; aham — I; ekaiva = eka — only one + eva — definitely; mūḍha-dhīḥ = mūḍha — fool + dhīḥ — intellect; yānyam = yā — who + anyam — another; icchanty = icchanti — those wishing for things; asaty = asatī — immoral; asmād = asmāt — other than him; ātma-dāt — one who gives realisation of the spiritual self; kāmam — enjoyment; acyutāt — from the infallible God.

Translation

"Indeed, of the people wishing for things in this city of Videha, I am the only fool, who being immoral, desires another enjoyer, other than the infallible God, who gives the realization of the spiritual self. (3.34)

Commentary:

Nearly every human being must come to this conclusion, that he or she is a fool, for having desired other things and persons besides the Supreme Being, the infallible God who gives the realization of the spiritual self.

सुहृत् प्रेष्ठतमो नाथ
आत्मा चायं शरीरिणाम् ।
तं विक्रीयात्मनैवाहं
रमे ऽनेन यथा रमा ॥ ३.३५ ॥

suhṛt preṣṭhatamo nātha
ātmā cāyaṁ śarīriṇām
taṁ vikrīyātmanaivāhaṁ
rame 'nena yathā ramā (3.35)

suhṛt — friend; preṣṭhatamo = preṣṭha – dear person + tamo (tamaḥ) — the most; nātha — Lord; ātmā — self; cāyam = ca — and + ayam — he; śarīrinām — of the embodied beings; taṁ — him; vikrīyātmanaivāham = vikrīya — winning him over + ātmanā — by myself + eva — only + aham — I; rame — will enjoy; 'nena = anena — with him; yathā — just as; ramā — Laksmi.

Translation

"He is the friend, the most dear person, and the soul of all beings. Winning Him over by offering myself, I will, like Ramā Lakṣmī, enjoy with Him. (3.35)

Commentary:

There is a difference between offering oneself to the Lord and doing so to a limited being. Generally in dealing with the Lord, He becomes the director of the self while in offering oneself to a limited being, one might bargain for a position of superiority or equality. By realizing that the Lord is the *nātha*, the ruler of the limited selves, *Piṅgalā* indirectly realized why she had avoided the Supreme Director all along. It was because she wanted to be the director. Now she understood that desire as an impossibility.

To encourage herself, she compared herself with the Lord's spouse *Lakṣmī*. She imagined that she would be enjoying just as *Lakṣmī* did.

In this respect *Piṅgalā* is speculative in trying to define what sort of relationship she would have with the Lord if she directly served Him. Still, she needed a self-image to encourage herself to surrender to Him. This means that initially one should be aware of a devotee who serves the Lord in a capacity one desires. By aspiring to be like that devotee, we take the first steps in approaching the Supreme Being.

कियत् प्रियं ते व्यभजन्
कामा ये काम-दा नराः ।
आद्य्-अन्तवन्तो भार्याया
देवा वा काल-विद्रुताः ॥ ३.३६ ॥

kiyat priyaṁ te vyabhajan
kāmā ye kāma-dā narāḥ
ādy-antavanto bhāryāyā
devā vā kāla-vidrutāḥ (3.36)

kiyat — how much; priyam — love; te — they, any of these; vyabhajan — have given; kāmā = kāmāḥ — attractive objectives; ye — these; kāma-dā = kāma-dāḥ — those who give pleasure; narāh — men; ādy-antavanto = ādy (ādi) — beginning + anta — ending + vanto (vantaḥ) — having; bhāryāyā — of a wife; devā = devāḥ — supernatural rulers; vā — or; kāla-vidrutah = kāla — time + vidrutāḥ — swept away.

Translation

"The attractive objects, the men who give pleasure or the supernatural rulers even, all have a beginning and end and are swept away by time. How much love have any of these given to a wife? (3.36)

Commentary:

This is true in marriage and in every type of social relationship. All limited beings fall short in some way or the other. The completion of any of these relationships comes when we get that feature from the Supreme Being or from one of His parallel divinities. Thus the attractive gross and subtle objects, as well as the men or women who give pleasure and the supernatural rulers who exert pressure from the psychic plane, all have a beginning and ending because they are all based on the usages of the material energy which is a temporary manifestation. Everything which is based on material energy will be swept away by time. Looking ahead, *Pińgalā* with her newly-found insight drew the proper conclusions.

नूनं मे भगवान् प्रीतो
विष्णुः केनापि कर्मणा ।
निर्वेदो ऽयं दुराशाया
यन् मे जातः सुखावहः ॥३.३७॥

nūnaṁ me bhagavān prīto
viṣṇuḥ kenāpi karmaṇā
nirvedo 'yaṁ durāśāyā
yan me jātaḥ sukhāvahaḥ (3.37)

nūnam — surely; me — with me; bhagavān — the Blessed Lord; prīto = prītaḥ — is pleased; viṣṇuḥ — Vishnu; kenāpi — by some; karmanā — by action; nirvedo = nirvedah — disgust; 'yam = ayam — this; durāśāyā = durāśāyāḥ — false expectation; yan = yat — what; me — in me; jātaḥ — has arose; sukhāvahaḥ = sukha — happiness + āvahaḥ — bringing.

Translation

"Surely, due to some action or the other, the Blessed Lord Vishnu is pleased with me, since from a false expectation, this happy disgust arose in me. (3.37)

Commentary:

Pińgalā rightly concluded that the Blessed Lord Vishnu was pleased, otherwise she could not gain such advancement from the disgust. Disgust comes repeatedly in the life of a limited being but in most instances, he or she cannot draw the proper conclusion nor derive the proper conscience through which one expresses a powerful curative repentant attitude which brings on the complete self-reform. *Pińgalā* rightly understood that it was an act of the Supreme Being which manifested in her life in such a wonderful way. Even though she previous condemned herself and realized that she was the most wretched person in Videha, still she could understand that by some sheer divine grace, she was at that moment the most fortunate human being.

मैवं स्युर् मन्द-भाग्यायाः
क्लेशा निर्वेद-हेतवः ।
येनानुबन्धं निर्हृत्य
पुरुषः शमम् ऋच्छति ॥३.३८॥

maivaṁ syur manda-bhāgyāyāḥ
kleśā nirveda-hetavaḥ
yenānubandhaṁ nirhṛtya
puruṣaḥ śamam ṛcchati (3.38)

maivam = mā — not + evam — thus, otherwise; syur = syuḥ — they could manifest; manda-bhāgyāyāḥ = manda – ill-fated, unlucky + bhāgyāyāḥ — of a woman who is fated; kleśā = kleśāḥ — miseries; nirveda-hetavaḥ = nirveda— disgust + hetavaḥ — the causes; yenānubandhaṁ = yena — through which + anubandham — entrapment; nirhṛtya — getting rid of; puruṣaḥ — a person; śamam — peace; ṛcchati — attains.

Translation

"Otherwise for an ill-fated woman, the miseries which are the cause of the disgust, through which one gets rid of entrapment, and attains peace, would not have manifested. (3.38)

Commentary:

Pińgalā rightly understood that the routine sufferings in material existence do not cause a person to become detached. In fact the miseries simply spur someone to further challenge and try to rule over the mundane energy. The miseries usually form a basis for encouraging one to continue in the struggle for existence, making the spirit focus more and more on some aspect of mundane happiness. But there is a special type of misery that brings on self-realization and causes the spirit to release its grasp on the mundane energy, and to be released from it. This misery *(nirveda-hetavah)* is experienced by the grace of the Supreme Being, when the spirit is in close proximity to and is being directly supervised by the Supreme Lord or by one of His parallel divinities. From such misery one suddenly sees the futility of mundane focus and gets away from it. As a man who is shocked by a strong electric current cannot release the wire and instead grasps it more firmly, holding it under an involuntary muscular contraction, so despite all suffering, the spirit usually holds on to the material nature. But just as another man can throw a switch and stop the current, thus causing the victim to be released, so the Supreme Being may act to release a spirit from mundane involvement.

Of course after such an act of grace the spirit must himself or herself strive to keep away from the mundane potency, otherwise he would again resume his shocked stupefied condition.

It is not just *Pińgalā*. Every other spirit who is involved with the mundane energy is ill-fated *(manda),* destined for a doomed life in material existence, being harassed continually by the demands of the mundane potency and being continually preyed on by social circumstances.

तेनोपकृतम् आदाय
शिरसा ग्राम्य-सङ्गताः ।
त्यक्त्वा दुराशाः शरणं
व्रजामि तम् अधीश्वरम् ॥ ३.३९ ॥

tenopakṛtam ādāya
śirasā grāmya-saṅgatāḥ
tyaktvā durāśāḥ śaraṇaṁ
vrajāmi tam adhīśvaram (3.39)

tenopakrtam = tena — by him + upakṛtam — favor given; ādāya — accepting; śirasā — on the head; grāmya-saṅgatāḥ = gramya — attractive object + saṅgatāḥ — pertaining to; tyaktvā — giving up; durāśāḥ — false expectation; śaranam — shelter; vrajāmi — I take; tam — him; adhīśvaram — Supreme Lord.

Translation

"Accepting on my head, the favor given by Him, I gave up the false expectation that pertains to the attractive objects, and take shelter in the Supreme Lord. (3.39)

Commentary:

The favor energy of the Supreme Lord is always all-pervading and always ready to find a loop hole in our attraction to what is not in our interest. But we are so occupied with the mundane power that we do not sense nor do we willingly respond to the grace of the Supreme Being. Here *Pińgalā* did respond by accepting that grace energy. It operated with her willing attitude, to deliver her from the delusions of thinking that she could manipulate the mundane potencies.

As a last resort, after all frustration and disappointment, a spirit might, like *Pińgalā*, surrender to the Lord, taking shelter of Him and so developing the required resistance to buffer the temptations of sensuality.

सन्तुष्टा श्रद्दधत्य् एतद्
यथा-लाभेन जीवती ।
विहराम्य् अमुनैवाहम्
आत्मना रमणेन वै ॥ ३.४० ॥

santuṣṭā śraddadhaty etad
yathā-lābhena jīvatī
viharāmy amunaivāham
ātmanā ramaṇena vai (3.40)

santuṣṭā — contented; śraddadhaty = śraddadhatī — having confidence; etad = etat — this; yathā-lābhena = yatha – as fate would have it + labhena — with what comes; jīvatī — I live; viharāmy = viharāmi — I will enjoy; amunaivāham = amunā — with that specific one + eva — only + aham — I; ātmanā — with the self; ramaṇena — with the lover; vai — surely.

Translation

"Having confidence, I will live contentedly on what comes by fate. I will surely enjoy with that Specific Self, the Lover. (3.40)

Commentary:

That specific self *(amuna...ātmanā),* the lover *(ramaṇena),* the Supreme Lord and His circuit of divine personalities, are factually enjoying their existence. We are not doing so. If however we come into the divine association like *Pińgalā*, then we too may enjoy in reality. We may note that

Pińgalā is not in a physical association with the Supreme Lord, and still she is in touch with Him. Thus *Pińgalā*, by the divine grace, perceived spiritually and was delivered into the continuous presence of the Lord. Her insecurities vanished.

Pińgalā did not assume an impersonal belief but thought of that Specific Self, the Supreme Lord, who is a specific infinite spirit.

ससार-कूपे पतितं
विषयैर् मुषितेक्षणम् ।
ग्रस्तं कालाहिनात्मानं
को ऽन्यस् त्रातुम् अधीश्वरः ॥ ३.४१ ॥

saṁsāra-kūpe patitaṁ
viṣayair muṣitekṣaṇam
grastaṁ kālāhinātmānaṁ
ko 'nyas trātum adhīśvaraḥ (3.41)

saṁsāra-kūpe = saṁsāra — repeated birth and death + kūpe — in the pit; patitam — fallen; viṣayair = viṣayaiḥ — by the senses; muṣitekṣaṇam = musita — stolen + īksanam — vision; grastam — seized; kālāhinātmānaṁ = kāla — time + ahinā —serpent + ātmānam — spiritual soul; ko = kaḥ — who; 'nyas = anyaḥ — other than, besides; trātum — to save; adhīśvaraḥ — Supreme Lord.

Translation

"Who besides the Supreme Lord can save the spiritual soul, who is fallen in the pit of repeated birth and death, being robbed of vision by the senses and seized by the serpent of time. (3.41)

Commentary:

The two aspects which command stupidity in the limited spirit, are the time factor and the sensual equipment. One is internal and one is external. Those who feel that it is internal put all the blame on the limited spirit himself, they suggest that he should create a better existence by realizing that he is the cause of perplexities.

The others who feel that it is an external problem put all the blame on the material nature and time, the admixture of the mundane reality. They say that the limited spirit cannot get out of material existence since other overwhelming realities command him and keep him spellbound.

Pińgalā learned to depend on the third factor, the Supreme Lord ,that specific spirit. She applied herself in accepting the mercy energy, the curative potencies emitted by that Supreme Being. Since the mundane environment is not much help to the limited spirit in his quest for freedom, and since the spirit himself is deluded by this own sensual nature, his psyche, then another independent agent must assist him. That agent is the Supreme Being.

आत्मैव ह्य् आत्मनो गोप्ता
निर्विद्येत यदाखिलात् ।
अप्रमत्त इद पश्येद्
ग्रस्तं कालाहिना जगत् ॥ ३.४२ ॥

ātmaiva hy ātmano goptā
nirvidyeta yadākhilāt
apramatta idaṁ paśyed
grastaṁ kālāhinā jagat (3.42)

ātmaiva = ātmā — the soul + eva — alone, itself; hy = hi — indeed; ātmano = ātmanaḥ — of the self; goptā — protector; nirvidyeta — turns away; yadākhilāt – yadā — when + akhilāt — from everything mundane; apramatta — watchful; idaṁ — this; paśyed = paśyet — can see; grastaṁ — seized; kālāhinā = kāla — time + ahinā — by the serpent; jagat — the world.

Translation

"When one sees this world which is seized by the serpent of time, and when one becomes watchful and turns the self away from everything mundane, then the self itself functions as the protector of itself." (3.42)

<u>*Commentary:*</u>

Here is a different opinion from the one she had before. *Piṅgalā* admited to and testified to the belief that the self must help itself. In the *Bhagavad Gītā* this is also attested:

uddharedātmanātmānaṁ nātmānamavasādayet
ātmaiva hyātmano bandhur ātmaiva ripurātmanaḥ
bandhurātmātmanastasya yenātmaivātmanā jitaḥ
anātmanastu śatrutve vartetātmaiva śatruvat

One should elevate his being by himself. One should not degrade the self. Indeed, the person should be the friend of himself. Or he could be the enemy as well.

The personal energies are the friend of the person by whom those energies are subdued. But for one whose personality is not self-possessed, the personal energies operate in hostility like an enemy. (B.G. 6.5-6)

However this is just one valid opinion, the idea that the Supreme Being must help the limited self is not nullified nor is it contradicted by this other view. The Supreme Being by His assistance to the limited self, reinforces the limited self's capacity for self-protection.

In one view if one does not help himself, he cannot be helped even by the Supreme Being. In another view, if one does everything to help himself then he cannot do much to elevate himself if he does not take help from the Supreme Being. How then does an atheist actually improve himself? The answer is that the assistance of the Supreme Being is not condescending. It is there to be used by anyone. It does not have to be personally awarded to anyone. Even though the sun is a specific planet, one does not have to recognize it, worship or praise it, to derive its benefit.

One other important realisation is this. The self (*ātma*) is not alone but is in the family of selves. These selves include the Supreme Being. Thus at any time, the self may in the association with the greater selves and in association with like-spirits who are divinely in tune, become the protector of itself *(ātmano goptā).*

The requirements are given by *Piṅgalā*, that one must absorb the mercy energy of the Supreme Lord, repent for one's stupidity, become watchful *(apramatta)* and turn the self away from distractions.

श्री-ब्राह्मण उवाच
एव व्यवसित-मतिर्
दुराशां कान्त-तर्ष-जाम् ।
छित्त्वोपशमम् आस्थाय
शय्याम् उपविवेश सा ॥ ३.४३ ॥

śrī-brāhmaṇa uvāca
evaṁ vyavasita-matir
durāśāṁ kānta-tarṣa-jām
chittvopaśamam āsthāya
śayyām upaviveśa sā (3.43)

śrī-brāhmaṇa – the elevated brahmin; uvāca —said; evam — thus; vyavasita-matir = vyavasita — determined + matir (matiḥ) — mind; durāśām — degrading fantasy; kānta-tarṣa-jām = kānta — lovers + tarṣa — hankering + jām — due to; chittvopaśamam = chittva — ceasing + upaśanam — composure; āsthāya — being situated in; śayyām — bed; upaviveśa — sat down; sā — she.

Translation

The elevated brahmin said: Having thus determined in her mind, she ceased the degrading fantasy which was due to hankering for lovers, she sat on the bed in composure. (3.43)

<u>*Commentary:*</u>

Even though this is one instance in the life of a prostitute, the elevated brahmin indicated that it produced permanent change. However we find that we go through this change from time to time and then return to the degrading fantasies repeated. Thus the technique of permanent change is required. *Piṅgalā* had it.

आशा हि परमं दुःखं
नैराश्यं परमं सुखम् ।
यथा सञ्छिद्य कान्ताशां
सुखं सुष्वाप पिङ्गला ॥ ३.४४ ॥

āśā hi paramaṁ duḥkhaṁ
nairāśyaṁ paramaṁ sukham
yathā sañchidya kāntāśāṁ
sukhaṁ suṣvāpa piṅgalā (3.44)

aśā — expectation; hi — indeed; paramam — greatest; duḥkham — misery; nairāśyam — giving up false hopes; paramam — greatness; sukham — happiness; yathā — as; sañchidya — ceasing; kāntāśām = kānta — lover (s) + āśām — hankering; sukham — happiness; suṣvāpa — she slept; piṅgalā — Piṅgalā .

Translation

Indeed, expectation is the greatest misery and the giving up of false hopes is the greatest happiness, as Piṅgalā slept happily, by ceasing the hankering for lovers. (3.44)

Commentary:

Even though this is a very simple explanation of how to get out of material existence, it is very hard to apply, because the psyche or psychic equipments are prone to the fantasies. They aspire for the false happiness which kept *Piṅgalā* spell bound for such a long time. When at last, we get a sufficient quantity of the mercy energy of the Supreme Being, then and only then, are we delivered from the dominating time factor which works in conjunction with the bewitching mundane potencies.

CHAPTER 4*

The Valuable Human Form**

labdhvā su-durlabham idaṁ bahu-sambhavānte mānuṣyam artha-dam anityam apīha dhīraḥ
tūrṇaṁ yateta na pated anu-mṛtyu yāvan niḥśreyasāya viṣayaḥ khalu sarvataḥ syāt

After many births, the person with a spiritually-perceptive intellect, having got the temporary but valuable human form, which is very difficult to obtain, strives for liberation, before the human body, which is subject to death, should get disease, for sense enjoyment is always available elsewhere. (Uddhava Gītā 4.29)

*Śrīmad Bhāgavatam Canto 11, Chapter 9

** The translator selected this chapter title.

श्री-ब्राह्मण उवाच
परिग्रहो हि दुःखाय
यद् यत् प्रियतम नृणाम् ।
अनन्तं सुखम् आप्नोति
तद् विद्वान् यस् त्व् अकिञ्चनः ॥४.१॥

śrī-brāhmaṇa uvāca
parigraho hi duḥkhāya
yad yat priyatamaṁ nṛṇām
anantaṁ sukham āpnoti
tad vidvān yas tv akiñcanaḥ (4.1)

śrī-brāhmana – the elevated brahmin; uvāca —said; parigraho = parigrahaḥ — acquisition of anything; hi — indeed; duhkhāya — leads to suffering; yad yat = yat yat — whatever; priyatamam — o most dear; nṛṇām — of men; anantam — endless; sukham — happiness; āpnoti — gets; tad = tat — that; vidvān — one who knows; yas = yat — who; tu — but; akiñcanaḥ — free from possesiveness.

Translation

The elevated brahmin said: The acquisition of anything whatsoever, which is most dear to men, leads to suffering, but a person who knows this and who is free from possessiveness, gets endless happiness. (4.1)

Commentary:

Whatever is most dear to a man and which is not his eternal quota or his natural development within his scope for eternity, will be taken away from him eventually. When he is deprived of it, he will suffer in proportion to his attachment. Even subtle items cause suffering, just as gross ones do.

Knowing this, is not sufficient to protect one from anxieties. One must actually know this and be freed from the sense of possessiveness. Since one is not absolute and since one is bound to be overruled by others wherever one's spirit may go and since one will have to take help from various gross, supernatural and spiritual environments, one cannot be completely isolated. One must, from time to time, bend to providence, and this means that one will have to assume possession and then relinquish things as induced by providence.

Thus the only real protection is to be free from possessiveness. That alone leads to endless happiness as one's spirit is moved from place to place in the material or spiritual creations.

The tendency for possessiveness will remain with the living being, even after he attained the attitude of freedom from grasping and freedom from keeping what providence does not want him to have, but still a person must ignore that tendency by regarding it as a function of providence. Thus one should be possessive by the order of the Supreme Being or by destiny and then suddenly become unattached by His order or by its order, as well. This gets one the endless happiness *(anantam sukham).*

The key terms in this verse are *priyataman nṛṇām*, what is most dear to men. If something is not very special, if one is not very much desirous of something, it is no threat to one's peace of mind. But what ever is most dear is the most threatening, thus if one learns not to take a strong hold of what is attractive, one will discover the underlying happiness of the self.

सामिषं कुररं जघ्नुर्
बलिनो ऽन्ये निरामिषाः ।
तदामिषं परित्यज्य
स सुखं समविन्दत ॥४.२॥

sāmiṣaṁ kuraraṁ jaghnur
balino 'nye nirāmiṣāḥ
tadāmiṣaṁ parityajya
sa sukhaṁ samavindata (4.2)

sāmisam — with flesh; kuraran — a hawk; jaghnuḥ — they tormented; balino = balinaḥ —strong; 'nye = anye — others; nirāmisāḥ — without flesh; tadāmiṣaṁ = tadā — then + āmiṣam — the flesh; parityajya — giving up; sa — it, the hawk; sukham — happiness; samavindata — got.

Translation

A hawk with some flesh was tormented by stronger birds, which had no meat. It gave up the flesh and got happiness. (4.2)

Commentary:

Even though that particular hawk gave up the flesh, other hawks accepted the torment for the sake of the meat. In other cases, a human being may try to hold on to a commodity or a social position and he may strive for it life after life. Then suddenly he might be inspired to release himself from such survival techniques.

The elevated brahmin reached the stage of giving up the quest for survival and prestige. For anyone who was wondering why he did not strive to make an income, to improve his social position, the answer is given in this verse. He took a lesson by observing a hawk who decided that a piece of meat was not worth the harassment of the stronger birds who desired it.

Those who give up something and who keep on desiring to have it or who will strive later to regain it, suffer from a resentment when they are overpowered by more powerful creatures or by time, circumstance, or supernatural force. This particular hawk which was observed by the brahmin got happiness because it assumed the right attitude about losing the meat. Thus one must not only give up things which draw competition from others but one must do so without resentment and then one will resume the natural state of happiness which is the fundamental mood of a spirit.

न मे मानापमानौ स्तो
न चिन्ता गेह-पुत्रिणाम् ।
आत्म-क्रीड आत्म-रतिर्
विचरामीह बाल-वत् ॥४.३॥

na me mānāpamānau sto
na cintā geha-putriṇām
ātma-krīḍa ātma-ratir
vicarāmīha bāla-vat (4.3)

na — not; me — in me; mānāpamānau = māna — honor + apamānau — dishonor; sto = staḥ — live; na — not; cintā — worry; geha-putriṇām = geha —house + putriṇām — children; ātma-krīḍa = ātma — self + krīḍa (krīḍaḥ) — playing; ātma-ratir = ātma — self + ratir (ratiḥ) — enjoying; vicarāmiha = vicarāmi — I roam + iha — here on earth; bāla-vat — like a child.

Translation

I do not live for honor or dishonor, nor have I any worry like those who possess house and children. I play with the self, enjoy in the self, and roam here on earth like a child. (4.3)

Commentary:

The issue is responsibility which is termed *dharma* in Sanskrit. The basic meaning of *dharma* is duty. Duty is responsibility. Those who have house and children have worries because they have the responsibility to maintain other bodies in the social setting. Those who have jobs and position strive for honor. They do so by maintaining their assigned duties. Those who like dishonor and infamy do so because they are opposed to specific responsibilities. They desire to rebel against the authority who assigns duties. The issue here is responsibility.

In the next verse the ascetic discussed the supreme happiness *(paramānanda)*. This supreme happiness cannot be gained by executing social responsibilities. There is a happiness one derives from executing responsibilities or righteous duties but that is not the supreme joy. Thus, the elevated brahmin did not mention it, because it does not give complete satisfaction. The brahmin was empowered with a carefree life. No one could impose any responsibility on him, nor was he liable to destiny for his care-free mood.How then did he attain such a position? This is what King Yadu inquired of formerly.

A child may be ignorant and awkward in doing duties but that does not mean that he is free of responsibilities. He will have responsibilities no matter how small. But if the child is retarded, he will be free of responsibilities since his supervisors will feel that he is incapable of accountability and will not assign duties.

Responsibility is the thing that brings unhappiness but even so this does not mean that one can just give up duties. It is not that easy. Unless one is actually retarded he is not allowed to give up responsibilities, and unless one is as elevated as the brahmin who discoursed with King Yadu, one will not be able to ward off pressures from others who will insist that one assume obligations. For most people it is best for them to perform prescribed duties. They would get worries but they are freed from harassment by family, government and society.

For real happiness one must be transferred to the supreme reality, a realm in which, responsibilities do not require endeavor for completion since it is a self-sufficient situation.

द्वाव् एव चिन्तया मुक्तौ
परमानन्द आप्लुतौ ।
यो विमुग्धो जडो बालो
यो गुणेभ्यः परं गतः ॥४.४॥

dvāv eva cintayā muktau
paramānanda āplutau
yo vimugdho jaḍo bālo
yo guṇebhyaḥ paraṁ gataḥ (4.4)

dvāv = dvau — two; eva — only; cintayā — from worry; muktau — both are freed; parama-ānanda — in great happiness; āplutau — emerged; yo = yaḥ — who; vimugdho = vimugdhaḥ — one who is ignorant; jaḍo = jaḍaḥ — retarded, inexperienced; bālo = bālaḥ — child; yo = yaḥ — who; guṇebhyaḥ — to the mundane influences; paraṁ — the Supreme Reality; gataḥ — gone to, transferred to.

Translation

Two people only are free from worries, and one is immerged in great happiness. There is the child, who is ignorant and inexperienced and the person who was transferred to the supreme reality. (4.4)

Commentary:

The similarity between the child and the person who was transferred to the Supreme Reality, is the factor of a lack of responsibility and a lack of accountability for being without responsibility.This is the issue which King Yadu brought up in the beginning of his conversation with the elevated brahmin.

क्वचित् कुमारी त्व् आत्मानं
वृणानान् गृहम् आगतान् ।
स्वयं तान् अर्हयाम् आस
क्वापि यातेषु बन्धुषु ॥४.५॥

kvacit kumārī tv ātmānaṁ
vṛṇānān gṛham āgatān
svayaṁ tān arhayām āsa
kvāpi yāteṣu bandhuṣu (4.5)

kvacit — once; kumārī — maiden; tv = tu — but; ātmānam — himself; vṛṇānām — a marriage suitor and his supporters; gṛham — home; āgatān — came; svayam — herself; tān — them; arhayām āsa — received; kvāpi — elsewhere; yāteṣu — of those who were gone; bandhuṣu — of the relatives.

Translation

Once when her relatives were gone elsewhere, a maiden received a marriage suitor and his supporters, who came to her home. (4.5)

Commentary:

In the times of King Yadu, the custom was that a maiden who was fit for marriage did not receive marriage suitors. Those persons first approached her relatives. After being certified as being fit, they were accepted or rejected by her elders. At the time of this visit, those elders were absent, and so the maiden greeted the guests directly. It was a sensitive issue. She was fearful that she would make a mistake that might deprive her of a well-to-do spouse.

तेषाम् अभ्यवहारार्थं
शालीन् रहसि पार्थिव ।
अवघ्नन्त्याः प्रकोष्ठ-स्थाश्
चक्रुः शङ्खाः स्वनं महत् ॥४.६॥

teṣām abhyavahārārthaṁ
śālīn rahasi pārthiva
avaghnantyāḥ prakoṣṭha-sthāś
cakruḥ śaṅkhāḥ svanaṁ mahat (4.6)

teṣām — their; abhyavahārātham = abhyavahāra – of a meal + artham — for the purpose; śālīn — paddy; rahasi — by herself; pārthiva — O King; avaghnantyāḥ — one who is husking; prakoṣṭha-sthāś = prakoṣṭha — wrist + sthas (sthāḥ) — situated on; cakruḥ — they made; śankhāḥ — conch bracelets; svanam — noise; mahat — great.

Translation

For their meals, O King, she husked some paddy. The conch bracelets on her wrist made a great noise. (4.6)

Commentary:

If the marriage suitors had given sufficient notice, her relatives would have prepared meals and would have been present to provide hospitality but this was not so. The maiden did everything herself. She became conscious of poverty and took notice of the noise made by the conch bracelets. Conch bracelets were used by poor women who could not afford gold, silver or pearl bracelets. In addition she wanted to husk the paddy without being noticed since having to husk it all by herself was another indication of poverty. Her visitors were of a higher class and had servants. She did not want to discourage them by exhibiting habits of poverty.

सा तज् जुगुप्सितं मत्वा
महती व्रीडिता ततः ।
बभञ्जैकैकशः शङ्खान्
द्वौ द्वौ पाण्योर् अशेषयत् ॥४.७॥

sā taj jugupsitaṁ matvā
mahatī vṛīḍitā tataḥ
babhañjaikaikaśaḥ śaṅkhān
dvau dvau pāṇyor aśeṣayat (4.7)

sā — she; taj = tat — that; jugupsitam — ashamed; matvā — thinking; mahatī — intelligent girl; vrīḍitā — put to shame; tatah — hence; babhañjaikaikasah = babhañja — broke + eka-ekaśaḥ — one by one; śaṅkhān — conches; dvau dvau — two and two; pāṇyor = pāṇyoḥ — on her hands; aśeṣayat — remained.

Translation

The intelligent shy girl, thinking that as a disgrace, was ashamed, hence she broke the conches one by one until only two remained on each hand. (4.7)

Commentary:

Even though she was poor financially, she was intelligent enough to determine her self interest. Thus she decided to destroy the conch bracelets which were dear to her. She decided that the value of a wealthy suitor was more than the conch bracelets. She broke them one by one until there were only two on each hand.

उभयोर् अप्य् अभूद् घोषो
ह्य् अवघ्नन्त्याः स्व-शङ्खयोः ।
तत्राप्य् एक निरभिदद्
एकस्मान् नाभवद् ध्वनिः ॥४.८॥

ubhayor apy abhūd ghoṣo
hy avaghnantyāḥ sva-śaṅkhayoḥ
tatrāpy ekaṁ nirabhidad
ekasmān nābhavad dhvaniḥ (4.8)

ubhayor = ubhayoḥ — from the two; apy = api — even; abhūd = abhūt — there was; ghoṣo = ghoṣaḥ — sound; hy = hi — indeed; avaghnantyāḥ — husking; sva-śaṅkhayoḥ — of the two conches; tatrāpy = tatra — there + apy (api) — also; ekam — one; nirabhidad = nirabhidat — removed; ekasmān — from one; nābhavad = na — not + abhavad (abhavat) — there was; dhvaniḥ — a sound.

Translation

As she continued husking, even the two remaining shells made sound. She then removed one of the two shells. From the one remaining, there was no sound. (4.8)

Commentary:

Due to an attachment to the conches which symbolized wealth to the financially-poor girl, she wanted to keep at least two on each wrist but even that jeapordize her. When two conchs mingle they create sound. Thus the girl decided to remove one of the two conches which remained on each forearm. In that way she sacrificed for a higher interest. And so it is in spiritual life, that when a serious ascetic gradually realizes the attachments which prevent him from advancement, he acts to eliminate them one by one.

अन्वशिक्षम् इमं तस्या
उपदेशम् अरिन्दम ।
लोकान् अनुचरन्न् एतान्
लोक-तत्त्व-विवित्सया ॥४.९॥

anvaśikṣam imaṁ tasyā
upadeśam arindama
lokān anucarann etān
loka-tattva-vivitsayā (4.9)

anvaśikṣam — learnt; imam — this; tasyā — of her; upadeśam — lesson; arindama — O subduer of the enemy; lokān — countries; anucarann — roaming; etān — these; loka-tattva-vivitsayā = loka — world + tattva — truth + vivitsayā — wanting to know.

Translation

Roaming over these countries, wanting to know the truth, I learnt this lesson from her. O subduer of the enemy. (4.9)

Commentary:

Even though the maiden was an inexperienced girl and even though her story was a social one concerning her interest in marriage to a well-to-do suitor, still the brahmin was perceptive enough to learn a special lesson which he described in the next verse.

वासे बहूनां कलहो
भवेद् वार्ता द्वयोर् अपि ।
एक एव वसेत् तस्मात्
कुमार्या इव कङ्कणः ॥४.१०॥

vāse bahūnāṁ kalaho
bhaved vārtā dvayor api
eka eva vaset tasmāt
kumāryā iva kaṅkaṇaḥ (4.10)

vāse — in the place; bahūnām — of many; kalaho = kalahaḥ — quarrel; bhaved = bhavet — will be; vārtā — talking; dvayor = dvayoḥ — of two; api — even; eka — alone; eva — indeed; vaset — one should live; tasmāt — therefore; kumāryā — of a maiden; iva — like; kaṅkaṇaḥ — the bracelet.

Translation

In the place where many reside, there will be quarrel. Even between two, there is talk. Therefore one should live alone, like the bracelet of the maiden. (4.10)

Commentary:

Just as the conches jingled when there were many, as well as when there were two on each wrist, so when there is more than one human being, there is quarrel and non-productive talk. There is much effort to create holy assembles of persons but generally, there are arguments and disagreements which detract from the spiritual disciplines which are necessary for advancement.

In his own time and place, the elevated brahmin found that for rapid advancement, he had to be alone. He learnt this objectively when he studied the story of the jingling conches which were a threat to the future security of the girl who wanted to be married to the well-to-do suitor.

The idea is this: One must make whatever sacrifices are required for spiritual advancement. One should deprive himself of anything that slows down, deters, or stops advancement, even if it means that one should be alone like the one conch on each arm of the unmarried girl.

मन एकत्र संयुञ्ज्याज्
जित-श्वासो जितासनः ।
वैराग्याभ्यास-योगेन
ध्रियमाणम् अतन्द्रितः ॥४.११॥

mana ekatra saṁyuñjyāj
jita-śvāso jitāsanaḥ
vairāgyābhyāsa-yogena
dhriyamāṇam atandritaḥ (4.11)

manaḥ — mind; ekatra — one focus; samyuñjyāt — one should collect; jita-śvāso = jita — controlling + svaso (śvāsaḥ) — breath; jitāsanaḥ = jita — mastering + āsanaḥ — haṭha Yoga postures; vairāgyābhyāsa-yogena = vairāgya — detachment + abhyāsa – systematic practice + yogena — by yoga; dhriyamāṇam — holding the mind steady; atandritaḥ — attentively.

Translation:

Conquering haṭha yoga postures, and controlling the breath, being attentive, one should collect the mind in one focus, holding it steady through detachment and systematic yoga practice. (4.11)

Commentary:

The initial aim of yoga practice is to control the mind which is the brain of the subtle body, for unless the mind is controlled, any type of gross or subtle activity will be haphazard. However to control the mind, one is usually required to begin by controlling the gross body, and for that a system of postures and their related exercises was developed by ancient sages. These procedures were taught specifically by Lord Shiva to great sages.

Mastery of *haṭha* yoga leads to a partial mastery of the subtle body, which is interspaced in the physical form. For controlling the subtle body one has to energize it with subtle breath by practicing physical breathing exercises known as *prāṇāyāma*. When the subtle body is sufficiently energized, one gets a higher degree of mind control. One can then do as the brahmin advised in this verse.

यस्मिन् मनो लब्ध-पदं यद् एतच्
छनैः शनैर् मुञ्चति कर्म-रेणून् ।
सत्त्वेन वृद्धेन रजस् तमश् च
विधूय निर्वाणम् उपैत्य् अनिन्धनम् ॥४.१२॥

yasmin mano labdha-padaṁ yad etac
chanaiḥ śanair muñcati karma-reṇūn
sattvena vṛddhena rajas tamaś ca
vidhūya nirvāṇam upaity anindhanam (4.12)

yasmin — in whose; mano = manaḥ — mind; labdha-padam = labdha — having got + padaṁ — existential position; yad = yat – which; etac = etat — that; chanaiḥ śanair = śanaiḥ śanaiḥ — step by step; muñcati — gives up; karma-renūn = karma — cultural activity + renūn — urges; sattvena — by the clarifying power; vṛddhena — by an increase; rajas — impulsive energy; tamaś — depressive forces; ca — and; vidhūya — throwing off; nirvāṇam — complete removal of mundane disturbance; upaity = upaiti — experiences; anindhanam — without fuel, without agitation.

Translation

Having got an existential position in which one gradually gives up the urges for cultural activity, and throwing off the impulsive energy and the depressive force by increasing the clarifying power, one experiences the complete removal of mundane disturbances without further agitation. (4.12)

Commentary:

If somehow or the other, one can realize that there is a need for self realization in terms of knowing exactly the difference between the gross body and the spirit, as well as between polluted psychological energies and the spirit, then it means that one should take the advantage to go all the way with spiritual disciplines which would cause one to be released from the chores of material existence.

The elevated brahmin described his own situation. From his position we can understand our position to some extent. Since King Yadu asked the brahmin about his status, of not aspiring for any type of social accomplishment, the brahmin explained that since he gave up the urges for cultural activity, and threw off the impulsive energy which drives the creatures of the world, it was to his advantage to attain the complete removal of mundane disturbances.

He had a technique by which he could avoid social responsibilities and be free of reactions for such avoidance. Generally if one foresakes responsibilities, one suffers more, but somehow this elevated brahmin got a technique which caused him to surpass those laws which penalize a man who evades social duties *(dharma)*.

तदैवम् आत्मन्य् अवरुद्ध-चित्तो
न वेद किञ्चिद् बहिर् अन्तरं वा ।
यथेषु-कारो नृपति व्रजन्तम्
इषौ गतात्मा न ददर्श पार्श्वे ॥४.१३॥

tadaivam ātmany avaruddha-citto
na veda kiñcid bahir antaraṁ vā
yatheṣu-kāro nṛpatiṁ vrajantam
iṣau gatātmā na dadarśa pārśve (4.13)

tadaivam = tadā — then + evam — thus; ātmany = ātmani — in the self; avaruddha-citto = avaruddha — focused + citto (cittaḥ) — the mind; na — not; veda — is attentive; kiñcid = kiñcit — anything; bahir = bahih — outside; antaraṁ — inside; vā — or; yatheṣu-kāro = yathā — as + iṣu — arrow + kāro (kāraḥ) — maker; nṛpatiṁ — king; vrajantam — passing; iṣau — in the arrow; gatātmā = gata – was gone + ātmā — self; na – no; dadarśa — did notice; pārśve — by the side.

Translation

Then, with the mind focused in the self, one is not attentive to anything outside or inside, just as the arrow maker, whose attention was gone into himself and who did not notice the King who passed nearby. (4.13)

Commentary:

This verse has to do with self focus, focus of the entire psyche on the core self of the spirit. This verse is not a description of focus on the supreme spirit, on Lord Krishna or any of the divinities but on the limited self itself, on the *ātma*. Just as an arrow maker, being intent on making an arrow perfect, will be totally absorbed on making the weapon and would notice no one, not even a king and his entourage which passed by, so one should be intently absorbed in the self to realize the spirit.

When one sits to meditate on the self and when one is determined to find out about the capacities of his limited spirit, he will have to develop a focus as consistent as the arrow maker, otherwise distractions will play havoc with the mind. A lack of concentration will deprive one of knowing the qualities of the spirit self.

The elevated brahmin spoke of not being attached to anything outside or inside. When, meditating on one's spirit, one has to be careful not to be distracted inside. Since there are foreign elements inside, one should ignore them and bypass them to get on to the core self. Everything within the psychology of a person is not the spirit, this is why one must not be distracted by anything inside but must effectively resists the accessory subtle energies.

एक-चार्य् अनिकेतः स्याद्
अप्रमत्तो गुहाशयः ।
अलक्ष्यमाण आचारैर्
मुनिर् एको ऽल्प-भाषणः ॥४.१४॥

eka-cāry aniketaḥ syād
apramatto guhāśayaḥ
alakṣyamāṇa ācārair
munir eko 'lpa-bhāṣaṇaḥ (4.14)

eka-cāry = eka — alone + cāry (cārī) — wandering; aniketaḥ — without a home; syād = syāt — should be; apramatto = apramattah — be alert; guhāśayah = guhā – secretly + āśayah — living; alakṣyamāna = alakṣyamānaḥ — no characteristics; ācārair = ācāraiḥ — through activities; manir = muniḥ — the yogi sage; eko = ekaḥ — alone; 'lpa-bhāṣaṇaḥ = 'lpa (alpa) — very little + bhāṣaṇaḥ — conversation.

Translation

The yogi sage, should wander alone, without a house, being alert, living secretly, like a tiger or lion, showing no characteristic through his activities, and being alone, having very little conversation. (4.14)

Commentary:

Even if one hides from society and pretends to be dumb, one will be discovered as soon as one exhibits some knowledge in a conversation. Then people will say that one should make oneself useful to society. People will inquire of one's background and try to connect one with family, friends and community. Thus if an ascetic reached the stage where he can effectively clear himself away from social dealings, he must hide himself from human beings.

It is said in the *Devī Purāṇa* that *Śrīla Vyāsadeva* tried to convince his elevated son, Shuka to become a householder. *Vyāsadeva* tried to prove the harmlessness of householder life and got help from King Janaka in convincing Shuka that a person can be a householder and still execute detachment from mundane concerns. At first Shuka did not believe that it was possible.

However, besides the arguments of *Śrīla Vyāsadeva* and King *Janaka*, as well as some arguments of other great sages, still it is usually impractical for an ascetic to consolidate his advancement while in the householder status. For this reason most of the successful ascetics were celibate bachelors. Many of them wandered alone. Persons like *Nārada*, the four *Kumāras* and *Jaḍa Bharata*, pursued their spirit interest as bachelors.

Generally companionship ruins spiritual life. There are very few ascetics who are able to liberate themselves and their spouse or spouses. Of course divinities like Lord *Rāma*, and Lord Krishna liberated many but generally an ascetic's own liberation is the most he can achieve.

Since one is apt to be used by society, one has to hide one's capacity just like a lion or a tiger. Some big cats hide in the daytime. If recognized, they would be killed by human beings. Similarly an ascetic, if he is not careful, will be drawn into social services and thus his spiritual self interest will be nullified by human beings, just as they would kill a tiger if they notice it in the day time.

For those ascetics whose providence does not allow them to be single, and who must maintain a householder format of life, they must be very intelligent to be successful. They must be even more intelligent and secretive with the practice, just as *Śrīla Vyāsadeva* and King *Janak* in the time of Shuka. Only a superhuman can be successful in spiritual life as a householder, otherwise it is impossible because the householder's life is based on continued social involvements. It is not designed for an exit from this situation. It sponsors repeated birth and death and keeps the spirits spellbound, transmigrating from one material body to another.

गृहारम्भो हि दुःखाय
विफलश् चाध्रुवात्मनः ।
सर्पः पर-कृत वेश्म
प्रविश्य सुखम् एधते ॥४.१५॥

gṛhārambho hi duḥkhāya
viphalaś cādhruvātmanaḥ
sarpaḥ para-kṛtaṁ veśma
praviśya sukham edhate (4.15)

gṛhārambho = gṛha — home + ārambho (ārambhaḥ) — construction; hi — surely; duḥkhāya — leading to misery; viphalaś = viphalaḥ — without consequences; cādhruvātmanaḥ = ca — and + adhruva — shifty situation + ātmanaḥ — of the spiritual self; sarpaḥ — snake; para-kṛtaṁ = para – other + krtam — made; veśma — home; praviśya — having entered; sukham — is happy; edhate — prospers.

Translation

Surely the construction of a house, leads to misery and is without consequence and the situation of the soul is shifty. Having entered the home made by another creature, the snake prospers and is happy. (4.15)

Commentary:

Generally a human being overlooks the hassles and frustrations of material existence. The ultimate hassle and frustration is having to lose a material body and having others assume proprietorship of one's belongings and prestige, just as a mouse, mole, or rabbit might carefully prepare a nest, store up nuts and desired food and then be killed by a snake which assumes the victim's residence.

The snake which kills another creature and takes its home is itself subjected to misery. In the material existence, one prospers and is happy for a while. Then one is made miserable after some time. This situation was not desired by the elevated brahmin. He stopped taking steps to cover up the embarrassment of being in material existence. So long as we do not find an alternative to this existence, we will continue enduring repeated births and deaths, trying to justify each of these shifty existences that we are forced to assume.

एको नारायणो देवः
पूर्व-सृष्टं स्व-मायया ।
संहृत्य काल-कलया
कल्पान्त इदम् ईश्वरः ॥४.१६॥

eko nārāyaṇo devaḥ
pūrva-sṛṣṭaṁ sva-māyayā
saṁhṛtya kāla-kalayā
kalpānta idam īśvaraḥ (4.16)

eko = ekaḥ — one; nārāyano = nārāyaṇa — Nārāyaṇa; devaḥ — God; pūrva-sṛṣṭaṁ = pūrva — previously + sṛṣṭam — produced; sva-māyayā = sva – own + māyayā — through bewildering potency; saṁhṛtya — withdraws; kāla-kalayā = kāla — time + kalayā — by a part of His Godhead; kalpānta = kalpa – creative era + ante — at the end; idam — this; īśvaraḥ — the Lord;

Translation

Previously the One God Nārāyaṇa produced, through His own bewildering potency, a part of His own Godhead who manifests through time, then withdraws this creation at the end of the creative era. (4.16)

Commentary:

The question as to how the spiritual self took residence in the material creation is answered here. Even though the spiritual self may not like to be in this creation, or even if he does like to be here or if he really does not like it but agrees to cope with it, then how did he get into this creation? Is there a personality who placed him in these creations or has this creation come about naturally by unconscious potent forces?

If we agree that the spiritual self does not really like this creation but has agreed to cope with it, or that he must cope with it, since he cannot find a way to completely transcend it, then still the question as to how this creation was produced arises. This question is answered in a theistic way by the elevated brahmin. He cites the one God *Nārāyaṇa (eko nārāyaṇo devah)*.

By stating that a part of *Nārāyaṇa*'s Godhead manifested through time, the elevated brahmin hints that the idea of one God *Nārāyaṇa* is not just speculation or a reasonable conclusion of a philosopher. It is factually since the Godhead manifested through time into a dimension in which He was seen and related to.

एक एवाद्वितीयो ऽभूद्
आत्माधारो ऽखिलाश्रयः ।
कालेनात्मानुभावेन
साम्य नीतासु शक्तिषु ।
सत्त्वादिष्व् आदि-पुरुषः
प्रधान-पुरुषेश्वरः ॥४.१७॥

eka evādvitīyo 'bhūd
ātmādhāro 'khilāśrayaḥ
kālenātmānubhāvena
sāmyaṁ nītāsu śaktiṣu
sattvādiṣv ādi-puruṣaḥ
pradhāna-puruṣeśvaraḥ (4.17)

eka = ekaḥ — one; evadvitiyo = eva — indeed + advitīyo (advitīyaḥ) — without an assistant; 'bhūd = abhūt — was; ātmādhāro = ātma – self + ādhāro (ādhāraḥ) — everything; 'khilāśrayaḥ = akhila — everything + āśrayah — shelter; kālenātmānubhāvena = kālena — by the time person + ātma – self (personal) + anubhāvena — by His own energy + sāmyam — equilibrium; nītāsu — being put; śaktiṣu — subtle mundane potencies; sattvādiṣu = sattva – clarifying influence of material nature + ādiṣu — and its other influences; ādi-purusaḥ — original person; pradhāna-puruṣeśvarah = pradhāna – primal mundane energy + puruṣa – spirit person + īśvarah — Lord (pradhāna-puruṣeśvaraḥ - Lord of spirit persons and primal mundane energy.

Translation

Indeed, the Lord is one, having no second assistant, being himself, the reservoir and shelter of everything. The clarifying influence of material nature and that nature's other influences, those subtle mundane potencies, was put into equilibrium by Time, which is a manifestation of His personal energy. He is the original person, the Lord of the primal mundane energy and the spirit persons. (4.17)

Commentary:

The elevated brahmin was not an atheist. Even though he did not advocate a religious sect, still he had a conviction about a Supreme Being, whom he described to King Yadu. That person, he said, was a single entity, having no second assistant in terms of needing help for creating the mundane universe.That person was the reservoir and shelter of everything.

The brahmin claimed that Time itself as a manifestation of the personal energy *(anubhāvena)* of that Original Person, who was the Lord of the primal mundane energy and the spirit persons whom abound in the creation.

परावराणां परम
आस्ते कैवल्य-सञ्ज्ञितः ।
केवलानुभवानन्द-
सन्दोहो निरुपाधिकः ॥४.१८॥

parāvarāṇāṁ parama
āste kaivalya-saṁjñitaḥ
kevalānubhavānanda-
sandoho nirupādhikaḥ (4.18)

parāvarāṇām = para — superior creatures + avarāṇām — of ordinary creature; parama = paramaḥ — Supreme Lord; āste — He exists; kaivalya-samjñitah = kaivalya — one who is segregated from subtle mundane energy + samjñitaḥ — known as; kevalānubhavānanda-sandoho = kevala — absolute + anubhava — personal evidence + ānanda — bliss + sandoho (sandohaḥ) — mass, totality; nirupādhikah — without mundane qualities.

Translation

He, the Supreme Lord of the superior and inferior creatures, exists as a mass of absoluteness, personal existence, and bliss, He is known to be segregated from subtle mundane energy, and is without mundane qualities. (4.18)

Commentary:

It is remarkable that some yogis and mystics, took these verses from this instruction to Uddhava and sideswiped the meanings, in an effort to award the limited spirits the same status as that of the supreme being, the *ādi-puruṣa*. It is a plain fact that the limited spirits could not have created this material world in any type of shape or form, even though, once it is produced, they can manipulate large or small parts of it, depending on their existential power *(anubhāvah).*

At the same time, some devotees of the Lord, took it upon themselves to completely ignore and even to deny the creative powers of the limited spirits who flourish after the Lord manifests the mundane energy. Some modern mystics and yogis, notably *Śrīman* Paramhansa Ramakrishna, as well as some *Kriyā* teachers in the lineage from the noted *Bābāji* and his disciple Lahiri *Mahāśaya*, have popularized the terms *kaivalya*, *kevala*, and *parama*. However, other important terms which they did not stress are *para* and *avarāṇām*. *Parama* in this verse is the Supreme Being Himself. He supervises the superior and inferior ones. *Kevala* pertains to the Supreme Being as an absolute and unique individual, Who is uninvolved with the subtle mundane energy. All spirits are unique, but they are not all absolute. *Śrīman Patañjali* distinguished the Supreme Being in a clear way. He stated:

kleśa karma vipāka āśayaih
aparāmṛṣṭaḥ puruṣaviśeṣaḥ īśvarah

The Supreme Lord is that special person, who is not affected by troubles, action, developments or by subconscious motivations. (Yoga Sūtra 1.24)

Patañjali did not write that this Supreme Being and the other *puruṣas* or spiritual persons are one *(eka)*, nor did he define the term *kaivalyam* as oneness. Here is his statement:

tad abhāvāt samyogābhāvaḥ
hānaṁ taddṛśeḥ kaivalyam

The elimination of the conjunction which results from the elimination of that spiritual ignorance is the withdrawal. That is kaivalyam, the total seperation of the perceiver from the mundane psychology.(Yoga Sūtra 2.25)

केवलात्मानुभावेन
स्व-माया त्रि-गुणात्मिकाम् ।
सङ्क्षोभयन् सृजत्य् आदौ
तया सूत्रम् अरिन्दम ॥४.१९॥

kevalātmānubhāvena
sva-māyāṁ tri-guṇātmikām
saṅkṣobhayan sṛjaty ādau
tayā sūtram arindama (4.19)

kevalātmānubhāvena = kevala — absolute + ātma — self + anubhāvena — by existential power; sva-māyām = sva –own + māyām — bewildering energy; tri-guṇātmikām = tri — three + guṇa — influences + ātmikām — formed of; saṅkṣobhayam — motivates; srjaty = srjati — projects; ādau — at the time of creation; tayā — that; sūtram — sexually-charge mundane energy; arindama — O subduer of the enemies

Translation

O subduer of enemies, He, by use of existential power, motivates into activity, His bewildering energy, which consists of three influences of material nature, and at the time of creation, though that, He projects the sexually-charged mundane energy. (4.19)

Commentary:

Every spirit has some existential power, for that is the complimentary status of a living being. Still, the ordinary spirits and the superior ones, are not the Supreme Being. They do not have His power. They cannot operate the vast material cosmos.

It cannot be said however that the ordinary spirits and the superior ones, were not there at the onset or prior to this creation. They were there. They were part of the Whole Energy but still the Supreme Spirit is one special individual as *Śrī Patañjali* defined.

There is a distinction between the Supreme Lord and others. Initially the Supreme Lord has the objectivity to do something, while the others do not have it, even though they existed as spiritual potency. An example may illustrate this. While a spirit is in the groin of the body of a father, that spirit does not usually have much objectivity. It is there. Its energies are intact, but still it is not as objective as the spirit who operates the father's form. Similarly, when that spirit is transferred to the mother's body, its embryo naturally develops into a human baby, even though it is not objectively aware, but the spirit who operates the mother's form is very objective, and knows that something foreign, some other psyche, develops in her body. That something is expelled from her body when the pregnancy matures.

The Supreme Lord remains objective throughout the creative cycle and when the creation disappears. That is one of His special features. We cannot be equated with Him. An attempt to do so is simply a form of stupidity. To say that the limited spirits are one with God is to speak only, because they do not have that status. At the same time, they are definitely reliant on Him. They are intimately connected. The embryo is not one with the spirit who uses the mothering form, but at the same time, the embryo is reliant on that spirit to a degree.

The status of energy is an important subject matter, since we may confuse the spirit using a form and the form used. Or in the case of the Lord, we may confuse His bewildering energies and useful potencies with His personality. Until we sort this out, we will remain in confusion. In this instruction to Uddhava, we get clarification, which could embark us on the mystic perception required to see the reality.

ताम् आहुस् त्रि-गुण-व्यक्तिं
सृजन्तीं विश्वतो-मुखम् ।
यस्मिन् प्रोतम् इदं विश्वं
येन संसरते पुमान् ॥४.२०॥

tām āhus tri-guṇa-vyaktiṁ
sṛjantīṁ viśvato-mukham
yasmin protam idaṁ viśvaṁ
yena saṁsarate pumān (4.20)

tām — that; āhus = āhuḥ — sages say; tri-guṇa-vyaktiṁ = tri – three + guna — influences + vyaktiṁ — manifestation; sṛjantīm — producing; viśvato-mukham = viśvato (viśvataḥ) – manifold + mukham — appearances; yasmin — in which; protam — strung; idam — this; viśvam — universe; yena — by which; saṁsarate — transmigrates; pumān — spirit soul.

Translation

The sages say that this is the manifestation of the three influences of material nature, which produces this manifold appearance, in which the universe is strung, and by which the spiritual soul transmigrates. (4.20)

Commentary:

The sages referred to, are yogi-sages of the Upanishadic period. These sages transmitted most of this information aurally. Some writing of their conversations remain in the form of the Upanishads. In the *Bṛhad Araṇyaka* Upanishad, *Yajñavalka*, a brahmin sage of repute, was challenged by some assembled sages, in the presence of King *Janak* of *Videha*. The challenge pertained to his knowledge of the Ultimate Cause, the item, person, energy or principle upon which this manifestation is based.

The elevated brahmin alerted King Yadu that such conclusions though standard knowledge were realized by the great sages of the Upanishadic period and should be realized by every wise man in turn as the centuries proceed.

The spirits transmigrate through various forms, which are created within the material nature, but the nature does not afford a permanency. Thus the soul is forced to relinquish, many forms. The soul instinctively continues relying on material nature for more and more forms, endlessly. This is technically called the Entwining Manifestations or the *samsāras*.

The God of the world is not mentioned in this verse, but that God is there in the background. In the forefront is the activated material nature, the sexually-charged mundane potency, the *Sūtram* (previous verse). This activated nature is so actual and powerful to the limited spirits, that they become totally absorbed in its transformations. They identify with it, make endeavors to regulate it and feel as if they are limited to and bound by it.

Some say that if the spirit was freed from material nature, or if it would or could liberate itself, then it would be unlimited, but that is not the issue here. If a person is imprisoned, we are not that concerned with how free he would be if he were to escape. Our main concern is his actual escape, rather than what would happen to him if he did come out. For indeed, if he does escape, his freedom may not increase unlimitedly.

The Upanishadic sages stressed the word *protam* which mean strung. They inquired of the item on which this universe is strung, just as one might inquire about the main yarn upon which a cloth is woven.

यथोर्णनाभिर् हृदयाद्
ऊर्णां सन्तत्य वक्त्रतः ।
तया विहृत्य भूयस् ता
ग्रसत्य् एवं महेश्वरः ॥४.२१॥

yathorṇanābhir hṛdayād
ūrṇāṁ santatya vaktrataḥ
tayā vihṛtya bhūyas tāṁ
grasaty evaṁ maheśvaraḥ (4.21)

yathorṇanābhir = yathā — as + ūrṇa – nābhiṛ (ūrṇa-nābhiḥ) — spider; hṛdayād = hṛdayāt — from the core of its body; ūrṇām — web; santatya — spreading; vaktrataḥ — through the mouth; tayā — by that; vihṛtya — playfully handling; bhūyas — again; tām — that; grasaty = grasati — swallows; evam — so; maheśvaraḥ — the Great Lord.

Translation

As a spider spreads web from the core of its body through its mouth, playfully handling it, and then again swallowing it, so the great Lord does with the world. (4.21)

Commentary:

This comparison should be studied carefully so as not to completely identify the Great God *(maheśvarah)* with the spider. Only in certain respects is the Supreme Lord similar to the spider. Here in these instructions, the ascetic explained where the similarity begins and where it ends, thus we should not be led off by philosophers who use this verse in a complete identification.

The composite form of a spider is made of several aspects, not just one feature which is labeled spider. Within the spider body there is a spirit, a mind, moods and material components. Thus the directive part of the spider's body is not the form in entirety. And thus when it is said that the spider created the web from within its body, it does not mean that the spirit created the web from spiritual materials.

यत्र यत्र मनो देही
धारयेत् सकलं धिया ।
स्नेहाद् द्वेषाद् भयाद् वापि
याति तत्-तत्-स्वरूपताम् ॥४.२२॥

yatra yatra mano dehī
dhārayet sakalaṁ dhiyā
snehād dveṣād bhayād vāpi
yāti tat-tat-svarūpatām (4.22)

yatra yatra — wherever whatever; mano = manaḥ — mind; dehi — the embodied soul; dhārayet — should concentrate; sakalam — together with the parts, all, whole; dhiyā — with intellect; snehād snehāt — from love; dvesād = dvesāt — from hate; bhayād = bhayāt — from fear; vapi = va api — either or; yāti — attains; tat-tat-svarūpatām – tat-tat — that or that, whatever whatsoever + svarūpatām — the same state of existence.

Translation

On whatever object, the embodied soul concentrates his whole mind with the intellect, either for love, hate or fear, he attains that same state of existence. (4.22)

Commentary:

This realization of the elevated brahmin was confirmed by Lord Krishna, who explained it to Arjuna in this way:

yaṁ yaṁ vāpi smaranbhāvaṁ tyajatyante kalevaram
taṁ tamevaiti kaunteya sadā tadbhāvabhāvitaḥ

Moreover, whatever texture of existence is recalled when a person abandons his body in the end, to that same type of life, he is projected, O son of Kuntī, always being transformed into that status of life. (B.G. 8.6)

These two verses explain the law of transmigration under which all embodied beings move from one body to another with their resultant psyche, which consists of the subtle mind *(mano ... sakalam)* along with the intellect, the subtle tool of focus and the emotional energy which is expressed as love, hate or fear.

Transmigration does not rely solely on one's religious faith or belief. It relies mostly on the general texture of the psychology at the time of departure from the body, and that texture is based on one's over-all posture during the recent life. It has little to do with last minute adjustments. Aspirations in the forms of prayers to the Supreme Being, to God or reliance on saintly people like pandits, yogis, ministers, devotees and the like, do have a bearing but if these are inconsistent with one's life style, one will again revert to old habits, since the emotional nature which takes the form of love, hate, and fear, always resumes its natural posture. There is an important verse in the *Bhagavad Gītā*, where Lord Krishna explained to Arjuna how a person operates by his essential nature *(sattvānurūpā):*

sattvānurūpā sarvasya śraddhā bhavati bhārata
śraddhāmayo'yaṁ puruṣo yo yacchraddhaḥ sa eva saḥ

Confidence becomes manifest according to the essential nature of the person, O man of the Bhārata family. A human being follows his trend of confidence. Whatever type of faith he has, that he expresses only. (B.G. 17.3)

कीटः पेशस्कृतं ध्यायन्
उड्या तेन प्रवेशितः ।
याति तत्-सात्मतां राजन्
पूर्व-रूपम् असन्त्यजन् ॥४.२३॥

kīṭaḥ peśaskṛtaṁ dhyāyan
uḍyāṁ tena praveśitaḥ
yāti tat-sātmatāṁ rājan
pūrva-rūpam asantyajan (4.23)

kītaḥ — insect; peśaskṛtam — wasp; dhyāyan — contemplates, constantly thinks of; kuḍyām — within a hive; tena — by it; praveśitaḥ — being confined; yāti — goes; tat-sātmatām = tat — of that sa – with ātmatām — with the same subtle form; rājan — o king; pūrva-rūpam = pūrva – old + rūpam — gross body; asantyajan — without discarding.

Translation

O King, the insect, being confined within a hive by a wasp, constantly thinks of its captor, until it attains the same subtle form, even without realizing that it discarded a gross body. (4.23)

Commentary:

For the captive insect, the operative principle of consciousness, is fear. Due to a strong fear in the struggle for existence, a captured insect constantly thinks of its captor. It loses focus on its recent activities. Due to being stung by a superior creature, as well as being intimidated by being imprisoned and not knowing the plan of its captor, the captured insect, constantly thinks of, dwells upon and concentrates on its kidnapper.

By this constant focus, its subtle body changes into a form, which is similar to that of the captor. Due to persistent contemplation, it takes the next birth as the larva of its captor. Even before it discards its old body, the captured insect goes through a transformation of subtle form. In this regard, we may study what Lord Krishna told Arjuna along the same lines:

antakāle ca māmeva smaranmuktvā kalevaram
yaḥ prayāti sa madbhāvaṁ yāti nāstyatra saṁśayaḥ

If at the end of one's life, one recalls Me in particular, as one gives up the body, one is elevated to My condition of existence. There is no doubt about this. (B.G. 8.5)

kaviṁ purāṇamanuśāsitāram aṇoraṇīyāṁsamanusmaredyaḥ
sarvasya dhātāram acintyarūpam ādityavarṇaṁ tamasaḥ parastāt
prayāṇakāle manasācalena bhaktyā yukto yogabalena caiva
bhruvormadhye prāṇam āveśya samyak sa taṁ paraṁ puruṣamupaiti divyam (8.10)

He who meditates on the Person Who knows everything, the most ancient of people, the Supreme Supervisor, the most minute factor, the one with unimaginable form, with a radiant body, free of grossness, (8.9)

...and that meditator who even at the time of death, with an unwavering mind, being connected devotedly, with psychological power developed through yoga practice, and having caused the energizing breath to enter between the eyebrows with precision, goes to the Divine Supreme Person. (8.10)

Thus if one could focus effectively, one could change status and attain a superior form while transmigrating. There is a great lesson taught here by the elevated brahmin. The captured insect did not desire to change species. Its actual interest was to continue in its own species. Through a strong fear of its captor, it was circumstantial1y forced to change its self-conception. This means that in the final analysis, our plans are not that significant but rather, the pressures from the environment which affect our emotions, will, more or less, determine what status we achieve.

एव गुरुभ्य एतेभ्य
एषा मे शिक्षिता मतिः ।
स्वात्मोपशिक्षितां बुद्धिं
शृणु मे वदतः प्रभो ॥४.२४॥

evaṁ gurubhya etebhya
eṣā me śikṣitā matiḥ
svātmopaśikṣitāṁ buddhiṁ
śṛṇu me vadataḥ prabho (4.24)

evaṁ — thus; gurubhya = gurubhyaḥ — from the teachers; etebhya = etebhyah — from these; eṣā — this; me — by me; śikṣitā — learned; matiḥ — knowledge; svātmopaśikṣitāṁ = sva – my + ātma — psyche + upaśikṣitām — learned; buddhim — wisdom; śṛṇu — hear; me — from me; vadataḥ — explain; prabho — o respected one

Translation

Thus, from these teachers, this knowledge was learned by me; Please hear from me, as I explain, O respected one, what wisdom I learned from my psyche. (4.24)

Commentary:

One important aspect of higher yoga practice, is to learn from the psyche. One must learn from the Supreme Lord and from superior entities who are situated between oneself and the Lord. One must also learn from spirits who are on par. One must learn from those who are below one self existentially. One must learn from the gross material elements and the subtle energies as well. Most of all, one must be self observant to know how best to operate the psyche. This knowledge comes from a careful study of how the personal energies function.

The key is to give up wishful thinking and to study exactly how the energies operate. One should cease hoping and fantasizing about the possibilities of life and learn reality through accurate perception of the psychological energies. One should not trust the intellect but should carefully regulate its operations, regarding it as a calculator mostly and not as a capable consultant.

देहो गुरुर् मम विरक्ति-विवेक-हेतुर्
बिभ्रत् स्म सत्त्व-निधनं सततार्त्य्-उदर्कम् ।
तत्त्वान्य् अनेन विमृशामि यथा तथापि
पारक्यम् इत्य् अवसितो विचराम्य् असङ्गः ॥४.२५॥

deho gurur mama virakti-viveka-hetur
bibhrat sma sattva-nidhanaṁ satatārty-udarkam
tattvāny anena vimṛśāmi yathā tathāpi
pārakyam ity avasito vicarāmy asaṅgaḥ (4.25)

deho = dehah — body; gurur = guruh — teacher; mama — my; virakti-viveka-hetur = virakti — of dispassion + viveka — of discrimination + hetur (hetuḥ) — cause of; bibhrat — being subject to; sma — definitely; sattva-nidhanam = sattva — existence, birth + nidhanam — non-existence, death; satatārty-udarkam = satata — always + ārty (ārti) — pain + udarkam — end; tattvāny = tattvāni — realities; anena — with this; vimṛśāmi — I reflect on; yathā — as; tathāpi = tathāapi — so also; pārakyam — belonging to others; ity = iti — thus; avasito = av*Asita*ḥ — being convinced; vicarāmy = vicarāmi — I roam; asaṅgaḥ — without attachment.

Translation

The body is my teacher, as the cause of dispassion and discrimination, and being subjected to birth and death, which always bring pain as the end. With this body, I reflect on the realities. As I am convinced that it belongs to others, I roam without attachment. (4.25)

Commentary:

The question as to why the elevated brahmin wandered like a child or an idiot, was answered in this verse. On the basis of an observation that his body did not belong to him, the brahmin became disinterested in extravagant desires.

It may be argued that the body belongs to the Supreme God or to the supernatural rulers who regulate the elements and the astronomical powers like the sun and moon, but practically we see that the body is regulated by earthly lords, by politicians and powerful employers, who create social laws and economy. Some politicians and businessmen may create situations to send this body to its death in war.

This body may be overpowered by stronger animals, like lions and tigers. Ultimately, unless it is burned, this body may be consumed by animals and insect larva. Thus this body does not really belong to the spirit who uses it.

For the most part, a householder's body is used by his departed ancestors who require rebirth and who possess the reproductive organs of the body. Usually a popular monk's body is possessed by departed people, who push him here and there to influence human society. In all cases, therefore, this body does not belong to the spirit who uses it.

Thus the elevated brahmin became detached from his own form. He roamed about, observing how the influence of the subtle body bore down on the gross form, and caused it to meet with varying circumstances which were due to instincts and past life activities.

The material body, though not the spirit, and though temporary, is a great teacher for the spirit to invoke its sense of dispassion as well as to cause the spirit to develop discrimination. And by bringing on pain in the end, the body serves to alert the spirit that it should not become attached to such a useful instrument as a body. It should learn the lessons well, by reflecting on the various experiences.

जायात्मजार्थ-पशु-भृत्य-गृहाप्त-वर्गान्
पुष्नाति यत्-प्रिय-चिकीर्षया वितन्वन् ।
स्वान्ते स-कृच्छ्रम् अवरुद्ध-धनः स देहः
सृष्ट्वास्य बीजम् अवसीदति वृक्ष-धर्मः ॥४.२६॥

jāyātmajārtha-paśu-bhṛtya-gṛhāpta-vargān
pusṇāti yat-priya-cikīrṣayā vitanvan
svānte sa-kṛcchram avaruddha-dhanaḥ sa dehaḥ
sṛṣṭvāsya bījam avasīdati vṛkṣa-dharmaḥ (4.26)

jāyātmajārtha-paśu-bhṛtya-gṛhāpta-vargān = jaya — wife + ātma-ja — children + artha — money + paśu — domestic animals + bhṛtya — servant + gṛha — home + āpta — relatives + vargān — all such things; puṣṇāti — maintains; yat-priya-cikīrṣayā = yat — that + priya-cikīrṣayā — desiring to please; vitanvan — expanding; svante = sva – own + ante — end; sa-kṛcchram — with great endeavor; avaruddha-dhanaḥ = avaruddha — accumulated + dhanah — wealth; sa — that; dehah — body (old body); sṛṣṭvāsya — having created; bījam — basis of a new body; avasīdati — withers; vṛkṣa-dharmaḥ = vṛkṣa — tree + dharmah — law of nature.

Translation

Desiring to please that body, by expanding activities, a person maintains a wife, children, domestic animals, servants, home, relatives and all such things. With great endeavor, he accumulates wealth. Then, having created the basis of a new body, that old one withers like a tree at the end by the law of nature. (4.26)

Commentary:

The desire to please the body is persistent. As it takes much endeavor to please the body, so it also takes much endeavor to keep the body under restrictions whereby one works the minimum to satisfy the body and simultaneously works out one's salvation. This body was created on the basis of the past body, and similarly, a future body may being founded on the basis of this body. This is the cycle of birth and death. Ideally we should use this body for attaining liberation so that we do not have to take another gross form. Generally, human beings do not understand this. Hence they follow the tendencies of a particular body even if those traits are destructive to spiritual realization.

It is ironic that the spirit, who is supposed to use this body and extract something from it, may be influence to please the body and take a new one on the basis of his efforts to please the old one. The modern civilization with its sophistication, is mostly dedicated to creature comforts. As such it serves the needs of the physical bodies and specializes in ignoring self-realization.

जिह्वैकतो ऽमुम् अपकर्षति कर्हि तर्षा
शिश्नो ऽन्यतस् त्वग् उदरं श्रवणं कुतश्चित् ।
घ्राणो ऽन्यतश् चपल-दृक् क्व च कर्म-शक्तिर्
बह्व्यः सपत्न्य इव गेह-पतिं लुनन्ति ॥४.२७॥

jihvaikato 'mum apakarṣati karhi tarṣā
śiśno 'nyatas tvag udaraṁ śravaṇaṁ kutaścit
ghrāṇo 'nyataś capala-dṛk kva ca karma-śaktir
bahvyaḥ sapatnya iva geha-patiṁ lunanti (4.27)

jihvaikato = jihvā — tongue + ekato (ekataḥ) — one pursuit; 'mum = amum — the person; apakarsati — attracts; karhi — at any time, sometimes; tarṣā — thirst; śiśno = śiśnaḥ — sex impulse; 'nyatas = anyataḥ — another pursuit; tvag = tvak — touching impulse; udaram — stomach; śravanaṁ — ears; kutaścit — somewhere else; ghrāno = ghrānaḥ — smelling sense; 'nyataś = anyatah — another pursuit; capala-dṛk = capala – roving + dṛk — eyes; kva – somewhere else; ca — and; karma-śaktir = karma – working + śaktir (śaktiḥ) — tendency; bahvyaḥ — many; sapatnya — co-wives; iva — like; geha-patim — the householder; lunanti — divide, split up, distract.

Translation

The tongue attracts the person to one pursuit; and thirst to another. The sex impulse draws him somewhere else, and the touching impulse, stomach and ears to other features. The smelling sense attracts him to another objective; the roving eyes elsewhere, and the working tendency to another aspect, just like many wives who distract a householder. (4.27)

Commentary:

Due to its lack of decisive power over the various senses which utilize the sensations of the psyche, the spirit is unable to fulfill the spiritual purpose of life. It is circumstantially forced to satisfy natural instincts. As such, it is constantly engaged serving the senses. The spirit, who should be a master of his psyche, functions as a servant of it.

In yoga practice, there is a course known as *pratyāhar*, which is the withdrawal of the spirit from the senses, to allow that spirit to develop sufficient detachment from the need for sensation. The objective is to be more deliberate and to properly analyze the influences which prevail on the self.

The ascetic used the example of co-wives. Each one has unique desires which she expects the husband to fulfill. And thus, each exerts a particular pressure. As the householder tries to fulfill the desire of one wife, another one distracts him with demands. As soon as he tries to tend to that other wife, yet another one demands his attention. One should control the senses, rule over them and keep order in one's nature, just as a capable householder might have more than one wife, and will tend to each in turn without allowing any of them to disorient him.

As the brahmin had learnt so many lessons from life, I learnt from yoga, that by feeding the various sensual impulses a higher grade of subtle and gross energy, one is more able to control them since they calm down and are not as demanding as when they operate on low grade energy. And this comes through mastery of *prāṇāyāma* yoga.

सृष्ट्वा पुराणि विविधान्य् अजयात्म-शक्त्या
वृक्षान् सरीसृप-पशून् खग-दन्दशूकान् ।
तैस् तैर् अतुष्ट-हृदयः पुरुषं विधाय
ब्रह्मावलोक-धिषणं मुदम् आप देवः ॥४.२८॥

sṛṣṭvā purāṇi vividhāny ajayātma-śaktyā
vṛkṣān sarīsṛpa-paśūn khaga-dandaśūkān
tais tair atuṣṭa-hṛdayaḥ puruṣaṁ vidhāya
brahmāvaloka-dhiṣaṇaṁ mudam āpa devaḥ
(4.28)

sṛṣṭvā — having created; purāṇi — living quarters; vividhāny = vividhāni — various; ajayātma-śaktyā = ajayā — caused by + ātma – his own + śaktyā — potency; vṛkṣān — trees; sarīsṛpa-paśūn = sarīsṛpa — reptiles + paśūn — animals; khaga-dandaśūkān = khaga — birds + danda-śūkān — snakes; tai stair = taih taih — by these, by these; atuṣṭa-hṛdayaḥ = atuṣṭa — not satisfied + hṛdayaḥ — heart; puruṣam — humanity; vidhāya — creating; brahmāvaloka-dhiṣaṇaṁ = brahma — spiritual existence + avaloka — realisation + dhiṣaṇam — intelligence, understanding; mudam — happy; āpā — became; devah — God.

Translation

Having by His potency, created the various living quarters such as trees, reptiles, animals, birds and snakes, God was not satisfied in His heart by any of these. He created humanity, with the intellect for realizing spiritual existence and then He became happy. (4.28)

Commentary:

The contrast between the various species of life and the human beings, is here given with emphasis on the satisfaction derived by God after creating humanity. Since humanity is especially capable of realizing spiritual existence, the creation of the human species, with that potential, gave the Creator a special fulfillment.

The elevated brahmin called the various species, *purāṇi* or living quarters. Such residences are mistaken by the spirits for themselves; but in the human form, the misconception can be resolved by self realization, either partially by being properly informed or fully by direct mystic perception.

Even though the human form has the potential for self-realization, and the lower species gives more inclination to ignorance of spiritual existence, still only specific spirits realize themselves, when they use the human habitat.

By analyzing the creation and assessing its worth in terms of self-realization, the God of the world, enthused the creation with the potential for spiritual awakening. It is left to the particular spirits to monopolize on that motivation of the Lord.

लब्ध्वा सु-दुर्लभम् इदं बहु-सम्भवान्ते
मानुष्यम् अर्थ-दम् अनित्यम् अपीह धीरः ।
तूर्णं यतेत न पतेद् अनु-मृत्यु यावन्
निःश्रेयसाय विषयः खलु सर्वतः स्यात्
॥४.२९॥

labdhvā su-durlabham idaṁ bahu-sambhavānte
mānuṣyam artha-dam anityam apīha dhīraḥ
tūrṇaṁ yateta na pated anu-mṛtyu yāvan
niḥśreyasāya viṣayaḥ khalu sarvataḥ syāt (4.29)

labdhvā — having got; su-durlabham — very difficult to obtain; idam — this; bahu-sambhavānte = bahu — many + sambhavānte — after births; mānuṣyam — human forms; artha-dam — that which gives a value; anityam — not eternal, temporary; apiha = api — even + iha — here; dhīraḥ — a person with a spiritually-perceptive intellect; tūrṇam — quickly; yateta — should strive; na — not; pated = patet — should get disease; anu-mṛtyu — subject to death; yāvan = yāvat — as long as; niḥśreyasāya — for liberation; viṣayaḥ — sense enjoyment; khalu — always; sarvatah — in all circumstances; syāt — is available.

Translation

After many births, the person with a spiritually-perceptive intellect, having got the temporary but valuable human form, which is very difficult to obtain, strives for liberation, before the human body, which is subject to death, should get disease; for sense enjoyment is always available elsewhere. (4.29)

Commentary:

Human beings usually think that they have a rare opportunity to enjoy the senses of their bodies. Thus they endeavor very hard to get as many sensual gratifications as possible. Many religious people believe that they have a right to moral sense gratification and that it is for that reason, that God gave the human form of life.

However a person with a spiritually-perceptive intellect, is never comfortable with the material body unless and until he or she uses it for self realization. Any other type of body yields sense enjoyment. Some forms give more sensual pleasures in particular ways. Thus the human being has no monopoly on pleasure. Its feature is self realization, especially the ability to perfect the eightfold yoga process.

If a man is really intelligent, he will hurry up and use his body to perfect yoga and then use the resulting purity of psyche to get into the spiritual sky. Knowing fully well that the body will perish sooner or later, that it will definitely get old if it does not die in a youthful stage, that it will develop an incurable disease or die in a fatal accident, a wise person tries to use it for self realization.

We have to understand that whatever we enjoy may be experienced in an animal or angelic form. Therefore the unique feature of the human body is its ability to do yoga and to study the lives of the ancient yogis, so that we may follow in their footsteps.

एव सञ्जात-वैराग्यो
विज्ञानालोक आत्मनि ।
विचरामि महीम् एता
मुक्त-सङ्गो ऽनहङ्कृतः ॥४.३०॥

evaṁ sañjāta-vairāgyo
vijñānāloka ātmani
vicarāmi mahīm etāṁ
mukta-saṅgo 'nahaṅkṛtaḥ (4.30)

evam — thus; sañjāta-vairāgyo = sañjāta — developed + vairāgyo (vairāgyaḥ) — the sense of dispassion; vijñānāloka = vigj vijñāna — mystic and spiritual experience + ālokah — having perception; ātmani — in the self; vicarāmi — I roam over; mahīm — earth; etām — this; mukta-sango = mukta — freed + sangah — attachment; 'nahaṅkṛtah = anahankṛtah — without misplaced identity.

Translation

The sense of dispassion being developed, having the spiritual perception in the self, I roam over this earth, being freed from attachment and without a misplaced identity. (4.30)

Commentary:

The ascetic brahmin explained his position, stating that he reached a stage of having the spiritual self-perception and thus he roamed over the earth, being freed from attachment and without an identity for cultural circumstances. His sense of dispassion, being fully developed, no social circumstances in this world, attracted him.

न ह्य् एकस्माद् गुरोर् ज्ञानं
सु-स्थिरं स्यात् सु-पुष्कलम् ।
ब्रह्मैतद् अद्वितीयं वै
गीयते बहुधर्षिभिः ॥४.३१॥

na hy ekasmād guror jñānaṁ
su-sthiraṁ syāt su-puṣkalam
brahmaitad advitīyaṁ vai
gīyate bahudharṣibhiḥ (4.31)

na — not; hy = hi — indeed; ekasmād = ekasmāt — from one; guror = guroḥ — from the teacher; jñānam — information; su-sthiram — very steady; syāt — can be, is; su-puṣkalam — very ample; brahmaitad = brahma — spiritual reality + etad (etat) — this; advitīyam — one whole without disunity; vai — certainly; gīyate — is sung; bahudharṣibhiḥ = bahudha — in different ways = ṛṣibhiḥ — by yogi sages.

Translation

Indeed, information from one teacher is neither very steady or very ample. Certainly, the spiritual reality, though one whole without disunity, is glorified in different ways by the yogi sages. (4.31)

Commentary:

The spiritual reality is one whole without disunity, just as this planet earth is one planet only and is not divided into two or more spheres. However, according to the realization and mystic perception, different teachers explain the Absolute Truth in different ways. Still, the disciple or student has to apply what he may learn from one or from many teachers, so that he reaches spiritual perfection in the shortest possible time.

Generally the information from a teacher is neither steady nor ample but we found out that King Yayati got steady and very amply instructions from the ascetic brahmin. Uddhava got the same from Lord Krishna. Thus if we can find one teacher who is satisfactory, we should adhere to him, and learn also from other circumstances and people. Wherever we find an instruction that aids in spiritual development, we should accept it and make progression.

The ascetic explained why he took lessons from many teachers. Very often, one finds that the teacher who represents a disciplic succession is not realized, even though he may be versed intellectually, have a deep loyalty to *Śrī* Krishna and be versed in the ritual worship. Thus one has to protect oneself by learning from anyone who helps in the spiritual progression.

श्री-भगवान् उवाच
इत्य् उक्त्वा स यदु विप्रस्
तम् आमन्त्र्य गभीर-धीः ।
वन्दितः स्व्-अर्चितो राज्ञा
ययौ प्रीतो यथागतम् ॥४.३२॥

śrī-bhagavān uvāca
ity uktvā sa yaduṁ vipras
tam āmantrya gabhīra-dhīḥ
vanditaḥ sv-arcito rājñā
yayau prīto yathāgatam (4.32)

śrī-bhagavān – the Blessed Lord; uvāca — said; ity = iti — thus; uktvā — having spoken; sah — he; yadum — to King Yadu; vipras = viprah — the learned brahmin; tam — to him; āmantrya —

saying goodbye; gabhīra-dhīḥ = gabhīra — penetrating + dhīḥ — insight; vanditaḥ — offered respects; sv-arcito = su-arcitaḥ — duty worshiped; rājñā — by the King; yayau — he went; prito = pritah — joyously; yathāgatam = yatha — as + āgatam — came.

Translation

The Blessed Lord said; Having said this to Yadu, the learnt brahmin with the penetrating insight, said goodbye, and being offered respect, being duly worshiped by the King, he joyously went away just as he came. (4.32)

Commentary:

It may be said that since the learned brahmin had a fully-developed sense of dispassion and was free from cultural obligations, why did he bother to instruct Yadu. The answer is that in all stages, one must comply with the requirements of the Universal Form.

This means that even great yogins, who have the waiver from cultural activities, must on occasion as inspired by providence, instruct others if they get an inspiration from the Universal Form of *Śrī* Krishna or if they feel that such an inspiration was given to someone to ask them for teaching, otherwise their advancement further will be curtailed.

अवधूत-वचः श्रुत्वा
पूर्वेषां नः स पूर्व-जः ।
सर्व-सङ्ग-विनिर्मुक्तः
सम-चित्तो बभूव ह ॥४.३३॥

avadhūta-vacaḥ śrutvā
pūrveṣāṁ naḥ sa pūrva-jaḥ
sarva-saṅga-vinirmuktaḥ
sama-citto babhūva ha (4.33)

avadhūta-vacaḥ = avadhūta — of the wandering yogi + vacaḥ — words; śrutvā — having heard; pūrveṣām — of the ancestors; naḥ — our; sa = sah — he; pūrva-jaḥ — a progenitor; sarva-saṅga-vinirmuktaḥ = sarva — all + saṅga — attachment + vinirmuktaḥ — being freed; sama-citto = sama-cittah — having a controlled and quieted mento-emotional energy; babhūva — he became; ha — surely.

Translation

Having heard the words of the wandering yogi, that progenitor of our forefathers, was freed from all attachment and became a person with a controlled and quieted mento-emotional energy. (4.33)

Commentary:

In their purport, *Hridayānanda dās Gosvāmī* and *Gopīparanadhana dās Adhikārī*, cited *Śrīla* Sridhara *Swāmī* in referencing to the *Śrīmad Bhāgavatam* Canto 2 chapter 7 verse 4, which states that Lord *Dattātreya* effected the purity in many Yadus and Haihayas. They gave evidence from the disciplic succession through *Śrila Viśvanātha Cakravartī Thākura*, identifying the ascetic brahmin as *Dattātreya*. In addition, Lord Krishna identified Himself and Uddhava as King Yadu's descendants.

CHAPTER 5*

States of Existence**

Terri Stokes-Pineda Art

evam apy aṅga sarveṣāṁ dehināṁ deha-yogataḥ
kālāvayavataḥ santi bhāvā janmādayo 'sakṛt

Thus, even so, O friend, all embodied beings repeatedly endure states of existence like birth and the ensuing aspects, being mystically unified with a body and due to sequences of time. (Uddhava Gītā 5.16)

* Śrīmad Bhāgavatam Canto 11, Chapter 10
** Translator's selected chapter title.

श्री-भगवान् उवाच
मयोदितेष्व् अवहितः
स्व-धर्मेषु मद्-आश्रयः ।
वर्णाश्रम-कुलाचारम्
अकामात्मा समाचरेत् ॥५.१॥

śrī-bhagavān uvāca
mayoditeṣv avahitaḥ
sva-dharmeṣu mad-āśrayaḥ
varṇāśrama-kulācāram
akāmātmā samācaret (5.1)

śrī-bhagavān— the Blessed Lord; uvāca - said; mayoditeṣv = mayā — by me + uditeṣu — said; avahitaḥ — taking great care; sva-dharmeṣu — in my recommendation for righteous duty; mad-āśrayaḥ = mat-āśrayaḥ — one who takes shelter of me; varṇāśrama — working tendency and life style; kulācāram = kula — of the family + ācāram — behavior; akāmātmā = akāma — without cravings + ātmā — spirit; samācaret — should perform.

Translation

The Blessed Lord said: The person who takes shelter of Me, takes great care in adhering to My recommendations for righteous duty. He performs work and executes the life style and family responsibility without cravings. (5.1)

Commentary:

By a careful study of the *Bhagavad Gītā*, one can know that Krishna's recommendation for righteous duty, has to do with what the Central Figure in the Universal Form stipulates as a man's or woman's approved activities. These acts are cultural activities done by the recommendation of God, for the purpose of satisfying the desire of God for law and order in this world. The scheme of it was laid out to Arjuna:

yadā yadā hi dharmasya glānirbhavati bhārata
abhyutthānamadharmasya tadātmānaṁ sṛjāmyaham
paritrāṇāya sādhūnāṁ vināśāya ca duṣkṛtām
dharmasaṁsthāpanārthāya saṁbhavāmi yuge yuge

Whenever there is a decrease of righteousness, O son of the Bharata family, and when there is an increase of wickedness, then I show Myself.

For protecting the saintly people, to destroy the wicked ones, and to establish righteousness, I come into the visible existence from era to era. (B.G. 4.7-8)

Many modern preachers label this righteous duty as devotional service, *bhakti*. This is all fine and dandy. However for Arjuna it meant unpalatable and ghastly work on the battlefield, killing opposing relatives and friends. For Uddhava it meant backing out of the world, eliminating attachments to relatives, even ones who were dear devotees of *Śrī* Krishna, and also forgetting his fondness for the special material body *Śrī* Krishna manifested. It is a wonder that such actions can be termed devotional service.

However, the authorities who used that definition, have done so with due reason, for indeed, Arjuna may not have complied with *Śrī* Krishna's directives, if he had not loved *Śrī* Krishna deeply, nor would Uddhava have gone through with the austerities, he performed at Badrinatha after *Śrī* Krishna dismissed him. In consideration then, *bhakti* or devotion to *Śrī* Krishna is a special emotion through which a devotee can bring himself to do even that which repulses him but which *Śrī* Krishna requires in compliance to divine will.

If a devotee, as this verse states, can perform work and execute the life style and family responsibilities without cravings, then certainly the Central Person in the Universal Form, *Śrī* Krishna Himself, would be pleased and would award a waiver from the *karma* yoga cultural activities which satisfy the divine will. That soul will then be able to perfect the yoga practice and take exit from the material world, being dismissed from here by the Supreme Person.

अन्वीक्षेत विशुद्धात्मा
देहिनां विषयात्मनाम् ।
गुणेषु तत्त्व-ध्यानेन
सर्वारम्भ-विपर्ययम् ॥५.२॥

anvīkṣeta viśuddhātmā
dehināṁ viṣayātmanām
guṇeṣu tattva-dhyānena
sarvārambha-viparyayam (5.2)

anvīkṣeta — his soul should see; viśuddhātmā = viśuddha — purified + ātmā — soul; dehinām — of the embodied beings; viṣayātmanām — of the souls who are lured by attractive objects; guṇeṣu — in the mundane energy; tattva — what is real; dhyānena — by dwelling upon, considering; sarvārambha — all endeavors; viparyayam — reverses.

Translation

A person with a purified psyche should see the reverses of all endeavors of the embodied beings, who are lured by attractive mundane objects, and who consider them to be real. (5.2)

Commentary:

Without a purified psyche one cannot see the *tattva*, the reality of this material situation in its subtle and gross formations. Most of the effects we produce, will be reversed. That is certain. We ought to know this and not give ourselves over entirely to these situations. So long as the psyche remains impure, we will be lured by the gross and subtle sensual objects which are created in the material energy.

सुप्तस्य विषयालोको
ध्यायतो वा मनोरथः ।
नानात्मकत्वाद् विफलस्
तथा भेदात्म-धीर् गुणैः ॥५.३॥

suptasya viṣayāloko
dhyāyato vā manorathaḥ
nānātmakatvād viphalas
tathā bhedātma-dhīr guṇaiḥ (5.3)

suptasya — of a sleeper; visayaloko = visaya — sense objects + alokah — sight; dhyāyato = dhyāyatah — of an imaginative person; vā — or; manorathaḥ — fantasy; nanatmakatvad = nānā — constantly changinh + ātmakatvāt — by the nature; viphalas — without consequence; tathā — as; bhedātma-dhīr = bheda ātma — divided in nature, diversity in a formation + dhir (dhīḥ) — idea; guṇaiḥ — by the influence of material nature.

Translation

As the sight of objects of a sleeper, or the fantasy of an imaginative person, are without consequence, since they are constantly changing by nature, so is the idea of a diversity in the influence of material nature. (5.3)

Commentary:

For a dreamer all sights seen in a dream are a fantasy and for an imaginative person, many whimsical and totally meaningless ideas, flash in the mind from moment to moment. Similarly, whatever appears in material nature is actually insubstantial. There is a verse in the *Bhagavad Gītā* which explains this:

nāsato vidyate bhāvo nābhāvo vidyate sataḥ
ubhayorapi dṛṣṭo'ntas tvanayostattvadarśibhiḥ

Of the non-substantial things, there is no enduring existence. Of the substantial things, there is no lack of existence. These two truths were perceived with certainty by the mystic seers of reality. (B.G. 2.16)

निवृत्तं कर्म सेवेत
प्रवृत्तं मत्-परस् त्यजेत् ।
जिज्ञासाया सम्प्रवृत्तो
नाद्रियेत् कर्म-चोदनाम् ॥५.४॥

nivṛttaṁ karma seveta
pravṛttaṁ mat-paras tyajet
jijñāsāyāṁ sampravṛtto
nādriyet karma-codanām (5.4)

nivṛttaṁ — that which terminates one's mundane existence; *karma* — cultural activity; seveta — one should perform; pravṛttam — that which promotes one's mundane existence; mat-paras — one who is dedicated to Me; tyajet — one should abandon; jijñāsāyām — in the quest for self realisation; sampravṛtto = sampravṛttah — being completely engaged; nadriyet = na — not + ādriyet — one should regard; karma — cultural activity; codanām — to scriptural injunctions.

Translation

Being dedicated to Me, one should perform the cultural activity which terminates one's mundane existence. One should abandon that which promotes it. Being completely engaged in the quest for self-realisation, one should not regard scriptural injunctions, which increase cultural acts. (5.4)

Commentary:

This is part of *Śrī* Krishna's criticism of the Vedas and other scriptures which promote cultural activity for its own sake. In the *Bhagavad Gītā* discourse, there was similar criticism:

traiguṇyaviṣayā vedā nistraiguṇyo bhavārjuna
nirdvaṁdvo nityasattvastho niryogakṣema ātmavān (2.45)

Three moody phases are offered by the Vedas. Be without the three modes, O Arjuna. Be without the moody fluctuations. Be always anchored to reality. Be free from grasping and possessiveness. (2.45)

Even if a scriptural injunction or a spiritual master, promotes an activity, which will promote more and more cultural activity and even if such activities are passed as devotional service or as religion, one has to analyze for oneself where the compliance will lead.

One should only perform cultural acts under the eye of the Universal Form of *Śrī* Krishna, for such acts are righteous in His opinion. They will free one from having to do more and more cultural acts in intertwining situations. It is only *Śrī* Krishna or alternately Lord *Balarāma* or Lord Shiva or their parallel divinities who can perform cultural acts and escape from the negative reactions.

Thus when a devotee acts for *Śrī* Krishna, as Arjuna did at *Kurukṣetra* or as Uddhava did after this discourse, he will be exempt from the cultural situations which are social dead-ends, and which lead to more and more haphazard rebirths.

यमान् अभीक्ष्ण सेवेत
नियमान् मत्-परः क्वचित् ।
मद्-अभिज्ञं गुरुं शान्तम्
उपासीत मद्-आत्मकम् ॥५.५॥

yamān abhīkṣṇaṁ seveta
niyamān mat-paraḥ kvacit
mad-abhijñaṁ guruṁ śāntam
upāsīta mad-ātmakam (5.5)

yamān — moral restraints; abhīkṣṇam — always; seveta — one should observe; niyamān — recommended behavior; mat-paraḥ — one who is devoted to me; kvacit — appropiately; mad-abhijñam — one who realised me thoroughly; gurum — teacher; śāntam — spiritually pacified; upāsīta — one should serve; mad-ātmakam — one who is similar in nature to Me.

Translation

One who is devoted to Me, should always observe the moral restraints and appropriately heed the recommended behaviors. He should serve the spiritually-pacified teacher who realized Me thoroughly and who is similar in nature to Me. (5.5)

Commentary:

If a devotee does not observe the moral restraints and if his non-compliance is authorized by everyone except the Central Person in the Universal Form, he will come to ruination. He will face difficulty as a result. One has to be sure that one follows the guidelines given from moment to moment by the Universal Form. One should not be misled by the mind or emotions, nor by other devotees, even by senior ones and even by a spiritual master. One must always be sure that the Universal Form approved one's behavior, otherwise there will be reversals.

A spiritually-pacified teacher is one who is not greedy for popularity and disciples. If one has a teacher who is overtaken by popularity and who will increase his following at any cost, one will come to ruination if one complies with his instructions, because such a teacher, even though he may be a devotee in high standing, will by necessity, lose touch with the Central Person in the Universal Form.

There are cases of disciples who rejected the instruction of a reputed spiritual master and who did not lose progression by the rebuttal. And there are cases of those who rejected and who fell down. Thus one should be careful with a spiritual master and with the Supreme Lord, to be sure that whatever the spiritual master might order is actually the will of the Lord.

It is not a good idea to disrespect or to confront an established spiritual master. The reason is this: Even though such an individual may issue totally crazy orders on occasion, still he has value, especially in terms of the progression of the mass of people. Therefore it is best to respect him when one is near him, and to keep a safe distance from him otherwise. The case of King *Indradyumna* stands out. When he did not show respect for the reputed *Ācārya Agastya*, he had to go down to some births in elephant species. He was rescued from that condition and he assumed a spiritual body, but the point remains that instead of getting salvation in the very life when he slighted the Sage *Agastya*, his salvation was forestalled for many, many years.

Therefore one should be on the look-out for the eyes of the Central Person in the Universal Form, to know what to do and what not to do, who to respect and who to avoid, otherwise one's course in material existence will be extended indefinitely.

अमान्य् अमत्सरो दक्षो
निर्ममो दृढ-सौहृदः ।
असत्वरो ऽर्थ-जिज्ञासुर्
अनसूयुर् अमोघ-वाक् ॥५.६॥

amāny amatsaro dakṣo
nirmamo dṛḍha-sauhṛdaḥ
asatvaro 'rtha-jijñāsur
anasūyur amogha-vāk (5.6)

amāny = amānī — without pride; amatsaro = amatsarah — without jealosy; dakṣo = dakṣaḥ — capable; nirmano = nirmamaḥ — without attachment; dṛḍha-sauhṛdaḥ — firmly devoted to the spiritual master; asatvaro = asatvaraḥ — not impatient; 'rtha-jijñāsur = artha jijñāsuḥ — eager to know the truth; anasūyur = anasūyuḥ — free from envy; amogha-vāk — not being talkative.

Translation

He should be without pride, without jealousy, capable, without attachment, firmly devoted to the spiritual teacher, patient, eager to know the truth, free from envy and not be talkative. (5.6)

Commentary:

It is only by systematic and consistent application that the devotee can meet up to these qualifications. These attributes, do not come to a devotee merely because he is a devotee nor merely because he chants the holy names of *Śrī* Krishna. Some persons are born displaying some of these tendencies consistently. Others, even after being trained, lectured to and corrected, fail to display the qualities.

Whatever is unnatural to a human being, becomes easy for him only by consistent and steady austerity to develop it.

जायापत्य-गृह-क्षेत्र-
स्वजन-द्रविणादिषु ।
उदासीनः समं पश्यन्
सर्वेष्व् अर्थम् इवात्मनः ॥५.७॥

jāyāpatya-gṛha-kṣetra-
svajana-draviṇādiṣu
udāsīnaḥ samaṁ paśyan
sarveṣv artham ivātmanaḥ (5.7)

jāyāpatya = jāyā — wife + apatya — children; gṛha — house; ksetra — land; svajana — relatives;

draviṇādiṣu = dravina — money + ādiṣu — and the life; udāsīnaḥ — remaining indifferent; samam — equally; paśyan — considering; sarveṣv = sarveṣu — in all; artham — value; ivātmanah = iva — like, in comparison + ātmanaḥ — of the spirit.

Translation

He should be indifferent to his wife, children, house, land, relatives, money and the like, considering the value of his spirit in comparison to everything else. (5.7)

Commentary:

In comparison to one's spirit, the body of wife, those of one's children, one's house, land and the bodies of other relatives, one's money and the like, are worthless. This does not mean that the spirits of one's wife, children and relatives are worthless, for indeed their spirits have just as much value as one's own.

Still in the proper consideration, one should not fall for the misconception regarding the self, which one's wife and relatives, may have. If they do not understand their spirits, then their self-conceptions would be their gross bodies. As such if one gages one's life by their views one will lose out spiritually and will sacrifice spiritual advancement needlessly.

The confusion about the body being the soul was straightened out for Arjuna in the *Bhagavad Gītā*, especially in chapter two, which should be thoroughly studied and put into practice by all readers of this discourse with Uddhava.

विलक्षणः स्थूल-सूक्ष्माद्
देहाद् आत्मेक्षिता स्व-दृक् ।
यथाग्निर् दारुणो दाह्याद्
दाहको ऽन्यः प्रकाशकः ॥५.८॥

vilakṣaṇaḥ sthūla-sūkṣmād
dehād ātmekṣitā sva-dṛk
yathāgnir dāruṇo dāhyād
dāhako 'nyaḥ prakāśakaḥ (5.8)

vilakṣanaḥ — is distinct; sthūla — gross; sūksmād = sūkṣmāt — from the subtle; dehād = dehāt — from the body; ātmekṣitā = ātmā — the spirit + īkṣitā — observer; sva – self; dṛk — perception; yathāgnir = yathā — as + agniḥ — fire; daruno = darunaḥ — firewood; dāhyād = dāhyāt — from combustibles; dahako = dahakaḥ — that which burns; 'nyaḥ = anyaḥ — other, different; prakāśakaḥ — that which illuminates.

Translation

The spirit, the self-perceptive observer, is distinct from the gross and subtle body, as a fire that burns and illuminates is different to combustive firewood. (5.8)

Commentary:

When a gross body is awake, the subtle body is fused into it, so that they act as one unit, even though in fact the subtle one, can and does separate from and will survive the gross form. Beyond both forms, Is the spirit who provides the essential power for the operation of those two forms, just as fire burns and illuminates the very wood which it consumes. The spirit uses the gross and subtle bodies but it is distinct from either of them.

निरोधोत्पत्त्य्-अणु-बृहन्-
नानात्व तत्-कृतान् गुणान् ।
अन्तः प्रविष्ट आधत्त
एवं देह-गुणान् परः ॥५.९॥

nirodhotpatty-aṇu-bṛhan-
nānātvaṁ tat-kṛtān guṇān
antaḥ praviṣṭa ādhatta
evaṁ deha-guṇān paraḥ (5.9)

nirodhotpatty = nirodha — destruction + utpatti — manifestation; anu — minuteness; bṛhan = brhat — hughness; nānātvam — diversity; tat – that; kṛtān — produced; guṇān — qualities; antaḥ — within; praviṣṭaḥ — having entered; ādhatta = ādhatte — asumes, mimics; evam — similarly; deha — body; gunān — characteristics; parah — that which is superior.

Translation

Having entered within, it mimics the qualities produced by the material it entered, such as destruction, manifestation, minuteness, hughness and diversity. Similarly, that superior factor, assumes the characteristics of the body. (5.9)

Commentary:

The subtle body of the living entity assumes the characteristics of the particular birth environment which it becomes attached to in the process of time. Thus various identities are assumed by it, as being destroyed, being manifested, being microscopic, being huge and being diverse. The spirit since it is linked to the subtle body, mimics whatever that body endures.

The superior factor is the spirit as defined in the *Bhagavad Gītā*:

indriyāṇi parāṇyāhur indriyebhyaḥ paraṁ manaḥ
manasastu parā buddhir yo buddheḥ paratastu saḥ

The ancient psychologists say that the senses are energetic, but in comparison to the senses, the mind is more energetic. In contrast to the mind, the intelligence is even more sensitive. But in reference, the spirit is most elevated. (B.G. 3.42)

यो ऽसौ गुणैर् विरचितो
देहो ऽयं पुरुषस्य हि ।
ससारस् तन्-निबन्धो ऽय
पुसो विद्या च्छिद् आत्मनः ॥५.१०॥

yo 'sau guṇair viracito
deho 'yaṁ puruṣasya hi
saṁsāras tan-nibandho 'yaṁ
puṁso vidyā cchid ātmanaḥ (5.10)

yo = yah — which; 'sau = asau — that; guṇair = guṇaiḥ — by the influence of material nature; viracito = viracitah — is created; deho = dehaḥ — body; 'yam = ayam — this; purusasya — of the spirit; hi — indeed; saṁsāras = samsārah — transmigration; tan = tat – that; nibandho = nibandhah — bondage; 'yam = ayam — this; pumso = pumsah — the person; vidyā — knowledge acquired by experience; cchid = chit — that which breaks or destroys; ātmanah — of the soul.

Translation

This body of the spirit, which is created by the influences of material nature, is the cause of transmigration and bondage. That knowledge acquired by experience of the spirit destroys this. (5.10)

Commentary:

The combination of subtle and gross configurations makes up what we call a body. When the gross body dies, the subtle one is forced to leave that gross form forever. It then seeks shelter in some psychological environment through which it can develop another gross form. This all happens by instinct. The energy in the subtle body automatically operates to create another form.

If however, one develops knowledge of the spirit on the basis of hearing of the qualities of the spirit and then realizing these by direct perception, he has a chance for stopping the impulsive operation of the subtle body. Thus one might, if one is able and if one gets the divine grace, free oneself from having to take temporary forms.

तस्माज् जिज्ञासयात्मानम्
आत्म-स्थं केवलं परम् ।
सङ्गम्य निरसेद् एतद्
वस्तु-बुद्धि यथा-क्रमम् ॥५.११॥

tasmāj jijñāsayātmānam
ātma-sthaṁ kevalaṁ param
saṅgamya nirased etad
vastu-buddhiṁ yathā-kramam (5.11)

tasmāj = tasmāt — therefore; jijñāsayātmānam = jijñāsayā — by philosophical and mystic inquiry + ātmānam — of the spirit; ātma — soul; stham — situated; kevalam — isolated from the psychic equipments; param — transcendent; saṅgamya — being unified; nirased = niraset — should give up; etad = etat — this; vastu — material objects; buddhim — intellect; yathā – as; kramam — step by step.

Translation

Therefore by philosophical and mystic inquiry, into the self, one should realize the transcendent self as isolated from the psychic equipments. Being unified in this, one should give up the materialistic intellect step by step. (5.11)

Commentary:

This is achieved by higher yoga, beginning with *pratyāhar* sensual energy withdrawal. In this process, step by step, one causes the intellect to abandon its materialistic tendencies. This intellect is a light in the head of the subtle body. One gives up the materialistic conclusions and figurings of this subtle psychic organ, curbs and redirects it, to view the chit *ākāśa*, the sky of consciousness.

Usually one begins by a philosophical interest into the nature of the spiritual self, but when one discovers that one cannot actually penetrate the mystery of spiritual reality by means of philosophy and reasoning, one seeks out a teacher who can show one a mystic means.

आचार्यो ऽरणिर् आद्यः स्याद्
अन्ते-वास्य् उत्तरारणिः ।
तत्-सन्धानं प्रवचनं
विद्या-सन्धिः सुखावहः ॥५.१२॥

ācāryo 'raṇir ādyaḥ syād
ante-vāsy uttarāraṇiḥ
tat-sandhānaṁ pravacanaṁ
vidyā-sandhiḥ sukhāvahaḥ (5.12)

ācāryo = ācāryaḥ — teacher; 'raṇir = araṇiḥ — kindling wood; ādyah — lower; syād = syāt — should be; ante-vāsy = ante-vāsī — disciple; uttarāraṇiḥ = uttara — upper + araṇiḥ — kindling wood; tat – that; sandhānam — connecting; pravacanām — instructions; vidyā — technique; sandhiḥ — combination; sukhāvahaḥ = sukha — happiness + āvahah — producing.

Translation

The teacher should be compared to the lower kindling wood, the disciple to the upper one, the instruction to the piece connecting them and the technique used, the combination of these which produces happiness. (5.12)

Commentary:

The teacher serves as the foundation for one's spiritual life. It is the teacher's austerities that one will hear of and which will inspire one to take up the same. The technique given by the teacher must be practiced by the disciple personally. The teacher cannot save the disciple without the disciple taking up the relevant practice. When all that happens timely, the student becomes happy from the success in spiritual life.

वैशारदी सातिविशुद्ध-बुद्धिर्
धुनोति मायां गुण-सम्प्रसूताम् ।
गुनांश् च सन्दह्य यद्-आत्मम् एतत्
स्वयं च शाम्यत्य् असमिद् यथाग्निः ॥५.१३॥

vaiśāradī sāti-viśuddha-buddhir
dhunoti māyāṁ guṇa-samprasūtām
gunāṁś ca sandahya yad-ātmam etat
svayaṁ ca śāṁyaty asamid yathāgniḥ (5.13)

vaiśāradī — precise; sāti-viśuddha = sā — that + ati-viśuddha — purified; buddhih — intellect; dhunoti — removes; māyām — misconception; guṇa — mundane influence; samprasūtām — produced; gunāṁs = gunān — mundane influence; ca — and; sandhaya — burning, nullifying; yad = yat — which; ātmam — self; etat — this; svayam — itself; ca — and; śāmyaty = śāmyati — becomes calm; asamid = asamit — without fuel; yathāgniḥ = yatha — as; agniḥ — fire.

Translation

By the precise highly purified intellect, he removes the misconception produced of the mundane influences, and nullifying those influences, of which the mundane objects consists, the self becomes calmed, just as a fire without fuel. (5.13)

Commentary:

This has to do with *kriyā* yoga and not by merely hearing from a spiritual master. One attains a calmed intellect only after perfecting *buddhi* yoga, which is described in the *Bhagavad Gītā* beginning in chapter two. That is attained by higher yoga only. It cannot be attained by merely hearing from a spiritual master, because neither Arjuna nor Uddhava attained it by mere hearing. Arjuna had to get a revelation to supplement the hearing. Uddhava had to perform end-of-life austerities.

It is totally false to think that a person can gain a consistently-calmed intellect by hearing. But what such a person may do is to adopt a mood of calmness. That is not the state which, *Śrī* Krishna described here.

The precise and highly purified intellect is created by doing higher yoga to perfection, not by chanting nor by devotional services in temple worship and missionary activities.

अथैषाम् कर्म-कर्तृणां
भोक्तृणा सुख-दुःखयोः भ्प् ।
नानात्वम् अथ नित्यत्वं
लोक-कालागमात्मनाम् ॥५.१४॥

athaiṣām karma-kartṝṇāṁ
bhoktṝṇāṁ sukha-duḥkhayoḥ
nānātvam atha nityatvaṁ
loka-kālāgamātmanām (5.14)

athaiṣām = atha — thus + eṣām — of those; karma — cultural activities; kartṝṇāṁ — of the performers; bhoktṝṇām — of the experiences; sukha - of happiness; duḥkhayoḥ — of distress; nānātvam — numerousness, many in number; atha — as well as; nityatvam — that which perpetually exists; loka — material world; kālāgamātmanām = kāla — time + āgama — Vedic scriptures which recommend cultural activities; ātmanām — spirit;

Translation

Concerning the concept of numerous performers of cultural activities and numerous experiences of happiness and distress as well as a perpetual material world, perpetual time, perpetual scriptures that recommend cultural activities and the perpetual spirits, (5.14)

Commentary:

This is completed in the next two verses. It gives a critique of the *Karma Mimamsaka* philosophy. That system of consideration states that everything is perpetual since everything that exists can be traced to a cause which carries itself over into a series of effects, endlessly.

मन्यसे सर्व-भावानां
सस्था ह्य् औत्पत्तिकी यथा ।
तत्-तद्-आकृति-भेदेन
जायते भिद्यते च धीः ॥५.१५॥

manyase sarva-bhāvānāṁ
saṁsthā hy autpattikī yathā
tat-tad-ākṛti-bhedena
jāyate bhidyate ca dhīḥ (5.15)

manyase — you think; sarva — all; bhāvānām — existence of things; saṁsthā — substantial; hy = hi — indeed; autpattikī — essential, inborn; yathā — as; tat-tad = tat tat — that that, a series; ākṛti — shape; bhedena — by shape; jāyate — is manifested; bhidyate — changes; ca — and; dhīḥ — intelligence;

Translation

...if you think that the existence of all things is substantial as a series and is essential, and that intelligence is manifested and changed by differences in shape, (5.15)

Commentary:

The philosophy of *Mimamsaka* is reasonable from the traditional view, in terms of perceiving everything through a material body, which has a dull intellect. However, when one sees through a mystically-charged intellect, one does not perceive in that way.

Śrī Krishna alerted Uddhava not to follow that traditional view because its conclusions which seem quite logical and true, are totally false. It does not account for the background influences which are imperceptible to the gross form, and to an intellect which came under the body's influence.

Even though the existence of things continues as a series, still those things in themselves continually lose their status, giving way to new formations. The essential parts of any material object are sub-atomic. The large conglomerations are actually a mock-up, a fantasy as it were. Even though the spirits, both the Supreme and limited ones, do have some control over the fluctuations of matter, and even though they can hold a formation in shape for sometime, none of them can hold any of these formations in a certain shape forever. Even *Śrī* Krishna, in the discourse with Arjuna stated flatly that the material nature is always changing, on and on endlessly. It cannot be controlled absolutely, either by Him or by anyone else.

Intelligence is manifested and it seems to change according to how shapes mutate. For instance, if a spirit moved from a human body to a cow form, then it will seem as if the spirit's intelligence decreased. Actually the intelligence used remains the same, but the facility for its expression was reduced.

A living being starts out in this creation with a set of psychological tools like sensual energy, mindal space, analytical intellect and a sense of identity. They remain with him for the duration of the creation. They do not change. Usually no one is allowed to change his psychological tools. The living being can show an upgrade in his tools by freeing them from contamination or he can show degradation when they are subjected to contamination. But usually, he remains with the same subtle and causal body for the duration of the creation.

Physically, a man uses the same body during one lifetime, even though by taking alcohol he would manifest vulgar behavior and by restraining from it, he would act respectably.

एवम् अप्य् अङ्ग सर्वेषां
देहिनां देह-योगतः ।
कालावयवतः सन्ति
भावा जन्मादयो ऽसकृत् ॥५.१६॥

evam apy aṅga sarveṣāṁ
dehināṁ deha-yogataḥ
kālāvayavataḥ santi
bhāvā janmādayo 'sakṛt (5.16)

evam — thus; apy = api — even; aṅga — O friend; sarveṣāṁ — of all; dehinām — embodied beings; deha – boby; yogataḥ — by mystic union with; kālāvayavataḥ = kāla — time + avayavatah — by sequence; santi — are; bhāvāḥ — states of existence; janmadayo = janma – birth + ādayaḥ — and the ensuing aspects; 'sakrt = asakrt — repeatedly.

Translation

...thus, even so, O friend, all embodied beings repeatedly endure states of existence like birth and the ensuing aspects, being mystically unified with a body and due to sequences of time. (5.16)

Commentary:

Even if one were to believe that this material world is eternal and that it goes through changes, but actually remains absolute, still then it must be admitted that all embodied beings are repeatedly enduring states of existence like birth of a body, growth of it, disease and death of it. This takes place because the living entities are helplessly subjected to the experiences of these alterations. This is mostly controlled by time and by interactions in the material energy.

तत्रापि कर्मणां कर्तुर्
अस्वातन्त्र्यं च लक्ष्यते ।
भोक्तुश् च दुःख-सुखयोः
को न्व् अर्थो विवशं भजेत् ॥५.१७॥

tatrāpi karmaṇāṁ kartur
asvātantryaṁ ca lakṣyate
bhoktuś ca duḥkha-sukhayoḥ
ko nv artho vivaśaṁ bhajet (5.17)

tatrāpi tatra — there, in this matter + api — even; karmaṇām — of cultural activities; kartur = kartuḥ — he performs; asvātantryam — no independence; ca — and; lakṣyate — is characteristic; bhoktuś = bhoktaḥ — the experiencer; ca — and; duḥkha-sukhayoḥ — of happiness and misery; ko = kaḥ — what; nv = nu — indeed; artho = arthaḥ — benefit; vivaśam — one who is dependent; bhajet — is shared out.

Translation

Even in this matter, the performer of cultural activity and the experiencer of happiness and misery, is characterized by a lack of independence. And what benefit is shared out to one who is dependent? (5.17)

Commentary:

The traditional view which is the materialistic way of life, is nothing to be proud of. In that case there is no independence for a spirit. Everyone is subjected to various compelling forces through his life. He must do this and he must do that, and accordingly, he enjoys or suffers a consequence.

No benefit or dividend is shared out to an infant, because the adults feel that infants cannot properly utilize property. Similarly no share of a profit of a business concern, is given to the ordinary employees who are wage earners, even though the profit is realized on the basis of their labor. And no wealth from a slaving enterprise is given to the slaves, even though they are the basis for success of the enterprise. Thus one should not take material existence for granted. One should not be proud of it, because one functions as its underdog. It is best to take heart, study the situation and try to get away from it.

न देहिनां सुखं किञ्चिद्
विद्यते विदुषाम् अपि ।
तथा च दुःखं मूढानां
वृथाहङ्करणं परम् ॥५.१८॥

na dehināṁ sukhaṁ kiñcid
vidyate viduṣām api
tathā ca duḥkhaṁ mūḍhānāṁ
vṛthāhaṅkaraṇaṁ param (5.18)

na — not; dehinām — of the embodied beings, of the human being; sukham — happiness; kiñcid = kiñcit — sometimes; vidyate — have; viduṣām — of wise men; api — even; tathā — so; ca — and; duḥkham — misery; mūdhānām — of foolish people; vṛthāhankaranaṁ = vṛthā — useless + ahaṅkaraṇam — pride; param — certainly.

Translation

Sometimes, even the wise person has no happiness, and the foolish one is without misery. Thus pride is useless. (5.18)

Commentary:

Pride in the material view of life, the traditional way of cultural dealings, is vain. Even if a man believes that this existence is reasonable, and fair, still he will be frustrated because we see that on occasion, a good person suffers heedlessly. Sometimes, a wicked person enjoys himself fittingly, even though he does nothing constructive for society.

The situation is so contrary, that one should not be proud of it. Many things which transpire make no sense when we think that perhaps there is just one life and that everything should be just and fair.

यदि प्राप्तिं विघातं च
जानन्ति सुख-दुःखयोः ।
ते ऽप्य् अद्धा न विदुर् योगं
मृत्युर् न प्रभवेद् यथा ॥५.१९॥

yadi prāptiṁ vighātaṁ ca
jānanti sukha-duḥkhayoḥ
te 'py addhā na vidur yogaṁ
mṛtyur na prabhaved yathā (5.19)

yadi — if; prāptim — achievement; vighātaṁ — removal; ca — and; jānanti — they know; sukha-duḥkhayoḥ — of happiness and distress; te — they; 'py = api — also; addhā — surely; na — not; vidur = viduh — know; yogam — the yoga technique; mṛtyur = mṛtyuh — death; na — not; prabhaved = prabhavet — could exert power; yathā — as, by which.

Translation

If they know the process of achieving happiness and removing distress, surely they do not know the yoga technique by which death could be made powerless. (5.19)

Commentary:

In the traditional way of developing cultural activities, people focus on achieving happiness and removing distress of the material body. But this is only superficial, for higher than the body is the mind. Higher than the mind and its apparatus, is the spirit.

Instead of focusing on the body, one should find the yoga technique *(yogam),* which would make death an advantage.

को ऽन्व् अर्थः सुखयत्य् एनं
कामो वा मृत्युर् अन्तिके ।
आघातं नीयमानस्य
वध्यस्येव न तुष्टि-दः ॥५.२०॥

ko 'nv arthaḥ sukhayaty enaṁ
kāmo vā mṛtyur antike
āghātaṁ nīyamānasya
vadhyasyeva na tuṣṭi-daḥ (5.20)

ko = kah — what; nv = nu — certainly; arthah — thing; sukhayaty = sukhayati — pleases; enam — this; kāmo = kāmah — enjoyment; vā — or; mṛtyur = mṛtyuḥ — death; antike — near; āghātam — place of execution; nīyamānasya — one who is pulled; vadhyasyeva = vadhyasya — of one who is to be killed + iva — like; na — no; tuṣṭi-daḥ — that which satisfies.

Translation

What thing or enjoyment pleases, when death is near. That which satisfies does not serve the purpose, just as an animal which is pulled to be killed at the place of execution. (5.20)

Commentary:

Whatever we may work for, to build up our cultural status, will become useless in the end. The persons who are related to us for cultural purposes, will all be useless when the time of death comes. It may be argued however, that by contributing services to a particular family, one acquires the merit through which one would take rebirth in that family. But even this argument is useless because no man or woman can guarantee that he or she will get an opportunity to take birth in the family of their present circumstance.

Materialistic life will end in frustration in one way or the other, because the body through which we enjoy that life is itself temporary. And without it, we cannot continue to enjoy in exactly the same way.

श्रुतं च दृष्ट-वद् दुष्टं
स्पर्धासूयात्यय-व्ययैः ।
बह्व्-अन्तराय-कामत्वात्
कृषि-वच् चापि निष्फलम् ॥५.२१॥

śrutaṁ ca dṛṣṭa-vad duṣṭaṁ
spardhāsūyātyaya-vyayaiḥ
bahv-antarāya-kāmatvāt
kṛṣi-vac cāpi niṣphalam (5.21)

śrutam — that which is heard of; ca — and; dṛṣṭa-vad = dṛṣṭa-vat — like what we experience; duṣṭam — is affected; spardhāsūyātyaya = spardhā — by rivalry + asūyā — by envy + atyaya — by destruction; vyayaiḥ — by waste; bahv = bahu — many; antarāya — obstacles; kāmatvāt — desire; kṛṣi-vac = kṛṣi-vat — like farming; cāpi = ca — and + api — even; nisphalam — fruitless, without produce.

Translation

That which is heard of is also affected, just as what we experience presently, is affected by rivalry, envy, destruction and wastage. The desire for it is hampered by obstacles, just as in farming, there may be no produce. (5.21)

Commentary:

The happiness we hear of in religious lectures, is the happiness gained by moving from here to the heavenly places, the Svargaloka places. Even there, the happiness is not consistent, just as presently we hear of how we could life in peace and happiness and due to rivalry, envy, destruction of our bodies and property, and wastage of the same, we are frustrated. It is not just what we plan but what will intercept or frustrate what we aim for. It is just like farming. One may plant seeds or shoots but one does not know if one will live to enjoy the produce, or even if the seedlings or mature trees will survive to fruition. So much of material existence, is left to chance, to nature and supernatural agency.

अन्तरायैर् अविहितो
यदि धर्मः स्व्-अनुष्ठितः ।
तेनापि निर्जित स्थानं
यथा गच्छति तच् छृणु ॥५.२२॥

antarāyair avihito
yadi dharmaḥ sv-anuṣṭhitaḥ
tenāpi nirjitaṁ sthānaṁ
yathā gacchati tac chṛṇu (5.22)

antarāyair = antarāyaiḥ — by obstacles; avihito = avihitah — is not affected; yadi — if; dharmaḥ — righteous duty; sv-anuṣṭhitaḥ = su-anuṣṭhitaḥ — well performed; tenāpi = tena — by that + api — even; nirjitam — attained; sthānam — status; yathā — as, in this way; gacchati — it takes place; tac = tat — that; chṛṇu = śṛṇu — hear.

Translation

If righteous duty is well-performed, and is not affected by obstacles, then what is the result of it? Hear how that takes place. (5.22)

Commentary:

There are cases where a performance of righteous duty was not affected by obstacles. However ultimately, there will be obstacles, because that is the underlying way of operation in material nature.

इष्ट्वेह देवता यज्ञैः
स्वर्-लोकं याति याज्ञिकः ।
भुञ्जीत देव-वत् तत्र
भोगान् दिव्यान् निजार्जितान् ॥५.२३॥

iṣṭveha devatā yajñaiḥ
svar-lokaṁ yāti yājñikaḥ
bhuñjīta deva-vat tatra
bhogān divyān nijārjitān (5.23)

iṣṭveha = iṣṭvā — having worshipped + iha — here on earth; devatā — supernatural rulers; yajñaiḥ — with religious ceremonies and disciplines; svar-lokam — heavenly places; yāti — goes; yājñikaḥ — the sacrificial performers; bhuñjīta — may enjoy; deva-vat — like a god; tatra — there; bhogān

— pleasures; divyān — celestial; nijārjitān = nija — by his endeavor + arjitān — achieved.

Translation

Having worshiped the supernatural rulers, the sacrificial performer goes to a heavenly place. Like a god, he enjoys the celestial pleasures which he achieved by endeavor. (5.23)

Commentary:

Sooner or later, every man or woman gets what was earned, all depending on the force of the endeavor and the assistance rendered by providence. Everything is transpired by the force of attraction to seen or unseen, known or unknown personalities, either consciously or sub-consciously.

स्व-पुण्योपचिते शुभ्रे
विमान उपगीयते ।
गन्धर्वैर् विहरन् मध्ये
देवीनां हृद्य-वेष-धृक् ॥५.२४॥

sva-puṇyopacite śubhre
vimāna upagīyate
gandharvair viharan madhye
devīnāṁ hṛdya-veṣa-dhṛk (5.24)

sva-puṇyopacite = sva — his own + punya — good luck derived from past endeavor + upacite — accumulated; śubhre — glowing; vimāna — in a conveyance; upagīyate — is praised by songs; gandharvair = gandharvaiḥ — by celestial musicians and songsters; viharan — enjoys; madhye — in the midst; devīnām — of celestial women; hṛdya-veṣa-dhṛk = hrdya — beautiful + vesa — clothing + dhṛk — dressed.

Translation

In a glowing flying conveyance, which was acquired by his accumulated good luck derived from past endeavors, he enjoys, being dressed in beautiful clothing, in the midst of celestial women and praised by celestial musicians and songsters. (5.24)

Commentary:

Each person moves about in the material world or in the subtle material heavens on the basis of his good or bad acts. Good acts when accumulated form into a piety, which results in good luck, while bad acts form a force which comes into one's life as bad luck and mishap.

The way of life in the material world conditions a person to *dharma* or righteous living, which is sponsored primarily by the clarifying mode of material nature, but this does not directly lead to liberation. Yogis of worth are not attracted to *dharma*. It is, however, better to perform righteous actions than it is to perform unrighteous ones.

In all respects a human being is conditioned either to do good or bad, or to be indifferent or to strive for liberation from all of material nature's concerns.

A person who acquired a heap of pious activities and who desires to be paid off by heavenly life, gets that sort of living condition after his or her body dies. At that time, suddenly and as if out of nowhere, some celestial persons come in glowing conveyances which move at the speed of one's thinking. They take the person to the world he or she earned. If that person has no companion, then one of the celestials becomes his or her companion for romantic affairs in the deserved heavenly place. Such is the heavenly life.

Many widows of pious men suffer after their husbands depart this earthly life. Subconsciously, they feel that their spouses have gone to heaven in the company of a celestial woman who affords him compatibility and pleasure. And similarly many widowers suffer, in the same way in relation to their departed wives, becoming heartbroken and depressed. Thus formerly there was a habit, whereby the widows entered the funeral pyres of their spouses, in order to pass on from this world at the same time as their beloved husbands.

Even if their bodies perish simultaneously, there is no guarantee that a husband and wife will remain together in the hereafter. Indeed, each of the spirits might slip into totally different dimensions. They might not see each other ever again or they might meet some hundreds or thousands of years after, under circumstances where a re-marriage has no possibility. It is not in all cases that a couple remains together in the afterlife.

स्त्रीभिः कामग-यानेन
किङ्किनी-जाल-मालिना ।
क्रीडन् न वेदात्म-पातं
सुराक्रीडेषु निर्वृतः ॥५.२५॥

strībhiḥ kāmaga-yānena
kiṅkinī-jāla-mālinā
krīḍan na vedātma-pātaṁ
surākrīḍeṣu nirvṛtaḥ (5.25)

strībhiḥ — with women; kāmaga = kāma-ga — going where desired; yānena — by flying conveyance; kiṅkinī – bells; jāla – small symbols; mālinā — trimmed loop; krīdan — sporting; na — not; vedātma-pātaṁ = veda — is aware + ātma — his own + pātam — fall; surākrīḍeṣu = sura — celestial people + ākrīḍeṣu — in the pleasure groves; nirvṛtah — being happy.

Translation

Sporting with the women, going wherever desired by that flying conveyance, which is trimmed with a loop of small cymbals and bells, the person is happy in the pleasure groves of the celestial people, and is not aware of his up-coming fall. (5.25)

Commentary:

Most of the celestial people are permanent residents of the Svargaloka heavenly places. The earthly people who go there on the basis of accumulated righteous acts, stay there only for as long as they are sustained by the force of such acts. Thus when that force is abated, one falls back to the earthly domain, all to one's disappointment. But the impetus sustains one to again try to live in a pious way, through which one would again return to those heavenly places. This manifests in the life of a human being as an inclination towards and an instinct for a righteous life-style.

तावत् स मोदते स्वर्गे
यावत् पुण्यं समाप्यते ।
क्षीण-पुन्यः पतत्य् अर्वाग्
अनिच्छन् काल-चालितः ॥५.२६॥

tāvat sa modate svarge
yāvat puṇyaṁ samāpyate
kṣīṇa-punyaḥ pataty arvāg
anicchan kāla-cālitaḥ (5.26)

tāvat — until; sa = sah — he; modate — enjoys; svarge — in heaven; yāvat — until; puṇyam — his merits of good behavior; samāpyate — are exhausted; kṣīṇa — expiration; puṇyah — his merits which will be converted into good luck; pataty = patati — he falls; arvāg = arvāk — down; anicchan — not wanting; kāla — by time; cālitaḥ — forced.

Translation

He enjoys in heaven until the merits of his good behavior are exhausted. On expiration of that force, he falls away from there, without desiring that, being forced to accept that by the time factor. (5.26)

Commentary:

The plan to live a good righteous life on earth and then to go to heaven or to the kingdom of God, is not a well-considered scheme. Even if one goes to heaven on the basis of good behavior on earth, one will have to return to the earth, when the force of one's good luck is terminated. Even though one would desire to stay in heaven as the celestial people do, one cannot remain there.

यद्य् अधर्म-रतः सङ्गाद्
असतां वाजितेन्द्रियः ।
कामात्मा कृपणो लुब्धः
स्त्रैणो भूत-विहिंसकः ॥५.२७॥

yady adharma-rataḥ saṅgād
asatāṁ vājitendriyaḥ
kāmātmā kṛpaṇo lubdhaḥ
straiṇo bhūta-vihiṁsakaḥ (5.27)

yady = yadi — if; adharma — irresponsible activity; rataḥ — as addicted; saṅgād = saṅgāt — due to company; asatām — wicked people; vājitendriyaḥ = vā — or + ajita — not controlling + indriyaḥ — sensual energy; kāmātmā = kāma — lusty + ātmā — self, nature; krpano = kṛpanaḥ — miserly; lubdhaḥ — greedy; straino = strainaḥ — womanizer; bhūta — creatures; vihiṁsakah — causing injury.

Translation

Or if due to wicked company, he is addicted to irresponsible acts, if he does not control his sensual energy and is lusty by nature, miserly, greed and is a womanizer, or one who causes injury to other creatures, (5.27)

Commentary:

This is part of the description of irresponsible living *(adharma)*. The same person who is responsible in one life, can become irresponsible and reckless in some other life. Sometimes we see that good people turn to bad ways suddenly as if they are forced to act to their detriment.

पशून् अविधिनालभ्य
प्रेत-भूत-गणान् यजन् ।
नरकान् अवशो जन्तुर्
गत्वा यात्य् उल्बण तमः ॥५.२८॥

paśūn avidhinālabhya
preta-bhūta-gaṇān yajan
narakān avaśo jantur
gatvā yāty ulbaṇaṁ tamaḥ (5.28)

paśūn — animals; avidhinālabhya = avidhinā — without scriptural sanction + ālabhya — killing; preta – ghost; bhūta — spirits; gaṇān — groups; yajan — worshipping; narakān —hells; avaśo = avaśaḥ — helpless; jantur = jantuḥ — a human being; gatvā — having gone; yāty = yāti — enters; ulbanam — dreadful; tamaḥ — mental darkness.

Translation

...if without scriptural sanction, he kills animals and worships ghosts and spirits, he goes helplessly to hellish dimensions, and enters dreadful mental darkness. (5.28)

Commentary:

According to a human being's mentality, he is drawn into a certain type of pleasant or unpleasant circumstance. One should control the sensual energy. If one does this, then the reserved energy will empower one to see what is right and what is wrong. It will give one the power to resist.

कर्माणि दुःखोदर्काणि
कुर्वन् देहेन तैः पुनः ।
देहम् आभजते तत्र
किं सुखं मर्त्य-धर्मिणः ॥५..२९॥

karmāṇi duḥkhodarkāṇi
kurvan dehena taiḥ punaḥ
deham ābhajate tatra
kiṁ sukhaṁ martya-dharmiṇaḥ (5.29)

karmāṇi — activities; duhkhodarkāni = duḥkha — misery + udarkāni — resulting; kurvan — doing; dehena — through a body; taiḥ — by those; punah — again; deham — a body; ābhajate — gets; tatra — there; kim — what; sukham — happiness; martya — that which is subject to death; dharminah — those who perform righteous actions.

Translation

Doing through those bodies, activities which result in misery, he again gets another form, there at the same hellish place. What happiness is there for those who perform righteous actions for the sake of bodies which are subjected to death? (5.29)

Commentary:

Even criminals think that they do good. The person who performs an irresponsible act is motivated for betterment just as the person who acts responsibly. Therefore it does not make sense to strive for the sake of the temporary body. One should not live merely for one's body nor for the body of others, since these forms are subjected to death.

लोकानां लोक-पालानां
मद् भय कल्प-जीविनाम् ।
ब्रह्मणो ऽपि भयं मत्तो
द्वि-परार्ध-परायुषः ॥५.३०॥

lokānāṁ loka-pālānāṁ
mad bhayaṁ kalpa-jīvinām
brahmaṇo 'pi bhayaṁ matto
dvi-parārdha-parāyuṣaḥ (5.30)

lokānām — in various dimensions; loka-pālānām — of the rulers of the living places; mad = mat — of me; bhayam — fear; kalpa-jīvinām = kalpa – a celestial day for the Procreator God + jīvinām - for those who live; brahmano = brahmanah — of Brahmā the Procreator; 'pi = api — even; bhayam — afraid; matto = mattah — from Me; dvi – two; parārdha — 100,000,000,000,000,000 human years; parāyusah = para — utmost + āyuṣaḥ — life span.

Translation

The fear of Me is present in the various dimensions and in the rulers of those places, who live for a celestial day of the Procreator God. Even that person, Brahmā, who lives the utmost life span of two time spans of 100,000,000,000,000,000 human years, is afraid of Me. (5.30)

Commentary:

Everything hinges on the minds of greater personalities. We rely on supernatural people, who in turn, rely on the Personality of Godhead. As the time limit, *Śrī* Krishna portrayed Himself as the most feared principle. No matter how long a life one may have, if the body one uses will be subjected to death in the near or distant future, one is not situated in a secure position. The solution is to acquire a spiritual form or to develop or realize one, for that would not be subjected to termination.

The mere fact, that the spirits are eternal, tells us that they have spiritual forms. But the question is left as to why they do not realize eternity.

गुणाः सृजन्ति कर्माणि
गुणो ऽनुसृजते गुणान् ।
जीवस् तु गुण-सयुक्तो
भुङ्क्ते कर्म-फलान्य् असौ ॥५.३१॥

guṇāḥ sṛjanti karmāṇi
guṇo 'nusṛjate guṇān
jīvas tu guṇa-saṁyukto
bhuṅkte karma-phalāny asau (5.31)

gunāḥ — the subtle sensual energies of material nature; sṛjanti — create; karmāṇi — cultural activities; guṇo = guṇaḥ — the mundane influence; 'nusṛjate = anusṛjate — motivate; guṇān — the subtle sensual energies of material nature; jīvas = jīvah — the individual limited spirit; tu — but; guṇa — the mundane influence; saṁyukto = saṁyuktaḥ — mixed up with; bhuṅkte — experiences; karma — action; phalāny = phalāni — consequences; asau — this.

Translation

The subtle sensual energy of material nature created cultural activities. The mundane influence motives the sensual energy. This individual limited spirit, being mixed up with the sensuality, experiences the consequences of actions. (5.31)

Commentary:

Everything in the material world is geared to further cultural activities. Thus it is very difficult to comprehend, much less to get out of the material situation. By predisposition, a limited being acts in a certain way either to advance cultural interest or to curtail it. But none of this adds to his spirituality. To pursue the spiritual path, one should segregate oneself from the sensual energy in one's psyche, since material nature is not just outside but is within the living being, as his sensuality. This process of segregation begins in the fifth stage of yoga, that of *pratyāhar* sensual energy withdrawal.

यावत् स्याद् गुण-वैषम्य
तावन् नानात्वम् आत्मनः ।
नानात्वम् आत्मनो यावत्
पारतन्त्र्यं तदैव हि ॥५.३२॥

yāvat syād guṇa-vaiṣamyaṁ
tāvan nānātvam ātmanaḥ
nānātvam ātmano yāvat
pāratantryaṁ tadaiva hi (5.32)

yāvat — so long; syād = syāt — there is; guṇa — influences of material nature; vaisamyam — diversification; tāvan = tāvat — as there will be; nānātvam — perceptible diverse formations; ātmanaḥ — for the spirit; nānātvam — perceptible diverse formations; ātmano = ātmanaḥ — concerning the spirit; yāvat — so long; pāratantryam — dependence on factors other than what is spiritual; tadaiva = tadā — then will be + eva — only, surely; hi — indeed.

Translation

So long as there is diversification of the influence of material nature, there will be perceptible formations in matter which attract the soul. As long as those formations attract the soul, surely there will be dependence on factors besides what is spiritual. (5.32)

Commentary:

Our conditioning in material nature occurs through innate attraction to her perceptible formation. If we can overcome that, we would be liberated instantly. Our dependence on non-spiritual factors would cease.

यावद् अस्यास्वतन्त्रत्वं
तावद् ईश्वरतो भयम् ।
य एतत् समुपासीरस्
ते मुह्यन्ति शुचार्पिताः ॥५.३३॥

yāvad asyāsvatantratvaṁ
tāvad īśvarato bhayam
ya etat samupāsīraṁs
te muhyanti śucārpitāḥ (5.33)

yāvat — as long; asyāsvatantratvaṁ = asya — of this + asvatantratvam — no independence; tāvad = tāvat — as; īśvarato = īśvaratah — from the Lord; bhayam — fear, apprehension; ya = yah — those who, they; etat — this; samupāsīrams = samupāsīran — being dedicated; te — they; muhyanti — are bewildered; śucārpitāḥ = sucā — in grief + arpitāḥ — smitten.

Translation

So long as there is no independence for this soul, it will have apprehension about the Supreme Lord. Those who are dedicated to the idea of mundane diversity, are bewildered and are smitten with grief. (5.33)

Commentary:

In this case of dependence, it hardly matters if a man is religious or not or as to whether he is a devotee of the very same *Śrī* Krishna or not. If he does not become detached from the material energy by a withdrawal of sensuality from it, he will have no independence. Being a devotee of Krishna is fine, being a yogi devotee is even better, but until one gets the sensual energy withdrawn from material nature, one cannot have full independence.

Apprehension or fear and doubts about the Supreme Lord will persists even in the lives of devotees so long as their sensual energies are not withdrawn from the material energies, as we can observe in the life of Uddhava who was fearful that he would become separated from the special material body of *Śrī* Krishna.

Fear will always be there as long as we are trapped in the material sensual way of perceiving. So long as we remain dedicated to enhancing this material energy for one reason or the other, for good or bad, religious or irreligious purposes, we will have apprehensions about the Supreme Lord, even if we are devotees and even if we deny that we are fearful. Only a total detachment from all forms of the material energy can free us from that anxiety.

काल आत्मागमो लोकः
स्वभावो धर्म एव च ।
इति मां बहुधा प्राहुर्
गुण-व्यतिकरे सति ॥५.३४॥

kāla ātmāgamo lokaḥ
svabhāvo dharma eva ca
iti māṁ bahudhā prāhur
guṇa-vyatikare sati (5.34)

kālā = kālāh — time; ātmāgamo = ātmā — spirit self + āgamaḥ — Vedic scripture; lokah — the habitat; svabhāvo = svabhāvah — inherent nature; dharma = dharmah — righteous duty; eva — indeed; ca — and; iti — thus, is called; mām — me; bahudhā — in many ways; prahur = prahuh — the authoritative sages address; guṇa — influences of material nature; vyatikare — blending; sati — when there is.

Translation

When there is the blending of the influences of material nature, the authoritative sages address Me in various ways as time, the spiritual self, the Vedic scripture, the habitat, the inherent nature and as righteous duty. (5.34)

Commentary:

The blending of the influences of material nature is brought on by an action of the Supreme Being. Thus the authoritative sages, identify Him either directly as the Supreme Person or indirectly as a primal cause. The Supreme Being is represented as time, which regulates what occurs. He is represented by the spirit self which is the highlighted feature in the various life forms. He is indicated by the Vedic scriptures which describe His existence and recommend His worship. He is indicated by the various habitats for living. He can be traced though the series of inherent natures. And He is definitely perceived as the ultimate source of righteous duty, *dharma*.

श्री-उद्धव उवाच
गुणेषु वर्तमानो ऽपि
देह-जेष्व् अनपावृतः ।
गुणैर् न बध्यते देही
बध्यते वा कथ विभो ॥५.३५॥

śrī-uddhava uvāca
guṇeṣu vartamāno 'pi
deha-jeṣv anapāvṛtaḥ
guṇair na badhyate dehī
badhyate vā kathaṁ vibho (5.35)

śrī-uddhava – the worthy Uddhava; uvāca — said; guṇeṣu — in the mundane influences; vartamāno = vartamānah — is mixed up; 'pi = api — since; deha — body; jesv = jesu — spring from; anapāvrtah — being not affected; gunair = gunaih — by the modes of material nature; na — not; badhyate — is bound; dehī — the embodied soul; badhyate — is entrapped; vā — or, alternately; katham — how; vibho — O Almighty Lord.

Translation

The worthy Uddhava said: O Almighty Lord, since the embodied soul is considered to be mixed up in the mundane influence, which comes from the body, how can he not be affected by those moods? And since the alternative view, is that the soul is not bound, then how can it be entrapped thereby? (5.35)

Commentary:

These are two very good questions, asked of the Supreme Lord by Uddhava. If we are subjected to or mixed up with the mundane influence through the avenue of the gross, subtle and causal bodies, which are presently in an inexplicable magical combination, then how would it be possible for any of us to transcend the moods which the admixture produce?

Since also, by the theory of the *Sāṅkhya* philosophy, which *Śrī* Krishna preached, the spirit is never bound in fact, then why does a particular spirit feel entrapped and seeks liberation? Why is it that when a spirit becomes liberated, only that particular one is freed?

कथं वर्तेत विहरेत्
कैर् वा ज्ञायेत लक्षणैः ।
किं भुञ्जीतोत विसृजेच्
छयीतासीत याति वा ॥५.३६॥

kathaṁ varteta viharet
kair vā jñāyeta lakṣaṇaiḥ
kiṁ bhuñjītota visṛjec
chayītāsīta yāti vā (5.36)

katham — how; varteta — he lives; viharet — he enjoys; kair = kaih — by what; vā — or; jñāyeta — could be recognised; lakṣaṇaiḥ — by what characteristics; kim — what; bhuñjītota = bhuñjīta — he would eat + uta — and; visṛjec = visṛjet — would operate his body; chayītāsīta = śayīta — would lie down + āsīta — would sit; yāti — go about; vā — or;

Translation

How does he live and enjoy? By what characteristics can he be recognized? What would he eat? How would he operate the body? How would he lie down, sit or go about? (5.36)

Commentary:

Śrī Uddhava wanted a detailed description of the spirit soul and of how it operates the bodily system which houses it. If one knows the characteristics of the spirit soul, one would remain objective and perceive the actions in a discriminative manner, which tallies with *Śrī* Krishna's views.

एतद् अच्युत मे ब्रूहि
प्रश्नं प्रश्न-विदां वर ।
नित्य-बद्धो नित्य-मुक्त
एक एवेति मे भ्रमः ॥५.३७॥

etad acyuta me brūhi
praśnaṁ praśna-vidāṁ vara
nitya-baddho nitya-mukta
eka eveti me bhramaḥ (5.37)

etad = etat — this; acyuta — O Acyuta; me — to me; brūhi — explain; praśnam — inquiry; praśna – inquire; vidām — of those who know; vara — o best person; nitya-baddho = nitya-baddhaḥ — eternally bound, nitya-mukta = nitya-muktah — eternally freed; eka = ekah — the one, the same; eveti = eva — indeed + iti — thus; me — my; bhramaḥ — uncertainty.

Translation

O Achyuta, best of those who know, explain to me this inquiry. Is the same spirit eternally bound or eternally freed? This is my uncertainty. (5.37)

Commentary:

This is a classic inquiry. It would be necessary in the course of self realization to find out for sure if the spirit is bound and freed repeatedly. If the same spirit may be bound today and then be freed tomorrow, and if this may happen perpetually, then there must be another controlling factor which dictates the application of a binding or a releasing force. Under what terms is a soul freed? Who or what may release it?

CHAPTER 6*

Devotion Offered by Yoga Expertise**

Terri Stokes-Pineda Art

prāyena bhakti-yogena sat-saṅgena vinoddhava
nopāyo vidyate samyak prāyaṇam hi satām aham

O Uddhava, as a general rule, there is no other functional method, except devotion that is offered by yoga expertise, and through the association of the reality-perceptive devotees. Indeed, I am the objective of the reality-perceptive persons. (Uddhava Gītā 6.48)

* Śrīmad Bhāgavatam Canto 11, Chapter 11
** Translator's selected chapter title.

श्री-भगवान् उवाच
बद्धो मुक्त इति व्याख्या
गुणतो मे न वस्तुतः ।
गुणस्य माया-मूलत्वान्
न मे मोक्षो न बन्धनम् ॥ ६.१ ॥

śrī-bhagavān uvāca
baddho mukta iti vyākhyā
guṇato me na vastutaḥ
guṇasya māyā-mūlatvān
na me mokṣo na bandhanam (6.1)

śrī-bhagavān – the Blessed Lord; uvāca — said; baddho = baddhaḥ — bound; mukta = muktah — liberated; iti — thus; vyākhyā — explanation, description; guṇato = guṇataḥ — in reference to the mundane energy; me — my; na — not; vastutaḥ — in fact; guṇasya — of the mundane influence; māyā — bewildering energy; mūlatvān = mūlatvāt — the root cause; na — not; me — my; mokso = moksaḥ — liberation; na — not; bandhanam — bondage.

Translation

The Blessed Lord said: It is described as being bound or freed in reference to the mundane influence. But in fact, there is neither liberation or bondage, since the bewildering energy is the root cause of the mundane influence. For Me, there is neither bondage nor freedom. (6.1)

Commentary:

The application of the bewildering energy causes the limited soul to become bound. Since the Supreme Being is not affected, and since He can see the subtle activity of material nature for what it is, He is neither bound nor freed.

शोक-मोहौ सुख दुःखं
देहापत्तिश् च मायया ।
स्वप्नो यथात्मनः ख्यातिः
ससृतिर् न तु वास्तवी ॥ ६.२ ॥

śoka-mohau sukhaṁ duḥkhaṁ
dehāpattiś ca māyayā
svapno yathātmanaḥ khyātiḥ
saṁsṛtir na tu vāstavī (6.2)

śoka — grief; mohau — and infatuation; sukham — happiness; duḥkham — distress; dehāpattiś = deha — body + āpattih — taking; ca - and; māyayā — due to the bewildering potency; svapno = svapnah — dream; yathātmanaḥ = yathā — just + ātmanaḥ — of the soul; khyātiḥ — imagination; samsṛtir = samsṛtiḥ — cyclic material existence; na — not; tu — indeed; vāstavī — reality.

Translation

Grief, infatuation, happiness, distress and the taking of a body, are due to the bewildering potency. Just as a dream is an imagination of the soul, so material existence is not a reality. (6.2)

Commentary:

A dream which occurs in the mind alone is definitely an imagination within the *buddhi* organ of the subtle body. Such a thing is not real but it can be spell-binding. Similarly, on a cosmic scale, the range of subtle, gross and causal material existence is an imagination of the Supreme Being. And thus it should not be taken too seriously. But this is easier spoken of, than it is realized.

विद्याविद्ये मम तनू
विध्द्य् उद्धव शरीरिणाम् ।
मोक्ष-बन्ध-करी आद्ये
मायया मे विनिर्मिते ॥ ६.३ ॥

vidyāvidye mama tanū
viddhy uddhava śarīriṇām
mokṣa-bandha-karī ādye
māyayā me vinirmite (6.3)

vidyāvidye = vidyā — correct perception of reality + avidye — misinterpretation of reality; mama — my; tanū — potencies; viddhy = viddhi — know; uddhava — Uddhava; śarīriṇām — of the creatures; mokṣa — liberation; bandha — bondage; karī — causing, creating; ādye — primordial;

māyayā — by the bewildering potency; me — my; vinirmite — created.

Translation

Know the correct perception of reality, and the misinterpretation of it, as My potencies, O Uddhava, which cause the liberation and bondage of the creatures. These are primordial, being created by My bewildering potency. (6.3)

Commentary:

Material existence is not such a serious force but we find that even in the religious field, people are spell-bound by it. Just read chapter one of the *Bhagavad-Gītā*, where Arjuna was mixed up and had given statements from scripture in a distorted manner. Arjuna was affected emotionally by the illusory potency.

The immediate cause of bondage is the illusory force, and *Śrī* Krishna, the Supreme Being, is the remote cause. This is because *Śrī* Krishna, by His proximity to the mundane potency, affords it the power to entertain us. Our liberation is caused by both material nature and by the Supreme Being, but the slackening of material nature's bewitchment upon us, occurs when the Supreme Being enthuses us with more of His transcendental energy.

A limited being cannot ever dictate as to whether he will be liberated or not, bound or not, because whenever material nature is allowed to expand, its potency may subdue him all over again.

एकस्यैव ममांशस्य
जीवस्यैव महा-मते ।
बन्धो ऽस्याविद्ययानादिर्
विद्यया च तथेतरः ॥६.४॥

ekasyaiva mamāṁśasya
jīvasyaiva mahā-mate
bandho 'syāvidyayānādir
vidyayā ca tathetaraḥ (6.4)

ekasyaiva = ekasya — of the one soul + eva — certainly; mamāmśasya = mama — my + amśasya — of the partner; jīvasyaiva = jīvasya — of the individual limited spirit + eva — certainly; mahā-mate — o talented one; bandho = bandhah — bondage; 'syāvidyayānādir = asya — of him + avidyayā — by misinterpretation of reality + anādiḥ — without beginning, perpetual; vidyayā — by correct perception of reality; ca — and; tathetarah = tathā — so + itarah — the opposite.

Translation

O talented one, for the one soul, my partner, there is perpetual bondage, caused by the misinterpretation of reality. When there is correct perception, he derives the opposite feature. (6.4)

Commentary:

The limited individual spirit, the partner of the Supreme Lord, was described to Arjuna in some other wording:

mamaivāṁśo jīvaloke jīvabhūtaḥ sanātanaḥ
manaḥṣaṣṭhānīndriyāṇi prakṛtisthāni karṣati

My partner is in this world of individualized conditioned beings. He is an eternal individual soul but he draws to himself the mundane senses of which the mind is the sixth detection device. (B.G. 15.7)

Śrī Krishna very tactfully informed Uddhava that the illusory potency would not be adjusted just for the convenience of people becoming liberated from it. That illusory force will remain the same. However, for those who are serious about liberation, the development of correct perception of reality would free them.

This same idea was expressed later by Lord Buddha about 500 years before the birth of Jesus Christ. Buddha stress the Noble Eightfold Path of which right views or conceptions was one of the eight means.

अथ बद्धस्य मुक्तस्य
वैलक्षण्यं वदामि ते ।
विरुद्ध-धर्मिणोस् तात
स्थितयोर् एक-धर्मिणि ६.५

atha baddhasya muktasya
vailakṣaṇyaṁ vadāmi te
viruddha-dharmiṇos tāta
sthitayor eka-dharmiṇi (6.5)

atha — moreover; baddhasya — of the bound soul; muktasya — of the freed souls; vailaksanyam — characteristics; vadāmi — I speak; te — to you; viruddha — opposite; dharminos = dharminoh — two behavioral tendencies; tāta — my dear; sthitayor = sthitayoh — of two who stay together; eka-dharmiṇi — in one situation.

Translation

Moreover, my dear, I speak to you of the characteristics of the bound and the freed soul, endowed with opposite behavioral tendencies and staying in one situation. (6.5)

Commentary:

The technicality as to why a limited being is bound and why the Supreme Being or an empowered entity, is liberated, is given in this verse. It is due to opposite behavioral tendencies. The Supreme Being and the limited soul have certain attributes which distinguish them. *Śrī* Krishna hinted at this when He lectured Arjuna in chapter four of the *Bhagavad Gītā*:

śrībhagavānuvāca
bahūni me vyatītāni janmāni tava cārjuna
tānyahaṁ veda sarvāṇi na tvaṁ vettha paraṁtapa
ajo'pi sannavyayātmā bhūtānāmīśvaro'pi san
prakṛtiṁ svāmadhiṣṭhāya saṁbhavāmyātmamāyayā

The Blessed Lord said: Many of My births transpired, and yours, Arjuna. I recall them all. You do not remember, O scorcher of the enemies. (4.5)

Even though I am birthless and My person is imperishable, and even though I am the Lord of the creatures, by controlling My material energies, I become visible by My supernatural power. (B.G. 4.5-6)

The Supreme Being not only remembers past births, but He effortlessly controls the material nature, while the limited entities can neither remember on a consistent basis nor control the mundane potency. This is not a fault of the limited spirit. However, something does not have to be one's fault, for it to affect one drastically.

The question remains as to what a limited being can do about this? Will we remain eternally bound? Will we be freed periodically and bound in turn from time to time? Do we have the potential for permanent release? If, as *Śrī* Krishna suggested, it is a matter of acquiring the correct perception of reality, then how can we attain that?

सुपर्णाव् एतौ सदृशौ सखायौ
यदृच्छयैतौ कृत-नीडौ च वृक्षे ।
एकस् तयोः खादति पिप्पलान्नम्
अन्यो निरन्नो ऽपि बलेन भूयान् ॥ ६.६ ॥

suparṇāv etau sadṛśau sakhāyau
yadṛcchayaitau kṛta-nīḍau ca vṛkṣe
ekas tayoḥ khādati pippalānnam
anyo niranno 'pi balena bhūyān (6.6)

suparnāv = suparnau — two birds; etau — these two; sadṛśau — alike; sakhāyau — two friends; yadṛcchayaitau = yadṛcchayā — somehow, by chance + etau — these two; kṛta-nīdau = kṛta — built + nīdau — nest; ca — and; vṛkṣe — in a tree; ekah — one; tayoh — of two; khādati — eats; pippalānnam = pippala — of the peepul tree + annam — fruit; anyo = anyah — other; niranno = nirannah — no fruit; 'pi = api — although; balena — by spiritual power; bhūyān — is superior.

Translation

Somehow, by chance, two birds of similar nature, who are friends, built a nest in a peepul tree. One of the two eats the fruit of the tree, while the other, although he takes

no fruit, is superior by virtue of spiritual power. (6.6)

Commentary:

This is a popular explanation of the difference between the Supreme Person, the *Paramātmā* and the limited person, the *jīvātma* individual spirit. The key to understanding this verse lies in studying the term *yadṛcchayā*, which means somehow or by chance.

Indeed it is by chance, by destiny, that this material world was created in the mind of the Supreme Being, just as by chance an ordinary man dreams. Even though the dreams come about by chance, still they have potency such that the dreamer may become fearful or very happy as a result.

The friendship of the two birds, is another predestined factor. Even though eternally they are friends, still on occasion, the limited bird becomes hostile and non-cooperative to the Infinite bird who is his senior and superior. Even though they were friends from time immemorial, still the limited bird does not have the intelligence to direct the friendship. Yet, it has a tendency to be directive. It gets annoyed at the other bird for not accepting its suggestions. We can study this in the discourse between Arjuna and *Śrī* Krishna in the *Bhagavad-Gītā*.

The Infinite bird does not enjoy anything in this world or as Krishna told Arjuna, He has no need to exploit this world, because there is nothing here that attracts Him in that way. But still, this lack of displaying an exploitive tendency, denotes superiority. The limited bird is confident of its indulgence in material nature.

The fact that both birds build a nest together, indicates that they are eternally in proximity to each other, and that they should work together no matter what. It also tells us that their relationship to material nature is eternal. From time to time, they take shelter in material nature but the limited bird goes a step further by eating the fruits of the tree or by endeavoring for exploitations. This weakens his psychology.

आत्मानम् अन्यं च स वेद विद्वान्
अपिप्पलादो न तु पिप्पलादः ।
यो ऽविद्यया युक् स तु नित्य-बद्धो
विद्या-मयो यः स तु नित्य-मुक्तः ॥६.७॥

ātmānam anyaṁ ca sa veda vidvān
apippalādo na tu pippalādaḥ
yo 'vidyayā yuk sa tu nitya-baddho
vidyā-mayo yaḥ sa tu nitya-muktaḥ (6.7)

ātmānam — the self; anyam — the other; ca — and; sa = sah — he; veda — knows; vidvān — a wise person; apippalādo = a – not + pippala – peepul + adaḥ — eating; na — not; tu — but; pippalādah = pippala – peepul fruit + adah — eating; yo = yah — who; 'vidyayā = avidyayā — with misconception; yuk — full of; sa = sah — he; tu — but; nitya — eternally always; baddho = baddhah — bound; vidyā – real perception; mayo = mayah — consisting of; yah — who; sa = sah — he; tu — but; nitya — always; muktah — liberated.

Translation

The one who does not eat the peepul fruit, knows himself and is wise, but not the one who eats it. The one who is full of misconception is always bound but the one who has real perception is always liberated. (6.7)

Commentary:

Lord Buddha also traced human suffering to craving and participation. For without involvement with the energies of material nature, one cannot suffer or be in bondage.

It is by a reliance on his divine friend, that the limited soul becomes liberated. But it is not a passive reliance. It is an active one with the bound soul taking up disciplines as recommended by the Supreme Person. The soul and the Supersoul are already in proximity as these verses attest. The proximity is there. What is not present is the active reliance and the compliance for austerity.

देह-स्थो ऽपि न देह-स्थो
विद्वान् स्वप्नाद् यथोत्थितः ।
अदेह-स्थो ऽपि देह-स्थः
कुमतिः स्वप्न-दृग् यथा ॥ ६.८॥

deha-stho 'pi na deha-stho
vidvān svapnād yathotthitaḥ
adeha-stho 'pi deha-sthaḥ
kumatiḥ svapna-dṛg yathā (6.8)

deha-stho = deha — body + sthah — situated, living; 'pi = api — even; na — not; deha-stho = deha-sthaḥ — materialistic demeanor based on a gross body; vidvān — a wise person; svapnād = svapnāt — from a dream; yathotthitah = yathā — just as + utthitaḥ — awaken; adeha — not in a body; stho = sthah — situated; 'pi = api — although; deha-sthah — one situated in a body; kumatih — a foolish person; svapna — dream; dṛg = dṛk — experiencing; yathā — just as.

Translation

The wise person, even though in a body, is not materialistic just like being awakened from a dream. But the foolish one, even though not identical with the body, is materialistic, just as experiencing a dream. (6.8)

Commentary:

A certain objectivity is required for spiritual realization, but it must be based on experiences and not only on knowledge given by an authority or heard in a scripture like this. One should experience the self separate from the body.

A foolish human being, you or me, due to not having daily experiences of total separation from the gross body, identifies with that form and feels that it is that form in fact. Actually the identity is separate from the body, because at death, the person and its identity is forced to leave the dead form and move to some other situation in the astral world. The key is to realize this by daily practice before the body dies. By regularly experiencing oneself in the subtle body, separate from the gross one, this realization comes about.

The spirit is distinct from the gross as well as from the subtle or astral body which is used in dreams but still the distinction is realized in degrees beginning with a separation from the gross form. One must first realize himself in the subtle body separate from the gross form. And when that experience is firmly rooted, one should strive for separation from the subtle one.

इन्द्रियैर् इन्द्रियार्थेषु
गुणैर् अपि गुणेषु च ।
गृह्यमाणेष्व् अहं कुर्यान्
न विद्वान् यस् त्व् अविक्रियः ॥ ६.९॥

indriyair indriyārtheṣu
guṇair api guṇeṣu ca
gṛhyamāṇeṣv ahaṁ kuryān
na vidvān yas tv avikriyaḥ (6.9)

indriyair = indriyaiḥ — by the sensual energy; indriyārtheṣu = indriya — of the sensual perception + artheṣu — in the attractive objects; guṇair = guṇaiḥ — by the mundane influence; api — also; guṇeṣu — in the mundane influences; ca — and; gṛhyamāneṣv = gṛhyamāneṣu — identification of, being forcibly attracted by; aham — I; kuryām — should act; na — not; vidvān — a wise man; yas = yah — who; tv = tu — indeed; avikriyaḥ — is not motivated to act.

Translation

When the sense organs perceive the objects and also when the mundane influence detect the mundane energies, a wise man who is not motivated to act, does not think, "I should act." (6.9)

Commentary:

Even though a *vidvān* or wise man, naturally restrains, others are motivated. One cannot do this merely by being a devotee of *Śrī* Krishna, unless he is a learned yogi who mastered the mystic *kriyās*. This is due to the subtleness of the motivating force.

This wise man is restrained because he disarmed his psyche, so that it can no longer push the subtle body to act. When the subtle body is motivated, the gross one follows suit to fulfill desires. Thus if the subtle body is curbed, the gross one can do no harm. On the other hand, external methods of sense control, do not necessarily affect the subtle body. A yogin checks his activities in dreams and in subtle encounters to test to see if his subtle body is compliant with preferred behavior. If it is not, he learns more difficult mystic practices from advanced souls. By applying these, he gains control of the subtle form.

The wise man does not think that he should act when there is a motivation which is not in his interest, because he gained a detachment from his *buddhi* organ's thinking faculty, and because he quieted that thinking organ, disenabling it from urging the body. This is done in higher yoga practice, particularly in the 6th stage of *dhāraṇā* linking of the attention to higher concentration forces. When doing the *dhāraṇā* practice, in the preliminary stage, a yogin must repeatedly wean the thinking faculty away from its attachment to the ideation energy, the *citta*. This is done by relocating the attention repeated to the back right side of the subtle head, to link it with the naad subtle sound which comes into the right subtle ear from the chit *ākāśa*, the sky of consciousness.

This is a big struggle for the yogin because the thinking faculty is very attached to the *citta* ideation energy. By an inbred instinct, it always goes there to activate and expand thought impressions.

Śrī Patañjali alerted all yogis that yoga practice is successful only when the *citta* energy is completely quieted or when the thinking faculty is divorced from the ideation energy, and no longer activates and expands its impression. The state reached when this is accomplished is called *śānti* or peace of mind.

For this instruction to Uddhava, there is a related statement made to Arjuna:

tattvavittu mahābāho guṇakarmavibhāgayoḥ
guṇā guṇeṣu vartanta iti matvā na sajjate

But, O powerful man, having considered that variations of material nature interact with variations of material nature, the reality-perceiving person is not attached to anything. (B.G. 3.28)

When a yogin detached himself from the cultural identity, he no longer is compelled to act on the basis of the motivational force within. The motivational forces, even though they comprise material nature, are subtle. These are converted into a personal psychological energy which is usually mistaken to be the nature of the person. A yogin, by clear mystic perception, frees himself from that energy and loses the confusion regarding what is spirit and what is subtle matter.

दैवाधीने शरीरे ऽस्मिन्
गुण-भाव्येन कर्मणा ।
वर्तमानो ऽबुधस् तत्र
कर्तास्मीति निबध्यते ॥६.१०॥

daivādhīne śarīre 'smin
guṇa-bhāvyena karmaṇā
vartamāno 'budhas tatra
kartāsmīti nibadhyate (6.10)

daivādhīne = daiva — destiny + adhīne — under the influence; śarīre — in the body; 'smin = asmin — in this; guna — mundane influence; bhāvyena — by production; karmanā — by cultural activities; vartamāno = vartamānaḥ — living; 'budhas = abudhah — a foolish person; tatra — there, within the body; kartāsmiti = kartā — doer + asmi — I am + iti — thus; nibadhyate — is implicated.

Translation

Living in this body under the influence of destiny, the foolish person by cultural activities produced by the mundane influence, is implicated by thinking, "I am the doer." (6.10)

Commentary:

It is hardly likely that any of us will be the beneficiaries of any cultural activities we perform. We are so many stooges of the energies which push the cultural formations in these worlds. This does not mean that any man can successfully avoid cultural duties, because Arjuna was unable to sidestep those activities on the battlefield of *Kurukṣetra*. For that matter, some of those activities were endorsed by the Supreme Being, by *Śrī* Krishna, the Central Person in the Universal Form.

However this still does not mean that cultural acts directly lead to freedom from material bondage. In fact they do not. The most we may get out of cultural activities, is a better opportunity in the future for exploitation and for increasing responsibilities.

Since we are motivated, it is stupid to think that we are doers. Still, by psychology, we have to identify the righteous duties as assigned tasks, being pressured to do these willingly or unwillingly by supernatural agency *(daiva).*

People usually criticize a genuine yogi who refuses to act in the cultural world, in the, *I-am-the-doer*, mood. This is because they cannot perceive how the yogi could act without a possessive mentality. There is a related verse in the *Bhagavad-Gītā*:

prakṛteḥ kriyamāṇāni guṇaiḥ karmāṇi sarvaśaḥ
ahaṁkāravimūḍhātmā kartāhamiti manyate

In all cases, actions are performed by variations of the primal mundane energy. But the identity-confused person thinks: "I am the performer." (B.G. 3.27)

एव विरक्तः शयन
आसनाटन-मज्जने ।
दर्शन-स्पर्शन-घ्राण-
भोजन-श्रवणादिषु ॥ ६.११ ॥

evaṁ viraktaḥ śayana
āsanāṭana-majjane
darśana-sparśana-ghrāṇa-
bhojana-śravaṇādiṣu(6.11)

evam — thus; viraktaḥ — detached; śayana = śayane — in lying down; āsanātana = āsana — in sitting + aṭana — in walking; majjane — in bathing; darśana — in seeing; sparśana — in touching; ghrāna — in smelling; bhojana — in eating; śravaṇādiṣu = śravaṇa — in hearing + ādiṣu — and related acts.

Translation

Thus by being detached, in lying down, sitting, walking, bathing, seeing, touching, smelling, eating, hearing and the related acts, (6.11)

Commentary:

This continues into the next verse, which completes the description of how a wise person does or should act.

न तथा बध्यते विद्वान्
तत्र तत्रादयन् गुणान् ।
प्रकृति-स्थो ऽप्य् असंसक्तो
यथा ख सवितानिलः ॥ ६.१२ ॥

na tathā badhyate vidvān
tatra tatrādayan guṇān
prakṛti-stho 'py asaṁsakto
yathā khaṁ savitānilaḥ (6.12)

na — not; tathā — in that way; badhyate — is implicated; vidvān — a wise person; tatra tatrādayan = tatra tatra — there, there, here or there + ādayan - noticing ; guṇān— the sensuous mundane energies; prakṛti-stho = prakṛti-sthaḥ - situated on material energy; 'py = api — even though; asaṁsakto = asaṁsaktaḥ — detached; yatha — as; kham— sky; savitānilaḥ = savitā – sun + anilaḥ — wind.

Translation

...the wise person is not implicated, because in that way, here or there, he notices the sensuous mundane energy. Even though situated in material nature, he is as detached as the sky, sun or wind. (6.12)

Commentary:

This is due to separation from the cultural motivational energy in the psyche of a yogi. An ordinary person cannot separate himself and by his inevitable identification with lower emotions, he is victimized and implicated accordingly.

वैशारद्येक्षयासङ्ग-
शितया छिन्न-सशयः ।
प्रतिबुद्ध इव स्वप्नान्
नानात्वाद् विनिवर्तते ॥६.१३॥

vaiśāradyekṣayāsaṅga-
śitayā chinna-saṁśayaḥ
pratibuddha iva svapnān
nānātvād vinivartate (6.13)

vaiśāradyekṣayāsaṅga-śitayā = vaiśāradyā - by accurate + īkṣayā –perception + asanga — by detachment + śitayā - made keen; chinna – removed; saṁśayaḥ - uncertainty; pratibuddha - awakened; iva — like; svapnān — from a dream; nānātvād = nānātvāt - from the multiplicity; vinivartate - turns away.

Translation

With his uncertainty removed by accurate perception, which is made keen by detachment, he turns away from multiplicity, like one who is awakened from a dream. (6.13)

Commentary:

This is done in higher yoga practice, during the perfection of the 6th stage of *dhāraṇā*, linking of one's attention with higher concentration forces. Usually when one begin to practise *dhāraṇā*, one has to take help from more advanced yogis, who are either physically present or astrally respondent. They instruct one in higher detachment, which concerns losing all interest in the affairs of the world.

The yogin practices this secretly in order to ward off resentments and hostilities which come from relatives, friends and other human beings. Even though he may act in the cultural world, still he practices the higher detachment and that frees his *buddhi* organ from the habit of refocusing into this world.

The yogi switches the *buddhi* to grasp concentration forms which are experienced during *prāṇāyāma* practice. He turns away from the multiple shapes and forms which usually pull his body here and there for fulfillments in this world.

यस्य स्युर् वीत-सङ्कल्पाः
प्राणेन्द्रिय-र्ननो-धियाम् ।
वृत्तयः स विनिर्मुक्तो
देह-स्थो ऽपि हि तद्-गुणैः ॥६.१४॥

yasya syur vīta-saṅkalpāḥ
prāṇendriya-rnano-dhiyām
vṛttayaḥ sa vinirmukto
deha-stho 'pi hi tad-guṇaiḥ (6.14)

yasya — of whom; syur = syuḥ — they are; vīta-saks — free from; saṅkalpāḥ — motivations; prāṇendriya = prāṇa — vital energy + indriya — sense organs; mano = manah — mind; dhiyām — intellect organ in the subtle body; vṛttayaḥ — functions; sa = sah — he; vinirmukto = vinirmuktaḥ — freed; deha-stho = deha-sthah — situated in the body; 'pi = api — though; hi — indeed; tad = tat — of that; guṇaiḥ — from the mundane influence.

Translation

The functions of one whose vital energy, sense organs, mind and intellect, are free of motivations, is indeed free from the mundane influence, even though he is situated in the body. (6.14)

Commentary:

This is the stage of *jīvan-mukta*, or being freed even while having a material body. By practicing kundalini yoga, one masters the life energy (*prāṇa*). When this is achieved one strives to control the sensual energies and the *citta* ideation force. When these are regulated properly, the yogin practicing *buddhi* yoga to control the intellect, which is the brain of the subtle body. When he masters the skill, he becomes a liberated soul.

यस्यात्मा हिंस्यते हिंस्रैर्
येन किञ्चिद् यदृच्छया ।
अर्च्यते वा क्वचित् तत्र
न व्यतिक्रियते बुधः ॥ ६.१५ ॥

yasyātmā hiṁsyate hiṁsrair
yena kiñcid yadṛcchayā
arcyate vā kvacit tatra
na vyatikriyate budhaḥ (6.15)

yasyatma = yasya — of whom + ātmā — the self; himsyate — is harmed; hiṁsrair = hiṁsraiḥ — violent creatures; yena — by someone; kiñcid = kiñcit — somewhat; yadrcchayā — somehow, by chance; arcyate — is worshiped; vā — or; kvacit — somewhere; tatra — there; na — not; vyatikriyate — is affected; budhah — a wise man.

Translation

He who is not affected, when by chance, his body is harmed by violent people or creatures, or when he is worshipped somewhere by someone, is a wise man. (6.15)

Commentary:

When a yogin reaches this stage, he becomes detached even from his own cultural identity, the one that it took many, many millions of years to develop while transmigrating through various life forms. He leaves aside the cultural world, because he took an exemption from it and no longer focuses on it. He is about to return his subtle and causal forms to the reservoirs of subtle and causal bodies, which are in other dimensions and from which those bodies were derived initially.

न स्तुवीत न निन्देत
कुर्वतः साध्व् असाधु वा ।
वदतो गुण-दोषाभ्या
वर्जितः सम-दृङ् मुनिः ॥ ६.१६ ॥

na stuvīta na nindeta
kurvataḥ sādhv asādhu vā
vadato guṇa-doṣābhyāṁ
varjitaḥ sama-dṛṅ muniḥ (6.16)

na – not; stuvīta — praise; na – not; nindeta — criticises; kurvatah — those who work; sadhv = sadhu — nice; asādhu — unpleasant; vā — or; vadato = vadataḥ — those who speak; guṇa –virtue; doṣābhyām — from faults; varjitaḥ — freed; sama-dṛn = sama-dṛk — impartial vision; muniḥ — a yogi philosopher.

Translation

The yogi philosopher with impartial vision, being freed from virtues and faults, should neither praise nor criticise those who perform or speak nicely or unpleasantly. (6.16)

Commentary:

In this, the 6th stage of *dhāraṇā* practice, the yogis gets an instruction from a higher yogi or alternately from one of the goddesses, like *Mā Durgā*, to adopt an attitude of non-interference into material affairs. This causes a great conservation of energies, so that he can perfect the *dhāraṇā* practice and move on to the 7th stage of *dhyāna* effortless linkage of the attention to higher concentration forces.

By interference in cultural activities, a yogi remains bound and does not advance beyond the *pratyāhar* 5th stage of practice. Thus he must, if he is serious, adopt the non-interference posture and stay away from all good or bad cultural affairs.

न कुर्यान् न वदेत् किञ्चिन्
न ध्यायेत् साध्व् असाधु वा ।
आत्मारामो ऽनया वृत्त्या
विचरेज् जड-वन् मुनिः ॥६.१७॥

na kuryān na vadet kiñcin
na dhyāyet sādhv asādhu vā
ātmārāmo 'nayā vṛttyā
vicarej jaḍa-van muniḥ (6.17)

na – not; kuryān = kuryāt — should do; na – not; vadet — should say; kiñcin = kiñcit — anything; na – not; dhyāyet — consider; sādhv = sādhu – good; asādhu – malicious; vā — or; ātmārāmo = ātmārāmaḥ — spiritual pleasure of the self; 'nayā = anayā — with this; vṛttyā — attitude; vicarej = vicaret — should wander; jaḍa-van = jaḍa-vat — like a retarded person; muniḥ — a yogi philosopher.

Translation

The yogi philosopher should neither do, say, nor consider anything as good or bad. Being absorbed in the spiritual pleasure of the self, he should wander with this attitude like a retarded person. (6.17)

Commentary:

It does not matter if anything is really good or bad in the subtle or gross material existence, because regardless it is all insubstantial. Actually it is none of the limited being's concern, as to what happens to this world. A limited being cannot at any stage take on the full responsibility for this existence. He should try to get out of it. That is all.

शब्द-ब्रह्मणि निष्णातो
न निष्णायात् परे यदि ।
श्रमस् तस्य श्रम-फलो
ह्य् अधेनुम् इव रक्षतः ॥६.१८॥

śabda-brahmaṇi niṣṇāto
na niṣṇāyāt pare yadi
śramas tasya śrama-phalo
hy adhenum iva rakṣataḥ (6.18)

śabda-brahmani — in Vedas; niṣṇāto = niṣṇātaḥ — one who is versed; na – not; niṣnāyāt — perceptive; pare — in the supreme reality; yadi — if; śramas = śramaḥ — labor; tasya — his; śrama-phalo = śrama-phalaḥ — result; hy = hi — indeed; adhenum — a cow without milk; iva — just as; rakṣataḥ — one who tends.

Translation

If one who is versed in the Vedas, is not perceptive of the supreme reality, then his labor only, is the result of the exertion, just as one who tends to a cow which has no milk. (6.18)

Commentary:

This description applies to many modern preachers, even many of those who are in disciplic succession, preaching the *Śrīmad Bhagavad-Gītā* and the *Śrīmad Bhāgavatam*. Since the public is satisfied and feels entertained by such preachers, they are quite successful.

One may be versed in the Veda or in the auxiliaries to the Veda, like the *Bhagavad-Gītā* which was taken from the *Mahābhārata* which is called the Fifth Veda or be versed in the *Śrīmad Bhāgavatam* from which this instruction to Uddhava was derived, and still one may not have the mystic and spiritual perception of reality. One may depend on an intellectual grasp with a pretence of devotion. But that is not sufficient for success, even though one might become famous as a pure devotee or as an incarnation of Godhead, or as an empowered somebody.

To be honest, a preacher must strive for spiritual perception of reality. Such perception must be direct and clear just as the perception of this material world is, through the gross body. His subtle body, his causal and spiritual forms must be perceptive of the corresponding realities, apart from the intellectual grasp of what he heard from scripture or from religious authorities. Then and only then is he really qualified to teach anybody.

गा दुग्ध-दोहाम् असतीं च भार्यां
देहं पराधीनम् असत्-प्रजां च ।
वित्तं त्व् अतीर्थी-कृतम् अङ्ग वाचं
हीनां मया रक्षति दुःख-दुःखी ॥६.१९॥

gāṁ dugdha-dohām asatīṁ ca bhāryāṁ
dehaṁ parādhīnam asat-prajāṁ ca
vittaṁ tv atīrthī-kṛtam aṅga vācaṁ
hīnāṁ mayā rakṣati duḥkha-duḥkhī
(6.19)

gām — cow; dugdha — milk; dohām — milked, drawn out; asatīm — disloyal; ca — and; bhāryām — wife; deham — body; parādhīnam = para — others + adhīnam — controlled by; asat — non-productive; prajām — children; ca — and; vittam — wealth; tv = tu — but; atīrthī - not worthy; kṛtam — granted; aṅga — O friend; vācam — speech; hīnām — lacking; mayā — concerning Me; rakṣati — cares for; duḥkha - misery; duḥkhī — one who suffers

Translation

O friend, one who cares for a cow whose milk was drawn out, or for a disloyal wife, or for a body which is controlled by others, or for non-productive children, or for wealth that is granted to an unworthy person, or for speech which lacks references to Me, is a person who suffers misery repeatedly. (6.19)

Commentary:

The point is that one should live in a spiritually-productive way, using the human body for attaining self realization. Otherwise no matter what one does or what one enjoys, it is to be understood that one is actually working in a way that is counterproductive. There are many ways to enjoy life, but many experiences are degrading and frustrating. One should be sensible enough or fortunate enough to avoid these.

By following this conversation between *Śrī* Krishna and the deserving Uddhava, we get some idea of the ideal lifestyle for a sensible human being.

यस्यां न मे पावनम् अङ्ग कर्म
स्थित्य्-उद्भव-प्राण-निरोधम् अस्य ।
लीलावतारेप्सित-जन्म वा स्याद्
वन्ध्यां गिरं तां बिभृयान् न धीरः ॥६.२०॥

yasyāṁ na me pāvanam aṅga karma
sthity-udbhava-prāṇa-nirodham asya
līlāvatārepsita-janma vā syād
vandhyāṁ giraṁ tāṁ bibhṛyān na
dhīraḥ (6.20)

yasyām — in which; na — not; me — My; pāvanam — purifying; aṅga — O dear; *karma* — activity; sthity = sthiti — maintenance; udbhava — origin; prāṇa - vital energy; nirodham — termination; asya — of this; līlāvatārepsita = līlā-avatāra — sportive incarnations + īpsita — cherished; janma — appearance; vā — or; syād = syāt — is; vandhyām — futile; giram — speech; tām — this; bibhṛyān — support; na — not; dhīraḥ— perceptive person.

Translation

My dear, a perceptive person, should not support futile speech in which there is no mention of My activities concerning the maintenance, origin and termination of this world, or those of My cherished appearances, as sportive incarnations. (6.20)

Commentary:

If one becomes preoccupied with the activities of this world, one will lose out in the end and have to take another body haphazardly. The Supreme Lord in His *līlā-avatāras*, His sportive lives in these gross dimensions, exhibits both cultural and spiritual acts for the benefit of the world, to help those in the clarifying mode and those who are beyond that. If one studies these pastimes of the Lord, one will get hints on how to take one's life to a higher level, where one can associate with the Supreme Lord and with superior living entities, who have His association continuously.

एव जिज्ञासयापोह्य
नानात्व-भ्रमम् आत्मनि ।
उपारमेत विरजं
मनो मय्य् अर्प्य सर्व-गे ॥ ६.२१ ॥

evaṁ jijñāsayāpohya
nānātva-bhramam ātmani
upārameta virajaṁ
mano mayy arpya sarva-ge (6.21)

evam — thus; jijñāsayāpohya = jijñāsayā — by thorough inquiry + apohya — removing; nānātva — diversity; bhramam — restlessness; ātmani — in the spirit; upārameta — should cease from social activities; virajam — without impurity; mano = manaḥ — mind; mayy = mayi — in Me, on Me; arpya — focusing; sarva-ge — all pervading.

Translation

Removing in the spirit, the restlessness caused by diversity by thorough inquiry, one should cease from social activities, focusing the mind which is free from impurity, on Me, the all-pervading one. (6.21)

Commentary:

This process has two parts, one of hearing from a realized authority who heard and also experienced, and the other part, being masterful practice of the higher yoga system which gives one the ability to purify the mind and focus it on higher concentration forces or personalities, the highest of which is *Śrī* Krishna Himself in His spiritual form in the sky of consciousness.

If one hears from an authority who states that he is realized but who in fact has only intellectual understanding and faith in the truths, but who has not experienced these, one will not come to the realized state described in this verses. One needs to practice and to master higher yoga, so that the supernatural and spiritual senses will be activated.

यद्य् अनीशो धारयितुं
मनो ब्रह्मणि निश्चलम् ।
मयि सर्वाणि कर्माणि
निरपेक्षः समाचर

yady anīśo dhārayituṁ
mano brahmaṇi niścalam
mayi sarvāṇi karmāṇi
nirapekṣaḥ samācara (6.22)

yady = yadi — if; anīśo = anīśaḥ — unable; dhārayitum — to link the attention to the higher concentration force; mano = manah — the mind; brahmani — on a purely spiritual feature; niścalam — steady; mayi — on Me; sarvāni — all; karmāṇi — activities; nirapekṣaḥ — without desiring results; samācara — perform.

Translation

If you are unable to link your attention to the higher concentration force which has a purely spiritual feature, then perform all activities in relation to Me, without desiring results. (6.22)

Commentary:

This remark was also made to Arjuna. We should know however, that this is in reference to the 6th stage of yoga, that of *dhāraṇā* linking of the attention to a higher concentration force which has a purely spiritual feature *(dhārayitum mano brahmaṇi).*

In the discourse with Arjuna, *Śrī* Krishna recommended:

atha cittaṁ samādhātuṁ na śaknoṣi mayi sthiram
abhyāsayogena tato māmicchāptuṁ dhanaṁjaya
abhyāse'pyasamartho'si matkarmaparamo bhava
madarthamapi karmāṇi kurvansiddhimavāpsyasi

If, however, you cannot steadily anchor your thoughts on Me, then by yoga practice, try to attain Me, O conqueror of wealthy countries.

But if perchance, you are incapable of such practice, then by being absorbed in My work, or even by doing activities for My sake, you will attain perfection. (B.G. 12.9-10)

The problem with the instruction *for dhārayitum mano brahmaṇi*, is the finding of the higher concentration force, which has a purely spiritual feature *(brahmaṇi)*. How does one find such a force within the psyche? Is it something to be found internally by focusing off from this subtle environment into the spiritual sky, the chit *ākāśa*? This is where we must master the higher yoga techniques, the mystic *kriyās*.

श्रद्धालुर् मत्-कथाः शृण्वन्
सु-भद्रा लोक-पावनीः ।
गायन्न् अनुस्मरन् कर्म
जन्म चाभिनयन् मुहुः ॥६.२३॥

śraddhālur mat-kathāḥ śṛṇvan
su-bhadrā loka-pāvanīḥ
gāyann anusmaran karma
janma cābhinayan muhuḥ (6.23)

śraddhālur = śraddhāluh — a person with full faith; mat-kathāh — stories about Me; śṛṇvan — listening; su-bhadrā = su-bhadrāh — very beneficial; loka — world; pāvanīḥ — purity; gāyann = gāyan — singing; anusmaran — remembering again and again; karma — activities; janma — life; cābhinayan = ca — and + abhinayan — acting in theatrical plays; muhuḥ — repeatedly.

Translation

A person with full faith, listening to the stories about Me, which are very beneficial for the purity of the world, singing and remembering My deeds, again and again, repeatedly, acting out My activities and lives in theatrical plays, (6.23)

Commentary:

This verse is completed in the following one. It explains the activities of devotees of *Śrī* Krishna who are ever occupied with His pastimes, which were enacted in this world. Such devotees usually build large temples and encourage the public to come and hear about *Śrī* Krishna. Ascetics also hear about *Śrī* Krishna and also repeatedly consider the activities of the Lord, but they may not do so with large audiences and they may not plan for large gatherings where the pastimes of *Śrī* Krishna are described. However such ascetics should not be subjected to criticism. After all, Uddhava was not instructed by *Śrī* Krishna to go to cities and towns, nor to build large temples and make large missions for preaching. Every devotee is not instructed in exactly the same way. It all depends on what is required for one's personal advancement.

मद्-अर्थे धर्म-कामार्थान्
आचरन् मद्-अपाश्रयः ।
लभते निश्चलां भक्तिं
मय्य् उद्धव सनातने ॥६.२४॥

mad-arthe dharma-kāmārthān
ācaran mad-apāśrayaḥ
labhate niścalāṁ bhaktiṁ
mayy uddhava sanātane (6.24)

mad-arthe = mat-arthe — for my sake; dharma — righteous duty; kāmārthān – sensual activities and business; ācaran — performing; mad-apāśrayaḥ = mat-apāśrayaḥ — relying on Me; labhate — gets; niścalām — steady; bhaktiṁ — devotion; mayy = mayi — in me; uddhava — Uddhava; sanātane — in the Primeval God.

Translation

...performing righteous duty, sensual activities and business for My sake, relying on Me, O Uddhava, that faithful person, gets steady devotion in Me, the Primeval God. (6.24)

Commentary:

A careful study of this verse and the two preceding ones, explains that if a person cannot do yoga in order to intensify his focus on *Śrī* Krishna and whatever is purely spiritual, then he would get steady devotion to *Śrī* Krishna *(niścalām bhaktim),* if he adopts the Krishna Conscious lifestyle. He should engage in Krishna Conscious activities in a temple environment and he must also do *karma* yoga as described in the *Bhagavad Gītā.*

सत्-सङ्ग-लब्धया भक्त्या
मयि मां स उपासिता ।
स वै मे दर्शितं सद्भिर्
अञ्जसा विन्दते पदम् ॥ ६.२५ ॥

sat-saṅga-labdhayā bhaktyā
mayi māṁ sa upāsitā
sa vai me darśitaṁ sadbhir
añjasā vindate padam (6.25)

sat-saṅga — association of the reality perceiving devotees; labdhayā — attaining; bhaktyā — by devotion; mayi — to me; mām — me; sa = sah — he; upāṣitā — worships; sa = sah — he; vai — indeed; me — My; darśitam — revealed; sadbhir = sadbhiḥ — by the reality-perceving devotees; añjasā — easily; vindate — finds; padam — status.

Translation

Attaining devotion to Me by the association of the reality-perceiving devotees, he worships Me. Indeed, he easily realizes My status, as revealed by those devotees. (6.25)

Commentary:

Arjuna got direct revelation *(darśitam).* But here *Śrī* Krishna suggested that it be acquired from his reality-perceiving devotees *(satsaṇga, sadbhir).* Arjuna got *svacakṣusa divyam*, divine and supernatural sight, when *Śrī* Krishna revealed *(darśayāmsa)* the Universal Form and the Four-handed divine form. Please check the Sanskrit carefully since we must understand the difference between those spiritual masters who have the divine vision and those who preach merely on the basis of devotional faith and intellectual absorption:

na tu māṁ śakyase draṣṭum anenaiva svacakṣuṣā
divyaṁ dadāmi te cakṣuḥ paśya me yogamaiśvaram
saṁjaya uvāca
evamuktvā tato rājan mahāyogeśvaro hariḥ
darśayāmāsa pārthāya paramaṁ rūpamaiśvaram

But you cannot see with your vision. I give you supernatural sight to look at My mystic majesty.

Sanjaya said: O King, having said that, the great Master of yoga, Hari, the God Vishnu, revealed to the son of Pṛthā, the Supreme Form, the supernatural glory. *(B.G. 11.8-9)*

An example of a person who got the association of the reality-perceptive devotees, is *Nārada.* Due to that he attained the vision of the spiritual form of *Śrī* Krishna and also attained a spiritual body, thus realizing a status for himself which is similar to the Lord's.

Here *Śrī* Krishna discussed devotion *(bhaktyā),* something that Uddhava kept pushing for, intending to get an easy course for the average human being. The difficulty here is finding a spiritual master like the one who inspired *Nārada.* One cannot get this type of devotion from an advanced devotee who has not mastered higher yoga or one who can not impart the spiritual vision.

श्री-उद्धव उवाच
साधुस् तवोत्तम-श्लोक
मतः कीदृग्-विधः प्रभो ।
भक्तिस् त्वय्य् उपयुज्येत
कीदृशी सद्भिर् आदृता ॥६.२६॥

śrī-uddhava uvāca
sādhus tavottama-śloka
mataḥ kīdṛg-vidhaḥ prabho
bhaktis tvayy upayujyeta
kīdṛśī sadbhir ādṛtā (6.26)

śrī-uddhava – the qualified Uddhava; uvāca — said; sādhus = sādhuḥ — saint; tavottama-śloka = tava — your + uttama – unsurpassed + śloka — glory; mataḥ — view; kīdṛg = kīdṛk –what kind; vidhah — kind; prabho — o lord; bhaktis = bhaktiḥ — devotion; tvayy = tvayi — to you; upayujyeta — is accepted; kīdṛśī — what type; sadbhir = sadbhiḥ — by the reality-perceiving devotees; ādṛtā — approved.

Translation

The qualified Uddhava said: O person of unsurpassed glorification, O Lord, in Your view, what kind of saint is preferred by You? What type of devotion, which is approved by the reality-perceptive devotees, is most acceptable to You? (6.26)

Commentary:

This is a very good question, since so many persons in the disciplic succession claim to give their followers the pure devotion to *Śrī* Krishna, the vision of Him and everything else. Even though Uddhava was most eager for an easy method, still he wanted clarification, so as to clear up the issue of who is qualified to be a spiritual master on behalf of *Śrī* Krishna. What type of devotion, actually gives one the association of Krishna?.

एतन् मे पुरुषाध्यक्ष
लोकाध्यक्ष जगत्-प्रभो ।
प्रणतायानुरक्ताय
प्रपन्नाय च कथ्यताम् ॥६.२७॥

etan me puruṣādhyakṣa
lokādhyakṣa jagat-prabho
praṇatāyānuraktāya
prapannāya ca kathyatām (6.27)

etan = etat — this; me — to me; puruṣādhyakṣa = purusa – person + adhyaksa — supervisor; lokādhyakṣa = loka – world + adhyakṣa — supervisor; jagat-prabho — o lord of the universe; praṇatāyānuraktāya = praṇatāya — prostrated + anuraktāya — one devoted; prapannāya — one who surrenders; ca — and; kathyatam — let it be explained.

Translation

O Lord of people, Lord of the worlds, Lord of the universe, explain this to Me, who am prostrated, who are devoted and who are surrendered to You. (6.27)

Commentary:

Uddhava begs for clarification on the subject of who is a truly qualified spiritual master, and what kind of devotion is the type that gets one the association of *Śrī* Krishna, and the divine status which is similar to the Lord's.

त्व ब्रह्म परम व्योग
पुरुषः प्रकृतेः परः ।
अवतीर्णो ऽसि भगवन्
स्वेच्छोपात्त-पृथग्-वपुः ॥६.२८॥

tvaṁ brahma paramaṁ vyoma
puruṣaḥ prakṛteḥ paraḥ
avatīrno 'si bhagavān
svecchopātta-pṛthag-vapuḥ (6.28)

tvam — you; brahma – spirit; paramam — supreme; vyoma — sky-like; purusaḥ — primal person; prakṛteḥ — to material nature; parah — beyond; avatīrno = avatīrnaḥ — incarnated; 'si = asi — you are; bhagavān — blessed Lord; svecchopātta = sva — your own + icchā — desire + upātta — assumed; prthag = prthak — seperate; vapuḥ — body.

Translation

Blessed Lord, You are the Supreme Spirit, who is like the sky, the Primal Person who is beyond material nature. You incarnated assuming a separate body by Your desire. (6.28)

Commentary:

Śrī Krishna assumed a body in addition to His spiritual Form, but that assumed body was a special supernatural form which was capable of superhuman activities. As stated in the *Bhagavad Gītā*, *Śrī* Krishna comes by His own desire and brings into existence, a special body, which controls material nature.

ajo'pi sannavyayātmā bhūtānāmīśvaro'pi san
prakṛtiṁ svāmadhiṣṭhāya saṁbhavāmyātmamāyayā (4.6)

Even though I am birthless and My person is imperishable, and even though I am the Lord of the creatures, by controlling My material energies, I become visible by My supernatural power. (4.6)

श्री-भगवान् उवाच
कृपालुर् अकृत-द्रोहस्
तितिक्षुः सर्व-देहिनाम् ।
सत्य-सारो ऽनवद्यात्मा
समः सर्वोपकारकः ॥६.२९॥

śrī-bhagavān uvāca
kṛpālur akṛta-drohas
titikṣuḥ sarva-dehinām
satya-sāro 'navadyātmā
samaḥ sarvopakārakaḥ (6.29)

śrī-bhagavān - the Blessed Lord; uvāca — said; kṛpālur = kṛpāluḥ - merciful; akṛta-drohas = akrta —without doing + drohaḥ — malicious; titikṣuḥ —forebearing; sarva-dehinām — to all creatures; satya-sāro = satya sāraḥ —with realism as his essential quality; 'navadyātma = anavadya ātmā - faultless spirit; samaḥ - impartial; sarvopakārakaḥ = sarva-upakārakaḥ — benefactor to all.

Translation

The Blessed Lord said: Being merciful, without tendency for malice, forebearing to all creatures, with realism as his essential quality, a faultless spirit, impartial, a benefactor to all, (6.29)

Commentary:

This begins the listing of the qualities of a reality-perceptive devotee.

कामैर् अहत-धीर् दान्तो
मृदुः शुचिर् अकिञ्चनः ।
अनीहो मित-भुक् शान्तः
स्थिरो मच्-छरणो मुनिः ॥६.३०॥

kāmair ahata-dhīr dānto
mṛduḥ śucir akiñcanaḥ
anīho mita-bhuk śāntaḥ
sthiro mac-charaṇo muniḥ (6.30)

kāmair = kāmaiḥ — with carving; ahata - unaffected; dhīr = dhīḥ - intellect; dānto = dāntaḥ — disciplined; mṛduḥ - mild; śucir = śuciḥ — hygenic; akiñcanaḥ — without possessiveness; anīho = anīhaḥ — without worldy ambition; mita-bhuk - with measured diet; śāntaḥ — pacified in nature; sthiro = sthirah — steady in objectives; mac-charano = mat-śaraṇaḥ - having me as his shelter; muniḥ — yogi philosopher.

Translation

...with the intellect unaffected by cravings, disciplined, mild, hygenic, without possessiveness, without worldly ambition, with measured diet, pacified in nature, steady in objectives, having Me as his shelter, being a yogi philosopher, (6.30)

<u>Commentary:</u>

These are more of the qualities of a reality-perceptive devotee of *Śrī* Krishna.

अप्रमत्तो गभीरात्मा धृतिमाञ् जित-षड्-गुणः । अमानी मान-दः कल्यो मैत्रः कारुणिकः कविः ॥६.३१॥	apramatto gabhīrātmā dhṛtimāñ jita-ṣaḍ-guṇaḥ amānī māna-daḥ kalyo maitraḥ kāruṇikaḥ kaviḥ (6.31)

apramatto = apramattaḥ — ever alert; gabhīrātmā — having a penetrating spirit; dhṛtimān — with fortitude; jita — mastering; ṣad = ṣaṭ — six; gunaḥ - influences; amānī — devoid of desire for fame; māna-dah - having the inclination to honor others; kalyo = kalyaḥ — expert; maitraḥ — friendly; kārunikaḥ — merciful; kaviḥ — learned.

Translation

...being ever alert, having a penetrating spirit, having fortitude, mastering the six influences, being devoid of desire for fame, having inclination to honor others, being expert, friendly, merciful and learned, (6.31)

<u>Commentary:</u>

Swāmī Mādhavānanda gave the six influences as hunger, thirst, grief, infatuation, decay and death.

आज्ञायैवं गुणान् दोषान् मयादिष्टान् अपि स्वकान् । धर्मान् सन्त्यज्य यः सर्वान् मां भजेत स तु सत्तमः ॥६.३२॥	ājñāyaivaṁ guṇān doṣān mayādiṣṭān api svakān dharmān santyajya yaḥ sarvān māṁ bhajeta sa tu sattamaḥ (6.32)

ajñāyaivam = ajñāya — knowing + evam — this; gunāṇ - virtues; doṣān — vices; mayādistān = mayā — by me + ādiṣṭan— sanctioned; api — even; svakān — giving up; dharmān — righteous duty; santyajya — giving up; yaḥ — who; sarvān — all; mām – me; bhajeta — worship; sa = sah — he; tu — indeed; sattamah — best of the reality- perceptive ones.

Translation

...he who, knowing the virtues and vices, gives up righteous duty, even that which was sanctioned by Me, and then worships Me is the best of the reality-perceptive sages. (6.32)

<u>Commentary:</u>

If a devotee is able to get a waiver from cultural activities, then he can really devote himself to *Śrī* Krishna, exclusively leaving aside all else, including his own cultural interest *(svakān dharmān)* and the cultural duties which are to be performed on behalf of *Śrī* Krishna *(mayādiṣṭān)*. Arjuna was not advised in this by *Śrī* Krishna. For Arjuna, Krishna recommended that he gave up his views about cultural activities *(svakān dharmān)* and just do whatever Krishna approved *(mayādiṣṭān)*. But for the greater devotee both types of cultural acts may be given up, provided one has the waiver from *Śrī* Krishna, the Central Person in the Universal Form.

ज्ञात्वाज्ञात्वाथ ये वै मां यावान् यश् चास्मि यादृशः । भजन्त्य् अनन्य-भावेन ते मे भक्ततमा मताः ॥६.३३॥	jñātvājñātvātha ye vai māṁ yāvān yaś cāsmi yādṛśaḥ bhajanty ananya-bhāvena te me bhaktatamā matāḥ (6.33)

jñātvājñātvātha = jñātvā — knowing + ajñātvā — not knowing + atha — thus, then; ye — those; vai

— surely; mām — me; yāvān — how extensive; yas = yah — who; cāsmi = ca — and + asmi — I am, I exist; yādṛśaḥ — how much; bhajanty = bhajanti — they worship; ananya – without anything; bhāvena — with their whole psyche; te — they; me — by me; bhaktatamā = bhaktatamāḥ — best of devotees; matāḥ — considered.

Translation

Those who surely realized or who do not know how extensive I am, or who I am or how I exist and who worship Me with their whole psyche, without focusing on anything else, are considered by Me to be the best of devotees. (6.33)

Commentary:

Śrī Krishna made a surprise pronouncement that if someone who realized Him or even someone who do not know how extensive He is or who He is or how He exist, if that person can worship Him with their whole psyche, their whole being *(bhāvena),* without focusing on anything else *(ananya),* then He considers that person to be the best of the devotees.

Persons of this caliber are like the *gopīs* and *gopas* of *Vṛndavān*. Lord *Śrī* Chaitanya *Mahāprabhu* also exhibited this devotion. Not a word is mentioned here about yoga practice but yogis are not excluded. Persons like *Dhruva*, and *Nārada* who did yoga practice to intensify their *bhakti* or love for Krishna, attain to such a state as being the best of the devotees. But here in this verse, *Śrī* Krishna spoke of *bhajanti* or worshiping Him exclusively with all of one's being *(bhāvena).*

मल्-लिङ्ग-मद्-भक्त-जन-
दर्शन-स्पर्शनार्चनम् ।
परिचर्या स्तुतिः प्रह्व-
गुण-कर्मानुकीर्तनम् ॥६.३४॥

mal-liṅga-mad-bhakta-jana-
darśana-sparśanārcanam
paricaryā stutiḥ prahva-
guṇa-karmānukīrtanam (6.34)

mal-liṅga = mat-liṅga - My Deity Form; mad—bhakta—jana = mat-bhakta-jana — my devotees; darśana — seeing; sparśanārcanam = sparśana – touching + arcanam — worshiping; paricaryā — serving; stutih — praise; prahva — granting obeisances; guṇa — characteristic; karmānukirtanam = karma – deeds + anukīrtanam - glories.

Translation

Seeing, touching, worshiping, serving, praising, granting obeisances to My Deity Form, and to My devotees as well as reciting our characteristics, deeds and glories, (6.34)

Commentary:

This verse and the verses through verse 41, are descriptions of devotional activities which are recommended by *Śrī* Krishna and which may cause a person to offer up his whole psyche to *Śrī* Krishna spontaneously. The idea is for the devotee to keep busy in Krishna consciousness and Krishna related activities by impulsions from within the psyche and by being instructed and inspired by someone who is attached to *Śrī* Krishna and who is trained in these activities.

मत्-कथा-श्रवणे श्रद्धा
मद्-अनुध्यानम् उद्धव ।
सर्व-लाभोपहरणं
दास्येनात्म-निवेदनम् ॥६.३५॥

mat-kathā-śravaṇe śraddhā
mad-anudhyānam uddhava
sarva-lābhopaharaṇaṁ
dāsyenātma-nivedanam (6.35)

mat-katha - stories about Me; śravane — in listening; śraddhā — faith; mad-anudhyanam = mat-anudhyanam - continuous linkage of one's attention to Me; uddhava — Uddhava; sarva — all, everything; lābhopaharanam = lābha — acquired + upaharanam—offering; dāsyenātma = dāsyena — by serving + ātma — se1f; nivedanam — surrender.

Translation

...faith in listening to stories about Me, continuous meditation on Me, O Uddhava, offering everything acquired to Me, and surrendering oneself by serving Me, (6.35)

Commentary:

The continuous meditation is the mastership of the 7th stage of yoga namely *dhyāna (mad-anudhyānam).* This might be done spontaneously in rare cases like that of the *gopīs* and Lord *Śrī* Chaitanya *Mahāprabhu*. Otherwise it has to be developed by yoga practice, as in the cases of *Śrī Nārada* and *Dhruva*. Uddhava will also have to practise this to perfection by yogic methods.

The state of offering everything to *Śrī* Krishna should not be interpreted to mean that *Śrī* Krishna will accept everything offered. All we know is that the devotee will offer everything in his possession, so that *Śrī* Krishna may accept or reject. He may instruct the devotee to use or discard it.

Uddhava for example offered up himself to *Śrī* Krishna, wanting to leave aside his life and body on earth, but *Śrī* Krishna instructed Uddhava to go to Badrinatha for performance of austerities. Because of love for *Śrī* Krishna, Uddhava could not reject what the Lord requested, even though it pained him emotionally. He wanted to stay with *Śrī* Krishna physically and to leave his body at the same time as *Śrī* Krishna would, to go wherever *Śrī* Krishna would travel in the hereafter.

Lord *Śrī* Chaitanya left some good advice, to the effect, that we should offer ourselves to *Śrī* Krishna, so that the Lord could do whatever He desires, including rejecting us. That is the proper understanding of what it is to offer everything to Krishna. One should not offer with a demand even though the *gopīs* did that. Their position is such that they can act in that way with the Lord.

मज्-जन्म-कर्म-कथनं
मम पर्वानुमोदनम् ।
गीत-ताण्डव-वादित्र-
गोष्ठीभिर् मद्-ग्रहोत्सवः ॥६.३६॥

maj-janma-karma-kathanaṁ
mama parvānumodanam
gīta-tāṇḍava-vāditra-
goṣṭhībhir mad-gṛhotsavaḥ (6.36)

maj = mat — me; janma — life; karma — activities; kathanam — narrative; mama — my; parvānumodanam = parva — special aniversary days + anumodanam — much delight; gīta — song; tāṇḍava — dance; vāditra — instrumental music; goṣṭhībhir = goṣṭhībhiḥ — by devotees; mad = mat - my; gṛhotsavaḥ = gṛha — in my ternple + utsavah — festivity.

Translation

...the narration of My lives and activities, observation of My special anniversary days, much delighting in the festivities in My temple, which comprise songs, dancing and instrumental music by devotees, (6.36)

Commentary:

These are descriptions of devotional activities done under the supervision of great devotees of *Śrī* Krishna. From time to time, some great devotees take birth, establish temples and promote Krishna-centered activities. However such great devotees need not contest the yogi devotees who seem to have no interest in these matters which are enacted for the benefit of the public.

One has to understand *Śrī* Krishna to know what a yogi should do as an alternative, if he is permitted and if he has the waiver from cultural activities and from these devotional activities. A yogi who has the permission of the Supreme Lord to complete higher yoga, should not be ridiculed, criticized nor blacklisted by the leading devotees who establish, organize and supervise temple activities. There should be no contest.

Yogi devotees who take to higher yoga, which requires isolation, should stay at a distance from the popular teachers of Krishna Consciousness who promote large-scale temple activities.

This is for peace sake, since generally those preachers are against yoga practice and have a tendency to shun and ridicule it.

Even though Uddhava repeatedly asked for an easy method, still in the end *Śrī* Krishna insisted that Uddhava take up yoga austerities at Badrinatha to get full control of the forces within the psyche and then to transcend these, while shifting himself off to his spiritual form.

There is no evidence in this discourse, nor in the one with Arjuna, that *Śrī* Krishna was against yoga. Somehow many charismatic and forceful preachers, have convinced the vast majority of devotees, that yoga practice is not positively related to Krishna Consciousness. This shows the power of those preachers. They are able to distort the Sanskrit language and translate it with that sort of view which is contrary to what *Śrī* Krishna initially intended.

However since they have the power to do this, a yogi should not tangle with them over the matter. He should instead take care of his cultural activities in a terminal way and with the blessings of *Śrī* Krishna, get a waiver from the same cultural acts and then complete the higher yoga discipline. All this should be done very quietly and secretly, while sidestepping confrontation, condemnation and discouragement from the yoga-hating devotees.

यात्रा बलि-विधानं च
सर्व-वार्षिक-पर्वसु ।
वैदिकी तान्त्रिकी दीक्षा
मदीय-व्रत-धारणम् ॥ ६.३७॥

yātrā bali-vidhānaṁ ca
sarva-vārṣika-parvasu
vaidikī tāntrikī dīkṣā
madīya-vrata-dhāraṇam (6.37)

yātrā = religious processions; bali-vidhānam - making ceremonial offering; ca — and; sarva — all; vārṣika — annual date; parvasu — according to the lunar cycle; vaidikī — Vedic; tāntrikī — ritual texts; dīkṣā — initiation rites; madīya — in My honor; vrata — vows; dhāraṇam — observing.

Translation

...religious processions, and making ceremonial offerings on all annual dates, according to the lunar cycle, initiation rites according to the Vedic and Tantric ritual texts, and observing vows in My honor, (6.37)

Commentary:

These pertain to temple and home worship which is conducted under the guidance of knowledgeable Vaishnava *pujārīs*, ceremonial priests. These activities are conducted with the gross body, but the *pujārīs* are supposed to be mystic yogins who mastered the 6th stage of yoga, namely that of *dhāraṇā* linking of the mind with higher concentration forces or persons.

Nowadays however, the yoga practice is not taught. It is believed to be a waste of time. This feeling is to be regretted. Without yoga there is superficiality in the performance of the rituals. The public being ignorant however, cannot detect the shallowness of the procedures.

ममार्चा-स्थापने श्रद्धा
स्वतः संहत्य चोद्यमः ।
उद्यानोपवनाक्रीड-
पुर-मन्दिर-कर्मणि ॥ ६.३८॥

mamārcā-sthāpane śraddhā
svataḥ saṁhatya codyamaḥ
udyānopavanākrīḍa-
pura-mandira-karmaṇi (6.38)

mamārcā = mama — my + arcā - Deity Form; sthāpane - installing; śraddhā — faith; svataḥ - by oneself; saṁhatya — with others; codyamah = ca — and + udyamaḥ — endeavor; udyanopavanakrida = udyana – gardens + upavana – orchards + ākrīda — play-ground; pura — compound walls; mandira — temples; karmani — in the construction.

Translation

...faith to install My deity Forms, and endeavor by oneself or with others, in the construction of gardens, orchards, play grounds, compound walls and temples, (6.38)

Commentary:

These activities can be carried out by oneself or by one's family or by one's village or community or by one's disciples. In all cases, the leading devotee should have an active part and should not merely be a supervisor. He should have a taste for service to the Lord and as such even menial service would be acceptable to him.

Arjuna had the honor to engage *Śrī* Krishna as a chariot driver, because that was the desire of the Lord to be in a position to advise Arjuna during the battle of *Kurukṣetra*. This served *Śrī* Krishna's purpose as the Central Person in the Universal Form. He wanted to make decisions from incidence to incidence. It was not really for Arjuna's convenience, nor merely because Arjuna was His friend. We hear that when Arjuna found it to be unbearable to fight at *Kurukṣetra*, *Śrī* Krishna scared Arjuna into submission. Of course Arjuna asked to see the Universal Form but he did not ask to be frightened nor to be shown the part of it that was hostile to the Kurus. Yet he was shown that to set the record straight.

Yogis should also engage in temple activities if they live close to the temples but they should not lose focus on the higher yoga practice. If they are harassed by non-yogi devotees, they should move away and go wherever they can practice without interference.

It is best not to argue with missionaries. The best way is to move to a remote place, otherwise, if one is a yogi devotee, the non-yogis will break down one's resolution and cause one to abandon higher yoga, thus forestalling one's spiritual perfection. One should not become annoyed because the non-yogi devotees ridicule. Instead, one should quietly go away from them.

सम्मार्जनोपलेपाभ्यां
सेक-मण्डल-वर्तनैः ।
गृह-शुश्रूषणं मह्यं
दास-वद् यद् अमायया ॥ ६.३९ ॥

sammārjanopalepābhyāṁ
seka-maṇḍala-vartanaiḥ
gṛha-śuśrūṣaṇaṁ mahyaṁ
dāsa-vad yad amāyayā (6.39)

sammārjana = sweeping; upalepābhyam - plantering; seka — watering; maṇḍala — patterns; vartanaiḥ — drawing; gṛha — house of God, temple; śuśrūṣaṇam — custodial care; mahyam — my; dāsa-vad = dāsa vat — like a loyal servant; yad = yat - which; amāyayā - without deceit.

Translation

...by sweeping and plastering, watering and drawing patterns, taking custodial care of My temple, just as a loyal servant would, without deceit, (6.39)

Commentary:

This concerns the ideal attitude of a *pujārī*. Such a person should be a mystic yogi but if he is not, then he should have the higher intuition working in his psyche. He may do his best to communicate with the Deity. Ideally he should be a yogi who is at least at the 6th stage of yoga, that of *dhāraṇā* linking of the attention to the higher concentration forces.

If one gets the opportunity to be a *pujārī*, either by getting a body which was born as the son of a knowledgeable *pujārī* or by being trained, one should realize that one has the mercy of the Supreme Lord. However, one should not be stagnant. One should realize one's short-comings and strive for advancement.

Even though the public assumes that a *pujārī* is a great mystic, that is not always the case. One should be honest with oneself and work to obtain a purified psyche through which one may perceive the spiritual world before the time of death of the body. The definite way to do this is to advance through yoga practice.

If perchance one is in a *sampradāya* disciplic succession, a *guru paramparā* lineage, which is hostile to yoga and which dedicates itself to erasing yoga and the value of it in these dialogues of *Śrī* Krishna with Arjuna and Uddhava, then one should leave such a *sampradāya* and join one which teaches and supports the yoga practice in a way that is consistent with what *Śrī* Krishna taught.

अमानित्वम् अदम्भित्वं
कृतस्यापरिकीर्तनम् ।
अपि दीपावलोकं मे
नोपयुञ्ज्यान् निवेदितम् ॥ ६.४० ॥

amānitvam adambhitvaṁ
kṛtasyāparikīrtanam
api dīpāvalokaṁ me
nopayuñjyān niveditam (6.40)

amānitvam - without pride; adambhitvam - without arrogance; kṛtasyāparikīrtanam = kṛtasya - of deeds; aparikīrtanam - not glorifying; api — also; dīpāvalokaṁ = dīpa – lamps + avalokam - the light; me - to me; nopayuñjyān = na – not + upayuñjyān - should use; niveditam - offered ceremonially.

Translation

...without pride, without arrogance, not glorying one's deeds, not using the light of a lamp which is offered ceremonially to Me. (6.40)

Commentary:

This refers to the attitude required by a *pujārī*. He should have such tendencies innate within him or he should be under the guidance of someone who has such qualities and who trains and reforms him.

A *pujārī* should generally be silent. It is seen sometimes that the *pujārī* is the main preacher at the temple. This is risky. In general preaching, one may be carried away by pride, by being honored and by experiencing increases in one's charismatic or persuasive powers. These are all dangers to the *pujārī*. A *pujārī* should be quiet and should spend his time worshiping and caring for the Deity.

A person who does *pujārī* work and who then leaves it aside or does it partially because he became a temple authority as a preacher or leading singer, will inevitably fall down. His body may become fat. His mind may be greedy for popularity. He may do many acts which are offensive to the spiritual interest and which cause neglect of full attention to the Deities.

There are many devotees who become very popular, after they abandon the *pujārī* services and take up preaching activities, and leading kirtans. These persons are all marching steadily down the road that leads to hell. Most of them do not understand how they are progressing in that direction. It is because they neglected the association of great yogi devotees. They feel that yoga is a waste of time. Such persons talk about going back to Godhead or going to the *Akṣar Dhām* at the time of death and people believe what they say. Since they are able to convince the public, they become even more confident of themselves. They neglect the association of someone who can help them to develop higher yoga, which is the sure way of going to the chit *ākāśa*, the spiritual world.

यद् यद् इष्टतमं लोके
यच् चाति-प्रियम् आत्मनः ।
तत् तन् निवेदयेन् मह्यं
तद् आनन्त्याय कल्पते ॥ ६.४१ ॥

yad yad iṣṭatamaṁ loke
yac cāti-priyam ātmanaḥ
tat tan nivedayen mahyaṁ
tad ānantyāya kalpate (6.41)

yad yad = yat yat - what, what, whatever; iṣṭatamam = ista - + tamam - most desired; loke - in the world; yac = yat -what; cāti-priyam = ca – and + ati-priyam - most dear; atmanah - one self; tat tan = tat tat - that, that indeed; nivedayen = nivedayet - should offer ceremonially; mahyam — to me; tad = tat - that; ānantyāya — eternity; kalpate — produces.

Translation

Whatever is most desired in this world, and what is most dear to the self, that very object should be offered ceremonially to Me. That bestowal produces eternity. (6.41)

Commentary:

It is for this reason that we take up higher yoga practice, because as *Yajñavalka* explained to his wife *Maitreyī*, the most dear object is the self. The self itself is most dear to itself and everything is done selfishly, including those things which are done selflessly.

When one realizes that he is related to everyone else, one begins to act selflessly but that is also a form of selfishness. It cannot be avoided. Therefore in yoga practice, we work hard for purity of the psyche, so that we can offer ourselves in purity to *Śrī* Krishna. That gives us eternity. The thing that is most desired in this world is the vision of the spiritual world. That view must be had by using the eyes of the spiritual body. Everyone hankers for the spiritual form of himself or herself. What is most dear to the self is someone who can be wholly loved by the self. But none of this can be gained without purity. And purity comes through higher yoga practice:

tatraikāgraṁ manaḥ kṛtvā yatacittendriyakriyaḥ
upaviśyāsane yuñjyād yogamātmaviśuddhaye

...being there, seated in a posture, having the mind focused, the person who controls his thinking and sensual energy, should practise the yoga discipline for self-purification. (B.G. 6.12)

सूर्यो ऽग्निर् ब्राह्मणा गावो
वैष्णवः ख मरुज् जलम् ।
भूर् आत्मा सर्व-भूतानि
भद्र पूजा-पदानि मे ॥६.४२॥

sūryo 'gnir brāhmaṇā gāvo
vaiṣṇavaḥ khaṁ maruj jalam
bhūr ātmā sarva-bhūtāni
bhadra pūjā-padāni me (6.42)

sūryo = sūryaḥ — the sun; 'gnir = agniḥ — fire; brāhmaṇā = brāhmaṇāḥ — brahmins; gāvo = gāvaḥ — cows; vaiṣṇavaḥ — devotee of Lord Vishnu; kham — sky; maruj = marut — wind; jalam — water; bhūr = bhūḥ — earth; ātmā — the spiritual self; sarva – all; bhūtāni — beings; bhadra — my good friend; pūjā — worship; padāni — objects, receptables; me — of me.

Translation

The sun, fire, a brahmin, cows, a devotee of Lord Visnnu, the sky, the air, water, the earth, the spiritual self and all beings, O my good friend, are receptables for worship of Me. (6.42)

Commentary:

This is the view of life of those who mastered higher yoga, otherwise one will maintain social prejudices.

सूर्ये तु विद्यया त्रय्या
हविषाग्नौ यजेत माम् ।
आतिथ्येन तु विप्राग्र्ये
गोष्व् अङ्ग यवसादिना ॥६.४३॥

sūrye tu vidyayā trayyā
haviṣāgnau yajeta mām
ātithyena tu viprāgrye
goṣv aṅga yavasādinā (6.43)

sūrye - in the sun; tu - but; vidyayā trayyā — by Vedic hymns; haviṣāgnau = havisā – with oblations of ghee + agnau - fire; yajeta — one should ceremonially worship; mām - me; ātithyena - by hospitality; tu - but; viprāgrye = vipra — of a Brahmin + agrye — in the best; goṣv = goṣu - in cows; anga — dear friend; yavasādina = yavasa — by grass + ādinā — by other appropiate items.

Translation

One should ceremonially worship Me in the sun by reciting Vedic hymns, in the fire with oblations of ghee, in the best of the brahmins by hospitality, and in the cows with grass and other appropiate items, (6.43)

Commentary:

Here we get instructions of how to worship *Śrī* Krishna in particular objects. However when a *pujārī* becomes expert in these procedures, especially in laying out the items recommended in the rules on Deity worship and in sacrifices, and in chanting the relevant mantras, he should not get in the habit of flaunting himself on the public nor putting himself forward as an authority. If he does so, he courts ruination.

वैष्णवे बन्धु-सत्-कृत्या
हृदि खे ध्यान-निष्ठया ।
वायौ मुख्य-धिया तोये
द्रव्यैस् तोय-पुरःसरैः ॥ ६.४४॥

vaiṣṇave bandhu-sat-kṛtyā
hṛdi khe dhyāna-niṣṭhayā
vāyau mukhya-dhiyā toye
dravyais toya-puraḥsaraiḥ (6.44)

vaiṣṇave — in the devotees of Lord Vishnu; bandhu-sat-kṛtyā — by realistic and cordial reception; hṛdi — in the core of his being; khe — in the sky; dhyāna — by effortless linkage of the attention to the higher concentration force; nisthayā — by constant, regular; vāyau — in the air; mukhya — chief sustainer of the body; dhiyā — by considering; toye — in water; dravyais = dravyaiḥ — by things; toya – water; puraḥ - by presenting; saraiḥ — with water.

Translation

...in the devotee of Lord Vishnu by realistic and cordial reception, in the sky of the core of being by regular effortless linkage of the attention to the higher concentration forces, in the air by considering it as the chief sustainer of the body, in water by presenting things such as water, (6.44)

Commentary:

These are the methods for worshiping and recognizing *Śrī* Krishna in the particular items. Many of these practices can only be done by mystic actions, by *kriyās*.

स्थण्डिले मन्त्र-हृदयैर्
भोगैर् आत्मानम् आत्मनि ।
क्षेत्र-ज्ञं सर्व-भूतेषु
समत्वेन यजेत माम् ॥ ६.४५॥

sthaṇḍile mantra-hṛdayair
bhogair ātmānam ātmani
kṣetra-jñaṁ sarva-bhūteṣu
samatvena yajeta mām (6.45)

sthaṇḍile — in consecrated ground; mantra – ritual sounds; hṛdayair = hṛdayaiḥ — with secrecy; bhogair = bhogaiḥ — by wholesome experiences; ātmānaṁ — the soul; ātmani — within the psyche; kṣetra-jñam — the experience of the psyche; sarva-bhūteṣu — within all beings; samatvena — with a comparatively similar view; yajeta — should worship; mām — me.

Translation

...in the consecrated ground with secret ritual sounds, in the psyche one should worship the soul by offering wholesome experiences and in all beings with a comparatively similar view, one should worship Me as the experiencer of the psyche. (6.45)

Commentary:

The comparatively similar view is explained elsewhere in this discourse and in the *Bhagavad Gītā* conversation with Arjuna. One has to develop mystic perception to see that each of the spirits using a body is harnessed in that form to a set of psychological equipments like sensual energy, private mind compartment, *buddhi* organ and a sense of identity. Each spirit takes help from the Supreme Being and from His agents. That is the comparatively similar view regarding all beings. One should worship the self within by offering experiences which would not endanger it nor cause it to become a slave to vices.

धिष्ण्येष्व् इत्य् एषु मद्-रूपं
शङ्ख-चक्र-गदाम्बुजैः ।
युक्तं चतुर्-भुजं शान्तं
ध्यायन्न् अर्चेत् समाहितः ॥ ६.४६ ॥

dhiṣṇyeṣv ity eṣu mad-rūpaṁ
śaṅkha-cakra-gadāmbujaiḥ
yuktaṁ catur-bhujaṁ śāntaṁ
dhyāyann arcet samāhitaḥ (6.46)

dhiṣṇyesv = dhiṣṇyesu — in these locations; ity = iti — thus stated; eṣu — in these; mad-rūpam = mat-rūpam — my form; śaṅkha — conch; cakra — disc; gadāmbujaiḥ = gadā — club + ambujaiḥ — with the lotus flower; yuktam — having; catur-bhujam = catuh-bhujam — four arms; śāntam — peaceful; dhyāyann = dhyāyan — one should link the attention to the higher concentration force; arcet — should worship; samāhitah — with effortless continuous linkage of the attention to the higher concentration force.

Translation

In these locations, one should link the attention to My peaceful form having four arms, with conch, disc, club and lotus flower. One should worship with effortless and continuous linkage of the attention to My form as described. (6.46)

Commentary:

This is mostly higher yoga, consisting of the 7th stage of *dhyāna* and the 8th stage of *samādhi* practice. This refers to reaching the spiritual forms of Lord Krishna in the chit *ākāśa*, the sky of consciousness.

Admittedly, one or two non-yogi devotees may do *dhyāna* meditation and *samādhi* fixation on *Śrī* Krishna's Deity Form in the temple or preferably on His spiritual Form in the spiritual world, but only a few people out of thousands of devotees can do this. Lord *Śrī* Chaitanya did this. The *gopīs* did, perfectly and continuously, reach *Śrī* Krishna.

इष्टा-पूर्तेन माम् एवं
यो यजेत समाहितः ।
लभते मयि सद्-भक्तिं
मत्-स्मृतिः साधु-सेवया ॥ ६.४७॥

iṣṭā-pūrtena mām evaṁ
yo yajeta samāhitaḥ
labhate mayi sad-bhaktiṁ
mat-smṛtiḥ sādhu-sevayā (6.47)

iṣṭa — self motivated sacrificial ceremonies; pūrtena — by constructing religious and socially-beneficial facilities; mām — me; evam — thus, as stated; yo = yah — who; yajeta — worships; samāhitaḥ — with effortless and continuous linkage of one's attention to a higher concentration force; labhate — gets; mayi — in me; sad-bhaktim = sat-bhaktim — purely spiritual devotion; mat-smṛtiḥ — rememberance of me; sādhu — elevated soul; sevayā — by service.

Translation

He who worships Me by effortless and continuous linkage of his attention to My spiritual form, as stated, with sacrificial ceremonies or by conducting religiously and socially-beneficial facilities, gets pure spiritual devotion to Me. The ability to remember Me, is obtained by service to elevated souls. (6.47)

Commentary:

The ability to remember *Śrī* Krishna comes directly by the contact with an elevated soul who is a great and pure devotee of the Lord. It cannot be otherwise. This is how the remembrance of *Śrī* Krishna, is distributed. Pure spiritual devotion to *Śrī* Krishna comes from the effortless and continuous linkage to His four-handed spiritual forms as described.

Even though one may worship the two-handed physical deity form of *Śrī* Krishna, as Govinda or as *Śyāmasundara*, or as the *Śrī Śrī* Radha Krishna Murtis, still when one takes to higher yoga, one will have to go step by step, first approaching the four-handed form in the spiritual sky (verse 46).

It is totally incorrect to hold the view that since one worships the beautiful two-handed *Mūrti* of *Śrī* Krishna in the temple, one will go to Him at the time of death without having to approach the four-handed form. Arjuna requested to see the four-handed form. That was not a fault in Arjuna. It is very appropriate to understand that first we will see the four-handed form. For some of us He will be our worshippable deity, even if we worshipped the two-handed Deity form in the temple. These details are revealed to the devotee as he progresses.

प्रायेण भक्ति-योगेन
सत्-सङ्गेन विनोद्धव ।
नोपायो विद्यते सम्यक्
प्रायणं हि सताम् अहम् ॥ ६.४८ ॥

prāyeṇa bhakti-yogena
sat-saṅgena vinoddhava
nopāyo vidyate samyak
prāyaṇaṁ hi satām aham (6.48)

prāyeṇa — as a general rule; bhakti-yogena — the devotion offered with yoga expertise; sat-saṅgena — by association with the reality perceptive devotees; vinoddhava = vinā — without + uddhava — Uddhava; nopāyo = na — not + upāyah — method; vidyate — there is; samyak — functional; prāyaṇam — the objective; hi — indeed; satām — of the reality-perceptive person; aham — I.

Translation

O Uddhava, as a general rule, there is no other functional method, except devotion that is offered by yoga expertise, and through the association of the reality-perceptive devotees. Indeed, I am the objective of the reality-perceptive persons. (6.48)

Commentary:

This is the only method of attaining perfection in terms of Krishna Consciousness. It does include yoga and the most advanced devotees are those who mastered yoga. Nowadays *bhakti* yoga is being defined as regulated *bhakti* or devotional relationship to *Śrī* Krishna which is regulated by prescribed services rendered by the advice of a leading devotee. Usually such leading devotees do not practice and do ridicule yoga at every opportunity. But in the time of *Śrī* Krishna, *bhakti* was *bhakti* and *bhakti* yoga was *bhakti* with yoga. Then the terms *bhakti* and *bhakti* yoga were not interchangeable.

Let us look at two verses from the dialogue with Arjuna:

tapasvibhyo'dhiko yogī jñānibhyo'pi mato'dhikaḥ
karmibhyaścādhiko yogī tasmādyogī bhavārjuna
yogināmapi sarveṣāṁ madgatenāntarātmanā
śraddhāvānbhajate yo māṁ sa me yuktatamo mataḥ

The yogi is superior to other types of ascetics; he is also considered to be superior to the masters of philosophical theory, and the yogi is better than the ritual performers. Hence, be a yogi, Arjuna.

Of all yogis, the one who is attracted to Me with his soul, who worships Me with full faith, is regarded as being most devoted to Me. (B.G. 6.46-47)

अथैतत् परमं गुह्यं
शृण्वतो यदु-नन्दन ।
सु-गोप्यम् अपि वक्ष्यामि
त्वं मे भृत्यः सुहृत् सखा ॥६.४९॥

athaitat paramaṁ guhyaṁ
śṛṇvato yadu-nandana
su-gopyam api vakṣyāmi
tvaṁ me bhṛtyaḥ suhṛt sakhā (6.49)

athaitat = atha — thus + etat — this; paramam — supreme; guhyam — secret; śṛṇvato = śṛṇvataḥ — one who is attentive; yadu-nandana — dear son of the Yadu family; su-gopyam — most private; api — even though; vakṣyāmi — I will tell; tvam — you; me — my; bhṛtyah — servant; suhṛt — companion; sakhā — friend.

Translation

Now I will tell you, O attentive one, the supreme secret, even though it is most private, for you are my servant, companion and friend. (6.49)

Commentary:

Such a dear relation with Uddhava and Arjuna, was affirmed by the Supreme Person.

CHAPTER 7*

Association of the Reality-Perceptive Persons**

Terri Stokes-Pineda Art

sat-saṅgena hi daiteyā yātudhānā mṛgāḥ khagāḥ
gandharvāpsaraso nāgāḥ siddhāś cāraṇa-guhyakāḥ
bahavo mat-padaṁ prāptās tvāṣṭra-kāyādhavādayaḥ

Indeed by the association of the reality-perceptive persons, some sons of Diti, some predominately evil persons, the animals, the birds, the celestial musicians, the angelic women, the snakes, the perfected yogis, the celestial singers,... the son of Tvastri, the son of Kayadhu and many others achieved My abode. (Uddhava Gītā 7.3,5)

* Śrīmad Bhāgavatam Canto 11, Chapter 12

** Translator's selected chapter title.

श्री-भगवान् उवाच
न रोधयति मां योगो
न साङ्ख्यं धर्म एव च ।
न स्वाध्यायस् तपस् त्यागो
नेष्टा-पूर्तं न दक्षिणा ॥७.१॥

śrī-bhagavān uvāca
na rodhayati māṁ yogo
na sāṅkhyaṁ dharma eva ca
na svādhyāyas tapas tyāgo
neṣṭā-pūrtaṁ na dakṣiṇā (7.1)

śrī-bhagavān – the Blessed Lord; uvāca — said; na – neither; rodhayati — forcibly attracks; mām — me; yogo = yogaḥ — yoga discipline; na — nor; sāṅkhyam = Sāṅkhya — analysis; dharmah — righteous duty; eva — indeed; ca — and; na — nor; svādhyāyas = svādhyāyaḥ — study of the Vedas; tapas = tapah — penances; tyāgo = tyāgah — disclaiming the results of one's actions; neṣṭā-pūrtaṁ = na — nor + iṣṭā – endearing worship, sacred mood + pūrtam — sincere act of piety (neṣṭā-pūrtaṁ = nor sincere ceremonial worship and construction of religious and social facilities with related services); na — nor; dakṣiṇā — charity.

Translation

The Blessed Lord said: Neither of these attracts Me, neither yoga discipline, Sāṅkhya analysis, religious duty nor the study of the Vedas, nor penances, nor the disclaiming of the results of one's activities, nor sincere ceremonial worship and the construction of religious and social facilities with related services, nor even charity, (7.1)

Commentary:

Śrī Krishna began a listing of those disciplines performed by pious human beings which do not really attract Him as much as the association of the reality-perceptive persons. He began the listing with an emphatic denial of any of the disciplines. In the next verse, He makes it clear that when compared to the association of the reality-perceptive persons, these activities are not as forceful in attracting Him. This means that any of these aspects might attract His attention but they would not do so as strongly as the divine association with the great souls who are perceptive of reality, of *sat*.

Sat-saṅga has come to mean the company of saintly persons, especially persons who lead religious groups, temples, *sampradāyas*, *maths* and the like, regardless of whether these persons have supernatural and spiritual perception. But actually the meaning in the time of Uddhava was the perception of *sat, spiritual reality,* by mystic and spiritual means. Let us go over the listing of the disciplines which are not so effective in attracting *Śrī* Krishna:

Yogo (yogah)

This is the *aṣṭanga* yoga process. This process is designed to yield purification of the psyche, which does not necessarily result in attraction to *Śrī* Krishna. It would all depend on one's spiritual category. If one succeeds at yoga, his psyche will be upgraded. He will realize his spiritual category. He might be directly connected to *Śrī* Krishna or he might not be, all depending on the group of spirits he is eternally aligned to. The purpose of yoga is given by *Śrī* Krishna in the *Bhagavad-Gītā* as soul or spirit purification, *ātmaviśuddhaye*. (B.*G*. 6.12)

Yoga like any other discipline, results in a specific benefit. If one knows the purpose one can complete a discipline thoroughly and get the benefit. But if one does a discipline with some other purpose in mind, something besides its purpose, one will inefficiently use that austerity and come to ruin and complexity.

Even though yoga is not especially meant to attract the Supreme Personality, it is related to that attraction. When one's psyche is purified, one begins to see the subtle beings, the *devas* and *siddhas*, the perfected yogis. One begins to see the supernatural persons who govern the Universal Form. One begins to see the divine beings like the Personalities of Godhead. Yoga is related since it takes one to the edge of higher association, the very same aspect which *Śrī* Krishna is attracted to. But yoga is not that aspect. We must be clear on this point.

Sāṅkhya analysis

Sāṅkhya is the high class philosophy which was described initially by Lord Kapila, the son of *Kardama* and *Devahūti*. Initially this philosophy was used as a text for guidance when doing mystic research by yogic techniques. Recently the yoga aspect was removed and the mere theoretical study of this philosophy with its detailed explanation of creation, evolution and dissolution, has come to be called *sāṅkhya* . We must put behind us the modern definition and adopt the initial one from the time of *Śrī* Krishna.

This sāṅkhya is another aspect which brings one closer to divine association but it does not do the job as well as yoga, in which the theory of sāṅkhya is realized in fact.

Dharma or righteous duty

Dharma is righteous duty. This is done under the auspices of the Universal Form of *Śrī* Krishna. Even though the Form sanctions it, *dharma* or righteous duty is not so accommodating to the association of the reality-perceptive persons. This is because righteous living is usually focused into the material world for lubrication of the frictional social relationships which occur here.

Dharma does attract *Śrī* Krishna but only as He functions as the Central Person in the Universal Form. To understand this one has to read the eleventh chapter of the *Bhagavad-Gītā* about the revelation given to Arjuna. *Śrī* Krishna as that Central Person has a different interest, to Himself as the Person who addressed *Śrī* Uddhava. In the revelation, Arjuna saw the Supernatural Universal Form and the divine four-handed Form, in turn. That four-handed Form has the interest of the *Śrī* Krishna who spoke to Uddhava. He has no interest in *dharma* or social righteous lifestyle in the material world.

Svādhyāyas or study of the Vedas

This study of the Vedas used to be tantamount to spiritual practice. It was done by recitation of Vedic verses. Nowadays it is broadened in scope to include scriptures which are supportive of the Vedic version, which are more in tune with our times and which are explanatory of the methods of salvation, which were explored after the Vedic era. From such study comes intellectual realization and from that comes the desire for supernatural and spiritual experience. Just as a person develops a desire to travel to a foreign country after reading of such a place, so one develops a desire for higher perception after hearing of higher dimensions in the Vedic literatures. Indirectly, the reading of scriptures is related to spiritual experiences and to the association of the Supreme Person.

Tapas or penances

These are the penances which are hinted at or stipulated in scripture. One hears of these and tries to practice them to the best of one's ability, hoping for a set result which was described in scripture. Since the usual purpose of such a penance is to get a certain result, these penances are not really geared to attracting the divine *Śrī* Krishna. Usually these are performed haphazardly, by persons who are not ascetic, but who want to get the same result attained by ascetics who practice long-ranged austerities.

Tyāgo (tyāgah), disclaiming the results of actions

The purpose of disclaiming consequences is to avoid and deter future complications. It is a tactic for side-stepping haphazard transmigrations in the course of material existence, and to develop the ability to phase out one's participation in the mundane histories.

When working in *dharma* righteous living under the rules of *karma* yoga, as they are enacted in the *Bhagavad-Gītā*, one is supposed to always disclaim the result of actions. In fact, *Śrī* Krishna insisted that Arjuna act as a *tyāgi* during the battle, as a person who was continually disclaiming the benefits of his activities, regardless of whether those compensations were appealing or reprehensible.

Even though it was advised by *Śrī* Krishna as a behavioral stance, as an indifference to consequences, still it does not attract the divine Krishna, because the purpose of it is to sidestep complications of destiny. It has its use for civilized living, but it is not designed specifically for attracting Him.

Iṣṭā-pūrtam or sincere ceremonial worship and the construction of religious and social facilities

This is designed to ease off our need for recognition as God-fearing pious people. That need is there in the psyche. Such worship, even if directed to the Supreme Person, to *Śrī* Krishna, or to one of His parallel divinities or agents, does not really attract *Śrī* Krishna, because it springs from our need for being recognized as devotees or as good religious people. It is more of a fulfillment of that need than it is anything else.

Dakṣiṇā or charity

Charity is defined in the *Bhagavad-Gītā*, where it is characterized according to the energy of the giver at the time of the donation. Even when it is offered from the clarifying mode it is not designed to attract the divine Krishna. The purpose is to shed off excess. One cannot give what he does not have or what he was not given. Charity concerns giving excess items or energies. It is good but it does not attract the divine *Śrī* Krishna. He does not need anything that we might possess in the mundane creations.

Even though *Śrī* Krishna is emphatic that these aspects do not attract Him, one should use these when they are appropriate. *Śrī* Krishna stressed these aspects elsewhere for other purposes. It is just that we should know what practice gives what effects. We should not mistake one practice for another or become frustrated by misapplication of one for another. We must be sensible in that regard.

व्रतानि यज्ञश् छन्दांसि
तीर्थानि नियमा यमाः ।
यथावरुन्धे सत्-सङ्गः
सर्व-सङ्गापहो हि माम् ॥७.२॥

vratāni yajñaś chandāṁsi
tīrthāni niyamā yamāḥ
yathāvarundhe sat-saṅgaḥ
sarva-saṅgāpaho hi mām (7.2)

vratāni — observation of vows; yajñaś = yajñah — sacrificial ceremonies and disciplines; chandāmśi — secretive ritual hymns; tīrthāni — making pilgrimage to shrines; niyamā = niyamāḥ — behavioral advisories; yamāḥ — moral restraints; yathāvarudhe = yathā — as well as + avarundhe — attracts attention; sat-saṅgah = sat— reality perceptive persons + sangaḥ - association; sarva-saṅgāpaho = sarva-saṅgāpahaḥ = sarva — all + saṅga — impulsive social attachment + apahah — removing; hi — indeed; mām — me.

Translation

...observation of vows, sacrificial ceremonies and disciplines, secretive ritual hymns, shrines, moral restraints, as well as behavioral advisories. These do not attract My attention as much as the association of the reality-perceptive persons, which removes all impulsive social attachment. (7.2)

Commentary:

Vratāni or the observation of vows

Vows are usually done in an haphazard way but with such confidence, that the observer thinks that what his vows will be fruitful. He feel that he makes a big sacrifice. This is because many pandits or priests, give audiences, the idea that they can follow what a great soul did to achieve a particular result. Besides this, certain stimulating statements in the scriptures, cause a person to perform penances and to take vows but without having to do everything that a great soul did in some past era, to achieve the particular aim. When one follows these rulings, one does not get the result that the great person achieved. One becomes frustrated instead. To cover the frustration, one borrows confidence from deceptive-faith-wielding priests.

The idea behind the observance of vows is to ease off certain difficulties, either ones encountered in this world or in the next. When it pertains in this world, it has to confirm the needs of the performer or his living family members, and when it pertains to the next world, it is usually because the performer is in doubt about the destination attained by his ancestors in the hereafter. As such, the vows cannot attract Lord Krishna.

Besides this common usage of vows, there are specific usages for fasting and other observances on the appearance and memorial days of Deities and religious figure-heads, and for regular fasting on days like *ekādaśī* and *dvādaśī* or on new moon and full moon day or eclipses. There are supposed to be done selflessly without expecting rewards. We find however that some observers are expectant of benefits. That is due to the reward-desiring nature of a human being. Such is that stubborn trait.

Yajñaś or sacrificial ceremonies and disciplines

These disciplines serve the purpose of giving facility for worship on the material level. It is for the purpose of covering over our lack of supernatural and spiritual perception, so that we can go on relating to God and to the supernatural people without having to see them directly in their supernatural and divine forms. To substantiate this, certain spiritual masters boldly declare that the deity form is actually a spiritual form and that it is not made of anything material. Some devotees accept such statements verbatim and deny their own gross sense perception for what it is. They emphatically declare that the Deity forms in marble, metal or paint is a spiritual form.

Sometimes there is no deity form. Then the performer accepts the ceremony as a definite way of reaching the divine personages. However, usually behind all this, is a motive for relief from material complexities, circumstances which are hurled into the human plane by an unalterable destiny. This is not for the purpose of reaching the divine *Śrī* Krishna for His own purposes, but rather to get His aid in buffering off unfavorable circumstances.

Chandāmsi or secretive ritual hymns

The secretive ritual hymns are still regarded as confidential words which are to be repeated by someone who is duty initiated. However, the effects of these mantras are not the same today as it is described in the Vedic history. Nowadays, one cannot pronounce such mantras and produce the physical or supernatural effects which the ancient yogis and ritual priest manifested. In the time of Uddhava, Lord Krishna stated that these secretive mantra were not effective in attracting Him, so we can deduce that today they have less potency to do so, because today times changed in the direction of reducing the potency of the mantras. These secretive hymns include the *Gāyatrī* and *mūla* mantras.

Tīrthāni or the making of pilgrimage to shrines

This is not that attractive to *Śrī* Krishna, because usually, pilgrimages are not the primary activity of the pilgrim. Usually one does annual pilgrimage as a matter of tradition or under a religious peer pressure, a sort of status-activity. Some do pilgrimage to get status in a certain religious group, so that they might be recognized as great devotees. Others perform pilgrimage on the spur of the moment as they are inspired or advised by religious leaders or as they are induced after hearing stories from scripture where others previously gained a certain result by making the trek.

Usually the pilgrim has a primary activity which has nothing to do with religion. Usually his mind is inwardly focused on that other activity even during the trek. It does happen from time to time, that the pilgrim sincerely and abruptly gives up his former activities and becomes a devotee or a serious ascetic but that is not usually the case. Making pilgrimage is good for the pilgrim but he should not expect that the Supreme Person would take a special interest in him because of it. There might be no grace-energy felt during, nor after making a sincere pilgrimage.

Niyamā or behavioral advisories

The advisories, when observed, do facilitate *dharma* or righteous living. These cause the being to overcome bad tendencies. These cause him to realize that he can exist without expressing features of his psyche which are antisocial to human society. This is good for the living being. It helps the Supreme Person in His effort to maintain law, order and equitable living.

Nevertheless, this is not as attractive to Him because this concerns our material existence. It is focused down into the material creation.

Even though it is of utmost important in community life, it does not of itself cause one to branch off for spiritual existence. In fact, when a living entity adopts the behavioral advisories, he becomes a good man or woman, being filled with kindness and piety. This causes him to become overly concerned with cultural life. Thus his whole focus beams into the goodness in material existence. He leaves aside spirituality.

There are examples of persons who by neglecting the behavioral advisories got a hint about the importance of cultivating spiritual life. They came upon that hint either by discovery or by realizing their wretched condition or by being chastised or advised by the Supreme Person or one of his agents, or even by chance from pressures put on by material existence itself. These persons then realized that the cultural life was an unnecessary detour on the spiritual path. Instead of perfecting such cultural existence, they went from a bad life to a spiritually-focused one, without investing time in becoming a good and pious person.

Generally however, a person who comes to repent his criminal and antisocial acts, usually takes to pious life to be a good person in human estimation. Since this is not a spiritual focus directly, it does not do much to attract the attention of the Supreme Person, nor of His more important agents.

Yamāh or moral restraints

These are for the benefit of the performer and for the sake of maintaining an orderly society. These fall under the jurisdiction of *dharma* or righteous living which is enacted under the watchful gaze of the Universal Form, a form which frightened Arjuna when he resisted the divine will for bringing some political deviants to justice in the Kuru civil war.

Even though one must apply moral restraints in spiritual life, still they are not that attractive to the Supreme Being. It concerns our cultural development in the material world. It has to do with these creature bodies which we assume from time to time. It is not especially geared for exclusive spiritual existence.

By discarding the moral restraints, one makes trouble for the Supreme Being. In other words, one becomes a nuisance. The Lord appreciates those who take up the moral values, and their corresponding behaviors. Still it is not that satisfying to God, because He is not primarily focused into the material world.

Sat-saṅgah or the association of reality-perceptive persons

This feature of the association of the reality-perceptive persons is greatly misunderstood. This is because every person who is a religious leader, tries to categorize himself as a *sat-saṅgī*, a fellow among the reality-perceptive personalities. The religious leaders promise their audiences membership in spiritual societies, claiming that such membership prepares one to be, and in fact converts one into being, a *sat-saṅgī*. This is the farce of religious institutions and their founders.

The confusion is there, because of the altered meaning of the word *sat*. The word *saṅga* means association or the keeping of company of a group of persons. *Saṅgī* is one such person in a group of affiliates. However the word *sat* has came to mean just a religious person or a person who is a member of a religious institution. This meaning, however, though quite suitable to our times, is not the meaning used by *Śrī* Krishna.

At the time of the discourse with Uddhava, *sat* meant, that which really exists, the really essential truth, or the person who perceives reality on a consistent and continuous basis. *Śrī* Krishna is attracted to anyone who keeps the association of reality-perceptive persons. And He is more attracted to that than anything else. This is related to the fact, that such association decreases and ultimately eliminates, attachments to impulsive social relationships.

The association of the reality-perceptive persons causes one to link up with the spiritual family system, a lineage which may or may not coincide with material social relations.

सत्-सङ्गेन हि दैतेया
यातुधाना मृगाः खगाः ।
गन्धर्वाप्सरसो नागाः
सिद्धाश् चारण-गुह्यकाः ॥७.३॥

sat-saṅgena hi daiteyā
yātudhānā mṛgāḥ khagāḥ
gandharvāpsaraso nāgāḥ
siddhāś cāraṇa-guhyakāḥ (7.3)

sat-saṅgena — by association of the reality-perceptive persons; hi — indeed; daiteyā = daiteyāḥ — the sons of Diti; yātudhānā = yātudhānāḥ — predominantly evil persons; mṛgāḥ — animals; khagāḥ — birds; gandharvāpsaraso = gandharvāpsarasaḥ = gandharva — celestial musicians + apsarasaḥ — angelic woman; nāgāḥ — snakes; siddhās = siddhāḥ — perfected yogis; cāraṇa-guhyakāh = cārana – celestial singers + guhyakāḥ — elemental spirits.

Translation

Indeed by the association of the reality-perceptive persons, some sons of Diti, some predominately evil persons, the animals, the birds, the celestial musicians, the angelic women, the snakes, the perfected yogis, the celestial singers, the elemental spirits, (7.3)

Commentary:

This begins the listing of those persons in the various species of life, who were affected by the reality-perceptive persons, in such a way, as to attain the abode of *Śrī* Krishna. This listing includes those who were good, those who were bad, those who were perfected psychologically, those who reached their spiritual potential, and those who were suppressed in animal bodies. It includes some in the celestial world and some elementary spirits in the lower subtle world.

विद्याधरा मनुष्येषु
वैश्याः शूद्राः स्त्रियो ऽन्त्य-जाः ।
रजस्-तमः-प्रकृतयस्
तस्मिंस् तस्मिन् युगे युगे ॥७.४॥

vidyādharā manuṣyeṣu
vaiśyāḥ śūdrāḥ striyo 'ntya-jāḥ
rajas-tamaḥ-prakṛtayas
tasmiṁs tasmin yuge yuge (7.4)

vidyādharā = vidyādharāḥ — the very knowledgeable celestial beings; manuṣyeṣu — among humanity; vaiśyāḥ — the productive sectors of human beings; śūdrāḥ — the working class human beings; striyo = striyaḥ — women; 'ntya-jāḥ = antya-jāḥ — the undesireable ethnic groups; rajas = rajah – impulsive influence of material nature; tamaḥ - depressive mode; prakṛtayas — of material nature; tasmims = tasmin — in this, in that; yuge yuge — era after era.

Translation

...the very knowledgeable celestial beings, and among humanity; the productive sector, the working class, women, and the undesirable ethnic groups, those of the impulsive and depressive modes of material nature, in this or in that era; (7.4)

Commentary:

This continues the listing of those who attained the association of *Śrī* Krishna, by gaining the company of the reality-perceptive persons.

बहवो मत्-पदं प्राप्तास्
त्वाष्ट्र-कायाधवादयः ७.५।

bahavo mat-padaṁ prāptās
tvāṣṭra-kāyādhavādayaḥ (7.5)

bahavo = bahavaḥ — many; mat-padam = mat – my + padam — abode; prāptās = prāptāḥ — achieved; tvāṣṭra — the son of Tvashtri, Vritra; kāyādhavādayaḥ = kāyādhava — son of Kayādhu, Prahlād + ādayah — and others.

Translation

...the son of Tvaṣṭri, the son of Kayādhu and many others achieved My abode. (7.5)

Commentary:

The son of *Tvaṣṭri* was known as *Vṛtra*. The son of *Kayādhu* was known as *Prahlād*. These were operating in atheistic families. By the grace of the reality perceptive persons like *Śrī Nārada Muni*, they got free from bad association and attained the company of *Śrī* Krishna.

वृषपर्वा बलिर् बाणो
मयश् चाथ विभीषणः ।
सुग्रीवो हनुमान् ऋक्षो
गजो गृध्रो वणिक्पथः ।
व्याधः कुब्जा व्रजे गोप्यो
यज्ञ-पत्न्यस् तथापरे ॥७.६॥

vṛṣaparvā balir bāṇo
mayaś cātha vibhīṣaṇaḥ
sugrīvo hanumān ṛkṣo
gajo gṛdhro vaṇikpathaḥ
vyādhaḥ kubjā vraje gopyo
yajña-patnyas tathāpare (7.6)

vṛṣaparvā — Vṛṣaparvā; balir = baliḥ — Bali; bano = bānah — Bana; mayas = mayah — Maya; catha = ca — and + atha — thus; vibhīṣaṇaḥ — Vibhisana; sugrīvo = sugrīvah — Sugriva; hanumān — Hanumān; ṛkṣo = ṛkṣah — the bear; gajo = gajah — the elephant; gṛdhro = gṛdhraḥ — the vulture; vaṇikpathaḥ — the trader; vyādhaḥ — the bird catcher; kubjā — the hunch-backed girl; vraje — in Vraja; gopya = gopyaḥ — the gopis; yajña-patnyas = yajña-patnyah — the wives of the brahmin priests; tathāpare = tathā — so + apare — others.

Translation

Vṛṣaparvā, Bali, Bāṇa, Maya, Vibhīṣaṇa, Sugrīva, Hanumān, the bear, the elephant, the vulture, the trader, the bird catcher, the hunchback woman, and in Vṛndāvan, the gopīs and the wives of the brahmin priests, as well as others: (7.6)

Commentary:

This concludes this listing of persons who got *Śrī* Krishna's association in the divine world merely by having the association of *Śrī* Krishna or of His devotee in this material world. These persons include those who used animal forms, vindictive kings, traders, hunters and women with deformed bodies. Each of the examples can be researched by reading the Vedic literatures like the *Mahābhārata*, the *Śrīmad Bhāgavatam* and the *Rāmāyaṇa*.

ते नाधीत-श्रुति-गणा
नोपासित-महत्तमाः ।
अव्रतातप्त-तपसः
मत्-सङ्गान् माम् उपागताः ॥७.७॥

te nādhīta-śruti-gaṇā
nopāsita-mahattamāḥ
avratātapta-tapasaḥ
mat-saṅgān mām upāgatāḥ (7.7)

te — they; nādhita = na — not + adhita — studied; śruti-gaṇa — the collection of Vedic verses; nopāsita = na — not + up*Asita* — attended; mahattamāḥ — great saints; avratātapta = avrata — without vows + atapta — not performed; tapasah — austerities; mat-sangān — due to association with; mat-sangāt - due to association with Me; mām — me; upāgatāh — they got.

Translation

They did not study the collection of Vedic verses, nor attended the great saints, or observed vows, nor performed austerities. Due to association with Me, they got Me. (7.7)

Commentary:

At the time of their receiving the mercy association of *Śrī* Krishna or of His representatives, who are the reality-perceptive persons, non of these devotees were performing austerities for a religious or purificatory purpose, nor were any of them in a religious process at the time, and still the association was effective in their lives to bring on permanently, the relationship with *Śrī* Krishna, which effected their deliverance from the material existence.

This does not mean however that none of these persons ever studied the Vedic literatures, before or after their effective contact with *Śrī* Krishna or with a saint. In fact some of the persons did so in previous lives. Therefore it is the particular association at the time which triggered the attraction of *Śrī* Krishna to the said personalities. Why at a particular time, did their association with a saintly person initiate their deliverance while at other times, prior, it did not? If we do not regard this question in all seriousness, then we will run away with a very shallow and incomplete understanding of the technique of these associations.

A person like *Prahlād* for example was in a Vaishnava brahmin family in the life just before he took birth as the son of the atheistic king, *Hiraṇyakaśipu*. But it was by the influence of *Nārada* in the new birth that *Prahlād* got the association of Lord *Nṛsiṅghadeva*. Why therefore did the previous association with great devotees not produce the same effect?

Jāmbavān also had the association of Lord *Śrī Rāmacandra*, and it was later in another life when he met Lord Krishna and fought with him over a jewel, that he became completely freed from the course of material existence. Thus it is not just the association of the Lord or of the reality-perceptive people, who are in touch with Him, but rather the type of that association. We will have to carefully consider this to understand these verses. If we follow translators who are writing on behalf of institutions or who want to promote themselves or their teachers as pure devotees of the Lord or as reality-perceptive persons, we will hardly understand this verse, and the actual way that this association is effected.

केवलेन हि भावेन
गोप्यो गावो नगा मृगाः ।
ये ऽन्ये मूढ-धियो नागाः
सिद्धा माम् ईयुर् अञ्जसा ॥७.८॥

kevalena hi bhāvena
gopyo gāvo nagā mṛgāḥ
ye 'nye mūḍha-dhiyo nāgāḥ
siddhā mām īyur añjasā (7.8)

kevalena — by that alone; hi — indeed; bhāvena — by emotional feelings; gopyo = gopyah — gopis; gāvo = gāvah — cows; nagā = nagāḥ — trees; mṛgāh — animals; ye — those; 'nye = anye — others; mūḍha-dhiyo = muḍha dhiyo (dhiyaḥ) — intelligence; nāgāḥ — snakes; siddhā = siddhāḥ — perfected; mām — to me; īyur = īyuḥ — they went; añjasā — easily.

Translation

By emotional feelings, the gopīs, the cows, some trees, animals and others like the snakes which had dull intelligence, were perfected and easily went to Me, (7.8)

Commentary:

The common element in all these conversions is a particular change in attitude in relation to the Supreme Person. This is substantiated by the extremely odd examples of the snakes like *Kāliya* and his reptilian mates. *Kāliya* was hostile to *Śrī* Krishna and to other persons who ventured into the part of the *Yamunā* River which he considered to be his territory. When *Śrī* Krishna began to chastise *Kāliya*, the serpent became more and more annoyed but the serpent mates, some female reptiles, took a liking to *Śrī* Krishna and begged that their husband be spared. After fighting with *Śrī* Krishna for some time, *Kāliya* experienced a change in attitude towards the Supreme Lord.

Exactly how that attitude came about is a mystery. There are many other cases of persons who fought with *Śrī* Krishna, and or with His agents like Arjuna and *Bhīma* and who did not experience any change of attitude towards the Lord, even at the time of their deaths at the hands of the Lord or Arjuna or *Bhīma* or others. Therefore the process is not that easy to understand. We should not present it in an over-simplified way just to attract disciples and converts to the Krishna Conscious Societies.

What we can say with certainty is that a person can become transformed suddenly by the association of *Śrī* Krishna or by that of His associate. It can happen. A person does not necessarily have to perform austerities of any type or even be worshippers of spiritual masters, or saints, to get the mercy of the Lord. It can be granted without an immediate cause. It can come suddenly or abruptly.

The other important point is that even if such a person gets that grace association, through which he begins to perceive divine reality, still he may not be transferred from this material world at the time of reception of the grace. *Hanumān* is an example of a person who got the direct association of the divine brothers, Lord *Śrī Rāma* and *Śrī Lakṣmanji*, along with the association of the supreme female, *Sītā*, and still *Hanumān* did not go to the spiritual provinces immediately. In fact, according to the narration, *Hanumān* is still in the vicinity of this planet, living somewhere in a parallel dimension in the Himalaya area. He is still using a subtle body which looks the way his gross form did when he served Lord *Rāma* on this earth, some thousands of years ago.

This association with *Śrī* Krishna, does not necessarily mean that the person will be transferred to the spiritual world but it does mean that he or she will have *Śrī* Krishna's association as a constant and continuous factor from then onwards.

य न योगेन साङ्ख्येन
दान-व्रत-तपो-ऽध्वरैः ।
व्याख्या-स्वाध्याय-सन्न्यासैः
प्राप्नुयाद् यत्नवान् अपि ॥७.९॥

yaṁ na yogena sāṅkhyena
dāna-vrata-tapo-'dhvaraiḥ
vyākhyā-svādhyāya-sannyāsaiḥ
prāpnuyād yatnavān api (7.9)

yam — the person whom; na — not; yogena — by yoga practice; sāṅkhyena — by Sāṅkhya philosophical analysis; dāna — charity; vrata — vows; tapo (tapaḥ) — austerity; 'dhvaraih = adhvaraiḥ — by Vedic ritual sacrifices; vyākhyā — by teaching the Vedas; svādhyāya — by study of the Vedas; sannyāsaiḥ — by renunciation of opportunities for cultural activity; prāpnuyād = prāpnuyāt — one who can attain; yatnavān — great endeavor; api — even.

Translation

...the person Who cannot be attained by with great endeavor, by yoga practice, Sāṅkhya philosophy, charity, vows, austerity, Vedic ritual worship, teaching the Vedas, study of the Vedas or by renunciation of oppurtunities. (7.9)

Commentary:

This remark which is connected to the previous verse, makes it quite clear that the association of *Śrī* Krishna is achieved through the association with the reality-perceptive persons. That alone is the cause. This does not mean that the rescued person would not have to perform yoga practice, nor study *Sāṅkhya* philosophy, nor give in charity, nor observe vows, nor perform austerities, nor perform Vedic ritual worship, nor teach and study the Vedas, or to take to renunciation of opportunities. Any or a combination of these might be required at some stage, even after getting *Śrī* Krishna's association. The gist of it is that to get His association, one has to achieve the well wishes of the reality-perceptive persons who are His devotees.

रामेण सार्धं मथुरां प्रणीते
श्वाफल्किना मय्य् अनुरक्त-चित्ताः ।
विगाढ-भावेन न मे वियोग-
तीव्राधयो ऽन्यं ददृशुः सुखाय ॥७.१०॥

rāmeṇa sārdhaṁ mathurāṁ praṇīte
śvāphalkinā mayy anurakta-cittāḥ
vigāḍha-bhāvena na me viyoga-
tīvrādhayo 'nyaṁ dadṛśuḥ sukhāya (7.10)

rāmena — with Rāma; sārdhaṁ — with; mathurām — to Mathurā ; pranīte — was taken; śvāphalkinā — by the son of Svaphalka; mayi — myself; anurakta — always attached; cittāḥ — mental and emotional nature; vigāḍha — with deep; bhāvena — with emotional feelings; na — no; me — beside me; viyoga — separation; tīvrādhayo = tīvra — intense + ādhayayo (ādhayah) — felt anguish; 'nyam = anyam — other; dadṛśuḥ — they saw; sukhāya — for happiness.

Translation

When Rāma and Myself were taken to Mathurā by the son of Śvalphaka, those whose minds were always attached with deep mento-emotional feelings, felt intense anguish because of My separation and saw no other source for happiness. (7.10)

Commentary:

Rāma is *Balarāma*, *Śrī* Krishna's elder brother. The son of *Śvaphalka* was *Akrūra*, who was sent to *Vṛndāvan* to take Krishna and *Balarāma* to the city of *Mathurā* , for participation in a wrestling match. Up to that point in his life, *Śrī* Krishna had not left the *Vṛndāvan* area. The cowherd girls who were his friends, were overtaken with feelings of intense anguish because Krishna was to go from the area.

This is *bhakti* or devotional love. In fact it is the most powerful, enduring and gripping type of *bhakti* or devotional love for *Śrī* Krishna. It is the most unusual and rare divine feeling towards the Lord. These were natural feelings for the *gopīs*. *Śrī* Krishna absorbed these feelings for He was in fact the object of their emotional focus.

There are two factors involved, in adopting the course of the *gopīs*. One must be capable of having such intense feelings either naturally or deliberate by will power inducement and *Śrī* Krishna must absorb the feelings. Even if one sends such feelings to Him or feels that way toward Him, He might not reciprocate.

तास् ताः क्षपाः प्रेष्ठतमेन नीता
मयैव वृन्दावन-गोचरेण ।
क्षणार्ध-वत् ताः पुनर् अङ्ग तासा
हीना मया कल्प-समा बभूवुः ॥७.११॥

tās tāḥ kṣapāḥ preṣṭhatamena nītā
mayaiva vṛndāvana-gocareṇa
kṣaṇārdha-vat tāḥ punar aṅga tāsāṁ
hīnā mayā kalpa-samā babhūvuḥ (7.11)

tās tāḥ = those those, in a particular; kṣapāḥ — nights; preṣṭhatamena = prestha— beloved + tamena – with their; nītā = nītāḥ — passed; mayaiva = maya — with me + eva — usually; vṛndāvana-gocareṇa = vrndāvana — Vṛndāvana + go-careṇa — within range of, in the area; kṣaṇārdha-vat = ksana— a moment + ardha – half + vat — like; tāḥ — those; punar = punah — again; anga — friend; tāsām — for them; hīnā = hīnāḥ — absence; mayā — my; kalpa-samā = kalpa — a day of the Procreator, an eternity + samā (samāḥ) — equal; babhūvuḥ — became.

Translation

O friend, in particular, the nights which they would spend with Me, as their Beloved in the area of Vṛndāvan, and which usually passed like moments, became in My absence like an eternity to them. (7.11)

Commentary:

This mento-emotional condition of the *gopīs* is highlighted as the strongest most enduring most powerful affiliation with *Śrī* Krishna. There is nothing, no sentiment, no process like it anywhere in existence. It is the most direct way of reaching *Śrī* Krishna. It is the closest and surest way to relate to Him.

The interesting feature is that what was nectar to the *gopīs* which was the night-time, by virtue of the fact that they met *Śrī* Krishna after leaving their material bodies each night, was converted into the supreme anguish for them, when *Śrī* Krishna along with His brother, *Balarāma* left *Vṛndavān*.

The mystery of it is this: Why did *Śrī* Krishna not continue those nightly trysts with the *gopīs* after He physically left *Vṛndavān*? It is the mystery of *Śrī* Krishna's independence in receiving the devotional feeling from a devotee.

ता नाविदन् मय्य् अनुषङ्ग-बद्ध-
धियः स्वम् आत्मानम् अदस् तथेदम् ।
यथा समाधौ मुनयो ऽब्धि-तोये
नद्यः प्रविष्टा इव नाम-रूपे ॥७.१२॥

tā nāvidan mayy anuṣaṅga-baddha-
dhiyaḥ svam ātmānam adas tathedam
yathā samādhau munayo 'bdhi-toye
nadyaḥ praviṣṭā iva nāma-rūpe (7.12)

tā = tāh — they; nāvidan = na — not + avidan — knew; mayy = mayi — on me; anuṣaṅga-baddha-dhiyaḥ = anusanga — attachment + baddha — bound + dhiyah — intelligence + svam — their own; ātmānam — of the self; adas = adah — that which is something else, any other person or thing; tathedam = tatha — thus, so + idam — this; yathā — as; samādhau — in superconscious absorption; munayo = munayaḥ — yogi philosophers; 'bdhi-toye = abdhi-toye = abdhi — of the ocean + toye — in water; nadyah — rivers; praviṣṭā — entered; iva — like; nāma-rūpe = nāma — name + rūpe — in form.

Translation

With their intelligence bound in attachment to Me, they knew neither their own self nor any other person or thing, just as the yogi philosophers enter into continuous effortless focus upon higher concentration forces, like rivers entering the waters of the ocean and knowing nothing else in name or form. (7.12)

Commentary:

What it took yogis years to develop by the eightfold practice of yoga, which culminates in continuous effortless focus upon higher concentration forces, was achieved by the *gopīs* merely by their instinct and natural focus on *Śrī* Krishna. This was due to the strong attachment to Him and to His absorption of their loving emotions.

As rivers enter the ocean naturally, flowing of their own accord without any sort of mechanical contrivance directing them, so the *gopīs* were focused on *Śrī* Krishna.

The contrast between the successful yogis and the *gopīs* reveals that for some living entities a deliberate process of austerity is required to shift off from this world while for others like the *gopīs*, the shift occurs naturally by an inborn attachment to the Supreme Being.

मत्-कामा रमणं जारम्
अस्वरूप-विदो ऽबलाः ।
ब्रह्म मां परमं प्रापुः
सङ्गाच् छत-सहस्रशः ॥७.१३॥

mat-kāmā ramaṇaṁ jāram
asvarūpa-vido 'balāḥ
brahma māṁ paramaṁ prāpuḥ
saṅgāc chata-sahasraśaḥ (7.13)

mat-kāmā = mat — me + kāmā (kāmāh) — those who yearned passionately; ramanaṁ — a lover; jāram — a married woman's lover, a secret lover; asvarūpa-vido = asvarūpa-vidaḥ — not knowing my real form; balāh = abalāh — women; brahma — spirit; māṁ — me; paramam — supreme; prāpuḥ — they achieved; saṅgāc = saṅgāt — due to association or attachment; chata-sahasraśaḥ = śata-sahasraśaḥ — hundred of thousands.

Translation

Not knowing My real form, the women yearned for Me as a secret lover, yet by association, hundred and thousands of them achieved Me, the Supreme Spirit. (7.13)

Commentary:

In contrast to the yogi philosophers, the *gopīs* did not know who *Śrī* Krishna really was. Some yogis get to understand the supreme power of *Śrī* Krishna and so their realization of Him is filled with the knowledge and experience of that. The *gopīs* however were unaware of the supreme power of *Śrī* Krishna, and still by intense affectionate attraction for Him they attained Him. This means that by such affection one can reach perfection, provided of course, *Śrī* Krishna absorbs one's love for Him in the way He related to the *gopīs*.

तस्मात् त्वम् उद्धवोत्सृज्य
चोदनां प्रतिचोदनाम् ।
प्रवृत्तिं च निवृत्तिं च
श्रोतव्यं श्रुतम् एव च ॥७.१४॥

tasmāt tvam uddhavotsṛjya
codanāṁ praticodanām
pravṛttiṁ ca nivṛttiṁ ca
śrotavyaṁ śrutam eva ca (7.14)

tasmāt — therefore; tvam — you; uddhavotṣṛjya = uddhava — Uddhava + utsṛjya — giving up; codanām — injunctions; praticodanām — prohibitions; pravṛttim — path of social fulfillment; ca — and; nivṛttim — path of restriction in curtailing social fulfillments; ca — and; śrotavyam — instructions to be received; śrutam — instructions granted; eva — indeed; ca — and.

Translation

Therefore Uddhava, giving up injunctions and prohibitions, the path of social fulfillment and that of curtailing such fulfillment, giving up also any instructions that are to be received as well as those already granted, (7.14)

Commentary:

Śrī Krishna advised Uddhava to give up any effort to follow scriptural injunctions, prohibitions, as well as recommendations for social fulfillment and even advisories for curtailing the fulfillments themselves, as well as any instruction, Uddhava might have received before or any that he was in the process of getting from any other authority.

माम् एकम् एव शरणम्
आत्मानं सर्व-देहिनाम् ।
याहि सर्वात्म-भावेन
मया स्या ह्य् अकुतो-भयः ॥७.१५॥

mām ekam eva śaraṇam
ātmānaṁ sarva-dehinām
yāhi sarvātma-bhāvena
mayā syā hy akuto-bhayaḥ (7.15)

mām — me; ekam — alone; eva — indeed; śaranam — take refuge; ātmānam — the self; sarva-dehinām — all of the embodied beings; yāhi — you go; sarvātma-bhāvena — all feelings of the self; mayā — by mercy; syā = syāḥ — you should be; hy = hi — indeed; akuto-bhayah = akutah – not from anywhere, freedom from all angles + bhayaḥ — fear.

Translation

...with all feelings take refuge in Me alone, as the self of all the embodied beings. By My mercy, you should be freed from fear. (7.15)

Commentary:

A similar promise was given to Arjuna. This means that if a person can take refuge directly in Lord Krishna, not through someone else but directly, just as Arjuna and Uddhava did, just as the *gopīs* did, then that person by the full reliance on Him, would be freed from all fears. It means that he or she would not have to worry about protecting themselves personally. By their affiliation with Krishna, they would be taken care of automatically or they would be motivated to do what is needful for soul protection.

In Arjuna's case, we know that this did not mean that Arjuna would become like a gopi. Arjuna had to live as a member of the Kuru family. He had to fight on the battlefield as directed by *Śrī* Krishna. Therefore it is not in all cases, that a surrender to *Śrī* Krishna brings about a palatable service. Arjuna's service on the war field was not a palatable task but it was what *Śrī* Krishna wanted. It was satisfying to the Central Person in the Universal Form, *Śrī* Krishna Himself in that personal disciplinarian feature.

The *gopīs* also anguished for *Śrī* Krishna after He physically left Vṛndāvan. From what *Śrī* Krishna told Uddhava in verse 11 of this chapter, the *gopīs* anguished because they felt that Krishna left their area, after His physical form departed for Mathurā. So even in that case, the nightly loving affairs were curtailed. The *gopīs* did not realize *Śrī* Krishna as the Supreme Spirit.

Somehow their divine nightly affairs with Him ceased for the time being when He left Vṛndāvan. As to why *Śrī* Krishna did not reveal His supreme position to the *gopīs*, so that they could continue those nightly affairs, remains a mystery to this very day.

श्री-उद्धव उवाच
सशयः शृण्वतो वाच
तव योगेश्वरेश्वर ।
न निवर्तत आत्म-स्थो
येन भ्राम्यति मे मनः ॥७.१६॥

śrī-uddhava uvāca
saṁśayaḥ śṛṇvato vācaṁ
tava yogeśvareśvara
na nivartata ātma-stho
yena bhrāmyati me manaḥ (7.16)

śrī-uddhava – the respected Uddhava; uvāca — said; saṁśayah — doubt; śṛnvato = śṛnvataḥ — hearing; vācam — words; tava — yours; yogeśvareśvara — master of the masters of the yoga discipline; na – not; nivartata — removed; ātma-stho = ātma-sthah – soul situated; yena — by which; bhrāmyati — is unsettled; me — my; manaḥ — mind.

Translation

The respected Uddhava said: O Master of the masters of the yoga disciplines, though hearing Your words, the doubt which is situated in my soul, is not removed. My mind is unsettled. (7.16)

Commentary:

Uddhava was already instructed in what to do when he first approached *Śrī* Krishna. Those instructions were given in the second chapter verse 6:

tvaṁ tu sarvaṁ parityajya snehaṁ sva-jana-bandhu ṣu
mayy āveśya mana ḥ saṁyak sama-d ṛg vicarasva gām

You should give up all affection for relatives and friends, fix your mind completely on Me and while wandering over the earth, perceive everything as having the same existential configuration. (U.G. 2.6)

Uddhava however rejected that counsel of the Supreme Lord. He could not stomach it. Thus he pleaded for an alternative, something which might be, in his view, more suited to his personality. (chap 2 texts 14,15,16)

Even though he was given so many instructions, Uddhava remains undetermined about what he should do. He admited that he has doubts. He is still hesitant to follow the instruction about wandering over the earth, while renouncing any opportunities for cultural life that destiny might present to him, just as the ascetic brahmin did.

In this chapter, *Śrī* Krishna gave Uddhava an important hint, but somehow Uddhava failed to take it, just as many modern devotees do not grasp the idea, which is that if one cannot follow the instruction of *Śrī* Krishna, then one has to lean on the strength of one's attachment to Him, just as the *gopīs* did in their yearning and anguish for *Śrī* Krishna, when he left *Vṛndāvan*, depriving them of His nightly association in the forest groves as their sweetheart.

Śrī Krishna hinted in verse 48 of the last chapter that one may develop an affection for him by associating with the reality-perceptive persons who are His devotees. By that developed devotion, one would willingly do whatever He requested. In other words, if one cannot automatically follow the order of *Śrī* Krishna, then one can do so if one develops an affection for Him. By that affection, one's nature would be all too willing to act on His behalf.

In the case of Arjuna, we learnt that initially he too was unwilling to do as *Śrī* Krishna requested at *Kurukṣetra*. When *Śrī* Krishna showed the Universal Form, Arjuna relented and agreed to act for Krishna, even though Arjuna still hesitated until *Śrī* Krishna explained much more and displayed a special affection towards Arjuna.

Arjuna was faced with an unpalatable task, that of killing relatives on the war field. Uddhava though he hesitated, was not assigned such an offensive task. He was directed to wander over the earth in a detached manner, standing apart from cultural activities of all sorts, while realizing the spiritual basis behind all this mundane display that is before us. Still, Uddhava did not like the idea. He wanted instead, to stay physically with *Śrī* Krishna and to part from his body, when *Śrī* Krishna would part from His. *Śrī* Krishna however, did not agree to Uddhava's preferences, no more than He did to Arjuna's.

Even though one may be emotionally attached to the Lord, just as Uddhava was, still that does not mean that *Śrī* Krishna will subject Himself to all desires which arise in one's emotions. At times, *Śrī* Krishna will reject those desires, just as He did to some *gopīs* during the rasa dance on his nightly trysts. It means that even though the devotional path is easy in a way, it is also troublesome in another way. It causes anguish and may even cause disagreement and disharmony with *Śrī* Krishna, when the devotee is unwilling to surrender to what *Śrī* Krishna wants and when the devotee is unable to detach himself or herself from those Krishna-rejected emotions and, their concomitant desires. This is the difficulty on the path of devotion. It is not all easy as some preachers would have us think.

श्री-भगवान् उवाच
स एष जीवो विवर-प्रसूतिः
प्राणेन घोषेण गुहां प्रविष्टः ।
मनो-मयं सूक्ष्मम् उपेत्य रूपं
मात्रा स्वरो वर्ण इति स्थविष्ठः ॥७.१७॥

śrī-bhagavān uvāca
sa eṣa jīvo vivara-prasūtiḥ
prāṇena ghoṣeṇa guhāṁ praviṣṭaḥ
mano-mayaṁ sūkṣmam upetya rūpaṁ
mātrā svaro varṇa iti sthaviṣṭhaḥ (7.17)

śrī-bhagavān – the Blessed Lord; uvāca — said; sa = sah – he; eṣa = eṣaḥ — this, he in particular; jīvo = jīvah — the individual person; vivara-prasūtiḥ = vivara — causal cavity + prasūtiḥ — manifest; prāṇena — with vitalizing energy; ghoṣeṇa — with subtle sound; guhām — subtle places; praviṣṭaḥ — penetrated; mano-mayam — produced by the mind; sūkṣmam — subtle body; upetya — is indicated; rūpam — form; mātrā — syllable; svaro = svarah — tone, pitch; varṇa = varṇaḥ — letter sound; iti — thus; sthaviṣṭhah — gross level.

Translation

The Blessed Lord said: That individual spirit, He in particular, who manifest Himself in the causal cavity, with the vitalizing energy and with subtle sound and who penetrated the subtle body which is produced by the mind, is on the gross level as syllable, tone and letter sound. (7.17)

Commentary:

This is a special person. *Śrī* Krishna stressed that this individual was one in particular. This is the *Paramātmā* or Supersoul, a parallel divine form of *Śrī* Krishna Himself. This Person, the Supreme Being, entered the causal cavity and had with Him a cosmic vitalizing-power and subtle sound. After a time He created and then penetrated the subtle cosmic body, which was produced by the cosmic mind with its *buddhi* sensing light. Then He manifested Himself by a projection of His authority and knowledge as sound intonations for the sake of communicating with the living entities who were to be produced in the creation.

In this reply, it appears that *Śrī* Krishna insisted that He would have His way to make Uddhava take up a path that was similar to what *Śrī* Krishna described as the life of the ascetic brahmin who instructed King Yadu. Uddhava has other ideas of what he wanted but *Śrī* Krishna insisted otherwise.

यथानलः खे ऽनिल-बन्धुर् उष्मा
बलेन दारुण्य् अधिमथ्यमानः ।
अणुः प्रजातो हविषा समेधते
तथैव मे व्यक्तिर् इयं हि वाणी ॥७.१८॥

yathānalaḥ khe 'nila-bandhur uṣmā
balena dāruṇy adhimathyamānaḥ
aṇuḥ prajāto haviṣā samedhate
tathaiva me vyaktir iyaṁ hi vāṇī (7.18)

yathānalaḥ = yathā — as + analaḥ — fire; khe — in interspaces; 'nila-bandhur = anila-bandhuḥ = anila – air + bandhuḥ — assisted by; uṣmā — heat; balena — with vigor; dāruṇy = dāruṇi — in wood; adhimathyamānaḥ — by friction; aṇuḥ — as spark; prajāto = prajātaḥ — is produced, becomes; haviṣā — with ghee; samedhate — blazes; tathaiva = tathā — so + eva — indeed; me — my; vyaktir = vyaktih — manifestation; iyam — this; hi — indeed; vāni — speech.

Translation

As fire is in the interspaces, as heat which by vigorous friction, assisted by the wind, becomes a spark in wood, as fire blazes with ghee, so speech is My manifestation, (7.18)

Commentary:

Śrī Krishna gave Uddhava detailed instructions on what realizations and experiences Uddhava should get when Uddhava took up the ascetic life. This explains how the sound feature of the material creation comes about. *Śrī* Krishna said that the initial sounds are a manifestation of Him. Or rather they are an indication of His existence. It is not that the sound is *Śrī* Krishna Himself but rather it indicates His presence. By supernatural power it is produced in the creation. It gives living beings the hint of His existence.

In the early part of this creation, the Supreme Being did not take a gross manifestation as for example manifestation as *Śrī* Krishna, the son of *Devakī* and *Vasudeva*, but then some living beings assumed His existence through sounds which He produced by supernatural means.

एवं गदिः कर्म गतिर् विसर्गो
घ्राणो रसो दृक् स्पर्शः श्रुतिश् च ।
सङ्कल्प-विज्ञानम् अथाभिमानः
सूत्रं रजः-सत्त्व-तमो-विकारः ॥७.१९॥

evaṁ gadiḥ karma gatir visargo
ghrāṇo raso dṛk sparśaḥ śrutiś ca
saṅkalpa-vijñānam athābhimānaḥ
sūtraṁ rajaḥ-sattva-tamo-vikāraḥ (7.19)

evam — thus; gadiḥ — speaking; karma — action, acting; gatir = gatiḥ — motion, moving about; visargo = visargaḥ — ejaculating semen; ghrāṇo = ghrāṇah — smelling; raso = rasaḥ — tasting; dṛk — seeing; sparśaḥ — touching; śrutiś = śrutiḥ — hearing; ca — and; saṅkalpa-vijñānam = sankalpa — intention + vijñānam — experience; athābhimānaḥ = atha — moreover + abhimānah — assertion; sūtraṁ — sexually-charged cosmic energy; rajaḥ-sattva-tamo-vikāraḥ = rajaḥ — passionate influence of material nature + sattva – clarifying influence of material nature + tamo (tamah) — retardative influence of material nature; vikārah — the changes.

Translation

...and so are speaking, acting, moving about, ejaculating, smelling, tasting, seeing, touching and hearing as well as in intending, experiencing and asserting the sexually-charged cosmic energy and the changes of the passionate, clarifying and retardative influences of material nature. (7.19)

Commentary:

All these, along with sound vibration, are indications that there was a particular person in the beginning, before this creation manifested. The sound vibrations which the human beings and animals produce are different from that which abounded in the creation initially. Even these human and animal sounds which we now hear, indicate that there was a particular individual who started the creation.

Everything listed above especially the *sūtram* or sexually-charged cosmic energy indicate that there is a particular individual who started the creation. That should be surmised by everyone. That person is the God, the Supreme Individual.

अयं हि जीवस् त्रि-वृद् अब्ज-योनिर्
अव्यक्त एको वयसा स आद्यः ।
विश्लिष्ट-शक्तिर् बहुधेव भाति
बीजानि योनिं प्रतिपद्य यद्वत् ॥७.२०॥

ayaṁ hi jīvas tri-vṛd abja-yonir
avyakta eko vayasā sa ādyaḥ
viśliṣṭa-śaktir bahudheva bhāti
bījāni yoniṁ pratipadya yadvat (7.20)

ayam — this; hi — indeed; jīvas = jīvaḥ — that particular individual; trivṛd = trivṛt — the conscious motivator of the three modes of material nature; abja-yonir = abja — cosmic lotus flower + yonir (yoniḥ) — cause; avyaktah — invisible reality; eko = ekaḥ — one; vayasā — in time; sa = saḥ — he; ādyaḥ — primeval; viśliṣṭa — differentiated; śaktir = śaktiḥ — potency; bahudheva = bahudha — diverse, multiple + iva — like; bhāti — he appears; bījāni — seeds; yonim — in fertile land; pratipadya — falling; yadvat = yat vat — just like.

Translation

Indeed, that individual, being one person, has potency which is differentiated by time and which appears to be multiple, like seeds in fertile land. He is the primeval one, the conscious motivator of the three modes of material nature, the cause of the cosmic lotus flower.(7.20)

Commentary:

The material creation in entirety is pictured to be a lotus flower of cosmic proportions. That is the Vedic version. It is said that this lotus flower was the source of the procreator *Brahmā*, who created the habitation and creatures. Just as seeds sprout in farmland, take nutrients from the soil and produce vegetation, so by the impetus from the Supreme Person, the material world, comes into being with its varied life-forms and dimensions.

यस्मिन्न् इदं प्रोतम् अशेषम् ओतं
पटो यथा तन्तु-वितान-सस्थः ।
य एष ससार-तरुः पुराणः
कर्मात्मकः पुष्प-फले प्रसूते ॥७.२१॥

yasminn idaṁ protam aśeṣam otaṁ
paṭo yathā tantu-vitāna-saṁsthaḥ
ya eṣa saṁsāra-taruḥ purāṇaḥ
karmātmakaḥ puṣpa-phale prasūte (7.21)

yasmin — on whom; idam — this; protam — warp, crosswise; aśeṣam — entire, whole; otam — woof, lengthwise; paṭo = paṭah — cloth; yathā — as; tantu — thread; vitāna — network; saṁsthaḥ — rest, is situated; ya = yah — which; eṣa = eṣah — this; saṁsāra-taruḥ = samsara — system of transmigration in material bodies + taruḥ — tree; purānaḥ — anciet; karmātmakaḥ = karma — cultural activities + ātmakaḥ — self, natural tendency; puspa-phale = puspa — flower-like, colorful object + phale — in the result; prasūte — produces.

Translation

He is the Person on Whom as its crosswise and lengthwise basis, this whole system is situated, as a cloth on a network of threads. This tree-like system of transmigration is ancient. Cultural activity is its tendency and it produces flower-like colorful objects as its end result. (7.21)

Commentary:

The mere fact that the supreme Individual began this creation and serves as its foundation, indicated that He lived somewhere else before this creation was formulated. Thus the question arises as to His current residence. What does He look like? What sort of body does He use? How does He divest the extensive powers?

The flower-like colorful objects which are produced by the tree-like system of material nature attracts the bee-like entities who become aware of themselves in the creation, and who are endowed with senses which seek out the colorful production. Thus the limited entities remain time bound as it were, being occupied pursuing objects. Only a handful of entities can make the decision to seek out that *Particular Individual* who began the creation.

द्वे अस्य बीजे शत-मूलस् त्रि-नालः
पञ्च-स्कन्धः पञ्च-रस-प्रसूतिः ।
दशैक-शाखो द्वि-सुपर्ण-नीडस्
त्रि-वल्कलो द्वि-फलो ऽर्कं प्रविष्टः ॥७.२२॥

dve asya bīje śata-mūlas tri-nālaḥ
pañca-skandhaḥ pañca-rasa-prasūtiḥ
daśaika-śākho dvi-suparṇa-nīḍas
tri-valkalo dvi-phalo 'rkaṁ praviṣṭaḥ (7.22)

dve — two; asya — of this; bīje — seeds; śata-mūlas = śata — hundred + mūlas — roots; tri-nālaḥ = tri — three + nālah — trunk; pañca-skandhaḥ = pañca — five + skandhaḥ — main branches; pañca-rasa-prasūtiḥ = panca — five + rasa — sap + prasūtiḥ — exudes; daśaika-śākho = daśa — ten + eka — one + sakho (sakhah) — minor branches, twigs; dvi-suparṇa-nīḍas = dvi — two + suparṇa — bird + nīḍas (nīḍah) — nest; tri-valkalo = tri-valkalaḥ = tri — three + valkalaḥ — bark; dvi-phalo = dvi-phalaḥ = dvi — two + phalaḥ — fruit; 'rkam = arkam — sun; pravistah — extending to.

Translation

Of this tree, there are two seeds, one hundred roots, three trunks, five branches, ten or more twigs. It exudes five saps. It has two bird nests, three layers of bark and two fruits. It extends to the sun. (7.22)

Commentary:

This is a metaphoric description of material nature. In the system of planets which we inhabit, one may go as high as the sun, which is centrally located. One may evolve up to having a body which is harmonious with that fiery place. That would be the highest material situation one may attain.

अदन्ति चैकं फलम् अस्य गृध्रा
ग्रामे-चरा एकम् अरण्य-वासाः ।
हंसा य एकं बहु-रूपम् इज्यैर्
माया-मयं वेद स वेद वेदम् ॥७.२३॥

adanti caikaṁ phalam asya gṛdhrā
grāme-carā ekam araṇya-vāsāḥ
haṁsā ya ekaṁ bahu-rūpam ijyair
māyā-mayaṁ veda sa veda vedam (7.23)

adanti — they eat; caikam = ca — and + ekam — one; phalam — fruit; asya — of this; gṛdhrā = gṛdhrāḥ — vultures; grāme-carā = grāme-carāḥ = grāme — in the village + carāḥ — frequenting wandering; ekam — one; araṇya-vāsāḥ = araṇya — forest + vāsāḥ — residents; haṁsā = haṁsāḥ — swan; ya = yaḥ — who; ekam — one; bahu-rūpam — many forms; ijyair = ijyaih — with the help of teaches; māyā-mayaṁ — bewildering potency; veda — know; sa = saḥ — he; veda — know; vedam — Vedas.

Translation

Vultures wandering in villages eat one fruit, while swans who reside in the forest, eat the other. He who, with the help of teachers, knows the One who appears as multiple forms and who produced the bewildering potency, knows the Vedas. (7.23)

Commentary:

The idea is to find out who that Particular Individual is, the Person who began this creation. His ways are certainly complex. Since He used supernatural power to produce this world, it is enigmatic. Since we appeared after this place was created, we have the handicap of limited sense perception. We have no factual vision of how this world was produced.

एवं गुरूपासनयैक-भक्त्या
विद्या-कुठारेण शितेन धीरः ।
विवृश्च्य जीवाशयम् अप्रमत्तः
सम्पद्य चात्मानम् अथ त्यजास्त्रम् ॥७.२४॥

evaṁ gurūpāsanayaika-bhaktyā
vidyā-kuṭhāreṇa śitena dhīraḥ
vivṛścya jīvāśayam apramattaḥ
sampadya cātmānam atha tyajāstram (7.24)

evaṁ — thus; gurūpāsanayaika-bhaktyā = guru — of the spiritual master + upāsanayā — by attendance to + eka — singular; bhaktyā — by devotion; vidyā — of effective technique; kuṭhārena — by the axe; śitena — by sharp; dhīraḥ — one whose intellect is steadied by mastering buddhi yoga; vivṛścya — cut down; jīvāsayam = jīva — individual limited spirit + āśayam — the causal body; apramattaḥ — vigilant; sampadya — having obtained; cātmānam = ca — and + ātmānam — the self; atha — then; tyajāstram = tyaja — abandon + astram — weapon.

Translation

Thus, one whose intellect is steadied by mastery of buddhi yoga, and who is vigilant, should with the axe of effective mystic technique, sharpened by attendance to the spiritual master, with singular devotion, dismember the causal body of the individual soul, and then having attained the self, abandon the weapon. (7.24)

Commentary:

Jīvāśayam is usually taken to mean the subtle body. This is so because the subtle body is the immediate basis for transmigration into gross forms. It is the subtle body which sponsors the numerous gross ones. One cannot move from one gross form to another without using a subtle body as the basis for the psychological energy around which gross bodies are formed.

Still, it is really the causal form which is the foundation; This causal body, though very subtle and elusive, is the cause of the subtle one. The spirit is more situated in the causal body than he is in the subtle one. Commentators who are not proficient in higher yoga and who have read about the subtle body, make the assumption that the word *āśayam* should be translated as subtle body. Actually the principle of objectivity in the subtle body is the *buddhi* intellect organ. It is not the spirit per se. The spirit is situated with the sense of initiative, *ahankāra*, in the causal body. It is the *buddhi* organ that wields directive power in the subtle form. It is not the spirit.

This is why *Śrī Ādi Śaṅkara* defeated an opponent in a debate, where he revealed to the opponent that in reference to the *buddhi* organ, the spirit is merely an observer and not a pursuer of sensual phenomena in this world. The spirit by itself cannot pursue anything here. He must be first hitched to or be connected to the *buddhi* organ mechanism. It is that mechanism that pursues this or that in the material world, according to the facilities it utilizes in various life forms.

The word *dhīrah* is given in the *Bhagavad-Gītā*, beginning in chapter two and *Śrī* Krishna explains the *buddhi* yoga process in brief. It is by this yoga that one can conquer the *buddhi* organ, bring it under control and use it to escape from sensual dominance. But some teachers claim that *buddhi* yoga is *bhakti* yoga. That is an amazing pronouncement, because it is not defined in *Bhagavad-Gītā* in that way. A *dhīrah* is a person who mastered *buddhi* yoga. He does not have to be a devotee of *Śrī* Krishna. He does not have to practice *bhakti* to Krishna necessarily, even though some praticioners are in fact the greatest of the *bhaktās* or devotees of *Śrī* Krishna.

CHAPTER 8*

Śrī Krishna's Swan Form**

Terri Stokes-Pineda Art

sa mām acintayad devaḥ praśna-pāra-titīrṣayā
tasyāham haṁsa-rūpeṇa sakāśam agamaṁ tadā

That Supernatural Creator thought of Me, as he really desired the final answer to the question. Then I became visible to him in the form of a swan. (Uddhava Gītā 8.19)

* Śrīmad Bhāgavatam Canto 11, Chapter 13

** Translator's selected chapter title.

श्री-भगवान् उवाच
सत्त्वं रजस् तम इति
गुणा बुद्धेर् न चात्मनः ।
सत्त्वेनान्यतमौ हन्यात्
सत्त्वं सत्त्वेन चैव हि ॥८.१॥

śrī-bhagavān uvāca
sattvaṁ rajas tama iti
guṇā buddher na cātmanaḥ
sattvenānyatamau hanyāt
sattvaṁ sattvena caiva hi (8.1)

śrī-bhagavān – the Blessed Lord; uvāca — said; sattvam — the clarifying influence; rajas = rajah — the passionate power; tama = tamah — the retardative influence; iti — thus, namely; gunā = gunāh — the influence of material nature; buddher = buddheh — relating to the intellect; na — not; cātmanah = ca – and + ātmanam — to the soul; sattvenānyatamau = sattvena — by the clarifying influence + anyatamau — the other two; hanyāt — should eliminate; sattvam — the clarifying influence; sattvena — by the clarifying influence; caiva = ca — and + eva — only; hi — indeed.

Translation

The Blessed Lord said: The modes of material nature, namely the clarifying influence, the passionate power and the retardative influence, relate to the intellect not the spirit, except indirectly. By using the clarifying influence, one should eliminate the other two, and by using the clarifying influence only one should conquer that influence itself. (8.1)

Commentary:

Some feel that one does not have to do this, but rather, that one can take to devotional service and develop devotional purity. The idea is that one should leave aside detailed procedures for purification and just follow the *gopīs* by surrendering completely to *Śrī* Krishna or to His pure devotee.

However Uddhava was not given that advice. The point is that one has to start where he is. Furthermore, one has to surrender to *Śrī* Krishna in the way that is natural for oneself. Everyone cannot surrender in the way the *gopīs* did, because everyone does not have that sentiment. It cannot be developed merely by joining an institution or by taking a spiritual master in the Vaishnava succession.

One has to start where he is, in whatever mode he is accustomed to and work his way up from there, gradually and steadily, from the retardative mode to the passionate one and then to the clarifying energy. By taking help from a higher mode one is gradually lifted to the higher one. When that higher one becomes the foundation for one's behavior, one can work to be elevated even higher. Eventually when one is situated in the clarifying influence in the greater percentage of the time, one can secure a footing there, and take steps to use that mode to go higher, leaving the zones which are permeated by the two lower energies and at last leaving aside the clarifying influence as well.

सत्त्वाद् धर्मो भवेद् वृद्धात्
पुंसो मद्-भक्ति-लक्षणः ।
सात्त्विकोपासया सत्त्वं
ततो धर्मः प्रवर्तते ॥८.२॥

sattvād dharmo bhaved vṛddhāt
puṁso mad-bhakti-lakṣaṇaḥ
sāttvikopāsayā sattvaṁ
tato dharmaḥ pravartate (8.2)

sattvād = sattvāt — from the clarifying influence; dharmo = dharmaḥ — righteous nature; bhaved = bhavet — becomes, is developing; vṛddhāt — from the reinforcement; puṁso = puṁsaḥ — of a person; mad-bhakti-lakṣaṇaḥ = mad (mat) – to me + bhakti — devotion + lakṣaṇaḥ — characterised; sāttvikopāsayā = sāttvika — things which reinforce the clarifying influence + upāsayā — by utilizing; sattvam — the clarifying influence; tato = tatah — from that, hense; dharmaḥ — righteousness; pravartate — manifests.

Translation

From the clarifying influence, the righteous nature of a person, who is characterized by devotion to Me, is developed. By utilizing only that which reinforces the clarifying influence, that influence develops further. And from that development, the righteous nature becomes manifest. (8.2)

Commentary:

This is the result of completing the first two steps of yoga, namely *yama* or moral restraints and *niyama*, or moral advisories. These two aspects of the eightfold stages of yoga, are used throughout the practice. At the higher states it is introvertedly used, so that the ascetic turns the critical energy on himself and attains the full righteous nature.

धर्मो रजस् तमो हन्यात्
सत्त्व-वृद्धिर् अनुत्तमः ।
आशु नश्यति तन्-मूलो
ह्य् अधर्म उभये हते ॥८.३॥

dharmo rajas tamo hanyāt
sattva-vṛddhir anuttamaḥ
āśu naśyati tan-mūlo
hy adharma ubhaye hate (8.3)

dharmo = dharmah — the righteous nature; rajas = rajah — the passion influence; tamo = tamah — the retardative influence; hanyāt — from the displacement of; sattva — the clarifying influence; vrddhir = vrddhih — increase; anuttamah — superior type; āśu — quickly; naśyati — is eliminated; tan-mūlo = tat-mūlaḥ — of that root cause; hy = hi — indeed; adharma = adharmah — irreligious nature; ubhaye – both; hate — are pushed out.

Translation

The righteous nature, the superior state, which results from an increase of the clarifying influence, displaces the passionate and retardative potencies. When both of these are pushed out, the irreligious nature which is the root cause, is also quickly eliminated. (8.3)

Commentary:

One cannot push out the retardative potency simply by following moral principles and restraining oneself from irreligious acts. Therefore by necessity, if one is to progress further, one has to advance through higher yoga. Generally people try to move directly from morality to meditation. This is the general trend. However this does not work because the potencies of material nature, do not budge by weak meditation. Thus in the yoga system, one has to take it step by step, to progress through moral principles and recommended social behaviors to performing bodily postures, gaining an efficient breath system for surcharging the subtle body with clarifying *prāṇa* or subtle airs, and then to retract the sensual interest. This retraction of the sensual interest is the 5th stage of practice, known as *pratyāhar*.

It is not a matter of external social behavior, even though initially, that has importance. One has to review his psychology to see that it is an internal problem. His internal intake and fostering of passionate and retardative potencies is what sponsors his immoral acts over and over. Thus he displaces these by increasing the clarifying power *(sattva-vrddhir)*. This requires mystic expertise.

Even though the *gopīs* were not required to do this, most others cannot follow in their footsteps. Most others cannot develop the intense attraction for *Śrī* Krishna. Thus they will have to perfect the yoga discipline. That is the bottom line. Avoidance of yoga by cute approaches to these statements of *Śrī* Krishna is so much of a maneuver by the weak intellect. When the intellect becomes strong by the proper association and by honest practice, then one will be able to do yoga. And then one leaves aside the imaginary religious systems, even some of which are called standardized devotion to *Śrī* Krishna, but which do not give the desired results.

Decorating the Krishna *Mūrti*, the Krishna idol in the temple, in a very attractive way, to satisfy our perverted senses, will work temporary to tame the senses, but the senses will soon realize that this is not what they are after. And then the said devotee will turn aside from such temple attractions and take the senses to what they really want which is vulgar mundane sensuality.

One has to purify the senses by yoga austerities, because the senses cannot really be fooled by devotional attractions, for that is not what they really want. They want vulgar and varied perverted contact with sensuality. Thus until the senses are changed deeply by inner austerity, one will fail at the devotional system. We experience this repeatedly, and have observed it in the lives of many *sannyāsi* preachers who take to devotional life with an idea to avoid yoga, which they consider to be difficult and useless.

आगमो ऽपः प्रजा देशः
कालः कर्म च जन्म च ।
ध्यानं मन्त्रो ऽथ संस्कारो
दशैते गुण-हेतवः ॥८.४॥

āgamo 'paḥ prajā deśaḥ
kālaḥ karma ca janma ca
dhyānaṁ mantro 'tha saṁskāro
daśaite guṇa-hetavaḥ (8.4)

āgamo = āgamaḥ — scripture; 'pah = apaḥ — water; prajā = prajāḥ — people, association; deśaḥ — location; kālaḥ — time; *karma* — activity; ca — and; janma — birth; ca — and; dhyānam — effortless linkage of the attention to a higher concentration force; mantro = mantraḥ — sacred words; 'tha = atha — and; saṁskāro = saṁskāraḥ — purificatory rituals with mystic connotations; daśaite = daśa — ten + ete — these; guṇa-hetavaḥ = guṇa — tendency + hetavaḥ — causes.

Translation

The scripture, the water, the association, the location, the time and the activity, the birth, the effortless linkage of the attention to a higher concentration force or person, the sacred words recited, the purificatory rituals with mystic connotations. These ten aspects are the causes of tendencies. (8.4)

Commentary:

The mundane influence is threefold. There are combinations of these three energies. They hardly occur in their isolated forms. One has to work his way out of that combined influence. It is found that even if one becomes situated in the highest of the modes, that of the clarifying influence, then if he is not careful he falls back to the lower levels, being compelled as it were to act on their behalf. That is the natural way. It takes a certain amount of endeavor to break out completely.

Each of the aspects described above, can lead a person to either of the modes. One has to be selective in dealing with any of the ten factors above.

Scriptures

Study of the scriptures, acceptance of their standards, may lead a person in the proper direction for an improvement in spiritual life, but the scriptures may cause a person to go downwards as well. This is because no matter how elevated a scripture is, if one has a bad motivation, one might be able to convert scriptural rulings into something that is troublesome to one and all.

This means that reading of scriptures results in actions which are based on the person's good or bad motivation. Thus purity of character is necessary for the proper motivation. The scriptures cannot be blamed. There are some scriptures which offer claims which cannot be substantiated in fact. They were written by not-so-perfect saints. But still if one has purity of character one will not exploit a scripture nor indulge in any fantasies which a scripture advocates.

Water

Water is used mainly for nutrition and hygiene. A human being must have a certain quantity of water. In the Vedic rituals, water is considered to be an essential ingredient. It is used for the sanctification of objects. However, water can be misused. If one misuses it, it will cause one to go downwards.

The human body is mostly liquid in mass. This liquids can cause the body to have good, impulsive or evil qualities. Liquids controls sex desire which is a strong enticement for the human beings.

Association

Association has a big effect on an ascetic who is about to turn away from the material world. Therefore one has to be careful with association. Arjuna for example, had some emotional problems when confronted with the battle situation at *Kurukṣetra*. It was a problem with facing people, regarding whether they approved or disapproved his actions.

An ascetic has to know how to handle his social interactions if he is at all to be successful in the spiritual quest, since such a pursuit will inevitably involve getting the disapproval of many persons in social interactions.

For success in yoga, psychological isolation is necessary, for so long as one's psyche is open to vibrations from persons who do not desire that one should leave the world, one will not be free to practice the higher yoga. And without such practice, one is condemned to remain in this existence.

Even though yogis are required to go into isolation, still it does not mean just a physical confinement. The yogi must have a psychological one, if he is to succeed. If he cannot isolate himself from the disturbing sensuality of others, he will fail in higher yoga.

Location

The location is important for a yogi, because if he is in a social vicinity where people can relate to him frequently, he will not be able to complete the yoga practice. This is because such social interaction is time-consuming. Therefore he must be located in hard-to-reach places. We have heard so many stories in the *Purāṇas*, the *Rāmāyaṇa* and the *Mahābhārata* which describe yogis who lived in remote forest or in remote mountainous areas like the Himalayas.

However if the *devas* or *devatas*, the supernatural people, object to a particular yogi's plans to go into isolation, he will find that they present effective obstacles which will force him back into civilization. Then he has to consider what demands they place on him. Unless one gets a waiver from the Universal Form of *Śrī* Krishna, one cannot go into isolation successfully, since many strokes of destiny will frustrate one's plan for isolation.

Time

The time for practice and the time used by the yogi when he decides to greatly reduce social interactions, must be properly selected otherwise the yogi will fail at the practice. In this respect the yogi must be authorized. He must have gained the approval of the Universal Form. Some feel that he needs the approval of a spiritual master, of a pure devotee of the Lord, but that is not the issue. I do not care about such approval in this instance, because the spiritual master has no authority to go against the grain of the Universal Form and if he does so, he will be ruined. It is quite possible for an endearing spiritual master to go against the wishes of the Universal Form.

Here we are talking about the direct approval of the Universal Form. If the spiritual master or pure devotee is actually in touch with that form, when the ascetic discusses this and if that person echoes the opinion of that Form, then their decision would be in order, but all too often such spiritual masters, such pure devotees, pretend that they are always in touch with the Universal Form positively, or they sincerely believe so and disrupt the supreme will by offering off-beat advices to the ascetic who is endeavoring.

The ascetic needs the approval of the Universal Form, the same form which Arjuna saw on the battlefield, when *Śrī* Krishna gave the awesome revelation. Once he gets the supreme approval he can be successful even if his spiritual master is against it and feels that he should remain in public for preaching and other missionary activities. By such sanction, he would have the time for practice, and would be blessed to be free from social disturbances. If the Universal Form declines permission, the ascetic must remain in the social field and complete duties. He should do so in the attitude of a *karma* yogi as taught by *Śrī* Krishna to Arjuna in the *Bhagavad-Gītā*.

The *Bhagavad Gītā* is the ultimate crash course in *karma* yoga. By a careful study of it, one can learn how to function in the social, cultural and political fields for the satisfaction of *Śrī* Krishna, to help God to impregnate this world with moral values. After one has done this sufficiently, one may get a release from Him, so that one can take yoga on a full time basis.

Activity

Activity is important because it is by activity that we become bound or freed. Inactivity is also a form of activity. That must be realized. *Śrīla* Lahiri *Mahāśaya* introduced the idea of *prāṇa karma* or the activity of *prāṇa*. This is not a new idea but he brought it to our attention, because we usually regard activity as being only what is done on the gross level. That is *śarīra karma* or activity of the flesh and bones, gross energy.

A yogi has to learn how to make movements with *prāṇa* or the subtle energy which is invested into the subtle body. He has to become more mystic and less of a gross human being. It is by mystic activity that one effects purity of the psyche. Gross activities cannot by their nature, bring on sufficient purity. A certain amount of gross activity does help but it must be done under the watchful gaze and approval of the Universal Form, otherwise such social, cultural and political involvement deters and postpones spiritual advancement. The definition is given in verse 11 of chapter 5 of the *Bhagavad Gītā*:

kāyena manasā buddhyā kevalairindriyairapi
yoginaḥ karma kurvanti saṅgaṁ tyaktvātmaśuddhaye

With the body, mind and intelligence, or even with the senses alone, the yogis, having discarded attachment, perform cultural acts for self-purification. (B.G. 5.11)

Apart from activity for social interaction, one must take up in earnest, *haṭha* yoga practice which covers the full course of the 3rd step of yoga which is the practice of *āsana* postures. These postures stir up and disturb the energies in the gross and subtle bodies, so that the ascetic can rearrange or displace those energies for facilitating higher yoga.

Birth

In a sense, we are continually being born and continually are dying to one thing or the other. The grand births occurs anytime an infant form is delivered from a mother's womb. Even that birth affects our display of tendencies.

By aspiring in spiritual life, we continually change the psychological environment we are in and by that we alter the tendencies. Most commentators explained that *janma* or birth means ritual birth through initiation. In India this means initiation into the brahmin way of life, as a disciple of a spiritual master in a lineage of teachers. This is usually highlighted by the assumption of special mantras or sacred sounds which are repeated at a certain time of the day. Sometimes such initiations are effective. Sometimes they serve no purpose whatsoever, other than award a status to a certain person as a member of a religious society with privileges.

Even though such initiations are given in yoga practice, they are not the focal point. The yogi should look for new birth or initiation in the form of perception of the subtle, super subtle and spiritual environments. His supernormal experiences are what is highlighted in yoga practice. Arjuna for example got a new birth when he saw the revelation of the Universal Form. It was not a sacred thread. It was not a mantra.

Effortless linkage of the attention to a higher concentration force

This type of meditation certainly determines the tendencies which the yogi will exhibit. It is through higher meditation that the yogi is able to displace the lower qualities with higher ones.

The sacred word

This is the mantra used by the ascetic. It is important that the ascetic receive the mantra from the teacher of the particular discipline which the mantra concerns. Mantra or sacred words which are for calling Deities or supernatural people should be used for that only and not for asking for things to ease one's material existence.

Purificatory process

The purificatory process is given in the *Bhagavad Gītā*:

kāyena manasā buddhyā kevalairindriyairapi
yoginaḥ karma kurvanti saṅgaṁ tyaktvātmaśuddhaye

With the body, mind and intelligence, or even with the senses alone, the yogis, having discarded attachment, perform cultural acts for self-purification. (B.G. 5.11)

tatraikāgraṁ manaḥ kṛtvā yatacittendriyakriyaḥ
upaviśyāsane yuñjyād yogamātmaviśuddhaye

...being there, seated in a posture, having the mind focused, the person who controls his thinking and sensual energy, should practise the yoga discipline for self-purification. (B.G. 6.12)

These ten aspects above affect our tendencies, either to upgrade or to degrade further or even to cause us to remain stagnant.

तत् तत् सात्त्विकम् एवैषां
यद् यद् वृद्धाः प्रचक्षते ।
निन्दन्ति तामसं तत् तद्
राजसं तद्-उपेक्षितम् ॥८.५॥

tat tat sāttvikam evaiṣāṁ
yad yad vṛddhāḥ pracakṣate
nindanti tāmasaṁ tat tad
rājasaṁ tad-upekṣitam (8.5)

tat tat — that that, those; sāttvikam — whatever is productive of the clarifying influence; evaisam = eva — alone + eṣām — of those; yad yad = yat yat — what what, whatever; vṛddhāḥ — the respected ancient authorities; pracakṣate — acclaim; nindanti — they condemn; tāmasam — whatever is productive of the retardative influence; tat tad = tat tat — that that, those; rājasam — whatever is productive of the passionate influence; tad-upekṣitam = tad (tat) — that + upeksitam — ignore.

Translation

Of those causes, whatever is productive of the clarifying influence, the respected ancient sages acclaim. Whatever is productive of the retardative influence, they condemn. Whatever is productive of the passionate influence, they ignore. (8.5)

Commentary:

We have no other recourse but to take help from the great yogi sages. By discovery alone, it would take too long for us to become liberated, apart from the fact, that we might never discover a terminal method. And since our material bodies do not last forever, we cannot afford to follow only the path of discovery. The problem however is that most of the great yogi sages are departed. How then, are we to contact them? The secret to this is to develop mystic perception.

Any of those ancient yogis can be reached if we have mystic perception. Hence the necessity for it. Mystic perception is also required if we are to understand the operation of the subtle body and causal form, an understanding which is necessary for the completion of higher yoga.

Each living entity has to work with his or her psyche to displace the passionate and retardative influences with the clarifying one. That is the first step. It is believed that this step is unnecessary, since a powerful spiritual master can bless the disciple to by-pass it. It is believed that he can alter the nature of the disciple or that he can give the disciple an easy way of doing so. However this commentary does not ascribe to such beliefs. The spiritual master can give techniques for displacing the lower influence. In my view that is all he can do. The disciple must put such techniques into practice to cause the displacement. That is what I feel.

सात्त्विकान्य् एव सेवेत
पुमान् सत्त्व-विवृद्धये ।
ततो धर्मस् ततो ज्ञानं
यावत् स्मृतिर् अपोहनम् ॥८.६॥

sāttvikāny eva seveta
pumān sattva-vivṛddhaye
tato dharmas tato jñānaṁ
yāvat smṛtir apohanam (8.6)

sāttvikāny = sāttvikāni — whatever is productive of the clarifying influence; eva — only; seveta — should cultivate; pumān — a person; sattva-vivṛddhaye = sattva — clarifying influence + vivṛddhaye — in the reinforcement; tato = tataḥ — hence, consequentially; dharmas = dharmaḥ — righteous nature; tato = tataḥ — from that; jnanam — objectivity; yāvat — until; smṛtir = smṛtiḥ — memory; apohanam — psychological power for the removal of what is not desired.

Translation

For the reinforcement of the clarifying influence, a person should cultivate only what is conducive to clarity. Consequently, righteousness is manifested and from that objectivity comes, until there is a constant memory and the psychological power for the removal of what is not desired. (8.6)

Commentary:

These are detailed instructions for the *kriyā* yogi. He has to clear off the lower influence of the passionate and retardative forces. That should be his primary concern in the beginning. He has to adopt whatever austerities or lifestyle curtails the lower influences and are supportive of the clarifying power .

When the righteous energy becomes predominant in one's nature, one should still take steps to reinforce it, so that one comes to a point where the passionate and retardative influences are completely squeezed out, being displaced by the righteous power. This occurs by psychological or mystic actions within the nature. Once this is completed one gains an objectivity of consciousness, whereby one sees clearly the various influences in one's life and in the life of others. From that one gains a constant memory of the objectives of spiritual life and one does not forget that one will have to transmigrate sooner or later and that the subtle body serves as the foundation for the transmigrations. Then one develops a psychological power to remove from within the nature, whatever is not desired.

This psychological power does not come on in full force initially. It comes little by little in an accumulation according to movements of destiny and the intensity of one's higher yoga practice.

A yogin has to work his way up from a lower mode to a higher one, until he is consistently situated in the mode of clarity. It is from that foundation that he may attain the transcendence consistently. Using clarity as a platform, he may practice the higher disciplines which cause his psyche to be shifted from the modes of material nature into the transcendental atmosphere, the chit *ākāśa*.

Each yogi has to endeavor according to the extent of impurity. He must systematically remove the bad habits which cause him to remain or to always be re-adjusted to a lower plane. When he does sufficient austerity and is vigilant in watching the imperfections and painstakingly corrected these, the full righteousness becomes established in him. This abolishes the passionate influence and causes a constant memory and a heightened conscience. Thus his intellect becomes clarified.

Devotion in the passionate mode of material nature is quite possible. In fact any devotee who does not have the purified nature, renders his devotion mostly through that passionate mode but *Śrī* Krishna is not attracted to that. Therefore such devotees must carefully elevate themselves through the mode of goodness and into the transcendence, before they are actually recognized by the Blessed Lord. It is up to each devotee to understand this.

वेणु-सङ्घर्ष-जो वह्निर्
दग्ध्वा शाम्यति तद्-वनम् ।
एवं गुण-व्यत्यय-जो
देहः शाम्यति तत्-क्रियः ॥८.७॥

veṇu-saṅgharṣa-jo vahnir
dagdhvā śāmyati tad-vanam
evaṁ guṇa-vyatyaya-jo
dehaḥ śāmyati tat-kriyaḥ (8.7)

veṇu-saṅgharsa-jo = venu — bamboo + sangharsa – friction + jo (jah) — produced; vahnir = vahnih — fire; dagdhvā — having burnt; śāmyati — is quieted; tad-vanam = tad (tat) — that + vanam — forest; evam — thus, similarly; guṇa-vyatyaya-jo = guṇa — mundane influence + vyatyaya – intermixture + jo (jah) — produced; dehaḥ — gross body; śāmyati — is curbed; tat-kriyah = tat — that + kriyah — special bodily actions.

Translation

Having burnt the forest, the fire that is produced by the friction of bamboos, is quieted. Similarly, the body which is produced from the intermixture of the mundane influences, is curbed by special bodily actions. (8.7)

Commentary:

A yogin must get rid of his affiliation with material nature by using the same nature. He has to work his way out of this creation by using the very same energy of the creation. Even though the intellect is a mundane tool, it is a very subtle one made from the subtle material elements. It must be used nevertheless in the quest for its own elimination.

As far as a living material body is concerned, it includes the subtle and causal forms. The yoga practice is designed to engage all three of these in eliminating the very same energies eventually, so that the yogi can be his spiritual self without the subtle mundane appendages which are a necessary add-on, so long as his consciousness is not transferred into the other sky, the spiritual world, the chit *ākāśa*.

Śrī Krishna, the Supreme Lord, advised that we must use the material, subtle and causal bodies and their sensing instruments to get rid of these very same bodies. For liberation, we have to use these bodies.

श्री-उद्धव उवाच
विदन्ति मर्त्याः प्रायेण
विषयान् पदम् आपदाम् ।
तथापि भुञ्जते कृष्ण तत्
कथं श्व-खराज-वत् ॥८.८॥

śrī-uddhava uvāca
vidanti martyāḥ prāyeṇa
viṣayān padam āpadām
tathāpi bhuñjate kṛṣṇa tat
kathaṁ śva-kharāja-vat (8.8)

śrī-uddhava – the deserving Uddhava; uvāca — said; vidanti — realise; martyāḥ — human beings whose bodies will surely die; prāyena — generally; viṣayān — attractive objects; padam — location; āpadām — dangerous situations; tathāpi — even so; bhuñjate — exploit; kṛṣṇa —Krishna; tat — that; katha — how is it; śva-kharāja-vat = śva — dog + khara — ass + aja — goat + vat — like.

Translation

The deserving Uddhava said: In general, the human beings, whose bodies will surely die, realise that the attractive objects are locations of danger. Even so, O Krishna, how is it that like a dog, ass or goat, they try to exploit them? (8.8)

Commentary:

The answer to this question will explain why we are repeatedly attracted to exploitation. There is something compelling that forces even a discriminative person to indulge in mundane experiences which implicate him deeper in material existence. The power which is held over us is the same power which operates in the life of the animals. But despite our superior discrimination, the power repeatedly compels us.

श्री-भगवान् उवाच
अहम् इत्य् अन्यथा-बुद्धिः
प्रमत्तस्य यथा हृदि ।
उत्सर्पति रजो घोरं
ततो वैकारिकं मनः ॥८.९॥

śrī-bhagavān uvāca
aham ity anyathā-buddhiḥ
pramattasya yathā hṛdi
utsarpati rajo ghoraṁ
tato vaikārikaṁ manaḥ (8.9)

śrī-bhagavān – the blessed Lord; uvāca — said; aham — I; ity = iti — thus thinking; anyathā –error-prone, inaccurate; buddhih — intellect; pramattasya — of an inattentive person; yathā — as; hrdi — in the core of being; utsarpati — spreads through; rajo = rajah — passionate influence; ghoram — terrible; tato = tatah — then; vaikārikam — pertaining to the clarifying mode originally; manah — mind.

Translation

The Blessed Lord said: The error-prone intellect of an inattentive person projects the idea of 'I' in the core of being. Hence the terrible passionate influence spreads through the mind which is essentially clarifying. (8.9)

Commentary:

In this respect, nearly every human being is inattentive, at least periodically. *Śrī* Uddhava, that deserving and great personality, was also inattentive, even in the presence of the most attentive person, *Śrī* Krishna. It hinges on the nature of the intellect. This subtle organ is itself error-prone. It is hardly likely that anyone who depends on it, will get out of material existence. The reliance on the intellect puts the living entity into a very touchy position of having to accept its conclusions. *Śrī* Krishna posited that passionate influence as being the direct cause of the misunderstanding, but this happens so quickly, that it is hardly likely that a common man could master his psychology.

What *Śrī* Krishna stated is complicated. We are by nature inattentive. That is the first flaw. By such inattentiveness, we naturally hold the mind in reliance for keeping track of our physical and psychological activities. This is like a wealthy man who has many concerns and who hires various employees to conduct his numerous businesses. By nature he will be liable for the mistakes and faulty decisions of the employees. Yoga concerns itself with increasing our attentive powers by getting rid of all unnecessary and spiritually-harmful concerns. When we reduce our interests, then we have a chance of increasing our attentiveness and taking direct control of the psyche. Otherwise we will have to continue in total or near-total reliance on the mind and its intellectual apparatus.

The second flaw is that the intellect, which we are endowed with, is error-prone. This intellect was awarded by the Cosmic God but nevertheless, He did not give us a perfect instrument. It is however not His fault because our inattentive nature could not attach itself to a perfect instrument. By necessity, He gave us an analyzing tool which perfectly matched our inattentive nature.

The third flaw is that as soon as there is contact between our spirit and the energy of material nature, there arises a sense of identity. Even though at the dawn of creation, that sense of identity was not applied, as soon as it was operated later, as described in this verse, the passionate influence was actuated. That force banished clarity of the already fault-prone intellect.

The intellect given to us by the Cosmic God is capable of showing us the Supreme Reality but it can only do that if it is saturated with the clarifying energy. If there is any other type of energy in it, it cannot show the Reality.

The innate tendency of the mind is to clarify. It will do this or attempt to do this, regardless of which type of energy saturates it. When it is surcharged with the clarity energy, it perceives the Supreme Reality. The automatic conversion of the mind's energy intake from a higher force to a lower one, makes it near-impossible for any of us to consistently see the Reality, because the speed with which the mind switches from one mode to another, rarely permits our interference in its operations. In that sense, it seems that our liberation would be indefinitely forestalled.

रजो-युक्तस्य मनसः
सङ्कल्पः स-विकल्पकः ।
ततः कामो गुण-ध्यानाद्
दुःसहः स्याद् धि दुर्मतेः ॥८.१०॥

rajo-yuktasya manasaḥ
saṅkalpaḥ sa-vikalpakaḥ
tataḥ kāmo guṇa-dhyānād
duḥsahaḥ syād dhi durmateḥ (8.10)

rajo-yuktasya = rajo (rajah) — the passionate influence + yuktasya — of that which is used; manasaḥ — of the mind; saṅkalpaḥ — intention; sa-vikalpakaḥ — with variation; tataḥ — consequently; kāmo = kāmah — craving; guṇa-dhyānād = guṇa — feature + dhyānād (dhyānāt) — from the linkage of the attention to a higher force or person; duḥsahaḥ — unbearable, irresistible; syād = syāt — it must be; dhi = hi — indeed; durmateḥ — of a foolish person.

Translation

The intentions of the mind of one who functions under the passionate influence, has variations. Hence from the linkage of his attention to the features, a foolish person experiences an unbearable craving. (8.10)

Commentary:

For the purpose of *kriyā* yoga, we have to understand that we are the persons being described in these verses. We are the ones whose minds function under the passionate influence with many variations. Our intentions have many variations, even in respect to what we aim for in yoga practice. It is yoga practice itself which causes our intentions to be narrowed eventually. The practice causes this. Even though we begin with vague, indirect and totally unreasonable objectives, as we practice, we get the clarity which shows us what we may actually attain.

The unbearable irresistible cravings which we endure in materialistic life, are transferred over into spiritual life, because we move into the spiritual field with impractical objectives. When we give up what is absurd, then we will be freed from the cravings. But that only happens after consistent steady practice.

Uddhava's defect, as well as our own, is shown here. He exerted himself to help others, while he himself required the very same assistance he tried to procure for the others. In fact, unless we fix ourselves we cannot carry the remedial process to anyone else. We must first take these instructions to heart and perfect them in our lives, before we can share with others. In fact, it might not be necessary for a particular yogin to help others, because unless that is the desire of *Śrī* Krishna, it would be detrimental to his advancement.

Truly speaking, spiritual practice is no place for a compassionate man, because he will invariably be unresponsive to his teachers and will in the course of time, come to take on an incompetent teacher who will indulge him in the business of converting others, using that endeavor as an excuse for avoiding self purification and self attentiveness.

करोति काम-वश-गः
कर्माण्य् अविजितेन्द्रियः ।
दुःखोदर्काणि सम्पश्यन्
रजो-वेग-विमोहितः ॥८.११॥

karoti kāma-vaśa-gaḥ
karmāṇy avijitendriyaḥ
duḥkhodarkāṇi sampaśyan
rajo-vega-vimohitaḥ (8.11)

karoti — performs; kāma — craving; vaśa — under the control; gah — having gone; karmāny = karmāni — activities; avijitendriyaḥ = avijita — lacking control + indriyah — senses; duḥkhodarkāni = duhkha — misery + udarkāni — consequences; sampaśyan — perceiving; rajo (rajah) — passionate influence; vega — forceful; vimohitaḥ — bewildered.

Translation

Being subjugated by craving, the person who lacks sense control, who is bewildered by the force of passion, performs activities, although perceiving that the consequence is misery. (8.11)

Commentary:

The key is to control the shifting mechanism which causes the passionate mode to take control of the psyche. This however brings on another problem: Can that mechanism be controlled? It is one thing to consider that if we would control this, we would not be put under the lower dominance, but it is an entirely different matter to face up to the reality of our inability to gain control. Can we actually get the shifting psychological mechanism under control?

In the practice of *pratyāhar* sense withdrawal and in our feeble awkward attempts at meditation, we quickly realize that something controls that shifting mechanism. It is not controlled by the self, otherwise it would simply be a matter of keeping the psyche in the clarifying influence. We see that we are forcibly shifted off from that clarifying zone and placed under the dominance of the lower influences.

In the preliminary practice of meditation, one finds out that one does not control the alterations in the mind. These transpire of their own accord by the laws of nature which govern the particular type of mental energy. Hence the necessity for *prāṇāyāma* practice to change out lower mental force. It is not a matter of controlling the mind but it is rather, taking the upper hand to regulate its energy intake. It operates on the basis of the type of energy which powers it. The example of a carburetor may assist in understanding this. If one uses a low grade of fuel he will get a low gas mileage. A higher octane fuel burns more efficiently and gives more mileage, provided the carburetor is designed for the increased heat produced. In the long run, one is better off with a higher grade. It turns out to be cheaper. Similarly if we can put a higher grade of subtle energy into the mind, if our intellect would be powered by a higher *prāṇa*, then we would experience a more favorable relationship with the mind. We would find it to be more obedient.

The mind and intellect, like a carburetor, is prebuilt. The only thing we can adjust is the grade of fuel and the type of mental energy intake. One must practice *prāṇāyāma* and thus cause the mind to shift itself into a higher mode.

As stated in this verse, when we are under the control of the passionate force, we exhibit cravings. Although we might perceive that the consequences of our actions would be miserable, still we would persists in procuring what is desired, because in that state our discrimination is not allowed to monitor our actions. This is the way it is. The secret therefore is not to try to control ourselves when we are under the passionate force but rather to work to put another higher grade of energy into the mind. Again, this means that we must practice *prāṇāyāma*. There is no other effective method for changing out a lower energy from the mind.

This may not be what *Śrī* Uddhava wished to hear because he asked for a method to be used by the average human being, who is unable to devout himself or herself to yoga practice.

रजस्-तमोभ्यां यद् अपि
विद्वान् विक्षिप्त-धीः पुनः ।
अतन्द्रितो मनो युञ्जन्
दोष-दृष्टिर् न सज्जते ॥८.१२॥

rajas-tamobhyāṁ yad api
vidvān vikṣipta-dhīḥ punaḥ
atandrito mano yuñjan
doṣa-dṛṣṭir na sajjate (8.12)

rajas = rajaḥ - by passionate influence; tamobhyām — by retardation; yad = yat – that; api — even;

vidvān — of a wise person; vikṣipta-dhīh = vikṣipta — distracted + dhīḥ — intellect; punaḥ — again; atandrito = atandritaḥ — carefully; mano = manaḥ — mind; yuñjan — engages, disciplines; doṣa — defects; dṛṣṭir = dṛṣṭiḥ — perceiving; na — not; sajjate — is attached.

Translation

Even though the intellect of a wise man is distracted by the passionate and retardative influences, he again, carefully disciplines the mind. He perceives the defects and is not attached. (8.12)

Commentary:

The wise man has no alternative but to repeatedly adjust the wayward mind. He cannot totally stop the mind from deviating, because so long as he is in this world, his mind will, by the nature of the world, have to enter lower modes, though as he advances, it does so less frequently. He must readjust it repeatedly but he must use the practical method of changing the lower energies for higher ones. A wise man trains himself to be detached from the advantages which accrue from the lower energies. When this training is complete, he automatically does *prāṇāyāma* and uses psychic actions, *kriyās*, to readjust the energy in the mind.

अप्रमत्तो ऽनुयुञ्जीत
मनो मय्य् अर्पयञ् छनैः ।
अनिर्विण्णो यथा-कालं
जित-श्वासो जितासनः ॥८.१३॥

apramatto 'nuyuñjīta
mano mayy arpayañ chanaiḥ
anirviṇṇo yathā-kālaṁ
jita-śvāso jitāsanaḥ (8.13)

apramatto = apramattah — attentive; 'nuyuñjīta = anuyuñjīta — one should focus; mano = manaḥ — the mind; mayy = mayi — on Me; arpayan — placing; chanaiḥ = śanaiḥ — methodically; anirviṇṇo = anirviṇṇah — without being depressed; yathā-kālam = yathā – as, regular + kālam — time; jita-svāso = jita — mastering + śvāso (śvāsah) — breath; jitāsanaḥ = jita — mastering + āsanaḥ — sitting postures.

Translation

Being attentive, one should focus methodically, placing the mind on Me, without being depressed and at the regular time and having mastered the breath and sitting postures. (8.13)

Commentary:

This is the method used in *kriyā* yoga for shifting the mind from the passionate level to the clarifying plane. When the mind is stationed in the clarifying energy, being saturated with it, the yogi can control and direct it in concentrated focus.

What does it mean to place the mind on *Śrī* Krishna? The answer to this depends on the level of advancement of the yogin, for if he has not mastered the āsana postures and the breath regulation methods, he will not be able to focus on *Śrī* Krishna in the ideal way, instead he will focus haphazardly or he will practice lower yoga, which will not allow him to have the proper degree of concentration, nor the ability to penetrate into the transcendence where *Śrī* Krishna exists.

This type of focus is not physical Deity worship which is done to the *Śrī* Krishna *Mūrti*, the properly installed idol of *Śrī* Krishna. A yogi must first master his mind by practicing lower yoga. When he learns *kriyā* yoga sufficiently, he may graduate to higher yoga and learn how to transfer his attention to the sky of consciousness, the chit *ākāśa*. From there he may properly focus on *Śrī* Krishna.

एतावान् योग आदिष्टो
मच्-छिष्यैः सनकादिभिः ।
सर्वतो मन आकृष्य
मय्य् अद्धावेश्यते यथा ॥८.१४॥

etāvān yoga ādiṣṭo
mac-chiṣyaiḥ sanakādibhiḥ
sarvato mana ākṛṣya
mayy addhāveśyate yathā (8.14)

etāvān = etāvāt— thus, so far, to such a degree; yoga = yogah — yoga process; ādiṣṭo = ādiṣṭaḥ — taught; mac-chiṣyaiḥ = mat-śiṣyaiḥ = mat — by me + śiṣyaiḥ – students; sanakādibhiḥ = sanaka – Sanaka + ādibhiḥ — by other students; sarvato = sarvatah — from everything; mana = manah — mind; ākṛṣya — withdrawing; mayy = mayi — in me; addhāveśyate = addhā — truly + āveśyate — is absorbed; yathā — as, accordingly.

Translation

Thus the yoga process was taught by My students, Sanaka and others, for withdrawing the mind from everything so that it is absorbed in Me. (8.14)

Commentary:

The yoga process taught to *Sanaka* and others, is the same process taught today as the *aṣṭanga* yoga, which is defined by *Śrī Patañjali* Maharshi. It is also called *kriyā* yoga, and it has other names. Sometimes, parts of the whole yoga process are given under the names of rāja yoga, kundalini yoga, or *brahma* yoga. It does not change from era to era. The primary purpose of it is self-purification as described in the *Bhagavad Gītā* (6.12).

One must withdraw one's interest from the world. This is known nowadays as *pratyāhar* or the 5th stage of yoga, given in this talk to Uddhava as *ākṛṣya*. To accomplish that one must master *āsana* postures and breath recharge methods, along with developing a disinterest in the material world, just as the ascetic brahmin exhibited to King Yadu.

श्री-उद्धव उवाच
यदा त्वं सनकादिभ्यो
येन रूपेण केशव ।
योगम् आदिष्टवान् एतद्
रूपम् इच्छामि वेदितुम् ॥८.१५॥

śrī-uddhava uvāca
yadā tvaṁ sanakādibhyo
yena rūpeṇa keśava
yogam ādiṣṭavān etad
rūpam icchāmi veditum (8.15)

śrī-uddhava – the deserving Uddhva; uvāca — said; yadā — when; tvam — you; sanakādibhyo = sanakādibhyah = sanaka — Sanaka + ādibhiyaḥ - and the others; yena — by which; rūpeṇa — by form; keśava — O Keśava Krishna; yogam — yoga process; ādiṣṭavān — taught; etad = etat — that; rūpam — form; icchāmi — I wish; veditum — to know.

Translation

The deserving Uddhava said: When, by which form, O Keshava Krishna, was the yoga process taught to Sanaka and the others. I wish to know. (8.15)

Commentary:

As He spoke to Uddhava, discussing the method for reforming the distracted mind, *Śrī* Krishna recalled a previous incident when He instructed some sages who were headed by *Sanaka* Rishi. This happened a long, long time ago. *Śrī* Krishna fittingly recalled it. Uddhava's mind was drawn to the memory.

श्री-भगवान् उवाच
पुत्रा हिरण्यगर्भस्य
मानसाः सनकादयः ।
पप्रच्छुः पितर सूक्ष्मां
योगस्यैकान्तिकीम् गतिम् ॥८.१६॥

śrī-bhagavān uvāca
putrā hiraṇyagarbhasya
mānasāḥ sanakādayaḥ
papracchuḥ pitaraṁ sūkṣmāṁ
yogasyaikāntikīm gatim (8.16)

śrī-bhagavān – the blessed lord; uvāca — said; putrā = putrāḥ — sons; hiraṇyagarbhasya — of Hiraṇyagarbha, the Procreator Brahmā; mānasāḥ — of the mind, of the will power; sanakādayah = sanaka – Sanaka + ādayaḥ — and others; papracchuḥ — asked; pitaram — from the father; sūkṣmām — subtle aspect of reality; yogasyaikāntikīm = yogasya — of yoga discipline + ekāntikīm — the ultimate; gatim — objective.

Translation

The Blessed Lord said: Sanaka and others, who were produced by the will power of Hiraṇyagarbha, the Procreator Brahmā, asked their father about the subtle aspect of reality and of the ultimate objective of the yoga discipline. (8.16)

Commentary:

Sanaka Rishi and the others were mind-born sons of *Brahmā*. Just as a father begets a son by sexual intercourse, so Lord *Brahmā* begat his mind born sons by will power only. Thus *Swāmī Mādhavānanda* in his translation wrote that *Sanaka* and the others were the spiritual sons of *Brahmā*. This is not necessarily so but it is very likely. The mental begetting process used by *Brahmā* does not necessarily consign the progeny produces as spiritual off-spring, but it is likely. If so, then it means that in some creations, those spiritual sons of *Brahmā* disobey his order as we read in the early part of *Śrīmad Bhāgavatam* when Sanaka and the others, the four *Kumāras*, did disobey *Brahmā*, when he instructed that they become householders, to beget progeny by sexual indulgence.

Sanaka Rishi and the others were born yogins. They asked their father about the subtle aspect of reality. They wanted a sketch of the ultimate objective of the yoga disciplines, so that they would not have to waste time discovering something their father already knew. They wanted to accelerate yoga austerities so that they could get out of the material world quickly and set the same course for others.

सनकादय ऊचुः
गुणेष्व् आविशते चेतो
गुणाश् चेतसि च प्रभो ।
कथम् अन्योन्य-सन्त्यागो
मुमुक्षोर् अतितितीर्षोः ॥८.१७॥

sanakādaya ūcuḥ
guṇeṣv āviśate ceto
guṇāś cetasi ca prabho
katham anyonya-santyāgo
mumukṣor atititīrṣoḥ (8.17)

sanakāda = sanaka – Sanaka + ādaya – others; ūcuḥ — said; guṇeṣv = guṇeṣu — in the mundane objects; āviśate — attached itself to; ceto = cetah — the mind; guṇās = guṇāḥ — the mundane objects; cetasi — in the mind; ca — and; prabho — o respected elder; katham — how; anyonya — one to another; santyāgo = santyāgaḥ — stop interacting; mumuksor = mumukṣoḥ — of one who wants liberation; atititīrṣoḥ — of one who wants to transcend the mundane influence.

Translation

Sanaka and the others said: O respected elder, the mind attaches itself to the mundane objects and the objects do likewise to the mind. How, for one who wants liberation, and who wants to transcend the mundane influence, do the objects and the mind stop inter-acting with one another. (8.17)

Commentary:

As soon as they were produced, *Sanaka* and the others saw the defect in the *buddhi* organ of the subtle body. It has the tendency for attracting itself to mundane objects. They also noticed that the objects are magnetically drawn to the mind. That was a problem for anyone who wanted to transcend the mundane world and work for liberation, even though it was an asset or a convenience, for those persons who wanted to get involved.

Seeing that the operational instincts in the mind were an inconvenience for the spiritually-minded people, *Sanaka* and the others challenged *Brahmā* about it. The odds for liberation were against anyone becoming freed if he were to use an intellect which was accommodative to material nature. More or less, *Sanaka* wanted to know why the intellect which they were endowed with, was created in a way which discouraged detachment from the material world.

श्री-भगवान् उवाच
एव पृष्टो महा-देवः
स्वयम्भूर् भूत-भावनः ।
ध्यायमानः प्रश्न-बीजं
नाभ्यपद्यत कर्म-धीः ॥८.१८॥

śrī-bhagavān uvāca
evaṁ pṛṣṭo mahā-devaḥ
svayambhūr bhūta-bhāvanaḥ
dhyāyamānaḥ praśna-bījaṁ
nābhyapadyata karma-dhīḥ (8.18)

śrī-bhagavān – the blessed lord; uvāca — said; evam — thus; pṛṣṭo = pṛṣṭaḥ — asked; mahā-devaḥ — the great supernatural creator; svayambhūr = svayambhūḥ — self-born, apparently parentless; bhūta-bhāvanaḥ = bhūta — beings + bhāvanaḥ — originator; dhyāyamānah — effortless linkage of the attention to higher concentration energies; praśna-bījaṁ = praśna — question + bījam — seed, jist of; nābhyapadyata = na – not + abhyapadyata — solve out; karma-dhīḥ = karma – cultural activities + dhīḥ - mentally absorded, the focus of the intellect.

Translation

The Blessed Lord said: Being thus asked, the great supernatural creator, who is apparently parentless, the originator of the beings, effortlessly linked his attention to higher concentration energies, but could not solve the gist of the question. Despite that attempt, his intellect maintained its focus on cultural activities. (8.18)

Commentary:

Lord *Brahmā*, being no ordinary living entity, was quite capable of answering the question but he was caught off guard. At the time he was completely absorbed in mundane cultural activities having to do with the production of creatures, for exploitation of the subtle and gross creation, which he engineered by sheer imagination.

He was so engaged in that on the supernatural plane, that he could not extract himself from that sort of thinking. Thus he could not penetrate the question. To him, at that time, it was enigmatic. Even though he was capable of explaining why the intellect is attracted to objects and why the objects themselves seem to have a magnetic grasp on the intellect, still because he was absorbed with the subtle material energy, he could not free himself from that involvement for a sufficient time to give the answer to those questions.

The meaning is that if one is reliant on *Brahmā* for liberation, one will not be freed if *Brahmā* is in such a mood. The very same observations of *Sanaka* and the others, about the mind's involvement with the subtle and gross mundane energy, caused *Brahmā*, their spiritual elder, to be stupefied to the extent that he has no idea about how to become self-realized.

In this verse *Brahmā* is called *mahādevah*, which is a title usually reserved for Lord Shiva. *Brahmā* is also called *svayambhūr* or the one person who is parentless, an ultimate supernatural being. He is addressed as *bhūta-bhāvanah* which means that he is the originator of the subtle and gross beings in this creation.

And still, because he was absorbed with subtle material energy, his intellect which is the cosmic intelligence, could not free itself from that involvement in order to give vital information about self-realization. It is an important topic, because unless one knows it, one cannot be liberated.

स माम् अचिन्तयद् देवः
प्रश्न-पार-तितीर्षया ।
तस्याह हंस-रूपेण
सकाशम् अगमं तदा ॥८.१९॥

sa mām acintayad devaḥ
praśna-pāra-titīrṣayā
tasyāhaṁ haṁsa-rūpeṇa
sakāśam agamaṁ tadā (8.19)

sa = sah — he; mām — me; acintayad = acintayat — thought of; devaḥ — the supernatural creator; praśna-pāra-titīrṣayā = praśna — question + pāra — final answer, conclusion + titīrṣayā — really desired; tasyāham = tasya — to him + aham — I; haṁsa-rūpeṇa = haṁsa - swan + rūpeṇa — with a form; sakāśam — visible; agamam — became; tadā — then.

Translation

That Supernatural Creator thought of Me, as he really desired the final answer to the question. Then I became visible to him in the form of a Swan. (8.19)

Commentary:

Even though Lord *Brahmā* was perplexed by the question, still as a transcendentalist, he really desired to gave the answer to it. Since he is a specially-protected agent of *Śrī* Krishna, he automatically reached the Supreme Lord by mystic telecommunications.

Brahmā realized that in his present state of mind, he could not fathom the question but he knew that it should be answered because even though he was engaged in mundane creation, self-realization was a valid purpose. Thus he mentally reached Lord Krishna to get help with the perplexing inquiry. Because *Brahmā* was unable to release himself from the social affairs, he could not be inspired with the answer and so the Lord of *Brahmā* manifested into that dimension in a swan body.

This proves conclusively that if one is engaged in a cultural activity which is assigned by the Supreme Lord, one will get assistance from the Lord if one is unable to complete another duty because of being absorbed in the cultural assignment. *Karma* yoga, as it is defined in the *Bhagavad-Gītā* is not the highest practice but if one is engaged in it for *Śrī* Krishna, He will assist one if one is called upon to perform a higher duty. The higher duty above *karma* yoga is *jñāna* yoga, which is the application of yoga disciplines to philosophical inquires, just as the Sanaka and others did.

They were repulsed from *karma* yoga, and were attracted causelessly to *jñāna* yoga which is higher. *Śrī* Krishna desire that both *karma* yoga and *jñāna* yoga should be promoted in the mundane creation. In the *Bhagavad-Gītā*, Arjuna was taught *karma* yoga, which is the application of yoga expertise to cultural life, but in these instructions to Uddhava, *jñāna* yoga is the main topic.

दृष्ट्वा माम् त उपव्रज्य
कृत्व पादाभिवन्दनम् ।
ब्रह्माणम् अग्रतः कृत्वा
पप्रच्छुः को भवान् इति ॥८.२०॥

dṛṣṭvā mām ta upavrajya
kṛtva pādābhivandanam
brahmāṇam agrataḥ kṛtvā
papracchuḥ ko bhavān iti (8.20)

dṛṣṭvā — after seeing; mām — me; ta = te — they; upavrajya — came foward; kṛtvā — making; pādābhivandanam = pāda — feet + abhivandanam — bowing; brahmānam — Brahmā; agratah — in front; kṛtvā — placing; papracchuḥ — they asked; ko = kah - who; bhavān — you, o sir; iti — thus.

Translation

After seeing Me, they came foward, bowing at My feet and placing Brahmā in front, they asked, "Who are You, O Sir?" (8.20)

Commentary:

Sanaka and his brothers, had no idea who the Swan was. They suspected that whosoever that person was, he was there to answer the question. In any case, they dared to ask the Lord of His identity. This is because they were affected by social seniority. Even though they had the tendency for self-realization, they were affected by the fact that their father was the first manifested person in the creation, an apparently parentless being. They assumed that aside from their father *Brahmā*, they were the only seniors. Thus, instead of first identifying themselves and then asking in a submissive way about the identity of the Swan, they questioned the Swan to declare his pedigree.

Suspecting that he was the senior of *Brahmā*, because *Brahmā* had somehow referred the question to Him, they placed *Brahmā* in front and approached Lord Svan.

इत्य् अहं मुनिभिः पृष्टस्
तत्त्व-जिज्ञासुभिस् तदा ।
यद् अवोचम् अहं तेभ्यस्
तद् उद्धव निबोध मे ॥८.२१॥

ity ahaṁ munibhiḥ pṛṣṭas
tattva-jijñāsubhis tadā
yad avocam ahaṁ tebhyas
tad uddhava nibodha me (8.21)

ity = iti — thus; aham — I; munibhih — by the yogi philosophers; pṛṣṭas = pṛṣṭaḥ — asked; tattva — reality; jijñāsubhis = jijñāsubhiḥ — by those who are eager to understand; tadā — then; yad = yat — what; avocam — spoke; aham — I; tebhyas = tebhyaḥ — to them; tad = tat — that; uddhava — Uddhava; nibodha — learn; me — from me.

Translation

Being thus asked by the yogi philsophers, who were eager to understand the reality, I spoke to them. Now Uddhava, you may learn this from Me. (8.21)

Commentary:

Even though Uddhava verbalized the question in a different way, still his inquiry aimed for the same answers which the divine Swan gave to *Sanaka* and his brothers. Therefore *Śrī* Krishna instructed Uddhava to learn about the answer to his own question by hearing what was told to *Sanaka*.

What the sons of *Brahmā* inquired of at the beginning of that time cycle, was being asked by Uddhava to Lord Krishna, and the answer remained the same. It is the same question. It has the same answer, regardless of the time of an inquiry. Even if this question was asked today, it would have the very same answer, because nothing changed in the way the intellect of a human being relates to the material energy.

We cannot at this stage get a new answer which is different to the one given to the *Kumāras*, because essentially nothing changed since the time when the *Kumāras* asked the question, so many thousand years prior.

वस्तुनो यद्य् अनानात्व
आत्मनः प्रश्न ईदृशः ।
कथं घटेत वो विप्रा
वक्तुर् वा मे क आश्रयः ॥८.२२॥

vastuno yady anānātva
ātmanaḥ praśna īdṛśaḥ
kathaṁ ghaṭeta vo viprā
vaktur vā me ka āśrayaḥ (8.22)

vastuno = vastunaḥ — reality; yady = yadi — if; anānātva = anānātve — in the matter of being undivided; ātmanah — of the spirit; praśna — question; īdṛśah — such; katham — how; ghateta — is possible; vo = vah — of you; viprā = viprāḥ — brahmins, educated ones; vaktur = vaktuḥ — of the speaker; vā — or; me — of me, of my identity; ka = kah — what is; āśrayah — the existential foundation.

Translation

(Swan Krishna said:) If your question concerns the spirit, then that reality, being undivided, how is such an inquiry possible? O educated ones, what is the existential foundation of the one who asked the question about My identity. (8.22)

Commentary:

Even though the sons of *Brahmā* were new to the mundane creation, still they carried with them from the previous time cycle, their cultivated knowledge of spiritual principles. Some of this knowledge was there as intuition only. Some was objective knowledge or *jñānam*. In order to bring their intuition forward into their conscious minds, they approached *Brahmā* to ask for the way of changing the wayward nature of their intellects.

They wanted the process of *kriyā* yoga which enables a yogi to change his intellectual nature so that he can be free from mundane affinity. However, Sanaka and his brothers were slightly disrespectful of *Brahmā* because he was involved in cultural activity or *karma* yoga, the application of yoga expertise to cultural life. Since they disrespect him, they were due for chastisement from the master of *Brahmā*, the person who inspired him to give up *jñāna* yoga and take up the lower *karma* yoga. *Sanaka* and his fellows did not at the time, appreciate the fact that their birth in the material world, was made possible not by *jñāna* yoga but by the very *karma* yoga which they shunned. Thus Lord Krishna in the supernatural swan form, had every reason to humble them. They were proud of birth as educated brahmins, *viprās*. Lord Krishna wanted to humble them in that regard, for without humility, they could not understand the answer to their questions.

Basically the Supreme Lord said,

"You boys have the potential for understanding the transcendence. Hence naturally you are bound to look down on this material creation, as being useless. Therefore the cultural activities which your father contemplates, seems nonsensical to you. But I must remind you that it is through the very same cultural energy, that you became aware of yourselves here. It is the avenue for manifesting the objective consciousness which you use.

"Try to understand that if your father did not first engage in this cultural life, you would not even exist consciously here to ask him or Me any such questions. In fact, the karma yoga activity of your father, may be said to be your mother. By that agency you took these bodies and developed the audacity to challenge both him and Me.

"Now regarding your question, since you boys are educated and since your father is the first authority in this world, how could you ask such stupid questions about My identity. In turn, I ask you the same: What exactly is My identity? Am I a body or am I a spirit? If I am a spirit, as you consider, then how can you ask about Me as if I am a reality apart from yourselves? What is your identity? Whatever is in fact your position, so is mine as well."

पञ्चात्मकेषु भूतेषु
समानेषु च वस्तुतः ।
को भवान् इति वः प्रश्नो
वाचारम्भो ह्य् अनर्थकः ॥८.२३॥

pañcātmakeṣu bhūteṣu
samāneṣu ca vastutaḥ
ko bhavān iti vaḥ praśno
vācārambho hy anarthakaḥ (8.23)

pañcātmakeṣu = pañca — five elements + ātmakeṣu — of its nature; bhūtesu — of the mundane beings; samānesu — of the similar; ca — and; vastutaḥ — in reality; ko = kaḥ — who; bhavān — you; iti — thus; vaḥ — your; praśno = praśnaḥ — question; vācārambho = vācārambhaḥ = vācā — speech + ārambhaḥ — effort; hy = hi — indeed; anarthakaḥ — without meaning.

Translation

There is a similarity in the five elements and in the mundane beings. Thus your question of, "Who are you?" is an effort of speech only and is without meaning. (8.23)

Commentary:

In a very tactful way, *Śrī* Krishna, that supernatural swan, dismissed the query of *Sanaka* by explaining that anyone who really perceives the reality of this world, would not address a person as his material body, since all bodies are similar in constitution being composed only of five material elements.

The separation into various bodies is superficial only, because all the bodies are formed of the elements of material nature in varying proportions. These elements are in a composite whole. To ask someone to identify himself by his body is actually absurd.

Sanaka and fellows, all being prompted by the knowledge of self realization from their past lives of austerity, wanted to belittle *Brahmā*'s *karma* yoga activities but they should have appreciated his endeavors instead. Therefore *Brahmā*'s master, Lord Krishna, insulted them.

Sometimes as *kriyā* yogis, we get this idea that we are in a better standing than the preachers who take on large missions for engaging people in *karma* yoga. Some of these preachers come to believe that what they do is *bhakti* yoga. But in any case, they should not be ridiculed, because they do a necessary service. Even though yogis should not take to the path of *karma* yoga, and we should remain on the high road of *jñāna* yoga, still we should appreciate others. Somehow, we have to proceed and still appreciate them side by side. Whenever we meet such religious or social leaders, we should offer respect.

मनसा वचसा दृष्ट्या
गृह्यते ऽन्यैर् अपीन्द्रियैः ।
अहम् एव न मत्तो ऽन्यद्
इति बुध्यध्वम् अञ्जसा ॥८.२४॥

manasā vacasā dṛṣṭyā
gṛhyate 'nyair apīndriyaiḥ
aham eva na matto 'nyad
iti budhyadhvam añjasā (8.24)

manasā — by the mind; vacasā — by speech; dṛṣṭyā — by vision; gṛhyate — is perceived; 'nyair = anyaiḥ — by others; apīndriyaiḥ = api — even + indriyaiḥ — by the sense organs; aham — I; eva — alone; na — not; matto = mattaḥ — besides me; 'nyad = anyat — another; iti — thus; budhyadhvam — you should understand; añjasā — by analysis.

Translation

Whatever is perceived by the mind, by speech, by vision or even by other sense organs, is based on I alone. And there is no other factor besides Me. You should understand this by analysis. (8.24)

Commentary:

The Supreme Lord clarified for Sanaka that they were overlooking a very important fact, which is His existence as the Primal Cause. Because of that they were allowing their minds to pry into the cause of the material energy in an haphazard manner. *Sanaka* and fellows should have realized that their ability to analyze came from *Brahmā*. *Brahmā* himself came from another person, the same person who appeared in the supernatural swan form. Whatever was produced by *Brahmā* was reliant on that Swan. That was the total meaning of the existence which Sanaka and others perceived.

Everything and everyone besides the Supreme Person is subsidiary and thus such other things or persons do not have relevance except in reference to the Supreme One. Thus the sons of *Brahmā* should not have superseded him, nor tried to embarrass him by asking rude questions, even about the origins of the creation or about the faulty interaction of the mind and the objects of perception. Even if the creation is faulty, one should respect the creator of it, especially the original God who produced any of the sub-agents. After all, it does not really matter if one sees faults or does not see any, because after all, one's ability to perceive anything comes from that Supreme God and one should be appreciative of Him.

गुणेष्व् आविशते चेतो
गुणाश् चेतसि च प्रजाः ।
जीवस्य देह उभयं
गुणाश् चेतो मद्-आत्मनः ॥८.२५॥

guṇeṣv āviśate ceto
guṇāś cetasi ca prajāḥ
jīvasya deha ubhayaṁ
guṇāś ceto mad-ātmanaḥ (8.25)

guṇeṣu — in the mundane objects; āviśate — pursues, influences; ceto = cetaḥ — the mind; guṇās = guṇāḥ — the mundane objects; cetasi — in the consciousness; ca — and; prajāḥ — dependents; jīvasya — of the individual souls; deha = dehaḥ — the body; ubhayam — both; guṇās = guṇāḥ — the mundane objects; cetaḥ — the consciousness; mad-ātmanaḥ = mad (mat) — from me +

ātmanah – the individual souls.

Translation

My dependents, the consciousness does pursue the mundane objects and the objects influence the consciousness. The objects and the consciousness both form the body of the individual soul. But the souls emanate from Me. (8.25)

Commentary:

Śrī Krishna informed Sanaka and the others, that the consciousness and the mundane energies are very inter-related. They have an attraction that cannot be broken. This is due to the inter-penetrating nature. Since both the consciousness and the mundane energy are within the gross, subtle and causal bodies, there cannot be any real change in the relationship between the consciousness and the energies, except that on various levels of consciousness, there would be variations in the way the consciousness relates to the material energy.

Apart from this, the souls themselves are totally different, being as *Śrī* Krishna claimed, emanations from Him. As He is detached from the interplay between the consciousness and the mundane energy, so it is possible for a particular limited soul to exhibit some indifference.

गुणेषु चाविशाच् चित्तम्
अभीक्ष्णं गुण-सेवया ।
गुणाश् च चित्त-प्रभवा
मद्-रूप उभयं त्यजेत् ॥८.२६॥

guṇeṣu cāviśac cittam
abhīkṣṇaṁ guṇa-sevayā
guṇāś ca citta-prabhavā
mad-rūpa ubhayaṁ tyajet (8.26)

guṇeṣu — in the mundane objects; cāviśac = ca — and + āviśac (āviśat) — penetrates, pursues, influences; cittam — the mento-emotional energy; abhīkṣṇam — constantly; guṇa-sevayā = guṇa – mundane energy + sevayā — by attending; guṇās = guṇāḥ — mundane energy; ca — and; citta — mento-emotional energy; prabhavā = prabhavāḥ — existence, energy, nature; mad-rūpa = mat-rūpah = mat — from Me + rūpah – form; ubhayam — both; tyajet — should abandon.

Translation

The mento-emotional energy, by constantly pursuing an interest in the mundane world, attends to it, and the mundane energy influences the nature of the consciousness. One should abandon both, and attend to My form. (8.26)

Commentary:

This is the advice for those of us who are exempt from having to perform *karma* yoga as it is described in the *Bhagavad-Gītā* discourse to Arjuna. Lord *Brahmā* was not exempt, for He had duties for the production and development of this mundane creation. He had to be involved. Sanaka and his brothers, were not to be involved at all, neither with their consciousness nor with the material nature at large. Even though their consciousness had an impulsion to interact with material nature inside and outside their psyche, they were to pay attention to *Śrī* Krishna's spiritual form.

The technique involved using the consciousness in pursuit of *Śrī* Krishna's spiritual form. How is that done? How does one use his consciousness and not be victimized by its natural attraction for the material energy?

Sanaka and the others, got definite advice about not being fascinated by the relationship between their consciousness and the material energy. They were to be apart from that and astutely pursue *Śrī* Krishna's spiritual form.

जाग्रत् स्वप्नः सुषुप्तं च
गुणतो बुद्धि-वृत्तयः ।
तासां विलक्षणो जीवः

jāgrat svapnaḥ suṣuptaṁ ca
guṇato buddhi-vṛttayaḥ
tāsāṁ vilakṣaṇo jīvaḥ

साक्षित्वेन विनिश्चितः ॥८.२७॥ sākṣitvena viniścitaḥ (8.27)

jāgrat — wakefulness; svapnaḥ — dream; suṣuptaṁ — deep sleep; ca — and; guṇato = guṇataḥ — caused by the mundane influences; buddhi-vṛttayaḥ = buddhi — intellect + vṛttayaḥ — function; tāsām — from those; vilakṣano = vilakṣanaḥ — characterised; jīvaḥ — the individual spirit; sākṣitvena — with the observing capacity; viniścitaḥ — proven conclusively.

Translation

Wakefulness, dream and deep sleep, which are caused by the mundane influence, are functions of the intellect. Being different from those functions, the individual spirit, as proven conclusively, is characterised by his observing capabity. (8.27)

Commentary:

Even though *Śrī* Krishna gave the instruction of attending to His Form, that is not an easy process. This is because from the situation of wakefulness in a material body, or even in a subtle one, like the ones Sanaka and others used, *Śrī* Krishna's spiritual form is abstract. In order to pursue that abstraction, the yogi has to know more about transcending the subtle and causal mundane energy. He would be required to transfer into an existential locale in which he would experience spiritual perception.

The first consideration in this regard is to understand at least mentally, that the individual spirit is different from the wakefulness, dream and deep sleep states which the psyche endures. These come on by the movement of the intellect in its relationship to the life force of the subtle body. A saturation of the life force energy and the intellect, causes the psyche to experience varying states of wakefulness, but if the life force is withdrawn from the intellect, then coma, trance or deep sleep ensues.

None of these states are the state of the spirit itself. Initially, the spirit gets some idea of itself by observing its observational tendency, this occurs during meditation. Usually the spirit uses this tendency of observation on itself subjectively. But when it detaches itself from the intellect, it can understand that it is an observer. When this is done, the yogi has taken the first step in the path of *jñāna* yoga.

Śrī Krishna chided *Sanaka* and the others, since, instead of challenging *Brahmā* about the defects of the intellect, they should have taken the first step in *jñāna* yoga to realize that as individual spirits, they were observers of the operations of the intellect and the life force of their individual psyches.

It was not *Brahmā*'s duty to have given us a better type of intellect, but if we are inclined to spiritual realization, it becomes our duty to separate ourselves from the intellect and so improve our relationship with the material energies which bewitch the intellect which we were bestowed with. That responsibility lies with us. It serves no purpose to challenge the creator on this issue.

यर्हि ससृति-बन्धो ऽयम्	yarhi saṁsṛti-bandho 'yam
आत्मनो गुण-वृत्ति-दः ।	ātmano guṇa-vṛtti-daḥ
मयि तुर्ये स्थितो जह्यात्	mayi turye sthito jahyāt
त्यागस् तद् गुण-चेतसाम् ॥८.२८॥	tyāgas tad guṇa-cetasām (8.28)

yarhi — because; samsṛti — consciousness and mundane energy in combination; bandho = bandhah — a forceful link; 'yam = ayam — this; atmano = atmanah — of the soul; guṇa — mundane influences; vṛtti-daḥ — that which gives mental or emotional objectives; mayi — in me; turye — in the fourth dimension of existence; sthito = sthitaḥ — situated; jahyāt — one should give up; tyāgas = tyāgaḥ — abandonment, seperation; tad = tat — that; guṇa — mundane influence; cetasām — of the ideas and feelings within the psyche.

Translation

Because of the forceful link between the consiousness and the mundane energy,

which converts the mundane influence into mental and emotional objectives for the spirit, one should, being situated in Me in the fourth dimension of existence, give up the strong link with the intellect. Then the seperation of the mundane influence and the ideas and feelings within the psyche will be manifested. (8.28)

Commentary:

In his yoga Sutras, *Śrī Patañjali* suggested this very accomplishment but he stated that one has to cause the complete separation or isolation *(kaivalyam)* between the seer and the psyche. However some persons disagree with *Patañjali* since within their experience there can be no separation since they feel that the seer and the psyche are the same.

It is higher yoga and higher yoga alone which comes to our rescue in sorting this out. Say what we like, believe what we like, this can only be accomplished through mystic actions in *kriyā* yoga. The forceful link *(bandho)* between the consciousness and the mundane energy is reinforced by the spirit's attachment in reliance on the intellect. Thus one must take up higher yoga in terms of *pratyāhar* sense withdrawal and *dhāraṇā* focus of the attention within the *prāṇa*-charged psyche, in order to detach oneself from the sticky intellect, as well as to cause the intellect to loose most of its sticky constitution.

This is effectively done only after one perceived the various parts of the subtle body. Those are the intellect organ, the various sensual orbs which surround it, the life force or kundalini power and the various *naḍi* tubes through which pranic energy flows to energize the subtle body. The mundane energy produces both mental and emotional objectives, which are enlarged, expanded and published by the imagination for the spirit to observe or be indulged in. Therefore if the intellect is restricted, the mundane energy is automatically curtailed, and the spirit can free itself from lower dominance. One has to practice higher yoga, in terms of *dhyāna* effortless linkage of the attention to higher concentration forces within the psyche. Some of these penetrate the psyche from outside, from a spiritual environment. One must practice further to attain *samādhi* which is continuous effortless linkage of the attention to higher concentration forces so as to use these to be situated with *Śrī* Krishna in the fourth dimension of existence. This fourth plane is beyond the wakeful, dream and sleep states which come over the intellect and cause clear or vague perceptions of the material world.

The detachment of one's mental energy from the mundane influences, occurs only after one masters the higher levels of yoga practice. It occurs only for the particular yogi who achieved that. Others, be they yogis or not, will continue under the dominance of the minds, emotions and the related sense objects, because for those spirits, their spiritual selves are still dominated by the intellect organ in the subtle body. By its very nature, that organ will pursue and link up with mundane sense objects, as the objects cling to it and enthrall it.

अहङ्कार-कृत बन्धम्
आत्मनो ऽर्थ-विपर्ययम् ।
विद्वान् निर्विद्य संसार-
चिन्तां तुर्ये स्थितस् त्यजेत् ॥८.२९॥

ahaṅkāra-kṛtaṁ bandham
ātmano 'rtha-viparyayam
vidvān nirvidya saṁsāra-
cintāṁ turye sthitas tyajet (8.29)

ahaṅkāra — the sense of initiative to act in this material world; kṛtam — caused by; bandham — bondage; ātmano = ātmanaḥ — of the spirit; 'rtha = artha — that which is desired; viparyayam — opposite; vidvān — a wise man; nirvidya — being disgusted; saṁsāra — mundane existence; cintām — subtle scheme; turye — in the fourth dimension of existence; sthitas = sthitah — situated; tyajet — one should give up.

Translation

The bondage of the spirit is caused by the sense of initiative to act in the material world, which gives just the opposite of what is desired. Thus a wise man being disgusted with the subtle scheme of mundane existence, should give it up and be

situated in the fourth dimension. (8.29)

Commentary:

Liberation from the material world, even from legitimate or divinely-ordained duties here, does not come about until one becomes disgusted with the subtle scheme of the material energy. Even if one is engaged in divinely-ordained assignment, one will find that anytime, one is lax or inattentive, the subtle material energy will influence the intellect and cause it to reproduce ideas which have nothing to do with the duties. Eventually one becomes disgusted with the course of material existence. One gives up related desires. Thus if the God of this world frees one from assignments, one would strive for liberation just as *Sanaka* and his brothers.

As soon as the spirit is turned in the direction of the material energy, it develops a sense of initiative to act. That sense detects the slightest movement in the subtle mental energy, *citta*, and from that detection, forceful ideas come into play. These are expanded by the intellect. When the spirit is exposed to the intellectual workings, it becomes involved in viewing and sanctioning activities which turn out to be the exact opposite of what is desired. Thus eventually all wise men, become disgusted with the schemes, and endeavor on the mystic plane for a transference into the fourth dimension of existence, the place from where *Śrī* Krishna manifested the swan form.

यावन् नानार्थ-धीः पुंसो
न निवर्तेत युक्तिभिः ।
जागर्त्य् अपि स्वपन्न् अज्ञः
स्वप्ने जागरणं यथा ॥८.३०॥

yāvan nānārtha-dhīḥ puṁso
na nivarteta yuktibhiḥ
jāgarty api svapann ajñaḥ
svapne jāgaraṇaṁ yathā (8.30)

yāvan = yāvat — until, if; nānārtha-dhīh = nānā — many + artha — valuable things + dhīḥ — ideas; puṁso = puṁsaḥ — person; na — no; nivarteta — ceases; yuktibhiḥ — by the standard disciplines; jāgarty = jāgarti — awake; api — even; svapann = svapan — sleep, dream; ajñah — one who does not perceive reality; svapne — in dream, in sleep; jāgaraṇam — being awake; yathā — as.

Translation

If a person's idea of many valuable things, does not cease by applying the standard disciplines, then he is asleep even though awake, for he does not perceive reality, just as one who thinks he is awake while in fact he dreams. (8.30)

Commentary:

If after applying the standard disciplines of yoga which were described to the sons of *Brahmā*, one still finds that one's perception is restricted to this dimension, then one must understand that one is still in a state of illusion under the influence of the material energy. It means that there was some defect in the application of the disciplines. There are many processes for self-realization and one must test each one until one finds a method that breaks through the illusion.

असत्त्वाद् आत्मनो ऽन्येषां
भावानां तत्-कृता भिदा ।
गतयो हेतवश् चास्य
मृषा स्वप्न-दृशो यथा ॥८.३१॥

asattvād ātmano 'nyeṣāṁ
bhāvānāṁ tat-kṛtā bhidā
gatayo hetavaś cāsya
mṛṣā svapna-dṛśo yathā (8.31)

asattvād = asattvāt — due to temporary existence; ātmano = ātmanaḥ — other than the spirit; 'nyeṣām = anyesām — of others; bhāvānām — objects; tat — by them; kṛtā — created; bhidā — diversity; gatayo = gatayaḥ — transport to various mundane dimensions; hetavaś = hetavaḥ — causes, whatever causes; casya = ca — and + asya — of that; mṛṣā — false, illusory; svapna —

dream; dṛśo = dṛśaḥ — the observer; yathā — just as.

Translation

As things other than the spirit have only temporary existence, the diversity created by them, is also illusory, and so is the transport of such phenomena to various dimensions, as well as whatever causes that, just as the observer has value and not his dream. (8.31)

Commentary:

This means that the whole range of mundane existence is illusory. None of it has lasting duration. All of it is based on the original cause which is the conjunction of the cosmic intelligence with the subtle mundane energy. The spirit itself, is an observer only. It needs to get itself detached from the intellect which is the subtle tool used to make the observations. So long as it peers into the material world, it will be affected by the interaction of the intellect with the material elements. It will be victimized by the ideas which are formulated by that interaction and which entertain it and involve it.

Even though dreams are flimsy in contrast to material life, a dreamer is affected by the dreamy perceptions. The dreamer has to get out of the dream if he wants to be free of its effects. The spirit can be free of the effects of the mundane energy if it becomes liberated from this world and escapes into the fourth dimension of existence.

यो जागरे बहिर् अनुक्षण-धर्मिणो ऽर्थान्
भुङ्क्ते समस्त-करणैर् हृदि तत्-सदृक्षान् ।
स्वप्ने सुषुप्त उपसंहरते स एकः
स्मृत्य्-अन्वयात् त्रि-गुण-वृत्ति-दृग् इन्द्रियेशः
॥८.३२॥

yo jāgare bahir anukṣaṇa-dharmiṇo 'rthān
bhuṅkte samasta-karaṇair hṛdi tat-sadṛkṣān
svapne suṣupta upasaṁharate sa ekaḥ
smṛty-anvayāt tri-guṇa-vṛtti-dṛg indriyeśaḥ
(8.32)

yo = yaḥ — who; jāgare — in waking state; bahir = bahiḥ — external; anukṣana — momentarily changing; dharmino = dharminaḥ — features; 'rthān = arthān — objects; bhuṅkte — experiences; samasta — all; karaṇair = karaṇaiḥ — through the sense organs; hṛdi — in the psyche; tat – that; sadṛkṣān — with experiences; svapne — in dream; suṣupta = suṣupte — in sound sleep; upasaṁharate — withdraws; sa = sah — he; ekaḥ — that same one; smṛty = smṛti — recall; anvayāt — from repeated, persistent; tri-guṇa — of the three features of material nature; vrtti — functions; dṛg = dṛk — perceiving, perception; indriyeśaḥ — the monitor of the senses.

Translation

He who in the waking state, experiences through the sense organs, objects with changing features in the external world, and who in dream is with experiences in the psyche, who withdraws in sound sleep, is that same spirit, who perceives the three aspects of material nature and the functions of perception. He is the monitor of the senses. This is evident by his persistent recall of this. (8.32)

Commentary:

The Lord provided evidence to show that the individual spirit is in a central position in reference to the sensual energies. The functions of perception are usually experienced through the intellect which is the monitor in the mind. The spirit is superimposed on the intellect. The recalling feature is operative only because the spirit is superimposed there. Even though the limited spirit does not control all psychological features, still those aspects, are operated on the basis of its central position in the mind.

At first, one understands this intellectually. Thereafter if one is serious enough to want to penetrate the psyche, one may experience this by introspection and meditation. Persons who attempt to penetrate deeply may not realize this by objective inner experiences, unless they practice *prāṇāyāma* to surcharge the mind so that it develops the ability for intuitive penetration and can change what is subjective into something objective, or change what is abstract into something perceptive.

एवं विमृश्य गुणतो मनसस् त्र्य्-अवस्था
मन्-मायया मयि कृता इति निश्चितार्थाः ।
सञ्छिद्य हार्दम् अनुमान-सद्-उक्ति-तीक्ष्ण
ज्ञानासिना भजत माखिल-संशयाधिम् ॥८.३३॥

evaṁ vimṛśya guṇato manasas try-avasthā
man-māyayā mayi kṛtā iti niścitārthāḥ
sañchidya hārdam anumāna-sad-ukti-tīkṣṇa
jñānāsinā bhajata mākhila-saṁśayādhim
(8.33)

evam — thus; vimṛśya — considering; guṇato = guṇataḥ — pertaining to the mundane influences; manasas = manasah — of the mind; try-avasthā = tri-avasthāh — three states; man-māyayā = mat-māyayā — of My bewildering energy; mayi — in me; krtā = krtāḥ — projected; iti — thus; niścitārthāh = niscita - being certain + arthāh — real substance (niścitārthāḥ - persons who certain of the real substance); sañchidya — destroying; hārdam — situated in the core of being; anumāna — by logical conclusion; sad-ukti = sat-ukti — by testimony; tīkṣṇa — sharpened; jñānāsinā = jñāna — of knowledge + asinā — by the sword; bhajata — worships; mākhila = mā — me + akhila — of all; saṁśayādhim = saṁśaya — doubts + ādhim — anxiety.

Translation

Thus considering that the three states of mind, which pertain to the mundane influences, are projected on Me by My bewildering potency, persons who are certain of the real substance, destroy with the sword of knowledge, sharpened by logical conclusions and testimony of the reality-perceptive persons, the anxiety which is full of doubts. They worship Me who is situated in the core of being. (8.33)

Commentary:

The gist of this is that as yogins who seek liberation, we have to accept the projection of the subtle material energy, as it is reinforced by the Supreme Lord. This projection predominates because it occurs in the mental and emotional nature of all the souls in this world. The potency of it cannot be denied because it is reinforced by God and it enforces itself upon limited spirits. We must accept it as a temporary manifestation in the least. However, since we are not inclined to remaining in the material universe, we have to side-step that energy by taking shelter of the method for escape given by the same God.

The real substance was declared by Him already as being the spirit, when it is detached from the intellect, and when it is in conjunction with Him, the God. As *Śrī* Krishna declared we should worship Him after becoming firmly convinced of this. The mode of that worship is not limited to Deity Worship. It includes the purificatory acts or *kriyās* which we do in yoga, and which cause our intellect to be freed from its preoccupations with the mundane energy.

ईक्षेत विभ्रमम् इद मनसो विलासं
दृष्टं विनष्टम् अति-लोलम् अलात-चक्रम् ।
विज्ञानम् एकम् उरुधेव विभाति माया
स्वप्नस् त्रिधा गुण-विसर्ग-कृतो विकल्पः ॥८.३४॥

īkṣeta vibhramam idaṁ manaso vilāsaṁ
dṛṣṭaṁ vinaṣṭam ati-lolam alāta-cakram
vijñānam ekam urudheva vibhāti māyā
svapnas tridhā guṇa-visarga-kṛto vikalpaḥ
(8.34)

īkseta — one should see; vibhramam — hallucination; idam — this; manaso = manasah — of the mind; vilāsam — theatrical presentation; dṛṣṭam — seen; vinaṣṭam — gone, disappeared; ati-lolam = ati – extremely + lolam — shifting; alāta – fire branch; cakram — whirling in a circle; vijñānam — consciousness; ekam — one; urudheva = urudha — many variations + iva — as if; vibhāti — appears; māyā — illusion; svapnas = svapnah — dream; tridhā - tripart consciousness; guṇa — of the mundane influence; visarga — by transformation; krto = krtah — produced; vikalpaḥ — transformation.

Translation

One should regard this existence as an hallucination, being a theatrical presentation of the mind, being seen and then disappearing, being extremely shifty like a firebrand whirling in a circle. The one consciousness appears in many variations. The tripart consciousness which is produced by transformation of the modes of material nature is illusion like a dream. (8.34)

Commentary:

This substantiates the existence of the individual spirit and his source for manifestation in this world, which is the Supreme Spirit, as described in the previous verses of this discourse between Lord Swan and the sons of *Brahmā*. Everything besides the limited spirits and the Supreme Spirit is illusory in this world. The one consciousness of all the spirits and the Supreme Spirit is the reality, upon which this shifty world is manifested. This must become our persistent vision if we are to be freed from the hypnotic effect of perceiving this world.

दृष्टिम् ततः प्रतिनिवर्त्य निवृत्त-तृष्णस्
तूष्णीं भवेन् निज-सुखानुभवो निरीहः ।
सन्दृश्यते क्व च यदीदम् अवस्तु-बुद्ध्या
त्यक्तं भ्रमाय न भवेत् स्मृतिर् आ-निपातात्
॥८.३५॥

dṛṣṭim tataḥ pratinivartya nivṛtta-tṛṣṇas
tūṣṇīṁ bhaven nija-sukhānubhavo nirīhaḥ
sandṛśyate kva ca yadīdam avastu-buddhyā
tyaktaṁ bhramāya na bhavet smṛtir ā-nipātāt
(8.35)

dṛṣṭim — perceptive interest; tatah — hence; pratinivartya — withdrawing; nivṛtta — abandoning; tṛṣṇas = tṛṣṇaḥ — craving; tūṣṇīm — silent; bhaven = bhavet — should become; nija — one's own; sukha — happiness; anubhavaḥ — experiencing; nirīhaḥ — free from cultural activity; sandṛśyate — is experienced; kva ca — sometimes and; yadīdam = yadi — if + idam — this; avastu — unreal; buddhyā — by the intellect; tyaktaṁ — give up the benefits; bhramāya — bewildering; na — not; bhavet — may become; smṛtir = smṛtiḥ — memory; ā – until; nipātāt — the fall of a body.

Translation

Hence withdrawing the perceptive interest, abandoning craving, one should be silent and by expercencing self-happiness, one should be free from cultural activity. Sometimes, if this existence is experienced, it will not be bewildering, being already discarded as unreal by the intellect, even though it will be as a memory until the death of the body. (8.35)

Commentary:

This is the instruction of how to exist in this world, even after one attains liberation. A yogi is not absolute and so he might not be able to give up his material body as soon as he attains liberation. Even if he can give up his material body, he might not be allowed to give up the subtle form. And even if he can discard that, he might not be able to give up the causal body. Therefore *Śrī* Krishna advised that the yogi should remain situated in the spiritual happiness of the self, until the time that he is allowed to discard all mundane forms to which he is harnessed.

He must mastered the 5th stage of yoga, which is *pratyāhar* sense withdrawal. This is listed in this verse as *dṛṣṭim pratinivartya* or the withdrawal of the perceptive interest in this world. He must also have removed from his subtle body, the craving for things in this world. This means the mastership of kundalini yoga to curb the life force which operates the survival instincts. He must be silent within by having thrown out of his psyche, all forces which force him to relate to this world. He must also be free from cultural activity, having got exemption from *karma* yoga, the very same yoga that *Brahmā* performed, when *Sanaka* approached him for instructions on how to adjust the mind to free it from mundane affinity.

The yogi's intellect should be purified of lower influences, so that it no longer clings to the mundane energy. If the yogi achieved all this, then the material world will be like a remote memory, a very slight impression, something long forgotten.

देहं च नश्वरम् अवस्थितम् उत्थितं वा
सिद्धो न पश्यति यतो ऽध्यगमत् स्वरूपम् ।
दैवाद् अपेतम् अथ दैव-वशाद् उपेतं
वासो यथा परिकृतं मदिरा-मदान्धः ॥८.३६॥

dehaṁ ca naśvaram avasthitam utthitaṁ vā
siddho na paśyati yato 'dhyagamat svarūpam
daivād apetam atha daiva-vaśād upetaṁ
vāso yathā parikṛtaṁ madirā-madāndhaḥ (8.36)

deham — body; ca — and; naśvaram — transient; avasthitam — sitting; utthitam — standing; vā — or; siddho = siddhaḥ — a perfect person; na - not; paśyati — sees, regards; yato = yatah — because; 'dhyagamat = adhyagamat — realised; svarūpam — own form; daivād = daivāt — due to providence; apetam — taken away; atha — or; daiva-vaśād = daiva — due to destiny + vaśād (vaśāt) — due to being controlled; upetam — acquired; vāso = vāsaḥ — garment; yathā — just as; parikṛtam — cover; madirā — liquor; madāndhaḥ = mada — drunk + andhah — insensitive.

Translation

The perfected person, who realizes the self's true form, does not regard the transient body, whether it is sitting or standing, or even if it is taken away by providence, or acquired by destiny, just as a man who is made drunk by liquor, does not regard the garment which covers his body. (8.36)

Commentary:

This is a person who perfected the yoga disciplines, and reached the culmination. Such a yogi cannot expect that he would be free of having to take or having to maintain a material body. Since he is not absolute, he may have to accept a body. But still, he remains in his own spiritual form, his *svarūpa*.

As a drunken man becomes unaware of garments, regarding whether they are dirty or clean, respectable or disapproving, so the perfected yogi, the *siddha*, may be unaware of the condition of his material body. We heard the story of the ascetic brahmin who exhibited that behavior.

देहो ऽपि दैव-वश-गः खलु कर्म यावत्
स्वारम्भक प्रतिसमीक्षत एव सासुः ।
त स-प्रपञ्चम् अधिरूढ-समाधि-योगः
स्वाप्नं पुनर् न भजते प्रतिबुद्ध-वस्तुः ॥८.३७॥

deho 'pi daiva-vaśa-gaḥ khalu karma yāvat
svārambhakaṁ pratisamīkṣata eva sāsuḥ
taṁ sa-prapañcam adhirūḍha-samādhi-yogaḥ
svāpnaṁ punar na bhajate pratibuddha-vastuḥ (8.37)

deho 'pi = dehaḥ api = dehaḥ — body + api — even; daiva — of destiny; vaśa-gaḥ — something controlled; khalu — indeed; karma — cultural activities; yāvat — until; svārambhakam = sva – own + ārambhakam — origination; pratisamīkṣata — waited on, tolerated; eva — only; sāsuḥ = sa – with + asuḥ — the vital energy; tam — that; sa – with; prapañcam — extensions; adhirūḍha — attained; samādhi — continous effortless linkage of the attention to higher concentration forces; yogaḥ — yoga practice; svāpnam — dream; punar = punah — again; na – no; bhajate — dedicate oneself; pratibuddha — realised; vastuḥ — reality.

Translation

The body is controlled by providence and along with the vital energy, it must be tolerated until the cultural activities which are the origin of it, have run their course. The person who attains continuous effortless linkage of the attention to a higher concentration force, by yoga practice, and who realized reality, never again dedicates himself to the body and its extensions, which are like a dream. (8.37)

Commentary:

Because the God refuses to absorb any of our pious or sinful consequences which are due in this creation, we have to face up to these even after realizing that this world is a mock-up or an illusion. The refusal of the God is declared in the *Bhagavad-Gītā* as follows:

nādatte kasyacitpāpaṁ na caiva sukṛtaṁ vibhuḥ
ajñānenāvṛtaṁ jñānaṁ tena muhyanti jantavaḥ

The Almighty God does not receive from anyone, an evil consequence nor a good reaction. The knowledge of this is shrouded by ignorance through which the people are deluded. (B.G. 5.15)

However, despite this disadvantage, a realized person is shown methods for greatly decreasing his affiliation with this world, in such a way that he might transpose many pious and impious reactions, leaving them in this world with the sum total destiny which concerns cultural existence.

Each of these bodies come about by the seed energy of cultural activities but this does not mean that the spirit who is subjected to the consequence, is the only cause of that seed force. Others are involved. Ultimately the Supreme Lord, the God Himself is involved. Thus the yogi must learn how to tolerate providence. He can only sidestep it totally if he gets an exemption from the God.

Due to transcendental experiences gained in *samādhi* practice, while continuously and effortlessly linking his attention to higher realities, the yogi can no longer focus deeply into the mundane consciousness. He can never again sincerely dedicate himself to the body and its extensions in the form of its relations and properties. However he may act as a family man if he is instructed to do so by the Supreme Lord or if he is pressured into that lifestyle by destiny.

मयैतद् उक्तं वो विप्रा
गुह्यं यत् साङ्ख्य-योगयोः।
जानीत मागतं यज्ञं
युष्मद्-धर्म-विवक्षया ॥८.३८॥

mayaitad uktaṁ vo viprā
guhyaṁ yat sāṅkhya -yogayoḥ
jānīta māgataṁ yajñaṁ
yuṣmad-dharma-vivakṣayā (8.38)

mayaitad = mayaitat = mayā — by me + etat — this; uktam — explained; vo = vaḥ — to you; viprā = viprāḥ — o educated brahmins; guhyam — secret; yat — which; sāṅkhya -yogayoḥ = sānkhya — Sāṅkhya philosophical analysis + yogayoh — of yoga practice; jānīta — know; māgatam = mā — me + āgatam — came; yajñam — Yajña Vishnu; yuṣmad = yuṣmat — your; dharma — righteous duty; vivakṣayā — desiring to inform.

Translation

O educated brahmins, I explained to you the secret of the Sāṅkhya philosophical analysis and the yoga process. Know Me as Yajña Vishnu, who came, desiring to inform you of righteous duty. (8.38)

Commentary:

The system of the *Sāṅkhya* philosophical analysis, and the practice of yoga, go hand in hand. One compliments the other, especially in the early stages of the development of the yogin. In the advanced stages, the yoga process supersedes philosophical analysis, because the yogi gets first hand experience of the transcendental personalities and their domains. He no longer relies on the analytical theories of *Sāṅkhya*. Initially he relies on that because he has little or no experience.

Lord *Yajña*, Lord Vishnu, otherwise known as Lord Krishna or as the supernatural Swan, informed the sons of *Brahmā* of their righteous duty which was to complete the yoga practice fully. Thus he revealed His identity to them sufficiently.

अहं योगस्य साङ्ख्यस्य
सत्यस्यर्तस्य तेजसः ।
परायणं द्विज-श्रेष्ठाः
श्रियः कीर्तेर् दमस्य च ॥८.३९॥

aharh yogasya sāṅkhyasya
satyasyartasya tejasaḥ
parāyaṇaṁ dvija-śreṣṭhāḥ
śriyaḥ kīrter damasya ca (8.39)

aham — I; yogasya — of the yoga process; sāṅkhyasya — of the Sāṅkhya philosophical analysis; satyasya — of realism; ṛtasya — of religious principles; tejasaḥ — of valor; parāyaṇam = para – supreme + ayanam — shelter; dvija – brahmin; śreṣṭhāḥ — best; śriyah — of opulence; kīrter = kīrteḥ — of fame; damasya — of self control; ca — and.

Translation

O best of the brahmins, I am the supreme shelter of the yoga process, the Sāṅkhya philosophical analysis, realism, religious principles, valor, opulence, fame and self control. (8.39)

Commentary:

In event, they would ask in the future, Lord Krishna informed *Sanaka* and the others, that He is the ultimate factor in terms of yoga expertise, philosophical analysis, the perception of truth or realism, considerations of what are religious principles, the exhibition of approved valor, lawful exhibition of opulence, the acquirement of fame and self control.

Whatever might interest a living being has its culmination in the Supreme Being. His approval or disapproval is final.

मां भजन्ति गुणाः सर्वे
निर्गुणं निरपेक्षकम् ।
सुहृदं प्रियम् आत्मानं
साम्यासङ्गादयो ऽगुणाः ॥८.४०॥

māṁ bhajanti guṇāḥ sarve
nirguṇaṁ nirapekṣakam
suhṛdaṁ priyam ātmānaṁ
sāmyāsaṅgādayo 'guṇāḥ (8.40)

mām — me; bhajanti — they are dedicated to; guṇāḥ — virtues; sarve — all; nirguṇam — free from mundane influence; nirapekṣakam — independent; suhṛdam — friend; priyam — beloved; ātmānam — the spiritual self; sāmyāsangādayo = sāmya — comparatively equal assessment of the spirits who use material bodies + asaṅga — detachment + ādayo (ādayaḥ) — and other required aspects; 'guṇāḥ = aguṇāḥ — beyond the mundane influences.

Translation

All virtues such as the comparatively equal assessment of the souls using material bodies, as well as detachment and other aspects, are dedicated to Me, who are beyond the mundane influences, who is independent and is the beloved friend and spiritual self. (8.40)

Commentary:

Śrī Krishna used two specific terms in this discourse, namely *artha* and *guṇa*, in an unusual way. Usually *artha* means a valuable item; *guṇa* means a quality or mood. *Śrī* Krishna used these terms in an entirely new sense, using *artha* in verse 33 *(niścitārthāḥ)* as the spiritual substance, the spirit and the Supreme Spirit. He used *guṇa* in this verse to mean the real virtues which concern spiritual development and the exhibition of spiritual life.

He stated that all such virtues which either facilitate spiritual development or assert spirituality, are dedicated to Him. The two transcendental virtues mentioned, are developed in the advanced yoga practice. These are *sāmya*, which is described in the *Bhagavad-Gītā* as the comparatively equal assessment of the spirits in their relationship to the psychological equipments they use in the material creation, and *asaṅga*, which is detachment from the material creation.

This detachment is keynoted by the spirit's distinction from the intellect, which is an organ in the head of the subtle body.

इति मे छिन्न-सन्देहा
मुनयः सनकादयः ।
सभाजयित्वा परया
भक्त्यागृणत सस्तवैः ॥८.४१॥

iti me chinna-sandehā
munayaḥ sanakādayaḥ
sabhājayitvā parayā
bhaktyāgṛṇata saṁstavaiḥ (8.41)

iti — thus; me — by me; chinna — removed; sandehā = sandehāḥ — doubts; munayaḥ — the yogi philosophers; sanakādayaḥ = sanaka – Sanaka + ādayaḥ — and others; sabhājayitva — with worshiping; parayā — by prime; bhaktyāgṛṇata = bhaktyā — by devotion + agṛṇata — sang, chanted; saṁstavaiḥ — with glorification hymns.

Translation

Having their doubts thus removed, the yogi philosophers, Sanaka and the others, began worshipping Me with prime devotion, and with the chanting of glorification hymns. (8.41)

Commentary:

Sanaka and his brothers experiences a change of attitude after Lord Krishna explained the process of how to get freed from the interacting tendency of the intellect. In great appreciation they worshiped the Supernatural Swan with prime devotion and by composing glorification hymns.

तैर् अहं पूजितः सयक्
सस्तुतः परमर्षिभिः ।
प्रत्येयाय स्वकं धाम
पश्यतः परमेष्ठिनः ॥८.४२॥

tair ahaṁ pūjitaḥ saṁyak
saṁstutaḥ paramarṣibhiḥ
pratyeyāya svakaṁ dhāma
paśyataḥ parameṣṭhinaḥ (8.42)

tair = taiḥ — by them; aham — I; pūjitaḥ — worshiped; saṁyak — duly; saṁstutaḥ — attentively praised; paramarṣibhiḥ = parama – greatest + ṛsibhiḥ — by the yogi sages; pratyeyāya — I returned; svakam — to My own; dhāma — place, domain; paśyatah – looked on; parameṣṭhinah — of Brahmā.

Translation

I was duly worshipped and attentively praised by them, the greatest of the yogi sages. I returned to My own place, as Brahmā looked on. (8.42)

Commentary:

Even though the Supreme Lord returned to His domain, the greatest of the yogi sages, were unable to follow Him. They had not perfected the yoga practice through which a limited being might be transferred out of this world into the fourth dimension of existence.

However, since the Lord gave them the method, it was left to Sanaka and the others to practice and attain to the supreme abode. Lord *Brahmā* for his part, then resumed his duties for creating various species in the material world and for establishing his other capable sons as figureheads for all other living entities.

CHAPTER 9*

Spirited Devotion**

Terri Stokes-Pineda Art

na sādhayati māṁ yogo na sāṅkhyam dharma uddhava
na svādhyāyas tapas tyāgo yathā bhaktir mamorjitā

Neither yoga practice, nor Sāṅkhya philosophical analysis, nor righteous duty, nor Vedic study, nor austerity, nor giving up results, would attract Me, as much as spirited devotion. (Uddhava Gītā 9.20)

* Śrīmad Bhāgavatam Canto 11, Chapter 14
** Translator's selected chapter title.

श्री-उद्धव उवाच
वदन्ति कृष्ण श्रेयांसि
बहूनि ब्रह्म-वादिनः ।
तेषां विकल्प-प्राधान्यम्
उताहो एक-मुख्यता ॥९.१॥

śrī-uddhava uvāca
vadanti kṛṣṇa śreyāṁsi
bahūni brahma-vādinaḥ
teṣāṁ vikalpa-prādhānyam
utāho eka-mukhyatā (9.1)

śrī-uddhava – the deserving Uddhava; uvāca — said; vadanti — they speak; kṛṣṇa — Krishna; śreyāṁsi — the means of well-being; bahūni — various; brahma-vādinaḥ — the teachers of spirituality; teṣām — of them, these; vikalpa-prādhāṇyam = vikalpa — options + prādhānyam — essential; utāho = uta — or + aho — indeed; eka — one; mukhyatā — most important.

Translation

The deserving Uddhava said: O Krishna, the teachers of spirituality speak of various means of well being. Are all of these options essential? Is one the most important? (9.1)

Commentary:

Śrī Krishna gave Uddhava the means of detaching the spirit from the intellect but that required practice in yoga. Merely understanding it intellectually will not give one the ability to experience the detachment. Previously, *Sanaka* and his brothers got the method from the supernatural swan. They gloried the swan in appreciation, even though at the time, they did not practice it sufficiently to experience the detachment and to penetrate into the fourth dimension. Uddhava asked another question about the value of various means of well-being, which were advocated by various teachers in his time.

भवतोदाहृतः स्वामिन्
भक्ति-योगो ऽनपेक्षितः ।
निरस्य सर्वतः सङ्गं
येन त्वय्य् आविशेन् मनः ॥९.२॥

bhavatodāhṛtaḥ svāmin
bhakti-yogo 'napekṣitaḥ
nirasya sarvataḥ saṅgaṁ
yena tvayy āviśen manaḥ (9.2)

bhavatodāhṛtaḥ = bhavatā — by you + udāhrtaḥ — explained; svāmin — o master; bhakti-yoga = bhakti – affectionate energies + yogo (yogah) — yoga (bhakti-yogah = yoga used to intensify and focus affectionate energies); 'napekṣitaḥ = anapekṣitaḥ — independent; nirasya — of the removal; sarvataḥ — all; sangam — attachment; yena — by which; tvayy = tvayi — on you; āviśen = āviśet — may focus; manaḥ — the mind.

Translation

O Master, the independent path of using yoga to intensify and focus affectionate energies was explained by You. By that system, the mind through the removal of all attachment may focus on You. (9.2)

Commentary:

Uddhava, leaving aside the path of *jñāna* yoga, taken up by *Sanaka* Rishi and others, reminded Lord Krishna that there is the independent path of using yoga techniques to intensify and focus one's affectionate energy. That is a different process, because it uses the affectionate energies which are curbed and greatly restricted by the *jñāna* yogis like *Sanaka* Rishi.

श्री-भगवान् उवाच
कालेन नष्टा प्रलये
वाणीयं वेद-सञ्ज्ञिता ।
मयादौ ब्रह्मणे प्रोक्ता
धर्मो यस्यां मद्-आत्मकः ॥९.३॥

śrī-bhagavān uvāca
kālena naṣṭā pralaye
vāṇīyaṁ veda-saṁjñitā
mayādau brahmaṇe proktā
dharmo yasyāṁ mad-ātmakaḥ (9.3)

śrī-bhagavān – the Blessed Lord; uvāca — said; kālena — by time; naṣṭā — lost; pralaye — at the dissolution of the universe; vānīyam — statement, speech; veda – Veda; samjñitā — known as; mayādau = mayā — by me + ādau — at the beginning; brahmaṇe — to Procreator Brahmā; proktā — told; dharmo = dharmaḥ — guidelines for the righteous way of life; yasyām — in which; mad-ātmakaḥ = mad (mat) – to me + ātmakaḥ — self-disposition.

Translation

The Blessed Lord said:, At the beginning of the creation, this statement known as the Veda was told to Procreator Brahmā. It consists of guidelines for the righteous lifestyle which would cause the self to be disposed towards Me. (9.3)

Commentary:

Śrī Krishna explained that in the last creation, the Veda was lost because of the collapse of time. Later, when this creation began, the same Veda was taught to Procreator *Brahmā*. The teaching gave guidelines, which if followed, cause the living entities to be attracted to *Śrī* Krishna, to have a devotional disposition towards Him.

तेन प्रोक्ता स्व-पुत्राय
मनवे पूर्व-जाय सा ।
ततो भृग्व्-आदयो ऽगृह्णन्
सप्त ब्रह्म-महर्षयः ॥९.४॥

tena proktā sva-putrāya
manave pūrva-jāya sā
tato bhṛgv-ādayo 'gṛhṇan
sapta brahma-maharṣayaḥ (9.4)

tena — by him; proktā — explained; sva-putrāya — to the son; manave — to Manu; pūrva-jāya — eldest; sā — it; tato = tatah — hence; bhṛgv-ādayo 'gṛhṇan = bhṛgu – Bhṛgu + ādayaḥ - and others + 'gṛhṇan (agṛhṇan) — took; sapta — seven; brahma — conscious of the unadulterated spiritual plane; mahārṣayaḥ — the great yogi sages.

Translation

It was explained by him to his eldest son, Manu, from whom the seven great yogi sages who were conscious of the unadulterated spiritual plane, as well as Bhṛgu and others, learnt it. (9.4)

Commentary:

Even though this was explained in disciplic succession, we should take note that these persons were related. *Manu* was the son of *Brahmā* and the other seven great yogi sages, were sons of *Brahmā*. These persons were in a family. Even though they were mind-born sons, still they were genetically related.

Another observation is this: These persons had to practice the yoga disciplines described to *Sanaka* and his brothers. It was a two-part education of hearing information, just as the Supernatural svan told it to *Sanaka* and then practicing it in fact. Without practice, most of those who hear, derive the theory. They have no practical application of it.

It is misleading to all concerned to say that a disciplic succession which does not practice yoga austerities is the same as that which was in vogue among these sons of *Brahmā*, what to speak of saying that such a yoga-less succession is even better. Those persons in the time of *Brahmā* were practicing yogins.

तेभ्यः पितृभ्यस् तत्-पुत्रा
देव-दानव-गुह्यकाः ।
मनुष्याः सिद्ध-गन्धर्वाः
स-विद्याधर-चारणाः ॥९.५॥

tebhyaḥ pitṛbhyas tat-putrā
deva-dānava-guhyakāḥ
manuṣyāḥ siddha-gandharvāḥ
sa-vidyādhara-cāraṇāḥ (9.5)

tebhyah — from those; pitṛbhyas — from the forefathers; tat — their; putrā = putrāḥ — sons; deva — supernatural rulers; dānava — sons of Danu; guhyakāḥ — supernatural guardians of natural resources; manuṣyāḥ — human beings; siddha – perfected yogis; gandharvāḥ — celestial songsters; sa – with; vidyādhara – skilled angelic beings; cāranāḥ — praisers of the supernatural rulers.

Translation

From those forefathers, it passed to their sons, namely the supernatural rulers, the sons of Danu, the supernatural guardians of natural resources, the human beings, the perfected yogis, the celestial songsters, the skilled angelic beings, the praisers of the supernatural rulers, (9.5)

Commentary:

This is a partial listing of the persons who were inducted into the disciplic succession. We must keep in mind that those persons were physically or supernaturally related, due to having bodies which were produced in families which were related.

The other factor to remember is that the tradition of that time, dictated that each person was taught elementary yoga practice. Each of the persons did not perfect the practice, only some did but they were all taught it. Thus their placement in the disciplic succession was different to some modern successions in which a spiritual master takes disciples without having any yoga expertise. Many spiritual masters in the modern version of the disciplic succession from *Śrī* Krishna, have absolutely no yoga practice to their credit in the present life. They cannot teach yoga to their students. Their commentaries on these verses are very dogmatic in regard to the information about yoga but they do succeed in presenting themselves as persons with full knowledge and experience on these matters.

किन्देवाः किन्नरा नागा
रक्षः-किम्पुरुषादयः ।
बह्व्यस् तेषा प्रकृतयो
रजः-सत्त्व-तमो-भुवः ॥९.६॥

kindevāḥ kinnarā nāgā
rakṣaḥ-kimpuruṣādayaḥ
bahvyas teṣāṁ prakṛtayo
rajaḥ-sattva-tamo-bhuvaḥ (9.6)

kindevāḥ — beings who are mistaken to be supernatural rulers; kinnarā = kinnarāḥ — species which are mistaken as human beings; nāgā = nāgāḥ — supernatural snakes; rakṣaḥ — cannibalistic mystics; kimpuruṣādayaḥ = kimpurusa — monkey-faced human beings + ādayaḥ — and other species; bahvyas = bahvyah — various; tesam — of them; prakrtayo = prakrtayah — tendencies; rajaḥ - passionate influence; sattva – clarifying influence; tamo = tamah – retardative influence; bhuvaḥ — manifestation, existential distribution.

Translation

...beings who are mistaken to be supernatural rulers, species which are mistaken as human beings, the supernatural snakes, the cannibalistic mystics, the monkey-faced human beings and others, all whose tendencies vary by the existential distribution of the passionate, clarifying and retardative influences, (9.6)

Commentary:

The information which was given to *Brahmā*, as well as the method for realizing it by yoga austerities, was handed down in the various families, being developed by the various sons, grandsons and other descendants of *Brahmā*. Many of these persons became perfected in yoga and understood the information by direct perception. Some only partially realized it. It may sound incredible that so many varying species did yoga practice, but if we check the Puranic literatures, there is sufficient evidence to support this.

If we go back further to the *Rāmāyaṇa*, which was written by *Śrīla Vālmīki* Rishi, we will see that *Hanumān*, a *kimpuruṣa*, a monkey-faced human being, was versed in *prāṇāyāma*, the 4th stage of yoga practice and so was *Jāmbavān*, a bear-faced human being, as well as Angad and others who were commissioned by *Sugrīva*, a golden-faced monkey-like human being.

The same *Rāmāyaṇa* describes *kindevas* like King *Rāvaṇa*, human beings who were mistaken to be supernatural rulers, as having mastered the yoga practice and having alliances with great yogi adepts like *Mārīca*. *Rāvaṇa* had alliances with many rakshasas, cannibalistic mystics, who were somewhat versed in yoga and the resulting mysticism. The tradition then, was to hear of the Veda and to practice yoga to realize what was beyond physical perception.

Each person has a disposition according to the percentage of clarifying, passionate or retardative energy which inhabites the psyche. Therefore the adherence to the disciplic succession varies.

याभिर् भूतानि भिद्यन्ते
भूताना पतयस् तथा ।
यथा-प्रकृति सर्वेषां
चित्रा वाचः स्रवन्ति हि ॥९.७॥

yābhir bhūtāni bhidyante
bhūtānāṁ patayas tathā
yathā-prakṛti sarveṣāṁ
citrā vācaḥ sravanti hi (9.7)

yābhir = yābhiḥ — by which; bhūtāni — beings; bhidyante — differentiated; bhūtānām — of the beings; matayas — opinions; tathā — so being; yathā – according; prakṛti — tendency; sarveṣām — of all; citrā = citrāḥ — various; vācaḥ — doctrines; sravanti — pass on; hi — indeed.

Translation

...by which the beings are differentiated as are their opinions. According to their tendencies, various doctrines pass to others. (9.7)

Commentary:

The religious diversity of India is hereby explained. Even though initially there was one Veda and according to *Śrī* Krishna, it was taught in such a way as to cause the living beings to develop devotional affection for Him, still in the end, there evolved various doctrines which were propagated by various teachers according to their particular tendencies which were based on their relationship to material nature.

It was unavoidable that there would be a clash between the original Veda and some of the teachers who came after, because each teacher becomes convinced on the basis of experience. *Śrī* Krishna explained this in a different way to Arjuna:

śrībhagavānuvāca
trividhā bhavati śraddhā dehināṁ sā svabhāvajā
sāttvikī rājasī caiva tāmasī ceti tāṁ śṛṇu
sattvānurūpā sarvasya śraddhā bhavati bhārata
śraddhāmayo'yaṁ puruṣo yo yacchraddhaḥ sa eva saḥ
yajante sāttvikā devān yakṣarakṣāṁsi rājasāḥ
pretānbhūtagaṇāṁścānye yajante tāmasā janāḥ

The Blessed Lord said: According to innate tendency, there are three types of confidences of the embodied souls. These are clarifying, motivating and depressing. Hear about this.

Confidence becomes manifest according to the essential nature of the person, O man of the Bhārata family. A human being follows his trend of confidence. Whatever type of faith he has, that he expresses only.

The clear-minded people worship the supernatural rulers. The impulsive ones worship the passionate sorcerors and the cannibalistic humans. The others, the retarded people, petition the departed spirits and the hordes of ghosts. (B.G. 17.2-4)

एव प्रकृति-वैचित्र्याद्
भिद्यन्ते मतयो नृणाम् ।
पारम्पर्येण केषाञ्चित्
पाषण्ड-मतयो ऽपरे ॥९.८॥

evaṁ prakṛti-vaicitryād
bhidyante matayo nṛṇām
pāramparyeṇa keṣāñcit
pāṣaṇḍa-matayo 'pare (9.8)

evam — thus; prakṛti — mundane tendency; vaicitryād = vaicitryāt — owing to difference; bhidyante — differ; matayo = matayah — beliefs; nṛṇām — among the human beings; pāramparyena — by a succession of Vedic teachers; keṣāñcit — of some; pāṣaṇḍa — non-Vedic, heritcal; matayo = matayaḥ — belief; 'pare = apare — others.

Translation

Thus, owing to different mundane tendencies, there are different beliefs among the human beings. Some differ by the influence of a succession of teachers. Others have non-Vedic beliefs. (9.8)

Commentary:

The contentions among different groups of spiritualists will continue until the end of time, because the dispositions vary according to how a person is influenced by the modes of material nature. It cannot be stopped. Besides the Vedic beliefs, there are others which developed independently, all based on various experiences of someone or another.

मन्-माया-मोहित-धियः
पुरुषाः पुरुषर्षभ ।
श्रेयो वदन्त्य् अनेकान्तं
यथा-कर्म यथा-रुचि ॥९.९॥

man-māyā-mohita-dhiyaḥ
puruṣāḥ puruṣarṣabha
śreyo vadanty anekāntaṁ
yathā-karma yathā-ruci (9.9)

man = mat – my; mayā — bewildering potency; mohita — muddle; dhiyah — intellect; purusāḥ — people; puruṣarṣabha — best of the human beings; śreyo = śreyaḥ — beneficial; vadanty = vadanti — speak of; anekāntam = aneka – numerous + antam — methods; yathā-*karma* — according to their activities; yathā-ruci — according to their preferences.

Translation

O best of the human beings, persons whose intellect are muddled by My bewildering potency, speak of numerous beneficial methods, according to their activities and preferences. (9.9)

Commentary:

Just as a government standardizes its currency, so Lord Krishna defines religious practice. However, just as a ruler or enterprising banker may create his own currency, so many charismatic teachers create doctrines which are at variance with Krishna's philosophy.

धर्मम् एके यशश् चान्ये
कामं सत्यं दमं शमम् ।
अन्ये वदन्ति स्वार्थं वा
ऐश्वर्यं त्याग-भोजनम् ।
केचिद् यज्ञं तपो दानं
व्रतानि नियमान् यमान् ॥९.१०॥

dharmam eke yaśaś cānye
kāmaṁ satyaṁ damaṁ śamam
anye vadanti svārthaṁ vā
aiśvaryaṁ tyāga-bhojanam
kecid yajñaṁ tapo dānaṁ
vratāni niyamān yamān (9.10)

dharmam — righteous duty; eke — some; yaśaś — popularity; cānye = ca — and + anye — others; kāmam — pleasure; satyam — realism; damam — discipline; śamam — peace of mind; anye — other; vadanti — say; svārtham = sva – own + artham — aim of life; vā — surely; aiśvaryam — political influence; tyāga — giving up of benefits; bhojanam — food consumption; kecid = kecit — some; yajñam — religious ceremony and disciplines; tapo = tapah — austerity; dānam — charity; vratāni — vows; niyamān — behavioral codes; yamān — moral restraints.

Translation

As for their aim of life, some say righteous duty; some say popularity; others say pleasure; some others say realism; some discipline; others say peace of mind; some say political influence; others say renunciation of benefits; others say food consumption; some say religious ceremony and discipline; some say austerity; some say charity; some say vows; some say behavioral codes, some say moral restraint. (9.10)

Commentary:

There are many religions in the world. Each has principles for the believers. It all depends on one's sense of conviction and how that is invested in the modes of material nature.

आद्य्-अन्त-वन्त एवैषां
लोकाः कर्म-विनिर्मिताः ।
दुःखोदर्कास् तमो-निष्ठाः
क्षुद्रा मन्दाः शुचार्पिताः ॥९.११॥

ādy-anta-vanta evaiṣāṁ
lokāḥ karma-vinirmitāḥ
duḥkhodarkās tamo-niṣṭhāḥ
kṣudrā mandāḥ śucārpitāḥ (9.11)

ady = ādi – beginning; anta – ending; vanta — having; evaisām = eva — certainly + esām — of them; lokāh — the situations derived; karma — cultural actvities; vinirmitāḥ — caused by; duhkhodarkas = duhkha — misery + udarkāḥ — resulting in; tamo = tamah — depression + nisthāḥ — situated; ksudrā — meager; mandāḥ — transient; śucārpitāḥ = śucā — with lamentation + arpitāḥ — filled.

Translation

The situations derived from these methods which are caused by cultural actvities, have a beginning and ending, producing misery and resulting in depression, being meager and transient, and filled with lamentation. (9.11)

Commentary:

Whatever we do for religion, for philosophy or for divinity, which is sponsored by cultural activity will pan out into depression. It is the way material nature operates. Whatever we do which is motivated for upliftment in cultural activities, will in the end be taken over by the depressive or retardative mood which is known as *tamo guṇa* in Sanskrit.

मय्य् अर्पितात्मनः सभ्य
निरपेक्षस्य सर्वतः ।
मयात्मना सुखं यत् तत्
कुतः स्याद् विषयात्मनाम् ॥९.१२॥

mayy arpitātmanaḥ sabhya
nirapekṣasya sarvataḥ
mayātmanā sukhaṁ yat tat
kutaḥ syād viṣayātmanām (9.12)

mayy = mayi — in me; arpitātmanaḥ = arpita — absorded on + ātmanah — of the self; sabhya — cultured one; nirapekṣasya — of one who is indifferent to objects; sarvatah — all; mayātmanā = mayā — with me + ātmanā — self; sukham — happiness; yat tat — which that; kutah — how; syad = syat — could it be; viṣayātmanām = viṣaya — sense objects + ātmanām — of the self.

Translation

O cultured one, how can a person who is attached to sense objects, have the happiness, which a person who is absorbed in Me, and who is indifferent to all sense objects, derive from Myself. (9.12)

Commentary:

This is in response to Uddhava's question:

śrī-uddhava uvāca
vadanti kṛṣṇa śreyāṁsi bahūni brahma-vādinaḥ
teṣāṁ vikalpa-prādhānyam utāho eka-mukhyatā

The deserving Uddhava said: O Krishna, the teachers of spirituality speak of various means of well being. Are all of these options essential? Or is one the most important? (U.G. 9.1)

The various methods for salvation do not give the same result. It depends on the method used. Each one yields particular advantages for the practitioner. It is not a matter of the claims of any teacher, but rather it is how it is practiced and what each follower derives.

Each religion, even the one advocated by *Śrī* Krishna, makes certain claims for its adherent. When all is said and done, each follower only reaps results according to how well he followed the disciplines which were recommended to him.

The satisfaction derived from a particular practice is appreciated differently by different persons. Each person has a similar or dissimilar psychology. Therefore even within a particular religion, there are differences of opinion among followers. Even though generally, persons from a religious group present a unity, still as soon as one joins the group, one finds that there is disunity. Even a person who claims to be a loyal follower of a specific teacher, may have essential and very strong disagreements with the teacher. This is all because of difference in the psychology. These differences may not disappear even in the mature stages of each person.

Of interest to us as *kriyā* yogis is the standard put forward for devotees of *Śrī* Krishna. The person must be His devotee. He must also be indifferent to all sense objects. This means that his absorption in *Śrī* Krishna must be total.

अकिञ्चनस्य दान्तस्य
शान्तस्य सम-चेतसः ।
मया सन्तुष्ट-मनसः
सर्वाः सुख-मया दिशः ॥९.१३॥

akiñcanasya dāntasya
śāntasya sama-cetasaḥ
mayā santuṣṭa-manasaḥ
sarvāḥ sukha-mayā diśaḥ (9.13)

akiñcanasya — of one who craves nothing; dāntasya — of one who is disciplined; śāntasya — of one who has peace of mind; sama-cetasaḥ — one who is equally disposed mentally and emotionally; mayā — with Me; santuṣṭa — satisfied; manasaḥ — mind; sarvāḥ — all; sukha – happiness; mayā = mayāḥ — full of; diśaḥ — circumstances.

Translation

All circumstances are full of happiness for the person who craves nothing, who is disciplined, who has peace of mind, who is equally disposed to all and whose mind is satisfied with Me. (9.13)

Commentary:

This describes a person who mastered himself by the eightfold process of yoga, otherwise one cannot find happiness in all circumstances. This is a trained cultivated habit of a person who is perfectly detached. This does not mean satisfaction with temple life among devotees, but rather it means satisfaction any and everywhere and being able to stay in touch with *Śrī* Krishna any and everywhere, not expecting anything good or bad from this material creation and being satisfied even with a perverse and disagreeable destiny.

न पारमेष्ठ्यं न महेन्द्र-धिष्ण्य
न सार्वभौमं न रसाधिपत्यम् ।
न योग-सिद्धीर् अपुनर्-भव वा
मय्य् अर्पितात्मेच्छति मद् विनान्यत् ॥९.१४॥

na pārameṣṭhyaṁ na mahendra-dhiṣṇyaṁ
na sārvabhaumaṁ na rasādhipatyam
na yoga-siddhīr apunar-bhavaṁ vā
mayy arpitātmecchati mad vinānyat 9.14

na — not; pārameṣṭhyam — the position of Procreator Brahmā; na — not; mahendra-dhiṣṇyaṁ = mahā – great + indra – ruler of the angelic world + dhiṣṇyam — position; na — not; sārvabhaumam — all the earth; na — not; rasādhipatyam — ruler of the nether region; na — no; yoga-siddhīr = yoga-siddhīḥ — skills resulting from yoga practice; apunah-bhavam — no more birth, liberation; vā — or; mayy = mayi — in Me; arpitātmecchati = arpita — fully absorded + ātmā — self + icchati — desires; mad = mat — me; vinānyat — without any other thing, nothing else.

Translation

The man who is fully absorbed in Me, desires nothing else not even the position of Procreator Brahmā, nor that of the great ruler of the angelic world, nor sovereignty of the nether regions, nor the skills resulting from yoga practice, nor the status of not being born again. (9.14)

Commentary:

Such full absorption is rarely experienced by a common living entity if he has not perfected yoga practice. But it is always possible for the eternal associates of the Supreme Lord. By virtue of their spiritual category, they can exhibit the full absorption. This is because, as stated before by Sanaka, the intellect is attached to the subtle material elements and such elements are forcibly attracted to the intellect.

A yogi devotee who has not completed the course of yoga, will not qualify by this verse, since until the completion he would be attracted to one or more of the mystic skills developed as he practices. When a yogi reaches the perfective stage, he is no longer attracted to the mystic skills, because he masters the technique of investing those abilities to reach the culmination of yoga, which is full absorption in *samādhi* practice.

The various attractions mentioned, do face the aspiring yogi. If he is unable to overcome them, he will not get success but will fall back to cultural activities.

The status of not being born again in this world is coveted by most yogis, and it serves well to make them serious about giving up the attraction to the material world. However a yogi soon finds out that it is not merely a matter of not desiring to be born here. One has to develop a nature that is resistant to the advantages of this type of birth. Thus, when the yogi, by austerity in mystic practice, can change his nature, he becomes resistant to these births. He gives up desires but exhibits a willingness to comply with the orders of the Supreme Personality Lord Krishna or with Lord Shiva, alternately.

A yogi is a limited being even in the liberated stage. Whatever he achieves is subject to alteration or denial by the Supreme Being. Thus in the final stage of practice, his psyche becomes compliant with the Supreme Lord, the Supreme Being, the Supreme Personality of Godhead.

As the yogi is an individual person, so the Supreme Being is also a person but the power difference between them is great. Thus the yogi leans on the Supreme Lord and complies with the divine will. That is the full course of yoga practice for those who are theistic.

न तथा मे प्रियतम
आत्म-योनिर् न शङ्करः ।
न च सङ्कर्षणो न श्रीर्
नैवात्मा च यथा भवान् ॥९.१५॥

na tathā me priyatama
ātma-yonir na śaṅkaraḥ
na ca saṅkarṣaṇo na śrīr
naivātmā ca yathā bhavān (9.15)

na — neither; tathā — so; me — to me; priyatamah — very dear; ātma-yonir = ātma-yoniḥ — Brahmā; na — nor; śaṅkaraḥ — Shiva; na — not; ca — and; saṅkarṣaṇo = Saṅkarṣaṇaḥ — Sankarshan Balarāma; na — no; śrīr = śrīḥ — the Lady Laksmi; naivātmā = na — nor + eva — indeed + ātmā — self; ca — and; yathā — as; bhavān — you

Translation

Neither Procreator Brahmā, nor Śaṅkara Shiva, nor Sankarshana Balarāma, nor the Lady Lakṣmī, nor myself even, is very dear to me as You are. (9.15)

Commentary:

There are various explanations of this verse, given out by the various lines of disciplic succession which came down from the Supreme Lord. In addition, many persons who became spiritual authorities for one reason or the other, by some influence or the other, explained this verse. However, this dearness, *(priyatama)* refers to Uddhava and others on par or greater than him, in terms of the qualities described in verses 12,13 and 14 above.

In a rare and very sensational announcement, *Śrī* Krishna declared that such devotees are even more dear to him than Procreator *Brahmā*, his dear servant who manages universal cultural activity, even Lord Shiva who supervises the liberations of the perfected beings, even *Śrī* Krishna's elder brother, the most prominent of His parallel divinities, Lord *Sañkarṣaṇa Balarāma*, and even Krishna's eternal spouse, the Goddess *Śrī Lakṣmī*, as well as *Śrī* Krishna Himself.

Such a statement has to be analyzed thoroughly, so that we do not risk ourselves into thinking that we are devotees of such a value to the Lord.

These are the qualifications of such endearing devotees:

Verse 12

- *mayy arpitātmanaḥ — absorption of the self on Śrī Krishna.*
- *nirapekṣasya sarvataḥ — being indifferent to all sense objects.*

Verse 13

- *akiñcanasya —craving nothing, being completely disinterested, being without ambitions.*
- *dāntasya — being disciplined.*
- *sama-cetasaḥ — being equally disposed mentally and emotionally.*
- *śāntasya — having peace of mind.*
- *mayā santuṣṭa-manasaḥ — having a mind which is satisfied with Śrī Krishna.*

Verse 14

- *na pārameṣṭhyam — one who does not aspire for the position of Procreator Brahmā.*
- *na mahendra-dhiṣṇyam — one who does not want the position of the ruler of the*
- *angelic world.*
- *na sārvabhaumani —not wanting rulership of all territories on earth.*
- *na rasādhipatyam —not wanting rulership of the nether region.*
- *na yoga-siddhīr —not aspiring for the skills resulting from yoga practice.*
- *apunar-bhavam —not caring even for the liberation.*
- *arpitātmecchati — being fully absorbed in Śrī Krishna.*

Such a devotee having all these qualifications is more dear to *Śrī* Krishna, than even the creator devotee of this world, or even Lord Shiva or Lord *Balarāma* or Goddess *Lakṣmī* or even *Śrī* Krishna Himself. Such a person is so dear because of his being completely free from desires and ambitions *(akiñcana)*, such that he is in reserve for usage by the Blessed Lord.

Śrī Krishna is so precise in the definition of that devotee, that even His own self *(naivatma* = na eva *ātma*) is down rated in comparison.

निरपेक्षं मुनिं शान्तं	nirapekṣaṁ muniṁ śāntaṁ
निर्वैरं सम-दर्शनम् ।	nirvairaṁ sama-darśanam
अनुव्रजाम्य् अहं नित्यं	anuvrajāmy ahaṁ nityaṁ
पूयेयेत्य् अङ्घ्रि-रेणुभिः ॥९.१६॥	pūyeyety aṅghri-reṇubhiḥ (9.16)

nirapekṣam — free from cravings, carefree; munim — philosophical; santam — peaceful; nirvairam — not hostile to anyone; sama-darśanam — seeing the comparative existential similarity between the embodied souls; anuvrajāmy = anuvrajāmi — follow; aham — I; nityam — always; pūyetety = pūyeya — I may be purified + iti — thus, so that; aṅghri-reṇubhiḥ = anghri — feet + renubhiḥ — by the dust.

Translation

I always follow that person who is carefree, philosophical, peaceful, having no hostility to anyone, and who sees the comparative existential similarity between the embodied souls. I do this to be purified by the dust of his feet. (9.16)

Commentary:

Śrī Krishna complied with this philosophy in the examples of devotee *Nārada* and devotee *Sudāma Vipra*. In both cases, *Śrī* Krishna took the dust of their feet upon His own head, sincerely and with confidence, feeling that He could purify Himself.

Śrī Nārada is the prime example of a devotee who is carefree. He wanders all over the various territories and dimensions in a very carefree mood. His discourses are philosophical. He is peaceful. By his influence many demons assumed a pacifist stance. *Nārada* has no hostility to anyone, even to those who are openly antagonistic or disbelieving in the Lord. He was very friendly and counseling to demons who were sworn enemies of *Śrī* Krishna. *Nārada* is an accomplished *mahāyogin* who continually sees the comparative similarity between the embodied souls in terms of their spirits being mystically linked to the *buddhi* organs in their subtle bodies and to a life force kundalini mechanism.

Such devotees are indeed great. In fact, the Lord states that they are greater than His primary associates, Lord *Brahmā*, Lord Shiva, Lord *Balarāma* and the Goddess *Śrī Lakṣmī*.

निष्किञ्चना मय्य् अनुरक्त-चेतसः
शान्ता महान्तो ऽखिल-जीव-वत्सलाः ।
कामैर् अनालब्ध-धियो जुषन्ति ते
यन् नैरपेक्ष्यं न विदुः सुखं मम ॥९.१७॥

niṣkiñcanā mayy anurakta-cetasaḥ
śāntā mahānto 'khila-jīva-vatsalāḥ
kāmair anālabdha-dhiyo juṣanti te
yan nairapekṣyaṁ na viduḥ sukhaṁ mama (9.17)

niṣkiñcanā = niṣkiñcanāḥ — penniless; mayy = mayi — in Me; anurakta – devoted; cetasaḥ — consciousness; śāntā = śāntāh — self composed; mahānto = mahāntaḥ — great souls; 'khila = akhila — all; jīva — individual soul; vatsalāh — those who have a caring interest; kāmair = kāmaiḥ — by pleasures; anālabdha — not urged by; dhiyo = dhiyah — intellect; juṣanti — they experience; te — they; yan = yat — in which case; nairapekṣyam — indifferent to the things of this world; na – not, not others; viduḥ — they know; sukham — happiness; mama — my.

Translation

Great souls, who are penniless, whose consciousness is devoted to Me, who are self-composed, who have a caring interest towards all souls, whose intellect is not urged by pleasures, in which case, since they are completely indifferent to the things of this world, do experience My type of happiness, not others. (9.17)

Commentary:

These great souls are penniless because they do not acquire or aspire for anything in the material world. That means any gross or subtle commodity. Their consciousness is singly devoted to *Śrī* Krishna as described. They are self-composed, not being addicted to nor compelled by the subtle intellect. They have a caring interest towards all souls but it is not an independent concern. It is an interest that remains dormant unless it is actuated by the Lord. They do not express a caring interest that runs contrary to the supreme will. As in the case of Arjun, at the onset of the battle of Kuruksetra, he expressed an interest which opposed the supreme will. But after *Śrī* Krishna preached and revealed, Arjuna relented and complied with the divine ideas.

One's intellect must be freed from all urges for pleasure. This means that it must be detached from its own sense of understanding so that it is not empowered for independent acts within the psyche. One must be completely indifferent to the things of this world, except when the Lord expresses His interest through oneself. This was epitomized by Arjuna, who developed an interest in warfare by the urging and under the influence of *Śrī* Krishna.

When a devotee attains these qualities, he experiences the spiritual happiness which is in the transcendental body of *Śrī* Krishna.

बाध्यमानो ऽपि मद्-भक्तो
विषयैर् अजितेन्द्रियः ।
प्रायः प्रगल्भया भक्त्या
विषयैर् नाभिभूयते ॥९.१८॥

bādhyamāno 'pi mad-bhakto
viṣayair ajitendriyaḥ
prāyaḥ pragalbhayā bhaktyā
viṣayair nābhibhūyate (9.18)

bādhyamāno = bādhyamānaḥ — tormented; 'pi = api — even; mad = mat – my; bhakto = bhaktah — devotee; viṣayair = viṣayaiḥ — by the alluring objects; ajitendriyaḥ — not conquered; prāyah — on the average; pragalbhayā — spirited; bhaktyā — by devotion; viṣayair = viṣayaiḥ — by the alluring objects; nābhibhūyate = na — not + abhibhūyate — is overcome.

Translation

Even a devotee of Mine, who has not conquered his senses and who is tormented by the alluring objects, is generally not overcome by them, because of spirited devotion. (9.18)

Commentary:

This means that even if a devotee of Krishna has not conquered his senses, his psychological energies and instruments, he will be tormented by the alluring objects, because his intellect will still be in a condition of attraction and dependence upon such objects. But still, because of his spirited or very forceful *(pragalbhayā)* devotion *(bhaktyā)* for *Śrī* Krishna, he will not give in to them in most instances.

Here we have to be careful that we do not abolish nor overlook, two important words. These are *prāyah* which means generally or on the average and *pragalbhayā*, which means spirited, powerful or forcefully enduring.

One must not only be a devotee of *Śrī* Krishna but one must be a devotee who has a spirited or very strong devotional attraction to Him. *Śrī* Krishna must Himself regard our devotion in that way. The definition of the strength of devotion must be made by Krishna Himself. Then we would qualify under the guarantee of this verse.

If the devotee qualifies, then still, he will overcome most of the temptation, not all. He will on occasion but over all, he will overcome the faults and stand out as a protected soul. His spirited devotion will cause a protective energy to rescue him in most instances. Providence itself will miraculously usher him safely away from many dangerous situations where otherwise he would surely give in and be degraded.

This is a case of the power of *bhakti*, not *bhakti* yoga. This is an example of the power of devotion all by itself without any application of yoga practice. It is based on a very powerful, strong, enduring and spirited devotion to *Śrī* Krishna.

Everyone does not have this intensity of devotion. Not every devotee has this. Nor can everyone get this merely by joining an institution nor by chanting *Śrī* Krishna's holy names or any such related method. This is an inborn spirited devotion to the Lord. In addition, this does not mean that such a devotee does not have to take up yoga practice to elevate himself. He might have to. It is totally misleading to suggest that merely because one is a devotee, one is in this category and hence does not have to do yoga austerities.

यथाग्निः सु-समृद्धार्चिः
करोत्य् एधांसि भस्मसात् ।
तथा मद्-विषया भक्तिर्
उद्धवैनांसि कृत्स्नशः ॥९.१९॥

yathāgniḥ su-samṛddhārciḥ
karoty edhāṁsi bhasmasāt
tathā mad-viṣayā bhaktir
uddhavaināṁsi kṛtsnaśaḥ (9.19)

yathāgniḥ = yathā — as + agniḥ — fire; su-samṛddhārciḥ = su-samṛddha — increasing intensely + arciḥ — blaze; karoty = karoti — converts; edhāṁsi — firewood; bhasmasāt — into ashes; tathā — as; mad = mat – me; viṣayā — object; bhaktir = bhaktiḥ — devotion; uddhavaināṁsi = uddhava — Uddhava + enāṁsi — sins, faults; kṛtsnaśaḥ — totally.

Translation

As fire which increases into an intense blaze, converts firewood into ashes, so O Uddhava, devotion with Me as the objective, totally destroys one's faults. (9.19)

Commentary:

The word *bhaktir* refers to the same spirited devotion in the previous verse. This must be understood in the context of these verses and not otherwise, as will be stressed in the next verse. However in the previous verse, there is the case of a devotee whose devotion to *Śrī* Krishna is spirited part of the time and lacking in intensity the rest of the time. He will get the coverage when he is in the spirited mood, not when there is a slack in the intensity of his attraction to *Śrī* Krishna.

The increase in intensity of a fire was cited by *Śrī* Krishna to show that it has to be the type of devotion that is spirited sufficiently to increase more and more to drive the devotee to be intensely attached to *Śrī* Krishna and to do whatever is necessary to satisfy the Lord. Then and only then, the devotion acts to destroy the faults of the devotee.

If we find that a devotee has an increase in his faults, obviously the increase in his devotion is not being effective. That would mean that his devotion is not the type described.

Sometimes we experience that a devotee appears to be increasing in devotion, and then we find out that he was involved in a very faulty life style and that he was misrepresenting the devotional profile. In that case, we must realize that such devotion was in the mode of passion and was not spirited by divine energy.

न साधयति मां योगो
न साङ्ख्यं धर्म उद्धव ।
न स्वाध्यायस् तपस् त्यागो
यथा भक्तिर् ममोर्जिता ॥९.२०॥

na sādhayati māṁ yogo
na sāṅkhyaṁ dharma uddhava
na svādhyāyas tapas tyāgo
yathā bhaktir mamorjitā (9.20)

na — neither; sādhayati — attracts; mām — Me; yogo = yogah — yoga practice; na — nor; sāṅkhyam — Sāṅkhya philosophical analysis; dharma = dharmah — righteous duty; uddhava — Uddhava; na — nor; svādhyāyas = svādhyāyah — Vedic study; tapas = tapaḥ — austerity; tyāgo = tyāgaḥ — giving up results; yathā — as; bhaktir = bhaktih — devotion; mamorjitā = mama — me + ūrjitā — spirited, enthusiastic.

Translation

Neither yoga practice, nor Sāṅkhya philosophical analysis, nor righteous duty, nor Vedic study, nor austerity, nor giving up results, would attract Me, as much as spirited devotion. (9.20)

Commentary:

By this declaration, it is clear that nothing we may practice for spiritual elevation at any stage, will attract *Śrī* Krishna to us as much as spirited devotion. This however does not give us the right to feel or to advocate that any other type of devotion will attract Him in the same way. Even though the other aspects of spirituality do attract *Śrī* Krishna, they do not attract Him with as much drawing force, but all the same, it does not mean that all these other methods are useless. Nor does it mean that they should not be practiced. Nor does it indicate that the spirited devotee, the same devotee accredited in these verses, will not have to practice any of these.

For that matter any of these, might be recommended to that same spirited devotee. It is a great injustice to state that a devotee would be spirited like this if he accepts one as a spiritual master or if he joins a certain sect. Certainly, that might be the opinion of the spiritual master who attracts such a person but it might not be the opinion of *Śrī* Krishna. All too often, converts to the Krishna Conscious Societies, are fooled by preachers who draw them into a certain sect by misrepresenting these verses. That is nothing less than manipulation.

In the case of *Prahlād*, the son of *Hiraṇyakaśipu*, he certainly had this spirited devotion to *Śrī* Krishna and *Śrī* Krishna did in an instant come to *Prahlād*'s rescue, not so much to save *Prahlād* from the violence of his father but rather to substantiate *Prahlād*'s word about Krishna being in every location everywhere, being capable of making an appearance anywhere. Even though *Śrī* Krishna appeared like that, still, though *Prahlād* was the ideal spirited devotee, *Śrī* Krishna asked *Prahlād* to take up righteous duty as the son of a king, to rule the territory which was governed by his deceased father, whom Krishna killed. *Prahlād* protested, but *Śrī* Krishna would have none of it. There are other examples. Thus even though one might be spirited in devotion, and even if that spirited devotion, tallies with what *Śrī* Krishna has in mind here, still it does not mean that *Śrī* Krishna, after He is attracted, will not request that one should take up the other disciplines listed in this verse. Arjuna is another example. He was attached to *Śrī* Krishna but he was told to do *karma* yoga, righteous duty for the son of king, which meant that Arjuna had to fight in a civil war.

When one tries to contrast the various methods for spirituality, and when one tries to put *bhakti* up as the ultimate process, one does an injustice if one does not make it clear to the hearers, that *bhakti* means to surrender to do whatever *Śrī* Krishna recommends. After such a complete surrender, the options are open to *Śrī* Krishna, not to the devotee. And that means that the devotee might have to do something that is not to his liking. *Prahlād* for instance was not much in favor of sovereignty. Arjuna was not much in favor of fighting a battle. *Dhruva* was not much in favor of ruling either, even though initially as a child that is what he desired.

भक्त्याहम् एकया ग्राह्यः
श्रद्धयात्मा प्रियः सताम् ।
भक्तिः पुनाति मन्-निष्ठा
श्व-पाकान् अपि सम्भवात् ॥९.२१॥

bhaktyāham ekayā grāhyaḥ
śraddhayātmā priyaḥ satām
bhaktiḥ punāti man-niṣṭhā
śva-pākān api sambhavāt (9.21)

bhaktyāham = bhaktyā — by devotional + aham — I; ekayā — only; grāhyaḥ — obtained; śraddhayātmā = śraddhayā — by faith + ātmā — self; priyaḥ — dear; satām — of the pious people; bhaktiḥ — devotion; punāti — purifies; man-niṣṭhā = mat-nisthā — fixed in Me; śva-pākān — dog-meat eaters; api — even; sambhavāt — from tendencies.

Translation

I, the dear self of the pious people, am obtained by devotion only, and by faith. Devotion that is fixed in Me, purifies even the dog-meat eaters of their tendencies. (9.21)

Commentary:

Śrī Krishna adds on faith *(śraddhayā)* but this is inclusive of the spirited devotion described in the previous verses. Spirited devotion has faith as a counterpart. Even a person who has sordid habits like flesh eating, even one who eats dog-meat, can, if he is overcome by spirited devotion to *Śrī* Krishna, be purified of barbaric tendencies. This illustrates the strength of spirited devotion and its cleansing power.

धर्मः सत्य-दयोपेतो
विद्या वा तपसान्विता ।
मद्-भक्त्यापेतम् आत्मानं
न सम्यक् प्रपुनाति हि ॥९.२२॥

dharmaḥ satya-dayopeto
vidyā vā tapasānvitā
mad-bhaktyāpetam ātmānaṁ
na samyak prapunāti hi (9.22)

dharmah — righteous duty; satya-dayopeto = satya — realism + dayā — mercy + upeto (upetaḥ) — coupled with; vidyā — learning; vā — or; tapasānvitā = tapasā — with austerity + anvitā — coupled with; mad-bhaktyāpetam = mad (mat) - to me + bhaktyā — devotion; apetam — devoid of; ātmānam — self; na — not; samyak — completely; prapunāti — purifies; hi — indeed.

Translation

Righteous duty, coupled with realism and mercy, or learning with austerity, does not completely purify a self without devotion to Me. (9.22)

Commentary:

These statements do not rule out the values of righteous duty, realism, mercy, learning and austerity. These aspects may or may not have to be developed by a devotee, but even if they are practiced, they would not completely purify the self if there is no devotion to *Śrī* Krishna. They would only partially purify. The person would then have to realize that he lacks devotion to the Lord and would have to cultivate that.

This also indicates that the potential for devotion is there in every person who strives for spiritual upliftment, but the person may not realize it. After he or she is improved by other methods, they would come to understand, either by being told or by inspiration, that for the completion of purify, the devotion must be cultivated.

Generally learning and austerity go together, because when one gets knowledge about spiritual life, he develops an inclination to perform austerities so that he can transcend bodily attachment to experience life in other dimensions of consciousness. Righteous duty is supplemented by realism and mercy, because in executing such tasks, one has to be realistic in considering the various circumstances, and one must express mercy according to the various situations of the persons who break morality. Still in executing righteous duty one becomes purified to a certain degree. Thus one realizes that it is insufficient for full purity.

Yogis who are expertly proceeding with righteous duty, perform *karma* yoga under the direction of the Central Figure in the Universal Form. An example of such a person is Arjuna, and he was in fact a yogi of worth. Another example is King *Prahlād*, who governed his father's domains justly. Another was King *Yudhiṣṭhira*. Yogis who take up learning and austerity, expertly, perform *jñāna* yoga. They serve under the auspices of *Śrīla Vyāsadeva*, Lord Shiva or Lord Kapila and other leaders of the ascetics.

However in either case, these persons will have to add the factor of *bhakti*, either with a natural intensity or deliberately by applying yoga concentration to the devotional focus upon *Śrī* Krishna. But this does not mean that one who has the spirited devotion will not have to take up either *karma* yoga or *jñāna* yoga. Some might have to take up either or both of these disciplines.

कथं विना रोम-हर्षं
द्रवता चेतसा विना ।
विनानन्दाश्रु-कलया
शुध्येद् भक्त्या विनाशयः ॥९.२३॥

kathaṁ vinā roma-harṣaṁ
dravatā cetasā vinā
vinānandāśru-kalayā
śudhyed bhaktyā vināśayaḥ (9.23)

katham — how; vinā — without; romaharsam — hairs becoming erect; dravatā — turned favorably; cetasā — consciousness; vinā — without; vinānandāśru-kalaya = vinā — without + ānanda — spiritual happiness + aśru – tears + kalayā — flowing; śudhyed = śudhyet — can be purified; bhaktyā — by devotion; vinā — without; āśayaḥ — emotions.

Translation

How, without the hairs becoming erect, without the consciousness being turned favorably, without the flowing of tears of spiritual happiness, how, in a gist, without devotion, can the emotions be purified? (9.23)

Commentary:

This is a very touching appraisal about the effects of intensified devotion, spirited devotion. In our experience, as far as we heard, Lord *Śrī* Krishna Chaitanya exemplified this statement of *Śrī* Krishna. In fact Lord Chaitanya stressed this kind of life for all devotees of *Śrī* Krishna. And He,

Chaitanya Mahaprabhu, saw this as the only means of reaching *Śrī* Krishna. He advocated this as the sum total salvation of the living beings.

Some symptoms of intensified devotion are given as the bristling of the hairs, the favorable conversion of the consciousness, and the flowing of tears, which are due to feelings of spiritual happiness. *Śrī* Krishna asked a very simply question as to how without such devotion could the emotions within the psyche be purified.

वाग् गद्गदा द्रवते यस्य चित्तं
रुदत्य् अभीक्ष्णं हसति क्वचिच् च ।
विलज्ज उद्गायति नृत्यते च
मद्-भक्ति-युक्तो भुवनं पुनाति ॥९.२४॥

vāg gadgadā dravate yasya cittaṁ
rudaty abhīkṣṇaṁ hasati kvacic ca
vilajja udgāyati nṛtyate ca
mad-bhakti-yukto bhuvanaṁ punāti (9.24)

vāg = vāk — speech; gadgadā — broken; dravate — melts; yasya — of whom; cittam — emotions; rudaty = rudati — weeps; abhīkṣṇam — profusely; hasati — laughs; kvacic = kvacit — sometime; ca — and; vilajja = vilajjah — ashamed; udgāyati — sings aloud; nṛtyate — dances; ca — and; mad-bhakti-yukto = mat-bhakti-yuktaḥ — a person who is absorded in devotion to Me; bhuvanam — world; punāti — purifies.

Translation

One whose speech is broken, whose emotions melts, who without shame, weeps profusely, laughs, sings aloud or dances, who is absorbed in devotion to Me, purifies the world. (9.24)

Commentary:

This brings to mind the life of Lord *Śrī* Chaitanya Mahaprabhu. He is the epitome of such devotion to *Śrī* Krishna. Unfortunately many unqualified persons imitate this behavior. There are many preachers who are all too willing to suggest that any human being can adopt this devotional mood, which they say is so easy. However this does not apply to everyone as they suggest.

Such a person as Lord *Śrī* Krishna Chaitanya Mahaprabhu, can certainly purify the world, but that is if His or Her influence is accepted by everyone in the world. It so happens that everyone is not as emotional about *Śrī* Krishna as Lord Chaitanya. There are various types of living entities in the creation, each being inclined to a particular path for spiritual life and that cannot be altered just for the convenience of spreading this intense affection, spirited devotion to *Śrī* Krishna. We have to be realistic or we will create a farce in the name of devotion to *Śrī* Krishna.

यथाग्निना हेम मलं जहाति
ध्मातं पुनः स्वं भजते च रूपम् ।
आत्मा च कर्मानुशयं विधूय
मद्-भक्ति-योगेन भजत्य् अथो माम् ॥९.२५॥

yathāgninā hema malaṁ jahati
dhmātaṁ punaḥ svaṁ bhajate ca rūpam
ātmā ca karmānuśayaṁ vidhūya
mad-bhakti-yogena bhajaty atho mām
(9.25)

yathāgninā = yathā — as + agninā — by fire; hema — gold; malam — impurities; jahāti — gives up; dhmātam — smelted; punaḥ — again; svam — own; bhajate — assumes; ca — and; rūpam — form; ātmā — spirit; ca — and; karmānuśayam = karma — of cultural activities + anuśayam — bad consequences; vidhūya — removing; mad-bhakti-yogena — devotion to Me, focused by the discipline of yoga; bhajaty = bhajati — worships; atho — thus; mām — me.

Translation

As gold smelted by fire, gives up impurities, and assumes its own form, so the spirit by yogically-focused devotion to Me, removes the bad conseqences of cultural activities and worships Me. (9.25)

Commentary:

Bhakti yoga is psychologically focused devotion to *Śrī* Krishna. This may be done with or without yoga practice. Those persons who naturally have the spirited focused devotion which is devoid of mundane passionate energy, have no need to practice yoga to refine their absorption on *Śrī* Krishna. But others must use yoga to develop that. This is certain. A person who is a scatter-brain and whose emotions are normally diffused, will not be able to develop the spirited focused just by hearing of the pastimes of Lord *Śrī* Chaitanya or of a devotee who exhibited that intense pure devotion, which is a divine and not a passionate energy.

Thus in this verse, *bhakti* yoga is highlighted. In the previous verse, some indication of the deliberately-focused devotion was given by the word *yukto (yuktah).* By learning how to apply yoga expertise to the focusing of devotion upon *Śrī* Krishna and the absorption in Him of the divine emotions, the bad consequences of cultural activities are gradually removed from one's life. One then spends all his time worshipping *Śrī* Krishna in one way or the other, by the continuous focus on the Supreme Lord.

यथा यथात्मा परिमृज्यते ऽसौ
मत्-पुण्य-गाथा-श्रवणाभिधानैः ।
तथा तथा पश्यति वस्तु सूक्ष्मं
चक्षुर् यथैवाञ्जन-सम्प्रयुक्तम् ॥९.२६॥

yathā yathātmā parimṛjyate 'sau
mat-puṇya-gāthā-śravaṇābhidhānaiḥ
tathā tathā paśyati vastu sūkṣmaṁ
cakṣur yathaivāñjana-samprayuktam
(9.26)

yathā yathā — as, frequently; ātmā — self; parimṛjyate — is cleansed; 'sau = asau — he; mat – about me; punya – sacred; gāthā — stories; śravana — listening; abhidhānaih — by reciting; tathā tathā — so so, the more; paśyati — it sees; vastu — reality; sūkṣmam — subtle; caksur = caksuh — eye; yathaivāñjana = yathā — just as + eva — indeed + añjana — sight-improving ointment; samprayuktam — application.

Translation

The more frequently, the self is cleansed by listening to and reciting sacred stories about Me, the more it sees the subtle reality just as the eye sees more clearly by the application of a sight-improving ointment. (9.26)

Commentary:

Two types of devotional practices were described. The first was the spirited type that required no assistance from anything else and which attracts *Śrī* Krishna more than anything else. The second is *bhakti*-yoga practice which is the application of yoga focus to the devotional cultivation in relationship to *Śrī* Krishna.

This verse gives more details about the second practice of deliberate *bhakti* yoga or yogically focused devotion. Some may do this without yoga practice but others must develop concentration and focus by yoga techniques and then use the expertise developed to focus their devotional love on *Śrī* Krishna.

In this verse, *Śrī* Krishna informs that this has for one of its component practices, the listening and reciting of sacred stories about Him. This is called Krishna *kathā*.

This verse attests to the fact that if a person practices *bhakti* yoga as described and if he also hears and recited the sacred stories about *Śrī* Krishna, then such recitation will in time cause him to see the reality of the spiritual world. We must not over-simplify nor depreciate the process, otherwise some will think that their imagination of Krishna's activity is itself the spiritual world, and so we would have done an injustice.

विषयान् ध्यायतश् चित्तं
विषयेषु विषज्जते ।
माम् अनुस्मरतश् चित्तं
मय्य् एव प्रविलीयते ॥९.२७॥

viṣayān dhyāyataś cittaṁ
viṣayeṣu viṣajjate
mām anusmarataś cittaṁ
mayy eva pravilīyate (9.27)

viṣayān — attractive objects; dhyāyatas = dhyāyataḥ — of one whose attention is linked to a concentration force; cittaṁ — the mental and emotional energies; viṣayeṣu — in the attractive objects; viṣajjate — is attached; mām — me; anusmarataś = anusmarataḥ — of one who constantly remembers; cittam — the mental and emotional energies; mayy = mayi — in Me; eva — alone; pravilīyate — is absorbed.

Translation

The mind and emotions of a person whose attention is linked to the attractive objects is attached to them. The mento-emotional energies of one who constantly remembers Me is absorbed in Me. (9.27)

Commentary:

This refers to both the spirited devotee and the devotee who takes steps to cultivate a spirited devotional interest in *Śrī* Krishna. Both of these devotees, by virtue of their constant remembrance, become absorbed in Him alone, just as when our consciousness, especially the emotional part of it, is saturated with images of attractive objects, we become attached to the objects and create a life style which promotes procuring and possessing such objects.

It sounds easy but if we consider deeply, we will admit that it is not natural for our consciousness to be always dwelling on *Śrī* Krishna. Imitating persons like *Śrī* Krishna Chaitanya or the *gopīs* of *Vṛndavān* does not change the nature of our consciousness. Our mind's natural means is to focus on the sense objects of this world. If perchance we develop a focus on *Śrī* Krishna, it is usually limited to focusing on objects which relate to Him in this world only. Hardly any of us, have experiences of *Śrī* Krishna in the transcendental world. This is because our focus through the mind is habituated and bend down into this world.

तस्माद् असद्-अभिध्यानं
यथा स्वप्न-मनोरथम् ।
हित्वा मयि समाधत्स्व
मनो मद्-भाव-भावितम् ॥९.२८॥

tasmād asad-abhidhyānaṁ
yathā svapna-manoratham
hitvā mayi samādhatsva
mano mad-bhāva-bhāvitam (9.28)

tasmād = tasmāt — therefore; asad = asat — temporary things; abhidhyānam — habit of dwelling upon; yathā — just as; svapna — dream; manoratham — fantasy; hitvā — giving up; mayi — in Me; samādhatsva — focused absorption; mano = manah — mind; mad = mat – for Me; bhāva — feelings; bhāvitam — saturated with.

Translation

Therefore, giving up the habit of dwelling on temporary things, which are like dreams and fantasies, assume a focused absorption of the mind, which is saturated with feelings for Me. (9.28)

Commentary:

This again is much easier said or conceived than can be done. Despite the high sounding words and the convincing statements of so many devotees of *Śrī* Krishna especially those with a Bengali or Vṛndāvan upbringing or training, still in our present condition, this is not as practical as it seems. But it was practical for Uddhava and was easy for him to apply. And we must not forget that *Śrī* Krishna addressed Uddhava here.

To perform this kind of absorbed focused devotion or *bhakti* either as spontaneous spirited devotion or as deliberated focused devotion, one has to be either born with the spirited love for

Śrī Krishna or one must have practiced yoga and reached the 6th, 7th and 8th stages of yoga practice, namely *dhāraṇā* focusing, *dhyāna* mystic contemplation and *samādhi* total out-of-this-dimension absorption. Otherwise it cannot be done in the way *Śrī* Krishna described to Uddhava.

One would do well if he were to try for this and then be honest with himself to realize if indeed he could give up the temporary things which are like dreams and fantasy. If he cannot give them up, despite his listening to and reading of the pastimes of *Śrī* Krishna, and despite his association with devotees of Krishna, then he would do well to develop his mind's detachment from this world and his mind's transferred focus to what is transcendental to this world.

स्त्रीणां स्त्री-सङ्गिनां सङ्गं
त्यक्त्वा दूरत आत्मवान् ।
क्षेमे विविक्त आसीनश्
चिन्तयेन् माम् अतन्द्रितः ॥९.२९॥

strīṇāṁ strī-saṅgināṁ saṅgaṁ
tyaktvā dūrata ātmavān
kṣeme vivikta āsīnaś
cintayen mām atandritaḥ (9.29)

strīnām — of women; strī — women; saṅginām — of those who associate with; saṅgam — association; tyaktvā — abandoning; dūrata = dūrataḥ — far; ātmavān — one who is self-controlled; kṣeme — at ease; vivikta — in isolation; āsīnaś = āsīnaḥ — sitting; cintayen = cintayet — one should think; mam — about Me; atandritaḥ — attentively.

Translation

Having abandoned far off, the company of women as well as of those who associate with them, the self-controlled person, should sit in a secluded place at ease and should attentively consider Me. (9.29)

Commentary:

The fact that it is not practical for most of us to use devotion alone, *bhakti* alone, becomes very evident when we regard these digressions by *Śrī* Krishna. Here He instructed that one should go into isolation *(vivikta)* and should sit considering Him attentively. One should already have mastered himself sufficiently to be self controlled and should abandon sexual association.

Undoubtedly most of the devotees of Krishna, will not be successful in the complete Krishna focus unless they develop concentration and absorption by yoga disciplines.

न तथास्य भवेत् क्लेशो
बन्धश् चान्य-प्रसङ्गतः ।
योषित्-सङ्गाद् यथा पुंसो
यथा तत्-सङ्गि-सङ्गतः ॥९.३०॥

na tathāsya bhavet kleśo
bandhaś cānya-prasaṅgataḥ
yoṣit-saṅgād yathā puṁso
yathā tat-saṅgi-saṅgataḥ (9.30)

na — not; tathāsya = tathā — so being + asya — of him; bhavet — should be; kleśo = kleśaḥ — misery; bandhaś = bandhaḥ — complication; canya = ca — and + anya – to other; prasaṅgataḥ — attachment; yoṣit — of women; saṅgāt — from association; yathā — as; puṁso = puṁsaḥ — of man; yathā — so; tat — that; saṅgi — of those who are attached; saṅgataḥ — of those association.

Translation

For a man, no other attachment causes so much misery and complication, as the association of women, and of those who are attached to them. (9.30)

Commentary:

It is interesting that *Śrī* Krishna, warns us about the shattering effects of the association of women and of those who are fascinated by females. These include females who are themselves fascinated with their own forms and with the forms, affections and charms of other females. *Śrī* Krishna informed that a major cause of our failure to cultivate the focus on Him is the attachment to female association. It is a wonder that in so many branches of His disciplic succession, the *Ācāryas* initiate many women and justify that on the strength of their ability to preach Krishna consciousness to one and all. Many of these same Acharyas down-play, ridicule, and abolish yoga practice and isolation as being against or contrary to Krishna Consciousness.

Bhakti, devotion, and *bhakti* yoga, application of yoga concentration to devotional focus, is recommended with isolation and with leaving aside the company of females. This is recommended by *Śrī* Krishna here so it is a wonder that many of the gurus shun such advice of *Śrī* Krishna and write purports to these verses, undervaluing this.

श्री-उद्धव उवाच
यथा त्वाम् अरविन्दाक्ष
यादृशं वा यद्-आत्मकम् ।
ध्यायेन् मुमुक्षुर् एतन् मे
ध्यानं त्वं वक्तुम् अर्हसि ॥९.३१॥

śrī-uddhava uvāca
yathā tvām aravindākṣa
yādṛśaṁ vā yad-ātmakam
dhyāyen mumukṣur etan me
dhyānaṁ tvaṁ vaktum arhasi (9.31)

śrī-uddhava – the deserving Uddhava; uvāca — said; yathā — as; tvām — you; aravindākṣa — o lotus-eyed one; yādṛśam — in what aspect; vā — or; yad = yat – which; ātmakam — spiritual feature; dhyāyen = dhyāyet — should meditate; mumukṣur = mumukṣuḥ — one who desires liberation; etan = etat — this; me — to Me; dhyānam — meditation; tvam — you; vaktum — to tell; arhasi — you can.

Translation

The deserving Uddhava said: O lotus-eyed one, in what aspect or what spiritual feature, should one who desires liberation, meditate on You? You can tell me this. (9.31)

Commentary:

There is a lot of twisting and turning in the devotional succession which came down from *Śrī* Krishna, in their explanation to this pointed question by Uddhava. But this is the stage at which Uddhava wants to be realistic and the stage at which he really began to listen to what *Śrī* Krishna informed. Uddhava pressed and pressed for an easy method of salvation but he gave up that quest, because the easy and most definite method which is spontaneous spirited devotion, is not practical for most people in this world. This is because their devotional feelings are sponsored mostly by the passionate mode in material nature. The focus of such feelings on *Śrī* Krishna will not cause the person to attain spiritual life, because Krishna is interested in divine emotions, something which is way beyond the reach of the common person.

People must first develop concentration before they can apply their devotion to *Śrī* Krishna. This is because presently the emotions we have are mundanely contaminated, mundanely formed. To go through transformation, we have to take up yoga austerities. That Is certain.

Śrī Uddhava had boldly brought up the point about persons who are desirous of liberation, the *mumukṣur*, because besides those who have the spontaneous spirited devotion, all others who want to get out of the material world will have to aspire for it in one way or the other, focusing on one aspect or the other. But if such people desire to meditate on *Śrī* Krishna, as the Lord suggested, what are the details on how they should go about doing that. In what specific aspect or feature, should that be done?

श्री-भगवान् उवाच
सम आसन आसीनः
सम-कायो यथा-सुखम् ।
हस्ताव् उत्सङ्ग आधाय
स्व-नासाग्र-कृतेक्षणः ॥९.३२॥

śrī-bhagavān uvāca
sama āsana āsīnaḥ
sama-kāyo yathā-sukham
hastāv utsaṅga ādhāya
sva-nāsāgra-kṛtekṣaṇaḥ (9.32)

śrī-bhagavān – the blessed lord; uvāca — said; sama = same — on a flat; āsana = āsane — on a seat;

āsīnah — sitting; sama – balanced; kāyo = kāyaḥ — body; yathā – as; sukham — easy posture; hastav = hastau — two hands; utsaṅga = utsaṅge — in the lap; ādhāya — placing; sva –own; nāsāgra = nāsa – nose + agra — highest point; kṛtekṣaṇaḥ = krta — applied, focused + īkṣaṇaḥ — visual energy;

Translation

The Blessed Lord said: Sitting on a flat surface, in an easy posture, with the body balanced, placing the hands on the lap, and with the visual energy applied to the highest point on the nose. (9.32)

Commentary:

Undoubtedly this is a *kriyā* yoga practice, which has to do with an *āsana* postures in *Haṭha* yoga and *prāṇāyāma* breath nourishment methods. This is for putting an end to the jumpy nature of the mind and for causing the mind to be saturated with a higher pranic energy which accelerates its focus out of material existence.

Even though the same Lord Krishna said that yoga disciplines are not as effective in attracting Him, when compared to the spontaneous spirited devotion, still for those of us who do not have that spirited love and atttraction, we should develop by first curbing the psyche by yoga methods, such as the one described in this verse.

The easy posture is not just any posture but a posture which has become easy for the body because it was practiced sufficiently in the 3rd stage of yoga which is the āsana practice. The body has to be balanced, and that itself restricts the posture to being a variation of the *padmāsana* or lotus pose. It may be *padmāsana*, *siddhāsana* or *sukhāsana*, lotus pose, perfected pose or easy pose. The hands are placed on the lap in a *mudrā* hand gesture, which was cultivated and which facilitates, the settling down of the life force energy. The visual energy is applied to the highest point on the nose in order to begin the preparation for internalizing the visual power into the *buddhi* organ of the subtle body, so that eventually the attentive focus of the soul can be relocated to *Śrī* Krishna or to the spiritual world where *Śrī* Krishna permanently resides.

प्राणस्य शोधयेन् मार्गं
पूर-कुम्भक-रेचकैः ।
विपर्ययेणापि शनैर्
अभ्यसेन् निर्जितेन्द्रियः ॥९.३३॥

prāṇasya śodhayen mārgaṁ
pūra-kumbhaka-recakaiḥ
viparyayeṇāpi śanair
abhyasen nirjitendriyaḥ (9.33)

prāṇasya — of the vitalizing energy; śodhayen = śodhayet — should purify; mārgam — the passage, route; pūra – inhalation; kumbhaka – retension; recakaiḥ — with exhalation; viparyayenapi = viparyayena — by the reverse order + api — also; śanair = śanaiḥ — by graduating; abhyasen = abhyaset — should practice; nirjitendriya = nirjita — having controlled + indriyah — the sensual energy.

Translation

One should purify the passage of the vitalizing energy by inhalation, retension and exhalation, and by graduation in the reverse order, having the sensual energy controlled. (9.33)

Commentary:

This is the 4th stage of yoga namely *prāṇāyāma*, which leads to the 5th stage of *pratyāhar* sensual energy withdrawal from the mundane objects and from forcibly indulging the mind in fantasy and ideas which relate to temporary objects. This frees the mind from having to engage in mundane sense objects of all sorts and causes it to become detached from the material world.

If one cannot exhibit the spontaneous spirited devotion, the type of devotion that propels one out of this material world, then one has to realize that one's mind is attached to the material world. One should take a drastic step to change the nature of the mind by purifying the passage of the vitalizing energy, so that the intake of mental and emotional force is changed to give one the desired results. This is done by mastering *prāṇāyāma* and *pratyāhar* practice.

हृद्य् अविच्छिनम् ओंकार	hṛdy avicchinam oṁkāraṁ
घण्टा-नाद् बिसोर्ण-वत् ।	ghaṇṭā-nādaṁ bisorṇa-vat
प्राणेनोदीर्य तत्राथ	prāṇenodīrya tatrātha
पुनः सवेशयेत् स्वरम् ॥९.३४॥	punaḥ saṁveśayet svaram (9.34)

hṛdy = hṛdi — in the heart chakra; avicchinnam — continuous without breakage; oṁkāram — Om sound; ghaṇtā — bell; nādam — sound; bisorṇa-vat = bisa – fibre + ūrna – lotus + vat — like; prāṇenodīrya = prāṇena — by the vitalizing energy + udīrya — raising; tatrātha = tatra — there + atha — thus; punaḥ — again; saṁveśayet — one should blend with; svaram — of musical notes, tones.

Translation

In the heart chakra, the Om sound which is like the continuous peal of a bell, resonates continually, like a fibre in a lotus stalk. Raising it by using the vitalizing energy, one should blend that sound with the musical tones. (9.34)

Commentary:

This is a combination of the practices of kundalini and *nāda* yogas. Both of these disciplines are part of the practice called *kriyā* yoga. Sometimes it is called *rāja* yoga.

In the practice of kundalini yoga, the ascetic uses the *prāṇāyāma* practice to strike the vitalizing life force which is at the bottom of the spine. He strikes that force by using *prāṇa*. When he compacts *prāṇa* into his subtle body, he pushes it down the front or center of that form into the pubic area. From there he forces it into the *mūlādhār* or base chakra. When this occurs the *apāna* energy which operated digestion, collection of nutrients and evacuation, tries to oppose the pranic energy but since that energy is compressed and sufficiently charged, it forces the *apāna* energy up the spine. This mixture of *apāna*, *prāṇa* and sexual force is called kundalini energy. When the *apāna* and *prāṇa* mix, they become ignited and a light flashes at the bottom of the spine. By applying locks, the yogi forces the energy to move upwards.

At first the yogi is taught these locks as if they were merely physical actions of muscle contraction but as he practices he realizes that they are also psychological actions taking place. Thus he gives up doubts and practices with more confidence. There are many gurus, who brandish the idea that *haṭha* yoga is merely physical exercise. They do a service to *haṭha* yoga by attracting insincere people away from the effective yoga practices. Without their knowledge those critical teachers help to keep *haṭha* Yoga in reserve for serious aspirants, persons who are very desirous of liberation, the *mumukṣus*.

When kundalini shakti is sufficiently aroused, it comes up into the brain of the physical body, and the intellect of the subtle one. But it descends back down the spine to the base as soon as it is able to. Thus it raises and falls repeatedly according to the frequency of practice and the ability to arouse it by various techniques which are a combination of *prāṇāyāma* and *āsana* postures. Collectively it is called *haṭha* Yoga. A yogi must carefully regulate diet to facilitate the practice.

After sometime the yogi realizes that kundalini shakti simply refuses to stay up on a permanent basis. Feeling frustrated in his effort to remain in higher consciousness continuously, he approaches senior yogis for a solution to the problem.

At that stage, the senior yogis usually tell their student that he has to strive for complete celibacy, which is called the *ūrdhva retā* stage. But the student becomes baffled because he thinks that he is already celibate. However it is explained to him that his celibacy was partial only.

The yogi must then take up celibacy yoga, which is the same *haṭha* yoga and *prāṇāyāma* practice with the aim to raise the seminal fluid and to eliminate both the gross and subtle bodies storage capacity, for sexual fluids. The yogi returns to his practice in a humble state of mind and continues to cause the sexual fluids to rise up.

Initially one is able to make it rise only to the heart chakra and into the central chest area. It is at that stage that the yogi might hear the Om sound which is like the continuous peel of a bell. It resonates in the *suśumnā naḍi* passage which is the central passage in the subtle spine. Because the chakras are cleared and because the central passage is open, the sound rises in it from the bottom. This Om sound is not a sound made by the yogi but is a sound which resonates in the central spinal area of the subtle body. It is like the continuous pealing sound which is heard from a bell or like the sound heard when a conch shell is put to one ear and a vibration within echoes continually of its own accord. When a bell is struck there remains a ringing sound after some time. That is similar to the continuous Om sound which is heard by a yogin.

Since he does not have to create nor to vibrate nor speak the sound with his vocal cord or even with his mind, the yogi is freed from the chore of chanting. He focuses on the sound and takes relief just by hearing it. This sort of relief sets the pace for his entry into the chit *ākāśa*, the sky of consciousness.

By the continual practice of kundalini yoga and celibacy yoga, the yogi is able to move the seminal force beyond the heart chakra on a permanent basis but he has to take help from the sound which is heard in the right ear. This sound comes from the chit *ākāśa*, the sky of consciousness. It pours in from the outside of the subtle right ear, which is a hearing orb which stays close to the intellect organ in the subtle body. By purity of intent, by proper diet, by very limited association with materialistic people, the yogi is able to cause the Om sound from the *suśumnā naḍi* to rise up and meet the Om sound which comes in from the subtle right ear. At that point he hears the Om sound as if it were a blend of musical tones and he finds himself to be saturated with its resonance.

This is the beginning of the *kriyā* yoga practice of being transferred into the chit *ākāśa*, the sky of consciousness.

एवं प्रणव-संयुक्तं
प्राणम् एव समभ्यसेत् ।
दश-कृत्वस् त्रि-षवणं
मासाद् अर्वाग् जितानिलः ॥९.३५॥

evaṁ praṇava-saṁyuktaṁ
prāṇam eva samabhyaset
daśa-kṛtvas tri-ṣavaṇaṁ
māsād arvāg jitānilaḥ (9.35)

evam — thus; praṇava — Om inner sound; saṁyuktam — premixed; prānam — vitalizing energy, eva — indeed; samabhyaset — should direct; daśa – ten; kṛtvas = kṛtvaḥ — procedures; tri-ṣavaṇam — three times; māsād = māsāt — month; arvāg = arvāk — after; jitānilaḥ = jita — conquer + anilah — the life air.

Translation

Thus, one should carefully direct the pre-mixed Oṁ sound and the vitalizing energy, ten times, thrice per day. (9.35)

Commentary:

This is the procedure for a special *Omkāra kriyā* practiced by advanced yogis who have purified the subtle body, the *suśumnā* central spinal passage and have freed-up their *buddhi* organ from mundane pursuits. One cannot do this procedure effectively if one is not advanced in celibacy yoga.

This procedure serves as a *kriyā omkāra Gāyatrī* procedure which is done three times per day, in the early morning, just after *haṭha* yoga and *prāṇāyāma* practice, at noon or earlier depending on when the yogi did his midday practice, and in the later afternoon. Some yogis set the timing for these practices at dawn, noon and at sunset.

This procedure was done ten times, not superficially nor as a matter of routine but with full concentration. If the yogi did not have the required concentration, he did more *prāṇāyāma* practice to bring his mind to focus. I gave two alternate procedures for this:

Technique 1

The yogi goes down through the suśumnā passage from the top of the neck. He reaches down as far as the heart chakra. He remains there and listens to the sound which is like the continuous after-ring of a bell. Once the sound is contacted he remains in it to identify with it. Then he moves up the suśumnā passage through the neck and reaches the sound blend of musical notes, which are heard on the right side of the subtle head. When the two sounds make contact, the yogi remains in them in stillness, causing his psyche to be saturated with that blend of supernatural sounds.

Technique 2

Other yogis may move into the causal cove which is in the front centre of the body. From there, they go backwards and enter the suśumnā passage. Once in there they listen for the Om sound. Then they look up and move through the upper passage. Thereafter they connect the upward and downward sounds and remain in the blend of musical tones.

The objective of either of these procedures is for the yogi to have vision in the sky of consciousness the chit *ākāśa*. From there he perceives the divine beings and can communicate with them regarding his spiritual development.

हृत्-पुण्डरीकम् अन्तः-स्थम्
ऊर्ध्व-नालम् अधो-मुखम् ।
ध्यात्वोर्ध्व-मुखम् उन्निद्रम्
अष्ट-पत्रं स-कर्णिकम् ॥९.३६॥

hṛt-puṇḍarīkam antaḥ-stham
ūrdhva-nālam adho-mukham
dhyātvordhva-mukham unnidram
aṣṭa-patraṁ sa-karṇikam (9.36)

hṛt — heart chakra; pundarīkam — lotus shaped; antaḥ-stham — situated within; ūrdhva – above; nālam — stalk; adho = adhah – downward; mukham — flower tips; dhyātvordhvamukham = dhyātvā — having conceived + ūrdhva-mukham — with flower tips upwards; unnidram — without becoming drowsy; aṣṭa – eight; patram — petal; sa-karṇikam — with the pericarp.

Translation

Situated within the heart chakra, there is a lotus with its stalks above and dropping downwards. Without becoming drowsy, one should conceive of the flower facing upwards with eight petals and a pericarp. (9.36)

Commentary:

This is experienced by any yogi who cleared out his *suśumnā* passage. Even though in advanced kundalini yoga, one succeeds in causing the kundalini energy to pierce through the *suśumnā* spinal channel to go upwards to energize the *buddhi* organ in the head of the subtle body, still as its habit, the kundalini energy subsides into the base chakra, again and again. Thus the yogi does *prāṇāyāma* with intentions for complete celibacy, so that the subtle sexual energy does not stay in the groin of the subtle body but rather it moves upwards always and keeps the *suśumnā* passage and central portion of the subtle body open and clear.

It so happens that even after clearing out the *suśumnā* passage, the passage has a tendency to remain cleared from the base to the heart chakra only. Special practice of *kriyā* yoga might cause a yogi to clear it further up on a permanent basis.

Normally the heart chakra points downwards and the energy flows between it and the base chakra for the operation of breathing, blood circulation, digestion, sexual expression, urination and evacuation. This includes the mobility of the thighs, legs and feet. Thus the yogi has to make an effort to change this process by causing the heart chakra to turn upwards as described in this verse. This is an entirely mystic practice. It can be done by mastering *haṭha* yoga and *prāṇāyāma*. Many persons try to do this mentally but they do not succeed because they have not mastered *haṭha* yoga and *prāṇāyāma*, which are preliminary and which cause the subtle energy to lighten up and to be surcharged with a higher level of pranic force.

A yogi may or may not see the eight petal lotus flower-shape of the heart chakra, but if he is proficient in the practice, he will see an eight-part energy gyrating disc which is curved downwards and which can be influenced to turn upwards and to remain open in the centre. Some may see this by *prāṇa* vision, rather than from a visual perspective. *Prāṇa* vision means that by energy, we can perceive energy, just as scientifically one can photograph by X-ray energy, or by light rays passing through a lense to a light sensitive surface.

कर्णिकायां न्यसेत् सूर्य-
सोमाग्नीन् उत्तरोत्तरम् ।
वह्नि-मध्ये स्मरेद् रूपं
ममैतद् ध्यान-मङ्गलम् ॥९.३७॥

karṇikāyāṁ nyaset sūrya-
somāgnīn uttarottaram
vahni-madhye smared rūpaṁ
mamaitad dhyāna-maṅgalam (9.37)

karnikāyām — within the pericarp; nyaset — should conceive; sūrya — sun; somagnim = soma — moon + agnīn — fire; uttarottaram = uttara uttaram — one after the other; vahni –fire; madhye — in the midst; smared = smaret — one should reflect; rūpam — form; mamaitad = mama — my + etad (etat) — this; dhyāna – effortless linkage of the mind; maṅgalam — what is auspicious.

Translation

One should conceive of the sun, moon, and fire, one after the other. In the midst of the fire one should reflect on My form which is auspicious for practicing the effortless linkage of one's attention. (9.37)

Commentary:

This is a special *kriyā* for transference to the meditation on the spiritual body of *Śrī* Krishna. It is assumed that the yogi transferred his attention out of this atmosphere to the chit *ākāśa*, the place from which that Omkara sound originated. The yogi has to pass through a plane of crystal white light, which may be compared to sunlight, moonlight and bright fire. When he passes through, he finds himself in the sky of consciousness. There he might reach the spiritual form of *Śrī* Krishna, a form which is auspicious and ideal for effortless and continuous linkage of one's attention.

Initially one experiences that one is unable to see into that sky of consciousness. The darkness which is in the head of the subtle body clears off after some time of sincere practice. Then one see through a clear sky into the spiritual world.

समं प्रशान्त सु-मुखं
दीर्घ-चारु-चतुर्-भुजम् ।
सु-चारु-सुन्दर-ग्रीवं
सु-कपोल शुचि-स्मितम् ॥९.३८॥

samaṁ praśāntaṁ su-mukhaṁ
dīrgha-cāru-catur-bhujam
su-cāru-sundara-grīvaṁ
su-kapolaṁ śuci-smitam (9.38)

samaṁ — symmetrical; praśāntam — serene; su-mukham — cheerful; dīrgha – long; cāru – beautiful; catur = catuḥ - four; bhujam — arms; su-cāru — charming; sundara — beautiful; grīvam — neck; su-kapolam — beautiful cheeks; suci-smitam — sincere smile;

Translation

Symmetrical, serene, cheerful, with four long beautiful arms, a beautiful neck, beautiful cheeks and a sincere smile, (9.38)

Commentary:

This is part of the description of the looks of the Supreme Lord Krishna in the spiritual sky. This is not the same as the Deity Form in the temple which is constructed on the basis of these descriptions. This form as seen by the yogi is the actual spiritual form of the Supreme Lord. It is not seen in this atmosphere but is seen only in the spiritual world. A yogi first sees this when his imagination orb converts into spiritual eyes and he peers beyond the darkness of consciousness normally experienced behind closed eyes. Only a yogin who perfected the *samādhi* continuous effortless linkage of the attention to Omkar subtle sound which was described in some preceding verses and who goes beyond that, can see such forms.

It is believe that one can do Deity Worship as an authorized *pujārī* and then one will see the spiritual form of *Śrī* Krishna but this is not correct, because one has to master the yoga process to develop the required spiritual vision. Some Acharyas who become authorized for one reason or the other, established that one can bypass the yoga described here by *Śrī* Krishna and just see Krishna in the spiritual sky through doing Deity Worship. They have also given the opinion that Uddhava is on the platform of love of Godhead and therefore yoga was redundant and unnecessary for him but that he asked questions which caused these detailed yoga explanations because he felt sorry for those who had to take to yoga because they did not have any love or devotion to *Śrī* Krishna.

However such explanations of these statements of Lord Krishna are construed because Uddhava did in fact need to perform yoga. This is why it was explained and this is why *Śrī* Krishna directed him to go to Badrinatha. If Uddhava had the natural spontaneous spirited devotion of the *gopīs*, he would not have been directed to go to Badrinath. And he did not go there just to preach to others and to explain Krishna *līlā* as some Acharyas have tried to convince us. In fact he went there for the very purpose of continuously and effortlessly linking his attention to *Śrī* Krishna in the transcendental world before passing from the body. This was also done by *Yudhiṣṭira*, Arjuna and others. Even Arjuna forget much of what *Śrī* Krishna revealed to him as the Universal Form and as the four handed divine spiritual-sky form of *Śrī* Krishna as Vasudeva. Arjuna's supernatural and spiritual senses did shut down and were again opened by the practice of yoga. It is totally misleading to state otherwise and to try to bleach out yoga from these discourses merely because one feels that one should not have to do it and that one can follow the *gopīs* or even Lord Chaitanya by attaining the divine vision and divine body without doing yoga. Why hawk yoga if it is effective?

The idea that one will go to see this form at the time of death, if one performs services at the Krishna temple to the Krishna *Mūrti*, which is designed according to these descriptions, is totally misleading and frustrating. It is a dead end for the devotee, because those who do Deity Worship and who do not develop the mystic *kriyās* will not be able to transfer their consciousness to the spiritual world at the time of death. Nor will they be transferred there by Lord Krishna nor by their spiritual master as they believe.

One is transferred on the basis of one's endeavor in *kriyā* yoga practice, not otherwise. The performance of Deity Worship to the properly installed deity form of Lord Krishna will either cause the devotee to again take a material body and again worship the Deity in this physical world, or it will show him that he cannot be transferred to the spiritual sky merely by that worship. He will realize that he must perfect the required mystic *kriyās*, one of which was described in the preceding verses.

समान-कर्ण-विन्यस्त-
स्फुरन्-मकर-कुण्डलम् ।
हेमाम्बरं घन-श्यामं
श्रीवत्स-श्री-निकेतनम् ॥ ९.३९ ॥

samāna-karṇa-vinyasta-
sphuran-makara-kuṇḍalam
hemāmbaraṁ ghana-śyāmaṁ
śrīvatsa-śrī-niketanam (9.39)

samāna — matched; karṇa — ear; vinyasta — situated; sphuran — shining; makara — fish-shaped; kuṇḍalam — earrings; hemāmbaraṁ = hema — golden + ambaram — cloth; ghana-śyāmam — color of a dark rain cloud; śrīvatsa — unique curl of hair; śrī – goddess Laksmi; niketanam — residence.

Translation

...with shining fish-shaped earrings, situated in matched ears, with a golden cloth, having the body color of a dark rain cloud, with the unique Śrīvatsa curl of hair and the residence of the Goddess Lakṣmī on the chest, (9.39)

Commentary:

This is more description of the transcendental body of Lord Krishna, as the body is seen in the spiritual sky. This cannot be seen with physical vision. It is not the Krishna *Mūrti* in the temple, even though the temple Deity may be designed to fit this description.

शङ्ख-चक्र-गदा-पद्म-
वनमाला-विभूषितम् ।
नूपुरैर् विलसत्-पादं
कौस्तुभ-प्रभया युतम् ॥९.४

śaṅkha-cakra-gadā-padma-
vanamālā-vibhūṣitam
nūpurair vilasat-pādaṁ
kaustubha-prabhayā yutam (9.40)

śaṅkha — conchshell; cakra — disc; gadā — club; padma — lotus flower; vanamālā —garland of forest flowers; vibhūṣitam — adorned; nūpuraur = nūpuraiḥ — with ankle-bells; vilasat — shimmering; pādam — feet; kaustubha — gem; prabhayā — effulgence; yutam — resplendent.

Translation

...adorned with conchshell, disc, club, lotus flower and a garland of forest flowers, with the feet adorned with shimmering ankle bells, and the chest resplendent with the effulgent kaustubha gem, (9.40)

Commentary:

This is more description of how the Supreme Lord looks when he is seen in the spiritual sky by the vision of a yogi. This does occur, that the yogi sees the Supreme God in this personal form. On some occasions, the yogi is not allowed an interview with the Lord and the vision may not last long. Thus with this description the yogi can identify what or who was seen by him while he was in the *samādhi* state. There are other persons seen in *samādhi*, all depending on the level of existence pierced by the yogi. Thus this description clarifies what the yogi would see. If his vision only opens to the subtle material plane, the plane of the mundane heavens, where the angelic persons reside, he would see certain celestial personalities. However by giving detailed descriptions of His spiritual body, *Śrī* Krishna, gave all yogis a definite way of identifying him.

द्युमत्-किरीट-कटक-
कटि-सूत्राङ्गदायुतम् ।
सर्वाङ्ग-सुन्दरं हृद्यं
प्रसाद-सुमुखेक्षनम् ॥९.४१॥

dyumat-kirīṭa-kaṭaka-
kaṭi-sūtrāṅgadāyutam
sarvāṅga-sundaraṁ hṛdyaṁ
prasāda-sumukhekṣanam (9.41)

dyumat — shining; kirīṭa — crown; kaṭaka — bracelets; kati – waist; sūtrāṅgadāyutam = sūtra — band + aṅgada — bracelets + āyutam — adorned with; sarvāṅga — all limbs; sundaram — beautiful; hrdyam — appealing, charming; prasāda — with mercy; sumukhekṣanam = sumukha — very nice facial appearance + īksanam — glance.

Translation

...adorned with a shining crown, bracelets, and a waist band, with all beautiful limbs, charming, with a nice facial appearance and a glance with mercy. (9.41)

Commentary:

This continues the description of the spiritual body of *Śrī* Krishna. This is one of His spiritual forms, one with four arms.

Usually a yogi sees the four-armed spiritual forms first. He may or may not progress to seeing the two-armed forms because it is not a matter of desire of the yogi. It is rather his existential category and the relationship he already has with a particular divinity. Thus if his relationship is with a four-armed form, he may not be permitted to see a two-handed form.

There are many teachers, sannyasis, who advertise the two-handed form of *Śrī* Krishna. Some of them erect temples, and install with appropriate mantras, the two-handed form of *Śrī* Krishna. They tell congregations that the two-handed form, Krishna with the flute, is the Supreme Form and should be worshiped leaving aside any four-handed Deities in other temples. But little do they know that a devotee is not allowed to select whom he will worship in fact. One may not go to the spiritual place where the two-handed divinities reside and one by existential arrangement may be aligned to a four-handed form.

In yoga the devotee progresses in the way that is natural for him. He leaves aside conceptions and all sorts of misleading and so-called authorized information which came down in the disciplic succession and which is hailed by excited preachers and their followers.

सु-कुमारम् अभिध्यायेत्
सर्वाङ्गेषु मनो दधत् ।
इन्द्रियाणीन्द्रियार्थेभ्यो
मनसाकृष्य तन् मनः ।
बुद्ध्या सारथिना धीरः
प्रणयेन् मयि सर्वतः ॥९.४२॥

su-kumāram abhidhyāyet
sarvāṅgeṣu mano dadhat
indriyāṇīndriyārthebhyo
manasākṛṣya tan manaḥ
buddhyā sārathinā dhīraḥ
praṇayen mayi sarvataḥ (9.42)

su-kumāram — very youthful; abhidhyāyet — one should effortlessly link one's attention; sarva-angeṣu — in all parts; mano = manah — mind; dadhat — placing; indriyāṇīndriyārthebhyo = indriyāṇi — sense organs + indriya-arthebhyo (indriya-arthebhyah) — from the sense objects; manasākṛṣya = manasā — by the mind + ākṛṣya — withdrawn; tan = tat — that; manah — mind; buddhyā — by intellect; sārathinā — by the driver, supervising; dhīrah — the person with a stabalised intellect; pranayen = pranayet — should direct; mayi — at me; sarvatah — at all parts.

Translation

One should meditate on this very youthful form, placing the mind on all limbs. The person with a stablised intellect, should by the mind, withdraw the organs from the sense objects. The mind should be directed to all My limbs by the supervising intellect. (9.42)

Commentary:

This is a *kriyā* yoga procedure. Many modern teachers in the disciplic succession, many of the popular and most successful ones, have all but left aside these procedures. As far as they are concerned, all this should be left aside until the time of death, when they claim that themselves as well as their staunch devotees, will see *Śrī* Krishna's spiritual forms, when all this will be rightly revealed. But the truth is that they have failed to see any such forms because for them the spirited devotional technique of reaching *Śrī* Krishna in full did not work. They are left now with the hope that the methods followed by them, the so-called adapted methods for this Age, will work and reveal *Śrī* Krishna at the time of death and in the meantime, everyone must be content to accept the Temple Deity as a spiritual form on par with the real spiritual form in the spiritual sky.

But such an approach confirms that yoga practice in *bhakti* yoga is actually the way to see the divine forms. It is the way for most human beings who are not like *Śrī* Chaitanya Mahaprabhu, not like the *gopīs* of *Vṛndavān*, for whom so many superhuman claims are made.

What was described in these verses to Uddhava is *kriyā* yoga procedure. It cannot be done unless one has mastered the *samādhi* continuous effortless linkage of one's attention to the spiritual places and persons in the spiritual sky. To get the stabilized intellect *(dhīrah)* one should master the stage of listening to the Omkar sound which was described by *Śrī* Krishna. Then the intellect sheds off its instability and is prepared to see the supernatural and spiritual worlds. These methods are precise and direct.

It is totally misleading to suggest to anyone, that by worshipping the Deity in the temple, he will suddenly at the time of death or otherwise, enter the spiritual sky. It does not usually happen like that, even though in very rare cases such an occurrence might occur. It cannot be guaranteed by a spiritual leader on this side of existence, especially by one who is not a master of the techniques given in these verses and who has not taught his disciples these methods.

तत् सर्व-व्यापकं चित्तम्
आकृष्यैकत्र धारयेत् ।
नान्यानि चिन्तयेद् भूयः
सु-स्मितं भावयेन् मुखम् ॥९.४३॥

tat sarva-vyāpakaṁ cittam
ākṛṣyaikatra dhārayet
nānyāni cintayed bhūyaḥ
su-smitaṁ bhāvayen mukham (9.43)

tat — that; sarva — all; vyāpakam — situated all over; cittam — mental and emotional energies; ākṛṣyaikatra = ākṛṣya — withdraw + ekatra — one part; dhārayet — should effortlessly link the attention; nānyāni = na — not + anyāni — other parts; cintayed = cintayet — one should contemplate; bhūyah — again; su-smitam — wonderfully smiling; bhāvayen = bhāvayet — one should convey one's psyche; mukham — face.

Translation

Withdrawing the consciousness from all over, one should convey one's psyche to one part and contemplate the wonderfully smiling face alone and no other feature. (9.43)

Commentary:

This is *kriyā* yoga practice, because the degree of control of the consciousness required, is not to be experienced if one has not practiced the 5th, 6th, 7th and 8th stages of yoga, except rarely for those with the spirited devotion described by *Śrī* Krishna. And such devotion cannot be imitated or adapted by others. It is a joke to think that one can do this without yoga expertise. It is not merely a matter of focusing the mind on the face of the Deity in the temple, because the sensual energies must be withdrawn *(ākṣṭya)* from everything else both internally and externally, including the Deities in the temple.

This is not a physical staring of the eyes. This is not an imagining of the temple Deities or a Deity-making in the mind of the devotee. This has nothing to do with the physical viewing or darshan of the Deity in the temple. This is an entirely different practice.

तत्र लब्ध-पदं चित्तम्
आकृष्य व्योम्नि धारयेत् ।
तच् च त्यक्त्वा मद्-आरोहो
न किञ्चिद् अपि चिन्तयेत् ॥९.४४॥

tatra labdha-padaṁ cittam
ākṛṣya vyomni dhārayet
tac ca tyaktvā mad-āroho
na kiñcid api cintayet (9.44)

tatra — there; labdha - obtained; padam — position; cittam — mental and emotional energies; ākṛṣya — withdrawing; vyomni — in the sky of consciousness; dhārayet — one should effortlessly link the attention; tac = tat — that; ca — and; tyaktvā — giving up; mad = mat — to me; āroho = ārohaḥ — having risen up; na — not; kiñcid = kiñcit — anything; api — also; cintayet — should contemplate.

Translation

Withdrawing the mental and emotional energy, which had obtained a position there, one should effortlessly link, the attention to the sky of consciousness. And then abondoing that, having risen up to Me, one should not conceive of anything. (9.44)

Commentary:

At first when one gets a focus on the spiritual form of the Lord, one becomes very pacified, for that is the culmination of so many austerities in yoga practice. Such a view of the divine form of *Śrī* Krishna in the spiritual sky, may last for seconds, minutes or hours, all depending on the depth of focusing power of the yogi. However one should practice more consistently to make that a permanent feature of one's psyche.

Thus the Lord instructed that the yogi should concentrate his mind on the sky of consciousness, the spiritual sky, *vyomni*, as a general environment. When the yogi is stabilized into that view, he sees transcendental forms in that spiritual environment. He understands that he has some rights to be there. His insecurities, which were derived from transmigrating in perishable bodies, go away.

By that steady absorption, time and time again, by repeated practice, the psychology of the yogi changes into being that of a transcendental being, a divine self. The yogi then rises up to the transcendental plane permanently.

एवं समाहित-मतिर्
माम् एवात्मानम् आत्मनि ।
विचष्टे मयि सर्वात्मन्
ज्योतिर् ज्योतिषि सयुतम् ॥९.४५॥

evaṁ samāhita-matir
mām evātmānam ātmani
vicaṣṭe mayi sarvātman
jyotir jyotiṣi saṁyutam (9.45)

evam — thus; samāhita — meditatively; matir = matih — consciousness; mām — Me; evātmānam = eva — alone + ātmānam — the spirit (objective case); ātmani — in the spirit; vicaṣṭe — sees; mayi — in Me; sarvātman = sarva – of all + atman — self; jyotir = jyotih — light; jyotiṣi — in light; saṁyutam — joined.

Translation

Thus, being meditatively absorbed, one sees Me alone in reference to the self and sees the self in reference to Me, who is the self of all, like a light joined into a light. (9.45)

Commentary:

The underlying basis of the mergence of the individual limited spirit with the Supreme Spirit is given here in no uncertain terms by *Śrī* Krishna. No one can whip around or dodge the Sanskrit of the last sentence namely *joytir jyotiṣi samyutam*, the joining *(samyutam)* of a light into a light.

However this does not mean that the limited spirit lost identity but it does signify that he assumed a spiritual form in total and has entered the environment where the Supreme Spirit is primarily situated.

There is a popular analogy of this as a drop of water entering the ocean and losing itself but that comparison is misleading. In this case the limited spirit maintains its identity. It is just that it is in the security of the spiritual environment in which the Supreme Spirit is permanently situated.

Such a spirit has left this atmosphere and has gone to the transcendental sky to be in association with the Supreme Person. From our perspective it is exactly as it is described, as a light going to join another light but in fact that is due to our lack of spiritual perception, where we cannot clearly distinguish spiritual forms. When a green bird enters the foliage of a tree, it might appear that it disappeared into the greenery but in fact the bird is still an individual creature there.

ध्यानेनेत्थ सु-तीव्रेण
युञ्जतो योगिनो मनः ।
सयास्यत्य् आशु निर्वाणं
द्रव्य ज्ञान-क्रिया-भ्रमः ॥९.४६॥

dhyānenettham̐ su-tīvreṇa
yuñjato yogino manaḥ
saṁyāsyaty āśu nirvāṇaṁ
dravya jñāna-kriyā-bhramaḥ (9.46)

dhyānenettham = dhyānena — by effortless linkage of the attention; ittham — thus; su-tīvreṇa — very keen; yunjato = yunjataḥ — of a practicioner; yogino = yoginaḥ — of a yogi; manaḥ — mind; saṁyāsyaty = saṁyāsyati — will go away; āśu — quickly; nirvāṇam — cessation of mundane information; dravya – mundane things; jñāna – mundane information; kriyā — cultural activities; bhramah — delusion.

Translation

Thus the mind of the practising yogi, is controlled by very keen effortless linkage of his attention to higher concentration forces. And quickly the delusive influence of mundane things, mundane knowledge and cultural action, goes away. This is the cessation of material existence. (9.46)

Commentary:

This indeed is the definition of *nirvāṇa*.

CHAPTER 10*

Mystic Skills**

Terri Stokes-Pineda Art

śrī-uddhava uvāca
kayā dhāraṇayā kā svit kathaṁ vā siddhir acyuta
kati vā siddhayo brūhi yoginām siddhi-do bhavān

The deserving Uddhava said: By what linking of the attention to a higher concentration force, does a mystic skill develop, O infallible Krishna? How many mystic skills are they? Tell me of it. Are You the giver of such skills to the yogis? (Uddhava Gītā 10.2)

* Śrīmad Bhāgavatam Canto 11, Chapter 15
** Translator's selected chapter title.

श्री-भगवान् उवाच
जितेन्द्रियस्य युक्तस्य
जित-श्वासस्य योगिनः ।
मयि धारयतश् चेत
उपतिष्ठन्ति सिद्धयः ॥ १०.१ ॥

śrī-bhagavān uvāca
jitendriyasya yuktasya
jita-śvāsasya yoginaḥ
mayi dhārayataś ceta
upatiṣṭhanti siddhayaḥ (10.1)

śrī-bhagavān – the blessed lord; uvāca — said; jitendriyasya — of one who conquered his senses; yuktasya — of one who has completed the required yoga disciplines; jita-śvāsasya — of one who has mastered the pranic energies; yoginaḥ — of the yogis; mayi — in me; dhārayataḥ — linking the attention; cetaḥ — consciousness; upatiṣṭhanti — attend; siddhayaḥ — mystic skills.

Translation

The Blessed Lord said: The mystic skills attend to the yogis who conquer the senses, who complete the required disciplines, who master the life force energies and whose consciousness is linked attentively to Me. (10.1)

Commentary:

The 4th, 5th, 6th, and 7th stages of yoga are mentioned in their completion in this verse. The 4th is listed as *jita-svāsasya*, the complete regulation of higher pranic force. The 5th stage is listed as *jitendriyasya*. This is *pratyāhar* sensual energy withdrawal. *Prāṇāyāma* results in the purification of the subtle body, the cleaning out of the *naḍi* channels. When that is achieved, the psyche of the yogi gains the ability to be internalized. Then the *pratyāhar* process becomes complete.

There are orbs of energy, which come out of the *buddhi* organ. These energize the various parts of the subtle body, which in turn activate energy in the gross form. When these orbs are retracted into the *buddhi* organ, the yogi is able to internalize. Thus he completes the 5th stage of yoga practice. Unless one's kundalini is cleaned up and made to course up continuously through the spine of the subtle body into the head, one cannot transcend the lower urges which force one to interact with the external world. Thus the 5th stage of yoga includes kundalini yoga. It also includes celibacy yoga for the retraction of the procreative energies. All this must be mastered before one can complete the 5th stage.

The sensual energies are retracted into the attentive power of the spirit. This attentive force is internalized upon the *I-sense*, the centralized sense of identity. When this occurs, the attentive power is quieted. Once this is achieved, the quieted attentive force, takes one direction or another into other dimensions. Then the yogi links his will with its focus into other dimensions. This linking of the will with the attentive power is the practice of the 6th stage of yoga called *dhāraṇā*.

The 7th stage of yoga, *dhyāna*, is listed here as *yuktasya* which means that the yogin has completed the elementary stages sufficiently to cause the effortless linkage of his core consciousness with the chit *ākāśa*, the sky of consciousness. This is no ordinary achievement for a yogi. Such a continuous link begins either in an audile, visionary or feeling way, either by hearing the continuous spiritual sounds, or by seeing into other dimensions, or by sensing the force of higher energy. For a neophyte yogi, this happens periodically without his control of its occurrences. For the advanced yogin, this happens because he knows how to put himself into a position from where he is automatically transferred into or connected to the sky of consciousness.

Śrī Yogiraja Lahiri *Mahāśaya* and great yogins like *Śrīla Yogeśwarānanda* and even the *Siddha Muktānanda*, took birth for the purpose of explaining these matters in detail and to give initiations for these processes. People are hungry for the information but descriptions alone will not cause one to achieve this. One has to practice ardently. After a certain amount of practice, one gets the experience.

As stated, once a yogi completed the 4th, 5th, 6th and 7th stages of yoga, the mystic skills attend him. This is because for him, the restrictions in the use of his subtle form, are removed. That body then functions freely and exhibits its dormant abilities. These are called *siddhis* or mystic perfective powers. For such a yogin, the *siddhis* are not a problem. They do not serve as a distraction. The yogi is not tempted to use them or to become distracted in exhibiting them.

श्री-उद्धव उवाच
कया धारणया का
स्वित् कथं वा सिद्धिर् अच्युत ।
कति वा सिद्धयो ब्रूहि
योगिनां सिद्धि-दो भवान् ॥ १०.२॥

śrī-uddhava uvāca
kayā dhāraṇayā kā
svit kathaṁ vā siddhir acyuta
kati vā siddhayo brūhi
yogināṁ siddhi-do bhavān (10.2)

śrī-uddhava – the deserving Uddhava; uvāca — said; kayā — by what; dhāraṇayā — linking of the attention to a higher concentration force; kā svit — which indeed; katham — how; vā — or; siddhir = siddhiḥ — mystic skill; acyuta — O infallible Krishna; kati — how many; vā — or; siddhayo = siddhayaḥ — mystic skills; brūhi — tell of it; yoginām — of yogis; siddhi-do = siddhi-daḥ — one who gives mystic skills; bhavān — you.

Translation

The deserving Uddhava said: By what linking of the attention to a higher concentration force, does a mystic skill develop, O infallible Krishna? How many mystic skills are they? Tell me of it. Are You the giver of such skills to the yogis? (10.2)

Commentary:

Dhāraṇā, the 6th stage of yoga was translated into English as concentration. However such a word does not fit the actual meaning. Concentration as we know it in the Western Society is not even part of yoga practice. At least it is not listed in the eight stages given by *Śrī Patañjali*. However some of the teachers who first translated the *Bhagavad-Gītā* and the *Patañjali Yoga Sūtras*, used that word. Thus it became standardized.

In the *Bhagavad-Gītā*, particularly in chapter two, *Śrī* Krishna spoke of *buddhi* yoga, the curbing of the *buddhi* organ in the head of the subtle body. This *buddhi* yoga concerns the curtailment and stoppage of concentration as we understand that word in English usage.

In English usage concentration is the deliberate application of the will power which is a directive muscle in the mind. But in Yoga, *dhāraṇā* occurs anytime, the will power is linked to a concentration force which flows of its own accord within or without the mind, or going into or flowing out of the mind chamber. In such a situation, the will power does not create the concentration. It is not used to form the concentration, but rather it is linked to an already existing concentration which is caused by another force. This already-existing concentration may be flowing within the mind from one place within it to another. Or it might occur in a concentration of energy which saturates the entire mind chamber. It might be a force which originates somewhere in the mind and flows out of it into another dimension. Or it might be in another dimension and flow into the mind. In any of these examples, the flow of that concentration must cause the mind to shift to a higher level, preferably to the sky of consciousness, the chit *ākāśa*.

When the will power is linked up to that flow of concentration, then we have the stage of *dhāraṇā*. Again it is important to understand that this is not a concentration of what is formed by the application of will power but rather by a higher energy or a higher personality force. But the will power is linked to it by the yogi himself. His only mystic action is to link his will power to that concentration force, which was not created by him and which cannot ultimately be controlled by him. He can control the linkage of his will with it but he cannot control it, because it is not created by him.

The deserving Uddhava asked *Śrī* Krishna some questions which are of interest to us. If yoga is something definite, then certainly there must be definite answers to certain questions. Any science functions like that. When the will power is linked to a certain concentration force, what sort of mystic skill will the yogi experience? Again we may ask how many of these abilities are there? Or stated differently; what abilities does the subtle body have, once that body is freed from internal impurities? We may also ask if *Śrī* Krishna gives the mystic skills to a yogi. Or stated differently: Can a yogi develop such skills without *Śrī* Krishna's interference or bestowal? Is God necessary as a giver of such skills or do they develop naturally?

श्री-भगवान् उवाच
सिद्धयो ऽष्टादश प्रोक्ता
धारणा योग-पार-गैः ।
तासाम् अष्टौ मत्-प्रधाना
दशैव गुण-हेतवः ॥१०.३॥

śrī-bhagavān uvāca
siddhayo 'ṣṭādaśa proktā
dhāraṇā yoga-pāra-gaiḥ
tāsām aṣṭau mat-pradhānā
daśaiva guṇa-hetavaḥ (10.3)

śrī-bhagavān – the blessed lord; uvāca — said; siddhayo = siddhayaḥ — mystic skills; 'ṣṭādaśa = aṣṭādaśa — eight and ten, eighteen; proktā — state; dhāraṇā — the linking of the attention to various concentration forces; yoga — yoga; pāra-gaiḥ — one whose interest has progressed the farthest; tāsām — of them; aṣṭau — eight; mat-pradhānā = mat-pradhānāḥ — prominent in me; daśaiva = daśa — ten + eva — indeed; guṇa – influences of material nature; hetavaḥ — causes.

Translation

Those who progressed the farthest in yoga, state that there are eighteen mystic skills, and eighteen types linkage of the attention to eighteen types of concentration forces. Eight of these are prominent in Me, the remaining ten are caused by a particular influence of material nature. (10.3)

Commentary:

Śrī Patañjali Mahārṣi, the expounder of the Yoga system, gave an analysis of the mystic skills and the linkage of the attention to the concentration forces in his *Yoga Sutras*. Serious students of yoga would do well to study what *Śrī* Krishna outlined here as well as what *Śrī Patañjali* wrote down. Readers should note that *Śrī* Krishna is a *mahāyogī* of repute and did take instruction from *Upamanyu* Rishi on the higher yoga disciplines. This is described in the *Mahābhārata* in the discourse with Bhishma, who asked Lord Krishna to recite the *Śiva Sahasranāma Stotra*.

What *Śrī* Krishna said above is very interesting. The conclusion is that the yogi develops the mystic *siddhis* by linking of his attention in particular ways to either *Śrī* Krishna's spiritual environment or to a particular influence or potency of material nature in the clarifying aspect of material nature.

The special eight mystic skills which are prominent or inherent in *Śrī* Krishna, pertains to the spiritual body of the yogi. The remaining ten skills pertain to the subtle and causal forms of the yogi. It is interesting that *Śrī* Krishna referenced this to yogins of his time and those before him who progressed the furthest in yoga. *Śrī* Krishna could have cited His own authority but He deliberately honored previous ascetics.

अणिमा महिमा मूर्तेर्
लघिमा प्राप्तिर् इन्द्रियैः ।
प्राकाम्यं श्रुत-दृष्टेषु
शक्ति-प्रेरणम् ईशिता ॥१०.४॥

aṇimā mahimā mūrter
laghimā prāptir indriyaiḥ
prākāmyaṁ śruta-dṛṣṭeṣu
śakti-preraṇam īśitā (10.4)

animā — becoming atomic; mahimā — becoming cosmic; mūrter = mūrteḥ — pertaining to form of the yogi; laghimā — technique of weightlessness; prāptir = prāptiḥ — acquiring or experiencing;

indriyaiḥ — through sense organs; prākāmyam — enjoying almost anything desired; śruta-dṛṣṭeṣu = śruta — of what is heard of only + dṛṣṭeṣu — what can be seen normally; śakti-preraṇam — the ability to manipulate mundane potency; īśitā — power of ruling others.

Translation

Becoming atomic, becoming cosmic, pertains to a form of the yogi, as well as being weightless, acquiring or experiencing through the sense organs of others, enjoying what was heard of and what was seen normally, manipulating mundane potency, ruling over others, (10.4)

Commentary:

Seven of the eight mystic skills which are prominent in *Śrī* Krishna are listed. These are abilities of the spiritual body but in the yoga tradition, these are listed as mystic skills or *siddhis*. Just as a human body has certain natural abilities like walking, talking and eating, so a spiritual body has these powers naturally. These same powers are reflected down into the gross and subtle material world, where they are experienced from time to time.

Here is an itemized list of the seven skills listed above:

1. *Using an atomic form*
2. *Using a cosmic form*
3. *Using a weightless form*
4. *Acquiring or experiencing through the body of another person*
5. *Enjoying something or someone who is in this or another dimension*
6. *Manipulating mundane potency*
7. *Ruling over others*

When a yogi experiences any of these seven powers or the one listed in the next verse, he should understand that he experiences himself as his spiritual body. Such experiences are a clear and definite indication that the yogi developed or is transferred into his spiritual body, even though it may be a momentary experience. Such experiences increase confidence in yoga practice.

There is a misunderstanding about the assumption of atomic, cosmic and anti-gravitational powers of a yogi. Some commentators of *Patañjali* Yoga and other related texts, indicate that the yogi can experience these to an absolute degree. However they are wrong. What is absolute to a yogi, is small wonder, when we consider that the galaxies floating in the sky are in one universe only. For that matter we have no idea of the extent of the space in which these galaxies float. We cannot say by our personal experience that there are not innumerable systems in other time zones and in other dimensions of existence. A yogi is limited. His temporary or permanent assumption of his spiritual body will not make him absolute in any case.

Śrī Krishna eased us by using the word *mūrter*, which means anything which has a definite shape or limits. *Mūrteh* in this case, means any of the forms which a yogi becomes aware of. These include his own psyche or the psyche of others. It also includes the linkage of his existential energy with the cosmic energy or with the energy of a divine being. It does not limit the yogi to his physical body, nor to his subtle or causal forms.

Anti-gravitational powers need not be exhibited by the gross body. It may be exhibited by the subtle form. For instance, around the year 1973, the Americans were putting satellites into orbit around this earth. They also put men in such metal containers. Once in my subtle body, I went to such a satellite, looked into the window of it and observed the astronaut who was within it. This is an exhibition of anti-gravitational force, but my gross body was not involved. It was laying in a room on the earth.

On another occasion, I experienced a cosmic expansion of the subtle body but it was not exhibited in my gross form. I also experienced atomic vision just as if I peered through a microscope but I used the brow chakra protrusion of the subtle body.

Experiences of this nature usually occur in the subtle body, but they indicate the proximity of the spiritual form. Rarely is a yogi able to experience the spiritual body objectively. He usually experiences it through its effect on the subtle form. *Śrī* Krishna graciously informed Uddhava of how a yogi can know that his spiritual form is in proximity by the eight special *siddhis* or perfective skills.

गुणेष्व् असङ्गो वशिता
यत्-कामस् तद् अवस्यति ।
एता मे सिद्धयः सौम्य
अष्टाव् औत्पत्तिका मताः ॥१०.५॥

guṇeṣv asaṅgo vaśitā
yat-kāmas tad avasyati
etā me siddhayaḥ saumya
aṣṭāv autpattikā matāḥ (10.5)

guṇeṣv = guṇeṣu — to the mundane influence; asaṅgo = asaṅgaḥ — non-attachment; vaśitā — technique of controlling one's nature; yat — what; kāmas = kāmaḥ — desire; tad = tat — that; avasyati — can obtain; etāḥ — these; me — my; siddhayaḥ — mystic skills; saumya — dear friend; aṣṭāv = aṣṭau — eight; autpattikā = autpattikāḥ — natural; matāḥ — considered.

Translation

...non-attachment to mundane influences, which results in the technique of controlling one's nature, and obtaining what is desired; these my dear friend, are considered to be the eight natural skills. (10.5)

Commentary:

The techniques of controlling one's nature are given in no uncertain terms as *asaṇgo*, or the non-attachment to mundane influences. Since a limited being cannot control the material nature in all of its forms and shapes, the only option for him, is to control his response to it. He can control himself by detachment only. Ultimately such detachment causes him to satisfy the requirement for isolation *(kevalam).* This is psychological isolation. By this he develops supernatural and spiritual insight into the fourth dimension of existence, the chit *ākāśa*, the sky of consciousness.

The yogi may obtain what is desired but that does not mean that he acquires this *siddhi* in an immature stage. The desires obtained pertain to spiritual aims only. Desires which are fulfilled in relation to material nature are different to those which come about from the development or assumption of the spiritual body.

अनूर्मिमत्त्व देहे ऽस्मिन्
दूर-श्रवण-दर्शनम् ।
मनो-जवः काम-रूपं
पर-काय-प्रवेशनम् ॥१०.६॥

anūrmimattvaṁ dehe 'smin
dūra-śravaṇa-darśanam
mano-javaḥ kāma-rūpaṁ
para-kāya-praveśanam (10.6)

anūrmimattvam = anūrmi – not wavering, not fluctuating, not being affected + mattvam — my-ness, possessiveness, the sense of identification; dehe – in the boby; 'smin = asmin — this; dūra — afar, at a distance; śravana — hearing; darśanam — seeing; mano = manaḥ - mind; javaḥ — speed; kāma – desire; rūpam — form; para – other; kāya — body; praveśanam — entering.

Translation

Being unaffected by the sense of self identification with the body, hearing from a distance, seeing from a distance, moving at the speed of the mind, assuming any desired form, entering anyone's body, (10.6)

Commentary:

Six of the mystic abilities of the subtle body are given. The remaining four will be given in the next verse. These are the mystic perfections experienced by a yogin who is able to fill his subtle body with the clarifying energy of material nature. If that body is only partially filled, the yogi will only experience some of these perfection, according to the quantity and quality of the clarifying energy in the subtle form.

It is mostly by the perfection of the 4th stage of yoga, that of *prāṇāyāma*, that the yogi can reach the stage of being unaffected by the sense of self-identification with the body. Actually it appears to a common man that the yogi is unaffected but in truth, by perfecting *prāṇāyāma* breath nutrition techniques, the yogi's body changes so that he does not experience normal food cravings. Thus people say that he is unaffected by hunger and thirst and other basic urges like sexual expression and the need for intoxication and excitement.

Hearing and seeing from a distance is experienced when the yogi perfects the 5th stage of yoga, that of sensual energy withdrawal which is called *pratyāhar*. Once his sensual energy is freed from gross pursuits, the yogi's sensual powers are extended to places near or far.

In the *pratyāhar* sensual energy internalization practice, the yogi is able to move at the speed of the mind, because by that practice, his perception of psychic actions and objects increases noticeably. Then the speedy thoughts, ideas and imaginations no longer baffles him.

The assumption of any desired form is gained by the *pratyāhar* practice also. Since by it, the yogi conserves sensual powers and greatly increases his psychological abilities. The ability to enter someone's body is attained in the first stages the 6th step of yoga, that of *dhāraṇā* linking of the attention to concentrations of higher energy in the psyche.

Some yogis are distracted by these powers. They try to develop these to perfection and waste much time using these. Instead a yogi should use these to accelerate the yoga progress. Otherwise he should ignore them and be attentive to the practice.

A person going on a long journey, should not stop in every town he meets, since it is likely that his journey will take longer or he may forget the destination and settle down in some town along the way.

स्वच्छन्द-मृत्युर् देवानां
सह-क्रीडानुदर्शनम् ।
यथा-सङ्कल्प-ससिद्धिर्
आज्ञाप्रतिहता गतिः ॥१०.७॥

svacchanda-mṛtyur devānāṁ
saha-krīḍānudarśanam
yathā-saṅkalpa-saṁsiddhir
ājñāpratihatā gatiḥ (10.7)

svacchanda-mṛtyur = svacchanda — own desire + mṛtyur (mṛtyuh) — death, dying; devānām — of the supernatural rulers; saha — with; krīḍānudarśanam = krida — sports + anudarśanam — participating; yathā — as; saṅkalpa — motive; saṁsiddhir = saṁsiddhiḥ — perfect fulfilment; ājñāpratihatā = ajna — command + apratihatā — unopposed; gatih — course.

Translation

...dying as desired, participating in the sports of the supernatural rulers, perfect fulfillment of one's motive, and to command circumstances from an unopposed course anywhere, (10.7)

Commentary:

The feature of dying as desired was exhibited by *Śrī* Bhishmadeva, the eldest Kuru in the time of Lord Krishna. Other able yogis also exhibited that. It has to do with controlling the life force's final exit from the body. If however a yogi mastered kundalini chakra, then he may kill his own body easily, by first weakening kundalini chakra, by reducing the food needs of the body and by increasing its pranic breath intake. Some yogis who master *prāṇāyāma* take an alternate method by making their lungs and brain more accommodating to the *apāna* energy, which we experience as carbon dioxide physically. Thus such yogis may practice living under water or living while being buried in the earth for some time.

The yogi may sport with the supernatural rulers when his subtle body is energized sufficiently to resonate on the same plane or dimension in which the supernatural people reside. Arjuna, for example, did this when he visited the *Svarga Loka* paradise and lived with the Indra demigod there. Serious yogis avoid such encounters because when the subtle body shifts to the heavenly world, it causes one to forget self-realization. In the heavenly association, the subtle form craves enjoyment. Arjuna however, because he was a superior soul, carefully avoided the pleasures to which the subtle body is prone. When one of Indra's girlfriends asked Arjuna to indulge in sexual intercourse, he politely declined. As a result, the angelic woman cursed him to be a eunuch later on.

The perfect fulfillment of one's motives is a petty desire but if a yogi has a strong impression deep within the mind, he will be faced with the fulfillment sooner or later. An example is the *Mahāyogī Dhruva*, who after perfecting yoga practice, and even after gaining an audience with *Śrī* Krishna, had to return to the gross existence, to satisfy the motive for which he began the yoga austerities. That desire was formed in his nature when he was insulted by his stepmother. In resentment and anger, he developed a strong desire to rule the world.

To command circumstances for an unopposed course anywhere, is another desire which one might develop. However the yogi should try his best to let all such desires rest in peace by the process of complete retraction of sensual energy and a retrogression of the samskara desire-seed energies into the causal body.

There are many trillions of desires in the causal form. Some of these are reactionary, being based on previous fulfillments and frustrations. Some others are new desires which were never expressed or felt before. These desires should stay put in the causal body. One should learn how not to interfere with any of them. A yogin should not become a stooge of such desires. He should carefully sidestep them if he is able to, or he should get help from superior souls on how to do so.

त्रि-काल-ज्ञत्वम् अद्वन्द्वं
पर-चित्ताद्य्-अभिज्ञता ।
अग्न्य्-अर्काम्बु-विषादीनां
प्रतिष्टम्भो ऽपराजयः ॥१०.८॥

tri-kāla-jñatvam advandvaṁ
para-cittādy-abhijñatā
agny-arkāmbu-viṣādīnāṁ
pratiṣṭambho 'parājayaḥ (10.8)

tri – three phases; kāla – time factor; jñatvam — know, knowing, knowledge of; advandvam — not being affected by the dualities of heat and cold, happiness and distress; para — of others; cittādy = citta — mental and emotional energy + ādy (ādi) — and related privacies; abhijñata — knowing; agny (agni) — fire; arkāmbu = arka — sun + ambu — water; viṣādīnām = visa — poison + ādīnām — and other dangers; pratiṣṭambho = pratiṣṭambhah — counteracting; 'parājayaḥ = aparājayaḥ = aparā – not others + jayah - being conquered.

Translation

...knowing the three phases of the time factor, not being affected by heat and cold, happiness and distress, knowing the mental and emotional energy and other related privacies of others, counteracting the influence of fire, sun, water, poison and other dangers, not being conquered by others: (10.8)

Commentary:

These are five other mystic skills which might be exhibited by a yogi. These are not so important as the eighteen which were mentioned before. A yogi should not focus on developing these. By their nature, these skills make the yogi prone to a preoccupation with popularity, which is a distraction from the objective.

These powers are minor skills because they pertain mostly to mundane existence. The knowledge of the three phases of time, namely the past, present and future, usually pertain to gross material existence. The ability of not being affected by cold or heat or by happiness or distress, is to be developed as prescribed by *Śrī* Krishna in his *Bhagavad-Gītā* instruction to Arjuna, but not as a mystic skill, only for the purpose of being detached from unfavorable and favorable circumstances which might use up the attention of the yogi.

The knowing of the mental and emotional energy of others, has some value. By it, the yogi may avoid restricting associations by knowing in advance what others think of him, how they feel about him and how they plan to use him. Other uses of telepathy and clairaudience cause the retardation of yoga practice.

The counteracting of the influence of fire, weather, poison and other dangers, is a distraction for the yogi. On occasion he might be circumstantially pressured to exhibit such powers. He should not become addicted to the use of it, because it has to do with material bodies for the most part. In *prāṇāyāma* practice, a yogi works to eliminate the negative influences which come on in bad weather but only so that he can complete the practice, not to exhibit power nor to adjust the climate.

A yogi avoids being used by others but only because he needs to be free to complete yoga practice. If pressured by time and circumstance, he accepts the restrictions which are placed on him by others.

एताश् चोद्देशतः प्रोक्ता
योग-धारण-सिद्धयः ।
यया धारणया या स्याद्
यथा वा स्यान् निबोध मे ॥ १०.९ ॥

etāś coddeśataḥ proktā
yoga-dhāraṇa-siddhayaḥ
yayā dhāraṇayā yā syād
yathā vā syān nibodha me (10.9)

etāś = etāḥ — these; coddeśataḥ = ca — and + uddeśatah — a brief description; proktāḥ — said to be; yoga — yoga practice; dhāraṇa — linking of the attention with the concentration force; siddhayaḥ — mystic skills; yayā — by which; dhāranayā — linking of the attention with the concentration force; yā — which; syād = syāt — will manifest; yathā — as; vā — or; syān = syāt — will manifest; nibodha — learn; me — from me.

Translation

These are a brief description of the mystic skills which manifest from the linking of the attention with the concentration force in yoga practice. Learn from Me, by which concentration linkage, particular skills are developed and how they will manifest. (10.9)

Commentary:

With yoga practice, there will be development of mystic powers. Some persons are born with certain abilities but usually these function by instinct. Deliberate control comes by doing yoga. *Śrī* Krishna began the description at the *dhāraṇā* stage. This is the 6th stage, where the yogi notices certain concentrations of energy within the psyche. He links his attention to these. Sometimes, these concentrations of higher energy come from outside the psyche. At other times, these flow from the inside and travel to the outside, into some other dimension or even into this dimension. In all cases, the yogi links his attention to the flow of concentration force. This happens by an increase in pranic energy in the psyche and by a shifting of his attention out of the material environment in which his gross body resides.

भूत-सूक्ष्मात्मनि मयि
तन्-मात्रं धारयेन् मनः ।
अणिमानम् अवाप्नोति
तन्-मात्रोपासको मम ॥ १०.१० ॥

bhūta-sūkṣmātmani mayi
tan-mātraṁ dhārayen manaḥ
aṇimānam avāpnoti
tan-mātropāsako mama (10.10)

bhūta – matter; sūkṣmātmani = sūkṣma — subtle + ātmani — in the self; mayi — in me; tan = tat – that; mātram — subtle matter; dhārayen = dhārayet — one should link his attention with the concentration force; manaḥ — mind; aṇimānam — assuming an atomic form; avāpnoti — acquires; tan = tat – that; mātropāsako = mātra — subtle matter + upāsako (upāsakaḥ) — the worshippers; mama — My.

Translation

By linking his attention with the concentration force of subtle matter, which is in his psyche, and in My subtle body, the worshipper of subtle matter, acquires the ability to assume an atomic form. (10.10)

Commentary:

Even though *Śrī* Krishna included Himself, the point being made is that a person who wants to be atomic, desires that because he is under the influence of subtle matter. *Śrī* Krishna accredited Himself as being the owner of all subtle matter. He uses the possessive pronoun, *mama* (my).

The subtle matter *(tan-mātram)* is within the psyche of the limited soul and within the supernatural psyche of the Supreme Being as well. But this psyche is not the spiritual body of the limited being or of God. It is in the subtle and causal forms. Both the limited soul and the Supreme Soul have subtle and causal forms, even though the Supreme Soul is in full knowledge of these psychological equipments.

People who worship subtle matter, and even great yogins who are irresistibly attracted to it, are not particularly interested in the Supreme Being, in *Śrī* Krishna. Their interest is in the subtle material elements, which to them might seem to be supreme. Some yogis mistake their subtle and causal bodies for something supreme. This is because these yogins are over-powered, fascinated as it were, by the powers exhibited by these forms.

By linking up one's attention with the concentrated psychic force within the psyche, one can develop in an instant, an atomic form (*mūrter* verse 4) of one's own, made or manufactured from psychic energy. Sometimes this occurs of its own accord, spontaneously even without being desired by the yogin. Sometimes he does it willfully. For such willful assumption of any atomic form, the yogi has to focus his will on the concentrated flow of subtle matter into or out of his psyche. This may occur during the practice of the 6th stage of yoga, that of *dhāraṇā* linkage of the attention to higher concentration forces or persons.

Great yogis and fortunate neophytes do ignore such powers and focus beyond that to attain higher accomplishments but sometimes, they are conveyed into atomic forms which develop suddenly in their supernatural bodies. In such forms they perceive the energies within an atom.

महत्-तत्त्वात्मनि मयि
यथा-सस्थ मनो द्धत् ।
महिमानम् अवाप्नोति
भूतानां च पृथक् पृथक् ॥ १०.११ ॥

mahat-tattvātmani mayi
yathā-saṁsthaṁ mano dadhat
mahimānam avāpnoti
bhūtānāṁ ca pṛthak pṛthak 10.11)

mahat-tattvātmani = mahat-tattva — total mundane potency + ātmani — in the psyche; mayi — on me; yathā — as; saṁstham — situation, condition; mano = manaḥ — mind; dadhat — linking the attention with the concentration force; mahimānam — assuming a cosmic form; avāpnoti — achieves; bhūtānām — of the material elements; ca — and; prthak prthak — distinctly, each seperately.

Translation

Linking the attention with the concentration force in the supersubtle total material energy, which is in his psyche and in Mine, the yogi becomes situated in that supersubtle condition and achieves the ability to experience a cosmic form of either of the super subtle elements. (10.11)

Commentary:

This is an application of the 6th stage of yoga, that of *dhāraṇā* linkage of the attention with various types of focused energy which enter into or pour out of the psyche of a yogi. In the *dhāraṇā* practice, these experiences are gained by the yogi. Some happen spontaneously. Some are done by the yogi's curiosity and his tendency for research.

In a successful yoga practice, one passes through these stages, because one shifts from one lower plane to another higher one, on and on and on. As one progresses, one encounters the various abilities of the various bodies and experiences the powers which are inherent in various energies.

परमाणु-मये चित्तं
भूतानां मयि रञ्जयन् ।
काल-सूक्ष्मार्थता योगी
लघिमानम् अवाप्नुयात् ॥ १०.१२ ॥

paramāṇu-maye cittaṁ
bhūtānāṁ mayi rañjayan
kāla-sūkṣmārthatāṁ yogī
laghimānam avāpnuyāt (10.12)

paramānu – atomic energy; maye — in the composition of; cittam — mental and emotional energy used for ideation; bhūtānām — of the material elements; mayi — in me; rañjayan — attaching; kāla — time; sūkṣmārthatām = sūkṣma — subtle + arthatām — substance; yogī — yogi; laghimānam — assuming a weightless form; avāpnuyāt — acquires.

Translation

Attaching the energy which is used for ideation, to Me, as I am related to the material elements, in the composition of atomic energy, the yogi assumes a weightless form, which is based on the subtle existence of time. (10.12)

Commentary:

A big part of mystic yoga has to do with neutralizing the energy which is used for ideation. This is the same energy which is used in imagining various ideas and in visualizing objects. It is called chitta *(citta)*. Unless one learns how to neutralize this ideation energy, the mental and emotional force which conveys feelings, one cannot be successful in yoga. In fact a yogi cannot be successful, without curtailing this energy.

One cannot free oneself from a low estimation of God merely by hearing of the highest view. One has to evolve up from low to high, step-by-step, deep within one's nature. The 7th stage of yoga, that of *dhyāna*, is the effortless linkage of the attention to higher concentration forces within the psyche. It depends on the level of energy in the psyche at the time of the concentration.

Śrī Krishna, the Supreme Being, is connected to the atomic composition of the material elements. Thus when a yogi links to concentration forces on the atomic level, he links up with the super subtle energy, which is connected to the Supreme Being. This causes the yogi to be transferred into a weightless form. Such forms cross the time barrier, causing the yogi to be transferred into the past or future or to slip to a parallel dimension nearby.

If a yogi's material body passes away while he has such an experience, he might be transferred out of this dimension and find himself in a totally different world, being transposed there permanently. A yogi may become frightened when he is temporarily transferred. By the power of fright, the life force draw the subtle body into the physical form in this world. Some stop mystic practice due to fear of losing a gross body. Other yogis, who are transferred into higher world systems, do not come back to this place. Some regret such transfers and exert themselves in the new environment, making efforts to return here.

धारयन् मय्य् अह-तत्त्वे
मनो वैकारिके ऽखिलम् ।
सर्वेन्द्रियाणाम् आत्मत्वं
प्राप्तिं प्राप्नोति मन्-मनाः ॥ १०.१३ ॥

dhārayan mayy ahaṁ-tattve
mano vaikārike 'khilam
sarvendriyāṇām ātmatvaṁ
prāptiṁ prāpnoti man-manāḥ (10.13)

dhārayan — linking of the attention to the concentration force; mayy = mayi — in me; aham-tattve — in the energy of assertion; mano = manaḥ — the mind; vaikārike — in the motivational powers of material nature; 'khilam = akhilam — whole, all; sarvendriyāṇām = sarva — all + indriyānām — of the sensual energy; ātmatvam — self identification; prāptim — the power to appropriate anything; prāpnoti — acquires; man = mat – on me; manāḥ — the mind.

Translation

Linking the attention to the concentration force which is focused on Me, on My energy of assertion and on the motivational powers of material nature, one feels self identification with sensual energies. By focusing the mind on Me in that way, one acquires the power of appropriation. (10.13)

Commentary:

This is a mystic skill which might be developed by a yogi who perfects the 6th stage of yoga that of *dhāraṇā* linking of the attention to a concentration force within or without the psyche. In this case, the concentration force must comprise the energy which is the motivational force and the assertive powers of the Supreme Being. When a yogi's attention links to that focused energy, he feels a self-identification with cosmic sensuality. From this comes the ability to appropriate anything in that existential locale.

महत्य् आत्मनि यः सूत्रे
धारयेन् मयि मानसम् ।
प्राकाम्यं पारमेष्ठ्यं मे
विन्दते ऽव्यक्त-जन्मनः ॥१०.१४॥

mahaty ātmani yaḥ sūtre
dhārayen mayi mānasam
prākāmyaṁ pārameṣṭhyaṁ me
vindate 'vyakta-janmanaḥ (10.14)

mahaty = mahati — in the mahat-tattva, in the primal conscious causal force; ātmani — the psyche; yah — who; sūtre — in the sexually polarized mahat tattva, in the sexually polarised conscious cosmic power; dhārayet — should link the attention with the concentration force; mayi — in me; mānasam — mind; prākāmyam — experiencing whatever is desired; pārameṣṭhyam — supreme, the greatest; me — from me; vindate — obtains; 'vyakta = avyakta – the abstract existence; janmanaḥ — origination.

Translation

One who applies his mind to Me by linking the attention with the concentration force, consisting of the sexually-charged conscious cosmic power and the primal conscious cosmic force which originated from the abstract existence, obtains the greatest mystic skill of being able to fulfill any desire. (10.14)

Commentary:

The *mahat-tattva* is the conscious cosmic force from which this gross manifestation was derived. This manifestation exists in that force and was produced from it, as well. It abounds in outer space and inner space. A portion of that conscious cosmic power is given a sexual charge by the Supreme Being. That is called the *sūtram*. On one hand, you have the *puruṣas* or persons, the exploiters and on the other hand you have the *sūtram* which is a sexually-charged conscious energy which exhibits lusty characteristics. This is also called Māyā or *Prakṛti* in Sanskrit.

All persons, the Supreme One as well as the innumerable limited beings, have relationship with this sexually-charged conscious cosmic force, but the Supreme Person regulates His attraction to it, while most of the limited individuals are irresistibly drawn to it and subsequently fall under its influence. Instead of exploiting it, they usually are exploited by it. It does however save them the embarrassment by giving them a sense of being its overlord. This is because it imparts to them a sense of selfness which is termed *ātmatvam* in the previous verse. When a yogi breaks this spell of selfness in relation to the sexually-charged force, he attains liberation by an acute detachment from it.

We should notice that in these verses, *Śrī* Krishna repeatedly interjects himself by using personal pronouns like *me* (verse 9), *mayi*, *mama* (verse 10) *mayi* (verse 11) *mayi* (verse 12), *mayi man* (verse 13), and *mayi*, me, in this verse 14. All these personal pronouns indicated Himself as my, me, in me and so on. *Śrī* Krishna showed that a yogi realizes God initially only in terms of God's connection with material nature. One cannot all of a sudden move from a materialistic view of oneself to the spiritual view. Therefore it is highly unlikely that anyone of us, will be able to relate to the spiritual body of the Supreme Personality, suddenly and abruptly.

It occurs by gradations, as a yogin moves up and up and up as described in these verses. First one connects with the Supreme Person through His mundane potencies, from the lower gross ones to the higher subtler ones as described.

At first when the Supreme Spirit contacts the mundane potency, there arises what is called the *Mahat Tattva*. From the contact of the two there arises a portion of that primeval mundane force, which becomes sexually charged. This is called the *Sūtram*. This *sūtram* carries with it, an irresistible attraction which lures the limited spirits. Initially the limited spirits enter into and are fully influenced by that sexually-charged conscious force. Some philosophers feel that the mundane potency is not conscious but they are all wrong. It is very conscious. Because of its proximity to the Supreme Being it absorbs consciousness. There was no time when it was not in His proximity, so there was no time when it was not conscious. The idea that it became conscious only after the Supreme Being made contact with it, and imparted living force to it, is only hypothetical. There was never a time when He was not in touch with it. Thus it is always a conscious and attractive power. Thus it is called *Māyā* or *Mahāmāyā*, the bewildering and irresistible potency, which keeps us time and space bound. It has got the power to control us and keep us ever occupied with its concerns.

In this verse, *Śrī* Krishna identified it as His own force. He said that when the yogi connects with the concentration power within it, that yogi, acquires the highest mystic power which is to fulfill any desire. This is because in terms of desires in any part of the material world, that sexually-charged force has the complete potential in it. Thus if a yogi gets in touch with it through meditation he may fulfill any desires it is capable of.

Even though this prerogative belongs to the Supreme Being, who is the master of the sum-total cosmic force, still because the Supreme Person does not use all of the force, there is ample room for others to engage it. Some yogis use it and then appear to be gods in their own right. They manipulate it in a masterful way.

In the tussle between the limited souls and that sexually charged conscious power, they, the limited beings, are used by that powerful force. But if someone takes help from the Supreme Being, from *Śrī* Krishna, as stated in this verse, that person can master a portion of it.

विष्णौ त्र्य्-अधीश्वरे चित्तं
धारयेत् काल-विग्रहे ।
स ईशित्वम् अवाप्नोति
क्षेत्रज्ञ-क्षेत्र-चोदनाम् ॥ १०.१५॥

viṣṇau try-adhīśvare cittaṁ
dhārayet kala-vigrahe
sa īśitvam avāpnoti
kṣetrajña-kṣetra-codanām (10.15)

viṣṇau — on Vishnu; try = tri – three influences of material nature; adhīśvare — on the supreme Lord; cittam — on the ideation energy of the psyche; dhārayet — should link the attention with the concentration force; kāla — time; vigrahe — in the form; sa = sah — he; īśitvam — skill of controlling; avāpnoti — gets; kṣetrajña — the individual spirit in a compartmentalized psyche; kṣetra — the psyche, the existential environment; codanām — dominion.

Translation

One who links his attention to his ideation energy which is focused on Vishnu, the Supreme Lord of the three influences of material nature, and the One who assumes the form of Time, obtains the skill of controlling, having dominion over spirits and their psyches. (10.15)

Commentary:

More precisely, *Śrī* Krishna used the term *viṣṇau* meaning Lord Vishnu, who is *Śrī* Krishna's parallel divinity. This Lord Vishnu is the one who expressed the manifested material world. Previously when *Śrī* Krishna used terms denoting Himself, He actually spoke of Lord Vishnu, His parallel divinity.

The *cittam* is not just the mind, nor even the intellect, but rather the energy of ideation which is experienced as emotions and ideas. This is the energy from which thoughts, images, inner sounds and imaginations are produced. It is the energy from which conceptions manifest. It is a charged mental and emotional force. The mind is a chamber. One of the energies within the mind is the *citta* force, or the substance of ideation, thinking, imagining and conceiving.

The question is: How can one focus such energy on Lord Vishnu or on Lord Krishna, since we hear that Lord Krishna is not within the purview of our present mentality. In other words, our present mind cannot reach the spiritual body of the God. The answer is that even though we cannot reach that spiritual form, we can reach God indirectly by making contact with His influence in the subtle material nature. By experiencing an ideation energy which is focused on the conscious cosmic powers in their three forms, we may make contact with the influence of the God. This is not a direct communication with His spiritual body.

नारायणे तुरीयाख्ये
भगवच्-छब्द-शब्दिते ।
मनो मय्य् आदधद् योगी
मद्-धर्मा वशिताम् इयात् ॥१०.१६॥

nārāyaṇe turīyākhye
bhagavac-chabda-śabdite
mano mayy ādadhad yogī
mad-dharmā vaśitām iyāt (10.16)

nārāyaṇe — on Lord Nārāyaṇa; turīyākhye = turīya – the fourth dimension of existence + ākhye — named, known as; bhagavac-chabda-śabdite = bhagavac (bhagavat) — the one with the most skills + chabda (śabda) – work + śabdite — known as; mano = manah — the mind; mayy = mayi — on Me; ādadhad — linking the attention; yogī — yogi; mad = mat – my; dharmā — sense of values; vaśitām — the skill of near-absolute self control; iyāt — does attain.

Translation

By attentively linking the mental force to Me, as Lord Nārāyaṇa, as the person who is in the fourth dimension, as the one with the most skills, Bhagavān, the yogi gets near-absolute self control and exhibits My sense of values. (10.16)

Commentary:

Even though this is a concentration of mental force *(manah),* it is not the normal mental energy which we experience. This is a superfine mental energy which has for its focus Lord *Nārāyaṇa*, the parallel divinity of *Śrī* Krishna, who is known the Person from the fourth dimension. He is outside of this material atmosphere, outside the space in which the material cosmos floats. The exterior locale in which He resides is an unearthly dimension.

When the yogi reaches Lord *Nārāyaṇa*, who is beyond the three dimensions of the material world, he has reached the spiritual locales. His yoga practice reached the culmination. Lord *Nārāyaṇa* is called *Bhagavān*, because He is the most skilled person in existence. In association with that Lord, the yogi exhibits divine virtues.

Śrī Krishna showed how a yogi devotee definitely progresses up through the subtle material energies, until he passes beyond this atmosphere (*ākāśa*) and enter into the spiritual realm (chit *ākāśa*), which is called the *para vyoma*, *Vaikuṇṭha* and *akṣara dhāma*.

निर्गुणे ब्रह्मणि मयि
धारयन् विशदं मनः ।
परमानन्दम् आप्नोति
यत्र कामो ऽवसीयते ॥१०.१७॥

nirguṇe brahmaṇi mayi
dhārayan viśadaṁ manaḥ
paramānandam āpnoti
yatra kāmo 'vasīyate (10.17)

nirguṇe — being without mundane influences; brahmani — in the spiritual existence; mayi — on Me; dhārayan — linking the attention with the higher concentration force; viśadam — cleansed; manaḥ — mind; paramānandam = parama - supreme + ānandam — happiness; āpnoti — obtains; yatra — wherefrom; kāmo = kāmah — the need for pleasure; 'vasīyate = avasīyate — is completely fulfilled.

Translation

By linking the attention, with the concentration force of the cleansed mind, which is focused on Me, Who is the spiritual existence beyond the mundane influence, one obtains the supreme happiness, wherefrom the need for pleasure is completely fulfilled. (10.17)

Commentary:

Śrī Krishna, who is the Spiritual Existence which is beyond the mundane influence, exists in a completely different dimension, which is in proximity to this material world. To connect with Him, the yogi must use a completely cleansed mind compartment, which contains spiritual potency only. When the yogi attains such a high state, having completed purity yoga, he obtains the supreme happiness, which is so fulfilling that it satisfies fully the need for enjoyment.

श्वेतद्वीप-पतौ चित्तं
शुद्धे धर्म-मये मयि ।
धारयञ् छ्वेतता याति
षड्-ऊर्मि-रहितो नरः ॥१०.१८॥

śvetadvīpa-patau cittaṁ
śuddhe dharma-maye mayi
dhārayañ chvetatāṁ yāti
ṣaḍ-ūrmi-rahito naraḥ (10.18)

śvetadvīpa — white island paradise; patau — in the lord; cittam — the ideation energy of the mind; śuddhe — on the person of full existential purity; dharma - righteous way of life; maye — composition, nature; mayi — on Me; dhārayan — linking the attention to the concentration force; chvetatām = śvetatām — pure; yāti — obtains; ṣaḍ = ṣaṭ - six types; ūrmi — agony; rahito = rahitaḥ — exemption; narah — a person.

Translation

A person obtains purity and gains exemption from the six agonies by linking the attention with the concentration force which is focused on Me, the Person of full existential purity, The Lord of the White Island Paradise, the One Whose nature is composed of the righteous way of life. (10.18)

Commentary:

This is a direct connection with the spiritual body of the Supreme Lord. Subsequently the yogi, if he remains in this world, will exhibit the righteous way of life which Lord Vishnu *Nārāyaṇa* would have exhibited if He were in a physical manifestation. This yogi gets an exemption from having to experience the six agonies.

Swāmī Mādhavānanda in his translation, listed those ailments as hunger, thirst, grief, delusion, decay and death. These agonies are experienced by all mundane life forms but the human being, because of his or her complicated life style, experiences more tribulations.

Hunger, thirst, decay and death are mostly related to the gross body. Grief and delusion are felt mostly in the emotional part of the subtle body. The hunger, thirst and decay potencies are transferred into the subtle body when the gross body dies. Death is not transferred from the gross form to the subtle one, except as an impression of having to be detached from the stability of the gross form. The subtle body experiences the death of the gross one, as an involuntary detachment or unhooking from the gross form.

By nature, the subtle body, when it is not highly energized, prefers to be in a gross form. Thus when it is forced to disconnect from a gross body, it experiences the disconnection in a negative way. This forms an impression of agony.

The subtle body suffers from decay just as the gross body does, but the subtle one does recover from such decay. Eventually however, after millions of years, the subtle body perishes. Then the soul is automatically transferred into its causal form. By nature the causal body likes to have a subtle form. Thus when the subtle body is destroyed, the causal form maintains a desire to create another subtle form. It is not allowed to do so immediately, but it does not grieve over the issue, because it has no facility for depression. It merely maintains its desire for another subtle body without endeavor or complaint.

The causal body is not affected by the six common agonies of hunger, thirst, grief, delusion, decay and death, but that does not mean that the causal body is immune to death. It does die eventually. Its death however is not like that of the subtle form. It simply becomes nonexistent at a certain time. Then the soul, the spirit, is left without any of these mundane forms.

When the causal body disappears, nothing is left to carry any impressions from this side of existence, and still when Lord *Nārāyaṇa* begins a new creation, the spirits again get new causal forms which are exact replicas of the ones they used in the previous time cycle. This is because the spirits are attracted to the material nature, in exactly the same way in which they were attuned to it at the end of the last creation.

A devotee should not confused the actual spiritual form of *Śrī* Krishna with the Deity Form in the temple. The Deity Form has great value but all the same it is not the actual spiritual form of the Lord. One should always remember this. One should not equate a person who sees or communicated with the spiritual form to another devotee who has access only to the Deity Form. Even though it is a good idea for the time being, to see the Deity Form as if Krishna were using that Form as a spiritual body, still one will not progress into the spiritual domains if one does not realize that more efforts are required to reach the actual spiritual body of *Śrī* Krishna.

मय्य् आकाशात्मनि प्राणे
मनसा घोषम् उद्वहन् ।
तत्रोपलब्धा भूतानां
हंसो वाचः शृणोत्य् असौ ॥ १०.१९ ॥

mayy ākāśātmani prāṇe
manasā ghoṣam udvahan
tatropalabdhā bhūtānāṁ
haṁso vācaḥ śṛṇoty asau (10.19)

mayy = mayi — on me; ākāśātmani = ākāśa – atmosphere + ātmani — on myself; prāṇe — on the energizing airs; manasā — with the mind; ghoṣam — subtle sound; udvahan — continuous linkage of the attention with the concentrating force; tatropalabdhā = tatra — there + upalabdhā (upalabdhāḥ) — directly hears; bhūtānām — the living beings; haṁso = haṁsaḥ — advanced yogi who is compared to a mythical swan; vācah — speeches, sounds; śṛṇoty = śṛṇoti — hear; asau — that.

Translation

By continuous linking of his attention with the concentration force which is focused on subtle sound within the mind, and on Me in the spiritual atmosphere and in the energising energy, the advanced yogin directly hears the sounds of distant 1iving beings. (10.19)

Commentary:

Hamsa means an advanced yogi who is compared to a mythical swan which extracts milk only from a mixture of milk and water. In this verse this is used to salute those advanced yogins who mastered the 6th stages of yoga and who practice the 7th stage of continuous linkage of their attention to higher concentration forces and divine persons.

The *ghoṣam* subtle sound is called naad. This sound may be heard on the right or left side of the subtle head. This sound may be heard outside the vicinity of the right or left physical ear. Sometimes it seems to enter into the left side of the subtle head. Sometimes yogis hear it in the *suśumnā* central spinal passage of the subtle form. This sound comes from the chit *ākāśa* or the sky of consciousness. It is used in many *kriyā* practices as an anchor point and as a stabilizing force for the jumpy attention.

Prāṇa is subtle life force. This is taken into the subtle body simultaneously when the physical body breathes air. By energizing their subtle forms with *prāṇa*, yogis cause their minds to become introverted. This introversion is the 5th stage of yoga, that of *pratyāhar* sensual energy withdrawal, containment and conservation. This verse described a lower stage of practice, when the yogi partially mastered *pratyāhar* sensual energy withdrawal and when he begins to practice the 6th stage of *dhāraṇā* linkage of the attention with naturally occurring concentration energies.

Due to being in touch with subtle sounds, the yogi might hear sounds from very far away, even sounds coming from other dimensions, which are physically out of reach, even sounds from the spiritual atmosphere. Such experiences, though preliminary are important for a neophyte's confidence in the results of yoga.

चक्षुस् त्वष्टरि संयोज्य
त्वष्टारम् अपि चक्षुषि ।
मां तत्र मनसा ध्यायन्
विश्वं पश्यति दूरतः ॥१०२०॥

cakṣus tvaṣṭari saṁyojya
tvaṣṭāram api cakṣuṣi
māṁ tatra manasā dhyāyan
viśvaṁ paśyati dūrataḥ (10.20)

cakṣus = cakṣuḥ — the visual power; tvaṣṭari — in the subtle light; samyojya — linking the attention with a certain focusing energy; tvaṣṭāram — subtle light; api — also; cakṣuṣi — in the visual energy; mām — me; tatra — there at that linkage; manasā — in the mind; dhyāyan — effortlessly meditating on the linkage of the attention with a certain focused energy; viśvam — everything; paśyati — sees; dūratah — what is far away.

Translation

Linking the visual power with subtle light and subtle light with the visual energy, while effortlessly meditating on the linkage and on Me, the yogin can, from within his mind, see whatever is far away. (10.20)

Commentary:

This describes a yogin who is somewhat successful with the 5th stage of yoga, that of *pratyāhar* sensual energy withdrawal and who begins to practice the 6th stage, which is *dhāraṇā* linkage of the attention with certain focusing energies in the psyche.

Initially, this yogi does not control this. As he practices, he experiences this haphazardly. Persistent practice brings him to the stage of deliberate control of his endeavors. The visual power *(cakṣuh)* is mentioned because it is very important to internalize this force. If this is not internalized, the yogi will have no lasting success. This power has to be completely internalized in the advanced stages of practice. *Śrīla Yogeśwarānanda* of Gangotri is a master of this visual focus.

Subtle light is not controlled by a neophyte yogi. At first he has to practice steadily until the light appears. When it appears it does so independently of his will power. After some practice, he may link his attention to it. Initially when a yogi tries to link or focus on the inner light or lights, it disappears from view, as if to tease him. This occurs because of the unsteady intellect. To steady the intellect further, he has to perfect the *prāṇāyāma* practice which causes the psyche to become purified by the full expulsion of the *apāna* de-energizing airs. Bhastrika breath exercises are a good method of causing psychic purification, but they are other *prāṇāyāmas* which achieve this.

A yogi has to practice detachment and must remove himself from all associations, which do not help to accelerate practice, otherwise he cannot be successful.

मनो मयि सु-सयोज्य
देहं तद्-अनुवायुना ।
मद्-धारणानुभावेन
तत्रात्मा यत्र वै मनः ॥१०.२१॥

mano mayi su-saṁyojya
dehaṁ tad-anuvāyunā
mad-dhāraṇānubhāvena
tatrātmā yatra vai manaḥ (10.21)

mano = manah — the mind; mayi — on me; su-samyojya — easily and continually connecting; deham — body; tad = tat — that; anuvāyunā — by the life air that trails; mad = mat – on me; dhāraṇānubhāvena = dhāraṇā — linking the attention with the concentration energy; anubhāvena — by the inner nature; tatrātmā = tatra — there + ātmā — spirit; yatra — wherever; vai — surely; manaḥ — the mind.

Translation

Easily and continually connecting to Me, the mind, the body and the life air that trails the mind, and by linking the attention with the concentration energy, which is operative in the inner nature, and which is focused on Me, the spirit surely goes wherever the mind travels. (10.21)

Commentary:

Difficult as these procedures sound, they are elementary to the practices mentioned before which are the advanced stages of yoga dealing with aspects of atomic, cosmic and spiritual importance. However, a neophyte benefits from these descriptions since he will have to progress through these basic stages after he masters *pratyāhar* practice.

Instead of saying samyojya, *Śrī* Krishna added the prefix *su*, which means easy. Thus this practice applies when the yogi can easily *(su)* and continually *(su-samyojya)* perform the 6th stage of yoga, that of *dhāraṇā*. In such practice, it is not that the yogi focuses the energy himself. The yogi energizes his subtle body and the energies within it, become focused of their own accord or alternately, energies from other dimensions begin to penetrate into his energized psyche in a focused way. The yogi then acts to link his will power, his attentive energy, to that focused force. It is very important to understand what *dhāraṇā* is, otherwise one may assume that it means the focusing of one's will power. It means the linking or joining of one's attention with a naturally focused force.

Śrī Krishna mentioned the mind, the body and the life force which trails the mind. This means that the yogi must have mastered kundalini yoga, since otherwise the mind will trail the life force instead. It does not matter whether one is a devotee or not, if one has not mastered kundalini yoga, his mind will have to trail his life force. Only those yogis who mastered kundalini chakra to cause it to rise up and out of the base chakra, the *mūlādhāra*, will have their life force trail the mind or precisely, trail the *buddhi* organ in the subtle head. They raise the kundalini energy up into the brain either to the back or to the frontal lobe or to the top of the head.

This applies to yogis who mastered the *āsana* posture and inner body purity by *prāṇāyāma*, because only such persons can make their body obey their will in this manner. Others cannot do it, even if they are devotees of *Śrī* Krishna. The traveling of the mind is mentioned, with the spirit following the mind. This is because at this stage of practice, the spirit remains behind the *buddhi* organ as it seeks out higher dimensions. Being behind the *buddhi* organ, actually means being centralized behind it or being in the centre of it directorially, with it before or on all sides spherically.

यदा मन उपादाय
यद् यद् रूपं बुभूषति ।
तत् तद् भवेन् मनो-रूपं
मद्-योग-बलम् आश्रयः ॥१०.२२॥

yadā mana upādāya
yad yad rūpaṁ bubhūṣati
tat tad bhaven mano-rūpaṁ
mad-yoga-balam āśrayaḥ (10.22)

yadā — when; mana = manaḥ — the mind; upādāya — applying; yad yad = yat yat — whatever; rūpam — form; bubhūṣati — one wishes to assume; tad tad = tat tat — that that, that specifically; bhaven = bhavet — may become; mano-rūpam — the form of the mental energy; mad = mat – on me; yoga – yoga; balam — power; āśrayaḥ — resorting.

Translation

When applying the mind, whatever form one wishes to assume, that specific form he becomes, by resorting to yoga power as concentrated on Me. (10.22)

Commentary:

It may be argued that some yogis experience such powers and they are not devotees of *Śrī* Krishna, nor are they aware of a reliance on Him. However if we follow *Śrī* Krishna's broad definition of Himself, we will understand that any sort of identification or reliance on any power in the material, supernatural or spiritual dimensions, was considered to be a reliance on Him.

He regards all energy and super-energy, to be His power and to be connected with Him in some way or the other. Therefore yogis who do not have the reliance on *Śrī* Krishna, would still be contacting or becoming linked with such energies. Thus they would experience these mystic faculties.

पर-कायं विशन् सिद्ध
आत्मान तत्र भावयेत् ।
पिण्डं हित्वा विशेत् प्राणो
वायु-भूतः षडङ्घ्रि-वत् ॥ १०.२३ ॥

para-kāyaṁ viśan siddha
ātmānaṁ tatra bhāvayet
piṇḍaṁ hitvā viśet prāṇo
vāyu-bhūtaḥ ṣaḍaṅghri-vat (10.23)

para — another; kāyam — body; viśan — desiring to enter; siddhaḥ — a skilled yogi; ātmānam — self; tatra — there; bhāvayet — should existentially position himself; piṇḍam — gross body; hitvā — leaving; viśet — should enter; prāṇo = prāṇah — the life force; vāyu-bhūtaḥ — the nature of the wind; ṣaḍaṅghri-vat — like the bee.

Translation

Desiring to enter another's body, a skilled yogi, should existentially relocate himself there. Leaving the gross body, his life force which is like the wind, should enter just like a bee. (10.23)

Commentary:

One yogi who performed this mystic skill was *Śrīpad Ādi Śaṅkarācārya*. In my own body, I experienced the demonstration of this mystic skill, whereby advanced yogis like *Śrīla Yogeśwarānanda Yogīrāj*, and *Siddha Swāmī* Muktananada entered through the *brahmarandra* of my subtle form using miniature forms which are about the size of a drone bee. They did this to converse with me and to demonstrate techniques.

By using the terms *siddha* which means a skilled and accomplished yogin, *Śrī* Krishna indicated that this mystic skill cannot be demonstrated by any yogi who has not mastered all eight stages of yoga practice.

पार्ष्ण्यापीड्य गुदं प्राणं
हृद्-उरः-कण्ठ-मूर्धसु ।
आरोप्य ब्रह्म-रन्ध्रेण
ब्रह्म नीत्वोत्सृजेत् तनुम् ॥ १०.२४॥ ॥

pārṣṇyāpīḍya gudaṁ prāṇaṁ
hṛd-uraḥ-kaṇṭha-mūrdhasu
āropya brahma-**randhreṇa**
brahma **nītvotsṛjet** tanum (10.24)

parsnyapidya = pārṣṇyā — with the heel + āpīḍya — blocking; gudam — anus; prānam — vital energy; hṛd = hṛt — heart chakra; uraḥ — chest; kaṇṭha — neck; mūrdhasu — to the head; āropya — listing; brahma-randhreṇa — by the hole at the top of the subtle head; brahma — to the spiritual existence; nītvotsṛjet = nītvā — taking + utsṛjet — should give up; tanum — the gross form.

Translation

Blocking the anus with the heel, and lifting the vital energy to the heart chakra, then through the chest, throat and head, and by taking it through the hole at the top of the head of the subtle body, one should transfer to the spiritual existence, while giving up the gross form. (10.24)

Commentary:

This is a description of the removal of kundalini shakti from the *mūlādhāra* place where it is usually stationed. This practice should be perfected long before departure from the body. For the final removal of this energy at the time of death, the yogi takes help from the time factor, to relocate himself to a higher dimension.

Because he practiced all along for many years prior to the final exit from the body, the skillful yogi definitely relocates to the chit *ākāśa* at the time of death. Mostly by his own endeavors, with the grace of mahayogis and Lord Krishna, he serves the purpose of having a material body, by having perfected himself while living in the material world.

विहरिष्यन् सुराक्रीडे
मत्-स्थं सत्त्वं विभावयेत् ।
विमानेनोपतिष्ठन्ति
सत्त्व-वृत्तीः सुर-स्त्रियः ॥१०.२५

viharisyan surākrīḍe
mat-sthaṁ sattvaṁ vibhāvayet
vimānenopatiṣṭhanti
sattva-vṛttīḥ sura-striyaḥ (10.25)

viharisyan — wishing to enjoy life; surākrīḍe = sura — the supernatural rulers + ākrīḍe — in the parks; mat-stham — based on me; sattvam — clarifying energy; vibhāvayet — one should contemplate; vimānenopatiṣṭhanti = vimānena — by aerial conveyances + upatiṣṭhanti — they appear; sattva — clarifying energy; vrttīḥ — productions; sura — of the celestial type; striyaḥ — women.

Translation

Wishing to enjoy life in the parks of the supernatural rulers, one should contemplate the clarifying energy as it is based on Me, then by aerial conveyances, the celestial women whose bodies are productions of the clarifying power, will appear in aerial conveyances. (10.25)

Commentary:

This applies to those yogis who perfected the eight-staged yoga process, *aṣṭanga* yoga, and who are still feeling a need for subtle enjoyment. Such yogis, by honesty, take help from more advanced ascetics to find out how long it would take for them to become mature enough to be totally detached from the pleasure facilities of the heavenly worlds.

It is not a matter of wishful thinking nor of telling oneself that since one is a devotee, one will not be attracted to subtle sensuality. It does not work like that in reality. The yogi as he advances, begins to experience the subtle material world. While doing yoga practice in astral projections, a yogi meets angelic women. Therefore he has first hand experience and can realize what level he is really on and what sort of nature he really has as contrasted to his guru's or his own ideas and religious aspirations.

Getting first hand experience about his nature, he can know for sure before the time of death, as to whether he will by-pass the angelic paradises or not. If a yogi knows before hand that he will not be able to avoid the temptations of such places, he can take advice from more advanced souls as to how he may be cured of the need for the enticements.

Many persons who feel that they will by-pass the angelic world and go the spiritual atmosphere, are just miscalculating. They grossly over-estimate themselves. Or they accepted statements from popularity-hungry teachers and from incentive scriptures which assured them of something that will not happen at the time of death. I have over the years tried to help many of these devotees of *Śrī* Krishna, *Śrī Rāma*, Lord Shiva and Lord *Swāmīnārāyaṇa*, but to no avail, because they are stubbornly attached to the misconceptions which they cherish so much.

The situation is this: If the yogi or even the non-yogi devotee who qualifies, has any tendencies for heavenly life, he will after death, enjoy in the subtle heavens for sometime. As soon as he leaves the body, he will find himself in a subtle form which has a keen enjoying interest in the heavenly world. Many angelic beings will appear around him. If the person is female, male angelic beings will come, other wise a human male will see female angelic beings. At the time of death, such a human being will find himself or herself enjoying life with such beings. This is usually highlighted by sexual intercourses. After a time, the human will again take rebirth on this planet or in a similar dimension with an earthly body.

Those who do not qualify will simply take ghostly subtle bodies after death and then after some time, they will again enter into the semina of a man to come out again from a woman's belly as an embryo in this world. Such a process of death and then subsequent birth takes place automatically by the grace of the subtle material nature, with or without the cooperation of any limited person.

यथा सङ्कल्पयेद् बुद्ध्या
यदा वा मत्-परः पुमान् ।
मयि सत्ये मनो युञ्जस्
तथा तत् समुपाश्नुते ॥ १०.२६ ॥

yathā saṅkalpayed buddhyā
yadā vā mat-paraḥ pumān
mayi satye mano yuñjaṁs
tathā tat samupāśnute (10.26)

yathā — accordingly; saṅkalpayed = saṅkalpayet — has an intention; buddhyā — with the intellect; yadā — when; vā — or; mat-paraḥ — one who is devoted to me; pumān — a person; mayi — on me; satye — on reality; mano = manah — the mind; yuñjams = yuñjan — linking the attention with the focused force; tathā — as; tat — that; samupāśnute — gets.

Translation

Accordingly, whenever a person who is devoted to Me, has an intention within the intellect and links his attention with the force which is focused on Me and on Reality, he gets that objective as desired. (10.26)

Commentary:

This is a general guideline. It is the basic procedure underlying most of the statements made by *Śrī* Krishna in this chapter. There are four aspects:

- *being devoted to Śrī Krishna, to the Supreme Being (mat parah).*
- *having some intention which is within the intellect of the a subtle body (saṅkalpayet buddhyā).*
- *linking the attention to an internal force which is focused on an aspect of reality (satye yuñjams).*
- *Linking the attention on an internal force which is focused on Śrī Krishna (mayi yuñjams)*

The aspect of reality, *satya*, which is contacted and which acts to convey the yogi's intention to *Śrī* Krishna, is important. That aspect will restrict or liberate the devotee, since it would make contact indirectly or directly with the Lord as He described in the previous verses of this chapter.

All in all the yogi is responsible for his development. As he advances more and more, he clears himself of impurities and lower stages.

वै मद्-भावम् आपन्न
ईशितुर् वशितुः पुमान् ।
कुतश्चिन् न विहन्येत
तस्य चाज्ञा यथा मम ॥ १०.२७ ॥

vai mad-bhāvam āpanna
īśitur vaśituḥ pumān
kutaścin na vihanyeta
tasya cājñā yathā mama (10.27)

yo = yah — he who; vai — indeed; mad = mat — my; bhāvam — nature; āpanna = āpannaḥ — assimilated; īśitur = īśituḥ — perfect ruler; vaśituḥ — perfect controller; pumān — person; kutaścin — in any way; na – not; vihanyeta — frustrated; tasya — his; cājñā = ca — and + ājñā — instruction, wish; yathā — just as; mama — mine (my desire).

Translation

A person who assimilated My nature, Me, who am the perfect ruler and controller, finds that his wish is not frustrated in any way, just as it is with My desire. (10.27)

Commentary:

This explains the similarity between a liberated devotee and *Śrī* Krishna. It does not in any way suggest that the devotee has merged into the existence of *Śrī* Krishna and has lost himself or herself, but rather that he adopted the nature of *Śrī* Krishna. Subsequently his spiritual self begins to function in a way that is similar to *Śrī* Krishna's psychology.

मद्-भक्त्या शुद्ध-सत्त्वस्य
योगिनो धारणा-विदः ।
तस्य त्रै-कालिकी बुद्धिर्
जन्म-मृत्यूपबृंहिता ॥१०.२८॥

mad-bhaktyā śuddha-sattvasya
yogino dhāraṇā-vidaḥ
tasya trai-kālikī buddhir
janma-mṛtyūpabṛṁhitā (10.28)

mad = mat – to me; bhaktyā — by devotion; śuddha – pure; sattvasya — of those who are reliant on the clarifying influence; yogino = yoginaḥ — of yogis; dhāranā – by linking the attention with a concentration force; vidaḥ — one who knows how; tasya — of him, his; trai – three phases; kālikī — concerning time; buddhir = buddhiḥ — the intellect; janma – birth; mṛtyūpabṛṁhitā = janma – birth + mṛtyu — death + upabṛṁhitā — encompassed, having an increased capacity.

Translation

The intellect of the yogi, whose is reliant on the pure clarifying influence by devotion to Me, and who knows how to link his attention to the concentration force in the clarifying energy, has an increase capacity to discern the three phases of time, as well as his births and deaths. (10.28)

Commentary:

This is another type of *dhāraṇā* linking of the attention to special focusing energies in the psyche. Here we hear of *mad-bhaktyā* which is devotion to *Śrī* Krishna. This must be achieved. Along with this, there are other aspects, such as the mastery of the *dhāranā* 6th stage of yoga practice. The yogi must also cause his subtle energy to consist of the purest type of clarifying energy *(śuddha sattvasya).* This is accomplished in two ways by *prāṇāyāma* practice and by adoption, of the right conduct which frees the yogi from lower influences.

When the intellect organ of the subtle body, ingest only the pure clarifying energy, the yogi, if he is a devotee, gets much closer to *Śrī* Krishna. He experiences a noticeable increase in the capacity to discern the three phases of time as well as to know of former births and deaths.

Yogis who are not devotees of *Śrī* Krishna are not barred from these benefits but their connection with the pure clarifying energy may not necessarily reveal to them anything about the existential position of *Śrī* Krishna. Thus they might remain ignorant of Him. Such yogis will however advance into the spiritual energy but they might not encounter any divine beings there.

अग्न्य्-आदिभिर् न हन्येत
मुनेर् योग-मयं वपुः ।
मद्-योग-शान्त-चित्तस्य
यादसाम् उदकं यथा ॥१०.२९॥

agny-ādibhir na hanyeta
muner yoga-mayaṁ vapuḥ
mad-yoga-śānta-cittasya
yādasām udakaṁ yathā (10.29)

agny = agni — fire; ādibhih — other dangerous factors; na — not; hanyeta — is destroyed; muner = muneḥ — of a yogi philosopher; yoga-maya — produced by or tempered by yoga austerities; vapuḥ — body; mad = mat - me; yoga — yoga discipline; śānta — pacified, made quiescent; cittasya — of the ideation energy in the mind; yādasām — of the aquatics; udakam — water; yathā — just as.

Translation

Provided that the yogi philosopher's ideation energy is tempered by yoga austerity and made quiescent by yogic discipline to Me, his body is not destroyed by fire or other dangerous factors, just as in the case of the aquatics and water. (10.29)

Commentary:

Some very important practices are divulged in these verses. Some commentators think that since these regard petty *siddhis*, one should not regard them. *Śrī* Krishna however, graced the sincere yogis by explaining these means of advancement. Nothing He says here should be taken lightly.

Let us consider some key Sanskrit terms:

Muner

This means a yogic philosopher not just a philosopher. It is a person who mastered the *aṣṭanga* yoga and who by nature is philosophically inclined. Because he has a philosophical interest, he will use yoga realization to test philosophical ideas. When he finds that his ideas are inconsistent with reality, he will drop or adjust them in accordance with the truth. This type of yogi is more systematic and is more likely to become a spiritual master, a *yogācārya*.

The temptation is his attraction to the teaching role. If he can overcome that risk, his advancement in yoga would be rapid. Otherwise, much will be spent teaching and explaining whatever little or great amount he knows about yoga. Such a person might take up the vocation of writing books. In that way he could efficiently fulfill the responsibility to teach and explain the path of yoga. Otherwise he might be forestalled by teaching, explaining and demonstrating.

Human beings are all too eager to worship, honor and glorify a proficient yogin. If one wants to maintain a steady progress, one has to avoid such prestige.

yoga-mayam vapuh

This means that the yogi tempered his body by yoga austerities. Subsequently he changed the nature of his body, changed some of its genetic tendencies. A person who gets a body from a father, who is himself a masterful yogin might not have to do this. Those of us who received bodies from parents who were not interested in yoga, should work to change the tendencies of the body.

Haṭha yoga is the process for changing such bodies. This includes all aspects of it, which are *āsana* posture, various bodily contractions called *bandhas*, change in diet, adjustment of the time of eating certain foods, practice of *prāṇāyāma* for mastering kundalini and celibacy yoga and mystic practice for adjusting the parts of the subtle body which prevail on the gross one in a negative way.

One cannot change the tendencies of the body merely by chanting mantras, even if such mantras consists of the holy name of God. This is because at this time, our material bodies do not readily respond to such sounds, except superficially. For deep and permanent changes one has to use *haṭha* Yoga. Because human beings are too lazy to take up *haṭha* Yoga they are being told that they can chant and that will adjust everything. However this will produce failure.

yoga-śānta-cittasya

This means that the ideation energy *(citta)* in the mind has to become quiescent *(śānta)* and that the yoga discipline should be done in accordance with the system taught by *Śrī* Krishna Himself. The quiescence of the mind is not the pacification or occupation of the mind by mantras. It is the changing of the energy in the mind to a higher type of energy. What is that higher type of energy? We must go to the previous verse to find the answer, by the terms *śuddha-sattvasya*, which is to say purified clarified energy. This is a material energy but it is the highest type of that potency, which is available to us under the present conditions. Various aspects of this energy were mentioned by *Śrī* Krishna in previous verses as follows:

vaikārike - verse 13; *mahat, sūtre* - verse 14; *brahmaṇi* - verse 17; *ākāśātmani, ghoṣam* - verse 19.

The pure and simple, the definite way of changing out the energy in the mind is *prāṇāyāma*. It is the direct straight forward method. But if you do not have the time to do it, if you are disagreeable to it, then you will have to use other methods which will not give you such a definite result. Many persons who chant mantras, feel that they changed the mind but it is the surface levels of the mind which are affected. Deep down, the energy remains the same, because the mantras do not penetrate to subconscious levels. Without mystic ability no one can penetrate deeply into the mind. It is impossible.

As soon as the yogi tempers his body sufficiently by yoga disciplines, and provided that his ideation energy is made quiescent, he acquires a harmony in respect to material nature. Subsequently fire and other energies which are dangerous to a material body, avoid attacking him. This does not mean that he will not lose the body, for he certainly will, but many of the common ailments and causes for alarm, do not bother him.

When material nature treats the yogi in this way, he is given a special exemption so that he can spend more time cultivating the practice to reach higher stages. Sometimes when a yogi reaches the stage of becoming harmonic with material nature, the goddess *Durgā* appears and blesses him directly but her appearance is not necessary in each case. If she appears to a yogi, he can assume that he is especially blessed to proceed to the higher stages without having to deal with impediments.

Śrī Krishna gave the example of aquatics in water, since even though water is a danger, it affords protection to some creatures. Hence a yogi who has a yogically-reformed material body and who has mastered the 5th and 6th stages of yoga, lives in the material world with a special protection, afforded to him by material nature and by its patron deity, the goddess *Durgā*.

मद्-विभूतीर् अभिध्यायन्
श्रीवत्सास्त्र-विभूषिताः ।
ध्वजातपत्र-व्यजनैः
स भवेद् अपराजितः ॥१०.३०॥

mad-vibhūtīr abhidhyāyan
śrīvatsāstra-vibhūṣitāḥ
dhvajātapatra-vyajanaiḥ
sa bhaved aparājitaḥ (10.30)

mad = mat — my; vibhūtīr = vibhūtīḥ — supernatural form; abhidhyāyan — effortlessly remaining in the linkage of the attention and the concentration force; śrīvatsāstra = śrīvatsa — Srivatsa curl of hair + astra — weapon; vibhūṣitāḥ — adorned; dhvajātapatra = dhvaja — banner + ātapatra — umbrella; vyajanaiḥ — with chowry fan; sa = sah — he; bhaved = bhavet — becomes; aparājitaḥ — unconquerable.

Translation

One who effortlessly remains in the linkage of his attention and the special concentration force which is focused on My supernatural form, which is adorned with the Śrīvatsa curl of hair, with a weapon, a banner, an umbrella and a chowry fan, becomes unconquerable. (10.30)

Commentary:

The general English equivalent of *dhyāna* and *abhidhyāyan* is meditation. I deliberately give the full meaning which is to effortlessly remain in the linkage of the attention and the concentration force within the psyche. It is important to use the correct meaning for abhidhyāyan since the word meditation, or even the word contemplation, does not convey the details of the *dhyāna* and *abhidhyāyan* yoga practice.

Śrī Patañjali grouped the last three stages of yoga, as a process of *samyama*. This is because these final states are inter-related. When a yogi masters the 6th stage of *dhāraṇā*, he might automatically enter the 7th stage of *dhyāna*. When practicing the 7th stage, he might effortlessly slip into the 8th stage of *samādhi*. Because these practices are related and because one might evolve into the other, or even devolve into the other, *Śrī Patañjali*, the fully experienced mystic yogi, placed them together as the process of *samyama*.

If the neophyte yogi does not understand what *dhāraṇā* is, he will waste much time in practice for weeks, months or years, and never achieve it, all because he misunderstands what *dhāraṇā* means. *Dhāraṇā* does not mean that one creates a concentration in the psyche or in the mind chamber or in the intellect proper. That is normal concentration for materialistic purposes and for emotional usages, but it is not *dhāraṇā*. A self-directed concentration force is not *dhāraṇā*.

Dhāraṇā is when the subtle body is surcharged to such a degree that there occurs in the psyche, a natural concentration which is not dependent on will power and which is not necessarily linked to one's will power. This concentration of energy would continue in a focused way, even if the will power is not linked to it. Conversely, in normal concentration, the focus collapses if one's will power does not maintain it.

While for ordinary concentration one does not have to surcharge the subtle body, one only has to apply his will to a certain idea, objective or place, in *dhāraṇā* focus, he has to surcharge the subtle form. That is the main action. As soon as the form is surcharged, he senses where the concentration energy is manifested. Observing it, he applies his attention to the formation. Therefore for *dhāraṇā*, a yogi has to know that the key practice is not concentration but is rather, the technique for surcharging the subtle body. What is that technique? It is *prāṇāyāma* and *pratyāhara*, which are the 4th and 5th stages of yoga, namely breath surcharging and sensual energy withdrawal.

Once the practice of *dhāraṇā* becomes established, the yogi moves on to *dhyāna* or *abhidhyāyan*, which is discussed in this verse. In *dhyāna*, the yogi drops his effort to link his will to the concentration force. He does this because he finds that after repeatedly linking his attention, it stays linked all by itself without any effort on his part. This effortless linkage with the concentration force, is appreciated by him, because it means that he is relieved from having to apply his will to the concentration force. He can then go deeply into the inner world.

Once he practiced *dhyāna* for sometime, he progresses into *samādhi* which is even deeper in the sense that in *samādhi* he is effortlessly conveyed into the linkage of his attention with the concentration force for long periods of time. This is why a yogi may instruct his disciple or the person watching his body, to bring it out of *samādhi* after a certain number of minutes, hours or days. Interestingly it is said in the *Mahābhārata* that Arjuna stayed in *samādhi* for nearly a year. That is quite amazing but it may be that he used to enter long samadhis during that year and did not necessarily stay in *samādhi* every second of the day.

Those persons who badgered me about yoga practice and about concentration and *samādhi* may get some clarification in this commentary. Apart from understanding what *dhyāna* is, one must also understand the idea conveyed about imagining the spiritual form of *Śrī* Krishna on the basis of seeing the Deity form in the temple. Such imagining is not the technique suggested in this verse. This practice has hardly anything to do with the Deity Form in the temple, except that after hearing of the Deity Form, one may develop the desire to do this practice. One cannot use the image of the Deity Form to develop this practice. That will not work for this. One has to drop all imagined images, even sacred ones. But one may get the impetus to practice after seeing the Deity Form in the temple. Then one has to take up the yoga austerities described by *Śrī* Krishna to Uddhava.

There are supernatural forms of the Lord which come into this world for special missions. These are not spiritual forms but these supernatural forms are capable of miraculous activities. Some of these are four-handed forms. Some are two-handed or six or eight-handed. Usually when these forms are seen in the supernatural worlds, they are four-handed. Arjuna for instance, requested that *Śrī* Krishna would allow the vision of a four-handed form but what Arjuna saw was the spiritual body which is higher than a supernatural form. When Arjuna saw the Universal Form which had thousands of arms, that was a supernatural and not spiritual form. There are two aspects to these forms which one should understand. The first is that these forms have a supernatural presentation of themselves and secondly they have spiritual forms as well. The supernatural one is not spiritual but it is so close in vibration to what is spiritual, as to be almost indistinguishable from it. In either case, when a devotee or yogi sees these forms, he has to be in a higher body. He must be in a supernatural body or he must be in his own spiritual form *(svarūpa).* Arjuna for instance is usually depicted in paintings as seeing the Universal Form and the four-armed spiritual form through physical eyes but that is not possible. The physical body cannot see such forms. Arjuna would have been transferred into his supernatural or spiritual form to perceive that, otherwise he could not view it. God cannot make a devotee see a spiritual form through material eyes. But God may energize a devotee's existence to such a degree, that the devotee experiences his own spiritual form and then sees spiritually.

Śrī Krishna in some of the earlier verses of this chapter, explained about the yogi's linkage of his attention to the concentration force of various levels of high energy, either high material energy or spiritual energy. When the yogi's psyche is surcharged sufficiently, and he is transferred to higher planes of consciousness, he observes certain concentration forces or focused forces on those planes, and he links to these or as in this verse, his attention is effortlessly linked to these.

If he is on the plane where the supernatural form or divine forms of *Śrī* Krishna are existing, he will see those forms, which are adorned with the *Śrīvatsa* curl of hair, with a weapon like a club or disc, with a banner, an umbrella of sorts, a chowry fan and other paraphernalia. When this happens on a consistent basis, the yogi becomes unconquerable. No one interferes with him, because there exudes from his presence an infallible nature. A momentary connection with the supernatural or spiritual plane, does not give the yogi the infallible radiance. Only consistent contact produces that.

उपासकस्य माम् एवं
योग-धारणया मुनेः ।
सिद्धयः पूर्व-कथिता
उपतिष्ठन्त्य् अशेषतः ॥१०.३१॥

upāsakasya mām evaṁ
yoga-dhāraṇayā muneḥ
siddhayaḥ pūrva-kathitā
upatiṣṭhanty aśeṣataḥ (10.31)

upāsakasya — of one who is worshiping; mām — me; evam — thus; yoga-dhāranayā = yoga – yoga + dhāranayā — by linking the attention with the concentration energy; muneḥ — of a yogi philosopher; siddhayaḥ — mystic skills; pūrva — before; kathitā = kathitāh — mentioned; upatiṣṭhanty = upatisthanti — come, are manifested; aśeṣatah — in full measure.

Translation

Thus, to the yogi philosopher who worships Me by yogic linkage of the attention with the concentration force, the mystic skills mentioned before, are manifested in their full measure. (10.31)

Commentary:

This is a blessing of *Śrī* Krishna upon all sincere yogi devotees. As they develop, all mystic skills will be manifested in their psyches. Such yogi devotees should not aspire for the mystic skills but should focus on the practice. Just by practice, each of the various mystic skills will develop automatically. They would not be a distraction but would aid the yogi in getting more firmly situated in higher stages.

जितेन्द्रियस्य दान्तस्य
जित-श्वासात्मनो मुनेः ।
मद्-धारणां धारयतः
का सा सिद्धिः सु-दुर्लभा ॥ १०.३२ ॥

jitendriyasya dāntasya
jita-śvāsātmano muneḥ
mad-dhāraṇāṁ dhārayataḥ
kā sā siddhiḥ su-durlabhā (10.32)

jitendriyasya — of one whose sensual energies are subdued; dāntasya — of one who is disciplined; jita – is controlled; śvāsātmano = śvāsa — breath + ātmano (ātmanah) — the self; muneḥ — of the yogi philosopher; mad = mat — on me; dhāraṇām — the linking of the attention to the concentration force; dhārayataḥ — one who effortlessly links his attention to a higher concentration force; kā — what; sā — that; siddhiḥ — mystic skill; su-durlabhā — very difficult to achieve.

Translation

What mystic skill is very difficult to achieve for the yogi philosopher whose sensual energies are subdued, who is disciplined, who controlled his breath and psyche, who linked his attention to the concentration force which is connected to Me, and who effortlessly links his attention to a higher concentration force. (10.32)

Commentary:

This concludes the issue of the life of a yogi philosopher. That can be explained by a verse from the *Bhagavad Gītā*:

tapasvibhyo'dhiko yogī jñānibhyo'pi mato'dhikaḥ
karmibhyaścādhiko yogī tasmādyogī bhavārjuna
yoginām api sarveṣāṁ madgatenāntarātmanā
śraddhāvānbhajate yo māṁ sa me yuktatamo mataḥ

The yogi is superior to other types of ascetics; he is also considered to be superior to the masters of philosophical theory, and the yogi is better than the ritual performers. Hence, be a yogi, Arjuna.

Of all yogis, the one who is attracted to Me with his soul, who worships Me with full faith, is regarded as being most devoted to Me. (B.G. 6.46-47)

अन्तरायान् वदन्त्य् एता
युञ्जतो योगम् उत्तमम् ।
मया सम्पद्यमानस्य
काल-क्षपण-हेतवः ॥ १०.३३ ॥

antarāyān vadanty etā
yuñjato yogam uttamam
mayā sampadyamānasya
kāla-kṣapaṇa-hetavaḥ (10.33)

antarāyān — obstacles; vadanty = vadanti — they say, the authoritive yogis say; etā = etāh — these (mystic perfections); yuñjato = yuñjatah — of one who habitually practices linking of the attention with higher concentration forces; yogam — yoga achievement; uttamam — highest; mayā — with me; sampadyamānasya = sampadya - spiritual well being + mānasya — of one whose mind is focused; kāla — time; kṣapaṇa — waste; hetavaḥ — cause.

Translation

The authoritative yogis say that these mystic perfections are obstacles. For one who habitually practices the linking of the attention with higher concentration forces, which are connected to Me, and who seeks the higher achievement, and whose mind is focused on spiritual well-being, they are a waste of time. (10.33)

Commentary:

If a yogi pushes on with practice and if he adheres as a student to advanced yogis, he will not be victimized by mystic perfections. The perfections will manifest as one advances. That cannot be stopped. But it is the yogi's misuse of the perfections that causes ruination. If he adheres to studentship under a great teacher, he will not be distracted.

जन्मौषधि-तपो-मन्त्रैर्
यावतीर् इह सिद्धयः ।
योगेनाप्नोति ताः सर्वा
नान्यैर् योग-गतिं व्रजेत् ॥१०.३४॥

janmauṣadhi-tapo-mantrair
yāvatīr iha siddhayaḥ
yogenāpnoti tāḥ sarvā
nānyair yoga-gatiṁ vrajet (10.34)

janmausadhi = janma — birth + ausadhi — herbs, drugs; tapo = tapah — austerities; mantrair = mantraiḥ — by special sounds; yāvatīr = yāvatīḥ — as much as; iha — in this world; siddhayaḥ — mystic skills; yogenāpnoti = yogena — by yoga practice + āpnoti — attain; tāḥ — those; sarvā = sarvāḥ — all; nānyair = nānyaiḥ = na — not + anyaiḥ — by other methods; yoga-gatim — objective of yoga; vrajet — one can achieve.

Translation

By yoga practice, one achieves all those mystic skills, which may otherwise be gained by birth, herbs or drugs, austerities, and special chants, but one cannot achieve the actual objective of yoga by those other means. (10.34)

Commentary:

In their commentary, to this verse, *Hridayānanda dās Gosvāmī* and *Gopīparanadhana dās Adhikārī*, followed closely in the footsteps of *Śrīla* A.C. *Bhaktivedānta Swāmī Prabhupāda*. They gave *yogena* as devotional service. They have consistently done so in the commentary by conveniently translating *yoga* as devotional service when it suits the purpose of the *sampradāya* and by translating *yoga* as yoga when they want to give it a negative connation. I am also in that *sampradāya* but I chose to follow an instruction of Lord *Balarāma* of my *Śrī Śrī* Krishna-*Balarāma* Deities. He advised that I not take the course of *Śrīla Bhaktivedānta Swāmī* in whitewashing and bombasting yoga nor in conveniently translating it as devotional service.

In the līla of *Śrī* Chaitanya Mahaprabhu, He, Lord Chaitanya, objected to these changes in the *Śrīmad Bhāgavatam*. There is the incidence in the *Śrī* Chaitanya Charitamrita, when devotees wanted to change the word *mukti* to *bhakti*. Lord Chaitanya even though he discouraged yoga, and extolled *bhakti* or devotion, objected and prohibited changes. In any case, as it is today, His instruction was neglected. That was the development in the *sampradāya*.

In the gradual progression which we faced in the translations and commentaries, given to us by *Śrīla Bhaktivedānta Swāmī*, the *Śrīmad Bhāgavatam* and the *Śrīmad Bhagavad Gītā* was adjusted in such a way as to blacklist yoga, even when Lord Krishna recommended and clearly explained and encouraged it. I was instructed by Lord *Balarāma* not to discourage yoga.

If one studies the Sanskrit of this verse, one will not be able to honestly come up with any word which is the equivalent of devotion or devotional service. This verse concerns a comparison regarding two types of yoga practice. In both cases, yoga is involved. In one case, the yoga is used to develop mystic skills which may otherwise be acquired by taking birth in a species or by taking herbs or drugs or by performing other types of austerities like fasting, staying awake for longer than necessary and by special chants or invocations.

In the second case, the yoga is used for the highest objective of yoga which was mentioned in the previous verse as *sampadya* or spiritual well being.

If yoga is used for the spiritual well-being, it is approved by Lord Krishna and we have His blessings, but if it is used merely for acquiring mystic skills, it will cause wastage of time, distraction and delay.

A person can work for birth in the angelic world by performing pious activities, or by ruling over human beings in a just and protective way. He does not have to do yoga for this. One can take drugs or herbs and experience subtle perception or enter into trances to see the past or future. He does not have to perform yoga for that. One can perform austerities like fasting, abstaining from sleep, remaining soaked in cold water during winter, for the purpose of getting special psychic abilities and to develop powers for ruling over others and for having one's desire prevail. Mahatma Gandhi for instance, fasted and brought British authorities to their knees. Nelson Mandella endured imprisonment and developed the determination to rid South Africa of White rule. One can chant special sounds or learn how to make invocations to achieve certain ends, but only by yoga *(yogena)*, can a person reach spiritual perfection and develop spiritual well-being permanently *(sampadya)*.

सर्वासाम् अपि सिद्धीना
हेतुः पतिर् अहं प्रभुः ।
अहं योगस्य साङ्ख्यस्य
धर्मस्य ब्रह्म-वादिनाम् ॥ १०.३५ ॥

sarvāsām api siddhīnāṁ
hetuḥ patir ahaṁ prabhuḥ
ahaṁ yogasya sāṅkhyasya
dharmasya brahma-vādinām (10.35)

sarvāsām — of all; api — also; siddhīnām — of the mystic skills; hetuḥ — cause; patir = patiḥ — master; aham — I; prabhuḥ — Lord; aham — I; yogasya — of yoga; sāṅkhyasya — of the Sāṅkhya philosophical analysis; dharmasya — of righteous duty; brahma-vādinām — of the teachers of spirituality.

Translation

I am the cause, the master and Lord of all mystic skills. I am the Lord of Yoga and of the Sāṅkhya philosophical analysis, of righteous duty and of the teachers of spirituality. (10.35)

Commentary:

Śrī Krishna declared Himself as the cause of the mystic skills. This answers a question Uddhava asked in the beginning of this chapter:

śrī-uddhava uvāca
kayā dhāraṇayā kā svit kathaṁ vā siddhir acyuta
kati vā siddhayo brūhi yogināṁ siddhi-do bhavān

The deserving Uddhava said: By what linking of the attention to a higher concentration force, does a mystic skill develop, O infallible Krishna? How many mystic skills are they? Tell me of it. Are You the giver of such skills to the yogis? (U.G. 10.2)

Śrī Krishna declared that He is the Lord even of the teachers of spirituality, the *brahma-vādinām*. Without naming *Śrī* Krishna, *Śrī Patañjali Mahārṣi* described the Supreme Lord as the teacher of the ancient instructors:

sa eṣaḥ pūrveṣām api guruḥ kālena anavacchedāt

He, that particular person, being unconditioned by time, is the guru even of the ancient teachers, the authorities from before. (Yoga sūtras l.26)

अहम् आत्मान्तरो बाह्यो
ऽनावृतः सर्व-देहिनाम् ।
यथा भूतानि भूतेषु
बहिर् अन्तः स्वयं तथा ॥ १०.३६ ॥

aham ātmāntaro bāhyo
'nāvṛtaḥ sarva-dehinām
yathā bhūtāni bhūteṣu
bahir antaḥ svayaṁ tathā (10.36)

aham — I; ātmāntaro = ātmā — self + āntaraḥ — interiorised; bāhyo = bāhyaḥ – outside; 'nāvṛtaḥ = anāvṛtah — unconfined; sarva – all; dehinām — of the embodied being; yathā — as; bhūtāni — the elements; bhūteṣu — among the living beings; bahir = bahih — exterior; antaḥ — interior; svayam — myself; tathā — in the same way.

Translation

I am the interiorized self of all embodied being. Being unconfined, I am outside of the bodies as well. As the elements are inside and outside the living beings, so am I. (10.36)

Commentary:

The limited selves, the *ātmas*, are here contrasted to the Supreme Being and to material nature. This is perceived in the advanced stages of practice as indicated in many verses of this chapter.

CHAPTER 11*

The Self of All Creatures**

Terri Stokes-Pineda Art

aham ātmoddhavāmīṣāṁ bhūtānāṁ suhṛd īśvaraḥ
ahaṁ sarvāṇi bhūtāni teṣām sthity-udbhavāpyayah

O Uddhava, I am the self of all these creatures, their friend and Lord. I am the cause of all creatures and of their living condition, birth and death. (Uddhava Gītā 11.9)

* Śrīmad Bhāgavatam Canto 11, Chapter 16
** Translator's selected chapter title.

श्री-उद्धव उवाच
त्व ब्रह्म परमं साक्षाद्
अनाद्य्-अन्तम् अपावृतम् ।
सर्वेषाम् अपि भावानां
त्राण-स्थित्य्-अप्ययोद्भवः ॥११.१॥

śrī-uddhava uvāca
tvaṁ brahma paramaṁ sākṣād
anādy-antam apāvṛtam
sarveṣām api bhāvānāṁ
trāṇa-sthity-apyayodbhavaḥ (11.1)

śrī-uddhava – the deserving Uddhava; uvāca — said; tvam — you; brahma — spirit; paramam — supreme; sākṣā = sākṣāt — directly, in person; anādy-antam = anādi-antam — without beginning or ending; apāvṛtam — unlimited; sarveṣām — of all; api — even; bhāvānām — of the beings; trāṇa — protector; sthithy = sthiti — maintainer; apyayodbhavaḥ = apyaya — destroyer + udbhavaḥ — creator.

Translation

The deserving Uddhava said: You are the Supreme Spirit in Person, without beginning or ending, and unlimited. You are the protector, maintainer, destroyer and creator of all beings. (11.1)

Commentary:

Arjuna made a similar declaration about *Śrī* Krishna, after seeing the Universal Form. He said:

tvamādidevaḥ puruṣaḥ purāṇas tvamasya viśvasya paraṁ nidhānam
vettāsi vedyaṁ ca paraṁ ca dhāma tvayā tataṁ viśvamanantarūpa

You are the First God, the most ancient spirit. You are the knower, You are the supreme refuge of all the worlds. You are that which is to be known. You are the ultimate sanctuary. By You, the universe is pervaded, O Person of Infinite Form. (B.G. 11.38)

For those of us who do not perceive this directly, we should accept this statement of Uddhava at face value, based on the conviction that *Śrī* Krishna is the Person He claims to be. Until we get direct evidence, as did Arjuna in the perception of the Universal Form, we should without fanaticism, assume this belief.

उच्चावचेषु भूतेषु
दुर्ज्ञेयम् अकृतात्मभिः ।
उपासते त्वां भगवन्
याथा-तथ्येन ब्राह्मणाः ॥११.२॥

uccāvaceṣu bhūteṣu
durjñeyam akṛtātmabhiḥ
upāsate tvāṁ Bhagavān
yāthā-tathyena brāhmaṇāḥ (11.2)

uccāvaceṣu = ucca — superior + avacesu — in the inferior; bhūteṣu — in created beings; durjñeyam — difficult to know; akṛtātmabhiḥ = akrt – impious + ātmabhiḥ — with spirits; upāsate — they worship; tvām — you; Bhagavān — lord; yathā-tathyena — in fact; brāhmanāḥ — brahmins.

Translation

O Lord, the brahmins worship You as You are in the superior and inferior created beings, but for the impious souls, You are difficult to know. (11.2)

Commentary:

The impious souls do not have the insight required to perceive the influence of *Śrī* Krishna. Some pious persons see an all-pervading influence but they do not trace it to *Śrī* Krishna. But those who are impious are usually not inclined to believing in a Supreme Being, since such an idea implies being accountable to that Person for one's misbehavior.

येषु येषु च भूतेषु
भक्त्या त्वां परमर्षयः ।
उपासीनाः प्रपद्यन्ते
संसिद्धिं तद् वदस्व मे ॥ ११.३॥

yeṣu yeṣu ca bhūteṣu
bhaktyā tvāṁ paramarṣayaḥ
upāsīnāḥ prapadyante
saṁsiddhiṁ tad vadasva me (11.3)

yeṣu yeṣu — in which, in which; ca — and; bhūteṣu — in the created forms; bhaktyā — by devotion; tvām — you; paramarṣayaḥ — highest yogi sages; upāsīnāḥ — worshiping; prapadyante — achieve; saṁsiddhim — perfection; tad = tat — that; vadasva — tell; me — me.

Translation

Tell me, in which created forms, do the highest yogi sages worship You with devotion and thus achieve perfection? (11.3)

Commentary:

This relates directly to what Uddhava said in the previous verse regarding the recognition of *Śrī* Krishna or of His influence in the superior and inferior forms in the material world. Uddhava wanted to know how the highest yogi sages worship *Śrī* Krishna.

गूढश् चरसि भूतात्मा
भूतानां भूत-भावन ।
न त्वां पश्यन्ति भूतानि
पश्यन्तं मोहितानि ते ॥ ११.४॥

gūḍhaś carasi bhūtātmā
bhūtānāṁ bhūta-bhāvana
na tvāṁ paśyanti bhūtāni
paśyantaṁ mohitāni te (11.4)

gūdhaś = gūdhaḥ — hidden; carasi — you roam; bhūtātmā = bhūta – created beings + ātmā — self; bhūtānām — of the beings; bhūta-bhāvana — O originator of the beings; na — not; tvām — you; paśyanti — they see; bhūtāni — the created beings; pasyantam — one who sees; mohitāni — those who are bewildered; te — by you.

Translation

O You, originator of the beings, O self of the created beings, Who roam about hidden in all beings, those Who are bewildered by You, do not see You but see the created beings. (11.4)

Commentary:

If that bewilderment were removed, all the living beings would see the truth about the formation of the world. But this is wishful thinking. At all times, some living beings are bewildered, and cannot see spiritual truth. This is ongoing. Because of being harnessed to a sensual mechanism, which only allows perception of external forms, the living entity denies that there is a spiritual person, Who is the Cause of all causes.

याः काश् च भूमौ दिवि वै रसायां
विभूतयो दिक्षु महा-विभूते ।
ता मह्यम् आख्याह्य् अनुभावितास् ते
नमामि ते तीर्थ-पदाङ्घ्रि-पद्मम् ॥ ११.५॥

yāḥ kāś ca bhūmau divi vai rasāyāṁ
vibhūtayo dikṣu mahā-vibhūte
tā mahyam ākhyāhy anubhāvitās te
namāmi te tīrtha-padāṅghri-padmam (11.5)

yāh kāś = yāh kāḥ — what, what; ca — and; bhūmau — on earth; divi — in heaven; vai — indeed; rasāyām — in hellish dimensions; vibhūtayo = vibhūtayaḥ — wondrous manifestations; dikṣu — in the directions, everywhere; mahā-vibhūte — O superperson of wonderful forms; tā = tāḥ — those; mahyam — unto me; ākhyāhi — tell of; anubhāvitās = anubhāvitāḥ — manifested; te — by you; namāmi — I respectfully bow; te — your; tīrtha – shrine; pada — position, location; anghri-padmam — lotus feet.

Translation

O Person of wonderful forms, tell me of Your wondrous manifestations that are produced by You on earth, in heaven, in hellish locations and elsewhere. I respectfully bow to Your lotus feet in which the shrines are located. (11.5)

Commentary:

This request of Uddhava is similar to the request of Arjuna in the *Bhagavad-Gītā*, a request which caused *Śrī* Krishna to impart supernatural vision to Arjuna.

श्री-भगवान् उवाच
एवम् एतद् अहं पृष्टः
प्रश्नं प्रश्न-विदां वर ।
युयुत्सुना विनशने
सपत्नैर् अर्जुनेन वै ॥ ११.६ ॥

śrī-bhagavān uvāca
evam etad ahaṁ pṛṣṭaḥ
praśnaṁ praśna-vidāṁ vara
yuyutsunā vinaśane
sapatnair arjunena vai (11.6)

śrī-bhagavān – the blessed Lord; uvāca — said; evam — thus; etad = etat — this; aham — I; pṛṣṭaḥ — was asked; praśnam — question; praśna-vidām = praśna – inquiry + vidām — one who knows; vara — the best; yuyutsunā — by one who desires to fight; vinaśane — in a battle; sapatnair = sapatnaiḥ — with his enemies; arjunena — by Arjuna; vai — indeed.

Translation

The Blessed Lord said: O best of those who know how to inquire, I was asked this question by Arjuna who desired to fight his enemies in battle. (11.6)

Commentary:

The questions of Arjuna had to do with *Śrī* Krishna's wondrous manifestations in this world. It was to substantiate *Śrī* Krishna's claims about supremacy over the world.

ज्ञात्वा ज्ञाति-वधं गर्ह्यम्
अधर्मं राज्य-हेतुकम् ।
ततो निवृत्तो हन्ताहं
हतो ऽयम् इति लौकिकः ॥ ११.७ ॥

jñātvā jñāti-vadhaṁ garhyam
adharmaṁ rājya-hetukam
tato nivṛtto hantāhaṁ
hato 'yam iti laukikaḥ (11.7)

jñātvā — perceiving; jñāti — of his relations; vadham — killing; garhyam — a sin; adharma — sinful actions; rājya — kingdom; hetukam — for the sake of; tato = tatah — hence; nivṛtto = nivṛttaḥ — turning away; hantāham = hanta — killer + aham — I am; hato = hataḥ — killed; 'yam = ayam — this; iti — thus thinking; laukikaḥ — ordinary.

Translation

Perceiving the killing of his relatives for the sake of a kingdom, as an evil sinful act, thinking in an ordinary way, that "I am a killer. This person will be killed," he turned away. (11.7)

Commentary:

Arjuna's perception of himself as an agent of death, caused him to regret that he came to the battlefield. Upon self-analysis he found himself to be a condemned man, about to do the most heinous of crimes, that of murdering relatives. He became pathetic. He then appealed to Krishna for clarification.

Terri Stokes-Pineda Art

स तदा पुरुष-व्याघ्रो
युक्त्या मे प्रतिबोधितः ।
अभ्यभाषत माम् एवं
यथा त्वं रण-मूर्धनि ॥ ११.८॥

sa tadā puruṣa-vyāghro
yuktyā me pratibodhitaḥ
abhyabhāṣata mām evaṁ
yathā tvaṁ raṇa-mūrdhani (11.8)

sa = saḥ — he; tadā — then; puruṣa-vyāghro = puruṣa-vyāghraḥ — tiger among men; yuktyā — by analysis; me — by my; pratibodhitaḥ — intellectually aroused; abhyabhāṣata — spoke to; mām — to me; evam — thus; yathā — just as; tvam — you; raṇa — battle; mūrdhani — before.

Translation

Then, by My analysis, that tiger among men, was intellectually aroused. Thus before the battle he spoke to Me just as you do. (11.8)

Commentary:

For eight chapters of discourse in *Bhagavad-Gītā*, from chapter two through chapter nine, *Śrī* Krishna riled Arjuna with information about the soul, the Supreme Soul, this world, the social conditions here and the rules which are involved. Then Arjuna asked for direct evidence, something that he could perceive, something that would verify what *Śrī* Krishna said.

अहम् आत्मोद्धवामीषां
भूतानां सुहृद् ईश्वरः ।
अहं सर्वाणि भूतानि
तेषां स्थित्य्-उद्भवाप्ययः ॥ ११.९॥

aham ātmoddhavāmīṣāṁ
bhūtānāṁ suhṛd īśvaraḥ
ahaṁ sarvāṇi bhūtāni
teṣāṁ sthity-udbhavāpyayaḥ (11.9)

aham — I; ātmoddhavāmīṣāṁ = ātmā — self; uddhava — Uddhava + amīṣām — of these; bhūtānām — of the creatures; suhṛd = suhṛt — friend; īśvaraḥ — Lord; aham — I; sarvāṇi – all; bhūtāni — creatures; teṣām — of them; sthity = sthiti — living condition; udbhavāpyayah = udbhava — birth + apyayah — death.

Translation

O Uddhava, I am the self of all these creatures, their friend and Lord. I am the cause of all creatures and of their living condition, birth and death. (11.9)

Commentary:

These claims were made by *Śrī* Krishna to Arjuna except that Arjuna pressed forward for evidence and got the revelation of the Universal Form. Arjuna asked Krishna to reveal how it was possible to control the world in the most minute details.

अहं गतिर् गतिमतां
कालः कलयताम् अहम् ।
गुनाणां चाप्य् अहं साम्यं
गुणिन्य् औत्पत्तिको गुणः ॥ ११.१०॥

ahaṁ gatir gatimatāṁ
kālaḥ kalayatām aham
gunāṇāṁ cāpy ahaṁ sāmyaṁ
guṇiny autpattiko guṇaḥ (11.10)

aham — I; gatir = gatiḥ — objective; gatimatām — of those seeking progress; kālaḥ — time; kalayatām — of the conquers; aham — I; guṇānām — of the modes of material nature; capy = ca — and + api — even; aham — I; sāmyam — equilibrium; guṇiny = guṇini — in what has attributes; autpattiko = autpattikaḥ — basic part; guṇah — quality, aspect.

Translation

I am the objective of those seeking progress. I am time amongst the conquerors. Of the modes of material nature, I am their state of equilibrium. And in what has attributes, I am the basis. (11.10)

Commentary:

Arjuna asked *Śrī* Krishna about these matters and got a similar explanation. Arjuna asked:

kathaṁ vidyāmahaṁ yogiṁs tvāṁ sadā paricintayan
keṣu keṣu ca bhāveṣu cintyo'si bhagavanmayā

How will I know You, Mystic Master, O Yogi? Is it by constantly meditating? In what aspects of existence are You to be considered by Me, O Blessed Lord? (B.G. 10.17)

It is not easy to understand or to accept all the examples without proof, but with due reason some of these examples are plausible. If *Śrī* Krishna is the objective of everyone everywhere who seeks some type of progress, then it means that He causes all motivational force, regardless of whether these urges result in constructive or destructive actions. Thus in fact, only God can make such claims and only God can be responsible for the whole domain.

Time regulates the life, even of conquerors. Thus time stands over all as supreme and reduces all prowess to nothing, causing all rulers to lose their conquests. Time has absolutely no regard for anyone. In as much as it presents opportunities to somebody, it also deprives that person of the same facilities. Time can be trusted only to award and then to confiscate opportunities.

The state of material nature's equilibrium, is the supreme stage of that subtle energy, a stage in which all urges, and desires come to nil. It is a stage in which, a limited being cannot exercise objective perceptions. Only the Supreme Being has sufficient objectivity and power to adjust it.

गुणिनाम् अप्य् अहं सूत्रं
महतां च महान् अहम् ।
सूक्ष्माणाम् अप्य् अहं जीवो
दुर्जयानाम् अहं मनः ॥ ११.११ ॥

guṇinām apy ahaṁ sūtraṁ
mahatāṁ ca mahān aham
sūkṣmāṇām apy ahaṁ jīvo
durjayānām ahaṁ manaḥ (11.11)

guṇinām — among the influences of material nature; apy = api — also; aham — I; sūtram — the sexually-charged mundane potency; mahatām — of the vast things; ca — and; mahān — the total mundane potency in equilibrium; aham — I; sūkṣmāṇām — of the subtle things; apy = api — even; aham — I; jīvo = jīvaḥ — the individual soul; durjayānām — things difficult to subdue; aham — I; manaḥ — mind.

Translation

I am the subtle sexually-charged mundane potency. On the cosmic scale, I am the total mundane potency in equilibrium. Of subtle things, I am represented by the individual spirit. Of that which is difficult to subdue. I am represented by the mind. (11.11)

Commentary:

The influences of material nature bear down on us as clarifying power, enticing force and depressing energy. These forces abound everywhere in varying proportions. Besides these, there is the sexually-charged cosmic force, which is a concentrated combination of the three influences. In the material world, that force is supreme. On the cosmic level, it creates universes, and at the local scene, it causes reproduction of bodies. *Śrī* Krishna regarded that sexually-charged potency as His representative.

Greater however, than the *Sūtram* sexually-charged cosmic force is the total mundane potency in equilibrium. This is a static stage of material energy. It is its ultimate stage.

Of the subtle things, *Śrī* Krishna claimed identity with the spirits which are the most minute of things. They have the ability to inhabit the smallest life forms and even atomic energy. Of that which is difficult to subdue, *Śrī* Krishna identified with the mind, because it is the mind which consistently resists one's determination. And when the same mind is subdued, we attain liberation.

In speaking to Arjuna, *Śrī* Krishna did not mention the *Sūtram*. This is because He intended to teach Arjuna only *karma* yoga, how to apply yogic skills to political work. With Uddhava *Śrī* Krishna taught *jñāna* yoga and *bhakti* yoga.

हिरण्यगर्भो वेदानां
मन्त्राणां प्रणवस् त्रि-वृत्
अक्षराणाम् अ-कारो ऽस्मि ।
पदानि च्छन्दुसाम् अहम् ॥११.१२॥

hiraṇyagarbho vedānāṁ
mantrāṇāṁ praṇavas tri-vṛt
akṣarāṇām a-kāro 'smi
padāni cchandusām aham (11.12)

hiranyagarbho = hiranyagarbhaḥ — procreator Brahmā; vedānām — regarding the advocates of the Vedas; mantrānām — of the technical sounds; praṇavas = praṇavah — om sound; tri-vṛt — consisting of three; akṣarāṇām — of the letters; akāro = akāraḥ — letter a; 'smi = asmi — I am; padāni — three lined Gāyatrī hymn; chandasām — sacred poetry; aham — I.

Translation

Regarding the advocates of the Vedas, I am represented by Procreator Brahmā. Of the technical sounds, I am represented by Om, which consists of three letters. Of the letters, I am represented by A. Of sacred poetry, I am represented by the three-lined Gāyatrī hymn. (11.12)

Commentary:

This is a training for elementary Krishna Consciousness in how to relate everything to *Śrī* Krishna, how to remember His connection with everything. Arjuna was given this training as well.

इन्द्रो ऽहं सर्व-देवानां
वसूनाम् अस्मि हव्य-वाट् ।
आदित्यानाम् अहं विष्णू
रुद्राणां नील-लोहितः ॥११.१३॥

indro 'haṁ sarva-devānāṁ
vasūnām asmi havya-vāṭ
ādityānām ahaṁ viṣṇū
rudrāṇāṁ nīla-lohitaḥ (11.13)

indro = indrah — Indra; 'ham = aham — I; sarva – all; devānām — among the supernatural rulers; vasūnām — of the Vasus; asmi — I am; havya-vāt — of the carriers of oblations; ādityānām — of the sons of Aditi; aham — I; viṣṇū — Vishnu; Rudrānām — of the Rudras; nīla-lohitaḥ — Nilalohita Shiva.

Translation

Among the supernatural rulers, I am represented by Indra. Of the Vasus I am the oblation carrier. Of the sons of Aditi, I am Vishnu. Of the Rudras, I am Nīlalohita Shiva. (11.13)

Commentary:

These examples were explained to Arjuna. I commented on most of these examples at length in the *Bhagavad-Gītā Explained*, as well as in the *Kriyā Yoga Bhagavad-Gītā* and *Brahma Yoga Bhagavad Gītā.*

Nīlalohita is Lord Shiva. The son of *Aditi* is a divinity known as *Vāmanadeva*.

ब्रह्मर्षीणां भृगुर् अहं
राजर्षीणाम् अह मनुः ।
देवर्षीणां नारदो ऽह
हविर्धान्य् अस्मि धेनुषु ॥११.१४॥

brahmarṣīṇāṁ bhṛgur ahaṁ
rājarṣīṇām ahaṁ manuḥ
devarṣīṇāṁ nārado 'haṁ
havirdhāny asmi dhenuṣu (11.14)

brahmarṣīṇām — the spirit-realised yogi sages; bhṛgur = bhṛguḥ — Bhrigu; aham — I; rājarṣīṇām — among the sagely yogi kings; aham — I; manuh — Manu; devarṣīṇām — of the supernatural yogi sages; nārado = nāradaḥ — Nārada; 'haṁ = aham — I am; havirdhāny = havirdhānī — Kamadhenu cow; asmi — I am; dhenuṣu — among the cows.

Translation

Among the spiritually-realized yogi sages, I am Bhṛgu. Of the sagely yogi kings, I am represented by Manu. Of the supernatural yogi sages, I am represented by Nārada. Among the cows, I am represented by Kāmadhenu. (11.14)

Commentary:

The supernatural yogi sages are yogis who live unaffectedly in the heavenly planets. *Nārada* is the chief among them. He is the son of *Brahmā*, the Procreator. Among cows, *Śrī* Krishna represented Himself in *Kāmadhenu*, a wish-fulfilling cow of repute.

Of the sagely-yogi kings, those who are masters of *karma* yoga, as it was taught to Arjuna, *Śrī* Krishna identified Himself with *Manu*, who is also mentioned in the *Bhagavad-Gītā*.

The *brahma* rishis, are the yogi sages who mastered the science of spirituality and are perfectly realized. *Bhṛgu* is the most famous of these.

सिद्धेश्वराणां कपिलः
सुपर्णो ऽहं पतत्रिणाम् ।
प्रजापतीनां दक्षो ऽहं
पितॄणाम् अहम् अर्यमा ॥ ११.१५ ॥

siddheśvarāṇāṁ kapilaḥ
suparṇo 'haṁ patatriṇām
prajāpatīnāṁ dakṣo 'haṁ
pitṝṇām aham aryamā (11.15)

siddheśvarāṇām — among the lordly perfected yogis; kapilaḥ — Kapila; suparṇo = suparṇah — Garuda; 'ham = aham — I; patatriṇām — among the birds; prajāpatīnām — among the procreators; dakṣo = dakṣaḥ — Dakṣa; 'ham = aham — I; pitṝṇām — among the departed spirits; aham — I; aryamā — Aryama.

Translation

Among the lordly perfected yogis, I am Kapila. Of the birds, I am represented by Garuḍa. Among the procreators, I am represented by Dakṣa. Among the departed spirits, I am identified with Aryamā (11.15)

Commentary:

Kapila is the authority of the *Sāṅkhya* analysis and is a *mahāyogīn* of repute. His activities are described in the third canto of the *Śrīmad Bhāgavatam.* This dialogue between *Śrī* Krishna and Uddhava occurs in the eleventh Canto of that text. Kapila Muni, a divine being, is rated as an incarnation of *Śrī* Krishna. Yoga and the *Sāṅkhya* analysis are closely linked. It is from the *Sāṅkhya* philosophy that we get the motivation to pursue yoga.

Garuḍa is a bird man, as described in the Vedic literature. He serves as the carrier of Lord Vishnu. There are many procreators, but the most important one is *Brahmā*. There is *Manu*, who had the required potency and sense of purpose. He cooperated with *Brahmā* to produce many life forms. There was *Dakṣa*. He was hostile to renunciation. He did not get along with *Nārada*, who personified detachment and spiritual realization.

Among the departed spirits, a supernatural person called *Aryamā* supervises their activities and helps to determine the families in which they would acquire new physical bodies.

मा विद्ध्य् उद्धव दैत्यानां
प्रह्लादम् असुरेश्वरम् ।
सोमं नक्षत्रौषधीनां
धनेशं यक्ष-रक्षसाम् ॥ ११.१६ ॥

māṁ viddhy uddhava daityānāṁ
prahlādam asureśvaram
somaṁ nakṣatrauṣadhīnāṁ
dhaneśaṁ yakṣa-rakṣasām (11.16)

mām — me; viddhy = viddhi — know; uddhava — Uddhava; daityānām — among the sons of Diti; prahlādam — Prahlād; asureśvaram = asura – opponents of the supernatural rulers + īśvaram

— king; somam — Soma, the moon; nakṣatrauṣadhīnām = nakṣatra – star + oṣadhīnām — among the herbs; dhaneśam = dhana – treasures of the earth + īśam — lord, patron deity; yaksa-raksasam — Yaksas and Raksasas.

Translation

Among the sons of Diti, know me, O Uddhava to be represented by Prahlād, the king of those who are inimical to the supernatural rulers. Among the stars and herbs, I am represented by the moon. Of the Yakshas and Rakshasas races, I am represented by Kubera, the patron deity of the earth's resources. (11.16)

Commentary:

Prahlād is a great devotee of Lord Krishna's parallel divinity named *Nārasińgha*. He is a leonine human form incarnation of divinity. *Prahlād* has enduring fame. *Śrī* Krishna posited Himself as being represented by the moon. The moon is not as big as the stars, but from our perspective, the moon is more prominent and effectual.

In the Vedic history, the Yakshas and Rakshas are considered to be barbaric races. Kubera, though a Yaksha, is the patron deity of natural resources.

ऐरावतं गजेन्द्राणा
यादसां वरुणं प्रभुम् ।
तपतां द्युमतां सूर्यं
मनुष्याणां च भू-पतिम् ॥११.१७॥

airāvataṁ gajendrāṇāṁ
yādasāṁ varuṇaṁ prabhum
tapatāṁ dyumatāṁ sūryaṁ
manuṣyāṇāṁ ca bhū-patim (11.17)

airāvatam — Airavat; gajendrāṇām — among lordly elephants; yādasām — among the aquatics; varunaṁ — Varuna; prabhum — lord, master; tapatām — of that which radiates heat; dyumatām — of the illuminators; sūryam — sun; manuṣyānām — among human beings; ca — and; bhū-patim — king.

Translation

Among the lordly elephants, I am represented by Airāvat. Of the aquatics, I am represented by Varuṇa. Of that which radiates heat and of the illuminators, I am represented by the Sun. And of human beings, I am represented by the king. (11.17)

Commentary:

Vedic literature lists *Airāvat* as a supernatural elephant which lives on heavenly planets and which serves as the mount of King Indra, the ruler of the angelic people. Thus *Śrī* Krishna identified Himself with this celestial animal. *Varuṇa* is listed in the Vedic pantheon as the ruler of the seas. And the sun, of course, is regarded by all as the chief source of heat and illumination.

उच्चैःश्रवास् तुरङ्गाणां
धातूनाम् अस्मि काञ्चनम् ।
यमः संयमतां चाहम्
सर्पाणाम् अस्मि वासुकिः ॥११.१८॥

uccaiḥśravās turaṅgāṇāṁ
dhātūnām asmi kāñcanam
yamaḥ saṁyamatāṁ cāham
sarpāṇām asmi vāsukiḥ (11.18)

uccaihśravās = uccaihśravāh — Uccaihsrava; turaṅgāṇām — among the horses; dhātūnām — among the metals; asmi — I am; kāñcanam — gold; yamaḥ — Yama; saṁyamatām — among the disciplinarians; caham = ca — and + aham — I; sarpāṇām — among the serpents; asmi — I am; vāsukiḥ — Vāsuki.

Translation

Among the horses I am represented by Uccaiḥśravā. Of the metals I am represented by gold. And among the disciplinarians, I am represented by Yama. Among the serpent I am represented by Vāsuki. (11.18)

Commentary:

Ucchaihśravā is a supernatural horse. The Vedic literature accredits this animal as a mount of King *Indra*, of the angelic world. Of metals *Śrī* Krishna selected gold, a metal which does not tarnish. Among the disciplinarians, *Yama*, the judge of the sinfully-departed souls, is the most exacting. Among the serpents, *Vāsuki*, is the largest.

नागेन्द्राणाम् अनन्तो ऽह
मृगेन्द्रः शृङ्गि-दंष्ट्रिणाम् ।
आश्रमाणाम् अहं तुर्यो
वर्णानां प्रथमो ऽनघ ॥ ११.१९ ॥

nāgendrāṇām ananto 'haṁ
mṛgendraḥ śṛṅgi-daṁṣṭriṇām
āśramāṇām ahaṁ turyo
varṇānāṁ prathamo 'nagha (11.19)

nāgendrānām — of the ruling many-hooded snakes; ananto = anantah — Ananta; 'haṁ = aham — I; mṛgendrah — the king of the beasts, the lion; śṛṅgi-daṁṣṭriṇām — of animals with sharp horns and teeth; āśramāṇām — among the life styles; aham — I; turyo = turyah — the fourth stage; varṇānām — of the occupational categories; prathamo = prathamah — the foremost type; 'nagha = anagha — O sinless one.

Translation

Of the ruling many-hooded snakes, I am represented by Ananta. Of animals with horns and teeth. I am by the lion, the king of the beasts. Of the lifestyles, I am represented by the fourth stage. Of the occupational categories, I am the foremost type, O sinless one. (11.19)

Commentary:

Ananta is a supernatural many-hooded snake, which according to the Vedic pantheon, is the king of such creatures. Among the animals, *Śrī* Krishna identified Himself with the lion, the king of the beasts. Of lifestyles, He selected the fourth stage, that of full renunciation for the purpose of contemplating and achieving spiritual realization. Of the occupational categories, *Śrī* Krishna picked out the foremost which is that of the brahmins, who educate human society and cultivate spiritual realization.

तीर्थानां स्रोतसा गङ्गा
समुद्रः सरसाम् अहम् ।
आयुधानां धनुर् अहं
त्रिपुर-घ्नो धनुष्मताम् ॥ ११.२० ॥

tīrthānāṁ srotasāṁ gaṅgā
samudraḥ sarasām aham
āyudhānāṁ dhanur ahaṁ
tripura-ghno dhanuṣmatām (11.20)

tirthānām — shrines; srotasām — among streams; gaṅgā — Ganges River; samudraḥ — the ocean; sarasām — among the reservoirs; aham — I; āyudhānām — among weapons; dhanur = dhanuh — the bow; aham — I; tripura-ghno = tripura-ghnah — the destroyer of the three cities; dhanuṣmatām — of those who wield the bow.

Translation

Among the streams which are regarded as shrines, I am represented by the Ganges River. Among the reservoirs of water, I am regarded as the ocean. Of the weapons, I am represented by the bow. And of those who wield the bow, I am present as Lord Shiva, the destroyer of the three cities. (11.20)

Commentary:

Even though there are other rivers, which are comparable to the Ganges, these rivers are not in India. Rivers like the Amazon and the Nile have a similar reputation in South America and

North Africa respectively. In India, the Ganges is considered to be the most important river. The Ganges is venerated by millions of Hindus. Its reputation has stood the test of time.

Of the reservoirs of water, none is as large as the Pacific Ocean. Among the weapons, *Śrī* Krishna identified with the bow which was a prominent weapon in His time. In the modern world, the firearm supersedes all ancient armaments. *Śrī* Krishna identified Himself with the destroyer of the three cities. That is Lord Shiva who is known as *Tripurāri*.

धिष्ण्यानाम् अस्म्य् अहं मेरुर्
गहनानां हिमालयः ।
वनस्पतीनाम् अश्वत्थ
ओषधीनाम् अहं यवः ॥ ११.२१ ॥

dhiṣṇyānām asmy ahaṁ merur
gahanānāṁ himālayaḥ
vanaspatīnām aśvattha
oṣadhīnām ahaṁ yavaḥ (11.21)

dhiṣṇyānām — of the dimensional regions; asmy = asmi — am; aham — I; merur = meruḥ — Meru; gahanānām — of the inaccessible places; himālayah — Himalaya; vanaspatīnām — of the trees; aśvattha — banyan tree; oṣadhīnām — of the annual plants; aham — I; yavaḥ — barley.

Translation

I am represented by Meru among the dimensional regions. Of the inaccessible places. I am represented by the Himalayas; Of trees, the banyan; of the annual plants, the barley. (11.21)

Commentary:

These comparisons show that *Śrī* Krishna selected the best of everything, the foremost, to be representative of Himself. This is training in Krishna Consciousness, using the ordinary and extraordinary facets of existence.

पुरोधसां वसिष्ठो ऽहं
ब्रह्मिष्ठानां बृहस्पतिः ।
स्कन्दो ऽहं सर्व-सेनान्याम्
अग्रण्यां भगवान् अजः ॥ ११.२२ ॥

purodhasāṁ vasiṣṭho 'haṁ
brahmiṣṭhānāṁ bṛhaspatiḥ
skando 'haṁ sarva-senānyām
agraṇyāṁ bhagavān ajaḥ (11.22)

purodhasām — of the priests; vasiṣṭho = vasiṣṭhah — Vasiṣṭha; 'ham = aham — I; brahmiṣṭhānām — of those who are situated in spiritual realisation; bṛhaspatiḥ — Bṛhaspati; skando = skandah — Skanda; 'ham = aham — I; sarva – all; senānyām — of the military commanders; agraṇyām — among the pioneers; bhagavān — one who is divinely endowed; ajaḥ — Brahmā.

Translation

Of the priests, I am represented by Vasiṣṭha. Of those who are situated in spiritual realization, I am represented by Bṛhaspati. Of the military commanders, I am Skanda. Of the pioneers, I am represented by the divinely-endowed Brahmā. (11.22)

Commentary:

Brahmā is here addressed as *Bhagavān*, an honorary title meaning a person who has complete facility by virtue of natural mystic power. *Brahmā* is the ultimate pioneer. According to the Vedic literature, he produced the planets and creatures.

Skanda, the son of Lord Shiva, otherwise known as *Karttikeya* or *Kumāra*, is said to be the military commander of the angelic hosts. *Bṛhaspati* is said to be the person with the most knowledge and realization in matters of brahman spiritual reality. This *Bṛhaspati* serves as the chief priest in the heavenly world. *Vasiṣṭha* Rishi is a renown priest from the time of Lord *Rāma*.

यज्ञानां ब्रह्म-यज्ञो ऽहं
व्रतानाम् अविहिंसनम् ।
वाय्व्-अग्न्य्-अर्काम्बु-वाग्-आत्मा
शुचीनाम् अप्य् अहं शुचिः ॥ ११.२३ ॥

yajñānāṁ brahma-yajño 'haṁ
vratānām avihiṁsanam
vāyv-agny-arkāmbu-vāg-ātmā
śucīnām apy ahaṁ śuciḥ (11.23)

yajñānām — of religious ceremonies and disciplines; brahma-yajño = brahma-yajñaḥ — the teaching and reciting of the Veda; aham — I; vratānām — of the vows; avihiṁsanam — nonviolence; vāyv = vāyu — wind; agny = agni — fire; arkāmbu — sun; vāg = vāk — speech; ātmā — spirit; śucīnām — of the cleansing agents; apy = api — also; aham — I; śuciḥ — cleanliness.

Translation

Of the religious ceremonies and disciplines, I am the teaching and recitation of the Vedas. Of the vows, I am represented by non-violence. Of the cleansing agents, I am represented by the wind, the fire, the sun, water, speech and the spirit itself. I am represented by cleanliness. (11.23)

Commentary:

The hardest vow to keep is to be sincerely nonviolent. This is different from non-violence for political purposes or for upholding pacifist principles. Non-violence means not to do harm to any creature, but that does not mean that it applies only to the physical bodies. Those who feel that nonviolence applies only to physical bodies, do not understand much about it. A living being is not just his material body nor even his emotional self.

Śrī Krishna is the supreme teacher regarding nonviolence. Thus if we disagree with him or with some of the things which He did in His life, it means that we do not understand non-violence.

In the time of *Śrī* Krishna, the teaching and recitation of the Vedas, was considered to be the foremost occupation. However, that society was structured. Those of the brahmin caste, were mostly persons who were born in brahmin families. They had a set of duties, the foremost of which was to teach and recite the Vedas and to engage in worship ceremonies.

Of the cleansing agents, Krishna selected the wind, the fire, the sun, the water, speech and the spirit itself. He said that cleanliness represented Him.

योगानाम् आत्म-सरोधो
मन्त्रो ऽस्मि विजिगीषताम् ।
आन्वीक्षिकी कौशलानां
विकल्पः ख्याति-वादिनाम् ॥ ११.२४ ॥

yogānām ātma-saṁrodho
mantro 'smi vijigīṣatām
ānvīkṣikī kauśalānāṁ
vikalpaḥ khyāti-vādinām (11.24)

yogānām — of the eight stages of yoga; ātma – self; saṁrodh = saṁrodhaḥ — complete restraint; mantro = mantraḥ — policy; 'smi = asmi — I; vijigīsatām — of those aspiring for victory; ānvīkṣikī — discriminating spirit from matter; kauśalānām — of the types of discernment; vikalpaḥ — diversity of opinion; khyāti – in hypothesis; vādinām — of those who specialise.

Translation

Of the stages of yoga, I am represented by complete restraint of the psyche. Of those aspiring for victory, I am represented by policy. Of the types of discernment, I am represented by the discrimination between spirit and matter. Of those who specialize in hypothesis, I am diversity of opinion. (11.24)

Commentary:

Ātma-samrodho is the complete restraint of the psyche. This is its restraint from engaging with the material energy. This is known as *samādhi*. There are different types of *samādhi* and differing stages of its practice. By stipulating *ātma-samrodho*, *Śrī* Krishna singled out the highest or deepest stage of that practice.

Policy or diplomacy is the superior method of politics. Sometimes it becomes necessary to discard it and substitute warfare. For instance, the Pandavas who were led by the just Prince *Yudhiṣţhira*, tried to enact a policy with their rival cousins. When they were unable to, they adopted a militant stance and that led to warfare. Even in such cases, however, when all is said and done, the victor has to develop some policy to rule subjects and some diplomacy to coordinate with foreign governments. In householder life, there is also ample opportunity to develop policy between the husband and wife and between the parents and children.

Since this is so essential in all phases of social life, *Śrī* Krishna singled it out as His representative. In this way He trained Uddhava in how to be Krishna Conscious in day-to-day affairs. This training should be absorbed by us.

Discernment is required in life. Even animals must discern one thing from the other. However the human beings are allowed a more advanced intellect. They can investigate the difference between spirit and matter. The animals and even the plants also have intellect. In fact, their intellect is just as proficient as ours but their bodies do not allow its full usage. In the human body, the intellect can reach its full capacity. *Śrī* Krishna identified Himself with the type of intellectual discrimination that reveals the soul to the soul, the distinction between spirit and matter.

Of those who specialize in hypothesis, *Śrī* Krishna identified Himself with diversity of opinion.

Wherever there is philosophy, there are differences of opinion. Every person is biased in a certain way.

स्त्रीणां तु शतरूपाहं
पुसां स्वायम्भुवो मनुः ।
नारायणो मुनीनां च
कुमारो ब्रह्मचारिणाम् ॥११.२५॥

strīṇāṁ tu śatarūpāhaṁ
puṁsāṁ svāyambhuvo manuḥ
nārāyaṇo munīnāṁ ca
kumāro brahmacāriṇām (11.25)

strīṇām — among ladies; tu — but; śatarūpāhaṁ = śatarūpā — Śatarūpā + aham — I; puṁsām — men; svāyambhuvo = svāyambhuvaḥ - Svāyambhuva; manuḥ — Manu; nārāyaṇo = Nārāyaṇah — *Nārāyaṇa;* munīnām — of the yogi philosophers; ca — and; kumāro = kumāraḥ — Kumara; brahmacāriṇām — of those who are focused on spiritual existence.

Translation

But of women, I am represented by Śatarūpā. Among men, I am represented by Svāyambhuva Manu. And of the yogi philosophers, I am Nārāyaṇa. Of those who are focused on spiritual existence, I am Kumāra. (11.25)

Commentary:

The Vedic literatures, gave *Śatarūpa* and *Manu* as the first man and wife in the creation. These were created directly by Lord *Brahmā* during his deliberation on how to sexually reproduce. These two engaged sexually, but only for the purpose of begetting offspring. Because of this *Manu* was highly respected in his own time.

Kumara, also known as *Sanat Kumār*, was a mentally-conceived son of *Brahmā*. Three other sons of *Brahmā* appeared simultaneously with *Sanat*. These were *Sanaka*, *Sanandana* and *Sanātana*. They were averse to sexual indulgence and female association. When they were requested to form households, they refused to do so, even though they were asked by their father Lord *Brahmā*. However even they respect persons like *Manu* and *Śatarūpa*, who engaged in sexual linkage with self-control. The term *brahmacārī* has come to mean a celibate male whose material body has never had sexual intercourse. Initially it meant a person who was focused on spiritual existence exclusively. Of course, to be focused in that way one must be celibate, since sexual indulgence reverses the focus of the living being and causes his vital energy to flow downward, causing varied interest in the material world.

Of the yogi philosophers, *Śrī* Krishna is directly *Nārāyaṇa* Rishi as confirmed by Bhishma in the *Mahābhārata*. Arjuna is supposed to be the incarnation of Nara Rishi, who was the companion of Lord *Nārāyaṇa* Rishi.

Sexual intercourse, and affectionate dealings go together. Therefore it is difficult for women, who are in fact, the personifications of affection, to be detached from sexual opportunities. Thus *Śatarūpa Devī* is highly respected by all great yogins and even by *Śrī* Krishna, the Supreme Being.

धर्माणाम् अस्मि सन्न्यासः
क्षेमाणाम् अबहिर्-मतिः ।
गुह्याना सु-नृत मौनं
मिथुनानाम् अजस् त्व् अहम् ॥ ११.२६ ॥

dharmāṇām asmi sannyāsaḥ
kṣemāṇām abahir-matiḥ
guhyānāṁ su-nṛtaṁ maunaṁ
mithunānām ajas tv aham (11.26)

dharmāṇām — of the righteous way of life; asmi — I am; sannyāsaḥ — renunciation of all exploitive opportunities; kṣemāṇām — of the sources of well being; abahir = abahiḥ - internalization; matiḥ — intellect; guhyānām — of secrets; su-nṛtam — agreeable speech; maunam — silence; mithunānām — of sexual partners; ajas = ajah — Brahmā; tv = tu — but; aham — I.

Translation

Of the righteous ways of life, I am the renunciation of exploitive opportunities. Of the sources of well-being, I am represented by the internalization of the intellect. Of secrets, I am represented by silence and agreeable speech. But of sexual partners, I am Ajah Brahmā. (11.26)

Commentary:

It is interesting that Krishna, identified Himself with *sannyāsa*, which is to the total renunciation of all exploitive opportunities. In the *Bhagavad-Gītā*, *Śrī* Krishna discouraged Arjuna from *sannyāsa* and practically forced the hero to be a *tyāgi*, which is a person who can only renounce the results of opportunities and not the opportunities themselves. Of course that person is expected to only accept righteous duties, harmless leisure and nothing else.

Here we see that *Śrī* Krishna does not push Uddhava in the direction of being a *tyāgi* but rather he wants Uddhava to take the high road of *sannyāsa*, a path that he barred Arjuna from traversing. It is very interesting that *Śrī* Krishna mentioned *sannyāsa* which is itself the rejection of cultural opportunities, He listed it as the supreme form of *dharma* or righteous duty. This shows another aspect, that ultimately it is our duty to reject all the cultural opportunities which destiny affords us, because otherwise we would never become liberated.

Of note to yogis, is the statement made by *Śrī* Krishna about well-being *(kṣemāṇām)*. To get that one has to internalize his intellect *(matih)*. This is the process of *pratyāhar* and *dhāraṇā*, which advances into *dhyāna* and *samādhi* practice. But the highlight of *samādhi* was listed in verse 24 as *ātma-samrodho*, the complete restraint of the psyche from mundane engagements.

Of secrets, *Śrī* Krishna identified Himself with silence and agreeable speech. This has to do with yoga practice in the advanced stages, when the yogi has to adopt silence on the internal and external levels for a decreased interaction with the creatures of this world. He must also use agreeable speech in order to reduce the resentments of those whom he interacts with. This is for closing off material existence and its resulting concerns. By the grace of *Śrī* Krishna, a yogin is allowed to do this not otherwise. The yogi does not have to believe in *Śrī* Krishna to get the grace of the Supreme Being. One acquires that grace not by identification as Krishna's devotee but rather by one's sincerity for closing out oneself from the material world.

Because a person who closed out his existence, stops being a bother to the Supreme Being, because that person's will power no longer runs contrary to the supreme, he is allowed the grace of God spontaneously. This is why we sometimes hear of great personalities who do not attest to a belief in Lord Krishna but who become liberated nevertheless. It is not that one has to be *Śrī* Krishna's accommodating devotee just to get His grace. *Śrī* Krishna is not biased. He is completely free to help anyone, even if the person does not acknowledge Him, provided the person takes a sincere path and becomes less and less bothersome to the Universal Form.

A person who learns how to put himself out of the way of the Universal Form, to live in a way which does not oppose the supreme will, will get the grace of the Supreme, even if he does not pay lip service to God, even if he does not specialize in praising *Śrī* Krishna or in chanting Krishna's name.

We are so lucky, that we do not have to rely on the devotees of *Śrī* Krishna, who are hostile to and inimical towards any of us who do not pay lip service to Krishna. If we were reliant on them, all yogis who do not understand *Śrī* Krishna's perspective as He presented it to Arjuna and Uddhava and who are disinclined from accepting *Śrī* Krishna's claims as the Supreme Being, would be doomed. Fortunately, a yogi is not doomed, and he will be successful if he sincerely strives to get out of the material world, and if he stays out of the way of the Universal Form.

A yogi should not be a botheration in the material world. He should not be like Duryodhana, the rival of the Pandavas, otherwise he will be checked by destiny. It is really irrelevant as to whether Lord Shiva, Lord Krishna or *Devī*, is the Central Person in the Universal Form. It is not so important if that Supreme Person is Shiva, *Devī* or Krishna or even Jesus Christ for that matter. The important thing is to work in a way that is cooperative to that Person. The Supreme Being cannot be a petty God who needs every living being to love Him or to join His religious institution.

Of those who are sexually-linked, *Śrī* Krishna identified Himself with *Brahmā*, a self-tantric sexist, a person who reproduces without a partner. *Brahmā* is sometimes called the supreme mystic, because he created living beings without taking help from females.

सवत्सरो ऽस्म्यु अनिमिषाम्
ऋतूनां मधु-माधवौ ।
मासानां मार्गशीर्षो ऽहं
नक्षत्राणां तथाभिजित् ॥ ११.२७॥

saṁvatsaro 'smy animiṣām
ṛtūnāṁ madhu-mādhavau
māsānāṁ mārgaśīrṣo 'haṁ
nakṣatrāṇāṁ tathābhijit (11.27)

saṁvatsaro = saṁvatsarah — the year; 'smy = asmi — I am; animiṣām — of the continuties; ṛtūnām — of the seasons; mādhavau — spring; māsānām — of the months; mārgaśīrṣo = mārgaśīrṣah — the November-December lunar month; 'haṁ = aham — I; nakṣatrāṇām — of the stars; tathābhijit = tathā — similarly + abhijit — Abhijit.

Translation:

Of the continuities, I am represented by the year; of seasons, the spring, of months, the November-December lunar month. And similarly, I am the Abhijit asterism among the stars. (11.27)

Commentary:

Of the continuous cycles of time, *Śrī* Krishna identified with the year. For seasons, He chose the spring, when whatever was dormant resumes growth again. Of the months, He chose November-December period. And among the constellations, he selected Abhijit.

अहं युगानां च कृतं
धीराणां देवलो ऽसितः ।
द्वैपायनो ऽस्मि व्यासानां
कवीनां काव्य आत्मवान् ॥ ११.२८॥

ahaṁ yugānāṁ ca kṛtaṁ
dhīrāṇāṁ devalo 'sitaḥ
dvaipāyano 'smi vyāsānāṁ
kavīnāṁ kāvya ātmavān (11.28)

aham — I; yugānām — of the trend cycles; ca — and; kṛtam — the Krta Age; dhīrānām — of the yogis with steady intellect; devalah — Devala; 'sitah = Asitah — Asita; dvaipāyano = dvaipāyanaḥ — Dvaipayana, who was born on an island; 'smi = asmi — I am; vyāsānām — of the editors of the Vedas; kavīnām — of the mystic poets; kāvya = kāvyah — Sukracarya; ātma-vān — self reliant.

Translation

Of the trend cycles, I am represented by the Age of Easy Attainment. Of the yogis, with steady intellect, I prefer Asita Devala. I am represented by Dvaipāyana among the editors of the Vedas. Of the mystic poets, I am represented by the self-reliant Śukrācārya. (11.28)

Commentary:

The Vedic literature, gave four trend cycles which are headed by the *Kṛta A*ge. This is also called the *Satya Yuga*. It is said that in that era most of the people were God-conscious. Because of a constant communication with God, persons in that era did not pray to God externally.

Of the yogis with steady intellect, there was *Asita Devala*. Of the brahmins who attempted to edit the Vedas, *Dvaipāyaṇa Vyāsa*, the one born on an island, is the most prominent.

Of the mystic poets, *Śukrācārya* is the greatest. He could revived dead bodies just by pronouncing Sanskrit sounds. He was totally self-reliant, because he discovered many effective mantra sounds without having to hear any of them from a guru.

वासुदेवो भगवतां
त्व तु भागवतेष्व् अहम् ।
किम्पुरुषानां हनुमान्
विद्याध्राणां सुदर्शनः ॥ ११.२९ ॥

vāsudevo bhagavatāṁ
tvaṁ tu bhāgavateṣv aham
kimpuruṣāṇāṁ hanumān
vidyādhrāṇāṁ sudarśanaḥ (11.29)

vāsudevo = vāsudevaḥ — Vasudeva; bhagavatām — of those displaying features of the Supreme Being; tvam — you; tu — but; bhāgavateṣu — among the great devotees; aham — I; kimpuruṣāṇām — among the monkey-faced humans; hanumān — Hanumān; vidyādhrāṇām — of the technically-skilled angelic leaders; sudarśanaḥ — Sudarsana.

Translation

Of those displaying the features of the Supreme Being, I am Vāsudeva. But of the great devotees, I am represented by you. Of the monkey-faced human beings, I am represented by Hanumān. Of those angelic people who are technically-skilled, I am represented by Sudarśan. (11.29)

Commentary:

Many persons are said to display the feature of the Supreme Being but *Śrī* Krishna identified Himself as *Vāsudeva*, the son of *Vasudeva* and *Devakī*. In India, every so often, someone is declared to be either God or an incarnation of God. It is amazing how in century after century, so many persons are declared by their followers to be either the Supreme Person Himself or His choice representative on earth. That is the Indian tradition. Subsequently the word *Bhagavān* is used loosely in India.

Even though *Śrī* Krishna's history of activities is unparalleled, still from time to time a sect forms which declares somebody else as the Supreme, even as being more supreme than *Śrī* Krishna. But all this is so much insecurity and self-delusion, because no matter who we declare to be God, if that person cannot change our habits and if he has to wait until our bodies die before he can change our behavior, then he is for us, a worthless God.

What are we to do with so many persons who are being declared in the various religions which come out of India, in which someone from recent history is declared as God, even as superior to *Śrī* Krishna? The whole argument and presentation of such ideas is ridiculous. It does not matter who God is. What matters is our life style and the changes in behavior which will cause us to view the transcendental world now, and not only at the time of death.

Among the great devotees of Krishna, He singled out his dear friend Uddhava. When *Śrī* Krishna spoke to Arjuna, he claimed identity with Arjuna as the leading Pandava. Of the monkey-faced humans, *Śrī* Krishna would of course, select *Hanumān*, a hero of the *Rāmāyaṇa*. Arjuna used *Hanumān* as his flag-pole insignia. Of the angelic people who are technically skilled, Krishna identified *Sudarśan*.

The angelic people have permanent status in angelic bodies, which do not die in one hundred years. While a human body dies in about one hundred years for the most, the subtle forms used by the angelic people live for hundreds of years and in the same youthful configuration. These are not spiritual bodies. Those angelic forms will perish after thousands of years but they are much more durable than the material forms we use.

A minor portion of the angelic hosts are elevated human begins who after leaving a dead form, ascended there, on the basis of pious activities by virtue of exhibiting godly qualities. Most of these elevated humans will have to take more human forms, before they can either be upgraded into the angelic world permanently or go on to the spiritual world where the body is the person himself or herself, and where there is no shell like a gross or subtle form.

Those who are permanent residents of the angelic world, have no needs for human existence. They do not feel that they should work hard for a living nor that they should endeavor for anything. Human existence is symbolized by a need for endeavor to acquire one thing or another or for aspiring for liberation or a higher status in this world, either as a struggle for existence here or as an endeavor to remove oneself from this situation. If however an angelic being adopts a human body, that person would experience the human emotions and would act as a human being.

Some angelic beings, like *Urvaśī* for instance, do take human birth, but they aspire to return to the angelic status, because they do not see any advantage in human life, which is full of endeavor for the very same things that the angelic people acquire without effort. However such persons as *Urvaśī* did overlook the one advantage of human existence, that is the capacity for liberation. A human being is easily motivated for liberation, while an angelic being never feels the need for it.

In the heavenly planet, there are varying grades of people. There are rulers like King Indra. There are supervisors who control the situation and act as deputy kings. There are the *Vidyādharas*, who are very knowledgeable. Even though there is no work in the angelic world, and one's needs are automatically fulfilled, still there is subtle discrimination there. The only needs fulfilled there, are the ones which arise in the subtle body. The need for liberation hardly arises there, because the subtle body as it is experienced in heaven, does not allow the manifestation of that need.

The yogis try to avoid the heavenly world but they are not always able to sidestep it. Hence, sometimes, after leaving a gross body, a yogi might spend years in the angelic kingdoms, mostly enjoying romances and sexually dalliances with the angelic women, who are especially attracted to yogins, particularly those yogins who have mastered celibacy to a degree. Such yogins, when they appear on the heavenly planets carry in their bodies, a special sex appeal which irresistibly attracts angelic women, who are all too eager to pair up with a yogi. The same applies to accomplished yogini women, who might be victimized by angelic males.

To save a yogi from this mishap, the process of yoga has a facility for a yogi to go to the angelic world, before his material body dies. By traveling there in his surcharged subtle form, the yogi gets a preview of how he would perform in the hereafter, as to whether he has the detachment and purity to bypass the angelic kingdoms. Thus if a yogi experiences that he is not able to resist the heavenly paradises, he can strive harder and keep testing himself until he feels that he can sidestep the sexual temptations. He should check his psyche carefully to see what it is capable of. Then he can work for improvement. In doing this, a yogi takes help from superior ascetics who guide him in special purificatory *kriyās*.

As far as women yoginis are concerned, they face the same challenges in the heavenly world, since the male angelic beings would be attracted to them, and would cause them to stop yoga practice in order to enjoy sexual and other sensual pleasures. They too, should test themselves before leaving the physical form, by going to the angelic paradises, through astral projections and dimensional switching.

There are devotees of Lord Krishna. There are devotees of Lord *Śrī* Chaitanya. There are devotees of Lord *Svāmīnārāyaṇa*. And there are devotee of others who are acclaimed as the Supreme Being. Many of these devotees feel that they will by-pass the Svarga heavenly worlds at the time of death and just be instantly transferred to the spiritual world. In this belief, the majority make a sad miscalculation. But what does it matter? Most of these devotees do not remember their past lives as devotees. Most of them will not know in their next birth, whether they lived before and had the same views before and just kept taking human rebirth and believing the same ideas about salvation for many lives before. But that is their predicament.

रत्नानां पद्म-रागो ऽस्मि
पद्म-कोशः सु-पेशसाम् ।
कुशो ऽस्मि दर्भ-जातीनां
गव्यम् आज्यं हविःष्व् अहम् ॥ ११.३० ॥

ratnānāṁ padma-rāgo 'smi
padma-kośaḥ su-peśasām
kuśo 'smi darbha-jātīnāṁ
gavyam ājyaṁ haviḥṣv aham (11.30)

ratnānām — of gems; padma-rāgo = padma-rāgah — ruby; 'smi = asmi — I am; padma-kośaḥ — lotus bud; su-peśasām — of beautiful things; kuśo = kuśaḥ — Kusha grass; 'smi = asmi — I am; darbha-jātīnām — of types of grasses; gavyam — dairy products; ājyam — ghee; haviḥṣv = haviḥṣu — of the oblations; aham — I.

Translation

Of the gems, I am represented by the ruby. Of the beautiful things, it is the lotus bud; of the grass plants, the kusha grass; of the oblations, the ghee and other dairy products. (11.30)

Commentary:

Even in terms of minerals and vegetation, *Śrī* Krishna identified Himself with particular things, like the ruby and kusha grass which is used in Vedic religious ceremonies. *Śrī* Krishna taught this method of Krishna Consciousness whereby we can remember Him when we deal with ordinary items.

व्यवसायिनाम् अह लक्ष्मीः
कितवाना छल-ग्रहः ।
तितिक्षास्मि तितिक्षूणा
सत्त्वं सत्त्ववताम् अहम् ॥ ११.३१ ॥

vyavasāyinām ahaṁ lakṣmīḥ
kitavānāṁ chala-grahaḥ
titikṣāsmi titikṣūṇāṁ
sattvaṁ sattvavatām aham (11.31)

vyavasāyinām — of the enterprising persons; aham — I; lakṣmīḥ — Laksmi; kitavānām — of the cheaters; chala-grahaḥ — fraud; titikṣāsmi = titikṣā — forgiveness + asmi — I am; titikṣūṇām — of tolerant; sattvam — of the clarifying influence; sattvavatām — of those who possess clarity; aham — I.

Translation

Of those who are enterprising, I am prosperity. Of the cheaters I am represented by fraud. Of those who are tolerant, I am represented by forgiveness. I am represented by the clarifying influence for those who possess clarity. (11.31)

Commentary:

We should consider that *Śrī* Krishna is represented by fraud, in the sense that one is victimized by cheaters because of ignorance of their motives and being misled by destiny. Since *Śrī* Krishna claims Himself as the Supreme Being, He assumes responsibility for everything, even for what is bad. Of course the liability for personal acts is focused on the actors, even though there is a Supreme Being who masterminded the cosmic situation.

Of the enterprising persons and outlaws, He is represented by opulence, the very thing they desire. Of those who are tolerant, He is represented by forgiveness. For those using the clarifying influence, they are reliant on an energy supply from that influence. *Śrī* Krishna identified Himself with that highest potency in material nature.

ओजः सहो बलवतां
कर्माहं विद्धि सात्वताम् ।
सात्वतां नव-मूर्तीनाम्
आदि-मूर्तिर् अहं परा ॥११.३२॥

ojaḥ saho balavatāṁ
karmāhaṁ viddhi sātvatām
sātvatāṁ nava-mūrtīnām
ādi-mūrtir ahaṁ parā (11.32)

ojaḥ — bodily strength; saho = sahaḥ — mental vigor; balavatām — of the strong; karmāham = karma — activities + aham — I; viddhi — know; sātvatām — of the *Sātvata* clan of devotees; nava-mūrtīnām — of the nine Deity forms; ādi-mūrtir = ādi-mūrtiḥ — foremost Deity form; aham — I; parā — Supreme.

Translation

Know that I am represented as the bodily energy and mental vigor of the strong. I am the activities of the Sātvata clan of devotees. I am the foremost of the nine Deity forms. (11.32)

Commentary:

Sātvata refers to a clan of devotees who were physically related to *Śrī* Krishna. They were a branch of the family dynasties which were with *Śrī* Krishna in *Dvārakā*. Such devotees worked under His direct supervision. Thus *Śrī* Krishna identified Himself with their cultural activities, just as He admitted Himself to be the work, which Arjuna did as *karma* yoga on the battlefield of *Kurukṣetra*. It is very misleading to translate *Sātvata* as any devotee or as devotees of a certain spiritual master in the disciplic succession, because here it refers to certain physical family members of *Śrī* Krishna who were in a certain clan and who did what *Śrī* Krishna said to the letter.

Nine Deities were worshipped by the *Sātvata* relatives of Lord Krishna. He identified Himself with the foremost of those forms who was known as *Vāsudeva*. *Śrī* Krishna said that he was represented by the bodily energy and mental vigor of the strong men.

विश्वावसुः पूर्वचित्तिर्
गन्धर्वाप्सरसाम् अहम् ।
भूधराणाम् अहं स्थैर्यं
गन्ध-मात्रम् अहं भुवः ॥११.३३॥

viśvāvasuḥ pūrvacittir
gandharvāpsarasām aham
bhūdharāṇām ahaṁ sthairyaṁ
gandha-mātram ahaṁ bhuvaḥ (11.33)

viśvāvasuḥ — Vishvavasu; pūrvacittir = pūrvacittiḥ — Purvacitti; gandharvāpsarasām = gandharva – male angelic singers + apsarasām — angelic women; aham — I; bhūdharāṇām — of the mountains; aham — I; sthairyam — stability; gandha – color; mātram — primary; aham — I; bhuvaḥ — of the earth.

Translation

Of the male angelic singers and the angelic women, I am Viśvāvasu and Pūrvacitti respectively. I am represented by the stability of the mountains and the primary smell of the earth. (11.33)

Commentary:

In the heavenly dimensions, there is diversity just as there is on earth. This means that we should prepare ourselves for that. One should not think that he is equal to everyone else in heaven or in the kingdom of God. The diversity and disparities which we face on this earth, will meet us elsewhere. Thus the only thing to do is to learn about our individual existential category and learn to adjust it accordingly. *Śrī* Krishna singled out *Viśvāvasu* and *Pūrvacitti*. It is said that

Pūrvacitti once came down to this earth and enticed a King named *Agnīdhra*. He took up yoga practice in order to get a wife from the higher dimensions. Just by hearing the ringing of an angel's ankle-bells, he gave up meditation and united with her.

Of the mountains, *Śrī* Krishna cited their stability, something that we take for granted. However when we consider that we live on a planet whose core is molten metal, it is amazing that there is any stability on the surface of the globe. In relation to the earth, *Śrī* Krishna cited its primary smell. All food nutrients originate from this primary odor. It is a very subtle pranic energy, which can be seen, and smelt by the subtle body.

अपां रसश् च परमस्
तेजिष्ठानां विभावसुः ।
प्रभा सूर्येन्दु-ताराणां
शब्दो ऽह नभसः परः ॥ ११.३४॥

apāṁ rasaś ca paramas
tejiṣṭhānāṁ vibhāvasuḥ
prabhā sūryendu-tārāṇāṁ
śabdo 'haṁ nabhasaḥ paraḥ (11.34)

apām — of water; rasah — taste; ca — and; paramas = paramaḥ — foremost, fine; tejiṣṭhānām — of the brillant things; vibhāvasuḥ — sun; prabhā — effulgence; sūryendu = sūrya — sun + indu — moon; tārāṇām — of the stars; śabdo = śabdaḥ — sound; 'ham = aham — I; nabhasaḥ — of the sky; parah — spiritual.

Translation

I am identified with the fine taste of water. Of the brilliant things, I am identified with the effulgence of the sun, moon and stars. And I am the sound of the spiritual sky. (11.34)

Commentary:

Śrī Krishna identified with the fine taste of drinking water, a taste that is greatly appreciated by many creatures. Of the brilliant things, He singled out the sun. He choose the effulgence of the sun, moon and stars. Of interest to yogis is the sound in the chit *ākāśa (śabdo nabhasah parah)*, a sound heard in the vicinity of the right ear mostly.

This sound is used in *dhāraṇā* practice, where the yogi links his attentive power to it. Sometimes a yogi is conveyed by this sound into the other atmosphere, the chit *ākāśa*. By listening to this sound, which is the un-expressed Om, a yogi attains *kaivalyam*, which is the separation of a spirit from its psychological equipments. By this he attains alone-ness not one-ness as it is often misnamed. A yogi also attains spiritual perception by adhering to this sound, since it causes the intellect to reach the *dhīrah* stage of quiescence.

ब्रह्मण्याना बलिर् अहं
वीराणाम् अहम् अर्जुनः ।
भूतानां स्थितिर् उत्पत्तिर्
अहं वै प्रतिसङ्क्रमः ॥ ११.३५॥

brahmaṇyanaṁ balir ahaṁ
vīrāṇām aham arjunaḥ
bhūtānāṁ sthitir utpattir
ahaṁ vai pratisaṅkramaḥ (11.35)

brahmanyānām — of those devoted to brahmins; balir = baliḥ — Bali; aham — I; vīrānām — of the heroes; aham — I; arjunah — Arjuna; bhūtānām — of the creatures; sthitir = sthitiḥ — maintenance; utpattir = utpattiḥ — origin; aham — I; vai — surely; pratisaṅkramaḥ — annihilation.

Translation:

Of those devoted to brahmins, I am represented as Bali. Of heroes, I am represented by Arjuna. Surely I am the maintenance, origination and annihilation of the creatures. (11.35)

Commentary:

King Bali was part of a demoniac dynasty, which opposed the supernatural rulers, but this king was devoted to the brahmins nevertheless. He respected brahmins and supported brahminical families even those which were opposed to his dynasty. *Śrī* Krishna considered such support to be essential to a righteous civilization. He appreciated the attitude of King *Bali*.

Of the heroes, *Śrī* Krishna identified Himself with Arjuna. This of course is a literal identification, for we know by reading the *Bhagavad-Gītā*, that *Śrī* Krishna empowered Arjuna to act on behalf of the Universal Form. *Śrī* Krishna's power functioned through the body of Arjuna.

गत्य्-उक्त्य्-उत्सर्गोपादानम्
आनन्द-स्पर्श-लक्षनम् ।
आस्वाद्-श्रुत्य्-अवघ्राणम्
अहं सर्वेन्द्रियेन्द्रियम् ॥ ११.३६ ॥

gaty-ukty-utsargopādānam
ānanda-sparśa-lakṣanam
āsvāda-śruty-avaghrāṇam
ahaṁ sarvendriyendriyam (11.36)

gaty = gati — movement; ukty = ukti — speech; utsargopādānam = utsarga — evacuation + upādānam — appropiation; ānanda — enjoyment; sparśa — touching sensation; lakṣaṇam — vision; āsvāda — tasting; śruty = śruti — hearing; avaghrāṇam — smelling; aham — I; sarvendriyendriyam = sarva-indriya — of all senses + indriyam — sensual power.

Translation

I motivate movement, speech, evacuations, appropriation, enjoyment, touch sensations, vision, taste, hearing, and smelling. I activate the sensual power of the senses. (11.36)

Commentary:

Directly, these aspects are driven by life force. These expressions are involuntary and voluntary, proving that the limited person can only control these to a nominal degree. Thus ultimately, these features are controlled by the Supreme Being. The psyche of the spirit was not created by that spirit itself, but by another more powerful and resourceful agency, by God, the Supreme Being.

पृथिवी वायुर् आकाश
आपो ज्योतिर् अहं महान् ।
विकारः पुरुषो ऽव्यक्त
रजः सत्त्व तमः परम् ।
अहम् एतत् प्रसङ्ख्यानं
ज्ञानं तत्त्व-विनिश्चयः ॥ ११.३७ ॥

pṛthivī vāyur ākāśa
āpo jyotir ahaṁ mahān
vikāraḥ puruṣo 'vyaktaṁ
rajaḥ sattvaṁ tamaḥ param
aham etat prasaṅkhyānaṁ
jñānaṁ tattva-viniścayaḥ (11.37)

prthivī — earth; vāyur = vāyuh — air; ākāśa — sky; āpo = āpaḥ — water; jyotir = jyotiḥ — light; aham — assertion of individuality, I; mahān = mahāt — the primal mundane energy; vikāraḥ — the natural modification; puruṣo = puruṣaḥ — person; 'vyaktaṁ = avyaktam — the imperceptible energy; rajaḥ — the impulsive energy of subtle material nature; sattvam — the clarifying influence of subtle material nature; tamaḥ — the retardative influence of subtle material nature; param — the Supreme Reality; aham — I; etat — this; prasaṅkhyānam — enumeration of essential principles; jñānam — knowledge; tattva – truth; viniścayaḥ — strong conviction.

Translation

I am represented as the earth, the air, the sky, water, light, the assertion of individuality, the primal mundane energy, the natural modifications, the personality, the imperceptible energy, the impulsive, clarifying and retardative subtle influences of material nature, as well as the Supreme Reality. I am represented as the enumeration of essential principles, as knowledge and as the strong convictions of these truths. (11.37)

Commentary:

In any direction, from any angle of consideration or perception, a devotee can become Krishna-aware by applying these teachings. In all respects, a devotee can conceive of a connection with *Śrī* Krishna, along the guidelines given in this chapter.

मयेश्वरेण जीवेन
गुणेन गुणिना विना ।
सर्वात्मनापि सर्वेण
न भावो विद्यते क्वचित् ॥ ११.३८॥

mayeśvareṇa jīvena
guṇena guṇinā vinā
sarvātmanāpi sarveṇa
na bhāvo vidyate kvacit (11.38)

mayeśvareṇa = mayā — by me + īśvareṇa — by the controller; jīvena — by the individual spirit; guṇena — by the influences of material nature; guṇinā — by the supersubtle influences of material nature; vinā — without; sarvātmanāpi = sarva – all + ātmanā — by the spirit + api — also; sarveṇa — by all; na — not; bhāvo = bhāvaḥ — existence; vidyate — there is; kvacit — whatever.

Translation:

There is no existence whatsoever, without Me, either I am represented as the controller, the individual spirit, the obvious and super subtle influences of material nature, or as the soul of all and or as everything there is. (11.38)

Commentary:

Śrī Krishna made a similar statement to Arjuna:

yaccāpi sarvabhūtānāṁ bījaṁ tadahamarjuna
na tadasti vinā yatsyān mayā bhūtaṁ carācaram

And O Arjuna, I am the origin of all created beings. There is nothing active or stationary which could exist without My influence. (B.G. 10.39)

सङ्ख्यानं परमाणूनां
कालेन क्रियते मया ।
न तथा मे विभूतीनां
सृजतो ऽण्डानि कोटिशः ॥ ११.३९॥

saṅkhyānaṁ paramāṇūnāṁ
kālena kriyate mayā
na tathā me vibhūtīnāṁ
sṛjato 'ṇḍāni koṭiśaḥ (11.39)

saṅkhyānam — counting; paramānūnām — of the atoms; kālena — in time; kriyate — is done; mayā — by me; na — not; tathā — so; me — of me; vibhūtīnām — of wondrous manifestations; sṛjato = sṛjataḥ — one who creates; 'ṇḍāni = andāni — universes; koṭiśah — millions.

Translation

In time, the counting of the atoms may be done by Me, but not that of My wondrous manifestations, for I am the One Who created millions of universes. (11.39)

Commentary:

This indeed Is an outlandish statement for any human being to make. After all, *Śrī* Krishna was a person of history. He did have a biological mother, *Devakī,* and father, Vasudeva. He was reared by a foster father, the dairy farmer Nanda Gopa. However a similar declaration was made to Arjuna:

nānto'sti mama divyānāṁ vibhūtīnāṁ paraṁtapa
eṣa tūddeśataḥ prokto vibhūtervistaro mayā

There is no end to My supernatural manifestations, O burner of the enemy forces. This was explained by Me as a sampling of My extensive opulence. (B.G. 10.40)

तेजः श्रीः कीर्तिर् ऐश्वर्यं
ह्रीस् त्यागः सौभगं भगः ।
वीर्यं तितिक्षा विज्ञानं
यत्र यत्र स मे ऽंशकः ॥ ११.४० ॥

tejaḥ śrīḥ kīrtir aiśvaryaṁ
hrīs tyāgaḥ saubhagaṁ bhagaḥ
vīryaṁ titikṣā vijñānaṁ
yatra yatra sa me 'ṁśakaḥ (11.40)

tejaḥ — prowess; śrīh — prosperity; kīrtir = kīrtih — popularity; aiśvaryam — sovereignty; hrīs = hrīḥ — modesty; tyāgaḥ — abandonment of benefits, renunciation; saubhagam — charm; bhagaḥ — luck; vīryam — strength; titikṣā — tolerance; vijñānam — realisation; yatra yatra — wherever; sa — that; me — my; 'ṁśakaḥ = amśakaḥ — partial manifestation.

Translation

Whenever there is prowess, prosperity, popularity, sovereignty, modesty, renunciation, charm, luck, strength, tolerance and realization, that aspect is My partial manifestation. (11.40)

Commentary:

This was explained by Arjuna in another way:

yadyadvibhūtimatsattvaṁ śrīmadūrjitameva vā
tattadevāvagaccha tvaṁ mama tejoṁśasaṁbhavam

You should realize that whatever fantastic existence, whatever prosperous or powerful object there is, in any case, it originates from a fraction of My splendor. (B.G. 10.41)

एतास् ते कीर्तिताः सर्वाः
सङ्क्षेपेण विभूतयः ।
मनो-विकारा एवैते
यथा वाचाभिधीय ते ॥ ११.४१ ॥

etās te kīrtitāḥ sarvāḥ
saṅkṣepeṇa vibhūtayaḥ
mano-vikārā evaite
yathā vācābhidhīyate (11.41)

etās = etāt — these; te — to you; kīrtitāh — described; sarvāh — all; saṅkṣepeṇa — in brief; vibhūtayaḥ — wondrous manifestation; mano-vikārā = manaḥ-vikārāḥ = manaḥ — of the mind + vikārāḥ — modifications; evaite = eva — indeed + ete — these; yathā — accordingly; vācābhidhīyate = vācā — by speech + abhidhīyate — is expressed.

Translation

All these wondrous manifestations, were described by Me to you in brief. These are modifications of the mind and accordingly, it is expressed by speech. (11.41)

Commentary:

The wondrous manifestations in this material world are all temporary. These include even the supernatural forms which *Śrī* Krishna produced for Himself in this world or which are produced by His parallel divinities. The supernatural forms have real power in so far as they divulge their will and desire into this creation but they are still temporary forms. We can understand then, that the ordinary manifestations have less value.

So long as we are time bound, we will have to take all those wondrous manifestations seriously. Hence it is necessary for us to become liberated if we are to be transferred out of the material world.

Śrī Krishna admitted here that these are modifications of the mind. The question is: Whose mind was He speaking of? The answer of course, is that He spoke of the Supreme Mind, the Cosmic Intelligence which gives the spirits their minute allotment of sensibility. Everything is relative until we shift to the cosmic level of activity. Then we get a glimpse of divine power. Arjuna got his view of it in the revelation which *Śrī* Krishna afforded him on the battlefield of *Kurukṣetra*.

वाच यच्छ मनो यच्छ
प्राणान् यच्छेद्रियाणि च ।
आत्मानम् आत्मना यच्छ
न भूयः कल्पसे ऽध्वने ॥ ११.४२॥

vācaṁ yaccha mano yaccha
prāṇān yacchedriyāṇi ca
ātmānam ātmanā yaccha
na bhūyaḥ kalpase 'dhvane (11.42)

vācam — speech; yaccha — control; mano = manaḥ — mind; yaccha — control; prāṇān — vital energy; yacchendriyani = yaccha — control + indriyāṇi — senses; ca — and; ātmānam — soul; ātmanā — by the soul; yaccha — control; na — not; bhūyaḥ — again; kalpase — you will fall into; dhvane = adhvane — in the course of material existence.

Translation

Control speech. Control the mind. Control the vital energy. Control the senses. Control the soul by the soul and You will not fall into the course of material existence. (11.42)

Commentary:

This is yoga practice. It is not the process of devotional service, unless we define devotional service as the execution of any instruction of *Śrī* Krishna. Uddhava wanted a non-yogic procedure for deliverance, something that was just based on *bhakti* or a loving attitude towards Lord Krishna, but the Lord gave these controlling procedures.

One controls his speech by *pratyāhar* practice, the 5th stage of yoga. One controls his vital energy by *prāṇāyāma*, the 4th stage of yoga. One controls his sensual energies and mind by *pratyāhar* and *dhāraṇā*, the 5th and 6th stages of yoga. One controls his soul by practicing the 7th stage of yoga, that of *dhyāna*. This all culminates in *samādhi* practice, which is the 8th and final stage.

This cannot be avoided because the other methods, even the method of affectionate relationship, are not specialized for certain particular controls. Devotion is a central issue for those persons who are so inclined but they will have to use it as an impetus to take up yoga practice, just as Uddhava did after he was instructed by Lord Krishna.

If you love *Śrī* Krishna, then you are required to comply with His demands, even though your spiritual master might tell you that all you need to do is to be a devotee for performance of temple related devotional service. It is what *Śrī* Krishna will request of you personally in the end, that will matter, not what someone else says.

Devotion is important for many devotees, but it will become *Śrī* Krishna's bargaining chip in the end. He will use it to make the devotee practice the yoga austerities, just as He did with King *Muchukunda*, who had performed a tremendous amount of devotional services, helping senior devotees like the *devatās* on the higher planets.

The devotee who feels that devotion is sufficient and that the matter ends there, is simply fooling himself. If a devotee's devotion is not powerful enough to make that devotee perform yoga for full purification, then that sort of devotion certainly can liberate the devotee. It is a very good idea to cite and lean on the example of Lord *Śrī* Chaitanya Mahaprabhu and that of the *gopīs* of *Vṛndavān*, but the fact remains that even though ordinary devotees try to follow their paths, they do not get the same results. What they get is frustration and continued existence in the material world. This is because their devotion is sponsored by materialistic passion, and thus it does not reach *Śrī* Krishna. But each devotee has to realize this for himself or herself, because no one will do yoga, unless he or she realizes how necessary it is. Some devotees prefer to go on with hopes of salvation, rather than to realize the impurity and to work with effective methods for its removal. And to booth, there are so many powerful devotional figures in the disciplic succession, who discourage yoga and push devotees into a dead end at the time of death. This occurs and it will continue to happen, because by nature, human beings want a cheap but very unrealistic method of salvation.

यो वै वाङ्-मनसी सयग्
असयच्छन् धिया यतिः
तस्य व्रतं तपो दान
स्रवत्य् आम-घटाम्बु-वत् ११.४३

yo vai vāṅ-manasī saṁyag
asaṁyacchan dhiyā yatiḥ
tasya vrataṁ tapo dānaṁ
sravaty āma-ghaṭāmbu-vat (11.43)

yo = yah — one who; vai — surely; vān = vāk – speech; manasī — mind; saṁyag = saṁyak — fully; asaṁyacchan — not controlling; dhiyā — by the intellect; yatiḥ — a yogi; tasya — his; vratam — vow; tapo = tapah — austerity; dānam — charity; sravaty = sravati — run out, are dissipated; āma — unbaked; ghaṭāmbu = ghata — pot; ambu – water; vat — like.

Translation

Surely, a yogi who has not fully controlled his speech and mind by the intellect, finds that his vows, austerity, and charity are dissipated, like water evaporating from an unbaked pot. (11.43)

Commentary:

In yoga practice, everything hinges on containment and conservation of vital energy. It is the vital energy which is expressed in various ways by speech and by all sensual orifices of the mind. Thus one should learn how to use intellect in a way as to curb personal energies *(ātmānam ātmanā verse 42*). These are techniques of yoga practice. The process of external devotional service does not effectively curb the inner psyche. Therefore, in the final analysis, one has to be honest and see that one needs an inner technique to clamp down on the psyche.

तस्माद् वचो मनः प्राणान्
नियच्छेन् मत्-परायणः ।
मद्-भक्ति-युक्तया बुद्ध्या
ततः परिसमाप्यते ॥ ११.४४॥

tasmād vaco manaḥ prāṇān
niyacchen mat-parāyaṇaḥ
mad-bhakti-yuktayā buddhyā
tataḥ parisamāpyate (11.44)

tasmād = tasmāt — therefore; vaco = vacah — speech; manaḥ — mind; prāṇān — vital energy; niyacchen = niyacchet — should control; mat-parāyaṇaḥ — one who is wholely devoted to Me; mad-bhakti-yuktayā — one who is endowed with devotion to Me; buddhyā — by the intellect; tataḥ — then; parisamāpyate — one who has become competent to complete the goal.

Translation

Therefore, one who is wholly devoted to Me, should control speech, mind and life energy, by the intellect, which is endowed by devotion to Me. Then one becomes competent to complete the goal. (11.44)

Commentary:

The combination of yoga control of the psyche and devotion to *Śrī* Krishna is *bhakti* yoga. Devotion itself is *bhakti*, but when it is combined with yoga, then we get *bhakti* yoga not otherwise, and that is a discipline. It is not yoga alone, nor is it devotion alone. Both must be combined.

The key is to understand that even though the fastest route to perfection is devotion, still that does not mean that the devotee will not have to take up any other discipline. He or she certainly may have to. In this case, Uddhava is advised to use both yoga and devotion. If devotion is there, then the yoga practice will be accelerated, because the person's devotion will motivate him to apply himself fully to the austerities, required to break down the independence of the mind and vital energy. Without devotion, the yoga practice might go slower unless the yogi has very strong motivation to retrieve his energies from material nature. Thus yoga does not have to be an obstacle to devotion. It is in fact, the right compliment for devotion, especially if the Lord recommended it as He did to Uddhava.

CHAPTER 12*

Righteous Lifestyle**

Terri Stokes-Pineda Art

śrī-śuka uvāca
itthaṁ sva-bhṛtya-mukhyena pṛṣṭaḥ sa bhagavān hariḥ
prītaḥ kṣemāya martyānāṁ dharmān āha sanātanān

The illustrious Shuka said: Thus, being questioned by his foremost servant, the Blessed Lord Hari was pleased. He spoke of the perpetual means of righteous life style, for the benefit of those whose bodies must die. (Uddhava Gītā 12.8)

* Śrīmad Bhāgavatam Canto 11, Chapter 17
** Translator's selected chapter title.

श्री-उद्धव उवाच
यस् त्वयाभिहितः पूर्वं
धर्मस् त्वद्-भक्ति-लक्षणः ।
वर्णाश्रमाचारवतां
सर्वेषां द्वि-पदाम् अपि ॥ १२.१ ॥

śrī-uddhava uvāca
yas tvayābhihitaḥ pūrvaṁ
dharmas tvad-bhakti-lakṣaṇaḥ
varṇāśamācāravatāṁ
sarveṣāṁ dvi-padām api (12.1)

śrī-uddhava – the deserving Uddhava; uvāca — said; yah — which; tvayābhihitaḥ = tvayā — by you + abhihitah — explained; pūrvam — before; dharmas = dharmaḥ — righteous duty; tvad = tvat – to you; bhakti – devotion; laksanah — characterized; varnāśamācāravatāṁ = varna – work tendencies + āśrama — lifestyle + ācāravatām — adherents; sarveṣām — of all; dvi-padām — two legged species, human beings; api — also;

Translation

The deserving Uddhava said: Righteous duty, which is characterised by devotion to You, and which applies to all human beings, either to the adherents of Vedically-defined work tendencies and lifestyles, or to others, was explained by you before. (12.1)

Commentary:

Actually this was explained in great detail even to Arjuna, because the gist of the *Bhagavad Gītā* is that one should stick to caste occupation, and work in that way as directed by the Central Figure in the Universal Form, by *Śrī* Krishna Himself. For Arjuna that meant he was to stay on the battlefield and complete duties as a senior government official. Uddhava was not a warrior. Therefore at this stage of his life when the question was asked, it was not appropriate for him to take up the *karma* yoga that Arjuna was instructed to perform at *Kurukṣetra*. However Uddhava asked *Śrī* Krishna for clarification on this issue of righteous duty according to caste.

This is *karma* yoga. It may be termed *dharma* yoga as well. It may also be termed *bhakti* yoga. However when we look at this carefully and painstakingly, it is *karma* or work done in a *dharmic* or righteous duty-bound way, on the basis of devotion or *bhakti* to *Śrī* Krishna. And it must be done with the mystic expertise and detached stance gained from doing yoga. Thus this is a mixture of *karma*, *dharma*, *bhakti* and yoga. It is not *bhakti* alone, because no one will, from a loving feeling, go out and kill as a proficient warrior on a battlefield as Arjuna did.

But this type of righteous duty which is characterized by devotion to *Śrī* Krishna cannot be done by any and every body, since it requires certain pre-qualifications like expertise in duty, pre-training in yoga, and a relationship with *Śrī* Krishna.

यथानुष्ठीयमानेन
त्वयि भक्तिर् नृणां भवेत् ।
स्व-धर्मेणारविन्दाक्ष
तन् ममाख्यातुम् अर्हसि ॥ १२.२ ॥

yathānuṣṭhīyamānena
tvayi bhaktir nṛṇāṁ bhavet
sva-dharmeṇāravindākṣa
tan mamākhyātum arhasi (12.2)

yathānuṣṭhīyamānena = yathā — accordingly, how by + anuṣṭhīyamānena — by the practice; tvayi — in you; bhaktir = bhaktih — devotion; nṛṇām — of humanity; bhavet — may be invested; sva – their; dharmeṇāravindākṣa = dharmeṇa — by righteous duty + aravindakṣa — o lotus-eyed one; tan = tat — that; mamākhyātum = mama — me + ākhyātum — to explain; arhasi — you can.

Translation

O lotus-eyed One, you can explain to me, how the devotion of human beings, may be invested in You merely by the practice of righteous duty? (12.2)

Commentary:

This is a very clear question. There is no ambiguity in it. *Śrī* Krishna recommended the *sva-dharma* or assigned righteous duty to Arjuna and gave a guarantee that Arjuna would be able to please *Śrī* Krishna by performance. But Uddhava wants more details. After all, the devotion of human beings *(bhaktir nṛṇām)* may not be pure. It may not be spirited or forceful and motivational enough. How therefore will they attain to a pure exchange with the divine Lord merely by performance of cultural activities in this world?

In the case of Arjuna, the perplexities of life did not end after he complied with *Śrī* Krishna for the performance of *karma* yoga. Later on Arjuna lost touch with the revelation of the Universal Form, as well as with the spiritual goal of life. Therefore how can a common person attain to the devotion for Krishna merely by sticking to his divinely-ordained duties for life on earth?

Śrī Krishna gave insight about yoga practice and its value as a supplement to devotion to Him, for the sake of wholesale purification of the inner self of the devotee, but most people are unable to take up such a painstaking process. Thus Uddhava wants the details about the other system of work by duty without yoga. This is not *karma* yoga as it was performed by King *Janak.* It is not the kind of *karma* yoga Arjuna performed, because Arjuna was a masterful yogin. This is *karma* itself without yoga. Uddhava wants to know the details of how it can be done in such a way as to cause the non-yogis, to invest their devotion in *Śrī* Krishna.

पुरा किल महा-बाहो
धर्मं परमकं प्रभो ।
यत् तेन हंस-रूपेण
ब्रह्मणे ऽभ्यात्थ माधव ॥ १२.३ ॥

purā kila mahā-bāho
dharmaṁ paramakaṁ prabho
yat tena haṁsa-rūpeṇa
brahmaṇe 'bhyāttha mādhava (12.3)

purā — previously; kila — indeed; mahā-bāho — o mighty-armed one; dharmam — system of righteous duty; paramakam = parama – supreme + kam — productive of happiness; prabho — o Lord; yat — which; tena — by that; haṁsa-rūpeṇa — by the Swan Form; brahmane — to Procreator Brahmā; 'bhyāttha = abhyāttha — you explained; mādhava — O Madhava;

Translation

Previously, O Mighty-armed One, O Lord, O Mādhava, when displaying the Swan Form, You explained to Procreator Brahmā, the supreme bliss-producing system of righteousness. (12.3)

Commentary:

Uddhava recalls that Lord Svan, explained the details to *Sanat Kumāra* and his brothers, as well as to *Brahmā* who was with them. The important thing is the details. What seems to be very simple, what seems to be a short-cut, and what seems to be elementary, might turn out to be very intertwining, detailed and complicated.

स इदानीं सु-महता
कालेनामित्र-कर्शन ।
न प्रायो भविता मर्त्य-
लोके प्राग् अनुशासितः ॥ १२.४ ॥

sa idānīṁ su-mahatā
kālenāmitra-karśana
na prāyo bhavitā martya-
loke prāg anuśāsitaḥ (12.4)

sa = saḥ — that; idānīm — now; su-mahatā — very long; kālenāmitra-karśana = kālena — due to time + amitra – enemy + karśana — subduer; na — not, cease; prāyo = prāyaḥ — generally; bhavitā — will exist; martya-loke — in the mortal world; prāg = prāk — previously; anuśāsitaḥ — explained.

Translation

O subduer of the enemy, due to the very long time, the information which was explained perviously, ceased to exist in the mortal world. (12.4)

Commentary:

Uddhava considered the information of righteous duty and devotion, to be vital. He was worried that if *Śrī* Krishna did not explain the details, such information would be lost to posterity.

वक्ता कर्ताविता नान्यो
धर्मस्याच्युत ते भुवि ।
सभायाम् अपि वैरिञ्च्यां
यत्र मूर्ति-धराः कलाः ॥१२.५॥

vaktā kartāvitā nānyo
dharmasyācyuta te bhuvi
sabhāyām api vairiñcyāṁ
yatra mūrti-dharāḥ kalāḥ (12.5)

vaktā — lecturer; kartāvitā = kartā — originator + avitā — defender; nānyo = nānyaḥ — no other; dharmasyācyuta = dharmasya — of righteous living + acyuta — Acyuta; te — you; bhuvi — on earth; sabhāyām — in the court; api — even; vairiñcyām — of Procreator Brahmā; yatra — where; mūrti-dharāḥ — having a visible form; kalāḥ — Vedic information.

Translation

O Achyuta, there is no other lecturer, originator or protector of righteous duty on earth, besides You, not even in the court of Procreator Brahmā, where the Vedic information appears in bodily form. (12.5)

Commentary:

This is quite an appraisal of the *līlās* of *Śrī* Krishna, the pastimes which He performed as the upholder of righteous duty. In fact, at *Śrī* Krishna's name-giving ceremony, the Vaishnava priest *Gargācārya*, told Nanda Gopa, that in previous lives, *Śrī* Krishna protected righteous duty and that He would protect it again in that incarnation.

As the Lord of the world, the Central Person in the Universal Form, no one can know more about the value of righteous duty. *Śrī* Krishna as that Supreme Being who is concerned about world order, is the right person to describe the ways and means of it.

कर्त्रावित्रा प्रवक्त्रा च
भवता मधुसूदन ।
त्यक्ते मही-तले देव
विनष्टं कः प्रवक्ष्यति ॥१२.६॥

kartrāvitrā pravaktrā ca
bhavatā madhusūdana
tyakte mahī-tale deva
vinaṣṭaṁ kaḥ pravakṣyati (12.6)

kartrāvitrā = kartrā — as the originator + avitrā — as the protector; pravaktrā — as the instructor; ca — and; bhavatā — respected sir; madhusūdana — o slayer of Madhu; tyakte — in the abandonment; mahī-tale — in the earth; deva — God; vinaṣṭam — what was lost; kaḥ — who; pravakṣyati — will explain.

Translation:

O slayer of Madhu, when you, respected sir, as the originator, protector and instructor of righteous living, will leave the earth, who will explain what was lost? (12.6)

Commentary:

Uddhava appealed to *Śrī* Krishna to explain the procedures of righteous living for human beings. Whatever Lord Svan said was lost to time. Therefore Uddhava requested that *Śrī* Krishna explain it afresh, just as He explained the process of *karma* yoga to Arjuna.

Karma yoga is not possible for persons who are not expert in yoga, but *karma* is. *Śrī* Krishna without giving details told Arjuna about a way of doing just *karma*, cultural activities, which would eventually result in spiritual perfection. *Śrī* Krishna said:

atha cittaṁ samādhātuṁ na śaknoṣi mayi sthiram
abhyāsayogena tato māmicchāptuṁ dhanaṁjaya
abhyāse'pyasamartho'si matkarmaparamo bhava

madarthamapi karmāṇi kurvansiddhimavāpsyasi
athaitadapyaśakto'si kartuṁ madyogamāśritaḥ
sarvakarmaphalatyāgaṁ tataḥ kuru yatātmavān

If, however, you cannot steadily anchor your thoughts on Me, then by yoga practice, try to attain Me, O conqueror of wealthy countries.

But if perchance, you are incapable of such practice, then by being absorbed in My work, or even by doing activities for My sake, you will attain perfection.

If you are unable to even do this, then resorting to My yoga process, abandoning all results of action, act with self restraint. (B.G. 12.9-11)

There are devotional services and there are yogic devotional services as well. Both have value. When yoga is added, the devotional service becomes more pure and more concentrated and acts in a more definite way for the objective of reaching *Śrī* Krishna at His spiritual place. Or when devotional impetus is added to yoga practice, the yogi's progress is greatly accelerated.

तत् त्वं नः सर्व-धर्म-ज्ञ
धर्मस् त्वद्-भक्ति-लक्षणः ।
यथा यस्य विधीयेत
तथा वर्णय मे प्रभो ॥ १२.७॥

tat tvaṁ naḥ sarva-dharma-jña
dharmas tvad-bhakti-lakṣaṇaḥ
yathā yasya vidhīyeta
tathā varṇaya me prabho (12.7)

tat — that; tvam — you; nah — of us; sarva – all; dharma – righteous living; jña — knower; dharmas = dharmah — righteous living; tvad = tvat – to you; bhakti — devotion; lakṣaṇaḥ — characterized; yathā — as; yasya — of whom; vidhīyeta — may practise; tathā — so; varnaya — describe; me — to me; prabho — o Lord.

Translation

Therefore, O knower of the methods of righteous living, you may describe to me, which of us is suited for the righteous way of life, which is characterised by devotion to you, and how any of us may practice it. (12.7)

Commentary:

Basically speaking, the contention is that most people cannot practice yoga in earnest. Most of them decline the effort. This is mostly because of the passionate and depressive modes of material nature, which cause a discouragement in the nature of the living beings. Thus Uddhava pressed on for something besides yoga. What else may be a central discipline, we may ask?

Since there are so many other activities, which of these can become central to a person's life in such a way as to cause him to attain spiritual perfection?

Devotion is there in the nature of all living beings in the form of affections. However at present these are impure because they are formed in the lower modes of material nature, namely *raja guṇa* impulsive energy and *tama guṇa* depressive force. Thus how can a person use his affection to get out of the material world? Yoga practice is difficult, especially the *āsana* postures which cause pain to the body because of having to stretch taut limbs and put pressure on the arthritis joints, and because of having to exert oneself for breath absorption methods. Therefore it would be easier if a person did no yoga to attain salvation. Hence people wonder if they can chant or sing the names of God or just be motivated to do normal day to day services at God's temple and in relation to God's advocates, the preachers and temple residents.

श्री-शुक उवाच
इत्थं स्व-भृत्य-मुख्येन
पृष्टः स भगवान् हरिः ।
प्रीतः क्षेमाय मर्त्यानां
धर्मान् आह सनातनान् ॥ १२.८॥

śrī-śuka uvāca
itthaṁ sva-bhṛtya-mukhyena
pṛṣṭaḥ sa bhagavān hariḥ
prītaḥ kṣemāya martyānāṁ
dharmān āha sanātanān (12.8)

śrī-śuka – the illustrious Shuka; uvāca — said; ittham — thus; sva – own; bhṛtya – servant; mukhyena — by the foremost; pṛṣṭaḥ — questioned; sa = sah — he; bhagavān — the Blessed Lord; harih — O Hari; prītaḥ — being pleased; kṣemāya — for the benefit; martyānām — of those whose bodies must die; dharmān — religious lifestyle; āha — spoke; sanātanān — eternal.

Translation

The illustrious Shuka said: Thus, being questioned by his foremost servant, the Blessed Lord Hari was pleased. He spoke of the perpetual means of righteous lifestyle, for the benefit of those whose bodies must die. (12.8)

Commentary:

Shuka, the son of *Śrīla Vyāsadeva*, speaking to King *Parīkṣit*, explained that *Śrī* Krishna was pleased by the pressing inquiry of Uddhava for something which common people, non-yogis, could do to attain perfection. It would be services which did not include the rigors of the eightfold path of yoga. It would be activities which could be performed in the usual social setting and which would not cause the devotee to leave off the cultural scene altogether. This was for the benefit of those persons who had not mastered the mystic procedures for transfer into other dimensions as described in the last chapter. These persons are said to be *martyānām*, persons whose bodies must die. Of course the yogis too will lose bodies, but due to the yogi's accomplishment in transference to other dimensions, the yogi leaves his body behind when it dies, while others are forcibly deprived of their bodies by disasters and terminal illnesses.

श्री-भगवान् उवाच
धर्म्य एष तव प्रश्नो
नैःश्रेयस-करो नृणाम् ।
वर्णाश्रमाचारवतां
तम् उद्धव निबोध मे ॥१२.९॥

śrī-bhagavān uvāca
dharmya eṣa tava praśno
naiḥśreyasa-karo nṛṇām
varṇāśramācāravatāṁ
tam uddhava nibodha me (12.9)

śrī-bhagavān – the Blessed Lord; uvāca — said; dharmya = dharmyah — what is righteous; eṣa = eṣaḥ — this; tava — you; praśno = praśnaḥ — inquiry; naiḥśreyasa – highest good; karo = karaḥ — cause; nṛṇām — of the human being; varṇāśramācāravatāṁ = varna – occupation + āśrama — life style + ācāra-vatām — those who adhere to; tam — that; uddhava — Uddhava; nibodha — learn; me — from me.

Translation

The Blessed Lord said: This, your inquiry, O Uddhava, is righteous, for it will cause the highest good for human beings, who adhere to the recommended occupations and life styles. Learn that procedure from Me. (12.9)

Commentary:

Even though the yoga process is definite. It is not followed by the majority of human beings. Thus something else has to be recommended. Human society has to progress. Therefore there must be a general procedure through which mankind can evolve to a higher stage. Human society should be structured and there is no better person to recommend the social divisions and the corresponding duties, besides Lord Krishna.

आदौ कृत-युगे वर्णो
नृणां हस इति स्मृतः ।
कृत-कृत्याः प्रजा जात्या
तस्मात् कृत-युगं विदुः ॥१२.१०॥

ādau kṛta-yuge varṇo
nṛṇāṁ haṁsa iti smṛtaḥ
kṛta-kṛtyāḥ prajā jātyā
tasmāt kṛta-yugaṁ viduḥ 12.10)

ādau — initially; kṛta-yuga — in the Age of Easy Achievemant; varṇo = varṇaḥ — job classification; nṛṇām — of the human beings; haṁsa = haṁsaḥ — named Hamsa; iti — thus; smṛtaḥ — was called; kṛta – performed, did + kṛtyāh — what should be done, what was required to be performed; prajā = prajāḥ — o people; jātyā — by birth, by genetics; tasmāt — therefore; kṛta-yugam — Easy Achievement time-cycle; viduḥ — was called.

Translation

Initially, in the Age of Easy Achievement, the job classification of human beings was called hamsa. The people did what was required from their very birth. Therefore it was called the Easy Achievement Era. (12.10)

Commentary:

This *Kṛta* time cycle was also called the *Satya Yuga*, the Realism Age. It was a time, when many human beings, were God-fearing and all cognizant of how to live in a material body and still derive spiritual experiences, so that at the time of death, one would not have to come back into another physical form, but could go on to the spiritual universe.

Since the people of that time were elevated transcendentalists, there was only one social status.

वेदः प्रणव एवाग्रे
धर्मो ऽहं वृष-रूप-धृक् ।
उपासते तपो-निष्ठा
हसं मां मुक्त-किल्बिषाः ॥१२.११॥

vedaḥ praṇava evāgre
dharmo 'haṁ vṛṣa-rūpa-dhṛk
upāsate tapo-niṣṭhā
haṁsaṁ māṁ mukta-kilbiṣāḥ (12.11)

vedah — Veda; pranavah — Causeless Oṁ Sound; evāgre = eva — indeed; agre — at first; dharmo = dharmaḥ — the standard for righteous living; 'haṁ = aham — I; vṛṣa-rūpa-dhṛk = vṛṣa – bull + rūpa – form + dhṛk — using; upāsate — they dutifully worship; tapo = tapaḥ - austerity; niṣṭhāh — fixed; haṁsaṁ — Lord Hamsa; mām — me; mukta-kilbiṣāḥ — those who are freed from faults.

Translation

At first the Causeless Oṁ Sound was the Veda. I, in the form of a bull was the standard for righteous living. Those who were freed from faults, those who were fixed in austerity, dutifully worshiped Me, Lord Hansa. (12.11)

Commentary:

This *Praṇava* Om sound which was the Veda or scripture in the first Age, was not a sound said by human beings, but rather a sound which the human beings tuned into. It was the sound which entered into their psyches from the sky of consciousness. At that time, the bull, the symbol of farming and conveyance was proved very serviceable to the human being. Merely by farming and by going here and there as little as required, the human beings stayed in tune with Lord Swan, Lord *Hamsa*, who appeared in the supernatural Swan Form to *Sanat Kumāra* and his brothers.

त्रेता-मुखे महा-भाग
प्राणान् मे हृदयात् त्रयी ।
विद्या प्रादुरभूत् तस्या
अहम् आसं त्रि-वृन् मखः ॥१२.१२॥

tretā-mukhe mahā-bhāga
prāṇān me hṛdayāt trayī
vidyā prādurabhūt tasyā
aham āsaṁ tri-vṛn makhaḥ (12.12)

tretā-mukhe — at the beginning of the Treta Time Cycle; mahā-bhāga — o noble soul; prāṇān — from vital energy; me — my; hṛdayāt — from the causal body; trayī — three; vidyā — techniques for righteous living; prādurabhūt — was manifested; tasyā — from that; aham — I; āsam — became; tri-vṛn = tri-vṛt — three fold; makhaḥ — sacrifice.

Translation

At the beginning of the Easy Achievement Period, O noble soul, the three techniques for righteous living, was manifested from the vital energy, from My causal form. From that, I became the threefold sacrifice. (12.12)

Commentary:

The Treta Time Cycle is the 2nd Age in which three manuals for righteous living were manifested. These came down to us as the Rig, *Sāma* and Yajur Vedas. According to *Śrī* Krishna, these manifested from the vital energy within the cosmic causal body (His causal form).

The three procedures required experts for performance of each and therefore a tri-part religious ceremony was developed. At that time, gone were the days when those human beings could just link with the Supreme Being and with the Supreme Energy. Only some of the human beings could do that in the 2nd Time Cycle. The rest relied on the tri-part sacrifice.

We know now from archeological evidence, that the primitive human beings, the various types of cave men, were on the earth for many thousands of years, along with beastly monsters, but at a certain time, a more refined type of human form was manifested. What *Śrī* Krishna described has to do with some of the refined human beings.

विप्र-क्षत्रिय-विट्-शूद्रा
मुख-बाहूरु-पाद-जाः ।
वैराजात् पुरुषाज् जाता
य आत्माचार-लक्षणाः ॥१२.१३॥

vipra-kṣatriya-viṭ-śūdrā
mukha-bāhūru-pāda-jāḥ
vairājāt puruṣāj jātā
ya ātmācāra-lakṣaṇāḥ (12.13)

vipra — brahmin; ksatriya — ruling class; viṭ — business class; śūdrā — working class; mukha — from the mouth; bāhūru = bāhu — arms + ūru — thigh; pāda — feet; jāh — was produced; vairājāt — from the Universal Form; puruṣāj — from the Primal Person; jātā — was generated; ye — who, each person; ātmācāra = ātma — self, own + ācāra — activities; lakṣaṇāḥ — categorized.

Translation

The brahmins, the ruling class, the business class, and the working class, were produced from the mouth, arms, thighs and feet respectively, being all generated from the activities of the Primal Person's Universal Form. Each person was categorized by activities. (12.13)

Commentary:

In the *Tretā* Age, society was divested into four kinds of vocations, with appropriate lifestyles. Out of the Cosmic Causal body, a subtle body was formed, just as out of the individual causal forms, there developed subtle forms. This cosmic subtle body was seen by Arjuna on the battlefield of *Kurukṣetra*.

Various types of limited living entities were situated in that Universal Form according to various functions of the parts of the form, but it was all parts of One Gigantic Body. This was on the subtle plane.

गृहाश्रमो जघनतो
ब्रह्मचर्यं हृदो मम ।
वक्षः-स्थलाद् वने-वासः
सन्न्यासः शिरसि स्थितः ॥१२.१४॥

gṛhāśramo jaghanato
brahmacaryaṁ hṛdo mama
vakṣaḥ-sthalād vane-vāsaḥ
sannyāsaḥ śirasi sthitaḥ (12.14)

Translation

Householder life sprang from My thighs; celibate student life from My heart; the life of living in the woods from my chest, and total retirement from cultural activities was situated on my head. (12.14)

Commentary:

Appropriately the householder lifestyle was produced from the thighs of the Universal Form. From the thighs, sexual interest develops. Celibate student life came from His heart. That is the place of concern for others. The life of living in the woods to do austerities which is preparation for leaving one's body at its death, emerged from the chest of the Universal body. The lungs which absorb vital energy, are situated in the chest. The vital energy must transmigrate from a person's dead body to that of his would-be parent. In the mother's body, it forms for itself another living body.

Specially produced was the stage of sannyas or total retirement from cultural activities, in preparation for leaving the course of transmigration. This was produced from the head of the Universal Form.

As I type this commentary on the 17th day of August of 2002, *Śrī* Krishna inspired me to include this statement, on His behalf:

> *"All the living entities as well as the supreme living entity, Myself, are related to one whole existence. This was realized by those persons in the first Age, the Krita Period or the Satya Yuga Time. However, there developed a divestment of everybody. Some came to oppose My supremacy and developed a resistance to Me and a sense to deny My part in the whole. Thus the supreme will or My ideas, seem to be at variance to those who deny Me. This evolved into a psychological struggle within the Universal Form, the Cosmic Subtle body.*
>
> *"A phase of this struggle was viewed by Arjuna on the battlefield as revealed to him by Me. Eventually when all puny wills are recalled by Me, the struggle ceases. The lives that are lived by so many creatures, will come to an end for the time being. But those who are advanced, should always know that it is one whole, just as in the Krita Age, the people were aware, and there was no tendency for opposition to Me."*

वर्णानाम् आश्रमाणां च
जन्म-भूम्य्-अनुसारिणीः ।
आसन् प्रकृतयो नृनां
नीचैर् नीचोत्तमोत्तमाः ॥ १२.१५॥

varṇānām āśramāṇāṁ ca
janma-bhūmy-anusāriṇīḥ
āsan prakṛtayo nṝṇāṁ
nīcair nīcottamottamāḥ (12.15)

varṇānām — of the work tendencies; āśramāṇām — of the lifestyles; ca — and; janma — birth; bhūmy = bhūmi — source, situation; anusāriṇīḥ — correspond to; āsan — were; prakṛtayo = prakṛtayaḥ — dispositions; nṝṇām — of human beings; nīcair = nīcaiḥ — by inferior source, location; nīcottamottamāḥ = nīca — interior + uttama — superior + uttamāh — superior natures.

Translation

Regarding the work tendencies and lifestyles, the dispositions of human beings correspond to their source situations. The superior ones are from superior source locations. The inferior ones come from the inferior sources. (12.15)

Commentary:

From this we can understand that there is predestination in terms of what a person might turn out to be in any given situation. With certain advantages, a particular human being would develop certain abilities, while another person, even with more opportunity, could not improve his status considerably. This is due to the respective source situations in the Universal Form of the Supreme Being.

One who emerged initially from the feet of the Universal Form would be unable to function mentally like another person who emerged from the head. Thus the idea that every living being is equal or that every human being is equal to the other, is totally denied by *Śrī* Krishna. It all depends on one's source situation in the Universal Form.

Some commentators interpreted this verse in terms of our current status but there is no need to go that far, because *Śrī* Krishna already gave the context for understanding this in the previous verse. It means therefore that regardless of where we are born, we will still be limited according to our source positions in the Universal Form. Those positions cannot change at this stage of the creation.

Even though material nature may offer a person who was sourced in the head of the Universal Form, a position in the working class sector of society, that person will still exhibit the higher tendencies to be philosophical and instructive. But if nature gives someone, who initially emerged from the thigh of the Lord, a birth in a situation where he cannot be a householder, he will still exhibit the tendencies of a family man. In other words, he will express a caring interest and sexual concerns. Such is the life. This is predestined.

At this stage of the creation, there is little we can do, just as a cell in the feet of a man's body, cannot shift itself into his brain. Thus we have to see what sort of facility is available to the various types of entities who are stigmatized by this destiny. What does *Śrī* Krishna have to say about this? Obviously, there will always be disparities. People may be unhappy with reality, because when a person comes out into the objective world and looks around him, he will find that everyone is not endowed equally.

शमो दमस् तपः शौचं
सन्तोषः क्षान्तिर् आर्जवम् ।
मद्-भक्तिश् च दया सत्यं
ब्रह्म-प्रकृतयस् त्व् इमाः ॥१२.१६॥

śamo damas tapaḥ śaucaṁ
santoṣaḥ kṣāntir ārjavam
mad-bhaktiś ca dayā satyaṁ
brahma-prakṛtayas tv imāḥ (12.16)

śamo = śamaḥ — tranquility; damas = damaḥ — self discipline; tapaḥ — austerity; śaucam — cleanliness; santoṣaḥ — contentment; kṣāntir = kṣāntiḥ — forebearance; ārjavam — straightforwardness; mad-bhaktiś = mat-bhaktiḥ — devotion to me; ca — and; dayā — mercy; satyaṁ — truthfulness, realism; brahma — brahmin; prakṛtayas — disposition; tv = tu — but; imāḥ — these.

Translation

Tranquility, self discipline, austerity, cleanliness, contentment, forebearance, straight-fowardness and devotion to Me as well as mercy, realism or truthfulness; these are the dispositions of the brahmins. (12.16)

Commentary:

The human being is so constituted, that devotion to God is not His only quality. Thus we find a human being has to learn how to apply all positive and constructive character traits to bring on spiritual perfection. Devotion to God is actually the most important aspect of a person's existence, since ultimately, all living beings are dependent on God, but still that does not mean that we can exist without expressing the other traits. Thus the key is to express those under God's direction for His approval.

At face value every aspect of brahminical disposition mentioned here, is admirable or is a virtue but on close inspection, each of these aspects can be abused by the brahmin. Even the foremost aspect of devotion to God, to Krishna, can be abused. For as soon as a man is recognized as a devotee of God, he may try to exploit those who honor him.

तेजो बलं धृतिः शौर्यं
तितिक्षौदार्यम् उद्यमः ।
स्थैर्यं ब्रह्मन्यम् ऐश्वर्यं
क्षत्र-प्रकृतयस् त्व् इमाः ॥१२.१७॥

tejo balaṁ dhṛtiḥ śauryaṁ
titikṣaudāryam udyamaḥ
sthairyaṁ brahmanyam aiśvaryaṁ
kṣatra-prakṛtayas tv imāḥ (12.17)

tejo = tejaḥ — valor; balam — strength; dhṛtiḥ — heroism, courage; śauryam — heroism; titikṣaudāryam = titikṣā — endurance + audāryam — generosity; udyamaḥ — endeavor; sthairyam — steadiness; brahmanyam — supportive of the brahmins; aiśvaryam — political leadership;

kṣatra — ruling class; prakṛtayas — dispositions; tv = tu — but; imah — in these.

Translation

Valor, strength, courage, heroism, endurance, generosity; endeavor, steadiness, being supportive of brahmins, exhibiting political leadership; these are the dispositions of those in the ruling class. (12.17)

Commentary:

Rulers are in a special position, from which they can misuse enterprising power. They need to take special precautions to keep themselves under control, otherwise they will develop a large quantity of sins. In addition, the actions of rulers affect many others. Thus their mishaps cause great inconvenience to many other living entities, not just to the human beings.

It is important that a ruler be devoted to the qualified brahmins, to be supportive of them and to take their advice but this does not mean that the ruler should blindly follow a brahmin. He has to use discrimination. He should be selective in picking an advisor. A ruler has the right to change his choice of brahmin advisor. He may have more than one such counselor.

There was a king who took advice from some brahmin priests, who advised the royal family. The advice however was not good. Therefore after his body died that king went to the hellish regions. His son, who assumed the throne, was worried about the departed king. Somehow, the son had an intuition that his father had not reached the heavenly places, and had not taken a earthly rebirth. He therefore questioned the counselors who advised his father. They could not determine the destination of his father.

Sometime after the mystic sage Lomash Rishi, came there and the son questioned him. The sage than said that he would use his astral body to search the world of the hereafter for the departed king. He found the king suffering in the hellish realms. Lomash Rishi questioned the king about the reason for the transfer to that hellish place. The king explained:

"O, it was because I took advice from those brahmins. You can do me a favor, ask my son not to accept their counsel."

Lomash Rishi asked the king for some more details and the King explained: " When I ruled I used to offer many sacrifices as instructed by the counselors but I paid for these with money from the State Funds. This is why I am suffering. Just you tell my son not to do this. If he wants to have religious ceremonies, he should finance them from his salary. The state funds belong to the population, not to him. Religious functions which are done for the benefit of the royal family should not utilize money from the government treasury.

"If he follows this advice, I would be released from this hell eventually. Whatever money I used from the State Treasury, must be paid back with interest, before I would be freed from that sin."

This example shows that a king should not blindly follow religious advisors. He must question them closely, read scriptures and use good judgment. This is due to the fact that even though the brahmins emitted from the head of the Universal Form, they sometimes fall under lowering influences which affect their decisions.

Another important aspect is this. Someone may take birth from a discerning capable and honest brahmin's body but that person may be dishonest and incapable. Even though he should be given credit for his pedigree or birth status, his advice should be censored. He should not be followed blindly merely because his father was an honest brahmin. On the other hand, a person who took birth in a non-brahmin family but who has the qualities of a brahmin should be given recognition if he consistently displays the brahmin temperament. It is a person's general disposition *(prakṛtaya)* which is important not the family background.

It is not the body of a man but his character which counts. But if a person has a higher body by virtue of taking birth in a higher caste, we should realize that providence placed him in that position because of piety in some other life. While in the case of an elevated person who took a lower birth, we should notice that a low body does not necessarily cover up someone's glory.

Fire which is hidden under thick ashes will still burn but wet earth under a blazing fire, may still remain cool. Each individual case must be checked separately. We should not hold a stereotyped view.

आस्तिक्यं दान-निष्ठा च
अदम्भो ब्रह्म-सेवनम् ।
अतुष्टिर् अर्थोपचयैर्
वैश्य-प्रकृतयस् त्व् इमाः ॥१२.१८॥

āstikyaṁ dāna-niṣṭhā ca
adambho brahma-sevanam
atuṣṭir arthopacayair
vaiśya-prakṛtayas tv imāḥ (12.18)

āstikyam — belief in God; dāna-niṣṭhā — determination to give in charity; ca — and; adambho = adambhaḥ — sincerity; brahma-sevanam — service to brahmins; atuṣṭir = atuṣṭiḥ — not being satisfied; arthopacayair = arthopacayaih = artha — wealth + upacayaiḥ — by the accumulation; vaiśya — merchantile people; prakṛtayas — tendencies; tv = tu — indeed; imah — these.

Translation

Belief in God, determination to give charity, sincerity, service to brahmins, not being satisfied by the accumulation of wealth; these indeed are the tendencies of the mercantile people. (12.18)

Commentary:

Usually the mercantile people give in charity as they are advised by the brahmins or priestly class. In other words, unless they are in association with such people, they are unable to control their quest for money. However, some mercantile people who are atheistic or who are instinctively distrustful of the priestly class, do have a charitable disposition regardless. They usually form Charitable Trusts to give to the poor or to create beneficial community activities.

In the capitalistic societies, the governments usually pressure the mercantile sector to support community activities and to give to non-profit organizations. This is done by creating tax laws which favor those who donate to charitable trusts. In that way, capitalistic governments induce wealthy citizens to help with the maintenance of society. The wealthy people benefit by giving charity to the less fortunate human beings, since by doing so they deter theft of their property and reduce the incidence of social unrest.

Persons who are in the mercantile mentality will, sooner or later, be upgraded to the governing class. It will happen in time, even though it might happen in thousands of years. No one remains this or that, because material nature itself creates pressure to cause living entities to move forward or backward in the mundane evolutionary cycle.

Even though by nature, a mercantile person does not have much spiritual insight, still it is natural for him to have a belief in God. This is because he has a strong sense of ownership which inspires him to think that there must be a supreme proprietor. Thus, from such an instinct, such a person becomes a devotee of God. Understanding that a thief can hurt him, a mercantile person who even though essentially a thief himself, appreciates the goodness through which the less fortunate people restrain from attacking him. Thus the wealthy people are usually religiously inclined, even though they exploit the lower class.

शुश्रूषणं द्विज-गवां
देवानां चाप्य् अमायया ।
तत्र लब्धेन सन्तोषः
शूद्र-प्रकृतयस् त्व् इमाः ॥१२.१९॥

śuśrūṣaṇaṁ dvija-gavāṁ
devānāṁ cāpy amāyayā
tatra labdhena santoṣaḥ
śūdra-prakṛtayas tv imāḥ (12.19)

śuśrūṣaṇam — attending to; dvija-gavām = dvija — brahmins + gavām — of the cows; devānām — of the supernatural rulers; cāpy = ca — and + apy (api) — also; amāyayā — without trickery, sincerely; tatra — there; labdhena — with what is acquired; santoṣaḥ — contentment; śūdra — worker; prakṛtayas — tendencies; tv = tu — indeed; imāḥ — these.

Translation

Attending to the brahmins, the cows and the supernatural rulers, and doing so sincerely, being content with whatever is acquired from them; are the tendencies of the workers. (12.19)

Commentary:

It was said that verses like this one, prove conclusively that the *Purāṇas* were written by brahmins in ancient India, for the purpose of making people subservient to them. On a careful study of this verse, this might seem to be true. However there is another way to consider this.

In ancient India, persons with a working class temperament had little chance to change status, because the social situation was clan-oriented. It was difficult if not near impossible for a person who was born to working class parents, to gain status on par with brahmin families. Even today in some parts of the world, the caste system holds its place and it is near impossible for a person to change his birth stigma.

But elsewhere this also functioned, even though in the developed countries, and in many undeveloped locales, a person could move from one occupation to another at his own risk.

Śrī Krishna's intention is to show how a person would develop spiritually even if he is born in low class family and even if the society does not permit him to change status. First of all, the description given by *Śrī* Krishna is idealistic. In a human society, it is hardly likely that we will find pure-hearted brahmins. Usually the brahmins are protective of their family clans and operate to maintain the security of their families by suppressing the other classes. That is our experience.

This verse makes sense only if we were dealing with ideal brahmins, people who had the mystic perception to be in touch with the supernatural rulers and people who did not have to use sly methods to protect their families and to keep their clans on top in human society.

Śrī Krishna had this in mind, because he began by describing the conditions in the Treta Age, the 2nd Vedic Era, when the human beings began to manifest four types of tendencies and life styles. Those were a different stock of brahmins.

Thus under those circumstances, of those highly elevated people, a working class person who was attentive to the brahmins, the cows and the supernatural rulers, and who related to them sincerely, who was satisfied with whatever he acquired from them, exhibited the qualities of an ideal worker. The person had to have the nature which caused him to operate in that manner. It was not merely birth as the son or daughter of a worker.

अशौचम् अनृतं स्तेयं
नास्तिक्यं शुष्क-विग्रहः ।
स कामः क्रोधश् च तर्षश् च
स भावो ऽन्त्यावसायिनाम् ॥ १२.२० ॥

aśaucam anṛtaṁ steyaṁ
nāstikyaṁ śuṣka-vigrahaḥ
sa kāmaḥ krodhaś ca tarṣaś ca
sa bhāvo 'ntyāvasāyinām (12.20)

aśaucam — uncleanliness; anrtam — dishonesty; steyam — theft; nāstikyam — atheism; śuṣka-vigrahaḥ = śuṣka – futile + vigraham — discussion; kāmaḥ — craving; krodhas = krodhaḥ — anger; ca — and; tarṣaś — greed; ca — and; sa = sah — this; bhāvo = bhāvaḥ — nature; 'ntyāvasāyinām = 'ntya (antya) — lowest category + avasāyinām — of those living.

Translation

Uncleanliness, dishonesty, theft, atheism, futile discussion, craving, anger and greed; this is the nature of those living in the lowest category. (12.20)

Commentary:

All such persons who exhibit all or any of these qualities, are placed in a 5th class by Lord Krishna, in the lowest category. This is not a matter of birth necessarily, even though if a person is born from parents of a low character, he or she might assume that nature by association.

We know for certain however, that in the ancient societies, if a person was born of parents who had a reputation for being undesirable, that person was regarded in exactly the same way for his entire lifetime. The only way he could elevate himself in the social strata was to move to another area, where people were not conversant with his background. And this holds true to a certain extent today.

There are many children who are insulted and mistreated merely because their parents or one of their relatives, is considered or in fact are, criminally involved in society. This happens frequently.

Even though *Śrī* Krishna told us that the brahmins, the ruling class, the mercantile people and the honest content workers, emerged from certain parts of the Universal Form, He did not say where the undesirables originated from but else here in the *Śrīmad Bhāgavatam*, there is information that some of them came from the backside of the Supreme Being, either from the backside of Lord *Brahmā* or from the darkness which occurs behind the Universal Form. That is a supernatural and not a physical darkness.

अहिसा सत्यम् अस्तेयम्
अकाम-क्रोध-लोभता ।
भूत-प्रिय-हितेहा च
धर्मो ऽय सार्व-वर्णिकः ॥१२.२१॥

ahiṁsā satyam asteyam
akāma-krodha-lobhatā
bhūta-priya-hitehā ca
dharmo 'yaṁ sārva-varṇikaḥ (12.21)

ahimsā — non-injury; satyam — truthfulness; asteyam — non-stealing; akāma = a – not + kāma – craving; krodha – being angry; lobhatā — being greedy; bhūta — beings; priya — agreeable; hitehā = hita — beneficial + īhā — being inclined; ca — and; dharmo = dharmaḥ — righteous duty; 'yam = ayam — this; sārva – all; varṇikaḥ — of the members of human society.

Translation

Non-injury, truthfulness, non-stealing, not craving, not being angry, not being greedy, being inclined to do what is agreeable and beneficial to all beings; this is the righteous duty of all members of human society. (12.21)

Commentary:

This is *Śrī* Krishna's general definition of *dharma* for all human beings. This is a generalization which pertains to each of the four higher classes, who should be capable of behaving in the way described.

In yoga practice, this behavior is required and it is listed as the two lowest steps of yoga, that of *yama* and *niyama*. In *kriyā* yoga, these qualities are developed on the subtle plane, since even if the gross body exhibits these behaviors, that might be a diplomacy. For sincerity, the *kriyā* yogi has to develop them in his subtle body and manifest them in subtle acts.

An important factor is the social environment. Even a person as gentle as Arjuna, a person who was non-violent in nature, had to exhibit violence as part of his duty on the battlefield. Thus for perfect exhibition of these qualities, one has to be in a particular environment. In the human setting, one might have to sacrifice one good quality in order to enforce another. People who are fanatical about non-injury and other aspects of high character, do not seem to grasp this idea. They feel that under no circumstance, should one sacrifice one of these qualities to protect another virtue.

The connection is responsibility. Let us take for example, the case of Arjuna. He was requested by his brother, King *Yudhiṣṭhira*, and by his friend Lord Krishna, to fight at *Kurukṣetra*. Arjuna, though a pacifistic non-violent personality, was a trained warrior. As a warrior on a battlefield, he would be required to injure others. That meant that he was asked to use injury to bring about non-injury or stated differently to use violence to stop violence. The violence was being perpetrated by Arjuna's cousin, Prince Duryodhana. What should Arjuna have done?

Actually the Pandavas, the brothers of Arjuna, especially Prince *Yudhiṣṭhira* exerted themselves in a non-violent way for a long time and endured twelve years of banishment, and still they were unable to change the violent policy of Duryodhana. Because they were responsible for the effects of Duryodhana's policy upon the citizens, they had to stop him with violence.

We must understand that subtle violence is greater than physical violence. Some of us have a responsibility to discipline others. At first, when he saw the armies, Arjuna changed his mind about using violence. He could not stomach the apparent effects of a war. When he saw *Śrī* Krishna's Universal Form, and understood that Krishna was in charge, as the Ultimate Responsible Agent, he decided to cooperate in the use of violence for the sake of stopping Duryodhana's subtle and gross manipulations.

Any of the negative qualities, implied in this verse, such as violence, untruthfulness, theft, craving, anger, greed and doing what is not agreeable, maybe used with discretion by a person who has the responsibility to keep human society in order. This has the risk of misuse. But to be realistic that is a risk one must take for the over-all benefit of society.

We do not have a society of perfect human beings. We must have some disciplinary policy, because if some individual takes pleasure in committing violence, we should stop him in an agreeable or disagreeable manner, depending on his persistence in violating human rights.

Tolerance is also a good quality but it has appropriate time and place. We cannot be endlessly tolerant of criminal elements and decadent influences. At some point, we have to draw a line. And we do not have to be perfect to administer this, but we should aspire to do our best. After-all only the Supreme Being is perfect.

द्वितीयं प्राप्यानुपूर्व्याज्
जन्मोपनयनं द्विजः ।
वसन् गुरु-कुले दान्तो
ब्रह्माधीयीत चाहूतः ॥ १२.२२ ॥

dvitīyaṁ prāpyānupūrvyāj
janmopanayanaṁ dvijaḥ
vasan guru-kule dānto
brahmādhīyīta cāhūtaḥ (12.22)

dvitīyam — second birth; prāpyānupūrvyāj = prāpya — receiving + ānupūrvyāj (ānupūrvyāt) — in sequence; janmopanayanam = janma — birth + upanayanam — sacred thread ceremony; dvijaḥ — a twice-born student; vasan — living; guru-kule — at the school of the teacher; dānto = dāntaḥ — self-controlled; brahmādhīyīta = brahma — Vedic literatures + adhīyīta — should study; cāhūtaḥ = ca — and + āhūtaḥ — summoned.

Translation

Receiving in sequence of rites, the second birth which is the sacred thread ceremony, a twice born student while living at the school of the teacher, being self controlled and being summoned by the master, should study the Vedic literature. (12.22)

Commentary:

This begins the description of the ideal student life in the Vedic times before and during the time of Lord Krishna. This is rarely followed today, even in India. There was a sequences of rites which each member of the three higher castes was supposed to observe in youth, during householder life, in early retirement and in the elderly years just before passing from the body. These rites were enacted in a certain sequence which began with a prenatal ceremony and ended with the *antyeṣṭi* funeral rites.

Those boys who were born in the three higher castes, and who got the approval of a brahmin teacher, were awarded a sacred thread at a certain stage. This signified their initiation in certain sacred mantras, into advanced meditation techniques and into the liturgy for worship and sacred rites. It depended on the approval of a senior brahmin. It was mostly bestowed through personal discretion. Thus it was important for the student to understand the idiosyncrasies of the teacher, as well as to learn whatever was taught. Generally the main duty of the student was to serve, do as told and absorb whatever education the teacher bestowed.

It appears from the Vedic history, that many ancient brahmins had some type of power, such that if a student was blessed, he was blessed indeed, and if he was cursed, then he was damned for certain. Thus today most of those stories are regarded as myths, because it does not necessarily hold true today that if a teacher curses, the student is finished, nor if he blesses, the student reaches some good.

Because the brahmins were teachers of the infants of the three higher castes, they acquired unprecedented importance in society. Thus they were regarded as being more authoritative than rulers. Today, this changed. Nowadays the person who enjoys more authority than the rulers are the jurors, the judges, magistrates and the like. In ancient times the rulers themselves were the jurors who took advice from the brahmins.

मेखलाजिन-दण्डाक्ष-
ब्रह्म-सूत्र-कमण्डलून् ।
जटिलो ऽधौत-दद्-वासो
ऽरक्त-पीठः कुशान् दधत् १२.२३

mekhalājina-daṇḍākṣa-
brahma-sūtra-kamaṇḍalūn
jaṭilo 'dhauta-dad-vāso
'rakta-pīṭhaḥ kuśān dadhat (12.23)

mekhalājina = mekhalā — belt + ajina — deer skin; daṇḍāksa = danda — staff + akṣa — akṣa prayer beads; brahma - brahmin; sūtra — thread; kamaṇḍalūn — water pot; jaṭilo = jaṭilah — matted hair; 'dhauta = adhauta — being very concerned with; dad = dat - teeth; vāso = vāsaḥ — clothing; 'rakta = arakta - not red; pīṭhaḥ — seat; kuśān — kusha grass; dadhat — carry.

Translation

He should wear a belt, deer skin, akṣa prayer beads, a brahmin thread, carry a staff, water pot and kusha grass. He should wear matted hair and not be very concerned with his teeth and clothing, and should use an unpainted seat. (12.23)

Commentary:

This was the tradition in those days. *Śrī* Krishna knows this well not only as a tradition but by his own behavior in acting as a student of Sandipani Muni and also of *Mahāyogi* Upamanyu. The *akṣa* beads are *rudrākṣa* beads, for it was customary for the *brahmacārī* assistant to be a devotee of Lord Shiva. Lord Krishna behaved as a devotee of Lord Shiva, when Krishna accepted studentship under Upamanyu Rishi.

स्नान-भोजन-होमेषु
जपोच्चारे च वाग्-यतः ।
न च्छिन्द्यान् नख-रोमाणि
कक्षोपस्थ-गतान्य् अपि ॥ १२.२४॥

snāna-bhojana-homeṣu
japoccāre ca vāg-yataḥ
na cchindyān nakha-romāṇi
kakṣopastha-gatāny api (12.24)

snāna — bath; bhojana — eating; homeṣu — while offering oblations in fire; japoccāre = japa — chanting holy names + uccāre — while evacuating; ca — and; vāg = vāk - speech; yataḥ — restraint; na — not; cchindyān = chindyāt — should trim; nakha — nail; romāni — hairs; kakṣopastha = kakṣa — armpit + upastha — pubic; gatāny = gatāni — in relation to; api — even.

Translation

He should restrain speech while bathing, eating and offering oblation in fire, chanting holy names and evacuating the body. He should not trim his nails, nor cut hairs, even in relation to his armpit and pubic area. (12.24)

Commentary:

If one does not restrain speech while bathing, eating, offering oblations, chanting holy names and evacuating, then one will not give these activities the proper attention. Subsequently, they will be done haphazardly. This will slow down the spiritual progress. Bathing, eating, and evacuating are merely bodily functions but there are important in the life of an ascetic. In some phases of yoga practice, bathing is prohibited and so is eating but generally an ascetic should perform these functions carefully and with due attention.

Offering oblations in fire and chanting holy names are religious activities. The offering of oblations used to be very important in the Vedic era, when it was necessary to serve the fire-god Agni, and to ask him to convey offerings to the ancestors and to the supernatural rulers and the Supreme Being. Chanting of holy names became even more important in this age, and so we find that many religious sects stress chanting as the only method for salvation.

The tending of the sacrificial fire was a big event in the home of the teachers in Vedic times. The fire was not supposed to go out at any time. If a disciple was assigned the duty of maintaining the flame, he had to be sure that he did so, otherwise he incurred the disfavor of his spiritual master who was responsible to keep the fire-god present in the hermitage or at the shrine. There were very strict rules in those times.

रेतो नावकिरेज् जातु
ब्रह्म-व्रत-धरः स्वयम् ।
अवकीर्णे ऽवगाह्याप्सु
यतासुस् त्रि-पदा जपेत् ॥ १२.२५॥

reto nāvakirej jātu
brahma-vrata-dharaḥ svayam
avakīrṇe 'vagāhyāpsu
yatāsus tri-padāṁ japet (12.25)

reto = retaḥ — semen; nāvakirej = nāvakiret = should not expell; jātu — even; brahma – attentiveness to brahman, implying celibacy; vrata – vow; dharaḥ — one who maintains; svayam — itself; avakīrne — having passed out; 'vagāhyāpsu = avagāhyāpsu — plunging in water; yatāsus = yata – control + asuḥ — breath; tri-padām — three lined Gāyatrī verse; japet — he should respect.

Translation

As a person maintains attentiveness to the brahman spiritual existence, which implies celibate vows, he should never expel semen. If by itself the semen is passed out, he should plunge in water, and after doing breath control exercises, he should repeat the three-lined Gāyatrī verse. (12.25)

Commentary:

Celibacy is the highlight of yoga austerities for without it, one can neither develop nor maintain his *brahma-randra* nor keep kundalini shakti in the subtle brain. An ascetic should understand that sex life is the anti-pole to spiritual development.

The life force in the body usually resides in the base chakra, the *mūlādhāra*. If it is not energized it will remain in that area, to use most of its energy for digestion, sexual expression and excretion. If it is to rise from there into the brain, the three activities of eating, sexual emission and excretion will have to be curtailed.

In the pubic area, kundalini shakti is experienced as a flash of bright light during sexual release, but this same power can be used in the head of the subtle body. One has to decide as to where one wants to use that energy, ether in the lower trunk of the body or in the head, in the *buddhi* intellect organ.

On occasion semen will pass out of the body or an ascetic might have sexual dreams through which either his subtle body alone or his subtle and gross forms will experience sexual emission. Then he should do penance by taking bath, doing *prāṇāyāma* practices and by repeating the Gāyatrī mantras sufficiently to restore his mind's focus on spiritual reality.

Prāṇāyāma practice is mentioned, because without it, there can be no true celibacy. It is by *prāṇāyāma* practice that one becomes an *ūrdhva-retā* or a person whose seminal energy links with the kundalini chakra and flows upward as electrified energy in the spine of the subtle body. Stagnant celibacy is done without *prāṇāyāma* but it does not have the same effects.

Semen sometimes spills out of the body because of lifting heavy items or because of straining the body in one way or the other. That sort of sexual emission is not related to sexual intercourse and is not a breach of celibacy, even though it does negatively affect the kundalini power in the body.

There are many *brahmacaris* who approach me about celibacy. Sometimes they admit in private that they cannot maintain celibacy because they have wet dreams. However these are usually persons who feel that by chanting holy names all such problems would go away, but they find that this is untrue. This verse makes it clear that one must also do *prāṇāyāma*. Just as a householder is supposed to take a bath after his legitimate morally-approved sexual intercourses with his wife, so if one passes off semina by chance, or after falling into a flirtation, one should take a bath but one should also resituate himself in his religious procedure by chanting the special mantra one was given by a spiritual master, after one has done some *prāṇāyāma* and has re-linked the sexual energy to the kundalini shakti. Those who do not know kundalini yoga are unfortunate, but they can make an effort to learn it.

अग्न्य्-अर्काचार्य-गो-विप्र-
गुरु-वृद्ध-सुराञ् शुचिः ।
समाहित उपासीत
सन्ध्ये द्वे यत-वाग् जपन् ॥ १२.२६ ॥

agny-arkācārya-go-vipra-
guru-vṛddha-surāñ śuciḥ
samāhita upāsīta
sandhye dve yata-vāg japan (12.26)

agny = agni — fire; arka — sun; ācārya — head of the spiritual lineage; go — cow; vipra — brahmin; guru — spiritual master; vṛddha — elders; surān — supernatural rulers; śuciḥ — one who cleanses his bodies; samāhita = samāhitaḥ — with the linking of the attention to the concentration force; upāsīta — he should offer worship; sandhye — at dawn and twilight; dve — two, both; yata-vāg = yata-vāk — restrained speech; japan — repetition of sacred holy names.

Translation

One who cleansed his bodies, should link his attention to the concentration force in the psyche, and then offer worship to fire, the sun, the head of the spiritual lineage, the cows, the brahmins, the spiritual master, the elders and supernatural rulers, doing so both at dawn and twilight. He should restrain speech while repeating the holy names. (12.26)

Commentary:

The Acharya is the head of the spiritual lineage. This person may or may not be the guru or spiritual master of the disciple. The head of the lineage is a powerful person who established or boosted the disciplic succession which one entered. This person may not be one's spiritual master. In any case, one has to honor that Acharya. If he is one's spiritual master, he is honored in two respects, both as head of the lineage, and as the personal teacher. In addition there could be more than one spiritual master and a disciple might be affiliated with more than one head of lineages, all depending on the disciplines and worship procedures adopted. Therefore one should honor all such persons.

Even if a spiritual master departed from his body, one may honor him in meditation by reaching him mystically, depending on the development of one's yoga practice.

Śucih or cleansing of the body, may be different for each student, depending on the level of practice. For those who do no yoga, bodily cleansing means taking bath and then sanctifying the body with sanctified water, *tilak* sanctified clay markings and holy names. For yogis, it is the same but they also do *āsana* postures, *prāṇāyāma*, kundalini yoga, celibacy yoga and purity yoga for making sure that the sexual energy is not being used sexually on the subtle plane, that the kundalini chakra is moving upwards and that the entire psyche is energized with fresh *prāṇa* through *prāṇāyāma* practice.

The fire and the sun are to be recognized. Thus before yoga practice in the early morning, one says mantras outdoors while observing the sky. This is done before sunrise, when it is dawn outside. With hands folded in prayer fashion, one looks at the moon or at the sky and says:

Om Somāya namah	- My obeisances to the moon deity
Om Suryāya namah	- My obeisances to the sun deity
Om Indrāya namah	- My obeisances to the weather deity
Om Prāṇavayave namah	- My obeisances to the vitalizing air deity
Jai Śrī Mahādeva	- All glories to Lord Shiva

This is salutation to the moon, then to the sun, then to the supernatural person who regulates rainfall, then to the energizing air which is to be used in *prāṇāyāma* practice, then to Lord Shiva, who is the patron deity of yogis.

One should then bow down to Mother Earth and to the cows. This means that one recognizes that Mother Earth gives facility by providing a body in which one may do the yoga austerities and attain perfection. Since the demigods want material bodies and cannot get them, one has to appreciate one's fortune in getting one. One bows down to Mother Cow because she has agreed in conjunction with her sister, Mother Earth, to provide nutrients so that one's body can survive for sometime on this earth. This is also the worship of *Mā Puṣţidevī*, who is the patron deity of nutrition.

Because of *Mā Puşţidevī*, one's infant body got milk from the mother's body, as soon as it was expelled by the womb. So we have got to appreciate her at all times, by always saying to her, "Yes Mother, whatever you say or do is alright. If it were not for you I would not be here to practice the austerities through which I may attain perfection. I should not mistreat my wife's breast because the breast is my mother but if I beget children, then the breast will be their mother, just as she was my mother in infancy."

One should offer respects to the brahmin priests even if they are arrogant and proud. These ritual experts, even if they are not yogis, do a tremendous amount of service to keep human society in order by their ritual expertise. If they address a yogi, he should always reply, "Yes sir". He should be cordial and friendly with them. This does not mean that he should be in too close association with them, because then he will be induced to take up ritual worship and his yoga practice will gradually and surely cease.

Elders of the community and family elders should be treated with care, because these people invested pious activities into one's life. One should always remember that during infancy and childhood, one was helpless. These people by their attachments and affections took care of one's body.

The supernatural rulers should always be respected. One should not at any time take sides with one group of worshippers against another. One should be cordial to all. Somewhere, a devotee of Lord Shiva, thinks that Lord Shiva is the *deva deva*, the God of the gods. At another place a worshipper feels that Lord Vishnu is the God of gods. Therefore when they meet, instead of respecting each other, they argue and part with bad feelings. One should side with neither of them but one should respect each of the spiritual authorities. Even the minor devas like Lord *Gaṇesh*, and Lord *Hanumān* should be respected.

Lord Ganesh was a *mahāyogīn* in many of the previous time cycles, but at this time, he acts just as a supernatural ruler. Lord *Hanumān* acted as a *mahāyogin* warrior during the time of Lord *Rāma*. One should always remember this. Without their assistance and good will one cannot be successful in yoga practice. Lord Shiva, Lord Krishna or anyone else, cannot protect one if one neglects persons like *Śrī Gaṇesh* and Lord *Hanumān*. One should not adopt the attitude of those who think that *Śrī Gaṇesh* is a nobody and who feel that the devas or demigods are useless. No yogi in his right mind will adopt such an attitude because it destroys yoga progression.

Samāhita does not mean sitting down in the morning to concentrate and meditate without doing *prāṇāyāma*. One should not fool oneself nor the public by sitting to meditate without having a daily consistent *prāṇāyāma* practice. By doing one or two daily sessions of *prāṇāyāma*, one energizes the subtle body. Then one can meditate properly because the energization with *prāṇa* will cause certain concentration forces to manifest naturally. Then one can link one's attention to such forces and do the *dhāraṇā* focus which develops into *dhyāna* effortless meditation, which in turn leads to *samādhi* continuous linkage into higher reality. In addition, after the subtle body is energized, one should link up to the great yogis in the subtle atmosphere. They will advise one accordingly.

After meditation practice, depending on the instructions of the spiritual master, one should do japa chanting and do worship ceremonies or scriptural reading and any other services stipulated. Those who are householders or those who are single practitioners, should get a procedure to follow from their spiritual master.

As far as a guru is concerned, one should try to avoid taking one who is ostentatious, even if he is a capable yogi. This is because a spiritual master who sets himself up for ceremonial worship by the general mass of people, will not have sufficient time to pay detailed attention to one's progression. One should try to find a spiritual master who has few disciples and who is caring enough and has time enough to give one detailed instruction. Such a teacher should be diligent with his own spiritual practice *(sādhanā)* and should not be too involved in teaching others. The main thing is to get the required techniques from a spiritual master. Worshipping a spiritual master ceremonially is good but too much of that causes the disciples to become stagnant, because then they neglect the disciplinary practice in yoga and mistake ceremonial worship of the guru for personal *sādhanā*. In addition, the spiritual master may be imperiled by such worship as he may begin to feel that he deserves to be the focus of it.

Even though I gave this advice, for myself personally, I prefer not to have disciples. This is because I am not empowered to take students nor to set myself up for ceremonial worship. I can however gave some techniques in so far as I practiced. Somebody asked me to accept him as a disciple but I am not interested. This is because my concern is self-mastery not fanfare. I know a little about yoga, but I do not know enough to be a figurehead spiritual master. That is the gist of it. Because I found some worthy yoga teachers, most in the astral world, I can advise someone but that is all.

One should not regret if one cannot find a guru who is worthy of ceremonial worship. There is not always a facility for such worship on this earth but there is ample opportunity in the subtle world. Therefore one should practice steadily, to develop and increase one's subtle perception.

Restrained speech is part of *pratyāhar* sensual restraint practice, which is the 5th stage of yoga. This means that one curtails the exteriorization profile of the mind. If one fails to do this, he will not be able to enter *samādhi* and that would be unfortunate.

Repetition of holy names should be done to keep the external mind in order, otherwise it will hunt for ordinary objects. However one should not mindlessly repeat holy names, nor should one regard it as just a routine. *Śrīla Bhaktivedānta Swāmī* who was not a practicing aṣṭanga yogi, and who stressed the holy names of *Śrī* Krishna, had full faith in those holy names which extol *Śrī* Krishna. One has to get a set of holy names from somebody like him, because then, a confidence in chanting will be acquired.

आचार्यं मां विजानीयान्
नावन्मन्येत कर्हिचित् ।
न मर्त्य-बुद्ध्यासूयेत
सर्व-देव-मयो गुरुः ॥१२.२७॥

ācāryaṁ māṁ vijānīyān
nāvanmanyeta karhicit
na martya-buddhyāsūyeta
sarva-deva-mayo guruḥ (12.27)

ācāryam — head of the spiritual lineage; mām — me, myself; vijānīyām — he should know; nāvanmanyeta = na – not + avamanyeta — should regard; karhicit — at any time; na — not;

martya – those with temporary bodies; buddhyāsūyeta = buddhyā — with the view + asūyeta — should envy; sarva – all; deva — supernatural rulers; mayo = mayah — representative; guruḥ — spiritual master.

Translation

He should regard the head of the spiritual lineage as being Myself. He should not hold a view of the teacher as being bound for death, nor disregard him at any time, nor envy him. The spiritual master is the representative of all supernatural rulers. (12.27)

Commentary:

There are basically two types of spiritual masters. The most respected ones are those who become head of the spiritual lineages. Such persons as *Śrīpad Śankarācārya, Śrīmad Madhvācārya, Śrīmad Rāmānujācārya* and recently persons like *Śrī Śrīmad Bhaktivedānta Swāmī Prabhupāda* and even *Śrī Śrīmad Pramukha Swāmī* of the *Swāmīnārāyaṇa Sampradāya*, are heads of lineages. These personalities descend with special missions to set up foundations for the spread of a specific spiritual method.

It is not always possible to get close to such teachers. Even if one comes into their confidential circle, one may not get instructions for detailed spiritual development. This is because their missions are broad, encompassing human society. If one needs a tailored instruction, one will have to find teachers who have the time to check the details of one's practice.

The nature of the disciple has much to do with it. If one feels satisfied in the association of a spiritual master who is mainly concerned with a world mission, with missionary activities and the increase of the following, then one is not required to locate a teacher who would give tailored instructions. Otherwise if one has a different nature and wants to complete the austerities, one will have to ease away from a popular teacher and find one who can give one the special techniques which cause one to advance in the desired way.

A teacher who is so charismatic that he can develop and manage a world mission, should be regarded just as empowered by God. Such a person has to be regarded in that way but that does not mean that we allow such a person to keep us at a mediocre level. It might be wise to avoid such a person so that he does not engage one in missionary activities, doing everything for everyone else and causing on neglect of one's spiritual development.

A spiritual master, either a popular one or another one from whom one can get tailored techniques, is in fact a representative of the supernatural rulers. We should always remember that. But that does not mean that he might not abuse himself not mislead his others. Despite the high rating given by Lord Krishna, that is possible.

If the disciple pays attention to his spiritual progress, it is hardly likely that he would be abused by a teacher. An interest in self development is itself the means of protection from any possible exploitation, manipulation and tomfoolery by a teacher.

साय प्रातर् उपानीय
भैक्ष्य तस्मै निवेदयेत् ।
यच् चान्यद् अप्य् अनुज्ञातम्
उपयुञ्जीत सयतः ॥१२.२८॥

sāyaṁ prātar upānīya
bhaikṣyaṁ tasmai nivedayet
yac cānyad apy anujñātam
upayuñjīta saṁyataḥ (12.28)

sāyam — evening; prātar = prātaḥ — morning; upānīya — brings; bhaikṣyam — begged for; tasmai — to him; nivedayet — should give; yac = yat — whatever; cānyad = ca anyat — and other; apy = api — also; anujñātam — what is instructed; upayuñjīta — should take; saṁyataḥ — controlled.

Translation

At evening, in the morning, he should bring food and other items begged for, to the teacher. He should take as instructed with a controlled attitude. (12.28)

Commentary:

There are certain attitudinal requirements which facilitate the transmission of knowledge and technique from a spiritual master. Even though there are general guidelines, one should work along with the idiosyncrasies of the teacher. By serving him for sometime, one gets to understand his habits and learns to avoid what aggravates him. Over all, a humble service mood is the best way to approach a spiritual master.

If the spiritual master makes a mistake, one should not bother with it, because after all, if one is serious about spiritual life, one should keep one's objective in mind and not be diverted by focusing on the real or apparent defects of the teacher.

Previously, the disciples went out in the early morning hours to beg alms from the neighborhood communities. Nowadays that is not such a practical method because the societies changed their attitude towards ascetic life. However one will have to perform service as instructed by the spiritual master. No matter what it is, if one does not have a willing attitude, one will not develop a close relationship with the guru.

Usually there is a certain method of eating and a certain type of food which is cooked at the place of the guru. There are usually restrictions about the time for meals. Thus one must comply.

In such a situation, it should always be; *yes Sir* or *no Sir*. If one cannot tolerate the situation of the guru, one should offer respects to him any way and then quietly go away. It is not expected that every person will accept any particular spiritual master. Therefore one should not think that one must accept a certain teacher. But if one accepts him and then feels that he is not suitable, one should leave his association quietly without quarrel or hard feelings.

शुश्रूषमाण आचार्यं
सदोपासीत नीच-वत् ।
यान-शय्यासन-स्थानैर्
नाति-दूरे कृताञ्जलिः ॥१२.२९॥

śuśrūṣamāṇa ācāryaṁ
sadopāsīta nīca-vat
yāna-śayyāsana-sthānair
nāti-dūre kṛtāñjaliḥ (12.29)

śuśrūṣamāna = śuśrūṣamānaḥ — service; ācāryam — the head of the spiritual lineage; sadopāsīta = sadā — always + upāsīta — should worship; nīca-vat — just as a menial servant; yāna — following; śayyāsana = śayyā — resting + āsana — sitting; sthānair = sthānaiḥ — by standing in attendance; nāti = na — not + ati — very; dūre — far off; kṛtāñjaliḥ — being with folded hands.

Translation

He should always worship the spiritual master, serving like a menial servant. He should always worship the teacher appropriately, by following, resting, sitting, standing in attendance with folded hands, never being far off. (12.29)

Commentary:

In this verse *ācārya* means the personal guru who gives the disciple techniques for advancement. This teacher might be the head of the lineage. In all cases or dealing with the spiritual master, this advice should be followed. But if one feels that one is not benefiting from the association, one should quietly go away without making a fuss and without resentments.

One should not stay with a spiritual master, while remaining at a distance from him, nor carry oneself in a resentful or negative mood. That will not satisfy Lord Krishna. Therefore if one feels uncomfortable, one might silently go away. One does not always have agreeable feelings in the presence of a spiritual master. But that does not mean that one should go way at the slightest inconvenience or even at minor loses of confidence in him. One should try one's best to serve the teacher. But if the disagreeability increases, one may go away without offense.

एवं-वृत्तो गुरु-कुले
वसेद् भोग-विवर्जितः ।

evaṁ-vṛtto guru-kule
vased bhoga-vivarjitaḥ

विद्या समाप्यते यावद्
बिभ्रद् व्रतम् अखण्डितम् ॥१२.३०॥

vidyā samāpyate yāvad
bibhrad vratam akhaṇḍitam (12.30)

evam — this, in that way; vṛtto = vṛttah — acting; guru-kule — in the house of the teacher; vased = vaset — he should live; bhoga — comforts; vivarjitaḥ — shunning; vidyā — education; samāpyate — is completed; yāvad = yāvat — until; bibhrad = bibhrat — maintain; vratam — vow; akhaṇḍitam — unbroken, consistent.

Translation

Acting in that way, he should live in the house of his teacher, shunning comforts and should maintain a consistent vow, until his education is completed. (12.30)

Commentary:

One goes to a spiritual master for vidyā or theoretical and practical spiritual education, but one does not necessarily understand this when one is first attracted to a guru. The guru himself may not realize the disciple's motive either. He might not perceive hidden objectives. There are examples. *Karṇa*, for instance took up discipleship under the great guru *Pāraśurāma*, but the guru did not at first, detect *Karṇa's* motive which was to use the knowledge he would be given for political purposes. Kacha also had motives which Shukracharya did not pay attention to initially.

Pāraśurāma had a policy of not giving information and techniques to politically-minded students. Therefore *Karṇa* pretended to be a priestly-minded, academically-inclined student. The ruse worked for a time, until *Karṇa* himself by an oversight acted in a way which revealed his martial temperament. Thus he was cursed by *Pāraśurāma* so that when he would try to use the technique in a battle he would forget the method of it.

There is a belief that a spiritual master knows everything and that because he represents the *deva* supernatural people, the gods, he can know anything at any time. Some students as encouraged by their self-conceited gurus, advertise the teachers as being omniscient or being always informed due to a connection with *Śrī* Krishna or with Lord Shiva or some other divine being. This invariably causes ruination for such spiritual masters and their sects.

Certainly some spiritual masters are that advanced that they can know just about everything but not every spiritual master is like that. Some spiritual masters cannot know the hidden motives in the nature of every disciple. And the disciple himself may not understand his own intentions, which might be hidden deeply within his psyche, but which will motivate him nevertheless.

Because one goes to a spiritual master for vidyā or for some kind of education and experience, one has to act in a way which facilitates the delivery of the information or experience, otherwise one will never get it and will be frustrated. In some instances, one goes to a spiritual master who cannot give one the vidyā, technique or experience required. In that case, one might serve for years and then leave that teacher in total frustration and disappointment, having wasted so much time serving him submissively. This happens frequently to persons on the spiritual path. However, despite such mishaps, a seeker should go on and keep trying until he achieves his aim or realizes the impracticality of his desire.

It is a very bad idea to go to a spiritual master and to try to live in his environment in a comfortable way. That will not work for the disciple. One should be very regulated at the place of the guru and should not try to compete with him in any way.

यद्य् असौ छन्दसां लोकम्
आरोक्ष्यन् ब्रह्म-विष्टपम् ।
गुरवे विन्यसेद् देहं
स्वाध्यायार्थं बृहद्-व्रतः ॥१२.३१॥

yady asau chandasāṁ lokam
ārokṣyan brahma-viṣṭapam
gurave vinyased dehaṁ
svādhyāyārthaṁ bṛhad-vrataḥ (12.31)

yady = yadi — if; asau — that; chandasām – the personified Vedas; lokam — planet; āroksyan — wanting to ascend; brahma-viṣṭapam — Brahmā's world; gurave — to the guru; vinyased =

vinyaset — hold off; deham — body; svādhyāyārthaṁ = sva – own + adhyāya — instruction + artham — for the value; bṛhad-vrataḥ — observance of perpetual celibacy.

Translation

If that student wants to ascend to Brahmā's planet, where the personified Vedas reside, he should, while observing the vow of perpetual celibacy, offer his body to the spiritual master for the value of the instruction. (12.31)

Commentary:

This is possible only if one has a guru who is a master of celibacy yoga. Otherwise it cannot be achieved merely by serving a guru who does not do yoga. One does not go to such planets, merely by worshiping any and every guru. The guru should have certain accomplishments himself, before he can share with the disciple.

This vow of perpetual celibacy has to do with the sexual energy in the subtle body. It is the subtle body which will ascend to *Brahmā*'s planet, not the gross one. Thus a display of gross physical celibacy will not qualify a person for ascension to *Brahmā*'s world. It has to be celibate in the subtle body. This is attained by *prāṇāyāma* practice.

It is a general rule, that a person whose sexuality is operative, cannot live on *Brahmā*'s planet. There is the incidence of King Mahabhisha, who somehow became qualified to be called with the devas to the court of *Brahmā*. When he entered that zone, he was fated to arrive there simultaneously with Goddess Ganga. As destiny would have it, her sheer clothing blew up by the force of a celestial wind. Seeing her beautiful sexually-appealing torso, the King immediately experience a sexual arousal, although the devas who arrived there just before him saw Ganga too, and looked away when she was exposed. Thus Mahabhisha took birth on this planet as King *Śantanu* and the goddess met him here to have sexual intercourses with him.

My own recent history which is behind the present series of births in human bodies, also testified to this fact. I too, used to be in the association with Lord *Brahmā*, but I was distracted by females at his court and subsequently I took many births on the earthly planets. Up to this day, I am unable to get back to his place. It may be that I was destined to take these lower births, because even when I am able to make my subtle body celibate, still something usually happens, as if I am fated to again take another earthly body.

Once when I discussed this with *Śrīla Yogeśwarānanda* who is one of the Vedas Personified, he said this:

> *"Do not worry about this. The important thing is to always restore your subtle form to a celibate status. After all what else can a limited being do. We do not always know what is motivating us to do a certain thing. We are not in absolute control of our destinies. As a slave does not regard himself as his own master, so you should not consider yourself as the master of your destiny.*
>
> *"As a prisoner's life is in the hands of a magistrate, so your existence is in the hands of people like Shiva, Krishna and Brahmā, so do not lose sleep over it. But at the same time, always keep yourself in order so that if they decide to grant your wish, you would be qualified to accept it."*

One has to offer his life to the proper spiritual master who can give one the required techniques. Then one will get results. If one offers one's life to someone who is a pretender, who does not really know the techniques, then one will become disappointed sooner or later. A spiritual master must himself have practiced the yoga techniques, otherwise, it is hardly likely that he could impart it, but the disciple might miscalculate or assume that the spiritual master can impart something he is incapable of.

अग्नौ गुराव् आत्मनि च
सर्व-भूतेषु मां परम् ।
अपृथग्-धीर् उपसीत
ब्रह्म-वर्चस्व्य् अकल्मषः ॥ १२.३२ ॥

agnau gurāv ātmani ca
sarva-bhūteṣu māṁ param
apṛthag-dhīr upasīta
brahma-varcasvy akalmaṣaḥ (12.32)

agnau — in fire; gurāv = gurau — in the spiritual teacher; ātmani — in the spirit; ca — and; sarva-bhūteṣu — in all beings; mām — me; param — supreme being; apṛthag-dhīr = apṛthak-dhīḥ — without any idea of being seperate; upāsīta — he should worship; brahma – spirtual realization; varcasvy = varcasvi — blowing; akalmaṣaḥ — sinless.

Translation

Being sinless, glowing with spiritual realization, he should worship Me, the Supreme Being, in the fire, in the spiritual teacher, in his spirit, and in all beings, without any idea of being separate. (12.32)

Commentary:

To become sinless one has to master the eight-staged *aṣṭanga* yoga. That is the only way to achieve the stage of having an aura that glows with spiritual realization *(brahma varcasvi)*. This comes about by developing a *brahma*-yoga body in which one eliminates the ordinary subtle form with its kundalini shakti and develops a brahma energy form. In that stage one does not see one-self as being an isolated existence. One sees that there is only one existence and one is merely a part of it, like a cog in a large machine. In the cosmic situation, a limited entity is merely a minute part of a colossal reality.

After mastering kundalini yoga, celibacy yoga and purity-of-the-psyche yoga, one graduates to *brahma* yoga. That is the stage of developing an aura which glows with spiritual energy.

स्त्रीणा निरीक्षण-स्पर्श-
सलाप-क्ष्वेलनादिकम् ।
प्राणिनो मिथुनी-भूतान्
अगृहस्थो ऽग्रतस् त्यजेत् ॥ १२.३३ ॥

strīṇāṁ nirīkṣaṇa-sparśa-
saṁlāpa-kṣvelanādikam
prāṇino mithunī-bhūtān
agṛhastho 'gratas tyajet (12.33)

strīnām — in relation to women; nirīkṣana — glancing; sparśa — touching; saṁlāpa — chatting with; kṣvelanādikam = ksvelana — joking + ādikam — and other casual ways of relating; prāṇino = prāṇinaḥ — creations; mithunī – sexual contact; bhūtān — creatures; agṛhastho = agṛhasthaḥ — not responsible for a household; 'gratas = agrataḥ — first of all; tyajet — should avoid.

Translation

First of all, in relation to women, persons who are not responsible for households, should avoid glancing at, touching, chatting, joking and other causal ways of relating, and should not see creatures who are engaged in sexual intercourse. (12.33)

Commentary:

The material world is such a place, that any sort of flirtation even the superficial type, serves as formative motivations for sexual contact. Those who are not responsible for a household, should avoid the dangers of householder life by not glancing at, not touching, not chatting, not joking, nor relating in any casual or intentional way with members of the opposite sex. This advice applies to yogins and yoginis. Because the material nature has the *Sūtram* sexually-charged force which we heard of in the previous chapters, any failure to take these precautions will cause us to extend the mundane transmigrations.

Seeing creatures engaged in sexual conduct may cause one to become sexually-aroused. There is the case of *Saubhari* Muni. He mastered celibacy to a degree by *prāṇāyāma*, which is the sure and definite way to do that, but still when he was in the river, being submerged, he happened to open his eyes and saw some fishes copulating. By this, his sexual urge was aroused. He was pressured from within to take wives.

Some teachers who deride yoga, explain that this is a clear example of the failure of yoga practice. They misunderstand, because whatever is achieved by yoga practice can be reversed if the yogi is not careful. And this applies to every effective method of spirituality. Arjuna for instance forgot all about what *Śrī* Krishna told him and revealed to him in the *Bhagavad-Gītā*. It was for that reason, that *Śrī* Krishna again explained certain things to Arjuna in what is known as the Anu-*Gītā* in the later part of the *Mahābhārata* when *Śrī* Krishna enjoyed His last holiday at the Pandavas palaces.

If we do not protect our advancement, we will regress. That is the law of nature which operates in all zones of the material world. Circumstantially, a householder has to engage in what is prohibited for a single ascetic, but even the householder has to understand that at some stage he must observe all prohibitions, otherwise he will not be successful in spiritual practice.

शौचम् आचमनं स्नानं
सन्ध्योपास्तिर् ममार्चनम् ।
तीर्थ-सेवा जपो ऽस्पृश्या-
भक्ष्यासम्भाष्य-वर्जनम् ॥ १२.३४॥

śaucam ācamanaṁ snānaṁ
sandhyopāstir mamārcanam
tīrtha-sevā japo 'spṛśyā-
bhakṣyāsambhāṣya-varjanam (12.34)

śaucam — cleanliness; ācamanam — ceremonial purification; snānam — bath; saṁdhyopāsranamarjavam = saṁdhya — prayers said at dawn, noon and dusk + upāsranam — religious service + arjavam — straightfowardness; tīrtha-sevā — serving at shrines; japo = japah — chanting holy names; 'spṛśyābhaksyāsambhāsya-saṁyamah = 'spṛśya (aspṛśya) — not to be touched + abhakṣya — not to be eaten + asambhāṣya — not to be discussed + varjanam — avoidance.

Translation

Cleanliness, ceremonial purification, performance of religious service at dawn, noon and dusk, straightforwardness, serving at shrines, chanting of holy names, avoidance of things not to be touched, eaten or discussed, (12.34)

Commentary:

This listing is completed in the next verse. Cleanliness is important because the mind is affected by the hygienic status of the body and environment. If one becomes careless with cleanliness, one's mind will become relaxed in other regards, and it will affect the spiritual disciplines in such a way as to cause one to abandon the practices.

The ceremonial purification of the body is required if one is to visit Deity Forms and if one is to perform Vedic religious ceremonies, as well as if one is to apply tilak sacred clay or scent marks to one's body. If one has not done the necessary purification and purificatory rites, one should not approach the deity. These rules should be followed by all. Some who practice austerity in isolation and who enter trance states may be exempt from these stipulations but only for as long as one engages in such practices, otherwise one should resume these since they are the order of the Supreme Lord. He wants us to set examples which are serviceable to all human beings, even to those who cannot take up yoga austerities. We must be careful in this regard.

One should be straightforward, otherwise one will become habituated to diplomacy and to polite but meaningless courtesies, and one's spiritual life will be deterred. All the same, one should avoid situations which would require an offensive straightforwardness.

Service should be performed at shrines, because these places are the spiritual life for the general public. Such places are charged effectively by the service of the advanced souls and their disciples. Shrines which became political arenas, should be avoided at all costs, but if such shrines are popular, and if the public has confidence in them, one should render services in such a way as to avoid becoming implicated in the political struggles which distracted ascetics engage in.

The chanting of holy names is a must for all ascetics. This chanting of holy names was declared by Lord Chaitanya and other divine personages, as the *Yuga-dharma* or as the general method of salvation for this Age. Thus all ascetics should in some way, support and contribute to the glorification of *Śrī* Krishna by chanting holy names. As yogis, we should not abandon yoga practice but we should chant nevertheless to add impetus to the general procedure.

One should be keen in spiritual life so that he avoids those things which are not to be touched, eaten or discussed.

सर्वाश्रम-प्रयुक्तो ऽयं
नियमः कुल-नन्दन ।
मद्-भावः सर्व-भूतेषु
मनो-वाक्-काय-संयमः ॥ १२.३५॥

sarvāśrama-prayukto 'yaṁ
niyamaḥ kula-nandana
mad-bhāvaḥ sarva-bhūteṣu
mano-vāk-kāya-saṁyamaḥ (12.35)

sarvāśrama — all life stages; prayukto = prayuktaḥ — recommended; 'yaṁ = ayam — this; niyamaḥ — observances; kula-nandana — joy of the clan; mat-bhāvaḥ — my existence; sarva-bhūteṣu — in all creatures; mano = manaḥ — of mind; vāk — of speech; kāya — body; saṁyamaḥ — control.

Translation

...O joy of the clan, this observance is recommended for all life styles, as well as the observance of My existence in all creatures and the control of the mind, speech and body. (12.35)

Commentary:

The disciplines mentioned are general principles to be followed by all ascetics, regardless of their variant lifestyles. Each must also endeavor to observe how *Śrī* Krishna exists in all creatures. Each must endeavor by the various methods of mind control, speech regulation and control of activities.

एवं बृहद्-व्रत-धरो
ब्राह्मणो ऽग्निर् इव ज्वलन् ।
मद्-भक्तस् तीव्र-तपसा
दग्ध-कर्माशयो ऽमलः ॥ १२.३६॥

evaṁ bṛhad-vrata-dharo
brāhmaṇo 'gnir iva jvalan
mad-bhaktas tīvra-tapasā
dagdha-karmāśayo 'malaḥ (12.36)

evam — thus; bṛhat-vrata — celibate vows; dharo = dharaḥ — one who maintains; brāhmaṇo = brāhmanaḥ — brahmin; 'gnir = agniḥ — fire; iva — like; jvalan — blazing; mad-bhaktas = mat-bhaktaḥ — one who is devoted to Me; tīvra-tapasā — by intense austerities; dagdha — burnt; karmāśayo = karmāśayaḥ = karma— implicating mundane activities + āśaya — tendency; 'malaḥ = amalaḥ — free from impurities.

Translation

Thus, the brahmin who maintains the celibate vow, is like a blazing fire. As a person who is freed from impurities, whose tendency for implicating activities is burnt by the intense austerities, he becomes devoted to Me. (12.36)

Commentary:

Only a certain type of person can cut himself away from implicating mundane activities. This is because almost all activities in the material world are intertwining. If one acts to solve complications, one's actions for a solution, creates another implication. Therefore it is near impossible to get out of the material world.

Celibacy is mentioned because without complete celibacy, through *prāṇāyāma* one cannot become liberated. It is impossible. One must be celibate and he must perfect the kundalini yoga practice if he wants to leave the material world completely. For that matter one cannot even make it to the court of Brahma if one is not in perfect celibacy of the subtle body.

Devotion to *Śrī* Krishna *(mad-bhaktas)* is one of the requirements. This is an important requirement for those yogis who want to be in *Śrī* Krishna's association specifically. By devotion to Him, their purification will be accelerated. They will be drawn closer and closer to *Śrī* Krishna and that pull will produce in them a willingness to take up the necessary austerity.

Devotion to Krishna which causes a devotee to avoid the austerities required, which cause him to hate yoga and to feel that it should not be required, is not the type of devotion that will lead to the success mentioned in this verse.

A person has to be very serious to cut himself off from the cultural activities, the *karmāśayo*. He has to take up very severe austerities and he must apply himself with intensity once and for all. *Śrī* Krishna called this *tīvra-tapasā*.

अथानन्तरम् आवेक्ष्यन्
यथा-जिज्ञासितागमः ।
गुरवे दक्षिणां दत्त्वा
स्नायाद् गुर्व्-अनुमोदितः ॥१२.३७॥

athānantaram āvekṣyan
yathā-jijñāsitāgamaḥ
gurave dakṣiṇāṁ dattvā
snāyād gurv-anumoditaḥ (12.37)

athānantaram = atha — then + anantaram — after that; āvekṣyan — wishing to enter householder life; yathā — as required; jijñāsitāgamaḥ = jijñāsita — having studied + āgamah — the Vedas; gurave — to the spiritual teacher; dakṣiṇām — appropiate fees; dattvā — having given, giving; snāyād = snāyāt — should take ritual bath; guru — spiritual teacher; anumoditaḥ — permitted.

Translation

Then, after having studied the Vedas as required, and wishing to enter the householder life, giving the teacher the appropriate fee, he should take ritual bath as permitted by the teacher. (12.37)

Commentary:

This was how the student life was terminated for those boys who were destined to be householders. Instead of staying on as single men all their lives, they took permission and then took leave of their guru's house and returned to the family circle in preparation for marriage. Because they were already trained in yoga austerities and in worship ceremonies and other related techniques, their assumption of householder life did not completely disrupt their spiritual advancement.

गृहं वनं वोपविशेत्
प्रव्रजेद् वा द्विजोत्तमः ।
आश्रमाद् आश्रमं गच्छेन्
नान्यथामत्-परश् चरेत् ॥१२.३८॥

gṛhaṁ vanaṁ vopaviśet
pravrajed vā dvijottamaḥ
āśramād āśramaṁ gacchen
nānyathāmat-paraś caret (12.38)

gṛham — householder life; vanam — forest life, ascetic life; vopaviśet = vā — or upaviśet — he should assume; pravrajed = pravrajet — he should renounce; vā — or; dvijottamaḥ — the best of the twice born; āśramād = āśramāt — from the life style; āśramam — to another life style; gacchen = gacchet — should go; nānyathāmat-paraś = na — not + anyathā — otherwise + mat-paras — being intensely devoted to Me; caret — should advance.

Translation

The brahmin may assume the householder life or the hermit life or he may renounce the world. Being intently devoted to Me, he may advance from one life style to another but not otherwise. (12.38)

Commentary:

This verse is for the brahmin caste person in the time of *Śrī* Krishna. It refers to the *dvijottamah*, the highest brahmin-trained people. It does not necessarily apply to others and even though some commentators chose to use it to explain their missions, still *Śrī* Krishna applied this to the highest *(uttamah)* of the twice born *(dvija)*. This means persons whose bodies came from brahmin parents and who were highly trained in all the techniques pertaining to yoga, religious ritual, chanting of Gāyatrī prayers, chanting of Holy Names and so on. This verse should not be used to justify modern missions which according to time and place, have developed different agendas.

If we understand this verse within its own historic context, we would better appreciate the social structure at the time of *Śrī* Krishna and before during the Upanishad period of Indian history. Then we can try to apply this to ourselves. *Śrī* Krishna gave options to a brahmin student as follows:

He may after the student years, take to householder life; or to hermit life. He may become completely renounced and not have any set habitation. That would mean that he would be a wandering ascetic without shelter. In that way, the brahmin may move from one life style to another but he was not permitted to change status whimsically. If for instance, he took hermit life, then he was not to marry at any time while he had that body. If on the other hand, he took to being a wanderer, then he would not marry nor live in any village, town or city. He was supposed to wander for the rest of his life. If he took to householder life however, he could later assume hermit life or the wanderer's life. We must also remember the option given in the previous verse, that of remaining as a celibate in the association of a teacher.

We must also observe that in all cases, *Śrī* Krishna stressed devotion to Himself. That is constantly recommended by the Lord.

गृहार्थी सदृशी भार्याम्
उद्वहेद् अजुगुप्सिताम् ।
यवीयसीं तु वयसा
य स-वर्णाम् अनु क्रमात् ॥ १२.३९ ॥

gṛhārthī sadṛśīṁ bhāryām
udvahed ajugupsitām
yavīyasīṁ tu vayasā
yaṁ sa-varṇām anu kramāt (12.39)

grhārthī — one who values householder responsibilities; sadṛśīm — a female with similar characteristics; bhāryām — a wife; udvahed = udvahet — should marry; ajugupsitām — unblemished; yavīyasīm — younger; tu — but; vayasā — by age; yām — another; sa-varnām — same tendency; anu — after; kramāt — from the succeeding order.

Translation

A person who values householder responsibilities, should marry an unblemished girl, of the same character as he, who is younger in age, but if he wishes to marry another, he should afterwards, take a wife from the succeeding order. (12.39)

Commentary:

This shows that these regulation are description of what took place in the time of *Śrī* Krishna, for today, even in India, a man is not allowed to register more than one wife. These verses should not be hijacked into the agendas of the modern disciplic successions which struggle for survival in the modern environment, otherwise some very inadvertent changes will be made in the translation and some very misleading and twisted commentaries will be the result.

The rule was that any person who was trained by a guru as described, and who was ready for marriage, could first accept a wife who was of the same disposition as he. She was supposed to be unblemished, meaning that she was to be sexually untouched, her body being virgin from the sexual viewpoint. And her body was supposed to be younger than his.

The disciple, if he felt the necessity to marry again, could do so once the first marriage was matured somewhat, but he was not allowed to take that second wife from his own caste. She was to be from the next lower one. In practice, this meant that a brahmin youth could take a brahmin girl as his first wife. After that marriage was established, he could take a girl from the administrative class. Later he could take a third wife from the mercantile caste. Then again, he could take a fourth wife from a working class family.

By the same practice, a man from the administrative class, a prince for instance, took his first wife from the same status. Then later he could take one from a business oriented family and yet another from a working class background. While the son of a businessman could take only two wives in succession, the first from his own caste and the second from a working class family.

Such a regulation which was in vogue in the time of *Śrī* Krishna, is a social rule only because it is not current today. Any person who does to this today, may be subjected to arrest by government officials, at least in the developed countries. However by studying this, we can understand the social situation in the time of Lord Krishna.

इज्याध्ययन-दानानि
सर्वेषां च द्वि-जन्मनाम् ।
प्रतिग्रहो ऽध्यापनं च
ब्राह्मणस्यैव याजनम् ॥ १२.४० ॥

ijyādhyayana-dānāni
sarveṣāṁ ca dvi-janmanām
pratigraho 'dhyāpanaṁ ca
brāhmaṇasyaiva yājanam (12.40)

ijyādhyayana = ijyā — performance of sacrifice + adhyayana — Vedic study; dānāni — offering charity; sarvesām — of all + ca — and + dvi-janmanām — pertaining to those who are twice-born; pratigraho = pratigrahaḥ — acceptance of gifts; 'dhyāpanaṁ = adhyāpanam — teaching; ca — and; brāhmaṇasyaiva = brāhmaṇasya — of the brahmin; eva — only; yājanam — conducting sacrifices for others.

Translation

The performance of sacrifice, Vedic study, offering charity, pertain to all those who are twice-born. The acceptance of gifts, teaching and conducting sacrifices for others, apply to the brahmin only. (12.40)

Commentary:

A distinction is made between all those who take initiation from a brahmin guru and the caste brahmin student himself. In other words, even though the three higher castes can take initiation from a brahmin guru, only the highest of the castes are permitted to teach, conduct sacrifices and accept fees for ceremonies. This means that in the time of *Śrī* Krishna, the society was caste-structured. This cannot be denied. There was prejudice in such a society, because the evidence is there in the Vedic histories. Exceptions of fairness or equality did occur but not frequently.

Students for celibate student life were taken from the three higher parentages, namely the brahmins, the administrative types and business types. All these were permitted to engage in the performance of sacrifices, to study the Vedic literatures and to offer in charity but only the persons of brahmin parentage were permitted licenses to officiate sacrifices, to teach religion and to accept fees for such services. This means that such a society was restricted in that respect and the occupations of the brahmin caste was reserved for certain families.

Some have tried to prove that this was not the case. They cite examples from the Vedic literatures, such as the case of the boy whose mother could not identify the father, because she had intercourses with several men when he was conceived. Gautama Rishi after questioning the boy, who applied for studentship, granted the boy a place at the ashram for Vedic initiation even though the boy could not identify his father's ancestry, and even though it was obvious that the boy's mother was sexually-permissive. However Gautama did this because the boy was honest in explaining his mother's background and the boy was humble by nature.

Such cases, however are the exceptions. Thus today, when such a caste-structured society has no place, spiritual masters even some of those who come from very protective and monopolistic brahmin families, take the chance to initiate any person from any type of background, provided the person agrees to render service and to accept the tenets of the teacher. But there is no necessity to try to change these verses to support the actions of such teachers. Times changed and therefore the spiritual masters today must use their intelligence and take whatever risks, they deem necessary. Of course their mistakes are costly.

प्रतिग्रहं मन्यमानस्
तपस्-तेजो-यशो-नुदम् ।
अन्याभ्याम् एव जीवेत
शिलैर् वा दोष-दृक् तयोः ॥ १२.४१ ॥

pratigrahaṁ manyamānas
tapas-tejo-yaśo-nudam
anyābhyām eva jīveta
śilair vā doṣa-dṛk tayoḥ (12.41)

pratigraham — acceptance of donation; manyamānas — considering; tapas — austerity; tejo = tejah — ability to resist material nature; yaśo = yaśaḥ — reputation; nudam — neutralisation; anyābhyām — by the other two recommended practices; eva — indeed; jīveta — he should live; śilair = śilaiḥ — by collecting unwanted produce from the fields; vā — or; doṣa — detrimental; dṛk — perceiving; tayoḥ — of the two.

Translation

A brahmin who considers that the acceptance of donations neutralizes his austerity, breaks down his resistance to material nature, and effaces his reputation, should live by either of the other two recommendations. Or if he perceives even these to be detrimental, he should live by collecting unwanted produce from the fields. (12.41)

Commentary:

This all depends on one's nature and on facilities of providence. For one thing, it depends on what sort of energy leaks over into one's conscious mind from the stock pile of impressions in his subconscious mind.

It is a fact that the acceptance of donations may neutralize the austerities of an ascetic. Or stated differently the energy conserved by the austerities are exchanged for the donation. Thus to accept donations might be counterproductive. It is frequently experienced that if one accepts a donation, even one that seems to be free of motive, still at a later date, the donor may be inspired to ask for a favor. In rendering such favors, the ascetic is required to use the energy which he conserved by the austerities.

Material nature, too, has a way about her, where if a donor grants an ascetic something, material nature takes note of it, in such a way as to demand from the ascetic some favor for the donor in some other situation at a future time. When that favor is rendered the equivalent energy is extracted or taken from the ascetic and in that way the energies are balanced.

Too much taking of donations, causes the ascetic to lose his *tejah*, which is his resistance to material nature. Subsequently he eventually loses it altogether and becomes a common human being. This happens frequently. And of course his reputation reduces. Even though people are all too willing to give donations to an ascetic, particularly in India, still the same people are all too eager to criticize him. This is due to human nature.

Śrī Krishna explained this verse to give some idea of how a person might live as an unemployed hermit and how a person might live as a wanderer. Of course in many countries, one is not permitted to wander about even on reserve lands. One may be arrested.

As a last resort, one may just live by picking up produce which was left behind by farmers in fields, but even this must be done with their permission, otherwise one could get arrested for trespassing. In the time of *Śrī* Krishna, this could be done freely, even without permission, because the Vedic society was accommodating to it.

In considering these recommendations of *Śrī* Krishna, the writer has decided not to live by begging nor by taking donations regularly but rather by living very simply so that my needs are the minimum. I could plant a little for my needs and take a little from the forest. Otherwise whenever I take donations, I must understand that there will be some compensation.

ब्राह्मणस्य हि देहो ऽयं
क्षुद्र-कामाय नेष्यते ।
कृच्छ्राय तपसे चेह
प्रेत्यानन्त-सुखाय च ॥ १२.४२ ॥

brāhmaṇasya hi deho 'yaṁ
kṣudra-kāmāya neṣyate
kṛcchrāya tapase ceha
pretyānanta-sukhāya ca (12.42)

brāhmanasya — of a brahmin; his — surely; deho = dehah — body; 'yam = ayam — this; ksudra — petty; kāmāya — for desires; neṣyate = na — not + iṣyate — is meant for fulfilling; kṛcchrāya — for rigorous; tapase — in austerity; ceha = ca — and + iha — here; pretyānanta = pretya — hereafter + ananta — endless; sukhāya — for happiness; ca — and.

Translation

Surely, the body of a brahmin, is not meant for fulfilling petty desires. It is for rigorous austerity here and endless happiness in the hereafter. (12.42)

Commentary:

This is the ideal for those who took birth in brahmin families. It is also relevant for anyone else from any parentage who takes spiritual life that seriously.

शिलोञ्छ-वृत्त्या परितुष्ट-चित्तो धर्मं
महान्त विरज जुषाणः ।
मय्य् अर्पितात्मा गृह एव तिष्ठन्
नाति-प्रसक्तः समुपैति शान्तिम् ॥ १२.४३ ॥

śiloñcha-vṛttyā parituṣṭa-citto dharmaṁ
mahāntaṁ virajaṁ juṣāṇaḥ
mayy arpitātmā gṛha eva tiṣṭhan
nāti-prasaktaḥ samupaiti śāntim (12.43)

śiloñcha — gathering unwanted produce; vṛttyā — by action; parituṣṭa — contented; citto = cittah — mind; dharmam — righteous duty; mahāntam — great; virajam — taintless; juṣāṇaḥ — observing; mayy = mayi — in me; arpitātmā — dedicated to the self; gṛha = gṛhe — at home; eva — even; tisṣṭhan — staying; nāti-prasaktaḥ = na — not + ati-prasaktah — overly attached; samupaiti — attains; śāntim — spirtual peace.

Translation

A brahmin whose mind is contented mentally by gathering unwanted produce left in fields, and by observing the taintless righteous duty, even while staying at home, and being dedicated to Me, not being overly attached, attains spiritual peace. (12.43)

Commentary:

This refers to exalted austere householder brahmins. These persons, though householders, live in such a way that they seem to be celibate ascetics. Their wives usually compliment them. Such persons do not endeavor for much material wealth. Subsequently they utilize a greater portion of their time for spiritual cultivation. Generally such persons are from the brahmin caste only. Those in the administrative field and those who are from the business class are hardly able to live in such an austere way. But there are exceptions.

The exalted householder brahmins must observe the great taintless righteous duties which are highlighted by the proper reception of guests. They must also be dedicated to *Śrī* Krishna. He stressed this in these verses. Then such persons would attain spiritual peace.

समुद्धरन्ति ये विप्रं
सीदन्तं मत्-परायणम् ।
तान् उद्धरिष्ये न चिराद्
आपद्भ्यो नौर् इवार्णवात् ॥ १२.४४ ॥

samuddharanti ye vipraṁ
sīdantaṁ mat-parāyaṇam
tān uddhariṣye na cirād
āpadbhyo naur ivārṇavāt (12.44)

samuddharanti — rescues, uplifts; ye — those; vipram — brahmin; sīdantam — misfortune; mat-parāyaṇam — one who is fully devoted to Me; tān — those; uddhariṣye — will deliver; na cirād = na cirāt — quickly; āpadbhyo = āpadbhyaḥ — from dangers; naur = nauh — boat; ivārṇavāt = iva — like as + arṇavāt — from the sea.

Translation

Just as a boat rescues one from the sea, I will quickly deliver from dangers, those persons who rescue from misfortune, a brahmin who is fully devoted to Me. (12.44)

Commentary:

This is an assurance that if someone should help a person who is fully devoted to *Śrī* Krishna, the helper will be assisted by *Śrī* Krishna in turn.

सर्वाः समुद्धरेद् राजा
पितेव व्यसनात् प्रजाः ।
आत्मानम् आत्मना धीरो
यथा गज-पतिर् गजान् ॥ १२.४५ ॥

sarvāḥ samuddhared rājā
piteva vyasanāt prajāḥ
ātmānam ātmanā dhīro
yathā gaja-patir gajān (12.45)

sarvāh — all; samuddhared = samuddharet — should deliver; rājā — king; piteva = pitā — father + iva — like; vysasnāt = vyasanāt — from callamities; prajāḥ — citizens; ātmānam — self; ātmanā — by himself; dhīro = dhīrah — very perceptive minded; yathā — just as; gaja-patir = jaga-patiḥ = bull elephant; gajān — elephants.

Translation

A king should deliver all citizens from calamities, like a father, and just as a bull elephant in relation to the elephant herd. Being perceptive, he should deliver his own self by himself. (12.45)

Commentary:

This is the ideal for a ruler, he is expected to save himself from danger and also to rescue the citizens from trouble.

एवं-विधो नर-पतिर्
विमानेनार्क-वर्चसा ।
विधूयेहाशुभं कृत्स्नम्
इन्द्रेण सह मोदते ॥ १२.४६ ॥

evaṁ-vidho nara-patir
vimānenārka-varcasā
vidhūyehāśubhaṁ kṛtsnam
indreṇa saha modate (12.46)

evam – thus; vidho = vidhah — manner, way; nara-patir = nara-patih — king; vimānenārka-varcasā = vimena — by flying conveyance + arka-varcasā — as the brillance of the sun; vidhūyehāśubhaṁ = vidhūya — nullifying + iha — here on earth + aśubham — sins; kṛtsnam — all; indreṇa — with Indra; saha — with; modate — enjoys.

Translation

Thus, in that way, nullifying all his sins on earth, a king by using a flying conveyance, which is brilliant as the sun, enjoys with Indra. (12.46)

Commentary:

This is the resulting life in the heavenly world, for a king whose profile fits the ideal described in the previous verse. After his body dies, he ascends to the angelic world and is offered honors there by the King of that place, by *Indra*.

सीदन् विप्रो वणिग्-वृत्त्या
पण्यैर् एवापदं तरेत् ।
खड्गेन वापदाक्रान्तो
न श्व-वृत्त्या कथञ्चन ॥ १२.४७॥

sīdan vipro vaṇig-vṛttyā
paṇyair evāpadaṁ taret
khaḍgena vāpadākrānto
na śva-vṛttyā kathañcana (12.47)

sīdan — needy; vipro = vipraḥ — brahmin; vaṇig-vrttyā = vaṇik-vrttyā = vaṇik — businessman + vrttyā — by working as; paṇyair = paṇyaiḥ — by selling; evapadam = eva — indeed + āpadam — misfortune; taret — should take recourse; khaḍgena — by weapon; vāpadākrānto = vāpadākrāntah = vā — or + āpadā — misfortune + ākrāntaḥ — overtaken; na — never; śva-vrttyā — by behaving like a dog; kathañcana — by any means.

Translation

A needy brahmin may support himself by working as a businessman, by selling or if he is still overtaken by misfortune, he may make a livelihood by using weapons but he should never behave like a dog by any means. (12.47)

Commentary:

If a brahmin cannot maintain himself by teaching and by performing religious ceremonies, then he is allowed to sell items which would not cause his degradation or which would not pile up sinful reactions on him. Alternately, if he cannot sell items, he may take the extreme measure of taking work as a soldier or as a government employee. But *Śrī* Krishna prohibited that the brahmin should enter the servile working class.

Actually there is a history of brahmins who circumstantially were forced into the working class and who by doing servile duties, were not degraded. The case of *Jaḍa Bharata* stands out. He had to work as a litter carrier without pay or recognition. More or less that meant that he had to work as a draught animal to carry the palanquin of King *Rahūgaṇa*. Because of detachment and because he understood the workings of destiny, he was not degraded by the menial service.

In my own case, not as a caste brahmin but as a devotee of *Śrī* Krishna, who was awarded a brahmin's status by the disciplic succession which came through *Śrīla Bhaktivedānta Swāmī Prabhupāda*, I was frequently compelled by destiny to do menial tasks, both in the devotee community and elsewhere. It has not hurt my spiritual life. For that matter it caused me to advance more rapidly. This is because in a menial position, one does not have to fatigue the intelligence. One can invest the mind in transcendental subjects and transcendental development all the more, while the physical body does the menial work.

I witnessed the degradation of many devotees who took to business and administrative work, because they became too preoccupied with the same, even in the name of *Śrī* Krishna and for the sake of their spiritual master, as they were told and as they believed.

This verse applies to emergencies. This instruction of *Śrī* Krishna applies for a temporary measure for the brahmin and not for prolonged activities. It applies to householder brahmins who for one reason or the other, were inconvenienced by social upheavals or haphazard rebirths. But as soon as the brahmin could, he was to resume teaching and religious activities.

A brahmin who becomes a businessman or a government man permanently will definitely ruin himself. He will be degraded in the mundane evolutionary cycle. For as much as we can go upwards, we can just as readily go down, even more so, because material nature sponsors descent more quickly.

वैश्य-वृत्त्या तु राजन्यो
जीवेन् मृगययापदि ।
चरेद् वा विप्र-रूपेण
न श्व-वृत्त्या कथञ्चन ॥ १२.४८ ॥

vaiśya-vṛttyā tu rājanyo
jīven mṛgayayāpadi
cared vā vipra-rūpeṇa
na śva-vṛttyā kathañcana (12.48)

vaiśya — merchandising; vṛttyā — by a job; tu — but; rājanyo = rājanyaḥ — a king; jīven = jīvet — may live; mṛgayayāpadi = mrgayayā — by hunting + āpadi — in adversity; cared = caret — may act; vā — or; vipra-rūpeṇa — in the format of a brahmin; na — not; śva-vṛttyā — by behaving like a dog; kathañcana — in any circumstance.

Translation

A king in adversity may live by merchandizing or by hunting. Or he may act in the format of a brahmin, but he should never behave like a dog in any circumstance. (12.48)

Commentary:

A king is allowed under special circumstances to assume the role of a brahmin. That means he may teach scripture and show yoga techniques which he mastered. He may also perform sacrifices. He can in adversity, under dire circumstances take to merchandising goods and to hunting animals, but he is prohibited from living as a servant of anyone just for meals.

The activity of a dog is to offer protection in exchange for shelter and meals. A dog agrees to protect the premises, provided he has a place to lay down and gets a daily meal. Such an existence is lowly and should not be accepted by a king nor by a businessman at any stage.

शूद्र-वृत्तिं भजेद्
वैश्यः शूद्रः कारु-कट-क्रियाम्
कृच्छ्रान् मुक्तो न गर्ह्येण ।
वृत्तिं लिप्सेत कर्मणा ॥ १२.४९ ॥

śūdra-vṛttiṁ bhajed
vaiśyaḥ śūdraḥ kāru-kaṭa-kriyām
kṛcchrān mukto na garhyeṇa
vṛttiṁ lipseta karmaṇā (12.49)

śūdra — worker; vṛttim — the job; bhajed = bhajet — may accept; vaiśyaḥ — businessman; śūdraḥ — member of the working class; kāru — jobber; kaṭa — handicrafts; kriyam — making, manufacturing; kṛcchrān — from adversity; mukto = muktaḥ — freed; na — never; garhyena — by anything inferior; vṛttim — livelihood; lipseta — should desire; karmanā — work.

Translation

A businessman may accept the job of a worker. A member of the working class may make handicrafts as a jobber. But once freed from adversity, no one should desire to work for a livelihood by any inferior method. (12.49)

Commentary:

One cannot expect that in each life one will be offered the ideal vocation, that is suited to one's nature. Therefore one must be willing to take a lesser role in human society. However, one should be ambitious enough and sensitive enough not to remain in an inferior position for long. Sometimes by a twist of fate, one has to spend an entire lifetime in a lowly position but as soon as one is freed from that, one should move to a higher status. However if one moves with false pride, providence will be sure to cause degradation.

In this verse, the course for moving upwards is indicated in that a member of the working class may elevate himself by beginning his own business as a handicraft manufacturer. Thus gradually he will become a jobber for a large financial concern or to supply traveling salesmen. In that way he will get an understanding of how to be a businessman, and in time, with the approval of providence, he will graduate from the worker status.

वेदाध्याय-स्वधा-स्वाहा-
बल्य्-अन्नाद्यैर् यथोदयम् ।
देवर्षि-पितृ-भूतानि
मद्-रूपाण्य् अन्व्-अहं यजेत् ॥ १२.५० ॥

vedādhyāya-svadhā-svāhā-
baly-annādyair yathodayam
devarṣi-pitṛ-bhūtāni
mad-rūpāṇy anv-ahaṁ yajet (12.50)

vedādhyāya — by recitation of the Vedas; svadhā — by saying Svadha; svāhā — by saying Svaha; baly = bali — by sacrificial offerings of grain; anna – food distribution; ādyair = ādyaiḥ — and related rites; yathodayam = yathā — as prescribed + udayam — income; devarṣi = deva — supernatural rulers + rsi — yogi sages; pitṛ — departed ancestors; bhūtāni — creatures; mat-rūpāny = mat-rūpāni — my forms; anv-aham = anu-aham — daily; yajet — should worship.

Translation

By recitation of the Vedas, by saying Svadhā, by saying Svāhā, by sacrificial offerings of grain, by sanctified food distributions and other related activities, prescribed according to one's income, one should on a daily basis, worship the supernatural rulers, the yogi sages, the departed ancestors, and the creatures as forms of Mine. (12.50)

Commentary:

Swāmī Mādhavānanda in his translation gave a notation about the use of *Svadhā* for the ancestors and *Svāhā* for the supernatural rulers. These words are said when offerings are made into a sacrificial fire.

Worship procedures, during the time of Lord Krishna were very elaborate affairs which required meticulous preparation and performance. Even small creatures like ants were considered in such worship. Sacred and very useful animals like mulch cows and domesticated bulls were specially fed in particular pujas or worship ceremonies.

यदृच्छयोपपन्नेन
शुक्लेनोपार्जितेन वा ।
धनेनापीडयन् भृत्यान्
न्यायेनैवाहरेत् क्रतून् ॥ १२.५१ ॥

yadṛcchayopapannena
śuklenopārjitena vā
dhanenāpīḍayan bhṛtyān
nyāyenaivāharet kratūn (12.51)

yadrcchayopapannena = yadṛcchayā — by chance, by good luck + upapannena — by funds; śuklenopārjitena = sukhena — by honest work + upārjitena — by what is acquired; vā — or; dhanenāpīḍayan = dhanena — by money + apīdayan — not causing strain; bhrtyān — dependents; nyāyenaivāharet = nyāyena — by due reason + eva — indeed + āharet — should perform; kratūn — sacrificial ceremonies.

Translation

By funds which come by good luck or which is acquired by honest work, he should by due reason, perform the sacrificial ceremonies, not putting a strain on his dependents. (12.51)

Commentary:

A householder should not get carried away, nor should a spiritual master become fame-crazy, to the extent of pressuring dependents or disciples to raise funds for sacrificial ceremonies and the like. One should not do this just to say that he is working under God's direction, under *Śrī* Krishna's desire for the sake of Krishna. This particular verse applies to any householder. He should not do this to his family nor allow a spiritual master to cause him to do this to his family. Some spiritual masters get carried away building temples and publishing books and do not care who they pressure to get funds for such activities, which they earmark as Krishna's devotional service or as *sevā* divine acts.

If one unduly pressures dependents or disciples, one will suffer a lapse in spiritual progression. Sometimes money comes of its own accord without it being planned or earned.

Such money is considered to be sent by good luck, by God or by providence. Sometimes one has to earn a livelihood. In either case the money should be managed properly. One should avoid burrowing money, since that causes stress in the family or in the spiritual lineage.

A spiritual master who borrows money frequently for large projects and who then pressures disciples to pay off loans and to raise more capital which would act as collateral for more loans, puts a burden on disciples unnecessarily but he may induce them to strain themselves by telling them that it is God's will. In that way, in the name of God, he creates hellish reactions.

A family man should not put his family under pressure. Each family member has a separate karmic account which will yield particular good and bad effects from fate. The householder should manage the family in such a way as not to implicate others in exorbitant desires. His sons should be free to form their own households. His daughters should be free to live with those men who become their husbands. In that way, by freeing dependents, the householder frees himself in turn and can earn liberation.

A spiritual master should free disciples, so that they can seek out and get techniques from other gurus who have skills which they require. If they are free to practice for spiritual perfection, then he too would be freed to complete austerities. If however a spiritual master poses as an incarnation of Godhead, then people will get the feeling that since he is already perfected, he does not need to take up any austerities and that he can bless them with all the spiritual advancement they might need. But this is not the right approach for a spiritual teacher. One should not fall into such a predicament.

कुटुम्बेषु न सज्जेत
न प्रमाद्येत् कुटुम्ब्य् अपि ।
विपश्चिन् नश्वरं पश्येद्
अदृष्टम् अपि दृष्ट-वत् ॥ १२.५२ ॥

kuṭumbeṣu na sajjeta
na pramādyet kuṭumby api
vipaścin naśvaraṁ paśyed
adṛṣṭam api dṛṣṭa-vat (12.52)

kuṭumbeṣu — to the family; na — not; sajjeta — should be attached; na — not; pramādyet — should not be confused; kuṭumby = kuṭumbī — a family man; api — even though; vipaścin = vipaścit — a wise man; naśvaram — temporary; paśyed = paśyet — should consider; adṛṣṭam — unseen future; api — indeed; dṛṣṭa-vat — just as what is perceived.

Translation

He should not get attached to the family and even though he is a family man, he should not get confused. A wise man should consider the unseen future to be just as temporary as what is currently perceived. (12.52)

Commentary:

This is the secret of how to form a philosophical basis for family life. If one can always remember that the future terminates in the death of one's body, and that one will definitely have to move on regardless of whether one likes it or not, one cannot become confused about family life.

The confusion is highlighted by feeling that once one is loved by one's family, they are dependent on oneself and one should remain centralized and focused on their well-being for as long as one might live. This is mostly a nonsensical view. No man is indispensable. No one man is necessary for the continuation of material existence. If a father were to die suddenly, his family would shed some tears for three or more days, but soon after they will go on with their lives just as if he never existed in the first place. This is because he was never essential. The essential factors are material nature and destiny. Otherwise a particular person is not needed.

Despite this seemingly pessimistic outlook, a man should do his duty, but he should do it with detachment while assessing the life situations as they are. He should know that he is just an agent of nature. If he departs from this world, having lost the body, nature will appoint others to fulfill its schemes.

As far as the future is concerned, it is even more uncertain than the present or past. The past is definite because it already occurred. We can rely on that. The present is before us. We react to it in one way or the other, according to how it facilitates or frustrates us. But the future may use and then discard us. It is therefore foolish to be inflexible. Of course a man should have a basic idea of what he aspires for but he should leave some leeway for providence, for as the saying goes: Man proposes and God disposes. Even though providence facilitates some of the time, it frustrates some of the time. So we should not set our minds on anything in the future because otherwise we would become depressed if we do not achieve it. One should move forward in time with an open mind, being submissive to providence.

पुत्र-दाराप्त-बन्धूनां
सङ्गमः पान्थ-सङ्गमः ।
अनु-देहं वियन्त्य् एते
स्वप्नो निद्रानुगो यथा ॥१२.५३॥

putra-dārāpta-bandhūnāṁ
saṅgamaḥ pāntha-saṅgamaḥ
anu-dehaṁ viyanty ete
svapno nidrānugo yathā (12.53)

putra — son, children; dārāpta — wife and relatives; bandhūnām — of friends; saṅgamah — association; pāntha — travelers; saṅgamaḥ — meeting; anu-deham — each body in succession; viyanty = viyanti — separate; ete — these; svapno = svapnah — dream; nidrānugo = nidrānugaḥ = nidrā — sleep + anugaḥ — occurance; yathā — just as.

Translation

The association of sons, wife, relatives and friends is like the meeting of travelers. These persons do seperate at the end of each body just as the occurrences end off in dreams. (12.53)

Commentary:

When assuming a boar form, *Śrī* Krishna killed *Hiraṇyakṣa*, subsequently there was much weeping and wailing among the women folk, who were *Hiraṇyakṣa's* relatives. And though *Hiraṇyakṣa's* brother, *Hiraṇyakaśipu*, was a vindictive man, still he understood what happens in the course of transmigration. He advised the women folk to cease lamentation since he said that the family members were like travelers who spent a night in a roadside inn. At daybreak such association comes to an end, as each traveler moves on to a different destination.

It is a fact however that some of the travelers will move on together but that does not mean that they will be travelling in company forever. They might not be. And even if two souls would be moving on together perpetually, it would mean that their spirits should be connected not their gross bodies, which must be left behind in this world, just as the hotel guests must leave the towels and utensils owned by the hotel.

Why is it then, that there is usually a great lamentation when someone departs from a body? It is because of a grief mechanism within the human psyche. That emotional energy exploits such situations. Thus in spiritual life, we curb and transform that emotional response.

इत्थं परिमृशन् मुक्तो
गृहेष्व् अतिथि-वद् वसन् ।
न गृहैर् अनुबध्येत
निर्ममो निरहङ्कृतः ॥१२.५४॥

ittham parimṛśan mukto
gṛheṣv atithi-vad vasan
na gṛhair anubadhyeta
nirmamo nirahaṅkṛtaḥ (12.54)

ittham — thus; parimṛśan — reflecting; mukto = muktaḥ — freed; gṛheṣv = gṛheṣu — at home; atithi-vad = atithi-vat — just like a guest; vasan — living; na — not; gṛhair = gṛhaiḥ — by home; anubadhyeta — should be bound; nirmamo = nirmamaḥ — with possessiveness; nirahaṅkṛtaḥ — without the feeling of "I am doing this".

Translation

Reflecting thus, one who is freed while living at home like a guest, is not bound by home and is without an attitude of possessiveness and without a feeling of "I am doing this".(12.54)

Commentary:

This is the attitude to be adopted by the *kriyā* yogi householder. We can live at home and still practice and develop ourselves spiritually. It is possible. The important thing is the daily yoga practice and the related disciplines like limited eating, eating at the right time, keeping ourselves out of sexual dalliances, and worshiping the Supreme Being Lord Krishna and Lord Shiva, the master of the yogins. If we adhere to this, we will see our way out of the material existence, even as householders.

A householder has ample opportunity to take up the spiritual disciplines because he does not have a preaching mission to manage. He can use spare time for spiritual practice. He does not have many people coming to see him for advices and religious services. He is free to advance spiritually. When *Swāmī Rāma* was appointed to be a *Śankarācārya* in India, he took up the position as a leading spiritual master, but after sometime he considered it an impediment to spiritual life because he spent most of the time seeing people to give blessings and advices, darshans. Therefore he gave up the position by disappearing from the temple compound where he was the spiritual master.

In the modern era, the householder ashram is a good hiding place in which to perfect the yoga *kriyās* and attain perfection. One only needs to practice in one's spare time and keep one's progress a secret from others. If people rate one as a nobody and only regard the temple devotees and *sannyāsis* as being important, it gives one ample opportunity to progress.

कर्मभिर् गृह-मेधीयैर्
इष्ट्वा माम् एव भक्तिमान् ।
तिष्ठेद् वनं वोपविशेत्
प्रजावान् वा परिव्रजेत् ॥ १२.५५॥

karmabhir gṛha-medhīyair
iṣṭvā mām eva bhaktimān
tiṣṭhed vanaṁ vopaviśet
prajāvān vā parivrajet (12.55)

karmabhir = karmabhiḥ — by activities; gṛha-medhīyair = gṛha-medhīyaiḥ — by householder duty; iṣṭvā — worshiping; mām — me; eva — indeed; bhaktimān — a devotee; tiṣṭhed = tiṣṭhet — may remain as; vanam — forest; vopaviśet = vā — or + upaviśet — may enter; prajāvān — having capable adult children; vā — or; parivrajet — may take full renuciation.

Translation

A devotee, who worships me by cultural activities and householder duties, may remain as a householder, or he may enter the forest. If he is a householder with capable adult children, he may take full renunciation. (12.55)

Commentary:

Some tricks of the trade for the advanced householder devotee are explained here by Lord Krishna. The first thing is that a householder has to begin his married life by completing two functions. These are *karma* and *kāma* functions. The details of *karma* yoga for a warrior are explained in the *Bhagavad-Gītā* but the one for householders who are not warriors is not given here in detail. The main idea is yoga. Once a person understands what yoga is, the application of it to whatever he does makes for that career and yoga. *Karma* means cultural activities, which includes the activities of politicians and warriors like Arjuna. Therefore when our cultural activities are tempered because we have mastered at least the 5th stage of yoga, that of *pratyāhar* sense withdrawal, then we are practicing *karma* yoga and we will get the approval of the Universal Form.

Gṛha-medhīyair means that which concerns the affectionate dealings in family life. These dealings are all highlighted by two aspects. The first is sexual indulgence. The second is the pride a parent feels when his or her child becomes successful in life. Needless to say, sexual indulgence is the single most important feature of family life, because through it, bodies are reproduced and through it, the partners experience the inside of the bodies of each other. This is not just a physical exchange but a subtle one as well. Both parties, the wife and husband are involved in the penetration of each other's psyche in the sexual indulgence. While they are occupied with sexual pleasure, an ancestor endeavors to come out of the wife's body in approximately nine months.

For the purpose of *kriyā* yoga, one has to curtail and eventually stop all sexual indulgence but this is easier discussed than it is accomplished in fact. By a steady practice of kundalini yoga, one gets to understand that the mixture of sexual energy, life force and deliberation, is interpreted by the mind as sexual pleasure. When one understands this, one is inspired to take steps to bring an end to sexual indulgences. The key is to cause the energy which is involved in a sexual release to come up the spine into the head of the subtle body to the *brahmarandra*.

Instead of the energy being released through the genitals, one has to painstakingly train it to be released through the top of the head of the subtle body. God will not do this for the devotee. The devotee has to take instructions from God or from the agent of God, the *kriyā* yoga teacher, on how to accomplish this in his own body.

All affections for wife, children, friends and the like are merely round about or subsidiary expressions of the sexual force. Therefore if one curbs the sexual energy, all the other forces are subdued. At that time, one can really chant the *sannyāsa* mantra which is *śivo-ham*. This means that I am auspicious. I am a little bit like Lord Shiva. Both the husband and wife can master their affections through kundalini yoga but that does not mean that they will work together for this. There might be disagreement.

For householders the second aspect to conquer is the pride felt when the children become successful and the discouragement and disappointment experienced when they turn out to be failures on the social plane. But if one masters the first aspect by stopping the sexual indulgence through a consistent yoga practice, one will not have to worry about this pride, because it will not manifest.

The concern for children is converted into a concern for one's spiritual self if one masters kundalini yoga and gets the sexual energy sublimated and raised out of the lower part of the body.

As soon as one takes up *kriyā* yoga practice in earnest, one's children are no longer a problem, because one's mind releases itself from their destiny. One then sees that the big problem before one, is the body's impending death. One then works hard to leave this material body with honor by yogic process. This yogic process is not a *sit-down-and-wait-for-salvation* procedure. It is an *up-and-at-it* endeavor, taking help from the Supreme Being and from the great yogins, to become perfected while the body lives and to attain salvation before the body deteriorates.

Thus if the householder completes *karma*, which is to get his children a basic education and if he completes *kāma*, which is to indulge sexually, and then to withdraw from it fully by yogic process, then he will be a successful householder.

Śrī Krishna said that one who worships Him by *karma* yoga cultural activities and by householder duties *(gṛha-medhīyair)* may remain as a householder all his life or he may take other options which we will discuss below. He can remain a householder and be a successful spiritualist, provided that he secretly uses spare time for the hard core austerities in yoga. There are examples of this like *Śrīla Vyāsadeva*, a life-long householder.

Alternately a householder might enter the forest with or without his wife, to be sure that he completes the yoga austerities. An example was King *Dhṛtaraṣṭra* who was encouraged to go to the forest by Vidura, and who completed the *aṣṭanga* yoga practice there, thus retrieving his spirituality before leaving the body.

Alternately the householder, if he has capable adult children, and if he is pre-trained in yoga, can take full renunciation. The yoga training is a prerequisite because without it, one will not be able to focus the mind in any deep way and one's superficial interest in spirituality will be ineffective, except by causing one to a take another body as soon as possible in some pious family on this earth, and to again come out and repeat the same disgusting history as a religious and kind head of household.

यस् त्व् आसक्त-मतिर् गेहे
पुत्र-वित्तैषणातुरः ।
स्त्रैणः कृपण-धीर् मूढो
ममाहम् इति बध्यते ॥१२.५६॥

yas tv āsakta-matir gehe
putra-vittaiṣaṇāturaḥ
straiṇaḥ kṛpaṇa-dhīr mūḍho
mamāham iti badhyate (12.56)

yas = yah — who; tv = tu — but; āsakta — attached; matir = matiḥ — mind; gehe — in household affairs; putra — son; vittaiṣaṇāturaḥ = vitta — money + eṣaṇa — desire + āturaḥ — is anxious; straiṇaḥ — if it is focused on females; kṛpaṇa — scheming; dhīḥ — intellect; mūḍho = mūḍhaḥ — foolish; mamāham = mama — mine + aham — I; iti — thus thinking; badhyate — is bound.

Translation

But he whose mind is attached in householder affairs, who is anxious about children and money, who is focused on women, whose intellect always schemes, is foolish. He is bound, thinking of "I" and "mine". (12.56)

Commentary:

This is the exact opposite of the objective for a yogin householder. *Śrī* Krishna obviously does not approve of a materialistic life for a householder but that does not mean that others agree with *Śrī* Krishna's preference. Hence, if one takes up yogic austerities and pleases the Lord, one will also aggravate those people who are opposed to a toned-down social life.

Most males are not strong enough to avoid fitting the description given in this verse. But the few ones who can resist this, should strive by effective means and break the pattern by not being materialistic and by acquiring spiritual experiences before the body dies.

अहो मे पितरौ वृद्धौ
भार्या बालात्मजात्मजाः ।
अनाथा माम् ऋते दीनाः
कथं जीवन्ति दुःखिताः ॥१२.५७॥

aho me pitarau vṛddhau
bhāryā bālātmajātmajāḥ
anāthā mām ṛte dīnāḥ
kathaṁ jīvanti duḥkhitāḥ (12.57)

aho — alas; me — my; pitarau — parents; vṛddhau — elderly; bhāryā — wife; bālātmajātmajāḥ = bāla – child + ātmajā — my baby + ātmājāh — my other children; anāthā — with a guardian; mām — me; ṛte — without; dīnāḥ — helpless dependents; katham — how; jīvanti — they live; duḥkhitāḥ — those who suffer.

Translation

Alas! My elderly parents, my wife, my baby and the other children, my helpless distressed dependents, how can they live without me, the guardian of the family. (12.57)

Commentary:

This is how we think when we are caught up with family life. Then, we do not have the strength of renunciation. We become confused regarding destiny. Even though death awaits us, we deny its presence by shifting our attention to the social scene around us. Most of our relatives are all too willing to indulge us.

In turn, in the tradition of the elderly parents, who passed away in ignorance, we assume an indispensible demeanor. Our children after us, usually adopt the same stance, as soon as they become guardians of families. Thus by tradition, we remain in ignorance.

एवं गृहाशयाक्षिप्त-
हृदयो मूढ-धीर् अयम् ।
अतृप्तस् तान् अनुध्यायन्
मृतो ऽन्धं विशते तमः ॥ १२.५८॥

evaṁ gṛhāśayākṣipta-
hṛdayo mūḍha-dhīr ayam
atṛptas tān anudhyāyan
mṛto 'ndhaṁ viśate tamaḥ (12.58)

evam — thus; gṛhāśayākṣipta-hṛdayo = gṛha — domestic affairs + āśaya — contemplating, focusing + ākṣipta — distracted + hṛdayo (hṛdayah) — seat of feelings, emotions; mūḍha — fool; dhīr = dhīḥ — intellect; ayam — this; atṛptas = atṛptaḥ — dissatisfied; tān — them, those; anudhyāyan — impulsively linking the attention to focused emotions; mṛto = mṛtaḥ — body dies; 'ndhaṁ = andham — destroy; viśate — enters; tamaḥ — darkness.

Translation

This person with a fool's intellect, whose emotions are distracted by focusing on domestic affairs, remains dissatisfied. While impulsively linking his attention to those emotions, his body dies and he enters mental darkness. (12.58)

Commentary:

This is the situation of any human being who lives with a preoccupation for family affairs. Such a person enters into mental darkness when the body dies, regardless of their religious affiliation or professed faith and regardless of how much money they donate or services they render to a religious institution.

However they do take rebirth in this world, according to the cultural contributions made. Such persons are not entirely lost. They do acquire a body again in this world, because most people in this world have similar natures. It is through their pious activities that they again take rebirth either in the family they departed from or in some other clan in which they deposited services.

Because such persons were focused on family members and because they invested their affection upon them, their spirits, even in the dark mental condition, are automatically attracted to their relatives and so again they enter into the emotions of those who were fond of them and they come out into this world again as babies and repeat their histories. Such is this material existence.

CHAPTER 13*

Becoming a Devotee**

Terri Stokes-Pineda Art

etat te 'bhihitam sādho bhavān pṛcchati yac ca mām
yathā sva-dharma-saṁyuktobhakto māṁ samiyāt param

I explained this, O saint, as you inquired from Me about the method of how being attentive to righteous duty, one becomes a devotee and attains to Me, the Supreme Being. (Uddhava Gītā 13.48)

* Śrīmad Bhāgavatam Canto 11, Chapter 18
** Translator's selected chapter title.

श्री-भगवान् उवाच
वनं विविक्षुः पुत्रेषु
भार्यां न्यस्य सहैव वा ।
वन एव वसेच् छान्तस्
तृतीयं भागम् आयुषः ॥ १३.१ ॥

śrī-bhagavān uvāca
vanaṁ vivikṣuḥ putreṣu
bhāryāṁ nyasya sahaiva vā
vana eva vasec chāntas
tṛtīyaṁ bhāgam āyuṣaḥ (13.1)

śrī-bhagavān – the blessed lord; uvāca — said; vanam — forest; vivikṣuḥ — wishes to retire; putreṣu — in care of the sons; bhāryām — wife; nyasya — leaving; sahaiva = saha — with + eva — indeed; vā — or; vana = vane — in the forest; eva — indeed; vasec = vaset — one should live; chāntas = śāntaḥ — peacefully; tṛtīyam — third; bhāgam — portion; āyuṣaḥ — of life.

Translation

The Blessed Lord said: One who wishes to retire into the forest, should leave his wife in care of sons; or she may, following him, assume the ascetic lifestyle. He should live peacefully in the forest, for that third portion of life. (13.1)

Commentary:

When a man understands that at the time of death, his children and relatives will not be able to assist, he may decide to make a run for it. One runs for the hereafter by developing awareness of the operations of the subtle body. This is *sukṣma karma* or cultural activities of the psyche in the subtle world.

Those who do not make a run for it, decide to stay on and let providence take its toll. They do not care as to what will happen to their bodies in old age or as to where they will be transferred in the hereafter. Subsequently they are careless in this regard and develop no desire to separate from the thriving domestic life of younger relatives.

Some men make a run for it with their wives and others do so alone, because their wives are reluctant to engage in such an uncertain enterprise as the hereafter. If a man runs off with his wife, with the idea to face death and get familiar with his subtle body, while his wife endeavors to know hers, he assumes a burden. Generally, women are not parry to austerities, but there are a few women who could successfully stand the rigors of ascetic life. The main handicap for a woman is her tendency to enjoy life among relatives, particularly among her children.

It is for this reason that generally women do not accompany men who decide to leave home to search out the hereafter. There are some men however who leave home in old age to live at a temple, to do temple services, to hear scriptural readings, and to chant holy names. Most of these men die in the same uncertainty about the hereafter that they had before leaving home. This is because they hardly get any hereafter experience or *sukṣma karma* before leaving their bodies. These individuals are usually conned by preachers who milk them for money and who assure them that merely by dying at a holy place, they will go to the kingdom of God.

A man who makes a run for the forest to complete or to begin yoga austerities and to develop subtle perception thereby and who does so with a wife, has got his job cut out for him. He can be successful but he will have to work a lot harder than a man who goes away and leaves his wife to complete her old body in the usual way of becoming more and more involved in family affairs.

In the old communities in India, during the time of Lord Krishna, there were many ascetics with wives in the forest reserve, but these were mostly persons who either lived there all their lives practicing or persons who practiced intensely in youth and then practiced some during the householder years. Nobody then, would go to the forest with his wife if she was not versed to an extent in the austerities. We hear that King *Dhṛtaraṣṭra* took his wife *Gāndhārī* to the forest and King *Yudhiṣṭhira* also took his wife *Draupadī*. There are examples. Otherwise only a crazy man would take his wife into isolation to begin austerities in yoga if they had not practiced previously.

At the beginning of the third stage of life, a man should have a little talk with himself, just as elderly people usually do. He should say, "I have married and raised children. Now what should I do? The best part of my life is over. It was invested in generating children and living with a spouse. Now with little time left, I will make a run for perfection. I have nothing to lose. If I do not complete it, then in my next life at least I will have the impetus to resume it again, otherwise if I do nothing then in the next body, I will become more reluctant to develop myself. I must step aside from materialistic life and realize the subtle world. "

कन्द्-मूल-फलैर् वन्यैर्
मेध्यैर् वृत्तिं प्रकल्पयेत् ।
वसीत वल्कलं वासस्
तृण-पर्णाजिनानि वा ॥ १३.२ ॥

kanda-mūla-phalair vanyair
medhyair vṛttiṁ prakalpayet
vasīta valkalaṁ vāsas
tṛṇa-parṇājināni vā (13.2)

kanda — tubers; mūla — roots; phalair = phalaih — with fruits; vanyair = vanyaih — with edible produce from the forest; medhyaih — with health, yielding food; vṛttim — substance; prakalpayet — should subsist; vasīta — should wear; valkalam — bark; vāsas — cloth; tṛṇa — straw; parṇājināni = parna — leaves + ajināni — deer skins; vā — or.

Translation

He should subsist on health-yielding tubers, roots, fruits and other edible produce of the forest. He should wear bark or cloth, straw garments, leaf garments or a deer skin. (13.2)

Commentary:

One goes to the forest to be away from relatives. If the relatives know one's whereabouts, it is likely that they will pester one to return home. Or they may insist on building a comfortable cabin. This happens frequently, where a yogin gives up austerity as soon as many disciples find him and build for him a luxurious residence. Regarding him as God or as an agent of God, the followers indulge him. His austere practices become adjusted into being just pleasant meditation sessions, or melodious singing programs.

When Vidura instructed King *Dhṛtaraṣṭra* to go to the forest, he told the king that they should go to a place which was unknown to relatives, and that to die at such a place, is a glorious departure from this world. Vidura cited a scriptural verse to prove the point.

केश-रोम-नख-श्मश्रु-
मलानि बिभृयाद् दतः ।
न धावेद् अप्सु मज्जेत
त्रि कालं स्थण्डिले-शयः ॥ १३.३ ॥

keśa-roma-nakha-śmaśru-
malāni bibhṛyād dataḥ
na dhāved apsu majjeta
tri kālaṁ sthaṇḍile-śayaḥ (13.3)

keśa — scalp hair; roma — body hair; nakha — nails; śmaśru — beard; malāni — evaculation; bibhṛyād = bibhṛyāt — should not restrict; dataḥ — teeth; na – not; dhāved = dhāvet — should scrub; apsu — in water; majjeta — should plunge; tri-kālam — three times daily; sthaṇḍile — on earth; śayah — lay down.

Translation

He should not restrict his scalp hair, body hair, nails, beard or evacuations. He should not scrub the teeth and should plunge into water three times daily and lay on the earth. (13.3)

Commentary:

Śrī Krishna gave details of the *vanaprastha* stage of life, when a man having seen the futility of raising a family, decides to get a footing in the hereafter, so that he may get a handle on his destiny. This is the real life, for a person who already raised a family. Most men are not interested in such a life. They regard these stories as a very amusing description of ancient Indian history.

It is a fact however, that at the time of death, we must migrate to the subtle world. Hence it is quite reasonable for any of us to prepare for it, by exploring that subtle existence beforehand. It is a sound proposal.

ग्रीष्मे तप्येत पञ्चाग्नीन्
वर्षास्व् आसार-षाड् जले ।
आकण्ठ-मग्नः शिशिर
एवं वृत्तस् तपश् चरेत् ॥ १३.४॥

grīṣme tapyeta pañcāgnīn
varṣāsv āsāra-ṣāḍ jale
ākaṇtha-magnaḥ śiśira
evaṁ vṛttas tapaś caret (13.4)

grīṣme — in summer; tapyeta — should practise austerity; pañcāgnīn — five types of heat; varsāsv = varsāsu — in the rainy season; āsāra — rain showers; sād = sāṭ — tolerating; jale — in water; ākaṇṭha — to the neck; magnaḥ — submerged; śiśira — in the winter; evam — thus; vṛttas — performed; tapaś = tapaḥ — penance; caret — should practice.

Translation

In summer, he should practice the austerity of the five types of heat, in the rainy season, he should tolerate rain showers, in water he should remain submerged up to the neck. Thus performed he should practice penance. (13.4)

Commentary:

Once the householder gets to the forest, he should begin the practice at the level of austerity which suits his nature. If he was habituated to comforts in the householder life, he will first have to subject himself to many types of discomforting situations until he adapts and becomes detached from the need for bodily comfort. When his mind gets accustomed to the penances, he advances. These penances are part of the process of getting immune to the dualities which we experience in nature, such as good or bad weather, soft or hard objects and so on.

In householder life one is usually subjected to comforts, thus one becomes timid in relation to austerities. And hence a timid man has to adapt himself by deliberately subjecting himself to discomforts. Needless to say, if a man took his wife into this phase of life, she too would be required to get accustomed to the inconveniences.

Lord Buddha after personally practicing similar austerities, came to the conclusion that ultimately these deprivations do not cause one to attain enlightenment, at least these do not bring on a spiritual vision. However he recommended what he called the Middle Way or the process of austerities without going to extremes and without going down the materialistic enjoying vice-ridden type of worldly life. However it depends on one's nature. One may have to take extreme austerities for a time, just as Lord Buddha did, just to attain detachment from the body and from its comfort-needs, even though one will not gain spiritual perception by such methods necessarily. Detachment must be attained by whatever means one finds to be expedient.

अग्नि-पक्वं समश्नीयात्
काल-पक्वम् अथापि वा ।
उलूखलाश्म-कुट्टो वा
दन्तोलूखल एव वा ॥ १३..५॥

agni-pakvaṁ samaśnīyāt
kāla-pakvam athāpi vā
ulūkhalāśma-kuṭṭo vā
dantolūkhala eva vā (13.5)

agni — fire; pakvam — cooked; samaśnīyāt — should heat; kāla — time; pakvam — ripened; athāpi = atha — or else + api — also; vā — or; ulūkhalāśma-kuṭṭo = ulūkhala — pestle + aśma — stone + kuṭṭo (kuṭṭaḥ) — pulverized; vā — or; dantolūkhala = danta — teeth + ulūkhala (ulūkhalaḥ) — grinding mortar; eva — also; vā — or.

Translation

He should eat food cooked by a fire or what is ripened by time, or he may pulverise foods with pestle or stone, or even using his teeth as the grinding mortar. (13.5)

Commentary:

The idea is that even if a householder has wealth, and even if he can afford servants, he should not have these in the forest life. He has to become his own servant in this case. He should not carry luxuries and other amenities.

स्वयं सञ्चिनुयात् सर्वम्
आत्मनो वृत्ति-कारणम् ।
देश-काल-बलाभिज्ञो
नाददीतान्यदाहृतम् ॥ १३.६ ॥

svayaṁ sañcinuyāt sarvam
ātmano vṛtti-kāraṇam
deśa-kāla-balābhijño
nādadītānyadāhṛtam (13.6)

svayam — himself; sañcinuyāt — should collect; sarvam — all; ātmano = ātmanaḥ — his own; vṛtti — sustenance; kāraṇam — means; deśa — place; kāla — time; balābhijño = balābhijñaḥ = bala — personal power + abhijñaḥ — knowing the application; nādadītānyadāhṛtam = na – not + ādadīta — should procure + anyadā — some other + āhṛtam — things.

Translation

Knowing the application of personal power in terms of place and time, he should collect his means of sustenance, and should not procure things from some other time. (13.6)

Commentary:

The ascetic has to learn how to live with the forest, in the forest and by the forest. If he wants to advance into subtle perception and to curb his subtle body for guiding it to a particular locale in the hereafter, he has to forget the conveniences of householder life. He should not arrange to get food from relatives who live a normal life in a village or town. He should not try to buy foods from people who came from the towns or from a foreign country, since the eating of such items would reduce the rate of his progress into the subtle countries which he would see if he sincerely maintains the austerities.

He should restrict the diet to what he can easily procure in the forest area and should get used to that kind of food. Realizing that death is certain and that he cannot avoid it, no matter what, and knowing that he cannot carry property to the hereafter, he should become determined to do whatever is necessary to become conscious of the subtle form, for it is that form into which he will be transferred when the gross body dies.

वन्यैश् चरु-पुरोडाशैर्
निर्वपेत् काल-चोदितान् ।
न तु श्रौतेन पशुना
मां यजेत वनाश्रमी ॥ १३.७ ॥

vanyaiś caru-puroḍāśair
nirvapet kāla-coditān
na tu śrautena paśuna
māṁ yajeta vanāśramī (13.7)

vanyaiś = vanyaiḥ — with items obtained from the forest; caru — oblations of grain; purodāśair = purodāśaiḥ — with wild grain from the forest; nirvapet — should perform; kāla-coditān — seasonal ritualistic ceremonies; na — not; tu — but; śrautena — with Vedic ritualistic observances; paśunā — with animal sacrifice; mām — me; yajeta — may worship; vanāśramī — one who retired to the ascetic forest life.

Translation

He should perform the seasonal ritualistic ceremonies, with oblations of wild

grain obtained from the forest. One who retired to ascetic forest life, should not worship Me with animal sacrifice. 13.7)

Commentary:

Here there is a prescription for using wild grain to continue the performance of sacrifice but if the householder was from a religion that permitted animal sacrifice, he should not continue the practice. *Śrī* Krishna rejects animal offerings. It should not be presented to His Deity Form. The householder who was used to sacrificing animals should discontinue the practice once he takes to the ascetic life.

अग्निहोत्रं च दर्शश् च
पौर्णमासश् च पूर्व-वत् ।
चातुर्मास्यानि च मुनेर्
आम्नातानि च नैगमैः ॥१३.८॥

agnihotraṁ ca darśaś ca
paurṇamāsaś ca pūrva-vat
cāturmāsyāni ca muner
āmnātāni ca naigamaiḥ (13.8)

agnihotram — fire sacrifice; ca — and; darśaś = darśaḥ — new moon ritual; ca — and; paurnamāsaś = paurnamāsaḥ — full moon ritualistic ceremony; ca — and; purva-vat — as done earlier in life; cāturmāsyāni — the four-month rainy season ritual observances and austerities; ca — and; muner = muneḥ — of the ascetic forest retirees; āmnātāni — traditionally enjoined; ca — and; naigamaiḥ — by the Vedic authorities.

Translation

The Agnihotra fire sacrifice, the Darśa new moon rituals and the Paurṇamāsa full moon ceremonies, as well as the Cāturmāṣa four-month rainy season observances, were traditionally enjoined by the Vedic authorities as obligations for the ascetic forest retiree, just as was done earlier in his life. (13.8)

Commentary:

These procedures were to be continued in the forest life, except that the retiree ascetic was to use forest grains and materials. He was not to acquire items from towns and villages, nor to invite the general public, as he did previously. Everything was to be continued on a smaller scale, without involvement.

एवं चीर्णेन तपसा
मुनिर् धमनि-सन्ततः ।
मां तपो-मयम् आराध्य
ऋषि-लोकाद् उपैति माम् ॥१३.९॥

evaṁ cīrṇena tapasā
munir dhamani-santataḥ
māṁ tapo-mayam ārādhya
ṛṣi-lokād upaiti mām (13.9)

evam — thus; cīrṇena — by practice; tapasā — of austerity; munir = munih — the ascetic retiree; dhamani – vein; santataḥ — stretched, prominently showing; mām — me; tapo-mayam — embodiement of austerity; ārādhya — worshiping; ṛṣi-lokād = ṛṣi-lokāt — from the planet of the yogi sages; upaiti — achieves; mām — me.

Translation

Thus the ascetic forest retiree, with his veins stretched, showing prominently over his body, by the practice of austerity and worshipping Me, who is the embodiment of austerities, attains Me when he is transferred to the planet of the yogi sages. (13.9)

Commentary:

From this description, we know that a forest retiree is not supposed to be eating sumptuous food preparations at least not if he expects to reach the planet of the yogi sages, a place in which he would finish the austerities and traverse the rest of the way to the spiritual place of *Śrī* Krishna.

यस् त्व् एतत् कृच्छ्रतश् चीर्णं
तपो निःश्रेयसं महत् ।
कामायाल्पीयसे युञ्ज्याद्
बालिशः को ऽपरस् ततः ॥१३.१०

Yas tv etat kṛcchrataś cīrṇaṁ
tapo niḥśreyasaṁ mahat
kāmāyālpīyase yuñjyād
bāliśaḥ ko 'paras tataḥ (13.10)

yas = yaḥ — one who; tv = tu — but; etat — this; kṛcchrataś = kṛcchrataḥ — great austerity; cīrṇam — time consuming; tapo = tapaḥ — austerity; nihśreyasam — designed for liberation; mahat — great; kāmāyālpīyase = kāmāya — for cravings + alpīyase — petty; yuñjyād = yuñjyāt — from the practices; bāliśaḥ — fool; ko = kaḥ — who; 'paras = aparaḥ — else; tataḥ — but.

Translation

Considering that these practices of this great time-consuming austerity are designed for liberation, who but a foolish person, would extract from them, the fulfillment of petty cravings? (13.10)

Commentary:

The key to not abusing an austerity is to be in isolation and not to attract anyone who would want to glorify and praise one for being an ascetic. The whole idea behind taking *vanaprastha* or forest retiree asceticism is to scale down involvement and to turn oneself to the world hereafter, in order to train the subtle body to get to a higher location.

यदासौ नियमे ऽकल्पो
जरया जात-वेपथुः ।
आत्मन्य् अग्नीन् समारोप्य
मच्-चित्तो ऽग्निं समाविशेत् ॥१३.११॥

yadāsau niyame 'kalpo
jarayā jāta-vepathuḥ
ātmany agnīn samāropya
mac-citto 'gniṁ samāviśet (13.11)

yadasau = yadā — when + asau — that (person); niyame — in the rules; 'kalpo = akalpaḥ — unable to observe; jarayā — by old age; jāta-vepathuḥ = jāta — manifested + vepathuḥ — trembling; ātmany = ātmani — in himself; agnīn — sacrificial fires; samāropya — place; mac-citto = mat-cittah — mental and emotional energy fixed on me; 'gnim = agnim — fire; samāviśet — should enter.

Translation

When there is a trembling manifested in the body, due to old age, that ascetic retiree is unable to observe the rules. Then he should place the sacrificial fires in himself and with his mind, mental and emotional energy fixed on Me, enter the fire. (13.11)

Commentary:

Instead of making elaborate plans to enter a hospital or to be cared for by servants in a hospice, the ascetic retiree should plan how to deal with his body when it reaches a stage of infirmity, whereby he cannot use it efficiently, because of the diseases and disabilities which come on in old age. A man who stays with relatives, has little chance of planning how to handle his old body. Usually such decisions are made by the relatives and he simply looks on and allows them to execute their decisions.

For those who become advanced in the yoga practice, particularly in *prāṇāyāma*, death is easily regulated by control of the life force mechanism which thrives on pranic intake during breathing. Others may adopt a meditative stance that may or may not work for them, depending on their good or bad luck.

In the case of King *Dhṛtaraṣṭra*, he had enough training. He completed enough of the practice in the retired stages, so that he could destroy his own body in a fire.

There is no point continuing in an incapacitated body but we see that many spiritual leaders nowadays adapt to the Western methods of entering hospitals, taking many surgeries and other treatments during their last years, in the effort of their followers to prolong their lives.

Nowadays, we hear that the guru allows this, so that the disciples can get an opportunity to render service.

यदा कर्म-विपाकेषु
लोकेषु निरयात्मसु ।
विरागो जायते सम्यङ्
न्यस्ताग्निः प्रव्रजेत् ततः ॥ १३.१२ ॥

yadā karma-vipākeṣu
lokeṣu nirayātmasu
virāgo jāyate samyaṅ
nyastāgniḥ pravrajet tataḥ (13.12)

yadā — when; karma — cultural activities; vipākeṣu — in the outcome; lokeṣu — in societies; nirayātmasu = niraya – miserable, hellish + ātmasu — essentially, inherently; virāgo = virāgaḥ — disgusted; jāyate — produced; samyan — completely; nyastāgniḥ = nyasta — cease performing + agniḥ — sacrificial fire ceremony; pravrajet — should become fully renounced; tataḥ — from then onwards.

Translation

When he is completely disgusted with life in societies, that are the outcome of cultural activity, knowing that they are essentially hellish, he should cease performing the sacrificial fire ceremony and from then onwards become fully renounced. (13.12)

Commentary:

This is easy for a yogi who practiced through his life, or for one who began the practice late in life but who by virtue of austerities in his past lives, instinctively understood that cultural activity in any society, is ultimately a creature affair and is merely a waste of time.

Even though mundane cultural life is necessary, and even though it has value in that it provides these bodies, still it is in a big way, a complete reversal of spiritual life. It is not easy to take a cultural opportunity and make something spiritual out of it. It is near impossible to do so. For that matter, any type of cultural birth that a living entity takes, automatically imperils his spiritual interest, because the cultural situations are such that they demand compensation by more intertwining cultural acts.

It is for this reason that a yogi assumes an extremist attitude and becomes repelled from cultural life. One cannot win spiritually in the cultural world. If one contributes culturally he will have to derive benefits, not spiritually but culturally only. Therefore what is done for cultural aims is lost in the spiritual sense.

We should perform our cultural duties to the satisfaction of the Central Person in the Universal Form but that does not mean that such performance will cause liberation. It will not. For liberation one must leave aside the cultural world at some point.

इष्ट्वा यथोपदेशं मां
दत्त्वा सर्व-स्वम् ऋत्विजे ।
अग्नीन् स्व-प्राण आवेश्य
निरपेक्षः परिव्रजेत् ॥ १३.१३ ॥

iṣṭvā yathopadeśaṁ māṁ
dattvā sarva-svam ṛtvije
agnīn sva-prāṇa āveśya
nirapekṣaḥ parivrajet (13.13)

iṣṭvā — having worshiped; yathopadeśam = yathā — according to + upadeśam — scriptural injunctions; mām — me; dattvā — having given; sarva-svam — all possessions; ṛtvije — to the officiating priest; agnīn — sacrificial fire; sva-prāṇe — in his own life force; āveśya — putting; nirapekṣah — without caring for anything; parivrajet — should renounce and wander about.

Translation

Having worshiped Me according to scriptural injunctions, and having given all possessions to the officiating priest, putting the sacrificial fire into his own life force, he should renounce and wander about without caring for anything. (13.13)

Commentary:

This is for those elderly persons whose bodies do not become diseased and infirmed. If a yogi's old body remains fit and can travel about, this is what he should do.

विप्रस्य वै सन्न्यसतो देवा दारादि-रूपिणः । विघ्नान् कुर्वन्त्य् अयं ह्य् अस्मान् आक्रम्य समियात् परम् ॥ १३.१४ ॥	viprasya vai sannyasato devā dārādi-rūpiṇaḥ vighnān kurvanty ayaṁ hy asmān ākramya samiyāt param (13.14)

viprasya — of the brahmin; vai — indeed; sannyasato = sannyasataḥ — intention to renounce completely; devāh — the supernatural rulers; dārādi = dāra – wife + ādi – and other relations; rūpiṇah — in the form of; vighnān — obstuctions; kurvanty = kurvanti — present; ayam — this person; hy = hi — indeed; asmān — us; ākramya — surpassing; samiyāt — attain; param — the supreme destination.

Translation

Noticing the brahmin's intention to renounce completely, the supernatural rulers would present obstructions in the form of his wife and other relations. The supernatural rulers think, "Surpassing us, this ascetic retiree may attain the supreme destination." (13.14)

Commentary:

This is the psychology of those angelic beings who are in the mundane paradises, and who are permanent residents there. Even though their bodies do not have any motivation to go beyond their spheres, they are conscious of the efforts of human beings who might surpass them.

Thus when a yogi performs sufficient austerities to refine his subtle form, so that it could by-pass the heavenly planets, the supernatural rulers detect and feel that he is being presumptuous. A yogin has to either hide his attainment from them or make friends with them by respecting them for the services they render to the Supreme Being, otherwise it is hardly likely that he would be successful, because they can place some very effective impediments on his path.

The supernatural rulers can invoke feelings of regret and lamentation in one's relatives. They may pester one with emotional pleas. A yogin gets a taste of this when as a householder, his wife or children beg him to desists from austerities. At each stage he might be checkmated by such feelings from relatives. Many persons who approach me about renunciation, specifically males, are unable to take up the disciplines in yoga, because they come down to social plane, being forcibly pushed back there by relatives. Some persons are drawn down by devotees and friends, persons who do no yoga, and who feel that salvation would be attained by an easy method like chanting holy names and eating temple foods.

The attitude of the *deva* supernatural rulers is that a human being should not surpass them in spiritual development. Their idea is simply this: That we should be elevated to their domains and then gradually in the process of time, get higher after they have evolved further. The problem with their view is this: It would take many, many millions of years before one could get away from such heavenly paradises. In fact only one in so many thousands of persons who ascend from the earth to the heavenly worlds, do not have to return again to the earth after their pious credits are exhausted.

Some Hindus feel that once you have a stock of pious credits, you will definitely see heaven in the hereafter, but they are mistaken because it has to be a particular type of pious credit. Some pious credits pay off only on this earth or in some similar type of hardship-dimension like the earth. For heavenly life, a special type of credit is applicable. When that is exhausted one will disappear from the heavenly place.

Supernatural rulers like *Indra* are to be respected. If one fails to respect such persons, one will not be successful even in bypassing their domains, but all the same one should be aware that Indra is not particularly concerned to see one go beyond his sphere. The supernatural rulers do work in the subtle atmosphere over the earth. They control weather situations. That is their part-time job. Therefore they feel that human beings owe them respect. Thus if an ascetic develops himself spiritually, they feel that he is being rude towards them. It is for this reason that one has to respect them and get their goodwill for advancement. One should not have a sour attitude towards them or be alienated or feel that they have no value. It is best to be cordial so that they can take pride if one attains a zone which is beyond theirs. A father might not be as educated as a son but that does not mean that the father is incapable of appreciating the success of the son in earning an engineering degree. We have to develop similar relations with the *devas*, and then they will not place before us impediments which might drag us back into cultural activities.

Even if the devas put obstructions before us, we should recognize their actions and not resent them but should say, "Yes Sir, I took seriously to the austerities. By your grace I had some luck. I appreciate you."

A yogin should never forget that when Arjuna saw the Universal Form, he saw the devas as parts of that Universal Body. They did their part for the Universal Form. As expansions of *Śrī* Krishna, they are deserving of respect. All the same, we should not allow them to keep us time-bound.

बिभृयाच् चेन् मुनिर् वासः
कौपीनाच्छादनं परम् ।
त्यक्तं न दण्ड-पात्राभ्याम्
अन्यत् किञ्चिद् अनापदि ॥१३.१५॥

bibhṛyāc cen munir vāsaḥ
kaupīnācchādanaṁ param
tyaktaṁ na daṇḍa-pātrābhyām
anyat kiñcid anāpadi (13.15)

bibhryāc = bibhryāt — would wear; cen = cet — if; munir = muniḥ — the ascetic philosopher; vāsaḥ — clothes; kaupīnācchādanam = kaupīna — loin cloth; ācchādanam — covering; param — other; tyaktam — discarded; na — not; danda — stall; pātrābhyām — water container; anyat — other; kiñcid = kiñcit — anything; anāpadi — in emergency.

Translation

If the ascetic philosopher wears clothings, it should be a loin cloth covering. Except in emergency, he should not have anything which he already discarded, other than his staff and water container. (13.15)

Commentary:

Whatever was formally discarded should not be taken up again merely for convenience. The ascetic should advance stage by stage and should not retrogress to the time when he was a householder and had conveniences. He should not fall for inducements which anyone might offer. People are apt to find such an ascetic and insist that he take it easy, instead of punishing himself in the forest with sparse utensils and hardly any conveniences.

दृष्टि-पूतं न्यसेत् पादं
वस्त्र-पूतं पिबेज् जलम् ।
सत्य-पूतां वदेद् वाचं
मनः-पूत समाचरेत् ॥१३.१६॥

dṛṣṭi-pūtaṁ nyaset pādaṁ
vastra-pūtaṁ pibej jalam
satya-pūtāṁ vaded vācaṁ
manaḥ-pūtaṁ samācaret (13.16)

dṛṣṭi — seeing; pūtam — cleared; nyaset — should place; pādam — foot; vastra — cloth; pūtam — filtered; pibej = pibet — should drink; jalam — water; satya — truthful; pūtām — substantiated; vaded = vadet — should speak; vācam — word; manaḥ — mind; pūtam — clarified; samācaret — should act.

Translation

He should place his foot after seeing that the path is cleared, should drink water filtered by a cloth, should speak words that are substantiated by truth, and should act as determined with a clarified mind. (13.16)

Commentary:

Being in the forest also means becoming more and more sensitive to subtle phenomena. This means an increase in mystic perception, because of an accelerated yoga practice, which gives one the ability to use the subtle senses even while having the gross form.

Thus the yogin sees living creatures everywhere and begins to understand that he does not have a right to intercept them. This yogi actually sees this. It is not just his belief because he was told about it from a saintly person, or because he read from a scripture.

There are living creatures everywhere, in the air, on the land and in the sea. They are entitled to development through assumption of life forms. Therefore one does not have a right to deprive them of the opportunities. A yogin takes precautions when he walks, when he eats and when he speaks.

Lord *Mahāvīra* and other Jain *tirthankaras*, brought it to our attention that there are microscropic creatures in water. They asked that water be strained through a tightly woven cloth. Of course we should not be fanatical but should try to understand what Lord *Mahāvīra* and others like Lord Buddha explained. Some persons tie a cloth to a modern tap and filter water through it. In the sect of *Swāmīnārāyaṇa* this is done by many of the devotees who migrated to the Western countries. However that is just a superficial application of what Lord *Swāmīnārāyaṇa* instituted. If one strains through a cloth, water which was already micro-filtrated and chlorinated, then one is wasting time. An ordinary cotton or polyester cloth cannot remove the tiniest bacteria and viruses. We have to be sensible. If for instance, I strain water from a river through a cloth, the creatures trapped in the cloth may die as soon as the cloth dries out, unless I take precautions to release them back into the water.

Another aspect of this is the entry of bacteria into one's body. There are two facets of this. One is that those creatures might be killed when they enter the human body by climatic and chemical situations in the stomach and intestines. If they are not killed they will begin to live in the body or they might be expelled from the anus at a later time. Just as we live in this atmosphere, other creatures live in our body. It cannot be prevented. Thus the instruction to strain off microscopic life, is a consideration for not disrupting the lives of other creatures.

Modern medical science has shown conclusively that certain bacteria and viruses are harmful to the human body. In fact, if some species get into the body, they multiply rapidly and kill the body. Others, like the ones which cause the common cold, make the body sick for a short time only.

One should avoid giving emotional pain to others because merely by speaking a harsh word, a person can be put to grief. The best way to avoid this, is to be alone.

मौनानीहानिलायामा
दण्डा वाग्-देह-चेतसाम् ।
न ह्य् एते यस्य सन्त्य् अङ्ग
वेणुभिर् न भवेद् यतिः ॥१३.१७॥

maunānīhānilāyāmā
daṇḍā vāg-deha-cetasām
na hy ete yasya santy aṅga
veṇubhir na bhaved yatiḥ (13.17)

maunānīhānilāyāma = mauna — silence + anīha — not striving for cultural improvement +; anila – breath + āyāmāḥ — regulations; daṇḍa = daṇḍāh — restraints; vāg = vāk — speech; deha — body; cetasām — of consciousness; na — not; hy = hi — indeed; ete — these; yasya — of whom; santi — are; aṅga — friend; veṇubhir = veṇubhiḥ — by bamboo rods; na — not; bhaved = bhavet — becomes; yatiḥ — accomplished yogi.

Translation

Silence, not striving for cultural improvement and regulation of breath, are restraints of speech, body and consciousness respectively. One who has not mastered these, O friend, never becomes an accomplished yogi, merely by having bamboo rods. (13.17)

Commentary:

The bamboo rods are used for making *dańḍas* or staffs, used by ascetics to denote their *sannyāsa* status. But one will not become an accomplished yogin, a *yatih*, if he does not master the sense of expression which operates speech. To do this one must adopt the technique of silence or *mauna*. This means one gets the intellect to retract its need for social dialogue. This is a purely a mystic technique, even though it can be faked by a pretense of not speaking externally. Without isolation one cannot do this, because as soon as one interacts, one is compelled to speak.

It was believed that *Śrī* Ramana Maharishi, a self realized Indian, mastered the *mauna* discipline. Some modern Vaishnavas however, including our Vaishnava spiritual master *Śrīla Bhaktivedānta Swāmī Prabhupāda*, preached that *mauna* or silence, means not speaking of anything which is unrelated to *Śrī* Krishna. That is a completely new definition. It is not what *Śrī* Krishna described to Uddhava, even though it is consistent with what Lord Chaitanya advocated.

To restrain the body, one has to stop all striving for cultural improvement. This is the most frightening of all the austerities, because to one's relatives this is a statement of hostility. It is, in fact, what is called *nivṛtti mārga*, the path of non-involvement externally and internally. *Iha* means wish, desire, effort, exertion of activity. When an is prefixed to *iha*, it is the opposite, meaning a lack of desire, lack of exertion, lack of activity. Thus to discipline the body, one has to stop the internal impetus for cultural life, by developing a disinterest in social affairs. This is called *vairāgya* or indifference but in this verse, *Śrī* Krishna used the synonym which is *anilāyāmāh*. *Anila* means air or wind and *āyāmāh* is the regulation or restraint.

The life air is controlled by *prāṇāyāma*. When that is achieved, the consciousness *(cetasam)* which is the mental and emotional force, shifts to a higher plane.

भिक्षां चतुर्षु वर्णेषु
विगर्ह्यान् वर्जयंश् चरेत् ।
सप्तागारान् असङ्कॢप्तांस्
तुष्येल् लब्धेन तावता ॥ १३.१८॥

bhikṣāṁ caturṣu varṇeṣu
vigarhyān varjayaṁś caret
saptāgārān asaṅkḷptāṁs
tuṣyel labdhena tāvatā (13.18)

bhikṣām — food acquired by begging; caturṣu — from the fourth; varṇeṣu — people in the work categories; vigarhyām — unworthy people; varjayamś = varjayan — excepting, excluding; caret — should visit; saptāgārān = sapta — seven + āgārān — houses; asaṅkḷptāms = asaṅkḷptān — without intending to get anything; tuṣyet — should be satisfied; labdhena — with what is obtained; tāvatā — with whatever.

Translation

He should acquire food by begging from people of the four work categories, except from those persons who are unworthy. Without intending to get anything, he should visit seven houses and be satisfied with whatever is obtained. (13.18)

Commentary:

This rule is such that an ascetic should not beg from persons outside the four castes. Persons who live in a very nasty way or who are hunters or fishermen, should be avoided. They are engaged in brutal methods of raising a livelihood.

When visiting homes for the sake of begging, the ascetic should have no expectation. If he is sent away, neglected or insulted, he should take no mind to it. He should visit no more than seven houses. If he obtains nothing he should accept that as a statement of providence.

Ideally the ascetic should drift around and not go to the same seven houses every day, nor be seen in the same village for long. This will protect him from falling under the control of others.

बहिर् जलाशयं गत्वा
तत्रोपस्पृश्य वाग्-यतः ।
विभज्य पावित शेषं
भुञ्जीताशेषम् आहृतम् ॥ १३.१९ ॥

bahir jalāśayaṁ gatvā
tatropaspṛśya vāg-yataḥ
vibhajya pāvitaṁ śeṣaṁ
bhuñjītāśeṣam āhṛtam (13.19)

bahir = bahih — outside, beyond; jalāśayam = jala — water + āśayam — place; gatvā — going; tatropaspṛśya = tatra — there + upaspṛśya — contacting, bathing; vāg-yataḥ = vāk-yataḥ — restrained speech; vibhajya — offering; pāvitam — sanctified; śeṣam — portion; bhuñjītāśeṣam = bhuñjīta — should eat + aśeṣam — without remainder; āhṛtam — collected.

Translation

Going to a water place beyond the village, bathing there, restraining speech, he should purify the food collected, and offer sanctified portions, then he should eat the remnants without leaving any. (13.19)

Commentary:

This means that this ascetic lives alone. This cannot mean that he lives at a temple and has disciples and invites the public to eat sanctified food. This applies to renunciants who have no disciples, hence no need to share food with others.

एकश् चरेन् महीम् एता
निःसङ्गः सयतेन्द्रियः ।
आत्म-क्रीड आत्म-रत
आत्म-वान् सम-दर्शनः ॥ १३.२० ॥

ekaś caren mahīm etāṁ
niḥsaṅgaḥ saṁyatendriyaḥ
ātma-krīḍa ātma-rata
ātma-vān sama-darśanaḥ (13.20)

ekaś = ekaḥ — alone; caren = caret — should come; mahīm — earth; etām — this; niḥsaṅgah — without attachment; saṁyatendriyaḥ = saṁyata – control + indriyaḥ — sensual energy; ātma-krīḍa — being sportive in the spirit; ātma-rata — being delighted in the spirit; ātma-vān — being situated in the spirit; sama-darśanaḥ — seeing the comparative psychological equipments.

Translation

He should roam the earth alone, without attachment and with controlled sensual energy, being sportive in spirit and delighted in it and being spirit-situated and perceiving the comparative similarity of each spirit which is harnessed to a similar set of psychological equipments. (13.20)

Commentary:

At the end of the body, one will be alone, no matter what anyone says. Each religion tries to assure the followers that the Supreme Being will save him or her at the end, but this is mostly a hoax. The Supreme Being if He is not interested in associating with the devotee during the life of the material body, will hardly do so at the body's death. In each body, a living being may throw his faith into a religion which promises salvation, but such a prospect is mostly fallacious. It is an effective ruse because in the new life, we may believe this and in each life, we will not remember the broken promise and will fall for the same farcical belief all over again.

Each person must face the death of his or her body alone. Death is a personal affair, like so many other psychological occurrences. In as much as one feels certain pleasures alone and suffers through certain agonies singularly, one will go through the death experience either consciously, semi-consciously or unconsciously, alone.

Therefore one does himself or herself a great favor by preparing for death, by studying the process of astral projection, by becoming familiar with the dimensions into which one's subtle body usually enters in dreams, by making a log of possible avenues one might take for reentry into this earthly domain and most of all by trying one's best to develop spiritual perception. This should be experienced while using the material body.

For all it may be, in terms of giving one confidence and in terms of causing one to be fearless in the face of death, a religion that cannot cause one to experience the subtle world before that time, and one that cannot allow its God to give the experience of salvation before death, is a questionable religion.

A person should work on inner self control, inner access to subtle and spiritual perception. These must develop within the psyche of the individual while his physical body lives. Then one can be assured of what will happen at the time of death, otherwise it is mostly belief and hope.

विविक्त-क्षेम-शरणो
मद्-भाव-विमलाशयः ।
आत्मानं चिन्तयेद् एकम्
अभेदेन मया मुनिः ॥ १३.२१ ॥

vivikta-kṣema-śaraṇo
mad-bhāva-vimalāśayaḥ
ātmānaṁ cintayed ekam
abhedena mayā muniḥ

vivikta — secluded; kṣema — suitable; śarano = śaranaḥ — taking shelter; mad-bhāva — having one's being invested in Me; vimalāśayaḥ = vimala — purified + āśayah — consciousness; ātmānam — on the spiritual self; cintayed = cintayet — should meditate; ekam — alone; abhedena — not apart; mayā — from me; muniḥ — the ascetic philosopher.

Translation

Taking shelter in a secluded and suitable place, with the consciousness purified by investing his being in Me, the ascetic philosopher should meditate on the spiritual self alone as not being apart from Me. (13.21)

Commentary:

This is the highest meditation practice. It should be done in a secluded place where there is no noise or disturbance. There is no mention here of chanting holy names, because the ascetic philosopher at this stage, will be making contact with *Śrī* Krishna on the spiritual plane. Thus there will be no need for him to chant holy names on the physical level. Because his attentive energies are sufficiently energized and were conveyed away from this world, there would be no question of forming devotional activities on this level.

Everything has its time, place and application. At that stage of the ascetic philosopher's life, his primary concern is to complete his connection with the supernatural and spiritual worlds and the realities which are contained there. He will not be interested in the temples and deity forms.

अन्वीक्षेतात्मनो बन्धं
मोक्षं च ज्ञान-निष्ठया ।
बन्ध इन्द्रिय-विक्षेपो
मोक्ष एषां च संयमः ॥ १३.२२ ॥

anvīkṣetātmano bandhaṁ
mokṣaṁ ca jñāna-niṣṭhayā
bandha indriya-vikṣepo
mokṣa eṣāṁ ca saṁyamaḥ (13.22)

anvīkṣetātmano = anvīkṣeta — should consider + ātmana (ātmanah) — the self; bandham — bondage; mokṣam — liberation; ca — and; jñāna — in analysis; niṣṭhayā — by steadiness; bandha = bandhaḥ — bondage; indriya — senses; vikṣepo = vikṣepaḥ — dispersal; mokṣa — liberation; eṣām — of these; ca — and; saṁyamaḥ — thorough control.

Translation

He should consider bondage and liberation, by steadiness in analysis. Bondage is the dispersal of the senses. Liberation is the thorough control of these. (13.22)

Commentary:

This again is a result of higher yoga practice. The 5th stage of yoga, that of *pratyāhar* sensual energy withdrawal from interest in this world, is the stage described. That 5th stage is never completed until one attains to the last stage, which is the 8th stage of *samādhi*, continuous effortless linkage of the attention to the higher concentration force. *Yogācārya Śrī Patañjali* Muni used the terms *samyama* to describe the final three stages of yoga, namely *dhāraṇā*, *dhyāna* and *samādhi*. If one completes the *pratyāhar* practice, proficiently, one progressed into the final three stages, one after the other in a gradual or rapid sequence.

For each yogi the progression varies but each goes through the stages one by one in sequence just as *Śrī Patañjali* stated. The dispersal of the senses is the actual cause of bondage. The senses do not voluntarily internalize for spiritual purposes except by yoga practice or by involuntary introversion of the subtle body into the causal form at the time of destruction of Lord *Brahmā*'s subtle form.

It is simply a fantasy of devotees if they think that by the external process of devotional services, they will become internalized or that they will be transferred into spiritual vision. It is a nonsensical and completely unscientific idea.

One must stop the dispersal *(vikṣepo)* of the senses from the *buddhi* organ. Hridayānanda dās Gosvami and Gopīparānadhaṇa dās Adhikārī gave the meaning of *vikṣepo* as deviation to sense gratification. But they are mistaken about this. They have not done any higher yoga in their present bodies and they have unnecessarily warped the *Śrīmad Bhāgavatam* verses they translated to make these suit into the profile of the Vaishnava philosophy of our *sampradāya*. Unfortunately they were empowered to do so by our spiritual master, His Divine Grace *Śrīla Bhaktivedānta Swāmī*, who himself was completing the tasks for his predecessors.

Vikṣepo means that the sensual energies are completely retracted into the *buddhi* organ in the subtle body and that means a full retraction from all forms of sensual interpolation in this world. It applies to all the gratifications that we receive from our senses on this plane of existence including all legitimate sensual intakes. All these must be curtailed for the 5th stage of yoga to be complete. All these must be curtailed before the supernatural and spiritual vision can open up.

Liberation is thorough control of these senses and their thorough internalization, so that they are completely shut down, having been retracted into the *buddhi* organ, which then develops the supernatural and spiritual sight. This is what is meant by *samyamah* which is mentioned by *Śrī* Krishna in this verse.

Unfortunately our *sampradāya* dedicated itself to the erasure of yoga practice. Its commentaries are contrary to what Śrī Krishna explained to Uddhava because so much of this concerns higher yoga.

तस्मान् नियम्य षड्-वर्गं
मद्-भावेन चरेन् मुनिः ।
विरक्तः क्षुद्र-कामेभ्यो
लब्ध्वात्मनि सुखं महत् ॥ १३.२३ ॥

tasmān niyamya ṣaḍ-vargaṁ
mad-bhāvena caren muniḥ
viraktaḥ kṣudra-kāmebhyo
labdhvātmani sukhaṁ mahat (13.23)

tasmān = tasmāt — therefore; niyamya — restraining; ṣaḍ-vargam = ṣaṭ-vargam — six passions; mad-bhāvena = mat-bhāvena — by his feelings given over to Me; caren = caret — should roam; muniḥ — ascetic philosopher; viraktaḥ — turned away; kṣudra — petty; kāmebhyo = kāmebhyah — from cravings; labdhvātmani = labdhvā — deserving + ātmani — in the spiritual self; sukham — happiness; mahat — great.

Translation

Therefore, the ascetic sage, while restraining the six senses, should roam with his feelings being given over to Me. Perceiving great happiness in the spiritual self, he should turn away from petty cravings. (13.23)

Commentary:

The entire material world is itself a petty craving for the spiritual self. One sees this only when one has steadied the self by higher yoga practice, otherwise one will keep on roaming around in various births as a devotee or as a non-devotee all depending on favorable or unfavorable acts of providence.

The term *ṣaḍ-vargam* means the six inner foes of a living being. These are; *kāma, krodha, lobha, harsha, mana* and *mada;* or lust, anger, greed, excitement, pride and intoxication. These are also called the *ṣaḍ-vikārah*. These are impurities within the mind. These are curbed by *pratyāhar* practice on the mystic level.

पुर-ग्राम-व्रजान् सार्थान्
भिक्षार्थं प्रविशंश् चरेत् ।
पुण्य-देश-सरिच्-छैल-
वनाश्रम-वतीं महीम् ॥ १३.२४ ॥

pura-grāma-vrajān sārthān
bhikṣārthaṁ praviśaṁś caret
puṇya-deśa-saric-chaila-
vanāśrama-vatīṁ mahīm (13.24)

pura — towns; grāma — villages; vrajān — cowherd settlements; sārthān — with well-to-do travellers; bhikṣārtham = bhikṣā – begging for food + artham — for the purpose; praviśaṁś = praviśan — approaching; caret — should wander; puṇya — holy; deśa — lands; saric = sarit — river; caila = śaila — mountain; vanāśrama – forest hermitage; vatīm — abounded by; mahīm — earth.

Translation

Approaching towns, villages, cowherd settlements, well-to-do travellers for the purpose of begging alms, he should wander over the earth which is abounded by holy lands, rivers, mountains, forests and hermitages. (13.24)

Commentary:

This applied to the condition of the earth before the Industrial Revolution. There are some places which might be called *puṇya*, holy and pure, places like virgin forests, which are untouched by human habitation and exploitation.

वानप्रस्थाश्रम-पदेष्व्
अभीक्ष्णं भैक्ष्यम् आचरेत् ।
संसिध्यत्य् आश्व् असम्मोहः
शुद्ध-सत्त्वः शिलान्धसा ॥ १३.२५ ॥

vānaprasthāśrama-padeṣv
abhīkṣṇaṁ bhaikṣyam ācaret
saṁsidhyaty āśv asammohaḥ
śuddha-sattvaḥ śilāndhasā (13.25)

vānaprasthāśrama = vānaprastha – ascetic forest retirees + āśrama — life style; padeṣv = padeṣu — those the position; abhīkṣṇam — mostly; bhaikṣyam — food obtained by begging; ācaret — he should acquire; saṁsidhyati — he becomes perfected; āśv = āśu — quickly; asammohaḥ — free from delusion; śuddha — pure; sattvah — clarified consciousness; śilāndhasā = śīla — picking up from farmlands + andhasā — by grains.

Translation

He should acquire food mostly from those in the position of being ascetic forest retirees, for by taking their food, which consists of grains picked up from fields, he becomes perfected quickly and is freed from delusion and attains the pure clarified consciousness. (13.25)

Commentary:

Mostly, an ascetic should stay in the forest community with similar yogis who practice to attain spiritual perfection, for if one mixes too much with persons who have the materialistic interest, one might imperil oneself. If one stays in the association of the ascetic devotees who are aspiring in a like manner and who would reinforce one practice, one will advance rapidly.

As soon as one associates with materialistic persons, one's spiritual progress will either slow down or come to a complete halt. In the times of Lord Krishna and before in the Upanishadic period, there were many ascetic communities here and there in the forests of India. That changed considerably. Still, an ascetic has to protect himself from undeserving associations which would cause spiritual progress to enter a reversal.

As we were conditioned before, and as we are striving to reverse that, so we can be conditioned again. We should never forget this. The protection of God is on-going. It is not something new nor something we might only get in this birth. It is always there but our associations either reinforce or neutralize it.

नैतद् वस्तुतया पश्येद्
दृश्यमानं विनश्यति ।
असक्त-चित्तो विरमेद्
इहामुत्र-चिकीर्षितात् ॥ १३.२६ ॥

naitad vastutayā paśyed
dṛśyamānaṁ vinaśyati
asakta-citto viramed
ihāmutra-cikīrṣitāt (13.26)

naitad = na — not + etat — this; vastutayā — as reality; paśyed = paśyet — should perceive; dṛśyamānam — what is perceived in the visible world; vinaśyati — is destroyed; asakta — unattached; citto = cittah — ideation energy in the mind; viramed = viramet — should desist; ihamutra = iha — in this world + amutra — in a future life here; cikīrṣitāt — from activities which yield enjoyments.

Translation

He should not perceive this world as reality, for what is perceived in this world, will be destroyed. With his ideation energy unattached to this world and to a future life here, he should desist from activities which yield enjoyments here. (13.26)

Commentary:

The procedure for causing the ideation energy in the mind, to be detached from this world is the 5th , 6th , 7th , and 8th stages of yoga practice. The 5th stage of *pratyāhar* is the withdrawal of the sensual energy *(indriyah)* and ideation *(citta)* energy from this world. It must also be withdrawn from conceptions about this world, relating to its past, present and future. These conceptions arise in the chitta *(citta)* energy of the mind and emotions. *Śrī Patañjali* in the second *sūtra* stated that yoga means the complete stoppage of the turmoil of the chitta energy. That is yoga indeed.

Activities which yield enjoyment will pan-out in depression, sooner or later, because that is the nature of the energy. It has to subside into nothingness or boredom at some point. In fact, the whole material world comprising of this gross dimension which we perceive and numerous other levels of manifestation, was formed from a quiescent energy. Ultimately all of it has to retrogress into that state, either gradually or suddenly, depending on the laws which govern mundane manifestation.

Therefore it is sensible not to invest our attention in this material manifestation. To say this is easy. To reason it out is also easy. To do so is an entirely different matter. Our ideation energy is itself attached and innately desirous of contemplating the mundane energy in one form or the other, to such a degree that even religious people find ways of legitimizing mundane focus by saying that sanctified or holy objects are transcendental forms. This is so much assurance only.

Actually the sanctified holy objects, have great value for bringing us to the point of desiring to be in the association of the spiritual forms they represent or reflect, still but they are not in fact spiritual forms. If God uses a material form to alert us to His existence on a spiritual plane, then the material form He uses, is still a material form. We still have to take God's advice to meet Him on the spiritual side of life. If we stagnate here and let others convince us that we do not have to develop ourselves spiritually, we will not achieve the aim.

Presently, we are at a great disadvantage, because our psychology is mostly mundane. It is very subtle but it is mundane nevertheless. Hence we must find a way to turn ourselves away from it. And that is the value of higher yoga practice. Anything that yields enjoyment on this side of existence is itself a big problem, because our minds are motivated by such excitation, which keeps us preoccupied with the objects of this world.

यद् एतद् आत्मनि जगन्
मनो-वाक्-प्राण-संहतम् ।
सर्वं मायेति तर्केण
स्व-स्थस् त्यक्त्वा न तत् स्मरेत् ॥ १३.२७॥

yad etad ātmani jagan
mano-vāk-prāṇa-saṁhatam
sarvaṁ māyeti tarkeṇa
sva-sthas tyaktvā na tat smaret (13.27)

yad = yat — which, whatever; etad = etat — this; ātmani — on the spiritual self; jagan = jagat — the world; mano = manaḥ — the mind; vāk — speech; prāṇa — vital energy; saṁhatam — projected; sarvam — all; māyeti = māyā — illusory formation + iti — thus considered; tarkeṇa — by analysis; sva-sthas = sva-sthat — self situated; tyaktvā — giving up; na — not; tat — that, it; smaret — should think.

Translation

Whatever there is, as this world, is an illusory formation, projected by the combination of mind, speech and vital energy on the spiritual self. Considering that by analysis, he should be self-situated, giving up the world and thinking no more of it. (13.27)

Commentary:

This is done by a fourfold method of analysis, an initial attempt to withdraw the mind from the world, actually acting in a way that shows renunciation of the cultural situation and finally by higher yoga, in bringing the mind to think no more of the world. This complete cessation of ideation of this world is hailed as *nirvāṇa* in the *Bhagavad-Gītā*:

eṣā brāhmī sthitiḥ pārtha naināṁ prāpya vimuhyati
sthitvāsyāmantakāle'pi brahmanirvāṇamṛcchati

This divine state is required, O son of Pṛthā. If a man does not have this, he is stupefied. At the time of death, the full stoppage of mundane sensuality and the attainment of divinity is attained by one who is fixed in this divine state. (B.G. 2.72)

The fourfold method of seeing the illusory formation of the world before us, is:

1. One first hears of the temporary nature of the world or one develops by himself an understanding that everything in the material world will be changed into another type of energy sooner or later. As the saying goes, all things must pass away. It is just a matter of time. This is easily analyzed. However such analysis does not stop one from investing in the world. Moreover many who understand this analytically still go on investing their energies, just as if they did not understand the impermanence.

2. If a person accepts that the world is temporary and if that acceptance strikes him deeply, he will, as a reaction, attempt to withdraw from the world. This is done in numerous ways. In all respects, it means that He tries to scale down social participation. However, when doing this, a person finds that he has mandatory desires. "The world might be temporary or it might not be," he thinks, "still I feel compelled to fulfill desires. I feel fulfilled when accomplishing desires. "

Thus the initial attempt to withdraw from the world usually ends there at the attempt. Most people try to withdraw and when they realize that they get fulfillment from desires, they gave up the effort and try to be pragmatic.

3. Some others after making an initial effort to withdraw from the world, and realizing that they must fulfill some desires, effectively restrain themselves in some aspects. These persons renounce some cultural opportunities and take others with full force. Some of these people gain a power over the sense of attachment. They gradually renounce more and more aspects of the cultural situations. If they are successful for the most part, they stumble upon or are shown a method for complete renunciation.

4. When one makes the bid for complete renunciation, he usually wants to get an instant result of total detachment from the world. Thus he might take an extreme measure such as going to an isolated place to live alone or entering a monastery to live a dull life as a religious monk. After trying and trying, he realizes that the effort for full renunciation, if it can be attained at all, will be a prolonged one. It will not be effective overnight.

From within the psyche there are forces which are against renunciation. And from without the psyche there are forces which draw the psyche into the cultural involvement. These are gross and subtle forces. They put up a struggle and refuse to release the individual who wants renunciation.

Seeing this, a person has to consider the matter in a more serious and scientific way, and plot or get help plotting an escape.

The main obstacle is the force within the psyche which is against renunciation. The ascetic has to find a way to evict this energy. If he finds that he cannot get rid of those potencies, then he must find a way to reform them. Or he has to find a way to remove the negative aspects. This is all to be done on the mystic plane. Hence the necessity for higher yoga. None of this can be achieved by wishful thinking nor will God do it for anybody. God advised us, just as He lectured Arjuna and Uddhava. God cannot do it for us because He is not in a position to effect it. We are the ones who are in that key position in the psyche. God will not be able to displace it and do it for us. But he will advise us.

Those devotees who feel that God will do this for them, make a great miscalculation. If God would have done it, He would have a long time ago. He did His part already, by making the method of purification available to us. We are not liberated because we are not taking the right actions to effect it. In that sense, God did His part. It is up to each individual to practice God's advisories.

ज्ञान-निष्ठो विरक्तो वा
मद्-भक्तो वानपेक्षकः ।
स-लिङ्गान् आश्रमांस् त्यक्त्वा
चरेद् अविधि-गोचरः ॥ १३.२८॥

jñāna-niṣṭho virakto vā
mad-bhakto vānapekṣakaḥ
sa-liṅgān āśramāṁs tyaktvā
cared avidhi-gocaraḥ (13.28)

jñāna — knowledge; niṣṭo = niṣṭhaḥ — firmly situated; virakto = viraktah — detached toward from the world; va — or; mad-bhakto = mat-bhaktaḥ — devoted to me; vānapekṣakaḥ = vā — or + anapeksakah — one who is completely indifferent to anything in this world; sa-lingān — with external marks; āśramāms = āśraman — life styles; tyaktvā — giving up; cared = caret — should act; avidhi – beyong traditional rulers + gocaraḥ — formalities.

Translation

He who is firmly situated in this knowledge, who is detached from this existence, who is devoted to me, and who is completely indifferent to anything in this world, should act, giving up the external marks of his life style. He is beyond traditional rules and formalities. (13.28)

Commentary:

In the advanced stages, the forest ascetic should put aside the mark of his lifestyle. This means that if he had formally taken *sannyāsa*, he should no longer use a *sannyāsa*-indicating dhoti. He should no longer carry a staff if that is the general indication of that status. He may also discard his neck beads and sacred thread and any other items like a shaven head and other bodily marks or clothing which indicate to the public that he is a monk or a religious retiree.

This has special importance if he lives among Hindus, since they are superstitious and naturally honor anyone who is dressed in a monk's clothes. There is a technical reason for this. In the most advanced stage, one has to shed connections with people and leave aside their reciprocation which is based on one's religious status. The energy of reciprocation does inhibit advancement.

If indeed one is detached from the world, and if indeed one's ideation energy is no longer focused into the subtle or gross material energy, one will not be able to maintain a status. Persons like *Jaḍa Bharata* found it expedient to discard all indications of their spiritual status, so that they would attain the full spiritual focus to be transferred completely out of the subtle and gross material world.

बुधो बालक-वत् क्रीडेत्
कुशलो जड-वच् चरेत् ।
वदेद् उन्मत्त-वद् विद्वान्
गो-चर्यां नैगमश् चरेत् ॥ १३.२९ ॥

budho bālaka-vat krīḍet
kuśalo jaḍa-vac caret
vaded unmatta-vad vidvān
go-caryāṁ naigamaś caret (13.29)

budho = budhah — enlightened person; bālaka-vat — like a child; krīḍet — he should play; kuśalo = kuśalaḥ — one who is skilled; jaḍa-vac = jaḍa-vat — like a retarded person; caret — should act; vaded = vadet — should speak; unmatta-vad = unmatta-vat — like an idiot; vidvān — one who is educated; go-caryām — one who exhibits a cow's behavior; naigamaś = naigamaḥ — one who is versed in scripture; caret — should behave.

Translation

The enlightened person should play like a child. Though skilled, he should act like a retarded person. Though educated, he should speak like an idiot. Though he is versed in scripture, he should exhibit a cow's behavior. (13.29)

Commentary:

This happens when the ascetic gets the full exemption from *karma* yoga. He cannot do this effectively if he does not get the approval of the Supreme Lord, for stopping all cultural involvement. Arjuna wanted this exemption from cultural acts, but he was not permitted before the battle of *Kurukṣetra*.

Once the exemption is acquired, the ascetic must take steps to ward off the public and to get rid of those disciples who are not advanced enough to become liberated in a short space of time. Here a short space of time, means in this time cycle. There are many persons who come to a spiritual master and who cannot under any circumstance become liberated in this time cycle. Such persons hang around an ascetic to get supernatural or natural favors from him. They divert him and attract his mind to the subtle and gross mundane potencies.

Once the ascetic gets the approval of the Central Figure in the Universal Form, he should dismiss such persons. They can pester other souls who strive for liberation but who have not acquired an exemption from cultural acts.

Thus the advanced ascetic becomes inspired by *Śrī* Krishna, or alternately by Lord Shiva or Lord *Balarāma*, to behave in an insane way. He acts like a simpleton and then certain persons leave his company, thinking that somehow he meditated too much or performed too much austerity or has lost sanity and realism.

Sometimes I talk to the *Mahāsiddha Swāmī Nityānanda*. He was such a person. He used to act in a crazy manner. Sometimes he would pelt visitors with stones. They came to see him to get blessings, but he would hurt them by throwing stones. In that way he was inspired to abandon the role of being a guru. Those who really knew that he was a *mahāsiddha* could not be fooled by his improper behavior but others went away with doubts.

In my own history, I used to have a fine time, when some people thought that I was a woman-hunter. Actually I did some things to justify the reputation but all the same, it served me well to cause some people to avoid me, thus saving me from *time-consuming go-no-where* discussions. Some persons however, managed to see though my disguise and still persisted, accepting me as a person of spiritual worth.

Presently as I write this, I received an exemption from cultural activities from Central Person in the Universal Form, from *Śrī* Krishna Himself. I write this during the month of August of the year 2002. However that exemption was given to me only on the supernatural plane, which means that it will take time to filter into the gross dimension. At present I can see that in the near future some persons will take steps to bar me from becoming fully renounced.

However by the grace of Lord Shiva, I will carefully sidestep them. Right now I act as if I am educated and scripturally conversant but the time may come when I will shut up and begin insulting anyone who comes near me. I will have to do so to complete the course for which I took this body, which is to show the sure way of becoming freed from this material world.

वेद्-वाद्-रतो न स्यान्
न पाषण्डी न हैतुकः ।
शुष्क-वाद्-विवादे न
कञ्चित् पक्षं समाश्रयेत् ॥ १३.३० ॥

veda-vāda-rato na syān
na pāṣaṇḍī na haitukaḥ
śuṣka-vāda-vivāde na
kañcit pakṣaṁ samāśrayet (13.30)

veda-vāda-rato = veda-vāda-rataḥ — one who enjoys expounding the ritualistic portion of the Vedas; na — not; syān = syāt — should be; na — nor; pasandi — heretic; na — nor; haitukaḥ — one who is skeptical; śuṣka – futile; vāda — discussion; vivāde — in argument; na — not; kañcit — any; pakṣam — side; samāśrayet — should support.

Translation

He should not enjoy expounding the ritual portion of the Vedas, nor be a heretic, nor be a skeptic, nor be involved in futile discussions or arguments. He should not support either side. (13.30)

Commentary:

The advanced ascetic should be indifferent to almost anything but that does not mean that he should adopt a skeptical or heretical attitude towards the Vedic scriptures. If he does anything like that he will gain the disapproval of the Universal Form. Subsequently he will be drawn back into the material world to do cultural activities to rectify the damage he did to righteous living or *dharma*. One should be careful not to interfere with *dharma*. A careful study of the *Bhagavad-Gītā* will make this idea become very clear.

If we make extra work for God, then it means that we ourselves will have to take birth to do such work. Thus we should be careful not to interfere with the *dharmic* responsibilities of the Supreme Being. An extreme renunciant has to put himself in a position whereby he does not have to act in a way that is counterproductive to the aims of the Universal Form, which means that even though he has the exemption from *karma* yoga, as it is defined in the *Bhagavad-Gītā*, still he has no right to impede *karma* yoga. His duty is to either facilitate it or stand apart without interference.

नोद्विजेत जनाद् धीरो
जन चोद्वेजयेन् न तु ।
अति-वादास् तितिक्षेत
नावमन्येत कश्चन ।
देहम् उद्दिश्य पशु-वद्
वैर कुर्यान् न केनचित् ॥ १३.३१ ॥

nodvijeta janād dhīro
janaṁ codvejayen na tu
ati-vādāṁs titikṣeta
nāvamanyeta kañcana
deham uddiśya paśu-vad
vairaṁ kuryān na kenacit (13.31)

nodivijeta = na — not + udvijeta — be annoyed; janād = janāt — because of people; dhīro = dhīraḥ — a person of steady intellect; janam — people; codvejayen = ca — and + udvejayet — should intimidate; na — not; tu — but; ativādāms = ati-vādān — abusive language; titikseta — should tolerate; nāvamanyeta = na — never + avamanyeta — should insult; kañcana — anyone; deham — body; uddiśya — for the sake of; paśu-vad = paśu-vat — like an animal; vairam — hostility; kuryān — should create; na — not; kenacit — anyone.

Translation

The person of steady intellect, should not be annoyed by people, nor should he intimidate them. He should tolerate abusive language and should not insult anyone. And just like an animal, he should not for the sake of the body, create hostility with anyone. (13.31)

Commentary:

This was epitomized in the life of *Jaḍa Bharata*. This is told in the fifth part of the *Śrīmad Bhāgavatam*. Material nature has a way about her, and the living entities have a tendency not to want anyone to become liberated. Thus a great soul who is on the verge of being granted full freedom to leave this world, may become an object of abuse. However he does not worry about it. He recognizes material nature's playful attitude towards him. He sees her as the mother on this side of existence. Besides that, there are the living entities in general who do not appreciate liberation. Sensing that a person is about to be liberated, they feel insecure. By instinct, they take steps to draw his attention to cultural activities. If he does not comply with their wishes they are likely to abuse him. The advanced ascetic understands this. He does not retaliate.

Sometimes, other great souls feeling sorry for those who abuse him, take steps to stop them for their own sake. But the advanced ascetic might tell them that it is alright for him to receive negative treatment. This is because he desires to endorse the release of their resentments.

एक एव परो ह्य् आत्मा
भूतेष्व् आत्मन्य् अवस्थितः ।
यथेन्दुर् उद-पात्रेषु
भूतान्य् एकात्मकानि च ॥ १३.३२ ॥

eka eva paro hy ātmā
bhūteṣv ātmany avasthitaḥ
yathendur uda-pātreṣu
bhūtāny ekātmakāni ca (13.32)

eka — one; eva — only; paro = paraḥ — supreme; hy = hi — indeed; ātmā — spiritual self; bhūteṣv = bhūteṣu — in all creature forms; ātmany = ātmani — in the spirit self; avasthitaḥ — situated; yathendur = yathā — just as + induḥ — moon; uda — water; pātreṣu — in reservoirs of water; bhūtāny = bhūtāni — all creatures; ekātmakāni = eka — one + ātmakāni — essential natures; ca — and.

Translation

Only one supreme spiritual self is situated in all creature forms and in the spirit soul as well, just as the moon is reflected in reservoirs of water. And all creatures have the same essential nature. (13.32)

Commentary:

A person who is self realized has to see that the various creatures have a similarity, in the sense that each of the spirits who dominate a particular body, is harnessed to a similar set of psychological equipments. This means that each predominating spirit in each living body, is linked up to a life force, and an intellect. Apart from that, there is a supreme soul *(paro ātma),* whose existence is reflected in each of the creatures as well. That supreme soul is also reflected into the individual spirits. All this must be realized spiritually by direct perception.

The forest ascetic who retired from worldly activities, who is devoted to *Śrī* Krishna and who practiced the yoga austerities as described, will experience this as he advances towards the spiritual plane.

अलब्ध्वा न विषीदेत
काले काले ऽशनं क्वचित् ।
लब्ध्वा न हृष्येद् धृतिमान्
उभयं दैव-तन्त्रितम् ॥ १३.३३ ॥

alabdhvā na viṣīdeta
kāle kāle 'śanaṁ kvacit
labdhvā na hṛṣyed dhṛtimān
ubhayaṁ daiva-tantritam (13.33)

alabdhvā — does not obtain; na — not; visīdeta — should be sorry; kāle kāle — in time, in time; 'śanam = aśanam — food; kvacit — whatever; labdhvā — getting; na — not; hṛṣyed = hṛṣyet — should be happy; dhrtimān — one who is steady in mind; ubhayam — both; daiva — supernatural power; tantritam — controlled by.

Translation

One who is steady in mind, should not be sorry when not obtaining food, nor be happy when getting any. Both circumstances are controlled by supernatural power. (13.33)

Commentary:

Even though *Śrī* Krishna described these facts of spiritual perception, each ascetic should reach a point where he can see this for himself by psychic and spiritual perception. At first one should believe this, then one should analyze to see if it makes sense. But then one still has to strive for spiritual vision to see this on the supernatural plane.

It is not merely a matter of faith in *Śrī* Krishna, because a serious ascetic has to put aside superstition at some stage if he really wants to achieve spiritual life. One begins with faith in *Śrī* Krishna but one must not end there. The ascetic should do whatever is necessary to develop psychic perception. He has to go further to bring on spiritual vision.

If one does not progress in that way one's application of these statements of *Śrī* Krishna will be sporadic based on beliefs, forceful application of adopted attitudes and pressures which force one to demonstrate that one has the realization. For such a person, it will never be a natural or ongoing application based on direct perception.

We have to improve the subtle perception and then open spiritual vision. Arjuna for instance, heard much from *Śrī* Krishna about the glories of the Supreme Being, the glories of *Śrī* Krishna Himself. Then Arjuna could not see what *Śrī* Krishna revealed. Thus he asked for direct perception. Fortunately for him, it was granted. We are not in that position. We have to get the vision by the austerities which would cause our subtle psychology to have the sight to see on the supernatural plane. That level of existence is there. Whatever it comprises is there, but we should get the vision to see what transpires on that level. In Arjuna's case, he lost that vision of the Universal Form which *Śrī* Krishna revealed. He later begged Lord Krishna to show divinity again but *Śrī* Krishna declined to reveal it.

It means therefore that a person has to develop supernatural perception, if he wants to verify this for himself, otherwise it will remain a matter of faith and belief only. The idea that we should have faith now and then later after death, we would see this by the grace of *Śrī* Krishna, after spending our lifetime serving Him and those who advocate Him, is an entirely baseless and unreasonable hoax. It has no value whatsoever. If Krishna is the Supreme Being as claimed, then why should He not allow a devotee the vision now. Further more why should He not allow the devotee the continuous vision forever. Why as in Arjuna's case, there was a loss of vision accompanied with forgetfulness of what was seen.

The reason is this: Until the individual limited being develops his own supernatural vision, no action of God can adjust his mentality on a permanent basis. Even if God acts to cause an energization in the psyche of the limited being, such that the subtle and spiritual perceptions becomes possible, still it will be a temporary revelation only. Hence the necessity for austerities through which we can develop our supernatural and spiritual psyches once and for all. We cannot rely on sporadic assistance from the Supreme Being. We need something permanent.

आहारार्थं समीहेत
युक्त तत्-प्राण-धारणम् ।
तत्त्वं विमृश्यते तेन
तद् विज्ञाय विमुच्यते ॥ १३.३४॥

āhārārthaṁ samīheta
yuktaṁ tat-prāṇa-dhāraṇam
tattvaṁ vimṛśyate tena
tad vijñāya vimucyate (13.34)

āhārātham — procuring food for the purpose; samīheta — one should strive; yuktam — appropiate; tat — that; prāna — vital energy; dhāraṇam — continuity; tattvam — essential truth; vimṛśyate — can reflect; tena — through this; tad = tat — which, that; vijñāya — knowing; vimucyate — is freed.

Translation

He should strive for procuring food, since the continuity of life is appropriate. Through the human body, one can reflect on the essential truth, knowing which one is freed. (13.34)

Commentary:

Even though the ascetic should not be attached to material existence, he still has to assess this situation for what it is and he may attempt to cull some value from it The human body is a special facility for attaining spiritual realization. Therefore once a spirit acquires that body he should use it to the fullest to go as far as he can on the spiritual path.

One should not attempt to kill the body, if it can still used it to advance self-realization. If the body is damaged and cannot be used, or if it is terminally ill, then the ascetic may discard it, otherwise he should use it so long as it is healthy and can be maintained. So long as it can help him to advance further on the spiritual path, he should protect it fittingly but without attachment.

यदृच्छयोपपन्नान्नम्
अद्याच् छ्रेष्ठम् उतापरम् ।
तथा वासस् तथा शय्यां
प्राप्तं प्राप्तं भजेन् मुनिः ॥ १३.३५॥

yadṛcchayopapannānnam
adyāc chreṣṭham utāparam
tathā vāsas tathā śayyāṁ
prāptaṁ prāptaṁ bhajen muniḥ (13.35)

yadṛcchayopapannānnam = yadṛcchayā — by chance + upapanna — comes, appears + annam — food; adyāc = adyāt — should eat; chreṣṭham = śreṣṭham — the very best; utaparam = uta — or + aparam — the worse; tathā — so; vāsas — clothes; tathā — so; śayyām — bedding; prāptam prāptam — what is obtained; bhajen = bhajet — should use; munih — the ascetic philosopher.

Translation

The ascetic philosopher should eat the best or the worse eatable, which come by chance. He should use clothes and bedding or whatever is obtained. (13.35)

Commentary:

Repeatedly, *Śrī* Krishna used the term *munih*, which means a yogi philosopher performing austerities in the time of *Śrī* Krishna. This person has to be a philosopher otherwise he would not be sustained in the austerities. One has to be able to think through this situation along the lines explained by the great sages of the Vedic era. One must be able to follow the reasoning of *Śrī* Krishna and perform austerities which bring on supernatural and spiritual perception, to directly verify and attest to these statements.

The ascetic must heed the stipulations of providence. He may have to accept the very best at times and the worse on other occasions, just as providence suggest to him or circumstantially pressures him.

No matter how great an ascetic is or how thoroughly his austerities are, still as a limited being he is subordinate to providence. He must see this on the supernatural plane. His compliance with the supreme will becomes manifested in various ways.

Even after a spirit is liberated, material nature will still throw reactions at him. This is because he still uses a mundane psyche in part. Whatever energies are due to come to such a psyche, will come to him. However he does not react as if it is his own. He separates himself from the psychological equipments which are the target of material nature's reactionary force.

Material nature will go on acting and reacting, regardless of whether an ascetic becomes liberated or not, regardless of whether his spiritual vision operates or not. The ascetic does not take her maneuvers seriously.

शौचम् आचमन स्नानं
न तु चोदनया चरेत् ।
अन्यांश् च नियमाञ् ज्ञानी
यथाहं लीलयेश्वरः ॥ १३.३६ ॥

śaucam ācamanaṁ snānaṁ
na tu codanayā caret
anyāṁś ca niyamāñ jñānī
yathāhaṁ līlayeśvaraḥ (13.36)

śaucam — bodily cleanliness; ācamanam — ritual cleanliness; snānam — bath; na — not; tu — but; codanayā — because of scriptural injunction; caret — should observe; anyāṁś = anyān — other; ca — and; niyamān — observance; jñānī — a knowledgeable person; yathāham = yathā — but, rather as + aham — I; līlayeśvaraḥ = līlayā — by desire + īśvaraḥ — the supreme Lord.

Translation

The knowledgeable person should observe bodily and ritual cleanliness. He should take bath, and do the other observances, not because of scriptural injunction, but rather as I, the Supreme Lord, act by free desire. (13.36)

Commentary:

At first one endeavors to follow scriptural rules and instructions from a teacher. Then after some practice when one develops insight, there is little need to be instructed. One develops the appropriate intuition. As stated before, an advanced soul develops Krishna's sense of values.

न हि तस्य विकल्पाख्या
या च मद्-वीक्षया हता ।
आ-देहान्तात् क्वचित् ख्यातिस्
ततः सम्पद्यते मया ॥ १३.३७ ॥

na hi tasya vikalpākhyā
yā ca mad-vīkṣayā hatā
ā-dehāntāt kvacit khyātis
tataḥ sampadyate mayā (13.37)

na — not; hi — surely; tasya — of him; vikalpākhyā = vikalpa — difference + ākhyā — perception; yā — which; ca — and; mad-vīkṣayā = mat-vīkṣayā — by direct perception of Me; hatā — are removed; ā — until; dehāntāt = deha — body + antāt — until death; kvacit — occasionally; khyātis = khyātiḥ — perception; tataḥ — then; sampadyate — becomes similar; mayā — with Me.

Translation

Surely for him, there is no difference of perception in reference to Me, and any such disparities are removed by direct perception of Me. Until the death of the body, he occasionally has that contrary perception, and then he becomes similar to Me. (13.37)

Commentary:

This is the status of a yogi devotee of *Śrī* Krishna. This yogi devotee must mastered the higher yoga practices of *pratyāhar* sense withdrawal, *dhāraṇā* linkage of his attention with higher concentration forces, which occur in his *prāṇa*-surcharged psyche, *dhyāna* effortless linkage of those concentration energies and *samādhi* absorption with the same. By this the devotee gets to sees into the sky of consciousness, the chit *ākāśa*. He therefore sees the supernatural and divine forms directly.

Unfortunately for humanity, many non-yogi preachers mislead audiences by assuring them that at the time of death, they will see the Supreme Lord or that He will grant them salvation, on the basis of their adherence to a particular faith. Nothing can be further from the truth.

Even for a yogi, who experienced the supernatural and spiritual visions, while using a material body and who experienced it frequently, there is no definite salvation for him unless he completely dissolves the subtle body before the time of death. And he must also relinquish his causal form, which is a super-subtle chamber. Therefore it is not possible for other limited beings, to suddenly assume a spiritual body at the time of death merely on the basis of faith in *Śrī* Krishna or any other divine personality.

The word *vīkṣayā* does not mean a realization in the mind nor hearing of such forms from teachers. It means direct perception of such forms. *Vīkṣam* means a visible object not a mental realization or a concept. *Vīkṣayā* means to look at, visibly or perceptibly. This is direct perception. This is gained by the higher yoga practice.

Because the ascetic still has a material body, and a set of psychological equipments which do revert back to mundane vision, he is prone to swaying back and forth between normal human vision and supernatural insight.

Subsequently whenever his vision changes back to the normal material perception, he has to remove that by again practicing higher yoga and by relying on the integration acquired by previous practice. But after giving up the material body, if he practiced sufficiently, he switches over to his supernatural or spiritual body and completely loses the normal mundane perception, due to having abandoned or dissolved the subtle form.

दुःखोदर्केषु कामेषु
जात-निर्वेद आत्मवान् ।
अज्ज्ञासित-मद्-धर्मो
मुनिं गुरुम् उपव्रजेत् ॥ १३.३८ ॥

duḥkhodarkeṣu kāmeṣu
jāta-nirveda ātmavān
ajjñāsita-mad-dharmo
munim̐ gurum upavrajet (13.38)

duḥkhodarkeṣu = duhkha — misery + udarkeṣu — in that which results in; kāmeṣu — in the fulfillments; jāta — produced; nirveda — disgusted; ātmavān — one who is self-directive; ajijñāsita — one who has not researched thoroughly; mad = mat — to me; dharmo = dharmah — righteous life; munim — ascetic philosopher; gurum — spiritual master; upavrajet — should approach.

Translation

A person who is disgusted with the fulfillment which results in misery, and who is self directive, but who researched thoroughly the method of righteous life style which leads to Me, should approach an ascetic philosopher as the spiritual master. (13.38)

Commentary:

This spiritual teacher must be a yogi devotee of *Śrī* Krishna. He must have a philosophical understanding of what *Śrī* Krishna explained so far. Some persons who have a self-directive nature, are unable to free themselves from implicating actions even though they repeatedly become disgusted with the intricacies of actions in the material world. It means then, that merely by becoming disgusted and merely by realizing that something is amiss in this world, a man may not be freed.

A self-directive person *(ātmavān)*, will more than likely avoid a spiritual master, but it becomes necessary to accept one if he cannot discover the righteous life style. In the *Bhagavad-Gītā* this righteous life was described to Arjuna. In a gist it is doing whatever is necessary to gain the approval of the Central Figure in the Universal Form. Therefore one should find a person who understands this and learn from him how to satisfy that Lord by completing the assignments given by Him.

One can do whatever he likes and whatever seems to him to be correct and appropriate, but if such preferences do not correspond with the ideas of the Universal Form, one will be frustrated. It is not just a matter of doing what one desires or what one prefers. And it is not a free-for-all, whereby anybody can do anything and get away with it. It is more a factor of recognizing superior authority. Ultimately it is the Supreme Being whom we must come to terms with.

It is really irrelevant if a person seeking liberation has a theistic bent of mind or not. What is important is his determination to do whatever is necessary to gain the spiritual freedom. If he has to get the approval of somebody, then he should be sensible enough and desperate enough to acquire it, otherwise liberation will elude him.

Śrī Krishna in a very open discussion with Uddhava, flatly indicated the reason why some who are disgusted, do not become liberated. They do not realize that there is a Supreme Being whose will has to be complied with. Thus we see that there are many ascetics who make the endeavor, and who realized that the material world is simply a waste of their valuable existence, and still they do not stumble upon or become inspired with the method for liberation.

तावत् परिचरेद् भक्तः
श्रद्धावान् अनसूयकः ।
यावद् ब्रह्म विजानीयान्
माम् एव गुरुम् आदृतः ॥१३.३९॥

tāvat paricared bhaktaḥ
śraddhāvān anasūyakaḥ
yāvad brahma vijānīyān
mām eva gurum ādṛtaḥ (13.39)

tāvat — until; paricared = paricaret — should save; bhaktaḥ — being devotee; śraddhāvān — having faith; anasūyakaḥ — being non-critical; yāvad = yāvat — until; brahma spiritual existence; vijānīyān — he realizes; mām — me; eva — indeed; gurum — the spiritual master; ādrtah — with respect.

Translation

Until he realized the spiritual existence, he should serve the teacher as he would serve Me, with respect, devotion, faith and a non-critical attitude. (13.39)

Commentary:

There are many people who pass for spiritual masters who are not qualified for the position. Some of these people are sincere but they have no spiritual vision whatsoever. Some became popular because human beings are all too eager to post a person as a spiritual teacher, to worship him, glorify him and assure others that he is this or that. Subsequently many who are self-directive stay away from such spiritual masters. They do not want to be place in a position to serve unworthy religious leaders.

However, without accepting a spiritual master one will not progress unless one has the intuition to decipher the supreme will. Of course if one surrenders to a fake guru, one will only make progress in terms of realizing the tricks of a false teacher. This will help in selecting someone better in the future. Generally human beings learn by the mistakes.

Some people feel that the whole occurrence of having to accept a false guru is itself evidence of God's failure to provide proper guidance to the human beings. But this is merely a reactive thought. The fact is that even if we were presented initially with a valid guru, still we would not accept him because of an impure psychology. A living being has within him his own learning mechanism. He has to follow his intuition and preferences. In addition one has to play along with providence. Thus to be reasonable, and to be realistic, a disciple might have to progress through one or more false gurus before finding a genuine one.

If a person has a self-directive nature and still cannot figure out the path of righteous living, he has no alternative but to find someone who understands the intricacies of action as they were explained to Arjuna in the *Bhagavad-Gītā*. Arjuna is an example of a person who did not know what to do. Fortunately for him, he had the perfect guru. We are not in that position. Still, if we endeavor and are willing to learn as we progress, we will eventually come in contact with a perfect teacher.

Such a person would invoke our respect, devotion, faith and a non-critical attitude. One's reliance on a guru, even a perfect teacher, is eased as soon as one can directly perceive the sky of consciousness, the supernatural and spiritual existences.

यस् त्व् असंयत-षड्-वर्गः
प्रचण्डेन्द्रिय-सारथिः ।
ज्ञान-वैराग्य-रहितस्
त्रि-दण्डम् उपजीवति ॥१३.४०॥

yas tv asaṁyata-ṣaḍ-vargaḥ
pracaṇḍendriya-sārathiḥ
jñāna-vairāgya-rahitas
tri-daṇḍam upajīvati (13.40)

yas = yah — who; tv = tu — but; asaṁyata — one who has not curbed; ṣaḍ = ṣaṭ — six; vargaḥ — passions; pracaṇḍendriya = pracaṇḍa — impulsive + indriya — of the senses; sārathiḥ — the monitor; jñāna — knowledge; vairāgya — detachment; rahitas — devoid; tri-daṇḍam — triple staff; upajīvati — for a livelihood.

Translation

But one who has not curbed the six passions, whose monitor of the senses is impulsive, who is devoid of knowledge and detachment, and who assumes the triple staff for a livelihood, (13.40)

Commentary:

This is a criticism of those who take to monk status for the privilege of it. The six passions are lust, anger, greed, excitement, pride and intoxication *(kāma, krodha, lobha, harṣa, mana and mada)*. One cannot curb these merely by following moral principles. This is why yoga practice regards the moral restraints and behavioral observances as the two preliminary stages. Beyond these, there are six stages which allows one to get to the subtle aspects of curbing passion.

The monitor of the senses is the intellect. This instrument in the subtle body can be restrained by *pratyāhar* practice which is the 5th step of yoga. By the mastery of pratyāhar, the sensual energies are contained and made to be introverted.

The triple staff is offered as an insignia by someone who formally adopts the sannyāsa or monk status. Many take it because they are attracted to the honor the sannyāsi receives. This is a mistake. Unfortunately, nowadays there are many religious leaders who took the monk status for that very purpose. They attract similar persons as disciples.

सुरान् आत्मानम् आत्म-स्थं
निह्नुते मां च धर्म-हा ।
अविपक्व-कषायो ऽस्माद्
अमुष्माच् च विहीयते ॥ १३.४१ ॥

surān ātmānam ātma-sthaṁ
nihnute māṁ ca dharma-hā
avipakva-kaṣāyo 'smād
amuṣmāc ca vihīyate (13.41)

surān — supernatural rulers; ātmānam — the self; ātma-stham — situated in the self; nihnute — cheats; mām — me; ca — and; dharma-hā — destroyer of righteous duty; avipakva — not removed; kaṣāyo = kaṣāyaḥ — character faults; 'smād = asmāt — from this world; amuṣmāc = amuṣmāt — from the next life; ca — and; vihīyate — is deprived.

Translation

...is a destroyer of righteous duty and cheats the supernatural rulers, himself and Me, who is situated in the self. Since his character faults are not removed, he is deprived of this world and the next. (13.41)

Commentary:

A person should not use the renounced order of life, or any sort of religious or ascetic status, as a means to acquire honor. He should not use it as a way of avoiding moral principles or to justify violations of the same, otherwise he will face certain ruination, either here in this world or in the hereafter or in both situations.

When a renunciant acts in a deviant way, he causes common people to distrust religion. Therefore a false *sannyāsi* is cited as being offensive to the supernatural rulers and to Krishna. This is because people form criticisms about righteous living as soon as they find a deviant religious man. One has to work internally to remove character faults, for only by their removal, can one truly represent God.

भिक्षोर् धर्मः शमो ऽहिंसा
तप ईक्षा वनौकसः ।
गृहिणो भूत-रक्षेज्या
द्विजस्याचार्य-सेवनम् ॥ १३.४२ ॥

bhikṣor dharmaḥ śamo 'hiṁsā
tapa īkṣā vanaukasaḥ
gṛhiṇo bhūta-rakṣejyā
dvijasyācārya-sevanam (13.42)

bhikṣor = bhikṣoḥ — of a full renunciant; dharmaḥ — righteous duty; śamo = śamaḥ — tranquility; 'hiṁsā = ahiṁsā — non-injury; tapa = tapaḥ — austerity; īksā — subtle perception; vanaukasaḥ — of the forest dweller; gṛhiṇo = gṛhiṇah — of a householder; bhūta – creature; rakṣejyā = rakṣā — protection + ijyā — performance of sacrifice; dvijasyācārya = dvijasya — of a celibate student + ācārya — teacher; sevanam — service.

Translation

The righteous duty of a full renunciant is the cultivation of tranquility and non-injury; that of a forest dwelling retiree is austerity and subtle perception; that of the householder is the protection of creatures and performance of sacrifice, that of a celibate student is service to the teacher. (13.42)

Commentary:

The basic objective and duties of a yogi in various states of life are explained in this verse. The full renunciant or *sannyāsi*, the person who is done with cultural opportunity should cultivate tranquility, and develop the sense of non-injury to all creatures. These are more than social objectives. Śamah or tranquility is the type which is achieved in *samādhi* practice. It is not the ordinary peace of mind attained by casual meditations. Non-injury applies to spiritual, emotional and physical interactions. It includes physical detachment from others or keeping a safe distance from such social involvements which would require an ascetic to discipline others.

Since he has an exemption from *karma* yoga, the advanced yogi does not have to be involved in the violent disciplinary activities, conducted under the supervision of the Universal

Form. Arjuna for instance, was pressured by *Śrī* Krishna to do battlefield work for the chastisement of the corrupt Kurus, but an ascetic who has an exemption, is not required to engage in such activity.

Undoubtedly there are people who feel that all sorts of violence is inappropriate but we have to listen to *Śrī* Krishna, to the Supreme Being, to understand His definition of this. When a yogi has the exemption from cultural acts, and when he is circumstantially out of touch with the cultural world of human beings, he can afford to honor nonviolence in the full sense.

A forest-dwelling retiree is supposed to cultivate the yoga austerities and the resulting subtle perception which is derived from that. That is his total duty. Thus he should make whatever adjustment and do whatever is necessary to facilitate yoga practice. He is in a crucial stage of his life, because soon, his body will pass away. He knows that whatever he attains in yoga practice will stay with him when he passes from the body. Thus if he progresses at a snail's pace, he would be doing himself an injustice. The big objective is to master *samādhi* practice and to become steady in it before the body passes away.

One who does not attain *samādhi* will more than likely have to take an haphazard rebirth. Some might go to a place in the astral world, where other yogis aspire to complete the austerities but usually the subtle body maintains a resistance to yoga practice in the subtle world and it is attracted to life in the angelic kingdoms, which are pleasure-yielding worlds. A yogi should make sure that he attains the *samādhis* before he leaves the body. That will guarantee that his subtle body will not shift to the angelic pleasure world after the gross form dies, nor will it automatically re-enter the form of a human parent for rebirth.

A householder yogi should protect the family and the domestic animals and do whatever he is required to do as social services in society. That is his *karma* yoga practice. However to do this as *karma* yoga and not just as *karma*, he must also practice yoga side by side. This practice of yoga, though part-time will give him the power to become a forest retiree when his children become adults.

The celibate student should serve the teacher. In doing so he gets training in yoga, scriptural readings and religious ceremony. The teacher also monitors his behavior so that he may master the first two steps of yoga at least. Those celibate students who have the capacity may develop the samādhi practice, even before they graduate from the student years.

ब्रह्मचर्यं तपः शौचं
सन्तोषो भूत-सौहृदम् ।
गृहस्थस्याप्य् ऋतौ गन्तुः
सर्वेषां मद्-उपासनम् ॥ १३.४३ ॥

brahmacaryaṁ tapaḥ śaucaṁ
santoṣo bhūta-sauhṛdam
gṛhasthasyāpy ṛtau gantuḥ
sarveṣāṁ mad-upāsanam (13.43)

brahmacaryam — celibacy with the pursuit of spiritual experiences; tapaḥ — austerity; śaucam — purity; santoṣo = santoṣaḥ — contentment; bhūta-sauhṛdam — kindness to creatures; gṛhasthasyāpy = grhasthasya — of the householder; api — even; ṛtau — at the appropriate time; gantuḥ — consorting with a wife; sarvesām — of all; mat-upasanam — worship of me.

Translation

Celibacy with the pursuit of spiritual experience, austerity, purity, contentment and being kind to creatures, are the duties of a householder, as well as consorting with his wife at the appropriate times. Worship of me is the duty of all human beings. (13.43)

Commentary:

A householder's big accomplishment is celibacy and responsible sexual engagement with the spouse. Celibacy and sexual indulgence are opposite features. Therefore the householder has to restrict the sexual contacts. His main objective for sexual intercourse should be to beget children to take care of his ancestral obligations. Once he concludes that, he should stop the sexual indulgence altogether. If one achieves this by yoga practice, one will seal off the sexual expressions of the kundalini force, and the *suśumnā* passage will open so that the vital energy will come into the brain. This is the actual meaning of *brahmacarya*.

Śrī Krishna gave worship of Himself *(mad-upāsanam),* as the righteous duty (*dharma*, verse 42) of all human beings. That is the common religion of the devotional ascetics at all stages of practice.

इति मा यः स्व-धर्मेण
भजेन् नित्यम् अनन्य-भाक् ।
सर्व-भूतेषु मद्-भावो
मद्-भक्ति विन्दते दृढाम् ॥ १३.४४ ॥

iti māṁ yaḥ sva-dharmeṇa
bhajen nityam ananya-bhāk
sarva-bhūteṣu mad-bhāvo
mad-bhaktiṁ vindate dṛḍhām (13.44)

iti — thus; mām — me; yaḥ — who; sva-dharmeṇa — by his righteous duty; bhajen = bhajet — worship; nityam — constantly; ananya-bhāk — no other object of worship; sarva-bhūteṣu — in all creatures; mad-bhāvo = mat-bhāvah — being conscious of me; mad-bhaktim = mat-bhaktim — being devoted to me; vindate — attains; dṛḍhām — steadfast.

Translation

He who thus worships Me constantly by performance of righteous duty, and having no other object of worship, being conscious of me as situated in all beings, attains a steadfast devotion to Me. (13.44)

Commentary:

This worship of *Śrī* Krishna is the worship of honoring His instruction for the performance of righteous duty. This means taking up the *karma* yoga duties which are assigned by the Universal Form. If this is done while having no other object of worship but *Śrī* Krishna and being conscious of Him as situated in all beings, one will in time attain a steadfast devotion to Him. The key factors are to perform righteous duty as prescribed by *Śrī* Krishna and to adhere to *Śrī* Krishna's sense of values.

Having no other object of worship means that the devotee executes *Śrī* Krishna's instructions. This could also mean that one performs worship of others, but only as directed by *Śrī* Krishna. One has to follow *Śrī* Krishna's instruction. That is the gist of it. One must not be misled by anyone, even by a spiritual master. The disciple must be free to open himself to *Śrī* Krishna. The spiritual master should not present himself as the only access to *Śrī* Krishna.

भक्त्योद्धवानपायिन्या
सर्व-लोक-महेश्वरम् ।
सर्वोत्पत्त्य्-अप्ययं ब्रह्म
कारणं मोपयाति सः ॥ १३.४५ ॥

bhaktyoddhavānapāyinyā
sarva-loka-maheśvaram
sarvotpatty-apyayaṁ brahma
kāraṇaṁ mopayāti saḥ (13.45)

bhaktyoddhavānapāyinyā = bhaktyā — through devotion + uddhava — Uddhava + anapāyinyā — non stopping, perpetual; sarva — all; loka — world; maheśvaram — great lord; sarvotpatty = sarva — all + utpatti — originator; apyayam — destroyer; brahma — spiritual existence; kāranam — cause; mopayāti = mā — to me + upayāti — comes; saḥ — he.

Translation

O Uddhava, through devotion, he comes to Me, the great Lord of all the world, the originator and destroyer of all, the cause and the spiritual existence. (13.45)

Commentary:

Devotion is undoubtedly the big pulling force which causes a limited being to make sacrifices and to take up austerities to reach the Supreme Personality. Devotion is operative in the life of all ascetics, but it is not always plainly revealed. Sometimes an ascetic cannot understand how he is motivated to practice but we can safely guess that it is devotion, which underlines his sincere endeavors.

इति स्व-धर्म-निर्णिक्त-
सत्त्वो निर्ज्ञात-मद्-गतिः ।
ज्ञान-विज्ञान-सम्पन्नो
न चिरात् समुपैति माम् ॥ १३.४६ ॥

iti sva-dharma-nirṇikta-
sattvo nirjñāta-mad-gatiḥ
jñāna-vijñāna-sampanno
na cirāt samupaiti mām (13.46)

iti — thus; sva – own; dharma — righteous duty; nirṇikta — having purified; sattvo = sattvah — existence; nirjñāta — knowing; mad-gatiḥ — my situation; jñāna — knowledge; vijñāna — realization; sampanno = sampannah — endowed with; na cirāt — soon; samupaiti — attains; mām — me.

Translation

Having his existence purified by performance of righteous duty and knowing My situation, being endowed with knowledge and realization, he soon attains Me. (13.46)

Commentary:

This makes clear the point that if one performs righteous duty, one will not be liberated by it. Such a person will soon attain Krishna. The purification of his existence by the performance of righteous duty has to do with solving out cultural equations. It is a purification in that sense only. For psychological purification, yoga practice has to be perfected. *Karma* yoga does not effect full internal purification of the psyche, even though it simplifies cultural complexities which keep us hog-tied to the material world. The solution of these complexities causes us to be free to pursue yoga and to gain an exemption for its full practice, so that we can make it a full time engagement.

Śrī Krishna's situation is that he is in this material world and He is outside of it simultaneously. His being in this world, has to do with *dharma* or righteous duties, to enforce these upon the limited beings who do not know their self-interest. However, once we clear the hurdle of cultural duties, we begin to understand that Krishna's primary existence is outside of this world. Understanding this, and having developed a likeness for Krishna, the person inquires further about transference into *Śrī* Krishna's spiritual domains. For being transferred, he has to effect in himself internal purification by yoga austerities.

Devotion is the highlight because if the person does not have or does not develop true devotion for *Śrī* Krishna, that person will be unwilling to do the austerities. Instead he will think that it is not worth the efforts or he will be indulged by others who advocate an easy but very impossible method for salvation, something that will get him nowhere.

वर्णाश्रमवतां धर्म
एष आचार-लक्षणः ।
स एव मद्-भक्ति-युतो
निःश्रेयस-करः परः ॥ १३.४७ ॥

varṇāśramavatāṁ dharma
eṣa ācāra-lakṣaṇaḥ
sa eva mad-bhakti-yuto
niḥśreyasa-karaḥ paraḥ (13.47)

varnāśramavatam = varna – work category + aśrama – life style + vatām — of those who adhere; dharma = dharmah — righteous duty; eṣa = eṣaḥ — this; ācāra — rites and conduct; lakṣanaḥ — specific; sa = sah — this; eva — indeed; mad-bhakti-yuto = mat-bhakti-yutaḥ — conducted with devotion to me; niḥśreyasa — conducive to liberation; karaḥ — is functional; paraḥ — supreme.

Translation

This performance of righteous duty, which is characterized by specific rites and conducts, of those who adhere to work category and pertinent life style, when conducted with devotion to Me, is functional for liberation and is supreme. (13.47)

Commentary:

To understand this one needs to carefully go over the details of the contract for *karma* yoga, which was given to Arjuna in the *Bhagavad-Gītā* discourse. One has to start by performing *karma* yoga, and gradually cease that as one is relieved of those cultural duties. All the while, one has to practice yoga austerity and religious life in one's spare time. After a time, the yogi will be given an exemption from all cultural duties, and he will be able to take up yoga for spiritual perfection on a full time basis.

The main aspect is to keep in touch with *Śrī* Krishna or with Him as the central figure in the Universal Form. He will instruct one in what to do for approvals in cultural responsibilities. Even though the issue of *karma* yoga concerns cultural duties, still one has to keep an eye on the Universal Form, otherwise one will perform the duties and become attached to one's dependents and to other recipients of the services. That is not the right way to do *karma* yoga. Even though in *karma* yoga, we have to tend to worldly concerns, still we should do so only in so far as *Śrī* Krishna approves, not otherwise.

एतत् ते ऽभिहितं साधो
भवान् पृच्छति यच् च माम् ।
यथा स्व-धर्म-संयुक्तो
भक्तो मां समियात् परम् ॥ १३.४८ ॥

etat te 'bhihitaṁ sādho
bhavān pṛcchati yac ca mām
yathā sva-dharma-saṁyukto
bhakto māṁ samiyāt param (13.48)

etat — this; te — to you; 'bhihitam = abhihitam — explained; sadho = sadhah — saintly man; bhavān — you; pṛcchati — inquired; yac = yat — which; ca — and; mām — from me; yathā — according to the method; sva-dharma — one's own righteous duty; saṁyukto = saṁyuktaḥ — attentive to; bhakto = bhaktaḥ — devotee; mām — to me; samiyāt — one attains; param — supreme being.

Translation

I explained this O saint, as you inquired from Me about the method of how being attentive to righteous duty, one becomes a devotee and attains to Me, the Supreme Being. (13.48)

Commentary:

Actually a person cannot get out of material existence, merely by adopting a religious lifestyle. If he does so it will not work. He will again be brought back to cultural activities. This is because any unfinished tasks which were assigned by the Universal Form will not be waived merely because a person has seen flaws in social interaction, nor because his spiritual master feels that missionary activities are more important than social obligations.

The example is Arjuna. He saw flaws in the social interactions. He was discouraged to participate in the dutiful way required of him by the Universal Form. The flaws in social interactions does not permit anyone to avoid the social scene and step over it to become liberated. One will not be able to do so, if one does not first fulfill the assignment given by the Universal Form.

All the same, it does not mean that by fulfilling those cultural duties, one will become liberated. It is a great miscalculation when devotees think that by doing this their spiritual life is sealed or if they imagine that Arjuna became liberated merely because he agreed to serve the Universal Form. One should read the *Mahābhārata* to find out what the Pandavas had to do in the end to release themselves from the material existence.

Compliance with the *karma* yoga requirements set up by the Universal Form will only give one an exemption from cultural activities, so that one can increase the yoga practice, through which one would attain perfection.

CHAPTER 14*

The Chief Cause of Devotion**

Terri Stokes-Pineda Art

bhakti-yogaḥ puraivoktaḥ prīyamāṇāya te 'nagha
punaś ca kathayiṣyāmi mad-bhakteḥ kāraṇaṁ paraṁ

O sinless one, previously I explained to you, who has affection, the technique of using yoga disciplines in applying devotion. And I will again relate the chief cause of devotion to Me. (Uddhava Gītā 14.19)

* Śrīmad Bhāgavatam Canto 11, Chapter 19

** Translator's selected chapter title.

श्री-भगवान् उवाच
यो विद्या-श्रुत-सम्पन्नः
आत्मवान् नानुमानिकः ।
मया-मात्रम् इदं ज्ञात्वा
ज्ञानं च मयि सन्न्यसेत् ॥ १४.१ ॥

śrī-bhagavān uvāca
yo vidyā-śruta-sampannaḥ
ātmavān nānumānikaḥ
mayā-mātram idaṁ jñātvā
jñānaṁ ca mayi sannyaset (14.1)

śrī-bhagavān – the blessed lord; uvāca — said; yo = yaḥ — who; vidyā — practical technique; śruta — scriptural knowledge; sampannaḥ — endowed; ātmavān — self-composed; nānumānikaḥ = na — not + ānumānikaḥ — analytical conclusions; māyā — illusion; mātram — merely; idam — this; jñātvā — knowing; jñānam — knowledge; ca — and; mayi — to me; sannyaset — should relinquish.

Translation

One who is endowed with scriptural knowledge and practical technique, who is self-composed, who is not reliant on mere analytical conclusion, should relinquish knowledge to Me, knowing that this world is merely an illusion. (14.1)

Commentary:

As a person transmigrates, he picks up various types of knowledge which are converted into cultural skills. These abilities are hindrances to spiritual perfection. However they are useful in the material world. In the performance of *karma* yoga, one is requested to use some of this knowledge in *Śrī* Krishna's service for bringing *dharma* or righteous life style into this world. Arjuna for instance was a skilled warrior. Thus he was requested to use his expertise in the service of the Universal Form.

Ultimately however, one has to give up such knowledge, becoming totally detached from it. When this act of detachment is matured, one's cultural body which is the subtle body, falls away. Then one can become liberated. *Śrī* Krishna instructed that we relinquish such knowledge to Him so that we may become free from the course of material existence, including its righteous capacity. This world is merely an illusion, as He said, so even though we may work for Him here, ultimately it is still an illusory formation.

The illusion is imposed by none other, than the Supreme Being. Therefore to get rid of it, one has to take help from Him.

ज्ञानिनस् त्व् अहम् एवेष्टः
स्वार्थो हेतुश् च सम्मतः ।
स्वर्गश् चैवापवर्गश् च
नान्यो ऽर्थो मद्-ऋते प्रियः ॥ १४.२ ॥

jñāninas tv aham eveṣṭaḥ
svārtho hetuś ca sammataḥ
svargaś caivāpavargaś ca
nānyo 'rtho mad-ṛte priyaḥ (14.2)

jñāninas = jñāninah — of the ascetic philosophers; tv = tu — but; aham — I; eveṣṭaḥ = eva — alone + iṣṭaḥ — desired goal; svārtho = svārthaḥ — his own objective; hetuś = hetuḥ — means; ca — and; sammataḥ — subject of consideration; svargaś = svargaḥ — paradise hereafter; caivāpavargaś = ca — and + eva — indeed + apavargaḥ — final objective; ca — and; nanyo = nanyaḥ = na — not + anyaḥ — other; 'rtho = arthaḥ — value; mad-ṛte = mat-ṛte — besides me; priyaḥ — dear.

Translation

I alone am the desired goal of the ascetic philosopher. I am his objective, his means of attainment. I am the subject of consideration. I am the paradise hereafter. Indeed, I am his final objective. There is no other aspect of value, which is dear to him besides Me. (14.2)

Commentary:

This means that ultimately, a limited being will have to give himself over to the Supreme Person. It is as simply as that. One may not realize this until one becomes very advanced.

It is based on a personality circuit which originates in the Supreme Being. Just as planets revolved around a sun, and just as that system moves in a galaxy which moves in a larger cosmos, so the limited beings are moving according to the shifts of the Supreme Being.

ज्ञान-विज्ञान-ससिद्धाः
पद् श्रेष्ठं विदुर् मम ।
ज्ञानी प्रियतमो ऽतो मे
ज्ञानेनासौ बिभर्ति माम् ॥ १४.३ ॥

jñāna-vijñāna-saṁsiddhāḥ
padaṁ śreṣṭhaṁ vidur mama
jñānī priyatamo 'to me
jñānenāsau bibharti mām (14.3)

jñāna — knowledge; vijñāna — mystic experiences; saṁsiddhāḥ — those who are perfected; padam — status; śreṣṭham — supreme; vidur = viduh — they know; mama — my; jñānī — yogi philosopher; priyatamo = priyatamaḥ — most dear; 'to = atah — thus; me — to me; jñānenāsau = jñānena — by virtue of factual knowledge + asau — that person; bibharti — cherishes; mām — me.

Translation

Those who are perfect in knowledge and mystic experience, know My supreme status. Thus the yogi philosopher is most dear to me. That person cherishes Me by factual knowledge. (14.3)

Commentary:

Lord Krishna told Arjuna something similar:

teṣāṁ jñānī nityayukta ekabhaktirviśiṣyate
priyo hi jñānino'tyartham ahaṁ sa ca mama priyaḥ
udārāḥ sarva evaite jñānī tvātmaiva me matam
āsthitaḥ sa hi yuktātmā māmevānuttamāṁ gatim

Of these, the informed man who is constantly disciplined in yoga, being singularly devoted, is distinguished indeed. I am fond of this person and he is fond of Me.

All these are exalted people. But the informed one is considered to be my personal representative. Indeed, he who is disciplined in yoga practice, is situated with Me as the Supreme Objective. (B.G. 7.17-18)

तपस् तीर्थं जपो दान
पवित्राणीतराणि च ।
नालं कुर्वन्ति तां सिद्धिं
या ज्ञान-कलया कृता ॥ १४.४ ॥

tapas tīrthaṁ japo dānaṁ
pavitrāṇītarāṇi ca
nālaṁ kurvanti tāṁ siddhiṁ
yā jñāna-kalayā kṛtā (14.4)

tapas = tapaḥ — austerity; tīrtham — making pilgrimage; japo = japaḥ — chanting holy names of God; dānam — offering charity; pavitrāṇītarāṇi = pavitrāṇi — purificatory activities; itarāṇi — other; ca — and; nālam = na — not + alām — sufficient, adequate, matching; kurvanti — they make; tām — this; siddhim — perfection; yā — which; jñāna — factual knowledge; kalayā — by a fraction; kṛtā — is yielded.

Translation

Austerity, making pilgrimage, chanting holy names of God, offering charity and other purificatory activities, do not make a match to the perfection which is yielded by a fraction of factual knowledge. (14.4)

Commentary:

There is a similar statement made to Arjuna in the *Bhagavad-Gītā*:

na hi jñānena sadṛśaṁ pavitramiha vidyate
tatsvayaṁ yogasaṁsiddhaḥ kālenātmani vindati

Nothing, indeed, can be compared with direct experience. No other purifier is as relevant in this world. That man who himself is perfected in yoga practice, will in time, locate the realization in himself. (4.38)

External religious activities and disciplines which cause the mind to be focused externally into the material world, have some value but these do not give one the spiritual experience. As such, ultimately they are unfulfilling and, misleading. People must start where they are and since most people are extroverted into the material world, they must begin with a religious process which caters to that demeanor. But that is not their perfection.

When austerity, the making of pilgrimage, the chanting of holy names, the offering of charity and other purificatory activities are designed to cause one to be introverted, then these activities force the intellect to leave aside this world and to retract itself in preparation for entry into the chit *ākāśa*, the sky of consciousness. Then one derives supernatural and spiritual experiences from one's endeavors, even from the external ones, because they influence the intellect to retreat from its interest in the gross manifestation. It begins with the development of subtle perception and gradually the ascetic becomes cured from the disease of constantly peering into the material world.

From this he gets factual knowledge by direct experience. And then he can stand on his own psychological strength. Otherwise a living being finds himself leaning this way and that way on religious faith and shallow hopes which lead nowhere else but back into another parent's body.

तस्माज् ज्ञानेन सहितं
ज्ञात्वा स्वात्मानम् उद्धव ।
ज्ञान-विज्ञान-सम्पन्नो
भज मां भक्ति-भावतः ॥ १४.५ ॥

tasmāj jñānena sahitaṁ
jñātvā svātmānam uddhava
jñāna-vijñāna-sampanno
bhaja māṁ bhakti-bhāvataḥ (14.5)

tasmāj = tasmāt — therefore; jñānena — by factual knowledge; sahitam — with; jñātvā — realising; svātmānam — your spiritual self; uddhava — Uddhava; jñāna — knowledge; vijñāna — mystic experience; sampanno = sampannah — endowed with; bhaja — worship; mām — my; bhakti-bhāvataḥ — the mood of devotion.

Translation

Therefore Uddhava, by factual knowledge, realize your spiritual self. Be endowed with knowledge and mystic experience. Worship Me in the mood of devotion. (14.5)

Commentary:

The first requirement is knowledge which is given by *Śrī* Krishna Himself and by spiritual teachers who preach the word of Krishna. Even though some of these spiritual teachers have not practiced sufficiently to have had the mystic experience of the spiritual self, their contribution to our development must be acknowledged.

A person can go ahead, jump the gun, so to speak, and begin worshiping *Śrī* Krishna with the mood of devotion, but unless he first hears properly about the reality of the spiritual self, about himself and other limited beings, and then take steps to get the experience of that self, his devotional worship will not go far.

This is because it will be a counterfeit of spiritual devotion. Such a person should be accredited with having practiced to apply himself to *Śrī* Krishna, especially to have applied his emotions but since the emotional energy is impure, he cannot be accredited as a pure devotee.

Of course, immature devotees might say that he is pure but that does not change his category. It only serves to mislead him further. To be a pure devotee one has to first move to the mystic-spiritual plane of consciousness and experience one's spirituality there. The process of doing this is to enter *samādhi*, which is the eight stage of yoga practice. It is possible for someone to enter *samādhi* without doing yoga but such an occurrence is rare. It does not happen frequently. And *samādhi* can be faked.

However if one is really serious about spiritual life and about reaching a stage of worshiping *Śrī* Krishna in the mood of devotion, then that is mainly one's concern and *Śrī* Krishna's. It is not the concern of one's disciples or of all the people in the material world who would honor and glorify one, if they knew that one was in fact a pure devotee.

We hear that Lord *Śrī* Chaitanya used to enter into *samādhi* and then His Self would be transferred into the chit *ākāśa*, the sky of consciousness, straight to the region where *Śrī* Krishna's abode is located but we do not hear that Lord Chaitanya was actively trying to make disciples. This was not his primary concern.

Many devotees become spiritual leaders in imitation of *Śrī* Chaitanya Mahaprabhu. Even though they gain recognition as pure devotees, they are in fact far from that. But this is the material world. These are the features of this misleading place.

A person can worship *Śrī* Krishna as much as he likes, and he can apply his emotional energy to the Lord as much as he can work himself into it, but that does not mean that he will be successful in this life. He has to first realize the spiritual level by direct experience. It is nobody's business how he reaches the spiritual plane, whether it be by yoga, by chanting holy names or by this or by that. But if he reaches it and actually gets the experience there, then his devotion to *Śrī* Krishna will pay off.

Underneath the application of devotional affection, there must be the spiritual quality of having experienced oneself as a spirit only and having touched down into the spiritual sky in fact.

ज्ञान-विज्ञान-यज्ञेन
माम् इष्ट्वात्मानम् आत्मनि ।
सर्व-यज्ञ-पतिं मां वै
ससिद्धिं मुनयो ऽगमन् ॥ १४.६ ॥

jñāna-vijñāna-yajñena
mām iṣṭvātmānam ātmani
sarva-yajña-patiṁ māṁ vai
saṁsiddhiṁ munayo 'gaman (14.6)

jñāna — knowledge; vijñāna — mystic experience; yajñena — by the sacrifice of; mām — me; iṣṭvātmānam = iṣṭvā — having worshiped + ātmānam — the self; ātmani — in the self; sarva — all; yajña — religious ceremony and discipline; patim — lord; mām — me; vai — surely; saṁsiddhim — perfection; munayo = munayah — the yogi philosopher; 'gaman = agaman — achieved.

Translation

By worshipping Me, the self in the spiritual self, the Lord of all religious ceremonies and disciplines, by the method of sacrificing knowledge and experience, the yogi philosopher achieves perfection. (14.6)

Commentary:

This type of worship is quite different to that of a devotee who did not mastered yoga. The worship of *Śrī* Krishna as the Self in the spiritual self, after having the spiritual vision to see that as it is, is not the same as doing that on the basis of being told so by an authority or by reading of it in this written discourse.

One achieves perfection after having many experiences on a consistent basis and in samādhi practice not otherwise. Certainly, those who heard of this and who have not gone to the spiritual level to experience this, should realize it further by mentally considering it and by trying to act in the world in a detached manner but that does not mean that they will achieve perfection thereby. They will not.

त्वय्य् उद्धवाश्रयति यस् त्रि-विधो विकारो
मायान्तरापतति नाद्य्-अपवर्गयोर् यत् ।
जन्मादयो ऽस्य यद् अमी तव तस्य किं स्युर्
आद्य्-अन्तयोर् यद् असतो ऽस्ति तद् एव मध्ये
॥ १४.७॥

tvayy uddhavāśrayati yas tri-vidho vikāro
māyāntarāpatati nādy-apavargayor yat
janmādayo 'sya yad amī tava tasya kiṁ syur
ādy-antayor yad asato 'sti tad eva madhye
(14.7)

tvayy = tvayi — in you; uddhavāśrayati = uddhava — Uddhava + āśrayati — is manifested; yas = yah — which; tri-vidho = tri-vidhah — three part; vikāro = vikārah — modifications; māyāntarāpatati = māyā — illusion + antarā — in the middle + āpatati — appears; nady = nadi = na — not + ādi — beginning; apavargayoh — in the end; yat — which; janmādayo = janmādayaḥ — birth and related aspects; 'sya = asya — of this; yad = yat — what; amī — this; tava — your; tasya — of him; kim — what; syur = syuḥ — could have; ādy = ādi — in the beginning; antayor = antayoh — in the end; yad = yat — what; asato = asatah — that which is temporary; asti — is there; tad = tat — that; eva — indeed; madhye — in the middle.

Translation

The three-part modification, O Uddhava, which is manifested in you, is an illusion. It appears in the middle but not at the beginning nor ending. Birth and related aspects, pertain to that. What is it to you? That which exists in the beginning and ending is there in the middle too. (14.7)

Commentary:

The three part modification is the three developments which came about by the spirit's contact with material nature. These are the causal body, the subtle body and the gross form. The gross form is at the end of the development. That is as far as a spirit can descend into matter. All three of these bodies disappear when the mundane energy reaches a state of quiescence. Hence these bodies are not the spirit itself. But this must be realized by supernatural and spiritual experiences individually. This should be experienced individually in order to be integrated. It is a good question that *Śrī* Krishna as Uddhava: What is it to you?

For indeed what are these bodies which we use and which charmed us into accepting them as ourselves?

श्री-उद्धव उवाच
ज्ञान विशुद्धं विपुल यथैतद्
वैराग्य-विज्ञान-युतं पुराणम् ।
आख्याहि विश्वेश्वर विश्व-मूर्ते
त्वद्-भक्ति-योगं च महद्-विमृग्यम् ॥ १४.८॥

śrī-uddhava uvāca
jñānaṁ viśuddhaṁ vipulaṁ yathaitad
vairāgya-vijñāna-yutaṁ purāṇam
ākhyāhi viśveśvara viśva-murte
tvad-bhakti-yogaṁ ca mahad-vimṛgyam (14.8)

śrī-uddhava – the qualified Uddhava; uvāca — said; jñānam — knowledge; viśuddham — faultless; vipulam — profound; yathaitad = yathā — just as it is + etat — this; vairagya — dispassion; vijñāna — mystic experience; yutam — coupled with; purāṇam — ancient; ākhyāhi — please explain; viśveśvara = viśva īśvara — Lord of the universe; viśva-mūrte — form of the universe; tvad = tvat — to you; bhakti – devotion; yoga — applied yoga; ca — and; mahad = mahat — great persons; vimṛgyam — that which is sought after.

Translation

The qualified Uddhava said: O Lord of the universe, O form of the universe, please explain just as it is, that faultless and profound knowledge which is applied with dispassion and mystic experience, and which is ancient. Explain the application of yoga to devotion to You, which is the process which the great souls seek out. (14.8)

Commentary:

This is a very complicated subject matter. Fortunately for us, it is not a simplistic matter as many preachers would have us believe. Even devotion to *Śrī* Krishna is not such a simple matter, because to be effective, it has to be yogically-applied. Uddhava repeatedly asked for this clarification about the faultless and profound knowledge and about the *bhakti* yoga process. If it were as simple as some persons make it out to be, he would not have persisted in questioning about it.

This calls to mind Arjuna, who asked for so many details in his effort to understand what *karma* yoga was. These matters are not simplistic. They are very intricate. Unfortunately for us, becoming freed from material existence is not as simple as continuing on in it.

ताप-त्रयेणाभिहतस्य घोरे
सन्तप्यमानस्य भवाध्वनीश ।
पश्यामि नान्यच् छरणं तवाङ्घ्रि-
द्वन्द्वातपत्राद् अमृताभिवर्षात् ॥ १४.९ ॥

tāpa-trayeṇābhihatasya ghore
santapyamānasya bhavādhvanīśa
paśyāmi nānyac charaṇaṁ tavāṅghri-
dvandvātapatrād amṛtābhivarṣāt (14.9)

tāpa — troubles; trayeṇābhihatasya = trayena — threefold + abhihatasya — of one who is harassed; ghore — in horribly; santapyamānasya — of one who is distressed or tormented; bhavādhvanīśa = bhava — of existence + adhvani — in the pathway + īśa — lord; paśyāmi — I see; nanyac = na — not + anyat — other; charanam = śaraṇam — refuge; tavanghri = tava — you + aṅghri — lotus feet; dvandvātapatrād = dvandva — two + ātapatrāt — than the umbrella; amṛtābhivarṣāt = amṛta — sweetener + abhivarṣāt — than the rain showers.

Translation

O Lord, for one who is harassed by the three fold troubles, and who is tormented in the horrible pathway of existence, I see no other refuge besides the umbrella of Your lotus feet, which gives sweetened rain showers. (14.9)

Commentary:

It seems that some people become adapted to the miseries of material existence. They resign themselves to it and accept it as normal, come what may. But a sensitive person can understand that both the subtle and gross material existence is a horror. There are some currents of happiness here and there but it is erratic. There is no certainty here. Hence a person who objectively looks at this situation, will come to the conclusion that he should endeavor to get out, in one way or the other. One should then see that one needs help.

Because of the over-whelming cosmic forces, one is victimized in this creation. Thus Uddhava suggested that we should take shelter under the lotus feet of *Śrī* Krishna.

दष्टं जनं सम्पतितं बिले ऽस्मिन्
कालाहिना क्षुद्र-सुखोरु-तर्षम् ।
समुद्धरैनं कृपयापवर्ग्यैर्
वचोभिर् आसिञ्च महानुभाव. ॥ १४.१० ॥

daṣṭaṁ janaṁ sampatitaṁ bile 'smin
kālāhinā kṣudra-sukhoru-tarṣam
samuddharainaṁ kṛpayāpavargyair
vacobhir āsiñca mahānubhāva(14.10)

daṣṭam — bitten; janam — person; sampatitam — fallen; bile — in the pit; 'smin = asmin — in this; kālāhinā = the snake of time; kṣudra — trivial; sukhoru — pleasure; tarsam — craving; samuddharainam = samuddhara — rescue + enam — this; kṛpayāpavargyair = kṛpayā — by mercy + āpavargyaiḥ — by what is conducive to liberation; vacobhir = vacobhiḥ — by words; āsiñca — sprinkle; mahānubhāva — great majestic personality.

Translation

O great majestic personality, please rescue this person who is fallen into the pit, being bitten by the snake of time, and forcefully craving trivial pleasures. Sprinkle him over with words which are merciful and conducive to liberation. (14.10)

Commentary:

The emotional and sympathetic nature of Uddhava is clearly displayed in so many of these verses, where he pleads to *Śrī* Krishna for solutions to the human problem, which is more or less the neglect of spiritual elevation, particularly of Krishna consciousness in terms of what *Śrī* Krishna advocated for the human beings to be devoted to Him under all circumstances, regardless of their lifestyles.

श्री-भगवान् उवाच
इत्थम् एतत् पुरा राजा
भीष्मं धर्म-भृता वरम् ।
अजात-शत्रुः पप्रच्छ
सर्वेषां नो ऽनुश्रृण्वताम् ॥ १४.११ ॥

śrī-bhagavān uvāca
ittham etat purā rājā
bhīṣmaṁ dharma-bhṛtāṁ varam
ajāta-śatruḥ papraccha
sarveṣāṁ no 'nuśṛṇvatām (14.11)

śrī-bhagavān – the blessed lord; uvāca — said; ittham — exactly; etat — this; purā — previously; rājā — the king; bhīṣmam — to Bhishma; dharma-bhṛtāṁ = upholders of righteous duty; varam — best; ajāta-śatruḥ — Yudhiṣṭhira, who was known as one whose enemy was never born; papraccha — asked; sarveṣām — of all; no = nah — of us; 'nuśṛṇvatām = anuśṛṇvatām — keenly listening.

Translation

The Blessed Lord said: Previously, King Yudhiṣṭhira, who was known as not having an enemy, asked this of Bhishma, the best of the upholders of righteous duty. We keenly listened to Bhishma's answers. (14.11)

Commentary:

After the battle of Kurukṣetra, Yudhiṣṭhira the victor, was advised by Lord Krishna to question Bhishma about approved methods of behavior.

निवृत्ते भारते युद्धे
सुहृन्-निधन-विह्वलः ।
श्रुत्वा धर्मान् बहून् पश्चान्
मोक्ष-धर्मान् अपृच्छत ॥ १४.१२ ॥

nivṛtte bhārate yuddhe
suhṛn-nidhana-vihvalaḥ
śrutvā dharmān bahūn paścān
mokṣa-dharmān apṛcchata (14.12)

nivṛtte — ended; bhārate — of the Bharatas; yuddhe — in war; suhṛn = suhṛt — of dear one; nidhana — death; vihvalaḥ — overwhelmed; śrutvā — after hearing; dharmān — righteous duties; bahūn — many types; paścān — afterwards; moksa — liberation; dharmān — righteous duties; aprcchata — asked what.

Translation

When the war of the Bhāratas ended, Yudhiṣṭhira, being overwhelmed by the death of dear ones, and after hearing of many types of righteous duties, did afterwards, ask about the righteous duty of liberation. (14.12)

Commentary:

When all is said, the ultimate aim of human life is to put an end to misery, sorrow and the like. However, to achieve this, one has to get out of the material world. This place cannot be changed, either by God or man. Man has to remove himself from here if he wants total happiness.

There are many duties of a living being according to the time, place and circumstance, but the ultimate obligation that the individual has to God and to himself is to become liberated *(mokṣa).*

तान् अहं ते ऽभिधास्यामि
देव-व्रत-मखाच् छ्रुतान् ।
ज्ञान-वैराग्य-विज्ञान-
श्रद्धा-भक्त्य्-उपबृंहितान् ॥ १४.१३॥

tān ahaṁ te 'bhidhāsyāmi
deva-vrata-makhāc chrutān
jñāna-vairāgya-vijñāna-
śraddhā-bhakty-upabṛṁhitān (14.13)

tān — those; aham — I; te — to you; 'bhidhāsyāmi = abhidhāsyāmi — will tell; deva-vrata — Bhisma; mukhāc = mukhāt — from the mouth; chrutān = śrutān — heard; jñāna — knowledge; vairāgya — detachment; vijñāna — mystic experience; śraddhā — faith; bhakty = bhakti — devotion; upabṛṁhitān — enriched with.

Translation

I will tell you of those actions which are enriched with knowledge, detachment, mystic experience, faith and devotion, and which were heard from the mouth of Bhishma Devavrata. (14.13)

Commentary:

To a certain extent we will have to act our way out of the material world. Thus we should take advice from expert souls like *Śrī* Bhishma *Devavrata*. They would give hints in how we may shorten the course of material existence.

नवैकादश पञ्च त्रीन्
भावान् भूतेषु येन वै ।
ईक्षेताथाकम् अप्य् एषु
तज् ज्ञानं मम निश्चितम् ॥ १४.१४॥

navaikādaśa pañca trīn
bhāvān bhūteṣu yena vai
īkṣetāthāikam apy eṣu
taj jñānaṁ mama niścitam (14.14)

navaikādaśa = nava — nine + ekādaśa — eleven; pañca — five; trīn — three; bhāvān — factors; bhūteṣu — in the beings; yena — that by which; vai — certainly; īkṣetāthāikam = īkṣeta — one may see + atha — thus + ekam — one; apy = api — also; eṣu — in these; taj = tat — that; jñānam — knowledge; mama — by me; niścitam — is considered.

Translation

One should perceive the nine, the eleven, the five and the three factors in all beings, and also the one factor which is in each of these other ones. That is considered by Me to be knowledge. (14.14)

Commentary:

This is the list of items enumerated in the *Sāṅkhya* philosophy, which are the twenty nine factors which comprise the material world. The nine are the primal material nature, personality, the sexually-charged portion of primal material nature, the sense of initiative of the personalities, and the five aspects of subtle matter which are sound, texture, color, flavor and odor.

The eleven factors are the active organs, namely the voice, hands, legs, genital and anus, plus the five perceiving senses which are the ear, skin, eye, tongue and nostril. Plus the one special sense which is the mind itself.

The three factors are the three influences of material nature, which are its clarifying energy, its impulsive force and its retardative power. The one factor which is all the above is the Supreme Being's manifestation as the Supersoul or *Paramātmā*.

एतद् एव हि विज्ञानं
न तथैकेन येन यत् ।
स्थित्य्-उत्पत्त्य्-अप्ययान् पश्येद्
भावानां त्रि-गुणात्मनाम् ॥ १४.१५॥

etad eva hi vijñānaṁ
na tathaikena yena yat
sthity-utpatty-apyayān paśyed
bhāvānāṁ tri-guṇātmanām (14.15)

etad = etat — this; eva — indeed; hi — because; vijñānam — mystic experience; na — not; tathaikena = tathā — in that way + ekena — by one; yena — by whom; yat — which; sthithy = sthiti — continuity; utpatty = utpatti — origination; apyayān — dissolution; paśyed = paśyet — should perceive; bhāvānām — of the essestial factors; tri-guṇātmanām = tri-guṇa — of the three influences of material nature + ātmanām — composed on, inherent in.

Translation

This information becomes mystic experience when one no longer sees that the factors are pervaded by one outstanding principle. One should then see the continuity, origination and dissolution of the essential factors related to the three influences of material nature. (14.15)

Commentary:

Śrī Krishna explained a key stage in the development of spiritual life, when the yogi no longer relies on mere knowledge. This knowledge which is explained in the *Sāṅkhya* philosophy and which is repeated by many teachers, states that there is the material world, along with the Puruṣa. When one asks who the Puruṣa is, one is usually told that He is the Supreme Personality. But some teachers say that it is the Supreme Personality along with the limited persons or *ātmas*. The Supreme Person is known as the *Paramātmā* or *antaryami* but the limited person is known as the *jīvātma* or compartmentalized minute eternal spiritual self.

However when one practices yoga and gets into the 6th stage of practice, which is the *dhāraṇā* practice, one no longer relies on this information, because one sees something else. It is not bookish knowledge nor what is heard physically. It is something that is seen directly by super-natural vision. This is developed when the yogi completes the 5th stage, that of *pratyāhar* sensual energy withdrawal into the *buddhi* organ. The completion of this, conveys him into the 6th stage of *dhāraṇā*, in which through *prāṇāyāma* he energizes his psyche sufficiently so that it shifts off from this level and reaches higher planes of reality in which certain concentrations of energy occur. There he links his attention to those concentration forces, and he develops the supernatural perception, as his intellect which before, was focused through the gross and subtle sense, now acts as a single sense.

With this single sense he perceives only the influences of material nature. These are subtle powers which cause origination, continuation and dissolution of the subtle and gross sense objects. In the background of this, there is one singular energizer which is the sum total spiritual force. It is always in proximity to material nature and to a greater or lesser degree it causes the sexually-charged cosmic force to operate.

This sort of realization was perfected by the sages during the Upanishadic period. This is why the Upanishads hail *brahman* as the supreme. Later on, when yoga was neglected, religious leaders did not factor it into their lectures but instead featured only *Bhagavān* or the Supreme Lord, who is also known as *Īśwara*.

Īśwara or the Supreme Person, is there along with the minute entities, the atom-like *jīvātmas* but still in the over-all sense, their collective power acts as a conjoint enthusing force to activate material nature in various ways. Feeling that the realization of *brahman* would contribute to atheism and that it would discourage theism or the worship of *Bhagavān*, the Supreme Person, many God-fearing teachers avoid stressing it. But these teachers are usually the ones who do not practice yoga and who do not get that deep into spiritual experiences. They remain in the world with their mental conceptions, picked up from the *Purāṇas* and from practical experience in day-to-day social affairs.

Brahman realization or the perception of the collective or sum total spiritual force, which motivated material nature at large, does not necessarily lead to atheism but it can do so in those individuals who have that disposition. Still, such persons have to come to terms with the Universal Form, the *Viśvarūpa* which Arjuna saw. If they become liberated, it is up to the Supreme Being, regarding if He desires their devotional services.

From a careful reading of the *Bhagavad-Gītā*, one comes to understand that *Śrī* Krishna is not particularly interested in making every living entity into a theist, but rather he wants all the living beings to aim for liberation. The discrimination about being a theist or being a non-believer in God, is pushed by some devotees. In the *Bhagavad Gītā*, we do not pick up that attitude from Lord Krishna. The Supreme Being is so fabulous that He does not express a craving to convert everyone to His influence. He does not bar a person from liberation, merely because that person does not believe in Him personally.

The one outstanding principle mentioned in verse 14 and in this verse, is the Supersoul *Paramātmā*. But when one actually sees on the supernatural plane, one notices that the Supersoul is absent as the background figure. One then detects the sum-total spiritual influence of all the *Puruṣas* as the background power.

आदाव् अन्ते च मध्ये च
सृज्यात् सृज्य यद् अन्वियात् ।
पुनस् तत्-प्रतिसङ्क्रामे
यच् छिष्येत तद् एव सत् ॥ १४.१६ ॥

ādāv ante ca madhye ca
sṛjyāt sṛjyaṁ yad anviyāt
punas tat-pratisaṅkrāme
yac chiṣyeta tad eva sat (14.16)

ādav = ādau — in the beginning; ante — in the end; ca — and; madhye — in the middle; ca — and; sṛjyāt — from creation; sṛjyam — to creation; yad = yat — which; anviyāt — persists through; punas = punaḥ — again; tat — that; pratisaṅkrāme — in the retrogression; tac = tat — which; chiṣyeta = śiṣyeta — remains; tad = tat — that; eva — indeed; sat — reality.

Translation

That which persist throughout from one creation to another, in the beginning, in the end and in the middle, and which again, remains after the retrogression of the essential elements, is indeed the Reality of the thing. (14.16)

Commentary:

One begins to see this directly in higher yoga. There are essentially two realities as stated in the *Bhagavad-Gītā*. These are the spiritual forces and the subtle material energy. Both of these are eternal. It is through their interaction, that the material world comes about.

श्रुतिः प्रत्यक्षम् ऐतिह्यम्
अनुमानं चतुष्टयम् ।
प्रमाणेष्व् अनवस्थानाद्
विकल्पात् स विरज्यते ॥ १४.१७ ॥

śrutiḥ pratyakṣam aitihyam
anumānaṁ catuṣṭayam
pramāṇeṣv anavasthānād
vikalpāt sa virajyate (14.17)

śrutiḥ — Vedic text; pratyaksam — sensory experience; aitihyam — traditional information; anumānam — logical analysis; catuṣṭayam — fourfold; pramāṇeṣv = pramāṇeṣu — based on the proofs of knowledge; anavasthānād = anavasthānāt — due to constant alteration; vikalpāt — from superficial diversity; sa = sah — he; virajyate — turns away.

Translation

On the basis of fourfold proof of knowledge, namely Vedic text, sensory experience, tradition and logical analysis, he turns away from it, due to its constant alteration and superficial diversity. (14.17)

Commentary:

A yogi takes help from the four sources, namely; Vedic knowledge, direct sensory experience, traditional views and logical analysis. Of these the most important is direct sensory experience. The other means of knowledge have value in the neophyte stages, when the yogi has no transcendental experience. One can only turn away from the material energy partially with

Vedic knowledge, traditional views and logical analysis. But with direct experience, one gets a power through which one can make an all-out effort to escape.

The problem with the material energy is its constant alteration and its superficial but very imposing diversity. If it were something permanent, it would not be such a disappointment for the limited entities. One comes down into the material world, because one has an instinct for locating permanence. But one does not find that here, even though one finds the promise of it in every direction. This promising power of material nature is called māyā or the force of bewilderment.

A yogin does turn away from material nature but that does not mean that it turns away from him. Thus he has to wean himself from dependence on it and also neutralize its attraction to him. He has to become a mystic.

कर्मणां परिणामित्वाद्
आ-विरिञ्च्याद् अमङ्गलम् ।
विपश्चिन् नश्वरं पश्येद्
अदृष्टम् अपि दृष्ट-वत् ॥ १४.१८॥

karmaṇāṁ pariṇāmitvād
ā-viriñcyād amaṅgalam
vipaścin naśvaraṁ paśyed
adṛṣṭam api dṛṣṭa-vat (14.18)

karmanām — regarding cultural action; parinämitvād = parinämitvāt — since it is subjected to change; a — up to; viriñcyāt — from Brahmā Virinci's planet; amaṅgalam — inconvenient; vipaścin — a wise man; naśvaram — temporary; paśyed = paśyet — should perceive; adṛṣṭam — that which is not yet experienced; api — also; dṛṣṭa-vat — just as what was already endured.

Translation

Regarding cultural activities, since it is subject to change, the wise man should perceive whatever is not yet experienced, even life up to the level of Brahmā Viriñci's planet, as being inconvenient and temporary, just as the experiences he already endured. (14.18)

Commentary:

Material existence is very tricky. This means that there will always be a horizon for success up ahead. Following this, a living entity repeats the same frustrating history. Thus one should understand that there is nothing to gain in the material world, except disgust or *nirvedah*. This was explained to Uddhava in the first part of this discourse in the story of the woman *Pińgalā*. She expected and expected, became frustrated and disappointed and then was freed through the energy of disgust.

Cultural activities, regardless of whether they are enacted by an ant or by a planetary creator, is a dead end. This does not mean that we can avoid it. If we do not get an exemption from the same Supreme Being who tells us of its futility, we will not be successful in spiritual life. Understanding that the world is a mock-up and a frustrating one at that, is no reason to overlook the controlling power of the Supreme Being. Whatever is enacted or imagined by a great personality, has force. Whatever was conceived by the Supreme Being has supreme force. To side-step that power, we must acquire His approval.

Viriñci is *Brahmā*, the planetary creator. Even his life is full of cultural activities. What can be said about others? It will all prove to be inconvenient and temporary. It is just like a pregnancy. It cannot last forever. And it is painfully and exhaustively concluded.

There is nothing else to see in this material world, because as *Śrī* Krishna stated, everything which occurs now, and everything that is to be, will be just like what was experienced already. When the yogi becomes convinced of this, he turns away permanently. By mastering higher yoga, the yogin travels into other dimensions and experiences what is to be experienced elsewhere in the higher and lower situations and even in various other species of life. Thus the yogi get first hand experiences and can draw correct conclusions.

भक्ति-योगः पुरैवोक्तः
प्रीयमाणाय ते ऽनघ ।
पुनश् च कथयिष्यामि
मद्-भक्तेः कारणं परं ॥ १४.१९ ॥

bhakti-yogaḥ puraivoktaḥ
prīyamāṇāya te 'nagha
punaś ca kathayiṣyāmi
mad-bhakteḥ kāraṇaṁ paraṁ (14.19)

bhakti-yogaḥ — yoga disciplines as applied to devotionship; puraivoktaḥ = purā — previously + eva — indeed + uktaḥ — explained; prīyamānāya — to one who has affection; te — to you; 'nagha = anagha — o sinless one; punaś = punah — again; ca — and; kathayisyāmi — I will relate; mad-bhakteḥ = mat-bhakteḥ — of devotion to me; kāraṇam — cause; param — best, chief.

Translation

O sinless one, previously I explained to you, who has affection, the technique of using yoga disciplines in applying devotion. And I will again relate the chief cause of devotion to Me. (14.19)

Commentary:

We have to understand that devotion and devotion applied with yoga disciplines are two different aspects. If a yogi takes to devotion, then his devotion will be of a more intense and direct nature. Some persons like the *gopīs* did not practice yoga in the life in *Vṛndāvan*, but still Uddhava was astonished with the intensity of their devotion which not only rivaled but surpassed the devotional focus of great yogins. Therefore it is a fact that someone can have that sort of devotion without doing yoga discipline.

However we understand that some *gopīs* used ascetic male bodies in the time of Lord *Rāmacandra*. They applied themselves to yoga in that former life time, when Lord *Śrī Rāma* blessed them to meet with *Śrī* Krishna in the future, for the intense application of loving devotion to Him. Other *gopīs* are supposed to have come with *Śrī* Krishna from the spiritual places, where yoga practice is unnecessary. These could apply themselves with great intensity in loving *Śrī* Krishna.

However this does not mean that other living entities can do so. When we speak of Uddhava and Arjuna and when we overlook or minimize their yoga expertise, we do ourselves a disfavor, because then we underestimate what we should do to attain pure devotion. The devotion has to be of a high quality. It has to reach *Śrī* Krishna's spiritual form, not just any of His material forms. This is why yoga is necessary in most cases. This is why there is *bhakti* and yoga are put together to make *bhakti* yoga otherwise *bhakti* itself would be sufficient.

Bhakti is being used day after day in human socially affairs. But that sort of energy when applied to *Śrī* Krishna does not reach him, because it is of a low vibration. One has to shift to a much higher level before one can successfully apply *bhakti* or devotional life and relationship to *Śrī* Krishna.

श्रद्धामृत-कथायां मे
शश्वन् मद्-अनुकीर्तनम् ।
परिनिष्ठा च पूजायां
स्तुतिभिः स्तवनं मम ॥ १४.२० ॥

śraddhāmṛta-kathāyāṁ me
śaśvan mad-anukīrtanam
pariniṣṭhā ca pūjāyāṁ
stutibhiḥ stavanaṁ mama (14.20)

śraddhāmṛta = śraddhā — faith + amṛta — sweetener; kathāyām — of tales; me — of my; śaśvan = śaśvat — constant; mad-anukīrtanam = mat-anukīrtanam — singing sons which glorify; pariniṣṭha — fixed attachment; ca — and; pūjāyām — in worship; stutibhiḥ — with praising hymns; stavanam — prayers; mama — in relation to me.

Translation

A constant faith for the sweet stories concerning Me, singing songs which glorify Me, a fixed attachment in worshipping Me and saying prayers with hymns in reference to Me, (14.20)

Commentary:

We should not forget that these words are being said to Uddhava a great yogin who was a personal associate of *Śrī* Krishna, who *Śrī* Krishna rated as His personal representative and highest devotee. It is the same with the *Bhagavad-Gītā* which was told to Arjuna, a person who was rated by *Śrī* Krishna as His reserved, non-envious friend and His personal representative for showing the ideal method of *karma* yoga. If we forget this, we will substitute ourselves in their place and make a serious blunder.

Some spiritual masters in the disciplic succession are all too eager to accredit us as being qualified to love *Śrī* Krishna effectively, merely on the basis of our acceptance of a discipleship under their authority. But that is a ploy only. It will not place us in the position we so much desire.

The worshipping activities mentioned in this verse and in some verses to follow are those activities which may be performed by a devotee who uses a physical body. These are activities which are primed by *Śrī* Krishna Himself by His mercy act of taking a body in this world and displaying activities here.

Uddhava's constant faith for the sweet stories concerning Krishna, his singing of songs which glorify Krishna, his fixed attachment in worshiping Krishna and his saying of prayers in reference to Krishna, will give the intended result, because of the quality of Uddhava's affections. But that does not mean that we are in a position to do this by merely attempting to do it. We will graduate to that position by taking up purificatory austerities.

In my own case, following the advice of authorities in the disciplic succession, I found that I was unable to improve my devotional focus, except superficially and in a very external way.

Of course when questioned about this, their answer was that I was offensive or that I was not fully surrendered unto them. But such excuses are useless because many who surrendered to them, who they displayed as their pure servants and fully surrendered devotees, continually exhibited a deviant character. History revealed later that many of the authorities were themselves in deviancy.

It means therefore that despite their fitting of themselves into the profile of purity, and despite their awarding their pet disciples the pure status, still they remained impure and were not qualified for those guarantees which are suited to person like Uddhava and Arjuna.

आदरः परिचर्यायां
सर्वाङ्गैर् अभिवन्दनम् ।
मद्-भक्त-पूजाभ्यधिका
सर्व-भूतेषु मन्-मतिः ॥१४.२१॥

ādaraḥ paricaryāyāṁ
sarvāṅgair abhivandanam
mad-bhakta-pūjābhyadhikā
sarva-bhūteṣu man-matiḥ (14.21)

ādaraḥ — reverence; paricaryāyām — zeal in regular performance of ceremonial worship; sarvāṅgair = sarvāṅgaiḥ — with all bodily limbs; abhivandanam — offering obeisances; mad-bhakta = mat-bhakta — my devotee; pūjābhyadhikā = pūjā — worship + abhyadhikā — very special; sarva – all; bhūteṣu — in all beings; man matiḥ = mat matiḥ — perception of me.

Translation

...reverence, zeal in regular performance of ceremonial worship, offering obeisances with all bodily limbs, giving very special worship to My devotees, having the perception of Me in all beings, (14.21)

Commentary:

Even though devotion became popular as an easy course for salvation, it is in application, a difficult one indeed. This is because there are many details and the quality of it has to be high. Anyone can throw around affections, even animals are capable of that, but it takes special persons to be cultured in the devotional purity and focus which causes one to go to *Śrī* Krishna.

The cheap advertisement about devotional love does serve to bring many persons who would otherwise not be interested in the devotional community. But since there is hardly any way to improve the quality of their love, most of these attracted persons are left in a stagnant condition. All too often, the spiritual teachers themselves become so preoccupied with increasing the number of followers, that they maintain a pretense of devotion while being fully engaged in the actions required to keep the following and to increase the membership.

What does that have to do with devotion? Interestingly, most of these spiritual leaders can explain away their political prowess as devotional service, and their staunch followers are all to eager to defend this.

मद्-अर्थेष्व् अङ्ग-चेष्टा च
वचसा मद्-गुणेरणम् ।
मय्य् अर्पणं च मनसः
सर्व-काम-विवर्जनम्

mad-artheṣv aṅga-ceṣṭā ca
vacasā mad-guṇeraṇam
mayy arpaṇaṁ ca manasaḥ
sarva-kāma-vivarjanam (14.22)

mad-artheṣu = mat-artheṣu — for the sake of me; aṅga – bodily limbs; ceṣṭā — physically activating; ca — and; vacasā — by speech; mad-guṇeraṇam = mat-guna — my qualities + īraṇam — declaring; mayy = mayi — on me; arpaṇam — focusing; ca — and; manasaḥ — of the mind; sarva – all; kāma — cravings; vivarjanam — banishing.

Translation

...physically motivating the limbs of the body for My sake, declaring My qualities by speech, focusing on Me, banishing all cravings of the mind, (14.22)

Commentary:

Too many of the spiritual masters substitute themselves for *Śrī* Krishna. Some do this openly. Some do it in an indirect way. However such a substitution will not work. It becomes necessary to substitute the spiritual master if one cannot directly see nor relate to *Śrī* Krishna nor to His Deity Form. However the substitution is not always applicable.

Who without yoga, has the ability to banish all cravings from the mind? We should be realistic and do whatever is necessary to attain our desire if we really love or want to reach a stage where we can love *Śrī* Krishna as described. In our case, the spiritual master is not *Śrī* Krishna but He was for Arjuna and Uddhava. We should never forget that. Therefore the substitution of a guru in *Śrī* Krishna's place, will not do. It is an effective method to a certain level only. At some point one has to deal with *Śrī* Krishna directly if it is one's aim to be His devotee. Otherwise both the disciple and the spiritual master should be honest and admit that *Śrī* Krishna is not the immediate focus, the spiritual master is.

In Arjuna's and Uddhava's cases, *Śrī* Krishna was both the Supreme Lord and guru, but it is not so in our case. Therefore if we treat the spiritual master as if he is God and guru, then we should not allow the teacher to indulge us in the belief that since he represents Krishna, the treatment of him as God has the same value as Arjuna's or Uddhava's relations with Krishna. These are misleading and totally fallacious procedures of a guru.

मद्-अर्थे ऽर्थ-परित्यागो
भोगस्य च सुखस्य च ।
इष्टं दत्तं हुतं जप्तं
मद्-अर्थं यद् व्रतं तपः ॥१४.२३॥

mad-arthe 'rtha-parityāgo
bhogasya ca sukhasya ca
iṣṭaṁ dattaṁ hutaṁ japtaṁ
mad-arthaṁ yad vrataṁ tapaḥ (14.23)

mad-arte = mat-arthe — for my sake; 'rtha = artha — wealth; parityāgaḥ — giving up; bhogasya — of enjoyment; ca — and; sukhasya — of happiness; ca — and; iṣṭam — desirable activities; dattam — charity; hutam — offering of oblations in sacrifice; japtam — chanting holy names of God; mad-artham = mat-artham — for my sake; yad = yat — which; vratam — vow; tapaḥ — austerities.

Translation

...giving up wealth, enjoyment and happiness, for My sake, doing desirable activities, giving charity, offering oblations in sacrifices, chanting of holy names of God, observing vows, doing austerities far My sake, (14.23)

Commentary:

These activities may be done for the sake of *Śrī* Krishna, provided this is what He really desired for a particular person. Then it will result in a devotional relationship with Him. Arjuna is an example of a person who gave up his own views, who parted with his own sympathies and even with his initial discretion, for the sake of Krishna. But Arjuna was directly advised by *Śrī* Krishna. He did not have to work with an in-between person. We have to either be directly inspired or be advised by an in-between.

In either case, we might be misled either by our intuition or by the spiritual master who served as the in-between. Many spiritual masters claim that they are transparent via-media for *Śrī* Krishna but it is discovered frequently that only some of their advices classify as what *Śrī* Krishna approved. Anyone can advise anyone else, even this writer can advise somebody but that does not mean, that if the advisor says that he is a pure devotee of Krishna and a perfect spokesman for the Lord, that all the advices would be approved by Krishna.

Therefore when dealing with go-betweens, the risk is there, that what is recommended, might not be what *Śrī* Krishna approved. This is the flaw of our lives in dealing with gurus. But it does not mean that we should not take one or more gurus. It is just that we must be conscious of the risks.

We should be extra-cautious when we taking advice from spiritual masters who become popular and who are well known as pure devotees or as transparent mediums for Krishna. Invariably, such popular spiritual masters give whimsical or general advice which are not approved by the Blessed Lord. We see that *Śrī* Krishna personally gave Arjuna advice and personally spoke to Uddhava. Even though *Śrī* Krishna is the Supreme Being, He did not have many followers around Him, praising Him when He gave these instructions. It was tailored to the two devotees concerned.

We should not think or be influenced to think, that what was said to Arjuna was for the general public or that what was said to Uddhava is for us. It is not like that. Certain parts of these discourses are relevant to one devotee and other parts are vital to another. Each devotee needs instructions which are suited for his development and which bring him specifically into *Śrī* Krishna's graces.

एवं धर्मैर् मनुष्याणाम्
उद्धवात्म-निवेदिनाम् ।
मयि सञ्जायते भक्तिः
को ऽन्यो ऽर्थो ऽस्यावशिष्यते ॥ १४.२४॥

evaṁ dharmair manuṣyāṇām
uddhavātma-nivedinām
mayi sañjāyate bhaktiḥ
ko 'nyo 'rtho 'syāvaśiṣyate (14.24)

evam — in that way; dharmair = dharmaiḥ — by righteous duty; manuṣyāṇām — among human beings; uddhavātma = uddhava — Uddhava + ātma – self; nivedinām — surrendered; mayi — to me; sañjāyate — acquire; bhaktiḥ — devotion; ko = kah — what; 'nyo = anyah — other; 'rtho = arthah — purpose; 'syāvaśiṣyate = asyāvaśiṣyate = asya — of this + avaśisyate — remains.

Translation

...in that way, O Uddhava, by righteous duties, the surrendered souls among human beings, acquire devotion to Me. What other aspect remains to be achieved by the devotee? (14.24)

Commentary:

In these discussions of *bhakti* and of *bhakti* yoga, *Śrī* Krishna always reached a point in the discussion and stopped. This is because devotion must improve in quality before it can be effective. There is no point in pushing the Lord for a devotional solution. The question still remains of how to purify the nature, so that the devotion will be accepted by Him.

The most difficult task is to purify devotion, affection and love. Even though love is the most spontaneous emotion, still by its innate position in the psyche, it is difficult to purify. Again, *Śrī* Krishna reached a point and stopped, telling Uddhava that by *dharma* or righteous duty, a person may acquire devotion. And once he gets that, it sustains him for everything else he must do to satisfy or gain the approval of *Śrī* Krishna. The devotion then serves as the main motivating force for making the sacrifice and taking up the austerities which are necessary for someone who has got that close to *Śrī* Krishna.

In Arjuna's case he had to serve more *dharma* or do more righteous duty as a warrior to please *Śrī* Krishna. Uddhava had to go to the Himalayas to perform austerities for the same purpose. They complied easily because they had devotion.

Those who do not have the devotional drive, find it difficult to adhere to austerities unless they have within them an innate and very powerful urge to seek out perfection. Devotion is not just devotion, it is in fact the strongest motivation for complying with the unpalatable instructions of *Śrī* Krishna. It is a compelling force and a necessary motivation for the non-philosophical human beings, who are the majority of the human population.

यदात्मन्य् अर्पितं चित्तं
शान्तं सत्त्वोपबृंहितम् ।
धर्मं ज्ञानं स वैराग्यम्
ऐश्वर्यं चाभिपद्यते ॥ १४.२५॥

yadātmany arpitaṁ cittaṁ
śāntaṁ sattvopabṛṁhitam
dharmaṁ jñānaṁ sa vairāgyam
aiśvaryaṁ cābhipadyate (14.25)

yadatmany = yada — when + ātmany (ātmani) — in the core self; arpitam — focused; cittam — the mental and emotional energy; śāntam — pacified; sattvopabṛmhitam = sattva — clarifying energy + upabṛmhitam — enriched; dharmam — righteous duty; jñānam — knowledge; sa = sah — he; vairāgyam — dispassion; aiśvaryam — spiritual majesty; cābhipadyate = ca — and + abhipadyate — achieves.

Translation

When the mental and emotional energy being pacified and enriched with the clarifying force, is focused on the core self, the person achieves the grasp on righteous duty, knowledge, dispassion and spiritual majesty. (14.25)

Commentary:

This is a higher yoga process. If you do not know what yoga does, then you may think that this can be done by other means. However that is the wrong idea. One cannot enrich the mental and emotional energy with the clarifying force without doing *prāṇāyāma* practice. It is not possible. Those who feel that they can do this by another method, such as chanting, going to temple programs, discussing Krishna *līla*, are fooling themselves. Since they have not done *prāṇāyāma* or have not done it properly, they do not know what they are missing.

The mental and emotional energy, the *cittam*, is shifted away from this level not by shifting it but by changing it to a higher type of energy, to the pure clarifying force. This occurs by *prāṇāyāma* only. When this is done, the mental and emotional force is no longer of the same ingredients as before. These assume a condition of pacification once they are sufficiently charge with higher pranic energy. In that consciousness, the yogi devotee naturally and effortlessly focuses within his psyche. After this, he develops the vision to know what his righteous duty is. That is his *karma* yoga activity which is stipulated by the Central Person in the Universal Form, who is *Śrī* Krishna Himself, not the spiritual master.

Such a yogi devotee with that first-hand knowledge, develops dispassion and spiritual majesty in the course of time. We must remember that *Śrī* Krishna spoke to Uddhava who is a great yogin. All these procedures were known to Uddhava. He is not a common human being of this modern era. Thus we should not adjust these procedures, downplay the yoga aspects of them and assure people who are not proficient in yoga.

यद् अर्पितं तद् विकल्पे
इन्द्रियैः परिधावति ।
रजस्-वलं चासन्-निष्ठं
चित्तं विद्धि विपर्ययम् ॥ १४.२६ ॥

yad arpitaṁ tad vikalpe
indriyaiḥ paridhāvati
rajas-valaṁ cāsan-niṣṭhaṁ
cittaṁ viddhi viparyayam (14.26)

yad = yat — when; arpitam — focused; tad = tat — that; vikalpe — in the many mundane objectives; indriyaiḥ — with the senses; paridhavati — pursues in every direction; rajas = rajah – impulsive energy; valam — reinforced; cāsan = ca — and + asan (asat) — temporary things; niṣṭham — tightly attached; cittam — the mental and emotional energy; viddhi — know; viparyayam — the opposite.

Translation

But when that mental and emotional energy is focused on many mundane objectives, pursuing these in every direction, it is reinforced by the impulsive energy and becomes attached to temporary things. Know that this gives the opposite result. (14.26)

Commentary:

If devotional service to *Śrī* Krishna is as easy as advocated, then why do we have to imbibe all this information about so many features of the operation of the mental and emotional energy, and the operation of our bodies in the social setting? Obviously, devotion is not that easy. In ordinary dealings, devotion is instinctual but it is not so in spiritual dealings unless we use impure affections. But that will not serve the purpose intended. The emotions and affections have to be of high quality, otherwise we are more or less wasting valuable time.

The impulsive energy also, operates a devotional affectionate force. Can that be applied to *Śrī* Krishna? Would its application give the devotee the opposite result of what is desired in the form of putting him at a further distance from the Lord?

धर्मो मद्-भक्ति-कृत् प्रोक्तो
ज्ञानं चैकात्म्य-दर्शनम् ।
गुणेस्व् असङ्गो वैराग्यम्
ऐश्वर्यं चाणिमादयः ॥ १४.२७ ॥

dharmo mad-bhakti-kṛt prokto
jñānaṁ caikātmya-darśanam
guṇesv asaṅgo vairāgyam
aiśvaryaṁ cāṇimādayaḥ (14.27)

dharmo = dharmah — righteous duty; mad-bhakti-kṛt = mad (mat) — to me + bhakti — devotion + kṛt — producing; prokto = proktah — is defined; jñānam — knowledge; caikātmya = ca — and + aikātmya — concerning the unity of the spirits; darśanam — perceiving; guṇeṣv = guṇeṣu — in the influences of material nature; asaṅgo = asaṅgaḥ — non-attachment; vairagyam — dispassion; aiśvaryam — spiritual majesty; cāṇimādayaḥ = ca — and + aṇimā — minuteness + ādayaḥ — and other mystic functions.

Translation

Righteous duty is defined as whatever produces devotion to Me. Knowledge is the perception of the unity of the spirits. Dispassion is the non-attachment to the influences of material nature. And spiritual majesty is the minuteness and other mystic functions. (14.27)

Commentary:

Śrī Krishna gave definitions; righteous duty being whatever produces devotion to Him. In other words, if we serve the Universal Form, we will by that association develop devotion to *Śrī* Krishna who is the Central Person therein. By working for Him we develop affection for Him. This was explained in chapter 12 of the *Bhagavad-Gītā*. This means that some of us do not feel devotion for *Śrī* Krishna. If however we are attracted to Him and want to attain Him, we can achieve that by complying with His request for social services.

abhyāse'pyasamartho'si matkarmaparamo bhava
madarthamapi karmāṇi kurvansiddhimavāpsyasi

But if perchance, you are incapable of such practice, then by being absorbed in My work, or even by doing activities for My sake, you will attain perfection. (B.G. 12.10)

The perception of the unity of the spirits which *Śrī* Krishna defines as knowledge, tallies with what he told Arjuna. But this is attained by mystic perception and not by receiving knowledge in the disciplic succession. This is attained by higher yoga. Fully integrated dispassion comes on by higher yoga. Partial dispassion is achieved by analysis and by peer pressure in the spiritual community. Spiritual majesty comes by opening up the kundalini chakra, so that the subtle body becomes purified. This is done by *prāṇāyāma* for the purpose of kundalini and celibacy yoga. I do not see how one can achieve these aspects by other means.

श्री-उद्धव उवाच
यमः कति-विधः प्रोक्तो
नियमो वारि-कर्षण ।
कः शमः को दमः कृष्ण
का तितिक्षा धृतिः प्रभो ॥१४.२८॥

śrī-uddhava uvāca
yamaḥ kati-vidhaḥ prokto
niyamo vāri-karṣaṇa
kaḥ śamaḥ ko damaḥ kṛṣṇa
kā titikṣā dhṛtiḥ prabho (14.28)

śrī-uddhava = the qualified Uddhava; uvāca — said; yamaḥ — moral restraints; kati-vidhaḥ — how many types; prokto = proktah — as declared; niyamo = niyamah — approved behaviors; vari = va — or + ari – enemy; karṣaṇa — chastiser; kaḥ — what; śamaḥ — spiritual peace; ko = kah — what; damaḥ — self-control; kṛṣṇa — Krishna; kā — what; titikṣā — tolerance; dhṛtiḥ — patience; prabho — lord.

Translation

The qualified Uddhava said: How many types of moral restraint and approved behaviors are declared, O chastiser of the enemy? What is spiritual peace? What is self control? What is tolerance? What is patience, O Lord? (14.28)

Commentary:

Uddhava asked these questions to get the definitions from *Śrī* Krishna, since it seemed that all this is involved in the practice of the *dharma* righteous living which would cause a person to develop the devotional relationship.

If a person has no devotion to *Śrī* Krishna or is not attracted in any way, but wants to advance spiritually, that person may develop a relationship by working under the direction of the Universal Form in a righteous life style. By that association with what is approved by Krishna, he would develop a divine relationship, through which perfection could be achieved.

किं दानं किं तपः शौर्यं
किम् सत्यम् ऋतम् उच्यते ।
कस् त्यागः किं धनं चेष्टं
को यज्ञः का च दक्षिणा ॥१४.२९॥

kiṁ dānaṁ kiṁ tapaḥ śauryaṁ
kim satyam ṛtam ucyate
kas tyāgaḥ kiṁ dhanaṁ ceṣṭaṁ
ko yajñaḥ kā ca dakṣiṇā (14.29)

kim — what; dānam — charity; kim — what; tapaḥ — austerity; śauryam — heroism; kim — what;

satyam — realism; ṛtam — truthfulness; ucyate — is stated; kas = kah — what; tyāgaḥ — renunciation of benefits; kim — what; dhanam — wealth; ceṣṭam = ca — and + iṣṭam — most desirable; ko = kah — what; yajñah — religious ceremony and disciplines; kā — what; ca — and; dakṣina — fee for teacher or priest.

Translation

What is charity? What is austerity? What is heroism? What is realism? What is truthfulness? What is renunciation of benefits? What is the most desired wealth? What is religious ceremony and disciplines? What is a fee for a teacher or priest? (14.29)

Commentary:

Uddhava requested clarification in terms of how different individuals might perform their cultural duties for *Śrī* Krishna's approval in order to qualify for developing the devotional relationship, through which they would eventually attain perfection.

पुसः किं स्विद् बलं श्रीमन्
भगो लाभश् च केशव ।
का विद्या ह्रीः परा का श्रीः
कि सुखं दुःखम् एव च ॥१४.३०॥

puṁsaḥ kiṁ svid balaṁ śrīman
bhago lābhaś ca keśava
kā vidyā hrīḥ parā kā śrīḥ
kiṁ sukhaṁ duḥkham eva ca (14.30)

puṁsaḥ — of a person; kim — what; svid = svit — what indeed; balam — strength; śrīman — O gracious one; bhago = bhagah — fortune; lābhas = lābhah — profit; ca — and; keśava = Keshava = Krishna; kā — what; vidyā — technique; hṛīḥ — shyness; parā — supreme; ka — what; śrīh — beauty; kim — what; sukham — happiness; duhkham — misery; eva — also; ca — and.

Translation

What indeed is the strength of a person, O gracious one? What is fortune? What is profit O Keśava Krishna? What is technique? What is shyness? What is supreme beauty? What is happiness? And also what is misery? (14.30)

Commentary:

A definition of any or all of these aspects would help us to understand the perspective of *Śrī* Krishna; so that we can bring ourselves closer into His association by stream-lining our life styles to gain His approval.

कः पण्डितः कश् च मूर्खः
कः पन्था उत्पथश् च कः ।
कः स्वर्गो नरकः कः स्वित्
को बन्धुर् उत किं गृहम् ॥१४.३१॥

kaḥ paṇḍitaḥ kaś ca mūrkhaḥ
kaḥ panthā utpathaś ca kaḥ
kaḥ svargo narakaḥ kaḥ svit
ko bandhur uta kiṁ gṛham (14.31)

kah — who; panditaḥ — a well-versed priest of scholar; kas = kah — who; ca — and; mūrkhaḥ — a fool; kaḥ — which; panthā = panthāḥ — path; utpathaḥ — the wrong process; ca — and; kaḥ — what, which; kaḥ — what; svargo = svargaḥ — heaven hereafter; narakaḥ — hell after death; kaḥ — what; svit — indeed; ko = kah — who; bandhur − bandhuh — friend; uta — and; kim — what; grham — home.

Translation

Who is a well-versed priest or scholar? Who is a fool? Which is the path? Which is the wrong process? What is heaven hereafter? And what is hell after death? Who is a friend? What is a home? (14.31)

Commentary:

By getting *Śrī* Krishna's definitions, a person who takes up the path of righteous living with intentions to develop the devotional relationship with Krishna, would know His view point and be able to discern what would be approved by Him. Such a person would take advices from others, but with these definitions he would be able to compare their advices to be sure that the counsels are approved by *Śrī* Krishna.

क आढ्यः को दरिद्रो वा
कृपणः कः क ईश्वरः ।
एतान् प्रश्नान् मम ब्रूहि
विपरीतांश् च सत्-पते ॥ १४.३२ ॥

ka āḍhyaḥ ko daridro vā
kṛpaṇaḥ kaḥ ka īśvaraḥ
etān praśnān mama brūhi
viparītāṁś ca sat-pate (14.32)

ka = kaḥ — who; āḍhyaḥ — wealthy; ko = kaḥ — who; daridro = daridrah — poor; vā — or; kṛpaṇaḥ — miserly person; kaḥ — who; ka = kah — who; īśvaraḥ — master, lord; etān — these; praśnān — questions; mama — my; brūhi — answer; viparītāṁś = viparītān — opposites; ca — and; sat-pate — of the protection of the great souls.

Translation

Who is wealthy? Who is poor? Who is miserly? Who is lordly? Please answer these questions and explain the opposites, O protector of the great souls? (14.32)

Commentary:

As the Protector of the great souls, *sat-pate*, *Śrī* Krishna is duty bound to clarify issues that pertain to the acquirement of divine approval. When He is not physically present, someone else has to assist others in getting His definitions. If these assistants give wrong explanations, people are misled. This happens frequently. Even persons who hail as pure devotees and who from all appearances seem to be so, are found to be offering incomplete, convenient and sometimes outright contrary definitions. Thus many devotees are misled and then discover that the recommendations had neither the approval of Lord Krishna nor even the support of material nature.

The answers to these pertinent questions of Uddhava, put a check on those who gave advice on Krishna's behalf.

श्री-भगवान् उवाच
अहिंसा सत्यम् अस्तेयम्
असङ्गो ह्रीर् असञ्चयः ।
आस्तिक्यं ब्रह्मचर्यं च
मौनं स्थैर्यं क्षमाभयम् ॥ १४.३३ ॥

śrī-bhagavān uvāca
ahiṁsā satyam asteyam
asaṅgo hrīr asañcayaḥ
āstikyaṁ brahmacaryaṁ ca
maunaṁ sthairyaṁ kṣamābhayam
(14.33)

śrī-bhagavān – the blessed lord; uvāca — said; ahiṁsā — non-injury; satyam — realism; asteyam — non-stealing; asaṅgo = asaṅgaḥ — non-attachment; hrīr = hrīḥ — modesty; asañcayah — non-accumulation of wealth; āstikyam — faith in God; brahmacaryam — celibacy with the pursuit of spirituality; ca — and; maunam — silence; sthairyam — patience; kṣamābhayam = kṣamā — forgiveness; abhayam — fearlessness.

Translation

The Blessed Lord said: Non-injury, realism, non-stealing, non-attachment, modesty, non-accumulation of wealth, faith in God, celibacy with the pursuit of spirituality, silence, patience, forgiveness, fearlessness, (14.33)

Commentary:

These are *Śrī* Krishna's enumeration of moral restraints which is the first step of yoga, that of yama, moral restraints.

शौचं जपस् तपो होमः
श्रद्धातिथ्यं मद्-अर्चनम् ।
तीर्थाटनं परार्थेहा
तुष्टिर् आचार्य-सेवनम् ॥ १४.३४॥

śaucaṁ japas tapo homaḥ
śraddhātithyaṁ mad-arcanam
tīrthāṭanaṁ parārthehā
tuṣṭir ācārya-sevanam (14.34)

śaucam — cleanliness; japas = japah — chanting of holy names; tapo = tapah — austerity; homah — offering of oblations in sacred fire; śraddhātithyaṁ = śraddhā — faith + ātithyam — hospitality; mad-arcanam = mat-arcanam — worship of me; tīrthāṭanam — touring shrines; parārthehā = para – others + artha – the interest + īha — endeavoring; tuṣṭir = tuṣṭiḥ — contentment; ācārya-sevanam — service to the spiritual master.

Translation

Cleanliness, chanting of holy names of God, austerity, offering of oblation in sacred fire, faith, hospitality, worship of Me, touring shrines, endeavoring for the good of others, contentment and service to the spiritual master; (14.34)

Commentary:

This is *Śrī* Krishna's listing of the observances which comprise the second stage of yoga, *niyama*.

एते यमाः स-नियमा
उभयोर् द्वादश स्मृताः ।
पुसाम् उपासितास् तात
यथा-कामं दुहन्ति हि ॥ १४.३५॥

ete yamāḥ sa-niyamā
ubhayor dvādaśa smṛtāḥ
puṁsām upāsitās tāta
yathā-kāmaṁ duhanti hi (14.35)

ete — these; yamāh — moral restraints; sa-niyama = sa-niyamāh — with approved behaviors; ubhayor = ubhayoḥ — each of both; dvādaśa — twelve; smrtāḥ — traditionally approved; puṁsām — by human beings; upāsitās = upāsitāḥ — properly practised; tāta — O friend; yathā-kāmam — according to desire; duhanti — yield results; hi — definitely.

Translation

...these are the moral restraints and approved behaviors. The twelve facets of each, are traditionally approved. O dear friend, if properly practiced by human beings, they definitely yield results according to what is desired. (14.35)

Commentary:

Even though this listing is given, still a devotee should know when to apply one facet and when to use another. The key term is *upāsitās* which means when properly practiced. One should have an advisor in this regard. Or one must have the correct intuition. The advisor must be aware of *Śrī* Krishna's preference at the time of the advisory, otherwise one will get contrary results.

An example of getting an advice from a spiritual master which is inconsistent with what *Śrī* Krishna said may be given from the life of this commentator. I was trained in the disciplic succession which came through *Śrīla Bhaktivedānta Swāmī*, to regard *Śrī Patañjali* Muni as an impersonalist yogi who was not a devotee and whose *Yoga Sūtras* was not to be read or taken seriously. On a careful checking I found that this attitude towards *Śrī Patañjali* and to some others, came about through Bengali influences which seeped into the disciplic succession. This also occurred because of the commentary of various Acharyas in the disciplic succession who were not yogis, who never practiced it and who never intended to but who set out to prove that yoga was useless and harmful to the devotional path.

However by the grace of Lord Baladeva, *Śrī* Krishna's elder brother, I was freed from that bias of the disciplic succession, a bias which is very harmful to those devotees who will need to succeed in yoga for their soul purification. On checking *Śrī Patañjali*, one will find that He is consistent with *Śrī* Krishna in more ways than he is accredited by some authorities in the disciple succession. Here is an example: *Śrī Patañjali* also defines *yama* and *niyama*: Let us see his definitions:

ahiṁsā satya asteya brahmacarya aparigrahāḥ yamāḥ
jāti deśa kāla samaya anavacchinnāḥ sārvabhaumāḥ mahāvratam
śauca santoṣa tapaḥ svādhyāya īśvarapraṇidhānāni niyamāḥ
vitarkabādhane pratipakṣabhāvanam

Non-violence, realism, non-stealing, sexual non-expressiveness which results in the perception of spirituality (brahman) and non possessiveness are the moral restraints.

These moral restraints are not to be adjusted by the status, location, time and condition. They are related to all stages of yoga, being the great commitment;

Purification, contentment, austerity and profound religious meditation on the Supreme Lord are the recommended behaviors.

In the case of the annoyance produced by doubts, one should conceive of what is opposite. (Yoga sutras 2. 30-33)

Ignorant teachers in the disciplic succession have criticize and will continue to carp on *Śrī Patañjali* for listing the profound meditation on the Supreme Lord to be a mere part of the recommended behaviors. But perhaps those authorities are unaware that *Śrī* Krishna listed *mad-arcanam* or worship of Me (of *Śrī* Krishna Himself) as one of the required behaviors. He also listed *japa* as such also. Thus one may free oneself from the prejudices of the succession when such ideas run contrary to what *Śrī* Krishna said.

शमो मन्-निष्ठता बुद्धेर्
दम इन्द्रिय-संयमः ।
तितिक्षा दुःख-सम्मर्षो
जिह्वोपस्थ-जयो धृतिः ॥१४.३६॥

śamo man-niṣṭhatā buddher
dama indriya-saṁyamaḥ
titikṣā duḥkha-sammarṣo
jihvopastha-jayo dhṛtiḥ (14.36)

śamo = śamaḥ — tranquility; man-niṣṭhatā = mat-niṣṭhatā — steady absorption in Me; buddher = buddheḥ — of the intellect; dama = damaḥ — self-control; indriya — senses; saṁyamaḥ — mastership; titikṣā — tolerance; duḥkha — distress; sammarṣo = sammarṣaḥ — bearing; jihvopastha = jihvā — the tongue + upastha — sex impulse; jayo = jayaḥ — perfect control; dhṛtih — steadiness.

Translation

Tranquility is the steady absorption of the intelligence in Me. Self-control is the mastership of the senses. Tolerance is the bearing of distress. Steadiness is the perfect control of the tongue and sex-impulse. (14.36)

Commentary:

Śrī Krishna defined the various terms used. This clarified His meanings. If we take the example of *dhṛtih* or steadiness, a Sanskrit dictionary gives the meaning as taking, holding, possessing, firmness, steadiness, satisfaction and contentment. Thus it would not be easy to know what *Śrī* Krishna meant. Any authority would search his mind for the meaning that he thought suited the definition. Since *Śrī* Krishna gave a definition, He clarified His usage.

How then can one attain perfect control of the tongue and sex impulse? That would be the next question. We do not need a seemingly easy but ineffectual and temporary remedy. In the time of *Śrī* Krishna such mastery of the tongue and sex impulse was achieved by yoga austerities.

Another example is tranquility, which He defined as steady absorption of the intellect in Him, in *Śrī* Krishna. That also is yoga practice for the deliberate focus of the intellect on *Śrī* Krishna, the divine person.

दण्ड-न्यासः पर दानं
काम-त्यागस् तपः स्मृतम् ।
स्वभाव-विजयः शौर्यं
सत्यं च सम-दर्शनम् ॥ १४.३७॥

daṇḍa-nyāsaḥ paraṁ dānaṁ
kāma-tyāgas tapaḥ smṛtam
svabhāva-vijayaḥ śauryaṁ
satyaṁ ca sama-darśanam (14.37)

daṇḍa — aggression; nyāsaḥ — relinguishing; param — highest; dānam — charity; kāma — cravings; tyāgas = tyāgah — abandoning; tapah — austerity; smṛtam — is defined as; svabhāva — one's nature; vijayah — conquest; śauryam — heroism; satyam — realism; ca — and; sama-darśanam — comparatively equal view of the relationship between the spirits and their bodies, and the Supreme Being.

Translation

The highest charity is to relinquish aggression. Austerity is defined as abandoning cravings. Heroism is the conquest of one's nature. Realism is having a comparatively equal view of the relationship between the spirits, their bodies, and the Supreme Being. (14.37)

Commentary:

To relinquish all aggression from one's nature, one has to completely withdraw from the material world. This is defined as *nirvāṇa* in the *Bhagavad-Gītā* (2:72). A person cannot do this while using the lower energies of material nature, even though the aggressive force may exhibit dormancy on lower levels from time to time.

Kriyā yoga dictates that one should be heroic in conquering one's nature, and that one should give up external fights with people and with the environment. The real enemy is discovered during *kriyā* practice, to be within one's nature. A *kriyā* yogin learns how to flex muscles internally to evict the self-destructive forces within.

ऋतम् च सुनृता वाणी
कविभिः परिकीर्तिता ।
कर्मस्व् असङ्गमः शौचं
त्यागः सन्न्यास उच्यते ॥ १४.३८॥

ṛtam ca sunṛtā vāṇī
kavibhiḥ parikīrtitā
karmasv asaṅgamaḥ śaucaṁ
tyāgaḥ sannyāsa ucyate (14.38)

ṛtam — truthfulness; ca — and; sūnṛtā — fine and agreeable; vāṇī — speech; kavibhiḥ — by the realized poets; parikīrtitā — is praised; karmasv = karmasu — in cultural activity; asaṅgamaḥ — non-attachment; śaucam — purity; tyāgaḥ — renunciation of benefits; sannyāsa = sannyāsaḥ — renunciation of cultural oppurtunities; ucyate — is defined as.

Translation

Truthfulness is true and agreeable speech, which is praised by the realized poets. Purity is non-attachment in the performance of cultural activity. Renunciation of cultural oppurtunities is the renunciation of benefits. (14.38)

Commentary:

Here again there are some very strange definitions, such as the one regarding *saucam* or purity. *Saucam* also means cleanliness. *Śrī* Krishna defined this as it pertains to keeping the emotional energies clear of cultural involvements. Was this what *Śrī* Krishna taught Arjuna as the technique for not becoming contaminated while doing *karma* yoga cultural work under His supervision?

Renunciation of opportunities is defined as *sannyāsa* in the *Bhagavad-Gītā* but *tyāgah* is not given the same meaning there. *Śrī* Krishna requested Arjuna to take the route of a *tyāgi* and not to aspire for *sannyāsa*. *Tyāga* was defined in the *Bhagavad Gītā* as being the renunciation of the benefits of actions performed. It was not explained as being the same as *sannyāsa* which was the renunciation of the duties along with whatever benefits they yield.

Here however *Śrī* Krishna lists *tyāga* and *sannyāsa* as the same. This might appear to be an ambiguity. However, it is not. It is simply that *tyāga* is the preliminary stage of renunciation and *sannyāsa* is the completion of it. *Tyāga* if performed correctly, would in the course of time develop into *sannyāsa*. And *sannyāsa* if it is relaxed, would digress into *tyāga*.

धर्म इष्टं धनं नृणां
यज्ञो ऽहं भगवत्तमः ।
दक्षिणा ज्ञान-सन्देशः
प्राणायामः परं बलम् ॥ १४.३९ ॥

dharma iṣṭaṁ dhanaṁ nṝṇāṁ
yajño 'haṁ bhagavattamaḥ
dakṣiṇā jñāna-sandeśaḥ
prāṇāyāmaḥ paraṁ balam (14.39)

dharma — righteous duty; iṣṭam — desirable; dhanam — wealth; nṝṇām — for human beings; yajño = yajñaḥ — religious ceremony and discipline; 'ham = aham — I; bhagavattamaḥ — supreme lord; dakṣiṇā — teacher's fee; jñāna – knowledge; sandeśaḥ — instruction; prāṇāyāmaḥ — control of vital energy by breath exercises; param — highest; balam — strength.

Translation

Righteous duty is that desirable wealth of human beings. I, the Supreme Lord am the religious ceremony and discipline. The instruction of knowledge is the teacher's fee. The highest strength is the control of the vital energy. (14.39)

Commentary:

Here we get some strange definitions, such as the one concerning righteous duty. It means that *Śrī* Krishna regards His approval of such acts as being like funds for the living entities. In the *Bhagavad-Gītā* also He identified Himself with religious ceremony and the related disciplines. Here He said that teaching what one learnt from a spiritual master is the real fee to be paid to the teacher.

भगो म ऐश्वरो भावो
लाभो मद्-भक्तिर् उत्तमः ।
विद्यात्मनि भिदा-बाधो
जुगुप्सा ह्रीर् अकर्मसु ॥ १४.४० ॥

bhago ma aiśvaro bhāvo
lābho mad-bhaktir uttamaḥ
vidyātmani bhidā-bādho
jugupsā hrīr akarmasu (14.40)

bhago = bhagaḥ — fortune; me — my; aiśvaro = aiśvarah — lordship; bhāvo = bhāvaḥ — nature; lābho = lābhaḥ — profit; mad-bhaktir = mat-bhaktih — devotion to me; uttamaḥ — greatest; vidyātmani = vidyā — technique + ātmani — in the self; bhidā-bādho = bhidā-bādhaḥ = bhidā — the idea of multiplicity + bādhaḥ — removal; jugupsā — abhorence; hrīr = hrīḥ — modesty; akarmasu — in irreligious activities.

Translation

Fortune is lordship which is My very nature. The greatest profit is devotion to Me. Technique is the removal of the idea of multiplicity in the self. Modesty is abhorence of doing irreligious activities. (14.40)

Commentary:

Śrī Krishna lists devotion to Himself as the greatest profit. This is because one can make the most advancement by getting a devotional relationship with Him. Arjuna asked a question about those yogis who are devoted to *Śrī* Krishna and the others who cherish the imperishable invisible existence. He wanted to know which of the two types of yogis have the highest yoga techniques. But *Śrī* Krishna explained that the yogi devotees are the most discipline. Those who cherish the imperishable, indefinable, invisible, all pervading, inconceivable, unchanging, immovable and constant reality, also attain Him, even though their mental exertion is greater, and they reach the goal with much difficulty. Because they take little assistance from the Supreme Being, they have to exert themselves in a much greater way.

Śrī Krishna defined modesty as being timid towards irreligious activities. One does this by instinct or by knowing fully well that one will not gain by immoral activity. The technique for the removal of the idea of multiplicity, is acquired by introspection in the higher stages of yoga.

A man who does not practice yoga and who does not surcharge his subtle body by *prāṇāyāma*, may also feel that there is no multiplicity, but that is a false feeling for there is multiplicity in terms of the distinction between the life force, the *buddhi* intellect organ and the sense of identity. There is also the compartmental space which is the causal body. This space is filled with charged subtle energy. There is the spirit which predominates over the body, whose energy is the main driving force for the psychology. These are distinct as seen by the yogi in meditations when his mystic perception is clarified.

However these energies are traced to the primal material energy, the *mahat tattva*. A yogi traces this in *samādhi*. Others cannot trace it, but they can believe Lord Krishna's or a great yogi's description of it.

श्रीर् गुणा नैरपेक्ष्याद्याः
सुखं दुःख-सुखात्ययः ।
दुःखं काम-सुखापेक्षा
पण्डितो बन्ध-मोक्ष-वित् ॥ १४.४१ ॥

śrīr guṇā nairapekṣyādyāḥ
sukhaṁ duḥkha-sukhātyayaḥ
duḥkhaṁ kāma-sukhāpekṣā
paṇḍito bandha-mokṣa-vit (14.41)

śrīr = śrīḥ — beauty; guṇā = guṇāḥ — virtue, qualities; nairapekṣyādyāḥ = nairapekṣya — dispassion + ādyāḥ — and the related factors; sukham — happiness; duḥkha — a pain; sukhātyayaḥ = sukha — pleasure + atyayah — transcending; duḥkham — misery; kāma-sukhāpekṣā — sense pleasure; paṇḍito = paṇḍitaḥ — a proficient priest or teacher; bandha — bondage; mokṣa — liberation; vit — one who can distinguish.

Translation:

Beauty is dispassion and other virtues. Happiness is transcending pleasure and pain. Misery is yearning for sense pleasure. A proficient priest or teacher is one who can distinguish between bondage and liberation. (14.41)

Commentary:

Some very strange definitions are given by *Śrī* Krishna, such as beauty being dispassion and related virtues. Even in the Krishna Conscious societies, in which I received training, I never heard any of the teachers say that beauty is dispassion. They have all said that beauty is the Krishna *Mūrti* form on the altar. Here however *Śrī* Krishna gave a definition which is needed by the yogi devotees who aspire for spiritual perfection. *Nairapekṣa* is indifference towards everything. This is supreme dispassion which is also known as *paravairāgya*. I was introduced to the practice of this by *Śrīla Yogeśwarānanda Yogīrāj*. He showed me that if one does not attain this, on cannot attain *samādhi*, because otherwise the sensual energies will not withdraw from this world completely.

In the eyes of the Supreme Being, a person who has withdrawn his interest from this world, has got the beauty. In the Vaishnava societies, happiness was never described to me as being the transcendence of pleasure and pain. In fact their idea is that one should get happiness from Krishna consciousness as it is taught by them. Here however we get another definition, which suits the yoga practice of complete internalization, the complete removal from the pleasure and pain which is pursued by and experienced by the intellect and life force of the psyche. This causes the yogi to advance into the 6th stage of yoga, that of *dhāraṇā* linking of his attention with higher concentration energies.

These definitions are very useful for yogi devotees who turn away from the material world in all its shapes or forms, sanctified or unsanctified.

मूर्खो देहाद्य्-अहं-बुद्धिः
पन्था मन्-निगमः स्मृतः ।
उत्पथश् चित्त-विक्षेपः
स्वर्गः सत्त्व-गुणोदयः ॥ १४.४२ ॥

mūrkho dehādy-ahaṁ-buddhiḥ
panthā man-nigamaḥ smṛtaḥ
utpathaś citta-vikṣepaḥ
svargaḥ sattva-guṇodayaḥ (14.42)

murkho = murkhah — a fool; dehādy = dehādi — the body and what is related to it; aham – I-identity; buddhiḥ — intellect; panthā = panthāḥ — path; man-nigamaḥ = mat-nigamaḥ — leading to me; smṛtaḥ — is defined; utpathaś = utpathaḥ — wrong path; citta — mental and emotional energy; vikṣepaḥ — distraction; svargaḥ — heavenly world; sattva – clarifying; guṇodayaḥ = guna — influence + udayah — predominance.

Translation

A fool is a person who identifies himself as being the intellect, the sense of initiative to act in the body and what is related to it. The path is that which leads to Me. The wrong path is the distraction which utilizes the mental and emotional energy. The heavenly world is the predominance of the clarifying force. (14.42)

Commentary:

These again are some strange definitions, which require careful study by a yogin. We can derive great impetus to practice by studying the meanings.

नरकस् तम-उन्नाहो
बन्धुर् गुरुर् अहं सखे ।
गृहं शरीरं मानुष्यं
गुणाढ्यो ह्य् आढ्य उच्यते ॥ १४.४३ ॥

narakas tama-unnāho
bandhur gurur ahaṁ sakhe
gṛhaṁ śarīraṁ mānuṣyaṁ
guṇāḍhyo hy āḍhya ucyate (14.43)

narakas = narakah — hell; tama — depressive mode; unnāho = unnāhaḥ — predominance; bandhuh — real friend; gurur = guruh — spiritual master; aham — I; sakhe — O friend; gṛham — home; śarīram — body; mānuṣyam — pertaining to a human being; guṇāḍhyo = guna — virtue + āḍhyaḥ — good; hy = hi — indeed; ādhya = ādhyaḥ — one who is wealthy; ucyate — is defined.

Translation

Hell is the predominance of the retardative mode. O friend, I am represented by the spiritual master, the true friend. The human body is the home. He indeed is wealthy who has good qualities. (14.43)

Commentary:

Some important *kriyā* yoga concepts are explained in this verse, especially the meaning of home as the human body. In the *Bhagavad-Gītā Śrī* Krishna used the word *kṣetra* for the internal environment of the gross, subtle and causal forms:

śrībhagavānuvāca
idaṁ śarīraṁ kaunteya kṣetramityabhidhīyate
etadyo vetti taṁ prāhuḥ kṣetrajña iti tadvidaḥ

The Blessed Lord said: This, the earthly body, O son of Kuntī, is called the living space. Those who are knowledgeable of this, declare the person who understands this to be the experiencer of the living space. (B.G. 13.2)

In *kriyā* yoga, hell is not a place where one suffers, even though there are such places in reality. It is considered to be a condition when the living entities are dominated or influenced by the depressive energies of material nature. Someone is considered to be wealthy, not if he has money but if he has trustworthy character. And the spiritual master, in so far as he represents *Śrī* Krishna is realized as being the true friend, who gives long-ranged advisories for attainment of spiritual perfection.

दरिद्रो यस् त्व् असन्तुष्टः
कृपणो यो ऽजितेन्द्रियः ।
गुणेष्व् असक्त-धीर् ईशो
गुण-सङ्गो विपर्ययः ॥ १४.४४॥

daridro yas tv asantuṣṭaḥ
kṛpaṇo yo 'jitendriyaḥ
guṇeṣv asakta-dhīr īśo
guṇa-saṅgo viparyayaḥ (14.44)

daridro = daridraḥ — pauper; yas = yah — who; tv = tu — but; asantuṣṭaḥ — contented; kṛpaṇo = kṛpaṇaḥ — a miserly person; yo = yah — who; 'jitendriyaḥ = ajitendriyah — not mastered; guṇeṣv = guṇeṣu — in the mundane objects; asakta — not attached; dhīr = dhīḥ — intellect; īśo = īśah — master; guṇa — mundane emotion; saṅgo = saṅgaḥ — attaches; viparyayaḥ — opposite.

Translation

But one who is discontent is a pauper. One who has not mastered his senses is a miser. One who is not attached to the mundane objects is a master. One whose intellect is attached to the mundane emotions is the opposite of a master. (14.44)

Commentary:

These definitions serve the purpose of *kriyā* yoga. These cause a person to take a look internally to reform and perfect the psyche.

एत उद्धव ते प्रश्नाः
सर्वे साधु निरूपिताः ।
किं वर्णितेन बहुना
लक्षणं गुण-दोषयोः ।
गुण-दोष-दृशिर् दोषो
गुणस् तूभय-वर्जितः ॥ १४.४५॥

eta uddhava te praśnāḥ
sarve sādhu nirūpitāḥ
kiṁ varṇitena bahunā
lakṣaṇaṁ guṇa-doṣayoḥ
guṇa-doṣa-dṛśir doṣo
guṇas tūbhaya-varjitaḥ (14.45)

eta = ete — these; uddhava — Uddhava; te — to you, your; prasnah — questions; sarve — all; sādhu — fully; nirūpitāḥ — defined; kim — what use; varṇitena — elaborating; bahunā — variously, with many details; lakṣaṇam — characteristics; guṇa-dosayoh — merits and demerits; guna – good feature; dosa — bad feature; dṛśir = dṛśiḥ — discerning; doṣo = doṣaḥ — defect; guṇas = guṇaḥ — virtuous; tūbhaya = tu — indeed + ubhaya — both of them; varjitaḥ — to be removed.

Translation

O Uddhava, all these questions of yours are fully defined. What is the use of elaborating with many details on the characteristics of merits and demerits? It is a defect to even distinguish between a good feature and a bad one. Indeed it is virtuous to be removed from both of them. (14.45)

Commentary:

Uddhava asked for details of a righteous life style, through which a man who could not do the yoga austerities, could gain the association of the Supreme.

Śrī Krishna however did not like the query. Even though He answered the questions, He criticized Uddhava, stating that it is a defect to distinguish between a good and bad feature. That attitude is usually based on a result-oriented demeanor which stifles the devotee and stagnates progression.

CHAPTER 15*

Three Applications of Yoga Discipline**

Terri Stokes-Pineda Art

śrī-bhagavān uvāca
yogās trayo mayā proktā nṝṇām śreyo-vidhitsayā
jñānam karma ca bhaktiś ca nopāyo 'nyo 'sti kutracit

Desiring to give perfection of the human being, three applications of yoga discipline were taught by me, namely the application to thinking experience, the application to physical experience and the application to emotions. Besides these, there is no other method whatsoever. (Uddhava Gītā 15.6)

* Śrīmad Bhāgavatam Canto 11, Chapter 20
** Translator's selected chapter title.

श्री-उद्धव उवाच
विधिश् च प्रतिषेधश् च
निगमो हीश्वरस्य ते ।
अवेक्षते ऽरविण्डाक्ष
गुणं दोषं च कर्मणाम् ॥ १५.१ ॥

śrī-uddhava uvāca
vidhiś ca pratiṣedhaś ca
nigamo hīśvarasya te
avekṣate 'raviṇḍākṣa
guṇaṁ doṣaṁ ca karmaṇām (15.1)

śrī-uddhava – the deserving Uddhava; uvāca — said; vidhiś = vidhiḥ — approved conduct; ca — and; pratiṣedhaś = pratiṣedhah — prohibited actions; ca — and; nigamo = nigamaḥ — Vedas; hīśvarasya = hi — indeed + īśvarasya — of the Lord; te — of you; avekṣate — reveals, shows, points out; 'raviṇḍākṣa = araviṇḍākṣa — lotus eyed; guṇam — assets; doṣam — faults; ca — and; karmaṇām — of activities.

Translation

The deserving Uddhava said: The Vedas is Your scripture, O Lotus-eyed Lord. It reveals approved conduct and prohibited actions, showing assets and faults of activities. (15.1)

Commentary:

Since *Śrī* Krishna minimized the inquiry made in the last chapter, Uddhava presented a counter-argument. *Śrī* Uddhava points out that these subjects were considered important in the Veda. Why is it that *Śrī* Krishna minimized these subject matters which defined right and wrong activities?

वर्णाश्रम-विकल्पं च
प्रतिलोमानुलोमजम् ।
द्रव्य-देश-वयः-कालान्
स्वर्गं नरकम् एव च ॥ १५.२ ॥

varṇāśrama-vikalpaṁ ca
pratilomānulomajam
dravya-deśa-vayaḥ-kālān
svargaṁ narakam eva ca (15.2)

varnāśrama — work tendency and life style; vikalpam — types; ca — and; pratilomānulomajam = pratiloma — high class mother and low class father + anuloma – high class father and low class mother + jam — birth; dravya — material; deśa — place; vayaḥ — age; kālān — time; svargam — heaven hereafter; narakam — hell hereafter; eva — as well as; ca — and.

Translation

It shows the type of work tendency and life style, the births through a high class mother and a low class father or through a high class father and a low class mother. It points out the material, place, age and time, as well as the heavenly or hellish destinations in the hereafter. (15.2)

Commentary:

Uddhava wanted clarification. Even though to *Śrī* Krishna this information concerned the social interactions, still Uddhava thought that it was important in facilitating the righteous methods of lifestyle.

Uddhava felt that a person's social life had much to do with his religious and spiritual bearing. If there is clarification of what is right or wrong and what is conducive to spiritual realization and what is not, then more human beings would become devotees of *Śrī* Krishna and would, by that relationship, have the opportunity for perfection.

गुण-दोष-भिदा-दृष्टिम्
अन्तरेण वचस् तव ।
निःश्रेयसं कथं
नृणां निषेध-विधि-लक्षणम् ॥ १५.३ ॥

guṇa-doṣa-bhidā-dṛṣṭim
antareṇa vacas tava
niḥśreyasaṁ kathaṁ
nṝṇāṁ niṣedha-vidhi-lakṣaṇam (15.3)

guṇa — virtues; doṣa — faults; bhidā — difference; dṛṣṭim — seeing, perceiving; antareṇa — without; vacas = vacaḥ — instructions; tava — your; niḥśreyasam — that which yields liberation; katham — how; nṛṇām — for humanity; niṣedha — prohibited activity; vidhi — approved conduct; lakṣaṇam — marking off.

Translation

Without perceiving the difference between virtues and faults, how can your instructions which mark-off the prohibited activities, from the approved conducts, yield liberation for humanity? (15.3)

Commentary:

This is a very good question. Practically speaking, no matter what God knows, an explanation in detail would be required by other persons who are not that conversant with spiritual life. They would not be able to determine the intricacies of action.

पितृ-देव-मनुष्यानां
वेदश् चक्षुस् तवेश्वर ।
श्रेयस् त्व् अनुपलब्धे ऽर्थे
साध्य-साधनयोर् अपि ॥ १५.४॥

pitṛ-deva-manuṣyānāṁ
vedaś cakṣus taveśvara
śreyas tv anupalabdhe 'rthe
sādhya-sādhanayor api (15.4)

pitṛ — departed relatives; deva — supernatural rulers; manuṣyānām — for humanity; vedaś = Vedas; cakṣus = cakṣuḥ — revelation; taveśvara = tava — your + īśvara — Lord; śreyas = śreyah — highest; tv = tu — but; anupalabdhe — in that which is imperceptible; 'rthe = arthe — in the objective; sādhya – the result accomplished; sādhanayor = sādhanayoḥ — of the method; api — as well as.

Translation

For the departed relatives, the supernatural rulers and humanity, the Vedas is Your best revelation in terms of the imperceptible objectives, as well as the methods and results accomplished. (15.4)

Commentary:

This is an appraisal of the value and service rendered by the Vedas up to the time of Uddhava. The Vedas rendered tremendous service for in it, the human beings got standards of conducts; a set of values regarding what was right or wrong. They got indications about the Supreme Being and how to get in touch with Him.

Uddhava made a statement to the effect that even the departed relatives in the hereafter as well as the supernatural rulers in the subtle world, and humanity, did up to that point, get much from the Vedas for spiritual and material well-being.

Śrī Uddhava in raising these points, made it clear that the Vedas contributed to the progress of human society. It should not be ridiculed. *Śrī* Krishna in the *Bhagavad-Gītā* gave a low profile to the Vedas. It appears that Uddhava objected to Krishna's appraisal of the Vedas.

गुण-दोष-भिदा-दृष्टिर्
निगमात् ते न हि स्वतः ।
निगमेनापवादश् च
भिदाया इति ह भ्रमः ॥ १५.५॥

guṇa-doṣa-bhidā-dṛṣṭir
nigamāt te na hi svataḥ
nigamenāpavādaś ca
bhidāyā iti ha bhramaḥ (15.5)

guṇa — virtues; doṣa — sins; bhidā — distinguishing; dṛṣṭir = dṛṣṭiḥ — that which is ascertained; nigamāt — by studying the Vedas; te — your; na — not; hi — indeed; svataḥ — by natural tendency; nigamenāpavādas = nigamena — by a new instruction + apavādah — refutation; ca — and; bhidāyā — of distinction; iti — thus stated; ha — quite; bhramah — confusion.

Translation

Sin is ascertained by studying Your Vedas and not by natural tendency. And thus, by a new instruction, you propose the refutation of the Vedas. This is quite confusing. (15.5)

Commentary:

Evidence of Lord Krishna's refutation of the Vedas is given in the *Bhagavad-Gītā*. In that text, *Śrī* Krishna also highly appraised and identified with the Vedas. Uddhava raised a good point. Here are some of the verses from the *Bhagavad-Gītā*.

yāmimāṁ puṣpitāṁ vācaṁ pravadantyavipaścitaḥ
vedavādaratāḥ pārtha nānyadastīti vādinaḥ (2.42)

This is poetic quotation which the ignorant reciters proclaim, O son of Pṛthā. Enjoying the Vedic verses, they say there is no other written authority. (B.G. 2.42)

traiguṇyaviṣayā vedā nistraiguṇyo bhavārjuna
nirdvaṁdvo nityasattvastho niryogakṣema ātmavān
yāvānartha udapāne sarvataḥ saṁplutodake
tāvānsarveṣu vedeṣu brāhmaṇasya vijānataḥ

Three moody phases are offered by the Vedas. Be without the three modes, O Arjuna. Be without the moody fluctuations. Be always anchored to reality. Be free from grasping and possessiveness.

For as much importance as there is in a well when suitable water flows in all directions, so much worth is in the entire Vedas for a perceptive brahmin. (25.45-46)

karma brahmodbhavaṁ viddhi brahmākṣarasamudbhavam
tasmātsarvagataṁ brahma nityaṁ yajñe pratiṣṭhitam

Cultural activity is produced from the Personified Veda. The Personified Veda comes from the unaffected Supreme Spirit. Hence the all-pervading Supreme Spirit is always situated in prescribed austerity and religious ceremony. (B.G. 3.15)

pitāhamasya jagato mātā dhātā pitāmahaḥ
vedyaṁ pavitramoṁkāra ṛksāma yajureva ca

I am the father of this universe, the mother, the creator, the grandfather, the subject of education, the purifier, the sacred syllable Oṁ, the Rig, Sāma, and Yajur Vedas. (B.G. 9.17)

vedānāṁ sāmavedo'smi devānāmasmi vāsavaḥ
indriyāṇāṁ manaścāsmi bhūtānāmasmi cetanā

Of the Vedas, I am represented by the Sāma Veda. Of the supernatural rulers, I am represented as Vāsava Indra. Of the senses, I am represented as the mind. In creature forms, I am represented as consciousness. (B.G. 10.22)

bṛhatsāma tathā sāmnāṁ gāyatrī chandasāmaham
māsānāṁ mārgaśīrṣo'ham ṛtūnāṁ kusumākaraḥ

Of the Sāma Veda chants, the Brihat Sāma melody represents Me. Of the poetic hymns, I am the Gāyatrī. Of months, I am best represented by the November-December lunar month. Of the seasons, I am best compared to Spring. (B.G. 10.35)

We know for certain that this Krishna who spoke to Arjuna was the same person who later instructed Uddhava, because the advisories are consistent in that respect. *Śrī* Krishna's baffling explanations occur in each of the discourses.

श्री-भगवान् उवाच
योगास् त्रयो मया प्रोक्ता
नृणां श्रेयो-विधित्सया ।
ज्ञानं कर्म च भक्तिश् च
नोपायो ऽन्यो ऽस्ति कुत्रचित् ॥ १५.६ ॥

śrī-bhagavān uvāca
yogās trayo mayā proktā
nṝṇāṁ śreyo-vidhitsayā
jñānaṁ karma ca bhaktiś ca
nopāyo 'nyo 'sti kutracit (15.6)

śrī-bhagavān – the blessed lord; uvāca — said; yogās = yogāḥ — application of yoga disciplines; trayo = trayaḥ — three; mayā — by me; proktā = proktāḥ — was taught; nṛṇām — of human beings; śreyo = śreyaḥ — perfection; vidhitsayā — desiring to give; jñānam — thinking experience; karma — physical experience; ca — and; bhaktis = bhaktiḥ — emotional experience; ca — and; nopāyo = na — no + upayah — method; 'nyo = anyah — other; 'sti = asti — is; kutracit — whatsoever.

Translation:

The Blessed Lord said: Desiring to give perfection of the human being, three applications of yoga discipline were taught by me, namely the application to thinking experience, the application to physical experience and the application to emotions. Besides these, there is no other method whatsoever. (15.6)

Commentary:

In a very direct and tactful way, *Śrī* Krishna indicated that whatever was stated in the Vedas which did not center on yoga practice, in its three-fold application, was of little value in terms of getting the perfection for the human beings.

In so far as the Vedas endorsed cultural life as an end in itself, *Śrī* Krishna distanced Himself from it, even though He said that He was the author of the Vedas and the *Vedānta.*

sarvasya cāhaṁ hṛdi saṁniviṣṭo mattaḥ smṛtirjñānam apohanaṁ ca
vedaiśca sarvairahameva vedyo vedāntakṛdvedavideva cāham

And I entered the central psyche of all beings. From Me comes memory, knowledge and reasoning. By all the Vedas, I am to be known. I am the author of Vedānta and the knower of the Vedas. (B.G. 15.15)

Basically speaking *Śrī* Krishna disavowed whatever is stated in the Vedas which does not concern yoga and its application to thinking experience, physical experience and emotional interplay.

निर्विण्णानां ज्ञान-योगो
न्यासिनाम् इह कर्मसु ।
तेष्व् अनिर्विण्ण-चित्तानां
कर्म-योगस् तु कामिनाम् ॥ १५.७॥

nirviṇṇānāṁ jñāna-yogo
nyāsinām iha karmasu
teṣv anirviṇṇa-cittānāṁ
karma-yogas tu kāminām (15.7)

nirviṇṇānām — for those who are disgusted; jñāna-yogo = jñāna-yogah — the yoga application to thinking experience; nyāsinām — for those who renounce cultural oppurtunities; iha — here, in reference; karmasu — in cultural activities; teṣv = teṣu — those; anirviṇṇa — those who are not disgusted; cittānām — for those who are attached to the mental and emotional energy; *karma*-yogas = karma-yogah — yoga application to physical experience; tu — but; kāminām — for those who crave the pleasure derived from cultural interactions.

Translation

In reference, the application of yoga to thinking experience is for those who are disgusted with cultural activities and have renounced those opportunities. But for those who are not disgusted, who are attached to the mental and emotional energy, who crave the pleasures derived from cultural interactions, the yoga application to physical experience is prescribed. (15.7)

Commentary:

The path of *bhakti* yoga is different from the path of *bhakti* by itself. *Bhakti* yoga is the most difficult path to take up and one can only do it after one passed through either of the paths listed in this verse. However *bhakti* by itself is very easy to practice. The confusion occurs because many of the spiritual masters in the authorized disciplic succession define *bhakti* as *bhakti* yoga. They interchange the terms so that the word yoga in the compound Sanskrit word, *bhakti*yoga, has absolutely no meaning in terms of the eightfold yoga process. The original *bhakti* yoga is not the same as the modern explanation of it which is *bhakti* without yoga. The modern usage is actually the preliminary steps for taking the path of *karma* yoga. But for some reason, due to a twist of time it is advocated and accepted as *bhakti* yoga. It is actually a shadow of the real *bhakti* yoga, which will be described in the next verse.

Śrī Krishna already made it clear to Uddhava that the easy path for the common people was the path of adoption of a righteous life style, *dharma*, on the basis of their work tendencies *(varṇa)* and the related life styles (āśrama).

For a common man, the emotional experiences are funneled through and sponsored by social interaction, which is *karma*, but an intellectual person uses an additional avenue which is analysis. The intellectual specializes in using the ideation energy of the mind as a cultural environment. He conceptualizes or is inspired from within the mind. Thus the two paths are available in yoga, either to use the austerities to figure life in the social field or to use it in the intellectual mind-space.

There is an idea that a person can stop applying his emotional needs and expressions to the social interactions and instead substitute Lord Krishna and His incarnations, but actually this cannot be done in fact. The reason is this: *Śrī* Krishna and His incarnations in the spiritual environment cannot be reached by low-level emotions. It is impossible. Even for Arjuna, his low-level feelings of depression were rejected by Lord Krishna, even though he was a dear friend of the Lord. Arjuna had to bring himself to order to perform *karma* yoga, so that he could serve in the cultural field under *Śrī* Krishna's direction.

Of the two paths, namely *jñāna* yoga and *karma* yoga, *jñāna* yoga is the highest. It is for people who became disgusted with cultural life, and who took steps to renounce these. Those who still crave the pleasures derived from cultural involvement can use the *karma* yoga process and by that, they would develop an attachment to *Śrī* Krishna. That however, depends on the condition that they work under the direction of the Universal Form, in a responsible cultural life as He dictates. It is not merely what their guru says, because if at any time their Guru is off-key, their actions will offend the Universal Form.

यदृच्छया मत्-कथादौ
जात-श्रद्धस् तु यः पुमान् ।
न निर्विण्णो नाति-सक्तो
भक्ति-योगो ऽस्य सिद्धि-दः ॥ १५.८॥

yadṛcchayā mat-kathādau
jāta-śraddhas tu yaḥ pumān
na nirviṇṇo nāti-sakto
bhakti-yogo 'sya siddhi-daḥ (15.8)

yadṛcchayā — if somehow; mat-kathādau = mat-kathā – stories about me + ādau — and other ways; jāta — develops; śraddhaḥ — faith; tu — but; yah — who; pumān — person; na — not; nirviṇṇo = nirviṇṇaḥ — disgusted; nati-sakto = na — not + ati-saktaḥ — very attracted; bhakti-yoga = bhakti-yogaḥ — application of yoga discipline to emotional experience; 'sya = asya — of him; siddhi-daḥ — that which will give perfection.

Translation

If somehow, a person develops faith in stories about Me, and is attracted to Me by other ways, but is not disgusted with cultural life, and is not very attached to it either, then the application of yoga disciplines to emotional experience will give that person perfection of life. (15.8)

Commentary:

This is a very interesting statement which gives us much clarification about the yogically-disciplined devotional path.

Some persons are neither completely disgusted with cultural life nor fully attached to it. By nature they are in their response to cultural life, neither abhorrent of it nor very attracted to it, These people are recommended to that the path of *bhakti* yoga.

For such a person to use *bhakti* yoga as it may be applied to Lord Krishna specifically and not to some other divine or supernatural person, he or she must develop faith in stories about *Śrī* Krishna or be attracted to Him in an approved way.

तावत् कर्माणि कुर्वीत
न निर्विद्येत यावता ।
मत्-कथा-श्रवणादौ वा
॥ श्रद्धा यावन् न जायते ॥ १५.९॥

tāvat karmāṇi kurvīta
na nirvidyeta yāvatā
mat-kathā-śravaṇādau vā
śraddhā yāvan na jāyate (15.9)

tāvat — until; karmāṇi — cultural activities; kurvīta — one should perform; na – not; nirvidyeta — becomes dissatisfied; yāvatā — as long as; mat-kathā — true stories about me; śravaṇādau = śravaṇa – hearing + ādau — and related methods; vā — or; śraddhā — faith, confidence; yāvan = yāvat — as long; na — not; jāyate — has developed.

Translation

One should perform cultural activities, until one becomes dissatisfied with it or until one developes confidence in hearing true stories about Me or any related method of contacting Me. (15.9)

Commentary:

This applies to those who are not disgusted with cultural life. Those persons should keep on acting and being interested in the world, until they have had their fill of it, to the point of disgust or until they develop confidence in *Śrī* Krishna by hearing of His activities or by some other approved way of making contact with His character and glories.

For those who would keep acting in the material world, they were advisories given in chapter 12 of the *Bhagavad-Gītā*, and in this discourse with Uddhava.

स्व-धर्म-स्थो यजन् यज्ञैर्
अनाशीः-काम उद्धव ।
न याति स्वर्ग-नरकौ
यद्य् अन्यन् न समाचरेत् ॥ १५.१०॥

sva-dharma-stho yajan yajñair
anāśīḥ-kāma uddhava
na yāti svarga-narakau
yady anyan na samācaret (15.10)

sva – his own; dharma — righteous duty; stho = sthah — routinely performs, steadily performs; yajan — religiously executes; yajñair = yajñaiḥ — by worship ceremonies and disciplines; anāśīh – no benefits; kāma = kāmaḥ — desiring; uddhava — Uddhava; na — not; yāti — go; svarga — heaven hereafter; narakau — hell hereafter; yadi — if; anyan = anyat — other; na — not; samācaret — should perform.

Translation

O Uddhava, a person who routinely performs his righteous duty and religiously executes ceremonies and related disciplines, while desiring no benefits, goes neither to heaven or hell hereafter, if he does not perform other contrary actions. (15.10)

Commentary:

Then what happens to that person, does he automatically go to the kingdom of God? Does he have to practice other austerities before his spirit would be manifested in God's world.

अस्मिल् लोके वर्तमानः
स्व-धर्म-स्थो ऽनघः शुचिः ।
ज्ञानं विशुद्धम् आप्नोति
मद्-भक्तिं वा यदृच्छया ॥ १५.११॥

asmiṁl loke vartamānaḥ
sva-dharma-stho 'naghaḥ śuciḥ
jñānaṁ viśuddham āpnoti
mad-bhaktiṁ vā yadṛcchayā (15.11)

asmin — in this; loke — in the world; vartamānaḥ — while being in a perishable body; sva-dharma-stho = sva-dharma-sthaḥ — routinely performing his righteous duty; 'naghaḥ = anaghah — sinless; śuciḥ — pure; jñānam — knowledge; viśuddham — divine; āpnoti — obtains; mad-bhaktim = mat-bhaktim — devotion to me; vā — or; yadṛcchayā — as destined.

Translation

While being in a perishable body in this world, routinely performing righteous duty, and being sinless and pure, he obtains divine knowledge or as destined he gets devotion to Me. (15.11)

Commentary:

This person has a long course to take; either to become sinless and pure over a period of lives of routinely and consistently performing righteous duty and then getting the divine information, which motivates him to make an all-out effort to relocate to the spiritual atmosphere; or as destined, by sheer divine good luck, he may just get devotion to Krishna, which is such a strong feeling that it motivates him to give up everything else and to do whatever is necessary to gain the transcendental association of the Lord.

One should make a careful study of the term *yadṛccchaya*, which means accidentally or by chance. Such a thing does not apply to every human being.

स्वर्गिणो ऽप्य् एतम् इच्छन्ति
लोकं निरयिणस् तथा ।
साधकं ज्ञान-भक्तिभ्याम्
उभयं तद्-असाधकम् ॥ १५.१२ ॥

svargiṇo 'py etam icchanti
lokaṁ nirayiṇas tathā
sādhakaṁ jñāna-bhaktibhyām
ubhayaṁ tad-asādhakam (15.12)

svargiṇo = svargiṇaḥ — residents of heaven in the hereafter; 'py = api — even; etam — this; icchanti — desire; lokam — world; nirayiṇas = nirayiṇah — residents of hell in the hereafter; tathā — so; sādhakam — that which yeilds achievements; jñāna – thinking experience; bhaktibhyām — of emotional experience; ubhayam — both; tad = tat — that; asādhakam — that which is incapable of yielding achievement.

Translation

The residents of heaven and those of hell hereafter, desire this world which yields the achievement of thinking and emotional experiences. Both heaven and hell are locations which are in incapable of yielding an achievement. (15.12)

Commentary:

This could be one motivation for those persons who do not have the divine luck described in the previous verse, that of getting devotion to *Śrī* Krishna. They may develop disgust with their inability to use this world to attain liberation. Even though the heavenly worlds and the hells hereafter give experiences, which are due on the basis of pious and impious activities performed on earth, those dimensions do not afford achievements. When a person is released or chased away from either heaven or hell, he or she has to generate more piety or impiety by getting an opportunity to live on an earthly planet.

The earths are designed in such a way as to allow persons to access the worth of physical, emotional and thinking experiences.

न नरः स्वर्-गतिं काङ्क्षेन्
नारकीं वा विचक्षणः ।
नेमं लोकं च काङ्क्षेत
देहावेशात् प्रमाद्यति ॥ १५.१३ ॥

na naraḥ svar-gatiṁ kāṅkṣen
nārakīṁ vā vicakṣaṇaḥ
nemaṁ lokaṁ ca kāṅkṣeta
dehāveśāt pramādyati (15.13)

na — neither; naraḥ — a human being; svar – heaven; gatim — course; kāṅkṣen = kāṅkṣet —

should pursue; nārakīm — hell; vā — or; vicakṣaṇaḥ — a wise man; nemam = na — nor + imam — this; lokam — world; ca — and; kāṅkṣeta — should desire; dehāveśāt = deha — body + āveśāt — from dwelling on; pramādyati — is bewitched.

Translation

A wise human being should pursue neither the course of heaven nor that of hell. And he should not desire this world either, for here he is bewitched from the habit of dwelling in a body. (15.13)

Commentary:

Even though living in this world has the advantage of causing a disgust for the whole range of material existence, still we should not desire to be perpetually reborn here. One should aspire for complete liberation. A living being is repeatedly bewitched because of the habit of dwelling in a body, particularly dwelling in a subtle form. Therefore a yogi tries to eliminate his subtle material form, since it impulsively sponsors future transmigrations.

एतद् विद्वान् पुरा मृत्योर्
अभवाय घटेत सः ।
अप्रमत्त इदं ज्ञात्वा
मर्त्यम् अप्य् अर्थ-सिद्धि-दम् ॥ १५.१४॥

etad vidvān purā mṛtyor
abhavāya ghaṭeta saḥ
apramatta idaṁ jñātvā
martyam apy artha-siddhi-dam (15.14)

etad = etat — this; vidvān — knowing; purā — before; mrtyor = mrtyoh — death; abhavāya — to be free of mundane existence; ghaṭeta — should strive for; saḥ — he; apramatta = apramattah — being without bewilderment; idam — this; jñātvā — knowing; martyam — something that will die, the body; apy = api — even though; artha-siddhi-dam = artha — goal + siddhi – perfection + dam — something capable of assisting.

Translation

Knowing this, and being without bewilderment, he should before death, strive to be free of mundane existence; knowing that even though the body will die, it is capable of assisting in the goal of perfection. (15.14)

Commentary:

If one does not become liberated before leaving the material body, it is hardly likely that one will be liberated in the hereafter. More than likely one will again have to take another gross form and strive again for liberation. When this is understood, one does not waste time with cultural activities. One consolidates the spiritual practice, which will cause one to experience deliverance before leaving the material body.

छिद्यमान यमैर् एतैः
कृत-नीडं वनस्पतिम्।
खगः स्व-केतम् उत्सृज्य
क्षेमं याति ह्य् अलम्पटः ॥ १५.१५॥

chidyamānaṁ yamair etaiḥ
kṛta-nīḍaṁ vanaspatim
khagaḥ sva-ketam utsṛjya
kṣemaṁ yāti hy alampaṭaḥ (15.15)

chidyamānam — what is cut down; yamaiḥ — by cruel persons; etaiḥ — by these; kṛta – built; nīḍam — nest; vanaspatim — tree; khagaḥ — bird; sva-ketam — his home; utsṛjya — abandons; kṣemam — well-being; yāti — achieves; hy = hi — indeed; alampaṭaḥ — being without attachment.

Translation

Observing that the tree, on which its nest was built, was being cut down by cruel persons, a bird, being without attachment abandons its home and achieves well-being. (15.15)

Commentary:

Presently, providence cuts down the tree of our present life time, by causing diseases and other negative factors to deteriorate our bodies. Therefore we should grow out of the attachment for these forms, realize the stupidity of ignoring providence's threatening actions, and make a decision to abandon these opportunities.

अहो-रात्रैश् छिद्यमानं
बुद्ध्वायुर् भय-वेपथुः ।
मुक्त-सङ्गः परं बुद्ध्वा
निरीह उपशाम्यति ॥ १५.१६ ॥

aho-rātraiś chidyamānaṁ
buddhvāyur bhaya-vepathuḥ
mukta-saṅgaḥ paraṁ buddhvā
nirīha upaśāmyati (15.16

aho = ahah — by days; rātraiś = rātraiḥ — by nights; chidyamānam — that which is being reduced; buddhvāyur = buddhvā — figuring + āyuḥ — life span; bhaya — with fear; vepathuḥ — trembling; mukta – freeing; saṅgaḥ — attachment; param — supreme; buddhvā — realizing; nirīha = nirīhah — without endeavoring for anything; upaśāmyati — becomes peaceful.

Translation

Figuring that his life span is being reduced by the passing days and nights, someone trembles in fear and freeing himself from attachment, he realizes the Supreme. Without endeavor for anything, he becomes peaceful. (15.16)

Commentary:

There are two ways to relieve the trembling of mind one gets when one realizes that his body is old and that one is losing the grip on life. The traditional method is to cling even more tenaciously to life and to show more interest in cultural affairs, to become even more attached and to enter a stage of denial of the vicious attack perpetrated by time upon one's existence in the material world. *Śrī Patañjali Mahārṣi* explained this as follows:

svarasavāhī viduṣaḥ api tatha ārūḍhaḥ abhiniveśaḥ

As it is, the strong focus on mundane existence, which is due to the instinctive fear of death, and which is sustained by its own potencies, which operates for self-preservation, is developed even in the wise man. (Yoga-sutras 2.9)

The other way to relieve the trembling mind is the one recommended by *Śrī* Krishna. That is to take steps to free oneself from attachment, and to endeavor to realize the Supreme. If one attempts this, one will over a time, cease endeavoring for anything on the material side, and one will have peace of mind.

नृ-देहम् आद्यं सु-लभं सु-दुर्लभं
प्लवं सु-कल्पं गुरु-कर्णधारम् ।
मयानुकूलेन नभस्वतेरितं
पुमान् भवाब्धिं न तरेत् स आत्म-हा ॥ १५.१७॥

nṛ-deham ādyaṁ su-labhaṁ su-durlabhaṁ
plavaṁ su-kalpaṁ guru-karṇadhāram
mayānukūlena nabhasvateritaṁ
pumān bhavābdhiṁ na taret sa ātma-hā
(15.17)

nṛ-deham — human body; ādyam — foremost form; su-labham — easily obtained; su-durlabham — very difficult to achieve; plavam — boat; su-kalpam — very useful; guru — teacher; karṇa – the rudder + dhāram — the holder (karṇadhāram – the steersman); mayānukūlena = mayā — by me + anukūlena — with favorable; nabhasvateritaṁ = nabhasvatā — winds + īritam — is pushed; pumān — a human being; bhavābdhiṁ = bhava — material existence + abdhim — ocean; na — not; taret — cross over; sa = sah — he; atmaha = ātma – self + hā — killer.

Translation

Seeing the foremost form, the human body which was easy to obtain, but which may be difficult to secure again, which is very useful like a boat, which has a teacher for the steersman, and which is pushed by Me, as by favorable wind, he who does not cross over the ocean of material existence, is a killer of his own soul. (15.17)

Commentary:

Somehow one has to determine the value of the human body and work hard for spiritual perfection. A man cannot guarantee the kind of opportunity he will get in the next transmigration. One should feel a sense of urgency about spiritual advancement. If one has a human body and a proficient spiritual master, and if *Śrī* Krishna approves of one's endeavor, then one will be successful undoubtedly.

यदारम्भेषु निर्विण्णो
विरक्तः सयतेन्द्रियः ।
अभ्यासेनात्मनो योगी
धारयेद् अचलं मनः ॥ १५.१८॥

yadārambheṣu nirviṇṇo
viraktaḥ saṁyatendriyaḥ
abhyāsenātmano yogī
dhārayed acalaṁ manaḥ (15.18)

yadārambheṣu = yadā — when + ārambheṣu — in cultural activities; nirviṇṇo = nirviṇṇaḥ — disgusted; viraktah — detached; saṁyatendriyaḥ = samyata — controlling + indriyaḥ — senses; abhyāsenātmano = abhyāsena — by practice + ātmano = ātmanaḥ — of the spirit; yogī — yogi; dhārayed = dhārayet — should link his attention to the concentration force; acalam — steady; manaḥ — mind.

Translation

When he is disgusted with cultural activities and attained detachment, having controlled the senses, the yogi should by practice, hold the mind steady on the spirit. (15.18)

Commentary:

This is the 6th stage of yoga of *dhāraṇā* practice. This has to do with yogis, not other transcendentalists. It is totally misleading to translate the word yogī as transcendentalist which is a very vague and misleading term. Efforts to translate yogī in that way are ways of hijacking what *Śrī* Krishna said, for using His words to support various new definitions of who would qualify as described in these verses.

Uddhava was a great yogin and so was Arjuna. These instructions were imparted to them because they were able to apply these advices which require yoga expertise.

धार्यमाणं मनो यर्हि
भ्राम्यद् अश्व् अनवस्थितम् ।
अतन्द्रितो ऽनुरोधेन
मार्गेणात्म-वश नयेत् ॥ १५.१९॥

dhāryamāṇaṁ mano yarhi
bhrāmyad aśv anavasthitam
atandrito 'nurodhena
mārgeṇātma-vaśaṁ nayet (15.19)

dhāryamāṇam — being linked to the higher concentration force; mano = manaḥ — mind; yarhi — when; bhrāmyad = bhrāmyat — wander off; āśv = āśu — quickly; anavasthitam — not situated at the desired place; atandrito = atandritaḥ — by its own waywardness; 'nurodhena = anurodhena — being alert; mārgeṇātma = mārgena — by a process + ātma — spirit; vaśam — control of; nayet — should bring.

Translation

When the mind is being linked to the higher concentration force, and it quickly wanders off, not being steadied on the desired place, then being alert, he would bring it under the control of the soul, by a process that takes into account its own waywardness. (15.19)

Commentary:

This above is an experience in higher yoga, when one completes the course for *pratyāhar* practice in sensual energy withdrawal and sensual energy conservation. One intensifies *prāṇāyāma* practice. After subduing and energizing the kundalini energy, one progresses into *dhāraṇā* practice which is the 6th stage.

Initially in the *dhāraṇā* practice, one does not have steadiness of mind. The mind acts just as *Śrī* Krishna described, where it repeatedly wanders off due to waywardness and thought-formation habits. But yoga, according to *Śrī Patañjali*, means the stoppage of the activities of the ideation energy in the mind. Therefore for success one has to do something to stop the mind from its wayward and thought-occupying tendencies.

It so happens that one cannot achieve this by will power, because the mind by nature is impulsive. The solution therefore is to be sure to energize the mind by *prāṇāyāma*. When the mind takes in higher pranic energy its natural tendency for extroversion changes. Instead of being jittery, the higher pranic energy causes it to be quiescent. When it is energized, there occurs in the mind, a concentration force. One links his attention to that force. This is *dhāraṇā* practice. There is more than one type of effective concentration force, but as a standard method a yogi links his mind to the sound which is usually heard on the left side of the subtle head. This is not a chanted sound. It is a high-pitched sound which comes from the chit *ākāśa*, the sky of consciousness.

The mind however will not retain the higher pranic charge of energy forever. It will again resume its normal troublesome activities as soon as the higher energy subsides, because then the mind will again attach itself to its usual low-level energy intake. Therefore a yogi finds that initially he has to repeatedly charge the mind.

I still have not figured out how commentators took these verses and stated that they pertain to devotional services at temples and ashrams. Something that is purely a mystic practice within the psyche has little to do with any sort of sacred external activity.

Śrī Uddhava, the compassionate person that he was, repeatedly took *Śrī* Krishna back to considerations about processes for the common person who do no yoga, or who find yoga to be hard and impractical. And repeatedly *Śrī* Krishna moved back to discussing techniques for yoga.

मनो-गतिं न विसृजेज्
जित-प्राणो जितेन्द्रियः ।
सत्त्व-सम्पन्नया बुद्ध्या
मन आत्म-वशं नयेत् ॥ १५.२० ॥

mano-gatiṁ na visṛjej
jita-prāṇo jitendriyaḥ
sattva-sampannayā buddhyā
mana ātma-vaśaṁ nayet (15.20)

mano = manah — of the mind; gatim — objective; na — not; visṛje = visrjet — should lose focus; jita – mastered; prāṇo = prāṇaḥ — life energy; jitendriyaḥ — one who has controlled the senses; sattva — clarifying energy of material nature; sampannayā — surcharged with; buddhyā — by the intellect; mana = manaḥ — mind; ātma – spirit; vaśam — under control; nayet — should bring.

Translation

He should not lose the focus on the objective set for the mind. Having mastered the life energy and conquered the senses, he should bring the mind under control by using the intellect, which is surcharged with the clarifying energy of material nature. (15.20)

Commentary:

No specific objective is given here because as one advances through the stages of yoga practice, one gets new instructions along the way. It is not a set or stagnant practice of just one technique. The yogi works on his level of advancement and applies relevant disciplines at particular stages.

He should master the life energy (*prāṇa*). This means *prāṇāyāma* for completing kundalini and celibacy yoga. He has to conquer the senses by means of *pratyāhar* or the 5th stage of yoga, to mystically draw in the sensual energies into their orbs of light in the head of the subtle body and then to draw those orbs close to the *buddhi* light in the head of the subtle form. This is the only way to cease the external sensual pursuits.

The mind is brought under the control of the surcharged intellect only *(sampannayā),* not otherwise. The surcharging act is done by *prāṇāyāma* not otherwise. After it is surcharged then the intellect co-operates with the desire of the yogi and he is then placed in a psychological location from which he can link his attention to concentration forces in higher dimensions.

This allows him to sip on and to imbibe higher energies and gradually after much practice, he is transferred out of this dimension.

एष वै परमो योगो
मनसः सङ्ग्रहः स्मृतः ।
हृदय-ज्ञत्वम् अन्विच्छन्
दम्यस्येवार्वतो मुहुः ॥ १५.२१ ॥

eṣa vai paramo yogo
manasaḥ saṅgrahaḥ smṛtaḥ
hṛdaya-jñatvam anvicchan
damyasyevārvato muhuḥ (15.21)

esa = esah — this; vai — indeed; paramo = paramaḥ — highest; yogo = yogah — yoga discipline; manasaḥ — of the mind; saṅgrahaḥ — tight control; smṛtaḥ — is said to be; hṛdaya – intimate; jñatvam — one who knows; anvicchan — trying to make; damyasyevārvato = damyasya — of the unruly + iva — like + arvato (arvatah) — of a horse; muhuḥ — always.

Translation

This tight control of the mind is said to be the highest yoga discipline like the curbing of an unruly horse, by one who knows the creature intimately and who tries to make it confirm always. (15.21)

Commentary:

Śrī Krishna revealed the process of yoga in very clear and easy-to-understand terms. Uddhava asked for an easy solution and the only ones he got so far were *bhakti*, *bhakti* yoga and *dharma*, but these were given with conditions attached, even though here and there one gets the idea that *bhakti* and *bhakti* yoga may be done independently. Still here, one sees on close inspection that elsewhere *Śrī* Krishna made it clear that many details, must be taken into consideration. These details make the *bhakti*, *bhakti* yoga and *dharma* to be not as easy as it seems. What is *bhakti*? What is *bhakti* yoga? What is *dharma*?

Bhakti is devotional love. This is the use of emotional energy to form a devotional approach to Lord Krishna. *Bhakti* however is fraught with problems because of the human impurities. It is therefore the most uncertain and most difficult path, because a human being is usually unable to rid himself or herself of emotional impurities.

Easy *bhakti* for a human being means that he or she applies impure emotions to *Śrī* Krishna and that will not work. Thus most devotees, who take the *bhakti* path are checkmated by their own impure emotions, feelings which are extremely difficult to clean up. External activities, even though they streamline and regulate the impure emotions do not cause purity. These activities do not in any way affect the impure status of the emotional energies.

However, human beings are easily fooled by the feel-good, smiley moods, which are induced by singing devotional songs, staying in association with like-minded devotees and attending worship ceremonies of the Krishna *Mūrti*. And many spiritual masters are all too eager to victimize human beings with false assurances of quickly-achieved purity.

Bhakti yoga is yoga and devotion combined and applied with psychological intensity to *Śrī* Krishna. This works if the yoga is the yoga described by *Śrī* Krishna, which is *aṣṭanga* yoga. However one cannot take up this path haphazardly. It can only be successfully practiced by those whose natures are predisposed towards it and who already have a devotional relationship with *Śrī* Krishna, from before this universe was created, or who are awarded a devotional relationship by *Śrī* Krishna, one which is made available to the devotee in his attempts to reach *Śrī* Krishna. The devotee should apply higher yoga expertise to guide his purified emotions into the groove of that relationship. This will take time and it is done only by intimate personal practice, not by a group effort. It may or may not have a thing to do with a spiritual master. In this respect the spiritual master may advise but he might not be an indispensable factor in the affair between the devotee and *Śrī* Krishna.

Dharma is righteous duty as assigned by the Universal Form. This is clearly explained in the instructions to Arjuna, because he had to comply with *dharma. Dharma* when it is done under the direction of the Universal Form for His approval, is called *karma* yoga which means *karma* with yoga expertise being applied in the cultural field.

Yoga practice is nicely described here by the comparison of the unruly horses. The trainer has to know the nature of the animal or he will not be successful. Each yogi must study the nature of the mind. General explanations will only help a little. The main thrust is to get inside the mind to practice restraining it. When one is attentive inside, one will see what is needed. No one else can do this for the yogi. He has to do it himself. It cannot be done for him by a yoga teacher, even though a great yogin may enter his mind in a minute form and show how the mind operates. He can be freed by the grace of God, when that grace manifests as instructions on what he may do to better understand how the mind operates so that he can become determined to take up the yoga austerities which curb it.

As a horseman has to know each horse intimately, so each yogi has to know his own mind in detail. He must practice in seclusion to know this. It cannot be done by a group effort or by chanting holy names and the like. These other aspects of spiritual life like chanting holy names give us some reprieve from the roving, dominating mind but they do not penetrate deep enough into the mind to cause its complete subjugation. Chanting was not designed for that purpose anyway.

साङ्ख्येन सर्व-भावानां
प्रतिलोमानुलोमतः ।
भवाप्ययाव् अनुध्यायेन्
मनो यावत् प्रसीदति ॥ १५.२२ ॥

sāṅkhyena sarva-bhāvānāṁ
pratilomānulomataḥ
bhavāpyayāv anudhyāyen
mano yāvat prasīdati (15.22)

sāṅkhyena — by Sāṅkhya analysis; sarva — all; bhāvānām — existential factors; pratilomānulomataḥ = pratiloma — by retrogression + anulomataḥ — by progression; bhavāpyayāv = bhava — origination + apyayāv (apyayāu) — dissolution; anudhyāyet — should remain in the stage where the attention is effortlessly linked to the concentration force; mano = manaḥ — mind; yāvat — till; prasīdati — stilled.

Translation

By the Sāṅkhya information on the origination and dissolution of all existential factors in their retrogression and progression, one should remain in the stage where the attention is effortlessly linked to the relevant concentration force, until the mind becomes stilled. (15.22)

Commentary:

These are details for higher yoga, before the yogi can enter *samādhis*. This had nothing to do with thinking out the *Sāṅkhya* theories and descriptions of creations, nor of getting intellectual realization of these and then feeling satisfied that one understood this.

These details of higher yoga can only be activated in the life of a yogin who mastered the 6th stage and advanced into the 7th stage. In the 6th stage, that of *dhāraṇā*, the yogi after perfecting sensual energy withdrawal from this world, energizes his subtle form sufficiently, as to cause his sensual energies to be completely withdrawn from this world. Then he finds that within his psyche there is a focused or concentrated higher force. He then links his attention to that energy. This linkage is called *dhāraṇā* practice. Some people feel that *dhāraṇā* is concentration of will power or concentration of the attention but they are incorrect.

The concentration does not come on by application of will power or attention but rather by natural polarizations within the higher energies, which are drawn into the psyche through *prāṇāyāma*. When those higher energies become manifested to the yogi, his linkage of his attention to them is called *dhāraṇā* practice.

The yogi's only effort is to first surcharge his subtle body with *prāṇāyāma*; And then to link his attention to the concentration force which occurs as a result of the surcharged of higher energy. However in the next stage, the 7th, that of *dhyāna*, the yogi only makes the first effort and the second act of linking his attention is sustained by the concentration force itself, which draws his attention to it of its own accord, just as the mind is effortlessly drawn to mundane sense objects in the case of a non-yogi.

Śrī Krishna graciously gave us another important *kriyā* here, which is for the yogi to keep referring to the *Sāṅkhya* information about the origination and dissolution of all existential factors in their retrogression and progression so that in his practice, that interest remains as a momentum force to cause him to perceive on the mystic plane how the mundane universe comes about. Once he perceives this, he becomes freed from the bewildering potency of the mundane energy in full, otherwise being a devotee or not, he will remain time-bound, and he will be bewildered periodically. These are internal meditation practices, having little or nothing to do with anything sacred or profane in the external world.

निर्विण्णस्य विरक्तस्य
पुरुषस्योक्त-वेदिनः ।
मनस् त्यजति दौरात्म्यं
चिन्तितस्यानुचिन्तया ॥१५.२३॥

nirviṇṇasya viraktasya
puruṣasyokta-vedinaḥ
manas tyajati daurātmyaṁ
cintitasyānucintayā (15.23)

nirviṇṇasya — of one who is disgusted with material existence; viraktasya — regarding one who assumed a detached attitude; puruṣasyokta = puruṣasya — regarding a person + ukta – teaching; vedinaḥ — teachings of an educated brahmin; manas = manah — mind; tyajati — gives up; daurātmyam — bad in inclinations; cintitasyānucintaya = cintitasya — of what comprises the concentration force + anucintaya — by repeatedly being absorbed into the concentration force.

Translation

Regarding a person who is disgusted with material existence, who assumed a detached mood, and who understood the teachings of an educated brahmin, his mind gives up its bad inclinations by his repeatedly being absorbed into the concentration force. (15.23)

Commentary:

This does not mean a mental analysis of the teachings of a guru. This is totally different to that. This concerns what was discussed in the previous verse, regarding the 7th stage of yoga.

By repeatedly engaging in such meditation where the higher concentration force becomes manifested in the psyche, and where that force draws the yogi's attention to it and holds his attention in linkage to it, the mind becomes so energized after long practice that it is no longer able to return to the basic level where it exhibits bad inclinations. This happens after sustained practice.

The teacher described in this verse is the *kriyā* yoga master, who can give the student yogi some idea of the practices. He is not a person who analyzed the *Sāṅkhya* philosophy, read it through, mastered it intellectually, contemplated it and has not done yoga, nor has surcharged his body with *prāṇāyāma*, and does not intent to do so.

यमादिभिर् योग-पथैर्
आन्वीक्षिक्या च विद्यया ।
ममार्चोपासनाभिर् वा
नान्यैर् योग्यं स्मरेन् मनः ॥१५.२४॥

yamādibhir yoga-pathair
ānvīkṣikyā ca vidyayā
mamārcopāsanābhir vā
nānyair yogyaṁ smaren manaḥ (15.24)

yamādibhir = yamādibhiḥ — with moral restraints and the other preliminary stages; yoga-pathair = yoga-pathaiḥ — by the path of yoga; ānvīkṣikyā — by logical analysis; ca — and; vidyayā — by effective technique; mamārcopāsanābhir = mama — me + arcā — worship + upāsanābhiḥ — by attentive service; vā — or; anyair = na — not + anyair (anyaiḥ) — by other; yogyam — the objective of yoga practice; smaren = smaret — should be absorbed in; manah — mind.

Translation

By moral restraints and other preliminary stages, by the path of yoga, by logical analysis, as well as by effective techniques or attentive service to My worship ceremony and by no other means, the mind should be absorbed in the objective of yoga. (15.24)

Commentary:

There are some persons who are convinced that if they perform devotional service in the Krishna *sampradāya*, they will never have to do yoga. They feel that if they do devotional service in relation to missionary activities for spreading Krishna Consciousness among the public, they will never be required to do yoga. These people make a blunder. There is no guarantee that a devotee who sincerely applies himself to temple service and missionary activities, will not have to take up yoga austerities in this or in some future life. The mere idea that certain devotees and their spiritual masters are dead set against yoga practice, indicate that they might have to take it up in the future. Their innate dislike of it, does not obligate *Śrī* Krishna from requiring it. And besides, if their devotional services are unable to purify their emotional nature, they will have to take it up if they are really serious about attaining *Śrī* Krishna.

No one in his right mind, would say that he knows for sure that he would not be required by *Śrī* Krishna to take up yoga practice, here or hereafter. Only a person who has a personal hatred for yoga austerities will say such a thing. But what does that dislike for yoga have to do with Lord Krishna?

If someone can get their mind to be totally absorbed not just on the surface level but on the deepest levels, such that the mind departs from the lower plane completely and moves into the spiritual level with full spiritual vision in a spiritual body then certainly he does not need to perform yoga. I accept this. Otherwise, one would be fool number one, not to take up yoga, which is itself recommended by *Śrī* Krishna.

यदि कुर्यात् प्रमादेन
योगी कर्म विगर्हितम् ।
योगेनैव दहेद् अंहो
नान्यत् तत्र कदाचन ॥ १५.२५॥

yadi kuryāt pramādena
yogī karma vigarhitam
yogenaiva dahed aṁho
nānyat tatra kadācana (15.25)

yadi — if; kuryāt — should do; pramādena — through carelessness; yogī — yogi; karma — activity, an act; vigarhitam — disapproved; yogenaiva = yogena — by yoga discipline + eva — alone; dahed = dahet — should completely remove; aṁho = aṁhah — offence; nanyat = na — not + anyat — other; tatra — there; kadācana — at any time.

Translation

If through carelessness, the yogi does a disapproved act, he should completely remove the offence by yogic discipline alone. There is no other effective method for this. (15.25)

Commentary:

Here again, *Śrī* Krishna stressed yoga. It can hardly be avoided because it is the sure way for self purification and for relating to higher levels. Yoga is so powerful that if through carelessness a yogi does a disapproved act, he may get instructions from higher yogis or he may be inspired within, on an austerity to nullify the offense. Yoga alone has that special facility because it works on a much deeper level than anything else. Because it goes to the core of the being and because it reaches into the level from which this material energy was formulated, it can nullify even the causal energies, which could cause a yogi to do things which would reverse progression.

स्वे स्वे ऽधिकारे या निष्ठा स गुणः परिकीर्तितः । कर्मणां जात्य्-अशुद्धानाम् अनेन नियमः कृतः । गुण-दोष-विधानेन सङ्गानां त्याजनेच्छया ॥ १५.२६ ॥	sve sve 'dhikāre yā niṣṭhā sa guṇaḥ parikīrtitaḥ karmaṇāṁ jāty-aśuddhānām anena niyamaḥ kṛtaḥ guṇa-doṣa-vidhānena saṅgānāṁ tyājanecchayā (15.26)

sve sve — one's own; 'dhikāre = adhikāre — in duty; yā — which; niṣṭhā — firm adherence; sa = saḥ — that; guṇaḥ — merit; parikīrtitah — is confidentially declared; karmaṇām — pertaining to cultural activities; jāty = jāti — nature; aśuddhānām — pertaining to impurity; anena — by this; niyamaḥ — restriction; kṛtah — is made; guṇa — of merit; doṣa — of demerit; vidhānena — by a declaration; saṅgānām — of social attachment; tyājanecchayā = tyājana — removal + icchayā — by desire.

Translation

Firm attachment to one's duty is definitely declared as merit. By this declaration of merits and demerits, a restriction is made pertaining to cultural activities, which are by nature impure. This is done by a desire for the removal of social attachment. (15.26)

Commentary:

Śrī Krishna regressed to the practical level for common human beings who will do no yoga, and who will lean to cultural activities, either those which pass as religious observances or those which cannot be disguised as religion.

Such a human being has to take *karma* yoga as defined in the *Bhagavad Gītā*, not in terms of what Arjuna had to do, which was battlefield work but in terms of whatever the Universal Form would stipulate as one's righteous duty. It might not be militant work.

Such people cannot do *bhakti* yoga effectively because their emotional energies are too impure to be of any worth to *Śrī* Krishna, but their working power which is sponsored by the same emotional force, could be used by *Śrī* Krishna for maintaining law and order in this human world, not for loving Him or anything like that.

The devotional service, which such people are said to perform, is mostly a farce but it passes for something divine in some segments of the Krishna *sampradāya*. This is going on because many powerful teachers have pushed it into human society and standardize it as *bhakti*, *bhakti* yoga, devotion or devotional services. Some say it is divine service or *sevā*.

The whole scope of cultural activity in this world is polluted. There is no doubt about it. But to be pragmatic, we must agree to do what is the least polluting. Such activities are regarded as merits. Those which carry the greater pollution are called demerits. Initially we should do *karma* yoga as *Śrī* Krishna stipulated to Arjuna. But if we cannot do that, then we can do *karma* alone or cultural activities without application of yoga, but under *Śrī* Krishna's direction as explained in the *Bhagavad Gītā,* especially in the chapter twelve instructions to Arjuna, where *Śrī* Krishna gave alternatives to *karma* and yoga being performed either separately or together.

Human beings, as we are, we are creatures of habit. Thus if we practice higher habits, either by force or willingness, it is likely that we will develop detachment from the enjoyments we get from sordid activities. That will move us up into a higher culture and cause us to get closer to *Śrī* Krishna and the great sages. This will open the door of higher association.

जात-श्रद्धो मत्-कथासु
निर्विण्णः सर्व-कर्मसु ।
वेद् दुःखात्मकान् कामान्
परित्यागे ऽप्य् अनीश्वरः ॥ १५.२७॥

jāta-śraddho mat-kathāsu
nirviṇṇaḥ sarva-karmasu
veda duḥkhātmakān kāmān
parityāge 'py anīśvaraḥ (15.27)

jāta — one who experiences; śraddho = śraddhaḥ — faith; mat-kathāsu — true stories about me; nirviṇṇah — disgusted; sarva-karmasu — in all cultural activities; veda — knows; duḥkhātmakān = duḥkha — misery + ātmakān — the nature; kāmān — cravings; parityāge — in giving up; py = api — although; anīśvarah — one who is unable.

Translation

One who has faith in true stories about Me, and who is disgusted in being involved in cultural activities, who knows that the nature of cravings is misery, but who also is unable to give up those cravings, (15.27)

Commentary:

This is a description of the devotee of Krishna who is disgusted with cultural activities. Such a person may know that these activities always pan out into misery but still he may not have the power to give them up. He tries but his nature acts in a contrary way to always keep him intertwined in social life.

The main aspect is that this particular devotee becomes attracted by hearing of true stories of *Śrī* Krishna's pastimes. This description is continued in the next verse.

ततो भजेत मां प्रीतः
श्रद्धालुर् दृढ-निश्चयः ।
जुषमाणश् च तान् कामान्
दुःखोदर्कांश् च गर्हयन् ॥ १५.२८॥

tato bhajeta māṁ prītaḥ
śraddhālur dṛḍha-niścayaḥ
juṣamāṇaś ca tān kāmān
duḥkhodarkāṁś ca garhayan (15.28)

tato = tataḥ — thence, at that stage; bhajeta — should worship; mām — me; prītah — lovingly; śraddhālur = śraddhāluḥ — a faithful person; dṛḍha — firm; niścayaḥ — conviction; jusamānaś = jusamānaḥ — continuing to satisfy; ca — and; tān — those; kāmān — cravings; duḥkhodarkams = duḥkha — misery + udarkān — all that, which ends; ca — also; garhayan — condemning.

Translation

...that faithful devotee, having firm conviction, should at that stage, lovingly worship Me, and should continue to satisfy those cravings, while condemning all that ends in misery. (15.28)

Commentary:

This makes a clarificatlon that a devotee, even if he is attracted to stories about *Śrī* Krishna, stories which are told in the tenth part of the *Śrīmad* -Bhagavatam, still he might not be able to stop himself from undesirable cravings. This is an admittance by *Śrī* Krishna, which explains that a devotee might not be free from the lower nature instantly. It might take time. *Śrī* Krishna recommended that the devotee in that predicament should still lovingly worship Him, while having to satisfy the lower cravings nevertheless. But the devotee should in his mind condemn the de-meritorious habits to which he is addicted.

प्रोक्तेन भक्ति-योगेन
भजतो मासकृन् मुनेः ।
कामा हृदय्या नश्यन्ति
सर्वे मयि हृदि स्थिते ॥ १५.२९॥

proktena bhakti-yogena
bhajato māsakṛn muneḥ
kāmā hṛdayyā naśyanti
sarve mayi hṛdi sthite (15.29)

proktena — with instructions; bhakti-yogena — by the yoga application to emotional experience;

bhajato = bhajatah — one who worships; māsakṛn = ma — me + asakṛt — always; muneḥ — regarding the yogi philosopher; kāmā = kāmāḥ — cravings; hṛdayyā = hṛdayyāh — in the core of being; naśyanti — are destroyed; sarve — all; mayi — in me; hṛdi — in the core of being; sthite — in position.

Translation

Regarding the yogi philosopher who constantly worships Me as instructed for the application of yoga to the emotional experiences, all cravings in the core of his being, are destroyed by me, who is positioned in his core self. (15.29)

Commentary:

Even though Uddhava repeatedly wanted a devotional solution for the common man, *Śrī* Krishna did not award this privilege to the common person. He described this for the *muneḥ*, the yogi philosopher. Without yoga, it is hardly likely that anyone would apply his or her emotions to *Śrī* Krishna successfully.

भिद्यते हृदय-ग्रन्थिश्
छिद्यन्ते सर्व-सशयाः ।
क्षीयन्ते चास्य कर्माणि
मयि दृष्टे ऽखिलात्मनि ॥ १५.३० ॥

bhidyate hṛdaya-granthiś
chidyante sarva-saṁśayāḥ
kṣīyante cāsya karmāṇi
mayi dṛṣṭe 'khilātmani (15.30)

bhidyate — penetrated; hṛdaya — of the causal body; granthiś = granthiḥ — knots; chidyante — sorted out; sarva — all; samśayāḥ — uncertainties; kṣīyante — dispelled; casya = ca — and + asya — his; karmaṇi — cultural obligations; mayi — on me; dṛṣṭe — having put his vision; 'khilātmani = akhilatmani = akhila — basis of all + ātmaṇi – on the self.

Translation

The blockage to his causal body is penetrated. All uncertainties are sorted out. His cultural obligations are dispelled, having put his vision on Me, the Self Who is the basis of all. (15.30)

Commentary:

This refers to higher yoga practice. One cannot penetrate into the causal body, in the core of being by ordinary means. It is only by mystic, supernatural and spiritual means that one can do this. No amount of external chanting or external repetition of any words will bring this about, even though those methods have value and do contribute to the purification of the being to a certain degree.

One cannot dispel cultural obligations by wishful thinking, nor by hopes, not by acceptance of promises of salvation and the like. Cultural obligations go away by their performance under the supervision of the Universal Form and by no other means. Such a surrender to Him causes the performer to get an exemption from the same cultural acts at some stage.

The exemption is the avenue to fulltime yoga practice, which leads to deep purification by *kriyā* yoga austerities. Putting one's vision on the Krishna *Mūrti* in the temple is not the same as seeing *Śrī* Krishna's spiritual form directly. Arjuna did not see the Supernatural Universal Form and the spiritual Four-handed Form while looking at *Śrī* Krishna's special material body on the battlefield of *Kurukṣetra*. His energy was boosted to allow him to use spiritual perception.

तस्मान् मद्-भक्ति-युक्तस्य
योगिनो वै मद्-आत्मनः ।
न ज्ञानं न च वैराग्यं
प्रायः श्रेयो भवेद् इह ॥ १५.३१ ॥

tasmān mad-bhakti-yuktasya
yogino vai mad-ātmanaḥ
na jñānaṁ na ca vairāgyaṁ
prāyaḥ śreyo bhaved iha (15.31)

tasmān = tasmāt — therefore; mad-bhakti = mat-bhakti – devotion to me; yuktasya — of one who is habituated; yogino = yoginah — of the yogis; vai — indeed; mad-ātmanah = mat-ātmanah — of the self who is focused on me; na — not; jñānam — knowledge; na — nor; ca — and; vairāgyam — dispassion; prāyaḥ — generally; śreyo = śreyaḥ — benefit; bhaved = bhavet — may be; iha — in this world.

Translation

Therefore for the yogis who are habitually practiced in devotion to Me, whose self is focused on Me; knowledge and dispassion may not be of a benefit in this world. (15.31)

Commentary:

This means the yogis who advanced through the preliminary practices. This is certainly a yogi devotee. It does not pertain to a devotee who is not a yogi, even if such a person is accredited as being most advanced by his followers. It is not that such a person might not be a divine being. He might be. But this verse is a description of an advanced yogi, otherwise *Śrī* Krishna would not have used the terms *yogino*.

Dispassion and knowledge are necessary at a lower stage but they are not needed on the very advanced levels. Even so, they are displayed by very advanced yogis, because for such persons, those skills are at their disposal.

यत् कर्मभिर् यत् तपसा
ज्ञान-वैराग्यतश् च यत् ।
योगेन दान-धर्मेण
श्रेयोभिर् इतरैर् अपि ॥ १५.३२ ॥

yat karmabhir yat tapasā
jñāna-vairāgyataś ca yat
yogena dāna-dharmeṇa
śreyobhir itarair api (15.32)

yat — whatever; karmabhiḥ — by cultural activities; yat — whatever; tapasā — by penance; jñāna — theoretical understanding; vairāgyataś = vairāgyataḥ — through dispassion; ca — and; yat — whatever; yogena — by yoga disciplines; dāna — charity; dharmena — by righteous duty; śreyobhir = śreyobhiḥ — by methods for well-being; itarair = itaraiḥ — by others; api — even.

Translation

Whatever is to be gained by cultural activities, by penance, by dispassion and by theoretical understanding, by yoga disciplines, charity, righteous duty and even by other methods designed for one's well-being; (15.32)

Commentary:

This listing is completed in the next verse, for a comparison with *bhakti* yoga. But this does not mean that one can discard all these and be successful in *bhakti* yoga or in *bhakti*. It means rather that *bhakti* yoga or *bhakti* can or may take such a central position in the devotee's or yogi's life, that it will act as the central motivation from which he performs everything else.

सर्वं मद्-भक्ति-योगेन
मद्-भक्तो लभते ऽञ्जसा ।
स्वर्गापवर्गं मद्-धाम
कथञ्चिद् यदि वाञ्छति ॥ १५.३३ ॥

sarvaṁ mad-bhaktī-yogena
mad-bhakto labhate 'ñjasā
svargāpavargaṁ mad-dhāma
kathañcid yadi vāñchati (15.33)

sarvam — all; mad-bhaktī-yogena = mat-bhaktī-yogena — by applying yoga disciplines to devotion to me; mad-bhakto = mat-bhaktaḥ — my devotee; labhate — gets; 'ñjasā = añjasā — easily; svargāpavargaṁ = svarga — heaven + apavargam — liberation; mad-dhāma = mat-dhāma — my abode; kathañcid = kathañcit — somehow, perchance; yadi — if; vañchati — desires.

Translation

...My devotees gets all of it by applying yoga techniques to devotion to Me, even if perchance he desires heaven and liberation to My Abode. (15.33)

Commentary:

This happens because the attraction to *Śrī* Krishna, acts to motivate him to do what is necessary to attain what he desires in reference to the Lord. The strongest motivation in a human being is love, even impure love. In the social setting we see that even the most perverted types of affection cause people to do extra-ordinary things and to take many risks for which they might be sorry about afterwards. Thus love, which is directed to Krishna, can cause a devotee to make any sacrifice or take up any austerity to get what is desired. This is what this means. It does not mean that because one loves *Śrī* Krishna purely or impurely, that love is sufficient to cause one to get what one desires. The love is the motivating force.

Arjuna loved *Śrī* Krishna and his love for the Lord served to make him do what *Śrī* Krishna desired, which was *karma* yoga. Uddhava, as we shall see, by the strength of his love for *Śrī* Krishna, did what Krishna designed for him. And it is the same with others.

This does not mean that *bhakti* or devotional love is the same as *bhakti* yoga which is yoga as it is applied to reinforce and fine tune devotional love. *Bhakti* yoga is stronger and more definite than *bhakti*, because yoga adds directness and purity to the devotional energy.

न किञ्चित् साधवो धीरा
भक्ता ह्य् एकान्तिनो मम ।
वाञ्छन्त्य् अपि मया दत्तं
कैवल्यम् अपुनर्-भवम् ॥ १५.३४ ॥

na kiñcit sādhavo dhīrā
bhaktā hy ekāntino mama
vāñchanty api mayā dattaṁ
kaivalyam apunar-bhavam (15.34)

na — not; kiñcit — anything; sādhavo = sādhavaḥ — saintly persons; dhīrā — persons who have accurately-perceiving intellects; bhaktā = bhaktāḥ — devotees; hy = hi — surely; ekāntino = ekāntinaḥ — those who are singularly devoted; mama — to me; vāñchanty = vāñchanti — desire; api — even; mayā — by me; dattam — offered; kaivalyam — isolation of the spirit from its psychological equipments; apunar-bhavam = apunah – not again + bhavam — existing in the material world.

Translation

Saintly persons who have accurately-perceiving intellects, who are devoted and who are singularly dedicated to Me, do not desire the complete isolation of their spirits from its psychological equipments, such that they are never to be existent in the material world again, even if such privileges were offered to them by Me. (15.34)

Commentary:

This does not apply to a common devotee nor to an aspiring yogi. No attempt should be made to imitate this nor to adopt this attitude prematurely or artificially. If this is genuine, it is produced from advancement and not by a desire force, nor by the need to exhibit superiority over other transcendentalists in or out of the devotee community.

This verse applies to the *dhīrās* who are described in the *Bhagavad-Gītā* particularly in chapters two and three. These are *mahāyogīs*. This is not for others. One should read the *Bhagavad-Gītā* to understand what *Śrī* Krishna meant by a *dhīra*. The singular dedication to *Śrī* Krishna is the one attained by advanced yogis who practice *bhakti* yoga using the highest stages of yoga to boost, direct and fine-tune their affection. This must be understood in that way, other-wise we will mislead many people, while making numerous followers out of naive human beings who are looking for an easy path to apply their impure affections to the Supreme Being without the proper purification.

Kaivalyam means the absolute and complete isolation of the spirit from its psychological equipments. What are these equipments? These are the life force and the mind apparatus. When a yogi achieves *kaivalyam*, he does not become one with God but rather he becomes singularly separated from his mind and life force, such that they do not influence him nor cause him to have prejudiced notions. *Śrī Patañjali* defined *kaivalyam* clearly. We need not be confused by that term or have a vague idea of it as being some type of oneness:

sva svāmi śaktyoḥ svarūpopalabdhi hetuḥ saṁyogaḥ
tasya hetuḥ avidyā
tad abhāvāt saṁyogābhāvaḥ hānaṁ taddṛśeḥ kaivalyam

There is a reason for the conjunction of the individual self and his psychological energies. It is for obtaining experience of his own form. The cause of the conjunction is spiritual ignorance.

The elimination of the conjunction which results from the elimination of that spiritual ignorance is the withdrawal. That is the total separation of the perceiver from the mundane psychology. (Yoga-Sūtra 2.23-25)

Kaivalyam has become a very popular term among yogis. Many of them say it means becoming absolute and become one with the absolute. Some say it means to become one with God. On the other hand, the devotees who are not yogis and who pass under the general grouping as being Vaishnavas, list *kaivalyam* as liberation. Many regard it as a negative term since they feel that one should only desire service to *Śrī* Krishna, devotional service and not even liberation.

One person who defined *kaivalyam* clearly is *Śrī Patañjali Mahāmuni*, but one must check his Sanskrit closely and not just accept any translation of the Yoga Sutras, since a translator might not be free of the motive to use *Patañjali*'s authority to underscore his missionary and popularity objectives. As far as I can see, *Śrī Patañjali* used the term kaivalyam for the condition of a spirit who became consciously separated from its impure and faulty psychological equipments, such that the said spirit became distant from the influences of those faulty equipments. He also defined *kaivalyam* as the condition of a spirit who was unified with the purified non-faulty psychological equipments such that the impure influences which usually go to the spirit from such equipments no longer are accepted or reflected within the equipments, leaving the spirit free of the mundane prejudices which come from material nature.

Each serious yogi should study *Śrī Patañjali's Yoga Sutras*. If you want to understand yourself and to overcome the impurities and existential handicaps, then it is in order that you study the lives and methods of successful yogis. Such study is never a waste of time. Otherwise if one does not study the course of the ancient yogis, one will be left to discover everything for one self. And unless one is as determined and as mystically-piercing as Lord Buddha, one will not be successful.

Śrī Krishna stated in this verse that those saintly persons who are His devotees and who have accurately-perceiving intellects, do not desire *kaivalyam* or the separation of their core self from the psychological equipments used for perception in the material world. Such persons have already purified the intellect and life force, and are not influenced by the subtle mundane energy. As *Śrī Patañjali* stated:

sattva puruṣayoḥ śuddhi sāmye kaivalyam iti

When there is equal purity between the intelligence energy of material nature and the spirit, then the there is total seperation from the mundane psychology. (Yoga Sutras 3.56)

Under the circumstances, there would be no need to want to be separated from one's mundane psychology, but otherwise the need is relevant. *Śrī* Krishna in this verse described the most advance, most accomplished of the yogis. This is a description of the divine beings who come down into the material world, persons like *Śrī* Krishna Himself. It does not apply to others who do no yoga, deride yoga and pretend that they understand these verses.

नैरपेक्ष्यं परं प्राहुर्
निःश्रेयसम् अनल्पकम् ।
तस्मान् निराशिषो भक्तिर्
निरपेक्षस्य मे भवेत् ॥ १५.३५॥

nairapekṣyaṁ paraṁ prāhur
niḥśreyasam analpakam
tasmān nirāśiṣo bhaktir
nirapekṣasya me bhavet 15.35)

nairapekṣyam — not caring for anything; param — highest; prāhuh — is called; nihśreyasam — well being; analpakam — fullest; tasmāt — therefore; nirāśiṣah — of one who has no desires; bhaktiḥ — devotion; nirapekṣasya — of one who does not care for anything specific; me — to me; bhavet — is developed.

Translation

Not caring for anything is called the highest and fullest well-being. Therefore the devotion of one who has no desires, of one who does not care for anything, is developed in relationship to Me. (15.35)

Commentary:

A person, specifically a yogi, who is capable of reaching a stage where he cares for nothing in the material world, where he is willing to take on anything and everything, by the order of providence, without resentment or remorse, can develop in relationship to *Śrī* Krishna very quickly. This is because he is reserved from personal preference. Due to having attained the higher *kaivalyam* by the purity of his psychological equipments, he does not absorb any prejudices from material nature and is not reactionary in a positive or negative way to that mundane power.

If we study the *Bhagavad-Gītā*, we will see that Arjuna had some problem surrendering to *Śrī* Krishna. Initially Arjuna had so many concerns of his own. Once he detached himself from his emotions, he readily accepted *Śrī* Krishna's suggestions. Under the antiseptic influence of *Śrī* Krishna, Arjuna became separated from the views of material nature and transcended its influences for the time being, but later on he again resumed its prejudices which again clung to him and influenced his demeanor. Subsequently he made an appeal to Krishna to again help him to overcome that. As a result the Anu-*Gītā* was told to him by the Blessed Lord.

न मय्य् एकान्त-भक्ताना
गुण-दोषोद्भवा गुणाः ।
साधूनां सम-चित्तानां
बुद्धेः परम् उपेयुषाम् ॥ १५.३६॥

na mayy ekānta-bhaktānāṁ
guṇa-doṣodbhavā guṇāḥ
sādhūnāṁ sama-cittānāṁ
buddheḥ param upeyuṣām (15.36)

na — not; mayy = mayi — on me; ekānta — singularly focused; bhaktānām — of the devotees; guṇa — virtue; doṣodbhavā = doṣa — flaw + udbhavāh — those things which are produced; guṇāḥ — mundane influences; sādhūnām — of the saints; sama-cittānām — of those whose mental and emotional energy are similar in purity to the spirit; buddheh — than the intellect; param — beyond, further; upeyuṣām — of those who have achieved.

Translation

Mundane influences which produce virtues and flaws, do not affect those devotees, who are singularly dedicated to Me. They are saintly. Their mental and emotional energy are similar in purity to their spirits, and they achieved what is beyond the intellect. (15.36)

एवम् एतान् मया दिष्टान्
अनुतिष्ठन्ति मे पथः ।
क्षेमं विन्दन्ति मत्-स्थानं
यद् ब्रह्म परमं विदुः ॥ १५.३७॥

evam etān mayā diṣṭān
anutiṣṭhanti me pathaḥ
kṣemaṁ vindanti mat-sthānaṁ
yad brahma paramaṁ viduḥ (15.37)

evam — thus; etān — these; mayā — by me; diṣṭān — taught; anutiṣṭhanti — those who practice; me — me; pathaḥ — methods of achieving; kṣemam — full well-being; vindanti — attain; mat-sthānam — my abode; yad = yat — which; brahma – spirit; paramam — supreme; viduḥ — realize.

Translation

Thus, those who practice these methods of achieving Me, which was taught by Me, attain My abode, which is full well-being. They realize the Supreme spirit. (15.37)

CHAPTER 16*

Vedic Incentives**

Terri Stokes-Pineda Art

phala-śrutir iyaṁ nṝṇāṁ na śreyo rocanaṁ param
śreyo-vivakṣayā proktaṁ yathā bhaiṣajya-rocanam

The Vedic statements in relation to benefits, do not facilitate the highest well-being of human beings but are mere incentives, stated in such a way, as to make one eventually endeavor for the said well-being, just as inducements are used in administering medicine. (Uddhava Gītā 16.23)

* Śrīmad Bhāgavatam Canto 11, Chapter 21
** Translator's selected chapter title.

श्री-भगवान् उवाच
य एतान् मत्-पथो हित्वा
भक्ति-ज्ञान-क्रियात्मकान् ।
क्षुद्रान् कामांश् चलैः प्राणैर्
जुषन्तः ससरन्ति ते ॥ १६.१ ॥

śrī-bhagavān uvāca
ya etān mat-patho hitvā
bhaktī-jñāna-kriyātmakān
kṣudrān kāmāṁś calaiḥ prāṇair
juṣantaḥ saṁsaranti te (16.1)

śrī-bhagavān – the blessed lord; uvāca — said; ya = ye — those; etān — these; mat-patho = mat-pathaḥ — method for reaching me; hitvā — abandoning; bhaktī — loving emotional expression; jñāna — thinking expression; kriyā — functional work; ātmakān — consisting of; kṣudrān — petty; kāmāṁś = kāmān — cravings; calaiḥ — by the restless; prānair = prānaiḥ — by the sensual energy; juṣantaḥ — facilitate; saṁsaranti — endure birth and death; te — they.

Translation

Those who, abandon these methods of reaching Me, which consist of loving emotional expression, thinking expression and functional work, do by their restless sensual energy, facilitate the petty cravings. They endure birth and death. (16.1)

Commentary:

Śrī Krishna did not blacklist either the path of loving emotional expression, that of thinking expression or that of functional work, but commends each process. He explained that persons who can take to neither of these three courses, do by their restless sensual energy, facilitate the petty cravings which arise in the nature of a human being. Subsequently, such entities facilitate the course of aimless birth and death.

स्वे स्वे ऽधिकारे या निष्ठा
स गुणः परिकीर्तितः ।
विपर्ययस् तु दोषः स्याद्
उभयोर् एष निश्चयः ॥ १६.२ ॥

sve sve 'dhikāre yā niṣṭhā
sa guṇaḥ parikīrtitaḥ
viparyayas tu doṣaḥ syād
ubhayor eṣa niścayaḥ (16.2)

sve sve — one's own; 'dhikāre = adhikāre — in performance of duty; yā — which; niṣṭhā — consistency; sa = saḥ — that; guṇaḥ — merit; parikīrtitaḥ — is defined as; viparyayas — the converse; tu — but; doṣaḥ — defect; syād = syāt — is; ubhayor = ubhayoḥ — of the two; eṣa = eṣaḥ — this; niścayah — criterion.

Translation

Consistency in performance of one's own duty is defined as merit. But the converse is defect. This is the criterion of the two. (16.2)

Commentary:

This was stated before to Uddhava. *Śrī* Krishna repeated it again. He explained many details which were presented in the Vedas, but which were not stated as directly as He presented it here. For the common man, there is no other way but the performance of righteous duty. Someone or the other, the common people must be made to perform *karma* under the direction of *Śrī* Krishna or *karma* yoga under His direction alternately. This is the easy path for them, not the *bhakti* path.

The *bhakti* path is good for a few persons who have divine luck and who can do it perfectly because they have the connection with *Śrī* Krishna as stated in the previous chapter as follows:

yadṛcchayā mat-kathādau jāta-śraddhas tu yaḥ pumān
na nirviṇṇo nāti-sakto bhakti-yogo 'sya siddhi-daḥ

If somehow, a person develops faith in stories about Me, and is attracted to Me by other ways, but is not disgusted with cultural life, and is not very attached to it either, then the application of yoga disciplines to emotional experience will give that person perfection of life. (U.G. 15.8)

Otherwise the common people have to do *karma*, functional work in terms of righteous duty which is dictated to them by God directly or by some agent of the divinity who is in touch with Him while giving the instruction. There is no other general path for common people. All else is a farce.

शुद्ध्य-अशुद्धी विधीयेते
समानेष्व् अपि वस्तुषु ।
द्रव्यस्य विचिकित्सार्थं
गुण-दोषौ शुभाशुभौ ॥ १६.३ ॥

śuddhy-aśuddhī vidhīyete
samāneṣv api vastuṣu
dravyasya vicikitsārthaṁ
guṇa-doṣau śubhāśubhau (16.3)

śuddhy = śuddhi — purity; aśuddhī — impurity; vidhīyete — are stipulated; samāneṣv = samāneṣu — of the same groupings; api — also; vastuṣu — with regards to things; dravyasya — of things; vicikitsārtham = vicikitsā — categorization + artham — for the sake of; guṇa - merit; doṣau — and demerit; śubhāśubhau = śubha – what contributes to well-being + aśubhau — what detracts from well-being.

Translation

Purity and impurity are stipulated in terms of things of the same groupings and also for the sake of categorizing things, and so is merit and demerit, as well as what contributes to well-being and what detracts from it, (16.3)

Commentary:

For the average human being there are all kinds of do's and don'ts, all depending on tradition and approved life styles. Even though Uddhava cited the Vedas as the Ultimate reference on human behavior, still whatever is in the Vedas has to be explained to a common human being. It must also be enforced by rulers, teachers and parents. Thus merely the presence of the Vedas does not do everything all by itself. Details for specific people must be explained in terms of their tradition by some one who exerts authority over them. Thus there is no easy path for a common human being. *Śrī* Krishna, the Supreme Being, will not be there to instruct everyone, even if He is asked to do so by a great devotee like Uddhava who is sympathetic to humanity.

धर्मार्थं व्यवहारार्थं
यात्रार्थम् इति चानघ ।
दर्शितो ऽयं मयाचारो
धर्मम् उद्वहतां धुरम् ॥ १६.४ ॥

dharmārthaṁ vyavahārārthaṁ
yātrārtham iti cānagha
darśito 'yaṁ mayācāro
dharmam udvahatāṁ dhuram (16.4)

dharmārtham — for the sake of righteous duty; vyavahārārthaṁ = vyavahāra – behavior + artha — for the sake of; yātrārtham = yātrā – basic surivival + artham — for the sake of; iti — thus; cānagha = ca — and + anagha — o sinless one; darśito = darśitaḥ — revealed; 'yaṁ = ayam — this; mayācāro = mayā — by me + ācāraḥ — method of behavior; dharmam — righteous duty; udvahatām — for those who are carrying; dhuram — burden, task.

Translation

...and for the sake of righteous duty, behavior and basic survival, O sinless one, for those experiencing righteous duty as a task, this method of behavior was revealed by Me. (16.4)

Commentary:

This explains the situation of the Vedas as well as of the law books of the Vedic era. Such law books like the rules of *Manu* are meant to regulate human behavior and to limit what a human being might do for survival, so that he does not infringe the right of others, while procuring resources for his well being. For people who cannot take to *karma* yoga, *jñāna* yoga or *bhakti* yoga, they should be guided along the lines of social conduct in terms of good behavior.

भूम्य्-अम्ब्व्-अग्न्य्-अनिलाकाशा
भूतानां पञ्च-धातवः ।
आ-ब्रह्म-स्थावरादीनां
शारीरा आत्म-सयुताः ॥१६.५॥

bhūmy-ambv-agny-anilākāśā
bhūtānāṁ pañca-dhātavaḥ
ā-brahma-sthāvarādīnāṁ
śārīrā ātma-saṁyutāḥ (16.5)

bhūmy = bhūmi — solid material; ambv = ambu — liquid; agny = agni — combustive; anilākāśā = anila — gas + ākāśā — space; bhūtānām — of the creature forms; pañca — five; dhātavah — essential part; ā – from; brahma — procreator Brahmā; sthāvarādīnāṁ = sthāvara – stationary creatures + ādīnām — beginning with; śārīrā = śārīrāḥ — bodies; ātma — spirit; saṁyutāḥ — furnished with.

Translation

From Procreator Brahmā down to the stationary creatures, the solid materials, the liquids, the combustives, the gases, and spaces, being the five essential parts of the creature forms, and the bodies themselves, are all furnished with a spirit. (16.5)

Commentary:

This is basic information from the *Sāṅkhya* philosophy. This can be taught to common people. Some of them will be motivated by this knowledge to seek spiritual perfection. Others will just listen and go away. The idea is to show that ultimately there is a spirit in each of the living creature forms, which are made up of five essential ingredients. Then the question may arise as to what is the purpose of the conjunction between the spirits and these materials.

वेदेन नाम-रूपाणि
विषमाणि समेष्व् अपि ।
धातुषूद्धव कल्प्यन्त
एतेषां स्वार्थ-सिद्धये ॥१६.६॥

vedena nāma-rūpāṇi
viṣamāṇi sameṣv api
dhātuṣūddhava kalpyanta
eteṣāṁ svārtha-siddhaye (16.6)

vedena — by the Vedas; nāma — names; rūpāṇi — forms; viṣamāni — different; sameṣv = sameṣu — that which is singular; api — although; dhātuṣūddhava = dhātaṣu — in the essential parts + uddhava — Uddhava; kalpyanta = kalpyante — are imposed; eteṣām — of them; svārtha-siddhaye = svārtha — of one's own interest + siddhaye — in the perfection of life.

Translation

O Uddhava, for their own interest in the perfection of life, many different names and forms are imposed by the Vedas, on those bodies which are similar. (16.6)

Commentary:

Even though the bodies are pretty much the same in constitution, still in the Vedas, there are gradations listed, even in relation to the human forms. For example, a different treatment is given to a brahmin's body than to one of a laborer. But this is imposed by the Vedas to initiate an evolution whereby people would develop interest in the perfection of life and not just accept that they are material bodies and nothing else.

Of course this information from the Vedas and from the *Manu Samhitā* and other such books, was frequently misused, whereby a higher caste unfairly predominated over a lower one.

Still the original motive was to elevate human beings and to cause those in the lower status to strive for perfection in a series of lives.

देश-कालादि-भावानां
वस्तूनां मम सत्तम ।
गुण-दोषौ विधीयेते
नियमार्थं हि कर्मणाम् ॥ १६.७॥

deśa-kālādi-bhāvānāṁ
vastūnāṁ mama sattama
guṇa-doṣau vidhīyete
niyamārthaṁ hi karmaṇām (16.7)

deśa — place; kālādi — time and other factors; bhāvānām — regarding material existence; vastūnāṁ — regarding things, commodities; mama — by me; sattama = sat – saint + tama — best; guṇa – merit; doṣau — and demerit; vidhīyete — are defined; niyamārthaṁ = niyama – regulating + artha — for the sake of; hi — indeed; karmaṇām — of cultural activities.

Translation

Regarding the place, time and other factors of material existence, merit and demerit are defined in relation to commodities for the purpose of regulating cultural activities, O best of the saints. (16.7)

Commentary:

There are many commodities in material nature. Each has usage to this or that species of life. However, human beings are given guidelines, either by *Śrī* Krishna directly or by prophets, great sages and other leaders. These guidelines stipulate that a certain commodity should only be used in a certain way. This is all for regulating cultural activities *(niyamārtham karmaṇām).*

If the human being had more discrimination, there would be no need for the Supreme Lord to lay down rules and regulations. But it is not so, because the human being is only equipped with a sense for survival at any costs. Thus he is given guidelines for the protection of himself and others. Human society is supervised by the Supreme Being in His configuration of the Universal Form which was seen by Arjuna.

Śrī Krishna is not always directly involved as He was on the battlefield with Arjuna, but ultimately He is responsible for what takes place. He admitted this to Arjuna:

yadi hyahaṁ na varteyaṁ jātu karmaṇyatandritaḥ
mama vartmānuvartante manuṣyāḥ pārtha sarvaśaḥ
utsīdeyurime lokā na kuryāṁ karma cedaham
saṁkarasya ca kartā syām upahanyāmimāḥ prajāḥ

If perchance, I did not perform attentively, then all human beings, O son of Pṛthā, would follow Me in all respects.

If I should not engage in cultural activity, these worlds would perish. And I would be a producer of social chaos. I would have destroyed these creatures. (B.G. 3.23-24)

ye yathā māṁ prapadyante tāṁstathaiva bhajāmyaham
mama vartmānuvartante manuṣyāḥ pārtha sarvaśaḥ

As they rely on Me, so I relate to them, O son of Pṛthā. All human beings, everywhere, are affected by My course of action. (B.G. 4.11)

अकृष्ण-सारो देशानाम्
अब्रह्मण्यो ऽसुचिर् भवेत् ।
कृष्ण-सारो ऽप्य् असौवीर-
कीकटासस्कृतेरिणम् ॥ १६.८॥

akṛṣṇa-sāro deśānām
abrahmaṇyo 'sucir bhavet
kṛṣṇa-sāro 'py asauvīra-
kīkaṭāsaṁskṛteriṇam (16.8)

akṛṣṇa-sāro = akṛṣṇa-sāraḥ — without spotted antelope; deśānām — of territories; abrahmaṇyo = abrahmaṇyah — with residents who are not devoted to brahmins; 'sucir = aśucih — impure; bhavet — should be; kṛṣṇa-sāro = kṛṣṇa-sāraḥ — black spotted antelopes; 'py = api — even; asauvīra — without righteous people; kīkaṭāsaṁskṛteriṇam = kīkata — Kikata country + asaṁskṛta — without Vedic purificatory procedures + īriṇam — province of barren land.

Translation

Of territories, those without black-spotted antelope and those with residents who are not devoted to the brahmins, should be considered as impure. Even a place with black-spotted antelope such as the Kīkaṭa country and places where Vedic purificatory procedures are not observed, or where the land is barren, is impure, if there are no righteous people present. (16.8)

Commentary:

There are basic guidelines to protect the common people from degressing to lower species of life, either lower human forms or animal forms. By association, one may go upward or downward. It is much easier to go downwards. Therefore one has to take precautions to protect oneself from lower rebirth.

कर्मण्यो गुणवान् कालो
द्रव्यतः स्वत एव वा ।
यतो निवर्तते कर्म
स दोषो ऽकर्मकः स्मृतः ॥ १६.९ ॥

karmaṇyo guṇavān kālo
dravyataḥ svata eva vā
yato nivartate *karma*
sa doṣo 'karmakaḥ smṛtaḥ (16.9)

karmaṇyo = karmaṇyah — for sanctioned activities; guṇavān — conducive to; kālo = kālaḥ — time; dravyataḥ — facility of having items required; svata = svataḥ — relating to itself; eva — indeed; vā — or; yato = yataḥ — relating to which; nivartate — is prohibited; *karma* — cultural activity; sa = saḥ — this; doṣo = doṣaḥ — unfit; 'karmakaḥ = akarmakaḥ — no approved cultural activity; smṛtaḥ — is considered.

Translation

The time is conducive to sanctioned activities when there is facility of having the items required, or when time itself facilitates, but is considered unfit when there is no approved cultural activity or when the action is prohibited. (16.9)

Commentary:

In practical terms, this means that one has to depend on reliable spiritual teachers and priests to inform of the correct type of cultural activity. Anything done is sponsored by and is productive of culture. Culture from the past is tradition. Based on tradition, a person acts either to support or oppose convention. Not all culture is sanctioned and approved by the Supreme Being.

If we adapt the culture which is recommended by *Śrī* Krishna, we get closer to Him, otherwise we are set at a distance and our progress towards Him will be deterred.

द्रव्यस्य शुद्ध्य्-अशुद्धी च
द्रव्येण वचनेन च ।
सस्कारेणाथ कालेन
महत्वाल्पतयाथ वा ॥ १६.१० ॥

dravyasya śuddhy-aśuddhī ca
dravyeṇa vacanena ca
saṁskāreṇātha kālena
mahatvālpatayātha vā (16.10)

dravyasya — of an object; śuddhy = śuddhi — purity; aśuddhī — impurity; ca — and; dravyeṇa — by another object; vacanena — by authoritive opinion; ca — and; saṁskāreṇātha = saṁskāreṇa — by sanctification in ceremony + atha — or; kālena — by time; mahatvālpatayātha vā = mahatva – vastness + alpatayā — by minuteness + atha + vā — or, either.

Translation

The purity or impurity of an object is determined by its relationship to another object, and by authoritative opinion or by its sanctification in ceremony, or either by time, by its vastness or minuteness. (16.10)

Commentary:

There are hard and fast rules but even these are variant, depending on the time, place, status or condition. Judgement relies on authoritative opinion of a superior person. If however that person makes a mistake, then it is an error nevertheless, and carries consequences for all concerned.

For instance, non-injury is a most noble quality, but its application on the battlefield of Kuruksetra was limited to spiritual and moral nonviolence. It was not applicable in its gross respect. Arjuna was corrected in his view since he wanted to apply bodily non-injury at the expense of moral and spiritual hazards.

This means that even though the Vedas have guidelines, still *Śrī* Krishna's opinion as it applies to particular places and times, is required. The question is: How may we get His view from moment to moment?

शक्त्याशक्त्याथ वा बुद्ध्या
समृद्ध्या च यद् आत्मने ।
अघं कुर्वन्ति हि यथा
देशावस्थानुसारतः ॥ १६.११ ॥

śaktyāśaktyātha vā buddhyā
samṛddhyā ca yad ātmane
aghaṁ kurvanti hi yathā
deśāvasthānusārataḥ (16.11)

śaktyāśaktyātha = śaktyā — by power + aśaktyā — by the lack of power + atha vā — either; buddhyā — by intellectual capacity; samṛddhyā — by wealth; ca — and; yad = yat — which; ātmane — to the self; agham — defect; kurvanti — the items cause; hi — indeed; yathā — according to; deśāvasthānusārataḥ = deśa — place + avasthā — circumstance + anusārataḥ — in accordance with, compliance.

Translation

Either by power or by a lack of it, by intellectual capacity or by wealth, the items cause a defect to the self, according to the place and circumstance. (16.11)

Commentary:

As stated in the *Bhagavad-Gītā*, actions are hard to evaluate as regarding their effects. One action in one place might be meritorious and the same action elsewhere might be condemned. Even though there are standards of conduct, still there is required to be adjustment, all depending on the circumstances and exigencies.

karmaṇo hyapi boddhavyaṁ boddhavyaṁ ca vikarmaṇaḥ
akarmaṇaśca boddhavyaṁ gahanā karmaṇo gatiḥ

Indeed, appropriate action should be known and one should also recognize the inappropriate type. The effect of no action should be understood. The course of action is difficult to comprehend. (B.G. 4.17)

धान्य-दार्व्-अस्थि-तन्तूनां
रस-तैजस-चर्मणाम् ।
काल-वाय्व्-अग्नि-मृत्-तोयैः
पार्थिवानां युतायुतैः ॥ १६.१२ ॥

dhānya-dārv-asthi-tantūnāṁ
rasa-taijasa-carmaṇām
kāla-vāyv-agni-mṛt-toyaiḥ
pārthivānāṁ yutāyutaiḥ (16.12)

dhānya — grain; dārv = dāru — wood; asthi — bone; tantūnām — of textiles; rasa — liquid; taijasa — smelted objects; carmanām — of skins; kāla — time; vāyv = vāyu — air; agni — fire; mṛt — earth; toyaiḥ — by water; pārthivānām — of earthen objects; yutāyutaiḥ = yuta — in combination + ayutaiḥ — by singularity.

Translation

The status of grains, wood, bone, textiles, liquids, smelted objects, skins, and earthen things, is affected by time, air, fire, earth, and water, either singly or in combination. (16.12)

Commentary:

This means that one has to get an expert opinion that tallies with Lord Krishna's idea in order to determine what is pure and what is impure, what is acceptable and what is not. This discrimination can be developed by a living entity through proper association.

अमेध्य-लिप्तं यद् येन
गन्ध-लेपं व्यपोहति ।
भजते प्रकृतिं तस्य
तच् छौचं तावद् इष्यते ॥ १६.१३॥

amedhya-liptaṁ yad yena
gandha-lepaṁ vyapohati
bhajate prakṛtiṁ tasya
tac chaucaṁ tāvad iṣyate (16.13)

amedhya — by a contaminant; liptam — smeared; yad = yat — what, whatever; yena — by which; gandha — smell; lepam — impure; vyapohati — removes; bhajate — restores; prakṛtim — natural state; tasya — of that; tac = tat — that; chaucaṁ = śaucam — purifying; tāvad = tāvat — until; iṣyate — is effected.

Translation

Whatever removes the smell from anything that was smeared by a contaminant, and restores it to its natural state, is the purifier of that item and should be applied until it is effective. (16.13)

Commentary:

Contamination can be nullified by various methods, one of which is listed in this verse. Some contaminants are removed by issuing sounds, others by the application of powdered earth or cow dung, by weathering, by sunlight or rainfall. There are other methods which might be approved by the Universal Form of the Supreme Lord. All this is under the jurisdiction of the Central Figure in the Universal Form and the supernatural persons who are allied to Him.

स्नान-दान-तपो-ऽवस्था-
वीर्य-संस्कार-कर्मभिः ।
मत्-स्मृत्या चात्मनः शौचं
शुद्धः कर्माचरेद् द्विजः ॥ १६.१४॥

snāna-dāna-tapo-'vasthā-
vīrya-saṁskāra-karmabhiḥ
mat-smṛtyā cātmanaḥ śaucaṁ
śuddhaḥ karmācared dvijaḥ (16.14)

snāna — bath; dāna — charity; tapo = tapaḥ — austerity; 'vasthā = avasthā — according to bodily age; vīrya — stamina; saṁskāra — purificatory rites; karmabhiḥ — with cultural activities; mat-smṛtyā — with remembrance of Me; cātmanaḥ = ca — and + ātmanaḥ — of the self, psyche; śaucam — cleanliness; śuddhaḥ — purified; karmācared = karma — appropiate actions + ācaret — should perform; dvijaḥ — duly initiated brahmin.

Translation

Bath, charity and austerity, performed according to bodily age and stamina with purificatory rites and cultural activities, as well as remembrance of Me, cause the purification of the psyche. A duly-initiated brahmin should perform the appropriate activities. (16.14)

Commentary:

This indicates that a duly initiated brahmin is qualified to effect self purification. He should be trained in the facets listed above. Remembrance of *Śrī* Krishna is necessary as listed but it is not the only requirement. Each of the methods have their particular applications to various aspects of the psychology.

मन्त्रस्य च परिज्ञानं
कर्म-शुद्धिर् मद्-अर्पणम् ।
धर्मः सम्पद्यते षड्भिर्
अधर्मस् तु विपर्ययः ॥ १६.१५ ॥

mantrasya ca parijñānaṁ
karma-śuddhir mad-arpaṇam
dharmaḥ sampadyate ṣaḍbhir
adharmas tu viparyayaḥ (16.15)

mantrasya — of a sacred recitation; ca — and; parijñānam — thoroughly-known subject; *karma* — cultural activities; śuddhir = śuddhiḥ — purity; mad-arpaṇam = mat-arpanam — offering to me; dharmaḥ — righteous duty; sampadyate — is accomplished; ṣaḍbhir = ṣaḍbhiḥ — by the six factors which cause purity to the self; adharmas = adharmaḥ — deviant activities; tu — but; viparyayaḥ — the converse, opposite, the absence.

Translation

The purity of a sacred recitation, rests on its being thoroughly-known; that of cultural activities relies on it being offered to Me. Righteous duty is sanctified according to the six factors which cause purity. But deviant activities result from the absence of these. (16.15)

Commentary:

A sacred recitation, a mantra, does not give the result if it is not thoroughly known by the chanter. He may get an initiation from a spiritual master regarding this. Or he may discover the value of the mantra by using it.

Cultural activities are under the jurisdiction of the Universal Form as described in the *Bhagavad-Gītā*. By a careful study of what *Śrī* Krishna told Arjuna, one can learn how to perfect cultural activities without becoming implicated in the involvements. Righteous duty depends on six factors which are the time, place, substance, agent, sacred sounds and purificatory act. These are listed in the *Śrīmad Bhāgavatam* Canto 10 chapter 5 verse 4.

क्वचिद् गुणो ऽपि दोषः स्याद्
दोषो ऽपि विधिना गुणः ।
गुण-दोषार्थ-नियमस्
तद्-भिदाम् एव बाधते ॥ १६.१६ ॥

kvacid guṇo 'pi doṣaḥ syād
doṣo 'pi vidhinā guṇaḥ
guṇa-doṣārtha-niyamas
tad-bhidām eva bādhate (16.16)

kvacid = kvacit — sometime; guṇo = guṇaḥ — praiseworthy act; 'pi = api — even; dosaḥ — mistake; syād = syāt — turns into; doṣo = doṣaḥ — faulty action; 'pi = api — also; vidhinā — by virtue of an injunction; guṇaḥ — merit; guṇa – pious acts; doṣārtha — for the sake of impious acts; niyamas = niyamaḥ — regulation; tad-bhidām = tat-bhidām = tat— of that + bhidām - destruction; eva — merely; bādhate — blurs, could confuse.

Translation

Sometimes a worthy act turns into a mistake and a faulty action manifests as a merit. Thus the regulation stated for the sake of defining pious and impious acts may confuse their distinctions. (16.16)

Commentary:

One has to check carefully as to whether an act is pious or impious. Arjuna for instance faced a dilemma when he tried to follow the stipulations of the Vedas in regards to how to deal with one's relatives. Because *Śrī* Krishna advised, Arjuna was freed from the confusion and took a course which superficially, appeared to be impious but which was in fact the most pious action that Arjuna could execute in such a situation. Therefore ultimately one has to check with the Universal Form of *Śrī* Krishna. It is not that the Supreme Being is an arbitrary operator or a mere dictatorial and whimsical power, but it is that since He has the over-all responsibility and since He carries universal liability, He knows best. No one's vision is superior to His at any time. The problem remains however as to how one should contact the Universal Form. That is a big issue if we are to perfect an activity.

समान-कर्माचरणं
पतितानां न पातकम् ।
औत्पत्तिको गुणः सङ्गो
न शयानः पतत्य् अधः ॥ १६.१७ ॥

samāna-karmācaraṇaṁ
patitānāṁ na pātakam
autpattiko guṇaḥ saṅgo
na śayānaḥ pataty adhaḥ (16.17)

samāna — identical; karmācaranaṁ = *karma* — deed + ācaraṇam — the doing; patitānām — of those who are degraded; na — not; pātakam — blemish; autpattiko = autpattikaḥ — tendency; guṇaḥ — an asset; saṅgo = saṅgah — association, social contact; na — not; śayānaḥ — a person who lays down; pataty = patati — falls; adhaḥ — lower, further.

Translation

The doing of an identical deed is no blemish for those who are degraded, but social contact on the basis of one's tendency, is an asset, since a person who lays down can fall no further. (16.17)

Commentary:

A person should elevate himself if he can or at least he should maintain the status. What can God do? If a person does not have the inner motivation nor the potential to be motivated by someone else, then he will by necessity, either remain as he is or become degraded.

Uddhava begged and begged for easy solutions to the human problems, but ultimately the human progression hinges on motivation, either for self-ambition or by being prodded by others.

यतो यतो निवर्तेत
विमुच्येत ततस् ततः ।
एष धर्मो नृणां क्षेमः
शोक-मोह-भयापहः ॥ १६.१८ ॥

yato yato nivarteta
vimucyeta tatas tataḥ
eṣa dharmo nṛṇāṁ kṣemaḥ
śoka-moha-bhayāpahaḥ (16.18)

yato yato = yatah yatah — from whatever; nivarteta — abstains; vimucyeta — is freed from; tatas = tatah — from that; eṣa = eṣaḥ — this; dharmo = dharmaḥ — righteous conduct; nṛṇām — for human beings; kṣemaḥ — well-being; śoka — grief; moha — delusion; bhayāpahaḥ = bhaya — fear + apahaḥ — removal.

Translation

From whatever one abstains, one is freed from that. This is the righteous conduct of human beings, which results in the removal of grief, delusion and fear. (16.18)

Commentary:

The technique for getting rid of bad tendencies is abstinence, but it does not work in each case. In the *Bhagavad-Gītā*, there are details which indicate that mere abstinence will not stop a tendency from manifesting, even though it will cause the impulse to be suppressed for a time.

Righteous conduct however is not concerned with total suppression but with partial suppression for social purposes in exhibiting moral conduct. If one does not observe morality, one will be subjected to large doses of grief, delusion and fear.

For the purpose of *kriyā* yoga, complete elimination of undesirable qualities is required. One has to do more than merely abstain, which is only a partial measure. One has to take up austerities which effect deep changes within the psyche.

विषयेषु गुणाध्यासात्
पुसः सङ्गस् ततो भवेत्
सङ्गात् तत्र भवेत् कामः ।
कामाद् एव कलिर् नृणाम् ॥ १६.१९ ॥

viṣayeṣu guṇādhyāsāt
puṁsaḥ saṅgas tato bhavet
saṅgāt tatra bhavet kāmaḥ
kāmād eva kalir nṛṇām (16.19)

viṣayeṣu — in objects; guṇādhyāsāt = guṇa – value + adhyāsāt — from assigning; puṁsaḥ — person; saṅgas = saṅgaḥ — attachment; tato = tatah — from that; bhavet — become manifest; saṅgāt — from the attachment; tatra — there, in that case; bhavet — develops; kāmaḥ — craving; kāmād = kāmāt — from craving; eva — also; kalir = kaliḥ — quarrel; nṛṇām — among human beings.

Translation

The attachment of a person becomes manifest from his assignment of values to objects. From that attachment craving develops. From craving, there is quarrel among the human beings. (16.19)

Commentary:

This was presented in a slightly different way to Arjuna:

dhyāyato viṣayānpuṁsaḥ saṅgasteṣūpajāyate
saṅgātsaṁjāyate kāmaḥ kāmātkrodho'bhijāyate

The act of considering sensual objects, creates in a person, an attachment to them. From attachment comes craving. From this craving, anger is derived. (B.G. 2.62)

Much of our biases are expressed impulsively without due reason or with justification for prejudices. In any case, craving develops according to the value of the objects. From cravings come desire, which if it is frustrated leads to quarrel. This is because the resources are not restricted to a particular person. Hence one human being thinks that he should enjoy the very same person or commodity that another has appropriated.

कलेर् दुर्विषहः क्रोधस्
तमस् तम् अनुवर्तते ।
तमसा ग्रस्यते पुसश्
चेतना व्यापिनी द्रुतम् ॥ १६.२० ॥

kaler durviṣahaḥ krodhas
tamas tam anuvartate
tamasā grasyate puṁsaś
cetanā vyāpinī drutam (16.20)

kaler = kaleh — from dispute; durviṣahaḥ — intense; krodha = krodhah — anger; tamas = tamaḥ — depressing influence; tam — that; anuvartate — follow; tamasā — by the retardative influence; grasyate — is overpowered; puṁsaś = puṁsah — of a human being; cetanā — conscience; vyāpinī — predominating; drutam — quickly.

Translation

Dispute brings on intense anger, which is followed by the depressive influence. Thus the predominating conscience of a person is quickly overpowered by the retarding influence of material nature. (16.20)

Commentary:

This was explained in the *Bhagavad-Gītā*:

krodhādbhavati saṁmohaḥ saṁmohātsmṛtivibhramaḥ
smṛtibhraṁśādbuddhināśo buddhināśātpraṇaśyati

From anger, comes delusion. From this delusion, the conscience vanishes. When he loses judgment, his discerning power fades away. Once the discernment is affected, he is ruined. (B.G. 2.63)

We have to realize that there are lower energies in the mind, emotions and life force. These must be curbed. Eventually they should be eliminated by shifting ourselves to higher planes of consciousness. So long as we are on the lower levels we will have to deal with these impulsive energies. They abound in the lower realms.

तया विरहितः साधो
जन्तुः शून्याय कल्पते ।
ततो ऽस्य स्वार्थ-विभ्रंशो
मूर्च्छितस्य मृतस्य च ॥१६.२१॥

tayā virahitaḥ sādho
jantuḥ śūnyāya kalpate
tato 'sya svārtha-vibhraṁśo
mūrcchitasya mṛtasya ca (16.21)

tayā — of that; virahitah — deprived; sādho = sādhah — o saint; jantuḥ — a person; śūnyāya — nothing; kalpate — becomes; tato = tataḥ — hence; 'sya = asya — of his; svārtha = sva – own self + artha — interest; vibhraṁśo = vibhraṁśah — deprived; mūrcchitasya — regarding one who is in a stupor; mṛtasya — regarding one who is like a dead body; ca — and.

Translation

O saint, a person who is deprived of that becomes like nothing. Hence, regarding that person in a stupor, regarding that person who is as good as a dead body, there is the ruination of his self-interest. (16.21)

Commentary:

A person who is deprived of his sense of right and wrong, his discernment, his conscience, is ruined. Without the proper sense of judgment, one cannot make the right decisions.

विषयाभिनिवेशेन
नात्मानं वेद नापरम् ।
वृक्ष जीविकया जीवन्
व्यर्थं भस्त्रेव यः श्वसन् ॥१६.२२॥

viṣayābhiniveśena
nātmānaṁ veda nāparam
vṛkṣa jīvikayā jīvan
vyarthaṁ bhastreva yaḥ śvasan (16.22)

viṣayābhiniveśena = viṣaya — in attractive objects + abhiniveśena — by being engrossed due to instinctive fear of death; nātmānaṁ = na — neither + ātmānam — self; veda — know; naparam = na — nor + aparam — another; vrksa — tree; jīvikayā — by the life-style; jīvan — living; vyartham — vainly; bhastreva = bhastra – bellows + iva — like; yaḥ — who; śvasan — breathing.

Translation

Engrossed in the attractive objects by an instinctive fear of death, he knows neither himself or any other person but lives in vain like a tree and breathes like bellows. (16.22)

Commentary:

The human life is capable of yielding liberation. A human being can exhibit keen discernment to realize that he is psychologically different from the gross body. A little of this realisation may lead to higher categorization of the various objects which are in the psychology. If however, a human being is unable to utilize the discernment, except for things of a purely physical nature, then his consciousness would be comparable to that of a tree and his vital energy would function like bellows in an air-forcing machine.

फल-श्रुतिर् इयं नृणां
न श्रेयो रोचनं परम् ।
श्रेयो-विवक्षया प्रोक्तं
यथा भैषज्य-रोचनम् ॥१६.२३॥

phala-śrutir iyaṁ nṛṇāṁ
na śreyo rocanaṁ param
śreyo-vivakṣayā proktaṁ
yathā bhaiṣajya-rocanam (16.23)

phala – benefits; śrutir = śrutiḥ — Vedic statements; iyam — this; nṛṇām — for human beings; na — not; śreyo = śreyaḥ — highest well-being; rocanam — incentive, inducement; param — merely;

śreyah — physical well-being; vivaksayā — with the aim of saying; proktam — stated; yathā — just as like; bhaisajya — administering medicine; rocanam — inducement.

Translation

The Vedic statements in relation to benefits, do not facilitate the highest well-being. They are mere incentives, stated in such a way, as to make one eventually endeavor for the said well-being, just as inducements are used in administering medicine. (16.23)

Commentary:

Many Vedic statements as well as statements in the *Purāṇas* are merely incentives to make a human being act in a moral way. In these statements there is an illusory promise of salvation, such that a human feels that if he follows a certain religion, he will get salvation at the time of death. What he gets is in fact is another material body, but in the mean time, he is induced to live in a pious way.

Human beings by their very nature, cause the creation of incentive religions which promise salvation by methods which cannot yield a spiritual result. Such methods only give them moral life or righteous duty. But if people take to such life and realize that it is not salvation, they are more likely to accept the austerity which is required for salvation.

For overcoming sickness, an unpalatable medicine is usually required, but children shy away from the cure. Thus doctors coat a medicine with a sweetener which as acts as an inducement.

However in terms of salvation, one should perform the proper austerities. The sweeteners or easy paths must be given up in the end. One must endeavor directly by austerities to achieve salvation. This is why *Śrī* Krishna repeatedly belittled the Vedas.

Unfortunately in this Age, there are so many religions which offer cheap or easy methods of salvation which will not yield what is promised. But this is due to the inherent dishonesty in human beings. When all is said and done however, no one will attain salvation by an easy path.

उत्पत्त्यैव हि कामेषु
प्राणेषु स्व-जनेषु च ।
आसक्त-मनसो मर्त्या
आत्मनो ऽनर्थ-हेतुषु ॥ १६.२४ ॥

utpattyaiva hi kāmeṣu
prāṇeṣu sva-janeṣu ca
āsakta-manaso martyā
ātmano 'nartha-hetuṣu (16.24)

utpattyaiva = utpattyā eva — by nature; hi — indeed; kāmeṣu — in pleasures; prāṇeṣu — in vital energy; sva – own; janeṣu — in folks; ca — and; āsakta – attachment; manaso = manasaḥ — of the mind; martyā — human beings who will definitely pass from their bodies; ātmano = ātmanaḥ — of the self; 'nartha = anartha — not in the interest; hetuṣu — in the causes.

Translation

Human beings by their very nature, are mentally attached to pleasure, vital energy and their relatives, although these are not in the interest of the self. (16.24)

Commentary:

Uddhava asked for an easy path. *Śrī* Krishna explained why it is not possible to have one and why it was instructed that human beings be made to take up righteous duties as directed by God through the great sages and other representatives of divinity.

By nature, we remain attached to mental pleasures, to what ever gives us physical life and to our relatives and friends, although such attachments are hardly proven to be in our spiritual interest.

नतान् अविदुषः स्वार्थं
भ्राम्यतो वृजिनाध्वनि ।
कथं युञ्ज्यात् पुनस् तेषु
तांस् तमो विशतो बुधः ॥१६.२५॥

natān aviduṣaḥ svārthaṁ
bhrāmyato vṛjinādhvani
kathaṁ yuñjyāt punas teṣu
tāṁs tamo viśato budhaḥ (16.25)

natān — those who submit; aviduṣaḥ — those who are without knowledge; svārtham — one's own interest; bhrāmyato = bhrāmyataḥ — wander; vṛjinādhvani = vṛjina — misery + adhvani — in the course; katham — how; yuñjyāt — put to task; punas = punaḥ — again; teṣu — in those (pleasures and attachment); tāṁs = tān — them; tamo = tamah — retardative influence; viśato = viśatah — those who become emerged; budhaḥ — enlightened person.

Translation

Considering the people who submit to the Vedic doctrine, but who are without knowledge of their self interest, who wander on the course of misery, and who subsequently become emerged in the retardative influence, how can an enlightened person again put them to the task in search of those same pleasures and attachments. (16.25)

Commentary:

This question of *Śrī* Krishna may be answered as follows. Many religious leaders pose as enlightened teachers. They are not realized, but they are sympathetic to human beings. They take to preaching activities, sincerely thinking that they can save human beings by presenting an easy path. These spiritual leaders take one or two agreeable statements from the scriptures and publicize these as paths to salvation.

Since the ordinary human beings does not know what salvation is, they are apt to be fooled by such preachers. One may be fooled life after life, because there is no memory of the former life and in each life, the false propositions for salvation are accepted with renewed fervor.

Since a human being derives satisfaction from the same pleasures and attachment which yield him no spiritual progress, he may be fooled repeatedly, provided he is given those satisfactions in a veiled form under the name of religion.

एवं व्यवसित केचिद्
अविज्ञाय कुबुद्धयः ।
फल-श्रुति कुसुमितां
न वेद-ज्ञा वदन्ति हि ॥१६.२६॥

evaṁ vyavasitaṁ kecid
avijñāya kubuddhayaḥ
phala-śrutiṁ kusumitāṁ
na veda-jñā vadanti hi (16.26)

evam — thus; vyavasitam — scheme of inducements; kecid = kecit — some persons; avijñāya — not knowing, unaware; kubuddhayah — perverted intellect; phala – result-motivating; śrutim — Vedic statements; kusumitām — poetic; na — not; veda-jñā — Veda knowers; vadanti — speak; hi — indeed.

Translation

Some persons, possessing a perverted intellect, and being unaware of the scheme of the inducement, glorify the result-motivated poetic Vedic statements. But the knowers of the Vedas do not speak like that. (16.26)

Commentary:

The incentives are there to induce the common people to begin the path of religion, so that gradually by orientation they would take up more and more austerities and admit that they must make a greater endeavor to achieve the ultimate aim of life, but some preachers do not understand this. They explain to audiences that the incentives are the actual austerities, and that anything more is unnecessary, since God does not require it and since He will give salvation easily.

However knowledgeable speakers do not say this. They do not redicule the incentive statements but all the same they do not convey the idea that those inducements are the whole path of salvation.

कामिनः कृपणा लुब्धाः
पुष्पेषु फल-बुद्धयः ।
अग्नि-मुग्धा धूम-तान्ताः
स्वं लोकं न विदन्ति ते ॥१६.२७॥

kāminaḥ kṛpaṇā lubdhāḥ
puṣpeṣu phala-buddhayaḥ
agni-mugdhā dhūma-tāntāḥ
svaṁ lokaṁ na vidanti te (16.27)

kāminah — people who crave pleasure; kṛpanā = kṛpanāh — those who are mean spirited; lubdhāh — those who are avaricious; puṣpeṣu — in the flowers, in the fantastic promises; phala-buddhayaḥ — those who are prone to thinking of benefits; agni — fire ceremony; mugdhā = mugdhāh — bewildered; dhūma – path of smoke; tāntāḥ — fatigued; svam — their own; lokam — destination hereafter; na – not; vidanti — know; te — they.

Translation

People who crave pleasures, who are mean-spirited and avaricious, who think that results are to be realized in fantastic promises, who are bewildered by fire ceremonies, and are fatigued while going on the path of smoke, do not know their deserved destinations hereafter. (16.27)

Commentary:

This is a condemnation of the Vedic fire sacrifices which cause the followers to take a human body or a subhuman one but which do not fulfill the fantastic promises about going to heaven or the kingdom of God. Unfortunately for human civilization at this time, there are many religious sects which do not use fire ceremonies but which advocate a fantastic life hereafter, either in the angelic or spiritual worlds, but such religions do serve the purpose of keeping many people in a moral life style for the time being.

न ते माम् अङ्ग जानन्ति
हृदि-स्थं य इद यतः ।
उक्थ-शस्त्रा ह्य् असु-तृपो
यथा नीहार-चक्षुषः ॥१६.२८॥

na te mām aṅga jānanti
hṛdi-sthaṁ ya idaṁ yataḥ
uktha-śastrā hy asu-tṛpo
yathā nīhāra-cakṣuṣaḥ (16.28)

na — not; te — they; mām — me; aṅga — dear friend; jānanti — know; hrdi – core of being; stham — situated; ya = yah — who; idam — this (world); yataḥ — from whom it is produced; uktha – those who acclaim; śastrā = śastrāḥ — scriptures; hy = hi — becomes; asu – living; tṛpo = tṛpaḥ — sensually satisfied; yathā — just as; nīhāra — restricted; cakṣuṣaḥ — those whose vision.

Translation

O dear friend, they do not know Me, who am situated in the core of their being, and who is the person from whence this world came into being, because they acclaim the scriptures but also live for sensual satisfaction just as people whose vision is restricted by fog. (16.28)

Commentary:

So long as we pursue sensual satisfaction in this world, we cannot have spirituality. It is as simply as that. Religion is there but it cannot help if we maintain sensual craving.

So long as we remain sensually-attached, we cannot attain salvation even if we believe in *Śrī* Krishna or in another divinity.

ते मे मतम् अविज्ञाय
परोक्षं विषयात्मकाः ।
हिंसायां यदि रागः स्याद्
यज्ञ एव न चोदना ॥ १६.२९ ॥

te me matam avijñāya
parokṣaṁ viṣayātmakāḥ
hiṁsāyāṁ yadi rāgaḥ syād
yajña eva na codanā (16.29)

te — they; me — my; matam — intention; avijñāya — not realising; parokṣam — secret; viṣayātmakāḥ = viṣaya – sensuality + ātmakāh — self-absorbed; hiṁsāyām — concerning the act of killing animals; yadi — if; rāgah — passion; syād = syāt — may be; yajña = yajñe — in sacrificial ceremonies; eva — only; na — no; codanā — rule (to authorize sacrificial killing).

Translation

These people who are self-absorbed in sensuality, do not realise my secret intention. For if one has a passion for killing animals, it may be fulfilled only in sacrifices, and it is not a rule to authorize killing. (16.29)

Commentary:

According to the Vedas one may engage in killing animals in sacrifices. In the Vedic period there were some scriptures which had procedures even for ritual killing of human beings, and it is well known that there were horse sacrifices performed by kings for the protection of their dynasties and kingdoms.

Śrī Krishna explained that in so far as He is the author of the Vedas, His intention was to regulate the violent nature of human beings, by allowing limited killing in the context of Vedic sacrifices but not otherwise. It was to accommodate and restrict the violent needs of some human beings, not to expand nor endorse their brutality.

हिंसा-विहारा ह्य् आलब्धैः
पशुभिः स्व-सुखेच्छया ।
यजन्ते देवता यज्ञैः
पितृ-भूत-पतीन् खलाः ॥ १६.३० ॥

hiṁsā-vihārā hy ālabdhaiḥ
paśubhiḥ sva-sukhecchayā
yajante devatā yajñaiḥ
pitṛ-bhūta-patīn khalāḥ (16.30)

hiṁsā – violence; vihārā — those who revel; hy = hi — indeed; ālabdhaiḥ — by sacrificing; paśubhiḥ — by animals; sva-sukhecchayā = sva-sukha — one's own happiness + icchayā — by desire; yajante — worship; devatā — supernatural rulers; yajnaih — by sacrificial ceremonies; pitr — departed ancestors; bhūta-patīn — leaders of the ghosts; khalāh — wicked people.

Translation

By a desire for their own happiness, those wicked people who revel in violence, worship the supernatural rulers, the departed ancestors and the leaders of the ghosts, in sacrificial ceremonies, by sacrificing animals. (16.30)

Commentary:

This is part of the reason why *Śrī* Krishna disavowed the Vedas, even though elsewhere He claimed to be its author. It was to discredit religiously justified violent acts and for not underwriting everything proclaimed and suggested in the Vedas.

स्वप्नोपमम् अमुं लोकम्
असन्तं श्रवण-प्रियम् ।
आशिषो हृदि सङ्कल्प्य
त्यजन्त्य् अर्थान् यथा वणिक् ॥ १६.३१ ॥

svapnopamam amuṁ lokam
asantaṁ śravaṇa-priyam
āśiṣo hṛdi saṅkalpya
tyajanty arthān yathā vaṇik (16.31)

svapnopamam = svapna — dream + upamam — resemblance, likeness; amum — that; lokam — world hereafter; asantam — imaginative; śravaṇa – to hear about; priyam — pleasing; āśiṣo = āśiṣaḥ — wish for the future, good will; hrdi — in central consciousness; sankalpya — imagining;

tyajanty = tyajanti — spend; arthān — money; yathā — just as, like; vanik — a trader.

Translation

Imagining in their central consciousness, a future world hereafter, which is like a dream, and which is pleasing to hear of, they spend money like a trader. (16.31)

Commentary:

Victims of cheap religions, of very impractical methods for attaining salvation, are just like traders who invest their money in risky business ventures in the hope of making lucrative profits. A trader may gain profits or he may be frustrated quickly and will then be able to analyze the miscalculation, but religious people are unable to do so, because their aspirations usually come after the death of their bodies, and unfortunately they are not conscious enough at that time in the after-world, to properly analyze what occured. Thus again when they take a new human form, they fall for the same schemes.

Such people do not like to speak to saintly persons who could show them the time-tested valid path in which they should perform honest austerities, because in such a path there appears to be no quick profits and no God who awards salvation as easily as they desire.

Invariably such people are victimized by preachers and religious leaders who use their hard-earned legally-obtained or criminally-acquired money, for building large temples, extensive preaching missions and whatever is required, to fulfill related desires. Such is this life.

रजः-सत्त्व-तमो-निष्ठा
रजः-सत्त्व-तमो-जुषः ।
उपासत इन्द्र-मुख्यान्
देवादीन् न यथैव माम् ॥ १६.३२ ॥

rajaḥ-sattva-tamo-niṣṭhā
rajaḥ-sattva-tamo-juṣaḥ
upāsata indra-mukhyān
devādīn na yathaiva mām (16.32)

rajah — impulsive mode of material nature; sattva — clarifying mode of material nature; tamo = tamaḥ — retardative mode of material nature; niṣṭhā = niṣṭhāh — situated in; rajaḥ — impulsive influence; sattva — clarifying influence; tamo = tamah — retardative influence; juṣah — who manifest; upāsate — they worship; indra – Indra; mukhyān — those who have a chief; devādīn — supernatural rulers and other supernatural providers; na — not; yathaiva = yathā eva — in the right way; mām — me.

Translation

Being situated in the impulsive, clarifying and retardative influences of material nature, they worship the supernatural rulers and other such providers who have Indra as their chief and who also resort to the impulsive, clarifying and retardative influences. They do not worship Me in the right way. (16.32)

Commentary:

This was discussed in the instructions to Arjuna, where *Śrī* Krishna said the same thing in another way, condemning the worship of the *devatas* who are headed by Indra, the ruler of the angelic world.

इष्ट्वेह देवता यज्ञैर्
गत्वा रंस्यामहे दिवि ।
तस्यान्त इह भूयास्म
महा-शाला महा-कुलाः ॥ १६.३३ ॥

iṣṭveha devatā yajñair
gatvā raṁsyāmahe divi
tasyānta iha bhūyāsma
mahā-śālā mahā-kulāḥ (16.33)

iṣṭveha = iṣṭvā — ceremonially worshiping + iha — here; devatā — supernatural rulers; yajñaiḥ — by Vedic ritualistic procedures; gatvā — going; raṁsyāmahe — we will enjoy; divi — in paradise hereafter; tasyānta = tasya — of that + anta — in the end, after which; iha — here on earth; bhūyāsma — we will be existing; mahā – large; śālā — homes; mahā – large; kulāḥ — families.

Translation

They think: "Ceremonially worshiping the supernatural rulers, while here on earth, by performing Vedic ritualistic ceremonies, we will go and enjoy in paradise hereafter. After which we will exist on earth in large homes in powerful families." (16.33)

Commentary:

This is the type of consciousness one derives from an easy religion. This also applies to those persons who worship Lord Krishna in an easy way, which will not get them His association, because their impurities are not removed. One will simply go to a heavenly world for a time or not go there at all, and then will again take another human body sometime after to repeat the same type of lifestyle with the same belief.

एव पुष्पितया वाचा
व्याक्षिप्त-मनसां नृणाम् ।
मानिनां चाति-लुब्धानां
मद्-वार्तापि न रोचते ॥ १६.३४॥

evaṁ puṣpitayā vācā
vyākṣipta-manasāṁ nṛṇām
māninām cāti-lubdhānāṁ
mad-vārtāpi na rocate(16.34)

evam — thus; puṣpitayā — by flowers, by poetic wording; vācā — by wording of the scripture; vyākṣipta – fascinated; manasām — of the minds; nṛṇām — people; māninām — of those who are arrogant; cāti-lubdhānāṁ = ca — and + ati-lubdhānām — of those who are very greedy; madvārtāpi = mat vārtā — references about me; api — also; na – no; rocate — like.

Translation

These people, whose minds are fascinated by the poetic wording of the scripture, who are arrogant and very greedy, never like even a reference about Me. (16.34)

Commentary:

We should not misunderstand this and think that everyone who is a devotee of *Śrī* Krishna is out of the category of those who hold much wishful thinking about how to attain salvation. Currently, there are many superficial religions which use *Śrī* Krishna as their one and only Deity. By twisting and contorting the *Śrīmad Bhagavad-Gītā*, and the *Śrīmad Bhāgavatam*, some religious leaders proclaim incentive-type Krishna-focused religions. Many scriptures which were produced in the disciplic succession over the centuries, which are in fact based on the Krishna *līla*, are cheapened versions of the Krishna Worship, which advocate an easy path which will take the followers to their end with similar fantasies, not regarding Indra and the angelic world but regarding Krishna and His spiritual world, or some other divine personality and His spiritual domain.

Advocates of such religions fight with tooth and nail to protect their religions from exposure. They take every step to ban any type of revealing commentaries. Such is the situation.

In India, in every region, a set of people have their *Avatār* or complete Personality of Godhead, who is an incarnation of *Śrī* Krishna and who brought to humanity a quick and easy process of salvation. It is simply amazing how many religions pop up in India repeatedly. The followers of each of these religions denounce the others and advocate their system as the only way for salvation and as the quickest and easiest method.

वेदा ब्रह्मात्म-विषयास्
त्रि-काण्ड-विषया इमे ।
परोक्ष-वादा ऋषयः
परोक्षं मम च प्रियम् ॥ १६.३५॥

vedā brahmātma-viṣayās
tri-kāṇḍa-viṣayā ime
parokṣa-vādā ṛṣayaḥ
parokṣaṁ mama ca priyam (16.35)

veda — Vedas; brahmātma = brahma spiritual existence; ātma — spirit; viṣayā = viṣayāḥ — subject maters; tri-kanda = three parts; viṣayā = viṣayāḥ — topics; ime — these; parokṣa – indirect; vada — statements; ṛṣayah — yogi sages; parokṣam — indirect explanations; mama — by me; ca — and; priyam — is appreciated.

Translation

The Vedas which consists of three parts deal with the subject of the spiritual existence and the spirit. These statements by the yogi sages, are indirect in meaning. And that indirectness is appreciated by Me. (16.35)

Commentary:

The Vedas were meant to explain the over-all spiritual existence as well as the individual spiritual person, the *ātma*, but the yogi sages only explained it indirectly, which *Śrī* Krishna appreciated. Thus an ordinary person cannot understand the spiritual import of the Vedas and instead, get the idea, that ceremonial procedures will give everything.

As applied to our modern situation, even Sanskrit literature like this talk with Uddhava as well as the *Bhagavad-Gītā* discourse which is very direct and which gives the spiritual explanations about the spiritual existence, and the limited spirits as well as material existence and its constituent parts, is not understood by common persons. And what is mentioned herein as being easy is taken out of context and explained to the common people as the total means of salvation.

Śrī Krishna appreciated the indirectness of the yogi sages who wrote the Vedas but He did not appreciate others who exploited that ambiguity by promising heaven to persons who did not qualify for it and who would certainly not achieve it by superficial means.

शब्द-ब्रह्म सु-दुर्बोध
प्राणेन्द्रिय-मनो-मयम् ।
अनन्त-पार गम्भीर
दुर्विगाह्यं समुद्र-वत् ॥१६.३६॥

śabda-brahma su-durbodhaṁ
prāṇendriya-mano-mayam
ananta-pāraṁ gambhīraṁ
durvigāhyaṁ samudra-vat (16.36)

sabda – sound, authoritive word text, the Vedas; brahma — the ultimate reality; su-durbodham — that which is very difficult to understand; prāṇendriya = prāṇa — vital energy + indriya — sensual energy; mano = manah — the mind; mayam — produced by manipulation; ananta – unlimited; pāram — transcendental; gambhīram — profound; durvigāhyam — O unfathomable; samudra-vat — like the ocean.

Translation

Describing the ultimate reality, the authoritive word-text, the Vedas, which was produced by the manipulation of vital energy, sensual energy and the mind, is very difficult to understand. It is unlimited, transcendental, profound and unfathomable like the ocean. (16.36)

Commentary:

The Vedas were an attempt to cross a barrier from the spiritual to the material. It involved the manipulation of vital energy, sensual power and the mind, all in an effort to explain something that was beyond mundane existence, something that was unlimited, transcendental, profound and unfathomable like the ocean. Thus there was bound to be misrepresentation by those who tried to use the Vedas but who were not on par with the yogi sages (*ṛṣayah* verse 35).

मयोपबृहितं भूम्ना
ब्रह्मणानन्त-शक्तिना ।
भूतेषु घोष-रूपेण
विसेषूर्णेव लक्ष्यते ॥१६.३७॥

mayopabṛṁhitaṁ bhūmnā
brahmaṇānanta-śaktinā
bhūteṣu ghoṣa-rūpeṇa
viseṣūrṇeva lakṣyate (16.37)

mayopabṛṁhitam = maya — by me + upabrmhitam — reinforced; bhūmnā — by the infinite; brahmaṇānanta = brahmaṇā — ultimate reality + ananta – endless; śaktinā — potency; bhūteṣu — in the living beings; ghosa – sound; rūpeṇa — by form; viseṣūrṇeva = viseṣu — in the lotus stalk + ūrṇā — fibre; iva — like; lakṣyate — is noticed.

Translation

Reinforced by Me, the Infinite Ultimate Reality of endless potency, it is noticed as the form of sound in all living beings, just like recognizing the slender fibers in a lotus stalk. (16.37)

Commentary:

Brahman or the ultimate reality was to be explained in the Vedas in a cryptic way which only the yogi sages could really understand. Others who attempted to tap into the Vedas got befooled by the poesy of the Sanskrit language. However, that Brahman Ultimate Reality is directly perceptible in its form of sound which is in all living beings.

Still, that is not easy to perceive. Some commentators have accredited it as the Om sound. Some suggested that it can be awakened by chanting various *mahāmantras*. However this is a purely mystic technique for those who do *kriyā* yoga. It cannot be realized on the external plane nor by any external methods which are used for attaining salvation. The indication of this was given before by Lord Krishna, when he explained a special *kriyā* for opening *suśumnā naḍi*:

hṛdy avicchinam oṁkāraṁ ghaṇṭā-nādaṁ bisorṇa-vat
prāṇenodīrya tatrātha punaḥ saṁveśayet svaram
evaṁ praṇava-saṁyuktaṁ prāṇam eva samabhyaset
daśa-kṛtvas tri-ṣavaṇaṁ māsād arvāg jitānilaḥ

In the heart chakra, the Om sound which is like the continuous peal of a bell, resonates continually, like a fibre in a lotus stalk. Raising it by using the vitalizing energy, one should blend that sound with the musical tones.

Thus, one should carefully direct the pre-mixed Om sound and the vitalizing energy, ten times, thrice per day. (U.G. 9.34-35)

Such a sound is only heard while practicing the 6th, 7th, and 8th stages of yoga, the higher practice. This sound leaks over into the psyche of a yogi from the chit *ākāśa*, the sky of consciousness. It is not a sound made by a person's mouth nor by his mental sounding apparatus. It is not heard when a person is focused on *japa* or *kīrtan* chantings. Those are completely different practices, which *Śrī* Krishna did not describe here.

यथोर्णनाभिर् हृदयाद्
ऊर्णाम् उद्वमते मुखात् ।
आकाशाद् घोषवान् प्राणो
मनसा स्पर्श-रूपिणा ॥ १६.३८॥

yathorṇanābhir hṛdayād
ūrṇām udvamate mukhāt
ākāśād ghoṣavān prāṇo
manasā sparśa-rūpiṇā (16.38)

yathorṇanābhir = yathā — as + ūrṇa-nābhiḥ — spider; hrdayād = hrdayāt — from within its body; ūrṇām — web; udvamate — projects; mukhāt — from its mouth; ākāśād = ākāśāt — from cosmic space; ghoṣavān — vibrates a sound; prāno = pranaḥ — cosmic vital force; manasā — through the mind; sparśa – lettered alphabet; rūpiṇā — by form.

Translation

As a spider projects a web, from within its body, through its mouth, so the cosmic vital force, from cosmic space, projects vibrating sound through the mind in the form of the lettered alphabet, (16.38)

Commentary:

There are two aspects of the Supreme Reality, one is the Supreme Person who is described in the previous verse, as the Infinite Ultimate Reality of Endless Potency and the other was described as the unlimited; transcendental, profound and unfathomable ultimate reality. These two aspects are related. One cannot be seperated from the other.

However various yogis consider either one or the other or both to be supreme. Thus there are various sects and various arguments to support the varied experiences and due speculations of the advanced mystics.

In this verse *Śrī* Krishna described why the Vedas was always considered to be revealed information. It was because, the cosmic vital force projected through the minds of the yogi sages, and produced by its appropriation of their vital energy, sensual energy and mind, the original Vedas (verse 36).

This might be hard to accept but we have to take it at face value for the time being, until we can prove otherwise. From this verse, it appears that the cosmic vital energy (*prāṇa*), which elsewhere was described as the *Sūtram* and or sexually-charged cosmic potency, acted on its own to invade the minds of those yogi sages who produced the Vedas in aural form.

छन्दो-मयो ऽमृत-मयः
सहस्त्र-पदवीं प्रभुः ।
ओकाराद् व्यञ्जित-स्पर्श-
स्वरोष्मान्तस्थ-भूषिताम् ॥ १६.३९ ॥

chando-mayo 'mṛta-mayaḥ
sahasra-padavīṁ prabhuḥ
oṁkārād vyañjita-sparśa-
svaroṣmāntastha-bhūṣitām (16.39)

chando = chandah – Vedic poetic meter; mayo = mayaḥ — comprising; 'mṛta = amṛta –delightful; mayaḥ — comprising, which is; sahasra – thousand; padavīm — issued; prabhuḥ — the master of this existence; omkārād = omkārāt — from Om; vyañjita — fashioned; sparśa — consonants; svaroṣmāntastha = svara — vowels + uṣma — sibilants + anta stha — semi-vowels; bhūṣitām — matched with.

Translation

...which produced the texts which comprise the Vedic poetic meter and which is delightful and which was issued in a thousand channels. That cosmic vital energy is the expression of the master of this existence. From Oṁ was fashioned the consonants, vowels, sibilants and semi-vowels, all matching suitably, (16.39)

Commentary:

The cosmic vital energy (*prāṇa* or *sūtram*) was charged by the Supreme Being. It induced the yogi sages to compose the Sanskrit language and the Vedas which they enunciated aurally.

विचित्र-भाषा-विततां
छन्दोभिश् चतुर्-उत्तरैः ।
अनन्त-पारां बृहतीं
सृजत्य् आक्षिपते स्वयम् ॥ १६.४० ॥

vicitra-bhāṣā-vitatāṁ
chandobhiś catur-uttaraiḥ
ananta-pārāṁ bṛhatīṁ
sṛjaty ākṣipate svayam (16.40)

vicitra — varied; bhāṣā — language; vitatām — elaborated; chandobhiś = chandobhiḥ — with poetic meters; catur – four; uttaraiḥ — with additional; ananta-pārām — endless; bṛhatīm — hugh vocabulary; sṛjaty = sṛjati — creates; ākṣipate — withdraws; svayam — himself.

Translation

...elaborated as varied language, with each having four additional syllables. He creates and withdraws the endless hugh vocabulary into Himself. (16.40)

Commentary:

This person is the *Hiraṇyagarbha* or Procreator *Brahmā*, who is the actual author of the Vedas. The yogi sages who were the original composers, were inspired by Him. Here again, we hear of personal and impersonal causes or stated more precisely personal and potent causes.

गायत्र्य् उष्णिग् अनुष्टुप् च
बृहती पङ्क्तिर् एव च ।
त्रिष्टुब् जगत्य् अतिच्छन्दो
ह्य् अत्यष्ट्य्-अतिजगद्-विराट् ॥ १६.४१ ॥

gāyatry uṣṇig anuṣṭup ca
bṛhatī paṅktir eva ca
triṣṭub jagaty aticchando
hy atyaṣṭy-atijagad-virāṭ (16.41)

gāyatry = gāyatrī – Gāyatrī ; uṣṇig = uṣṇik – Usnik; anuṣṭup – Anuṣṭup; ca — and; bṛhatī – Bṛhati; paṅktir = paṅktih — Pankti; eva – also; ca — and; triṣṭub = Tristub; jagaty = jagatī – Jagati; aticchando = aticchandaḥ — Aticchanda; hy = hi — indeed; atyaṣti – Atyaṣṭi; atijagat –Atijagati; virāṭ — Ativirāt.

Translation

There are the Gāyatrī. Uṣṇik, and Anuṣṭup, as well as the Bṛhatī and Paṅkti, the Tristup, Jagatī and Aticchanda, the Atyaṣṭi, Atijagatī and Ativirāṭ Vedic verses. (16.41)

किं विधत्ते किम् आचष्टे
किम् अनूद्य विकल्पयेत् ।
इत्य् अस्या हृदयं लोके
नान्यो मद् वेद कश्चन ॥ १६.४२ ॥

kiṁ vidhatte kim ācaṣṭe
kim anūdya vikalpayet
ity asyā hṛdayaṁ loke
nānyo mad veda kaścana (16.42)

kim — what; vidhatte — enjoin; kim — what; ācaṣṭe — states; kim — what; anūdya — categorising; vikalpayet — presents as an alternative; ity = iti — thus; asya — of this; hrdayam — the secret; loke — in this world; nānyo = na — no + anyaḥ — other; mad = mat — except Me; veda — know; kaścana — anyone.

Translation

What the Vedic text enjoins, what it states by categorizing, it presents as an alternative, no one in this world knows the secret of this but Me. (16.42)

Commentary:

We will have to accept this at face value. However we can surmise it by accepting *Śrī* Krishna as the source of the sexually-charged cosmic energy which manifested personally as Procreator *Brahmā*. He in turn presented the Vedas to his mind-born sons. However even they do not understand it in full, although it was revealed directly into their minds. As the person behind the *Sūtram*, sexually-charge cosmic potency, *Śrī* Krishna alone would be in a position to understand the intent of it completely.

मां विधत्ते ऽभिधत्ते मां
विकल्प्यापोह्यते त्व् अहम् ।
एतावान् सर्व-वेदार्थः
शब्द आस्थाय मा भिदाम् ।
माया-मात्रम् अनूद्यान्ते
प्रतिषिध्य प्रसीदति ॥ १६.४३ ॥

māṁ vidhatte 'bhidhatte māṁ
vikalpyāpohyate tv aham
etāvān sarva-vedārthaḥ
śabda āsthāya māṁ bhidām
māyā-mātram anūdyānte
pratiṣidhya prasīdati (16.43)

mām — me; vidhatte — enjoins; 'bhidhatte = abhidhatte — proclaims; mam — me; vikalpyāpohyate = vikalpya — presenting as an alternative proposition + apohyate — negates; tv = tu — but; aham — I; etāvān — thus; sarva – all; vedārthah — meaning of the Vedas; śabda — sound; āsthāya — establishing; mām — me; bhidām — difference; māyā-mātram — as based on supernatural misrepresentation; anūdyānte = anūdya — categorises + ante — at the end, finally; pratiṣidhya — refuting itself; prasīdati — is satisfied, is concluded.

Translation

It is Me that it enjoins, Me it proclaims. It is about Me that it presents alternative propositions, and what it negates is I. Thus this is the meaning of all the Vedas. The Vedic sound is established on Me. It categorizes differences as being based on supernatural misrepresentation. And finally by refuting itself it is concluded. (16.43)

CHAPTER 17*

The Contributing Factors**

Terri Stokes-Pineda Art

iti nānā-prasaṅkhyānaṁ tattvānām ṛṣibhiḥ kṛtam
sarvaṁ nyāyyaṁ yuktimattvād viduṣām kim aśobhanam

Thus the various listings of the contributing factors was proposed by the yogi sages. All of these are logical because of their scientific research. What lacks relevance in the ideas of those who are learned? (Uddhava Gītā 17.25)

* Śrīmad Bhāgavatam Canto 11, Chapter 22

** Translator's selected chapter title.

श्री-उद्धव उवाच
कति तत्त्वानि विश्वेश
सङ्ख्यातान्य् ऋषिभिः प्रभो ।
नवैकादश पञ्च त्रीण्य्
आत्थ त्वम् इह शुश्रुम ॥ १७.१ ॥

śrī-uddhava uvāca
kati tattvāni viśveśa
saṅkhyātāny ṛṣibhiḥ prabho
navaikādaśa pañca trīṇy
āttha tvam iha śuśruma (17.1)

śrī-uddhava – the qualified Uddhava; uvāca — said; kati — how many; tattvāni — essential factors; viśveśa = viśva – universe + īśa — lord; sankhyātāny = sankhyātāni — were explained; ṛṣibhiḥ — by the yogi sages; prabho — o lord; navaikādaśa = nava — nine + ekākaśa — eleven; pañca — five; trīny = trīṇi — three; āttha — spoke; tvam — you; iha — here in this world; śuśruma — I heard.

Translation

The qualified Uddhava said: How many essential factors, were explained by the yogi sages, O Lord of the Universe? Here in this world, I heard that You spoke of nine, eleven, five and three contributory causes. (17.1)

Commentary:

There are many expositions about the essential cause of this world. In modern times, we have scientific expositions. Uddhava asked for clarification.

केचित् षड्-विंशतिं प्राहुर्
अपरे पञ्च-विंशतिं ।
सप्तैके नव षट् केचिच्
चत्वार्य् एकादशापरे ।
केचित् सप्तदश प्राहुः
षोडशैके त्रयोदश ॥ १७.२ ॥

kecit ṣaḍ-viṁśatiṁ prāhur
apare pañca-viṁśatiṁ
saptaike nava ṣaṭ kecic
catvāry ekādaśāpare
kecit saptadaśa prāhuḥ
ṣoḍaśaike trayodaśa (17.2)

kecit — some; ṣaḍ = ṣaṭ - six; viṁśatim — twenty-six; prāhur = prāhuḥ — they explain; apare — others; pañca – five; viṁśatim — twenty; saptaike = sapta — seven + eke — some; nava — nine; ṣaṭ — six; kecic = kecit — some; catvāry = catvāri — four; ekādaśāpare = ekādaśa — eleven + apare — others; kecit — some; saptadaśa — seventeen; prāhuḥ — they explain; ṣoḍaśaike = ṣoḍaśa — sixteen + eke — some; trayodaśa — thirteen.

Translation

Some explain twenty-six and others twenty-five, some say seven, some nine or some six, some four and others eleven. Some explain seventeen, some sixteen and some thirteen. (17.2)

Commentary:

Different mystics and researchers explain the primal causes in different ways according to how they are inspired or according to how it is revealed to or perceived by them. My first yoga teacher, Mr. Arthur Beverford declared one, which he termed as the Primal Creative Cause.

एतावत्त्वं हि सङ्ख्यानाम्
ऋषयो यद्-विवक्षया ।
गायन्ति पृथग् आयुष्मन्न्
इदं नो वक्तुम् अर्हसि ॥ १७.३ ॥

etāvattvaṁ hi saṅkhyānām
ṛṣayo yad-vivakṣayā
gāyanti pṛthag āyuṣmann
idaṁ no vaktum arhasi (17.3)

etāvattvam — so many essential factors; hi — indeed; saṅkhyānām — of the listings; ṛṣayo = ṛṣayaḥ — the yogi sages; yad = yat – what; vivakṣayā — with the intention; gāyanti — they declared; pṛthag = pṛthak — in various ways; āyuṣmann = āyuh man — immortal one; idam —

this; no = nah — to us; vaktum — to explain; arhasi — you should.

Translation

What is the intention of the yogi sages, in declaring so many varied listings of the essential factors, O immortal One? You may tell us. (17.3)

Commentary:

The various philosophies, cosmologies and religious beliefs are very confusing to someone who tries to find a correlation in them.

श्री-भगवान् उवाच
युक्तं च सन्ति सर्वत्र
भाषन्ते ब्राह्मणा यथा ।
मायां मदीयाम् उद्गृह्य
वदतां किं नु दुर्घटम् ॥ १७.४॥

śrī-bhagavān uvāca
yuktaṁ ca santi sarvatra
bhāṣante brāhmaṇā yathā
māyāṁ madīyām udgṛhya
vadatāṁ kiṁ nu durghaṭam (17.4)

śrī-bhagavān – the blessed Lord; uvāca — said; yuktam — proper; ca — and; santi — are; sarvatra — all categories; bhāsante — say; brāhmaṇā = brāhmaṇāh — brahmins; yathā — accordingly; māyām — bewildering energy; madīyam — my; udgṛhya — reliant on; vadatām — of those who speak; kim — what; nu — after all; durghaṭam — is possible.

Translation

The Blessed Lord said: According to what the brahmins say; it is proper, since all categories are represented. And what is impossible for those who speak since they are reliant on My bewildering energy; (17.4)

Commentary:

Some explain that it does not matter how many categories are listed, provided the whole existence is taken into account. But *Śrī* Krishna felt that the differences of opinion are caused by a reliance on His bewildering energy.

Undoubtedly the mind of a limited person, is reliant on the intake of mental energy from the subtle material nature. Thus one's vision is reliant on that, at least in so far as one must use the mundane power.

नैतद् एव यथात्थ त्वं
यद् अहं वच्मि तत् तथा ।
एवं विवदतां हेतुं
शक्तयो मे दुरत्ययाः ॥ १७.५॥

naitad evaṁ yathāttha tvaṁ
yad ahaṁ vacmi tat tathā
evaṁ vivadatāṁ hetuṁ
śaktayo me duratyayāḥ (17.5)

naitad = na — not + etat — this; evam — thus; yathāttha = yathā — as + āttha — say; tvam — you; yad = yat — which; aham — I; vacmi — explain; tat — that; tathā — so; evam — was said; vivadatām — for those who argue; hetum — cause; śaktayo = śaktayaḥ — the potencies; me — my; duratyayāḥ — difficult to transcend.

Translation

"This is not as you say. It is as I explain." So it is said by those who argue over the causes, and who are influenced by My potencies which are difficult to transcend. (17.5)

Commentary:

Arguments about the Cause of the material creation and about the origination of the spirits in contact with this creation, are endless, all based on varying perspectives. There is no simple solution to such a problem. Such arguments will continue endlessly in human society. It is unrealistic to expect that the controversy will ever cease.

यासा व्यतिकराद् आसीद्
विकल्पो वदता पदम् ।
प्राप्ते शम-दमे ऽप्येति
वादस् तम् अनु शाम्यति ॥ १७.६ ॥

yāsāṁ vyatikarād āsīd
vikalpo vadatāṁ padam
prāpte śama-dame 'pyeti
vādas tam anu śāmyati (17.6)

yāsām — of which; vyatikarād = vyatikarāt — from the cosmic disturbance; āsīd = āsīt — was; vikalpo = vikalpaḥ — contention; vadatām — of the disputants; padam — subject; prāpte — when one attains; śama — tranquility; dame — sense control; 'pyeti = apyeti — vanished; vādas = vādaḥ — argument; tam – that; anu — after; śāṁyati — ends.

Translation

From the cosmic disturbance, the contention of the disputants regarding the subject, is caused. When one attains tranquility and sense control, the argument vanishes. And after that the dispute ends. (17.6)

Commentary:

All the arguments arose because we found ourselves in this creation and we desire to know how this was caused. Why are we involved here? Can we terminate the inconveniences?

Since we cannot stop the cosmic productions, we may try to control the reactions to it. And even that, may be an impossibility When a spirit realizes this and when it dedicates itself to gain freedom from this world, for it the arguments and disputations stop, because then it will have no time except to gain the required purification and insights that would empower it to make an exit from this world.

परस्परानुप्रवेशात्
तत्त्वानां पुरुषर्षभ ।
पौर्वापर्य-प्रसङ्ख्यानं
यथा वक्तुर् विवक्षितम् ॥ १७.७ ॥

parasparānupraveśāt
tattvānāṁ puruṣarṣabha
paurvāparya-prasaṅkhyānaṁ
yathā vaktur vivakṣitam (17.7)

parasparānupraveśāt = paraspara — mutual + anupraveśāt — due to interpenetration; tattvānām — of the essential factors; purusarṣabha — of best of the persons; paurvāparya = paurva — cause + aparya — effects; prasaṅkhyānam — enumeration; yathā — according to; vaktur = vaktuḥ — the speaker; vivakṣitam — desiring to explain.

Translation

O best of the personalities, it is due to mutual inter-penetration of the essential factors, that the enumeration of cause and effect is described according to the particular speaker who desires to explain it. (17.7)

Commentary:

It is not that all philosophers are nut-heads. But rather that they are seeing things as they are able to perceive, according to their respective abilities. It depends on their penetration into causes and into causes of causes, all the way to the ultimate source.

The living beings have a certain right to expression of their ideas. Thus it is not possible to outlaw them just for the sake of having only one view. The Supreme Being has His view. Each of us have ours according to insight. Thus there will always be differences of opinion.

एकस्मिन्न् अपि दृश्यन्ते
प्रविष्टानीतराणि च ।
पूर्वस्मिन् वा परस्मिन् वा
तत्त्वे तत्त्वानि सर्वशः ॥ १७.८ ॥

ekasminn api dṛśyante
praviṣṭānītarāṇi ca
pūrvasmin vā parasmin vā
tattve tattvāni sarvaśaḥ (17.8)

ekasminn = ekasmin — in one category; api — even; dṛśyante — are seen; praviṣṭānītarāṇi = praviṣṭāni — are within, included; itarāṇi — others; ca — and; pūrvasmin — in the previous cause; vā — either; parasmin — in a later effect; vā — or; tattve — in a factor; tattvāni — other factors; sarvaśaḥ — in all.

Translation

Even in one category, all other factors are seen to be included, either in the previous cause or in the latter effect. (17.8)

Commentary:

There is bound to be disagreement about something as complicated as material existence. It is not a simple matter. The various combinations are effects which are present directly or indirectly in their effects and in the effects of those effects. The situation is inexplicable.

पौर्वापर्यम् अतो ऽमीषां
प्रसङ्ख्यानम् अभीप्सताम् ।
यथा विविक्तं यद्-वक्त्रं
गृह्णीमो युक्ति-सम्भवात् ॥ १७.९ ॥

paurvāparyam ato 'mīṣāṁ
prasaṅkhyānam abhīpsatām
yathā viviktaṁ yad-vaktraṁ
gṛhṇīmo yukti-sambhavāt (17.9)

paurvāparyam = paurva — previous cause + aparyam — latter effect; ato = ataḥ — therefore; 'mīṣāṁ = amīṣām — of these; prasaṅkhyānam — of the listing; abhīpsatām — those who are eagerly contending; yathā — just as; viviktam — figured out; yad = yat – who; vaktram — mouth; gṛhṇīmo = grhṇīmaḥ — we accept; yukti — reason; sambhavāt — due to relativity.

Translation

Therefore we accept the previous cause and latter effect given by those who are eagerly contending, just as it is figured out by their mouth due to the reasons of relativity. (17.9)

Commentary:

If we follow the line of thought of the various philosophers, we will have to agree that they are seeing what they conceive, all depending on relative psychological positions in relation to material nature. As the saying goes: *To each, his own idea.*

अनाद्य्-अविद्या-युक्तस्य
पुरुषस्यात्म-वेदनम् ।
स्वतो न सम्भवाद् अन्यस्
तत्त्व-ज्ञो ज्ञान दो भवेत् ॥ १७.१० ॥

anādy-avidyā-yuktasya
puruṣasyātma-vedanam
svato na sambhavād anyas
tattva-jño jñāna-do bhavet (17.10)

anādy = anādi — beginningless; avidyā — ignorance; yuktasya — of one who is endowed with; puruṣasyātma = puruṣasya — of a person + ātma – spirit; vedanam — indept knowledge; svato = svataḥ — by his own ability; na = not – lack of; sambhavād = sambhavāt — due to mystic experience of or intuition; anyas = anyat — another; tattva-jño = tattva-jñaḥ — knower of the factors of reality; jñāna-do – jñāna daḥ — giver of true information; bhavet — must be.

Translation

Due to a lack of mystic experience or accurate intuition, a person who is endowed with a beginningless ignorance, must acquire the in-depth knowledge of the spirit, from another person who knows the factors of reality and who gives true information. (17.10)

Commentary:

If one does not know and still needs to find out, he will have to get the information from someone who has true information. The trouble is that there are so many people who pose as having the truth. Some persons say that they are experienced. Others say that their teachers are experienced. In any case, with good luck one might find someone who actually knows, just as Uddhava took recourse to Lord Krishna.

Of interest is the statement about those who have a beginningless ignorance *(anādy-avidyā-yuktasya)*. This implies that some of us might perpetually have to rely on others for true information, due to our being perpetually without spiritual vision.

पुरुषेश्वरयोर् अत्र
न वैलक्षण्यम् अण्व् अपि ।
तद्-अन्य-कल्पनापार्था
ज्ञानं च प्रकृतेर् गुणः ॥१७११॥

puruṣeśvarayor atra
na vailakṣaṇyam aṇv api
tad-anya-kalpanāpārthā
jñānaṁ ca prakṛter guṇaḥ (17.11)

puruṣeśvarayor = puruṣa — of the individual spirit + īśvarayoh — of God; atra — here in this case; na — no; vailakṣaṇyam — different to, characteristic marks; aṇv = aṇu — least; api — even; tad = tat — of that; anya — another factor, a separate factor; kalpanāpārthā = kalpanā — idea + apārthā — futile; jñānam — knowledge; ca — and; prakṛter = prakṛteḥ — of material nature; guṇaḥ — feature.

Translation

In this case, there is not the least difference, between the individual soul and God. This idea of a separate factor is considered futile. And knowledge is regarded as a feature of material nature. (17.11)

Commentary:

One view point as listed above is that there is no distinguishing marks between the individual soul and the God. The idea of their separation is considered futile by this view. Knowledge is regarded as a feature of material nature, since most information concerns the relation of either God or the limited soul, in conjunction with material nature. And besides, the means of perceiving such experience are tools which were furnished in material nature.

प्रकृतिर् गुण-साम्यं वै
प्रकृतेर् नात्मनो गुणाः ।
सत्त्वं रजस् तम इति
स्थित्य्-उत्पत्त्य्-अन्त-हेतवः ॥१७.१२॥

prakṛtir guṇa-sāmyaṁ vai
prakṛter nātmano guṇāḥ
sattvaṁ rajas tama iti
sthity-utpatty-anta-hetavaḥ (17.12)

prakṛtir = prakṛtiḥ — primal material nature; guṇa — diversified mundane energy; sāmyaṁ — equilibrium; vai — definitely; prakṛter = prakṛteḥ — of material nature; nātmano = na – not + ātmanaḥ — of the spirit; guṇāḥ — of the diversified mundane influences; sattvam — the clarifying influence; rajas = rajah — the impulsive mode; tamah — the retardative influence; iti — thus stated; sthity = sthiti — maintenance; utpatty = utpatti — origin; anta — destruction; hetavaḥ — causes.

Translation

The Primal Material Nature is the equilibrium of the diversified mundane energy, which is not a part of the spirits, and which is defined as the clarifying, impulsive and retardative influences. These are the causes of maintenance, origination and destruction respectively. (17.12)

Commentary:

These statements need to be accepted directly from Lord Krishna, until we reach a point where we can see this directly, provided our ignorance is not perpetual, in which case, we will not be able to ever verify nor deny this.

सत्त्वं ज्ञानं रजः कर्म
तमो ऽज्ञानम् इहोच्यते ।
गुण-व्यतिकरः कालः
स्वभावः सूत्रम् एव च ॥ १७.१३॥

sattvaṁ jñānaṁ rajaḥ karma
tamo 'jñānam ihocyate
guṇa-vyatikaraḥ kālaḥ
svabhāvaḥ sūtram eva ca (17.13)

sattvam — clarifying energy influence; jñānam — knowledge; rajaḥ — impulsive force; karma — cultural activity; tamo = tamah — retardative influence; 'jñānam = ajñānam — ignorance; ihocyate = iha — in this case + ucyate — is stated; guna — the tripart mundane energies; vyatikaraḥ — agitation; kālaḥ — time; svabhāvaḥ — personal tendencies; sūtram — the sexually-charged cosmic force; eva — indeed; ca — also.

Translation

It is stated that knowledge is the outcome of the clarifying influence. Cultural activity comes from the impulsive force. Ignorance is derived from the retardative influence. Time is regarded as the agitator of the mundane energy. Personal tendency springs from the sexually-charged cosmic force. (17.13)

Commentary:

At present our personal tendencies *(svabhāvah)* were derived from the sexually-charged cosmic force, which *Śrī* Krishna listed as the *Sūtram*. Each of the limited entities are endowed with a microscopic part of that *Sūtram* potency. It causes the formation of character. Most of what we think we are, is based on the psychological mundane energy. When divested in the psyche this sexually-charged force is known as emotion and mental energy for the formation of feelings and ideas.

पुरुषः प्रकृतिर् व्यक्तम्
अहङ्कारो नभो ऽनिलः ।
ज्योतिर् आपः क्षितिर् इति
तत्त्वान्य् उक्तानि मे नव ॥ १७.१४॥

puruṣaḥ prakṛtir vyaktam
ahaṅkāro nabho 'nilaḥ
jyotir āpaḥ kṣitir iti
tattvāny uktāni me nava (17.14)

puruṣah — spirit; prakṛtir = prakṛtiḥ — imperceptive material nature; vyaktam — perceptible material nature; ahamkāro = ahankāraḥ — the sense of assertion which is manifested in material nature; nabho = nabhaḥ — outer space; 'nilaḥ = anilaḥ — planetary atmosphere; jyotir = jyotiḥ — light; āpah — liquid; ksitir = ksitiḥ — solid substances; iti — as stated; tattvāny = tattvāni — the factors; uktāni — were declared; me — by me; nava — nine.

Translation

Spirit, imperceptive material nature, perceptible material nature, the sense of assertion, outer space, planetary atmosphere, light, liquid and solid substances, are the nine factors declared by Me. (17.14)

Commentary:

In any gross or subtle association with material nature, a spirit automatically develops a sense of assertion to identify with or to deny the material which he perceives.

श्रोत्र त्वग् दर्शनं घ्राणो
जिह्वेति ज्ञान-शक्तयः ।
वाक्-पाण्य्-उपस्थ-पाय्व्-अङ्घ्रिः
कर्माण्य् अङ्गोभयं मनः ॥ १७.१५॥

śrotraṁ tvag darśanaṁ ghrāṇo
jihveti jñāna-śaktayaḥ
vāk-pāṇy-upastha-pāyv-aṅghriḥ
karmāṇy aṅgobhayaṁ manaḥ (17.15)

śrotram — hearing ability; tvag = tvak — touching sense; darśanam — vision; ghrāṇo = ghrāṇaḥ — smelling sense; jihveti = jihvā — tasting sense + iti — as stated; jñāna – detecting; śaktayaḥ — potencies; vāk — vocal cord; pāny = pāni — hands; upastha — sexual organ; pāyu — anus;

aṅghriḥ — legs; karmāṇy = karmāṇi — working organs; aṅgobhayaṁ = anga — friend + ubhayam — belonging to both; manaḥ — mind.

Translation

Hearing ability, touching sense, vision, smelling sense, tasting sense are detecting potencies. Vocal cords, hands, sexual organ, anus and legs are working organs, O friend. The mind belongs to both categories. (17.15)

Commentary:

The mind mechanism operates both the detecting senses and the working organs. In *kriyā* yoga, one withdraws these when one masters *pratyāhar* practice. It is however, not a gross action in its completion. Even though one begins with physical restraint, it terminates in pulling in the sensual orbs which are subtle facilities.

शब्दः स्पर्शो रसो गन्धो
रूपं चेत्य् अर्थ-जातयः ।
गत्य्-उक्त्य्-उत्सर्ग-शिल्पानि
कर्मायतन-सिद्धयः ॥ १७.१६ ॥

śabdaḥ sparśo raso gandho
rūpaṁ cety artha-jātayaḥ
gaty-ukty-utsarga-śilpāni
karmāyatana-siddhayaḥ (17.16)

śabdaḥ — sound; sparśo = sparśaḥ — surface; raso = rasaḥ — flavor; gandho = gandhaḥ — odor; rūpam — shape; cety = ceti = ca — and + iti — as stated; artha — sensual pursuit, value; jātayah — categories; gaty = gati — movement; ukty = ukti — speech; utsarga — sexual arousal and excretion; śilpāni — manual skill; karmāyatana = *karma* – working + āyatana — organs; siddhayah — skills.

Translation

Sound, surface, flavor, odor and shape are the categories of sensual pursuit. Movement, speech, sexual arousal, excretion and manual dexterity are the skills of the working organs. (17.16)

Commentary:

In the material world, we pursue sounds, surfaces, flavors, odors and shapes, relentlessly by the impulses which dictate that we satisfy the senses. To do this, we execute movements, vocalizations, sexual acts, excretory functions and manual skills. This is mostly done for the sake of material nature. A turning point comes when we begin to curtail the material senses and limbs for the sake of spiritual realization.

सर्गादौ प्रकृतिर् ह्य् अस्य
कार्य-कारण-रूपिणी ।
सत्त्वादिभिर् गुणैर् धत्ते
पुरुषो ऽव्यक्त ईक्षते ॥ १७.१७॥

sargādau prakṛtir hy asya
kārya-kāraṇa-rūpiṇī
sattvādibhir guṇair dhatte
puruṣo 'vyakta īkṣate (17.17)

sargādau — creation; prakṛtir = prakṛtiḥ — material nature; hy = hi — indeed; asya — of this; kārya — produced from; kāraṇa — causal energy; rūpinī — forming, appearing as; sattvādibhir = sattvadibhih — clarifying force and other features; guṇair = guṇaiḥ — through the varied mundane influence; dhatte — exhibits itself; puruso = puruṣaḥ — the primal spirit; 'vyakta = avyakta — unmodified; īkṣate — observes.

Translation

In the beginning of this creation, material nature appearing as causal energy and producing forms, through the varied mundane influences, such as the clarifying force and the other features, exhibited itself. But the primal spirit, unchanged as it is, observes this. (17.17)

Commentary:

In the beginning of creation, the limited spirits do not have the objective awareness of themselves as they are in contrast to material nature. Hence the term *puruṣah* means the Supreme Spirit. This is because only He has the objective awareness to view nature in a dispassionate way at that time.

Later on, when the limited spirits separate out into the mundane creation, some find themselves looking on and experiencing as observers. Others find themselves attached to material nature as involvers.

व्यक्तादायो विकुर्वाणा
धातवः पुरुषेक्षया ।
लब्ध-वीर्याः सृजन्त्य् अण्डं
सहताः प्रकृतेर् बलात् ॥ १७.१८॥

vyaktādāyo vikurvāṇā
dhātavaḥ puruṣekṣayā
labdha-vīryāḥ sṛjanty aṇḍaṁ
saṁhatāḥ prakṛter balāt (17.18)

vyaktādāyo = vyaktādayaḥ — causal energy and other componets; vikurvānā = vikurvānāḥ — being transformed; dhātavaḥ — essential factors; puruṣekṣayā = purusha — primal person + īkṣayā — by the glance or observational powers; labdha — being surcharged; vīryāḥ — potencies; sṛjanty = sṛjanti — form; aṇḍam — enclosed universe; saṁhatāh — combined; prakṛter = prakṛteḥ — of material nature; balāt — due to potency.

Translation

The essential factors such as the causal energy and the other components, while being transformed, and being surcharged with potencies by the observational powers of the Primal Person, combine and form the enclosed universe. This is due to the potency which developed in material nature. (17.18)

Commentary:

The causal energy *(vyakta)* is the same *Sūtram* sexually-charged force. It is surcharged by the observational powers of the Primal Person, the Supreme Being for that universe. Subsequently the energy combines and forms an enclosed cosmos.

Some modern astronomers do not agree with this idea, since their telescopes show no border to the universe which we reside in. They do not see a membrane and they feel that space and time are elastic materials.

सप्तैव धातव इति
तत्रार्थाः पञ्च खादयः ।
ज्ञानम् आत्मोभयाधारस्
ततो देहेन्द्रियासवः ॥ १७.१९॥

saptaiva dhātava iti
tatrārthāḥ pañca khādayaḥ
jñānam ātmobhayādhāras
tato dehendriyāsavaḥ (17.19)

saptaiva = sapte — seven + eva — indeed; dhātava = dhātavaḥ — essential factors; iti — it is said; tatrārthāḥ = tatra — there in that other view + arthāḥ — physical states; pañca — five; khādayaḥ = kha – outer space + ādayaḥ — beginning with; jñānam — knowledge of the factors; ātmobhayādhāras = ātmā — self + ubhaya — of both + ādhāraḥ — one who is the fundation; tato = tataḥ — from these; dehendriyāsavaḥ = deha — body + indriya — sense organs + asavaḥ — vital energy.

Translation

It is said in yet another view, that there are seven factors, consisting of five physical states beginning with outer space, together with mental knowledge and the self who is the reference point of both factors. From these seven factors, the body, sense organs and vital energy emerges. (17.19)

Commentary:

Some commentators give *jñānam* as the individual spirit and *ātma* as the Supreme Soul. However I have stuck to the regular meaning and to the context, giving *jñānam* as knowledge of the factors.

The seven factors are as follows: solids, liquids, combustives, gases, spaces, knowledge of these materials and the spirit itself. The spirits act as a reference point for observation.

षड् इत्य् अत्रापि भूतानि
पञ्च षष्ठः परः पुमान् ।
तैर् युत आत्म-सम्भूतैः
सृष्ट्वेदं समपाविशत् ॥ १७.२० ॥

ṣaḍ ity atrāpi bhūtāni
pañca ṣaṣṭhaḥ paraḥ pumān
tair yuita ātma-sambhūtaiḥ
sṛṣṭvedaṁ samapāviśat (17.20)

ṣaḍ = ṣaṭ — six; iti — it is said; atrāpi = atra — in this other view + api — also; bhūtāni — physical states; pañca — five; ṣaṣṭhah — sixth; paraḥ — supreme; pumān — person; tair = taiḥ — with those; yukta = yuktaḥ — endowed with; ātma — self, from himself; sambhūtaiḥ — with the production; sṛṣṭedam = sṛṣṭvā — creating + idam — this world; samupāviśat — entered it.

Translation

It is said in this other view, that there are six factors, namely the five physical states and the sixth which is the Supreme Person. Being endowed with those five elements, which were produced from Himself, and having created this world, He entered it. (17.20)

Commentary:

There are two ways of looking at this, either as in the previous verse or in this verse. In the previous explanation, the Supreme Person is not accredited, but rather it is the limited soul and his knowledge along with the five elements. This is the spirit and his individual psyche alone. In this other explanation, the Supreme Person is considered along with the physical states, which were produced by Him, and which formed into the cosmic space which He entered.

My translation in the previous verse of *jñānam* as knowledge is substantiated by a statement made by *Śrī* Krishna in the *Bhagavad-Gītā*, when He described our status as His small partners in the venture of experiencing this mundane world:

mamaivāṁśo jīvaloke jīvabhūtaḥ sanātanaḥ
manaḥṣaṣṭhānīndriyāṇi prakṛtisthāni karṣati

My partner is in this world of individualized conditioned beings. He is an eternal individual soul but he draws to himself the mundane senses of which the mind is the sixth detection device. (B.G. 15.7)

चत्वार्य् एवेति तत्रापि
तेज आपो ऽन्नम् आत्मनः ।
जातानि तैर् इदं जातं
जन्मावयविनः खलु ॥ १७.२१ ॥

catvāry eveti tatrāpi
teja āpo 'nnam ātmanaḥ
jātāni tair idaṁ jātaṁ
janmāvayavinaḥ khalu (17.21)

catvāry = catvāri — four; eveti = eva — only + iti — thus, as some state; tatrāpi = tatra — in that verse + api — even; tejah — light producing combustion; āpo = āpaḥ — liquids; 'nnam = annam — solids; ātmanah — from the self; jātāni — were produced; tair = taiḥ — by them; idam — this; jātam — emerged; janmāvayavinah = janma — birth, manifestation + avayavinaḥ — of production; khalu — indeed.

Translation

If even as some state, there are four factors, like light producing-combustion, liquids, solids, together with the self from which they are produced; then by these the manifestation of the productions emerged. (17.21)

Commentary:

In yet another view, there is supposed to be one self, from which influences emanated to produce fire, liquids and solids, which interacted and produced other effects. Modern Science denies the existence of any such self. They begin with nuclear energy or atomic fire from which the other materials are produced. They do not regard personality as being primal to creation.

सङ्ख्याने सप्तदशके
भूत-मात्रेन्द्रियाणि च ।
पञ्च पञ्चैक-मनसा
आत्मा सप्तदशः स्मृतः ॥ १७.२२ ॥

saṅkhyāne saptadaśake
bhūta-mātrendriyāṇi ca
pañca pañcaika-manasā
ātmā saptadaśaḥ smṛtaḥ (17.22)

sankhyāne — in the listing; saptadaśake — in the seventeen factors; bhūta — the gross element; mātrendriyāṇi = mātra — subtle elements + indriyāni — sense organs; ca — and; panca – five; pancaika = panca — five + eka – one; manasā — with mind; ātmā — spirit; saptadaśa = saptadaśah — seventeen; smrtah — are traditionally accounted as.

Translation

In the listing of seventeen factors, the gross elements, subtle ones, the five sense organs, the five working organs, the one mind and the soul, are traditionally accounted as the seventeen components. (17.22)

Commentary:

This is the traditional view *(smṛtah),* because each of the individual spirits is hooked up to psychological and physical equipments in a similar way. This is called the comparatively similar view of the creatures *(śama).*

तद्वत् षोडश-सङ्ख्याने
आत्मैव मन उच्यते ।
भूतेन्द्रियाणि पञ्चैव
मन आत्मा त्रयोदश ॥ १७.२३ ॥

tadvat ṣoḍaśa-saṅkhyāne
ātmaiva mana ucyate
bhūtendriyāṇi pañcaiva
mana ātmā trayodaśa (17.23)

tadvat — similarly; ṣoḍaśa – sixteen; saṅkhyāne — in the listing; ātmaiva = ātmā — spirit + eva — only; mana = manaḥ — mind; ucyate — is said to be; bhūtendriyāṇi = bhūta — gross elements + indriyāni — sense organs; pañcaiva = panca — five of each + eva — indeed; mana = manaḥ — mind; ātmā — spirit, soul; trayodaśa — thirteen.

Translation

Similarly, in the listing of sixteen factors, there is the spirit which is identified only as the mind. Then there is the listing of thirteen factors which are the five gross elements, the five sense organs, the mind and the soul. (17.23)

Commentary:

Some philosophers identify the mind as the self and the self as the mind. Some feel that the intellect is the mind and that the mind is the intellect. Then there is the listing of thirteen factors, the five senses, the gross objects desired by those senses, the mind itself, the individual spirit and the combination of these as a living body. Some commentators listed *ātma* or soul as a soul/Supreme Soul combination, making the Supreme Soul one of the thirteen factors.

एकादशत्व आत्मासौ
महा-भूतेन्द्रियाणि च ।
अष्टौ प्रकृतयश् चैव
पुरुषश् च नवेत्य् अथ ॥ १७.२४ ॥

ekādaśatva ātmāsau
mahā-bhūtendriyāṇi ca
aṣṭau prakṛtayaś caiva
puruṣaś ca navety atha (17.24)

ekādaśatva = ekādaśatve — in the listing of eleven factors; ātmāsau = ātmā — spirit + asau — this; mahā-bhūtendriyāṇi = mahā-bhūta — five universal gross elements + indriyāṇi — sensory powers; ca — and; aṣṭau — eight; prakṛtayaś = prakṛtayaḥ — exhibition of material nature; caiva = ca — and + eva — alone; puruṣas = puruṣaḥ — primal person; ca — and; navety = nava — nine + iti — are accounted; atha — while.

Translation

In the list of eleven factors, this soul, the five universal gross elements, and the five sensory powers are accounted, while the eight exhibitions of material nature and the primal personality alone are accounted as nine factors. (17.24)

Commentary:

The eight exhibitions of material nature, are its primal quiescent state, its charged state, the sense of identity the spirit utilizes in it *(ahankāra),* and the five subtle elements which are odor, flavor, shape, surface and sound.

Some philosophers seem to think that there is only one person in existence, the Primal Person or the Supreme Being. They do not give credence to the individual limited spirits, who they regard as only a temporary reflection of the one Supreme.

इति नाना-प्रसङ्ख्यानं
तत्त्वानाम् ऋषिभिः कृतम् ।
सर्वं न्याय्यं युक्तिमत्त्वाद्
विदुषां किम् अशोभनम् ॥ १७.२५ ॥

iti nānā-prasaṅkhyānaṁ
tattvānām ṛṣibhiḥ kṛtam
sarvaṁ nyāyyaṁ yuktimattvād
viduṣāṁ kim aśobhanam (17.25)

iti — thus; nānā — various; prasaṅkhyānaṁ — listing; tattvānām — of the contributing factors; ṛṣibhiḥ — by the yogi sages; kṛtam — were proposed; sarvam — all; nyāyyam — logical; yuktimattvād = yuktimattvāt — because of scientific research presented; vidusam — of those who are learned; kim — what; aśobhanam — lacking relevance.

Translation

Thus the various listings of the contributing factors was proposed by the yogi sages. All of these are logical because of scientific research. What lacks relevance in the ideas of those who are learned? (17.25)

Commentary:

Even though He is the Supreme Philosopher, still Lord Krishna does not ridicule the various yogi sages who gave their analysis of the causes of the mundane creation. Each was presented from a specific angle of vision, after due reflection and mystic research.

श्री-उद्धव उवाच
प्रकृतिः पुरुषश् चोभौ
यद्य् अप्य् आत्म-विलक्षणौ ।
अन्योन्यापाश्रयात् कृष्ण
दृश्यते न भिदा तयोः ।
प्रकृतौ लक्ष्यते ह्य् आत्मा
प्रकृतिश् च तथात्मनि ॥ १७.२६ ॥

śrī-uddhava uvāca
prakṛtiḥ puruṣaś cobhau
yady apy ātma-vilakṣaṇau
anyonyāpāśrayāt kṛṣṇa
dṛśyate na bhidā tayoḥ
prakṛtau lakṣyate hy ātmā
prakṛtiś ca tathātmani (17.26)

śrī-uddhava – the qualified Uddhava; uvāca — said; prakṛtiḥ — primordial material nature; puruṣaś = puruṣaḥ — personality; cobhau = ca — and + ubhau — both; yady apy = yadi api — if even, although; ātma — by their nature; vilakṣaṇau — distinction in both; anyonyāpāśrayāt = anyonya — mutual + apāśrayāt — because of a dependent relationship; kṛṣṇa — Krishna; dṛśyate – is seen, appears; na — not; bhidā — difference; tayoḥ — between the two; prakṛtau — in material nature; lakṣyate — is characterized, is indicated; hy = hi — indeed; ātmā — spirit; prakṛtiś = prakṛtiḥ — material nature; ca — and; tathātmani = tathā — likewise + ātmani — in the soul.

Translation

The qualified Uddhava said: Although material nature and the personality are mutually distinct by their very nature, yet there appears to be no difference between them. Indeed, the spirit is characterized in material nature. Therefore material nature is indicated in the spirit. (17.26)

Commentary:

The relationship between material nature and the spirits is eternal. To speak of a permanent distinction while sharing existence with material nature, is to a degree, fallacious. Since the two realities are in eternal proximity and since when viewing the connection of their mutual influence, a spirit has got to be seeing it from being in material nature, he or she should realize that one is characterized by or indicated in the other.

When we look at the involved spirit, we see material nature's influence and when we view the sexually-charged material nature, we see the spirit's power. That is the way it is.

Uddhava wanted this matter cleared up so that the vagueness which appears to overshadow the distinction between the spirits and material nature, can be removed.

एव मे पुण्डरीकाक्ष
महान्त सशयं हृदि ।
छेत्तुम् अर्हसि सर्व-ज्ञ
वचोभिर् नय-नैपुणैः ॥ १७.२७॥

evaṁ me puṇḍarīkākṣa
mahāntaṁ saṁśayaṁ hṛdi
chettum arhasi sarva-jña
vacobhir naya-naipuṇaiḥ (17.27)

evam — this; me — my; pundarīkākṣa — lotus-eyed one; mahāntam — great; saṁśayam — contradiction; hṛdi — in my consciousness; chettum — to dispell; arhasi — you can; sarva-jña — omniscient one; vacobhir = vacobhiḥ — by words; naya — logical; naipuṇaiḥ — with precision.

Translation

O lotus-eyed One, O omniscient One, you can dispell this great contradiction in my consciousness with precise logical words. (17.27)

Commentary:

Words alone cannot completely dispel the contradiction of the feelings of being unified with matter as contrasted to being distinct from it. But words can set one on the course of getting the experience of that distinction and then doubts would be removed. Arjuna had doubts about *Śrī* Krishna. It was not until he saw the Universal Form that the misgivings were removed.

त्वत्तो ज्ञान हि जीवानां
प्रमोषस् ते ऽत्र शक्तितः ।
त्वम् एव ह्य् आत्म-मायाया
गतिं वेत्थ न चापरः ॥ १७.२८॥

tvatto jñānaṁ hi jīvānāṁ
pramoṣas te 'tra śaktitaḥ
tvam eva hy ātma-māyāyā
gatiṁ vettha na cāparaḥ (17.28)

tvatto = tvattaḥ — from you; jñānam — true information; hi — surely; jīvānām — by the people; pramoṣas = pramoṣaḥ — are robbed; te — your; 'tra = atra — in this case; śaktitaḥ — by potency; tvam — you; eva — only; hy = hi — surely; ātma — your own; māyāyā — of the bewitching energy; gatim — course; vettha — you know; na — no; cāparaḥ = ca — and + aparaḥ — any other.

Translation

Surely the true information acquired by the people comes from You and by Your potency, they are robbed of it. You alone and no other person, know the course of Your bewitching power. (17.28)

Commentary:

As the Supreme Being, *Śrī* Krishna is the ultimate source of true information but at the same time, since He is responsible for surcharging the *Sūtram* Cosmic Energy, He is also indirectly the source of the bewilderment which prevents people from getting the true information and from developing direct vision.

श्री-भगवान् उवाच
प्रकृतिः पुरुषश् चेति
विकल्पः पुरुषर्षभ ।
एष वैकारिकः सर्गो
गुण-व्यतिकरात्मकः ॥ १७.२९ ॥

śrī-bhagavān uvāca
prakṛtiḥ puruṣaś ceti
vikalpaḥ puruṣarṣabha
eṣa vaikārikaḥ sargo
guṇa-vyatikarātmakaḥ (17.29)

śrī-bhagavān – the Blessed Lord; uvāca — said; prakṛtiḥ — material nature; puruṣaś = puruṣaḥ — personality; ceti = ca — and + iti — thus; vikalpaḥ — totally distinct; puruṣarṣabha — best of the personalities; eṣa = eṣaḥ — this; vaikārikaḥ — subject to changes; sargo = sargaḥ — creation; guṇa — of the mundane influence; vyatikarātmakaḥ = vyatikara — agitation + ātmakaḥ — by nature.

Translation

The Blessed Lord said: O best of the personalities, material nature and personality are totally distinct. This creation is subject to changes, for it was produced from agitation of the mundane influences. (17.29)

Commentary:

The *puruṣa* is the original spiritual person who was subjected to the admixture of the material energy. Once a limited spirit is subjected to this, it has some difficulty identifying itself apart from it.

In material existence, the cultural personality is usually accepted as the total person, thus the confusion regarding who that person really is, continues in full force. Each ascetic should strive to experience the distinction between his spiritual core self and his cultural identity which was adopted for traditional usage.

ममाङ्ग माया गुण-मय्य् अनेकधा
विकल्प-बुद्धीश् च गुणैर् विधत्ते ।
वैकारिकस् त्रि-विधो ऽध्यात्मम् एकम्
अथाधिदैवम् अधिभूतम् अन्यत् ॥ १७.३० ॥

mamāṅga māyā guṇa-mayy anekadhā
vikalpa-buddhīś ca guṇair vidhatte
vaikārikas tri-vidho 'dhyātmam ekam
athādhidaivam adhibhūtam anyat (17.30)

mamāṅga = mama — my + aṅga — friend; māyā — bewildering potency; guṇa – mundane influence; mayy = mayī — my; anekadhā — innumerable; vikalpa — variation; buddhīś = buddhīḥ — intellect, perception; ca — and; guṇair = guṇaiḥ — through mundane influence; vidhatte — create produce; vaikārikas = vaikārikaḥ — created world; tri-vidho = tri-vidhaḥ — three fold; 'dhyatmam = adhyatmam — pertaining to personal initiative; ekam — one; athādhidaivam = atha — then + adhidaivam — pertaining to supernatural influences; adhibhūtam — pertaining to other creatures; anyat — another aspect.

Translation

My friend, My bewildering potency consisting of mundane influences creates through those powers, innumerable modifications and varied intellectual perceptions. The created world is threefold, consisting of one impact pertaining to personal initiative, and then another pertaining to supernatural influences and another due to other creatures. (17.30)

Commentary:

The material energy which comes as the sexually-charged force, called the *Sūtram* in the previous verses, is divested out into three types of influences, which are the perceptive, impulsive and de-energizing forces. These powers are within all life forms in varying proportions. They create innumerable modifications on the intellectual, emotional and physiological planes.

Besides this we have to deal with another threefold harassment for good or bad. That is our personal initiative, supernatural drives and social influences. These might act together or in opposition and might cause our upliftment or degradation. Since as limited beings we are not infallible, we are to a greater extent subjected to those influences.

Our personal initiative, our preferences and the resulting endeavors, might be faulty. The social influences which bear upon us might not be in our interest. And the supernatural forces which manipulate us might be reckless. Therefore there is hardly any likelihood that we would become liberated so long as we remain under that type of dominance. To be freed, we have to take shelter or be allowed to take shelter under a totally different type of influence. Even our self interest is faulty. Thus we have to rely on someone who is, by far superior.

दृग् रूपम् आर्कं वपुर् अत्र रन्ध्रे
परस्परं सिध्यति यः स्वतः खे ।
आत्मा यद् एषाम् अपरो य आद्यः
स्वयानुभूत्याखिल-सिद्ध-सिद्धिः ।
एवं त्वग्-आदि श्रवणादि चक्षुर्
जिह्वादि नासादि च चित्त-युक्तम् ॥ १७.३१ ॥

dṛg rūpam ārkaṁ vapur atra randhre
parasparaṁ sidhyati yaḥ svataḥ khe
ātmā yad eṣām aparo ya ādyaḥ
svayānubhūtyākhila-siddha-siddhiḥ
evaṁ tvag-ādi śravaṇādi cakṣur
jihvādi nāsādi ca citta-yuktam (17.31)

dṛg = dṛk — vision; rūpam — form; ārkam — sunshine; vapur = vapuḥ — portion of sunlight; atra — here, in this; randhre — in the pupil of the eye; parasparam — being interdependent; sidhyati — by its own potency; yaḥ — which; svataḥ — by its own potency; khe — in the sky; ātmā — the spirit; yad = yat — which; eṣām — of these; aparo = aparaḥ — that which is, distinction; yah — who; ādyaḥ — original cause; svayānubhūtyākhila = svayā — by its own + anubhūtyā — giving consciousness + akhila — all; siddha — production; siddhiḥ — creative technique, the very power that creates; evam — thus, it is, the same; tvag = tvak – skin; ādi — and related factors; śravanādi = sravana –ear + ādi — and related factors; cakṣur = cakṣuḥ — vision; jihvādi = jihvā – tongue + adi — and related factors; nasadi = nasa – nose + ādi — and related factors; ca — and; citta – mento-emotional energy; yuktam — combined with.

Translation

Vision, form, sunshine and the sunlight entering the eye, each are interdependent to operate efficiently. But that which is in the sky functions, by its own potency. The spirit which is the original cause of these is distinct. It is the very power which creates all production by giving its own consciousness to all. Thus it is the same in the case of the skin, the ear, the vision, the tongue, the nose and related factors along with the energy which comprise mental power and emotions. (17.31)

Commentary:

In terms of seeing materially, the most independent object is the sun. We can make use of it as a facility to help in seeing but we cannot command it to appear and not to appear. Still the sun itself is a material object and this is why we can perceive it by its own assistance of providing sunlight for vision of itself and other objects.

It is the same in the case of other means of sensual perception. Touch and feelings are for instance dependent on a membrane which we call a skin, but that also depends on air and on the producer of air. Of course we do not see a large scale producer of air as easily as we see the large generator of light which is the sun. But still, we should assume that there is such a producer.

Elsewhere in the Vedic literature we are informed of *Anila or Prāṇavāyu*, as the producer of air. Hearing for instance, depends on reception of sound, and on the flow through a material to transmit sound. Tasting depends on the tongue as well as the flavor and the supernatural causes of flavor. Gross flavors come from the earth and are divested in various ways.

Śrī Krishna informed that the spirit is the cause of these distinctions and developments, since it is the spiritual proximity to material nature, that empowers nature to mutate.

यो ऽसौ गुण-क्षोभ-कृतो विकारः
प्रधान-मूलान् महतः प्रसूतः ।
अहं त्रि-वृन् मोह-विकल्प-हेतुर्
वैकारिकस् तामस ऐन्द्रियश् च ॥ १७.३२ ॥

yo 'sau guṇa-kṣobha-kṛto vikāraḥ
pradhāna-mūlān mahataḥ prasūtaḥ
ahaṁ tri-vṛn moha-vikalpa-hetur
vaikārikas tāmasa aindriyaś ca (17.32)

yo = yah – that; 'sau = asau — this; guṇa — of the energies of material nature; ksobha — agitation; kṛto = kṛtaḥ — caused; vikāraḥ — modification; pradhāna – primal quiescent mundane energy; mūlān — from the most basic form, from the original; mahataḥ — from the primal mundane energy; prasūtaḥ — produced from; aham — the sense of assertion; tri-vṛn = tri-vṛt — threefold; moha — delusion; vikalpa — doubt; hetur = hetuh — cause; vaikārikas = vaikārikaḥ — initial change, initial response; tāmasa = tāmasaḥ — depression, lack of motivation; aindriyaś = aindriyaḥ — sensuality, enthusiam; ca — and.

Translation

That specific modification which is caused by the agitation of the energies of material nature is produced from the most basic form of the primal quiescent mundane energy. The sense of assertion which is the cause of delusion and doubt, is threefold, manifesting as initial response, lack of motivation and enthusiam. (17.32)

Commentary:

This is complicated but it will suffice to say that on our level of existence, we experience the divestment and development of material nature, as an initial response to consider, then as a lack of motivation to act, then as an enthusiasm to do something. This produced, ultimately, delusion and doubt on our part. Whatever we do as motivated by material nature exclusively, always will turn out to be incorrect. It is the nature of that energy to work in a direction which will ultimately contravene our desire.

आत्मापरिज्ञान-मयो विवादो
ह्य् अस्तीति नास्तीति भिदार्थ-निष्ठः ।
व्यर्थो ऽपि नैवोपरमेत पुसां
मत्तः परावृत्त-धियां स्व-लोकात् ॥ १७.३३ ॥

ātmāparijñāna-mayo vivādo
hy astīti nāstīti bhidārtha-niṣṭhaḥ
vyartho 'pi naivoparameta puṁsāṁ
mattaḥ parāvṛtta-dhiyāṁ sva-lokāt
(17.33)

ātma — individual spirit; aparijñāṇa – not objectively experiencing; mayah — based on, hinges on; vivādo = vivādaḥ — dispute; hy = hi — indeed; astiti = asti — is + iti — thus, it is said; nāstīti = na – not + asti — is + iti — it is said; bhidārtha-niṣṭhaḥ = bhidā — difference + artha – values + niṣṭhaḥ — based on; vyartho = vyarthaḥ — baseless; 'pi = api — even though; naivoparameta = na — never + eva — merely + uparameta — cease; puṁsām — for persons; mattaḥ — from me; parāvṛtta — turned away; dhiyām — intellects; sva – self; lokāt — from perception.

Translation

The dispute as to whether the individual spirit is distinct or not, hinges on a difference based on values merely. It is based on not objectively experiencing the individual spirit. Even though the argument is baseless, it never ceases for those persons whose intellects are turned away from Me and from their own self perception. (17.33)

Commentary:

Most of the experiences and resulting theories about oneness, has to do with a lack of distinction, with not being objective during the experiences. For objectivity one requires the proper perception to see with clarity the various objects. Of course when we enter the subtle and super-subtle dimensions there is more of a likelihood that there will be no distinction because to see there we would require finer and finer tools of perception.

Modern science has clearly shown that in the atoms, there are distinct electro-magnetic charges. This means therefore that even though we are not sensually equipped to peer into the most subtle objects, still we should not draw rash conclusions about oneness.

One has to strive for self-perception and then for a vision of the Supreme Self, the person whom *Śrī* Krishna claims to be. Disputes will continue among philosophers, mystics and religious leaders, and among various scientifically-minded persons but for one individual these disputes come to an end, when he decides to acquire clarity. This is the art of *kriyā* yoga.

श्री-उद्धव उवाच
त्वत्तः परावृत्त-धियः
स्व-कृतैः कर्मभिः प्रभो ।
उच्चावचान् यथा देहान्
गृह्णन्ति विसृजन्ति च ॥ १७.३४॥

śrī-uddhava uvāca
tvattaḥ parāvṛtta-dhiyaḥ
sva-kṛtaiḥ karmabhiḥ prabho
uccāvacān yathā dehān
gṛhṇanti visṛjanti ca (17.34)

śrī-uddhava – the deserving Uddhava; uvāca — said; tvattaḥ — from you; parāvṛtta — gravitated away from; dhiyaḥ — those whose intellects; sva – their own; kṛtaiḥ — by what is done deliberatedly; karmabhiḥ — by cultural activities; prabho — lord; uccāvacān = ucca – higher + avacān — lower; yathā — according to what rule; dehān — material bodies; grhṇanti — acquire; visṛjanti — lose; ca — and

Translation

The deserving Uddhava said: O Lord, regarding those whose intellects are gravitated away from You, by their own cultural activities, according to what rule do they acquire and lose higher or lower material bodies. (17.34)

Commentary:

This is an interesting question, because we see that even though a human being might not believe in *Śrī* Krishna and might deliberately or unknowingly gravitate from what *Śrī* Krishna desires, still sometimes that person attains a higher status in life. A person is not necessarily degraded just because he or she does not patronize the desire of *Śrī* Krishna. What therefore is the force which controls those who are detached from Him? What rule of existence governs the lives of those people?

Of course, we have to be clear by what we define as *Śrī* Krishna's preferences. If we mistake something for His preference, our judgment would be faulty and we would not answer the question. The only guarantee that someone followed *Śrī* Krishna is that person's reception of a direct instruction from the Lord, just as Arjuna or Uddhava received; or an instruction from someone who truly relays the instruction of *Śrī* Krishna.

तन् ममाख्याहि गोविन्द
दुर्विभाव्यम् अनात्मभिः ।
न ह्य् एतत् प्रायशो लोके
विद्वांसः सन्ति वञ्चिताः ॥ १७.३५॥

tan mamākhyāhi govinda
durvibhāvyam anātmabhiḥ
na hy etat prāyaśo loke
vidvāṁsaḥ santi vañcitāḥ (17.35)

tan = tat — that; mamākhyāhi = mama — to me + ākhyāhi — explain; govinda — Govinda Krishna; durvibhāvyam — difficult to realise; anātmabhih — by those who are not perceptive of their spiritual self; na — not; hy = hi — indeed; etat — this; prāyaśo = prāyaśaḥ — majority of people; loke — in this world; vidvāṁsaḥ — knowledgeable; santi — are; vañcitāh — deluded.

Translation

Explain that to me, O Govinda Krishna. The distinction of the spirit is difficult to realize by those who are not perceptive of the spiritual self. The majority of people in this world are not knowledgeable about this for they are deluded. (17.35)

Commentary:

Perhaps if people would understand what protection is afforded to those who gravitate towards Krishna and what is available to those who are adverse to Him, more persons would agree to accept Him.

श्री-भगवान् उवाच
मनः कर्म-मय णृणाम्
इन्द्रियैः पञ्चभिर् युतम् ।
लोकाल् लोकं प्रयात्य् अन्य
आत्मा तद् अनुवर्तते ॥ १७.३६ ॥

śrī-bhagavān uvāca
manaḥ karma-mayaṁ ṇṝṇām
indriyaiḥ pañcabhir yutam
lokāl lokaṁ prayāty anya
ātmā tad anuvartate (17.36)

śrī-bhagavān – the blessed lord; uvāca — said; manaḥ — the mind; karma – cultural activities; mayam — conditioned by; nṝṇām — of human beings; indriyaiḥ — with the senses; pañcabhir = pañcabhiḥ — with five; yutam — linked with; lokāl = lokāt — from one circumstance; lokam — to another circumstance; prayāty = prayāti — moves; anyah — other, something apart from; ātmā — individual spirit; tad = tat — that (mind); anuvartate — follows.

Translation

The Blessed Lord said: The mind of human beings, being conditioned by cultural activity, moves from one existence to another, accompanied by the five senses. The individual spirit, which is something apart, follows that mind. (17.36)

Commentary:

This is the sad situation of how we normally transmigrate in material existence. It is usually done at the whim of the mind. Thus the necessity to interrupt the natural process by developing mind control.

ध्यायन् मनो ऽनु विषयान्
दृष्टान् वानुश्रुतान् अथ ।
उद्यत् सीदत् कर्म-तन्त्र
स्मृतिस् तद् अनु शाम्यति ॥ १७.३७ ॥

dhyāyan mano 'nu viṣayān
dṝṣṭān vānuśrutān atha
udyat sīdat karma-tantraṁ
smṝtis tad anu śāmyati (17.37)

dhyāyat — linking the attention; mano = manaḥ — the mind; 'nu = anu — repeatedly; viṣayān — to attractive objects; dṛṣṭān — things seen in this world; vānuśrutān = vā — or + anusrutan — things heard of in the Veda; atha — then; udyat — draws near to; sīdat — retracts from; karma – cultural activities; tantram — complication; smṛtis = smṛtiḥ — memory; tad = tat – that (life); anu — after; samyati — is forgotten.

Translation

By repeatedly linking the attention to the attractive objects, which are seen in this world or heard of in media, the mind draws near to or retracts from the complications of cultural activity but after that life, the memory of those experiences is forgotten. (17.37)

Commentary:

The attractive objects have a drawing or a repelling power of their own. In most cases the mind is attracted helplessly, and the spirit has little to do with it, except to be the liable observer. After one life of being in the thick of things, the mind forgets the experiences which become compressed impressions in the subconscious. Thus in the next life, the same cycle of liable involvement and necessary retractions, followed by forgetfulness, occurs again.

विषयाभिनिवेशेन
नात्मानं यत् स्मरेत् पुनः ।
जन्तोर् वै कस्यचिद् धेतोर्
मृत्युर् अत्यन्त-विस्मृतिः ॥ १७.३८॥

viṣayābhiniveśena
nātmānaṁ yat smaret punaḥ
jantor vai kasyacid dhetor
mṛtyur atyanta-vismṛtiḥ (17.38)

viṣayābhiniveśena = viṣaya — attractive object + abhiniveśena — by being intensely absorbed due to an instinctive fear of death; nātmānam = na — not + ātmānam — the self, himself; yat — which; smaret — remembers; punaḥ — any more; jantor = jantoḥ — of a human being; vai — indeed; kasyacid = kasyacit – any whatever; dhetor = hetoḥ — for the reason; mṛtyur = mṛtyuḥ — death; atyanta — total; vismṛtiḥ — forgetfulness.

Translation

Due to an intense absorption of the attractive objects, he no more remembers himself. Indeed the total forgetfulness of a human being, for whatever reason, is called death. (17.38)

Commentary:

In each life, we become intensely absorbed in the attractive objects which pull us into the complications of social life. While doing this we forget ourselves. We identify instead with the social role afforded us by time and circumstance. Then there is a total forgetfulness after death of our bodies, because the mind of necessity withdraws completely from the social environment which it held so dearly. This forgetfulness is called death. In the *Bhagavad-Gītā*, this is explained in another way.

avyaktādīni bhūtāni vyaktamadhyāni bhārata
avyaktanidhanānyeva tatra kā paridevanā

The living beings are undetected in the beginning of a manifestation, visible in the interim stages, and are again undetected at the end of a manifestation. (B.G. 2.28)

जन्म त्व् आत्मतया पुसः
सर्व-भावेन भूरि-द ।
विषय-स्वीकृतिं प्राहुर्
यथा स्वप्न-मनोरथः ॥ १७.३९॥

janma tv ātmatayā puṁsaḥ
sarva-bhāvena bhūri-da
viṣaya-svīkṛtiṁ prāhur
yathā svapna-manorathaḥ (17.39)

janma — birth; tv = tu — however; ātmatayā — by self identity; puṁsah — of a person; sarva –all; bhāvena — with feeling; bhūri-da — generous one; viṣaya — attractive objects; svīkṛtiṁ — acceptance; prāhur = prāhuḥ — is called; yathā — as, in case of, svapna — dream; manorathaḥ — imagination.

Translation

O generous one, the birth of a person is the acceptance of an attractive object with all feelings and with self identification, as in the case of a dream or imagination. (17.39)

Commentary:

Birth for us, normally means that we completely identify with a sense object which is the body. This begins as an embryo. It has feelings. It has self-identification because it is actually a spirit with psychological equipments. It is similar to dreams, where a person completely identifies with the surroundings he finds himself in or in an imagination where one becomes engrossed in a fantasy.

Both in this verse and in the previous one, *Śrī* Krishna did not use the word for the human body which is *deha* or *śarīra*. Instead, He used the word for an attractive object or sense object. This is because the material body is more than just itself. When any of us pass away from this world, that particular spirit is usually drawn into a new body by a continued attraction to the complications of cultural life in this world (*karma-tantram* verse 37). Due to that one gets into a father's feelings, somehow or the other by some reason or the other (*dhetor-hetoh* verse 38). This is the beginning of one's new body, because one is transferred quite easily into that man's semina after being housed in his emotions. Thereafter one assumes the identity of a sexual urge and the romantic feelings which accompany that. Thus one is transferred by the force of sexual attraction into a woman's body. And she becomes one's mother, nine months thereafter.

It begins with the acceptance of feelings and self-identification *(ātmatayā sarva-bhāvena)*. And it ends when one is forced to retreat from this world at the time of death of one's body. At that time, the mind goes into its instinctive method of folding up all memories of that past life, dropping them or relinquishing them as it were, in order to focus on the new priority which is to acquire another body. Since the mind was focused into the social world, it again by the force of that pre-focus, takes another body to come out again in this world.

A preoccupation with this world, for whatever purpose, even for a religious one, will cause a particular spirit to again return here for cultural activities. This is a law of psychology.

स्वप्नं मनोरथ चेत्थं
प्राक्तनं न स्मरत्य् असौ ।
तत्र पूर्वम् इवात्मानम्
अपूर्वम् चानुपश्यति ॥ १७.४० ॥

svapnaṁ manorathaṁ cetthaṁ
prāktanaṁ na smaraty asau
tatra pūrvam ivātmānam
apūrvam cānupaśyati (17.40)

svapnam — dream; manoratham — imagined circumstance; cettham = ca — and + ittham — similarly; prāktanam — previously; na – no; smaraty = smarati — remembers; asau — he; tatra — in that situation; pūrvam — previous; ivātmānam = iva — as if + ātmānam — spirit; apūrvam — having no past existence; cānupaśyati = ca — and + anupaśyati — considers.

Translation

And similarly he does not remember the previous dream and imagined circumstance. In that situation, he considers his spiritual self as if it had no past existence. (17.40)

Commentary:

As soon as one take a new body, one feels as if one exists for the first time. Since the conscious mind lost its reference from the past life, it assumes that it is new and that everything about it, is perceived for the first time.

Because the mind was forced to relinquish any objective knowledge from the past life, it approaches everything in the new life with ignorance or innocence, and the spirit follows behind.

इन्द्रियायन-सृष्ट्येद
त्रै-विध्यं भाति वस्तुनि ।
बहिर्-अन्तर्-भिदा-हेतुर्
जनो ऽसज्-जन-कृद् यथा ॥ १७.४१ ॥

indriyāyana-sṛṣṭyedaṁ
trai-vidhyaṁ bhāti vastuni
bahir-antar-bhidā-hetur
jano 'saj-jana-kṛd yathā (17.41)

indriyāyana = indriya – senses + ayana — repository; sṛṣṭyedam = srstya — creation + idam — this; trai-vidhyam — threefold division; bhāti — appears; vastuni — in the real spirit; bahir = bahih — what is objective; antah — and internal; bhidā — division; hetur = hetuḥ — cause; jano = janaḥ

— person; 'saj-jana = asat-jana — wicked progeny; kṛd = kṛt — cause, parent; yathā — just as.

Translation

This creation of the repository of the senses, which is of a threefold division, appears in the real soul. It is the cause of the division of what is objective and what is subjective, just as a person who is a parent of a wicked child. (17.41)

Commentary:

The mind is the repository of the senses but the mind has within it many hidden and strange places. Usually when we take a new body, the old storage places are pushed into the subconscious, and appear as if they are non-existent. This happens in the interim between losing a body and gaining a new one. It is the way of nature to cause the conscious or objective mind to separate itself completely from all its recent experiences and to be completely empty on the surface level, for the purpose of accepting a new cultural identity.

नित्यदा ह्य् अङ्ग भूतानि
भवन्ति न भवन्ति च ।
कालेनालक्ष्य-वेगेन
सूक्ष्मत्वात् तन् न दृश्यते ॥ १७.४२ ॥

nityadā hy aṅga bhūtāni
bhavanti na bhavanti ca
kālenālakṣya-vegena
sūkṣmatvāt tan na dṛśyate (17.42)

nityadā — continually; hy = hi — indeed; aṅga — friend; bhūtāni — living bodies; bhavanti — are appeasing; na – no; bhavanti — are appearing; ca — and; kālenālakṣya = kālena — through time factor + alakṣya — imperceptible; vegena — with the swiftly moving; sūkṣmatvāt — because of subtlety; tan = tat — that (time force); na – not; dṛśyate — is seen.

Translation

O friend, through the imperceptible swiftly moving time factor, creature bodies are continually appearing and disappearing. But due to subtlety that time force is not seen. (17.42)

Commentary:

The spirit, though it is transcendental to the material body in all gross and subtle phases, still does not usually understand what transpires on the subtle level of material nature. In fact, even from the gross point of view, its purview is limited. Thus it is at a disadvantage, because material nature keeps on working on manifested and unmanifested levels at all times, producing numerous changes with or without the spirit's observations.

The only thing a person is allowed to carry from one life to another is instinct. This manifests as a predisposition in the new life. Otherwise the living entity is not allowed to carry any memories or anything else mental for that matter. The death experience and the interim period before acquiring a new baby form, is so thorough, that it might be compared to a very strict customs department through which all travelers are subjected before entering a country. As a customs officer may confiscate certain items from the travelers, so material nature by its process of subjection of the mind, removes from it many memories. Thus much of the psychological baggage which one intends to carry through the hereafter into the next life, is confiscated in the interim period while one stays in the hereafter as a wandering spirit or confused ghost. And for that matter, there is hardly anything that can be done about this.

In the new life, because his psychological knowledge was deleted from his conscious mind, the living entity finds himself with a seemingly new mind that appears to be clean of impressions. Thus he assumes that he lives for the first time. This is the great mystery of nature's magic of reincarnation.

As a man becomes responsible for the activities of any wicked children he might have, so the spirit becomes liable for any ignorant activities the mind enacts, because it has lost its acquired discrimination from the immediate and distant past lives. Thus in each life, one is liable to commit the same mistakes all over again. This is repeated over and over and over, because of the ability of material nature, to delete one's acquired discernment.

The only way to break out of this is to develop subtle vision, supernatural eyesight and spiritual vision. There is no other method for transcending this.

यथार्चिषां स्रोतसां च
फलानां वा वनस्पतेः ।
तथैव सर्व-भूतानां
वयो-ऽवस्थादयः कृताः ॥ १७.४३ ॥

yathārciṣāṁ srotasāṁ ca
phalānāṁ vā vanaspateḥ
tathaiva sarva-bhūtānāṁ
vayo-'vasthādayaḥ kṛtāḥ (17.43)

yathārciṣām = yathā — as in this case + arciṣām — of flames; srotasām — of streams; ca — and; phalānām — of fruits; vā — or; vanaspateḥ — of a tree; tathaiva = tathā — so, also + eva — surely; sarva – all; bhūtānām — of creature forms; vayo = vayaḥ — of age; 'vasthādayaḥ = avasthā — condition + ādayaḥ — and other; kṛtāḥ — are produced.

Translation

As in the case of flames and streams or of the fruits of a tree, surely also the age and other conditions of the creature forms, are produced. (17.43)

Commentary:

Every thing is changing from moment to moment, because that is the nature of these manifestations. The flames of a fire might seem to be of the same shape and intensity from moment to moment but there is variation no matter how minute. The waters of a stream all seem to remain the same but actually it changes at every moment. The fruits of a tree, which appear to be the same, go through continual transformation. This subtlety causes us confusion.

सो ऽयं दीपो ऽर्चिषां यद्वत्
स्रोतसां तद् इदं जलम् ।
सो ऽयं पुमान् इति नृणां
मृषा गीर् धीर् मृषायुषाम् ॥ १७.४४ ॥

so 'yaṁ dīpo 'rciṣāṁ yadvat
srotasāṁ tad idaṁ jalam
so 'yaṁ pumān iti nṛṇāṁ
mṛṣā gīr dhīr mṛṣāyuṣām (17.44)

so = saḥ — this; 'yam = ayam — this, the very same; dīpo = dīpaḥ — lamp; 'rciṣāṁ = arciṣām — of the flames; yadvat — as in the case; srotasām — of the streams; tad = tat — that; idam — that very same; jalam — water; so = sah — this; 'yam = ayam — this, the very same; pumān — human being; iti — thus, it is stated; nṛṇām — of people; mṛṣā — false; gīr = gīh — statement; dhīr = dhīḥ — intellect; mṛṣāyuṣām = mrsā – wrong perception + āyuṣām — of those whose life.

Translation

As in the case of flames, where it is stated, "This is the very same flame", or in the case of streams, where it is said, "This is the very same water."; so in the case of people it is stated, that "This is the very same human being." These are false statements, relating to the intellect of those who lives are based on wrong perception. (17.44)

Commentary:

This sums up the general culture of human existence.

मा स्वस्य कर्म-बीजेन
जायते सो ऽप्य् अयं पुमान् ।
म्रियते वामरो भ्रान्त्या
यथाग्निर् दारु-सयुतः ॥ १७.४५ ॥

mā svasya karma-bījena
jāyate so 'py ayaṁ pumān
mriyate vāmaro bhrāntyā
yathāgnir dāru-saṁyutaḥ (17 45)

mā — not; svasya — of his own; karma – cultural activities; bījena — by the instrumentality; jāyate — is born; so = sah — he; 'py = api — also; ayam — this; pumān — human being; mriyate — dies; vāmaro = vā — or + amaraḥ — deathless; bhrāntyā — by a misconception; yathāgnir = yathā — as + agniḥ — fire; dāru — wood; samyutaḥ — connected.

Translation

It is not born, nor does it die. It is not by the instrumentality of its cultural activities, that this human being is born or dies, for it is deathless. It is perceived so, by misconception, just as the fire is regarded when burning wood. (17.45)

Commentary:

The theory of *karma* as the ultimate cause of a man's cultural status is denied. Even though there is some interplay between one's actions and their results, still that is merely incidental. There is a higher function, which causes the birth and death of the various bodies and one's cultural responses are superficially intertwined with these.

Even though it appears that fire is dependent on wood, the chemicals in the wood, which mix with air to produce the fire, are actually independent of the wood. This is why there could be a flash of fire without wood.

निषेक-गर्भ-जन्मानि
बाल्य-कौमार-यौवनम् ।
वयो-मध्यं जरा मृत्युर्
इत्य् अवस्थास् तनोर् नव ॥ १७.४६ ॥

niṣeka-garbha-janmāni
bālya-kaumāra-yauvanam
vayo-madhyaṁ jarā mṛtyur
ity avasthās tanor nava (17 46)

niṣeka — impregnation; garbha — embryonic stage; janmāni — and birth; bālya — infancy; kaumāra — childhood; yauvanam — youth; vayo-madhyam = vayah-madhyam — middle age; jara — old age; mṛtyur = mṛtyuh — death; ity = iti — as listed; avasthās = avasthāḥ — stages; tanor = tanoḥ — of the body; nava — nine.

Translation

Impregnation, embryonic stage, birth, infancy, childhood, youth, middle age, old age, and death are listed as the nine stages of the body. (17.46)

Commentary:

These are physical stages which indicate the presence of a spirit. Besides these, there are emotional and mental stages, which are much more important and much more indicative of the spirit.

एता मनोरथ-मयीर्
हान्यस्योच्चावचास् तनूः ।
गुण-सङ्गाद् उपादत्ते
क्वचित् कश्चिज् जहाति च ॥ १७.४७ ॥

etā manoratha-mayīr
hānyasyoccāvacās tanūḥ
guṇa-saṅgād upādatte
kvacit kaścij jahāti ca (17.47)

eta = etaḥ — those; manoratha – imaginative power of the mind; mayīr = mayīh — that which is created by; hānyasyoccāvacās = ha — clearly + anyasya — of something else + ucca — superior + avacāḥ — inferior; tanūḥ — bodily status; guṇa – influences of material nature; saṅgād = saṅgāt — due to attachment; upādatte — assumes; kvacit — sometimes; kaścij = kaścit — someone; jahāti — gives up, casts away; ca — and.

Translation

The superior or inferior bodily status is created by the imaginary power of the mind, and are of something pertaining to something else. Due to attachment to the influence of material nature, the spirit assumes these. Sometimes however, someone does cast that aside. (17.47)

Commentary:

The superior and inferior positions of each of the various species and each of the various capabilities of particular bodies in the same species, has to do with the body actually and not with the spirit who is harnessed to it. But since the spirit is influenced by material nature, it holds a prejudiced view of itself in terms of the status the mind assumed in a particular body. There are some persons however who break the spell of the mind and perceive the utility of the various bodies without having to identify totally with the advantages and disadvantages of a particular species.

आत्मनः पितृ-पुत्राभ्याम्
अनुमेयौ भवाप्ययौ ।
न भवाप्यय-वस्तूनाम्
अभिज्ञो द्वय-लक्षणः ॥ १७.४८॥

ātmanaḥ pitṛ-putrābhyām
anumeyau bhavāpyayau
na bhavāpyaya-vastūnām
abhijño dvaya-lakṣaṇaḥ (17.48)

ātmanaḥ — one's own; pitṛ — father; putrābhyām — of the son; anumeyau — can be figured; bhava — birth + apyayau — and death; na — no; bhavāpyaya = bhava – affected by birth + apyaya – affected by death; vastūnām — of things; abhijño = abhijñaḥ — the observer; dvaya — by those two features; lakṣaṇaḥ — characterized.

Translation

One's own birth and death can be figured from those of one's son and father. The observer of things affected by birth and death is not characterized by those two features. (17.48)

Commentary:

By the youth of the son's body, and the aged condition of the father's, one can realize that one's body was in a youthful stage. If spared untimely death, it will exhibit old age. Since one observes the transit of time, one can understand that as the observer one is not time-conditioned. This is how one begins to study the nature of the soul. This is the preliminary course.

तरोर् बीज-विपाकाभ्यां
यो विद्वाञ् जन्म-सयमौ ।
तरोर् विलक्षणो द्रष्टा
एवं द्रष्टा तनोः पृथक् ॥ १७.४९॥

taror bīja-vipākābhyāṁ
yo vidvāñ janma-saṁyamau
taror vilakṣaṇo draṣṭā
evaṁ draṣṭā tanoḥ pṛthak (17.49

taror = taroḥ — of a plant; bīja — seed; vipākābhyām — from the final stage; yo = yaḥ — he who; vidvān — one in knowledge; janma — birth; samyamau — and death; taror = taroḥ — from a tree; vilakṣaṇo = vilakṣaṇaḥ — distinct; draṣṭā — he who sees; evam — similarly; draṣṭā — witness; tanoḥ — of the body; pṛthak — is separate.

Translation

A person in knowledge who sees the birth and death of a plant, from seed to final stage, is distinct from the plant. Similarly the witness of the body is separate from it. (17.49)

Commentary:

One has to start understanding one's existential perspective and from that, deduce that one is different from the body which changes continually. This is the basic lesson in self-realization.

प्रकृतेर् एवम् आत्मानम्
अविविच्याबुधः पुमान् ।
तत्त्वेन स्पर्श-सम्मूढः
ससारं प्रतिपद्यते ॥ १७.५० ॥

prakṛter evam ātmānam
avivicyābudhaḥ pumān
tattvena sparśa-sammūḍhaḥ
saṁsāraṁ pratipadyate (17.50)

prakṛter = prakṛteḥ — from material nature; evam — thus; ātmānam — spirit; avivicyābudhaḥ = avivicya — failing to correctly ascertain + abudhaḥ — the ignorant person; pumān — person; tattvena — by the substances; sparśa — by sensual conduct; sammūḍhaḥ — one who is deluded; saṁsāram — the process of birth and death; pratipadyate — is drawn into.

Translation

The ignorant person, failing to correctly ascertain his spirit from material nature, is deluded by sensual contact and by the substances. He is drawn into the process of birth and death. (17.50)

Commentary:

This ignorant person is not the exceptional human being but the average human being. Failing to discern our spirits from material nature, and being carried away by sensuality and by the subtle and gross substances which ours senses appreciate, we are continually drawn into the process of birth and death, as we are led here and there by the prejudices of the mind.

सत्त्व-सङ्गाद् ऋषीन् देवान्
रजसासुर-मानुषान् ।
तमसा भूत-तिर्यक्त्वं
भ्रामितो याति कर्मभिः ॥ १७.५१ ॥

sattva-saṅgād ṛṣīn devān
rajasāsura-mānuṣān
tamasā bhūta-tiryaktvaṁ
bhrāmito yāti karmabhiḥ (17.51)

sattva – perceptive mode; saṅgād = saṅgāt — by affiliation with; ṛṣīn — yogi sage; devān — supernatural rulers; rajasāsura = rajasā — impulsive mode, motivation + asura — wicked beings; mānuṣān — human beings; tamasā — by the confusing influence; bhūta — ghost; tiryaktvam — animal species; bhrāmito = bhrāmitaḥ — made to transmigrate; yāti — he goes; karmabhiḥ — by cultural activities.

Translation

Being made to transmigrate, by the force of cultural action, a person by affiliation with the perceptive energy in material nature, goes to the yogi sages or to the supernatural rulers; or by affiliation with the impulsive motivations he goes to the wicked personalities or the human beings; or by absorbing the depressive energies, he goes to the ghosts and animal species. (17.51)

Commentary:

There is a similar statement in the discourse with Arjuna:

yajante sāttvikā devān yakṣarakṣāṁsi rājasāḥ
pretānbhūtagaṇāṁścānye yajante tāmasā janāḥ

The clear-minded people worship the supernatural rulers. The impulsive ones worship the passionate sorcerors and the cannibalistic humans. The others, the retarded people, petition the departed spirits and the hordes of ghosts. (B.G. 17.4)

Before one can get out of the material world, one has to divest himself of the two lower modes, namely the depressive influence and the impulsive motivational force. When that is accomplished and one has to consistently relocated one's psyche for dependence on the perceptive energies of material nature, then one can make a dart for the transcendence. One cannot under any circumstance, maintain a consistent hold on the transcendence, if one does not relinquish one's affiliation with the two lower modes.

नृत्यतो गायतः पश्यन्
यथैवानुकरोति तान् ।
एवं बुद्धि-गुणान् पश्यन्न्
अनीहो ऽप्य् अनुकार्यते ॥१७.५२॥

nṛtyato gāyataḥ paśyan
yathaivānukaroti tān
evaṁ buddhi-guṇān paśyann
anīho 'py anukāryate (17.52)

nṛtyato = nṛtyataḥ — troupe of dancers; gāyataḥ — choir singers; paśyan — seeing; yathaivānukaroti = yathā — just as + eva — indeed + anukaroti — imitates; tān — them; evam — just so; buddhi — organ of the intellect; guṇān — operations; paśyann = paśyan — perceiving; anīho = anīhaḥ — that which is indifferent and neutral; 'py = api — also; anukāryate — patterns itself after.

Translation:

Just as when seeing a troupe of dancers or a choir of singers, one imitates them, just so upon observing the operations of the organ of the intellect, that factor, which is indifferent and essentially neutral, patterns itself after them. (17.52)

Commentary:

Even though this can be understood intellectually, to put this advice into practice, one has to master higher yoga, to perceive the intellect as an organ in the head of the subtle body.

The factor which is indifferent and essentially neutral is the spirit. This verse confirms what *Śrīpad Ādi Śaṅkarācārya* explained in the debate with Mandana Mishra where *Śrīpad* said that the spirit should be regarded as the detached bird on the tree of life, and the intellect should be considered as the reward-seeking creature of plumage. The two aspects, the spirit and its intellect live in the psyche together like two intimate friends. Since the spirit cannot directly interact with the subtle material nature, it takes cues from the intellect. If it is not careful it is conveyed through haphazard transmigrations by that intellectual dependence.

Despite this, the spirit does not become the intellect at any time, nor does the intellect ever become the spirit. Still the spirit, if it is not detached, is forced to observe the fantasies of the intellect and to endorse its willy-nilly plans.

यथाम्भसा प्रचलता
तरवो ऽपि चला इव ।
चक्षुसा भ्राम्यमाणेन
दृश्यते भ्रमतीव भूः ॥१७.५३॥

yathāmbhasā pracalatā
taravo 'pi calā iva
cakṣusā bhrāmyamāṇena
dṛśyate bhramatīva bhūḥ (17.53)

yathāmbhasā = yathā — as + ambhasā — by water; pracalatā — moving; taravo = taravaḥ — trees; 'pi = api — also; calā = calāḥ — moving; iva — as if, seems to be; cakṣusā — by eyes; bhrāmyamāṇena — by whirling; dṛśyate — is seen; bhramatīva = bhramatī — moving about + iva — as if; bhūḥ — landscape.

Translation

As trees reflected in moving water, seem to be moving so that landscape is seen moving about by whirling eyes. (17.53)

Commentary:

The spirit is influenced by his means of perception which is the intellect. This is why it is necessary to master *buddhi* yoga as described in the *Bhagavad-Gītā*, beginning in chapter two. This causes the stilling of the intellect, so that one can see clearly. Otherwise, no matter what a person does, no matter what spiritual path he takes, he will be affected by the wavy unstill nature of an intellect, which is energized by lower pranic force.

यथा मनोरथ-धियो
विषय्षानुभवो मृषा ।
स्वप्न-दृष्टाश् च दाशार्ह
तथा संसार आत्मनः ॥ १७.५४॥

yathā manoratha-dhiyo
viṣayṣānubhavo mṛṣā
svapna-dṛṣṭāś ca dāśārha
tathā saṁsāra ātmanaḥ (17.54)

yathā — as; manoratha — imagination; dhiyo = dhiyah — intellectual conception; viṣayānubhavaḥ = viṣaya — sensual + anubhavaḥ — experience; mṛṣā — unreal; svapna –dream; dṛṣṭaś = dṛṣṭaḥ — that which is seen; ca — and; dāśārha — o son of the Dasharha; tathā — so, also; saṁsāra — transmigration; ātmanaḥ — of the spirit.

Translation

As imagination, the intellectual conception and sense experience are also false, so also, O son of the Dāśārha, is the transmigrating existence of the soul. (17.54)

Commentary:

Underlying all mundane experience, is the material energy. Thus everything it is based on, is temporary, and ultimately unreal. Therefore even our transmigrations do not make for anything of lasting significance. A person who passes through many dreams in one night and who experiences joys and sufferings in these, still does not consider those experiences to be very significant once he awakens. Even though at present we are enthralled by these transmigrations which are spread out in the medium of time, still finally they will all seem to be meaningless once we become freed.

अर्थे ह्य् अविद्यमाने ऽपि
संसृतिर् न निवर्तते ।
ध्यायतो विषयान् अस्य
स्वप्ने ऽनर्थागमो यथा ॥ १७.५५॥

arthe hy avidyamāne 'pi
saṁsṛtir na nivartate
dhyāyato viṣayān asya
svapne 'narthāgamo yathā (17.55)

arthe — in the value, in fact; hy = hi — surely; avidyamāne — in what is unreal; 'pi = api — even though; saṁsṛtir = saṁsṛtiḥ — the material existence of changing bodies in ignorance of previous ones; na – not; nivartate — ceases; dhyāyato = dhyāyataḥ — one who links his attention with a concentration force; viṣayān — attractive mundane objects; asya — of him; svapne — in dream; 'narthāgamo = anartha — undesireable circumstances + āgamaḥ — appearance; yathā — just as.

Translation

Even though it is in fact, unreal, the material existence of changing bodies in ignorance of previous ones, does not cease for one whose attention is linked to the attractive mundane objects, just as the undesirable circumstances continue in a dream. (17.55)

Commentary:

So long as we remain connected to the attractive objects on this side of existence, we must continue in the aimless transmigrations helplessly. It is just like when a person is in an undesirable dream, he cannot get out of it if he is not permitted some objectivity. He is forced to endure it until it expends its potency.

तस्माद् उद्धव मा भुङ्क्ष्व
विषयान् असद्-इन्द्रियैः ।
आत्माग्रहण-निर्भात
पश्य वैकल्पिक भ्रमम् ॥ १७.५६॥

tasmād uddhava mā bhuṅkṣva
viṣayān asad-indriyaiḥ
ātmāgrahaṇa-nirbhātaṁ
paśya vaikalpikaṁ bhramam (17.56)

tasmād = tasmāt — therefore; uddhava — Uddhava; mā – stop; bhuṅkṣva — experiencing; viṣayān — attractive mundane objects; asad = asat — temporary; indriyaiḥ — with the senses; ātmāgrahaṇa

= ātma — spiritual self + agrahaṇa — non-perception; nirbhātam — without brightness, lack of clarity; paśya — see; vaikalpikam — varied world; bhramam — delusion.

Translation

Therefore, O Uddhava stop experiencing the attractive mundane objects with the temporary senses. See the perception of the delusive varied world as being the cause of the lack of clarity and the non-perception of the spiritual self. (17.56)

Commentary:

This is a general instruction for all *kriyā* yogins, to somehow put an end to the mind's interaction with this world, to internalize the mind and its instruments which are the sensual energy and the intellect. If one does this, he will in due course, develop supernatural and spiritual perception. This can only be done by higher yoga which culminates in *samādhi*. And it means turning away even from attractive sacred objects like Deities of *Śrī* Krishna even, just as Uddhava will have to turn away from the super-physical body of Lord Krishna and from the bodies of the *Yadu* devotees of the Yadu dynasty. At some point a devotee, if he is at all serious about going to the spiritual world, will have to turn away from every sacred and profane mundane object, even those which were produced by the Divinities.

क्षिप्तो ऽवमानितो ऽसद्भिः
प्रलब्धो ऽसूयितो ऽथ वा ।
ताडितः सन्निरुद्धो वा
वृत्त्या वा परिहापितः ॥ १७.५७॥

kṣipto 'vamānito 'sadbhiḥ
pralabdho 'sūyito 'tha vā
tāḍitaḥ sanniruddho vā
vṛttyā vā parihāpitaḥ (17.57)

kṣipto = kṣiptaḥ — scolded; 'vamānito = avamānitaḥ — insulted; 'sadbhiḥ = asadbhiḥ — materialistic people; pralabdho = pralabdhaḥ — ridiculed; 'sūyito = asūyitaḥ — resented; 'tha vā = atha vā — otherwise; tāḍitaḥ — beaten; sanniruddho = sanniruddhaḥ — arrested; vā — or; vṛttyā — of his means of livelihood; vā — or; parihāpitah — deprived.

Translation

Even though scolded and insulted by the materialistic people, rediculed and otherwise resented, beaten or arrested, or deprived of his means of livelihood, (17.57)

Commentary:

This is part of the description of how an advanced ascetic reacts to social circumstance in which he is harassed by the public and even by other devotees who feel that he should not take these extreme advisories of Lord Krishna but should instead take up easy methods which are dovetailed for human emotions. Sensing that he turned himself away from material existence, materialistic people even devotees feel insecure and so they react unfavorably to him.

Instead of facilitating and wishing him well, the materialistic devotees who follow the general path of salvation will condemn such a serious yogi devotee. They will do everything possible to turn him away from the definite path laid down by *Śrī* Krishna in this discussion with Uddhava.

निष्ठ्युतो मूत्रितो वाज्ञैर्
बहुधैव प्रकम्पितः ।
श्रेयस्-कामः कृच्छ्र-गत
आत्मनात्मानम् उद्धरेत् ॥ १७.५८॥

niṣṭhyuto mūtrito vājñair
bahudhaivaṁ prakampitaḥ
śreyas-kāmaḥ kṛcchra-gata
ātmanātmānam uddharet (17.58)

niṣṭhyuto = niṣṭhyutah — spat upon; mūtrito = mūtritah — pissed on; vājñair = vājñaih = va — or + ajñaih — by ignorant people; bahudhaivaṁ = bahudha — variously, in many ways + evam — thus; prakampitaḥ — aggravated; śreyas = śreyaḥ - well-being; kāmaḥ — one who desires; kṛcchra – difficulty; gata = gatah — going through; ātmanātmānam = ātmanā — by himself, by his own effort + ātmānam — himself; uddharet — should deliver.

Translation

...spat upon, or pissed on by ignorant people, being thus aggravated in many ways, and going through difficulties, the person who desires well-being should save himself by his own effort. (17.58)

Commentary:

One has to endeavor to save his own self, with the help of the Almighty God and with the help of advanced yogis. One should not be lax in spiritual austerities and should do whatever is necessary to reach the goal of spiritual perfection. One should not go hunting for cheap religions, which promise to reverse the effects of a long, long course of mundane evolution overnight. Such methods simply stall an ascetic and deprive him of a rapid progress in a worthy and sure path.

श्री-उद्धव उवाच
यथैवम् अनुबुध्येय
वद नो वदतां वर ।
सु-दुःषहम् इमं मन्य
आत्मन्य् असद्-अतिक्रमम् ॥ १७.५९॥

śrī-uddhava uvāca
yathaivam anubudhyeyaṁ
vada no vadatāṁ vara
su-duḥṣaham imaṁ manya
ātmany asad-atikramam (17.59)

śrī-uddhava – the deserving Uddhava; uvāca — said; yathaivam = yathā — according to how + evam — thus; anubudhyeyam — I may understand; vada — instruct; no = nah — to us; vadatām — of teachers; vara — best; su-duḥsaham — very difficult to tolerate; imam — this; manya — I think; ātmany = ātmani — oneself; asad = asat — by the materialistic people; atikramam — insult.

Translation

The deserving Uddhava said: According to how I may understand, instruct me, O best of teachers. I think that this insult by the materialistic people is very difficult to tolerate. (17.59)

Commentary:

This is why it is best to live far away from them if one can do so, otherwise one must be very patient and forbearing. If one is not determined, one will succumb and give up the path of yoga as being difficult and take to the general paths of salvation, paths which lead no where besides rebirth without any memory of former lives.

विदुषाम् अपि विश्वात्मन्
प्रकृतिर् हि बलीयसी ।
ऋते त्वद्-धर्म-निरतान्
शान्तांस् ते चरणालयान् ॥ १७.६० ॥

viduṣām api viśvātman
prakṛtir hi balīyasī
ṛte tvad-dharma-niratān
śāntāṁs te caraṇālayān (17.60)

viduṣām — for those who are learned; api — even; viśvātman — universe soul; prakṛtir = prakṛtiḥ — material nature; hi — definitely; balīyasī — very strong,domineering; ṛte — excepting; tvad = tvat – your; dharma — righteous duty; niratān — devoted; śāntāṁs = śāntān — those who are free from passions; te — your; caraṇālayān = caraṇa – lotus feet + ālayān — those who take refuge.

Translation

O Soul of the universe, the material nature is definitely domineering, excepting for those who are learned, those who are devoted to Your style of righteous duty, those who are freed from passions and those who take refuge at Your Lotus feet. (17.60)

Commentary:

Material nature cannot be transcended easily. It is near impossible. Further more the material manifestation of Divinity, when used as a subject of focus, does not cause a full transcendence in respect to material nature. One should give up easy paths of salvation and take up *kriyā* yoga in earnest so that one can perfect oneself within and go to the spiritual atmosphere by one's endeavors, by the grace of the Almighty God, *Śrī* Krishna, and with the help of those *mahāyogīns* who succeeded before.

CHAPTER 18*

The Supreme Lord Releases the Avanti Brahmin**

Terri Stokes-Pineda Art

nūnaṁ me bhagavāṁs tuṣṭaḥ sarva-deva-mayo hariḥ
yena nīto daśām etāṁ nirvedaś cātmanaḥ plavaḥ

Surely, being pleased with me, the Supreme Lord, the God Hari, who empowers all the supernatural rulers, is the one by Whom this crisis was manifested as well as the disgust which is a saving grace for my soul. (Uddhava Gītā 18.28)

* Śrīmad Bhāgavatam Canto 11, Chapter 23
** Translator's selected chapter title.

श्री-बादरायणिर् उवाच
स एवम् आशासित उद्धवेन
भागवत-मुख्येन दाशार्ह-मुख्यः ।
सभाजयन् भृत्य-वचो मुकुन्दस्
तम् आबभाषे श्रवणीय-वीर्यः ॥ १८.१ ॥

śrī-bādarāyaṇir uvāca
sa evam āśaṁsita uddhavena
bhāgavata-mukhyena dāśārha-mukhyaḥ
sabhājayan bhṛtya-vaco mukundas
tam ābabhāṣe śravaṇīya-vīryaḥ)18.1)

śrī-bādarāyaṇir = śrī-bādarāyaṇiḥ - the accomplished son of Badarāyana; uvāca — said; sa = saḥ — he; evam — thus; āśaṁsita = āśaṁsitaḥ — was asked; uddhavena — by Uddhava; bhāgavata — of the devotees; mukhyena — by the leader; dāśārha — of the Dasarha family; mukhyaḥ — chief; sabhājayan — praised; bhṛtya — of servant; vaco = vacaḥ — statement; mukundas = mukundah — Mukunda Krishna; tam — to him; ābabhāṣe — spoke; śravanīya — worthy of hearing; vīrya — of heroic activities.

Translation

The accomplished son of Badarāyana said: As he was asked by Uddhava, the leader of the devotees, that chief of the Dāśārha family, Mukunda Krishna, whose heroic activities are worth hearing, praised the statement of his servant and spoke. (18.1)

Commentary:

Bādarāyaṇa is *Śrīla Vyāsadeva*, who was known also as Krishna *Dvaipāyaṇa*, the son of *Parāśar Muni*. His son was Shuka. This Shuka told this story to King *Parīkṣit*, the grandson of Arjuna.

श्री-भगवान् उवाच
बार्हस्पत्य स नास्त्य् अत्र
साधुर् वै दुर्जनेरितैः ।
दुरक्तैर् भिन्नम् आत्मानं
यः समाधातुम् ईश्वरः ॥ १८.२ ॥

śrī-bhagavān uvāca
bārhaspatya sa nāsty atra
sādhur vai durjaneritaiḥ
duraktair bhinnam ātmānaṁ
yaḥ samādhātum īśvaraḥ (18.2)

śrī-bhagavān – the blessed lord; uvāca — said; bārhaspatya — disciple of Bṛhaspati; sa = sah — he, that person; nāsty = na – no + asti — does exist; atra — in this world; sādhur = sādhuḥ — a saint; vai — indeed; durjaneritaiḥ = durjana — wicked people + īritaiḥ — by that which is uttered; duruktair = duruktaiḥ — by harsh words; bhinnam — pierced, affected; ātmānam — himself; yah — who; samādhātum — to remain calm; īśvaraḥ — is able.

Translation

The Blessed Lord said: O disciple of Bṛhaspati, that saint does not exist in this world, who can remain calm when affected by the harsh words uttered by wicked people. (18.2)

Commentary:

A very interesting declaration is made here by Lord Krishna.

न तथा तप्यते विद्धः
पुमान् बाणैस् तु मर्म-गैः ।
यथा तुदन्ति मर्म-स्था
ह्य् असतां परुषेषवः ॥ १८.३ ॥

na tathā tapyate viddhaḥ
pumān bāṇais tu marma-gaiḥ
yathā tudanti marma-sthā
hy asatāṁ paruṣeṣavaḥ (18.3)

na — not; tathā — as much; tapyate — hurts; viddhaḥ — penetrating; pumān — a human being; bānais = bānaiḥ — by arrows; tu — but; marma – bossom; gaiḥ — by going; yathā — as; tudanti — cause anguish; marma – bossom; stha = sthāh — permanently lodged; hy = hi — indeed; asatām —

of the materialistic people; paruṣeṣavaḥ = paruṣa — harsh words + iṣavaḥ — shafts.

Translation

A human being is not hurt as much by penetrating arrows as he is anguished by the shafts of harsh words of materialistic people which going into his bossom becomes permanently lodged therein. (18.3)

Commentary:

Arrows and in modern times, bullets, penetrate the physical body, but harsh words go into the subtle form and disrupt the pranic energy. The stir of emotional force is more heart-rending than physical injury.

कथयन्ति महत् पुण्यम् इतिहासम् इहोद्धव तम् । अहं वर्णयिष्यामि निबोध सु-समाहितः ॥१८..४॥	kathayanti mahat puṇyam itihāsam ihoddhava tam ahaṁ varṇayiṣyāmi nibodha su-samāhitaḥ (18.4)

kathayanti — they tell; mahat — greatly; punyam — beneficial; itihāsam — story; ihoddhava = iha — in the same subject + uddhava — Uddhava; tam — that; aham — I; varṇayiṣyāmi — will narrate; nibodha — listen; su-samāhitaḥ — very attentively.

Translation

O Uddhava, they tell a greatly beneficial story of the same subject. I will narrate that to you. Listen very attentively. (18.4)

Commentary:

The system of teaching is to use history to explain points which illustrate how an ascetic should act. If someone endured difficulties which are relevant to one's progress, one benefits from hearing of it.

When we carefully study the path of the successful yogis, we get hints which accelerate progress.

केनचिद् भिक्षुणा गीतं परिभूतेन दुर्जनैः । स्मरता धृति-युक्तेन विपाकं निज-कर्मणाम् ॥१८.५॥	kenacid bhikṣuṇā gītaṁ paribhūtena durjanaiḥ smaratā dhṛti-yuktena vipākaṁ nija-karmaṇām (18.5)

kenacid = kenacit — by a certain; bhikṣuṇā — by the ascetic beggar; gītam — recited; paribhūtena — by mistreatment or abuse; durjanaiḥ — by wicked people; smaratā — remembering, considering; dhṛti – patience; yuktena — by linking the attention yogically; vipākam — effects; nija – one's own; karmanam — cultural activities.

Translation

This was recited by a certain ascetic beggar, who was abused by wicked people. Linking his attention yogically with patience, he considered that it was due to the effects of his past activities. (18.5)

Commentary:

This ascetic beggar was a great yogin. Thus he could divine his past life and assess clashes with the common people or with circumstances which destiny presented to him. A great yogin will hardly make an effort to fight destiny. Usually he agrees to whatever proposal providence might present.

अवन्तिषु द्विजः कश्चिद्
आसीद् आढ्यतमः श्रिया ।
वार्ता-वृत्तिः कदर्यस् तु
कामी लुब्धो ऽति-कोपनः ॥ १८.६ ॥

avantiṣu dvijaḥ kaścid
āsīd āḍhyatamaḥ śriyā
vārtā-vṛttiḥ kadaryas tu
kāmī lubdho 'ti-kopanaḥ (18.6)

avantiṣu — in Avanti ; dvijaḥ - duly-initiated brahmin; kaścid = kaścit - certain; āsīd = āsīt - there was; ādhyatamaḥ - very wealthy; śriyā - with riches; vārtā – business; vṛttiḥ — business; kadaryas – mean-hearted; tu - but; kāmī - avaricious ; lubdho = lubdhaḥ - greedy; 'ti-kopanaḥ = ati-kopanaḥ — very irritable.

Translation

There was a certain brahmin in Avanti, who was very wealthy with opulences, and who subsisted by doing business, but who was mean-hearted, avaricious, greedy and very irritable. (18.6)

Commentary:

It is normal for a wealthy person to be mean-hearted or at least to be superficially kind. It is the nature of wealth to make a person shrink in terms of kindness. This brahmin was duly-initiated. *Śrī* Krishna explained that he was a *dvijah*, a person who was trained in good conduct and spiritual realization. The contradiction is that such a person was a businessman. However in the material world, anyone can become degraded at anytime. It is the nature of this place.

ज्ञातयो ऽतिथयस् तस्य
वाङ्-मात्रेणापि नार्चिताः ।
शून्यावसथ आत्मापि
काले कामैर् अनर्चितः

jñātayo 'tithayas tasya
vāṅ-mātreṇāpi nārcitāḥ
śūnyāvasatha ātmāpi
kāle kāmair anarcitaḥ (18.7)

jñātayo = jñātayaḥ — relatives; 'tithayas = atithayah — guests; tasya — his; vān = vāk – words; mātreṇāpi = mātreṇa — with courtesy + api - even; nārcitāḥ = na – not + arcitāḥ — greeted; śūnya-avasathe — in his home deprived of religiosity and sense gratification; ātmāpi = ātmā — himself + api — even; kāle — in time, seasonal; kāmair = kāmaiḥ — with comforts; anarcitaḥ — not presented with.

Translation

Even his relatives and guests were not greeted with courteous words. In that desolate house, even his own self was not presented with seasonable comforts. (18.7)

Commentary:

For a human being, wealth is a strange bedfellow. It has to be acquired. It has to be maintained. It has to be protected. And it has to be invested. Some wealthy persons make sure that they have all comforts at their disposal. They eat the tastiest food. But some others are not concerned with that. It all depends on the energy, which drove one to acquire the wealth.

In my experiences in this life, traveling through one or two countries on this planet, I met many wealthy persons. To tell the truth, I can remember only one wealthy person who was spiritually-realized. This means that wealth discourages spiritual life. Of course there are many wealthy persons who are superficially religious. Some try to achieve self-realization by various valid and invalid means. Over-all, wealthy persons are a sorry lot. On one hand some saintly person may have assured them of salvation and on the other hand, salvation is very, very far away from them.

After seeing what wealth does to the human being, I am dead scared of it. Still that does not imply that poor people are self-realized. Unfortunately for them, they spend most of their time acquiring wealth. So there again their focus is also wealth, which damages them and blanks out the opportunity for simple living and self-realization.

Lord Jesus Christ explained that it was easier to push a camel through the eye of a needle than it was for a wealthy man to enter the Kingdom of God. It is a very important point. He would not have said this if he thought that wealth facilitated God consciousness. It is a distraction for any rich or poor human being.

दुह्शीलस्य कदर्यस्य	duhśīlasya kadaryasya
द्रुह्यन्ते पुत्र-बान्धवाः ।	druhyante putra-bāndhavāḥ
दारा दुहितरो भृत्या	dārā duhitaro bhṛtyā
विषण्णा नाचरन् प्रियम् ॥ १८.८॥	viṣaṇṇā nācaran priyam (18.8)

duḥśīlasya — of me who is unkind; kadaryasya — of one who had a bad disposition; druhyante — they disliked; putra — son; bāndhavāḥ — relatives; dārā — his wife; duhitaro = duhitaraḥ — daughter; bhṛtyā = bhṛtyāh — servants; viṣaṇṇā = viṣaṇṇāḥ — sad; nācaran = na acaran — not act; priyam — agreeable.

Translation

The sons and relatives of that ill-disposed mean-hearted brahmin, disliked him. His wife, daughter and servants were sad and did not act in an agreeable way. (18.8)

Commentary:

Householder life is very troublesome not just for a miserly rich man, but even for a generous householder. This is because if one does not accommodate the desires of the relatives, they will be disagreeable. If one accommodates them to the fullest, they will be unappreciative. Therefore in either case, one will see trouble.

If one has money, one should spend some of it. Once a man has money, and once his relatives and friends know about it, it itches their minds. Therefore he should spend the money if they know about it. That is the nature of wealth. If one has servants they will, sooner or later, become familiar with one's lifestyle. They are bound to think about it. Thus one will have to respond accordingly or face resentment.

तस्यैवं यक्ष-वित्तस्य	tasyaivaṁ yakṣa-vittasya
च्युतस्योभय-लोकतः ।	cyutasyobhaya-lokataḥ
धर्म-काम-विहीनस्य	dharma-kāma-vihīnasya
चुक्रुधुः पञ्च-भागिनः ॥ १८.९॥	cukrudhuḥ pañca-bhāginaḥ (18.9)

tasyaivam = tasya — his + evam — in this way; yakṣa – money; vittasya — of one who hoards; cyutasyobhaya = cyutasya — of one who is fallen + ubhaya — both; lokataḥ — worlds; dharma — righteous duty; kāma — sensual satisfaction; vihīnasya — of one who lacks; cakrudhiḥ — they were annoyed; pañca – five; bhāginah — shareholders.

Translation

In this way, five shareholders of that brahmin who hoarded money, who was fallen from both worlds, who lacked righteous duty and sensual satisfaction, were annoyed. (18.9)

Commentary:

Householder life is very troublesome but that does not mean that every man can avoid it. Most will be penalized by providence if they do not become responsible householders. *Śrī Bābāji Mahāśaya* began a program of encouraging most of the ascetic-minded young men to take up householder life while continuing their *kriyā* yoga practice side by side. These persons should not, under any circumstance, leave aside *kriyā* practice but at the same time, they should not leave aside their righteous duty as householders. They must strike a balance, at least until their children reached maturity in adulthood. This is the instruction of *Śrī Bābāji Mahāśaya*.

As yogis, we are in a crisis, because society becomes more and more hostile to us. Even some devotees of *Śrī* Krishna are hostile to us. They ban us from temples. Their leaders sit on honored seats, then ridicule and belittle us. Unless we stick to householder life, we will have more and more difficulty getting human forms on this planet, if we require any of these in the near future. Most of the ascetic yogis should take to householder life and practice the *kriyās* side by side. This is the order of *Śrī Bābāji Mahāśaya*. I did this myself. I left many books for the benefit of those householder yogi-devotees who will have to struggle to achieve celibacy.

Lord Shiva is not privy to this Kali Yuga. He did His best to prevent it, but some of the other devas were eager to expand the human population and so we are in this fix. Now we must do something about it. Remaining as celibate persons all our lives will do little to help us just in case we have to take another body in the near future. Therefore we should cooperate with *Śrī Bābāji Mahāśaya,* take up householder life if we can, and practice yoga side by side. The important thing is the practice of *prāṇāyāma* every day without fail and to engage our family members in Deity Worship in the home or at the temple. But when the children are gone, one should greatly accelerate the *kriyā* practice by increasing the *prāṇāyāma* practice and graduating to higher yoga for meditation and *samādhi*.

Personally I do not plan to take another body in the near future but then again I may have to, all depending on the will of the superior souls. But still, others would definitely require bodies in families of *kriyā* yogis. Therefore we should take steps to increase our numbers as householders.

For a householder there are five share-holders. These are the supernatural rulers, the yogi ascetics of repute, the ancestors, human beings in general and the domestic animals.

It does not matter if one is an ascetic or not, devotee or not, if one neglects the supernatural people like Lord Shiva, Lord Krishna, Lord Indra and others, one will not be successful neither in the spiritual or material environments. Therefore one should be very careful about this.

There are yogi ascetics of repute, both from the hoary past, and in the present. Some will come in the future. One should not fail to respect them and to take help from them, otherwise one will not advance in spiritual life. There are many persons nowadays who pose as knowledgeable learned holy men. Most of them are pretenders. One has to learn how to recognize an accomplished ascetic.

The ancestors are taken care of by providing bodies for them as one's children and by making sure that their infantile forms are given the proper religious training and educational orientation. One should not feel that he can help all the ancestors. There are too many of them. However, if one begets sufficient children, some of the ancestors will become their children in turn. Therefore an ascetic householder should in consultation with greater yogis have a cut-off point when he will beget no more children and when his sexual involvement will come to an end. Then he should resume or adopt a full celibate practice and perfect the *kriyā* yoga obligation he has to Lord Shiva.

The human beings are to be respected and to be treated kindly and fairly. An ascetic should not socialize, otherwise he will increase the social obligations. That will cause a reduction in austerity and in ascetic association. All the same, he should not be totally callous either. If he feels the necessity to getaway from the hustle bustle of human civilization, he should go to a remote place. Human beings will hardly visit a remote location.

A householder yogi should be kind to domestic animals. But he should not keep any animal if he can avoid that. The maintenance of animals takes time. However if one is circumstantially obligated to do so, one should do that very efficiently and should not cause the animals any inconvenience. A brahmin should not keep dogs, or cats. He may keep dairy animals like cows and nanny goats.

Over all, householder life is full of obligations. If one does not play the game right, one becomes fallen in the next life. Still, we cannot avoid mistakes altogether. People will invariably become annoyed with a householder. His priority has to be to please the Universal Form, just as

Arjuna was inspired to do by Lord Krishna. If a householder tries to please all dependents, he will be ruined. He should get hints from *Śrī* Krishna as to how far he should go in satisfying relatives. A householder who has a knowledgeable guru should consider himself to be a very fortunate human being.

तद्-अवध्यान-विस्रस्त-
पुण्य-स्कन्धस्य भूरि-द ।
अर्थो ऽप्य् अगच्छन् निधनं
बह्व्-आयास-परिश्रमः ॥ १८ १० ॥

tad-avadhyāna-visrasta-
puṇya-skandhasya bhūri-da
artho 'py agacchan nidhanaṁ
bahv-āyāsa-pariśramaḥ (18 10)

tad = tat — of them, of the share-holders; avadhyāna — by disregard of them; visrasta — depleted, was used up; punya — accumulated merits; skandhasya — of part; bhūri-da — o generous one; artho = arthah — wealth; 'py = api — too; agacchan – was done; nidhanaṁ — lost; bahv = bahu — much; āyāsa — of endeavor; pariśramaḥ — was fatigued very much.

Translation

By this disregard of those share-holders, a part of his accumulated merit was depleted. The wealth for which he became fatigued with much endeavor, that too, was dissipated. (18.10)

Commentary:

No one can amass a fortune by himself. Or stated differently; a man has to take help from the supernatural people, from the great sages, from the ancestors, from human beings and from the earth. There is no way around it. Even to eat, we take help from insects who might have contributed to the fertility of the soil. These insects might have lived millions of years ago on earth, before the fertile soil which our crops use today, was even created. In all respects we are obligated to so many creatures, to supernatural agency and to our ancestors. These obligations stare us in the face continuously.

As far as the supernatural people are concerned, they are in a position to deprive us at any time. Under no circumstance should we neglect them. We should also be careful with the ancestors. Even if one is a devotee of *Śrī* Krishna and even if one has the most powerful spiritual master in the world, or even the purest, still if one does not balance out one's debts to the ancestors, one will not be successful in the social or spiritual domains.

Many spiritual masters assure their disciples that the ancestors do not matter. These gurus are over-excited because they feel that they can nullify the pressure of the ancestors, which affect their disciples. But that is a big miscalculation. They do this however because they have no mystic vision. These gurus exhibit a pretense of advancement.

ज्ञात्यो जगृहुः किञ्चित्
किञ्चिद् दस्यव उद्धव ।
दैवतः कालतः किञ्चिद्
ब्रह्म-बन्धोर् नृ-पार्थिवात् ॥ १८.११ ॥

jñātyo jagṛhuḥ kiñcit
kiñcid dasyava uddhava
daivataḥ kālataḥ kiñcid
brahma-bandhor nṛ-pārthivāt (18.11)

jñātyo = jñātayaḥ — relative; jagṛhuḥ — took; kiñcit — some; kiñcid = kiñcit — some; dasyava = dasyavah — thieves; uddhava — Uddhava; daivataḥ — by providence; kālataḥ — by time; kiñcid = kiñcit — some; brahma-bandhor = brahma-bandhoḥ — of the descendants of a genuine brahmin; nṛ — by common citizens; pārthivāt — government officials.

Translation

Some wealth of this descendant of a genuine brahmin, was taken by relatives, some by thieves, O Uddhava, some by providence, some by time, some by common citizens and some by government officials. (18.11)

Commentary:

The whole idea behind becoming a householder is to take a position for managing the cultural activities of a family. Otherwise there is no need to become a married man. One should not become a father just to make money as many others do. Even if one is born in a mercantile family, still one's mission as a householder should not be a business. It should be to manage the cultural assets of the children, one might produce.

Money is always involved in any household, regardless of whether the family is rich or poor, but money is not the correct objective. If one considers wealth to be the objective, one will lose out in the end, just as this Avanti brahmin did.

The big asset to manage a family, is not money but piety. The piety comes from the ancestors who departed and who logged many services into the family lineage in past lives. Thus the father should be aware of that. He should gather his intuitional powers, get advice from senior yogis and manage the piety of the family efficiently. When the children reached maturity and can fend for themselves, he should reduce his family involvement.

स एव द्रविणे नष्टे
धर्म-काम-विवर्जितः ।
उपेक्षितश् च स्व-जनैश्
चिन्ताम् आप दुरत्ययाम् ॥ १८.१२ ॥

sa evaṁ draviṇe naṣṭe
dharma-kāma-vivarjitaḥ
upekṣitaś ca sva-janaiś
cintām āpa duratyayām (18.12)

sa = sah — he; evam — thus; dravine — in relation to property; naṣṭe — in relation to what was; dharma — righteous duty; kāma — sensual satisfaction; vivarjitah — one who had neglected; upekṣitaś = upekṣitaḥ — one who has rejected; ca — and; sva – his own; janais = janaiḥ — by his folks; cintām — thoughts; āpa — he experienced; duratyayām — very unbearable.

Translation

Thus in relation to the lost property, he who neglected righteous duty and sensual satisfaction, and who was rejected by his folks, experienced some very unbearable thoughts. (18.12)

Commentary:

This happens in householder life, where a householder is resented by relatives. A householder does not have to be miserly and neglectful to be mentally-harassed by relatives. In fact, even if one does everything possible for their sensual satisfaction, there will still be occasions of frustration which will cause the relatives to insult, undermine and criticize the father of the family. This is because of the way of material nature.

तस्यैवं ध्यायतो दीर्घं
नष्ट-रायस् तपस्विनः ।
खिद्यतो बाष्प-कण्ठस्य
निर्वेदः सु-महान् अभूत् ॥ १८.१३ ॥

tasyaivaṁ dhyāyato dīrghaṁ
naṣṭa-rāyas tapasvinaḥ
khidyato bāṣpa-kaṇṭhasya
nirvedaḥ su-mahān abhūt (18.13)

tasyaivam = tasya — of his + evam — thus; dhyāyato = dhyāyataḥ — by reflecting deeply; dīrgham — for a long time; naṣṭa – lost; rāyas = rāyaḥ — wealth; tapasvinaḥ — a person in agony; khidyato = khidyataḥ — being depressed; bāṣpa – tears; kaṇṭhasya — of the throat; nirvedaḥ — disgust; su-mahān — tremendous; abhūt — was experiencing.

Translation

Reflecting deeply for a long time over his lost wealth, being in agony, being depressed, a tremendous disgust was experienced in that brahmin whose throat choked as he shed tears. (18.13)

Commentary:

This type of mental depression may cause a householder to get serious about spiritual life. It all depends on his association. Some commit suicide or take to intoxication. Some become wretched, giving up responsibilities. Some live in abject poverty, wandering around aimlessly as if they were animals.

स चाहेदम् अहो कष्टं
वृथात्मा मे ऽनुतापितः ।
न धर्माय न कामाय
यस्यार्थायास ईदृशः ॥ १८.१४॥

sa cāhedam aho kaṣṭaṁ
vṛthātmā me 'nutāpitaḥ
na dharmāya na kāmāya
yasyārthāyāsa īdṛśaḥ (18.14)

sa = sah — he; cahedam = ca — and + āha — said; idam — this; aho — what a condition; kaṣṭam — wretchedness, being in calamities; vṛthātma = vṛthā — for nothing + ātmā — self; me — my; 'nutāpitaḥ = anutāpitaḥ — tormented; na — neither; dharmāya — for righteous duty; na — nor; kāmāya — for satisfaction sake; yasyārthāyāsa = yasya — whose + artha — money + āyāsa — endeavor; īdṛśaḥ — such.

Translation

And he said thus, "What a condition! What wretchedness! Having tormented myself for nothing, neither for righteous duty, nor for satisfaction's sake. Such an endeavor was made only for money's sake. (18.14)

Commentary:

In taking up householder life, a yogi takes a risk. But that does not mean that it should not be ventured. One has to take risk in one way or the other in material existence. Let us say for example that a yogi does not take the householder life style. Then it means that he cannot play the game with material nature. He has to aspire for full celibate life. But let us assume that he cannot complete the celibate training, then it means that he will be penalized by material nature in the next life. He will have difficulty getting a decent body. That is how it works. In any case, risks are involved.

There is no guarantee that if one takes to celibate life, one will be successful. The odds are against it. If one takes to celibate yogic life and if one was supposed to take up householder life, then it is not possible for one to be successful, because other powers will thwart progress and cause one to fail in the celibate endeavor. Many others have investments in one's life. If one offends any of them, one might find that spiritual progress is deterred, just as the brahmin even though he worked hard for money and got it, still he did not please his relatives, because he overlooked their destined satisfactions and lost track of righteous duty.

Money is a special danger because by its very nature, it causes one to become absorbed in it, to reflect on it deeply (*dhyāyato* verse 13). It steals away one's attention and makes one forget, its proper usage.

प्रायेणाथाः कदर्याणां
न सुखाय कदाचन ।
इह चात्मोपतापाय
मृतस्य नरकाय च ॥ १८.१५॥

prāyeṇāthāḥ kadaryāṇāṁ
na sukhāya kadācana
iha cātmopatāpāya
mṛtasya narakāya ca (18.15)

prāyeṇāthāḥ = prāyeṇa — usually + arthāḥ — riches; kadaryāṇām — of the miserly people; na — not; sukhāya — to happiness; kadācana — at any time; iha — here in this world; cātmopatāpāya = ca — and, but + ātma — self + upatāpāya — to distress; mṛtasya — concerning one who is departed; narakāya — to hell hereafter; ca — and.

Translation

"Usually, the riches of miserly people never lead to happiness. But in this world, it leads to distress of the self and concerning one who departed, it leads to hell hereafter. (18.15)

Commentary:

Because the brahmin was trained in spiritual life, he could draw the proper conclusions and the disgust (*nirvedah* verse 13) brought him to a point of realization such that he could do something to cause himself to take up spiritual life in earnest. If one has some training in spiritual realizations, one can retrieve the self if the family falls apart.

Wealth cannot be of any good use to a miserly person unless and until that person suffers a change of heart either by having lost the assets, or by coming to a status of kindness whereby one donates to the right persons at the right time. In general, wealthy ruins character.

यशो यशस्विना शुद्ध
श्लाघ्या ये गुणिना गुणाः ।
लोभः स्व्-अल्पो ऽपि तान् हन्ति
श्वित्रो रूपम् इवेप्सितम् ॥ १८.१६ ॥

yaśo yaśasvinām̐ śuddham̐
ślāghyā ye guṇinām̐ guṇāḥ
lobhaḥ sv-alpo 'pi tān hanti
śvitro rūpam ivepsitam (18.16)

yaśo = yaśaḥ — reputation; yaśasvinām — of a famous person; śuddham — untarnished; ślāghyā = ślāghyāḥ — praiseworthy; ye — which; guṇinām — of those with good qualities; guṇāḥ — virtues; lobhaḥ — greed; sv-alpo = su-alpah — a tiny bit; 'pi = api — even; tān — these; hanti — destroys; śvitro = śvitraḥ — white leprosy; rūpam — features, beauty; ivepsitam = iva — just as + īpsitam — enviable.

Translation

"There is the untarnished reputation of the famous people, and the praiseworthy virtues of those with good qualities. But even a tiny bit of greed destroys these, just as white leprosy nullifies enviable beauty. (18.16)

Commentary:

No matter how famous one may be or how good one's character is, if one displays a tiny bit of greed, one becomes condemned for It. For that matter one does not even have to display such greed but if any act of a famous or charitable man, appears to be an act of greed, he might be ruined. This is because people make their appraisal on the basis of sensual assessment. It is just like having enviable beauty and then exhibiting with a blotchy skin disease.

अर्थस्य साधने सिद्धे
उत्कर्षे रक्षणे व्यये ।
नाशोपभोग आयासस्
त्रासश् चिन्ता भ्रमो नृणाम् ॥ १८.१७ ॥

arthasya sādhane siddhe
utkarṣe rakṣaṇe vyaye
nāśopabhoga āyāsas
trāsaś cintā bhramo nṛṇām (18.17)

arthaysa — of wealth; sādhane — in the endeavor to acquire; siddhe — in the acquirement itself; utkarse — in the increase; rakṣaṇe — in the safeguarding; vyaye — in the utilizing; nāśopabhoga = nasa — in losing + upabhoge — in enjoying; āyāsas = āyāsaḥ — exertion; trāsaś = trāsaḥ — fear; cintā — anxiety; bhramo = bhramah — delusion; nṛṇām — for human beings.

Translation

"In the endeavor to acquire money, in the acquirement itself, in the increase of it, in safe-guarding it, in utilizing, losing and enjoying it, there is exertion, fear, anxiety and delusion for human beings. (18.17)

Commentary:

In all respects, money is a danger to the human being. Only a few people are not affected adversely by it. Once I questioned a wealthy medical doctor about money. He said that he observed that if he kept it, he found that it he could not enjoy it and if he spent it, he lost it. His conclusion was that money did not bring happiness.

स्तेय हिंसानृतं दम्भः
कामः क्रोधः स्मयो मदः ।
भेदो वैरम् अविश्वासः
सस्पर्धा व्यसनानि च ॥ १८.१८॥

steyaṁ hiṁsānṛtaṁ dambhaḥ
kāmaḥ krodhaḥ smayo madaḥ
bhedo vairam aviśvāsaḥ
saṁspardhā vyasanāni ca (18.18)

steyam — theft; hiṁsānṛtam = hiṁsā — violence + anṛtam — falsehood; dambhaḥ — fraud; kāmaḥ — lust; krodhaḥ — anger; smayo = smayaḥ — pride; madaḥ — arrogance; bhedo = bhedaḥ — contention; vairam — enmity; aviśvāsaḥ — distrust; saṁspardhā — rivalry; vyasanāni — vices; ca — and.

Translation

"Theft, violence, falsehood, fraud, lust, anger, pride, arrogance, contention, enmity, distrust, rivalry and vices, (18.18)

Commentary:

This listing continues in the next verse.

एते पञ्चदशानर्था
ह्य् अर्थ-मूला मता नृणाम् ।
तस्माद् अनर्थम् अर्थाख्यं
श्रेयो-ऽर्थी दूरतस् त्यजेत् ॥ १८.१९॥

ete pañcadaśānarthā
hy artha-mūlā matā nṛṇām
tasmād anartham arthākhyaṁ
śreyo-'rthī dūratas tyajet (18.19)

ete — these; pañcadaśānarthā = pañcadaśa — fifteen + anarthā — undesireable tendencies; hy = hi — indeed; artha - money; mūlā — to be rooted; matā = matāḥ — are considered; nṛṇām — of human beings; tasmād = tasmāt — therefore; anartham — undesirable aspect; arthākhyaṁ = artha - wealth + ākhyam — known as; śreyo = śreyaḥ - well-being; 'rthī = arthī — one who values; dūratas = dūratah — at a distance; tyajet — should leave aside.

Translation

"these fifteen undesirable tendencies of human beings, are considered to be rooted in money. Therefore a person who values well-being should leave at a distance that undesirable aspect which is known as wealth. (18.19)

Commentary:

On one hand, one cannot function as a householder without some money. And on the other hand, money sponsors its total absorption, so that one becomes so preoccupied acquiring it, that one forgets to enjoy it, to allow one's family to enjoy it and to complete one's righteous duty in relation to the supernatural people, the great yogi sages, the ancestors, humanity and the domestic animals.

भिद्यन्ते भ्रातरो दाराः
पितरः सुहृदस् तथा ।
एकास्निग्धाः काकिणिना
सद्यः सर्वे ऽरयः कृताः ॥ १८.२०॥

bhidyante bhrātaro dārāḥ
pitaraḥ suhṛdas tathā
ekāsnigdhāḥ kākiṇinā
sadyaḥ sarve 'rayaḥ kṛtāḥ (18.20)

bhidyante — are alienated; bhrātaro = bhrātaraḥ — brother; dārāḥ — wife; pitaraḥ — parents;

suhṛdas — friends; tathā — so and also; ekāsnigdhāh = eka — one, someone + āsnigdhāḥ — very dear to someone; kākininā — by a small sum of money; sadyaḥ — instantly; sarve — all; 'rayaḥ = arayaḥ — enemies; kṛtāh — are converted.

Translation

"Brothers, wife, parents, friends, all who are very dear to someone, are instantly converted into enemies for a small sum of money. (18.20)

Commentary:

That is the nature of money, that even a tiny bit of it causes persons who are dear, to become enemies. This is due to the attachment, which any kind of wealth, invokes in a personality.

अर्थेनाल्पीयसा ह्य् एते
सरब्धा दीप्त-मन्यवः ।
त्यजन्त्य् आशु स्पृधो घ्नन्ति
सहसोत्सृज्य सौहृदम् ॥ १८.२१ ॥

arthenālpīyasā hy ete
saṁrabdhā dīpta-manyavaḥ
tyajanty āśu spṛdho ghnanti
sahasotsṛjya sauhṛdam (18.21)

arthenālpīyasā = arthena — by money + alpīyasā — by a small amount; hy = hi — even; ete — these; saṁrabdhā = saṁrabdhāḥ — become annoyed; dīpta — inflame; manyavaḥ — anger (dīpta-manyavaḥ = become enraged); tyajanty = tyajanti — they reject one another; āśu — immediately; spṛdho = spṛdhaḥ — being quarrelsome; ghnanti — they kill; sahasotsṛjya = sahasā — suddenly + utsṛjya — rejecting; sauhṛdam — good relations.

Translation

"Even for a small amount of money, these relatives become annoyed and enraged. They immediately reject one another. Being quarrelsome, they even kill suddenly, rejecting good relations. (18.21)

Commentary:

Instead of becoming depressed over incidences pertaining to money, a yogi should study the situation, noting how influential money is. One looses his sense of discrimination and good will, if he comes under the influence of finances or of any commodity of wealth. Money represents the power to fulfill desire. Desires are sponsored by the emotional nature. Thus underneath the operations of social life is the emotions of the various persons concerned. A yogi should study this and then curb himself from emotional usages and participations.

लब्ध्वा जन्मामर-प्रार्थ्यं
मानुष्यं तद् द्विजाग्र्यताम् ।
तद् अनादृत्य ये स्वार्थं
घ्नन्ति यान्त्य् अशुभां गतिम् ॥ १८.२२ ॥

labdhvā janmāmara-prārthyaṁ
mānuṣyaṁ tad dvijāgryatām
tad anādṛtya ye svārthaṁ
ghnanti yānty aśubhāṁ gatim (18.22)

labdhvā — attained; janmāmara = janma — birth + amara — the supernatural rulers; prārthyam — something begged for; mānuṣyam — human being; tad = tat — that; dvijāgryatām = dvija – trained Brahmin + āgryatām — of the status; tad = tat — that; anādrtya — unappreciating; ye — those who; svartham — their own interest; ghranti — ruin; yānty = yānti — they go; aśubhām — uncomfortable; gatim — destination.

Translation

"Attaining a human birth, which is begged for by the supernatural rulers, and having the status of a trained brahmin; those who are unappreciative and who ruin their interest, go to an uncomfortable destination. (18.22)

Commentary:

The brahmin became self-critical. This is a symptom of getting back to the path of *kriyā* yoga. It is this self-critical energy that causes a yogi to turn upon himself and be successful in spiritual life. This causes him to stop trying to save others, while in fact he is in need of deliverance himself.

स्वर्गापवर्गयोर् द्वारं प्राप्य लोकम् इमं पुमान् । द्रविणे को ऽनुषज्जेत मर्त्यो ऽनर्थस्य धामनि ॥ १८.२३ ॥	svargāpavargayor dvāraṁ prāpya lokam imaṁ pumān draviṇe ko 'nuṣajjeta martyo 'narthasya dhāmani (18.23)

svargāpavargayor = svarga — angelic world + apavargayoḥ — of liberation; dvāram — gate oppurtunity; prāpya — achieving; lokam — this world; imam — this; pumān — person; draviṇe — in wealth; ko = kah — who; 'nuṣajjeta = anuṣajjeta — will become attached; martyo = martyaḥ — one whose body must die; 'narthasya = anarthasya — of what has no real value; dhāmani — in the location.

Translation

"Achieving this world, which is an oppurtunity for the angelic world or for liberation, which person whose body must die, will become attached to wealth, which is the location of what has no value? (18.23)

Commentary:

Assessing his own stupidity for allowing himself to be influenced by the potency of money, the brahmin reasoned that since the body must die, there is no sense in sacrificing oneself and family for the sake of funds. After all, in any case, one must leave money behind in this world. In fact, this world is a facility for liberation or for going to the angelic world.

देवर्षि-पितृ-भूतानि ज्ञातीन् बन्धूश् च भागिनः । असविभज्य चात्मानं यक्ष-वित्तः पतत्य् अधः ॥ १८.२४ ॥	devarṣi-pitṛ-bhūtāni jñātīn bandhūṁś ca bhāginaḥ asaṁvibhajya cātmānaṁ yakṣa-vittaḥ pataty adhaḥ (18.24)

devarsi = deva — supernatural rulers + ṛṣi — yogi sages; pitṛ — ancestors; bhūtāni — creatures in general; jñātīn — immediate family members; bandhūṁs = bandhūn — other relatives; ca — and; bhāginaḥ — to partners; asamvibhajya — not alloting; catmanam = ca — and + ātmānam — to oneself; yakṣa-vittah — one who guards his wealth but cannot utilize it; pataty = patati — moves down; adhah — lower existence.

Translation

"By not giving shares to the supernatural rulers, the yogi sages, the ancestors, the creatures in general, the relatives, and the partners as well as to himself, the person who guards wealth but does not utilize it, moves down to a lower existence. (18.24)

Commentary:

If one neglects to use wealth responsibly, he becomes degraded. This is because wealth represents the pious activity of the living entities. A father gets wealth on the basis of the piety of himself and of his relatives and ancestors. He represents all of them, and so destiny opens opportunities to him for getting commodities of value. However if he does not utilize the wealth in the interest of all concerned, he becomes accountable.

A yogi householder should therefore tune into the mind of the Universal Form of the Lord, so that he can execute righteous duty without making mistakes and without becoming subjected to the demands of the family. In that way, he would not convert any piety into funds unless that is the instruction of the Central Figure in the Universal Form. But if on the other hand, he does not have any input from *Śrī* Krishna, and if he takes advice from relatives, he will more than likely misuse their piety and become degraded thereby. This is because a limited entity cannot properly determine how to use piety.

One should make a careful study of the *Bhagavad-Gītā* to get an understanding of what is approved behaviors, Arjuna had to go against many relatives in order to do the righteous duty which was approved by the Universal Form. Sometimes the wishes of the Lord pleases the relatives and causes the fulfillment of their desires. Sometimes it displeases and frustrates them. A yogi householder should be attentive to or stayed attuned to the Universal Form so that later, when that Lord approves of his cultural activities in the art of *karma* yoga, he can get an exemption from cultural life and take to full renunciation for spiritual perfection.

व्यर्थयार्थेहया वित्तं
प्रमत्तस्य वयो बलम् ।
कुशला येन सिध्यन्ति
जरठः किं नु साधये ॥१८.२५॥

vyarthayārthehayā vittaṁ
pramattasya vayo balam
kuśalā yena sidhyanti
jaraṭhaḥ kiṁ nu sādhaye (18.25)

vyarthayārthehayā = vyarthayā — disappated uselessly + artha — wealth + īhayā — by the quest; vittam — wealth; pramattasya — of a crazy man; vayo = vayah — vitality; balam — strength; kuśalā = kuśalāh — wise men; yena — that by which; sidhyanti — they achieve; jarathaḥ — old man; kim — what; nu — indeed; sādhaye — I accomplish.

Translation

"That vitality, strength, and wealth, by which the wise men are perfected, is dissipated uselessly in a crazy man's quest for money. Indeed, as an old man what can I accomplish for myself? (18.25)

Commentary:

If one makes a fool of himself by dedication to cultural activities only, he will regret it at the end, but only if he has spiritual training. Those who have no spiritual aspirations, have nothing to regret except that at death, they are forced to leave their dear loved ones and the related cultural interests.

Whatever energy a man has, be it vitality, strength or money, it may all be used to help him with spiritual realization and internal transcendental experience, but if he is unable to use it for that sublime purpose, then of necessity, he will expand himself culturally. But if a person with potential for *kriyā* yoga practice, does not complete the disciplines all through his life, then he may not be able to advance much if he begins the practice in an old body. We hear that King *Dhṛtaraṣṭra* did retrieve his spirituality at the end, just before the death of his body, but generally people are unable to accomplish this.

कस्मात् सङ्क्लिश्यते विद्वान्
व्यर्थयार्थेहयासकृत् ।
कस्यचिन् मायया नूनं
लोको ऽयं सु-विमोहितः ॥१८.२६॥

kasmāt saṅkliśyate vidvān
vyarthayārthehayāsakṛt
kasyacin māyayā nūnaṁ
loko 'yaṁ su-vimohitaḥ (18.26)

kasmāt — why; saṅkliśyate — harassed; vidvān — wise man; vyarthayārthehayāsakṛt = vyarthayā — fruitless + artha – wealth + īhayā — by the quest + asakṛt — constantly; kasyacin — of someone; māyayā — by a fascinating energy; nūnam — surely; loko = lokaḥ — world; 'yaṁ = ayam — this; su-vimohitaḥ — utterly bewildered.

Translation

"What causes a wise man to be constantly harassed by the fruitless quest for wealth? Surely this world is utterly bewildered by the fascinating energy of someone else. (18.26)

Commentary:

If it were not for a greater power or a greater power of a greater personality, a wise man would never act in a way that is contrary to self interest. The brahmin concluded that there was a higher power which caused even the wise men to be diverted from their interest. Arjuna asked Lord Krishna a similar question:

arjuna uvāca
atha kena prayukto'yaṁ pāpaṁ carati pūruṣaḥ
anicchannapi vārṣṇeya balādiva niyojitaḥ

Arjuna said: Then explain, O family man of the Vṛṣṇis, by what is a person forced to commit an evil unwillingly, just as if he were compelled to do so? (B.G. 3.36)

किं धनैर् धन-दैर् वा किं
कामैर् वा काम-दैर् उत ।
मृत्युना ग्रस्यमानस्य
कर्मभिर् वोत जन्म-दैः ॥१८.२७॥

kiṁ dhanair dhana-dair vā kiṁ
kāmair vā kāma-dair uta
mṛtyunā grasyamānasya
karmabhir vota janma-daiḥ (18.27)

kim — what can be done; dhanair = dhanaih — with wealth; dhana-dair = dhana-daih — with givers of wealth; vā — or; kim — what use could there be; kāmair = kāmaiḥ — with desires; vā — or; kāma-dair = kāma-daiḥ — with the fulfillers of desire; uta — or; mṛtyunā — by death; grasyamānasya — concerning one who is seized; karmabhir = karmabhiḥ — with cultural activities; vota = vā – or + uta — even; janma-daiḥ — by that which results in rebirth.

Translation

"Concerning one who is already seized by death, what can be done with wealth or with those who gave it? What use could there be with desires or with the fulfillers of these; even with cultural activities which result in rebirth? (18.27)

Commentary:

If a discriminant person does not ask these questions early on in life, and if he asks these only at the end of his life, he will more than likely have to take another body haphazardly. One should ask these questions early on in life, and work in such a way as to answer them satisfactorily at the end of one's body.

Cultural activities should be performed by everybody without exception but their value is limited to the material world. A person cannot convert his cultural contributions to the spiritual environment at any time, even the cultural acts which are done and which pass as religious activities or as devotional services.

नून मे भगवांस्
तुष्टः सर्व-देव-मयो हरिः ।
येन नीतो दशाम् एतां
निर्वेदश् चात्मनः प्लवः ॥१८.२८॥

nūnaṁ me bhagavāṁs
tuṣṭaḥ sarva-deva-mayo hariḥ
yena nīto daśām etāṁ
nirvedaś cātmanaḥ plavaḥ (18.28)

nūnam — surely; me — with me; bhagavāṁs = bhagavān — the supreme lord; tuṣṭaḥ — is pleased; sarva – all; deva – supernatural rulers; mayo = mayah — powers, empowers; hariḥ — Hari, the God Hari; yena — by whom; nīto = nītaḥ — was brought, was manifested; daśām — crisis; etām — this; nirvedaś = nirvedaḥ — disgust; cātmanaḥ = ca — and + ātmanaḥ — of the self + plavaḥ — boat, saving mechanism, saving grace.

Translation

Surely, being pleased with me, the Supreme Lord, the God Hari, who empowers all the supernatural rulers, is the one by Whom this crisis was manifested as well as the disgust which is a saving grace for my soul. (18.28)

Commentary:

The Avanti brahmin appreciated the grace of the Supreme Lord, which caused him to come to his senses. It is not in all cases of ruination, that a wealthy man can convert his financial and domestic troubles into disgust of social life, and subsequently reflect on the contrast between spirituality and materialistic living. Thus the brahmin concluded that only by the grace of God, he was able to transcend the bewildering influence of material nature.

सो ऽहं कालावशेषेण
शोषयिष्ये ऽङ्गम् आत्मनः ।
अप्रमत्तो ऽखिल-स्वार्थे
यदि स्यात् सिद्ध आत्मनि ॥ १८.२९ ॥

so 'haṁ kālāvaśeṣeṇa
śoṣayiṣye 'ṅgam ātmanaḥ
apramatto 'khila-svārthe
yadi syāt siddha ātmani (18.29)

so = sah – he; 'ham = aham — I; kālāvaśeṣeṇa = kāla – time + avaśeṣeṇa — with the remaining; śoṣayisye — will discipline; 'ṅgam = aṅgam — body; ātmanaḥ — of the self or mind; apramatto = apramattah — without confusion; 'khila = akhila — full; svārthe — in the interest of myself; yadi — if; syāt — there is, is possible; siddha — being satisfied; ātmani — with the spiritual self.

Translation

"With the remaining time, I will discipline this body of mine. Being without confusion and in full interest of myself, and if it is possible, I would be satisfied with the spiritual self. (18.29)

Commentary:

One should make a decision like that at some stage of the life of the body, preferably at the first part of it. But if one makes it at the last minute, then that is better than not doing it at all, because then one might take that motivation to the next transmigration.

तत्र माम् अनुमोदेरन्
देवास् त्रि-भुवनेश्वराः ।
मुहूर्तेन ब्रह्म-लोकं
खट्वाङ्गः समसाधयत् ॥ १८.३० ॥

tatra mām anumoderan
devās tri-bhuvaneśvarāḥ
muhūrtena brahma-lokaṁ
khaṭvāṅgaḥ samasādhayat (18.30)

tatra — there, in this regard; mām — with me; anumoderan — may they bless me; devās = devāḥ — the supernatural rulers; tri – three; bhuvaneśvarāḥ — the controllers of the three worlds; muhūrtena — within forty-eight minutes; brahma – spirit; lokam — world; khaṭvāngah — Khaṭvāṅgaḥ; samasādhayat — attained.

Translation

"In this regard, may the supernatural rulers, the controllers of the three worlds, bless me. After all, Khaṭvānga attained the spiritual world within forty-eight minutes." (18.30)

Commentary:

King *Khaṭvānga*, did that but it is doubtful if others are so equipped by virtue of the blessings of the supernatural rulers and their own spiritual prowess. Still *Khaṭvānga's* example must be taken into consideration. King *Khaṭvāṅga* who is also known as *Dilīpa*, was a *mahāyogī*.

श्री-भगवान् उवाच
इत्य् अभिप्रेत्य मनसा
ह्य् आवन्त्यो द्विज-सत्तमः ।
उन्मुच्य हृदय-ग्रन्थीन्
शान्तो भिक्षुर् अभून् मुनिः ॥ १८.३१ ॥

śrī-bhagavān uvāca
ity abhipretya manasā
hy āvantyo dvija-sattamaḥ
unmucya hṛdaya-granthīn
śānto bhikṣur abhūn muniḥ (18.31)

śrī-bhagavān – the blessed lord; uvāca — said; ity = iti — thus; abhipretya — forming the conclusion; manasā — in his mind; hy = hi — indeed; āvantyo = āvantyaḥ — of Avanti; dvija – duly trained brahmin; sattamaḥ — most realized person; unmucya — unravelled; hṛdaya — in the core of his existence; granthīn — the entertwing energies; śānto = śāntah — spiritual peace; bhikṣur = bhikṣuḥ — ascetic beggar; abhūn = abhūt — became; muniḥ — yogi philosopher.

Translation

The Blessed Lord said: Thus forming that conclusion in his mind, that most realized and trained brahmin of Avanti, unraveled the intertwining energies in the core of his being. He became a peaceful, ascetic and philosophical yogi who begged for his needs. (18.31)

Commentary:

Persons like *Khaṭvānga* and the Avanti brahmin were pre-trained in yoga austerities. That is the main reason why they could complete the spiritual perfection with rapidity. It is totally unfair to the public to suggest that any ordinary devotee would be this successful in the end. It is hardly likely.

स चचार महीम् एतां
सयतात्मेन्द्रियानिलः ।
भिक्षार्थं नगर-ग्रामान्
असङ्गो ऽलक्षितो ऽविशत् ॥ १८.३२ ॥

sa cacāra mahīm etāṁ
saṁyatātmendriyānilaḥ
bhikṣārthaṁ nagara-grāmān
asaṅgo 'lakṣito 'viśat (18.32)

sa = sah — he; cacāra — wandered; mahīm — over the earth; etām — this; saṁyatātmendriyānilaḥ = saṁyata — controlled + ātma — spirit + indriya — sensual energies + anilaḥ — vital air; bhikṣārtham — for the sake of begging for food; nagara — towns; grāmān — villages; asaṅgo = asaṅgaḥ — without social connections; 'lakṣito = alakṣitaḥ — without the characteristic appearance of a saintly man; 'viśat = aviśat — he entered.

Translation

As a person with his spirit, sensual energies and vital air controlled, he wandered over the earth, entering towns and villages, for the sake of begging for food, without social connections and without the characteristic appearance of a saintly man. (18.32)

Commentary:

Thus the Avanti brahmin did not dress in a way as to be recognized as a saint or devotee. He was free to do spiritual practice without having to take care of disciples. He was not obligated to the public. In this way we can tell that he got an exemption from cultural activities from the Universal Form. The fact that he practiced *samyam*, the higher stages of yoga *(samyata)* means that he was definitely a yogin, for he also got his sensual energy controlled by *pratyāhar* and he mastered his vital energy by *prāṇāyāma*.

तं वै प्रवयसं भिक्षुम्
अवधूतम् असज्-जनाः ।
दृष्ट्वा पर्यभवन् भद्र
बह्वीभिः परिभूतिभिः ॥ १८.३३ ॥

taṁ vai pravayasaṁ bhikṣum
avadhūtam asaj-janāḥ
dṛṣṭvā paryabhavan bhadra
bahvībhiḥ paribhūtibhiḥ (18.33)

tam — him; vai — indeed; pravayasam — old; bhiksum — acetic beggar; avadhūtam — shabby-looking ascetic; asaj-janāḥ = asat-janāḥ — materialistic people; dṛṣṭvā — seeing; paryabhavan — insulted; bhadra — o friend; bahvībhiḥ — with various; paribhūtibhiḥ — indignities.

Translation

O friend, seeing the old shabby-looking ascetic beggar, the materialistic people insulted him with various indignities. (18.33)

Commentary:

People usually insult such a person because they are instinctively scared of his influence. They sense that he may convince them to give up temporary things. Their strong attachments to things of this world, cause them to shun him. Many such attached persons are religiously-inclined. Some are devotees of *Śrī* Krishna, who feel that a saint should dress well and should remain as a member of a recognized spiritual society. However if one is serious about spiritual retrieval, he has to make an all-out endeavor for perfection.

केचित् त्रि-वेणु जगृहुर्
एके पात्रं कमण्डलुम् ।
पीठं चैके ऽक्ष-सूत्रं च
कन्थां चीराणि केचन ॥ १८.३४॥

kecit tri-veṇuṁ jagṛhur
eke pātraṁ kamaṇḍalum
pīṭhaṁ caike 'kṣa-sūtraṁ ca
kanthāṁ cīrāṇi kecana (18.34)

kecit — some persons; tri-veṇum — his triple staff; jagṛhur = jagṛhuḥ — took; eke — some; pātram — bowl; kamandalum — water pot; pīṭham — seat; caike = ca — and + eke — some; 'kṣa-sūtraṁ = akṣa – beads + sūtram — thread; ca — and; kanthām — clothing; cīrāṇi — tattered; kecana — some.

Translation

Some took his triple staff; some his bowl and water pot. Some took his seat and string of akṣa beads. And some took his tattered clothing. (18.34)

Commentary:

Akṣa are *rudrākṣa* chanting beads, used by ascetics when chanting prayers having to do with Lord Shiva. *Tulasī* beads are used in reference to Lord Vishnu. We should note here that *Śrī* Krishna did not hold a bias against this Shaivite devotee.

Previously in these verses, Lord Krishna explained that this brahmin realized that it was by the mercy of Lord Hari, Lord Krishna, that he was endowed with the kind of disgust that gives one spiritual impetus for liberation. This was also the case with *Piṅgalā*, the woman whom *Śrī* Krishna spoke on early on in the discourse.

It is a fact that yogi devotees take help from both Lord Krishna and Lord Shiva and they do not form biases towards any religious affiliation.

Once a person decides to shun human civilization and to completely give over himself to austerities in preparation for liberation, he has to either hide from human beings or be prepared to tolerate insults. If one avoids cultural activities, one must be prepared for harassment.

प्रदाय च पुनस् तानि
दर्शितान्य् आददुर् मुनेः ।
अन्नं च भैक्ष्य-सम्पन्नं
भुञ्जानस्य सरित्-तटे ॥ १८.३५॥

pradāya ca punas tāni
darśitāny ādadur muneḥ
annaṁ ca bhaikṣya-sampannaṁ
bhuñjānasya sarit-taṭe (18.35)

pradāya — to return; ca — and; punas = punaḥ — again; tāni — they; darśitāny = darśitāni — were showing; ādadur = ādaduḥ — took; muneḥ — yogi philosopher; annam — food; ca — and; bhaiksya — begging; sampannam — what was got; bhuñjānasya — of one who was to eat; sarit — of a river; taṭe — on the river side.

Translation

After showing them, they returned the items, but again took them from the yogi philosopher. When on the riverside, he ate the food acquired by begging, (18.35)

Commentary:

People who are motivated by cultural energies, will tease an ascetic yogi who is anti-social. Most of this is unconsciously done, therefore a really-advanced yogi does not react to it. He knows that the vagabonds involved are being manipulated by subtle forces.

It is best therefore to be away from human society if one decides to live in this way, since in isolation one will hardly come in contact with the culture-hungry human beings.

मूत्रयन्ति च पापिष्ठाः
ष्ठीवन्त्य् अस्य च मूर्धनि ।
यत-वाचं वाचयन्ति
ताडयन्ति न वक्ति चेत् ॥ १८.३६ ॥

mūtrayanti ca pāpiṣṭhāḥ
ṣṭhīvanty asya ca mūrdhani
yata-vācaṁ vācayanti
tāḍayanti na vakti cet (18.36)

mūtrayanti — they pissed on; ca — and; pāpiṣṭhāḥ — vagabonds; sthīvanty = sthīvanti — they spat upon; asya — his; ca — and; mūrdhani — head; yata – vow of restraining; vācam — speech; vācayanti — they made him speak; tāḍayanti — they beat; na – not; vakti — he speaks; cet — if.

Translation

...the vagabonds pissed on him and spat on his head. They made him speak regardless of his silence vows. They beat him if he did not verbally respond. (18.36)

Commentary:

The only way to avoid this is to live in isolation. However if providence does not permit seclusion, it means that one is destined for harassment. Under the circumstance, one should offer all respects to providence by tolerating this. As soon as one is released from this, one should go into isolation. These pestering vagabonds, may slow down the progress of an ascetic. Yet, in another way, they hasten his advancement by causing him to develop tolerance by his absorption of reactions, which are due to come to him before he becomes liberated.

तर्जयन्त्य् अपरे वाग्भिः
स्तेनो ऽयम् इति वादिनः ।
बध्नन्ति रज्वा तं केचिद्
बध्यतां बध्यताम् इति ॥ १८.३७॥

tarjayanty apare vāgbhiḥ
steno 'yam iti vādinaḥ
badhnanti rajjvā taṁ kecid
badhyatāṁ badhyatām iti (18.37)

tarjayanty = tarjayanti — condemned; apare — other; vāgbhiḥ — with words; steno = stenah — thief; 'yam = ayam — this; iti — thus; vādinaḥ — saying; badhnanti — they bind; rajjvā — with rope; taṁ — him; kecid = kecit — some; badhyatām – tie him; badhyatām — tie him; iti — thus saying.

Translation

Others condemned him with words, saying, "This man is a thief." Some bound him with ropes. Some said, "Tie him! Tie him!" (18.37)

Commentary:

If one assumes an antisocial stance, one must expect to be mistreated. Thus it is best to be in isolation. On the other hand if one takes the alternative to live at a large temple compound or in a spiritual community, one runs the risk of stagnation in spiritual life and of getting involved in the political schemes of monks who pretend that their main interest is spiritual advancement.

क्षिपन्त्य् एके ऽवजानन्त
एष धर्म-ध्वजः शठः ।
क्षीण-वित्त इमां वृत्तिम्
अग्रहीत् स्व-जनोज्झितः ॥ १८.३८॥

kṣipanty eke 'vajānanta
eṣa dharma-dhvajaḥ śaṭhaḥ
kṣīṇa-vitta imāṁ vṛttim
agrahīt sva-janojjhitaḥ (18.38)

kṣipanty = kṣipanti — taunted; eke — some; 'vajānanta = avajānanta — insultingly; eṣa = eṣaḥ — this person; dharma – righteous duty; dhvajaḥ — hypocritical; śaṭhaḥ — cheater; kṣīna – having lost; vitta — wealth; imām — this; vṛttim — means of livelihood, a way of procuring money; agrahīt — took up; sva – own; janojjhitaḥ = jana — family + ujjhitaḥ — abandoned.

Translation

Some taunted him insultingly saying, "This person is a hypocrite to righteous duty, a cheater. Having lost wealth and being abandoned by family, he took this up as a way of procuring money. (18.38)

Commentary:

It is for this reason that one is supposed to go far away from one's home to take up severe austerity. If one remains in a familiar neighborhood, one will be criticized because of lingering resentments. When *Mahātma* Vidura advised the old King *Dhṛtaraṣṭra* to adopt forest life, Vidura suggested retirement to an unknown place.

People are accustomed to treating a person in a certain way. Thus if one is in the neighborhood, it will be difficult to curb human opinion. One should therefore move to another area if one desires success. Sometimes however, people are empowered to harass a saintly person or a reformed person who has sincerely turned to asceticism for purificatory purposes. In such a case, the ascetic should bear the brunt of abuse.

अहो एष महा-सारो
धृतिमान् गिरि-राड् इव ।
मौनेन साधयत्य् अर्थं
बक-वद् दृढ-निश्चयः ॥ १८.३९॥

aho eṣa mahā-sāro
dhṛtimān giri-rāḍ iva
maunena sādhayaty arthaṁ
baka-vad dṛḍha-niścayaḥ (18.39)

aho — o; eṣa = eṣaḥ — this man; mahā – exceptionally; sāro = sāraḥ — strong; dhṛtimān — steady; giri – Himalaya; rād = rāt — like; iva — just as; maunena — with silence; sādhayaty = sādhayati — strives; artham — objective; baka – heron; vad = vat — like; dṛḍha — firm; niścayaḥ — determination, ambition.

Translation

"O, he is exceptionally strong, and steady just like the Himalaya Mountains. With silence, he strives for his objective, being firm in his ambition like a heron," (18.39)

Commentary:

The Avanti brahmin could not leave human society completely because of forces of providence that kept him in the vicinity of his home. Thus he was destined to endure insults from resentful human beings.

इत्य् एके विहसन्त्य् एनम्
एके दुर्वातयन्ति च ।
तं बबन्धुर् निरुरुधुर्
यथा क्रीडनकं द्विजम् ॥ १८.४०॥

ity eke vihasanty enam
eke durvātayanti ca
taṁ babandhur nirurudhur
yathā krīḍanakaṁ dvijam (18.40)

ity = iti — thus; eke — some; vihasanty = vihasanti — ridicule; enam — that man; eke — some; durvātayanti — farted on; ca — and; tam — him; babandhur = babandhuḥ — tied up; nirurudhur = nirurudhuḥ — confined; yathā — just as; krīḍanakam — circus animal; dvijam — trained brahmin.

Translation

Thus they rediculed that man. Some farted at him. Some tied him up. Some criticized that trained brahmin just as if he were a circus animal. (18.40)

Commentary:

Much of this happened because of a back-log of resentments which the particular persons had for him from their current and previous lives. However, an ascetic would never become liberated if it were necessary for him to clear off all fair and unfair resentments which developed in others, due to his good or bad relationships with them. An ascetic must get away from this type of environment, and become liberated from the material world.

एवं स भौतिकं दुःखं
दैविकं दैहिकं च यत् ।
भोक्तव्यम् आत्मनो दिष्टं
प्राप्तं प्राप्तम् अबुध्यत ॥ १८.४१ ॥

evaṁ sa bhautikaṁ duḥkhaṁ
daivikaṁ daihikaṁ ca yat
bhoktavyam ātmano diṣṭaṁ
prāptaṁ prāptam abudhyata (18.41)

evam — thus; sa = sah — he; bhautikam — that which is caused by other creatures; duḥkham — troubles; daivikam — that which is caused by supernatural agency; daihikam — that which is caused by personal mistakes; ca — and; yat — that which, whatever; bhoktavyam — must be experienced, endured; ātmano = ātmanaḥ — of the self; diṣṭam — predestined; prāptam prāptam — received in sequence; abudhyata — he understood.

Translation

Thus, whatever troubles he received, whether it was caused by other creatures, by supernatural agency or by personal mistakes, he understood that it must be endured as it was the predestination of the self. (18.41)

Commentary:

In such situations, one has to come to such conclusions. A perceptive ascetic understands which influence caused which difficulty. He does not become annoyed. He does not fret over such matters. Sometimes however he might explain this to others for their education regarding the operations of destiny.

परिभूत इमां गाथाम्
अगायत नराधमैः ।
पातयद्भिः स्व धर्म-स्थो
धृतिम् आस्थाय सात्त्विकीम् ॥ १८.४२ ॥

paribhūta imāṁ gāthām
agāyata narādhamaiḥ
pātayadbhiḥ sva dharma-stho
dhṛtim āsthāya sāttvikīm (18.42)

paribhūta = paribhūtaḥ — insulted; imām — this; gāthām — meaningful lyric; agāyata — sang; narādhamaiḥ — by those who are demeaning; pātayadbhiḥ — by those who intimidate; sva-dharma-stho = sva-dharma-sthaḥ — remained situated in one's righteous duty; dhṛtim — steadiness; āsthāya — applying; sāttvikīm — in the perceptive influences.

Translation

Being insulted by demeaning persons who intimidated him, he sang a meaningful lyric and remained situated in righteous duty, applying himself steadily in the perceptive influence. (18.42)

Commentary:

The Avanti brahmin was duty-bound to beg. That was his *karma* yoga activity. He was to make himself available to receive the resentments which many people held against him. In that way he eased the tension in the neighborhood.

द्विज उवाच
नाय जनो मे सुख-दुःख-हेतुर्
न देवतात्मा ग्रह-कर्म-कालाः ।
मनः परं कारणम् आमनन्ति
ससार-चक्रं परिवर्तयेद् यत् ॥१८.४३॥

dvija uvāca
nāyaṁ jano me sukha-duḥkha-hetur
na devatātmā graha-karma-kālāḥ
manaḥ paraṁ kāraṇam āmananti
saṁsāra-cakraṁ parivartayed yat (18.43)

dvija – the trained brahmin; uvāca — used to sing; nāyam = na — not + ayam — these; jano = janaḥ — people; me — my; sukha — happiness; duhkha — distress; hetur = hetuḥ — cause; na — nor; devatātmā = devatā — supernatural rulers + ātmā — my spiritual self; graha — influential planets; karma — cultural activities; kālāh — time; manaḥ — mind; param — supreme, ultimate; kāranam — cause; āmananti — the yogi sages declare; samsāra — changing from body to body in confusion; cakram — cycle; parivartayed = parivartayet — sets into motion; yat — that which.

Translation

The trained brahmin used to sing: "Neither are these people, nor the supernatural rulers, nor my spiritual self, nor the influential planets, nor cultural activities, nor time, the cause of my happiness and distress. The mind is the ultimate cause as the yogi philosophers declare. It is that which sets into motion the cycle of changing body after body in confusion. (18.43)

Commentary:

Even though circumstances are brought about by various direct and indirect, personal and impersonal agencies, still we must understand that we are exposed and subjected to the circumstances by our connection to the mind.

As soon as one can disconnect the mind from this world, all pleasant and unpleasant events become imperceptible. They continue for others but they cease for the individual who has that absolute detachment *(kaivalyam).* Because we are linked to the *buddhi* organ and the sensual energy and because these subtle equipments are focused into this world, we must by necessity, take on the experiences which pertain to this place.

Thus as a classic *kriyā* yogi, the brahmin ascetic diagnosed the problem.

मनो गुणान् वै सृजते बलीयस्
ततश् च कर्माणि विलक्षणानि ।
शुक्लानि कृष्णान्य् अथ लोहितानि
तेभ्यः स-वर्णाः सृतयो भवन्ति ॥१८.४४॥

mano guṇān vai sṛjate balīyas
tataś ca karmāṇi vilakṣaṇāni
śuklāni kṛṣṇāny atha lohitāni
tebhyaḥ sa-varṇāḥ sṛtayo bhavanti (18.44)

mano = manah — mind; gunān — influences of material nature; vai — indeed; sṛjate — promotes; balīyas = balīyah — forceful; tataś = tataḥ — subsequently; ca — and; karmāṇi — cultural activities; vilakṣaṇāni — varying types; śuklāni — pious types; kṛṣṇāny = kṛṣṇāni — abominable types; atha — and, then; lohitāni — mixed types; tebhyah — from these; sa-varṇāḥ — with the same texture; sṛtayo = sṛtayaḥ — birth circumstances; bhavanti — become manifest.

Translation

"Indeed, the forceful mind promotes the influences of material nature. And subsequently, various cultural activities of a pious, abominable or mixed nature are produced. From these, birth circumstances become manifest with the same corresponding texture. (18.44)

Commentary:

This explains in brief how a spirit becomes involved in material nature. The cause therefore is the spirit's irresistible attraction to the mind. Here is a verse from the *Bhagavad-Gītā*:

mamaivāṁśo jīvaloke jīvabhūtaḥ sanātanaḥ
manaḥṣaṣṭhānīndriyāṇi prakṛtisthāni karṣati

My partner is in this world of individualized conditioned beings. He is an eternal individual soul but he draws to himself the mundane senses of which the mind is the sixth detection device. (B.G. 15.7)

A question arises as to how a spirit can overcome his attraction to the mind. We know however, that until a particular spirit can master his mind, he cannot be freed from material nature.

अनीह आत्मा मनसा समीहता
हिरण्-मयो मत्-सख उद्विचष्टे ।
मनः स्व-लिङ्गं परिगृह्य कामान्
जुषन् निबद्धो गुण-सङ्गतो ऽसौ ॥१८.४५॥

anīha ātmā manasā samīhatā
hiraṇ-mayo mat-sakha udvicaṣṭe
manaḥ sva-liṅgaṁ parigṛhya kāmān
juṣan nibaddho guṇa-saṅgato 'sau
(18.45)

anīha = anīhah — not exerting himself; ātmā — spirit; manasā — the mind; samīhatā — with that which endeavors, with the every-active factor; hiraṇ - effulgence; mayo = mayaḥ — made of; mat – my; sakha — friend; udvicaṣṭe — looks on; manaḥ — mind; sva – myself; lingam — image; parigṛhya — accepting; kāmān — sensual influences; juṣan — exploiting; nibaddho = nibaddhaḥ — becomes bound; guṇa – material nature; saṅgato = saṅgataḥ — due to association with; 'sau = asau — that (indulgent spirit).

Translation

"The spirit who does not exert himself, who is self effulgent and who is my friend, looks on, while the mind endeavors. But accepting the mind as my self-image, while it exploits the sensual influences, I become bound by the association with material nature. (18.45)

Commentary:

In this verse, the trained brahmin, who nearly completed the austerities required for spiritual perfection, came to realize that he neglected his dear friend, the self-effulgent one. This person, the Supreme Spirit, is not dependent on material nature and does not have a reliance upon that mundane power. He supervises the activities of his partner, the dependent reliant spirit, who acts as though he is unified with the subtle and gross mundane potencies.

By not paying attention to the Supreme Spirit, and by remaining attached to the mind, which exploits the sensual energies, the limited spirit becomes bound by virtue of the over-riding influence of material nature.

दान स्व-धर्मो नियमो यमश्
च श्रुतं च कर्माणि च सद्-व्रतानि ।
सर्वे मनो-निग्रह-लक्षणान्ताः
परो हि योगो मनसः समाधिः ॥१८.४६॥

dānaṁ sva-dharmo niyamo yamaś
ca śrutaṁ ca karmāṇi ca sad-vratāni
sarve mano-nigraha-lakṣaṇāntāḥ
paro hi yogo manasaḥ samādhiḥ (18.46)

dānam — charity; sva-dharmo = sva-dharmaḥ — one's own righteous duty; niyamo = niyamaḥ — approved behaviors; yamaś = yamaḥ — moral restraints; ca — and; śrutam — hearing of scripture; ca — and; karmāni — cultural activities; ca — and; sad-vratāni = sat-vratāni — vows for attaining a purified psyche; sarve — all; mano = manaḥ - mind; nigraha — control; lakṣaṇāntāḥ = lakṣaṇa — indicative + antāḥ — their end result; paro = paraḥ — highest; hi — indeed; yogo = yogaḥ — yoga discipline; manasaḥ — of the mind; samādhiḥ — effortless, continuous linking of the attention with the higher concentration force.

Translation

"Charity, one's righteous duty, approved behaviors, moral restraints, as well as hearing of scriptures, cultural activities, vows for attaining a purified psyche, all are indicative of the end result of mind control. Indeed, the absorption in the continuous effortless linking of the attention with the higher concentration force is the supreme yoga discipline (18.46)

Commentary:

Undoubtedly *samādhi* is the ultimate accomplishment for a yogi.

समाहितं यस्य मनः प्रशान्तं
दानादिभिः किं वद तस्य कृत्यम् ।
असयतं यस्य मनो विनश्यद्
दानादिभिश् चेद् अपरं किम् एभिः ॥ १८.४७॥

samāhitaṁ yasya manaḥ praśāntaṁ
dānādibhiḥ kiṁ vada tasya kṛtyam
asaṁyataṁ yasya mano vinaśyad
dānādibhiś ced aparaṁ kim ebhiḥ (18.47)

samāhitam — restrained by the self; yasya — whose; manah — mind; praśāntam — stilled by focus on a spiritual dimension; dānādibhiḥ — charity and related features; kim — what; vada — say; tasya — of that; kṛtyam — be done; asamyatam — not controlled by the self; yasya — whose; mano = manaḥ — mind; vinaśyad = vinaśyat — is distracted; dānādibhiś = dānādibhiḥ — charity and related courtesies; ced = cet — if; aparam — further more; kim — what; ebhih — by such.

Translation

"To one whose mind is restrained by the self and stilled by focus on a spiritual dimension, what can he do with charity and its related courtesies? Furthermore, to one whose mind is distracted and not controlled by the self, what can he do with the same charity and related customs? (18.47)

Commentary:

Both persons, the yogi who attained *samādhi*, and the very disturbed unruly human being, have no use for charity. The masterful yogi does not have to engage in elementary religious practices. The uncontrolled human beings who do not know what to give, who to contribute to and when to offer, do not benefit by offering charity. They do not know when to offer it appropriately.

मनो-वशे ऽन्ये ह्य् अभवन् स्म देवा
मनश् च नान्यस्य वश समेति ।
भीष्मो हि देवः सहसः सहीयान्
युञ्ज्याद् वशे तं स हि देव-देवः ॥ १८.४८॥

mano-vaśe 'nye hy abhavan sma devā
manaś ca nānyasya vaśaṁ sameti
bhīṣmo hi devaḥ sahasaḥ sahīyān
yuñjyād vaśe taṁ sa hi deva-devaḥ (18.48)

mano = manaḥ — of the mind; vaśe — under the control; 'nye = anye — other; hy = hi — indeed; abhavam — were; sma — supposedly before; devā — supernatural rulers; manaś = manah — mind; ca — and; nānyasya = na — never + anyasya — of another; vaśam — under an influence; sameti — was; bhīṣmo = bhīṣmaḥ — fierce; hi — indeed; devaḥ — mystic ruler; sahasaḥ — stronger; sahīyān — stronger; yuñjyāt — consistently disciplined; vaśe — under control; tam — that (mind); sa = sah — he, the person; hi — indeed; deva-devaḥ — master of the mystic rulers.

Translation

"Supposedly before, the other supernatural rulers who were supposed to regulate the senses, were under the control of the mind, but the mind never was influenced by anyone else. Indeed, the mind is a fierce mystic ruler, which is stronger than the strongest. The person who consistently disciplines the mind, is the master of the mystic rulers. (18.48)

Commentary:

This is the idea in *kriyā* yoga that we must come to terms with our inner nature, not with anything on the outside. If the inner nature is brought to order, all problems will be solved in so far as our response to what happens on the outside.

The Avanti brahmin realized that his troubles had to do with the psyche and not with the persons who harassed him.

तम् दुर्जयं शत्रुम् असह्य-वेगम्
अरुन्-तुदं तन् न विजित्य केचित् ।
कुर्वन्त्य् असद्-विग्रहम् अत्र मर्त्यैर्
मित्राण्य् उदासीन-रिपून् विमूढाः ॥ १८.४९ ॥

tam durjayaṁ śatrum asahya-vegam
arun-tudaṁ tan na vijitya kecit
kurvanty asad-vigraham atra martyair
mitrāṇy udāsīna-ripūn vimūḍhāḥ (18.49)

tam — that; durjayam — difficult to subdue; śatrum — enemy; asahya — unbearable; vegam — urge; arum-tudam — that which agonises the psyche; tan = tat — therefore; na – not; vijitya — having conquered; kecit — someone; kurvanty = kurvanti — formulate, creating; asad-vigraham — meaningless quarrels; atra — here in this life; martyair = martyaiḥ — with those who use temporary bodies; mitrāny = mitrāni — friends; udāsīna — neutral people; rupūn — enemies; vimūdhāḥ — foolish people.

Translation

"Therefore having not conquered that hard to subdue enemy, which has unbearable urges, and which agonizes the psyche, some foolish people formulate whimsical quarrels here in this life, with others who use temporary bodies, thus creating friends, neutrals and enemies. (18.49)

Commentary:

People do not like to hear about *kriyā* yoga, much less take lessons and take up the practice. They follow general religions which are concerned with an external enemy. The real enemy which is the mind, which has unbearable urges and which agonizes the psyche, is greatly ignored by them. In that way as he said in the previous verse, the minds acts as the mystic of mystics to rule the psyche.

देहं मनो-मात्रम् इमं गृहीत्वा
ममाहम् इत्य् अन्ध-धियो मनुष्याः ।
एषो ऽहम् अन्यो ऽयम् इति भ्रमेण
दुरन्त-पारे तमसि भ्रमन्ति ॥ १८.५० ॥

dehaṁ mano-mātram imaṁ gṛhītvā
mamāham ity andha-dhiyo manuṣyāḥ
eṣo 'ham anyo 'yam iti bhrameṇa
duranta-pāre tamasi bhramanti (18.50)

deham — body; mano = manaḥ - mind; mātram — figment, idea; imam — this; grhītvā — having accepted, assumed; mamāham – me and I; ity = iti — thus thinking; andha — blind; dhiyo = dhiyah — intellect; manuṣyāḥ — human beings; eṣo = eṣaḥ — this; 'ham = aham — I; anyo = anyaḥ — another person; 'yam = ayam — this; iti — thus; bhramena — by confusion of mind; duranta-pāre — in limitless; tamasi — in ignorance; bhramanti — they wander.

Translation

"Having assumed this body, which is a figment of the mind, and thinking of it in terms of me and I, human beings who possess a blind intellect, think, 'This is another person.' By that confusion of mind, they wander in limitless ignorance. (18.50)

Commentary:

The material body we use was formed in the belly of the mother through our mental condition which was fused into our mother's psyche. The nutrients from the mother's body were drawn through the placenta, which was attached to the embryo but only on the basis of our mental image which we carried from the past life. Thus the material body is created on the basis of the mental energy.

The mind is capable of supernatural insight but only if it is defocused out of the gross existence and is applied to higher dimensions. Otherwise the intellect within the mind remains blind to the supernatural and spiritual worlds and becomes reliant on the physical body for vision in this gross existence.

We wander in limitless ignorance when we rely on the mind for vision. We assume the lower habits of the mind, the chief of which is its sense of possessiveness and its biases, which result from prejudices.

जनस् तु हेतुः सुख-दुःखयोश् चेत्
किम् आत्मनश् चात्र हि भौमयोस् तत् ।
जिह्वां क्वचित् सन्दशति स्व-दद्भिस्
तद्-वेदनायां कतमाय कुप्येत् ॥ १८.५१ ॥

janas tu hetuḥ sukha-duḥkhayoś cet
kim ātmanaś cātra hi bhaumayos tat
jihvāṁ kvacit sandaśati sva-dadbhis
tad-vedanāyāṁ katamāya kupyet (18.51)

janaḥ — people; tu — but; hetuḥ — cause; sukha – happiness; duhkhayoḥ — of distress; cet — if; kim — what; ātmanaś = ātmanaḥ — for the spirit; cātra = ca — and + atra — in this; hi — indeed, for; bhaumayos = bhaumayoḥ — concerning material nature; tat — that; jihvām — tongue; kvacit — sometimes; sandaśati — bites; sva-dadbhis = sva-dadbhiḥ — with one's teeth; tad = tat — that; vedanāyām — in the agony; katamāya — by which of the factors; kupyet — one should get angry.

Translation

"But if the people are the cause of happiness and distress, then what is it to the spirit, for in this case, that concerns material nature. And if sometimes one bites the tongue with his own teeth, which of the factors should be blamed for the agony? (18.51)

Commentary

It is customary to think that someone causes happiness and distress, but in that case, this is due to social interaction, which is mostly enacted by and in material nature. The spirit, a mere by-stander, is not involved in this.

Sometimes a man regrets an action on his body, such as when he eats and accidentally bites the tongue, or attempts to cut a foodstuff and accidentally cuts the finger. What should be blamed in that case, the teeth or the hand which wielded the knife?

दुःखस्य हेतुर् यदि देवतास् तु
किम् आत्मनस् तत्र विकारयोस् तत् ।
यद् अङ्गम् अङ्गेन निहन्यते क्वचित्
क्रुध्येत कस्मै पुरुषः स्व-देहे ॥ १८.५२ ॥

duḥkhasya hetur yadi devatās tu
kim ātmanas tatra vikārayos tat
yad aṅgam aṅgena nihanyate kvacit
krudhyeta kasmai puruṣaḥ sva-dehe (18.52)

duḥkhasya — of misery; hetur = hetuḥ — cause; yadi — if; devatās = devatāḥ — the mystic supervisors of sensual energy; tu — but; kim — what; ātmanas = ātmanaḥ — of the spirit; tatra — in that case; vikārayos = vikārayoḥ — relating to the two mystic supervisors who cause bodily changes; tat — that; yad = yat — which however; aṅgam — limb; aṅgena — by a limb; nihanyate — is struck; kvacit — now and then; krudhyeta — should be angry; kasmai — to whom; puruṣaḥ — the person; sva-dehe — in one's body.

Translation

"But if the mystic supervisors of sensual energy, are the cause of misery, then in that case what may be said of the spirit, since the incidence relates only to those two mystic supervisors who cause the changes? However, if now and then a limb is struck by another limb, to whom should the person be angry? (18.52)

Commentary:

Each of the limbs of the body and its various parts are controlled by a supernatural personality. Therefore if one limb hits another, at least the two supernatural people are affected. The spirit has nothing to do with this. If on the other hand, one does not believe in mystic supervision, even then in that case, the limbs of the body should take responsibility. If one foot tangles the other and causes the body to fall, it is that offensive foot which may be blamed but to no avail.

आत्मा यदि स्यात् सुख-दुःख-हेतुः
किम् अन्यतस् तत्र निज-स्वभावः ।
न ह्य् आत्मनो ऽन्यद् यदि तन् मृषा स्यात्
क्रुध्येत कस्मान् न सुखं न दुःखम् ॥ १८.५३ ॥

ātmā yadi syāt sukha-duḥkha-hetuḥ
kim anyatas tatra nija-svabhāvaḥ
na hy ātmano 'nyad yadi tan mṛṣā syāt
krudhyeta kasmān na sukhaṁ na duḥkham
(18.53)

ātmā — individual spirit; yadi — if; syāt — is regarded; sukha – pleasure; duḥkha — pain; hetuḥ — cause; kim — what; anyatas = anyatah — other factor; tatra — in that case; nija — his own, individual; svabhāvaḥ — inherent tendency; na — not; hy = hi — because; ātmano = ātmanaḥ — besides the soul; 'nyad = anyat — any other factor; yadi — if; tan = tat — that; mṛṣā — false; syāt — should be; krudhyeta — should be angry; kasmān = kasmat — besides whom; na — neither; sukham — happiness; na — nor; duhkham — misery.

Translation

"If the individual spirit is regarded as the cause of pleasure and pain, then what other factor is responsible? It would be reliant on the individual's inherent tendency, and there is no other factor besides the individual spirit. If there should be such a factor, it is false. Then who should one be angry with? Neither happiness nor distress is real. (18.53)

Commentary:

The brahmin reasoned that if one puts the blame on the spirit self, then even that makes no sense, because the spirit would be required to have an inherent nature, which has within it the duality of pleasure and pain. Therefore that argument would fall apart.

ग्रहा निमित्तं सुख-दुःखयोश् चेत्
किम् आत्मनो ऽजस्य जनस्य ते वै ।
ग्रहैर् ग्रहस्यैव वदन्ति पीडां
क्रुध्येत कस्मै पुरुषस् ततो ऽन्यः ॥ १८.५४ ॥

grahā nimittaṁ sukha-duḥkhayoś cet
kim ātmano 'jasya janasya te vai
grahair grahasyaiva vadanti pīḍāṁ
krudhyeta kasmai puruṣas tato 'nyaḥ (18.54)

grahā — influential planets; nimittam — cause; sukha – happiness; duḥkhayoś = duḥkhayoh — and of distress; cet — if; kim — what; ātmano = ātmanaḥ — concerning the self; 'jasya = ajasya — of that which is birthless; janasya — of what is produced; te — those; vai — indeed; grahair = grahaiḥ — by the planets, grahasyaiva = grahasya — of a planet + eva — only; vadanti — they say; pīḍām — misfortune; krudhyeta — should direct the anger; kasmai — at whom; puruṣas — person; tato = tatah — thence, from that; 'nyah = anyaḥ — separate factor.

Translation

"If the influential planets are the cause, then what concern is it to the birthless spirit, since that concerns those planets which are produced. They say however that the misfortune of one planet is caused by another. Since the person is a separate factor, to whom should one direct the anger? (18.54)

Commentary:

Again, if one believes in astrology or even if that can be proven beyond any doubt, still that would concern the struggle between different planets. And then where would one direct one's anger, since those spheres are not within the reach of human endeavor. In that case it would be wise to abandon anger.

कर्मास्तु हेतुः सुख-दुःखयोश् चेत्
किम् आत्मनस् तद् धि जडाजडत्वे ।
देहस् त्व् अचित् पुरुषो ऽयं सुपर्णः
क्रुध्येत कस्मै न हि कर्म मूलम् ॥ १८.५५ ॥

karmāstu hetuḥ sukha-duḥkhayoś cet
kim ātmanas tad dhi jaḍājaḍatve
dehas tv acit puruṣo 'yaṁ suparṇaḥ
krudhyeta kasmai na hi karma mūlam (18.55)

karmāstu = karma — cultural activity + astu — let it be assumed; hetuḥ — cause; sukha-duḥkhayoś = sukha-duhkhayoḥ — happiness and distress; cet — if; kim — what; ātmanas = ātmanaḥ — for the individual spirit; tad = tat — that; dhi = hi — factually; jaḍājaḍatve = jaḍa – inert principle, insensible principle + ajaḍatve — and the sensible principle; dehas = dehaḥ — body; tv = tu — but; acit — not conscious; puruṣo = puruṣaḥ — the person; 'yaṁ = ayam — this; suparṇaḥ — a ray of the sun, what is spiritually enlivening; krudhyeta — should be angry; kasmai — at whom; na — cannot be; hi — since; karma — cultural activities; mūlam — the basis.

Translation

"If it is assumed that cultural activity is the cause of happiness and distress, then what does the spirit have to do with that, since surely cultural acts are involved in the insensible and sensible objects. The body itself is not the generator of its own awareness, only the spirit who uses the body is spiritually-enlivening. Thus to whom should one direct anger since the cultural activity cannot be the basis? (18.55)

Commentary:

Cultural activity is going on as a contribution from several factors. It is a potpourri of the sensible and insensible objects. One cannot direct one's anger to that since there is no one factor that is involved in any given activity. The body of a man cannot be blamed in fact, because if isolated from the spirit, the body is dead matter. Therefore only the spirit would be left in that case. And ultimately it is a detached factor, so it cannot be blamed.

By the reasoning powers of the brahmin, we can see that even though he got trapped by wealth, he was not an ordinary personality. It was his oversight that cause him to become lax in spirituality. Therefore it was possible for him to retrieve himself once he was ruined by wealth and was rejected by relatives.

कालस् तु हेतुः सुख-दुःखयोश् चेत्
किम् आत्मनस् तत्र तद्-आत्मको ऽसौ ।
नाग्नेर् हि तापो न हिमस्य तत् स्यात्
क्रुध्येत कस्मै न परस्य द्वन्द्वम् ॥ १८.५६ ॥

kālas tu hetuḥ sukha-duḥkhayoś cet
kim ātmanas tatra tad-ātmako 'sau
nāgner hi tāpo na himasya tat syāt
krudhyeta kasmai na parasya dvandvam (18.56)

kālas = kālaḥ — time; tu — supposing; hetuh — cause; sukha-duḥkhayos = sukha-duḥkhayoh — happiness and distress; cet — if; kim — which; ātmanas = ātmanah — for the spirit; tatra — in that case; tad = tat – that; ātmako = ātmakaḥ — being of the same nature; 'sau = asau — that; nāgner = na — not + agneḥ — from fire; hi — hence; tāpo = tāpaḥ — burning; na — not; himasya — of snow; tat — that; syāt — becomes; krudhyeta — should the anger be directed to; kasmai — at whom; na — not; parasya — concerning that which is supreme; dvandvam — duality.

Translation

"Supposing that time is assumed as the cause of happiness and distress, then what is that to the spirit? In that case, that same time has the same nature of the soul. And factually fire is not affected by burning nor snow by the cold. Thus to whom should the anger be directed, for there is no duality in that which concerns the supreme?" (18.56)

Commentary:

Since time is an aspect of the supreme and since the spirit is too, then it makes no sense to blame time no more than fire is blamed for its inherent nature of burning or snow for chilling. Thus again there is no point in anger.

न केनचित् क्वापि कथञ्चनास्य
द्वन्द्वोपरागः परतः परस्य ।
यथाहमः ससृति-रूपिणः स्याद्
एवं प्रबुद्धो न बिभेति भूतैः ॥ १८.५७॥

na kenacit kvāpi kathañcanāsya
dvandvoparāgaḥ parataḥ parasya
yathāhamaḥ saṁsṛti-rūpiṇaḥ syād
evaṁ prabuddho na bibheti bhūtaiḥ (18.57)

na — not; kenacit — by anything; kva api — anywhere; kathañcanāsya — in anyway; dvandvoparāgaḥ = dvandva — opposite feature in the material world + uparāgaḥ — influence; parataḥ - which is transcendental; parasya — regarding the superior principle; yathā — as, in this case; ahamaḥ — the assertive sense; samsṛti — material existence; rūpinaḥ — that which formulates; syād = syāt — is; evam — thus; prabuddho = prabuddhaḥ — one who is enlightened; na – not; bibheti — becomes frightened; bhūtaiḥ — by any creatures.

Translation

"Regarding the superior principle which is transcendental, it is not subjected in any way to the duality of happiness and distress, by anything anywhere, as in the case of the assertive sense which formulates the material existence. Thus an enlightened person is not frightened by any creature. (18.57)

Commentary:

It is a mistake to think that because this brahmin or any other person can reason this out, he or she is able to transcend the bothersome emotions of material nature. The ability to reason this out, only gives the person the impetus to get the realizations through which he or she may be freed. That comes from actually experiencing the spirit apart from the psychic equipments like the *buddhi* organ, the sensual energies which are derived from it, the mind, the assertive power, the vital energy and the over-all emotional make-up (*citta*) of the psyche. One has to go within to sort through these energies and see them in distinct forms, otherwise even if one can conceptualize this, one will still be subjected to the pleasures and pains.

The problem arises because the spirit has too close of a relationship to the assertive principle which is termed, the *ahamah*, in this verse. This principle is a seed energy, a very small point of subtle power in the psyche. It should be isolated from the self. Even though the self has to use it to function in the material world, it will have to leave the assertion behind when it enters the chit *ākāśa*, the sky of consciousness. So long as the self remains in confidence with this *ahamah* power it is influenced to identify with ideas, which are expanded by the *buddhi* organ in the mental and emotional energy fields.

एतां स आस्थाय परात्म-निष्ठाम्
अध्यासितां पूर्वतमैर् महर्षिभिः ।
अहं तरिष्यामि दुरन्त-पारं
तमो मुकुन्दाङ्घ्रि-निषेवयैव ॥ १८.५८॥

etāṁ sa āsthāya parātma-niṣṭhām
adhyāsitāṁ pūrvatamair maharṣibhiḥ
ahaṁ tariṣyāmi duranta-pāraṁ
tamo mukundāṅghri-niṣevayaiva (18.58)

etām — this; sa = saḥ — that; āsthāya — becoming established; parātma – supreme spirit; niṣṭhām — permanent awareness of; adhyāsitām = adhiāsitām — was settled upon, focused on; pūrvatamair = pūrvatamaiḥ — by those who were in the retardative influence previously; maharṣibhiḥ — by the great yogi sages; aham — I; tarisyama — will cross over, get beyond; duranta – that which is difficult to overcome; pāram — very; tamo = tamah — the retardative energy; mukundāṅghri — the feet of Mukunda Krishna; niṣevayaiva = niṣevayā — by devotionally serving; eva — only.

Translation

"Becoming established in that permanent awareness of the Supreme Spirit, that was focused on by the great yogi sages, who were under the retardative influence long ago, I will, by devotionally serving the feet of Mukunda Krishna, get beyond that retardative energy which is difficult to overcome." (18.58)

Commentary:

The trick is to follow the methods used by the ancient yogi sages. The influence which they were under and which they eventually overcame, is similar to that which keeps us under its control. If we could apply their techniques, we would get out of the perceptive darkness which prohibits us from accurately gauging the situation.

By devotionally serving Lord Krishna, we would have the impetus to do whatever He recommends as necessary for progression. As we heard previously in this discourse, the prostitute *Piṅgalā* expressed a similar sentiment:

tenopakṛtam ādāya śirasā grāmya-saṅgatāḥ
tyaktvā durāśāḥ śaraṇaṁ vrajāmi tam adhīśvaram

"Accepting on my head, the favor given by Him, I gave up the false expectation that pertains to the attractive objects, and take shelter in the Supreme Lord. (U.G. 3.39)

श्री-भगवान् उवाच
निर्विद्य नष्ट-द्रविणे गत-क्लमः
प्रव्रज्य गां पर्यटमान इत्थम् ।
निराकृतो ऽसद्भिर् अपि स्व-धर्माद्
अकम्पितो ऽमूं मुनिर् आह गाथाम् ॥ १८.५९ ॥

śrī-bhagavān uvāca
nirvidya naṣṭa-draviṇe gata-klamaḥ
pravrajya gāṁ paryaṭamāna ittham
nirākṛto 'sadbhir api sva-dharmād
akampito 'mūṁ munir āha gāthām (18.59)

śrī-bhagavān – the blessed lord; uvāca — said; nirvidya — being disgusted; naṣṭa – having lost; draviṇe — wealth; gata – pushed off; klamaḥ — troubles; pravrajya — becoming renounced; gām — earth; paryatamāna — wandering around; ittham — in that way; nirākṛto = nirākṛtaḥ — insulted; 'sadbhir = asadbhiḥ — by wicked materialistic people; api — even though; sva-dharmād = sva-dharmāt — from his righteous duty; akampito = akampitaḥ — cannot be budged; 'mūṁ = amūm — this; munir = muniḥ — ascetic philosopher; āha — sang; gāthām — song.

Translation

The Blessed Lord said: Becoming disgusted, having lost wealth, pushing off troubles, becoming renounced, wandering over the earth, the ascetic philosopher, sang that song and was not budged from righteous duty, even though he was insulted by materialistic people. (18.59)

Commentary:

At that time of his life, his righteous duty was to live as an ascetic. He did not desist from it, because of pressure put on him by materialistic people. He rightly wandered around from place to place, causing a reduction in the social hassles.

सुख-दुःख-प्रदो नान्यः
पुरुषस्यात्म-विभ्रमः ।
मित्रोदासीन-रिपवः
ससारस् तमसः कृतः ॥ १८.६० ॥

sukha-duḥkha-prado nānyaḥ
puruṣasyātma-vibhramaḥ
mitrodāsīna-ripavaḥ
saṁsāras tamasaḥ kṛtaḥ (18.60)

sukha-duḥkha-prado = sukha – happiness + duḥkha – distress + pradaḥ — that which is productive of; nānyaḥ = na — no + anyaḥ — other; puruṣasyātma = puruṣasya — concerning the personality + ātma — individual spirit; vibhramaḥ — delusion; mitrodāsīna = mitra — friends + udāsīna — neutral persons; ripavaḥ — enemies; saṁsāras = samsārah — haphazard course of births and deaths; tamasaḥ — concerning the retardative influence; kṛtaḥ — caused by.

Translation

That which is productive of pleasure and pain, the delusion concerning the identity of the person, the concept of friends, neutral persons and enemies, and the haphazard course of births and deaths, was caused by and concerns no other force, besides the retardative influence. (18.60)

Commentary:

We have to realize that we are under an influence. So long as we remain under the retardative influence, we will be forced to do things which are counterproductive to our spiritual concerns.

तस्मात् सर्वात्मना तात
निगृहाण मनो धिया ।
मय्य् आवेशितया युक्त
एतावान् योग-सङ्ग्रहः ॥ १८ ६१ ॥

tasmāt sarvātmanā tāta
nigṛhāṇa mano dhiyā
mayy āveśitayā yukta
etāvān yoga-saṅgrahaḥ (18 61)

tasmāt — therefore; sarvātmanā — by all your soul; tāta — dear friend; nigṛhāna — restraining; mano = manaḥ — mind; dhiyā — by the intellect; mayy = mayi — in me; āveśitayā — being absorbed; yukta = yuktaḥ — connected; etāvān — thus; yoga – yoga practice; saṅgrahaḥ — the gist.

Translation

Therefore my dear friend, with all your soul, restrain the mind by the intellect and be connected by being absorbed in Me. This much is the gist of yoga practice. (18.61)

Commentary:

This is the definition of *bhakti* yoga, which is the application of affections for Krishna by the psychological control gained through yoga. *Nigṛhāṇa mano dhiyā* is the yoga process in practice to completion. And mayy āveśitayā yukta is the *bhakti* process being applied to *Śrī* Krishna. When the two are put together we get yoga and *bhakti*, or *bhakti* yoga.

य एतां भिक्षुणा गीतां
ब्रह्म-निष्ठां समाहितः ।
धारयञ् छ्रावयञ् छृण्वन्
द्वन्द्वैर् नैवाभिभूयते ॥ १८ ६२ ॥

ya etāṁ bhikṣuṇā gītāṁ
brahma-niṣṭhāṁ samāhitaḥ
dhārayañ chrāvayañ chṛṇvan
dvandvair naivābhibhūyate (18 62)

ya = yah — he, who; etām — this (song); bhikṣuṇā — by the ascetic beggar; gītām — sung, recites; brahma — spiritual reality; niṣṭhām — steadily focusing; samāhitaḥ — with continuous absorption; dhārayan — effortlessly applying the attention to the higher concentration force; chṛāvayañ = śrāvayan — tells the story of; chṛṇvan = śṛnvan — listens to; dvandvair = dvandvaiḥ — by the two phases of happiness and distress; naivābhibhūyate = na — not + eva — indeed + abhibhūyate — is affected.

Translation

He who recites this song of the ascetic beggar, and who can effortlessly apply his attention to the higher concentration force, steadily focussing on spiritual reality with continuous absorption, and who tells this and listens to this story, is not affected by the two phases of happiness and distress. (18.62)

Commentary:

One must not only recite this story and tell it to others as well as to listen to explanations of more elevated souls, but one must also master the 7th.stage of yoga *(dhārayan)* and the 8th stage *(samāhitah)* of yoga practice.

CHAPTER 19*

Sāṇkhya Theory of Creation**

Terri Stokes-Pineda Art

śrī-bhagavān uvāca
atha te sampravakṣyāmi sāṅkhyam pūrvair viniścitam
yad vijñāya pumān sadyo jahyād vaikalpikaṁ bhramam

The Blessed Lord said: Now I will explain to you, the Sāṅkhya theory of creation, which was figured out by the ancient sages. By knowing that, any person may immediately give up the misconception, which is based on the multiplicity seen in this creation. (Uddhava Gītā .19.1)

* Śrīmad Bhāgavatam Canto 11, Chapter 24
** Translator's selected chapter title.

श्री-भगवान् उवाच
अथ ते सम्प्रवक्ष्यामि
साङ्ख्यं पूर्वैर् विनिश्चितम् ।
यद् विज्ञाय पुमान् सद्यो
जह्याद् वैकल्पिक भ्रमम् ॥ १९.१ ॥

śrī-bhagavān uvāca
atha te sampravakṣyāmi
sāṅkhyaṁ pūrvair viniścitam
yad vijñāya pumān sadyo
jahyād vaikalpikaṁ bhramam (19.1)

śrī-bhagavān – the blessed lord; uvāca — said; atha — now; te — to you; sampravakṣyāmi — I will explain; sāṅkhyam — Sāṅkhyaṁ theory of creation; pūrvair = pūrvaiḥ — by ancient sages; viniścitam — figured out; yad = yat — that; vijñāya — knowing; pumān — any person; sadyo = sadyah — immediately; jahyād = jahyāt — can give up; vaikalpikam — that which is based on multiplicity seen in this creation; bhramam — misconception.

Translation

The Blessed Lord said: Now I will explain to you, the Sāṅkhya theory of creation, which was figured out by the ancient sages. By knowing that, any person may immediately give up the misconception, which is based on the multiplicity seen in this creation. (19.1)

Commentary:

The *Sāṅkhya* theory of creation was explained by the yogi mystics who by spiritual perception saw the truth behind this creation. Acceptance of it and integration of their information may set one on the path of mystic yoga, wherein one sees the realities directly. One cannot become self-realized in fact, merely by hearing this information, from anybody, even from the Supreme Person. The purpose of divulging the *Sāṅkhya* information is truly served only when one completes yoga practice and can see directly what is described by the great yogi sages.

आसीज् ज्ञानम् अथो अर्थ
एकम् एवाविकल्पितम् ।
यदा विवेक-निपुणा
आदौ कृत-युगे ऽयुगे ॥ १९.२ ॥

āsīj jñānam atho artha
ekam evāvikalpitam
yadā viveka-nipuṇā
ādau kṛta-yuge 'yuge (19.2)

āsīj = āsīt — there existed; jñānam — knowledge; atho = athau — thus; artha = arthaḥ — object known; ekam — one consistency; evāvikalpitam = eva — only + avikalpitam — without distortion; yadā — when; viveka — discrimination, perception; nipuṇā — people with accurate; ādau — at the beginning; kṛta-yuga — in the age of Easy Realisation; 'yuge = ayuge — during the time prior to this manifestation.

Translation

Once, the knowledge gained and the object known were of one consistency only, without distortion. That was when there were people with accurate perception at the beginning of the Age of Easy Realization, and during the time prior to this manifestation. (19.2)

Commentary:

For those people, language was not a barrier. They had direct perception of the supernatural and spiritual worlds.

तन् माया-फल-रूपेण
केवलं निर्विकल्पितम् ।
वाङ्-मनो-ऽगोचरं सत्य
द्विधा समभवद् बृहत् ॥ १९.३ ॥

tan māyā-phala-rūpeṇa
kevalaṁ nirvikalpitam
vāṅ-mano-'gocaraṁ satyaṁ
dvidhā samabhavad bṛhat (19.3)

tan = tat — that primal reality; māyā — productive enterprise; phala — product; rūpena — by the form of; kevalam — unified existence; nirvikalpitam — what is without ambiguity; vān = vāk — description; mano = manaḥ — mind; 'gocaraṁ = agocaram — beyond the capacity; satyam — reality; dvidhā — twofold; samabhavad = samabhavat — that became; bṛhat — the extensive primat existence.

Translation

That unified existence, which was without ambiguity, which is beyond the capacity of description and the mind, the Reality, that extensive Primal Existence, did by taking the form of productive enterprise and product, become twofold. (19.3)

Commentary:

The famous *kevalam-nirvikalpitam* is the Sum Total Reality as it was before this creation was manifested. It is what we would perceive if we could vacate ourselves from this creation and see the Primal Reality. This would be the Supreme Being with the limited spirits, and the material nature in proximity. That is beyond description because what happens now, which causes our vocabulary, is not totally appropriate to what was existent before. It is a fact however that the original condition can be observed by great yogins in *samādhi*.

Their spirits are transferred out of this zone into existential places where some of the material nature is still in quiescence. Such places are there in the chit *ākāśa*, the sky of consciousness.

Some yogins seeking relief from this varied but temporary existence, endeavor in austerities of higher yoga and reach the stage of *kevalam nirvikalpitam*, a stage in which they do, for the time being, quiet off their troubled existence here.

तयोर् एकतरो ह्य् अर्थः
प्रकृतिः सोभयात्मिका ।
ज्ञानं त्व् अन्यतमो भावः
पुरुषः सो ऽभिधीयते ॥ १९.४॥

tayor ekataro hy arthaḥ
prakṛtiḥ sobhayātmikā
jñānaṁ tv anyatamo bhāvaḥ
puruṣaḥ so 'bhidhīyate (19.4)

tayor = tayoh — of the two; ekataro = ekataraḥ — one; hy = hi — definitely; arthah — aspect; prakṛtiḥ — material nature; sobhayātmikā = sā — that (submissive factor) + ubhaya – two-fold + ātmikā — of the nature of; jñānam — knowledge, awareness; tv = tu — but; anyatamo = anyatamah — the other; bhāvah — conscious aspect; puruṣaḥ — personality; so = sah — that (predominating factor); 'bhidhīyate = abhidhīyate — is called.

Translation

Of the two, one aspect is material nature, which has a two-fold nature. But the other conscious aspect is awareness. That predominating factor is called the personality.(19.4)

Commentary:

In the previous verse, *Śrī* Krishna listed two aspects as *māyā* or productive enterprising power and *phala* or the product or result of such enterprise. Now He tells us that these two aspects are *jñānam* or the experiencer, otherwise known as the *puruṣa* or personality and the *prakṛtih* or material nature. This becomes very complicated, because a person could then ask why that *māyā* is correlated as the *jñānam* and the *puruṣa*. And why the *phala* is not labeled as *prakṛtih*? However these matters are complicated. This cannot be oversimplified without distorting the explanation. The reason for the variation in terminology is this: There is the time factor and the universal and local developments which cause one thing to be transformed into another and which causes one type of influence to appear different in newer transformations.

When water is added to clay, a potter makes pottery. After the pottery is baked, it appears to be different to water and clay because of transformation. While the potter fashions the pottery, his knowledge is put to work in creating the item. At that time, the potter, water, clay and the potter's wheel, are connected as a mechanism. Thus the terminology can get confusing, if we do not realize that at different stages the same item assumes a different function.

Initially when a section of material nature shifts from its state of quiescence, there is just the influence of the Supreme Spirit upon it. Thus it can be said that everything started from there. Everything began with the material nature and the proximity influence of the Supreme Spirit. Of course by Supreme Spirit, in this case, it would be the Supreme Lord Himself as well as the individual spirits. There are all there at that time. None of the individual spirits would be in the material creation then, because there was no manifestation due to material nature's non-responsive status in the quiescent state.

By God's proximity, a portion of the material nature assumed the attitude of a productive enterprise. From that, a product was produced. Previously Lord Krishna called that product, the *Sūtram*, or the sexually-charge, emotionally-responsive primal potency. This *Sūtram* divested even further until gross energies were manifested.

In the material nature, in the sexually-charged portion of it, there is knowledge but it is living knowledge and so it forms into the cosmic awareness (jñānam). That cosmic awareness is used by the Supreme Being to produce what is known as the Universal Form and from that Form, the limited entities take minute portions of the cosmic intellect for usages in the creation.

तमो रजः सत्त्वम् इति
प्रकृतेर् अभवन् गुणाः ।
मया प्रक्षोभ्यमाणायाः
पुरुषानुमतेन च ॥ १९.५॥

tamo rajaḥ sattvam iti
prakṛter abhavan guṇāḥ
mayā prakṣobhyamāṇāyāḥ
puruṣānumatena ca (19.5)

tamo = tamah — the retardative energy; rajaḥ — the impulsive force; sattvam — the perceptive ability; iti — thus, namely; prakṛter = prakṛteḥ — from material nature; abhavan — were produced; guṇāḥ — the modes; mayā — by me; prakṣobhyamāṇāyāḥ — was agitated; puruṣānumatena = puruṣa — the collective personality + anumatena — with approving urge; ca — and.

Translation

The mundane influences were produced from material nature, namely the retardative energy, the impulsive force and the perceptive ability. And with the approval urge of the collective personality, it was agitated by Me. (19.5)

Commentary:

The question of how we got into material existence, is very tacitly explained in this verse. If we are to accept this, then the question arises as to why *Śrī* Krishna put us in this creation in the first place. Did He get our approval for doing that? The answer lies in the Sanskrit term *anumatena* which means that *Śrī* Krishna got permission or approval from the *puruṣa* or the Collective Person.

I translated *puruṣa* as Collective Person, rather than as the Person, since in fact, the translation as Person is greatly misunderstood. Person in this verse means not just the Primal Person, Procreator *Brahmā*, but all the living entitles who are in his body at the start of the manifestation. Therefore it is not just one person but many individuals. In fact it is many trillions of living entities who inhabit the form of *Brahmā*. We can understand this by our nomenclature of a pregnant woman. Usually we address her as a person, even though we know that there is another person in her body, who will be expelled from it at delivery. Thus to clarify the issue, she should be addressed as two persons, because in fact that is what is present before us in a pregnant body.

The question remains as to how *Śrī* Krishna got that approval from procreator *Brahmā* and from us, the individual tiny souls. The answer is that He did not get formal permission. What he got was our instinct for manifestation. That instinct was so strong, that it might be compared to a sexual approval of the body of a desiring woman. Such an approval is there by force of the sex urge and not so much by the woman's deliberation.

The next question is: Could *Śrī* Krishna have not permitted that instinct to enter into this manifestation? The obvious answer is that He could not. It is a natural development that He can regulate. He cannot stop it altogether.

It may be argued that God seems to have no independence in the matter of initiating this creation. This is the fact. Both God and the limited spirits have eternal relationships with material nature. This relationship must be expressed from time to time. At some stage God has to release us into this type of creation. At some stage He has to act to release us out of it, either as liberated entities in full objective consciousness or as liberated entities with subjective awareness only. Then again, he has to re-release us into another development of material nature. This is an ongoing cyclic occurrence. It will never stop, because the whole range of existence is eternally set up like that. If we want to be released, we should strive for objective liberation.

तेभ्यः समभवत् सूत्रं
महान् सूत्रेण संयुतः ।
ततो विकुर्वतो जातो
यो ऽहङ्कारो विमोहनः ॥ १९.६ ॥

tebhyaḥ samabhavat sūtraṁ
mahān sūtreṇa saṁyutaḥ
tato vikurvato jāto
yo 'haṅkāro vimohanaḥ (19.6)

tebhyah — from those; samabhavat — developed; sūtram — sexually-charge cosmic energy; mahān — the mahat-tattva, primal cosmic energy; sūtreṇa — with the sexual-charge cosmic energy; samyūtaḥ — was mixed; tato = tataḥ — from that; vikurvato = vikurvataḥ — transformation; jāto = jātaḥ — was generated; yo = yah — which; 'haṅkāro = ahaṅkāraḥ — the cosmic assertive sense; vimohanaḥ — that which bewilders.

Translation

From those mundane potencies, the sexually-charged cosmic energy developed. The primal cosmic energy and that sexually-charged cosmic force were mixed. From the admixture, the cosmic assertive sense which bewilders, emerged. (19.6)

Commentary:

The sequence of events described so far is as follows. First there is the Supreme Spirit along with the limited spirits who are to govern a particular material manifestation. The manifestation is not yet produced but the energy for it, is in existence in a quiescent state. Even in that state, the material nature is in proximity with the Supreme Spirit and His companions, the limited spirits. Thus even in the quiescence, the material energy is emotionally-charged, even though the potency, is relatively speaking, static. Material nature even though alive and electrically-charge at the time, might be compared to a sleeping man. In the sleeping condition we cannot say that he is dead but all the same he does not exhibit activity. Because we detect symptoms, we know that he is alive.

Thus the first stage of material nature is its proximity state in which there is no movement. That is the stage of quiescence. The second stage is sometimes called *pradhāna*, which means the charge in material nature is somehow increased. This might be compared to a sleeping man who is on the verge of waking up. Because we see that his eyelids are opening and that his arms and legs are moving, we conclude that he is capable of movement. When God gives a tiny bit more attention to material nature, something more than just His proximity to it, it is called *prakṛti*. But after that, the God actually focuses a little on material nature and when this is done, a part of it becomes emotionally-charged. Wherever He deliberately gives his attention; that part becomes emotionally-charged. This is called the *Sūtram*, in these verses. That *sūtram* emotionally-charged force, draws energy from the uncharged force around it, from the *mahān* or *mahat tattva*. The admixture of those two forces produces a cosmic assertive sense which is known as the cosmic *I*, or the cosmic *I am*.

From this cosmic assertive sense, minute portions are divested and are awarded to the limited entities, who draw it to themselves (according to the language of the *Bhagavad-Gītā*) and who are bewildered by it, because it frees them from a totally-subjective existence into an objective one, in which they depart from the Supreme Being and are able to tell the difference between themselves and the Lord.

This is something like a pregnancy. Even though the mother and child are very close, the child by innate urges, takes help from the mother in order to become separated from her. Similarly the limited beings take help from the *Puruṣa*, the Primal Person, for the purpose of objectifying themselves from Him, to separate themselves later, when they adopt individual identity.

वैकारिकस् तैजसश् च
तामसश् चेत्य् अहं त्रि-वृत् ।
तन्-मात्रेन्द्रिय-मनसां
कारणं चिद्-अचिन्-मयः ॥ १९.७॥

vaikārikas taijasaś ca
tāmasaś cety ahaṁ tri-vṛt
tan-mātrendriya-manasāṁ
kāraṇaṁ cid-acin-mayaḥ (19.7)

vaikārikas = vaikārikaḥ — pertaining to the perception-forming energy; taijasaś = taijasaḥ — pertaining to the motivating energy; ca — and; tāmasaś = tāmasaḥ — pertaining to the inertia energy; cety = ca — and + iti — as declared; aham — the sense of assertion; tri-vṛt — threefold; tan-mātrendriya-manasāṁ = tat-mātra — subtle sense objects + indriya — sensual energy + manasam — of mindal energy; kāraṇam — cause; cid = cit – self awareness; acin = acit — that which has no self awareness; mayah — comprising.

Translation

As declared, the sense of assertion is threefold; as pertaining to the perception-forming energy, the motivational force and the inertial energy. These in turn serve as the subtle sense objects, the sensual power and the mind compartment. Part of it comprise a self awareness and part has no self consciousness. (19.7)

Commentary:

The sense of assertion is experienced by us through the minute portions of it which we use. This is the sense of, *I exist*. That however is threefold, depending on which of the three energies promote it. In the material world, the sense of assertion is not independent, for it is always aligned with or overcome by a certain energy, either by the perception-forming energy, the motivational force or the inertial dulling power. These three energies produce the subtle sense objects, sensual power and mindal space.

The situation is such that self awareness tries to experience itself. To accomplish that it references itself to energies which exhibit no self awareness. This satisfies the urge for exploitation through which we become time bound.

Śrī Patañjali Mahārṣi gave a very concise explanation:

eva svāmi śaktyoḥ svarūpopalabhi hetuḥ saṁyogaḥ

There is a reason for the conjunction of the individual self and his psychological energies. It is for obtaining the experience of his own form. (Yoga Sutras 2. 23)

अर्थस् तन्-मात्रिकाज् जज्ञे
तामसाद् इन्द्रियाणि च ।
तैजसाद् देवता आसन्न्
एकादश च वैकृतात् ॥ १९.८॥

arthas tan-mātrikāj jajñe
tāmasād indriyāṇi ca
taijasād devatā āsann
ekādaśa ca vaikṛtāt (19.8)

arthas — gross matter; tan-mātrikāj = tan-mātrikāt — from the subtle objects; jajñe — developed; tāmasād = tāmasāt — from the non-energetic assertive force; indriyāṇi — the sensual energies; ca — and; taijasād = taijasāt — from the energetic assertive potency; devatā — the supernatural rulers; āsann = āsan — emerged; ekādaśa — eleven; ca — and; vaikṛtāt — from the perception-oriented assertive potency.

Translation

Gross matter developed from the subtle objects, which developed from the non-energetic assertive force. The senses developed from the energetic assertive potency. The eleven supernatural rulers emerged from the perception-oriented potency. (19.8)

Commentary:

The perception-oriented potency is known as sattva-guna, the clarifying energy through which we perceive gross and subtle objects. The subtle objects are five perceptions namely subtle sound, subtle surfaces, subtle shapes, subtle flavors and subtle odors. These subtle perceptions were developed from the non-energetic assertive force, which is a form of subtle matter in quiescence.

The sensual energy developed from the energetic assertive potency, known otherwise as *raja guṇa*. And the eleven supernatural rulers emerged from the perception-oriented potency, hence they have mystic perception.

मया सञ्चोदिता भावाः
सर्वे संहत्य-कारिणः ।
अण्डम् उत्पादयाम् आसुर्
ममायतनम् उत्तमम् ॥ १९.९ ॥

mayā sañcoditā bhāvāḥ
sarve saṁhatya-kāriṇaḥ
aṇḍam utpādayām āsur
mamāyatanam uttamam (19.9)

mayā — by me; sañcoditā = sañcoditāḥ — as motivated; bhāvāh — the factors; sarve — all; saṁhatya — combining together; kārinaḥ — reacting; aṇḍam — cosmic egg-shaped enclosure; utpādayām āsur = utpādayām āsuḥ — produced; mamāyatanam = mama — of mind + āyatanam — habitat; uttamam — most suitable.

Translation

As motivated by Me, all the factors by combining together and reacting accordingly, produced a cosmic egg-shaped enclosure, which is a most suitable habitat of Mine. (19.9)

Commentary:

The Supreme Being exists both inside and outside the material existence. For *kriyā* yoga, the research, investigation and subsequent visitation concerns the existence which is dimensionally outside of this enclosed material world.

तस्मिन्न् अहं समभवम्
अण्डे सलिल-संस्थितौ ।
मम नाभ्याम् अभूत् पद्मं
विश्वाख्यं तत्र चात्म-भूः ॥ १९.१० ॥

tasminn ahaṁ samabhavam
aṇḍe salila-saṁsthitau
mama nābhyām abhūt padmaṁ
viśvākhyaṁ tatra cātma-bhūḥ (19.10)

tasmin — in that; aham — I; samabhavam — manifested form; aṇḍe — in the cosmic enclosure; salila — water; saṁsthitau — situated within, floating; mama — my; nābhyām — from the navel; abhūt — developed; padmam — lotus; viśvākhyam — known as the universal; tatra — from there; cātma-bhuh = ca — and + ātma-bhūḥ — self-produced person.

Translation

In that cosmic enclosure, which floated in water, I manifested a form. From My navel, a lotus developed, which is called the universe. And from there, the self-produced one emerged. (19.10)

Commentary:

So far astronomers have found no evidence of a lotus-shaped configuration of the universe. They have not found an edge to it, nor a membrane containing it. They have not found the Universal Form nor a self-produced person. However their evidence does not disprove this statement since that evidence has to do with what is perceptible from this dimension, either through bodily sense perception or through sensing mechanisms.

सो ऽसृजत् तपसा युक्तो
रजसा मद्-अनुग्रहात् ।
लोकान् स-पालान् विश्वात्मा
भूर् भुवः स्वर् इति त्रिधा ॥ १९.११ ॥

so 'sṛjat tapasā yukto
rajasā mad-anugrahāt
lokān sa-pālān viśvātmā
bhūr bhuvaḥ svar iti tridhā (19.11)

so = sah — he; 'sṛjat = asrjat — created; tapasā — by rigid sensual restraint; yukto = yuktaḥ — endowed; rajasā — with the impulsive potency; mad-anugrahāt = mat-anugrahāt — due to my grace; lokān — the world; sa-pālān — with the supernatural rulers; viśvātmā — universal soul; bhur – Bhur lower zone; svar – Svar higher zone; iti — namely; tridhā — three regions.

Translation

Due to My grace, by his rigid sensual restraint, and by being endowed with the impulsive potency, he, the soul of the universe, created the worlds, in three regions, namely the Bhūr lower zone, the Bhuva middle area and the Svar higher region. (19.11)

Commentary:

This is a description of *Brahmā*, the procreator. By the blessings of the Almighty God and being empowered with the sum total passionate force, he functions as the soul of the universe. Having within his causal form, all limited entities who were to come out in the creation and all their motivational powers. Thus as compelled by the energies, *Brahmā* created a three-fold regioned world.

देवानाम् ओक आसीत् स्वर्
भूतानां च भुवः पदम् ।
मर्त्यादीनां च भूर् लोकः
सिद्धानां त्रितयात् परम् ॥ १९.१२ ॥

devānām oka āsīt svar
bhūtānāṁ ca bhuvaḥ padam
martyādīnāṁ ca bhūr lokaḥ
siddhānāṁ tritayāt param (19.12)

devānām — of the supernatural rulers; oka = okah — zone; āsīt — became; svar — Svar higher region; bhūtānām — of the spirits; ca — and; bhuvah — Bhuva middle zone; padam — habitation; martyādīnām — of humans and other species using short-term bodies; ca — and; bhūr – Bhūr lower zone; lokaḥ — region; siddhānām — of the perfected beings; tritayāt — in reference to the three; param — beyond.

Translation

The Svar higher region became the zone of the supernatural rulers. The Bhuva middle zone is the habitation of the spirits. And the Bhūr lower zone is that of the humans and other species using short-term bodies. Beyond the three, is the zone of the perfected beings. (19.12)

Commentary:

These are four dimensional divisions, each higher than the other. If we start with the lowest one, which is this physical world, it is called *Bhūr*. This is the dimension which we inhabit. According to our astronomers, the planets nearby the earth are uninhabited physically. They do not account for any other dimension. Despite technological sophistication, scientists are unable to detect the numerous spirits in the air around us in the *Bhūva* dimension, which is the middle zone.

The *Bhūva* middle dimension is the location where we enter as soon as we leave our bodies at death. We go there in dream-like subtle forms, even while using these gross bodies. However most people by their addictive focus into this physical world are unaware of their entry into that world. In the *Bhagavad-Gītā*, the *bhūva* middle zone is said to be an undetected place (avyakta); the interim location where the spirits stay in the hereafter:

avyaktādīni bhūtāni vyaktamadhyāni bhārata
avyaktanidhanānyeva tatra kā paridevanā

The living beings are undetected in the beginning of a manifestation, visible in the interim stages, and are again undetected at the end of a manifestation. (B.G. 2.28)

Some spirits however, by-pass that place and go to the higher Svar world, which is the place where the supernatural rulers have their super-subtle bodies. Beyond their place is the place for the *Siddha* perfected beings. This is the place to which many *kriyā* yogis are transferred. Or if they are totally successful, they go farther than that location. Since these places are not in this dimension, one cannot journey to any of them physically. One has to learn the supernatural geography to understand how these places are located in reference to each other. This is what is done in the 7th and 8th stages of yoga.

अधो ऽसुराणां नागानां
भूमेर् ओको ऽसृजत् प्रभुः ।
त्रि-लोक्यां गतयः सर्वाः
कर्मणां त्रि-गुणात्मनाम् ॥ १९.१३ ॥

adho 'surāṇāṁ nāgānāṁ
bhūmer oko 'sṛjat prabhuḥ
tri-lokyāṁ gatayaḥ sarvāḥ
karmaṇāṁ tri-guṇātmanām (19.13)

adho = adhah — below; 'surāṇāṁ = asurānām — of the powerful wicked spirits; nāgānām — of the subtle snakes; bhūmer = bhūmeh — from the earth; oko = okah — habitat; 'sṛjat = asṛjat — created; prabhuḥ — Procreator Brahmā; tri-lokyām — three dimensions; gatayah — destination, environment; sarvāh — all; karmanām — of cultural activities; tri-guṇātmanām = tri-guṇa – three influences of material nature + ātmanām — comprising.

Translation

Procreator Brahmā created the habitats of the powerful wicked spirits and the subtle snakes below the earth. All environments in the three dimensions are based on the three influences of material nature which comprise cultural activities. (19.13)

Commentary:

This below the earth is below in the subtle sense. It not in the physical geography. This is a mystic geography which may or may not correspond to physical locations. In all respects however, all these environments are created on the basis of material nature and thus the cultural activities we enact, cause us to be attracted to a particular place.

योगस्य तपसश् चैव
न्यासस्य गतयो ऽमलाः ।
महर् जनस् तपः सत्यं
भक्ति-योगस्य मद्-गतिः ॥ १९.१४ ॥

yogasya tapasaś caiva
nyāsasya gatayo 'malāḥ
mahar janas tapaḥ satyaṁ
bhaktī-yogasya mad-gatiḥ (19.14)

yogasya — by yoga practice; tapasaś = tapasaḥ — by austerity; caiva = ca — and + eva — indeed;

nyāsasya — of the renunciation of cultural oppurtunities; gatayo = gatayah — that which leads to; 'malāḥ = amalāh — pure; mahar — Mahar; janas — Jana; tapah — Tapa; satyam — Satya; bhaktī-yogasya — by devotion as it is applied with the yoga discipline; mad-gatiḥ = mat-gatiḥ — My region.

Translation

The practice of yoga, austerity and the renunciation of cultural oppurtunities, causes one to achieve the pure worlds, namely Mahar, Jana, Tapa and Satya zones. While the practice of devotion as it is applied with yoga disciplines leads to My region. (19.14)

Commentary:

In each case yoga is involved, either as those who do the *aṣṭanga* yoga process, those who do other austerities along with it, those who renounce all cultural opportunities while doing it, and those who master it and use yoga to intensify their devotion to *Śrī* Krishna. Accordingly, the ascetic achieves a particular world which is flawless or pure *(amalāh).*

But it is not that every yogi, every ascetic yogi, every renunciant yogi or every devotee yogi, will achieve any of these objectives. One has to complete the particular course. Those who fall short of the completion, will go to a place where they can finish out their practice, either to be born on earth or to attain a place within this world in a dimension where they would get the opportunity to continue the process. This is described in the *Bhagavad-Gītā*:

śrībhagavānuvāca
pārtha naiveha nāmutra vināśastasya vidyate
na hi kalyāṇakṛtkaścid durgatiṁ tāta gacchati
prāpya puṇyakṛtāṁllokān uṣitvā śāśvatīḥ samāḥ
śucīnāṁ śrīmatāṁ gehe yogabhraṣṭo'bhijāyate
atha vā yogināmeva kule bhavati dhīmatām
etaddhi durlabhataraṁ loke janma yadīdṛśam
tatra taṁ buddhisaṁyogaṁ labhate paurvadehikam
yatate ca tato bhūyaḥ saṁsiddhau kurunandana
pūrvābhyāsena tenaiva hriyate hyavaśo'pi saḥ
jijñāsurapi yogasya śabdabrahmātivartate
prayatnādyatamānastu yogī saṁśuddhakilbiṣaḥ
anekajanmasaṁsiddhas tatoyāti parāṁ gatim

The Blessed Lord said: O son of Pṛthā, it is realized that neither here on earth nor above in the celestial regions, does the unaccomplished yogi lose his skill. Indeed, O dear Arjuna, no performer of virtuous acts, goes down permanently into misfortune.

After obtaining the celestial places where the virtuous souls go, having lived there for many, many years, the fallen yogi is born into the social circumstances of the purified and prosperous people.

Alternately, he is born into a family of enlightened people. But such a birth is very difficult to attain in this world.

In that environment, he is inspired with the cumulative intellectual interest from a previous birth. And from that time, he strives again for yoga perfection, O dear son of the Kurus.

Indeed, by previous practice, he is motivated, even without conscious desire. He who persistently inquires of yoga, instinctively sees beyond the Veda, the spoken description of the spiritual reality.

From a steady effort and a consistently controlled mind, the yogi who is thoroughly cleansed of bad tendencies, who is perfected in many births, reaches the supreme goal. (B.G. 6.40-45)

The yoga practice is described in detail in chapter six of the *Bhagavad-Gītā* and elsewhere, but some say that it is impractical and that another divine person deleted it as a requirement for salvation.

मया कालात्मना धात्रा
कर्म-युक्तम् इद् जगत् ।
गुण-प्रवाह एतस्मिन्न्
उन्मज्जति निमज्जति ॥ १९.१५॥

mayā kālātmanā dhātrā
karma-yuktam idaṁ jagat
guṇa-pravāha etasminn
unmajjati nimajjati (19.15)

mayā — by me; kālātmanā = kāla – time + ātmanā — by the self, by itself; dhātrā — origin of the world; karma – cultural activities; yuktam — devoted to; idam — this; jagat — universe; guṇa – mundane energies; pravāha = pravāhe — in the flow; etasminn = etasmin — in this; unmajjati — develops; nimajjati — subsides.

Translation

By Me, who is time itself, who is the originator of the world, this universe which is devoted to cultural activity, develops and subsides in this flow of mundane energies. (19.15)

Commentary:

Śrī Krishna claimed to be time itself. If we are to accept His premises, it would mean that His mind controls when the universe began, how it continues and when it will end. This is done by supernatural connection to the world. The material world is undoubtedly devoted to cultural activity *(karma yuktam),* of causing the elevation of the individual spirits who had no objective awareness in the spiritual sky. It is for causing them to develop objectivity.

In considering modern scientific ideas about the formulation, continuation and possible ending of this creation, we must always bear in mind that the supernatural factor is not ruled out by science. It is just that science has neither proven nor disproven it. Everything may proceed for a time as science predicts but science itself admits that it cannot foresee every angle. If we take, for instance, the disappearance of the dinosaurs on earth, we can see that for sure, some-thing might happen in the future that could radically change the nature of the universe as we currently perceive it and all the normal laws which science discovered recently might be suddenly abolished.

अणुर् बृहत् कृशः स्थूलो
यो यो भावः प्रसिध्यति ।
सर्वो ऽप्य् उभय-सयुक्तः
प्रकृत्या पुरुषेण च ॥ १९.१६ ॥

aṇur bṛhat kṛśaḥ sthūlo
yo yo bhāvaḥ prasidhyati
sarvo 'py ubhaya-saṁyuktaḥ
prakṛtyā puruṣeṇa ca (19.16)

aṇur = aṇuḥ — tiny; bṛhat — large; kṛśaḥ — thin; sthūlo = sthūlaḥ — thick; yo yo = yaḥ yaḥ — whatever; bhāvaḥ — object; prasidhyati — is manifested; sarvo = sarvah — all; 'py = api — surely; ubhaya — both; saṁyuktah — is mixed; prakṛtyā — with material nature; puruṣeṇa — with the spirit; ca — and.

Translation

Whatever there is in a tiny, large, thick or thin object, which is manifested, all of it surely, is mixed with both the material nature and spirit. (19.16)

Commentary:

This has to do with whatever we might encounter in the three zones of the material world, the gross levels, the immediate hereafter and the heavenly worlds.

यस् तु यस्यादिर् अन्तश् च स वै मध्यं च तस्य सन् । विकारो व्यवहारार्थो यथा तैजस-पार्थिवाः ॥१९.१७॥	yas tu yasyādir antaś ca sa vai madhyaṁ ca tasya san vikāro vyavahārārtho yathā taijasa-pārthivāḥ (19.17)

yas = yah — whatever; tu — but; yasyādir = yasya — of which + ādiḥ — beginning; antaś = antaḥ — end; ca — and; sa = sah — that; vai — indeed; madhyam — middle state; ca — as well as; tasya — concerning that; san — reality of the thing; vikāro = vikāraḥ — changed form; vyavahārārtho = vyavahāra – that which is practical, customary + arthah — value; yathā — as; taijasa — that which is produced by ore, metallic objects; pārthivaḥ — that which is produced from clay, ceramic objects.

Translation

That which is present as the beginning and ending, and which is the same in the middle stage, alone is the reality of the thing. The changed forms are a utility only as in the case of metallic or ceramic objects. (19.17)

Commentary:

This point is very difficult to apply because we have customary usages. These usages, being predominant in the material world, cause us to overlook the realty of things *(san)*. By a steady focus on the *Sāṅkhya* philosophy and by taking yoga practice to the internal planes, we can begin to see the reality as something substantial. It is abstract but it is the essence of everything.

यद् उपादाय पूर्वस् तु भावो विकुरुते ऽपरम् । आदिर् अन्तो यदा यस्य तत् सत्यम् अभिधीयते ॥१९.१८॥	yad upādāya pūrvas tu bhāvo vikurute 'param ādir anto yadā yasya tat satyam abhidhīyate (19.18)

yad = yat — that which; upādāya — obvious cause, raw material; pūrvas = pūrvaḥ — previous cause, primal element; tu — but; bhāvo = bhāvaḥ — object; vikurute — created thing occurring due to changes made in an original; 'param = aparam — the effect or changed appearance of an original element; ādir = ādih — beginning; anto = antaḥ — ending; yadā — when; yasya — of which; tat — that cause; satyam — real; abhidhīyate — is identified.

Translation

That which is the raw material, which is the primal element, but which produces an object, is the real thing. That cause is identified as real which is there in the beginning and end of an object, which survived the changes. (19.18)

Commentary:

Due to admixtures, there is constant bewilderment in the material world. And due to our external sensual orientation, we are unable to find the Cause of all causes. However, the serious yogis do research into the Cause of all causes, using these hints given by *Śrī* Krishna, hints which are part of the *Sāṅkhya* theory.

प्रकृतिर् यस्योपादानम् आधारः पुरुषः परः । सतो ऽभिव्यञ्जकः कालो ब्रह्म तत् त्रितयं त्व् अहम् ॥१९.१९॥	prakṛtir yasyopādānam ādhāraḥ puruṣaḥ paraḥ sato 'bhivyañjakaḥ kālo brahma tat tritayaṁ tv aham (19.19)

prakṛtir = prakṛtiḥ — primal material nature; yasyopādānam = yasya — of which, of this world + upādānam — the substance used, raw material; ādhāraḥ — the person who sustains; puruṣaḥ — person; paraḥ — supreme; sato = satah — of what is real; 'bhivyañjakaḥ = abhivyañjakah — that which causes a manifestation; kālo = kālah — time; brahma — spiritual reality; tat — that specifically; tritayam — the three aspects; tv = tu — but; aham — I am.

Translation

Primal Material Nature, which is the raw material of this world, the Supreme Person Who is the one who sustains it, Time which causes the manifestations, and which is real, these three aspects are the spiritual reality. But I am all of this. (19.19)

Commentary:

Śrī Krishna defined *brahma* in three ways as the Primal Material Nature, the Supreme Person who sustains material nature in its manifested form and Time which causes history. Stating that these three are real, He accredits Himself as being these three combined.

Material nature is the gross cause and effect. The Supreme Person is the remote manipulator and background influence. Time is the functional supervisor. *Śrī* Krishna made a claim while talking to Arjuna, where He said that the God of this manifestation was merely a fraction of Himself.

atha vā bahunaitena kiṁ jñātena tavārjuna
viṣṭabhyāhamidaṁ kṛtsnam ekāṁśena sthito jagat

But Arjuna, what is the value of this extensive information? As the foundation, I support this entire universe with a fraction of Myself. (B.G. 10.42)

सर्गः प्रवर्तते तावत्
पौर्वापर्येण नित्यशः ।
महान् गुण-विसर्गार्थः
स्थित्य्-अन्तो यावद् ईक्षणम् ॥ १९.२० ॥

sargaḥ pravartate tāvat
paurvāparyeṇa nityaśaḥ
mahān guṇa-visargārthaḥ
sthity-anto yāvad īkṣaṇam (19.20)

sargaḥ — mundane creation; pravartate — persists; tāvat — so long as; paurvāparyeṇa = paurva – causes + aparyeṇa — through the effects; nityaśaḥ — continuation; mahān — vast, bountiful; guṇa – influences of material nature; visargārthaḥ = visarga — the created object in the mundane creation + arthah — for the purpose; sthity = sthiti – manifested existence; anto = antah — end; yāvad = yāvat — till; īkṣaṇam — glance, mystic interest, developing interest.

Translation

The mundane creation persists as long as there is a continuation through effects and causes. The vast world, which is for the purpose of producing created mundane objects, exists till the end of this manifested existence, which is reliant on the developing interest. (19.20)

Commentary:

Eventually the material world will terminate. The effects will no longer be permitted to evolve. Then it will be the end of time. Of course elsewhere other universes will come into being. But all of these will endure for sometime only and then will go out of existence as exhausted energy. These worlds rely on the developing interest of the *Puruṣa*, who is God. The *Puruṣa* here does not mean God alone, however. It means God plus all the innumerable spirits who are to come out in that creation in one way or the other to enliven it and to be stimulated into objectivity by it.

Furthermore, many commentators do not understand the word *puruṣa* because that term as used in this chapter refers mostly not to one person, not to the Supreme Being alone, but to Himself and others. Some commentators steer away from this, because they are afraid to deal with anything which presents a unity of personalities. They are deadly afraid of *advaita* or a unity of limited souls and the Supreme Soul. They want to be sure that the distinction between these is always maintained.

However it is a fact, like it or not, that initially the limited souls were in the supernatural body of God. In that status they remained as spiritual urges only, for many trillions of years. They were factually merged into His consciousness even though their individualities remained in tact for manifestation into objective existence in the future.

विराण् मयासाद्यमानो
लोक-कल्प-विकल्पकः ।
पञ्चत्वाय विशेषाय
कल्पते भुवनैः सह ॥ १९.२१ ॥

virāṇ mayāsādyamāno
loka-kalpa-vikalpakaḥ
pañcatvāya viśeṣāya
kalpate bhuvanaiḥ saha (19.21)

virān = virāt — contained universe; mayāsādyamāno = mayāsādyamānh = mayā — by me + āsādyamānaḥ — held in check (Sanskrit root words: asad – to attack; asedhah – are arrested, hold in custody; asadanam – attacking); loka — world; kalpa — comprising creative duration; vikalpakah — phase of dissolution; pañcatvāya — of the five material elements; viśeṣāya — types; kalpate — is brought to the stage; bhuvanaiḥ — with the planetary zones; saha — along with.

Translation

As held in check by Me, the contained universe which comprise the creative durations and phases of dissolution of the world, is brought along with its planetary zones, to the stage of becoming merely the five types of material elements. (19.21)

Commentary:

The development of the material elements from a very subtle stage, from the atomic or particle level to the very gross objects, occurs under time schedule. Physicists seem to think that it is controlled by natural laws governing quantum energy. Still, we have to accept that it is regulated by certain forces. Physicists do not figure in anything supernatural but that is due to their inability to detect and categorize the supernatural aspects.

The five types of material elements exist in various dimensions. It is not just the physical world which has these factors. They are there on the atomic or particle level in this dimension and in others.

अन्ने प्रलीयते मर्त्यम्
अन्नं धानासु लीयते ।
धाना भूमौ प्रलीयन्ते
भूमिर् गन्धे प्रलीयते ॥ १९.२२ ॥

anne pralīyate martyam
annaṁ dhānāsu līyate
dhānā bhūmau pralīyante
bhūmir gandhe pralīyate (19.22)

anne — in food; pralīyate — is converted; martyam — the short-term bodily existence; annam — food; dhānāsu — in the seeds; līyate — is converted; dhānā = dhānāḥ — seeds; bhūmau — in the soil; pralīyante — are turned into; bhūmir = bhūmiḥ — the soil; gandhe — into gas; pralīyate — is turned into.

Translation

The short term bodily existence is converted into food. The food is converted into seeds. The seeds are turned into soil which is turned into gas. (19.22)

Commentary:

Eventually the material bodies are converted into soil, which in turn is converted into seed, which in turn are converted into soil which is ultimately converted into odor or gas. We have to understand that there will come a time, when we will not be able to utilize the material world any longer.

This may be understood by the epochal disasters, such as the extinction of the dinosaurs, a history which the anthropologists described. Those creatures were all converted into soil, once and for all. Their bodies were used by plants and other creatures as food. In the process some of the bodies just rooted away as odor. Ultimately the gross material elements are converted into a smoky gas which the ancient sages categorized as *gandha*.

अप्सु प्रलीयते गन्ध
आपश् च स्व-गुणे रसे ।
लीयते ज्योतिषि रसो
ज्योती रूपे प्रलीयते ॥ १९.२३ ॥

apsu pralīyate gandha
āpaś ca sva-guṇe rase
līyate jyotiṣi raso
jyotī rūpe pralīyate (19.23)

apsu — in liquid; pralīyate — is converted; gandha — odor, gas; āpaś = āpaḥ — liquid; ca — and; sva-guṇe — its own characteristic; rase — in flavor; līyate — is converted; jyotiṣi — in fire; raso = rasaḥ — flavor; jyotī = jyotiḥ — fire; rūpe — in shape; pralīyate — turns into.

Translation

Gas is converted into liquid. Liquid is turned into its own characteristic flavor, which is converted into fire, which turns into shape. (19.23)

Commentary:

Odor, smoke or vapor is converted into a liquid which turns into a concentrate which has a particular flavor. The concentrate eventually becomes flammable because of its absorption of combustive chemicals. Under particular circumstances, a flammable liquid exhibits spontaneous combustion, which assumes a certain shape.

रूपं वायौ स च स्पर्शे
लीयते सो ऽपि चाम्बरे ।
अम्बरं शब्द-तन्-मात्र
इन्द्रियाणि स्व-योनिषु ॥ १९.२४ ॥

rūpaṁ vāyau sa ca sparśe
līyate so 'pi cāmbare
ambaraṁ śabda-tan-mātra
indriyāṇi sva-yoniṣu (19.24)

rūpam — shape; vāyau — into air; sa = sah — it; ca — and; sparśe — in contact; līyate — turns into; so = sah — it; 'pi = api — also; cāmbare = ca — and + ambare — in space; ambaram — space; śabda — sound; tan-mātra = tan-mātre — in its subtle aspect; indriyāni — sensual energies; sva-yoniṣu — their own sources.

Translation

Shape is converted into air, which turns into contact, which converts into space. This space is converted into the subtle aspect of sound. The sensual energies revert to their own sources. (19.24)

Commentary:

When a liquid is burnt, it is converted into air, which in turn is converted into the sense of contact, which converts into space. The space changes into the subtle aspect of sound, which is a vibration heard on the natural and supernatural levels. That break down of the gross elements causes the sensual energies to revert to their sources.

योनिर् वैकारिके सौम्य
लीयते मनसीश्वरे ।
शब्दो भूतादिम् अप्येति
भूतादिर् महति प्रभुः ॥ १९.२५ ॥

yonir vaikārike saumya
līyate manasīśvare
śabdo bhūtādim apyeti
bhūtādir mahati prabhuḥ (19.25)

yonir = yoniḥ — the sensual sources; vaikārike — in the perceptive assertive sense; saumya — my friend; līyate — is converted; manasīśvare = manasi — in the mind + īśvare — in the regulator;

śabdo = śabdaḥ — sound; bhūtādim = bhuta – mundane sensation + ādim — to the first; apyeti — reverted; bhūtādir = bhūtādiḥ = bhuta – mundane sensitivity + ādiḥ — the first; mahati — in the Primal Mundane Potency; prabhuḥ — director.

Translation

Into the perceptive assertive sense, the sensual sources are reverted as these enter into their regulator, the mind. Sound is reverted into the first mundane sensitivity. That is reverted into the directive primal mundane potency. (19.25)

Commentary:

The mechanism of the mind, consists of the senses, the general mind field and the intellect. These are retrogressed one into the other, beginning with the senses which are retracted into the intellect and the intellect which is phased out along with its general compartment, the mind. To phase these out they have to be retracted into the assertive sense, the feeling of, *I exist to relate to mundane potencies.* Sound or vibration which is the last manifested foothold of the material nature, is reverted into the first mundane sensibility which is called mento-emotional energy (*prāṇa, citta).* This *potency* is converted into the subtle form of itself, which is the *mahat tattva*, the primal mundane potency.

स लीयते महान् स्वेषु
गुणेसु गुण-वत्तमः ।
ते ऽव्यक्ते सम्प्रलीयन्ते
तत् काले लीयते ऽव्यये ॥१९.२६॥

sa līyate mahān sveṣu
guṇesu guṇa-vattamaḥ
te 'vyakte sampralīyante
tat kāle līyate 'vyaye (19.26)

sa = sah — that; līyate — reverted; mahān — primal mundane potency; sveṣu — in its own; guṇeṣu — in the mundane potencies; guṇa – characteristic; vattamaḥ — endowed with the best; te — these; 'vyakte = avyakte — in the unmanifested mundane energy; sampralīyante — are reverted; tat — that, which; kāle — in the time energy; līyate — reverts; 'vyaye = avyaye — in the unchangeable energy.

Translation

That total mundane potency reverts into its own best characteristic, which in turn, reverts into the mundane influence, which reverts into the unmanifested mundane potency, which reverts into the time energy, which converts into the unchangeable energy. (19.26)

Commentary:

This process can be seen by a yogi with supernatural vision. That the material world evolved out of an unchangeable energy is amazing. For it seems paradoxical that an unchangeable energy can be changed into being a manifested creation. But all this is possible by supernatural force. A yogin may view this by *prāṇa*-vision.

कालो माया-मये जीवे
जीव आत्मनि मय्य् अजे ।
आत्मा केवल आत्म-स्थो
विकल्पापाय-लक्षणः ॥१९.२७॥

kālo māyā-maye jīve
jīva ātmani mayy aje
ātmā kevala ātma-stho
vikalpāpāya-lakṣaṇaḥ (19.27)

kālo = kālaḥ — time energy; māyā – bewildering mundane potency; maye — in he who motivates potency; jīve — in the specific spirit; jīva — specific spirit; ātmani — in that spirit, in itself; mayy = mayi — in me; aje — in the birthless person; ātmā — self, itself; kevala = kevalaḥ — one who is not influenced by sensing mechanisms; ātma-stho = ātma-sthaḥ — situated in itself; vikalpāpāya = vikalpa — varied creation; apāya — dissolution; lakṣaṇaḥ — one who is indicated.

Translation

Time reverts into the Specific Spirit, who motivates the bewildering potency. That Specific Spirit into his own Self. And He into Me, the birthless person. That Specific Spirit who is not influenced by sensing mechanisms and is self-situated, is the one who is indicated by the varied creation and its dissolution. (19.27)

Commentary:

Śrī Patañjali Maharshi gave a definition of that Specific Spirit as follows:

kleśa karma vipāka āśayaiḥ
aparāmṛṣṭaḥ puruṣaviseṣaḥ īśvaraḥ

The Supreme Lord is that special person who is not affected by troubles, actions, developments or by subconscious motivations. (Yoga-Sūtra 1. 24)

When all is said and done, the limited spirits who do not gain objective awareness, of their spiritual natures before the dissolution occurs, do revert back into the Supreme Being. They remain unified in His supernatural body, until the time for the next creation, when they again are let loose in individual forms.

एवम् अन्वीक्षमाणस्य
कथं वैकल्पिको भ्रमः ।
मनसो हृदि तिष्ठेत
व्योम्नीवार्कोदये तमः ॥ १९.२८॥

evam anvīkṣamāṇasya
kathaṁ vaikalpiko bhramaḥ
manaso hṛdi tiṣṭheta
vyomnīvārkodaye tamaḥ (19.28)

evam — in this way; anvīkṣamānasya — of one who mystically researches the matter; katham — how; vaikalpiko = vaikalpikah — the mundane diversity; bhramaḥ — misconception; manaso = manasaḥ — from the mind; hṛdi — in the center of feelings; tiṣṭheta — can stay; vyomnīvārkodaye = vyomni — in the sky + iva — just as + arka — sun + udaye — of the rising; tamah — darkness.

Translation

How can the misconception which is mundane diversity come from the mind or remain in the seat of a person's feelings if he mystically researches the matter in this way, just as darkness would not remain at the rising of the sun? (19.28)

Commentary:

One remains with the concept of mundane diversity, so long as one has not got the supernatural vision to see this directly. One may understand this intellectually but still, one will be prone to misconceptions. It is by mystic means and mystic means alone, that one can understand this thoroughly. That is the value of higher yoga practice.

एष साङ्ख्य-विधिः प्रोक्तः
सशय-ग्रन्थि-भेदनः ।
प्रतिलोमानुलोमाभ्यां
परावर-दृश मया ॥ १९.२९ ॥

eṣa sāṅkhya-vidhiḥ proktaḥ
saṁśaya-granthi-bhedanaḥ
pratilomānulomābhyāṁ
parāvara-dṛśa mayā (19.29)

eṣa = eṣaḥ — this; sāṅkhya – Saṅkhya mystic analysis; vidhiḥ — method; proktaḥ — method described; saṁśaya — doubt; granthi — tangle; bhedanaḥ — that which dismantles; pratilomānulomābhyāṁ = pratiloma – regression + anulomābhyām — and in progression; parāvara = para — supreme + avara — relative; dṛśā — one who perceives; mayā — by me.

Translation

This method of Sāṅkhya mystic analysis which dismantles the tangle of doubt, was described by Me, the one who perceives it, in terms of its regression and progression. (19.29)

Commentary:

As the Supreme Being, *Śrī* Krishna always has the supernatural vision. But we can attain it by austerities.

CHAPTER 20*

The Unmixed Mundane Energies**

Terri Stokes-Pineda Art

śrī-bhagavān uvāca
guṇānām asammiśrāṇāṁ pumān yena yathā bhavet
tan me puruṣa-varyedam upadhāraya śaṁsataḥ

The Blessed Lord said: In regards to the unmixed mundane energies, by which a person is influenced, hear of that from Me, as I explain it, O best of personalities. (Uddhava Gītā 20.1)

* Śrīmad Bhāgavatam Canto 11, Chapter 25
** Translator's selected chapter title.

श्री-भगवान् उवाच
गुणानाम् असम्मिश्राणां
पुमान् येन यथा भवेत् ।
तन् मे पुरुष-वर्येदम्
उपधारय शसतः ॥२०.१॥

śrī-bhagavān uvāca
guṇānām asammiśrāṇāṁ
pumān yena yathā bhavet
tan me puruṣa-varyedam
upadhāraya śaṁsataḥ (20.1)

śrī-bhagavān – the blessed lord; uvāca — said; guṇānām — in regards to the mundane energies; asammiśrāṇām — in regards to that which is unmixed; pumān — person; yena — by which; yathā — by how; bhavet — becomes; tan = tat — that; me — by me; puruṣa-varyedam = puruṣa-varya — best of the personalities + idam — this; upadhāraya — learn; śaṁsatah — I explain.

Translation

The Blessed Lord said: In regards to the unmixed mundane energies, by which a person is influenced, hear of that from Me, as I explain it, O best of personalities. (20.1)

Commentary:

Śrī Krishna explained the three primary influences of material nature, regarding how they affect the behavior of a human being. This clarification informs us of our mental and emotional condition, so that we can gage which influence motivates us to act at any given circumstances. This was explained to Arjuna in detail.

शमो दमस् तितिक्षेक्षा
तपः सत्यं दया स्मृतिः ।
तुष्टिस् त्यागो ऽस्पृहा श्रद्धा
ह्रीर् दयादिः स्व-निर्वृतिः ॥२०.२॥

śamo damas titikṣekṣā
tapaḥ satyaṁ dayā smṛtiḥ
tuṣṭis tyāgo 'spṛhā śraddhā
hrīr dayādiḥ sva-nirvṛtiḥ (20.2)

śamo = śamaḥ — mental calmness; damas = damaḥ — sense control; titikṣekṣā — patience; tapaḥ — austerity; satyam — realism; dayā — compassion; smṛtiḥ — recollection; tuṣṭis = tuṣṭih — contentment; tyāgo = tyāgaḥ — donation of benefits, generosity in practice; 'spṛhā = aspṛhā — non attachment; śraddhā — faith; hrīr = hrīḥ — shame; dayādiḥ — charity and related actions; sva-nirvṛtiḥ — taking happiness in oneself.

Translation

Mental calmness, sense control, patience, austerity, realism, compassion, recollection, contentment, donation of benefits, non-attachment, faith, shame, charity and related actions, as well as taking happiness in the self; (20.2)

Commentary:

This is the listing of the clarifying or perceptive influence.

काम ईहा मदस् तृष्णा
स्तम्भ आशीर् भिदा सुखम्
मदोत्साहो यशः-प्रीतिर् ।
हास्यं वीर्यं बलोद्यमः ॥२०.३॥

kāma īhā madas tṛṣṇā
stambha āśīr bhidā sukham
madotsāho yaśaḥ-prītir
hāsyaṁ vīryaṁ balodyamaḥ (20.3)

kāma = kāmaḥ — craving; īhā — endeavor; madas = madaḥ — pride; tṛṣṇa — coveteousness; stambha = stambhaḥ — stubbornness; āśīr = āśīḥ — praying for mundane fulfillment; bhidā — prejudice; sukham — sense pleasure; madotsāho = madotsāhaḥ — courage based on pride; yaśaḥ-prītir = yaśaḥ-prītiḥ — love of popularity; hāsyam — making fun of others, ridiculing others; vīryam — displaying heroism; balodyamaḥ = bala-udyamah — being motivated to act by strength or power.

Translation

Craving, endeavor, pride, coveteousness, stubborness, praying for mundane fulfillment, prejudice, sense pleasure, courage based on pride, love of popularity, ridiculing others, heroism and being motivated to act by strength or power, (20.3)

Commentary:

These are the qualities which are sponsored by the motivational energy of material nature.

क्रोधो लोभो ऽनृतं हिंसा
याच्ञा दम्भः क्लमः कलिः ।
शोक-मोहौ विषादार्ती
निद्राशा भीर् अनुद्यमः ॥२०.४॥

krodho lobho 'nṛtaṁ hiṁsā
yācñā dambhaḥ klamaḥ kaliḥ
śoka-mohau viṣādārtī
nidrāśā bhīr anudyamaḥ (20.4)

krodho = krodhaḥ — anger; lobho = lobhaḥ — greed; 'nṛtam = anṛtam — untruth; hiṁsā — cruelty; yācñā — begging; dambhaḥ — hypocrisy; klamaḥ — fatigue; kaliḥ — quarrel; śoka – grief; mohau — and confusion; viṣādārtī = visada – disillusionment + ārtī — and misery; nidrāśā = nidrā — drowsiness + āśā — fantasy; bhīr = bhīḥ — fear; anudyamah — lack of vitality.

Translation

...anger, greed, untruth, cruelty, begging, hyprocricy, fatigue, quarrel, grief, and confusion, disillusionment and misery, drowsiness and fantasy, fear and lack of vitality; (20.4)

Commentary:

These are the manifestations of the influence of the depressive energy.

सत्त्वस्य रजसश् चैतास्
तमसश् चानुपूर्वशः ।
वृत्तयो वर्णित-प्रायाः
सन्निपातम् अथो श‍ृणु ॥२०.५॥

sattvasya rajasaś caitās
tamasaś cānupūrvaśaḥ
vṛttayo varṇita-prāyāḥ
sannipātam atho śṛṇu (20.5)

sattvasya — of the perceptive influence; rajasaś = rajasaḥ — of the motivational influence; caitās = ca — and + etāḥ — these; tamasaś = tamasaḥ — of the depressive force; cānupūrvaśaḥ = ca — and + ānupūrvaśaḥ — in order; vṛttayo = vṛttayaḥ — functions; varṇita — was described; prāyāḥ — generally; sannipātam — combination; atho = athoḥ — now; śṛnu — hear.

Translation

...these are, in order, the perceptive influence, the motivational energy and the depressive force, the functions of which was described in general. Now hear of the combination of these. (20.5)

Commentary:

We have to recognize these influences in our behavior. We must also recognize their various combinations.

सन्निपातस् त्व् अहम् इति
ममेत्य् उद्धव या मतिः ।
व्यवहारः सन्निपातो
मनो-मात्रेन्द्रियासुभिः ॥२०.६॥

sannipātas tv aham iti
mamety uddhava yā matiḥ
vyavahāraḥ sannipāto
mano-mātrendriyāsubhiḥ (20.6)

sannipātas = sannipātaḥ — combination; tv = tu — moreover; aham – I; iti — as though; mamety = mameti = mama – my + iti — as though; uddhava — Uddhava; ya — which; matiḥ — ideas; vyavahāraḥ — social life; sannipāto = sannipātaḥ — combination; mano = manah — by the mind;

mātrendriyāsubhiḥ = mātrā — subtle matter + indriya — sensual energy + asubhiḥ — vital power.

Translation

Moreover, the idea of I and Mine, is based on the influence of a combination of these modes of material nature, O Uddhava. Social life, which is sponsored by the mind, subtle matter, the sensual energy and the vital power, is based on a combination also. (20.6)

Commentary:

More or less, all our involvements are sponsored by material nature. A very small portion is naturally dedicated to spiritual life. Hence the need for a deliberate shift to cultivate spirituality.

धर्मे चार्थे च कामे च
यदासौ परिनिष्ठितः ।
गुणानां सन्निकर्षो ऽयं
श्रद्धा-रति-धनावहः ॥२०.७॥

dharme cārthe ca kāme ca
yadāsau parinișṭhitaḥ
guṇānāṁ sannikarṣo 'yaṁ
śraddhā-rati-dhanāvahaḥ (20.7)

dharme — in righteous duty; cārthe = ca — and + arthe — in financial gain; ca — and; kāme — in sensuous filfillment; ca — and; yadāsau = yadā — when + asau — someone; parinișṭhitaḥ — focused on; gunānām — of the mundane influences; sannikarṣo = sannikarṣaḥ — intermixture, drawing together; 'yaṁ = ayam — this; śraddhā — confidence; rati — enjoyment; dhanāvahaḥ = dhana — wealth + āvahaḥ — that which contributes.

Translation

When someone is focused on righteous duty, financial gain and sensuous fulfillment, this is the result of an intermixing of the mundane influences. These contribute to confidence, wealth and enjoyment accordingly. (20.7)

Commentary:

Śrī Krishna did not gave Arjuna so many details about the admixture of the modes of material nature. Uddhava, a more advanced *kriyā* yogi, was given more information. One has to practice *kriyā* to this extent, so that one is able to understand the admixture of the modes of material nature and their respective influences, otherwise it will be impossible to absorb the energies which would cause salvation.

Righteous duty for all it is, produces confidence in the cultural skills, which in turn causes the person to be arrogant. Even though righteous duty was mandatory for Arjuna and even though it was predestined into his life by the Universal Form, still righteous duty has flaws. Therefore one has to combine it with yoga expertise, for using a detached attitude. This is called *karma* yoga or *dharma* yoga. It is explained in great detail in the *Bhagavad-Gītā*. One cannot safely avoid cultural activity which was assigned by the Universal Form. Somehow by intuition, revelation or instruction, one should perform it. If in doing so, one does not remain detached, one will develop a sense of confidence in *dharma*, or responsible living. That will eventually lead to arrogance, which will cause one's downfall.

Arjuna for instance, became very confident in himself and when his son was killed by warriors he made a vow to kill *Jayadratha* but that was due to an arrogance. Fortunately, *Śrī* Krishna rescued him. *Śrī* Krishna chided Arjuna for making a promise to kill Jayadratha, a vow that Arjuna could not fulfill on his own, even though he made the vow on the basis of self-confidence. Therefore one should be careful not to embrace *dharma* but only to serve it in the most efficient way.

Financial gain brings money, but only by conniving in one way or the other, either in this life or a past one. A man who gets an inheritance gets that on the basis of his unseen work in the past, his unseen history. Nobody gets money easily because material nature does not release herself to anyone without their endeavor to acquire her. In such an exertion, one gives himself over to material nature. That is the flaw. Anytime someone gives himself over to material nature, his release will come only if he exerts himself with just as much power as he invested himself in the first place. No God will be able to extricate him either, for he will have to retract his energies by himself, with God's support aiding him. Ultimately the endeavor for financial gain results in a painful austerity called *pratyāhar* which is the withdrawal of one's sensual power from the realm of material nature.

Sensual fulfillment is caused by the outreaching of the subtle senses which came out of the *buddhi* organ in the head of the subtle body. This sensual outreaching is inhabited by the energy of greed. There is only one thing that can be done with greed in *kriyā* yoga. That is to pull it in and divest it of its powers and its appetite for exploitation. This can only be done by the individual spirit himself. No God, no guru, can do this for the disciple but the guru and God can help by setting an example, by giving advices and by sharing confidences in the long-winded exertion required to complete this. It is for this reason that so many people remain trapped in cheap religions, some of which carry even Lord Krishna's name. It is because they are unable to retract the greedy senses. Hence they follow leaders who tell them that rigid yoga austerities are totally unnecessary.

Whatever we enjoyed through the senses which came out of the *buddhi* organ, will have to be regretted by us, before we can gain salvation. And the regret will have to be a sincere one, so sincere, that we will have to become very repentant and agree to finish out the long-winded austerities in *aşţanga* yoga practice. Those who feel that they can avoid *aşţanga* yoga and follow in the footsteps of the *gopīs* are simply marching steadily on the way to more and more bondage in the material energy but since they do so happily and with great confidence, they do not feel the degradation. They are so naive.

प्रवृत्ति-लक्षणे निष्ठा
पुमान् यर्हि गृहाश्रमे ।
स्व-धर्मे चानु तिष्ठेत
गुणाना समितिर् हि सा ॥२०.८॥

pravṛtti-lakṣaṇe niṣṭhā
pumān yarhi gṛhāśrame
sva-dharme cānu tiṣṭheta
guṇānāṁ samitir hi sā (20.8)

pravṛtti — social well-being; lakṣaṇe — on that which is indicative; niṣṭhā — focused on; pumān — person; yarhi — when; gṛhāśrame — in family affairs; sva-dharme — in the righteous life style; canu = ca — and + anu — after that consequence; tiṣṭheta — he persistently maintains an interest; guṇānām — of the mundane influences; samitir = samitiḥ — admixture; hi — definitely; sā — this.

Translation

When a person is focused on a life which is indicative of social well-being and family affairs, and when consequently he persistently maintains an interest in his righteous duty, this attitude, is definitely due to an admixture of the mundane influences. (20.8)

Commentary:

Here again we see that *dharma* is a regulation for social living. It is not a spiritual gain, even though it may free the individual to pursue spiritual life, if the Universal Form decides to grant him a waiver from such cultural involvement.

पुरुषं सत्त्व-सयुक्तम्
अनुमीयाच् छमादिभिः ।
कामादिभी रजो-युक्तं
क्रोधाद्यैस् तमसा युतम् ॥२०.९॥

puruṣaṁ sattva-saṁyuktam
anumīyāc chamādibhiḥ
kāmādibhī rajo-yuktaṁ
krodhādyais tamasā yutam (20.9)

puruṣam — person; sattva – the perceptive influence; saṁyuktam — unified with; anumīyāc = anumīyāt — should be figured, may be inferred; śama – mental control; adhibhih — and related qualities; kamadhibhih = kāma ādhibhiḥ — craving and other related tendencies; rajo-yuktaṁ = rajah – impulsive energy + yuktam — being possessed by; krodhādyais = krodha – anger + ādyaiḥ — and related dispositions; tamasā — by the depressive energy; yutam — being possessed by.

Translation

By mental calmness and the related qualities a person should be figured as being unified with the perceptive influence. By cravings and related tendencies, one may be inferred as being possessed by the impulsive energy. And by anger and related dispositions, one may be inferred as being possessed by the depressive energy. (20.9)

Commentary:

A person is gauged by his general disposition, even though he may exhibit higher or lower qualities on occasion.

यदा भजति मां भक्त्या
निरपेक्षः स्व-कर्मभिः ।
त सत्त्व-प्रकृतिं विद्यात्
पुरुषं स्त्रियम् एव वा ॥ २०.१० ॥

yadā bhajati māṁ bhaktyā
nirapekṣaḥ sva-karmabhiḥ
taṁ sattva-prakṛtiṁ vidyāt
puruṣaṁ striyam eva vā (20.10)

yadā — when; bhajati — worship; mām — me; bhaktyā — with devotion; nirapekṣaḥ — regardless of benefits; sva-karmabhiḥ — by performance of one's own righteous duty; tam — that person; sattva – clarifying mode; prakṛtim — material nature's influence; vidyāt — should be recognized; puruṣam — person; striyam — woman; eva — definitely; vā — or.

Translation

When one worships Me with devotion, by performance of his or her own righteous duty, regardless of the benefits, that person should definitely be recognized as being in the clarifying mode. (20.10)

Commentary:

Arjuna is the example of a person who worshipped *Śrī* Krishna in this way. This worship is not going to a temple, nor chanting rounds of holy names, necessarily. In Arjuna's case, it was battlefield work.

It is clear that devotion to *Śrī* Krishna is successful when it is used by *Śrī* Krishna to get the devotee to do what *Śrī* Krishna desires of him or her. For devotion to be effective in real terms, *Śrī* Krishna has to get a handle on it, so that He may use it to cause the devotee to attain perfection. That is the sort of devotion that *Kriyā* yoga advocates.

यदा आशिष आशास्य
मां भजेत स्व-कर्मभिः ।
त रजः-प्रकृतिं विद्यात्
हिसाम् आशास्य तामसम् ॥ २०.११ ॥

yadā āśiṣa āśāsya
māṁ bhajeta sva-karmabhiḥ
taṁ rajaḥ-prakṛtiṁ vidyāt
hiṁsām āśāsya tāmasam (20.11)

yadā — when; āśiṣa = āśisaḥ — favors; āśāsya — prompted by a need; mām — me; bhajeta — worships; sva-karmabhiḥ — his or her cultural activities; tam — that person; rajah – impulsive energy; prakṛtim — material nature; vidyāt — should be recognised; hiṁsām — injury to others; āśāsya — prompted by a need; tāmasam — of the depressive energy.

Translation

When one worships Me by righteous duty, as prompted by a need for favors, that person should be recognized as being under the impulsive influence. A devotee who is prompted by a need for injuring others, is possessed by the depressive force. (20.11)

Commentary:

Each devotee has to analyze for himself and upgrade the motives. It is all due to the varying energies of material nature. Thus if the devotee recognizes what force dominated him, he can, by taking help from *Śrī* Krishna and from more advanced devotees, elevate himself so that he can worship *Śrī* Krishna from a higher motive. Of course, in all cases of such worship, the devotee should surrender to *Śrī* Krishna's desire. The devotion to Krishna has to be given to *Śrī* Krishna in such a way, that Krishna can use it to cause the devotee to make spiritual advancement in the long run.

A person who offers his devotion to *Śrī* Krishna, but who by nature needs favors, will be reluctant to allow *Śrī* Krishna to control the situation. One who offers devotion and who has a need to injure others, will be even more reluctant and will want to get *Śrī* Krishna's sanction and assistance in the venture for cruelties.

Success with devotion depends on the level of purity of the devotee. It does not improve automatically without endeavor, except superficially. It is totally misleading to think or to have someone convince you that your devotion will improve merely because you applied it to Lord Krishna, for unless you respond to Him with improvement, you will remain stagnant or even regress into even worse behavior.

सत्त्वं रजस् तम इति
गुणा जीवस्य नैव मे ।
चित्त-जा यैस् तु भूतानां
सज्जमानो निबध्यते ॥२०.१२॥

sattvaṁ rajas tama iti
guṇā jīvasya naiva me
citta-jā yais tu bhūtānāṁ
sajjamāno nibadhyate (20.12)

sattvam — the clarifying energy; rajas = rajah — the impulsive force; tama = tamah — the retardative power; iti — as stated; guṇā = guṇāh — the mundane influences; jīvasya — concerning the individual spirit; naiva = na — not + eva — indeed; me — to me; citta – in the mental and emotional energy; jā = jāh — occurring within, manifesting; yais = yaiḥ — by which, by these same energies; tu — but; bhūtānām — the mundane creations; sajjamāno = sajjamānah — becomes attached; nibadhyate — is captivated.

Translation

The clarifying energy, the impulsive force, and the retardative power, as stated, are the mundane influences which concern the individual spirit but they do not apply to Me. These are the energies manifesting as mental power and emotions in his mind, by which he becomes attached to the mundane creations and is captivated. (20.12)

Commentary:

This type of categorization of the living entity, made by Lord Krishna, who exempts Himself, shows clearly the need for yoga practice as the definite way to curb the mental and emotional energy in the mind. So long as the material nature comprises the energy of our ideas and feelings, we will be under its sway. Sentimental devotion will not help us to conquer this. We should practice austerities for mind and ideation control and to change out the energy in the mind, so that the ideas formed there, originate in a higher energy.

यदेतरौ जयेत् सत्त्वं
भास्वरं विशदं शिवम् ।
तदा सुखेन युज्येत
धर्म-ज्ञानादिभिः पुमान् ॥२०.१३॥

yadetarau jayet sattvaṁ
bhāsvaraṁ viśadaṁ śivam
tadā sukhena yujyeta
dharma-jñānādibhiḥ pumān (20.13)

yadetarau = yadā — when + itarau — the other two; jayet — prevails over; sattvam — the clarifying energy; bhāsvaraṁ — bright; viśadam — pure; śivam — serene; tadā — then; sukhena —

with happiness; yujyeta — is endowed; dharma — virtue; jñānādibhiḥ — knowledge and other related qualities; pumān — person.

Translation

When the clarifying energy, which is bright, pure and serene, prevails over the other two influences, then a person is endowed with happiness, virtue, knowledge and its related qualities. (20.13)

Commentary:

Even though so many spiritual masters hawk about transcendental energy, the fact remains that a living entity has to work his way up gradually from a lower to higher mode. We will first have to rely heavily on the clarifying mode, the perception-yielding energy of material nature for some time, before we can cross to the supernatural level. And for that matter we will have to stay on that level for a time, before finally we can get to the spiritual plane. No amount of great expectations, hoping, praying, chanting or assuring can change this.

One must first become adapted to this bright, pure and serene level of the material energy before he can move further up. No spiritual master with his assurances and high sounding words can adjust this. One has to work his way up through the modes of material nature and exert as much personal endeavor as would be required in his own individual case. Otherwise his religious aspiration will remain something dreamed of by him and his guru.

All along in this discourse, Uddhava kept asking for any easy method for the common people, and this is what he got from *Śrī* Krishna. But others in these modern times, are telling us that some other incarnation came with a really easy method that pushes aside all these statements of Lord Krishna as being out of date and unnecessarily at this time. Spiritual life and its attainment have not changed since the time of Lord Krishna, neither have the methods of attainment. Thus it is our false hopes which have caused us to believe in the methods which depreciate what Krishna presents here.

यदा जयेत् तमः सत्त्वं
रजः सङ्गं भिदा चलम् ।
तदा दुःखेन युज्येत
कर्मणा यशसा श्रिया ॥२०.१४॥

yadā jayet tamaḥ sattvaṁ
rajaḥ saṅgaṁ bhidā calam
tadā duḥkhena yujyeta
karmaṇā yaśasā śriyā (20.14)

yadā — when; jayet — prevails over; tamaḥ - depressive energy; sattvam — perceptive energy; rajaḥ — motivational force; saṅgam — attachment; bhidā — prejudices; calam — unstable mental focus; tadā — then; duhkhena — with misery; yujyeta — is possessed; karmaṇā — with cultural activity; yaśasā — with popularity; śriyā — with prosperity.

Translation

When the impulsive force, which fosters attachment, prejudices and unstable mental focus, prevails over the depressive energy and the perceptive power, then one is possessed with misery, cultural activity, popularity and prosperity. (20.14)

Commentary:

This is true even if one is a devotee and even if one's activities are done for and in a spiritual society of repute. Material nature does not regard one's religious affiliation. It penetrates anything anywhere. One must be aware of its influences and not gloss oneself over with false views and imaginary assurances, even if these are given out by a spiritual master of repute.

Would this impulsive energy foster attachment to *Śrī* Krishna? Yes, it certainly would. And then the devotee might think that his devotion is pure and that it is enthusiastic and firm, while in fact, it is functioning under the impulsive force, and is not being accepted by *Śrī* Krishna as a divine sentiment.

The impulsive energy can use an unstable focus, the very type of mental demeanor it uses to focus on *Śrī* Krishna's pastimes in one aspect now, and then in another aspect a second later, but that does not mean that such a devotee is a pure devotee or even a mediocre devotee. It certainly does not mean that this devotee is accepted by *Śrī* Krishna.

यदा जयेद् रजः सत्त्वं
तमो मूढं लय जडम् ।
युज्येत शोक-मोहाभ्यां
निद्रया हिंसयाशया ॥२०.१५॥

yadā jayed rajaḥ sattvaṁ
tamo mūḍhaṁ layaṁ jaḍam
yujyeta śoka-mohābhyāṁ
nidrayā hiṁsayāśayā (20.15)

yadā — when; jayed = jayet — prevails over; rajaḥ - impulsion; sattvam — perceptive energy; tamo = tamaḥ — depressive mental force; mūḍham — infatuation; layam — lack of objectivity, unconsciousness; jaḍam — stupidity; yujyeta — is possessed; śoka — grief; mohābhyām — and with bewilderment; nidrayā — with sleep; hiṁsayāśayā = hiṁsayā — cruelty; āśayā — with false expectation.

Translation

When the depressive mental force which is characterized by infatuation, unconsciousness and stupidity, prevails over impulsion and clarity, then one is possessed by grief, bewilderment, sleep, cruelty and false expectation. (20.15)

Commentary:

Each of these influences are studied in the higher yoga practice. There, one gets an intimate understanding of the nature of consciousness. This is perfected in the 7th and 8th stages of yoga. Without understanding this, knowing the mechanisms of one's consciousness, one cannot live in the sky of consciousness which is beyond this dimension. One cannot just go to the spiritual world, just because one is devoted to *Śrī* Krishna in some way or the other, but rather if Krishna approves of the quality of devotion and arranges for one to experience the various grades of consciousness objectively. He must arrange for one to be taught how to recognize them and avoid those levels which deter spiritual progression.

यदा चित्तं प्रसीदेत
इन्द्रियाणां च निर्वृतिः ।
देहे ऽभयं मनो-ऽसङ्गं
तत् सत्त्वं विद्धि मत्-पदम् ॥२०.१६॥

yadā cittaṁ prasīdeta
indriyāṇāṁ ca nirvṛtiḥ
dehe 'bhayaṁ mano-'saṅgaṁ
tat sattvaṁ viddhi mat-padam (20.16)

yadā — when; cittam — mental and emotional energy; prasīdeta — becomes serene; indriyāṇām — of the sensual energy; ca — and; nirvṛtiḥ — non-excitation; dehe — in the body; 'bhayaṁ = abhayam — fearlessness; mano = manah — of the mind; 'saṅgaṁ = asaṅgam — detachment; tat — that; sattvam — perceptive influence; viddhi — know; mat-padam — of my status.

Translation

When the mental and emotional energy becomes serene and there is a suspension of sensual excitation, when there is fearlessness in the body and detachment of mind, know that to be the clarifying influence which is My situation. (20.16)

Commentary:

This is a description of what *Śrī Patañjali* Muni called *samyama* which is the 7th and 8th stages of yoga. This is experienced after the mastery of *prāṇāyāma, pratyāhar* and *dhāraṇā* practice, which causes one to be in the states of *dhyāna* and *samādhi*. This can be experienced haphazardly from time to time but if one is to experience it definitely, one has to practice higher yoga. By this, one enters into the sky of consciousness. That is the situation of *Śrī* Krishna *(mat-padam).*

At first one hears a sound which leaks into one's mind space from the sky of consciousness. But after much practice the density of one's mind space is dissipated and one sees into the chit *ākāśa*, the sky of consciousness. This does not happen if the mental and emotional energy does not become serene *(prasīdeta)* by a complete suspension of all the sensual excitations in respect to everything on this side of existence. The *kriyā* technique for the leakage of the spiritual sound was given to Uddhava in this discourse.

hṛdy avicchinam oṁkāraṁ ghaṇṭā-nādaṁ bisorṇa-vat
prāṇenodīrya tatrātha punaḥ saṁveśayet svaram
evaṁ praṇava-saṁyuktaṁ prāṇam eva samabhyaset
daśa-kṛtvas tri-ṣavaṇaṁ māsād arvāg jitānilaḥ

In the heart chakra, the Om sound which is like the continuous peal of a bell, resonates continually, like a fibre in a lotus stalk. Raising it by using the vitalizing energy, one should blend that sound with the musical tones.

Thus, one should carefully direct the pre-mixed Om sound and the vitalizing energy, ten times, thrice per day. (U.G. 9.34-35)

विकुर्वन् क्रियया चा-धीर्
अनिवृत्तिश् च चेतसाम् ।
गात्रास्वास्थ्यं मनो भ्रान्तं
रज एतैर् निशामय ॥२०.१७॥

vikurvan kriyayā cā-dhīr
anivṛttiś ca cetasām
gātrāsvāsthyaṁ mano bhrāntaṁ
raja etair niśāmaya (20.17)

vikurvan — being over-occupied; kriyayā — by working; cā-dhīr = ca — and + ā — up to including + dhīḥ — intellect; anivṛttiś = anivṛttiḥ — that which is super active, restless; ca — and; cetasām — energies of consciousness; gātrāsvāsthyaṁ = gātra — organs of action + asvāsthyam — in a frenzy; mano = manaḥ — the mind; bhrāntam — wandering about; raja = rajah — the influence of impulsion; etair = etaiḥ — by these; niśāmaya — know.

Translation

When one is over-occupied by working, with the energies of consciousness including the intellect being restless, with the organs of action in a frenzy and the mind wandering about, know this as the influence of impulsion. (20.17)

Commentary:

This is the common state of a human being. Even devotional activities which are performed in this world in this way are mostly conducted and used by the mode of passion, the impulsive motivational force of material nature. We have to understand, we must accept, that these modes can use the devotional energies which we direct to *Śrī* Krishna.

In fact, being in any of these modes, except for the higher aspects of the perceptive one, we are force to relate to *Śrī* Krishna on this side of existence. That would mean that we relate to His idol form in the temple or at the home where it is properly installed. Or we offer our services to a teacher who claims to be His representative. But it is not an offering to *Śrī* Krishna on the spiritual side of existence. It is being conducted by and through the material energy.

In the case of conducting our devotions through the higher aspect of the perceptive mode, *sattva guṇa*, we may do so effectively reaching *Śrī* Krishna on the spiritual side, if we conduct our consciousness out of this dimension into the sky of consciousness. And that is done in the 6th, 7th and 8th stages of yoga practice.

सीदच् चित्तं विलीयेत
चेतसो ग्रहणे ऽक्षमम् ।
मनो नष्टं तमो ग्लानिस्
तमस् तद् उपधारय ॥२०.१८॥

sīdac cittaṁ vilīyeta
cetaso grahaṇe 'kṣamam
mano naṣṭaṁ tamo glānis
tamas tad upadhāraya (20.18)

sīdac = sīdat — lethargic, cloudy; cittam — mental and emotional energy; vilīyeta — unable to be objective; cetaso = cetasah — energies of consciousness; grahane — in being utilised; 'kṣamam = aksamam — incapable; mano = manah — mind; naṣṭam — spaced out; tamo = tamaḥ — depressive energy; glānis = glāniḥ — mental exhaustion; tamas = tamaḥ — depressive energy; tad = tat — that; upadhāraya — know.

Translation

When the lethargic mental and emotional energy is unable to be objective, when the sensual energy is incapable of being utilized, when the mind is spaced out, when there is depression and mental exhaustion, know these as symptoms of the depressive mode. (20.18)

Commentary:

We should recognize these states in our minds as well as in others.

एधमाने गुणे सत्त्वे
देवानां बलम् एधते ।
असुराणां च रजसि
तमस्य् उद्धव रक्षसाम् ॥२०.१९॥

edhamāne guṇe sattve
devānāṁ balam edhate
asurāṇāṁ ca rajasi
tamasy uddhava rakṣasām (20.19)

edhamāne — in the increasing; guṇe — in the influence; sattve — in clarity of consciousness; devānām — of the supernatural rulers; balam — strength; edhate — expands; asurāṇām — of the rivals of the supernatural rulers; ca — and; rajasi — in the impulsive influence; tamasy = tamasi — in the retardative force; uddhava — Uddhava; rakṣasām — of the cannibalisitic humans.

Translation

In the increase of the clarifying influence, the strength of the supernatural rulers expands. In the increase of the impulsive influence, that of their rivals expands. And when, O Uddhava, there is an increase in the retardative influence the power of the cannibalistic humans increase. (20.19)

Commentary:

When human beings take energy from the clarifying influence, their psychic perception of the angelic world increases. Subsequently they become more submissive to the supernatural rulers. Alternately when the impulsive influence increases, then the rivals of the angelic people hold sway. But when the retardative power spreads, the criminals and other undesireable association prevail.

सत्त्वाज् जागरणं विद्याद्
रजसा स्वप्नम् आदिशेत् ।
प्रस्वापं तमसा जन्तोस्
तुरीयं त्रिषु सन्ततम् ॥२०.२०॥

sattvāj jāgaraṇaṁ vidyād
rajasā svapnam ādiśet
prasvāpaṁ tamasā jantos
turīyaṁ triṣu santatam (20.20)

sattvāj = sattvāt — from clarity; jāgaraṇam — alertness; vidyāt — know; rajasā — by impulsion; svapnam — dream; ādiśet — is indicated; prasvāpam — deep sleep; tamasā — by the retardative influence; jantos = jantoḥ — of the creature; turīyam — the fourth state of consciousness; triṣu — through the three mundane influences; santatam — continually present.

Translation

Know that from clarity, alertness results; by dream, impulsion is indicated; by the retardative influence, the sleep of the creatures prevail. The fourth state of consciousness is continually present along with the three mundane influences. (20.20)

Commentary:

There is a fourth state of consciousness which is indicated here and which exists side by side with the three states which we are familiar with. This is in another dimension. One attains it by doing the higher yoga and piercing into the sky of consciousness.

उपर्य् उपरि गच्छन्ति
सत्त्वेन ब्राह्मणा जनाः ।
तमसाधो ऽध आ-मुख्याद्
रजसान्तर-चारिणः ॥२०.२१॥

upary upari gacchanti
sattvena brāhmaṇā janāḥ
tamasādho 'dha ā-mukhyād
rajasāntara-cāriṇaḥ (20.21)

upary upari = upari upari — higher and higher; gacchanti — become elevated; sattvena — through the clarifying influence; brāhmaṇā = brāhmaṇāḥ — those dedicated to Vedic principles; janāḥ — people; tamasādho 'dha = tamasā — through the retardative mode + adhah adhah — lower and lower; ā-mukhyād = ā – from + mukhyāt — from the head; rajasāntara-cāriṇaḥ = rajasā — through the impulsive force + antara-cāriṇaḥ — one who transmigrates in-between.

Translation

Those dedicated to the Vedic principles, become elevated higher and higher through the clarifying energy. But through the retardative mode one moves head first, lower and lower. Through the impulsive force, one transmigrates in-between the two. (20.21)

Commentary:

These are the methods of elevation, degradation or remaining in the earthly transmigrations.

सत्त्वे प्रलीनाः स्वर् यान्ति
नर-लोकं रजो-लयाः ।
तमो-लयास् तु निरयं
यान्ति माम् एव निर्गुणाः ॥२०.२२॥

sattve pralīnāḥ svar yānti
nara-lokaṁ rajo-layāḥ
tamo-layās tu nirayaṁ
yānti mām eva nirguṇāḥ (20.22)

sattva — in the clarifying influence; pralīnāḥ — those whose bodies are destroyed; svar = svah — to the angelic world; yānti — go; nara-lokam — to the human world; rajo-layāḥ — those who pass on in the impulsive mode; tamo-layās = tamo-layāḥ — those who pass on in the retardative influence; tu — but; nirayam — hellish places; yānti — go; mām — to me; eva — however; nirgunāḥ — those who transcend the influence of material nature.

Translation

Those whose bodies are destroyed while they are in the clarifying influence, go to the angelic world. Those whose forms pass on while in the impulsive mode, go to the human world. Those who pass on from the depressive retardative influence, go to hellish places. But those who transcend the subtle influences of material nature go to Me. (20.22)

Commentary:

Most human beings come back into this world at the time of death. They remain in the subtle presence of their relatives and friends. Then gradually they are absorbed into or amalgamated into the emotional feelings of a dear one, who becomes the parent. By sexual intercourse, their emotional make-up is transferred into the would-be mother. And then they develop a baby form in her womb. This is conducted automatically by the subtle material nature, which is very sensitive to the presence of the spirits.

A few human beings who develop the clarifying influence, go to the angelic world. Those who feed on the retardative influence, go to a hellish destination either in the hereafter or by taking birth in the animal and vegetable kingdoms.

Only one or two human beings transcend all three modes of material nature. This is done by the practice of higher yoga, to get the spirit to focus into the sky of consciousness, before the time of death. If one does this, he would go to a spiritual world.

मद्-अर्पण निष्फलं वा
सात्त्विकं निज-कर्म तत् ।
राजसं फल-सङ्कल्पं
हिंसा-प्रायादि तामसम् ॥२०.२३॥

mad-arpaṇaṁ niṣphalaṁ vā
sāttvikaṁ nija-karma tat
rājasaṁ phala-saṅkalpaṁ
hiṁsā-prāyādi tāmasam (20.23)

mad-arpanam = mat-arpanam — offerings to satisfy me; nisphalam — with desire for benefits; vā — or; sāttvikam — consisting of the clarifying energy; nija — one's own; karma — cultural activities; tat — that which; rājasam — consisting of the impulsive force; phala – benefits; saṅkalpam — intentions; himsā – cruelty; prāyādi = prāya – as a rule, more than likely + ādi — and related demeanors; tāmasam — consisting of the retardative mode.

Translation

One's own cultural activities which are done to satisfy Me or done without a desire for benefits, consists of the clarifying energy. That which is done with intentions for a benefit consists of the impulsive force. That which is done with cruelty and related attitudes, does consist, more than likely, of the retardative energy. (20.23)

Commentary:

The concept that religious work done for *Śrī* Krishna is a transcendental form of work, and that ordinary work done for Him is in the clarifying mode of material nature, is questionable, because it would depend on the level of the person who does the religious work. Actually there is no such thing as ordinary work done for *Śrī* Krishna, because whatever is done for Him in fact, must be sanctioned by the Universal Form before it is accepted by Him. As soon as the performer gets the divine approval, those activities, even if they appear to be ordinary, fall into a devotional category. But that does not mean that all such devotional work is free from the modes of material nature.

Arjuna for instance, did battlefield work, which involved cruelty to others, and still that work was identified by *Śrī* Krishna as being sanctioned by the Universal Form, as *karma* yoga. But that was not done on the basis of spiritual energy but on the basis of cultural involvements in this world, which are supervised by the Universal Form, for the sake of *dharma* or righteous living.

Any work which is based on the clarifying energy of material nature, is just what it is, even if it is done under the direct guidance of *Śrī* Krishna. A religious-over-coating or devotional labeling does not change anything.

Similarly, if one works for Krishna but has a reward-seeking attitude, still even though the work was done that He assigned, one's reward-seeking demeanor will cause the work to be evaluated only as something based on impulsion. This is why Lord *Balarāma* was offended when Bhima broke the legs of Duryodhana, even though Bhima was advised by *Śrī* Krishna to do so. It was because Bhima was in the passionate mode when he followed that instruction. There were some incidences on the battlefield of *Kurukṣetra* where Arjuna was taken over by impulsion and wanted to get a specific result from his battle performance. Also initially, before he was lectured on the *Bhagavad-Gītā*, that was the mentality of Arjuna.

Śrī Krishna mentioned the Sanskrit term *prāya* which means as a rule or more than likely. This is because some cruel activities might not be in the depressive mode. We all know that Arjuna had to do some cruel things at *Kurukṣetra* but these activities, being done on-behalf of the Universal Form, were not in the depressive nor impulsive mode but in the clarifying influence, at least in so far as the cosmic mind of the Universal Form was concerned.

कैवल्यं सात्त्विकं ज्ञानं
रजो वैकल्पिकं च यत् ।
प्राकृतं तामसं ज्ञानं
मन्-निष्ठं निर्गुणं स्मृतम् ॥२०.२४॥

kaivalyaṁ sāttvikaṁ jñānaṁ
rajo vaikalpikaṁ ca yat
prākṛtaṁ tāmasaṁ jñānaṁ
man-niṣṭhaṁ nirguṇaṁ smṛtam (20.24)

kaivalyam — state of being isolated from subtle mundane influences; sāttvikam — that which is promoted by the clarifying energy; jñānam — knowledge; rajo = rajah — concerning the impulsive force; vaikalpikam — varied mundane world; ca — and; yat — which; prākṛtam — that which is the very basic or and ordinary; tāmasam — concerning the retardative mode; jñānam — knowledge; man-niṣṭham = mat-niṣṭham — focused on me; nirguṇam — that which transcends the mundane influence; smṛtam — is considered.

Translation

Knowledge relating to the spirit in isolation from the subtle mundane influences is promoted by the clarifying energy. Knowledge of the varied mundane world is promoted by the impulsive force. Knowledge which is very basic and ordinary is promoted by the retardative energy. But knowledge relating to Me is considered to be transcendental to the mundane influences. (20.24)

Commentary:

Kaivalyam means that a spirit experiences itself without its intellectual and vital force sheathing. When this is experienced, the spirit is said to be isolated from or is alone without its psyche. This is *kevala* or *kaivalyam*. According to *Śrī Patañjali*, one must first experience the spirit itself without its psyche and then after advancing further to purify the psyche, one can again be linked with it in its pure state and not fall under the subtle prejudices which come from an impure intellect and life force.

Information about the varied mundane world is promoted by the impulsive motivational force in material nature, which sponsors and enlarges the multiplicity of objects in this world.

Whatever is outside of the material energy is called *nirguṇah*. Even the spirits are *nirguṇah* when they are totally detached from the mundane involvements and when their intellects are fully detached as well and do not retain prejudices.

We heard initially that there was the *Puruṣa* or the Supreme Being who was not in the material energy but was in proximity to it. That Supreme Being is the Supreme Person and the limited beings combined. These can only be understood by completely transcending the material energy. And that cannot be done without higher yoga. It is not done just by receiving knowledge from *Śrī* Krishna nor from His representative in the disciplic succession. Arjuna, even in the presence of *Śrī* Krishna, could not understand it, until the four-handed divine form was revealed to him.

वन तु सात्त्विको वासो
ग्रामो राजस उच्यते ।
तामस द्यूत-सदनं
मन्-निकेतं तु निर्गुणम् ॥२०.२५॥

vanaṁ tu sāttviko vāso
grāmo rājasa ucyate
tāmasaṁ dyūta-sadanaṁ
man-niketaṁ tu nirguṇam (20.25)

vanam — forest; tu — but; sāttviko = sāttvikah — concerning the clarifying energy; vāso = vāsaḥ — residence; grāmo = grāmaḥ — town; rājasa = rājasaḥ — concerning the impulsive energy; ucyate — it is regarded; tāmasam — concerning the retardative mode; dyūta – gambling; sadanam — place; man = mat – my; niketam — residence; tu — but, and; nirguṇam — that which transcends the mundane influences.

Translation

But the forest as a residence is regarded as being in the clarifying mode; the town is in the impulsive mode; the place for gambling is in the retardative mode; and My residence transcend the mundane influences. (20.25)

Commentary:

This particular verse has to do with certain relative considerations. The forest for instance is a place of the retardative energy, for those who use it for hunting animals. However for a spiritually-aspiring ascetic like the Avanti brahmin it is in the clarifying mode, since he could use it for the isolation required to complete yoga practice.

For human beings, cities and towns are of the impulsive energy, since these locations keep them busy in cultural activities. The place of gambling is obviously in the retardative mode.

Śrī Krishna listed his residence as being transcendental to the mundane influence. At the time of His speaking to Uddhava He departed from His physical residence. That place could not be transcendental to material nature, otherwise it would not have been destroyed just as any other part of the material energy. His actual residence is in the spiritual sky. It is not a location in this material world, because whatever can be destroyed here is under the laws of material nature.

सात्त्विकः कारको ऽसङ्गी
रागान्धो राजसः स्मृतः ।
तामसः स्मृति-विभ्रष्टो
निर्गुणो मद्-अपाश्रयः ॥२०.२६॥

sāttvikaḥ kārako 'saṅgī
rāgāndho rājasaḥ smṛtaḥ
tāmasaḥ smṛti-vibhraṣṭo
nirguṇo mad-apāśrayaḥ (20.26)

sāttvikah — concerning the clarifying energy; kārako = kārakaḥ — one who functions; 'saṅgī = asaṅgī — one who is consistently free from attachment; rāgāndho = rāga – attachment + andhah — one who is blinded; rājasah — concerning the impulsive energy; smṛtaḥ — is regarded; tāmasaḥ — concerning the depressive force; smṛti-vibhraṣṭo = smṛti — sense of conscience + vibhraṣṭaḥ — lost; nirguṇo = nirguṇaḥ — that which transcends the mundane influence; mad-apāśrayaḥ = mat-apāśrayaḥ — one who relies on me.

Translation

One who functions in a manner which is consistently free from attachment is regarded as being in the clarifying energy. One who is blinded by attachment is regarded as being in the impulsive energy. One who has lost the sense of conscience is in the depressive energy. And one who relies on Me transcends the mundane influences. (20.26)

Commentary:

By reaching a stage of behavior whereby one consistently functions in freedom from attachment, one moves permanently into the clarifying energy. Persons who are usually blinded by attachment, are predominantly in the impulsive force. Those who have lost their sense of conscience or who did not seem to have one in the first place, are possessed by the depressive mental force.

However a person who relies completely on *Śrī* Krishna at all times, has transcended the mundane influence. One who relies part-time, moves into the transcendence periodically. Arjuna for instant did not rely on *Śrī* Krishna initially in the *Bhagavad-Gītā*, when he first began to complain about disagreeable duties at *Kurukṣetra*. After he was shown the Universal Form, he became completely reliant on the Lord. Later however, in Arjuna's life, from time to time, he found himself out of that reliance. But in the end he regained it.

सात्त्विक्य् आध्यात्मिकी श्रद्धा
कर्म-श्रद्धा तु राजसी ।
तामस्य् अधर्मे या श्रद्धा
मत्-सेवायां तु निर्गुणा ॥२०.२७॥

sāttviky ādhyātmikī śraddhā
karma-śraddhā tu rājasī
tāmasy adharme yā śraddhā
mat-sevāyāṁ tu nirguṇā (20.27)

sāttviky = sāttvikī — in the clarifying energy; ādhyātmikī — in the supreme spirit; śraddhā — faith; karma — cultural activities; śraddhā — faith; tu — but; rājasī — in the impulsive energy; tāmasy = tāmasī — of the depressive force; adharme — in irreligious activities; yā — which; śraddhā — confidence; mat-sevāyām — my service and worship; tu — however; nirguṇā — that which transcends the mundane influence.

Translation

Faith in the Supreme Spirit is in the clarifying mode. But faith in cultural activities is in the impulsive mode; while faith in the irreligious acts is of the depressive energy. However faith in My service and worship transcends the mundane influence. (20.27)

Commentary:

Normal faith in the Supreme Spirit is in the clarifying mode but if it is qualified by service and worship under His direction, then it moves beyond the mundane energy and enters into the transcendental energy.

पथ्यं पूतम् अनायस्तम्
आहार्यं सात्त्विकं स्मृतम् ।
राजसं चेन्द्रिय-प्रेष्ठं
तामसं चार्ति-दाशुचि ॥२०.२८॥

pathyaṁ pūtam anāyastam
āhāryaṁ sāttvikaṁ smṛtam
rājasaṁ cendriya-preṣṭhaṁ
tāmasaṁ cārti-dāśuci (20.28)

pathyam — wholesome; pūtam — pure; anāyastam — obtained without much endeavor; āhāryam — food; sāttvikam — concerning the clarifying influence; smṛtam — is regarded; rājasam — concerning the impulsive energy; cendriya = ca — and + indriya – sensual energy; preṣṭham — that which is cherished dearly; tāmasam — concerning the retardative force; cārti-dāśuci = ca — and + ārti – misery + da — that which produces + aśuci — impure.

Translation

Food which is wholesome, pure and which is obtained without much endeavor, concerns the clarifying mode. That which is cherished dearly by the sensual energy concerns the impulsive energy. That which produces misery and which is impure, concerns the retardative force. (20.28)

Commentary:

Śrī Krishna explained foods in the *Bhagavad-Gītā*:

āyuḥsattvabalārogya-sukhaprītivivardhanāḥ
rasyāḥ snigdhāḥ sthirā hṛdyā āhārāḥ sāttvikapriyāḥ
kaṭvamlalavaṇātyuṣṇa-tīkṣṇarūkṣavidāhinaḥ
āhārā rājasasyeṣṭā duḥkhaśokāmayapradāḥ
yātayāmaṁ gatarasaṁ pūti paryuṣitaṁ ca yat
ucchiṣṭamapi cāmedhyaṁ bhojanaṁ tāmasapriyam

Foods which increase the duration of the life, the spiritual well-being, strength, health, happiness and satisfaction, which are juicy, milky, sustaining and palatable, are eatables which are dear to the clear-minded people.

Foods which are pungent, sour, salty, peppery, acidic, dry and overheated, are desired by the passionate people. These foods cause pain, misery and sickness.

Food which is stale, tasteless, and rotten, which was left over, as well as that which is rejected or unfit for religious ceremony, is cherished by the depressed people. (B.G. 17.8-10)

सात्त्विकं सुखम् आत्मोत्थं
विषयोत्थं तु राजसम् ।
तामसं मोह-दैन्योत्थं
निर्गुणं मद्-अपाश्रयम् ॥२०.२९॥

sāttvikaṁ sukham ātmotthaṁ
viṣayotthaṁ tu rājasam
tāmasaṁ moha-dainyotthaṁ
nirguṇaṁ mad-apāśrayam (20.29)

sāttvikam — concerning the clarifying energy; sukham — happiness; ātmotthaṁ = ātma + uttham — that which is produced from the spirit self; viṣayotthaṁ = viṣaya + uttham — that which is caused by the attractive objects; tu — but; rājasam — concerning the impulsive force; tāmasam — concerning the retardative force; moha — delusion; dainyotthaṁ = dainya + uttham — that which is derived from misery; nirgunah — that which is beyond the mundane influences; mad-apāśrayam = mat-apāśrayam — reliance on me.

Translation

Happiness which is produced from the spirit itself is of the clarifying energy, but that which is caused by the attractive objects is of the impulsive force, and that which is derived from delusion and misery is of the retardative power. Happiness which is based on reliance on Me is beyond the mundane influences. (20.29)

Commentary:

Even though the spirit is spiritual, still while it has a gross, subtle and causal body, it remains attuned to these to a greater or lesser degree. As such its happiness is always connected to the modes of material nature, either slightly, partially or near-fully. When the spirit is focused on itself, it might derive some happiness from the highest modes of material nature. And when it is focused on the subtle or gross objects, it digresses to the impulsive energy. But when it is involved in delusion and misery, it descends to the lowest stage.

If however a spirit is able to have a complete reliance on *Śrī* Krishna it is elevated in happiness to the transcendental mode which prevails in the spiritual atmosphere. So long as a limited being is in the material world, he cannot experience himself as a spirit in essence, unless he enters into *samādhi* continuous effortless linkage of his attention to the transcendental domains. Generally however the spirit's happiness is reliant on the subtle emotional mundane energy, the *Sūtram* which is the sensually, sexually, emotionally-charged cosmic force.

द्रव्यं देशः फलं कालो
ज्ञानं कर्म च कारकः ।
श्रद्धावस्थाकृतिर् निष्ठा
त्रै-गुण्यः सर्व एव हि ॥२०.३०॥

dravyaṁ deśaḥ phalaṁ kālo
jñānaṁ karma ca kārakaḥ
śraddhāvasthākṛtir niṣṭhā
trai-guṇyaḥ sarva eva hi (20.30)

dravyam — object; deśaḥ — place; phalam — result; kālo = kālaḥ — time; jñānam — knowledge; karma — cultural activity; ca — and; kārakaḥ — agent; śraddhāvasthākṛtir = śraddhā — confidence + avasthā — state of mind; ākṛtiḥ — form; niṣṭhā — objective; trai-gunyah — concerning the three mundane influences; sarva = sarvah — all; eva hi — surely.

Translation

The object, the place, the result, time, knowledge and cultural activity, as well as the agent, the confidence applied, the state of mind, the form and the objective, all of this, surely do pertain to the three mundane influences. (20.30)

Commentary:

When all is said and done, material nature is material nature. Its influence is just that only. Even though we can cull off some motivation to be liberated from it, still it is what it is. Therefore in summary, Lord Krishna said this to Arjuna:

na tadasti pṛthivyāṁ vā divi deveṣu vā punaḥ
sattvaṁ prakṛtijairmuktaṁ yadebhiḥ syāttribhirguṇaiḥ

There is no object on earth nor even in the subtle mundane domains, that can exist without these three modes which were produced from material nature. (B.G. 18.40)

सर्वे गुण-मया भावाः
पुरुषाव्यक्त-धिष्ठिताः ।
दृष्टं श्रुतं अनुध्यातं
बुद्ध्या वा पुरुषर्षभ ॥२०.३१॥

sarve guṇa-mayā bhāvāḥ
puruṣāvyakta-dhiṣṭhitāḥ
dṛṣṭaṁ śrutaṁ anudhyātaṁ
buddhyā vā puruṣarṣabha (20.31)

sarve — all; guṇa-mayā = guna-mayāḥ — comprising of the mundane influences; bhāvāḥ — status, states of existence in the material world; puruṣāvyakta = puruṣa — spirit + avyakta — abstract energy; dhiṣṭhitāḥ — governed; dṛṣṭam — seen; śrutam — heard; anudhyātam — conceived; buddhyā — by the intellect; vā — or; puruṣarṣabha — best of the personalities.

Translation

O best of the personalities, whatever is seen, heard, or conceived by the intellect, are the states of existence in the material world, comprising of the mundane influences and are governed by the spirits and the abstract energy. (20.31)

Commentary:

There are many, many dimensions in the material world, some are gross as this one, many are subtle. There is the causal level. All of this comprise of the mundane influences in varying proportions. Thus whatever is seen, heard of and conceived of in relation to this is actually the same mundane energy. It is energized by the spirits who are in the creation and function under the great primal energy of material nature, which is abstract to gross sense perception.

एताः संसृतयः पुंसो
गुण-कर्म-निबन्धनाः ।
येनेमे निर्जिताः सौम्य
गुणा जीवेन चित्त-जाः ।
भक्ति-योगेन मन्-निष्ठो
मद्-भावाय प्रपद्यते ॥२०.३२॥

etāḥ saṁsṛtayaḥ puṁso
guṇa-karma-nibandhanāḥ
yeneme nirjitāḥ saumya
guṇā jīvena citta-jāḥ
bhaktī-yogena man-niṣṭho
mad-bhāvāya prapadyate (20.32)

etāḥ — these; saṁsṛtayah —transmigrating through various bodies; puṁsaḥ — of a person; guna — material nature; karma — cultural activity; nibandhanāḥ —that which is formed; yena — by whom + ime — these; nirjitāḥ — is not conquered; saumya — o good man; guṇah — mundane influence; jīvena — by the spirit; citta – mental and emotional energy + jāḥ — produced; bhaktī-yogena — by the application of yoga expertise to devotion; mat-niṣṭhaḥ — for being dedicated to me; mat-bhāvāya — for intimate existential linkage to me; prapadyate — is fit, qualified.

Translation

All this which concerns a person's transmigration through various bodies, are formed through cultural activity which is sponsored by material nature. O good man, a person who is not subdued by these mundane influences which occur in the mental and emotional energy, is by virtue of application of yoga expertise to devotion, qualified for being dedicated to Me and for the intimate existential linkage with Me (20.32)

Commentary:

The technique is to become resistant to material nature's influences which reach the spirit, through its mental and emotional energy. This energy is in the mind and feelings and it is used by the intellect for visualization and by the feelings for focusing on affections. So long as a living entity is spell bound by such energy he has to remain in the material world. And it does not matter if he is a devotee or not.

Even a devotee if he wants to get out and if he wants to be situated on the spiritual level, has to come to terms with the aggressive and impulsive nature of the mental and emotional energy in terms of its acceptance of material nature's suggestions.

This has to be done by the three higher stages of yoga practice, namely *dhāraṇā*, *dhyāna* and *samādhi*. The intellect has the power of *dhyāna* but unfortunately it has a natural propensity to use this power to promote the impressions which come from material nature. It does not automatically use that power to pursue the transcendence. Thus the individual spirit has to put himself or herself to the task of causing this power to be focused into the transcendence.

If God had given us a mind which was predisposed to the transcendence, we would not have been in this predicament in the first place. And even though *Śrī* Krishna said that in the Krita Age, the Time of Easy Enlightenment, most persons were inclined to the transcendence, and their mental and emotional energy were impressionable to it, it is not so at this time. Therefore an endeavor in higher yoga would be necessary to re-indoctrinate our minds and emotions, so that we can turn to the transcendence.

The intimate existential linkage with *Śrī* Krishna *(mad-bhāvāya)* cannot be attained by wishful thinking or by a mere expression of confidence in *Śrī* Krishna. It is a deep accomplishment which is attained by turning inwards and getting pass the mental and emotional forces, so that the insight of the spirit can be used to focus into the transcendence. From this perspective, a yogi sees that all those superficial methods of devotion are useless.

If one is serious at all, he should apply his devotion with yoga expertise. This means higher yoga. Otherwise his love for Krishna, being of a low nature, being mundane in fact, will get him nowhere. He will then hope for salvation. He will again have to rely on material nature and again he will be born again, and again he will be a devotee of *Śrī* Krishna with that low level of energy. He will again struggle with material nature's invasion of his privacy, her forceful utilization of his attention for investment in the prejudiced mental and emotional force.

तस्माद् देहम् इम लब्ध्वा
ज्ञान-विज्ञान-सम्भवम् ।
गुण-सङ्गं विनिर्धूय
मा भजन्तु विचक्षणाः ॥२०.३३॥

tasmād deham imaṁ labdhvā
jñāna-vijñāna-sambhavam
guṇa-saṅgaṁ vinirdhūya
māṁ bhajantu vicakṣaṇāḥ (20.33)

tasmād = tasmāt — therefore; deham — body; imam — this; labdhvā — having acquired; jñāna — information; vijñāna — actual experience; sambhavam — that which is productive; guna-saṅgam — association with the mundane influence; vinirdhūya — thoroughly shake off, shed off, discard; mām — me; bhajantu — should worship affectionately; vicakṣaṇāḥ — persons with spiritual insight.

Translation

Therefore, having acquired the body, which is productive of information and actual experience, having thoroughly discarded the association with material nature, persons with spiritual insight should worship Me (20.33)

Commentary:

Ideally, everyone should worship *Śrī* Krishna, but we know that everyone is not inclined to this. Among those who worship Him, many have not discarded the association of material nature, nor have they developed the spiritual insight, even though they have the information about Him and about the dangers of continuing in the association with material nature.

The key aspect is to thoroughly discard the association of material nature. This should be done by an effective method and not merely by faith or belief.

निःसङ्गो मां भजेद् विद्वान्
अप्रमत्तो जितेन्द्रियः ।
रजस् तमश् चाभिजयेत्
सत्त्व-ससेवया मुनिः ॥२०.३४॥

niḥsaṅgo māṁ bhajed vidvān
apramatto jitendriyaḥ
rajas tamaś cābhijayet
sattva-saṁsevayā muniḥ (20.34)

nihsaṅgo = nihsaṅgaḥ — being devoid of attachment; mām — me; bhajed = bhajet — should worship; vidvān — wise person; apramatto = apramattah — without bewilderment; jitendriyaḥ — having mastered the senses; rajas = rajah — the impulsive energy; tamaś = tamaḥ — the retardative force; cābhijayet = ca — and + abhijayet — should effectively suppress; sattva – clarifying influence; samsevayā — by the cultivation of; muniḥ — the yogi philosopher.

Translation

Being devoid of attachment, the wise person should worship Me, without bewilderment. Having mastered the senses, the yogi philosopher should effectively suppress the impulsive energy and retardative force by cultivation of the clarifying influence. (20.34)

Commentary:

This advice is for all devotees. Those who are advanced yogis can complete this instruction to the fullest. One cannot get out of the material nature without moving gradually from a lower stage to a higher one. One must start where he is and gradually by effective yogic methods in *aṣṭanga* yoga, move from one lower mode to a higher one, until one is situated permanently in the highest mundane level. From there when one becomes stabilized, one will begin to contact the spiritual energy and the divine persons in the spiritual world.

Some preachers in the Krishna disciplic successions, like to cite the example of King *Khaṭvāṅga* who is mentioned in the *Śrīmad Bhāgavatam*, as an example of a devotee who in less than one hour, switched himself over to the transcendence, after he was told by the supernatural rulers that he had only a little time to live in a mundane form. But such an example is not as fantastic as it seems, nor is it a demonstration of instant salvation as some would have us believe. Kings like *Khaṭvāṅga* were expert yogis. Thus they could instantly free themselves. Many others who pride themselves in citing his example will not be able to follow in his footsteps. Their attempt at such instant transference to the spiritual world at the time of death, will prove to be a failure.

सत्त्वं चाभिजयेद् युक्तो
नैरपेक्ष्येण शान्त-धीः ।
सम्पद्यते गुणैर् मुक्तो
जीवो जीवं विहाय माम् ॥२०.३५॥

sattvaṁ cābhijayed yukto
nairapekṣyeṇa śānta-dhīḥ
sampadyate guṇair mukto
jīvo jīvaṁ vihāya mām (20.35)

sattvam — clarifying influence; cābhijayed = ca — and + abhijayet — should effectively conquer over; yukto = yuktaḥ — having rigidly practised; nairapekṣyena — by neutrality to mundane pressures; śānta — tranquil; dhīḥ — intellect (śānta-dhīḥ - an intellect which is free from mental and emotional urgings and ideas); sampadyate — attains; gunair = gunaiḥ — by the mundane influence; mukto = muktaḥ — liberated; jīvo = jīvah — spirit; jīvam — the mundane life force; vihāya — giving up; mām — me.

Translation

Having rigidly practiced and by an attitude of neutrality towards mundane pressures, the person whose intellect is free from mental and emotional urgings and ideas, should effectively conquer over the clarifying influence. Thus being freed, and by giving up the mundane life force, the spirit attains Me. (20.35)

Commentary:

This is a description of higher yoga practice. The intellect becomes tranquilized in the 7th stage of yoga that of *dhyāna* effortless linkage of the attention to higher concentration forces, especially to the energy in the sky of consciousness or to a divine personality there. It is not possible to tranquilize the intellect in any other way, except superficially, but those who have not practiced higher yoga, do not understand this. Even devotees who did not practice yoga, or who disliked the practice of it, comment on these verses, and give completely misleading purports.

In every respect, each time Uddhava asked questions, *Śrī* Krishna repeatedly mentioned these yoga practices. It is not possible to practice devotion perfectly without adding yoga expertise to it. Thus yoga and *bhakti* is a good combination which is called *bhakti*-yoga. *Bhakti* is alright but by itself in its impure stage, it is unable to rid itself of the material energy. Hence the need for yoga, to internally shed off the modes of material nature, one by one, effectively.

जीवो जीव-विनिर्मुक्तो
गुणैश् चाशय-सम्भवैः ।
मयैव ब्रह्मणा पूर्णो
न बहिर् नान्तरश् चरेत् ॥२०.३६॥

jīvo jīva-vinirmukto
guṇaiś cāśaya-sambhavaiḥ
mayaiva brahmaṇā pūrṇo
na bahir nāntaraś caret (20.36)

jīvo = jīvah — the spirit; jīva – the mundane life force; vinirmukto = vinirmuktah — being completely freed; guṇais = gunaiḥ — by the mundane influence; cāśaya = ca — and + āśaya – causal body; sambhavaiḥ — by that which emerged from; mayaiva = mayā — by me + eva — indeed; brahmanā — by the supreme reality; pūrṇo = pūrṇah — wholly filled; na — not; bahir = bahiḥ — external; nāntaras = na — not + antaraḥ — internal; caret — should wander about.

Translation

The spirit, being completely freed from the mundane life force, and from the mundane influence which emerged from the causal body, is wholly filled by Me, the Supreme Reality and should not let his attention wander about internally or externally. (20.36)

Commentary:

This is a clear-cut description of higher yoga practice. This cannot be what was taught by Lord *Śrī* Chaitanya Mahaprabhu about chanting the holy names of *Śrī* Krishna. It is incredible that our authorities in the disciplic succession were able to somehow redesign these verses to make them fit into the mission of Lord Chaitanya.

However those of us who are practicing *kriyā* yogis, need not ponder over this any longer. We have full support from Lord Krishna. One has to practice kundalini yoga, master it so that he can shed off the lower part of the subtle body, which in effect means to get rid of the individualized kundalini survival force *(jīva)*. Then one has to take care of the causal form. If all this is done, one is sure to make contact with the sky of consciousness. From there, one can be transferred away from this plane of existence permanently. It can be done.

CHAPTER 21*

Purūravā, That Brillant Person**

Terri Stokes-Pineda Art

śrī-bhagavān uvāca
evaṁ pragāyan nṛpa-deva-devaḥ sa urvaśī-lokam atho vihāya
ātmānam ātmany avagamya māṁ vai upāramaj jñāana-vidhūta-mohaḥ

The Blessed Lord said: Thus musing to himself, that brilliant person who was prominent among the angelic people and the human beings, abruptly gave up the dimensional residence of Urvaśī. Realizing Me as the Spirit in himself, he through knowledge, dispelled the infatuation and attained peace. (Uddhava Gītā 21.25)

* Śrīmad Bhāgavatam Canto 11, Chapter 26
** Translator's selected chapter title.

श्री-भगवान् उवाच
मल्-लक्षणम् इमं कायं
लब्ध्वा मद्-धर्म आस्थितः ।
आनन्दं परमात्मानम्
आत्म-स्थं समुपैति माम् ॥२१.१॥

śrī-bhagavān uvāca
mal-lakṣaṇam imaṁ kāyaṁ
labdhvā mad-dharma āsthitaḥ
ānandaṁ paramātmānam
ātma-sthaṁ samupaiti mām (21.1)

śrī-bhagavān – the blessed lord; uvāca — said; mal-lakṣaṇam = mat-lakṣaṇam — that which gives the indication; imam — this; kāyam — human body; labdhvā — having acquired; mad-dharma = mat-dharme — in performance of righteous duty to me; āsthitaḥ — being established; ānandam — spiritual happiness; paramātmānam — the Supreme Spirit; ātma-stham — being situated in the spirit itself; samupaiti — reaches; mām — me.

Translation

Having acquired the human body, which gives the indication of Me, and being established in the performance of righteous duty to Me, one reaches Me, who is the supreme happiness, the Supreme Spirit and who is spirit-situated. (21.1)

Commentary:

This is the only easy method given thus far in this discourse. If one honestly and truly checks each and every verse, he will find that when Uddhava wanted a simply method for the common people, this is all that *Śrī* Krishna gave. The only simpler offer was devotion to *Śrī* Krishna which would be powerful enough to cause the person to do whatever Krishna would demand. If one carefully checks chapter twelve of the discourse with Arjuna (*Bhagavad-Gītā*), one will find that at one point, *Śrī* Krishna laid out a series of alternatives, from higher to lower until He was unable to go any lower, and then He resumed the explanation of the higher courses. In that discourse, it is the same offer of doing work for *Śrī* Krishna with or without yoga practice; but, ultimately with yoga practice *(karma + yoga = karmayoga)*.

Here again in this conversation with Uddhava, *Śrī* Krishna re-iterated the *mad dharma* which is the performance of righteous duty to Him. This is the personal righteous duty which may or may not be related to missionary activities, spreading Krishna Consciousness. For Arjuna this was battlefield work, for Uddhava it was something else. It has little to do with gurus in temples with disciples fanning them on their lofty seats. It has to do with what the Universal Form wants a man to do for the establishment of righteous living in the cultural realm.

By doing this one does not reach *Śrī* Krishna in the spiritual world in a jiffy but rather one gets the approval of the Universal Form, an approval which gives one the permission to take up full time yoga practice, which if completed, will result in transference to the spiritual world. Reaching *Śrī* Krishna by this method of performing righteous duty to His approval is a slow process. It is not necessary to glamorize it to trick anybody to join the spiritual path. People should be told the plain truth about it. Arjuna did not go to the spiritual world by its performance alone, because the *Mahābhārata* history does not say that. But ultimately, it did assist his passage there.

गुण-मय्या जीव-योन्या
विमुक्तो ज्ञान-निष्ठया ।
गुणेषु माया-मात्रेषु
दृश्यमानेष्व् अवस्तुतः ।
वर्तमानो ऽपि न पुमान्
युज्यते ऽवस्तुभिर् गुणैः ॥२१.२॥

guṇa-mayyā jīva-yonyā
vimukto jñāna-niṣṭhayā
guṇeṣu māyā-mātreṣu
dṛśyamāneṣv avastutaḥ
vartamāno 'pi na pumān
yujyate 'vastubhir guṇaiḥ (21.2)

guṇa-mayyā — by what consists of the mundane energies; jīva – mundane life force; yonyā — by the generating cause; vimukto = vimuktah — freed from; jñāna — information; niṣṭhayā — by having a permanent hold; guṇeṣu — in the mundane influence; māyā – composed by bewildering energy; mātreṣu — in the subtle material nature; dṛśyamāneṣv = dṛśyamāneṣu — in what is perceived; avastutah — that which lacks substantiality; vartamāno = vartamānaḥ — lives, living; 'pi = api — although; na — not; pumān — person; yujyate — become involved; 'vastubhir = avastubhiḥ — with what is insubstantial; guṇaiḥ — with the mundane energy.

Translation

Being freed by having a permanent hold on this information, regarding the generating cause of the mundane life force, which consist of the mundane influence, a person, even though living in the material world, which is composed of bewildering mundane energy, which is perceived but which lacks substantiality, does not become involved with the insubstantial mundane force. (21.2)

Commentary:

We have to leave aside the cheap get-nowhere paths and move forward, picking up the pieces of our illusions and moving on to real progression. Yoga practice might be difficult. It is the only thing that will work because it is strong enough to cause us to slip away from the bewildering energy.

Śrī Krishna petitions us. Whatever little attraction or affection (*bhakti*) we have for Him, even if it is impure, could help in this quest for freedom. It could motivate us to follow His directions.

सङ्गं न कुर्याद् असतां
शिश्नोदर-तृपा क्वचित् ।
तस्यानुगस् तमस्य् अन्धे
पतत्य् अन्धानुगान्ध-वत् ॥२१.३॥

saṅgaṁ na kuryād asatāṁ
śiśnodara-tṛpāṁ kvacit
tasyānugas tamasy andhe
pataty andhānugāndha-vat (21.3)

saṅgam — association; na – not; kuryād = kuryāt — should function with; asatām — of those who do not perceive reality; śiśnodara = śiśna — genitals + udara — belly; tṛpām — those who are devoted to satisfying; kvacit — anytime (na … kvacit not at any time); tasyānugas = tasya — of him of such a person + anugaḥ — follower; tamasy = tamasi – in mental darkness; andhe — in mental blindness; pataty = patati — falls; andhānugāndha-vat = andha – a blind man + anuga — following + andha-vat — like a blind man.

Translation

One should never function in the association of those who do not perceive reality, and who are devoted to satisfying the genitals and body. The followers of such a person falls into the blinding mental darkness just as one blind man who follows another. (21.3)

Commentary:

Basically speaking we have to move away from those who follow paths which lead nowhere. But that does not mean that we should alert such persons to their folly. Unless it is our duty, alerting them about it, would slow our progression. We have to quietly slip away. It is not their fault but it is in fact our mental blindness, which causes us to be in their association in the first place. Those who do not take up the austerities to control the genitals, and then to control diet, cannot be successful on this path. They have to follow the prescriptions which were given in chapter four of the *Bhagavad-Gītā* discourse where *Śrī* Krishna explained *prāṇāyāma* and diet control:

apāne juhvati prāṇaṁ prāṇe'pānaṁ tathāpare
prāṇāpānagatī ruddhvā prāṇāyāmaparāyaṇāḥ
apare niyatāhārāḥ prāṇānprāṇeṣu juhvati

sarve'pyete yajñavido yajñakṣapitakalmaṣāḥ

Some offer inhalation into the exhalation channels; similarly others offer the exhalation into the inhalation channels, thus being determined to restrain the channels of the energizing and de-energizing airs.

Others who were restrained in diet, impel fresh air into the previously inhaled air. All these ascetics whose impurities were removed by austerity and religious ceremony understand the value of an act of sacrifice. (B.G. 4.29-30)

Without diet control, there can be no genital control or celibacy, even though there might be superficial celibacy which is shown to the public as external sexual restraint.

ऐलः सम्राड् इमां गाथाम्
अगायत बृहच्-छ्रवाः ।
उर्वशी-विरहान् मुह्यन्
निर्विण्णः शोक-सयमे ॥२१.४॥

ailaḥ samrāḍ imāṁ gāthām
agāyata bṛhac-chravāḥ
urvaśī-virahān muhyan
nirviṇṇaḥ śoka-saṁyame (21.4)

ailah — Ila's son; samrād = samrāt — emperor; imām — this; gāthām — song; agāyata — sang; bṛhac = bṛhat — immensely; chravāḥ = śravāḥ — popularity; urvaśī; – Urvaśī; virahān = virahāt — from seperation; muhyan — become crazy; nirviṇṇah — being disgusted; śoka — grief; samyame — in subduing.

Translation

The immensely popular Emperor, Ilā's son, sang this song when he became crazy with the seperation from Urvaśī, and became detached in the act of subduing his grief. (21.4)

Commentary:

Ilā's son, the immensely popular Emperor, was *Purūravā*. Being a devotee, will not necessarily save a person from fall down. Being a *sannyāsi* will not do it, even if one is a devotee of Krishna in a large and famous mission. These are not the means for overcoming the procreative power which manifest itself in our bodies as sex desire.

त्यक्त्वात्मानं व्रयन्तीं तां
नग्न उन्मत्त-वन् नृपः ।
विलपन्न् अन्वगाज् जाये
घोरे तिष्ठेति विक्लवः ॥२१.५॥

tyaktvātmānaṁ vrayantīṁ tāṁ
nagna unmatta-van nṛpaḥ
vilapann anvagāj jāye
ghore tiṣṭheti viklavaḥ (21.5)

tyaktvātmānaṁ = tyaktvā — was leaving + ātmānam — himself; vrajantīm — she who was going away; tām — to her; nagna — naked; unmatta – mad man; van = vat — like; nṛpah — the king; vilapann = vilapan — crying out; anvagāj = anvagāt — went after; jāye — o wife; ghore — o cruelty incarnate; tiṣṭheti = tiṣṭha — stop + iti — thus saying; viklavaḥ — agonized.

Translation

When she was going away, abandoning him, the king went after her like a mad man, naked and crying out , agonized, and saying, "O my wife, stop! O cruelty incarnate!" (21.5)

Commentary:

Many false *sannyāsis* who pretend that they are saving the world on behalf of this *Avatār* of *Śrī* Krishna and that Divine Personality, will cry out when their fame leaves them. Fame is cruel because it is the force which attracts their sexual energy, just as *Urvaśī* attracted King *Purūravā* romantically.

These sannyasis will tell any lie and abuse any divine person, by advertising something cheap which will help no one in truth. Thus in the end, they will be frustrated.

Devotion is there in our nature, but in the impure stages, it is a crazy energy without discrimination. It will cause us pain even when and if we direct it to *Śrī* Krishna. This is because it is an unreasonable energy. It will want *Śrī* Krishna to do what it says. It will try to define devotion to *Śrī* Krishna. It will not want to be curbed and refined by yoga practice. It will influence us to avoid the true path.

कामान् अतृप्तो ऽनुजुषन्
क्षुल्लकान् वर्ष-यामिनीः ।
न वेद यान्तीर् नायान्तीर्
उर्वश्य्-आकृष्ट-चेतनः ॥२१.६॥

kāmān atṛpto 'nujuṣan
kṣullakān varṣa-yāminīḥ
na veda yāntīr nāyāntīr
urvaśy-ākṛṣṭa-cetanaḥ (21.6)

kāmān — desires; atṛpto = atṛptaḥ — unfulfilled; 'nujuṣan = anujuṣan — indulging repeatedly; kṣullakān — vulgar; varṣa-yāminīḥ = varṣa — years + yāminīḥ — nights; na – not; veda — know; yāntīr = yāntīḥ — the passing; urvaśy = urvaśī — Urvaśī; ākṛṣṭa — irresistibly drawn; cetanah — feeling, emotions.

Translation

He whose emotions were irresistibly drawn to Urvaśī, did not realize the passing nor approach of those nights, having his vulgar desires unfulfilled, but indulging repeatedly for many nights through the years. (21.6)

Commentary:

King *Purūravā* was so preoccupied *(akṛṣṭa)* with vulgar sexual indulgence, and its romantic overtones that he did not realize the aging of his body, and that he neglected the mission for which he got the human form.

For a householder, in the early part of marriage, sexual indulgence is a must but it should not become a preoccupation otherwise one will forget righteous duty and become carried away with romantic overtones which are supportive of and which cause the build up of more sexual desires endlessly.

What then is the righteous duty of a householder? It is to beget and raise children with godly behavior. His mission is not sexual indulgence but rather, the raising of children. Thus in the *Gītā*, *Śrī* Krishna identified Himself with restricted sexual indulgence. Once the sexual energy is used to beget bodies, it has no more proper usage, except to be channeled into the energy needed to raise children with godly values.

Thus any other sexual expression which does not produce children and which is not converted into parental-guiding energy for good behavior in children, is for all practical purposes, outlawed. It was for this reason that this commentator took this body, to make this point perfectly clear. Of course an ascetic might struggle for sometime before he can comply with this ruling. Still it is his duty to endeavor to attain it.

ऐल उवाच
अहो मे मोह-विस्तारः
काम-कश्मल-चेतसः ।
देव्या गृहीत-कण्ठस्य
नायुः-खण्डा इमे स्मृताः ॥२१.७॥

aila uvāca
aho me moha-vistāraḥ
kāma-kaśmala-cetasaḥ
devyā gṛhīta-kaṇṭhasya
nāyuḥ-khaṇḍā ime smṛtāḥ (21.7)

aila – the son of Ilā; uvāca — said; aho — o what a spectacle; me — my; moha — infatuation; vistārah — the extent; kāma — by lusty cravings; kaśmala — polluted; cetasaḥ — consciousness; devyā — by the goddess; grhīta — embraced; kaṇṭhasya — of the neck; nāyuḥ = na — not + āyuḥ — life span; khaṇḍā — portions; ime — these; smṛtāh — did observe.

Translation

The son of Ilā said: "What a spectacle. Hey look at the extent of my infatuation. My consciousness was polluted by lusty cravings. Being embraced at the neck, by the goddess, I did not observe the portions of my life span. (21.7)

Commentary:

The sadness of this, is that when we become infatuated, we neglect the Universal Form. That is dangerous. Our time is His time. Thus if we waste time or engage in activities which are of low priority to Him or which oppose His intentions, we corrupt His time. And that is inappropriate, because He is our master and teacher.

It is interesting that *Purūravā* addressed *Urvaśī* respectfully as goddess, as *devī*, because the angelic women like *Urvaśī* are our superiors. Still, that does not mean that we should indulge sexually with them. We heard of King Mahabhisa who indulged with the goddess Ganga, but that activity, sweet as it was, was not approved by Lord *Brahmā*, who is one of our spiritual masters. Therefore we have to be careful that we are not drawn into the sexual needs of the goddesses or of their servants, the angelic women. This is important.

This is advice for *kriyā* yogins, that when all is said and done, we should not under any circumstance, be caught fulfilling the vulgar desires of any of these ladies. It is best to stay with Lord Shiva and not get involved in the vulgar needs of the vaginas of these respectable women. One will bring a lot of trouble on one's head, if one does not understand what I explained in this commentary. I took this birth, just to warn you about this. This was a risky birth, still I took it for that sole purpose.

नाहं वेदाभिनिर्मुक्तः
सूर्यो वाभ्युदितो ऽमुया ।
मूषितो वर्ष-पूगाना
बताहानि गतान्य् उत ॥२१.८॥

nāhaṁ vedābhinirmuktaḥ
sūryo vābhyudito 'muyā
mūṣito varṣa-pūgānāṁ
batāhāni gatāny uta (21.8)

nāham = na — not + aham — I; vedābhinirmuktah = veda — know + abhinirmuktah — did set; sūryo = sūryah — sun; vābhyudito = vā — or + abhyuditaḥ — did rise; 'muyā = amuyā — by her; mūṣito = mūṣitah — being tricked; varṣa — years; pūgānām — amounting to; batāhāni = bata — o my; ahāni — days; gatāny = gatāni — had gone; uta — this is a fact.

Translation

"Being tricked, I did not know if the sun set or rose, O my, the days amounting to years went by. This is what happened. (21.8)

Commentary:

This is exactly what occurs to householders. Being tricked into serving the romantic notions which they share with women, male ascetics forget all about the passing of time, which features in our lives as the rising and setting of the sun.

After marriage, one should continue yoga practice, doing it at least twice daily in the early morning and before resting. One should, little by little, advance, so that as soon as the responsibilities to children are taken care of, one can increase the practice to reach perfection.

As for one's wife, if she has interest in austerities, she should strive alongside as one endeavors. Otherwise, one should allow her to maintain her interest in domestic affairs, and one should quietly and definitely ease away from the household duties.

An ascetic who takes care of children in terms of giving them behavioral training before they reach maturity, will get the grace of the Almighty in the form of a waiver from such cultural activities which were beneficial to those ancestors who took bodies, and thus he will be able to step aside from the world of *karma* and *karma* yoga, and take directly to higher yoga for perfection. That is happens by the grace of the Supreme Person, *Śrī* Krishna.

अहो मे आत्म-सम्मोहो
येनात्मा योषिता कृतः ।
क्रीडा-मृगश् चक्रवर्ती
नरदेव-शिखामणिः ॥२१.९॥

aho me ātma-sammoho
yenātmā yoṣitāṁ kṛtaḥ
krīḍā-mṛgaś cakravartī
naradeva-śikhāmaṇiḥ (21.9)

aho — what a wonder; me — of me, my; ātma — self; sammoho = sammohaḥ — infatuation; yenātmā = yena — through which + ātmā — self; yoṣitām — of women; kṛtaḥ — was made; krīḍā – toy; mṛgaś = mṛgaḥ — animal; cakravartī — emperor; naradeva — king; śikhāmaṇiḥ — crown jewel.

Translation

"What a wonder O my soul! The infatuation through which myself the emperor, the crown jewel of kings, was made the toy animal of women! (21.9)

Commentary:

In all respects, a yogi has to analyze his condition and criticize himself fittingly. This provides a platform from which to jump away from cultural activities, which bring on involvements which leads to sexual contact. It is no exaggeration that a householder yogi comes to realize that he was made a pawn by the sexual organ of his own and of his wife's body as well.

स-परिच्छदम् आत्मानं
हित्वा तृणम् इवेश्वरम् ।
यान्ती स्त्रियं चान्वगमं
नग्न उन्मत्त-वद् रुदन् ॥२१.१०॥

sa-paricchadam ātmānaṁ
hitvā tṛṇam iveśvaram
yāntīṁ striyaṁ cānvagamaṁ
nagna unmatta-vad rudan (21.10)

sa – with; paricchadam — royal servants and priveleges; ātmānam — myself; hitvā — was discarded; tṛṇam — piece of straw; iveśvaram = iva — as if + īśvaram — lord of the land; yāntīm — she who went away; striyam — woman; cānvagamam = ca — and + anvagaman — I followed; nagna = nagnaḥ — naked; unmatta – mad man; vad = vat — like; rudan — weeping.

Translation

"Even though, myself, who is lord of the land, along with royal servants and privileges, were discarded just as if I were a piece of straw, still naked and weeping, like a mad man, I followed the woman who went away. (21.10)

Commentary:

Attachment to any agreeable or pleasing objects, causes one to loose discretion. Sexual attraction in particular causes a person to lose moral values and any other assets he might have in the field of cultural existence. Sexual attraction is perhaps the most powerful urge other than political status and popularity.

Urvaśī did not think anything of leaving *Purūravā* and his royal staff with the associated privileges. She was more attracted to life in the angelic world, where she held a privileged position. She disliked the struggles of life on earth. She had some attraction to *Purūravā* but she did not consider him to be much of a man, even though he rated her as the perfect companion.

In retrospect, after he came to his senses, *Purūravā* evaluated the situation in the proper way, because the infatuation which overcame him had worn away.

कुतस् तस्यानुभावः स्यात्
तेज ईशत्वम् एव वा ।
यो ऽन्वगच्छं स्त्रियं यान्तीं
खर-वत् पाद-ताडितः ॥२१.११॥

kutas tasyānubhāvaḥ syāt
teja īśatvam eva vā
yo 'nvagacchaṁ striyaṁ yāntīṁ
khara-vat pāda-tāḍitaḥ (21.11)

kutas = kutaḥ — where; tasyānubhāvaḥ = tasya — of him, of that person + anubhāvaḥ — charm; syāt — is; teja = tejaḥ — valor; īśatvam — political power; eva — indeed; vā — or; yo = yah — who; 'nvagacchaṁ = anvagaccham — followed; striyam — woman; yāntīm — she who left; khara – donkey; vat — like; pāda — hoof; tāditaḥ — kicked.

Translation

"Where indeed is the charm, valor, or political power, of that person who followed a woman who left him, just as a donkey follows while being kicked by the hoof of a she-ass? (21.11)

Commentary:

The charm, valor or political power, of such a person is suppressed by the sexual needs which over-powered his psyche. Therefore he has to study his nature. Taking help from Lord Shiva, he should rearrange his personal energies, so that they come under control and do not lead him to shameful activities.

किं विद्यया किं तपसा
किं त्यागेन श्रुतेन वा ।
किं विविक्तेन मौनेन
स्त्रीभिर् यस्य मनो हृतम् ॥२१.१२॥

kiṁ vidyayā kiṁ tapasā
kiṁ tyāgena śrutena vā
kiṁ viviktena maunena
strībhir yasya mano hṛtam (21.12)

kim — what; vidyayā — with learning; kim — what; tapasā — with austerity; kim — what; tyāgena — with leaving aside benefits; śrutena — with scriptural study; vā — or; kim — what; viviktena — with isolation; maunena — with restraint of speech; strībhir = strībhiḥ — by women; yasya — whose; mano = manah — mind; krtam — was captivated.

Translation

"What would be done with the learning, the austerity, the discarding of benefits, the scriptural study, the isolation or the restraint of speech, of a person whose mind is captivated by women? (21.12)

Commentary:

Anyone who is captivated by sexual desire, be he a man or be she a woman, becomes so preoccupied with romantic notions and vulgar sexual contacts, that nothing else at all matters to that person.

Urvaśī was somewhat detached from her sexual connections with King *Purūravā* but the king was very involved, more than he should have been, since he was of noble lineage. But all the same with some other males in the angelic world, *Urvaśī* would have been very attached in turn.

Sexual attraction though mutual is not always of an equal infatuation. One partner might be more spellbound than the other. Or one party might be more pleasure-extracting than the other.

स्वार्थस्याकोविदं धिङ् मां
मूर्खं पण्डित-मानिनम् ।
यो ऽहम् ईश्वरतां प्राप्य
स्त्रीभिर् गो-खर-वज् जितः ॥२१.१३॥

svārthasyākovidaṁ dhiṅ māṁ
mūrkhaṁ paṇḍita-māninam
yo 'ham īśvaratāṁ prāpya
strībhir go-khara-vaj jitaḥ (21.13)

svārthasyākovidam = sva – own + arthasya — of welfare + akovidam — one who does not understand; dhiṅ = dhik — shame; mām — me; mūrkham — fool; paṇḍita – educated man; māninam — one who imagines; yo = yaḥ — who; 'ham = aham — I; īśvaratām — one having political power; prāpya — having attained; strībhir = strībhiḥ — by women; go – bull; khara – male donkey; vaj = vat — like; jitaḥ — subdued.

Translation

"Shame on me! Being a person who does not understand his interest, the fool that I am and imagining myself as being educated, I who attained political control, was subdued by a female, just like a bull or male donkey. (21.13)

Commentary:

This same type of reasoning should be used by those *sannyāsis*, religious leaders and spiritual masters, who became attracted to popularity and who pose as saviors of the world or as agents of the real saviors, but who are themselves not liberated in fact. They need to consider what fools they are, that they became subdued by popularity and now have become pawns of the dictates of the vain mind and the naive disciples, who honor them as if in fact they were liberated, while they know in their hearts that they are afraid of death, and are doubtful about salvation.

A yogi householder should not come under the control of *karma* which is cultural activities, for that would mean that he came under the control of his materialistic ancestors, who operated within his mind and emotions to cause him to abandon the practice. He should instead take lessons from the *Bhagavad-Gītā* discourse given to Arjuna, to understand how to mix *karma* and yoga. In that way, yoga can control *karma* and he will not succumb to being controlled by the materialistic persons to whom he has obligations because of taking birth in their family.

If one is agreeable with *Śrī* Krishna, cooperates with Him and hears Him out, one will not sacrifice one's spiritual development just to please the ancestors. All the same, one will not deny them their due but would instead would compensate them the exact amount due according to the calculation in the mind of the Universal Form of *Śrī* Krishna.

सेवतो वर्ष-पूगान् मे
उर्वश्या अधरासवम् ।
न तृप्यत्य् आत्म-भूः कामो
वह्निर् आहुतिभिर् यथा ॥२१.१४॥

sevato varṣa-pūgān me
urvaśyā adharāsavam
na tṛpyaty ātma-bhūḥ kāmo
vahnir āhutibhir yathā (21.14)

sevato = sevataḥ — by an attendant; varṣa – year; pūgān — many; me — myself; urvaśyā — of Urvaśī; adharāsavam = adhara — lips + āsavam — intoxicating nectar; na – not; tṛpyaty = tṛpyati — is satisfied; ātma-bhūh — that which arose from my soul, life force; kāmo = kāmaḥ — lusty urges; vahnir = vahniḥ — fire; āhutibhir – āhutibhiḥ — by ceremonial fuels; yathā — just as.

Translation

"Being an attendant of the intoxicating nectar of the Urvaśī lips for many years, lusty urges which arose from the life force, were not satisfied, just like the fire with the ceremonial fuels. (21.14)

Commentary:

Śrī Krishna explained this to Arjuna in a similar way:

āvṛtaṁ jñānametena jñānino nityavairiṇā
kāmarūpeṇa kaunteya duṣpūreṇānalena ca

The discernment of educated people is adjusted by their eternal enemy which is the sense of yearning for various things. O son of Kuntī, the lusty power, is as hard to satisfy as it is to keep a fire burning. (B.G. 3.39)

पुंश्चल्यापहृतं चित्तं
को न्व् अन्यो मोचितुं प्रभुः ।
आत्मारामेश्वरम् ऋते
भगवन्तम् अधोक्षजम् ॥२१.१५॥

puṁścalyāpahṛtaṁ cittaṁ
ko nv anyo mocituṁ prabhuḥ
ātmārāmeśvaram ṛte
bhagavantam adhokṣajam (21.15)

puṁścalyāpahṛtaṁ = puṁścalyā — by a seductive woman; apahṛtam — was captivated; cittam —

the mind and emotions; ko = kaḥ — who; nv = nu — indeed; anyo = anyaḥ — other person; mocitum — to release; prabhuḥ — is able, can; ātmārāmeśvaram = ātma-ārāma — delighting in the spiritual self + īśvaram — master; ṛte — except for; bhagavantam — the exalted supreme lord; adhokṣajam — the one who is beyond mundane sense perception.

Translation

"Who other than the Exalted Supreme Lord Adhokṣaja who is beyond mundane sense perception, and who is the master of those who delight in their spiritual selves, can release the mind and emotions of one who is captivated by a seductive woman. (21.15)

Commentary:

Purūravā could understand that even though God was not present before him physically, still it was God who freed his mind and emotions from attraction to the seductive form of *Urvaśī*. He was grateful for this.

One who is inspired by Lord Krishna or by Lord Shiva or by Lord *Balarāma*, should take steps to repay by taking up the austerities which would solidify yoga practice, otherwise one will suffer a relapse, due to not reinforcing the grace of the Lord.

बोधितस्यापि देव्या मे
सूक्त-वाक्येन दुर्मतेः ।
मनो-गतो महा-मोहो
नापयात्य् अजितात्मनः ॥२१.१६॥

bodhitasyāpi devyā me
sūkta-vākyena durmateḥ
mano-gato mahā-moho
nāpayāty ajitātmanaḥ (21.16)

bodhitasyāpi = bodhitasya — of one who is informed + api — even though; devyā — by the supernatural woman; me — regarding me; sukta = su-ukta — well-worded; vākyena — by advice; durmateḥ — of one who is dull-witted; mano-gato = manah-gataḥ — passing through the mind; mahā-moho = mahā-mohah — great fantasy; nāpayāty = na – not + apayāti — cease; ajitātmanaḥ = ajita – not subdued + ātmanah — of the self (ajitātmanah – one whose psyche is not subdued).

Translation

"Regarding me; who, even though informed by the supernatural woman's well-worded advice, but who was dull-witted nevertheless, since the great fantasy passing through my mind did not cease; I am the one whose psyche is not subdued. (21.16)

Commentary:

One who is hung up on romantic sexual affairs, does not listen to anything else, even if he or she is advised to desist from it by the very partner who engages with detachment in such sexual affairs. It is as if the senses reject even the good advice given by a spouse.

In the part nine of the *Śrīmad Bhāgavatam*, the story of *Purūravā*'s encounter and subsequent sellout of his life, honor and everything to *Urvaśī*, is told. Initially *Urvaśī* tried to explain to *Purūravā* that women are very mean in getting what they desired. Still *Purūravā* heard those words like so much nectar not for their meaning but for the sweet sound of her voice. In retrospect *Purūravā* condemned himself for his absorption in *Urvaśī*'s sensuality.

किम् एतया नो ऽपकृतं
रज्ज्वा वा सर्प-चेतसः ।
द्रष्टुः स्वरूपाविदुषो
यो ऽहं यद् अजितेन्द्रियः ॥२१.१७॥

kim etayā no 'pakṛtaṁ
rajjvā vā sarpa-cetasaḥ
draṣṭuḥ svarūpāviduṣo
yo 'haṁ yad ajitendriyaḥ (21.17)

kim — what; etayā — by her; no = nah — to us; 'pakṛtaṁ = apakṛtam — insult committed by; rajjvā — by a rope; vā — or; sarpa – snake; cetasaḥ — conception; draṣṭuḥ — an observer; svarūpāviduṣo = svarūpa — actual form + aviduṣaḥ — one who does not realize; yo = yah — who; 'ham = aham

— I; yad = yat — because; ajitendriyah — one who has not subdued his sensuality.

Translation

"What insult was committed by her; or by a rope which an observer who did not realize its actual form, considered to be a snake? It is because I am the person who did not subdued his sensuality. (21.17)

Commentary:

This is part of the *kriyā* yoga practice, when one turns the critical energy on oneself. By that one can help himself and make the full exertion required for salvation. One has to look within, critique one's nature and take steps for reform.

क्वाय मलीमसः कायो
दौर्गन्ध्याद्य्-आत्मको ऽशुचिः ।
क्व गुणाः सौमनस्याद्या
ह्य् अध्यासो ऽविद्यया कृतः ॥२१.१८॥

kvāyaṁ malīmasaḥ kāyo
daurgandhyādy-ātmako 'śuciḥ
kva guṇāḥ saumanasyādyā
hy adhyāso 'vidyayā kṛtaḥ (21.18)

kvāyam = kva — what + ayam — this; malīmasaḥ — filth; kāyo = kāyah — body; daurgandhyādi = daurgandhya — of a bad odor + ādi — and such aspects; ātmako = ātmakaḥ — consisting of; 'śuciḥ = aśuciḥ — unclean; kva — what; gunāḥ — good aspects; saumanasyādyā = saumanasya — of the pleasing feelings or nice things + ādyāh — and such aspects; hy = hi — surely; adhyāso = adhyāsaḥ — misconception; 'vidyayā = avidyayā — by ignorance; kṛtaḥ — produced.

Translation

"What is this filthy body, which consist of bad odors and such aspects, and which is unclean? And what are good aspects or pleasing feelings or nice things? Surely the misconception regarding the comparison is produced by ignorance. (21.18)

Commentary:

Purūravā realized that he was misled by the sensual selections which were made by his own psyche, his own mental and emotional energy. It differentiated between one type of sensuous phenomena and another; when in fact all of material nature originated from one Primal Energy which was in proximity to the Supreme Being.

So long as one is focused externally, one cannot understand what to do for self-realization. One has to curb the sensuality completely, so that the mental and emotional feelings stop giving the intellect definitions regarding what is right or wrong, ugly or beautiful. When one is freed from the dictatorial sensuality, then one can make progress in terms of entering the other sky, the transcendental world.

पित्रोः किं स्वं नु भार्यायाः
स्वामिनो ऽग्नेः श्व-गृध्रयोः ।
किम् आत्मनः किं सुहृदाम्
इति यो नावसीयते ॥२१.१९॥

pitroḥ kiṁ svaṁ nu bhāryāyāḥ
svāmino 'gneḥ śva-gṛdhrayoḥ
kim ātmanaḥ kiṁ suhṛdām
iti yo nāvasīyate (21.19)

pitroḥ — of parents; kim — is it; svam — property; nu — or; bhāryāyāḥ — of the wife; svāmino = svāminaḥ — of the employer; 'gneḥ = agneḥ — of fire; śva – dog; gṛdhrayoḥ — of vultures; kim — is it; ātmanaḥ — of the self itself; kim — is it; suhṛdam — of relatives; iti — thus; yo = yah — who, someone; nāvasīyate = na – not + avasīyate — can figure out.

Translation

"Is it the property of the parents or the wife, or of the employer or the fire, or of the dog or the vulture? Is it of the self itself? Or is it of the relatives? No one can figure this out. (21.19)

Commentary:

The body belongs to material nature, as is conclusively proven at the time of the body's dissolution. Neither the soul, the relatives nor anyone else, not even God, can use the body as a living form after it dies. All the same there are relative users or claimants of a living body. Many agents take turns controlling the body. It is not assigned to just one person. In a sense, the body belongs to whatever power takes control of it.

Jaḍa Bharata was a king in a recent past life but he was circumstantially compelled to carry the palanquin of another king in a subsequent life. There was nothing he could do about it, because he was put into the situation providentially.

Śrī Krishna, the Supreme Being was requested by the mother of His physical body, to bring back her dearly departed sons. Because *Devakī* was his mother, and had certain rights in His life, *Śrī* Krishna complied with her request.

तस्मिन् कलेवरे ऽमेध्ये
तुच्छ-निष्ठे विषज्जते ।
अहो सु-भद्रं सु-नसं
सु-स्मितं च मुखं स्त्रियः ॥२१.२०॥

tasmin kalevare 'medhye
tuccha-niṣṭhe viṣajjate
aho su-bhadraṁ su-nasaṁ
su-smitaṁ ca mukhaṁ striyaḥ (21.20)

tasmin — to that; kalevare — body; 'medhye = amedhye — abominable; tuccha – vile; niṣṭhe — in the end; viṣajjate — becomes attached; aho — O; su-bhadram — very nice; su-nasam — nice nose; su-smitam — beautiful smile; ca — and; mukham — face; striyaḥ — of a woman.

Translation

"O, one becomes attached to that abominable body, which reaches a vile end, saying 'O the face of that woman is very nice, with its very nice nose and beautiful smile.' (21.20)

Commentary:

This is the profile of the sensual energy and not by the spirit directly. Since the spirit is reliant on the opinion of the sensual energy, it accepts such conclusions. One must curb the sensual energy by withdrawing it from this world. It does not make the proper decisions. In fact the sensual energy is destined to continue in this spiritually-destructive decision-making process. One has to perfect the 5th stage of yoga to withdraw the sensual energy and conserve it, so that one can focus into the spiritual dimension, forsaking this material location.

त्वङ्-मांस-रुधिर-स्नायु-
मेदो-मज्जास्थि-सहतौ ।
विण्-मूत्र-पूये रमतां
कृमीणां कियद् अन्तरम् ॥२१.२१॥

tvaṅ-māṁsa-rudhira-snāyu-
medo-majjāsthi-saṁhatau
viṇ-mūtra-pūye ramatāṁ
kṛmīṇāṁ kiyad antaram (21.21)

tvaṅ = tvak — skin; māṁsa — flesh; rudhira — blood; snāyu — muscle; medo = medah — fat; majjāsthi = majjā — marrow + asthi — bone; saṁhatau — combined; vin = vit — stool; mūtra — urine; pūye — pus; ramatam — those who delight; kṛmīṇām — in relation to maggots; kiyad = kiyat — how much, what; antaram — difference.

Translation

"What difference is there, between maggots and those who delight in the combined form of skin, flesh, blood, muscles, fat, marrow, bone, stool, urine and pus? (21.21)

Commentary:

In both cases, that of the human beings and that of the worms which eat flesh, the basic principle of consumption and enjoyment is there. It is the same exploitation.

अथापि नोपसज्जेत
स्त्रीषु स्त्रैणेषु चार्थ-वित् ।
विषयेन्द्रिय-संयोगान्
मनः क्षुभ्यति नान्यथा ॥२१.२२॥

athāpi nopasajjeta
strīṣu straiṇeṣu cārtha-vit
viṣayendriya-saṁyogān
manaḥ kṣubhyati nānyathā (21.22)

athapi = atha – therefore + api — even; nopasajjeta = na – no + upasajjeta — should associate; strīṣu — with women; straiṇeṣu — with those who crave to be with women; cārtha-vit = ca — and + artha-vit — one who knows his interest; viṣayendriya = viṣaya — attractive objects + indriya — sensual energy; saṁyogān = saṁyogāt — besides contact; manaḥ — mind; kṣubhyati — is agitated; nānyathā = na — not + anyathā — any other thing.

Translation

"Therefore, even a person who knows what is in his interest, should not associate with women, nor with those who crave their association, for the mind is agitated by no other factor besides the contact of the sensual energy with the attractive objects. (21.22)

Commentary:

This is the very best advice for all yogins. The sensual energy will remain the same, so long as the mind takes in lower pranic force. This cannot be changed. By surcharging the mind, the sensuality departs from this plane and becomes attracted to other realities. But when again the mind is lowered back to this level, the senses again resume the pursuit of this reality. When the mind is de-energized a yogi should know that and keep himself out of contact with the lower sense objects, particularly the alluring and compelling ones.

Saubhari Muni and others did not consider these matters initially. Therefore they fell from yoga practice when their minds were de-energized and had returned to the normal plane of consciousness. Of course such yogis did not give up, rather they resumed the practice and achieved spiritual perfection.

A yogi should surcharge the mind by *prāṇāyāma* and then he can focus into the supernatural and spiritual environments, but he should not be fooled into thinking that his mind will remain there. By nature, it will hustle back to the ordinary level. When it does, he should protect it by not exposing it to the attractive objects which lower it further.

अदृष्टाद् अश्रुताद् भावान्
न भाव उपजायते ।
असम्प्रयुञ्जतः प्राणान्
शाम्यति स्तिमित मनः ॥२१.२३॥

adṛṣṭād aśrutād bhāvān
na bhāva upajāyate
asamprayuñjataḥ prāṇān
śāmyati stimitaṁ manaḥ (21.23)

adṛṣṭād = adṛṣṭāt — from what was never seen; aśrutād = aśrutāt — from what was never heard of; bhāvān — from something; na — not; bhāva — emotional need; upajāyate — is experienced; asamprayuñjataḥ — that which is not connected; prāṇān — the sensual energy; śāmyati — is stilled; stimitam — stays in peace; manaḥ — the mind.

Translation

"An emotional need is not experienced for anything that was never seen nor heard of. The mind which is not connected to the sensual energy is still and stays at peace. (21.23)

Commentary:

This happens in the 6th and 7th stages of yoga practice, where the mind compartment is sectioned off so that the sensual energy *(citta)* stays put, stays without ideas or pictures and the intellect organ focuses out of this dimension completely. One does not experience a need for something to which the mind has no instinctive reference. Therefore once the mind is quieted, once the previous impressions are neutralized, the intellect makes no efforts to procure anything in this creation.

तस्मात् सङ्गो न कर्तव्यः
स्त्रीषु स्त्रैणेषु चेन्द्रियैः ।
विदुषां चाप्य् अविस्रब्धः
षड्-वर्गः किम् उ मादृशाम् ॥२१.२४॥

tasmāt saṅgo na kartavyaḥ
strīṣu straiṇeṣu cendriyaiḥ
viduṣāṁ cāpy avisrabdhaḥ
ṣaḍ-vargaḥ kim u mādṛśām (21.24)

tasmāt — therefore; saṅgo = saṅgaḥ — contact; na – never; kartavyaḥ — should be made; strīṣu — with women; straiṇeṣu — with those who crave women; cendriyaiḥ = ca — and + indriyaiḥ — through the senses; viduṣām — knowledgeable people; cāpy = ca – and + api — even; avisrabdhaḥ — that which is untrustworthy; ṣaḍ = ṣaṭ - six; vargaḥ — passions; kim – what to speak?; mādṛśām — of persons like me.

Translation

"Therefore contact through the senses, should never be made with women, or with those who crave them. And even for knowledgeable people, the six passions are untrustworthy, what to speak of their effect on people like me?" (21.24)

Commentary:

The six passions are lust, anger, greed, bewilderment, intoxication and envy. These should be curbed by emotional purification through higher yoga. If these are just curbed by observance of moral principles, they will remain dormant, and will give trouble when there is opportunity. For a deep effective cure, one should apply yoga process.

We cannot avoid women completely, either in this world nor anywhere in the hereafter. Therefore we should learn how to do our righteous duty in relation to them as directed by the Universal Form. Otherwise we should realize that we have little to do with them. Conversely, this same opinion should be used by yogini women when dealing with men and with sensually-inclined, spiritually-resistant females.

श्री-भगवान् उवाच
एवं प्रगायन् नृप-देव-देवः
स उर्वशी-लोकम् अथो विहाय ।
आत्मानम् आत्मन्य् अवगम्य मां वै
उपारमज् ज्ञान-विधूत-मोहः ॥२१.२५॥

śrī-bhagavān uvāca
evaṁ pragāyan nṛpa-deva-devaḥ
sa urvaśī-lokam atho vihāya
ātmānam ātmany avagamya māṁ vai
upāramaj jñāna-vidhūta-mohaḥ (21.25)

śrī-bhagavān – the blessed lord; uvāca — said; evam — thus; pragāyan — singing to himself; nṛpa-deva-devaḥ — that brilliant person among the angelic people and human beings; sa = saḥ — he; urvaśī-lokam — the dimensional residence of Urvaśī; atho = athau — then and there, abruptly; vihāya — gave up; ātmānam — spirit; ātmany = ātmani — in the spirit; avagamya — realizing; mām — me; vai — indeed; upāramaj = upāramat — attained peace; jñāna — knowledge; vidhūta — dispelled; mohaḥ — infatuation.

Translation

The Blessed Lord said: Thus musing to himself, that brilliant person who was prominent among the angelic people and the human beings, abruptly gave up the dimensional residence of Urvaśī. Realizing Me as the Spirit in himself, he through knowledge, dispelled the infatuation and attained peace. (21.25)

Commentary:

Purūravā was not supposed to become a pawn of *Urvaśī*, the very attractive and sexually appealing angelic woman. Even though *Urvaśī* was produced from the thighs of God *Nārāyaṇa*, still *Purūravā* should not have become subjugated by her. Thus in time, when his real self manifested, he took steps to ease himself away from the goddess *(devī).*

Even though one may be an associate of the Supreme Lord, or even though one may be an associate of Lord *Brahmā* or Lord Shiva, still one should not fall under the influence of the women who are expansions of these divine personalities. One must take care to stick to one's position as a servant or son of the divine persons and not fall under other influences.

Śrī Krishna saluted *Purūravā* as a god among the gods and the human beings, *nara-deva-devah*. That means that *Purūravā* was an eternal associate of *Śrī* Krishna. Somehow, he got lost in the material world, when he met *Urvaśī* who is another eternal associate of the Lord, who somehow emerged from the thigh of Lord *Nārāyaṇa* in the presence of the angelic hosts. Still *Urvaśī* and *Purūravā* were not meant for each other, but rather they were meant to be servants of Lord Krishna. They should not have taken it upon themselves to form a romance without considering themselves as associates of the Lord.

A person becomes befooled when he enters this material world. This applies to the eternal conditioned souls, who just do not know any better, as well as to the near-liberated ones, like *Urvaśī* and *Purūravā*. By seeing the example of *Purūravā*, the conditioned entities get hints on how they might be extricated from this dangerous situation of the attraction of the mind to the attractive objects which the sensual energy so desperately seeks.

Purūravā was able to snap out of it, because he was an eternal associate of the Lord. Such people usually do an abrupt reversal at some point in their degraded life. They never return to the life they endured before the realization. This is because their original identity surfaces in their objective minds permanently thereafter. Others however, have to make much more endeavor for a permanent release.

ततो दुःसङ्गम् उत्सृज्य
सत्सु सज्जेत बुद्धिमान् ।
सन्त एवास्य छिन्दन्ति
मनो-व्यासङ्गम् उक्तिभिः ॥२१.२६॥

tato duḥsaṅgam utsṛjya
satsu sajjeta buddhimān
santa evāsya chindanti
mano-vyāsaṅgam uktibhiḥ (21.26)

tato = tatah — therefore; duḥsaṅgam — bad company; utsṛjya — abandoning; satsu — in the company of saintly devotees; sajjeta — should make friendship; buddhimān — one who has a sharp intellect; santa — saintly people; evāsya = eva — only + asya — his; chindanti — dispell; mano = manaḥ — of the mind; vyāsaṅgam — unwarranted attachment; uktibhiḥ — by their advice.

Translation

Therefore abandoning bad company, the one who has a sharp intellect should make friendship with saintly people. They only, by their advice, can dispel the unwarranted attachment. (21.26)

सन्तो ऽनपेक्षा मच्-चित्ताः
प्रशान्ताः सम-दर्शिनः ।
निर्ममा निरहङ्कारा
निर्द्वन्द्वा निष्परिग्रहाः ॥२१.२७॥

santo 'napekṣā mac-cittāḥ
praśāntāḥ sama-darśinaḥ
nirmamā nirahaṅkārā
nirdvandvā niṣparigrahāḥ (21.27)

santo = santaḥ — saintly people; 'napekṣā = anapekṣāh — not reliant on favors; mic-cittaḥ = mat-cittāḥ — those whose mental and emotional energy is centered on me; praśāntāḥ — fully calmed; sama-darśinaḥ — those having the comparatively equal vision, those who perceive the similarity in each body of a spirit linked to a set of psychological equipments under God's supervision; nirmama = nirmamaḥ — from the tendency of possessiveness; nirahaṅkārā = nirahaṅkārāḥ — from the tendency of inappropriate self-assertion; nirdvandvā = nirdvandvāḥ — from reacting to happiness and distress; niṣparigrahāḥ — from grasping.

Translation

Those saintly persons are not reliant on favors. Their mental and emotional energy is centered on Me. They are fully calmed and have the perception of the comparatively equal similarity in each body, of a spirit linked to a set of psychological equipments under God's supervision. They are free from possessiveness, free from inappropriate self-assertion, free from reacting to happiness or distress, and free from grasping. (21.27)

Commentary:

Each of these aspects must be developed separately by the ascetic. He should not think that just by being in the company of the saints he will develop these. One will certainly exhibit these tendencies from time to time if one remains with the advanced souls but one must also aspire and observe one's psyche so that by self-critique one can recognize and eliminate unwanted tendencies.

तेषु नित्य महा-भाग
महा-भागेषु मत्-कथाः ।
सम्भवन्ति हि ता नृणां
जुषतां प्रपुनन्त्य् अघम् ॥२१.२८॥

teṣu nityaṁ mahā-bhāga
mahā-bhāgeṣu mat-kathāḥ
sambhavanti hi tā nṝṇāṁ
juṣatāṁ prapunanty agham (21.28)

teṣu — among them; nityam — constant; mahā-bhāga — o blessed man; mahā-bhāgeṣu — in the association with those who have much godilness; mat-kathāḥ — discussions about my activities; sambhavanti — there is; hi — indeed; tā — these; nṝṇām — of people; juṣatām — of those who delight; prapunanty = prapunanti — purge off; agham — bad tendency.

Translation

O blessed one, in the association of those who are blessed with much godliness, there is constant discussion about My activities. These dialogues of the people who delight in hearing of Me, purge off bad tendencies. (21.28)

Commentary:

Any discussion about the activities of *Śrī* Krishna is good for people, because it draws their minds away from petty things and puts their mind in focus on Him. However, when such discussions are held among those who are blessed with much godliness, the discussions have more potency.

Some people feel that if we sit down and talk about *Śrī* Krishna from now till the end of time, we will become liberated automatically and will not have to do anything else, but such ideas are offensive to Lord Krishna, because the discussion should bring on a submissive attitude to Him, whereby we would practice His advisories. It is not meant that we should only speak about *Śrī* Krishna and do nothing else. By a careful study of the *Bhagavad-Gītā* discourse to Arjuna and this talk to Uddhava, we can come to the conclusion that ultimately, after we are drawn to *Śrī* Krishna, we have to agree to do what He says. This is submissiveness towards Him.

Uddhava for instance wanted to stay with *Śrī* Krishna where he met the Lord sitting down with a wounded foot but the Lord insisted that Uddhava go to the Badrinatha Pilgrimage Site in the Himalayas. Uddhava wanted to leave this world at exactly the same time, that *Śrī* Krishna would, to be with the Lord wherever He would go but that was not allowed. Thus love of Krishna, hearing of His pastimes, chanting of His holy names and other related activities and services will culminate in having to follow an instruction even if that order is not agreeable to the devotee. On occasion, neither Arjuna or Uddhava preferred to do what Krishna desired of them, but due to their respect and love for Him they gladly complied.

ता ये श्रृण्वन्ति गायन्ति
ह्य् अनुमोदन्ति चादृताः ।
मत्-पराः श्रद्दधानाश् च
भक्तिं विन्दन्ति ते मयि ॥२१.२९॥

tā ye śṛṇvanti gāyanti
hy anumodanti cādṛtāḥ
mat-parāḥ śraddadhānāś ca
bhaktiṁ vindanti te mayi (21.29)

tā — those; ye — they who; śṛṇvanti — hear; gāyanti — chant; hy = hi — indeed; anumodanti — appreciate; cādṛtāḥ = ca — and + ādṛtāḥ — reverentially; mat-parāḥ — those who become attached to me; śraddadhānās = śraddadhānāḥ — those who acquire faith; ca — and; bhaktim — devotion; vindanti — attain; te — they; mayi — to me.

Translation

Those who reverentially chant and appreciate information about Me, become attached to Me and acquire faith in Me. They attain devotion to Me. (21.29)

Commentary:

It is often quoted that Lord *Śrī* Chaitanya Mahaprabhu said that there are no hard and fast rules for chanting the holy name of *Śrī* Krishna. Some seem to think that this means that any chanting of the holy names will bring about perfection immediately. However regardless of what *Śrī* Chaitanya Mahaprabhu said, and regardless of what He really meant, this instruction to Uddhava, does attest that reverential chanting will cause devotion to *Śrī* Krishna.

If one does not chant with respect one will lose out, because one's mind will make a joke of the holy names, by trivializing them. If we want *Śrī* Krishna's association, we have to heed His instructions. Someone cannot twist or turn these guidelines. A human being does not take something seriously if he deals with it in a whimsy.

Anybody can start where he is, but to reach *Śrī* Krishna, one has to change one's attitude to make advancement. Whatever compromise or incentive one was given by any other person, must be dropped if one really wants to reach *Śrī* Krishna, otherwise one will remain as a superficial devotee forever.

भक्तिं लब्धवतः साधोः
किम् अन्यद् अवशिष्यते ।
मय्य् अनन्त-गुणे ब्रह्मण्य्
आनन्दानुभवात्मनि ॥२१.३०॥

bhaktiṁ labdhavataḥ sādhoḥ
kim anyad avaśiṣyate
mayy ananta guṇe brahmaṇy
ānandānubhavātmani (21.30)

bhaktim — devotion; labdhavataḥ — one who has attained; sādhoḥ — for the purified person; kim — what; anyad = anyat — else, more; avaśisyate — remains to be achieved; mayy = mayi — to me; ananta – unlimited; gune — virtues; brahmaṇy = brahmaṇi — to the spiritual reality in person; ānandānubhavātmani = ānanda — spiritual happiness + anubhava — experience + ātmani — in the self, in essence.

Translation

What more is to be achieved for the purified person who attained devotion to Me. That person has unlimited virtues, and is the spiritual reality in person. He is essentially the experience of spiritual happiness itself. (21.30)

Commentary:

If a person is emotionally purified and if he has devotion for Krishna, then everything spiritual will be achieved by him. His motivational energies will work for the same objective. His whole self will be compelled to go in the spiritual direction. He is the spiritual reality in person. His existence is a sample of the experience of spiritual happiness. Because of inner purity, he perfectly reflects unlimited virtues of divinity.

यथोपश्रयमाणस्य
भगवन्तं विभावसुम् ।
शीतं भयं तमो ऽप्येति
साधून् ससेवतस् तथा ॥२१.३१॥

yathopaśrayamāṇasya
Bhagavantaṁ vibhāvasum
śītaṁ bhayaṁ tamo 'pyeti
sādhūn saṁsevatas tathā (21.31)

yathopaśrayamāṇasya = yathā — just as + upaśrayamāṇasya — of one who resorts to; Bhagavantam — powerful; vibhāvasum — fire; śītam — cold; bhayam — fear; tamo = tamah — darkness; 'pyeti = apyeti — goes away; sādhūn — purified persons; saṁsevatas = saṁsevatah — one who serves and worships; tathā — so.

Translation

Just as cold, fear and darkness go away from a person who resorts to a powerful fire, even so is one relieved who serves and worships with purified people. (21.31)

Commentary:

To get out of material existence, one will have to take assistance not only from *Śrī* Krishna but from the purified persons who have already taken deeper and more sincere shelter of Him. That sort of association causes one to lose bad tendencies and their resulting insecurities.

If one makes a mistake in selecting the advanced purified devotees of the Lord, then one should not give up but should instead search out a purified soul. If one cannot find such a person, one should do his best to follow the rules and regulations one hears of and reads of in the scriptures like the *Bhagavad-Gītā*. One should be confident that sooner or later, one will be shown a definite way to reach *Śrī* Krishna and one should be prepared to take any discipline which would cause one to draw nearer to Him.

निमज्ज्योन्मज्जतां घोरे
भवाब्धौ परमायणम् ।
सन्तो ब्रह्म-विदः शान्ता
नौर् दृढेवाप्सु मज्जताम् ॥२१.३२॥

nimajjyonmajjatāṁ ghore
bhavābdhau paramāyaṇam
santo brahma-vidaḥ śāntā
naur dṛḍhevāpsu majjatām (21.32)

nimajjyonmajjatām = nimajjya — of those who are losing their footing + unmajjatām — of those who are gaining their stance; ghore — in the dreadful; bhavābdhau = bhava — material existence + abdhau — in the ocean; paramāyaṇam = parama — supreme + ayanam — in the ocean; santo = santaḥ — saintly people; brahma-vidaḥ — those who realized the spiritual existence; śāntā = śāntāh — those who are spiritually pacified; naur = nauḥ — boat; dṛḍhevāpsu = dṛḍhā — sturdy + iva — just as + apsu — water; majjatām — those who are drowning.

Translation

The saintly people are the supreme refuge of those who lose their footing and of those who are gaining their stance, in the dreadful ocean of material existence, just as a sturdy boat is for those who are in water. (21.32)

Commentary:

The question may be asked, that since all along *Śrī* Krishna mentioned Himself only and no one else, why is it that all of a sudden, he includes the saintly purified devotee as the supreme refuge (paramāyanam). The answer is that *Śrī* Krishna does not in every case, take care of the devotee, as He did for Arjuna and Uddhava. In many cases, it is Arjuna or Uddhava or someone similar who has to rescue somebody. *Śrī* Krishna may use a great devotee to administer the mercy.

अन्नं हि प्राणिनां प्राण
आर्तानां शरणं त्व् अहम् ।
धर्मो वित्तं नृणां प्रेत्य
सन्तो ऽर्वाग् बिभ्यतो ऽरणम् ॥ २१.३३ ॥

annaṁ hi prāṇināṁ prāṇa
ārtānāṁ śaraṇaṁ tv aham
dharmo vittaṁ nṛṇāṁ pretya
santo 'rvāg bibhyato 'raṇam (21.33)

annam — food; hi — indeed; prāṇinām — of the living creatures; prāṇa = prāṇaḥ — vital energy; ārtānām — of those who are distressed; śaranam — refuge; tv = tu — and; aham — I; dharmo = dharmah — righteous duty; vittam — bargaining asset; nṛṇām — of people; pretya — pertaining to the hereafter; santo = santaḥ — the purified saints; 'rvāg = arvāk — of being degraded; bibhyato = bibhyataḥ — for those who are afraid; 'raṇam = aranam — means of safety.

Translation

As food is the sustenance of the living creatures, and as I am the refuge of those who are distressed, as righteous duty performed is the bargaining asset of those people in the hereafter, so the purified saints are the means of safety for those who are afraid of being degraded. (21.33)

Commentary:

It may be argued that if a person could get in touch with *Śrī* Krishna directly, then he would not have to take shelter of the purified saints, since His association with Krishna would be the complete shelter for him. However the argument may not hold up in all cases, because *Śrī* Krishna would have to be agree to be available on a full time basis to that devotee. If *Śrī* Krishna decided that such a devotee should take shelter of a purified saint, then the devotee would have no choice but to do so. This is why devotion to *Śrī* Krishna is a technical matter. The devotion must be so compelling that the devotee is prepared to be directed by *Śrī* Krishna.

The purified saintly devotees of *Śrī* Krishna are very important people, because they have the practical means of how a person can avoid degradation. Their advice is serviceable and humanly applicable. Since they use human forms and live at the time of the devotee, they may give up-to-date advice on how to apply rules and regulations for accelerated progression.

सन्तो दिशन्ति चक्षूंसि
बहिर् अर्कः समुत्थितः ।
देवता बान्धवाः सन्तः
सन्त आत्माहम् एव च ॥२१.३४॥

santo diśanti cakṣūṁsi
bahir arkaḥ samutthitaḥ
devatā bāndhavāḥ santaḥ
santa ātmāham eva ca (21.34)

santo = santaḥ — purified saint; diśanti — furnish; cakṣūṁṣi — eyes, many types of vision; bahir = bahiḥ — external; arkah — sun; samutthitaḥ — is fully risen; devatā = devatāḥ — worshipable deities; bāndhavāḥ — relatives; santah — purified saints; santa = santaḥ — purified saints; ātmāham = ātmā — spiritual self + aham — I; eva – only; ca — and.

Translation

The purified saints, furnish many types of vision. The fully risen sun gives external sight. These saints are to be regarded as worshipable deities and as one's own relatives, even as the spiritual self and as I myself. (21.34)

Commentary:

By studying the guidelines given to Uddhava and Arjuna, one may learn how to recognize a purified saint.

वैतसेनस् ततो ऽप्य् एवम्
उर्वश्या लोक-निष्पृहः ।
मुक्त-सङ्गो महीम् एताम्
आत्मारामश् चचार ह ॥२१.३५॥

vaitasenas tato 'py evam
urvaśyā loka-niṣpṛhaḥ
mukta-saṅgo mahīm etām
ātmārāmaś cacāra ha (21.35)

vaitasenas = vaitasenaḥ — Purūravā the son of the king whose army was subdued by a much stronger force; tato = tataḥ - hence, from then onwards; 'py = api — also; evam — thus; urvaśyā — of *Urvaśī*; loka — place of dimensional residence; niṣpṛhaḥ — from sensuous desires; mukta-saṅgo = mukta-sangaḥ — liberated from social attachment; mahīm — earth; etām — this; ātmārāmaś = ātmārāmaḥ — spiritually self-satisfied; cacāra — roamed about; ha — indeed.

Translation

From then onwards the son of the king whose army was subdued by a much stronger force, that Purūravā, who was freed from the desire to be in the dimensional residence of goddess Urvaśī, and who was liberated from social attachment, roamed over this earth, in a spiritually self-satisfied condition. (21.35)

Commentary:

Purūravā was called *Vaitasena*, because his father's army *(sena)* was subdued by Goddess *Durgā*, when it entered her forest territory without permission. By a charm all those soldiers and their king, the father of *Purūravā*, were transformed into women. That narration is told in the 9th canto of the *Śrīmad Bhāgavatam*.

CHAPTER 22*

Kriyā Yoga:

Application of Yoga to Mystic Activity**

Terri Stokes-Pineda Art

śrī-uddhava uvāca
kriyā-yogaṁ samācakṣva bhavad-ārādhanaṁ prabho
yasmāt tvāṁ ye yathārcanti sātvatāḥ sātvatarṣabha

The deserving Uddhava said: O Lord, please explain the application of yoga to mystic activity. On what basis and in what manner did the Sātvata clan devotees worship you, O leader of the clan. (Uddhava Gītā 22.1)

* Śrīmad Bhāgavatam Canto 11, Chapter 27

** Translator's selected chapter title.

श्री-उद्धव उवाच
क्रिया-योगं समाचक्ष्व
भवद्-आराधन प्रभो ।
यस्मात् त्वां ये यथार्चन्ति
सात्वताः सात्वतर्षभ ॥२२.१॥

śrī-uddhava uvāca
kriyā-yogaṁ samācakṣva
bhavad-ārādhanaṁ prabho
yasmāt tvāṁ ye yathārcanti
sātvatāḥ sātvatarṣabha (22.1)

śrī-uddhava – the deserving Uddhava; uvāca — said; kriyā – mystic activity; yogam — yoga discipline; samācakṣva — please describe; bhavad = bhavat — your; ārādhanam — duly worship; prabho — o Lord; yasmāt — from what, on what basis; tvām — you; ye — who; yathārcanti = yathā — in what manner + arcanti — they worship; sātvatāḥ — devotees of the Sātvata clan; sātvatarṣabha — the best of the Sātvata people.

Translation

The deserving Uddhava said: O Lord, please explain the application of yoga to mystic activity. On what basis and in what manner did the Sātvata clan devotees worship you, O leader of the clan. (22.1)

Commentary:

When *Śrī* Uddhava spoke of the *Sātvatas*, he spoke of a particular clan of persons who were related to *Śrī* Krishna's physical body. This does not mean that they were not spiritually related to the Supreme Lord, but we should not warp the meanings of the word *Sātvata* by translating it as devotee. It is really disgusting when leading members of our *Sampradāya* disciplic succession, make suggestions which imply that *Sātvata* means a devotee or any devotee in good standing in the succession. The meaning here is the family members in certain clans who were present with Lord Krishna. In the time of Uddhava the modern disciplic successions, did not exist as part of the *Sātvata* clan.

Satvaka was a king in the Yadava dynasty which descended from the famous King Yadu. These kings were related physically. King *Satvata's* sons established four distinct lineages of rulers and clans namely the *Bhojas*, *Andhakas*, *Kukuras* and *Vṛṣṇis*. The *Bhojas* ruled at Martikavat. The *Kukuras* were the ruling tribe of Shurasena country, which was ruled by the famous Ugrasena who was taken advantage of by his step-son Kansa, who was killed by *Śrī* Krishna. The *Andhaka* clan was headed by *Kṛtavarma* who was implicated in the killing of the sons of the Pandavas just after the *Kurukṣetra* war. The *Vṛṣṇi* clan took Lord Krishna as their leader. All of these are *Sātvata* people.

King *Sātvata* was the son of *Ayu*. These *Sātvata* people had a special technique for relating to, serving and worshiping *Śrī* Krishna. But their special qualification was that they hardly ever hesitated to follow any of *Śrī* Krishna's suggestions.

Uddhava extols them as prime examples of what it is to be a devotee of *Śrī* Krishna. Uddhava wants to know the secret of these *Sātvata* family members, because they had a knack for pleasing *Śrī* Krishna. Theirs is the ideal example. *Bhakti* yoga is great but in *bhakti* yoga, there is a section called *kriyā* yoga, which is exact and precise. Uddhava wants that revealed directly by *Śrī* Krishna.

एतद् वदन्ति मुनयो मुहुर्
निःश्रेयस नृणाम् ।
नारदो भगवान् व्यास
आचार्यो ऽङ्गिरसः सुतः ॥२२.२॥

etad vadanti munayo muhur
niḥśreyasaṁ nṛṇām
nārado bhagavān vyāsa
ācāryo 'ṅgirasaḥ sutaḥ (22.2)

etad = etat — this; vadanti — they say; munayo = munayaḥ — the yogi philosopher; muhur = muhuh — repeatedly; nihśreyasam — the highest well-being; nṛṇām — for human beings; nārado = nāradaḥ — Nārada; bhagavān – divine and highly respected; vyāsa = vyāsaḥ — Vyāsa; ācāryo = ācāryaḥ — spiritual master; 'ṅgirasaḥ = aṅgirasaḥ — of Angiras; suta — the son.

Translation

The yogi philosophers such as Nārada, the divine and respected Vyāsa, and my teacher, the son of Aṅgira, repeatedly describe this as being the highest well-being for human beings. (22.2)

Commentary:

The son of *Aṅgiras*, Uddhava's teacher, is *Bṛhaspati*. This person, as well as *Nārada* and *Nārada*'s disciple, the divine and highly respected *Vyāsa*, did extol the value of *kriyā* yoga, stating that it was the highest well-being of the human beings.

निःसृतं ते मुखाम्भोजाद्
यद् आह भगवान् अजः ।
पुत्रेभ्यो भृगु-मुख्येभ्यो
देव्यै च भगवान् भवः ॥२२.३॥

niḥsṛtaṁ te mukhāmbhojād
yad āha bhagavān ajaḥ
putrebhyo bhṛgu-mukhyebhyo
devyai ca bhagavān bhavaḥ (22.3)

niḥsṛtam — spoken; te — your; mukhāmbhojād = mukha – mouth; ambhojāt — from the lotus-shaped; yad = yat — which; āha — spoke; bhagavān — the lord; ajaḥ — Procreator Brahmā; putrebhyo = putrebhyaḥ — to his sons; bhṛgu – Bhṛgu; mukhyebhyo = mukhyebhyah — to those headed by; devyai — to Devi; ca — and; bhagavān – lord; bhavaḥ — Bhava Shiva.

Translation

The instruction spoke from Your lotus-shaped mouth, which the Lord Aja Brahmā spoke to his sons, who were headed by Bhṛgu and which Lord Bhava Shiva explained to the goddess Devī; (22.3)

Commentary:

Kriyā yoga is a series of techniques which was imparted to the yogis from Lord Shiva. As far as women are concerned, the first student of *kriyā* yoga is Devi, the wife of Lord Shiva. But we understand from the *Purāṇas* that *Vāk* or *Sarasvatī* who is also known as *Arundhati* discovered some *kriyās* by herself and took lessons from *Vasiṣṭa* in one of her life times. Other goddess such as *Savitri* and *Gāyatrī* are prime *kriyā* yoginis. It is described in the *Nārada Pañcaratra* that Lord Shiva explained much about its application to Deity worship, to Goddess *Devī*.

From what we heard in the *kriyā* yoga lineage, it appears that Goddess *Devī* was the first woman, in fact the first person to perfect the yoga *kriyās*. Her teacher is Lord Shiva. One of the *siddhas* of the eighteen special mahayogis is *Matsyendranath*, who is said to have taken birth as a fish and to have overheard what Lord Shiva told *Devī* about *kriyā* yoga. Subsequently that fish took human birth and perfected the *kriyās*. He took a disciple who become famous as Gorakhnatha.

Lord Krishna as the supreme teacher of *kriyā* yoga, taught it to many others. *Śrī* Krishna did not teach Arjuna *kriyā* yoga but that instruction was given to Arjuna by none other than *Yudhiṣṭhira* who was taught by the divine and highly respected *Vyāsa*, who was in fact their physical grandfather.

As far as *Nārada* is concerned, he is the teacher of *Śrīla Vyāsadeva* but he did not instruct *Vyāsa* in *kriyā* yoga because *Vyāsa* was endowed with the instinct for it. However, previously *Nārada* was cursed to assume the demeanor of an angelic playboy. He was known then as Upabarhana. When *Nārada* was freed from that curse, he mastered *kriyā* yoga and completely freed himself from all lower transmigrations.

From the very beginning of creation, Lord Shiva manifested with *kriyā* yoga practice but initially the supernatural people were, for the most part, disapproving of Lord Shiva's *kriyā* process. This is because His austerities were spearheaded by absolute celibacy. With celibacy to an absolute degree there can be no expansion of population. Since the supernatural people felt the necessity to bring out various species of life, they objected to Lord Shiva's perpetual preoccupation with *kriyā* yoga. This objection was brought to fore in the story of King *Dakṣa*, the father of Lord Shiva's wife.

एतद् वै सर्व-वर्णानाम् आश्रमाणां च सम्मतम् । श्रेयसाम् उत्तमं मन्ये स्त्री-शूद्राणां च मान-द ॥२२.४॥	etad vai sarva-varṇānām āśramāṇāṁ ca sammatam śreyasām uttamaṁ manye strī-śūdrāṇāṁ ca māna-da (22.4)

etad = etat — this; vai — indeed; sarva-varṇānām — by all job categories; āśramāṇām — by the life styles; ca — and; sammatam — approved; śreyasām — of that which is conducive to the highest well-being; uttamam — best procedure; manye — I feel; strī — women; śūdrānām — for the working class people; ca — and; māna-da — one who gives respect to others.

Translation

...That procedure is for all job categories and life styles. It is approved. I feel that it is the best process which is conducive to the higher well-being for women and the working class people, O You who are the giver of honor (22.4)

Commentary:

Actually *kriyā* yoga can hardly be done by the working class people. It can hardly be done by most women, even though some exceptional women can master it. Therefore Uddhava's request has to be explained. We must remember that in the time of Uddhava the *kriyā* yoga was not learnt by everyone and anyone. In fact the persons mentioned by Uddhava namely *Nārada*, *Vyāsa* and Guru *Bṛhaspati*, were the caliber of persons who mastered *kriyā*. Only they could do it, because it requires mastership of higher yoga practice. The leading teachers mentioned, namely Lord Krishna, Lord *Brahmā* and Lord Shiva did not teach it to any and every body. In fact Uddhava explained that it was taught to *Bṛhaspati* and *Devī*, the goddess *Durgā*. *Bṛhaspati* learnt it from his father *Aṅgiras* who learnt it from *Brahmā.* Goddess *Durgā* learnt it from Lord Shiva, even though on occasion she discovered some of the techniques herself.

The statement by Uddhava that it may be taught to the women and laboring class cannot mean that they were taught it normally. They were not, due to its complexity. However Uddhava felt that they could benefit from its usage in worship ceremonies. This is very important since today Deity worship is performed in many temples without *kriyā* yoga as a prerequisite. Generally the *pujārīs* do not know the techniques but after becoming familiar with the external procedures of worship, they operate with a pretence. Since the public is not mystically-aware, these false *pujārīs* function as authorities in many temples.

I myself, having carried many mystic skills from past lives, and doing *aṣṭanga* yoga in this life, learned some procedural Deity Worship techniques in the succession which came through *Śrīla Bhaktivedānta Swāmī*. But he was a person who was against yoga practice. In his *sampradāya*, yoga is conspicuous by its absence and there is a belief there, that what they do, covers all yogas. Such was his opinion.

एतत् कमल-पत्राक्ष कर्म-बन्ध-विमोचनम् । भक्ताय चानुरक्ताय ब्रूहि विश्वेश्वरेश्वर ॥२२.५॥	etat kamala-patrākṣa karma-bandha-vimocanam bhaktāya cānuraktāya brūhi viśveśvareśvara (22.5)

etat — this; kamala-patrāksa — one whose eyes are shaped like lotus petals; karma - cultural activities; bandha — liability; vimocanam — the means of absolving; bhaktāya — to the devotee; cānuraktāya = ca - and + anuraktāya — very devoted, sincere and loyal; brūhi — explain; viśveśvareśvara — lords of the lords of the universe.

Translation

O Lord, whose eyes are shaped like lotus petals, O Lord of the lords of the universe, explain to me, your very sincere and loyal devotee, the means of absolving the liabilities of cultural activity. (22.5)

Commentary:

Uddhava here tactfully suggested that there is a connection between the application of *kriyā* yoga to cultural life and the settling of the liabilities or complications of cultural activities for the common man. Since the common man cannot successfully perform *kriyā* yoga, he will have to depend on the experts to perform it on his behalf. This of course will mean that he has to attend the worship ceremonies which are conducted by the great yogis like *Nārada* or by their competent students.

A complication in this teaching arises, because *Śrī* Krishna explained earlier that a common man can, by execution of righteous duty which is approved by *Śrī* Krishna, get out of material existence, or at least develop an attachment or devotional sentiment to *Śrī* Krishna, which would be the cause of his getting the opportunity to work for deliverance from material existence. Now Uddhava suggested something else, that a person should absolve the cultural complications, just by taking the benefit of the *kriyā*-yoga-applied ceremonies which are carried out by great yogis like *Nārada* or by their students.

श्री-भगवान् उवाच
न ह्य् अन्तो ऽनन्त-पारस्य
कर्म-काण्डस्य चोद्धव ।
सङ्क्षिप्तं वर्णयिष्यामि
यथावद् अनुपूर्वशः ॥२२.६॥

śrī-bhagavān uvāca
na hy anto 'nanta-pārasya
karma-kāṇḍasya coddhava
saṅkṣiptaṁ varṇayiṣyāmi
yathāvad anupūrvaśaḥ (22.6)

śrī-bhagavān – the blessed lord; uvāca — said; na — there is no; hy = hi — factually speaking; anto = antaḥ — end; 'nanta-pārasya = ananta-pārasya — regarding what is unlimited; karma-kāṇḍasya — regarding the explanations of chapters in the Vedas which describe ritual acts; coddhava = ca — and + uddhava — Uddhava; saṅkṣiptam — brief description; varnayisyāmi — I will give; yathāvad = yathāvat — accordingly; anupūrvaśaḥ — in order, orderly.

Translation

The Blessed Lord said: O Uddhava, factually speaking there is no end in regards to the explanation of the chapters in the Vedas which describe ritual acts, for the scope of it is unlimited. But I will give a brief but accurate and orderly description. (22.6)

Commentary:

Even though Uddhava is pressing for something simply, he gets something detailed which requires in-depth explanation. The scope of mystic ritual acts (*kriyā*) is varied, because it depends on the motivation, the objective, the skill used and the destiny. Since there are so many variables, it has to be done according to time and place. It is not stereotype. There is a prescribed way, but variables must be taken into consideration for the performance of the mystic and corresponding physical acts.

वैदिकस् तान्त्रिको मिश्र
इति मे त्रि-विधो मखः ।
त्रयाणाम् ईप्सितेनैव
विधिना मां समर्चरेत् ॥२२.७॥

vaidikas tāntriko miśra
iti me tri-vidho makhaḥ
trayāṇām īpsitenaiva
vidhinā māṁ samarcaret (22.7)

vaidikas = vaidikaḥ — according to the procedures given in the Vedas; tāntriko = tāntrikaḥ —

according to the tantric procedures; miśra = miśraḥ — according to the mixture of the two; iti — thus; me — in regards to me; tri-vidho = tri-vidhaḥ — three kinds; makhaḥ — ceremonial worship; trayāṇām — three; īpsitenaiva = īpsitena — by what is most appealing + eva — indeed; vidhinā — by method; mām — me; samarcaret — one should worship properly.

Translation

There are three kinds of ceremonial worship in regards to Me. These are procedures given in the Vedas, those given in the Tantric texts, and those which are effective mixtures of the two. One should properly worship Me by whatever method is most appealing. (22.7)

Commentary:

The person who carries out the physical and mystic acts for the other person who cannot do it himself, should be versed in *kriyā* yoga. On the spur of the moment, he should be capable of selecting a suitable procedure. He must also know how to use part of the Vedic procedure with a part of the tantric way of ceremony and technique. This means that an uniformed person cannot do this. Thus there is no question that this can be directly used by a common man. Secondly those who are not expert yogins like *Nārada*, *Vyāsa*, *Bṛhaspati* or their capable students, cannot do this either, but they can make a mockery of it by fooling the gullible public. Thus we see that many sannyasis, priests, preachers, acharyas and the like, make presentation of being knowledgeable. After people try their system, it is proven to be useless for absolving the complications of social life. Of course many of these leaders assure their clients that everything will be satisfactorily settled at the time of death or they just instruct that the cultural situations should be ignored or neglected.

यदा स्व-निगमेनोक्तं
द्विजत्वं प्राप्य पूरुषः ।
यथा यजेत मां भक्त्या
श्रद्धया तन् निबोध मे ॥२२.८॥

yadā sva-nigamenoktaṁ
dvijatvaṁ prāpya pūruṣaḥ
yathā yajeta māṁ bhaktyā
śraddhayā tan nibodha me (22.8)

yadā — when; sva — one's selection; nigamenoktam = nigamena — by the Vedic or tantric procedure used + uktam — what is stated; dvijatvam — brahminical certification; prāpya — achieving; pūruṣaḥ — person; yathā — accordingly; yajeta — should do ceremonial worship; mām — to me; bhaktyā — with devotion; śraddhayā — with faith; tan = tat — that; nibodha — learn from me; me — from me.

Translation

When according to what is stated in one's selected Vedic or Tantric scripture, a person obtains the brahminical certification, he should accordingly, do ceremonial worship to Me, with devotion and faith. Learn that from Me. (22.8)

Commentary:

As far as the general public is concerned, they cannot directly do these physical and mystic ceremonies to God, because they do not have the *kriyā* yoga training required. Only a trained person, in this case Lord Krishna cites a duly trained, properly certified brahmin, should attempt this. Nowadays the gurus are saying that their disciples can do it, even though some of these followers are not trained in *kriyā* yoga and are not brahmins by nature.

In addition, the priest must use a scripture that is harmonious with the cultural upbringing of the persons concerned, because their faith must be consistently applied. If they are hijacked from their tradition and brought over to another religion, they might not be able to lift their faith from the customary way. Thus the ceremony will lack potency due to lack of attention and disinterest, as they go through the procedures.

However many preachers, cite scriptures and incarnations of Godhead to prove that their religion is the supreme one and that it is not an imposition on the minds of any followers. All of this however is only manipulation.

अर्चायां स्थण्डिले ऽग्नौ वा
सूर्ये वाप्सु हृदि द्विजः ।
द्रव्येण भक्ति-युक्तो ऽर्चेत्
स्व-गुरुं माम् अमायया ॥२२.९॥

arcāyāṁ sthaṇḍile 'gnau vā
sūrye vāpsu hṛdi dvijaḥ
dravyeṇa bhaktī-yukto 'rcet
sva-guruṁ mām amāyayā (22.9)

arcāyām — in the Deity Form; sthaṇḍile — in the earth; 'gnau = agnau — in fire; vā — or; sūrye — in the sun; vāpsu = vā — or + apsu — in water; hṛdi — in the core of his being; dvijah — the certified brahmin; dravyeṇa — with ceremonial items; bhaktī-yukto = bhaktī-yuktaḥ — endowed with devotion; 'rcet = arcet — should worship; sva-gurum — his spiritual master; mām — me; amāyayā — without deception.

Translation

Being endowed with devotion, the certified brahmin should worship me, as well as his spiritual teacher, without deception, and with the ceremonial items, as I am situated in the Deity form, in the earth, the fire, the sun, the water and in the core of his being. (22.9)

Commentary:

There is no prescription here for the common man to worship the Deity of *Śrī* Krishna on his own. Such a person has to take help from a certified brahmin. Or he has to convince such a brahmin to train him to do so. In the past, Gautama Rishi trained a boy whose mother was once engaged in sexually-permissive life. The boy was trained as a brahmin even though his pedigree was in question. If there is any deception by the priest or by the person for whom the ceremony is conducted, it will fail to bring the desired results. The brahmin must honor both *Śrī* Krishna and the spiritual master who trained him. And he must work with providence not against it.

पूर्वं स्नानं प्रकुर्वीत
धौत-दन्तो ऽङ्ग-शुद्धये ।
उभयैर् अपि च स्नानं
मन्त्रैर् मृद्-ग्रहणादिना ॥२२.१०॥

pūrvaṁ snānaṁ prakurvīta
dhauta-danto 'ṅga-śuddhaye
ubhayair api ca snānaṁ
mantrair mṛd-grahaṇādinā (22.10)

pūrvam — first; snānam — bath; prakurvīta — should properly take; dhauta — cleansing; danto = dantaḥ — teeth; 'nga = anga — body parts; śuddhaye — in the cleaning; ubhayair = ubhayaiḥ — with both; api – also; ca — and; snānam — bath; mantrair = mantraiḥ — with sacred sounds; mṛd-grahaṇādinā = mṛt – earth + grahaṇa – smearing clay + ādinā — and such.

Translation

In terms of cleaning the bodily limbs, he should cleanse the teeth and diligently take bath. He should also take bath with both procedures, using the Vedic and Tantric sacred sounds and by smearing clay and doing other ceremonial actions. (22.10)

Commentary:

A priest has to clean his body externally by cleaning teeth and taking bath. While doing so he is supposed to chant certain mantras, then while dressing he should put sacred marks on his body while chanting the appropriate mantras.

सन्ध्योपास्त्यादि-कर्माणि
वेदेनाचोदितानि मे ।
पूजा तैः कल्पयेत् सम्यक्-
सङ्कल्पः कर्म-पावनीम् ॥२२.११॥

sandhyopāstyādi-karmāṇi
vedenācoditāni me
pūjāṁ taiḥ kalpayet samyak-
saṅkalpaḥ karma-pāvanīm (22.11)

sandhyopāstyādi = sandhyā — dawn, early morning, noon and later evening + upāsti — worship + ādi — and such; karmāṇi — ritual acts; vedenācoditāni = vedena — through the Vedas + ācoditāni — standard procedures; me — me; pūjām — worship; taiḥ — by these; kalpayet — should perform; samyak – correct; saṅkalpaḥ — intentions; karma — cultural activity + pāvanīm — that which purifies one.

Translation

Through the Vedas, procedures consisting of ritual acts for worship at dawn, in the early morning, at noon and in the late afternoon, were given by Me. With these, one should worship with the correct intention, which results in the purification of cultural activity. (22.11)

Commentary:

This is done for patrons by the brahmin people who are duly qualified. If however those brahmins are not fit, the patrons will not get the benefits promised by *Śrī* Krishna, even if the *pujārī*, priest, pandit or devotee attests to it.

For householders, the purification of cultural activity is required, because to make a livelihood, one must be involved in some type of violence, no matter how subtle and therefore one has to counterbalance it or go on with the reactions in one's life. The correct intention in performing ritual ceremonies is required. In fact the entire ceremony is either validated or condemned by either the correct intention or the pretension.

शैली दारु-मयी लौही
लेप्या लेख्या च सैकती ।
मनो-मयी मणि-मयी
प्रतिमाष्ट-विधा स्मृता ॥२२.१२॥

śailī dāru-mayī lauhī
lepyā lekhyā ca saikatī
mano-mayī maṇi-mayī
pratimāṣṭa-vidhā smṛtā (22.12)

śailī — stone; dāru – book; mayī — composed of; lauhī — metal; lepyā — clay; lekhyā — paint; ca — and, or; saikatī — sand; mano – in the mind; mayī — conceived of, made of; maṇi – jewel; mayī — made of; pratimāṣṭa-vidhā = pratimā — Deity figure or picture + aṣṭa-vidhā — eight kinds; smṛtā — approved.

Translation:

Eight kinds of Deity figures, or pictures are approved, namely those composed of stone, wood, metal, clay, paint, sand, mental energy and jewel. (22.12)

Commentary:

This gives the ruling for the materials which may be used in constructing a Deity of *Śrī* Krishna.

चलाचलेति द्वि-विधा
प्रतिष्ठा जीव-मन्दिरम् ।
उद्वासावाहने न स्तः
स्थिरायाम् उद्धवार्चने ॥२२.१३॥

calācaleti dvi-vidhā
pratiṣṭhā jīva-mandiram
udvāsāvāhane na staḥ
sthirāyām uddhavārcane (22.13)

calācaleti = calā — movable + acalā — immovable + iti — thus namely; dvi-vidhā — two kinds; pratiṣṭā — installation; jīva-mandiram = jīva – the particular Deity + mandiram — temple of God; udvāsāvāhane = udvāsa — dismissal + āvāhane — invitation; na – not; stah — there is; sthirāyām

— permanently installed figure; uddhavārcane = uddhava — Uddhava + arcane — in the worship.

Translation

Two kinds of sanctified Deities Figures of the particular Deity worship exists, namely one which is movable and one immovable. O Uddhava, there is no invitation or dismissal in the worship ceremony of the permanently installed Figure. (22.13)

Commentary:

For very large Deities or for small ones which are permanently affixed, the *pujārī* is prohibited from making efforts to move the figure. Such Deities are installed permanently at established shrines or at new shrines which are designed for daily worship by trained priests.

The small deities may be moved from temple to temple or they can be taken out of the temple for special mobile programs. These deities are invited and are dismissed, according to the scriptural procedures.

अस्थिरायां विकल्पः स्यात्
स्थण्डिले तु भवेद् द्वयम् ।
स्नपनं त्व् अविलेप्यायाम्
अन्यत्र परिमार्जनम् ॥२२.१४॥

asthirāyāṁ vikalpaḥ syāt
sthaṇḍile tu bhaved dvayam
snapanaṁ tv avilepyāyām
anyatra parimārjanam (22.14)

asthirāyām — in regard to moveable figures; vikalpaḥ — option; syāt — there is; sthaṇḍile — in the case of a figure drawn on the ground; tu — but; bhaved = bhavet — should be done; dvayam — two; snapanam — bathing; tv = tu — moreover; avilepyāyām — in relation to a figure not made of clay; anyatra — other cases; parimārjanam — through dry cleaning.

Translation

There is an option in regards to the movable figures, but in the case of a figure drawn on the ground, the two greetings should be done. Moreover bathing is performed for those figures not made of clay. And in other cases, thorough dry cleansing is done. (22.14)

Commentary:

When performing ceremonies outdoors, the priest is required to call the deity to enter the deity form or to be present mystically in a physically-unseen dimension nearby. When the ceremony is near completion, he should ask the Deity for permission to close it and greet the deity as the deity withdraws from that place. One should not pour bath water over a deity which is made of clay or any dissolvable material. But such deities may endure ceremonial bathing by pouring the bath liquids into a container which is placed before them.

द्रव्यैः प्रसिद्धैर् मद्-यागः
प्रतिमादिष्व् अमायिनः ।
भक्तस्य च यथा-लब्धैर्
हृदि भावेन चैव हि ॥२२.१५॥

dravyaiḥ prasiddhair mad-yāgaḥ
pratimādiṣv amāyinaḥ
bhaktasya ca yathā-labdhair
hṛdi bhāvena caiva hi (22.15)

dravyaiḥ — with items; prasiddhair = prasiddhaiḥ — with the most perfect; mad-yāgaḥ = mat-yāgaḥ — worship ceremony; pratimādiṣv = pratima – sanctified figure + ādiṣu — and the like; amāyinaḥ — a person who is without deception; bhaktasya — of the devotee; ca — and; yathā –as; labdhair = labdhaiḥ — with what is available; hṛdi — within his feelings; bhāvena — by sentiments; caiva = ca — and + eva hi — surely.

Translation

My worship ceremony conducted through sacrificial figures and the like, by the devotee, should be conducted with the most perfect items according to what is available and by his deep feelings. (22.15)

Commentary:

The sacrificial priest or *pujārī* has to versed in worship procedures. He should be a mystic yogi, for if he is not, his performance will be devoid of the required mystic perception which is needed to call a deity and to request leave of one when the ceremony is concluded. If the sacrificial priest or *pujārī* is not a yogi, the person may do the best he can without having the mystic clarity.

Others attending the ceremony should be attentive to it, should have followed the requirements for cleanliness before approaching the ceremonial area. They should have selected the best items and should have deep feelings for the Deity. In other words, one should worship a Deity to which one has become endearingly involved.

स्नानालङ्करणं प्रेष्ठम्
अर्चायाम् एव तूद्धव ।
स्थण्डिले तत्त्व-विन्यासो
वह्नाव् आज्य-प्लुतं हविः ॥२२.१६॥

snānālaṅkaraṇaṁ preṣṭham
arcāyām eva tūddhava
sthaṇḍile tattva-vinyāso
vahnāv ājya-plutaṁ haviḥ (22.16)

snānālaṅkaraṇaṁ = snāna — bathing + alaṅkaraṇam — decorating; preṣṭham — prime activity, choice function; arcāyām — in the worship of figures; eva — in fact; tūddhava = tu — but + uddhava — Uddhava; sthaṇḍile — in the figures drawn on the ground; tattva –principal factors and worshipped personalities; vinyāso = vinyāsaḥ — inscribing letters; vahnāv = vahnau — in fire ceremonies; ājya-plutaṁ = ājya — ghee + plutam — drenched; haviḥ — oblations of seeds.

Translation

In the worship of figures, bathing and decorating are the prime activity. But, O Uddhava for figures drawn on the ground, inscribing letters and putting indications of principal factors and worshipped personalities, is the choice function, while in fire ceremonies, it is the oblation of seeds, drenched in ghee. (22.16)

Commentary:

Each type of religious ritual has its highlight. These features carry full meanings if one has a mystic priest and if the attendants cleansed themselves properly and performed the required preparatory austerities.

सूर्ये चाभ्यर्हणं प्रेष्ठं
सलिले सलिलादिभिः ।
श्रद्धयोपाहृतं प्रेष्ठं
भक्तेन मम वार्य् अपि ॥२२.१७॥

sūrye cābhyarhaṇaṁ preṣṭhaṁ
salile salilādibhiḥ
śraddhayopāhṛtaṁ preṣṭhaṁ
bhaktena mama vāry api (22.17)

sūrye — in the sun; cābhyarhaṇam = ca — and + abhyarhanam — mystic worship with prayers; preṣṭham — what is the choice function, what is precious; salile — in water; salilādibhiḥ — by water and such procedures; śraddhayopāhṛtaṁ = śraddhayā — with faith + upāhṛtam — offered; preṣṭham — most dear; bhaktena — by the devotee; mama — my; vāry = vāri — water; api — even.

Translation

And in worshiping the sun, mystic worship with prayers is the choice function. For worship in water, the offering of water and such procedures is precious. Even water offered with faith by My devotee is most dear to Me. (22.17)

Commentary:

Some ceremonies require that *Śrī* Krishna be worshipped as the Sun God, others as the form of pure water. In some cases sunlight is offered by the mystic priest or an attempt is made to do that by a non-mystic *pujārī*. Provided the devotee is qualified and provided that *Śrī* Krishna does in fact accept the ceremony, it would have the result of *Śrī* Krishna's presence, His observation of it and His decision to grant, or not to give whatever is desired by the devotee.

Without a mystic priest who has perfected the yoga disciplines, and who sees spiritually, it is hard for anyone to know if a ceremony really did get the approval of the Supreme Personality. It is not that the devotees should be doubtful but rather, they should have an open mind towards this, so that they do not develop a self-righteous attitude which would cause the formation of false pride.

There was a famous *sannyāsi* who was in the disciplic succession which was expanded by *Śrīla Bhaktivedānta Swāmī*. Once that *sannyāsi* got a well-trained formally-initiated brahmin priest to do a large opulent ceremony which was done with due regard for all the Vedic and tantric stipulations. However, despite the ritual formality, that *sannyāsa* fell into a terrible misery and was jailed by government authorities in the United States. When he did the ceremonies, his pride knew no bounds. He was so confident because he had the approval of his spiritual master and it was done mainly in the honor of that guru, but still it all failed, even though he chanted holy names at every moment and he was careful to cause everyone who attended to do so. He had the formally-installed Krishna *Mūrti*, and still he was disgraced soon after.

भूर्य् अप्य् अभक्तोपाहृतं
न मे तोषाय कल्पते ।
गन्धो धूपः सुमनसो
दीपो ऽन्नाद्यं च किं पुनः ॥२२.१८॥

bhūry apy abhaktopāhṛtaṁ
na me toṣāya kalpate
gandho dhūpaḥ sumanaso
dīpo 'nnādyaṁ ca kiṁ punaḥ (22.18)

bhūry = bhūri — abundance of items; apy = api — even; abhaktopāhṛtam = abhakta — one who is not a devotee + upāhṛtam — offered; na — not; me — my; toṣāya — to please; kalpate — is able; gandho = gandhaḥ — fragrance; dhūpaḥ — incense; sumanaso = sumanasaḥ — flowers; dīpo = dīpaḥ — flame; 'nnādyaṁ = annādyam — food and such things; ca — and; kim – what? How dear; punah — again, in reference to just water.

Translation

Even an abundance of items, offered by one who is not a devotee, is unable to please Me. But in reference to just water being offered by My devotee, how dear to me would it be, for offerings of fragrance, incense, flames, food and such items? (22.18)

Commentary:

There is no point in performing a ceremony to *Śrī* Krishna if one does not have a feeling for Him, even a normal feeling of affection which is merely social and not specifically spiritual love. One should not worship a deity just to make a show nor to compete with others.

Devotees make serious offence when they make ceremonies to show that they are of a certain sect, or because their spiritual master is famous, or because their temple has the best-dressed mostly opulently-adorned Deities.

The stress is on the proper motivation. If someone starts out with an impure or materialistic emotion, then if he is sincere from that position, as much as he can be, he will improve gradually by taking disciplines and austerities which cause elevation. Any person can start from any stage but one should not think that Krishna accepts offerings merely because one is in a certain institution or because one has a famous spiritual master. It depends on motivation.

शुचिः सम्भृत-सम्भारः
प्राग्-दर्भैः कल्पितासनः ।
आसीनः प्राग् उदग् वार्चेद्
अर्चायां त्व् अथ सम्मुखः ॥२२.१९॥

śuciḥ sambhṛta-sambhāraḥ
prāg-darbhaiḥ kalpitāsanaḥ
āsīnaḥ prāg udag vārced
arcāyāṁ tv atha sammukhaḥ (22.19)

śucih — being clean; sambhṛta — after collecting; sambhāraḥ — the ceremonial articles; prāg = prāk — eastward; darbhaiḥ — with kusha grass; kalpitāsanaḥ — have prepared; āsīnaḥ — seat; prāg = prāk — eastward; udag = udak — northward; vārced = vārcet = vā — or + arcet - should worship; arcāyām — on the sanctified figure; tv = tu — but; atha — alternately; sammukhah — face directly.

Translation:

Being clean, collecting the ceremonial articles, with kusha grass facing east, having a seat prepared, sitting eastward or northward, he should worship the Deity Form but alternately he should face the sanctified figure directly. (22.19)

Commentary:

The placing of the Deity in a certain direction is important, but there are exceptions to the rule. Therefore *Śrī* Krishna stated that alternately, no matter what direction the Deity is situated in, the *pujārī* and the audience are required to face the Figure.

Sometimes, when a mystic priest takes a Deity to a particular location, the Deity seems to want to turn away from the scripturally recommended direction, then the *pujārī* will allow the Deity to have His own way and will just face whatever direction the Deity indicates.

It is said that except in death rites, the *pujārī* should not under any circumstance face the southern direction, nor should he cause the audience to do so, since to face south is indicative of death of a body. It is said that *Yamarāja* the supernatural person who imprisons the subtle bodies of the departed souls, always comes from the south. Therefore one should do whatever one can to avoid him.

For advanced yogis such stipulations are meaningless. Instead they are friendly with *Yamarāja* and do not fear meeting him. However, as a general rule and for custom sake, and formality, no *pujārī* should cause an audience to face the south while worshipping a deity. The exception for this was the meeting between the yogi sages of the *Naimiśa* Forest Reserve and Suta, the son of Romaharshana. When they met, the sages said they were confident that *Yamarāja* would arrest no one there while they were engaged in lectures about the divine beings.

In the congregation of non-yogis, things are done in the traditional way. If for example a man's body was destined to drop dead five minutes after he were to leave a temple program or a home program, then if the *pujārī* was to make him face south during the ceremony, people might draw the conclusion that the man was killed because the *pujārī* arranged for the audience to face south. They will then slander the *pujārī*. People will lose faith in him and in the Deity. A *pujārī* should observe the scriptural rules, abiding by tradition and not doing anything which might seem to be variant or whimsical. It is different for ascetics who live in isolation. They do not have to follow customs.

When dealing with the public one has to observe certain restrictions which though traditional, may not be effective for anybody's spiritual life but that is the way it is for the general path of religion. The *pujārīs* who are attached to the public are thus blighted by this.

कृत-न्यासः कृत-न्यासां
मद्-अर्चां पाणिनामृजेत् ।
कलशं प्रोक्षणीयं च
यथावद् उपसाधयेत् ॥२२.२०॥

kṛta-nyāsaḥ kṛta-nyāsāṁ
mad-arcāṁ pāṇināmṛjet
kalaśaṁ prokṣaṇīyaṁ ca
yathāvad upasādhayet (22.20)

kṛta – having done; nyāsaḥ — methodical sanctification of his body; kṛta – having done; nyāsām — methodical sanctification of the worshipped figure; mad-arcām = mat-arcām — my sanctified form; pāṇināmṛjet = pāṇinā — with hand + āmṛjet — should clean; kalaśam — ceremonial water pot; prokṣaṇīyam — sanctifying water; ca — and; yathāvad = yathāvat — procedure; upasādhayet — should prepare.

Translation

Having done the methodical sanctification of his body and having performed the methodical sanctification of the worshipped figure, he should clean My sanctified form with his hands. And by that procedure, he should prepare the ceremonial water pot and the sanctified water. (22.20)

Commentary:

This has to do with the initial procedures in approaching the Deity in the early morning. At first the *pujārī* has to cleanse his body, then he offers prayers and performs purificatory actions on the body of the Deity. After this he takes away items used the previous day, and prepares a fresh set of items. If this is done at a temple it is done in private with the altar area closed to the public. If it is done in someone's home, it might be done in the presence of family members and other special guests.

There are many persons who become *pujārīs* due to being born in pandit or devotee families, or because of a burning desire from their previous lives. Most of these persons have no yoga expertise. Formerly all persons doing Deity Worship were mystics. This is why *Nārada*, *Vyāsa* and *Bṛhaspati* were mentioned in the beginning by Uddhava. One must master mystic yoga to gain supernatural and spiritual insight, before one can effectively do *pujārī* services.

Nowadays most of the spiritual masters are not yogis and did not do yoga in their present lives, yet, citing evidence from Lord Chaitanya's *līlās*, and other acts of other divine personages, they say that they are qualified. They go so far as to train their disciples in the Deity worship procedure, even though most of these students have no mystic insight.

The result of this is play-house Deity Worship. But the members of the public like this. Thus the non-mystic non-yogic *pujārīs* are successful in drawing large crowds by having pleasing music and attractively-dressed Deities.

Many persons with great ambitions for leading human beings towards salvation, come forward and accept these non-yogi gurus, get a certification from them as being brahmin trained devotees, get on an altar, turn their backs to the public and worship the Deities just as if there were a *Nārada*, a *Vyāsa* or a *Bṛhaspati* in person. We see this all over the world nowadays. It is a most wonderful farce.

At the same time, there is another group of persons who took birth in the traditional brahmin families, which had a history of doing pandit and *pujārī* work. Most of these persons do no yoga but they eat sumptuously the gheed-up, sugar-saturated and exotically spiced preparations which are made for the Deity. Because of gorging on these food offerings which are regarded as God Himself in the form of food, their bodies become bloated, especially around the belly area. They pose as priests, a claim made on the basis of their current ancestry. They exploit the gullible public. It is all pathetic, but it seems that this is the best we can do as human beings when we take birth in such brahmin families.

तद्-अद्भिर् देव-यजनं
द्रव्याण्य् आत्मानम् एव च ।
प्रोक्ष्य पात्राणि त्रीण्य् अद्भिस्
तैस् तैर् द्रव्यैश् च साधयेत् ॥ २२.२१ ॥

tad-adbhir deva-yajanaṁ
dravyāṇy ātmānam eva ca
prokṣya pātrāṇi trīṇy adbhis
tais tair dravyaiś ca sādhayet (22.21)

tad = tat — of that (container); adbhir = adbhiḥ — with water; deva-yajanam — place where the deity is installed; dravyāny = dravyāni — ceremonial items; ātmānam — on himself; eva — indeed, in fact; ca — also; prokṣya — purified ceremonially; pātrāṇi — containers; trīny = trīni — three; adbhis = adbhiḥ — with water; tais tair = taih taih — with these and those, with various; dravyaiś = dravyaiḥ — with ceremonial items; ca — and; sādhayet — should fill.

Translation

He should purify ceremonially the place where the Deity is installed, the ceremonial items and his own body with the water of that container, and should fill the three containers with water and the various ceremonial items. (22.21)

Commentary:

The procedures for worshiping the Deities are to be found in the particular regulatory scriptures. Some of these are Vedic texts and others are Tantric. Some are commentaries and corollaries which were adapted from the Vedas and Tantras. A *pujārī* should be literate enough to study these scriptures directly, so that he can understand the original texts and know any adaptation which was made by ancient or modern authorities.

Deity Worship is no joking matter, nor is it child's play. Therefore one should take it seriously, and perform it with due care. It is to be regretted that nowadays many *pujārīs* have no training in yoga. They feel that it is difficult and unnecessary. They claim that just being a devotee is sufficient, provided one takes initiation from a spiritual master in the Krishna lineage of teachers and provided one chants Krishna's names daily. However *Nārada, Vyāsa* and *Bṛhaspati* were great accomplished yogis and took time to maintain the practice. It is totally untrue that one cannot learn yoga or that it is too difficult. It can be learned, one can master it. And one's spiritual life would be greatly enhanced by the proficiency.

After all, in this chapter *Śrī* Krishna speaks about *kriyā* yoga, not just about *kriyā*. It is *kriyā* and yoga or yoga as it is applied to validate *kriyā* or mystic ritual actions in Deity Worship.

पाद्यार्घ्याचमनीयार्थं
त्रीणि पात्राणि देशिकः ।
हृदा शीर्ष्णाथ शिखया
गायत्र्या चाभिमन्त्रयेत् ॥ २२.२२ ॥

pādyārghyācamanīyārthaṁ
trīṇi pātrāṇi deśikaḥ
hṛdā śīrṣṇātha śikhayā
gāyatryā cābhimantrayet (22.22)

pādyārghyācamanīyārthaṁ = pādya — foot purification water + arghya — welcoming presentations + ācamanīya — mouth wash + artham — for the purpose; trīṇi — three; pātrāṇi — containers; deśikaḥ — conductor of worship ceremony; hṛdā — by the bosom; śīrṣṇātha = śīrṣṇā — by the head + atha — then; śikhayā — by the hair; gāyatryā — and by the Gāyatrī verses; cābhimantrayet = ca — and + abhimantrayet — should purify by chanting special stanzas.

Translation

The conductor of the worship ceremony should sanctify the three containers used for the purpose of foot purification, welcoming presentation and mouth wash, by chanting the special stanzas for the chest, head and hair respectively for each container in order, along with chanting the Gāyatrī verses for each. (22.22)

Commentary:

There are many pandits, *pujārīs, sannyāsis* and spiritual masters, who seek to keep the Deity worship procedure a secret. This is the traditional way of handling the canons or sacred procedures. However, secret or not, if the person who conducts the ceremony is not really qualified to do it, there will not be a perfect outcome. This does not mean that the public will detect the deficiencies. One benefit of keeping the procedures confidential is the continued ignorance of the public, as well as the unfamiliarity of those intelligent people in the audience who could detect discrepancies if they knew the procedures.

The conductor of the worship ceremony is responsible for the ceremony but if his audience is an ignorant one, then no one will recognize a deviation. In addition if his audience is enchanted by him, even a knowledgeable person in the audience will have to maintain silence about his lack of expertise.

Over the years attending Hindu Functions, as well as many Vaishnava Worship Ceremonies, I observed many discrepancies but do not say anything for two reasons. The first is the arrogance of the leaders, either of the pandit or of the devotee or *sannyāsis*. The second is the simplistic attitude of the audience. There is a two way discrepancy consisting of the cheating habits of the leaders and the indulgent attitude of the audiences.

Sometimes in private, when asked, I discuss the discrepancies with a certain member of the audience but only on the condition that he does not tell anybody what I pointed out to him. I have many friends who are *pujārīs*, pandits and *sannyāsis*. And I can say truly, that most of them are fake authorities. Basically speaking they do not know a thing about *kriyā* yoga but they pose as spiritual leaders.

The question is: What is my part in the scam? What is my responsibility, since after all, if one sees a fault one is liable to correct it? The answer is that if one sees a fault one is only liable to correct it, if one is ordered to do so by the Central Figure in the Universal Form. For instance, we heard that Arjuna was made responsible to help in the reform of the Kuru rulers but we do not hear that Uddhava had to do anything like that. Therefore it is not that every clear seeing person should correct faults.

Many of you might be surprised that I wrote this. For me personally I could care less as to whether the public is cheated or not. This is because the public itself wants to be indulged in a farce. The public itself wants to get a religious system that will not work. Hence if I bring it to their attention, the public will be annoyed with me. The real reason for my silence is the lack of authority to correct anybody.

Unless one is given the mission to do so by the Universal Form, one will get into karmic difficulty if one reveals the trickeries. In the *Bhagavad-Gītā*, there is a relevant verse:

na buddhibhedaṁ janayed ajñānāṁ karmasaṅginām
joṣayetsarvakarmāṇi vidvānyuktaḥ samācaran

One should not produce indetermination in the minds of the simpletons. A wise person should inspire them to be satisfied by action. The wise one should be disciplined in behavior. (B.G. 3.26)

That means that a person of my caliber should not interfere with religious leaders. If a religious leader is submissive to me, I may help him and by so doing, help his audience but I cannot usually interfere.

The secrecy about the procedures and mantras is for weaning out non-serious students but unfortunately it is used for monopoly. Hence it is not functioning in the proper way. But what can be done about that?

पिण्डे वाय्व्-अग्नि-सशुद्धे
हृत्-पद्म-स्था परा मम ।
अण्वीं जीव-कलां ध्यायेन्
नादान्ते सिद्ध-भाविताम् ॥२२.२३॥

piṇḍe vāyv-agni-saṁśuddhe
hṛt-padma-sthāṁ parāṁ mama
aṇvīṁ jīva-kalāṁ dhyāyen
nādānte siddha-bhāvitām (22.23)

piṇḍe — in the body; vāyv = vāyu — air; agni — fire; saṁśuddhe — in performing purification; hṛt — chest; padma — lotus; sthām — situated; parām — supreme; mama — my, of my; aṇvīm — subtle; jīva-kalām = jīva – specific divine individual + kalām — partial manifestation; dhyāyen = dhyāyet — should experience the effortless linking of the attention to the higher concentration force; nādānte = nāda – resonation of subtle sound + ante — at the end; siddha — perfected yogi; bhāvitām — experienced.

Translation

In performing full purification within his body, by air and by fire, he should meditate on the effortless linking of his attention to the concentration force which connects with My subtle but supreme partial manifestation, which is situated on a lotus in the bosom area, and which the perfected yogis experience at the end of their progression through nada subtle sound resonation. (22.23)

<u>*Commentary:*</u>

In the purpose to this verse, the ISKCON commentators, the humble servants of His Divine Grace A. C. *Bhaktivedānta Swāmī Śrīla Prabhupāda*, named *Hridayānanda dās Gosvāmī* and *Gopīparanadhana dās Adhikārī*, explained that according to *Śrī Śrīla* Sridhara *Swāmī*, the *prāṇava* or *omkāra*, has five parts: A, U, M, the nasal bindu and the reverberation nada. They state that liberated souls meditate upon the Lord at the end of that reverberation.

This sort of purport makes a lot of sense if one has no expertise in *kriyā* yoga practice. However it is a fact that these practices were to be used by *kriyā* yogis like *Nārada*, *Vyāsa*, *Bṛhaspati* and others on par with them. As far as *Śrī* Sridhara *Swāmī* is concerned, he is reputed as the first commentator of the *Śrīmad Bhāgavatam*. Therefore when there was some criticism about his commentary, Lord *Śrī* Chaitanya Mahaprabhu blocked his ears and did not want to hear it. He rebuked anyone who dared to even suggest that *Śrīla* Sridhara *Swāmī Mahārāja*, could be wrong. In that mood, most of the Acharyas regard Sridhara *Mahārāja* as infallible.

Śrī Krishna already informed us of the *kriyā* used by the *siddha* yogis. That was mentioned previously. This has nothing to do with sounding the Sanskrit letters AUM. It is not a practice of vibrating Om with any part of the material body. This is purely a tuning-into the sound which comes over from the chit *ākāśa*, the sky of consciousness, as well as the Om sound which is heard deep in the *suśumnā naḍi* canal of the subtle body. This has nothing to do with chanting holy names with the mouth, tongue and vocal chords.

The purification within the body by air is a purely yogic technique which cannot be done in fact by *pujārīs* who are not yogis. This is *prāṇa vāyu* and bhasvara *agni* purification which is done by *prāṇāyāma*, especially the bhastrika *prāṇāyāma* or by *viloma pratiloma* alternate breathing. The effortless linking of the concentration force to the sky of consciousness is the mastership of the 7th stage of yoga, that of *dhyāna (dhyāyen)*. This cannot be done by non-yogi *pujārīs*. Therefore they will not see but they will imagine that there is a subtle but supreme partial manifestation *(jīva-kalām)* of *Śrī* Krishna in the heart area. Their sounding of Om will not take them to Krishna.

Basically speaking, only a yogi can do this procedure. It cannot be done by common people unless such persons take up and master *kriyā* yoga practice. It cannot be done by people coming out of brahmin families or people who are initiated in the Vaishnava disciplic succession and who have not mastered yoga.

To say that this means the reverberation of Om with the mouth is to honor *Śrīla* Sridhar *Swāmī Mahārāja*, that first and perhaps greatest of the *Śrīmad Bhāgavatam* commentators, but still that does not mean that what he explained was what *Śrī* Krishna told Uddhava, even though the *Swāmī Mahārāja* had the proper intention and meant all well-being for humanity.

तयात्म-भूतया पिण्डे
व्याप्ते सम्पूज्य तन्-मयः ।
आवाह्यार्चादिषु स्थाप्य
न्यस्ताङ्गं मां प्रपूजयेत् ॥ २२.२४ ॥

tayātma-bhūtayā piṇḍe
vyāpte sampūjya tan-mayaḥ
āvāhyārcādiṣu sthāpya
nyastāṅgaṁ māṁ prapūjayet (22.24)

tayātma-bhūtayā = tayā — by that + ātma-bhūtayā — by that which one's spirit has contacted; piṇḍe — in the body; vyāpte — in being pervaded; sampūjya — completely worshiping; tan-mayaḥ = tat-mayaḥ — surcharged by that; āvāhyārcādiṣu = āvāhya — inviting + arcādiṣu — in deity figures; sthāpya — establishing, installing; nyastāṅgaṁ = nyasta – methodical santification + angam — limbs of the deity; mām — to me; prapūjayet — should worship in all respects.

Translation

By being in touch with that form of Mine, which his spirit contacted in his body, and being pervaded by that influence, completely worshiping that form of Mine, being surcharged by that influence, inviting that form of Mine to enter the Deity Figure, and other sanctified forms, establishing the entry by methodical sanctification of the limbs of the Deity Figure, he should worship Me. (22.24)

Commentary:

Nowadays we have everything except the yogic practice and its application to *kriyā*. We have *kriyā* but we do not have *kriyā* and yoga just as we have *karma* but no *karma* and yoga, and we have *bhakti* but no *bhakti* and yoga, as well as *jñāna* but no *jñāna* and yoga. We have methodical sanctification of the Deity Figure but we do not have the entry of the yogi into his subtle and causal bodies and the application made there for the Supersoul Personality to enter the Deity Form.

Some preachers even say that we are not worshipping just *Śrī* Krishna's partial manifestation as the *Paramātmā*, Supersoul, but rather we worship *Śrī* Krishna as *Bhagavān*, the Supreme Personality of Godhead who is complete. But no one has gone into the sky of consciousness by mystic entry and invited Him to come here and enter the Deity Form. We just assume that He enters.

After the yogi enters the *suśumnā* central passage and connects the Om sound that he hears in the sky of consciousness with the vibrational energy in the *suśumnā* subtle space, and after he entered into the dimension where the Supersoul exists, then he will, after he saturates himself with the influence of the Lord and with the vibration of that dimension, request that Lord to enter the Deity form. He will accompany the Lord to that form if the Lord accepts the invitation.

If for some reason, the Lord disagrees, He will indicate to the yogi devotee the reason for this. If there was an offence, the devotee would come out of meditation to correct the defect and begin the ceremony again. Of course if a devotee already invited hundreds of people as devotees do nowadays, he would be in quite a fix, since such an audience would expect the installation to take place as planned. It is obvious then, that these procedures are a world apart from the ones which are conducted nowadays.

पाद्योपस्पर्शार्हणादीन्
उपचारान् प्रकल्पयेत् ।
धर्मादिभिश् च नवभिः
कल्पयित्वासनं मम ॥२२.२५॥

pādyopasparśārhaṇādīn
upacārān prakalpayet
dharmādibhiś ca navabhiḥ
kalpayitvāsanaṁ mama (22.25)

pādyopasparśārhaṇādīn = pādya — foot wash + upasparśa — mouth wash + arhaṇa — welcoming presentations + ādīn — and other items; upacārān — ceremonial items; prakalpayet — should offer; dharmādibhiś = dharma – Dharma + ādibhiḥ — and other male supernatural authorities; ca — and; navabhiḥ — with the nine supernatural female authorities; kalpayitvāsanam = kalpayitvā — having offered + āsanam — seat; mama — for me.

Translation

He should offer the ceremonial items, namely foot wash, mouth wash, welcome presentations and other items, having offered a seat for Me, as attended by Dharma and other supernatural male authorities with the nine supernatural goddesses, (22.25)

Commentary:

The *pujārī* must also call other personalities from the supernatural world. These include *Dharma* the *deva* supervising righteous duty. He must also call supernatural female authorities as stipulated in the particular canon for the installation. If one has no mystic perception, this may be done superficially.

पद्मम् अष्ट-दल तत्र
कर्णिका-केसरोज्वलम् ।
उभाभ्यां वेद-तन्त्राभ्यां
मह्यं तूभय-सिद्धये ॥२२.२६॥

padmam aṣṭa-dalaṁ tatra
karṇikā-kesarojjvalam
ubhābhyāṁ veda-tantrābhyāṁ
mahyaṁ tūbhaya-siddhaye (22.26)

padmam — lotus; aṣṭa - eight; dalam — eight petalled; tatra — there; karnikā — pericarp; kesarojjvalam = kesara — stamens + ujjvalam — effulgent; ubhābhyām — by both; veda - Veda; tantrābhyām — of the Tantra; mahyam — to me; tūbhaya = tu — but, and + ubhaya — of both fulfillments; siddhaye — for the perfection.

Translation

...and there on the seat, an eight-petalled lotus with effulgent pericarp and stamens, all offered to Me according to both scriptures, the Veda and Tantra, for the perfection of both fulfillments. (22.26)

Commentary:

The fulfillments are for cultural and spiritual life. Thus the Deity worship is done for either or both of these.

सुदर्शनं पाञ्चजन्यं
गदासीषु-धनुर्-हलान् ।
मुषलं कौस्तुभं मालां
श्रीवत्सं चानुपूजयेत् ॥२२.२७॥

sudarśanaṁ pāñcajanyaṁ
gadāsīṣu-dhanur-halān
muṣalaṁ kaustubhaṁ mālāṁ
śrīvatsaṁ cānupūjayet (22.27)

sudarśanam — disc; pāñcajanyam — conchshell; gadāsīṣu = gadā — club + asi — sword + iṣu — arrows; dhanur = dhanuh — bow; halān — plow; muṣalam — mace; kaustubham — jewel; mālām — garland; śrīvatsam — curl of hair on the chest; cānupūjayet = ca — and + anupūjayet — he should worship in sequences.

Translation

He should worship in sequences, the disc named Sudarśan, the conchshell named Pāñcajanya, the club, sword, arrows, bow, plow, mace, the jewel named Kaustubha, the garland and the Śrīvatsa curl of hair on the chest. (22.27)

Commentary:

These are various paraphernalia of *Śrī* Krishna or of His parallel divinities. Accordingly, the *pujārī* would invoke the particular items during the installation ceremony.

नन्दं सुनन्दं गरुडं
प्रचण्डं चण्डं एव च ।
महाबलं बलं चैव
कुमुदं कमुदेक्षणम् ॥२२.२८॥

nandaṁ sunandaṁ garuḍaṁ
pracaṇḍaṁ caṇḍaṁ eva ca
mahābalaṁ balaṁ caiva
kumudaṁ kamudekṣaṇam (22.28)

nandaṁ - Nanda; sunandam – Sunanda; garuḍam — Garuda; pracaṇḍam – Pracaṇḍa; candam — Caṇḍa; eva — indeed; ca — and; mahābalam – Mahabala; balam — Bala; caiva = ca — and + eva — indeed; kumudam – Kumuda; kumudeksanam — Kamudeksana.

Translation

One should worship Nanda, Sunanda, Garuḍa, Pracaṇḍa, Caṇḍa, as well as Mahābala, Bala, Kumuda and Kamudekṣana. (22.28)

Commentary:

These are associates of *Śrī* Krishna who reside with Him in a certain part of the spiritual sky. Take note that *Śrī* Krishna did not instruct Uddhava to worship *Śrī Śrī Rādhā Kṛṣṇa*, even though formerly *Śrī* Krishna sent Uddhava with a message for the *gopīs* of *Vṛndavān*.

दुर्गां विनायकं व्यासं
विष्वक्षेनं गुरून् सुरान् ।
स्वे स्वे स्थाने त्व् अभिमुखान्
पूजयेत् प्रोक्षणादिभिः ॥२२.२९॥

durgāṁ vināyakaṁ vyāsaṁ
viṣvakṣenaṁ gurūn surān
sve sve sthāne tv abhimukhān
pūjayet prokṣaṇādibhiḥ (22.29)

durgām — Durgā; vināyakaṁ — Vinayaka Gaṇeśa; vyāsam — *Vyāsa;* viṣvaksenam — Viṣvaksena; gurūn — spiritual masters; surān — supernatural authorities; sve sve — each in his own; sthāne — in position; tv = tu — but; abhimukhān — all facing; pūjayet — should worship; prokṣaṇādibhiḥ = prokṣaṇa + ādibhiḥ — sprinkling sanctified water and along with other procedures.

Translation

One should worship Durgā, Vināyaka Gaṇeśa, Vyāsa, Visvakṣena, the spiritual masters and the supernatural authorities each in his or her own position, but facing me, by sprinkling sanctified water and applying the other procedures. (22.29)

Commentary:

Each of the incarnations of Godhead have personal associates who accompany them when they come across the time barrier to be in the material world. Some of the Lord's associates do not cross over. Only some do. Some others who are permanent residence of this material world, the supernatural authorities, join him when He appears here.

For accomplished yogi devotees, Deity worship is not a personal necessity. This is because such devotees regularly cross over to the sky of consciousness by virtue of higher yoga practice. However, some of these yogi devotees are assigned by *Śrī* Krishna as *pujārīs*. They render a valuable service to the human population by inviting the Supreme Lord to enter the Deity Forms.

The Lord's entry into such forms is a great boon for humanity. Its value cannot be over-estimated. Since the average human being cannot go to the spiritual world, even the majority of devotees of *Śrī* Krishna, then it is important for them if the Lord appears in this creation in the Deity Form.

चन्दनोशीर-कर्पूर-
कुङ्कमागुरु-वासितैः ।
सलिलैः स्नापयेन् मन्त्रैर्
नित्यदा विभवे सति ॥२२.३०॥

candanośīra-karpūra-
kuṅkumāguru-vāsitaiḥ
salilaiḥ snāpayen mantrair
nityadā vibhave sati (22.30)

candanośīra = candana — sandalwood paste + uśīra — Ushira Kush root; karpūra — camphor; kuṅkumāguru = kuṅkuma — vermillion + aguru — aloe wood; vāsitaih — which that which is scented; salilaih — with water; snāpayen = snāpayet — should bathe the Deity Figure; mantrair = mantraiḥ — with recitation of appropiate stanzas; nityadā — daily; vibhave — facility; sati — as there is, having.

Translation

Having the facility, he should bathe the Deity figure daily while reciting appropriate stanzas using water which is scented by sandalwood paste, Uśīra root, camphor, vermillion and aloe wood. (22.30)

Commentary:

The procedures for relating to the Deities came down to us from the instructions of *Nārada*, *Vyāsa* and *Bṛhaspati*. Lord Shiva gave specific instructions even regards worshipping *Śrī Śrī Rādhā-Kṛṣṇa*. These occur in the *Nārada Pāñcarātra*. These procedures mimic some of what is done in the spiritual world. Some of the formalities were adopted from activities of the various incarnations of Lord Krishna who exhibited themselves through material forms in this world. Some were brought over from their appearance elsewhere in other dimensions in the subtle world, the angelic kingdoms.

स्वर्ण-घर्मानुवाकेन
महापुरुष-विद्यया ।
पौरुषेणापि सूक्तेन
सामभी राजनादिभिः ॥२२.३१॥

svarṇa-gharmānuvākena
mahāpuruṣa-vidyayā
pauruṣeṇāpi sūktena
sāmabhī rājanādibhiḥ (22.31)

svarṇa-gharmānuvākena = svarṇa-gharma = Svarṇa-gharma + anuvākena — by reciting the Vedic hymn; mahāpuruṣa – Mahapurusha; vidyayā — by the Vidyā hymn; pauruṣeṇāpi = pauruṣeṇa — by the Puruṣa + api — also; sūktena — by the Sūkta hymn; sāmabhī — by the Sāma Veda hymn; rājanādibhiḥ — by the Rājana and corresponding hymns.

Translation

He should recite the Svarṇa-gharma, Mahāpuruṣa Vidyā, Puruṣa-sūkta, the Sāma Veda as well as the Rājana and corresponding hymns. (22.31)

Commentary:

In Deity worship specific hymns should be chanted. These cited, are ancient hymns used in the time of *Śrī* Krishna and Uddhava. Nowadays some of these hymns are ignored. Some *sampradāyas* stress hymns which glorify their spiritual masters and hymns which are extracted from the *Śrīmad Bhāgavatam* in which these instructions to Uddhava occur. Some also use new hymns which were recently composed to glorify particular incarnations of Godhead who descended since the time of *Śrī* Krishna.

वस्त्रोपवीताभरण-
पत्र-स्रग्-गन्ध-लेपनैः ।
अलङ्कुर्वीत स-प्रेम
मद्-भक्तो मां यथोचितम् ॥२२.३२॥

vastropavītābharaṇa-
patra-srag-gandha-lepanaiḥ
alaṅkurvīta sa-prema
mad-bhakto māṁ yathocitam (22.32)

vastropavītābharaṇa = vastra — clothing + upavīta — sacred thread + ābharaṇa — ornaments; patra — leaf pattern sandalwood paste imprints; srag = srak — garlands; gandha – fragrance; lepanaiḥ — by offering ointments; alaṅkurvīta — he should decorate; sa-prema — with purified affections; mad-bhakto = mat-bhaktaḥ — my devotee; mām — me; yathocitam = yathā – as + ucitam — as recommended.

Translation

While offering clothing, sacred thread, ornaments, leaf pattern sandalwood imprints, garlands, fragrance and ointments, My devotee having purified affection, should decorate Me as recommended. (22.32)

Commentary:

This pertains the yogi *pujārī* who perfected the higher yoga and could enter into the sky of consciousness. He should be capable of *prema* which is purified affections or spiritual love. Other devotees who assist him or even those who merely observe the ceremony would derive benefit and would obtain the impetus to strive to get a relationship with the Deity.

पाद्यम् आचमनीयं च
गन्धं सुमनसो ऽक्षतान् ।
धूप-दीपोपहार्याणि
दद्यान् मे श्रद्धयार्चकः ॥२२.३३॥

pādyam ācamanīyaṁ ca
gandhaṁ sumanaso 'kṣatān
dhūpa-dīpopahāryāṇi
dadyān me śraddhayārcakaḥ (22.33)

pādyam — sanctified foot wash; ācamanīyam — sanctified mouth wash; ca — and; gandham — fragrant substances; sumanaso = sumanasaḥ — flower; 'kṣatān = aksatān — unbroken grains; dhūpa — incense; dīpopahāryāṇi = dīpa — flame + upahāryāṇi — selected items; dadyan = dadyat — should offer; me — to me; śraddhayārcakaḥ = śraddhayā — with faith + arcakaḥ — the worshipper.

Translation

The worshipper should with faith, offer me sanctified foot wash and mouth wash, fragrant substances, flowers, unbroken grains, incense, flame and other selected items. (22.33)

Commentary:

These items are offered in a particular order and in a particular way, in a particular frequency. The methods are in the regulative scriptures. A learned priest can teach these to submissive devotees.

गुड-पायस-सर्पींषि
शष्कुल्य्-आपूप-मोदकान् ।
सयाव-दधि-सूपांश् च
नैवेद्यं सति कल्पयेत् ॥२२.३४॥

guḍa-pāyasa-sarpīṁṣi
śaṣkuly-āpūpa-modakān
saṁyāva-dadhi-sūpāṁś ca
naivedyaṁ sati kalpayet (22.34)

guḍa — sugar candy; pāyasa — sweet rice; sarpīṁsi — ghee; śaṣkuly = śaṣkulī — rice-flour cake; āpūpa — sweet cakes; modakā — sweet rice-flour dumplings; saṁyāva — a special sweet cake; dadhi — yogurt; sūpāṁś = sūpān — vegetable sauces; ca — and; naivedyam — sanctified meals; sati — having sufficient means; kalpayet — should offer.

Translation

Having sufficient means, he should offer me sanctified meals consisting of sugar candy, sweet rice, ghee, rice-flour cakes, sweet cakes, sweet rice-flour dumplins, other special sweet cakes, yogurt and vegetable sauces. (22.34)

Commentary:

In cases where there is a mystic yogi *pujārī*, he can see if the Deities accepted the offerings or if the Deity only accepted some and rejected others. He can then recommend changes in the preparation and detect offensive involvements like uncleanliness or omissions in the procedures.

Those who have no mystic vision must rely on intuition and intellectual assessment of what they read in scriptures as well as their faith in the procedure, in their spiritual master and in the devotional process which they adhere to. They make assumptions as to the acceptance of the offerings. The Sanskrit term *sati* means gift or donation, which indicates that the *pujārī* should get a contribution. He should be maintained by a congregation. They should provide whatever is needed for the offering. This does not mean however, and it is nowhere indicated, that the *pujārī* should apply artificial pressure on the public for funds. If he does this, the donations will come to him with resentment and the offerings will be ruinous to him and the congregation. Many modern devotees fail to take this into consideration.

Even though a *pujārī* prepares many sweet items to offer to the Deity of *Śrī* Krishna, he himself might not take these or he might honor a sample. It depends on the requirements for personal practice. Those who do no yoga hardly have any sense of what to eat to sustain their bodies in good health. We find that they eat as much of the remnants as they can procure, believing that since the food was placed before the deity and the relevant prayers were said, it is sanctified and would cause no inconvenience to their bodies.

Yogi devotees who are not in public temples and who live in isolated places, are not victimized by justifications for over-eating offerings. They do not eat in a way that harms health. As such they are able to push forward with the perfective practices of *kriyā* yoga.

अभ्यङ्गोन्मर्दनादर्श-
दन्त-धावाभिषेचनम् ।
अन्नाद्य-गीत-नृत्यानि
पर्वणि स्युर् उतान्व्-अहम् ॥ २२.३५ ॥

abhyaṅgonmardanādarśa-
danta-dhāvābhiṣecanam
annādya-gīta-nṛtyāni
parvaṇi syur utānv-aham (22.35)

abhyaṅgonmardanādarśa = abhyaṅga — ointment + unmardana — rubbing of scented powders + ādarśa — presenting a mirror; danta – teeth; dhāvābhiṣecanam = dhāva — washing + abhiṣecanam — bathing; annādya = anna — food + ādya — dainties; gītā — songs; nṛtyāni — dancing; parvaṇi — on special days; syur = syuḥ — should be offered; utanv-aham = uta — or + anu-aham — every day.

Translation

Ointments, rubbing of special powders, presenting a mirror, washing the teeth, bathing, foods, dainties, songs, and dancing should be offered on special days or every day. (22.35)

Commentary:

A temple requires, first of all, a mystic *pujārī*. It is best if this person was born in a brahmin family. He should be a masterful yogi, who was trained sufficiently to be advanced in higher yoga, the process through which one can break out of this dimension in *samādhi* and peer into the transcendental world. With such a person one can start a temple.

The temple requires a congregation of persons who were cultivated over a period of time or persons who by tradition are familiar with Deity Worship. If one has both a qualified priest and a congregation, then one can fulfill the *kriyā* yoga Deity Worship which is described in this chapter.

विधिना विहिते कुण्डे
मेखला-गर्त-वेदिभिः ।
अग्निम् आधाय परितः
समूहेत् पाणिनोदितम् ॥ २२.३६ ॥

vidhinā vihite kuṇḍe
mekhalā-garta-vedibhiḥ
agnim ādhāya paritaḥ
samūhet pāṇinoditam (22.36)

vidhinā — according to scriptural regulations; vihite — lighting; kuṇḍe — in the fireplace; mekhalā — with a sacred belt; garta — cavity; vedibhiḥ — with the altar; agnim — fire; ādhāya — establishing; paritaḥ — on all sides; samūhet — one should tend; pāṇinoditam = pāṇinā — with hand + uditam — blaze.

Translation

Lighting a fire in a fireplace, according to the scriptural regulations, with a sacred belt, a cavity, and the altar, he should tend the fire on all sides with his hands, establishing it as a blaze. (22.36)

Commentary:

Even though the sacrificial fire was considered to be essential to all religious ceremonies in the time of *Śrī* Krishna, He Himself departed from that by establishing the *Annakūṭa* Ceremony and the *Govardhana Pūjā*. *Śrī* Krishna's idea is that one does not necessarily have to use the fire ceremony for each function. However the items must still be sanctified and the sacrificial fire is there in the form of a flame of a ghee lamp.

परिस्तीर्याथ पर्युक्षेद्
अन्वाधाय यथा-विधि ।
प्रोक्षण्यासाद्य द्रव्याणि
प्रोक्ष्याग्नौ भावयेत माम् ॥२२.३७॥

paristīryātha paryukṣed
anvādhāya yathā-vidhi
prokṣaṇyāsādya dravyāṇi
prokṣyāgnau bhāvayeta mām (22.37)

paristīryātha = paristīrya — spreading kusha grass + atha — then; paryukṣed = paryukṣet — he should sprinkle water all around; anvādhāya — putting wood in the fire while reciting prescribed sounds; yathā-vidhi — as prescribed in scripture; prokṣaṇyāsādya = prokṣaṇyā — by sanctified water + āsādya — placing; dravyāṇi — ceremonial items; prokṣyāgnau = prokṣya — sprinkling + agnau — in the fire; bhāvayeta — should meditate, feelingly; mām — on me.

Translation

Then spreading kusha grass, putting wood in the fire, reciting sounds prescribed in scripture, and placing the ceremonial items, he should sprinkle sanctified water on the fire and meditate feelingly on Me, (22.37)

Commentary:

These procedures may be learned from a brahmin priest who is conversant with their performance. Through higher yoga, the *pujārī* should feelingly connect with *Śrī* Krishna's divine nature because of having already awakened his own spiritual status by *samādhi* methods.

तप्त-जाम्बूनद-प्रख्यं
शङ्ख-चक्र-गदाम्बुजैः ।
लसच्-चतुर्-भुज शान्तं
पद्म-किञ्जल्क-वाससम् ॥२२.३८॥

tapta-jāmbūnada-prakhyaṁ
śaṅkha-cakra-gadāmbujaiḥ
lasac-catur-bhujaṁ śāntaṁ
padma-kiñjalka-vāsasam (22.38)

tapta — molten; jāmbūnada — gold; prakhyam — complexion; śaṅkha — conchshell; cakra — disc; gadāmbujaiḥ = gadā — club + ambujaih — and with lotus flower; lasac = lasat — shining; catur = catuḥ - four; bhujam — arms; śāntam — serene; padma — lotus; kiñjalka — stamen; vāsasam — cloth.

Translation

...who has a complexion like molten gold, with conch, disc, club, and lotus flower, shining and four-armed, serene, wearing a cloth of the color of a lotus stamen, (22.38)

Commentary:

Śrī Krishna did not describe His two-handed form but instead described one of His parallel four-handed divinities, who has a golden rather than bluish complexion. This means that the mystic *pujārī* may reach a parallel divinity when he crosses over into the transcendental world. This description is of the Four-handed supernatural Vishnu Form which might be seen at the heart chakra in the *suśumnā naḍi* passage of a yogi's purified subtle body.

स्फुरत्-किरीट-कटक
कटि-सूत्र-वराङ्गदम् ।
श्रीवत्स-वक्षसं भ्राजत्-
कौस्तुभं वन-मालिनम् ॥२२.३९॥

sphurat-kirīṭa-kaṭaka
kaṭi-sūtra-varāṅgadam
śrīvatsa-vakṣasaṁ bhrājat-
kaustubhaṁ vana-mālinam (22.39)

sphurat — shining; kirīta — crown; kataka — bracelets; kati-sūtra — belt; varāṅgadam = vara – fine + aṅgadam — armlets; śrīvatsa — Śrīvatsa curl of hair; vakṣasam — on the chest; bhrājat — radiant; kaustubham — Kaustubha jewel; vana – forest; mālinam — flower.

Translation

...with a shining crown, bracelets, belt and fine armlets, with the Śrīvatsa curl of hair on the chest, which is radiant with the Kaustubha jewel, and wearing a garland of forest flowers. (22.39)

Commentary:

These descriptions are what is seen by the yogi *pujārī* in trance. He installs a deity that was seen spiritually by him and not just a deity he read of in the *Purāṇas*. Of course, in many cases one sees a Deity in the sky of consciousness who was described by another yogi devotee in the *Purāṇas*, or even by *Śrī* Krishna Himself as well in this narration.

It is important to distinguish between the method described here and the tradition as it is understood now, which is to create a *Mūrti* form according to these descriptions and to install it, without having any yoga expertise, and without ever seeing *Śrī* Krishna or His parallel divinity in the spiritual locales in *samādhi* meditation in advanced yoga practice.

ध्यायन्न् अभ्यर्च्य दारूणि
हविषाभिघृतानि च ।
प्रास्याज्य-भागाव् आघारौ
दत्त्वा चाज्य-प्लुतं हविः ॥२२.४०॥

dhyāyann abhyarcya dārūṇi
haviṣābhighṛtāni ca
prāsyājya-bhāgāv āghārau
dattvā cājya-plutaṁ haviḥ (22.40)

dhyāyann = dhyāyan — experiencing the effortless linking of one's attention to higher concentration forces which is linked to the spiritual form of the Deity and to the spiritual place from which the Deity descended; abhyarcya — worshipping; dārūṇi — dried wood kindling; haviṣābhighṛtāni = haviṣā — ghee + abhighṛtāni — dipped; ca — and; prāsyājya = prāsya — offer into fire + ājya — ghee; bhāgav = bhāgau — two parts; āghārau — in performing the Aghara procedure; dattvā — making an offer; cājya = ca — and + ājya — ghee; plutam — soaked; haviḥ — oblations.

Translation

After experiencing the effortless linkage of his attention with the higher concentration force which is linked to the spiritual form of the Deity and to the spiritual place from which the Deity descended, and by worshipping, he should offer into the fire, pieces of kindling that are dipped in ghee, and should perform the two Āghāra procedures, making oblations that are soaked in ghee. (22.40)

Commentary:

For the *Āghāra* procedure, the priest offers pieces of wood into the fire, while saying various mantras which invoke and are supposed to appease various supernatural and spiritual beings. All this should be done while performing higher yoga mystic actions (kriyās), to properly connect with super-natural and spiritual worlds accordingly.

जुहुयान् मूल-मन्त्रेण
षोडशर्चावदानतः ।
धर्मादिभ्यो यथा-न्यायं
मन्त्रैः स्विष्टि-कृत बुधः ॥२२.४१॥

juhuyān mūla-mantreṇa
ṣoḍaśarcāvadānataḥ
dharmādibhyo yathā-nyāyaṁ
mantraiḥ sviṣṭi-kṛtaṁ budhaḥ (22.41)

juhuyān — should offer into fire; mūla – Deity identification; mantreṇa — with special calling sounds; ṣoḍaśarcāvadānataḥ = ṣoḍaśa-ṛcā — with the sixteen lined Purushasukta hymn; avadānataḥ — pouring an oblation after each line; dharmādibhyo = dharmādibhyaḥ — to Dharma and other supernatural authorities; yathā-nyāyam — as stipulated; mantraiḥ — with hymns; sviṣṭi-kṛtaṁ — offering; budhaḥ — the intelligent worshipper.

Translation

The intelligent worshipper, should offer oblations into the fire, using the Deity identification sounds and the sixteen-lined Puruṣa Sūkta hymn, pouring an oblation after each line as stipulated, offering to Dharma and other supernatural beings, as well as making the Sviṣṭi-kṛta offering. (22.41)

Commentary:

The Deity identification mantras are called *mūla* mantras. These are used to call the various authorities. Here no bias is applied to the *devatās*, the supernatural people who hold relative authority over human nature. They are called in the proper sequence. They are not harassed as being nobody demigods.

अभ्यर्च्याथ नमस्कृत्य
पार्षदेभ्यो बलिं हरेत् ।
मूल-मन्त्रं जपेद् ब्रह्म
स्मरन् नारायणात्मकम् ॥ २२.४२ ॥

abhyarcyātha namaskṛtya
pārṣadebhyo baliṁ haret
mūla-mantraṁ japed brahma
smaran nārāyaṇātmakam (22.42)

abhyarcyātha = abhyarcya — worshipping + atha — then; namaskṛtya — making respectful obeisances; pārṣadebhyo = pārsadebhyah — to my attendants; balim — food; haret — he should offer; mūla-mantram — Deity identification sounds; japed = japet — she should murmur; brahma — spiritual reality; smaran — remember; nārāyaṇātmakam = Nārāyaṇa – Nārāyaṇa + ātmakam — self manifested as.

Translation

Then worshipping and making respectful obeisances, he should offer food to My attendants. He should murmur the Deity identification prayers, as he remembers the spiritual reality which manifests personally as Lord Nārāyaṇa. (22.42)

Commentary:

This remembrance is based on higher yoga in *samādhi* experience, where the yogi devotee enters into the *brahman* atmosphere, the spiritual sky, and sees Lord *Nārāyaṇa* there. Later he journeys there and invites Lord *Nārāyaṇa* to enter the Deity Form. In the meditations in higher yoga, one first hears a sound coming from the supernatural world. This practice was described by *Śrī* Krishna previously in the discourse. After linking one's attention to that sound repeatedly, one becomes stabilized in it, and then one is transferred out of this dimension into the sky of consciousness. From there more developments occur which leads to the perception of and meeting with divine beings on the other side of existence. The linking with the supernatural Om sound leads the yogi into *brahma*, the spiritual atmosphere. After sufficient linkage with the higher levels of existence, one makes contact with the personal *brahman*, Lord *Nārāyaṇa* in person *(nārāyaṇātmakam)*.

दत्त्वाचमनम् उच्छेष
विष्वक्षेनाय कल्पयेत् ।
मुख-वास सुरभिमत्
ताम्बूलाद्यम् अथार्हयेत् ॥ २२.४३ ॥

dattvācamanam uccheṣaṁ
viṣvakṣenāya kalpayet
mukha-vāsaṁ surabhimat
tāmbūlādyam athārhayet (22.43)

dattvācamanam = dattvā — having offered + ācamanam — sanctified mouth wash; ucchesaṁ — food which was ceremonially offered; viṣvaksenāya — to Visvaksena; kalpayet — should give; mukha-vāsam — chewing substances for the mouth; surabhimat — fragrant; tāmbūlādyam = tāmbūla-ādyam — betel nut and such items; athārhayet = atha — then + arhayet — should present.

Translation

Having offered sanctified mouth wash, he should give the food which was ceremonially offered to Viṣvakṣena. Then he should present to the mouth, fragrant substances for chewing, like betel nut and such. (22.43)

Commentary:

Viṣvakṣena is one of the associates of Lord *Nārāyaṇa* who come over with Him from the spiritual environment. The mystic *pujārī* should have met that associate in the other world, after inviting that divine person to attend with the Lord on this side of the existential divide. The *pujārī* should offer remnants of Lord *Nārāyaṇa* to him first, and should share those remnants with other devotees and with himself.

The items like fragrant substances and betel nut are offered according to the advisories in the scriptural texts.

उपगायन् गृणन् नृत्यन्
कर्माण्य् अभिनयन् मम ।
मत्-कथाः श्रावयन् शृण्वन्
मुहूर्तं क्षणिको भवेत् ॥२२.४४॥

upagāyan gṛṇan nṛtyan
karmāṇy abhinayan mama
mat-kathāḥ śrāvayan śṛṇvan
muhūrtaṁ kṣaṇiko bhavet (22.44)

upagāyan — singing; gṛṇan — praising; nṛtyan — dancing; karmāṇy = karmāṇi — deeds; abhinayan — performing a theatrical play; mama — my; mat-kathāḥ — stories about me; śrāvayan — narrating; śṛṇvan — listening to; muhūrtaṁ — for sometime; kṣaṇiko = kṣaṇikaḥ — for a time; bhavet — should be occupied.

Translation

Singing, praising, dancing, performing My deeds in a theatrical play, narrating stories about Me, listening to such stories, he should be occupied for sometime. (22.44)

Commentary:

This chapter described the complete procedure for administering large temples, like those which the *Sātvata* clan of devotees supervised in *Dvārakā* in the time of *Śrī* Krishna. This is why none of the Deities mentioned here is that of the two-handed *Śrī* Krishna, but rather, these are Deities of Lord *Nārāyaṇa*, the parallel divine form of *Śrī* Krishna, who was the patron deity of the *Sātvatas*.

स्तवैर् उच्चावचैः स्तोत्रैः
पौराणैः प्राकृतैर् अपि ।
स्तुत्वा प्रसीद भगवन्न्
इति वन्देत दण्ड-वत् ॥२२.४५॥

stavair uccāvacaiḥ stotraiḥ
paurāṇaiḥ prākṛtair api
stutvā prasīda bhagavann
iti vandeta daṇḍa-vat (22.45)

stavair = stavaiḥ — with scriptural hymns; uccāvacaiḥ = ucca-avacaiḥ — by greater and by lesser; stotraiḥ — with hymns; paurānaiḥ — by the ancient authorities; prākṛtair = prākṛtaiḥ — by the modern authorities; api — also; stutvā — having praised; prasīda — please shower grace; bhagavann = Bhagavan — o blessed lord; iti — thus saying; vandeta — he should submit himself; danda-vat — like a rod on the ground.

Translation

Having praised Me with greater or lesser scriptural hymns, and with hymns composed by the ancient and also the modern authorities, he should submit himself like a rod on the ground, saying "O Blessed Lord, please shower the grace upon me." (22.45)

Commentary:

The modern authorities in this verse, were those in the time of *Śrī* Krishna. The ancient ones were those before His time. Modern devotees from our time, may use more concurrent prayers, provided these do not undermine the meaning of these verses, and provided those do not misrepresent the history as it was in the time of *Śrī* Krishna.

शिरो मत्-पादयोः कृत्वा बाहुभ्या च परस्परम् । प्रपन्नं पाहि माम् ईश भीत मृत्यु-ग्रहार्णवात् ॥ २२.४६ ॥	śiro mat-pādayoḥ kṛtvā bāhubhyāṁ ca parasparam prapannaṁ pāhi mām īśa bhītaṁ mṛtyu-grahārṇavāt (22.46)

śiro = śiraḥ — head; mat-pādayoh — at my two feet; kṛtvā — placing; bāhubhyām — with hands; ca — and; parasparam — correspondingly, right with right, left with left; prapannam — one who took shelter; pāhi — please rescue; mām — me; īśa — o lord; bhītam — afraid; mṛtyu — death; grahārṇavāt = graha — crocodile + arṇavāt — from the ocean of material existence.

Translation

Having placed his head at my feet and holding them with both hands, right with right, left with left, he should say, "O Lord, as I take shelter of You, please rescue me, who are afraid of the ocean of material existence, which has within it, the crocodile of death." (22.46)

Commentary:

Many non-yogi devotees use this or a similar prayer when offering respect to the Krishna Deity Form. However for a yogi, this has special meaning. For the purpose of yoga, the yogi devotee understands that even though he mastered the higher yoga practice, or is in the process of doing so, there is no guarantee that he will not have to take birth in the material world again, even after practicing the *samādhi*. Unless Lord Krishna or alternately Lord *Balarāma*, Lord Shiva or Lord *Nārāyaṇa*, assures personally, one cannot know for sure where one's next body will be. This is because the yogi still remains as a limited being even after perfecting yoga. Yoga perfection for all it is, does not mean that one will command destiny. But it does mean that one has the transcendental experience as a fact. One has moved beyond faith and belief.

Thus the yogi-devotee asks the Lord to rescue him, meaning to give him the opportunity to get out of this material existence completely. Uddhava as we heard also wanted to leave with *Śrī* Krishna because he was fearful of having to stay behind in the material world. But Uddhava had to perform yoga austerities to assist his journey out of this world.

इति शेषां मया दत्ता शिरस्य् आधाय सादरम् । उद्वासयेच् चेद् उद्वास्यं ज्योतिर् ज्योतिषि तत् पुनः ॥ २२.४७॥	iti śeṣāṁ mayā dattāṁ śirasy ādhāya sādaram udvāsayec ced udvāsyaṁ jyotir jyotiṣi tat punaḥ (22.47)

iti — thus; śeṣām — items already used in the ceremony; mayā — by me; dattām — given; śirasy = śirasi — on the head; ādhāya — placing; sādaram = sa-ādaram — with respect; udvāsayec = udvasayet — he should dismiss the inhabiting divine personality; ced = cet — if; udvāsyam — a farewell ceremony; jyotir = jyotih — the effulgent presence; jyotiṣi — in the effulgent locale; tat — that; punaḥ — again, relocate.

Translation

Placing on his head, with respect, the items already used in the ceremony, which are given by Me, he should dismiss the inhabiting divine personality, by a farewell ceremony, relocating the effulgent presence into the effulgent locale. (22.47)

Commentary:

When the ceremony is concluded, in cases where the Deity must be dismissed, the mystic *pujārī* must return the Deity's effulgence in the reverse order of which it was done in verses 23 and 24 of this chapter.

अर्चादिषु यदा यत्र
श्रद्धा मां तत्र चार्चयेत् ।
सर्व-भूतेष्व् आत्मनि च
सर्वात्माहम् अवस्थितः ॥२२.४८॥

arcādiṣu yadā yatra
śraddhā māṁ tatra cārcayet
sarva-bhūteṣv ātmani ca
sarvātmāham avasthitaḥ (22.48)

arcādiṣu = arcā ādisu — in the Deity figure and related representations; yadā — whenever; yatra — wherever; śraddhā — according to faith; mām — me; tatra — there; cārcayet = ca — and + arcayet — he may worship; sarva-bhūteṣv = sarva-bhūteṣu — in all beings; ātmani — in the spirit; ca — and; sarvātmāham = sarva – all + ātmā — soul + aham — I; avasthitaḥ — situated.

Translation

One may worship Me according to faith in a Deity figure and in related representations, whenever and wherever, since I am situated in all beings, in the spirit itself and as the soul of all beings. (22.48)

Commentary:

This is the first verse of this chapter which covers worship of the Deity by non-yogi devotees. The preceding verses are particular to yoga devotees who mastered higher yoga. Anyone who has some faith in a particular deity of *Śrī* Krishna, either as Lord *Nārāyaṇa* or any other parallel divinity of *Śrī* Krishna may worship, and should know at least theoretically, that *Śrī* Krishna is somehow or the other situated in all beings and is in each spirit itself and is the soul of all beings. Such worship though not of the same potency as that done by the advanced yogi devotee, is accepted by *Śrī* Krishna according to the degree of faith and other factors which are meaningful to the Lord.

क्रिया-योग-पथैः
पुमान् वैदिक-तान्त्रिकैः ।
अर्चन्न् उभयतः सिद्धि
मत्तो विन्दत्य् अभीप्सिताम् ॥२२.४९॥

kriyā-yoga-pathaiḥ
pumān vaidika-tāntrikaiḥ
arcann ubhayataḥ siddhiṁ
matto vindaty abhīpsitām (22.49)

evam — in this way; kriyā-yoga-pathaiḥ — by the method of applying the yoga discipline to physical and mystic ritual activities; pumān — person; vaidika – Vedic; tāntrikaiḥ — according to Tantra; arcann = arcan — worshipping; ubhayatah — both here and hereafter; siddhim — perfection; matto = mattah — from me; vindaty = vindati — gets; abhīpsitām — desired.

Translation

In this way by the method of applying the yoga discipline to mystic and physical ritual activities, according to the Vedic and Tantric systems, a person gets Me, his desired goal, both here and hereafter. (22.49)

Commentary:

That is perfectly clear after understanding what was said by *Śrī* Krishna before. In their translation of this verse, *Śrīla Bhaktivedānta*'s disciples used *kriyā* yoga as regulated Deity worship. In their view this *kriyā* yoga is what they were taught by the honored *svāmī*, who was not a yogi, who bad-mouthed yoga at all opportunities, and who maintained that yoga was unnecessary. How on earth the word *kriyā* yoga could mean the modern regulated Deity worship which is done without any yoga expertise, only heaven knows.

मद्-अर्चां सम्प्रतिष्ठाप्य
मन्दिरं कारयेद् दृढम् ।
पुष्पोद्यानानि रम्याणि
पूजा-यात्रोत्सवाश्रितान् ॥ २२.५० ॥

mad-arcāṁ sampratiṣṭhāpya
mandiraṁ kārayed dṛḍham
puṣpodyānāni ramyāṇi
pūjā-yātrotsavāśritān (22.50)

mat-arcām = mat-arcām — my Deity form; sampratiṣṭhāpya — properly installing; mandiram — temple building; kārayed = kārayet — should construct; dṛḍham — sturdy; puṣpodyānāni = puṣpa-udyānāni — flower gardens; ramyāni — beautiful; pūjā — regular worship; yātrotsavāśritān = yātrā — devotional gatherings + utsava — special religious festivals + āśritān — having in reserve.

Translation

For properly installing My Deity Form, he should construct a sturdy temple building, which has beautiful flower gardens in reserve, for regular worship, devotional gatherings and special festivals. (22.50)

Commentary:

This is required for public temples. We should understand that *Śrī* Krishna meant for a temple to be established by an advance yogi devotee, even though today many large well-established temples were constructed by devotees who have much *bhakti* or devotion to *Śrī* Krishna obviously, but no current record of yoga practice.

पूजादीनां प्रवाहार्थं
महा-पर्वस्व् अथान्व्-अहम् ।
क्षेत्रापण-पुर-ग्रामान्
दत्त्वा मत्-सार्ष्टिताम् इयात् ॥ २२.५१ ॥

pūjādīnāṁ pravāhārthaṁ
mahā-parvasv athānv-aham
kṣetrāpaṇa-pura-grāmān
dattvā mat-sārṣṭitām iyāt (22.51)

pūjādīnām — regular worship and special festivals; pravāhārtham = pravāha – continuation + artham — for the purpose; mahā-parvasv = mahā – very + parvasu — on special religious occasions; athānv-aham = atha — and + anu-aham — day after day; kṣetrāpaṇa = kṣetra — land + āpaṇa — shop; pura — town; grāmān — villages; dattvā — donating; mat-sārṣṭitām — a majestic and divine status that is relatively equal to mine; iyāt — gains.

Translation

Donating lands, shops, towns and villages for the day to day continuation of regular worship and special festivals, and doing so on very special religious occasions, he gains a majestic and divine status that is relatively equal to Mine. (22.51)

Commentary:

This applies to those very advanced devotees who have the means to do so. This should not inspire poor men, to do irreligious acts to raise money to purchase lands, shops, towns and villages. Nor should this inspired wealthy persons to acquire more money by hook or crook, hoping to exploit the guarantee of this verse. If anyone is so encouraged, the advisor and the person donating, will not get what they aspire for.

I must at this point offer appreciation to the *Śrī Śrī Kṛṣṇa-Balarāma* Deities, particularly Lord *Balarāma* who ordered that I no longer write commentaries on the basis of those which came down in the disciplic succession but which have either whitewashed, distorted or hid the yoga practice and substituted temple services, missionary activities and guru worship in yoga's place.

Around the year 1994, Lord *Balarāma* instructed me to throw away hundreds of pages of commentary and summary study of the *Śrīmad Bhāgavatam* which I composed and began publishing under the title of *Krishna Divinities*. I complied with His order even though some devotee friends objected. Most of these were persons who did no yoga.

However now I see that I was correct in what I heard from Lord *Balarāma*. It would have been a continuation of an offense to Lord Krishna, if I published those writings. *Bhakti* is *bhakti*. Yoga is yoga. *Bhakti* yoga is *bhakti* and yoga combined. The redefinition of *bhakti* yoga as just *bhakti* is a distortion and deviation from what *Śrī* Krishna originally explained to both Arjuna and Uddhava. Similarly *karma* is *karma* and yoga is yoga. *Karma* yoga is *karma* plus yoga. This must be understood.

Śrī Balarāmji, the *Mahāpuruṣa*, guided me all the way to this translation and commentary of *Śrī* Krishna's advice to *Śrī* Uddhava, that most deserving and exalted yogi devotee. I am grateful on this date of September 8th of 2002.

To hide Uddhava's yoga austerities which were done at Badarinatha, the modern Vaishnava authorities say that Uddhava was sent there by *Śrī* Krishna only to tell the glories of the Lord. But this is not the full story. But after all if one does not do yoga, if one is afraid of it, if one does not like it, if one is convinced that it is no longer a requirement, then it is natural for one to minimize it.

प्रतिष्ठया सार्वभौमं
सद्मना भुवन-त्रयम् ।
पूजादिना ब्रह्म-लोक
त्रिभिर् मत्-साम्यताम् इयात् ॥ २२.५२ ॥

pratiṣṭhayā sārvabhaumaṁ
sadmanā bhuvana-trayam
pūjādinā brahma-lokaṁ
tribhir mat-sāmyatām iyāt (22.52)

pratiṣṭhayā — by establishing a Deity figure; sārvabhaumam — political control of the whole earth; sadmanā — by building a temple; bhuvana – worlds; trayam — three; pūjādinā — by worship and related services; brahma-lokam — the dimension of Procreator Brahmā; tribhir = tribhiḥ — by the three; mat-sāmyatām — a bodily resemblance to me; iyāt — gets.

Translation

By establishing a Deity Form, one gains political control of the earth. By building a temple, one gets sovereignty of the three worlds. By performing worship and other related services, one transfers to the dimension of Procreator Brahmā. And by completing all of these, one gets a bodily resemblance that is similar to Mine. (22.52)

Commentary:

These guarantees, if taken in the context of this chapter, apply to the advanced yogi devotee. It is the same in the *Bhagavad-Gītā* discourse. One has to read the guarantee very carefully and not project into it one's aspirations without considering all details laid out by *Śrī* Krishna.

Only verse 48 mentions those devotees who have no yoga practice and who rely on faith alone. Let us review that verse:

arcādiṣu yadā yatra śraddhā māṁ tatra cārcayet
sarva-bhūteṣv ātmani ca sarvātmāham avasthitaḥ

One may worship Me according to faith in a Deity figure and in related representations, whenever and wherever, since I am situated in all beings, in the spirit itself and as the soul of all beings. (U.G. 22.48)

However there is detailed information in this verse 52 about the motivations of various devotees who aspire to do the devotional services in temples. One who is eager to establish a Deity Form is usually motivated by political aspiration. Actually we find this to be true, because in most of the temples, the controllers assume the demeanor of politicians with a religious and devotional sentiment, of course. They rake and scrape their brains on how to control the public and the devotees who are under their supervision. They eventually reach a stage whereby all the temple programs are used for politically and socially controlling their respective congregations. Such devotees forget spiritual progress, while thinking day and night of schemes for getting the people to come to the temple and to support it with large donations.

Generally those who plan and supervise the building of temples, secretly regard themselves as the greatest of human beings, because of their large planning ability. These persons may be architects by nature or they maybe persons who finance the architects. Many of them are *sannyāsis* or wealthy business men. Their evolution will be eventually convey them to be super-controllers in the material world.

Those who specialize in worship ceremonies and who consider the rituals as the be-all and end-all, are motivated by a need to be in the dimension of Lord *Brahmā*, the master of these mundane creations. These people are more attracted to the material world than anything else. By nature, they focus on bringing the Almighty God into this creation, with themselves as the most important, most prominent, benediction-giving *pujārī* or priest.

But those devotees who have a balanced desire in Deity worship, temple construction and devotion service, will eventually attain either a material or spiritual form which looks like Lord *Nārāyaṇa*. Their attainment will be based on what level of yoga practice they attained. Such a person might appear as a permanent resident among the supernatural demigods but his body there will look just like that of Lord *Nārāyaṇa*.

माम् एव नैरपेक्ष्येण
भक्ति-योगेन विन्दति ।
भक्ति-योग स लभत
एवं यः पूजयेत माम् ॥ २२.५३ ॥

mām eva nairapekṣyeṇa
bhaktī-yogena vindati
bhaktī-yogaṁ sa labhata
evaṁ yaḥ pūjayeta mām (22.53)

mām — me; eva — in fact; nairapekṣyena — by being free from motivation; bhaktī-yogena — by applying yoga discipline to one's affections for *Śrī* Krishna; vindati — achieves; bhaktī-yogam — applied yoga discipline to devotion; sa = sah — that same person; labhata = labhate — gets; evam — thus; yaḥ — whosoever; pūjayeta — worship; mām — me.

Translation

In fact, by being freed from motivation, and by affection for Me, which is applied with yoga discipline, a person achieves Me. Whosoever worships Me in this way, that same person gets the techniques of applying the yoga discipline to devotion. (22.53)

Commentary:

What more can be said about the value of yoga as it is applied to devotion *(bhakti-yogam)*. It is the most glorious discipline indeed.

यः स्व-दत्ता परैर् दत्तां
हरेत सुर-विप्रयोः ।
वृत्तिं स जायते विड्-भुग्
वर्षाणाम् अयुतायुतम् ॥ २२.५४ ॥

yaḥ sva-dattāṁ parair dattāṁ
hareta sura-viprayoḥ
vṛttiṁ sa jāyate viḍ-bhug
varṣāṇām ayutāyutam (22.54)

yah — he who; sva-dattām — donated himself; parair = paraiḥ — by others; dattām — donate; hareta — takes; sura – supernatural authorities; viprayoḥ — and of the brahmins; vṛttim — property; sa = saḥ — he; jāyate — takes birth; viḍ-bhug = viṭ-bhuk — dung-eating worm; varṣāṇām — for years; ayutāyutam = ayuta — ten thousand + ayutam — multiplied by ten thousand.

Translation

He who takes the property of the supernatural authorities or that of a duly qualified brahmin, which was donated by himself or by others, takes birth as a dung-eating worm for 100 million years. (22.54)

Commentary:

The temple is considered to be the property of the supernatural authorities, the *devās* or *devatās*. One is not supposed to appropriate their property nor that of a duly-qualified brahmin who serves at a temple or who lives separately practicing spiritual disciplines which cause him to have spiritual perfection. If a person takes such property he will be degraded down to an insect level and will remain there for a long, long time, because of the low mentality which he acquired by the theft.

Even if one gives an item to the temple, one should not try to repossess it, even if it is misused by temple authorities. One should feel that any donation given to a temple was given to the supernatural authorities, even if such a donation is misused later by priests. The punishment of a priest who misuses such donations rests with the supernatural authorities and with *Śrī* Krishna. One should leave the matter to providence and go on in spiritual life without harboring resentments.

कर्तुश् च सारथेर् हेतोर्
अनुमोदितुर् एव च ।
कर्मणां भागिनः प्रेत्य
भूयो भूयसि तत्-फलम् ॥२२.५५॥

kartuś ca sārather hetor
anumoditur eva ca
karmaṇāṁ bhāginaḥ pretya
bhūyo bhūyasi tat-phalam (22.55)

kartuś = kartuh — the perpetration; ca — besides; sārather = sāratheh — of the accomplice; hetor = hetoh — of the instigator; anumoditur = anumodituh — of the approver; eva – also; ca — and; karmanām — of the actions; bhāginah — of the partners; pretya — in the hereafter; bhūyo = bhūyaḥ — greater; bhūyasi — proportionately greater; tat-phalam — of the consequence of it.

Translation

Besides the perpetrator, it applies to the accomplice, the instigator, and also the approver, all being partners in the act. The greater the theft, proportionately greater would be the consequence in the hereafter. (22.55)

Commentary:

This applies when a temple is installed by a duly qualified brahmin devotee who is a *mahāyogīn* in practice. It also applies, though in a lesser proportion to temples which are installed by devotees who are not yogis and who cannot execute the mystic procedures described by Lord Krishna.

CHAPTER 23*

This Yoga Process**

Terri Stokes-Pineda Art

yoga-caryām imām yogī vicaran mad-apāśrayaḥ
nāntarāyair vihanyeta niḥspṛhaḥ sva-sukhānubhūḥ

The yogi who practices this yoga process and who is reliant on Me, is free from sensuality, is not thwarted by obstacles and experiences the happiness of his spiritual self. (Uddhava Gītā 23.44)

* Śrīmad Bhāgavatam Canto 11, Chapter 28

** Translator's selected chapter title.

श्री-भगवान् उवाच
पर-स्वभाव-कर्माणि
न प्रशंसेन् न गर्हयेत् ।
विश्वम् एकामकं पश्यन्
प्रकृत्या पुरुषेण च ॥२३.१॥

śrī-bhagavān uvāca
para-svabhāva-karmāṇi
na praśaṁsen na garhayet
viśvam ekāmakaṁ paśyan
prakṛtyā puruṣeṇa ca (23.1)

śrī-bhagavān – the blessed lord; uvāca — said; para — another; svabhāva — own tendencies; karmāṇi — activities; na – not; praśaṁsen = praśaṁset — should appraise; na – not; garhayet — should condemn; viśvam — world; ekāmakaṁ = eka – one + ātmakam — comprising an essential nature; paśyan — perceiving; prakṛtyā — with material nature; puruṣeṇa — with the spiritual personality; ca — and.

Translation

The Blessed Lord said: One should not appraise nor condemn the actions and tendencies of oneself nor of another. One should perceive the world as comprising one essential nature produced with material nature and the spiritual personality. (23.1)

Commentary:

A theory of *Advaita* or oneness is here approved by *Śrī* Krishna in no uncertain terms by use of the term *ekātmakam*; that the world is one essential nature, regardless of the approvals and disapprovals of anyone. The terms *puruṣa (puruṣeṇa)* in this verse, related to what *Śrī* Krishna spoke of previously about the *puruṣa* as a class or reality which is linked to the material nature *(prakṛtyā)*.

When a yogin reaches the advanced stages, after being allowed exemption from *karma* yoga or approved cultural activities, he is instructed in a new use of the critical energy. Usually this energy is used to constructively or maliciously criticize others, but after getting an exemption from the cultural world, the yogi gets counsels on how to turn his critical energy upon himself. He advances further into the stages of non-interference into the material world.

This has to do with not interfering into Goddess *Durgā*'s affairs. She is the personified attractive material potency. The yogi gets an advice from her on how to avoid clashes with her energy. He can then follow the advice given in this verse. Such a yogi is on the brink of entering the chit *ākāśa*, the sky of consciousness, by using the same *kriyās* given by *Śrī* Krishna in previous chapters of this discourse.

पर-स्वभाव-कर्माणि
यः प्रशसति निन्दति ।
स आशु भ्रश्यते स्वार्थाद्
असत्य् अभिनिवेशतः ॥२३.२॥

para-svabhāva-karmāṇi
yaḥ praśaṁsati nindati
sa āśu bhraśyate svārthād
asaty abhiniveśataḥ (23.2)

para — others, another; svabhāva — own tendency; karmāṇi — activities; yah — he who; praśaṁsati — appraises; nindati — condemns; sa = sah — he; āśu — quickly; bhraśyate — becomes degraded; svārthād = sva – his own + arthāt — from his interest; asaty = asati — in what is non-substantial; abhiniveśatah — by reason of being absorbed.

Translation

He who appraises or condemns, the activities or tendencies of himself or of others, quickly becomes degraded away from his interest by reason of being obsessed in what is non-substantial or temporary. (23.2)

Commentary:

This was explained in a different way to Arjuna, using the same term *asaty*:

nāsato vidyate bhāvo nābhāvo vidyate sataḥ
ubhayorapi dṛṣṭo'ntas tvanayostattvadarśibhiḥ

Of the non-substantial things, there is no enduring existence. Of the substantial things, there is no lack of existence. These two truths were perceived with certainty by the mystic seers of reality. (B.G. 2.16)

Everything in the material world which comprise material nature and the spirits, is non-substantial, because the combinations are temporary. No one, not even God can make such combinations to be permanent. Eventually one understands this and forsakes the material energy altogether. One must first get an exemption from cultural activities and get the relevant mystic means for perceiving spiritual objects in the sky of consciousness. So long as we are interested in anything on this side of existence, we will have to remain here in a degradation. Of course there are varying degrees of involvement but any percentage is still a degradation. We need to go to the place where there is no material nature mixed in.

तैजसे निद्रयापन्ने
पिण्ड-स्थो नष्ट-चेतनः ।
मायां प्राप्नोति मृत्युं वा
तद्वन् नानार्थ-दृक् पुमान् ॥२३.३॥

taijase nidrayāpanne
piṇḍa-stho naṣṭa-cetanaḥ
māyāṁ prāpnoti mṛtyuṁ vā
tadvan nānārtha-dṛk pumān (23.3)

taijase — for that which consists of the vital energy, the senses; nidrayāpanne = nidrayā — by sleep + āpanne — are overpowered; piṇḍa-stho = piṇḍa — body + sthaḥ — he who is situated; naṣṭa-cetanaḥ = naṣṭa – having lost + cetanaḥ — objective consciousness, objectivity; māyām — bewildering scenes; prāpnoti — experiences; mrtyum — death-like slumber; vā — or; tadvan = tadvat — similarly; nānārtha-dṛk = nānā – many + artha — objects + drk — perceives; pumān — a person.

Translation

For when the senses which consists of the vital energy, are overcome by sleep, the one who is situated in the body, having lost objectivity, experiences bewildering scenes or death-like slumber. Similarly a person perceives many objects in the material world. (23.3)

Commentary:

A brash comparison is made to our waking and sleeping states. One has objective consciousness while awake in a material body. But that objectivity is lost during sleep. In sleep, the physical senses become inactive. Sometimes the subtle senses become inactive as well. While the subtle senses cease interacting, one experiences deep sleep or a death-like type of sleep in which there is no memory of actvities, even of subtle activities. When however only the physical senses are inactive and the subtle ones remain involved, one experiences imaginations and subtle actions in dreams.

This is compared to being inside and outside the material energy. When the soul is inside the material energy, even in his wakeful state, he is in a sense, dreaming and imagining so many insubstantial things. Thus he needs to get rid of that condition, to wake up on the spiritual side completely.

कि भद्रं किम् अभद्रं वा
द्वैतस्यावस्तुनः कियत् ।
वाचोदितं तद् अनृतं
मनसा ध्यातम् एव च ॥२३.४॥

kiṁ bhadraṁ kim abhadraṁ vā
dvaitasyāvastunaḥ kiyat
vācoditaṁ tad anṛtaṁ
manasā dhyātam eva ca (23.4)

kim — who; bhadram — good; kim — who; abhadram — bad; vā — or; dvaitasyāvastunaḥ = dvaitasya — of this duality + avastunaḥ — lacking durability; kiyat — to what extent; vācoditaṁ = vācā — by speech + uditam — formulated; tad = tat — that; anṛtam — false; manasā — by the mind; dhyātam — meditated upon; eva — surely; ca — and.

Translation

Regarding the duality which lacks durability, what is good in it or what is bad and to what extent? That which is formulated by speech; that which is meditated upon by the mind is surely false. (23.4)

Commentary:

To understand what *Śrī* Krishna means by duality *(dvaitasya)* we have to refer to the first verse of this chapter where He mentioned the one essential nature *(ekātmakam).* If anything, one should begin seeing the material world as a combination of matter and spirit (*prakṛtyā and puruṣeṇa*, verse 1). Once this is clearly seen by mystic vision, one can no longer look for a duality. The superficial but convincing fusion of matter and spirit occurred. If one wants to take exit from it, he will have to forget all about it, just like a man who wakes up and no longer dreams.

As stated in this verse, the duality of matter and spirit lacks durability. Therefore there is really no point in discussing the value of it, as to whether it is good or bad or to what degree it is useful or useless. Whatever we create in relation to this world, is actually baseless, even though so long as we exist here, we have to organize ourselves in terms of speech and the activities which speech describe. Furthermore whatever is conceived by the mind that has to do with this world is baseless ultimately.

This is why *Śrī Patañjali* addressed the problem in a summary way by stating that the success of yoga means the stoppage of the vrittis, the mental and emotional energies which entertain and afflict one in the mind. It is these ideas, because these ideas have to do with what the mind encountered in this world. So long as the mind is preoccupied with these images, the living entity who is linked to the involving mind will remain bound into the material energy. This calls for higher yoga practice. It is an individual skill because the mass of people cannot do it except by individual efforts to free the mind from its impulsive considerations. Each person must endeavor for this.

छाया-प्रत्याह्वयाभासा
ह्य् असन्तो ऽप्य् अर्थ-कारिणः ।
एव देहादयो भावा
यच्छन्त्य् आ-मृत्युतो भयम् ॥२३.५॥

chāyā-pratyāhvayābhāsā
hy asanto 'py artha-kāriṇaḥ
evaṁ dehādayo bhāvā
yacchanty ā-mṛtyuto bhayam (23.5)

chāyā — shadow; pratyāhvayābhāsā = pratyāhvaya — echo + ābhāsāḥ — mirage; hy = hi — in fact; asanto = asantaḥ — that which is unreal; 'py = api — although; artha — something; kāriṇaḥ — which causes; evaṁ — similarly; dehādayo = deha – body + ādayaḥ — and so forth; bhāvāḥ — mundane existence; yacchanty = yacchanti — they cause; ā-mṛtyuto = ā – until + mṛtyutaḥ — death; bhayam — fearfulness.

Translation

Even though unreal, a shadow, an echo or a mirage, is in fact the cause of something else. Similarly mundane existences like the body and so forth, cause fearfulness until the time of death. (23.5)

Commentary:

Though it is unreal and very insubstantial, in fact, still the material existence has a power by which it influences the spirit into accepting mundane manifestations as being substantial. A shadow cannot directly harm anyone but it can cause fearfulness. A mirage cannot give anyone fulfillment but it can cause one to hope for and to believe falsely. The question is: What is the mechanism through which a particular soul is fooled into thinking that the material world is real and substantial? How can that mechanism be changed to depict the actual condition?

आत्मैव तद् इदं विश्वं
सृज्यते सृजति प्रभुः ।
त्रायते त्राति विश्वात्मा
ह्रियते हरतीश्वरः ॥२३.६॥

ātmaiva tad idaṁ viśvaṁ
sṛjyate sṛjati prabhuḥ
trāyate trāti viśvātmā
hriyate haratīśvaraḥ (23.6)

ātmaiva = ātmā — soul + eva — only; tad = tat – that; idam — this; viśvaṁ — universe; sṛjyate — is indicated by what is created; sṛjati — creates; prabhuḥ — the God; trāyate — is maintained; trāti — maintains; viśvātmā — soul of the world; hriyate — is withdrawn; haratīśvarah = harati — withdraws + īśvaraḥ — the supreme lord.

Translation

The soul alone is involved in the universe. The God is indicated by what is created and what creates. The soul of the world is maintained and maintains. The Supreme Lord is withdrawn and withdraws. (23.6)

Commentary:

The movement of energy, the display of anything energetic, anything that demands our attention, is based ultimately on God, the Supreme Lord. Even in cases where a particular manifestation is traceable to a limited soul, still we should understand and surmise that the Supreme Lord is in the background as the Ultimate Motivator.

The material energy is never by itself because of its eternal proximity to God. We have to realize that our attraction to it, is ultimately, a search for the Prime Mover. Whatever is created, maintained or withdrawn has an energy background and ultimately if one traces it, he will find the Prime Mover, hidden behind a series of causes.

तस्मान् न ह्य् आत्मनो ऽन्यस्माद्
अन्यो भावो निरूपितः ।
निरूपिते ऽयं त्रि-विधा
निर्मूल भातिर् आत्मनि ।
इदं गुण-मयं विद्धि
त्रि-विधं मायया कृतम् ॥२३.७॥

tasmān na hy ātmano 'nyasmād
anyo bhāvo nirūpitaḥ
nirūpite 'yaṁ tri-vidhā
nirmūla bhātir ātmani
idaṁ guṇa-mayaṁ viddhi
tri-vidhaṁ māyayā kṛtam (23.7)

tasmān = tasmāt — therefore; na — no; hy = hi — in fact; ātmano = ātmanaḥ — besides the soul; 'nyasmād = anyasmāt — besides any other; anyo = anyah — other; bhāvo = bhāvaḥ — prominent factor; nirūpitah — is proved; nirūpite — is proven; 'yam = ayam — this; tri-vidhā — threefold; nirmūlā — without basis; bhātir = bhātiḥ — manifested in; ātmani — in the soul; idam — this; guna – mundane influence; mayam — caused by; viddhi — know; tri-vidham — threefold; māyayā — bewildering energy; kṛtam — produced by.

Translation

Therefore no other prominent feature is proven, besides the soul. This threefold manifestation which is projected in the soul is proven to be without a basis. Know that this threefold manifestation which was produced by the bewildering energy, is caused by the mundane influences. (23.7)

Commentary:

Since the soul becomes preoccupied or entertained by material nature's reactions to its presence, the soul loses objectivity and can hardly account for itself.

एतद् विद्वान् मद्-उदितं
ज्ञान-विज्ञान-नैपुणम् ।
न निन्दति न च स्तौति
लोके चरति सूर्य-वत् ॥२३.८॥

etad vidvān mad-uditaṁ
jñāna-vijñāna-naipuṇam
na nindati na ca stauti
loke carati sūrya-vat (23.8)

etad = etat — this; vidvān — knowledgeable person; mad-uditam = mat — by me + uditam — which is described; jñāna — theoretical understanding; vijñāna — factual experience; naipunam — a proficient person; na – not; nindati — criticizes; na – nor; ca — and; stauti — congratulates; loka — in this world; carati — moves about; sūrya-vat — just like the sun.

Translation

A knowledgeable person, who is proficient in the theoretical understanding and factual experience, of what is described by Me, does not criticize nor congratulate anyone. He moves about in this world, just like the sun. (23.8)

Commentary:

This is a stage of advanced practice, when a yogin no longer reacts to anything in the material world. At that stage he moves about like the sun. Having controlled and mastered his critical energy, he no longer applies it to others but only to himself. He adopts an attitude of non interference. He is completely unconcerned about the course of material existence. He does not see anything essentially wrong in the souls who are captivated by the material energy.

प्रत्यक्षेणानुमानेन
निगमेनात्म-सविदा ।
आद्य्-अन्तवद् असज् ज्ञात्वा
निःसङ्गो विचरेद् इह ॥२३.९॥

pratyakṣeṇānumānena
nigamenātma-savidā
ādy-antavad asaj jñātvā
niḥsaṅgo vicared iha (23.9)

pratyakṣeṇānumānena = pratyakṣeṇa – by mystic vision + anumānena - by analysis; nigamenātma-saṁvidā = nigamena- by scriptural evidence + ātma-samvidā – by spirit experience; ādy (ādi) – from beginning; antavad (antavat) –from ending; asaj = asat – temporary existence; jñātvā – knowing; niḥsaṅgo – without attachment (association); vicared (vicaret) - wander; iha - here on earth

Translation

Using mystic vision, analysis, scriptural evidence and spirit experience, knowing this temporary existence as having a beginning and ending, he should without association, wander on this earth. (23.9)

श्री-उद्धव उवाच
नैवात्मनो न देहस्य
ससृतिर् द्रष्ट्-दृश्ययोः ।
अनात्म-स्व-दृशोर् ईश
कस्य स्याद् उपलभ्यते ॥२३.१०॥

śrī-uddhava uvāca
naivātmano na dehasya
saṁsṛtir draṣṭṛ-dṛśyayoḥ
anātma-sva-dṛśor īśa
kasya syād upalabhyate (23.10)

śrī-uddhava – the deserving Uddhava; uvāca — said; naivātmano = na — not + eva — in fact + ātmanaḥ — of the spirit, pertaining to the spirit; na — nor; dehasya — of the body, pertaining to the body; saṁsṛtir = saṁsṛtiḥ — temporary existence, the course of transmigration; draṣṭṛ - perceiver; dṛśyayoḥ — pertaining to what is perceived; anātma — that which is not spirit, the non-animating factor; sva – self; dṛśoḥ — pertaining to that which is perceptive; īśa — lord; kasya — of whom; syād = syāt — it is; upalabhyate — experienced.

Translation

The deserving Uddhava said: O Lord, temporary existence does not pertain to the spirit nor the body, which are the perceiver and the perceived items respectively, and which are the perceptive self and the non-animating factor in turn. Who then experiences what it is? (23.10)

Commentary:

Uddhava asked a very important question, in order to understand the mechanisms of perception. If the spirit is indeed eternal, then how is it possible for it to experience what is temporary and to experience that to such a degree as to be fooled repeatedly? On the other hand if as *Śrī* Krishna said that the material energy is not the animated or energized of itself, then certainly, the material energy is not capable of even its own temporary manifestations. In both cases, one is prompted to look for a third reality but *Śrī* Krishna only described two factors, namely the spirits and the material energy.

आत्माव्ययो ऽगुणः शुद्धः
स्वयं-ज्योतिर् अनावृतः ।
अग्नि-वद् दारु-वद् अचिद्
देहः कस्येह ससृतिः ॥२३.११॥

ātmāvyayo 'guṇaḥ śuddhaḥ
svayaṁ-jyotir anāvṛtaḥ
agni-vad dāru-vad acid
dehaḥ kasyeha saṁsṛtiḥ (23.11)

ātmāvyayo = ātmā — individual spirit + avyayaḥ — changeless; 'guṇaḥ = agunaḥ — without mundane expression; śuddhaḥ — pure spirit; svayam – self; jyotir = jyotiḥ — luminous; anāvṛtaḥ — that which cannot be covered up; agni-vad = agni-vat — like fire; dāru-vad = dāru-vat — like firewood; acid = acit — lacking objective awareness; dehaḥ — body; kasyeha = kasya — of which pertaining to which + iha — in this world; saṁsṛtiḥ — the course of material existence.

Translation

The individual spirit is changeless and is without mundane expression. It is pure spirit, self-luminous. It cannot be covered. It is like fire. The body however lacks objective awareness. It is like firewood. To which of these, does the course of material existence pertain? (23.11)

Commentary:

The apparent contradictions are reconciled when we understand that material nature is always in proximity to the spirits. The nature of the spirits is reflected in material nature and visa versa. Neither actually adopts the nature of the other but there is a give and take, as it were, when the spirit's energy is focused into the subtle matter.

Neither the spirit nor matter is temporary. Both are eternal but the conjunction of the two which gives rise to this manifested world is periodic and thus temporary.

श्री-भगवान् उवाच
यावद् देहेन्द्रिय-प्राणैर्
आत्मनः सन्निकर्षणम् ।
ससारः फलवांस् तावद्
अपार्थो ऽप्य् अविवेकिनः ॥२३.१२॥

śrī-bhagavān uvāca
yāvad dehendriya-prāṇair
ātmanaḥ sannikarṣaṇam
saṁsāraḥ phalavāṁs tāvad
apārtho 'py avivekinaḥ (23.12)

śrī-bhagavān – the blessed lord; uvāca — replied; yāvad = yāvat — so long as; dehendriya = deha — body + indriya — senses; prāṇair = prāṇaiḥ — and with the vital energy; ātmanaḥ — of the spirit; sannikarṣaṇam — connection; saṁsāraḥ — the changing scenes of material existence; phalavāṁs = phala – result, worth + vān — yielding of (phala-van = potentially worthwhile); tāvad = tāvat — until such time; apārtho = apārthaḥ — not having long ranged value; 'py = api — even although; avivekinaḥ — for the indiscriminating person.

Translation

The Blessed Lord replied: So long as the connection of the spirit with the body, senses and vital energy remains, the changing scenes of the material existence, which have no long-ranged value, will be potentially worthwhile for the indiscriminating person. (23.12)

Commentary:

The term *sannikarṣaṇam* means drawing near, bringing near, vicinity, proximity, and presence. It also means connection, relation or the connection of a sense organ with an attractive object. Unfortunately the linkage of the spirit's attention with the material energy takes place effortlessly. Merely by being in proximity, the spirit becomes linked to the material energy, through a sensual mechanism which favors relationship with that energy. Thus liberation is for any limited being a near-impossibility.

अर्थे ह्य् अविद्यमाने ऽपि
ससृतिर् न निवर्तते ।
ध्यायतो विषयान् अस्य
स्वप्ने ऽनर्थागमो यथा ॥२३.१३॥

arthe hy avidyamāne 'pi
saṁsṛtir na nivartate
dhyāyato viṣayān asya
svapne 'narthāgamo yathā (23.13)

arthe — the objective world; hy = hi — in fact; avidyamāne — that which is unreal; 'pi = api — although; saṁsṛtir = saṁsṛtiḥ — material existence; na — not; nivartate — does cease; dhyāyato = dhyāyatah — one whose attention is impulsively linked; visayān — attractive objects; asya — of this; svapne — in dream; 'narthāgamo = anartha — undesirable circumstance + āgamaḥ — appearance; yatha — as.

Translation

Although the objective world is unreal, the material existence does not cease for a person whose attention is impulsively linked to the attractive objects, just as the appearance of undesirable circumstances come up in a dream. (23.13)

Commentary:

Telling someone that this world is insubstantial and proving this by reason, does not effect this world, for the person whose attention remains impulsively linked to the attractive objects. This is why the idea of hearing transcendental knowledge and becoming liberated by such hearing is nonsensical. Even after one hears, one still have to overcome the impulsive involuntary linkage of the sensual energy to the desirable objects.

Hearing alone does not remove nor abolish the impulsive linkage, for it is as if our minds were created with the inherent fault of having to become linked up to the attractive objects which the senses do appreciate.

Śrī Krishna cited the example of dreams. These may be analyzed as being unreal but while a person endures them he acts in that subtle environment just as if they were real. His information about the unreality of dreams does not protect him from experiencing them. Knowledge alone will not free a soul from the course of material existence.

यथा ह्य् अप्रतिबुद्धस्य
प्रस्वापो बह्व्-अनर्थ-भृत् ।
स एव प्रतिबुद्धस्य
न वै मोहाय कल्पते ॥२३.१४॥

yathā hy apratibuddhasya
prasvāpo bahv-anartha-bhṛt
sa eva pratibuddhasya
na vai mohāya kalpate (23.14)

yathā — as; hy = hi — indeed; apratibuddhasya — of one who is enlightened; prasvāpo = prasvāpaḥ — sleep; bahv = bahu — many; anartha — undesirable experiences; bhṛt — contains; sa

= saḥ — that condition; eva — indeed; pratibuddhasya — of one whose intellect functions correctly; na — not; vai — surely; mohāya — confusion; kalpate — leads to.

Translation

The sleep of an un-awakened person contains many undesirable experiences, but that condition does not lead to confusion once the person awakes and his intellect functions correctly. (23.14)

Commentary:

A limited being, be he a devotee of *Śrī* Krishna or a non devotee, a great yogin or not, cannot altogether stop the illusions from forming around him, even in his consciousness. This is because the operations of the senses and vital energy continue whenever one's vigilance becomes relaxed.

Until one is completely disconnected from the subtle body and its psychological sensing equipments, one will be subjected to the confusions and illusions which occur because material nature is highly energized. However if one develops the truth-bearing intellect, one will know when an illusion arises and will be able to see it for what it is.

There is ample evidence that even great devotees who are dear to *Śrī* Krishna, do fall into illusions and are fooled by such confusions from time to time, even in the presence of the Blessed Lord. Arjuna is such an example and there are others. In some past lives, as great a devotee as *Nārada,* was an example of this. Therefore those who say that this confusion does not arise for a devotee or for a pure devotee, are untruthful or naive.

शोक-हर्ष-भय-क्रोध-
लोभ-मोह-स्पृहादयः ।
अहङ्कारस्य दृश्यन्ते
जन्म-मृत्युश् च नात्मनः ॥२३.१५॥

śoka-harṣa-bhaya-krodha-
lobha-moha-spṛhādayaḥ
ahaṅkārasya dṛśyante
janma-mṛtyuś ca nātmanaḥ (23.15)

śoka — grief; harsa — uncontrollable enjoyment; bhaya — fear; krodha — anger; lobha — greed; moha — confusion; spṛhādayaḥ = spṛhā — desire + ādayaḥ — and other negative aspects; ahaṅkārasya — in relation to the assertive sense; dṛśyante — they are noticed; janma — birth; mṛtyus = mṛtyuḥ — death; ca — and; nātmanaḥ = na — not + ātmanaḥ — in reference to the spirit soul.

Translation

Grief, uncontrollable enjoyment, fear, anger, greed, confusion, desire and other negative aspects, as well as birth and death, are noticed in relation to the assertive sense but not in reference to the spirit. (23.15)

Commentary:

Each spirit should discover the various links between itself and whatever is a botheration to it. If upon discovery one can curtail, restrict or even eliminate the linkage, one would have partial or full freedom from the undesirable effects.

In higher yoga, one can see the assertive sense, which is a tiny red-blue light. When this is controlled in deep meditation, one gains the required freedom not otherwise. This same assertive sense is usually experienced as an all surrounding ever-active and responsive space around the core self in the head of the subtle body. It must be kept in strict allegiance to the core self, otherwise it will function as a servant or agent of the intellect which will function as an agent of its sensual outshoots, which will work in cahoots with the life force survival and reproduction mechanisms. And the result of that alliance is disaster for the self.

देहेन्द्रिय-प्राण-मनो-ऽभिमानो
जीवो ऽन्तर्-आत्मा गुण-कर्म-मूर्तिः ।
सूत्र महान् इत्य् उरुधेव गीतः
ससार आधावति काल-तन्त्रः ॥२३.१६॥

dehendriya-prāṇa-mano-'bhimāno
jīvo 'ntar-ātmā guṇa-karma-mūrtiḥ
sūtraṁ mahān ity urudheva gītaḥ
saṁsāra ādhāvati kāla-tantraḥ (23.16)

dehendriya = deha — body + indriya — senses; prāṇa — life force, vital energy; mano = manaḥ — mind; 'bhimāno = abhimānah — claimant; jīve = jīvah — the individual spirit; 'ntar = antaḥ — being inside the psyche; ātmā — spirit; guṇa — mundane tendencies; karma — cultural activities; mūrtiḥ — form; sūtram — emotionally-charged cosmic potency; mahān — primal mundane energy; ity = iti — thus; urudheva = urudha — various + iva — indeed, as if; gītaḥ — called; saṁsāre — in material existence; ādhāvati — transmigrated; kāla — time; tantraḥ — as regulated.

Translation

The individual spirit, the spirit soul who is inside the psyche, is assertive of the body, senses, life force and mind which appear as a form that was based on mundane tendencies and cultural activities. The claimant does, as regulated by time, transmigrate in material existence, which is called by various names, either as the emotionally-charged cosmic potency or the Primal Mundane Energy. (23.16)

Commentary:

The individual spirits impulsively adopted the assertive sense without any deliberation or selection on their part. This sense will not leave them unless they strive for and attain liberation from it. In this world since the beginning of time, the entities have acted as claimants in order to satisfy a sense of a proprietorship. Since the material nature changes and changes, all the claimants are forced to transmigrate to either possess new territories or to change their damaged bodies in order to continue exploiting the old lands.

अमूलम् एतद् बहु-रूप-रूपितं
मनो-वचः-प्राण-शरीर-कर्म ।
ज्ञानासिनोपासनया शितेन
च्छित्त्वा मुनिर् गां विचरत्य् अतृष्णः ॥२३.१७॥

amūlam etad bahu-rūpa-rūpitaṁ
mano-vacaḥ-prāṇa-śarīra-karma
jñānāsinopāsanayā śitena
cchittvā munir gāṁ vicaraty atṛṣṇaḥ (23.17)

amūlam — without basis; etad = etat — this; bahu – many; rūpa — form; rūpitam — is manifested, took shape; mano = manah — mind; vacah — speech; prāna — life force; śarīra — body; karma — cultural activity; jñānāsinopāsanayā = jñāna — knowledge + asinā — by the sword + upāsanayā — through service to a spiritual master; śitena — by sharpened; chittvā — cutting off; munir = muniḥ — a yogi philosopher; gām — earth; vicaraty = vicarati — roams; atṛṣṇaḥ — free from desires.

Translation

Cutting off with the sword of knowledge, sharpened by service to the spiritual master, this assertion, which though without a basis, took shape in many forms, the yogi philosopher roams over the earth being freed from desires. (23.17)

Commentary:

The yogi philosopher in the advanced stages of practicing yoga on the mystic level, does eventually perceive the sense of assertion, the *ahamkāra* (verse 15). This is a supernatural object. It is not just our sense of possession or our sense of wanting to do something in material existence. It is an object to be seen on the mystic plane. The yogi takes steps to disconnect himself from it. When this action is completed he remains free from the afflictions which come to one who is connected to cultural activities in this world. *Munir (munih)* is the yogi philosopher and not just any philosopher. He may or may not be recognized as a great devotee. This cannot be a sober sage nor just a philosopher who does not practice yoga. Non-yogis cannot perceive the assertive sense on the mystic plane, nor can they separate the core self from it. To them these subtle tools like the intellect, the sensual energies and the assertive sense are all one personality. They cannot segregate these merely by beliefs nor by getting the kind of information that is in this book. For that separation one has to master higher yoga.

ज्ञानं विवेको निगमस् तपश् च
प्रत्यक्षम् ऐतिह्यम् अथानुमानम् ।
आद्य्-अन्तयोर् अस्य यद् एव केवलं
कालश् च हेतुश् च तद् एव मध्ये ॥२३.१८॥

jñānaṁ viveko nigamas tapaś ca
pratyakṣam aitihyam athānumānam
ādy-antayor asya yad eva kevalaṁ
kālaś ca hetuś ca tad eva madhye (23.18)

jñānam — factual understanding; viveko = vivekaḥ — discrimination; nigamas — Vedic study; tapaś = tapaḥ — austerity; ca — and; pratyakṣam — direct perception; aitihyam — study of scriptural history; athānumānam = atha — and + anumānam — reasoning; ādy = ādi — beginning; antayoh — and in the end; asya — of this; yad = yat — that which; eva — indeed; kevalam — what is isolated from the psychic equipments; kālah — time; ca — and; hetuś = hetuh — cause; ca — and; tad = tat — that; eva — alone; madhye — in the interim stage.

Translation

Factual understanding is the discriminating ability, based on Vedic study and austerity, as well as on direct perception, study of scriptural history and application of reason, which discerns that what existed before the beginning and which will exist beyond the end of this creation, which is time and which is the cause. That which is isolated from the psychic equipments exists in reality in the interim stage. (23.18)

Commentary:

Jñānam or knowledge is defined as a discriminating ability developed from Vedic study, austerity, direct mystic perception, study of scriptural history, and the application of reason, and which shows us the underlying spiritual cause of the world. That reality is there while the creation is manifested but it is there as well when the creation terminates and it was there before the creation was produced. These are purely mystic matters. This is not apprehended by merely hearing from a spiritual master, nor by reading scripture. One must have direct perception. Each person must himself develop the relevant mystic ability to see this directly, not through reasoning nor through conceptions derived from reading and hearing.

यथा हिरण्यं स्व्-अकृत पुरस्तात्
पश्चाच् च सर्वस्य हिरण्-मयस्य ।
तद् एव मध्ये व्यवहार्यमाणं
नानापदेशैर् अहम् अस्य तद्वत् ॥२३.१९॥

yathā hiraṇyaṁ sv-akṛtaṁ purastāt
paścāc ca sarvasya hiraṇ-mayasya
tad eva madhye vyavahāryamāṇaṁ
nānāpadeśair aham asya tadvat (23.19)

yathā — as; hiraṇyam — gold; sv = su – beautiful; akṛtam — formed object; purastāt — before being formed; paścāc = paścāt — afterwards; ca — and; sarvasya — of all; hiraṇ - gold; mayasya — of what is made of; tad = tat — that; eva — only; madhye — in the middle, between manufacture and melt down; vyavahāryamānam — when utilized; nānāpadeśair = nānā — various + apadeśaiḥ — by means; aham — I; asya — in reference to this; tadvat — just so, similarly.

Translation

As gold is the same material in beautifully-formed objects, before being formed and afterwards, and is the same also though attributed with various names, when utilized in the period between manufacture and melt down, so also, I am the same in reference to this material creation. (23.19)

Commentary:

Even though we may understand this mentally or follow this or accept it on the basis of love for and faith in *Śrī* Krishna, still the material creation will baffle us so long as the connection with the senses and vital energy remains (verse 12). We should perform mystic actions in higher yoga to change this.

Even though we do understand clearly that gold ore, refined gold and gold jewels are gold, still we remain baffled by the various uses and shapes of the metal. Merely by convincing ourselves that it is the same, does not change the psychology which causes an attraction to golden objects. It is only an inner adjustment, a mystic change, that can correct the psychology.

विज्ञानम् एतत् त्रिय्-अवस्थम् अङ्ग
गुण-त्रय कारण-कर्य-कर्तृ ।
समन्वयेन व्यतिरेकतश् च
येनैव तुर्येण तद् एव सत्यम् ॥२३.२०॥

vijñānam etat triy-avastham aṅga
guṇa-trayaṁ kāraṇa-karya-kartṛ
samanvayena vyatirekataś ca
yenaiva turyeṇa tad eva satyam (23.20)

vijñānam — organ of perception; etat — this; triy = tri – three; avastham — phases of consciousness; aṅga — my dear; guṇa – mundane influences; trayam — three; kāraṇa — cause; kārya — effect; kartṛ — agency; samanvayena — by sequential combination; vyatirekataś = vyatirekataḥ — when existing distinctly from; ca — and; yenaiva = yena — by which + eva — in fact; turyeṇa — by the fourth state of consciousness; tad = tat — that; eva — alone; satyam — reality.

Translation

That organ of perception used to perceive the three phases of consciousness, the three mundane influences, the cause, effect and agency by sequential combination and which also perceives the fourth state of consciousness, when it is distinct from the rest, that alone is the perception of the Reality. (23.20)

Commentary:

This verse has baffled many commentators, simply because most of them have not practiced higher yoga. If one tries to translate or to comment upon these verses, without first having practiced higher yoga and having gained success thereby, one will not be able to render the meanings, because one would have ventured into a territory that is beyond one's reach. In higher yoga, one develops and then utilizes what is called the *ṛtambharā buddhi*. This means the truth or reality-perceiving instrument in the subtle body. This same subtle tool for perceiving was mentioned in the *Bhagavad-Gītā* as *jñāna-dīpena*:

teṣāmevānukampārtham ahamajñānajaṁ tamaḥ
nāśayāmyātmabhāvastho jñānadīpena bhāsvatā

In the interest of assisting them, I who am situated within their beings, cause the ignorance, produced by the stupefying influence of material nature, to be banished by their clear realized insight. (B.G. 10.11)

The jñāna-dīpena organ of perception is described in this verse as being capable of analyzing the three phases of ordinary consciousness which are wakefulness, dream and sleep. Dream means low level subtle activities procured by the mind. Wakefulness means subtle and gross activities which are done objectively. Sleep means a lack of memory.

The organ of perception is there in the head of the subtle body. It is called *buddhi* in Sanskrit. In the *Bhagavad-Gītā* Lord Krishna gave a course in the latter part of chapter two on how to curb the *buddhi* by doing *buddhi* yoga. When that organ of perception is curbed and refined when it is weaned from this world, it develops the ability to perceive into the fourth state of consciousness, the chit *ākāśa*, the sky of consciousness, the spiritual world.

Previously in this discourse, *Śrī* Krishna gave some preliminary practices for transferring into that fourth dimension. He spoke of the *ghoṣa* or sound which comes in from that dimension. If one learns this practice by mentally linking his intellect to that sound, he would develop the higher perception to see into the fourth dimension. He would then perceive the Reality.

न यत् पुरस्ताद् उत यन् न पश्चान्
मध्ये च तन् न व्यपदेश-मात्रम् ।
भूत प्रसिद्ध च परेण यद् यत्
तद् एव तत् स्याद् इति मे मनीषा ॥२३.२१॥

na yat purastād uta yan na paścān
madhye ca tan na vyapadeśa-mātram
bhūtaṁ prasiddhaṁ ca pareṇa yad yat
tad eva tat syād iti me manīṣā (23.21)

na — not; yat — that which; purastād = purastāt — existing before; uta — or; yan = yat — that, which; na — not (uta na = nor); paścān = paścāt — afterwards; madhye — in the interim state; ca — and; tan = tat — that; na — not; vyapadeśa - a designation; mātram — what is merely; bhūtam — something produced; prasiddham — something manifested; ca — and; parena — by another factor; yad yat = yat yat — what what, whatever; tad = tat — that; eva — alone; tat — that; syād = syāt — is; iti — thus; me — my; manīsā — opinion.

Translation

That which is neither before nor after, is non-existent in the interim state. It is merely a designation. My opinion is this: Whatever is produced and whatever is manifested by another factor is that factor only. (23.21)

Commentary:

To see what is continuous, what is real, one has to develop the faculty of perception which enters the fourth dimension, the sky of consciousness. This is not an understanding, but rather it is a perception or vision. It is a spiritual sensual perception, not an analytical conception. Ultimately we should directly see what is behind this creation. That ultimate cause is in another sky. It is not in this sky which we currently perceive. It is not an understanding or theoretical draft of something higher while we are in this world. It is an actual view of the fourth dimension.

The first dimension is the sensual perceptions we have of this world. That is normal sense perception. The second dimension is the sensual perceptions we have of the subtle material world. That is a type of psychic perception. The third dimension is what we perceive as imagination. And the fourth dimension is what we perceive of in the supernatural and spiritual worlds. These are all different types of perception, not different understandings or concepts.

अविद्यमानो ऽप्य् अवभासते यो
वैकारिको राजस-सर्ग एसः ।
ब्रह्म स्वयं ज्योतिर् अतो विभाति
ब्रह्मेन्द्रियार्थात्म-विकार-चित्रम् ॥२३.२२॥

avidyamāno 'py avabhāsate yo
vaikāriko rājasa-sarga esaḥ
brahma svayaṁ jyotir ato vibhāti
brahmendriyārthātma-vikāra-citram (23.22)

avidyamāno = avidyamānaḥ — that which is unreal; 'py = api — even though; avabhāsate — manifested; yo = yaḥ — which; vaikāriko = vaikārikaḥ — transforming creation; rājasa — impulsive energy; sarga = sargaḥ — creation; eṣaḥ — this world; brahma — spiritual reality; svayam — self, itself; jyotir = jyotiḥ — effulgent principle; ato = atah — therefore, hence, for that reason; vibhāti — exhibits; brahmendriyārthātma = brahma — random spiritual energy + indriya — sensual energy + artha — objects of value + ātma — individual spirit; vikāra — alteration; citram — variety.

Translation

Even though it is unreal, this transforming creation which is produced from the impulsive energy, is manifested because the spiritual reality itself, the effulgent principle, exhibits the variety which consists of random spiritual energy, sensual power, objects of value, individual spirits and alterations. (23.22)

Commentary:

The power of the creation comes from the spiritual reality which empowers it with a certain energy causing it to exhibit mobility and colorful transformations, which are perceived by the sensual energy which the individual spirits are endowed with. However that same sensual energy, if it is restrained and retracted by *pratyāhar* practice in the fifth stage of yoga, and if it is focused properly by techniques of higher yoga, would reveal the fourth dimension, the vision of which undermines our belief in this creation.

एव स्फुतं ब्रह्म-विवेक-हेतुभिः
परापवादेन विशारदेन ।
छित्त्वात्म-सन्देहम् उपारमेत
स्वानन्द-तुष्टो ऽखिल-कामुकेभ्यः ॥२३.२३॥

evaṁ sphutaṁ brahma-viveka-hetubhiḥ
parāpavādena viśāradena
chittvātma-sandeham upārameta
svānanda-tuṣṭo 'khila-kāmukebhyaḥ (23.23)

evam — by this method; sphutam — clearly; brahma — spiritual reality; viveka – discrimination; hetubhih — by means; parāpavādena = para — of other aspects + apavādena — by critical analysis; viśāradena — by skillful means; chittvātma = chittvā — removing + ātma — individual spirit; sandeham — doubt; upārameta — one should turn away; svānanda = sva –spiritual self + ānanda — happiness; tuṣṭo = tuṣṭaḥ — being satisfied; 'khila = akhila — all; kāmukebhyaḥ — from sense pleasures.

Translation

By this method, clearly removing any doubt about the individual spirit, by means which give discrimination regarding the spiritual reality and by skillful critical analysis of the other aspects, one should turn away from all sense pleasure, being satisfied with the spiritual self happiness. (23.23)

Commentary:

One has to use yoga practice, to get rid of the attraction to objects of this world. In this place there are good and bad objects, but one should abandon all of them by yoga practice if one is serious about relocating to the fourth dimension, otherwise one will merely come back into this world as a devotee, a yogi or this or that, according to how the mind was absorbed into this existence.

The sense pleasures in this world keep one preoccupied and when one becomes a devotee of the Lord, one follows the advice from religious leaders who feel that by restricting the senses to sacred material objects, one will reach the transcendence. When after a long practice, following these teachers one realizes that their methods simply will not work, one takes to higher yoga and in all seriousness, one weans oneself away from all mundane objects and retracts oneself into *svānanda-tuṣṭa*, the satisfaction gained by dwelling on one's spirit as it is, apart from the objects of this world, and developing the higher perception which views into the fourth dimension.

नात्मा वपुः पार्थिवम् इन्द्रियाणि
देवा ह्य् असुर् वायुर् जलम् हुताशः ।
मनो ऽन्न-मात्रं धिषणा च सत्त्वम्
अहङ्कृतिः खं क्षितिर् अर्थ-साम्यम् ॥२३.२४॥

nātmā vapuḥ pārthivam indriyāṇi
devā hy asur vāyur jalam hutāśaḥ
mano 'nna-mātraṁ dhiṣaṇā ca sattvam
ahaṅkṛtiḥ khaṁ kṣitir artha-sāmyam (23.24)

nātmā = na — nor + ātmā — individual spirit; vapuḥ — body; pārthivam — made of matter; indriyāni — senses; devā = devāḥ — supernatural controllers; hy = hi — in fact; asur = asuḥ — life air; vāyur = vāyuh — atmosphere; jalam — water; hutāśaḥ = huta āśah — fire; mano = manah — mind; 'nna-mātraṁ = anna – nutrients + mātram — what is merely, what is reliant; dhiṣaṇā — intellect; ca — and; sattvam — the clarifying energy of material nature; ahankṛtiḥ — sense of assertion; kham — outer space; kṣitir = kṣitiḥ — earth; artha — mundane objects; sāmyam — quiescent state of mundane energy.

Translation

The body which is made of matter, is not the spirit; nor are the senses, nor the supernatural controllers, the life air or the atmosphere. It is not the water,or fire or the mind which is reliant on nutrients. Neither is it the intellect, nor the clarifying energy of material nature, nor the sense of assertion, nor outer space, nor the earth, nor the state of quiescence of material nature. (23.24)

Commentary:

It may be argued that the gods must certainly be spirits, just as the human beings, but actually what we call a human being is a gross body in which spirit is represented by a subtle form. The *devās* or supernatural people use subtle bodies in which the spirit is represented by a causal form. Both the physical body and the subtle form are reliant on nutrients, even though the subtle one uses very subtle matter for its intake.

समाहितैः कः करणैर् गुणात्मभिर्
गुणो भवेन् मत्-सुविविक्त-धाम्नः ।
विक्षिप्यमाणैर् उत किं नु दूषण
घनैर् उपेतैर् विगतै रवेः किम् ॥२३.२५॥

samāhitaiḥ kaḥ karaṇair guṇātmabhir
guṇo bhaven mat-suvivikta-dhāmnaḥ
vikṣipyamāṇair uta kiṁ nu dūṣaṇaṁ
ghanair upetair vigatai raveḥ kim (23.25)

samāhitaih — by having stilled in meditation; kah — what; karanair = karanaiḥ — by the senses; gunātmabhir = guna – mundane influence + ātmabhiḥ — by what is essential; guṇo = guṇah — virtue; bhaven = bhavet — should be added; mat — my; suvivikta — easily and clearly perceived; dhāmnaḥ — splendor; vikṣipyamānair = vikṣipyamānaiḥ — by what is distracted; uta — or, alternately; kim — what; nu — in fact; dūṣaṇam — flaw; ghanair = ghanaiḥ — by clouds; upetair = upetaih — by assemblage; vigatai — by dispersion; raveḥ — of the sun; kim — what effect is there?

Translation

What virtue is there in having stilled the senses in meditation, for the senses are essentially productions of material nature? What attribute would be added to a person who clearly perceives My splendor? Or alternately, if the senses are distracted, what flaw is there? What effect is there on the sun by the assemblage or dispersal of clouds. (23.25)

Commentary:

There is really no credit for someone who becomes liberated. After all the spirit is liberated even when it seems to be under the influence of material nature, just as the sun is never covered by clouds even though it appears to be so affected. However the individual has to realize this by resituating its attention in the core-self and thereby causing it to be withheld from material nature. This requires endeavors in higher yoga.

यथा नभो वाय्व्-अनलाम्बु-भू-गुणैर्
गतागतैर् वर्तु-गुणैर् न सज्जते ।
तथाक्षर सत्त्व-रजस्-तमो-मलैर्
अह-मतेः ससृति-हेतुभिः परम् ॥२३.२६॥

yathā nabho vāyv-analāmbu-bhū-guṇair
gatāgatair vartu-guṇair na sajjate
tathākṣaraṃ sattva-rajas-tamo-malair
ahaṃ-mateḥ saṃsṛti-hetubhiḥ param (23.26)

yathā — as; nabho = nabhaḥ — sky; vāyv = vāyu — gas; analāmbu = anala — combustives + ambu — liquids; bhū — solid substances; guṇair = guṇaiḥ — by qualities; gatāgatair = gata – disappearing + āgataiḥ — by manifesting (gatāgatair – changing); vartu = vā — or + ṛtu –season; guṇair = guṇaiḥ — by the features; na – not; sajjate — affected; tathākṣaram = tatha — so + akṣaram — unaffected reality; sattva – clarifying energy; rajas – impulsive force; tamaḥ — retardative influence; malaiḥ — by impurities; aham – I, assertive sense; mateḥ — of the idea, view; saṁsṛti – material existence; hetubhiḥ — by the causes of; param — supreme, that is beyond.

Translation

As the sky is not affected by the qualities of gases, combustives, liquids, solids nor by the changing features of the seasons, so the Unaffected Reality, which is beyond the assertive sense, is not affected by the impurities of the clarifying, impulsive and retardative influence which are the causes of material existence. (23.26)

Commentary:

To reach beyond the assertive sense *(aham mateh)* one has to use a mystic method to reach back and situate the attention in the sky of consciousness, which consist of the Unaffected Energy *(akṣaram).* This cannot be done by mere conception after hearing a description of the process. One has to practice higher yoga in the last three stages which *Śrī Patañjali* Rishi explained as *samyama*, which is a combination of *dhāraṇā*, *dhyāna* and *samādhi*, with the least of these methods developing into the other, until one reaches the *samādhi*.

So long as the mind deals with the materials of this world, and regardless of whether such materials are sanctified with mantras or not, one will not be able to reach the chit *ākāśa*, the sky of consciousness, which is described as being *akṣaram* in this verse. The mystic process is as follows. First one focuses his attention on the sound which comes into the head of the subtle body on the right side. After sometime, one's *buddhi* organ will be taken to that sound because one's attention has gone there. There might be many thoughts. These should come into the *buddhi* organ very slowly. As they burst open with pictures and sounds, one should suppress them by totally ignoring them and by placing a small portion of one's attention at the place in the mind space where they appeared. Once the attention is placed there, the same idea will not arise again, but another idea might arise somewhere else in the mind.

After a short while in such meditation, one should find that a diffused light dawns of its own accord in the mind space. If this does not happen, then it means that the mind is not surcharged enough with *prāṇa* and the life force was not energized with fresh *prāṇa*, which means that even if one meditated like this for thousands of years, still he will not make progress beyond merely hearing the sound in the right side of the head and linking his attention to it, periodically.

The sound which is heard in the right side of the head comes into the subtle body from the spiritual sky, from the *akṣaram brahma*, the sky of consciousness. By the grace of the Almighty God, we have that facility. If we link our attention to it we are on our way to the spiritual world, but the subtle body has to be surcharged with *prāṇāyāma*, otherwise we might hear the sound, link to it sporadically and not advance any further.

There is a development with this sound. Sometimes, it is heard on the left side, sometimes on the left and right simultaneously, and sometimes in the entire head area of the subtle body. Some yogis experience it in the subtle spine, the *suśumnā naḍi*. *Śrī* Krishna in this discourse did give Uddhava a *kriyā* for taking this down to the heart chakra, where it is linked to the base chakra, the *mūlādhāra*.

There are many different ways of practicing *dhāraṇā* linkage of one's attention to a higher concentration force. Sometimes when the subtle body is surcharged by *prāṇa*, some other higher concentration force arises of its own accord. A yogi attaches his attention to the concentration force. This gives the yogi transcendental experiences. These are all *dhāraṇā*, which is the 6th stage. *Dhāraṇā* means uplifting one's attention from ideas in the chita mind-stuff energy and placing it on a higher concentration energy. *Dhāraṇā* is not just concentration. It must be connection with a higher concentration force. The force must be concentrated all by itself. The yogi's only action is to put his attention on it. Of course the yogi may also have to surcharge his subtle body so that he would reach the zones where those concentration forces occur naturally but once he perceives it, he merely has to link his attention to it.

The next stage of practice is *dhyāna* which is the 7th stage of yoga. In that stage, one merely remains in the linkage of one's attention and the concentration force to which it is connected. This happens by the pulling energy of the concentration force and by the natural attraction of one's attention to it. Just as when a young man wants a young woman and when the damsel also hungers for his sexual company, they stay together impulsively, so when one's attention has in it an attraction for the concentration force to which it is linked, one no longer has to apply will power to keep the linkage, just as parents of lovers do not have to supervise the love affairs. When the linkage occurs effortlessly on the part of the yogi, then it is *dhyāna*. This means that *dhyāna* is a progression from *dhāraṇā*.

The next stage is *samādhi*. In *samādhi* there is a further progression such that the yogi loses track of everything but the linkage of his attention and the concentration force. He loses reference to everything else.

Because these three stages are connected in a progression. *Śrī Patañjali* rightly labeled them as *samyama*. It is a fact however that one cannot do this unless the subtle body is surcharged by *prāṇāyāma* but it is not merely a matter of doing *prāṇāyāma* because to be successful with *prāṇāyāma* one has to regulate diet and do *āsana* postures so as to facilitate the breath exercises. The *āsana* postures, *prāṇāyāma* breath nutrition methods, *pratyāhar* sensual energy retraction, *dhāraṇā* linkage of the attention with the higher concentration force, *dhyāna* effortless linkage with the concentration force and *samādhi* total absorption with the same, are all required. It is not merely a matter of sitting down to meditate because if the mind is not surcharged and if the life force is not fed a purified pranic energy, one will not reach the higher concentration force consistently nor with sufficient purity to relax the mind away from the lower mind-stuff which creates mundane impressions in the form of ideas, pictures and feelings which pertain to the names and forms of this world.

From the comparison of the sky not being affected by random objects which float in it, we can get an idea that the spiritual sky is not affected by the little material clouds which are produce by its influence from time to time. However the limited entities who enter such clouds, appear to be affected. Their vision is blinded by the mundane manifestation. If a living entity can pierce through the opaque mental material energy, then he would connect himself with the spiritual sky and be able to defocus himself. This is done by higher yoga.

Remaining in the cloud and shouting God! God! God! will not help anyone. One has to get out of the cloud by first projecting one's attention to the outside of it into the spiritual world. This is made easy for us by the fact that vibrations from the spiritual sky come into our subtle bodies. If we connect through higher yoga, we can begin the course of getting away from the material existence.

तथापि सङ्गः परिवर्जनीयो
गुणेषु माया-रचितेषु तावत् ।
मद्-भक्ति-योगेन दृढेन यावद्
रजो निरस्येत मनः-कषायः ॥२३.२७॥

tathāpi saṅgaḥ parivarjanīyo
guṇeṣu māyā-raciteṣu tāvat
mad-bhakti-yogena dṛḍhena yāvad
rajo nirasyeta manaḥ-kaṣāyaḥ (23.27)

tathāpi = tathā – even + api — also; saṅgaḥ — contact; parivarjanīyo = parivarjanīyaḥ — should be avoided; guṇeṣu — in the mundane influence; māyā – bewildering energy; raciteṣu — in the production of; tāvat — for as long as; mad = mat – me; bhakti – devotion; yogena — through the application of yoga discipline; dṛḍhena — firm; yāvad = yāvat — until; rajo = rajah — impulsive tendency; nirasyeta — is removed; manaḥ — of the mind; kaṣāyaḥ — a stain, habit.

Translation

Even so, contact with the mundane influence, which is produced by the bewildering potency, should be avoided, until the impulsive tendency which is a habit of the mind, is removed, by a firm practice of devotion to Me as applied through yoga discipline. (23.27)

<u>*Commentary:*</u>

Advancement does not come easy for a human being, regardless of whether he is a devotee of *Śrī* Krishna or not. This is because it hinges on control of the psyche. Since the psyche is by nature unruly and resistant to will power, and since it has an impulsive tendency which forcibly attracts it to the mundane energies, self control is not easy to attain. There is no short cut for self control because each part of the psyche has a particular way in which it is to be curbed.

If a human being falls ill, the best course is for him to consult with a doctor but that does not mean that there is one single medicine that cures all diseases. There is no such thing because there are varying diseases that require varying treatments. Similarly in spiritual life, one has to get a particular method to achieve a particular type of control of a particular part of the psyche. If a doctor convinces his patients that he has one cure that will fix everything, then we understand that as a caption only.

In chapter four of the *Bhagavad-Gītā*, *Śrī* Krishna gave details of the various specialized fields for treating the human beings so that they can attain liberation. The verses are 24 through 30 of chapter 4. All of these have relevance. Each should be applied according to the particular type of control the yogi should achieve. The advice in this verse concerns the use of *bhakti* yoga, devotion as it is applied to *Śrī* Krishna with yoga reinforcement. When devotion is applied in this way, it will in the course of time, depending on the intensity of practice, cause the devotee to be free of the impulsive tendency of the mind which forced him to act in a spiritually counterproductive way. While doing this, one has to avoid the bewildering potency in all forms and shapes especially in the form to which one is helplessly attracted.

Śrī Krishna recommended *bhakti* yoga and not just *bhakti*. This means both *bhakti* and yoga. If *bhakti* is not reinforced by yoga, then it is hardly likely that it will effect the change required. The mind has an ingrained tendency for attachments to this world. Such a tendency can only be removed by a forceful process. This is why it is *bhakti* yoga and not just *bhakti* or devotion by itself. Some commentators however seem to think that *bhakti* yoga is devotional service without yoga. How they arrived at that conclusion is a mystery.

A devotee should not underestimate the mind's need for mundane attachments to things like palatable food, sexual indulgence, imaginative thinking, colorful objects and the like. These are deep-seated tendencies. None of the our minds will abandon these attachments merely because we are devotees or because we have an attraction to *Śrī* Krishna's pastimes, nor because we accepted a distinguished devotee as a teacher. This is why one has to use higher yoga to rid the mind of the unwanted tendencies. The mind, unless it is surcharge by higher energy in *prāṇāyāma*, will not completely leave aside the attachments. A devotee has to be honest with himself or herself to realize this. The devotee should leave aside all so-called easy processes which in fact lead nowhere but into another woman's womb.

यथागयो ऽसाधु चिकित्सितो नृणा
पुनः पुनः सन्तुदति प्ररोहन् ।
एव मनो ऽपक्व-कषाय-कर्म
कुयोगिन विध्यति सर्व-सङ्गम् ॥२३.२८॥

yathāmayo 'sādhu cikitsito nṛṇāṃ
punaḥ punaḥ santudati prarohan
evaṃ mano 'pakva-kaṣāya-karma
kuyoginaṃ vidhyati sarva-saṅgam
(23.28)

yathāmayo = yathā — as + āmayaḥ — disease; 'sādhu = asādhu — improperly; cikitsito = cikitsitaḥ — treated; nṛṇām — of human beings; punaḥ punaḥ — again and again; santudati — gives distress; prarohan — crops us; evam — so; mano = manaḥ — mind; 'pakva = apakva — half-baked, partially destroyed; kaṣāya — sensual vice; karma — activity; kuyoginam — of a badly motivated yogi; vidhyati — torment; sarva – everything; saṅgam — that which is attached.

Translation

As a disease which is improperly treated, crops up again and again, and gives distress, so the badly-motivated yogi's mind, in which sensual vice and related activity are only partially destroyed, remains attached to everything. (23.28)

Commentary:

Here again we see that these verses concern yogis and yoga practice. Yoga is clearly defined in chapter six of the *Bhagavad-Gītā*. There is no need to adjust the definition. One needs to accept it, take up its practice and use it to assist in the venture for perfection either as a *karma* yogi, *jñāna* yogi or *bhakti* yogi. In each area, yoga should be mastered and applied, either to working power *(karma)*, thinking energy (*jñāna*) or emotional feelings (*bhakti*).

Failure at spiritual life comes because of bad motivation. A yogi who is badly motivated is called a *ku-yogī*. Actually one cannot help but be badly-motivated in the beginning of spiritual life. This is because the material nature is full of bad motivation, and initially this nature causes the impetus for spiritual life. Since initially one is reliant on it, even if one realizes that it causes misery, one will still have to be badly motivated. Thus for honesty sake, we have to realize this. Once a yogi recognizes his faults one by one, he can apply the particular discipline to remove them step-by-step over a period of time. He will not do it all at once. He has to apply a particular discipline to rid himself of a particular fault *(kaṣāya).*

Sensual vices will not go away by wishful thinking nor by chanting of holy names. The most chanting will do is to cause their dormancy. This is why we see that they surface in the lives of the devotees, time and again in this life, in the past one and in the one to come. Sensual vice is deeply rooted as part of the nature of the mind and as an essential need of the life force. The mind must first be surcharged with *prāṇa* so that it is pushed out of the zones where the vices are manifest.

If one remains in those zones and chants holy names, still he will be afflicted with bad habits. Even though one may stall the vices for a while, they will reassert themselves with greater force at another time. The mind is to be surcharged with *prāṇa* which is reinforced with holy names. The mind feeds on *prāṇa* as its main nutrient, not sound. One has to improve the quality of the *prāṇa*.

Just as many devotees restrict themselves to vegetarian foods and eat these, because food is essential for the gross body, so one should improve the quality of pranic energy which enters the mind. Food is not the only area which needs to be improved. Breathing should be improved as well because breath is more important than food.

कुयोगिनो ये विहितान्तरायैर्
मनुष्य-भूतैस् त्रिदशोपसृष्टैः ।
ते प्राक्तनाभ्यास-बलेन भूयो
युञ्जन्ति योग न तु कर्म-तन्त्रम् ॥२३.२९॥

kuyogino ye vihitāntarāyair
manuṣya-bhūtais tridaśopasṛṣṭaiḥ
te prāktanābhyāsa-balena bhūyo
yuñjanti yogaṁ na tu karma-tantram (23.29)

kuyogino = kuyoginaḥ — badly-motivated yogis; ye — who; vihitāntarāyair = vihita — frustrated + antarāyaiḥ — by obstacles; manuṣya – of a human being; bhūtais = bhūtaiḥ — by the shape or form; tridaśopasṛṣṭaiḥ = tridaśa — supernatural people + upasṛṣṭaiḥ — those who are prompted; te — they; prāktanābhyāsa = prāktana — previous + abhyāsa — spiritual discipline; balena — by the momentum; bhūyo = bhūyah — again; yuñjanti — they practice; yogam — yoga; na — not; tu — but; karma – cultural activity; tantram — complicated course.

Translation

The badly-motivated yogis who were frustrated by obstacles in the form of human beings, who were prompted by the supernatural people, do, by the momentum of previous spiritual discipline, practice yoga again, but they are not attracted again to the complicated course of cultural activities. (23.29)

Commentary:

This applies to very advanced yogis and not to beginners nor to other persons who do not practice yoga. Those who are neophyte yogis, who play around with yoga practice using it for health, beauty and charisma and those who are on the spiritual path without doing yoga, will again go into the complicated course of cultural activities, even though they will do so in the name of religion. These persons are expert at converting mere cultural activity into religiously-sanctified actions which they claim will sponsor their journey to the kingdom of God.

If a yogi is so advanced that he received a waiver from cultural activities from the Universal Form, then if he falls back, he will take up yoga in this or some future life and will finish out the course of it to perfection then or in some future time. There is no telling how long it will take to gain perfection, because so much of our lives is in the hands of other persons like the super-natural controllers who regulate the world. These super people cannot always be thwarted. Sometimes they created diversions for a yogi, some of which he cannot avoid.

Some authorities say that if one is a devotee of *Śrī* Krishna, one cannot be diverted by another authority but that is not necessarily true. We heard of greater devotees who the supernatural people diverted and confused. One such case was King *Bharat* who was the son of Lord *Ṛṣbha*. *Śrī* Krishna does not always interfere to protect the devotee from being controlled by other powerful persons.

If a yogi gets the exemption from *karma* yoga, he can side step the supernatural people, not otherwise, but even if he does not play the game right to respect them cordially, and to cooperate with them now and again, his efforts will be frustrated for the time being at least until *Śrī* Krishna, Lord Shiva or alternately Lord *Balarāma* or a great yogin advises him on how to relate to the demigods.

Karma-tantram or the complicated zigzag course of cultural activities is supervised by the Universal Form of Lord Krishna, the same form which Arjuna saw on the battlefield and which practically forced him to do warfare. However this *karma tantram* is also known as *dharma* or righteous living. It is presided over by *Dharma*, a demigod who supervises it, for those who want to cooperate with the Universal Form. A yogin is supposed to get a waiver from having to serve King *Dharma* as that demigod is so aptly called. *Dharma* is the king of law in this world. If we go against him, our path will be very curvy. To sidestep him one must first do as ordered by him while taking hints from the Universal Form on how to serve him in an efficient way so that one can terminate that service responsibly.

करोति कर्म क्रियते च जन्तुः
केनाप्य् असौ चोदित आ-निपतात् ।
न तत्र विद्वान् प्रकृतौ स्थितो ऽपि
निवृत्त-तृष्णः स्व-सुखानुभूत्या ॥२३.३०.

karoti karma kriyate ca jantuḥ
kenāpy asau codita ā-nipatāt
na tatra vidvān prakṛtau sthito 'pi
nivṛtta-tṛṣṇaḥ sva-sukhānubhūtyā (23.30)

karoti — works; karma — cultural activity; kriyate — is affected; ca — and; jantuḥ — creature form; kenāpy = kena api — by some force or the other; asau — he; codita — urges; ā-nipatāt = a – not + nipātāt — death; na — not; tatra — there, in the same type of circumstance; vidvān — the knowledgeable person; prakṛtau — in material nature; sthito 'pi = sthitah — situated + api — even though; nivṛtta — having ceased; tṛṣṇaḥ — one who has sensual desire; sva — own; sukhānubhūtyā = sukha — happiness; anubhūtyā — experiencing.

Translation

Until its death, the creature form, urged by some force or the other, performs cultural activity, and is affected in turn, but although he is situated in material nature, the knowledgeable person whose sensual desire ceased by his experience of spiritual happiness, is not affected in the same type of circumstances as before. (23.30)

Commentary:

The creature form has innate tendencies. Some of these may be suppressed. Some cannot be interfered with. However despite the necessity of what that form must do so long as it survives, a knowledgeable person whose sensual desire ceased, and who was transferred into spiritual happiness by higher yoga, is not really affected by the circumstances which used to trouble him and which caused him to act against his interest before.

Such a yogin reaches a stage where he can safely ignore many of the urges which occur within material nature in the bodies of others and even in his own form. He is no longer troubled by these just as a man who sits on a conveyance which takes him out of a city from where he would relocate. Since he no longer has to deal with people in that place, he no longer reacts to them and they ignore him as well, feeling that he has no place in their cultural engagements.

तिष्ठन्तम् आसीनम् उत व्रजन्तं
शयानम् उक्षन्तम् अदन्तम् अन्नम् ।
स्वभावम् अन्यत् किम् अपीहमानम्
आत्मानम् आत्म-स्थ-मतिर् न वेद ॥२३.३१॥

tiṣṭhantam āsīnam uta vrajantaṁ
śayānam ukṣantam adantam annam
svabhāvam anyat kim apīhamānam
ātmānam ātma-stha-matir na veda (23.31)

tiṣṭhantam — standing; āsīnam — sitting; uta — or; vrajantam — walking; śayānam — lying down; ukṣantam — urinating; adantam — eating; annam — food; svabhāvam — its own natural function; anyat — other; kim apīhamānam = kim api — whatever + īhamānam — performs; ātmānam — self, psyche; ātma – spirit; stha — reposes; matir = matiḥ — mind; na – not; veda — know, give undue attention.

Translation

While standing or sitting, walking, lying down, urinating, eating food, or while performing other natural functions, the person whose mind reposes in his spirit, does not give undue attention to that portion of the psyche which engages in those natural functions. (23.31)

Commentary:

This was explained to Arjuna in a slightly different way:

naiva kiṁcitkaromīti yukto manyeta tattvavit
paśyañśṛṇvanspṛśañjighrann aśnangacchansvapañśvasan
pralapanvisṛjangṛhṇann unmiṣannimiṣannapi
indriyāṇīndriyārtheṣu vartanta iti dhārayan

"I do not initiate anything." Being proficient in yoga, this is what the knower of reality thinks. While seeing, hearing, touching, smelling, eating, walking, sleeping and breathing,

...while talking, evacuating, holding, opening and closing the eyelids, he considers, "The senses are interlocked with the attractive objects." (B.G. 5.8-9)

यदि स्म पश्यत्य् असद्-इन्द्रियार्थं
नानानुमानेन विरुद्धम् अन्यत् ।
न मन्यते वस्तुतया मनीषी
स्वाप्नं यथोत्थाय तिरोदधानम् ॥२३.३२॥

yadi sma paśyaty asad-indriyārthaṁ
nānānumānena viruddham anyat
na manyate vastutayā manīṣī
svāpnaṁ yathotthāya tirodadhānam (23.32)

yadi — if; sma — ever; paśyaty = paśyati — sees; asad = asat — temporary; indriyārtham = indriya – senses + artham — objects; nānānumānena = nānā — multiplicity + anumānena — by analysis; viruddham — rejection; anyat — other than, separate from; na – not; manyate — considers; vastutayā — as being substantial; manīṣī — perceptive person; svāpnam — dream; yathotthāya = yathā — just + utthāya — waking person; tirodadhānam — disappearing.

Translation

If he ever sees the temporary sense objects, the perceptive person does not consider them as being substantial. By analysis of their multiplicity, he rejects them as being other than the reality, just as a waking person regards a fading dream. (23.32)

Commentary:

The main hang-up of a yogin in terms of regarding material objects as reality, is his considerations about other human beings. He has to abandon the conventional usages of regarding a human body as a person. The human body certainly has a person within it but the body itself, along with its subtle counterpart and its causal forces, are not the person. The so called conventional person is a cultural mock-up of various forces and a spirit.

However, merely understanding this by analysis of given facts, does not give one the ability to transcend the conventional usage. One has to realize this through mystic insight so that one dissects the psyche by intuition and mystic vision, which is developed in higher yoga practice. One must first work on the self. Then one will see how others are a mock-up of spiritual and material forces, passing under conventional usage as personalities.

While under impressions in a dream, one has a tendency to lose discrimination and to accept whatever is presented as reality but when the dream fades, one snaps out of it and realizes that one was fooled. This happens as soon as one resumes possession of discriminative insight. Similarly for a yogin, there are occasions when he is drawn into cultural activities and when he behaves just as the average human being who believes that the body is the soul, but the yogin snaps out of the conventional usage when his developed intuition and mystic vision takes possession of the psyche.

पूर्वं गृहीतं गुण-कर्म-चित्रम्
अज्ञानम् आत्मन्य् अविविक्तम् अङ्ग ।
निवर्तते तत् पुनर् ईक्षयैव
न गृह्यते नापि विसृज्य आत्मा ॥२३.३३॥

pūrvaṁ gṛhītaṁ guṇa-karma-citram
ajñānam ātmany aviviktam aṅga
nivartate tat punar īkṣayaiva
na gṛhyate nāpi visṛyya ātmā (23.33)

pūrvam — prior to enlightenment; gṛhītam — was accepted; guṇa — mundane influence; karma — cultural activities; citram — diversity, spectrum; ajñānam — the temporary energies; ātmany = ātmani — in the spirit; aviviktam — indiscriminately; aṅga — my friend; nivartate — ceases; tat — that; punar = punaḥ — afterwards; īkṣayaiva = īkṣayā — by vision + eva — alone; na - not; gṛhyate — accepted; nāpi = na — nor + api — also; visṛjya — being rejected; ātmā — spirit.

Translation

Prior to enlightenment, temporary energies as a spectrum of cultural activities and mundane influences, were accepted indiscriminately as being in the spirit. Afterwards, that assumption ceases by vision. Then the spirit is neither accepted nor rejected.(23.33)

Commentary:

At first when one appears in human existence, one adopts the conventional mood under which one joins in for the development of the cultural world. This means taking possession of resources and regulating the same on the basis of survival needs.

However, long after, when one is done with the temporary energies, one gets an exemption from such culture. This occurs after one serves the Universal Form in His management of cultural affairs. The assumption that cultural activities are a necessity and that we must endure them until death is totally profane and silly but one cannot understand this initially. However as soon as one becomes disgusted with the pains of that cultural life, which once was so sweet to be involved in, one begins to see things in a different perspective. At that stage, one realizes that one's spirit was neither accepted nor really rejected by material nature at any stage. The moody variations for agreeable, disagreeable and indifferent sensations pertains to the *citta* mental and emotional energy.

Before completing higher yoga however, one may accept this but one cannot really understand nor perceive this. Therefore one must be involved in farcical religions, which pass as systems for salvation. They are not what they are advertised to be, because by such systems one will again come out in this world to continue in the performance of high class cultural acts with a religious over-coating.

In the material world, the spirit is neither accepted nor rejected and for that matter no limited spirit is indispensable. If anyone is liberated and is remove from the confines of the material energy, it will continue just as if he never existed here at all. Such is the status of the limited spirits in this world.

All the same, when one is involved, one feels that one has an important role to play. Even tiny creatures, like microbes and ants, feel important, even though their presence is not at all necessary.

When a yogin understands how dispensable he really is, he shifts his attention to be liberated. Before that he approaches the topic of liberation in a half-hearted manner, and follows spiritual masters who feel that they can and must save all living entities in the material world, a task that they cannot complete at any stage, a vain-glorious and very petty aspiration.

यथा हि भानोर् उदयो नृ-चक्षुषां
तमो निहन्यान् न तु सद् विधत्ते ।
एवं समीक्षा निपुणा सती मे
हन्यात् तमिस्रं पुरुषस्य बुद्धेः ॥२३.३४॥

yathā hi bhānor udayo nṛ-cakṣuṣāṁ
tamo nihanyān na tu sad vidhatte
evaṁ samīkṣā nipuṇā satī me
hanyāt tamisraṁ puruṣasya buddheḥ (23.34)

yathā — just as; hi — factual; bhānor = bhānoḥ — of the sun; udayo = udayah — rising; nṛ — human being; cakṣuṣām — of the vision; tamo = tamah — darkness; nihanyān = nihanyāt — banishes; na — not; tu — but; sad = sat — permanent objects; vidhatte — creates; evam — so; samīkṣā — thorough inspection; nipuṇā — accurate; satī — true; me — of me; hanyāt — takes away, removes; tamisram — mental darkness; puruṣasya — of a human being; buddheḥ — in the intellect.

Translation

Just as the rising of the sun banishes the darkness which affects vision but it does not produce the permanent objects seen, so a thorough inspection of Me which is accurate and true, dispels the mental darkness in the intellect of a human being. (23.34)

Commentary:

Such a thorough inspection can only be performed by one who mastered the higher yoga, and who developed supernatural vision. Arjuna was temporarily bestowed such vision by *Śrī* Krishna on the battlefield of *Kurukṣetra*. By it, Arjuna could assess *Śrī* Krishna's Universal and Four-handed forms.

एष स्वयं-ज्योतिर् अजो ऽप्रमेयो
महानुभूतिः सकलानुभूतिः ।
एको ऽद्वितीयो वचसां विरामे
येनेषिता वाग्-असवश् चरन्ति ॥२३.३५॥

eṣa svayaṁ-jyotir ajo 'prameyo
mahānubhūtiḥ sakalānubhūtiḥ
eko 'dvitīyo vacasāṁ virāme
yeneṣitā vāg-asavaś caranti (23.35)

esa = esaḥ — this; svayam – self; jyotir = jyotiḥ — effulgent; ajo = ajah — birthless; 'prameyo = aprameyah — immeasurable, unknowable; mahānubhūtiḥ = mahā – greatest + anubhūtiḥ — consciousness; sakalānubhūtiḥ = sakala – with knowing, with the knowledge, comprehensive of + anubhūtiḥ — all experience; eko = ekaḥ — absolute, one reality; 'dvitīyo = advitīyaḥ — without any other principle; vacasām – of speech; virāme — in the cessation; yeneṣitā = yena — by whom; īṣitāḥ — motivated; vāg = vāk — speech; asavaś = asavaḥ — vital energy; caranti — operate.

Translation

This self effulgent, birthless, unknowable, the greatest consciousness, that which is comprehensive of all experience, the Absolute, that which has no other principle to contend with, and which may be realized in the stoppage of speech, this is the one by whom speech and vital energy operate. (23.35)

Commentary:

At this point in a yogi's development, all sorts of earthly religious concepts stop. At this point all the previous considerations come to an end. All arguments stop for the yogin who advanced this far in the spiritual quest.

एतावान् आत्म-सम्मोहो
यद् विकल्पस् तु केवले ।
आत्मन् ऋते स्वम् आत्मानम्
अवलम्बो न यस्य हि ॥२३.३६॥

etāvān ātma-sammoho
yad vikalpas tu kevale
ātman ṛte svam ātmānam
avalambo na yasya hi (23.36)

etāvān — to such a degree; ātma — spiritual self; sammoho = sammohah — delusion; yad = yat — which; vikalpas = vikalpah — concept of a double reality; tu — but; kevale — in that which is indivisible; ātman — in the spirit; ṛte — without, besides; svam — one's own; ātmānam — self; avalambo = avalambah — foundation; na — there is no; yasya — of that, for that; hi — in fact.

Translation

The delusion of the self exists to the degree that there is the concept of a double reality in the indivisible spirit, for besides one's own self, there is no foundation for that concept. (23.36)

Commentary:

According to this, the delusion about the reality of spiritual and material existence, arises only because particular spirits have a misconception. Besides their proneness to illusion, there is really no misunderstanding. Even though the sun is never covered by clouds which we see in the sky, still because of our perspective, we pick up an idea that the sun is shrouded.

There was never a time when the sun was covered by the clouds which float above the earth. Still, we repeatedly feel that it is covered because we perceive it to be so, even though in fact that is untrue. By convention we accepted a double reality in terms of feeling that maybe the spirit is eternal and maybe it is not, maybe the person is his body or maybe he transcends his body. The solution is to get free from the false means of perception.

यन् नामाकृतिभिर् ग्राह्यं
पञ्च-वर्णम् अबाधितम् ।
व्यर्थेनाप्य् अर्थ-वादो ऽयं
द्वयं पण्डित-मानिनाम् ॥२३.३७॥

yan nāmākṛtibhir grāhyaṁ
pañca-varṇam abādhitam
vyarthenāpy artha-vādo 'yaṁ
dvayaṁ paṇḍita-māninām (23.37)

yan = yat — which; nāmākṛtibhir = nāma — names + ākṛtibhiḥ — and by forms; grāhyam — that which is distinguished; pañca – five; varṇam — elements; abādhitam — that which is irrefutable, that which is definite; vyarthenapy = vyarthena — by those whose views are meaningless + api — in fact; artha-vādo = artha-vādaḥ — thesis of a subject; 'yam = ayam — this; dvayam — double reality; paṇḍita – educated person; māninām — of those who are conceited.

Translation

That which is distinguished by names and forms, which consist of five elements and which is regarded as being definite by those whose views are meaningless, this double reality is the subject of a thesis by some educated but conceited people. (23.37)

Commentary:

In the time of *Śrī* Krishna some educated pandits who were conceited towards their own spiritual selves, presented an idea that the material world had all value and that statements to the contrary were meaningless. They explained that if the world was not real, was not *sat* or reality, then we would not perceive it. They established that it has the most value and that cultural activities were the most important function for human beings.

योगिनो ऽपक्व-योगस्य
युञ्जतः काय उत्थितैः ।
उपसर्गैर् विहन्येत
तत्रायं विहितो विधिः ॥२३.३८॥

yogino 'pakva-yogasya
yuñjataḥ kāya utthitaiḥ
upasargair vihanyeta
tatrāyaṁ vihito vidhiḥ (23.38)

yogino = yoginaḥ — concerning a yogi; 'pakva = apakva – only partially completed; yogasya — of yoga procedures; yuñjataḥ — pertaining to one who engages in a routine practice; kāya = kāyaḥ — body or psyche; utthitaiḥ — by what cropped up; upasargair = upasargaiḥ — by troubles; vihanyeta — is affected; tatrāyam = tatra — in this case + ayam — this; vihito = vihitaḥ — is prescribed; vidhih — remedy.

Translation

Concerning a yogi who engages in routine practices, and whose yoga procedures are only partially completed, if his body or psyche is affected by troubles which crop up, then this remedy is prescribed for him: (23.38)

Commentary:

The word kāya means more than just the material body. Furthermore *Śrī* Krishna gave advice for a serious yogi who is properly motivated, not for a *ku-yogī* who has the wrong objective. Sometimes a yogi gets trouble with disease in the physical form. At other times, it might be trouble in his subtle or causal forms. Such trouble might divert him from practice.

Śrī Krishna issued no biased statement about such a yogi, but others who pose as Krishna's pure devotees and who say that they are authorized in the disciplic succession, give biases and totally distort the text and its meaning.

योग-धारणया काश्चिद्
आसनैर् धारणान्वितैः ।
तपो-मन्त्रौषधैः काश्चिद्
उपसर्गान् विनिर्दहेत् ॥२३.३९॥

yoga-dhāraṇayā kāṁścid
āsanair dhāraṇānvitaiḥ
tapo-mantrauṣadhaiḥ kāṁścid
upasargān vinirdahet (23.39)

yoga – yoga; dhāraṇayā — by linking the attention to the higher concentration force; kāṁścid — some; āsanair = āsanaiḥ — by *āsana* postures of haṭha yoga; dhāraṇānvitaih — followed by techniques for linking the attention to higher concentration force; tapo = tapah — austerities; mantrauṣadhaiḥ = mantra — chanting special sounds + ausadhaih — by medicines; kāṁścid — some; upasargān — all afflictions; vinirdahet — should be eradicated.

Translation

Some afflictions should be eradicated by yogic process in linking the attention to the higher concentration force, some by āsana postures of haṭha yoga, which is followed by techniques for linking the attention to higher concentration forces. Some are removed by austerities or by chanting special sounds or by medicines. (23.39)

Commentary:

This verse shows that the afflictions experienced by a sincere yogin may not be physical. Some are psychological. Some are supernatural. Thus those which are physical might be removed by taking medicinal foods. Usually the advices for this are given by Lord Shiva or alternately by a yogin who studied from Him. There are also special *āsana* postures in *Haṭha* Yoga which are used to affect the subtle body for its purification, so that the yogi can energize his mind and *buddhi* intellect organ sufficiently with a cleanse life force. By that he can develop a clear-seeing *buddhi* with which to peer into the sky of consciousness.

To advance from *āsana* postures to *dhāraṇā* linkage of the attention to higher concentration forces, one has to practice *prāṇāyāma* and *pratyāhar* successfully, otherwise one will find that even though he meditates he is unable to bypass the subtle material energy, even though he might get relief from stress and might have some awareness of the intellectual and emotional energy.

Various austerities must be performed especially in regards to what should be eaten and when it should be eaten. One must also keep oneself away from non-yogic association. It also requires that certain special sounds be chanted. These are given by the spiritual teachers from time to time.

काश्चिन् ममानुध्यानेन
नाम-सङ्कीर्तनादिभिः ।
योगेश्वरानुवृत्त्या वा
हन्याद् अशुभ-दान् शनैः ॥२३.४०॥

kāṁścin mamānudhyānena
nāma-saṅkīrtanādibhiḥ
yogeśvarānuvṛttyā vā
hanyād aśubha-dān śanaiḥ (23.40)

kāṁścin — some; mamānudhyānena = mama — of me, on me + anudhyānena — by the continuous and effortless linkage of the attention; nāma — name; saṅkīrtanādibhiḥ = saṅkīrtana — chanting in a group; ādibhiḥ — and related practices; yogeśvarānuvṛttyā = yoga īśvara — great masters of yoga discipline + anuvṛttyā — by continuously attending; vā — or; hanyād = hanyāt — may be eliminated; aśubha - unsuitable conditions; dān — factors which produce; śanaiḥ — gradually.

Translation

Some of the factors which produce unsuitable conditions, may gradually be eliminated, by continuous linkage of the attention to Me, by chanting about Me in a group and by other related practices or by continuously attending to the great masters of the yoga discipline. (23.40)

Commentary:

Each process gives a particular result. Thus no one process is recommended since the yogi should use the appropriate method. Each process mentioned is potent in a specific way, for eliminating certain unfavorable factors which curtail or disrupt spiritual progression.

केचिद् देहम् इमं धीराः
सु-कल्पं बयसि स्थिरम् ।
विधाय विविधोपायैर्
अथ युञ्जन्ति सिद्धये .२३.४१॥

kecid deham imaṁ dhīrāḥ
su-kalpaṁ vayasi sthiram
vidhāya vividhopāyair
atha yuñjanti siddhaye (23.41)

kecid = kecit — some; deham — body; imam — this; dhīrāḥ — persons with steady mind capable of spiritual concentration; su-kalpam — very fit; vayasi — in youthfulness; sthiram — tough; vidhāya — having made; vividhopāyair = vividha — various + upāyaiḥ — by means of; atha — beginning then; yuñjanti — they practice yoga; siddhaye — for developing a mystic skill.

Translation

Having by various means, made the body tough and very fit in terms of youthfulness, and sturdy, some persons who have a steady mind which is capable of great concentration, begin to practice yoga for developing a mystic skill. (23.41)

Commentary:

In yoga practice as in anything else, the motivation may undermine the development of the objective. Thus those who practice yoga for reasons other than psyche purification, even for becoming charismatic or influential, do misuse yoga. Despite this, yoga practice eventually curbs the practitioner. It leads him into circumstances through which he becomes reformed. The purpose of yoga is given by *Śrī* Krishna in verse twelve of chapter six in the discourse with Arjuna:

tatraikāgraṁ manaḥ kṛtvā yatacittendriyakriyaḥ
upaviśyāsane yuñjyād yogamātmaviśuddhaye

...being there, seated in a posture, having the mind focused, the person who controls his thinking and sensual energy, should practise the yoga discipline for self-purification. (B.G. 6.12)

Even though this definition is there from the mouth of the Supreme Person, still if a practitioner is impure, he will be badly-motivated and will strive to use yoga to gain subtle or gross material powers, just as such a person would misuse anything else.

न हि तत् कुशलादृत्यं
तद्-आयासो ह्य् अपार्थकः ।
अन्तवत्त्वाच् छरीरस्य
फलस्येव वनस्पतेः ॥२३.४२॥

na hi tat kuśalādṛtyaṁ
tad-āyāso hy apārthakaḥ
antavattvāc charīrasya
phalasyeva vanaspateḥ (23.42)

na — not; hi — in fact; tat — that; kuśalādṛtyaṁ = kuśala — expert + ādṛtyam — respectibility; tad-āyāso = tat — of that + āyāsaḥ — the endeavor; hy = hi — surely; apārthakaḥ — useless; antavattvāc = anta – terminal + vattvāt — due to the quality; charīrasya = śarīrasya — of the body; phalasyeva = phalasya — pertaining to a fruit + iva — just as; vanaspeteḥ — of a tree.

Translation

In fact, that is not approved by those who are expert and deserving of respectability. Surely that sort of endeavor is useless, since the body has the quality of being terminal, just as pertaining to the fruit of a tree. (23.42)

Commentary:

Since the purpose of planting fruit trees is to acquire fruits, one may assume that the fruits are more important than the tree which produces them. Thus someone after drawing that conclusion, may take one or two fruits from a tree and then destroy the tree as being useless. This is a short-termed consideration. For long-ranged purposes, one should care for and protect the tree so that it may yield fruits seasonably. Similarly, in considering the spirit and the cultural personality, which it adopts in each of the lives it assumes, one should take care of the spirit being sure that the cultural endeavors will in the long run help the spirit to realize itself and to free itself from the very same cultural situations.

योगं निषेवतो नित्यं
कायश् चेत् कल्पताम् इयात् ।
तच् छ्रद्दध्यान् न मतिमान्
योगम् उत्सृज्य मत्-परः ॥२३.४३॥

yogaṁ niṣevato nityaṁ
kāyaś cet kalpatām iyāt
tac chraddadhyān na matimān
yogam utsṛjya mat-paraḥ (23.43)

yogam — yoga; niṣevato = niṣevatah — in the practices; nityam — regularly; kāyas = kāyah — the body; cet — if; kalpatām — state of being fit and healthy; iyāt — becomes; tac = tat — that condition; chraddadhyān = śraddadhyāt — should apply faith; na — not; matimān — the perceptive person; yogam — yoga process; utsṛjya — giving up; mat-paraḥ — one who is devotee to me.

Translation

If in the regular practices of yoga, the body becomes fit and healthy, the perceptive person who is devoted to Me, should not give up yoga and transfer his confidence to that healthy condition. (23.43)

Commentary:

Because of a bias towards yoga, the Vaishnava commentators who finished the translation and commentary of *Śrīmad Bhāgavatam* on behalf of *Śrīla Bhaktivedānta Swāmī*, did in the tradition of that Acharya mistranslate this verse, for the convenience of further deriding yoga. In the next verse where the terms *yoga-caryām* and *yogī* occur, he was then forced to avoid the actual meaning of the verse by citing *Śrīla* Sridhara *Swāmī* and *Śrīla Bhaktisiddhānta Sarasvatī*, two previous authorities in the disciplic succession who maintained the same bias towards yoga. Thus in that purport, *haṭha* yogis and *rāja* yogis were condemned and ridiculed while non-yogi devotees who surrender to the Supreme Lord, were appraised. And not a word was said about the terms *yoga-caryām* and *yogī*.

Leaving aside *Śrī* Krishna's attitude towards yogis of all sorts, His caring concern for them, these disciplic authorities established their own biases and pass these views to the public as *Śrī* Krishna's opinions.

In this verse *mat-parah* applies to the *matimān*, the person who practices yoga under *Śrī* Krishna's yoga system as explained to Uddhava, but somehow the Vaishnava commentator suggested that this person is not a yogi. His view is that a yogi is foolish because he practiced yoga to keep fit while a devotee who is dedicated to *Śrī* Krishna and who is intelligent keeps his body fit by eating nourishing Krishna *prasādam*, the sanctified food remnants.

Leaving aside all this, let us look at this verse and not maintain the prejudice which we inherited in the *Madhva-Gaudiya-Bhaktivedānta* Vaishnava *sampradāya*. This verse means that a yogi who notices that his body becomes fit and healthy because of his performance of yoga, should not give up the actual purpose of yoga but should instead overlook those benefits and not be distracted by them. He should continue the practice to achieve what yoga should yield. He should not divert himself even if his body become healthy and fit and his psyche gains vast amounts of subtle and supernatural perception, otherwise he will go off-course and cashed in on the yoga progress to get a strong and healthy body to rule over others. *Hiraṇyakaśipu* is an example of a person whose body became fit and healthy by yoga and who was ill-motivated just the same.

The body will get healthy and fit by doing yoga but one should not be concerned with the physical form, because it is the purification of the subtle form that counts. For subtle purification, one gets to enter into the causal form, from which position one is able to change the quality of the *citta* emotional energy which drives our haphazard transmigrations.

Now let us look at the last verse of this chapter to see how supportive of and how consistent Lord Krishna is about His instruction for yoga practice.

योग-चर्याम् इमां योगी
विचरन् मद्-अपाश्रयः ।
नान्तरायैर् विहन्येत
निःस्पृहः स्व-सुखानुभूः ॥२३.४४॥

yoga-caryām imāṁ yogī
vicaran mad-apāśrayaḥ
nāntarāyair vihanyeta
niḥspṛhaḥ sva-sukhānubhūḥ (23.44)

yoga-caryām — yoga process; imām — this; yogī — yogi; vicaran — practicing; mad-apāśrayaḥ = mat – on me + apāśrayaḥ — one who is reliant; nāntarāyair = na — not + antarāyaiḥ — by obstacles; vihanyeta — is thwarted; niḥspṛhaḥ — free from sensuality; sva-sukhānubhūḥ = sva — spirit self + sukha — happiness + anubhūḥ — experiences.

Translation

The yogi who practices this yoga process and who is reliant on Me, is free from sensuality, is not thwarted by obstacles and experiences the happiness of his spiritual self. (23.44)

Commentary:

If a yogi sticks to the purpose of yoga which is for psychic and spiritual purification *(ātmaviśuddhaye B.G. 6.12),* he will not be thwarted by obstructions and distractions. He will gain the badly-needed freedom from subtle mundane sensuality. To serve the purpose of yoga, one must take help from Lord Krishna and from Lord Shiva too, otherwise one cannot be successful. One should get a waiver from the Universal Form of *Śrī* Krishna, so that one side-steps *dharma* or righteous cultural activities, and one must take the necessary disciplines required for psyche purification.

These include chanting the holy name of Lord Krishna, as well as completing the *aṣṭanga* yoga process. Both of these are required along with diet control, restricted association and whatever else *Śrī* Krishna recommended in this discourse with Uddhava and in the talk with Arjuna.

CHAPTER 24*

Go Uddhava**

Terri Stokes-Pineda Art

śrī-bhagavān uvāca
gacchoddhava mayādiṣṭo badary-ākhyaṁ mamāśramam
tatra mat-pāda-tīrthode snānopasparśanaiḥ śuciḥ

The Blessed Lord said: Go Uddhava, as instructed by Me to My hermitage named Badari. There by bathing and touching, purification will be attained in the water of the sacred river, which sprang from My feet. (Uddhava Gītā 24.41)

* Śrīmad Bhāgavatam Canto 11, Chapter 29

** Translator's selected chapter title.

श्री-उद्धव उवाच
सु-दुस्तराम् इमां मन्ये
योग-चर्याम् अनात्मनः ।
यथाञ्जसा पुमान् सिध्येत्
तन् मे ब्रूह्य् अञ्जसाच्युत ॥२४.१॥

śrī-uddhava uvāca
su-dustarām imāṁ manye
yoga-caryām anātmanaḥ
yathāñjasā pumān siddhyet
tan me brūhy añjasācyuta (24.1)

śrī-uddhava – the deserving Uddhava; uvāca — said; su-dustarām — very difficult; imām — this; manye — I think; yoga-caryām — yoga process; anātmanah — for one who has not curbed his nature; yathāñjasā = yathā — according to, by which + añjasā — by a single method; pumān — person; siddhyet — may achieve; tan = tat — that; me — to me; brūhy = brūhi — please tell; añjasācyuta = añjasā — easily; acyuta — unaffected personality.

Translation

The deserving Uddhava said: I think that the yoga process is very difficult. Please tell me that simple procedure by which a person may easily achieve the objective, O Unaffected Personality. (24.1)

Commentary:

Here again after so much discourse and after so much is given in answer to his request, Uddhava keeps asking for an easy method. He inquired about that in every pause of *Śrī* Krishna. The Lord stressed unmotivated yoga which is done by His directions for purification of the psyche. *Śrī* Krishna also stated that the devotion to Him will make the process of spiritual perfection rapid and easy. This is because if one develops an attachment to *Śrī* Krishna, by the force of that affection for Him, one might be willing to do whatever *Śrī* Krishna would request. Arjuna is an example of a person who by His loving friendliness with *Śrī* Krishna, did battlefield work which Arjuna was very reluctant to perform, before *Śrī* Krishna explained much and showed the Universal Form. To convince Arjuna, *Śrī* Krishna had to display Arjuna's most worshippable Deity, the four handed parallel divine form of *Śrī* Krishna.

After seeing that four-handed divine form, Arjuna was so confident that he did whatever *Śrī* Krishna requested of him. He realized that the two-handed Krishna in the human body before him was His own worshippable Deity, the infallible and flawless *Nārāyaṇa* Vasudeva.

Uddhava, in this final chapter, asked for an easier method. Uddhava knows well that those who have not curbed their natures and who are not on the verge of doing so, cannot take up the yoga practice. This is because they are extroverted by nature. They are unable to retract the sensual energy.

Many commentators in the Vaishnava disciplic successions feel that this objection by Uddhava as well as similar objections raised to *Śrī* Krishna by persons like Arjuna, shows clearly that yoga is not a practical process. Their view is that there must be and there is some simpler process whereby one can gain spiritual perfection. They downplay and ridicule yoga as being physical bodily exercises.

However I have this to say: The only simple process besides yoga is the process which will prepare one to accept yoga. This would either be a process which will discourage you from yoga completely and then frustrate you, and by that frustration cause you to understand that you must do yoga even though you dislike it; or a process which gradually causes you to give up your dislike for yoga.

प्रायशः पुण्डरीकाक्ष
युञ्यन्तो योगिनो मनः ।
विषीदन्त्य् असमाधानान्
मनो-निग्रह-कर्शिताः ॥२४.२॥

prāyaśaḥ puṇḍarīkākṣa
yuñyanto yogino manaḥ
viṣīdanty asamādhānān
mano-nigraha-karśitāḥ (24.2)

prāyaśaḥ — generally, more than often; puṇḍarīkākṣa = puṇḍarīka – lotus + akṣa — eye (puṇḍarīkākṣa – lotus-eyed lord); yuñjanto = yuñjantaḥ — concerning those who practice yoga to grain self control; yogino = yoginah — of yogis; manaḥ — mind; viṣīdanty = viṣīdanti — become disillusioned; asamādhānān = asamādhānāt — because of attaining total fixation of their attention into the sky of consciousness, the spiritual world; mano = manah – mind; nigraha — control of; karśitāḥ — those who are exhausted.

Translation

O Lotus-eyed Lord, more often than not, the yogis who practice to gain self control become disillusioned because of not attaining total fixation of their attention into the sky of consciousness, the spiritual world. These yogis are the ones who become exhausted in the effort to control the mind. (24.2)

Commentary:

The answer to this implication was given by *Śrī* Krishna in the last chapter as follows:

yogino 'pakva-yogasya yuñjataḥ kāya utthitaiḥ
upasargair vihanyeta tatrāyaṁ vihito vidhiḥ
yoga-dhāraṇayā kāṁścid āsanair dhāraṇānvitaiḥ
tapo-mantrauṣadhaiḥ kāṁścid upasargān vinirdahet
kāṁścin mamānudhyānena nāma-saṅkīrtanādibhiḥ
yogeśvarānuvṛttyā vā hanyād aśubha-dān śanaiḥ

Concerning a yogi who engages in routine practices, and whose yoga procedures are only partially completed, if his body or psyche is affected by troubles which crop up, then this remedy is prescribed for him:

Some afflictions should be eradicated by yogic process in linking the attention to the higher concentration force, some by āsana postures of haṭha yoga, which is followed by techniques for linking the attention to higher concentration forces. Some are removed by austerities or by chanting special sounds or by medicines.

Some of the factors which produce unsuitable conditions, may gradually be eliminated, by continuous linkage of the attention to Me, by chanting about Me in a group and by other related practices or by continuously attending to the great masters of the yoga discipline. (U.G. 23.38-40)

yogaṁ niṣevato nityaṁ kāyaś cet kalpatām iyāt
tac chraddadhyān na matimān yogam utsṛjya mat-paraḥ

If in the regular practices of yoga, the body becomes fit and healthy, the perceptive person who is devoted to Me, should not give up yoga and transfer his confidence to that healthy condition. (U.G. 23.43)

If a yogi reaches a point of frustration, it means that he is not staying in touch with Lord Krishna and Lord Shiva, otherwise he would get the proper advice and be recommended with procedures for overcoming the frustrations. The key is to consult with higher yogins and with Lord Krishna, Lord *Balarāma* and Lord Shiva.

अथात आनन्द-दुघं पदाम्बुजं
हसाः श्रयेरन्न् अरविन्द-लोचन ।
सुखं नु विश्वेश्वर योग-कर्मभिस्
त्वन्-माययामी विहता न मानिनः ॥२४.३॥

athāta ānanda-dughaṁ padāmbujaṁ
haṁsāḥ śrayerann aravinda-locana
sukhaṁ nu viśveśvara yoga-karmabhis
tvan-māyayāmī vihatā na māninaḥ (24.3)

athāta = atha — thence + ataḥ — moreover; ānanda – spiritual happiness; dugham — source, that which yeilds; padāmbujaṁ = pada – feet + ambujam — lotus flower; haṁsāḥ — highly advanced yogis who are compared to swans; śrayerann = śrayeran — rely on; aravinda – lotus + locana — eye; sukham — happiness; nu — in fact; viśveśvara = viśva īśvara — lord of the universe; yoga – yoga proficiency; karmabhis = karmabhiḥ — and by cultural activity; tvan = tvat – your; māyayāmī = māyayā — by the bewildering potency + amī — these; vihatā = vihatāḥ — predominated by; na — not; māninaḥ — those who are arrogant.

Translation

Hence, O lotus-eyed Lord, the highly advanced yogis are reliant on Your lotus feet, which yields spiritual happiness. In fact, O Lord of the universe, these persons are not predominated by Your bewildering potency, and do not become arrogant by the yoga proficiency or by cultural activity. (24.3)

Commentary:

Yoga is not to be condemned nor eliminated, nor discouraged, but persons should be alerted that the proper motivation for doing it, is psyche purification, so that one can hem up and solidify one's relationship with the Supreme Person. Yoga has great value in accelerating the formation of that relationship.

Yoga does not make anyone God. God is God, regardless of accomplishments. One does not become God merely by doing yoga or by achieving anything else, but yoga can bring on a greater purity of psyche, so that one can understand one's spiritual nature and perceive how one is related to God.

किं चित्रम् अच्युत तवैतद् अशेष-बन्धो
दासेष्व् अनन्य-शरणेसु यद् आत्म-सात्त्वम् ।
ऽरोचयत् सह मृगैः स्वयम् ईश्वराणां
श्रीमत्-किरीट-तट-पीडित-पाद-पीठः ॥२४.४॥

kiṁ citram acyuta tavaitad aśeṣa-bandho
dāseṣv ananya-śaraṇesu yad ātma-sāttvam
'rocayat saha mṛgaiḥ svayam īśvarāṇāṁ
śrīmat-kirīṭa-taṭa-pīḍita-pāda-pīṭhaḥ (24.4)

kim — what; citram — the wonder; acyuta — o unaffected one; tavaitad = tava — Your + etat — this; aśeṣa-bandho = aśeṣa – everyone + bandhaḥ — friend; dāsesu — servants of servants; ananya – no one; śaraṇeṣu — of those who rely; yad = yat — which; ātma-sāttvam = ātma –self + sāttvam — in possession; yo 'rocayat = yah — who + arocayat — related on friendly terms; saha — with; mṛgaiḥ — with animals; svayam — yourself, your own; īśvarāṇām — of the supernatural rulers; śrīmat — effulgent; kirīta — crown; taṭa — edge; pīḍita — lay; pāda –foot; pīṭhaḥ — stool.

Translation

O Unaffected One, O friend of everyone, what is the wonder that You place Yourself in possession of the servants who rely on no one else but You. It is You, who related on friendly terms with the animals, even though the edges of the effulgent crowns of the supernatural rulers were laid at Your foot stool. (24.4)

Commentary:

Śrī Krishna is available to one and all, even to the monkey-like and bear-like human beings, as was demonstrated in the pastimes of His parallel divinity, *Śrī Rāma*, who formed intimate friendships with humans who used very crude bodies, resembling cavemen. *Śrī Rāma* even allowed himself to become reliant on those monkey-like men to discover and then rescue His dear wife *Sītā*.

It is no wonder that He would guide to perfection the *hansas*, the swan-like highly advanced yogis. *Śrī* Krishna made a similar appraisal in different wording in his discourse with Arjuna:

kiṁ punarbrāhmaṇāḥ puṇyā bhaktā rājarṣayastathā
anityamasukhaṁ lokam imaṁ prāpya bhajasva mām
manmanā bhava madbhakto madyājī māṁ namaskuru
māmevaiṣyasi yuktvaivam ātmānaṁ matparāyaṇaḥ

How much more accessible then, is it for the piously-inclined brahmins and yogi kings? Having acquired an opportunity in this temporary, miserable world, you should devote yourself to Me.

With the mind fixed on Me, being devoted to me, performing ceremonial worship to Me, make obeisance to Me. Being thus disciplined, with Me as the Supreme Objective, you will come to Me. (B.G. 9.33-34)

तं त्वाखिलात्म-दयितेश्वरम् आश्रितानां
सर्वार्थ-दं स्व-कृत-विद् विसृजेत को नु
को वा भजेत् किम् अपि विस्मृतये ऽनु भूत्यै
किं वा भवेन् न तव पाद-रजो-जुषां नः २४५

taṁ tvākhilātma-dayiteśvaram āśritānāṁ
sarvārtha-daṁ sva-kṛta-vid visṛjeta ko nu
ko vā bhajet kim api vismṛtaye 'nu bhūtyai
kiṁ vā bhaven na tava pāda-rajo-juṣāṁ naḥ (24.5)

tam — that; tvākhilātma = tvā — you + akhila — everyone + ātma — spirit; dayiteśvaram = dayita — beloved + īśvaram — supreme lord; āśrītānām — of those who rely on; sarvārtha-daṁ = sarva – all + artha — boons + dam — giver; sva – your own; kṛta — what was done; vid — one who knows; visṛjeta — would reject; ko = kah — a person who; nu — indeed; ko = kah — who; vā — or, and; bhajet — would experience, become; kim api — anything; vismṛtaye — in forgetfulness; 'nu = anu — afterwards, after which; bhūtyai — for material well being; kim — what; vā — and, or; bhaven = bhavet — would be available; na — not; tava — your; pāda — foot; rajo = rajaḥ — dust; juṣām — those who adore; nah — ourselves, us.

Translation

Indeed, would a person who knows what You did, reject You, who are the soul of everyone, the Beloved Supreme Lord, the giver of all boons to those who rely on You? And who would take anything for material well-being after which they would be in forgetfulness? And what would not be available for us, who adore the dust of Your feet? (24.5)

Commentary:

Here the hint is the reliance on *Śrī* Krishna.

नैवोपयन्त्य् अपचितिं कवयस् तवेश
ब्रह्मायुषापि कृतम् ऋद्ध-मुदः स्मरन्तः ।
यो ऽन्तर् बहिस् तनु-भृताम् अशुभं विधुन्वन्न्
आचार्य-चैत्त्य-वपुषा स्व-गतिं व्यनक्ति
॥२४.६॥

naivopayanty apacitiṁ kavayas taveśa
brahmāyuṣāpi kṛtam ṛddha-mudaḥ smarantaḥ
yo 'ntar bahis tanu-bhṛtām aśubhaṁ vidhunvann
ācārya-caittya-vapuṣā sva-gatiṁ vyanakti (24.6)

na – not + eva — certainly + upayanti — they repay; apacitim — obligation; kavayaḥ — poetic genius; taveśa = tava — your + īśa — lord; brahmāyuṣāpi = brahma – Procreator Brahmā + āyuṣā — in the life time + api — even; kṛtam — what was done, a deed; ṛddha — increase; mudaḥ — joy; smarantaḥ — in remembering; yo 'ntar = yah — who + antar — inside; bahih — outside; tanu – body; bhṛtām — of those who are born (tanu-bhṛtām - of the body-borned beings); aśubham — handicap; vidhunvann = vidhunvan — removing; ācārya — spiritual teacher; caittya — supreme mystic consultant; vapuṣā — by form; sva — own; gatim — course of living; vyanakti — reveals.

Translation

O Lord, poetic geniuses, whose joys increase as they remember Your deeds, certainly cannot, even with the lifetime of Brahmā, repay the obligation to You, who are inside as the Supreme Mystic Consultant, and outside as the spiritual teacher, who reveals Your course of living by removing the handicap of the body-borned beings. (24.6)

Commentary:

The Supreme Lord is met on the inside of the psyche and on the outside as well. Contacting the Lord on the inside is more valuable than contacting him with the material senses when He takes a material body or if He is inspired to make Himself available as the sanctified object known as the Deity or *Mūrti* in the temple.

The Lord was directly the spiritual master of Uddhava, and of Arjuna and others but He also represented Himself through limited beings who function as spiritual teachers. However it is very important for us to realize that we need to meet the Supreme Lord in the supernatural and spiritual dimensions. These realms supersede this physical world which we have grown used to.

श्री-शुक उवाच
इत्य् उद्धवेनात्य्-अनुरक्त-चेतसा
पृष्टो जगत्-क्रीडनकः स्व-शक्तिभिः ।
गृहीत-मूर्ति-त्रय ईश्वरेश्वरो
जगाद स-प्रेम-मनोहर-स्मितः .२४.७॥

śrī-śuka uvāca
ity uddhavenāty-anurakta-cetasā
pṛṣṭo jagat-krīḍanakaḥ sva-śaktibhiḥ
gṛhīta-mūrti-traya īśvareśvaro
jagāda sa-prema-manohara-smitaḥ (24.7)

śrī śuka – the illustrious Shuka; uvāca — said; ity = iti — thus; uddhavenati = uddhavena — by Uddhava; ati – very + anurakta — much devoted; cetasā — by one whose consciousness; pṛṣṭo = pṛṣṭaḥ — questioned; jagat — world; krīḍanakaḥ — one whose plaything; sva – own; śaktibhiḥ — through potencies; grhīta — assured; mūrti — forms; traya = trayah — three; īśvareśvaro = īśvareśvaraḥ — lord of lords; jagāda — spoke; sa-prema — with loving; manohara — attractive; smitah — assuming a smile.

Translation

The illustrious Shuka said: Being questioned by Uddhava whose consciousness was very devoted, the Lord of lords whose plaything is the world, and who by potency assumes a triple form, displayed a loving and attractive smile and spoke. (24.7)

Commentary:

Śrī Krishna smiled because through out the discourse, Uddhava persisted in trying to get a solution to the problem of mundane existence for the common people who are resistant to hard-core austerities of yoga and who avoid yoga at all costs. What should those people do? Now in this final chapter, let us hear the final instruction given to Uddhava.

श्री-भगवान् उवाच
हन्त ते कथयिष्यामि
मम धर्मान् सु-मङ्गलान् ।
यान् श्रद्धयाचरन् मर्त्यो
मृत्युं जयति दुर्जयम् ॥२४.८॥

śrī-bhagavān uvāca
hanta te kathayiṣyāmi
mama dharmān su-maṅgalān
yān śraddhayācaran martyo
mṛtyuṁ jayati durjayam (24.8)

śrī-bhagavān – the blessed lord; uvāca — said; hanta — well; te — to you; kathayiṣyāmi — I will describe; mama — my; dharmān — righteous conduct; su-maṅgalān — very auspicious; yān = yāt — which; śraddhayācaran = śraddhayā — with faith + ācaran — practicing; martyo = martyah — a person with a temporary body; mṛtyum — death; jayati — surpass; durjayam — that which is hard to breach.

Translation

The Blessed Lord said: I will describe some very sublime righteous conducts which if practiced with faith, results in the surpassing of death by a person who has a temporary body. And that is something that is hard to breach. (24.8)

Commentary:

The Vaishnava commentators after the authority of His Divine Grace *Bhaktivedānta Swāmī*, gave the principles of devotion for the meaning of the word *dharma*. In his word for word meanings he gave religious principles but somehow in the translation of the verse, he used principles of devotion.

Actually here we see that *Śrī* Krishna stuck to His presentation just as Uddhava stuck to the question about an easy means of salvation. *Śrī* Krishna made it clear all along that such persons would have to take up righteous duties under His direction, to develop a liking for Him through *bhakti* or devotion. By this one would easily do whatever was required for salvation. The *Bhagavad-Gītā* summary of this is given in chapter twelve, where *Śrī* Krishna regressed and gave alternate methods.

Basically speaking, this means that if I cannot do the yoga austerities as they are approved by *Śrī* Krishna, I should take up *karma* yoga as it is dictated by the Universal Form to Arjuna, such that I support *dharma* or righteous lifestyle. This goes right back to the *Bhagavad Gītā*. We have a choice either to do yoga or to do *dharma* righteous living under *Śrī* Krishna's direction. This is elaborated in chapter four of the *Bhagavad-Gītā* instructions to Arjuna. There is no other course to take and no other easy salvation.

कुर्यात् सर्वाणि कर्माणि
मद्-अर्थं शनकैः स्मरन् ।
मय्य् अर्पित-मनश्-चित्तो
मद्-धर्मात्म-मनो-रतिः ॥२४.९॥

kuryāt sarvāṇi karmāṇi
mad-arthaṁ śanakaiḥ smaran
mayy arpita-manaś-citto
mad-dharmātma-mano-ratiḥ (24.9)

kuryāt — should work; sarvāṇi — all; karmāṇi — works; mad-artham — for my sake; śanakaiḥ — calmly; smaran — remembering; mayy = mayi — in Me; arpita — investing; manaś = manaḥ - mind; citto = cittaḥ — mental and emotional energy; mad = mat – my; dharmātma = dharma — righteous duty + ātma – self; manah — mind; ratiḥ — being delighted.

Translation

Investing the mind and the mental and emotional energy in Me, while being delighted in spirit and mind over My righteous duty, one should, while remembering Me, calmly do all work for My sake. (24.9)

Commentary:

Again in this verse, the commentators as cited in the previous purport, gave *mat-dharma* as My devotional service. I cite this to show how the Vaishnava tradition developed over the years, with a certain adjusting of the meanings of the Sanskrit words.

There is really no reason to avoid yoga practice, nor to hate it nor to deride it, put it down and discourage all persons from it. There is really no sound reason to try to abolish it. We have to understand that the human being has not changed since the time of *Śrī* Krishna. The basic profile of a human being has remained the same. The human being has to attain salvation by the exact same means as he did in the time of *Śrī* Krishna. What has changed is not the means but the rapidity. Today a human being must endeavor longer for salvation. He must start the course at a lower point.

Śrī Krishna smiled upon Uddhava because if He could not convince Uddhava about this over so many discourses, then He would not be able to convince common people who are even more anxious to go to paradise and who do not want to work aggressively for it. They want to motivated God to do something miraculous to bring about their purification.

If one studies this verse and then goes back to chapter twelve of the *Bhagavad Gītā* discourse with Arjuna one will see that it is consistent with what *Śrī* Krishna explained there. Here are some verses:

mayyeva mana ādhatsva mayi buddhiṁ niveśaya
nivasiṣyasi mayyeva ata ūrdhvaṁ na saṁśayaḥ
atha cittaṁ samādhātuṁ na śaknoṣi mayi sthiram
abhyāsayogena tato māmicchāptuṁ dhanaṁjaya
abhyāse'pyasamartho'si matkarmaparamo bhava
madarthamapi karmāṇi kurvansiddhimavāpsyasi

Placing your mind on Me alone, causing your intellect to be absorbed in Me alone, you will be focused on Me from now onward. There is no doubt about this.

If, however, you cannot steadily anchor your thoughts on Me, then by yoga practice, try to attain Me, O conqueror of wealthy countries.

But if perchance, you are incapable of such practice, then by being absorbed in My work, or even by doing activities for My sake, you will attain perfection. (B.G. 12.8-10)

Here the term *cittah* does not mean thinking but rather the mental and emotional energy, the energy in which thoughts and feelings transpire. One has to learn how to invest both the mind chamber, the thought energy within it, as well as the feelings and emotions, upon *Śrī* Krishna. Some great devotees did this naturally from the start. The *gopīs* of Vṛndāvan are examples. This ability comes from having an intense loving feeling towards *Śrī* Krishna. If one's emotional nature is attracted to Him, one's mind, thought energy and emotions will be conveyed to Him by impulsion. This is because our minds take directions from the vital force which form the content of our emotions. However, that is not enough because in many cases, the vital force directs the mind in an unfavorable way. Thus one must have the emotional attachment to *Śrī* Krishna and also have a nature that is responsive or submissive to Him. Arjuna struggled with this and so did Uddhava, whereby their emotional nature was attracted to and simultaneously resistant to *Śrī* Krishna, where it wanted to control and use *Śrī* Krishna in its interest, in its view of what was right or wrong, acceptable or unacceptable, reasonable or unreasonable.

The example of a person who could not cooperate initially and who did so later on, was Arjuna. This is why *Śrī* Krishna spoke of being delighted *(ratih)* in spirit and mind over the performance of righteous duty. At first Arjuna was pained by the idea of performing such duty but after hearing the *Bhagavad Gītā*, and especially after getting two very important revelations, he went through a transformation and found delight in the very same duties which frightened him initially.

देशान् पुण्यान् आश्रयेत
मद्-भक्तैः साधुभिः श्रितान् ।
देवासुर-मनुष्येषु
मद्-भक्ताचरितानि च ॥२४.१०॥

deśān puṇyān āśrayeta
mad-bhaktaiḥ sādhubhiḥ śritān
devāsura-manuṣyeṣu
mad-bhaktācaritāni ca (24.10)

deśān — places; puṇyān — sacred; āśrayeta — should resort; mad = mat – to me; bhaktaiḥ — by those who are devoted; sādhubhiḥ — by saintly persons; śritān — taken shelter of; devāsura = deva — supernatural rulers + asura — opponents of the appointed supernatural rulers; manuṣyesu — and among human beings; mad-bhaktācaritāni = mat-bhakti — my devotee + ācaritāni — activities conduct; ca — and.

Translation

One should resort to sacred places which were taken shelter of by saintly persons who are devoted to Me. And among the supernatural rulers, their opponents and the human beings, one should follow the activities of My devotees. (24.10)

Commentary:

These procedures are not a replacement for yoga, but are rather being recommended for those who are not inclined to yoga practice and who feel that it is too hard or impractical or that it is a waste of time. Yoga was not a waste of time for saintly persons like *Nārada*, *Vyāsa*, *Dhruva* and others, and therefore the idea that it is merely bodily gymnastics is a slogan only, otherwise the same persons who discredit it would not be using the authority of *Nārada*, *Vyāsa* and other *mahāyogins* of repute. In fact Arjuna and Uddhava themselves are great yogins, even though the history of their yoga austerities, especially Arjuna's, is never mentioned by popular preachers who discredit yoga.

Within the context of Uddhava's question, we understand that these advisories are given because Uddhava claimed that the average human being cannot do the strenuous and pain-staking yoga austerities which require so much attention and concentration.

In the time of *Śrī* Krishna many saintly persons who were devoted to Him were expert yogins. Thus in their association one would get to like *Śrī* Krishna or to love Him all the more as the case may be and one would give up the resistance to the necessarily austerities. *Śrī* Krishna recommended that in the *deva* society of the supernatural world, in the society of their opponents even, and in human society, a person should follow the activities of His devotees. In the time of *Śrī* Krishna some of those activities included yoga practice, which *Śrī* Krishna Himself as well as *Śrī Balarāma* performed.

पृथक् सत्रेण वा मह्यं
पर्व-यात्रा-महोत्सवान् ।
कारयेद् गीत-नृत्याद्यैर्
महाराज-विभूतिभिः ॥२४.११॥

pṛthak satreṇa vā mahyaṁ
parva-yātrā-mahotsavān
kārayed gīta-nṛtyādyair
mahārāja-vibhūtibhiḥ (24.11)

pṛthak — alone; satreṇa — with others; vā — either; mahyam — for me; parva — monthly observances; yātrā — pilgrim sessions; mahotsavān = mahā-utsavān — festivals; kārayed = kārayet — should arrange; gīta — singing; nṛtyādyair = nṛtya – dancing + ādyaiḥ — and with related entertainment; mahārāja — king; vibhūtibhiḥ — with opulence.

Translation

Either alone or with others, the devotee should arrange the monthly observances, the pilgrim sessions, and the festivals which are for Me, done with singing, dancing and related entertainment, as well as with opulences which are fit for a king. (24.11)

Commentary:

There is an instruction in Chapter Twelve of the directions given to Arjuna:

mayyeva mana ādhatsva mayi buddhiṁ niveśaya
nivasiṣyasi mayyeva ata ūrdhvaṁ na saṁśayaḥ

Placing your mind on Me alone, causing your intellect to be absorbed in Me alone, you will be focused on Me from now onward. There is no doubt about this. (B.G. 12.8)

If we cannot place our mind on *Śrī* Krishna alone, then we may associate with devotees who do. By using the facilities created by them, we may become attuned to Krishna Consciousness in the way which was introduced by *Śrīla Bhaktivedānta Swāmī* and his predecessors, the process which is mentioned in this verse. They arrange monthly observances, pilgrim sessions and festivals which are done with much singing of *kīrtan* and with dancing in the styles introduced by Lord *Śrī* Chaitanya Mahaprabhu. They do so with arrangements which are fit for a king and which are offered to the *Śrī Śrī* Gour-Nitai, *Śrī Śrī Kṛṣṇa-Balarāma* and *Śrī Śrī Rādhā-Kṛṣṇa* Deities.

माम् एव सर्व-भूतेषु
बहिर् अन्तर् अपावृतम् ।
ईक्षेतात्मनि चात्मानं
यथा खम् अमलाशयः ॥२४.१२॥

mām eva sarva-bhūteṣu
bahir antar apāvṛtam
īkṣetātmani cātmānaṁ
yathā kham amalāśayaḥ (24.12)

mām — me; eva — indeed; sarva – all; bhūteṣu — in beings; bahir = bahiḥ — outside; antar — inside; apāvṛtam — not being covered or surrounded; īkṣetātmani = īkṣeta — one should observe +

ātmani — in the personal psyche; cātmānaṁ = ca — and + ātmānam — the spirit; yathā — just as; kham — sky; amalāśayaḥ = amala – pure + āśayaḥ — consciousness.

Translation

With a pure consciousness, he should observe Me, the spirit who cannot be covered, who is outside and inside all beings, and who is particularly in the personal psyche, just as the sky. (24.12)

Commentary:

Again, after giving an instruction for associating with devotees who excel in presenting temple worship, *Śrī* Krishna returned to the topic of higher yoga, mystic practice under His direction. But some feel that this can be realized fully by hearing of it from an authority in the disciplic succession, someone who is defined as a pure devotee or as a pure servant of a pure devotee.

In the *Bhagavad Gītā* however, Arjuna had mystic experiences of the controlling power of the Universal Form and of the four-handed parallel divine form of *Śrī* Krishna as *Vāsudeva Nārāyaṇa*. In the *Bhagavad-Gītā* also, *Śrī* Krishna after giving alternate methods in chapter twelve, returned to the topic of the accomplishments of the yogis:

saṁtuṣṭaḥ satataṁ yogī yatātmā dṛḍhaniścayaḥ
mayyarpitamanobuddhir yo madbhaktaḥ sa me priyaḥ (12.14)

...the yogi who is always content, who has a controlled self, who is determined, whose mind and intellect are focused on Me, who is devoted to Me, is dear to Me. (B.G. 12.14)

The devotee has to work for a pure consciousness *(amalāśayah)*. How is he to achieve that? And what should he see when he has achieved that? Such is the discussion in this verse. For he should observe *Śrī* Krishna, the spirit Who is not covered by the material energy, who is outside and inside all beings and who in particular is in the personal psyche of all beings. This is a mystic perception not an understanding of the mind or a belief based on what was heard or written.

इति सर्वाणि भूतानि
मद्-भावेन महा-द्युते ।
सभाजयन् मन्यमानो
ज्ञानं केवलम् आश्रितः ॥२४.१३॥

iti sarvāṇi bhūtāni
mad-bhāvena mahā-dyute
sabhājayan manyamāno
jñānaṁ kevalam āśritaḥ (24.13)

iti — thus perceiving; sarvāṇi — all; bhūtāni — beings; mad-bhāvena = mat-bhāvena — with my presence; mahā-dyute — o great effulgent one; sabhājayan — along with honoring; manyamāno = manyamānaḥ — regarding; jñānam — knowledgeable experience; kevalam — the spirit alone not being influenced by its psychic equipments; āśritaḥ — resorting to.

Translation

O great effulgent one, thus honoring and regarding all beings as being touched by My presence and resorting to the status of one's spirit being isolated from the influence of its psychic equipments. (24.13)

Commentary:

The meaning of *kevalam* as defined by *Śrī* Krishna is given in this verse and it tallies with what *Śrī Patañjali* defined. *Śrī Patañjali* gave two definitions; the preliminary and the advanced. According to him, when a yogin reaches the stage where he experiences his spirit isolated from its psychic equipments, that is *kaivalyam*. Further in more advanced practice, when the yogi purified the psychic equipments, they do not contaminate and thus his vision is pure because then the equipments are as pure as the spirit and they do not distort nor prejudice what is perceived.

Śrī Krishna told Arjuna about the comparative similarity between the various beings in this world:

sarvabhūtasthamātmānaṁ sarvabhūtāni cātmani
īkṣate yogayuktātmā sarvatra samadarśanaḥ
yo māṁ paśyati sarvatra sarvaṁ ca mayi paśyati
tasyāhaṁ na praṇaśyāmi sa ca me na praṇaśyati
sarvabhūtasthitaṁ yo māṁ bhajatyekatvamāsthitaḥ
sarvathā vartamāno'pi sa yogī mayi vartate
ātmaupamyena sarvatra samaṁ paśyati yo'rjuna
sukhaṁ vā yadi vā duḥkhaṁ sa yogī paramo mataḥ

With a spirit existing in every creature, and with every creature based on a spirit, a person who is proficient in yoga, perceives the same existential arrangement in all cases.

To him who sees Me in all forms and who sees all creatures in reference to Me, I am never out of range, and he is never out of My view.

Although moving in various circumstances, the yogi who is established in that harmony, who honors Me as being existentially situated in all creatures, remains in touch with Me.

He who, in reference to himself, sees the same facilities in all cases, regardless of pleasure or painful sensations, he, O Arjuna, is considered as the highest yogi. (B.G. 6.29-32)

Arjuna did not perceive that sort of vision when he was told about it. He said honestly that he did not see it at all:

arjuna uvāca
yo'yaṁ yogastvayā proktaḥ sāmyena madhusūdana
etasyāhaṁ na paśyāmi cañcalatvātsthitiṁ sthirām

Arjuna said: O slayer of Madhu, due to a shifty vision, I do not see this standard position of a comparatively similar view which is yielded by this yoga practice, declared by You. (B.G. 6.33)

But Lord Krishna insisted on the practice of yoga:

cañcalaṁ hi manaḥ kṛṣṇa pramāthi balavaddṛḍham
tasyāhaṁ nigrahaṁ manye vāyoriva suduṣkaram
śrībhagavānuvāca
asaṁśayaṁ mahābāho mano durnigrahaṁ calam
abhyāsena tu kaunteya vairāgyeṇa ca gṛhyate
asaṁyatātmanā yogo duṣprāpa iti me matiḥ
vaśyātmanā tu yatatā śakyo'vāptumupāyataḥ

Unsteady indeed is my mind, O Krishna. It is troublesome, impulsive and resistant. I think that controlling it is comparable to controlling the wind. It is very difficult to accomplish.

The Blessed Lord said: Undoubtedly, O powerful man, the mind is difficult to control. It is unsteady. By practice, however, O son of Kuntī, by indifference to its responses, also, it is restrained.

For the undisciplined person, yoga is difficult to master. This is My opinion. For the disciplined one, however, by endeavor, it is possible to acquire the skill by an effective means. (B.G.6.34-36)

Sooner or later, one will have to do yoga to effect the full purification of the psyche. It cannot be avoided but if one feels that he cannot do it or, if one dislikes it or if it seems to be an unfair requirement, then by developing a love or liking for *Śrī* Krishna, one will sooner or later, become convinced about the importance of it, especially when one realizes that other methods, even though they effect certain types of purifications, do not cause all the purifications required.

The experience of *jñānam kevalam*, the purified state of being isolated from the prejudices of the intellect and life force energies, has to be experienced on the supernatural and spiritual planes, just as Arjuna experienced it when he saw the Universal Form of *Śrī* Krishna and the four-handed divine form. A person who is to be liberated soon, will have to acquire that experience somehow or the other. Sanjaya saw it when he declared:

tatraikasthaṁ jagatkṛtsnaṁ pravibhaktamanekadhā
apaśyaddevadevasya śarīre pāṇḍavastadā

There the entire universe existed as one reality divided in many ways. Arjuna Pandava then saw the God of gods in that body. (B.G. 11.13)

One has to do whatever is necessary to get the supernatural and spiritual eyesight. It is not a matter of what we want to do or what someone else recommends. It is what we must do to get this *cakṣu divyam*, divine and supernatural vision.

ब्राह्मणे पुक्कसे स्तेने
ब्रह्मण्ये ऽर्के स्फुलिङ्गके ।
अक्रूरे क्रूरके चैव
सम-दृक् पण्डितो मतः ॥२४.१४॥

brāhmaṇe pukkase stene
brahmaṇye 'rke sphuliṅgake
akrūre krūrake caiva
Sama-dṛk paṇḍito mataḥ (24.14)

brāhmaṇe — in the brahmin; pikkase — in the tribesman; stene — in the thief; brahmaṇye — in the patron of brahmins; 'rke = arke — in the sun; sphulingake — in the spark of the fire; akrūre — in the gentle person; krūrake — in a cruel person; caiva = ca — and, or + eva — indeed; sama-dṛk — comparatively equal; paṇḍito = paṇḍitaḥ — a learned yogin; matah — is considered.

Translation

One who has the comparatively equal view in reference to a brahmin, a Pukkasa tribesman, a thief, a patron of brahmins, the sun, the spark of fire, the gentle or cruel person, is considered to be a learned yogin. (24.14)

Commentary:

This was elaborated upon in the instruction given to Arjuna. But it is not merely based on hearing and understanding. One has to experience this continually on the mystic plane by the psychic purification which comes about through higher yoga practice.

नरेष्व् अभीक्ष्णं मद्-भावं
पुसो भावयतो ऽचिरात् ।
स्पर्धासूया-तिरस्काराः
साहङ्कारा वियन्ति हि ॥२४.१५॥

nareṣv abhīkṣṇaṁ mad-bhāvaṁ
puṁso bhāvayato 'cirāt
spardhāsūyā-tiraskārāḥ
sāhaṅkārā viyanti hi (24.15)

nareṣv = nareṣu — in human beings; abhīkṣnam — always; mad-bhāvam = mat-bhāvam — my presence; puṁso = puṁsaḥ — regarding the person; bhāvayato = bhāvayataḥ — concerning one who keeps in touch; 'cirāt = acirāt — quickly; spardhāsūyā = spardhā — rivalry + asūyā — envy; tiraskārāḥ — the tendency of intimidation; sāhaṅkārā = sa — along with + ahaṅkārāḥ — inappropriate assertion; viyanti — depart from; hi — indeed.

Translation

Regarding the person who always keeps in touch with My presence in the human beings, tendencies of rivalry, envy, intimidation, along with inappropriate assertion, quickly depart from him. (24.15)

Commentary:

This means in mystic and spiritual touch with *Śrī* Krishna, based on spiritual experience, not based or hearing about and reading about *Śrī* Krishna. It has to be a mystic experience *(bhāvam)*, just as Arjuna had in the *Bhagavad-Gītā*. Otherwise one will on occasion fall away from the ideal behavior due to being overpowered by material nature and its views which come from either of the three modes.

विसृज्य स्मयमानान् स्वान्
दृश व्रीडां च दैहिकीम् ।
प्रणमेद् दण्ड-वद् भूमाव्
आ-श्व-चाण्डाल-गो-खरम् ॥ २४.१६ ॥

visṛjya smayamānān svān
dṛśaṁ vrīḍāṁ ca daihikīm
praṇamed daṇḍa-vad bhūmāv
ā-śva-cāṇḍāla-go-kharam (24.16)

visṛjya — ignoring, leaving aside; smayamānān — of those who redicule; svān — one's own friends; dṛśam — view; vrīḍām — embarrassment; ca — and; daihikīm — that which pertains to the body, that which is materialistic; praṇamed = pranamet — one should give respects; daṇḍa-vad = danda-vat — falling like a rod; bhūmāv = bhūmau — on the ground; ā — down to, even; śva — dog; cāṇḍāla — cannibalistic human being; go — cow; kharam — donkey.

Translation

Ignoring friends who redicule, and discarding the materialistic view as well as any embarrassment, one should give respects by lying down like a rod on the ground, before even a dog, a cannibalistic human being, a cow, or a donkey. (24.16)

Commentary:

These views or attitudes must be based on mystic and spiritual experience. If one has no such experience, one may try to behave in this way whenever possible but it would not be consistent unless one has got a purified psyche through yoga practice.

This is not a practical vision unless one stepped aside from society and attained yoga expertise. One who is still involved in society even in preaching, cannot do this consistently, because no matter what he thinks or believes, he still has to maintain a certain status to attract well-to-do human beings for the purpose of getting funds and other favors which are necessary in preaching missions. This type of vision, as described by *Śrī* Krishna is for the fully-detached yogin who has a waiver from cultural activities.

Arjuna was told about it, but at the time Arjuna did not have the waiver from cultural activities, and thus he had to discriminate on the basis of *dharma* righteous life style. He had to do violent war on the Kauravas.

यावत् सर्वेषु भूतेषु
मद्-भावो नोपजायते ।
तावद् एवम् उपासीत
वाङ्-मनः-काय-वृत्तिभिः ॥ २४.१७ ॥

yāvat sarveṣu bhūteṣu
mad-bhāvo nopajāyate
tāvad evam upāsīta
vāṅ-manaḥ-kāya-vṛttibhiḥ (24.17)

yāvat — until; sarveṣu — in all; bhūteṣu — in beings; mad-bhāvo = mat-bhāvaḥ — my presence; nopajāyate = na – not + upajāyate — acquired; tāvad = tāvat — for as long, for that length of time; evam — thus, as described; upāsīta — one should worship; vān = vāk — speech; manaḥ — mind; kāya — body; vṛttibhiḥ — with functions.

Translation

As long as one has not acquired the vision of My presence in all beings, that is the length of time for which one should worship as described with all functions of speech, mind and body. (24.17)

Commentary:

The point is that as long as one has not got the mystic and spiritual experience which is seen when the perception of the higher subtle body is opened, one should continue with ordinary worship and the like and with beliefs and opinions which tally with what Lord Krishna explained.

The human being cannot by-pass yoga purification at any stage but he can avoid it for as long as he likes, while in the meantime, he associates with devotees at temples, hearing the Krishna Conscious philosophy explained in perfect and imperfect ways by various speakers who are or are not realized in the mystic and spiritual vision.

When he has got the spiritual vision, everything will change for him, because there is nothing higher than personal experience.

na hi jñānena sadṛśaṁ pavitramiha vidyate
tatsvayaṁ yogasaṁsiddhaḥ kālenātmani vindati

Nothing, indeed, can be compared with direct experience. No other purifier is as relevant in this world. That man who himself is perfected in yoga practice, will in time, locate the realization in himself. (B.G. 4.38)

सर्वं ब्रह्मात्मकं तस्य
विद्ययात्म-मनीषया ।
परिपश्यन्न् उपरमेत्
सर्वतो मुत-सशयः ॥२४.१८॥

sarvaṁ brahmātmakaṁ tasya
vidyayātma-manīṣayā
paripaśyann uparamet
sarvato muita-saṁśayaḥ (24.18)

sarvam — everything; brahmātmakaṁ = brahma – spiritual reality + ātmakam — essestial being, based on; tasya — regarding that person; vidyayātma = vidyayā — by the technique + ātma –self; manīṣayā — by mystic perception; paripaśyann = paripaśyan — seeing all around; uparamet — should cease cultural activities; sarvato = sarvatah — in all respects; mukta-saṁśayaḥ = mukta – being freed + saṁśayah — doubts.

Translation

Regarding that person, by that mystic perceptual technique of seeing the spirit, everything is essentially the spiritual Reality. Seeing that all around, he would in all cases cease cultural activities and remain free from doubt. (24.18)

Commentary:

Arjuna had to continue in cultural activities, even though he doubted that there would be a positive outcome at *Kurukṣetra*, even with *Śrī* Krishna's participation there. But a person who has the waiver from cultural acts, has no doubts about the good in the world. He does not feel that he is essential to the cultural development. This type of person, who masters higher yoga, is on the highest level.

अय हि सर्व-कल्पानां
सध्रीचीनो मतो मम ।
मद्-भावः सर्व-भूतेषु
मनो-वाक्-काय-वृत्तिभिः ॥२४.१९॥

ayaṁ hi sarva-kalpānāṁ
sadhrīcīno mato mama
mad-bhāvaḥ sarva-bhūteṣu
mano-vāk-kāya-vṛttibhiḥ (24.19

ayam — this; hi — indeed; sarva — all; kalpānām — methods; sadhrīcīno = sadhrīcīnaḥ — best; mato = mataḥ — in regards; mama — by me; mad-bhāvah = mat-bhāvah — my presence; sarva – all; bhūteṣu — in beings; mano = manaḥ - mind; vāk – speech; kāya – body; vṛttibhiḥ — with the function.

Translation

In fact, this perception of My presence in all beings, along with service of the functions of mind, speech and body, is the best process of all. (24.19)

Commentary:

This is the highest utility of a human being. This is reached by the *paramhansa* yogins who have the full waiver from cultural activities and who wander about with a completely disinterested and detached mood in regards to the cultural functions of this world.

न ह्य् अङ्गोपक्रमे ध्वंसो
मद्-धर्मस्योद्धवाण्व् अपि ।
मया व्यवसितः सम्यङ्
निर्गुणत्वाद् अनाशिषः ॥२४.२०॥

na hy aṅgopakrame dhvaṁso
mad-dharmasyoddhavāṇv api
mayā vyavasitaḥ samyaṅ
nirguṇatvād anāśiṣaḥ (24.20)

na — not; hy = hi — indeed; aṅgopakrame = anga — my dear friend + upakrama — in the effort; dhvaṁso = dhvaṁsaḥ — destruction; mad-dharmasyoddhavāṇv = mat-dharmasu — of my righteous duty + uddhava — Uddhava + anv (anu) — least; api — even; mayā — by me; vyavasitah — is rated; samyaṅ = samyak — perfect; nirguṇatvād = nirguṇa – not being initiated by the mundane influences + tvāt — because of the quality; anāśiṣah — without bad motive.

Translation

My dear Uddhava, in the effort of participating in My righteous duty, there is no destruction, not even the least. It is rated by Me as being perfection, because of its quality of not being initiated by the mundane influence, and it is free from bad motive. (24.20)

Commentary:

This was told to Arjuna in different wording:

nehābhikramanāśo'sti pratyavāyo na vidyate
svalpamapyasya dharmasya trāyate mahato bhayāt

In this insight, no endeavor is lost nor is there any reversal. Even a little of this righteous practice protects from the great danger. (B.G. 2.40)

Here is given the underlying reason why one should not be afraid of working under *Śrī* Krishna's direction which comes down through the Universal Form. Of course if we are taking directions from a spiritual master in the disciplic succession or from any of His assistants, such persons might make mistakes and might on occasion mislead us. That risk is there. However we see that persons like Arjuna and Uddhava functioned directly under *Śrī* Krishna without a go-between. There is always a risk with any go-between personality, who might mislead a devotee on occasion.

Śrī Krishna's righteous duty in relation to this world is conducted through material nature and in it, but is initiated by Him and so it is free from bad motive towards anyone. It is for the best interest of all those involved in a cultural activity in which *Śrī* Krishna participates or in which He functions through an agent. *Śrī* Krishna again returned to the basic premise, which is that if we cannot do yoga, then we should try to take up His righteous duty in this world, something that was stressed to Arjuna in the *Bhagavad-Gītā*. By doing the righteous duty, we would in time, be able to practice yoga, because material nature's hold on us would be slackened considerably and our fear of the austerities would be lifted.

duḥkhamityeva yatkarma kāyakleśabhayāttyajet
sa kṛtvā rājasaṁ tyāgaṁ naiva tyāgaphalaṁ labhet

He who abandons action because of difficulty or because of a fear of bodily suffering, performs impulsive renunciation. He would not obtain the desired result of that renunciation. (B.G. 18.8)

यो यो मयि परे धर्मः
कल्प्यते निष्फलाय चेत् ।
तद्-आयासो निरर्थः स्याद्
भयादेर् इव सत्तम ॥२४.२१॥

yo yo mayi pare dharmaḥ
kalpyate niṣphalāya cet
tad-āyāso nirarthaḥ syād
bhayāder iva sattama (24.21)

yo yo = yah yah — whatever, any quantity; mayi — to me; pare — the supreme; dharmah — righteous duty; kalpyate — is suitable; nisphalāya — being from the motive for benefits; cet — if; tad = tat — of that; āyāso = āyāsah — the effort; nirarthaḥ — that which has no value; syād = syāt

— is; bhayāder = bhaya – fear + ādeḥ — and of such pressures; iva — as; sattama — o best of the realistic people.

Translation

O best of the realistic people, whatever is done for Me, the Supreme, is suitable as righteous duty, as it is free from motive for benefits. Even if the effort is prompted by fear and other such pressures, it has value. (24.21)

Commentary:

Here *Śrī* Krishna extols His path of righteous duty, which is Krishna-inspired activity. If indeed *Śrī* Krishna inspired an action, then even if one does it because of fear or through some other pressure, it will have value to *Śrī* Krishna. Since it is based on His motivation, it will be free from hassles.

Some person might act for Krishna fearing that if he did not comply his spiritual life would be jeopardized or that he would be punished by the Universal Form. That is alright because when complying, it does not matter how a person feels about what Krishna wants him to do. The important thing is for him to comply. Arjuna for example was fearful of the Universal Form and asked *Śrī* Krishna to please make the apparition disappear:

nabhaḥspṛśaṁ dīptamanekavarṇaṁ vyāttānanaṁ dīptaviśālanetram
dṛṣṭvā hi tvāṁ pravyathitāntarātmā dhṛtiṁ na vindāmi śamaṁ ca viṣṇo

Having seen You, sky extending, blazing, multi-colored, with gaping mouths and blazing vast eyes, there is a shivering in my soul. I find no courage, nor stability, O God Vishnu. (B.G. 11.24)

It is best if one does the work for *Śrī* Krishna with joy and that is recommended in the *Bhagavad Gītā* but if one cannot do so, still that work will give the proper result of drawing one closer to Him. The preferred mood for performing righteous duty is to do so in a detached manner, for if one is attached to limited persons, one will identify with their defiance or indifference towards the Supreme Person and then one will feel a reluctant to act for the Universal Form.

एषा बुद्धिमतां बुद्धिर्
मनीषा च मनीषिणाम् ।
यत् सत्यम् अनृतेनेह
मर्त्येनाप्नोति मामृतम् ॥२४.२२॥

eṣā buddhimatāṁ buddhir
manīṣā ca manīṣiṇām
yat satyam anṛteneha
martyenāpnoti māmṛtam (24.22)

eṣā — this; buddhimatām — of those who are considered to be intelligent; buddhir = buddhiḥ — intellect; manīṣā — cleverness; ca — and; manīṣiṇām — of the geniuses; yat — which, whereby; satyam — reality; anṛteneha = anṛtena — by the temporary + iha — here; martyenāpnoti = martyena — by what is mortal, the body + āpnoti — attains; māmṛtam = mā — me + amṛtam — the immortal.

Translation

This is a demonstration of those who are considered to be intelligent. It shows the cleverness of geniuses, whereby a person attains Me, the Immortal Reality, by use of the temporary and mortal body. (24.22)

Commentary:

By using this body to serve the Supreme Lord either by doing His righteous work or by getting a waiver from Him and by taking up higher yoga to gain complete purity of the psyche, one demonstrates great intelligence.

एष ते ऽभिहितः कृत्स्नो
ब्रह्म-वादस्य सङ्ग्रहः ।
समास-व्यास-विधिना
देवानाम् अपि दुर्गमः ॥२४.२३॥

eṣa te 'bhihitaḥ kṛtsno
brahma-vādasya saṅgrahaḥ
samāsa-vyāsa-vidhinā
devānām api durgamaḥ (24.23)

eṣa = eṣaḥ — this; te — to you; 'bhihitaḥ = abhihitaḥ — was taught; kṛtsno = kṛtsnaḥ — complete; brahma – spiritual reality; vādasya — of the science; saṅgrahaḥ — thesis; samāsa — in a concise way; vyāsa — in detail; vidhinā — methodically; devānām — of the supernatural people; api — even; durgamaḥ — hard to acquire.

Translation

The complete thesis of the science of the Spiritual Reality was taught to you, methodically in a concise way and in detail. It is hard to acquire even for the supernatural people. (24.23)

Commentary:

Basically speaking, this is the end of knowledge the real *Vedānta*. There is nothing else to know by a human being, besides what was taught here by *Śrī* Krishna. There is no other method of salvation which may be explained by anyone and which in fact would turn out to be true.

What was taught to Arjuna was incomplete in so far as *Śrī* Krishna did not elaborate on the process beyond *karma* yoga cultural duties for this world under His supervision, using yoga expertise to execute duties flawlessly. Here to Uddhava, *Śrī* Krishna laid out the whole process of salvation for human beings, by explaining *jñāna* yoga and *bhakti* yoga in detail.

अभीक्ष्णशस् ते गदितं
ज्ञानं विस्पष्ट-युक्तिमत् ।
एतद् विज्ञाय मुच्येत
पुरुषो नष्ट-सशयः ॥२४.२४॥

abhīkṣṇaśas te gaditaṁ
jñānaṁ vispaṣṭa-yuktimat
etad vijñāya mucyeta
puruṣo naṣṭa-saṁśayaḥ (24.24)

abhīkṣṇaśas = abhīkṣṇaśah — repeatedly; te — to you; gaditam — explained; jñānam — knowledge; vispaṣta — clear; yuktimat — reasoning fully; etad = etat — this; vijñāya — integrating; mucyeta — will be freed; puruṣo = puruṣaḥ — person; naṣṭa — dispelled; saṁśayaḥ — doubts.

Translation

I repeatedly explained the knowledge to you with clear reasons of analysis. By integrating this, a person is freed from material existence. His doubts are dispelled. (24.24)

Commentary:

The process of salvation is clearly laid out. There are no loop holes but a person is allowed to start where he is. One may begin by adopting the righteous duty of *Śrī* Krishna as defined by Him or as explained by His agent. The only risk is that an agent may, on occasion, misguide followers.

सु-विविक्तं तव प्रश्नं
मयैतद् अपि धारयेत् ।
सनातनं ब्रह्म-गुह्यं
परं ब्रह्माधिगच्छति ॥२४.२५॥

su-viviktaṁ tava praśnaṁ
mayaitad api dhārayet
sanātanaṁ brahma-guhyaṁ
paraṁ brahmādhigacchati (24.25)

su – very; viviktam — thoroughly analysed; tava — your; praśnam — question; mayaitad = maya — by me; etat — this; api — even; dhārayet — dwells upon, becomes absorbed in; sanātanam — eternal; brahma – Vedas; guhyam — secret; param — supreme; brahmādhigacchati = brahma — spiritual reality + adhigacchati — attains.

Translation

He who concentrates on your questions which were thoroughly analyzed by Me, attains the Eternal Supreme Spiritual Reality which is a secret in the Vedas. (24.25)

Commentary:

By dwelling upon, thinking of seriously and deeply, the questions of Uddhava and the answers given by Lord Krishna, a human being can gage where he or she fits into the plan of salvation, which is offered by *Śrī* Krishna. One should not be fooled by offers which circumvent and undermine what *Śrī* Krishna said nor which substitute other processes.

Each of the systems which He explained has particular value. No one can add to nor detract from these. One should not indulge in fantasies which lead nowhere. In the Vedas there are hints about salvation but when the Vedas were initially composed, the rishis who did so were preoccupied with survival on the physical level. Their main concern was how to safely continue reproducing human beings. The earthly environment was threatening to them. Thus in the Vedas one cannot easily find the path of salvation. Here *Śrī* Krishna laid it out clearly, showing where a person might start and how he should progress to higher courses.

य एतन् मम भक्तेषु
सम्प्रदद्यात् सु-पुष्कलम् ।
तस्याहं ब्रह्म-दायस्य
ददाम्य् आत्मानम् आत्मना ॥२४.२६॥

ya etan mama bhakteṣu
sampradadyāt su-puṣkalam
tasyāhaṁ brahma-dāyasya
dadāmy ātmānam ātmanā (24.26)

ya = yah — who; etan = etat — this; mama — my; bhakteṣu — among the devotees; sampradadyāt — thoroughly explain; su-puṣkalam — great detail; tasyāhaṁ = tasya — to him + aham — I; brahma – science of spiritual reality; dāyasya — one of one who imparts; dadāmy = dadāmi — I give; ātmānam — myself; ātmanā — by myself, of my own choosing.

Translation

Because of his imparting of the science of spiritual reality, I do, of My own choosing, give myself to the person who thoroughly explains this in great detail to My devotees. (24.26)

Commentary:

A similar declaration was given to Arjuna at the end of the *Bhagavad-Gītā* discourse:

ya idaṁ paramaṁ guhyaṁ madbhakteṣvabhidhāsyati
bhaktiṁ mayi parāṁ kṛtvā māmevaiṣyatyasaṁśayaḥ
na ca tasmānmanuṣyeṣu kaścinme priyakṛttamaḥ
bhavitā na ca me tasmād anyaḥ priyataro bhuvi

Whosoever, having performed the highest devotion to Me, will explain this supreme secret to My devotees, will certainly come to Me.

And no one among human beings is more pleasing to Me in performance than he. And no one on earth will be more dear to Me than he, (B.G. 18.68-69)

य एतत् समधीयीत
पवित्रं परमं शुचि ।
स पूयेताहर् अहर् मां
ज्ञान-दीपेन दर्शयन् ॥२४.२७॥

ya etat samadhīyīta
pavitraṁ paramaṁ śuci
sa pūyetāhar ahar māṁ
jñāna-dīpena darśayan (24.27)

ya — he who; etat — this; samadhīyīta — reads; pavitram — purifying; paramam — supremely; śuci — flawless; sa = saḥ — he; pūyetāhar = pūyeta — is purified + ahah ahah — day by day; mām — me; jñāna – knowledge; dīpena — by the illuminating intellect; darśayan — showing.

Translation

He who reads this purifying and flawless discourse, is purified day after day by showing Me through the use of the illuminating intellect which gives knowledge. (24.27)

Commentary:

This discourse as it was given to Uddhava and Arjuna, is the course for self-realization for all times. It was valid in the time of the *Dvāpara Yuga*. It is valid now in the time of the *Kali Yuga*. This Age may not be as favorable for its performance but that does not mean that it is not valid. It should not be adjusted. One has to discover one's level of advancement and proceed from there with sincerity.

Jñāna-dīpena means by the illuminating intellect which gives the yogi first hand mystic and spiritual insight into the Absolute Reality. It is developed in higher yoga practice. Without this development one cannot be successful in spiritual life. If a person tries to teach this to others and he has not developed the illuminating intellect in his subtle body, he will of necessity mislead others into a cheap theoretical religion. Arjuna got divine vision *(divyam cakṣu)* or stated differently his intellect was illuminated *(dīpena)* so that he could see these truths directly and with spiritual eyesight.

य एतच् छ्रद्धया नित्यम्
अव्यग्रः श्रृणुयान् नरः ।
मयि भक्तिं परां कुर्वन्
कर्मभिर् न स बध्यते ॥२४.२८॥

ya etac chraddhayā nityam
avyagraḥ śṛṇuyān naraḥ
mayi bhaktiṁ parāṁ kurvan
karmabhir na sa badhyate (24.28)

ya = yah — he who; etac = etat — this; chraddhayā = śraddhayā — with faith; nityam — regularly; avyagraḥ — without distraction; śṛṇuyān = śṛṇuyāt — listens; naraḥ — a person; mayi — to me; bhaktim — devotion; parām — highest; kurvan — cultivates; karmabhir = karmabhiḥ — by cultural activities; na — not; sa = sah — he; badhyate — is implicated.

Translation

The person who regularly with faith and without distraction, listens to this discourse, cultivates the highest devotion to Me. He is not implicated by cultural activities. (24.28)

Commentary:

To Arjuna a slightly different guarantee was given:

śraddhāvānanasūyaśca śṛṇuyādapi yo naraḥ
so'pi muktaḥ śubhāṁllokān prāpnuyātpuṇyakarmaṇām (18.71)

Even the person who hears with confidence, without ridiculing is freed. He should attain the happy worlds where persons of pious actions reside. (B.G. 18.71)

अप्य् उद्धव त्वया ब्रह्म
सखे समवधारितम् ।
अपि ते विगतो मोहः
शोकश् चासौ मनो-भवः ॥२४.२९॥

apy uddhava tvayā brahma
sakhe samavadhāritam
api te vigato mohaḥ
śokaś cāsau mano-bhavaḥ (24.29)

apy = api — also; uddhava — Uddhava; tvayā — by you; brahma — spiritual reality; sakhe — of friend; samavadhāritam — completely understood; api — whether; te — your; vigato = vigataḥ — is removed; mohah — bewildered; śokaś = śokaḥ — grief; cāsau = ca — and + asau — this; mano-bhavaḥ = manah-bhavah — production of the mind.

Translation

And also Uddhava, was the Spiritual Reality completely understood by you? Was your bewilderment and grief, the production of your mind, removed? (24.29)

Commentary:

Arjuna was told something similar:

kaccidetacchrutaṁ pārtha tvayaikāgreṇa cetasā
kaccidajñānasaṁmohaḥ pranaṣṭaste dhanaṁjaya

Was this heard by you, O son of Pṛthā, with a one-pointed mind? Was your ignorance and confusion removed, O conqueror of wealthy countries? (B.G. 18.72)

Uddhava's bewilderment was two fold, in relation to Lord Krishna and in relation to how the common people could be awarded salvation by an easy process other than yoga. Uddhava wanted to pass from this world at the same time with Lord Krishna and to remain in proximity to Krishna in a similar way to which his physical body was in proximity to Lord Krishna's specially-produced physical form. His misgivings and doubts were cleared up by the discourse.

नैतत् त्वया दाम्भिकाय
नास्तिकाय शठाय च ।
अशुश्रूषोर् अभक्ताय
दुर्विनीताय दीयताम् ॥२४.३०॥

naitat tvayā dāmbhikāya
nāstikāya śaṭhāya ca
aśuśrūṣor abhaktāya
durvinītāya dīyatām (24.30)

naitat = na — not + etat — this; tvayā — by you; dāmbhikāya — to a conceited person; nāstikāya — to an atheist; śathāya — to a deceitful person; ca — and; aśuśrūṣor = aśuśrūṣoḥ — to one who is not submissive; abhaktāya — to one lacking devotion; durvinītāya — to one who lacks modesty; dīyatām — should be shared.

Translation

This information should not be shared by you to a conceited person nor to an atheist, nor to one who is insubmissive nor to one who is a not a devotee, nor to one who lacks modesty. (24.30)

Commentary:

Something similar was said to Arjuna:

idaṁ te nātapaskāya nābhaktāya kadācana
na cāśuśrūṣave vācyaṁ na ca māṁ yo'bhyasūyati

This should not be told by you to anyone who does not perform austerity or is not devoted at anytime, or does not desire to hear what is said or is critical of Me. (B.G. 18.67)

एतैर् दोषैर् विहीनाय
ब्रह्मण्याय प्रियाय च ।
साधवे शुचये ब्रूयाद्
भक्तिः स्याच् छूद्र-योषिताम् ॥२४.३१॥

etair doṣair vihīnāya
brahmaṇyāya priyāya ca
sādhave śucaye brūyād
bhaktiḥ syāc chūdra-yoṣitām (24.31)

etair = etaiḥ — with these; dosair = dosaiḥ — by faults; vihīnāya — to one who lacks; brahmaṇyāya — to one who is a patron of brahmins; priyāya — to one who is endearing; ca — and; sādhave — to one who is saintly; śucaye — to one who is pure in nature; brūyād = brūyāt — one should explain; bhaktiḥ — devotee; syāc = syāt — there is; chūdra-yoṣitām = śūdra — working class people + yoṣitām — and to women.

Translation

One should explain this to a person who lacks faults, but who is a patron of brahmins and is endearing, to one who is saintly and pure-natured and even to the working class people and to women if they have devotion. (24.31)

Commentary:

Here the devotion is stressed in the case of working class persons who might not be educated and to women as well. In the *Bhagavad-Gītā*, there is a similar declaration:

māṁ hi pārtha vyapāśritya ye'pi syuḥ pāpayonayaḥ
striyo vaiśyāstathā śūdrās te'pi yānti parāṁ gatim

O son of Pṛthā, by relying on Me, even persons from sinful parentage, even women, businessmen, even laborers, do move towards the supreme goal. (B.G. 9.32)

नैतद् विज्ञाय जिज्ञासोर्
ज्ञातव्यम् अवशिष्यते ।
पीत्वा पीयूषम् अमृतं
पातव्यं नावशिष्यते ॥२४.३२॥

naitad vijñāya jijñāsor
jñātavyam avaśiṣyate
pītvā pīyūṣam amṛtaṁ
pātavyaṁ nāvaśiṣyate (24.32)

naitad = na — not + etat —this; vijñāya - realizing; jijñāsor = jijñāsoḥ - of, for the inquisitive student; jñātavyam — what is to be known, information; avaśiṣyate – remains; pītvā – having drunk; pīyūṣam – delicious; amṛtam - nectar; pātavyam —to be drunk; nāvaśiṣyate = na – not + avaśiṣyate – remains.

Translation

For the inquisitive student, after realizing this, no more information remains to be known. Having drunk this delicious nectar, no other beverage remains to be tasted. (24.32)

Commentary:

This discourse with Uddhava does give the full course of self and God realization, not deleting nor avoiding any part of it. It gives the essential parts for serious students who want spiritual perfection in touch with the Supreme Person.

ज्ञाने कर्मणि योगे च
वार्तायां दण्ड-धारणे ।
यावान् अर्थो नृणां तात
तावांस् ते ऽहं चतुर्-विधः ॥२४.३३॥

jñāne karmaṇi yoge ca
vārtāyāṁ daṇḍa-dhāraṇe
yāvān artho nṛṇāṁ tāta
tāvāṁs te 'haṁ catur-vidhaḥ (24.33)

jñāne — in procuring knowledge; karmaṇi — in performing cultural activities; yoge — in practicing yoga; ca — and; vārtāyām — in conducting business; daṇḍa-dhāraṇe — in maintaining political control; yāvān — as much as; artho = arthah — benefit; nṛṇām — of human beings; tāta — o dear; tāvāṁs = tāvān — that, much; te — to you; 'ham = aham — I; catur = catuḥ - four; vidhaḥ — sectioned.

Translation

My friend, in terms of procuring knowledge, performing cultural activities, practicing yoga, conducting business and maintaining political control, whatever benefit there is for human beings, that fourfold gain I am to you dear Uddhava. (24.33)

Commentary:

Here *Śrī* Krishna definitely stressed Himself, saying that whatever a person might get from any sensible course of life, would be achieved by his devotee Uddhava. The fourfold gain is *dharma*, *artha*, *kāma* and *mokṣa*. *Dharma* is righteous life style through which one acquires pious credits for assisting the Universal Form of *Śrī* Krishna. *Artha* is prosperity and wealth, through which a human being fulfills desires. *Kāma* is lust and desire which is a prime driving force. *Mokṣa* is liberation from the course of haphazard birth and death.

By procuring knowledge one gets some know-how about achieving one's aims, be they spiritual or material objectives. By performing cultural activities properly one gets a foothold in the world of the human beings and can advance culturally. By practicing yoga in the way that *Śrī* Krishna recommends, one gets purification of his or her own psychological nature. This leads to supernatural and spiritual insight which sets one firmly on the spiritual path. By conducting business, one acquires money and gets an understanding of the value of rendering some useful service to human society. This causes promotion in the cultural field. By maintaining political control one learns how to work under the direction of higher authority. This leads to serving the Universal Form of *Śrī* Krishna, as Arjuna and his brothers, the Pandavas, did.

But *Śrī* Krishna told Uddhava personally that whatever benefit he might aspire for from any of these, he would get in the friendly association with Krishna. This meant that in the course of such association whatever was required for perfection would be facilitated automatically. It does not mean that yoga or any other aspect would be deleted or cancelled and just the friendship in devotion would be required, but rather the friendship would facilitate and urge on the quick completion of all purificatory techniques.

मर्त्यो यदा त्यक्त-समस्त-कर्मा
निवेदितात्मा विचिकीर्षितो मे ।
तदामृतत्वं प्रतिपद्यमानो
मयात्म-भूयाय च कल्पते वै ॥२४.३४॥

martyo yadā tyakta-samasta-karmā
niveditātmā vicikīrṣito me
tadāmṛtatvaṁ pratipadyamāno
mayātma-bhūyāya ca kalpate vai (24.34)

martyo = martyaḥ — of a human being; yadā — when; tyakta — having relinquished; samasta — all; karmā — cultural activities; niveditātmā = nivedita – offering commiting + ātmā — his spirit, himself; vicikīrṣito = vicikīrṣitaḥ — wishing to elevate; me — by me; tadāmṛtatvam = tadā — then + amṛtatvam — immortality; pratipadyamāno = pratipadyamānaḥ — attaining; mayātma-bhūyāya = mayā — with me, my + ātma-bhūyāya — to the status of the spirit; ca — and; kalpate — is fit; vai — indeed.

Translation

When a human being relinquishes all cultural activity, and commits himself to be Me, I wish to elevate him. Then attaining immortality, he becomes fit to acquire My existential status. (24.34)

Commentary:

To move into the spiritual atmosphere, means to acquire an existential status somewhat like that of *Śrī* Krishna. To do this, one is required to relinquish cultural activities in this world. This means even religious activities or pretence devotional activities which are in fact, cultural means of operation in disguise.

A human being may be committed to *Śrī* Krishna and still remain in the cultural operations of the world but that sort of commitment only gives him the opportunity to be *Śrī* Krishna's devotee, life after life in the material world. If he desires to go farther or if *Śrī* Krishna selects him for closer association, then he must take the first step in that direction by seeking and then obtaining a waiver from acts which concern this world.

Committing himself to *Śrī* Krishna's affairs outside of this world, he becomes inspired in higher yoga practice. He is given the appropriate mystic means, either by *Śrī* Krishna Himself, by Lord *Balarāma*, by Lord Shiva or by a *mahāyogī* who mastered the techniques. Then by practice, gradually he becomes fit to acquire the divine status.

श्री-शुक उवाच
स एवम् आदर्शित-योग-मार्गस्
तदोत्तमःश्लोक-वचो निशम्य ।
बद्धाञ्जलिः प्रीत्य्-उपरुद्ध-कण्ठो
न किञ्चिद् ऊचे ऽश्रु-परिप्लुताक्षः ॥२४.३५॥

śrī-śuka uvāca
sa evam ādarśita-yoga-mārgas
tadottamaḥśloka-vaco niśamya
baddhāñjaliḥ prīty-uparuddha-kaṇṭho
na kiñcid ūce 'śru-pariplutākṣaḥ (24.35)

śrī-śuka – the illustrious Shuka; uvāca — said; sa = sah — he; evam — thus; ādarśita — shown; yoga – yoga; mārgas = mārgaḥ — path; tadottamaḥśloka = tadā — then + uttamah – best + śloka — the one who the verses glorify; vaco = vacaḥ — speech; niśamya — listening; baddhāñjaliḥ = baddha añjaliḥ — with hands in prayer gesture; prīty = prīti — with endearing emotions; uparuddha — choked, blocked; kaṇṭho = kaṇṭhaḥ — throat, voice; na – not; kiñcid = kiñcit — anything; ūce — say; 'śru = aśru — tears; pariplutākṣah = paripluta — overflowing + akṣaḥ — eyes.

Translation

The illustrious Shuka said: Being thus shown the path of yoga, and listening to the speech of the one who the best verses glorify, he whose hands were in prayer gesture, and whose voice was blocked off with endearing emotions, could not say anything, as even his eyes were overflowing with tears. (24.35)

Commentary:

This teaching of *Śrī* Krishna to Uddhava consists for the most part of the application of yoga *(yoga-mārgah).* Most of the verses concern just that. Therefore one cannot avoid this nor override this with something else. As *Śrī* Krishna told Uddhava in the discourse:

śrī-bhagavān uvāca
yogās trayo mayā proktā nṝṇāṁ śreyo-vidhitsayā
jñānaṁ karma ca bhaktiś ca nopāyo 'nyo 'sti kutracit

The Blessed Lord said: Desiring to give perfection of the human being, three applications of yoga discipline were taught by me, namely the application to thinking experience, the application to physical experience and the application to emotions. Besides these, there is no other method whatsoever. (U.G. 15.6)

विष्टभ्य चित्तं प्रणयावघूर्णं
धैर्येण राजन् बहु-मन्यमानः ।
कृताञ्जलिः प्राह यदु-प्रवीरं
शीर्ष्णा स्पृशंस् तच्-चरणारविन्दम् ॥ २४.३६ ॥

viṣṭabhya cittaṁ praṇayāvaghūrṇaṁ
dhairyeṇa rājan bahu-manyamānaḥ
kṛtāñjaliḥ prāha yadu-pravīraṁ
śīrṣṇā spṛśaṁs tac-caraṇāravindam
(24.36)

viṣṭabhya — restraining; cittam — mental and emotional energy; praṇayāvaghūrṇaṁ = praṇaya — by life force, vital energy; avaghūrṇam — uncontrollably stirred; dhairyeṇa — with steadiness; rājan — o king; bahu – very much; manyamānaḥ — blessed; kṛtañjaliḥ — one with hands for praying; prāha — spoke; yadu – Yadu; pravīram — great chief; śīrṣṇā — with his head; spṛśaṁs = spṛśan — touching; tac = tat — that; caraṇāravindam — lotus feet.

Translation

O king, restraining the mental and emotional energy, which was uncontrollably stirred by his life force, by steadying himself and considering that he was very blessed, he touched the lotus feet of the chief of the Yadus, with his head and spoke with hands set for offering prayers. (24.36)

Commentary:

This reaction of Uddhava shows clearly that *bhakti* or emotional endearment was prominent in his nature. Some have physical energy or working power, prominent. And others have thinking experience prominent. Accordingly one gravitates or prefers *bhakti*, *karma* or *jñāna*. But to these must be added yoga. The path of yoga which *Śrī* Krishna taught has three entry points accordingly.

Uddhava had to restrain his mental and emotional energy, particularly his emotional force, which was stirred by his vital energy. Some commentators derive the meaning that he was overwhelmed with love and had to steady his mind. The truth of the matter is that Arjuna was also in a similar state except that his *prāṇa* or life force, had caused his emotional energy to be nervous about complying with his battle duties, just as Uddhava had difficulty going to

Badarinatha initially and complied after this discourse, which gave him the power to discipline his emotional energy and vital power.

Whereas Arjuna was not to be physically separated from *Śrī* Krishna during the battle, Uddhava was to be. This physical separation caused fear to Uddhava's life force with its physical attachment habits, and so it broke down his mental and emotional energies. Uddhava however could resist because *Śrī* Krishna's lectures strengthened the *buddhi* organ in the head of Uddhava's subtle body. Uddhava steadied his mind and emotions *(dhairyena)* even though his *prāṇa* or life force moved to cause tears to come to his eyes.

Because some devotees cannot sort the psyche, they see it as one organism, as themselves. They mistake their emotions for their spiritual selves and make commentaries to suit their lack of clarity. These commentaries go well with others who have no insight.

Uddhava would have to perfect yoga practice to the degree that the physical presence of *Śrī* Krishna's special material body does not mean much to him, due to linking up with *Śrī* Krishna's transcendental form. To do this, Uddhava would transfer his attention to his own spiritual form and thus he would cause its full development and manifestation objectively. That is the purpose for which Uddhava was sent to Badarinatha in the Himalayas in order to perfect yoga practice to bring on a full purification of the psyche, so that the life force would cease its preference for physical presences.

It is very interesting that in the *Bhaktivedānta* purports the word *praṇaya* was translated as "with love". How on earth this word could mean that, only heaven knows.

श्री-उद्धव उवाच
विद्रावितो मोह-महान्धकारो
य आश्रितो मे तव सन्निधानात् ।
विभावसोः किं नु समीप-गस्य
शीतं तमो भीः प्रभवन्त्य् अजाद्य ॥२४.३७॥

śrī-uddhava uvāca
vidrāvito moha-mahāndhakāro
ya āśrito me tava sannidhānāt
vibhāvasoḥ kiṁ nu samīpa-gasya
śītaṁ tamo bhīḥ prabhavanty ajādya (24.37)

śrī-uddhava = the deserving Uddhava; uvāca — said; vidrāvito = vidrāvitaḥ — was driven away; moha — bewilderment; mahāndhakāro = mahā – great + andhakāraḥ — mental darkness, depression; ya = yaḥ — which; āśrito = āśritaḥ — was resorted to; me — by me; tava — your; sannidhānāt — due to the presence; vibhāvasoḥ — of the sun; kim — can; nu — factually; samīpa – near; gasya — of one who goes; śītam — cold; tamo = tamaḥ — darkness; bhīḥ — fear; prabhavanty = prabhavanti — suppress; ajādya = aja — the unborn one, Procreator Brahmā + ādya — o source.

Translation

The deserving Uddhava said: The great depression of bewilderment, which was resorted to by me, was driven away by Your presence, O source of Procreator Brahmā, can cold, darkness and fear suppress one who goes near the sun. (24.37)

Commentary:

Formerly Uddhava thought that if his physical body would die at the same time, that *Śrī* Krishna's physical one would, then he would be assured of going wherever *Śrī* Krishna's spirit would go but that thinking ceased. Uddhava is no longer fearful of not being in the physical presence of *Śrī* Krishna at the time of death or at any other time.

प्रत्यर्पितो मे भवतानुकम्पिना
भृत्याय विज्ञान-मयः प्रदीपः ।
हित्वा कृत-ज्ञस् तव पाद-मूलं
को ऽन्यं समीयाच् छरणं त्वदीयम् ॥२४.३८॥

pratyarpito me bhavatānukampinā
bhṛtyāya vijñāna-mayaḥ pradīpaḥ
hitvā kṛta-jñas tava pāda-mūlaṁ
ko 'nyaṁ samīyāc charaṇaṁ tvadīyam
(24.38)

pratyarpito = pratyarpitaḥ — restored; me — to me; bhavatānukampinā = bhavatā — by your good self + anukampinā — by one who is gracious; bhṛtyāya — to a servant; vijñāna –realisation; mayah — that which produces; pradīpah — lamp, source infinitely of illumination; hitvā — having abandoned; kṛta – deed; jñas = jñaḥ — one who is aware; tava — your; pāda – foot; mūlam — bottom sole; ko = kaḥ — who; 'nyam = anyam — another; samīyāc = samīyāt — seek; charaṇam = śaranam — sanctuary; tvadīyam — your.

Translation

The illumination which produced realization was restored to me by Your infinitely gracious and good self. Who, being aware of Your deeds, would abandon the sole of Your feet and seek another sanctuary? (24.38)

Commentary:

This is a wonderful appraisal by Uddhava. *Śrī* Krishna took steps to make Uddhava conquer over his materialistic emotional energies which were urged on and which consisted in part of the *prāṇa* life force, the *citta* sensual and thinking energy, combined into a compulsive emotional force, which tried to force *Śrī* Krishna to act on its motivations.

वृक्णश् च मे सु-दृढः स्नेह-पाशो
दाशार्ह-वृष्ण्य्-अन्धक-सात्वतेषु ।
प्रसारितः सृष्टि-विवृद्धये त्वया
स्व-मायया ह्य् आत्म-सुबोध-हेतिना ॥२४.३९॥

vṛkṇaś ca me su-dṛḍhaḥ sneha-pāśo
dāśārha-vṛṣṇy-andhaka-sātvateṣu
prasāritaḥ sṛṣṭi-vivṛddhaye tvayā
sva-māyayā hy ātma-subodha-hetinā
(24.39)

vṛkṇaś = vrknaḥ — severed; ca — and; me — my; su-dṛḍhaḥ — very touching; sneha – affection; pāśo = pāśaḥ — rope, bond; dāśārha – Dasarha; vṛṣṇy = vṛṣṇi – Vrishna; andhaka – Andhaka; sātvateṣu — and for the Satvatas; prasāritaḥ — spread over; sṛṣṭi — creation; vivṛddhaye — for the increase; tvayā — by you; sva – your own; māyayā — by the bewildering potency; hy = hi — indeed; ātma — soul; subodha — accurate perception; hetinā — by the sword.

Translation

You severed with the sword of accurate perception of the soul, the very bond of affection for the Dāśārhas, Vṛṣṇis, Andhakas and Sātvatas. It was spread by You for the increase of the creation, by means of Your bewildering potency. (24.39)

Commentary:

As I mentioned in these purports, the term *Sātvatas* means a clan of persons who were physically related to *Śrī* Krishna. That word does not mean devotee in general. This clan of persons were a group of devotees who lived in the time of *Śrī* Krishna. This is very clear to one who knows the history of those dynasties as related in the *Bhāgavata Purāṇa* and elsewhere. It is totally misleading to indicate that initially in this discourse, *Sātvata* meant devotee and now it means a member of the clan of families around *Śrī* Krishna. In all cases in this usage of this discourse it means a member of those clans.

The materialistic view of family members is solidly supported by, encouraged and prolonged by the life force which is called *prāṇa* in verse 36. This life force is primarily concerned with survival of one's own and one's relatives bodies. This same force kept Arjuna in a mind-set to resist *Śrī* Krishna's desire for the *Kurukṣetra* war. It wanted to maintain the Kuru family at all costs, even at the costs of corrupt government which worked against *dharma* or righteous life style as it is defined and desired by *Śrī* Krishna.

It worked on Uddhava in a different way, but nevertheless by the association of *Śrī* Krishna, Uddhava experienced a permanent detachment from it. Thus all of crying and pleading for solutions based on the materialistic outlook of his emotions, came to an end. At last he was freed to work for purifications of his psyche, shedding off the influence of the passionate mundane energy.

नमो ऽस्तु ते महा-योगिन्
प्रपन्नम् अनुशाधि माम् ।
यथा त्वच्-चरणाम्भोजे
रतिः स्याद् अनपायिनी ॥२४.४०॥

namo 'stu te mahā-yogin
prapannam anuśādhi mām
yathā tvac-caraṇāmbhoje
ratiḥ syād anapāyinī (24.40)

namo = namaḥ - all due respects; 'stu = astu — let there be; te — unto you; mahā-yogin — great yogi; prapannam — one who took shelter; anuśādhi — instruct; mām — me; yathā — according to, as to the method; tvac = tvat — your; caraṇāmbhoje = caraṇa ambhoje — at the lotus feet; ratiḥ — love; syād = syāt — is; anapāyinī — unending, constant.

Translation

Let there be all due respects to You, O great yogin. Instruct me, a person who took shelter of you, as to the method for applying constant love to Your lotus feet. (24.40)

Commentary:

This is the problem in this existence. It is the factor of not being able to apply one's attention continuously to Lord Krishna. Uddhava titled Lord Krishna fittingly as a *mahāyogin*.

श्री-भगवान् उवाच
गच्छोद्धव मयादिष्टो
बदर्य्-आख्य ममाश्रमम् ।
तत्र मत्-पाद-तीर्थोदे
स्नानोपस्पर्शनैः शुचिः ॥२४.४१॥

śrī-bhagavān uvāca
gacchoddhava mayādiṣṭo
badary-ākhyaṁ mamāśramam
tatra mat-pāda-tīrthode
snānopasparśanaiḥ śuciḥ (24.41)

śrī-bhagavān – the blessed lord; uvāca — said; gacchoddhava = gaccha — go + uddhava — Uddhava; mayādiṣṭo = mayā — by me + ādiṣṭah — as instructed; badary = badarī – Badari; ākhyam — named; mamāśramam = mama — my + āśramam — hermitage; tatra — there; mat – my; pāda — feet; tīrthode = tīrtha — sacred river + ude — in the water; snānopasparśanaiḥ = snāna — bathing + upasparśanaiḥ — and by touching; śuciḥ — cleansed.

Translation

The Blessed Lord said: Go Uddhava, as instructed by Me to My hermitage named Badari. There by bathing and touching, purification will be attained in the water of the sacred river, which sprang from My feet. (24.41)

Commentary:

Uddhava got his emotions in order and did as he is told.

ईक्षयालकनन्दाया
विधूताशेष-कल्मषः ।
वसानो वल्कलान्य् अङ्ग
वन्य-भुक् सुख-निःस्पृहः ॥२४.४२॥

īkṣayālakanandāyā
vidhūtāśeṣa-kalmaṣaḥ
vasāno valkalāny aṅga
vanya-bhuk sukha-niḥspṛhaḥ (24.42)

īkṣayālakanandāyā = īkṣayā — by glancing + alakanandāyāḥ — the Alakananda River; vidhūtāśeṣa = vidhūta — cleansed + aśeṣa — of all; kalmaṣaḥ — bad tendencies; vasāno = vasānaḥ — wearing; valkalāny = valkalāni — bark; aṅga — my dear; vanya — forest produce; bhuk — eating; sukha — happy; niḥspṛhaḥ — free of craving.

Translation

By glancing at the Alakananda River, you will be cleansed of all bad tendencies. Wear tree bark, my dear Uddhava, eat forest produce and be happy by being freed of craving. (24.42)

Commentary:

This is the path of a *sannyāsi*, which was recommended to Uddhava before but which Uddhava very tactfully tried to reject. Uddhava said previously in protest:

śrī-uddhava uvāca
yogeśa yoga-vinyāsa yogātman yoga-sambhava
niḥśreyasāya me proktas tyāgaḥ sannyāsa-lakṣaṇaḥ
tyāgo 'yaṁ duṣkaro bhūman kāmānāṁ viṣayātmabhiḥ
sutarāṁ tvayi sarvātmann abhaktair iti me matiḥ

The deserving Uddhava said: O Supreme Master of yoga, O treasure of yoga practice, O Yoga in person, O origin of the yoga discipline, for my salvation, you recommend the renunciation of the results of action, the objective of which is the renunciation of exploitive opportunities. (2.14)

O infinite Lord, for those who are absorbed in sense enjoyment and especially for those who are not devoted to you, who are the soul of all beings, this renunciation of cravings is difficult to accomplish. This is my view. (U.G. 2.14-15)

This type of *sannyāsi* is not a preaching *sannyāsi* but is one which matches the original definition of a *sannyāsi* who has little or nothing to do with the public. However some modern acharyas of repute, gave the opinion that Uddhava went to Badrinatha to preach to the ascetics there, to explain to them the glories and pastimes of *Śrī* Krishna. Still, Badarinatha is an isolated place of pilgrimage, even more so in the time of *Śrī* Krishna when the public did not have access to modern means of transportation. Traditionally Badrinatha was for yogis, for lone ascetics in the method used by Lords *Nara-Nārāyaṇa*.

तितिक्षुर् द्वन्द्व-मात्राणां
सुशीलः सयतेन्द्रियः ।
शान्तः समाहित-धिया
ज्ञान-विज्ञान-सयुतः ॥२४.४३॥

titikṣur dvandva-mātrāṇāṁ
suśīlaḥ saṁyatendriyaḥ
śāntaḥ samāhita-dhiyā
jñāna-vijñāna-saṁyutaḥ (24.43)

titikṣur = titikṣuḥ — tolerant; dvandva – dual conditions; mātrāṇām — of the impact; suśīlaḥ — well-behaved; saṁyatendriyaḥ = saṁyata – controlled + indriyaḥ — senses; śāntah — serene; samāhita — perfectly withdrawn from mundane sensations, being endowed with knowledge and mystic experience; dhiyā — with the intellect; jñāna — knowledge; vijñāna — and realization; saṁyutaḥ — endowed.

Translation

Being tolerant of the impact of dual conditions, well-behaved, with controlled senses, being serene, with the intellect perfectly withdrawn from mundane sensations, being endowed with knowledge and mystic experience, (24.43)

Commentary:

Anyone who is unbiased towards yoga, who wants to know the truth of what *Śrī* Krishna requested of Uddhava, will understand that this is higher yoga practice, which is done in personal isolation. This is not temple activities of singing and dancing in front of the Krishna *Mūrti*. This is definitely higher yoga practice to be mastered by Uddhava so that he can free himself from this material world in all its forms and shapes, so that he can catch up with the transcendental form of *Śrī* Krishna and also develop his own spiritual self.

मत्तो ऽनुशिक्षितं यत् ते
विविक्तम् अनुभावयन् ।
मय्य् आवेशित-वाक्-चित्तो
मद्-धर्म-निरतो भव ।
अतिव्रज्य गतीस् तिस्रो
माम् एष्यसि ततः परम् ॥२४.४४॥

matto 'nuśikṣitaṁ yat te
viviktam anubhāvayan

mayy āveśita-vāk-citto
mad-dharma-nirato bhava
ativrajya gatīs tisro
mām eṣyasi tataḥ param (24.44)

matto = mattaḥ — from me; 'nuśikṣitam = anuśikṣitam — what was learned; yat — what; te — to you; viviktam — deliberation; anubhāvayan — repeatedly reflecting upon; mayy = mayi — in, on me; āveśita — invested; vāk — speech; citto = cittaḥ — mental and emotional energy; mad = mat – my; dharmo = dharmaḥ — righteously; nirato = nirataḥ — being dedicated to; bhava — being in that state of experience; ativrajya — pass beyond; gatīs = gatīh — the range; tisro = tisraḥ — three; mām — to me; eṣyasi — you will reach; tataḥ - then; param — supreme.

Translation

...deliberating and repeatedly reflecting on what you learned from Me, with your speech and mento-emotional energy invested in Me, living like that; then passing beyond the range of the three mundane influences, you will reach Me, the Supreme. (24.44)

Commentary:

This is a description of a *kriyā* yoga process of transferring one's attention out of all things and manifestations of the material energy into the chit *ākāśa*, the sky of consciousness, the spiritual world. This cannot be done by any other means but by higher yoga. One has to withdraw his expressing power *(vāk)* and his mento-emotional energy *(citto)* by the process of *pratyāhar*, the 5th stage of yoga.

Once this energy is withdrawn from its sensual pursuits in this world, it will follow one's attention into the chit *ākāśa*, provided one is able to shift the focus there. In that place one meets the divine beings of whom *Śrī* Krishna is the Supreme Personality of Godhead.

This was to be done by Uddhava by higher yoga practice at Badrinatha. Uddhava was not to wait until death to go back home back to Godhead, as the modern acharyas term it today. He was to get himself transferred by his personal efforts in yoga practice before passing off from the material body. It is interesting that some preachers gave us the idea that all of *Śrī* Krishna's associates went to the spiritual world, merely by their association with *Śrī* Krishna, while here we get details of how that association worked in the life of Uddhava, a most confidential servant of the Lord. What then did others who were not as confidentially-related to *Śrī* Krishna do? And why did *Śrī* Krishna Himself as well as Lord *Balarāma* execute yoga on their departures from the bodies which they used on this plane.

In the *Mahābhārata*, we read that Arjuna and his brothers along with their wife *Draupadī*, had to situate themselves in yoga practice in the end. *Yudhiṣṭhira*, the senior, finished his practice in a classic way. The others finished partially before their bodies perished.

श्री-शुक उवाच
स एवम् उक्तो हरि-मेधसोद्धवः
प्रदक्षिणं त परिसृत्य पादयोः ।
शिरो निधायाश्रु-कलाभिर् आर्द्र-धीर्
न्यषिञ्चद् अद्वन्द्व-परो ऽप्य् अपक्रमे ॥२४.४५॥

śrī-śuka uvāca
sa evam ukto hari-medhasoddhavaḥ
pradakṣiṇaṁ taṁ parisṛtya pādayoḥ
śiro nidhāyāśru-kalābhir ārdra-dhīr
nyaṣiñcad advandva-paro 'py apakrame
(24.45)

śrī-śuka – the illustrious Shuka; uvāca — said; sa = saḥ — he; evam — thus; ukto = uktaḥ — addressed; hari – Hari the one who takes away the material existence; medhasoddhavah = medhasa — by the one, the memory of whom + uddhava — Uddhava; pradakṣinam —

reverentially facing; tam — to him; parisṛtya — encircling; pādayoḥ — at the two feet; śiro = śiraḥ — head; nidhāyāśru-kalābhir = nidhāya — placing + aśru-kalābhiḥ — tears with drops; ārdra — melted, emotional breakdown; dhīr = dhīḥ — intellect; nyaṣiñcad = nyaṣiñcat — bathe; advandva – without dual condition; paro = paraḥ — affection; 'py = api — even; apakrame — in deporting, at departure.

Translation

The illustrious Shuka said: Thus being addressed by Lord Hari, the memory of Whom takes away material existence, Uddhava reverentially encircled the Lord, facing as he went around clockwise. In departing, he placed his head at Krishna's feet, and bathe them with teardrops. Even though normally he was without the dual emotional condition, his intellect did emotionally break down. (24.45)

Commentary:

Even though Uddhava is a great devotee of the Lord and a *mahāyogin* in his own right, still the emotional nature in his subtle material body, broke down. This is not the same as the spiritual emotional nature but it is stated to be so by some authorities in the line of disciplic succession.

On the spiritual plane, the spiritual body of Uddhava would not have broken down since it would keep in touch with *Śrī* Krishna and would not have been threatened with separation from the Lord. The intricacies of these matters are explained in an erroneous way by some disciplic authorities. This is because of mistaking the subtle material body for the spiritual one, and mistaking the emotions of the subtle form for those of the spiritual one.

Uddhava, as a great devotee and a great yogin too, was normally without the dual emotional condition of subtle pleasure and pain which transpires in the subtle form. This is why *Śrī* Krishna engaged him in many confidential services, but still, Uddhava's subtle material form was pained to be separate from *Śrī* Krishna's superfine physical body. This is why Uddhava suffered these pains of separation.

The authorities in the disciplic succession who do not distinguish between the various bodies used by a devotee, confuse these issues. They gave a very simple explanation of these matters and their lectures are agreeable to the common people who have little or no mystic experiences and who rely on a theoretical and sentimental grasp of these scriptures.

सु-दुस्त्यज-स्नेह-वियोग-कातरो
न शक्नुवंस् तं परिहातुम् आतुरः ।
कृच्छ्रं ययौ मूर्धनि भर्तृ-पादुके
बिभ्रन् नमस्कृत्य ययौ पुनः पुनः ॥२४.४६॥

su-dustyaja-sneha-viyoga-kātaro
na śaknuvaṁs taṁ parihātum āturaḥ
kṛcchraṁ yayau mūrdhani bhartṛ-pāduke
bibhran namaskṛtya yayau punaḥ punaḥ (24.46)

su – very; dustyaja — being difficult to part with; sneha — one who is loved; viyoga — separation; kātaro = kātaraḥ — beside himself; na – not; śaknuvaṁs = śaknuvan — being capable, could do; tam — him; parihātum — to leave; āturaḥ — overwhelmed; krcchran – painful emotions; yayau — he experienced; mūrdhani — on the head; bhartṛ — master; pāduke — the sandals; bibhran — placing; namaskṛtya — bow down, respectfully; yayau — went away; punah punah — again and again.

Translation

Being besides himself because of separation from the Beloved, one whom it is very difficult to part with, and being overwhelmed with painful emotions, he could not leave. Placing the master's sandals on his head, bowing down again and again, he went away. (24.46)

Commentary:

Uddhava did finally agree to do what *Śrī* Krishna requested. Uddhava was pained emotionally in his subtle body which become attached to *Śrī* Krishna's physical presence, but Uddhava took courage and moved on to perfect yoga practice, for his own and for *Śrī* Krishna's sake.

There are several illusions which Uddhava will have to purify himself of. The first is his attachment to *Śrī* Krishna's physical presence. The second is his attachment to *Śrī* Krishna's subtle body which is made of subtle mundane energy. And the third is his attachment to *Śrī* Krishna's causal form. All these will have to become insignificant to Uddhava, through mastership of higher yoga, in which he would progressively shift his attention from the physical to the subtle, from the subtle to the causal and then to the spiritual at last.

Other authorities fail to distinguish between the various bodies of *Śrī* Krishna, because they cannot admit that He had or can have any other body besides His spiritual form. And so for them the confusion will go on.

ततस् तम् अन्तर् हृदि सन्निवेश्य
गतो महा-भागवतो विशालाम् ।
यथोपदिष्टां जगद्-एक-बन्धुना
तपः समास्थाय हरेर् अगाद् गतिम् ॥२४.४७॥

tatas tam antar hṛdi sanniveśya
gato mahā-bhāgavato viśālām
yathopadiṣṭāṁ jagad-eka-bandhunā
tapaḥ samāsthāya harer agād gatim (24.47)

tatas = tataḥ — then; tam — him (lord Krishna); antar = antah — in; hṛdi — in the core of his being; sanniveśya — investing; gato = gatah — went; mahā – great; bhāgavato = bhāgavataḥ — devotee; viśālām — to Badarikāśrama; yathopadiṣṭāṁ = yathā — as + upadiṣṭām — instructed; jagad = jagat — world; eka — one; bandhunā — by the friend; tapaḥ — austerity; samāsthāya — properly practicing; harer = hareḥ — of Lord Hari Krishna; agād = agāt — reached; gatim — abode.

Translation

Then investing Lord Krishna in the core of his being, the great devotee went to Viśālā Badarinath Shrine, just as instructed by the one friend of the world. By properly practicing the austerities he reached the abode of Lord Hari, Krishna. (24.47)

Commentary:

If the yoga austerities *(tapah)* were necessary for a person like Uddhava, one who was described as the best of the devotees of *Śrī* Krishna, then we can just imagine that these austerities would be required for most other devotees. If Uddhava could not by himself detach himself from the influence of his physical and subtle material forms and their mental and emotional energies *(prāṇa-citta)*, then how can anyone else?

It is wishful thinking if we feel that we can become perfected or that we may go to the kingdom of God without doing yoga practice. It is simply a big joke played on us by the great preachers, who are themselves under the influence of the subtle material nature.

य एतद् आनन्द-समुद्र-सम्भृतं
ज्ञानामृतं भागवताय भाषितम् ।
कृष्णेन योगेश्वर-सेविताङ्घ्रिणा
सच्-छ्रद्धयासेव्य जगद् विमुच्यते ॥२४.४८॥

ya etad ānanda-samudra-sambhṛtaṁ
jñānāmṛtaṁ bhāgavatāya bhāṣitam
kṛṣṇena yogeśvara-sevitāṅghriṇā
sac-chraddhayāsevya jagad vimucyate (24.48)

ya = yah — he who; etad = etat — this; ānanda — spiritual happiness; samudra — ocean; sambhṛtam — imbibes; jñānāmṛtaṁ = jñāna — knowledge + amṛtam — nectar; bhāgavatāya — to one who is devoted; bhāṣitam — was imparted; kṛṣṇena — by Krishna; yogeśwara — masters of yoga disciplines; sevitāṅghriṇā = sevita — is served + aṅghriṇā — by whose feet; sac = sat — real; chraddhayāsevya = śraddhayā — with faith + āsevya — serving; jagad = jagat — world; vimucyate — frees himself.

Translation

He who absorbs this ocean of spiritual happiness, this nectar of knowledge, which was imparted to the devotee Uddhava, by Krishna, whose feet is served by the lordly masters of yoga, and who does so with real faith while serving, frees himself and the world as well. (24.48)

Commentary:

This has to do with the devotees who mastered the higher yoga practice. *Bhakti* or devotion and yoga austerities go good together. Both compliment each other. A concerted effort should be made by all devotees of *Śrī* Krishna to perfect yoga, while loving *Śrī* Krishna, just as Uddhava was instructed in this discourse. There is no point trying to avoid yoga or in trying to cause *Śrī* Krishna to change the path of salvation to suit our dislike of yoga. What we need is to change our attitude and accept the suggestions of the Lord, instead of trying to change His view. Actually the Lord's views cannot be changed because the requirements for salvation remain the same from Age to Age, even though the beginning point changes. One may begin from a lower point in a more degraded Era but still again one will have to reach a level where one accepts the higher course of salvation, just as Uddhava had to accept and agree to perform the austerities.

भव-भयम् अपहन्तुं ज्ञान-विज्ञान-सारं
निगम-कृद् उपजह्रे भृङ्ग-वद् वेद-सारम् ।
अमृतम् उदधितश् चापाययद् भृत्य-वर्गान्
पुरुषम् ऋषभम् आद्यं कृष्ण-सञ्ज्ञं नतो ऽस्मि
॥२४.४९॥

bhava-bhayam apahantuṁ jñāna-vijñāna-sāraṁ
nigama-kṛd upajahre bhṛṅga-vad veda-sāram
amṛtam udadhitaś cāpāyayad bhṛtya-vargān
puruṣam ṛṣabham ādyaṁ kṛṣṇa-saṁjñaṁ nato 'smi (24.49)

bhava — of relative existence; bhayam — fear; apahantum — to take away; jñāna – knowledge; vijñāna — mystic and spiritual experience; sāram — highest aspect; nigama — of the Vedas; kṛd = kṛt — revealer; upajahre — extracted; bhṛṅga – bee; vad = vat — like; veda – Veda; sāram — essential part; amṛtam — nectar; udadhitaś = udadhitaḥ — from the ocean; cāpāyayad = ca — and + apāyayat — cause to be drunk, fed; bhṛtya – servant; vargān — groups; puruṣam — person; ṛṣabham — best; ādyam — the first; kṛṣṇa – Krishna; saṁjñam — known; nato = nataḥ — obeisances; 'smi = asmi — I.

Translation

That revealer of the Vedas, who takes away the fear of relative existence, did like a bee extract the essential part of the Vedas which is the highest aspect of knowledge, mystic and spiritual experiences, as He did remove nectar from the ocean and fed it to the groups of His servants. I make obeisances to that first and best, the Person known as Krishna. (24.49)

Commentary:

Śrī Krishna is specifically the person who removes our fear of relative existence, of our own or anyone else's relative body, just as He did for Uddhava who was fearful of parting from *Śrī* Krishna's temporary forms (bhava).

We should not be fearful of leaving our own nor anyone else's material forms. If we experience such fear and if it overpowers our emotions, it means that those emotions are not spiritual feelings. As *Śrī* Krishna tried to teach Arjuna the most basic lesson as follows:

na tvevāhaṁ jātu nāsaṁ na tvaṁ neme janādhipāḥ
na caiva na bhaviṣyāmaḥ sarve vayamataḥ param

There was never a time when I did not exist, nor you, nor these rulers of the people. Nor will we cease to exist from now onwards. (B.G. 2.12)

One should not think that he can be separated from anyone but if one is overcome with those emotions, in regards to *Śrī* Krishna just as Uddhava was, then one's only reprieve is to put to use these instructions which were given to Uddhava. Ultimately, apart from hearing and reading of this, one has to apply yoga practice in order to gain the purification which would cause one to transcend the mental and emotional impurities, which we derived from subtle material nature.

This takes us back to the *Bhagavad-Gītā* instruction which was given to Arjuna. Once we master that, we can apply these instructions for higher yoga which were given to *Śrī* Uddhava. There are many mystic actions which we need practice to perfection. They were given in this discourse. A devotee has to bring himself to a level where he can become proficient in these. Thus following in the footsteps of the deserving Uddhava we may fairly and squarely, truly and definitely, attain perfection.

OM TAT SAT

Jai Śrī Krishna!

Hare Kṛṣṇa Hare Kṛṣṇa Kṛṣṇa Kṛṣṇa Hare Hare
Hare Rāma Hare Rāma Rāma Rāma Hare Hare

Indexed Names of Uddhava

aṅga —dear friend
anuvrataḥ - devoted follower
bārhaspatya — disciple of Bṛhaspati
bhadra —friend
bhāgavata mukhyena – leader of devotees
bhūri-da — generous one
dāśārha —son of the Dāśārha family
mahā-bhāga — blessed person
mahā-mate —talented one
purusarṣabha — best of the persons
sabhya — cultured one
sādhah, sādho —saint
sattama —best of the realistic people.
śrī – the deserving, the worthy

Indexed Names of Krishna

acyuta — Acyuta, unaffected one
adbhuta-darśanam — one who was spectacular to see
adhokṣajam — one who is beyond mundane sense perception
ādyam — the first
ajādya — source of Procreator Brahmā
ajah — birthless person
ajita — unconquerable one
akhiladhara — support of the whole world
akhilatmani — the Self Who is the basis of all
akuṇṭha vikuṇṭha-dhiṣṇyam – one whose residence is the changeless Vaikuntha paradise
amitra-karśana — subduer of the enemy
amṛtam — the immortal reality
anādy-antam apāvṛtam — without beginning or ending, unlimited
ananta-pāraṁ — infinite beyond everything
anavadyam — flawless
apavargaḥ — final objective
aravindākṣa — lotus-eyed one
aravinda-locana — lotus-eyed Lord
aśeṣa-bandho — friend of everyone
aśeṣātman — Complete Spirit
ātma amīṣāṁ bhūtānāṁ suhṛd īśvaraḥ — the self of these creatures, their friend and Lord
ātmānam ātmani — self in the spiritual self
ātmāntaro — interiorized self of all embodied beings
ātmārāmeśvaram — the master of those who delight in their spiritual selves
ātma-stham — spirit situated
avyakta-jīva-mahatām — the ruler of the Unmanifested Energy, of the individual souls and of the reservoir of manifestible mundane potency
bhagavan — O Blessed Lord
bhagavantam — the exalted Supreme Lord
bhagavat — one with the most skills
bhavatā — respected sir
bhūman — O Almighty God
bhūmnā brahmaṇānanta-śaktinā — Infinite Ultimate Reality of endless potency
bhūta-bhāvana — originator of the beings
bhūtānāṁ sthitir utpattir pratisaṅkramaḥ — the maintenance, origination and annihilation of the creatures
bhūtātmā — self of the created beings
brahma paramaṁ sākṣād — Supreme Spirit in Person
brahma paramaṁ vyoma — Supreme Spirit, Who is like the sky
deva — God
deva-deveśa — O God of the greatest rulers of the supernatural kings
devakī-sutaḥ — the son of Devaki
dharma-maye — One Whose nature is composed of the righteous way of life
dharmasya brahma-vādinām — Lord of Yoga of the Samkhya philosophical analysis, of righteous duty and of the teachers of spirituality
dhātrā — origin of the world
dhvajātapatra-vyajanaiḥ — supernatural form, which is adorned with the śrīvatsa curl of hair, with a weapon, a banner, an umbrella and a chowry fan
gatir gatimatāṁ — objective of those seeking progress
govinda — Govinda
gūḍhaś carasi – One Who roams about hidden in all beings
gunāṇāṁ sāmyaṁ — the state of equilibrium of the modes of material nature
haṁsa-rūpa —the Swan Form
harih — Hari
hetuḥ patir ahaṁ prabhuḥ — the cause, the master and Lord of all mystic skills
hetur udaya-sthiti-saṁyamānām — cause of creation, continuation and annihilation of this manifestation
hṛṣīka-pate — master of the senses
īdya — worshipable one
īśa — Lord
īśvaram — Lord of the world
īśvareśvaraḥ — Lord of lords
jagad-īśvaram — Lord of the universe
jagat-krīḍanakaḥ — One whose plaything is the world
jagat-prabho — Lord of the universe
jñāninas iṣṭaḥ — the desired goal of the ascetic philosopher
kālaḥ kalayatām – One who is time amongst the conquerors
kālam tri-ṇābhir – One who is time with its three partitions
kālātmanā — time itself
kāla-vigrahe — One who assumes the form of Time

kamala-patrāksa — one whose eyes are shaped like lotus petals
kartrāvitrā pravaktrā — the originator, protector and instructor of righteous living
keśava — Keśava
kevalaḥ — one who is not influenced by sensing mechanisms
lokādhyakṣa — Lord of the worlds
loka-nāthena — Lord of the world
mādhava — Madhava
madhusūdana — slayer of Madhu
mahānubhāva — great majestic personality
mahā-vibhūte — superperson of wonderful forms
mukundah — Mukunda
nara-sakhaṁ — the friend of the human being
nārāyaṇaṁ — Nārāyaṇā
nārāyaṇātmakam - Nārāyaṇā Himself
nātha — Lord
nirguṇe brahmaṇi — the spiritual existence beyond the mundane influence
param — Supreme Being
paramātmānam — the Supreme Spirit
parasya — One who is superior
yogasya sāṅkhyasya satyasyartasya tejasaḥ parāyaṇaṁ dvija-śreṣṭhāḥ śriyaḥ kīrter damasya ca — the supreme shelter of the yoga process, and of the Samkhya philosophical analysis, realism, religious principles, valor, opulence, fame and self control.
prabho — Lord
prakṛti-pūruṣayoḥ — exploiter of material nature
prāyaṇaṁ satām — objective of the reality-perceptive persons
protam aśeṣam otaṁ paṭo yathā tantu-vitāna-saṁsthaḥ — Person on Whom as its crosswise and lengthwise basis, this whole system, is situated, as a cloth on a network of threads.
pumān — Primal Male Being
pundarīkākṣa — lotus-eyed one
puṇya-śravaṇa-kīrtana — person of whom it is auspicious to hear of and chant of
puruṣādhyakṣa — Lord of people
puruṣaḥ prakṛteḥ paraḥ — Primal Person who is beyond material nature
puruṣekṣayā — Primal Person
purusottama — Supreme Person
ṛṣabha — best, greatest of all
sanātane — Primeval God
sarva-dharma-jña — knower of the methods of righteous living
sarva-jña — omniscient one
sarvāṇi bhūtāni teṣāṁ sthity-udbhavāpyayaḥ — cause of all creatures and of their living condition, birth and death.
sarvāsām siddhīnāṁ patir prabhuh—master and lord of all mystic skills
sarvātman — self of all, soul of all beings
sarva-yajña-patiṁ — Lord of all religious ceremonies and disciplines
sṛjato 'ṇḍāni koṭiśaḥ — One Who created millions of universes
śuddhe — Person of full existential purity
sva-dṛśa — self-revealing
svāmin — master
śvetadvīpa-patau — Lord of the White Island Paradise
tasthūṣaś ca jagataś ca bhavān adhīśo — Supreme Lord of the movable and immovable objects the Infinite Ultimate Reality of endless potency
trāṇa-sthity-apyayodbhavaḥ — the protector, maintainer and destroyer and creator of all beings
try-adhīśvare — Supreme Lord of the three influences of material nature
turīya — person in the fourth dimension of existence
uccāvaceṣu bhūteṣu – one who is in the superior and inferior created beings
uttama-pūruṣa — Supreme Person
uttama-śloka — person of unsurpassed glorification
vadatāṁ vara — best of teachers
vibho — Almighty Lord
viṣṇau — Vishnu
viśva-mūrte — form of the universe
viśvātman — Soul of the universe
viśveśa — Lord of the Universe
viśveśvara = viśva īśvara — Lord of the universe
viśveśvareśvara — Lords of the lords of the universe
yogātman — Yoga in person
yoga-sambhava — origin of the yoga discipline
yogeśa — Supreme Master of yoga
yoga-vinyāsa — treasure of yoga practice
yogeśvareśvara — Master of the masters of the yoga discipline

Index to Translation

A

A, Krishna as, 11.12
abandonment, 9.10
Abhijit, 11.27
abhisheka, 22.30
absence of Krishna, 7.11
absorption in Krishna, 9.14, 28
absorption of intelligence, 14.36
abstract energy, 20.31
abstract existence, 10.14
abusive language, 13.30-31
accomplice, 22.55
achievement, 15.12
acquisitions, 4.1
acting, 6.23
activity, 6.22, 8.4
adhibhūtam, 17.30
Adhokṣaja, 21.15
adhyatmam, 17.30
adidaivam, 17.30
Aditi, 1.1; 11.13
administrators, 12.17
advanced soul, 21.30-31
adversity, 12.49
aerial conveyances, 10.25
affected, 5.21
affection,
  energies, 9.2
  problematic, 2.52
  severed, 24.39
  Vishnu's energy, 2.61
Age of Easy Achievement, 12.10
Age of Easy Realization, 19.2
agent, 20.30
aggression,
  motivational influence, 20.3
  relinquished, 14.37
Āghāra, 22.41
agitation, 17.13, 32
Agnihotra, 13.8
agonies, 10.18
agreeable nature, 12.21
agreeable speech, 11.26
aim of life, 9.10
air,
  effects, 16.12
  Krishna as, 11.37
  production, 19.24
  teacher, 2.33
  worship, 6.42-6.44
Ajah Brahmā, 11.26
Ajah succession, 22.3
Akrura, 7.10
akṣa beads, 12.23; 18.34
Alakananda, 24.42
alertness, clarity, 20.20
Almighty God, 2.47
alms, 3.11
aloe wood, 22.30
alphabet, 16.38
altar, 22.36
alternatives, 6.22
ambitions, 9.10
analysis,
  body's 21.20
  proof, 14.17
  required, 13.27; 15.23; 23.9
  retiree's, 13.22
ancestor,
  shareholder, 18.24
  worship, 1.37; 12.50; 16.30
Andhaka, 24.39
angelic beings, 1.3
angelic females, 7.3; 11.33
angelic world, 20.21-22
anger,
  assertive sense, 23.15
  depressive energy, 20.4,9
  tendency, 12.20; 18.18-19
Angira,1.1; 22.2
animal, 4.28; 7.3,8
animal sacrifice, 5.28; 13.7; 16.29-30
animal species, 17.51
animal world, 20.22
annihilation, 11.35
anniversaries, 6.36
annual plants, 11.21
anus, 17.15
anus lock, 10.24
Anuṣṭup, 16.41
anxiety, destroyed, 8.33; 18.18
appraisal, 23.1
appropriation power, 10.13; 11.36
approval urge, 19.5
approved behaviors, 2.11; 14.34
approver, 22.55
aquatics, 10.29; 11.17
arguments, 17.5-6
Arjuna, 11.6-8, 35
armpit, 12.24
arrogance, 18.18-19
arrow, 22.27
arrow-maker, 2.34; 4.13
art, 6.39
artist, 22.38
Aryamā, 11.15
āsana, 8.13; 23.39
ascertainment, 17.50
ascetic,
  attitude, 13.23
  beggar, 18.5
  devotional passage, 13.45
  dispassion, 4.30
  food, 13.25
  responsibility free, 4.4
  socially-separated, 2.25
  teachers of, 2.32
  unaffected, 2.29
  wanderings, 13.24
  worry-free, 4.3
  Yadu met, 2.24
asceticism,
  elderly years, 18.29
  lifestyle, 18.32
ashes, 9.19
ashram
  approved, 6.38
  regulations, 12.22-32
ass, 8.8
assertion
  destroyed, 23.17
  details, 17.32
  energy, 10.13
  factor, 17.14
  Krishna as, 11.37
assertive sense,
  cosmic, 19.6
  limitations, 23.15
  non-energetic, 19.8
  source, 19.25
  three-fold, 19.7
assessment, 23.1
association,
  advanced, 21.28
  desired, 6.25
  devotees, 6.48
  effects, 7.3
  Krishna prefers, 7.2-3
  restrictions, 21.3
  saint's, 21.26
  sexual type, 21.22
  temporary? 12.53
  tendency producing, 8.4
  vital, 21.33

asterism, 11.27
Aśvini, 1.1
atheism, 12.20
atheist, 24.30
Aticchanda, 16.41
Atijagati, 16.41
Ativirāṭ, 16.41
atmosphere, 17.14
atomic form, 10.10
atomic size, 10.4
attachment,
association effective, 7.2
conventional, 16.24
counterproductive, 15.16
impulsive, 20.14
removal of, 9.2
Uddhava's, 2.16
value based, 16.19
attention, linkage, 10.10, 11
attitude, 2.11; 13.39
attractive objects, 3.36; 8.8
Atyaṣṭi, 16.41
austerity,
aim of life? 9.10
approved behavior, 14.3
brahmin's mission, 12.42
compared, 1.9
defined, 14.37
disposition, 12.16
dissipation of, 11.43
effective, 23.39
experience compared, 14.4
householder's, 13.43
insufficient, 9.22
Krishna not attained by, 7.9
mystic skills gained, 10.34
perceptive influence, 20.2
purificatory, 16.14
purpose preferred, 13.10
required, 12.36; 23.18
result ultimate, 19.14
retiree's duty, 13.42
spirited devotion, 9.20
Uddhava's path, 24.47
unnecessary, 7.7
authority, 16.10
Avanti brahmin, 18.6, 31
awareness, 19.4

B

baby birds, 2.63
Bādarāyaṇa, 1.20; 18.1
Badarīnātha shrine, 24.41, 47
Bala, 22.28
Balarāma, 7.10
Bali, 7.6; 11.35
Bamboo, 8.7
Bāna, 7.6
banner, 10.30
banyan tree, 11.21
bark, 7.22; 13.2
barley, 11.21
basic survival, 16.4
bath,
Deity, 22.14
offerings, 22.35
purificatory, 16.14
regulation, 22.10
retiree's, 13.3
speech restraint, 12.24
bear, 7.6
beard, 13.3
beauty, 14.41
bed, 13.3
bee keeper, 2.34
bee,
eating habit, 3.9
hoarder, 3.11
teacher, 2.33
yogi entry compared, 10.23
begging,
Avanti brahmin, 18.32
depressive energy, 20.4
student's, 12.28
behavior,
categories, 20.26
codes, 9.10
listing, 14.34
mind control, 18.46
tendencies, 6.5
belief, 9.8
belief in God, 12.18
bell, 5.25; 9.34
bellows, 16.22
belt, 12.23; 22.36
benefits renounced, 14.38
best for Krishna, 6.41
betel nut, 22.43
bewildering objects, 3.8
bewilderment, 20.15
Bhagavan, 10.16
bhakti yoga,
all-inclusive, 15.33
applicants, 15.8
defined, 15.6
destination, 19.14
details, 20.32
effectiveness, 15.29
functional, 6.48
independent, 9.2
meditation, 6.47
practice, 23.27
simple, 6.22
technique, 22.53
Bhava Shiva, 22.3
Bhishma, 14.11, 13
Bhṛgu,
Krishna as, 11.14
Manu instructed, 9.4
succession, 22.3
Bhūr, 19.11-12
Bhūva, 19.11-12
bird, 4.28; 6.6; 11.15
bird catcher, 2.63, 72; 7.6
bird nest,
abandoned, 15.15
material existence, 7.22
birds liberated, 7.3
birth
assertive sense, 23.15
body stage, 17.46
death, 2.49
defined, 17.39-41
God's powers, 2.58
human, 18.22-23
Krishna as, 11.9
mystic skills, 10.34
tendency, 8.4
birthless person, 19.27
blame, 18.51-57
blood, 21.21
boat, 21.32
bodily energy, 11.32
body
bewitching, 15.13
control, 12.35
decomposition, 19.22
Deity worship, 22.22
destiny controlled, 8.37
detachment, 23.31
deteriorates, 4.26
entry, 10.23
existential dwelling, 3.33
factor, 17.19
nine stages, 17.46
owners? 4.25; 21.19
perfection, 15.14
Pingalā critiques, 3.33
preference, 2.22
regard for, 8.36
restraint, 13.17
satisfying it, 4.26
spirit furnished, 16.5
teacher, 4.25
tolerated, 8.37
transmigration, 5.10
type attained, 17.34
yoga curbs, 8.7
body-borne souls, 2.17
bond of affection, 24.39
bondage,
perception causes, 6.4
sensual dispersion, 13.22
bone, 3.33; 16.12; 21.21
boundaries, 1.30
bow, 11.20; 22.27
bracelets, 4.6, 7
Brahmā,
austerity, 19.11
baffled, 8.18
court of, 12.5
emergence, 19.10
entourage, 1.1

Brahmā, continued,
Krishna as, 11.12, 22
Krishna connected to, 8.19
Krishna feared by, 5.30
Krishna production, 24.37
Krishna visited by, 1.1; 2.1
life span, 5.30
master of supernaturals, 1.28
meditation, 8.18
obeisances by, 1.32
planet, 12.31; 14.18
position unwanted, 9.14
residence attained, 22.52
Sanaka's father, 8.16
snakes created, 19.13
spirit furnished, 16.5
succession, 22.3
Swan instructed, 12.3
Uddhava compared, 9.15
Uddhava criticized, 2.17
Veda told to, 9.3
vocabulary producer, 16.40
wicked spirits, 19.13
world creator, 19.11
brahmacari, 12.22
brahmarandra, 10.24
brahmin,
assistance to, 12.44
Avanti merchant, 18.6
birth, 18.22-23
curse, 1.31
dispositions, 12.16
duties, 12.40
food acquirement, 12.42, 43
independence of, 12.41
insulted, 18.33-40
Krishna worship, 11.2
livelihood rules, 12.47
offence to, 22.54
origin, 12.12-13
purpose, 12.42
rites, 12.22
ruler as, 12.48
student worships, 12.26
super-strict, 12.41
thread, 12.23
wives, 7.6
worship facility, 6.42-43
branches, 7.22
breath control, 4.11
Bṛhaspati, 11.22; 18.2; 22.2-3
Bṛhati, 16.41
buddhi yoga, 7.24
bull, standard, 1.14; 12.11-13
business, 6.24
businessman,
brahmin as, 12.47
career options, 12.49
origin, 12.12-13

C

calamity,
Dvāraka, 1.33
king's responsibility, 12.45
call prayer, 22.41
camphor, 22.30
Canda, 22.28
cannibal, 20.19; 24.16
careers, source of, 12.14, 15
carefree person, 9.16
casino, 20.25
caste system, 12.47-49
cāturmāsa, 13.8
causal body,
abandonment, 20.36
blockage, 15.30
dismembered, 7.24
indicated, 22.23
Supersoul within, 7.17
causal cavity, see causal body
causal energy,
origination, 17.17
Primal Person, 17.18
cause / effect, 17.7-8; 19.20
Causeless Om Sound, 12.11
causes, three-fold, 17.12,30
cavity, 22.36
celestial musicians, 7.3
celestial singers, 7.3
celestial spirit, 7.4
celestial women, 10.25
celibacy,
Brahmā's planet, 12.31
effective, 12.36
householder's, 13.43
moral restraint, 14.33
origin, 12.14
regulations, 12.25
ceremonial purification, 12.34
ceremonial water pot, 22.20
ceremonial worship, 7.1; 22.7
chakra, 9.34,36
chance, destiny, 2.63; 3.2; 6.6
Chandra, 1.36
chanting,
advanced, 21.29-31
approved, 6.36; 14.3
Deity worship, 22.22
effective, 23.39
experience compared, 14.4
householder's, 13.43
niyama rule, 12.34
speech restraint, 12.24
chants, mystic skills, 10.34
character faults, 13.41
character, wealth, 14.43
charisma, mystic skill, 10.7
charitable nature, 12.18
charity,
aim of life, 9.10
compared, 1.9
compensation, 1.38
dissipation of, 11.43
evaluated, 18.47
experience compared, 14.4
householder's, 13.43
Krishna not attained by, 7.9
Krishna's regard for, 7.1
mind control process, 18.46
perceptive influence, 20.2
purificatory, 16.14
charm, 11.40
cheaters, 11.31
chewing, 22.43
child care, 2.59
child, teacher, 2.34
childhood, 17.46
childlike behavior, 13.29
children,
focus on, 12.56
indifference towards, 5.7
nonproductive type, 6.19
choir, 17.52
chowry fan, 10.30
circumstance, 9.13; 16.11
circumstantial detachment, 10.8
citta vritti nirodhah, 17.56
clairaudience, 10.6, 19
clairvoyance, 10.6, 20
clarifying energy/influence,
described, 20.10
details, 20.2
effects, 20.13
Krishna as, 11.31, 37
mastery of, 8.1
required, 8.2
transmigration, 20.21-22
clarifying power, 4.12
clarity,
development, 8.6
heaven, 14.42
highest, 14.37
clay, 22.10, 12, 14
cleanliness,
approved behavior, 14.3
disposition, 12.16
Krishna as, 11.23
niyama rule, 12.34
cleansed mind linkage, 10.17
cloth,
compared, 7.21
retiree's, 13.2
clothing, 3.8; 22.32
clouds, 2.43
club, 6.46; 22.27
collecting produce, 12.41
combustion, 17.21
combustives, 2.43

commodities, 16.7
community influence, 17.30
comparative assessment, 8.40
comparative similarity, 9.16; 13.20; 14.37; 24.14
compassion, 20.2
competence, 11.44
components, 17.22
composite world, 19.16
conceited person, 24.30
concentration,
details, 15.18-22
tendency producing, 8.4
conception,
basis, 2.8
false, 17.54
concepts, 5.14
conch, 6.46
conch bracelets, 4.6, 4.7
conclusions, 2.20
condemnation, 23.1
conditioned soul, 6.8
confidence,
Krishna, 15.9
mundane influence, 20.30
righteous duty causes, 20.7
confusion,
assertive sense, 23.15
depressive energy, 20.4
congregational singing, 13.43
connotations, 8.4
conscience, 16.20-21
consciousness,
objects pursue, 8.25
restraint, 13.17
consecrated ground, 6.45
consequences,
destroyed, 2.46
proportional, 22.55
removal, 9.25
consonants, 16.39
consumptive disease, 1.36
contact,
Krishna, 15.9
production, 19.24
containment, 16.13
contemplation, 4.23
contention,
philosophers, 17.5-6
tendency, 18.18-19
contentment,
approved behavior, 14.34
disposition, 12.16
householder's, 13.43
perceptive influence, 20.2
continuity, 11.27; 14.15
contrary actions, 15.10
contributions, 22.51
control, 11.42
controller, 11.38
controlling mystic skill, 10.15
convention of attachments, 16.24
conventional considerations, 23.33
conviction, Krishna as, 11.37
core self, 14.25
cosmic assertive sense, 19.6
cosmic egg, 19.9
cosmic form, 10.11
cosmic lotus flower, 7.20
cosmic potency, 10.14; 23.16
cosmic size, 10.4
cosmic vital force, 16.38
cosmos, 19.21
counting of atoms, 11.39
courage,
disposition, 12.17
motivational influence, 20.3
courtesy, evaluated, 18.47
covetousness, 20.3
cow,
behavior, 13.29
compared, 6.18
Kāmadhenu, 11.14
liberated, 7.8
respected, 24.16
value of, 6.19
worship, 6.42-43; 12.26
craving,
abandonment, 14.37
attachment, 16.19
development, 8.10
impulsive, 20.9
motivational, 20.3
renunciation, 2.15
tendency, 12.20
creation,
change essential, 17.29
higher stage, 4.28
lower stage, 4.28
residual energy, 14.16
creative durations, 19.21
creature forms,
essential nature, 13.32
spirit furnished, 16.5
Supersoul inhabits, 13.32
criminals,
impulsive influence, 20.19
thief of wealth, 18.11
crisis, 18.28
critique, 23.1
crocodile of death, 22.46
crosswise/lengthwise, 7.21
cruelty,
depressive energy, 20.4,15
retardative influence, 20.23
cultural activity,
absorbing, 22.5
all pervasive, 19.15
attitude towards, 2.11
categorized, 20.23
cultural activity, continued,
death baffles, 5.19
decreased, 5.4
evolution related, 17.34, 36
family life, 4.26
forced? 5.17
heavenly results, 5.24
impulsion, 17.13; 20.14
impure, 15.26
incidental, 18.43, 55
liberation, 1.7
limit, 15.9, 32
material nature's tendency, 7.21
mind control, 18.46
mind promotes, 18.44
miserable, 9.11
mistake? 16.16
mundane influence, 20.30
on-going, 23.30
purity of, 16.14
rejected, 14.18
relinquishment, 24.34
removal of, 9.25
renounced, 7.14; 14.38
renunciation gradual, 4.12
renunciation of results, 2.14
ritual purification, 22.11
sensual energy creates, 5.31
terminal type, 5.4
transmigration, 17.51; 20.32
Vedic regulations, 16.7
cultural identity, 17.44
cymbals, 5.25

D

dainties, 22.35
dairy products, 11.30
Dakṣa, curse, 1.36; 11.15
dancers, 17.52
dancing,
approved, 6.36
Deity related, 22.44
offerings, 22.35
danda, 13.17, 40
dangers, 10.8
Danu, 9.5
dark rain cloud, 9.39
Darśa, 13.8
Dāśārha, 17.54; 18.1; 24.39
death,
assertive sense, 23.15
attainment, 4.22
body stage, 17.46
forgetfulness, 17.38, 40
instinctive fear, 16.22
Krishna as, 11.9
kundalini departure, 10.24
retiree's, 13.11
satisfaction? 5.20
December, 11.27
decomposition, 19.22

decorate Deity, 22.32
deduction, 17.47
deep sleep, 8.27
deer skin, 12.23; 13.2
deer,
music captures, 3.17
teacher, 2.34
defect,
conditional, 16.11
defined, 16.2
degradation,
discussed, 16.17
worm species, 22.54
Deity Form,
bath, 22.30
called, 22.41
conception, 22.38
decorating, 22.15
deliverance by self, 2.19
description, 22.38
dismissal, 22.13, 47
ingredients, 22.15
installation, 6.38
invitation, 22.13
Krishna as, 11.32
link to, 6.46
materials, 22.12
movable? 22.13
ornaments, 22.39
prayer, 22.42
Deity Worship,
daily procedure, 12.50
devotional reward, 22.52
opulence, 24.11
recommended, 6.34
regulations, 22.8-52
sanctification, 22.24
set-up, 22.19
delusion,
cause, 17.32
money causes, 18.18
removal, 16.18
demerit,
defined, 16.2
elaboration, 11.45
departed ancestors,
Aryamā, 11.15
worship, 12.50; 16.38
worship for, 1.37
dependence, 5.32
dependents, 12.51
depressive energy, 20.4, 15, 18
depressive persons, 7.4
desire,
assertive sense, 23.15
Krishna compared, 9.14
mystic skill, 10.14, 26
destinations hereafter, 17.51
destiny,
controller, 2.37
design of, 4.26
food controlled, 13.33-35
inconveniences, 18.41
destroyer of three cities, 11.20
destroyer of world, 13.45
destruction, 5.21
detachment,
clarifying, 20.16
effective, 5.22
ideal type, 2.40
Krishna dedication, 8.41
mystic skill, 10.6
practical, 6.11-12, 15-16
ultimate, 21.2; 23.8
yoga practice, 4.11
detecting potencies, 17.15
deva worship, 16.32-33
Devakī, 1.50
Devala Asita, 11.28
devatāh, 1.1
Devavrata, 14.13
Devī, 22.3
devotee,
activities, 24.11
advanced type, 6.25; 20.34-36; 21.27, 30; 27.18-19
Arjuna, 11.29
association, 7.2-3
best type, 6.33
compared, 9.16, 17
competence, 11.44
family indifference, 5.7
Krishna focus, 6.33
moral restraint, 5.5
neophyte, 15.27
process inclusive, 15.32
qualities, 5.6
recommended behavior, 5.5
requirements, 5.6
resignation, 15.34
rewards, 22.51-52
self-controlled type, 1.10
separation, 1.45
spiritual teacher served by, 5.5
worship facility, 6.42-6.44
devotion,
advanced, 21.29-31
all-inclusive, 15.33
control added, 11.44
desirelessness, 15.35
disciple's, 13.39
dispassion, 15.35
disposition, 12.16
faults destroyer, 9.19
methods, 14.20-24
necessary, 9.22
devotion, continue,
passage to Krishna, 13.45
profit as, 14.40
protective, 9.18
required, 7.24
result ultimate, 19.14
righteous duty, 12.1, 7; 13.44; 15.11
spirited type, 9.20-21
steady, 6.25
types, 6.26
worship develops, 13.44
yoga application, 14.8, 19; 20.32; 22.53; 23.27
yoga expertise, 6.48
yogically-focused, 9.25
devotional activities, 14.20-24
devotional excitement, 9.23
devotional service,
assumed, 18.58
Deity related, 22.44
mode, 20.10-11
niyama rule, 12.34
option, 6.22, 24
required, 15.23
righteous duty? 24.20
devotional worship, 6.34
Dharma Deity, 22.25, 41
dhiya lamp, 6.40
dhyāna practice,
Krishna linkage, 10.21
procedure, 9.37
proficiency, 9.43, 45
diet, 12.43
difference, God/individual, 17.11
dimension, 4th, 8.28-29; 10.16
direct perception, 2.20; 23.18
disc, 6.46; 22.27
discernment, 11.24
disciple,
comparison, 5.12
duty, 13.42
fees, 12.37
menial servant, 12.29
requirements, 12.22-32
services, 13.39
teacher interaction, 5.12
disciplic succession,
Manu's, 9.4-6
updated, 12.4
discipline,
aim of life? 9.10
supreme one, 18.46
discontentment, 14.44
discrimination,
defective, 11.45
dream, 23.3
required, 23.18
spirit/matter, 11.24
discussions of Krishna, 1.48

disease compared, 23.28
disguised yogi, 2.46
disgust,
Avanti brahmin's, 18.13, 28
cultural activities, 15.7, 18
extreme type, 13.12-13
Pingalā, 3.27
special type, 18.28
total, 13.38
Vishnu produces, 3.37
dishonesty, 12.20
disillusionment, 20.4; 24.2
dismissal of Deity, 22.13
dispassion,
ascetic's, 4.30
beauty, 14.41
clarity enriches, 14.25
defined, 14.27
limited, 15.32
disposition, 1.9
dispute, 16.20
dissolution, 14.15; 19.21
distraction, 14.42
distress,
cause, 6.2
tendency, 18.18-19
tolerated, 14.36
types, 5.14
Diti, 11.16
diversity,
attractive, 5.32
bewildering, 5.33
detachment from, 6.13
illusion, 23.4-7
inconsequential, 5.3
mundane energy, 17.12
Sāṇkhya explained, 19.1-29
divine knowledge, 15.11
doctrines, 9.7
doe, 3.18
doer mentality, 6.10
dog,
body scavenger, 21.19
brahmin compared, 12.47
human compared, 8.8
respected, 24.16
ruler compared, 12.48
dog-meat eaters, 9.21
domestic animals, 4.26
donation,
approved, 22.51
detrimental? 12.41
donation of benefits, 20.2
donkey,
husband, 12.13; 21.11
respected, 24.16
double reality, 23.26-27
doubt,
cause of, 17.32
destroyed, 8.33
dream,
bewildering, 23.3
birth compared, 17.39-41
imagination, 6.2
impulsion, 20.20
intellect operation, 8.27
life compared, 12.53
drowsiness, 20.4
drugs, 10.34
drunk man, 8.36
dumplings, 22.34
dung-eating worm, 22.54
Durgā, 22.3, 29
duty,
abandoned/waiver, 6.32
details, 12.1
God as, 5.34
insufficient, 9.22
Krishna's regard for, 7.1
lifestyle, 13.42
merit, 15.26; 16.2
required, 5.1
spirited devotion, 9.20
Dvaipāyaṇa, 11.28
Dvāraka, 1.4-5, 33; 2.3
dying as desired, 10.7

E

ears, 4.27
earth,
burden reduced, 1.21
effects, 16.12
Krishna as, 11.37
stability, 2.37
smell, 11.33
teacher, 2.33
worship facility, 6.42-6.44
earthen things, status, 16.12
Easy Achievement time cycle, 12.10
eating,
patience in, 3.3
speech restraint, 12.24
echo, 23.5
editors of Vedas, 11.28
effects/causes, 19.20
effortless linkage, 8.4
egg, 1.16; 2.57
eight-petaled lotus, 22.26
elderly years,
asceticism, 18.29
defaulted, 18.25
elders, 12.26
elemental spirits,
Krishna visited by, 1.1-2
liberated association, 7.3
elements,
factor, 17.22
spirit furnished, 16.5
elephant,
Airāvat, 11.17
ascetic compared, 2.29
captured, 3.13
king compared, 12.45
liberated, 7.6
teacher, 2.33
eleven factors, 17.24
embryonic stage, body stage, 17.46
emotion,
achievement, 15.12
purification, 9.23
yoga applied, 15.6, 8, 29; 22.53
emotional detachment, 10.8
emotional feelings, 7.8, 10
emotionally-charged cosmic potency, 23.16
endeavor,
disposition, 12.17
Krishna transcends, 7.9
motivation, 20.3
endless happiness, 12.42
endurance, 12.17
energizing air, 2.39
enjoyment
abandoned, 13.26
assertive sense, 23.15
householder's, 13.43
human objective, 2.27
Krishna motivates, 11.36
sensuous fulfillment, 20.7
enmity, 18.18-19
entering bodies, 10.6, 23
enterprising persons, 11.31
enthusiasm,
details, 17.32
householder's, 13.43
enumeration cause / effect, 17.7-8
environmental cause, 11.9
envy,
affects of, 5.21
eliminated, 24.15
equal assessment, 8.40
equilibrium, 11.10; 17.12
essential nature, 13.32
essential principles, 11.37
evacuation,
Krishna motivates, 11.36
speech restraint, 12.24
evaporation, 11.43
everything, 11.38
evil persons, 7.3
evolution,
action-based, 16.17
human's, 17.34, 36
excitation, 20.16
excretion, 17.16
execution, 5.20

exemption, 10.18
exertion, 18.18
exhaustion, 20.18
exhibition/material nature, 17.24
existence,
enigmatic, 8.2
hallucination, 8.34
existential conditions, 2.48
existential distribution, 9.6
existential place, 3.33
existential similarity, 9.16
expectation,
great misery, 3.44
renounced, 3.39
experience,
forgotten, 17.37
numerous? 5.14
perfection yielded by, 14.4-5
exploitive tendency, 8.8
external body, 17.44
External Reality, 24.25
eye,
self pulled by, 4.27
subtle sight, 9.26

F

factors,
details, 14.14
listed, 17.14; 19.24
inquiry, 17.1-12
faith,
advanced, 21.29-31
approved behavior, 14.33
categories, 20.27
devotion compliments, 9.21
disciple's, 13.39
effective, 15.27; 20.27
Krishna stories, 6.35
perceptive influence, 20.2
worship requires, 22.33
yoga application, 15.8
fall from heaven, 5.25
falldown, 11.42
false expectation, 20.15
falsehood, 18.18-19
fame,
greed destroys, 18.16
human objective, 2.27
family,
attachment, 12.52
causes, 20.8
fallen state, 2.74
purpose of life? 2.70
ruined, 2.68
fantasy,
ceasing, 3.43
depressive energy, 20.4
disgust, 3.28
farming, 5.21
fat, 21.21
fate, 3.40
fatigue, 20.4
fault,
analyzed, 18.51-57
basis, 2.8
defined, 16.2
devotion destroyed, 9.19
merit conversion, 16.16
favors, 20.11
fear,
assertive sense, 23.15
beneficial type, 24.21
death, 16.22
depressive energy, 20.4
Krishna, 5.30
money causes, 18.18
removal, 16.18
fearlessness,
clarifying, 20.16
moral restraint, 14.33
fee of teacher, 12.37; 14.39
feelings for Krishna, 9.28
fertile land, 7.20
festivals, 6.36; 24.11
fetus, 1.16
fiber, 9.34; 16.37
filtered water, 13.16
financial gain, 20.7
fire,
compared, 2.47
counteracting, 10.8
devotion compared, 9.19, 25
effects, 16.12
fuel-less, 5.13
Krishna as, 11.23
meditation, 9.37
offering, 22.36
priest set-up, 22.36
production, 19.23
self compared, 5.8
student worships, 12.26
Supersoul compared, 7.18
Supreme Being in, 12.32
teacher, 2.33
women compared, 3.7
worship facility, 6.42-43
yoga compared, 8.7
firebrand, 8.34
fire sacrifice, 14.3
firewood,
body compared, 5.8
faults compared, 9.19
fish,
compared, 3.19-21
lesson, 2.34
flagpole, 1.13
flames, 22.18, 33
flavor,
lure, 3.19
production, 19.23
sensual pursuit, 17.16
flaws transcended, 15.36
flesh, 21.21
flirtation, 3.14; 12.34
flower chakra, 9.36
flower-like objects, 7.21
flowers, offerings, 22.33
flying conveyance, 5.24
focus,
transformation, 4.22
on Krishna, 13.43
fog comparison, 16.28
follow devotees, 24.10

food,
acquirement, 13.25, 34-35
brahmin's, 12.43
categories, 20.28
consumption, 9.10
control, 3.20
decomposition, 19.22
destined, 13.33-35
indifference, 3.2
offering, 22.18, 35
procurement, 2.62
fool,
defined, 14.42
miserable? 5.18
foot purification, 22.22
foot wash, 22.25, 33
forbearance, 12.16
forefathers, 1.3
forest flower, 22.39
forest residence, 20.25
forgiveness,
Krishna as, 11.31
moral restraint, 14.33
form,
assumption, 10.6, 22
interactive, 17.31
mundane influence, 20.30
formations, 5.32
fortune, 14.40
four factors, 17.21
four-armed Deity, 6.46
fourth dimension, 8.28-29, 10.16
fourth state, 20.20; 23.20
fragrance,
offering, 22.18, 32-33
Krishna's, 1.46
fraud,
Krishna as, 11.31
tendency, 18.18-19
frenzy, 20.17
friction of bamboo, 8.7

friend,
everyone's, 2.12; 24.47
Krishna, 11.9
temporary, 12.53
spiritual master, 14.43
fruit-eating bird, 6.6
fruits,
body compared, 17.43
material existence, 7.22
retiree's, 13.2
fulfillment, 10.5
functional work, 16.1
functions, 6.36
funds, 12.51
futile discussion, 12.20
future, 12.52
future world hereafter, 16.31

G

gajah, 7.6
Ganesh, 22.29
Ganges River,
elephant, 2.29
Krishna as, 11.20
Krishna's feet, 1.13
garden, temple, 6.38
gardens, 1.6, 10.25
garland, 1.6, 46; 22.32
Garuḍa, 11.15; 22.28
gas, production, 19.22
Gāyatrī, 11.12; 16.41; 22.22
gems, 11.30
generosity, 12.17
genitals, 21.3
ghee,
oblations, 11.30; 22.16
offering, 24.34
worship requires, 6.43-45
ghee lamp, 6.40
ghost,
hereafter, 17.51
worship of, 5.28; 16.30
gift,
brahmin's, 12.40
teacher, 2.34
gist of yoga, 18.61
giving up of benefits, 9.10
glance of mercy, 9.41
glorifying, 1.49; 13.43
goal, 14.2
goat, 8.8
God,
concepts about, 5.34
creator/destroyer, 23.6
details, 19.27
enjoying with, 3.35
inscrutable powers, 2.58
manifestations, 2.47; 19.10
mass of absoluteness, 4.18
mass of personality, 4.18
subtle segregatation, 4.18
time energy, 4.17
goddess, Urvaśī, 21.7
Godhead, 4.16
gods, 16.32
gold,
bewildering, 3.8
Krishna as, 11.18
primal cause compared, 23.19
purification compared, 9.25
golden egg, 1.16
good behavior, 7.2
good luck, 12.51
good of others, 2.38
gopis,
liberated, 7.6
nights with Krishna, 7.11
yearning effective, 7.13
government, thief, 18.11
Govinda, 1.20
grace, requested, 22.45
grain, 16.12; 22.33
grass plant, 11.30
grass, 6.43-45; 11.30
greed,
assertive sense, 23.15
depressive energy, 20.4
disposition, 12.18
fall down, 18.16
hell, 5.27
scorches, 2.29
tendency, 12.20
grief,
assertive sense, 23.15
cause, 6.2
depressive energy, 20.4, 15
female bird's, 2.65
removal, 16.18
gross elements, 17.22-24
gross matter, 19.8
groves, 5.25
guidelines, Veda, 9.3
guru,
Krishna as, 12.27
status superior, 12.27
student worships, 12.26
gurukula, 12.22-32

H

habit, elimination, 15.23
habitat, God as, 5.34
hair,
body part, 3.33
erection, 9.23
retiree's, 13.3
trimming, 12.24
hallucination, 8.34
hamsa class, 12.10
Hamsa, Lord, 12.11
hands, 17.15
Hanumān, 7.6; 11.29
happiness,
aspiration, 3.1
categories, 20.29
cause, 6.2
clarifying energy, 20.13
compared, 9.12
defined, 14.41
detached type, 9.13
disgust produced, 3.27
endless type, 4.1
Krishna's type, 9.17
questioned, 5.29
renunciation, 4.2; 13.43
spiritual type, 2.30
types, 4.4; 5.14
Hari, 1.20; 2.58; 12.8; 18.28; 24.45
hassles, 18.49
haṭha yoga, 4.11; 23.39
haunted, 3.28
havya-vāt, 11.13
hawk, 4.2
hearing,
detecting potency, 17.15
effective, 1.24
Krishna pastimes, 14.24
Krishna motivates, 11.36
mystic skill, 10.6, 19
praised, 1.9
purification, 1.19
scripture, 18.46
heart chakra, 9.34, 36; 22.23
heat, 13.4
heaven,
achievement absent, 15.12
astral world, 3.1
belief in, 2.69
by-passed, 1.10
defined, 14.42
fall from, 5.25
hereafter, 5.23-25
hell,
achievement absent, 15.12
astral world, 3.1
defined, 14.43
hereafter, 5.27-28; 20.22
helpless family? 12.57
herbs,
moon, 11.16
mystic skills, 10.34
hereafter,
destinations, 17.51
godly life, 5.23
imagined, 16.31
mental darkness, 12.58
righteous duty asset, 21.33
senses present, 17.36
yogi planet, 13.10
hermit life, 12.38
hero, 11.35

heroism,
defined, 14.37
disposition, 12.17
motivational influence, 20.3
heron, 18.39
Himālaya, 11.21; 18.39
Hiranyagarbha, 8.16
history, ascetic/Yadu, 2.24
hive, 4.23
hoarder, 3.11
hoarding, 3.12, 15
holiness, 2.44
home, 14.43
honest work, 12.51
honey bee,
eating habit, 3.9
teacher, 2.33
honey gatherer, 2.34
honey thief, 3.15
honored yogi, 2.46
hooks, 3.19-21
hopes,
disgust, 3.28
false type, 3.44
happiness, 3.44
horse,
Krishna,11.18
mind compared, 15.21
horse-faced beings, 1.3
hospitality, 6.43-45; 14.3
hostility, 13.30-31
house
construction, 4.15
indifference towards, 5.7
householder (life),
affections, 2.54
conceit of, 12.57
death of, 12.58
detachment, 12.54
devotee lifestyle, 12.55
duties, 13.43
entry into, 12.37
objectivity, 12.56
origin, 12.14
shareholders, 18.9, 24
stressful, 18.6-10
human being,
exploitive, 8.8
hereafter, 17.51
objectives, 2.27
psychology, 16.24
human birth, 2.74
human body,
defined, 14.43
Krishna prefers, 2.22
obligation, 20.33
preferred usage, 4.29
value of, 15.17
human world hereafter, 20.22
humanity,
bewildered, 18.26
God's preference, 4.28
humility, 24.16
hunchback woman, 7.6
hundred sacrifices, 1.20
hunter, 2.72
husband/wife relation, 2.56
hygiene, 13.36
hymns,
Deity, 22.31
householder's, 13.43
hypocrisy, 20.4
hypothesis, 11.24

I

I, 8.9; 12.56
I am a killer, 11.7
I and mine, 20.6
ideation energy,
detachment of, 13.26
linkage, 10.12
mystic control of, 10.29
idiot, samnyasi role, 13.29
ignorance,
described, 18.50
retartive force, 17.13
Ilā, 21.4
image, 2.9
imagination,
birth compared, 17.39-41
creative force, 17.47
dream type, 6.2
false, 17.54
mind construction, 2.7
Pingalā, 3.25
imitation, 17.52
immodest person, 24.30
Immortal Reality, 24.22
impact, 17.30
imperceptible nature, 17.14
impious souls, 11.2
impregnation, 17.46
impulsion,
mental effects, 20.17
transmigration, 20.21-22
impulsive energy,
effects, 20.14
Krishna as, 11.37
impulsive persons, 7.4
impurity, 16.3, 10
incarnation, 6.20, 28
incense, 22.18, 33
independence, 5.17
indifference
food acquirement, 13.33-35
yogi's, 3.6; 6.17
indispensible factor, 11.38
individual spirit, 11.11
Indra,
king meets, 12.46
Krishna visited by, 1.1
Krishna as, 11.13
leading god, 16.32-33
inducement, 16.23, 26
inertial energy, 19.7
infancy, 17.46
infatuation,
cause, 6.2
depressive influence, 20.15
food, 13.25
mystic skill, 10.7
removal, 5.13
three-fold, 17.30
information, 17.28
inherent nature, 5.34
initiative, 17.30, 32; 20.6
injunctions, 7.14
injury, 20.11
inquiry,
about self, 23.25
desired, 6.21
necessary, 5.11
insect, 4.23
insignia, 22.27
inspection of Krishna, 23.34
instigator, 22.55
instinctive fear of death, 16.22
instruction,
renounced, 7.14
teacher's fee, 14.39
insubmissive person, 24.30
insult, 18.2
intellect,
clarity-surcharged, 15.20
control, 11.43
emotional attachment, 11.44
evolution related, 17.34
I projection, 8.9
material existence perceptive, 20.31
material nature affects, 8.1
materialistic? 5.11
meditation resistant, 8.18
purified type, 5.13
spirit imitates, 17.52
stability of, 2.37; 9.42
useful, 2.32
intelligence,
adjustable? 5.15
Krishna bound, 7.12
intentions, 8.10
interaction, 8.17
interest,
essential ingredient, 19.20
withdrawn, 8.35
interiorized self, 10.36
internalization, 11.26
interpenetration, 17.7-8

intimate linkage, 20.32
intimidation, 24.15
intuition, 17.10
investing in Krishna, 24.9
invocation, 22.41
irreligion, 14.40
irreligious nature, 8.3
irresponsibility, 5.27
isolation
bhakti yoga, 9.29
desired, 4.10
required, 4.14; 21.3; 23.9

J

Jagati, 16.41
Jana zone, 9.14
jealousy, 1.12
jewel, 22.12
jñāna yoga, 15.6, 7;
jñānam, explained, 23.18
job classification, 12.10
jumpiness, 20.17

K

kaivalyam, 15.34
Kali, 2.4, 5
Kamadhenu, 11.14
Kamudekśana, 22.28
karma yoga,
applicants, 15.6-7
preliminary type, 24.9
waivered, 6.32
Kaustubha, 9.40; 22.27, 39
Kayadhu, 7.5
Khaṭvānga, 18.30
kikata, 16.8
killer of self, 15.17
kindness, 13.43
king,
career options, 12.48
hereafter life, 12.46
ignored, 4.13
Krishna as, 11.17
mission, 12.45
kirtan, 13.43
knowledge,
categories, 20.24
clarifying energy, 14.25; 17.13; 20.13
defined, 14.27
experience, 5.10
four-fold proof, 14.17
Krishna as, 11.37
mundane influence, 20.30
profound type, 14.8
relinquished, 14.1
Krishna, Lord,
Abhijit, 11.27
abode, 19.14
absence, 7.11
Achyuta, 5.37; 12.5
acting as, 7.16

Krishna, Lord, continued,
activation as, 11.36
activities attractive, 1.44
acts freely, 13.36
agreeable speech, 11.26
air as, 11.37
Airāvat, 11.17
Ajah Brahmā, 11.26
all-pervading, 6.21; 22.48
alternatives, 6.22
Ananta as, 11.19-20
angelic beings visit, 1.1-3
angelic singers, 11.33
animals as, 11.19
annihilation, 11.35
Arjuna as, 11.29, 35
Aryamā as, 11.15
assertion as, 11.37
association preferred by, 7.2-3
attractions of, 7.1
Bali, 11.35
banyan tree, 11.21
barley, 11.21
basis as, 11.10
beasts, 11.19
beginningless, 11.1
Beloved, 24.5
best of teachers, 17.59
Bhrigu as, 11.14
birth cause, 11.9
birthless, 19.27
body beautiful, 1.4
body preference, 2.22
body separate, 6.28
bound/free, 6.1
bow, 11.20
Brahmā as, 11.12, 22, 26
Brahmā connected to, 8.19
Brahmā fears, 5.31
Brahmā visited by, 1.31
Brahmā's source, 24.37
Bṛhaspati, 11.22
bull form, 12.11
causal form, 12.12
cause of creatures, 11.9
cause of environment, 11.9
cause supreme, 1.14; 13.45
celestial visitors, 1.1-3
charm as, 11.40
chief of Dāśārhas, 18.1
clarifying energy as, 7.19 ; 11.31, 37
comparative attractions, 7.1
Complete Spirit, 1.21,
concepts about, 5.34
controller, 11.38
convictions as, 11.37
creative power, 1.8
creator of all beings, 11.2
curse counteracted? 1.42

Krishna, Lord, continued,
dairy products, 11.30
Dakṣa as, 11.15
dancers visit, 1.1-3
dear to ascetic, 14.2
death cause, 11.9
December, 11.27
dedication to, 5.4
Deity Forms, 11.32
Deity Worship, 6.34, 42-47; 22.8-52
delight of society, 1.4
departure, 1.26
destroyer, 13.45
destroyer of beings, 11.2
Devala Asita, 11.28
devotion awards, 9.21
disciplinarians, 11.18
discrimination as, 11.24
Dvaipāyaṇa, 11.28
earth as, 11.37
earth smell, 11.33
ejaculating as, 7.16
emotions for, 7.10
endless, 11.1
environmental cause, 11.9
equilibrium as, 11.10
essential factor, 23.19
essential principles, 11.37
Everything, 11.38
exemptions, 20.12
existential linkage, 20.32
existential purity, 10.18
experiencer of psyche, 6.45
experience as, 7.19
exploiter, 1.14
feet, 1.10, 12, 13; 14.9
fire as, 11.23
first and best, 24.49
flawless, 2.18
form of universe, 14.8
form, matchless, 1.23
fraud, 11.31
free to act, 13.36
friend of creatures, 11.9
friend, 2.18; 24.4
friend of the world, 24.47
Ganges as, 11.20
Garuḍa as, 11.15
Gāyatrī as, 11.12
ghee, 11.30
glories, 1.9; 6.34
goal, 14.2
gold, 11.18
Hamsa form, 12.11
Hanumān as, 11.29
happiness related, 20.29
Hari, 24.45
hearing as, 7.19
heroes, 11.35
hidden, 11.4

Krishna, Lord, continued,
Himālayas, 11.21
horses, 11.18
Immortal Reality, 24.22
immunity, 1.8
imperceptible energy, 11.37
impulsive energy as, 11.37
incarnated, 6.28
inconceivable, 11.39
indispensible, 11.38
individual spirit as, 11.11
Indra as, 11.13
Infinite Reality, 2.18; 16.37
influence as, 11.38
intending as, 7.19
interiorized self, 10.36
internalization as, 11.26
Kāmadhenu as, 11.14
Kapila as, 11.15
Keśava, 14.30
king as, 11.17
knowledge as, 11.37
knowledge of, 20.24
Lord of White Island, 10.18
mind modifications, 11.41
Krita Age, 11.28
Kumara, 11.25
kusha grass, 11.30
Kuvera as, 11.16
havya-vāt as, 11.13
lecturer supreme, 12.5
life-span, 1.25
lifestyle, 11.19
light as, 11.37
lion as, 11.19, 20
location in all beings, 11.4
location, 10.36
Lord of all, 13.45
Lord of creatures, 11.9
Lord of lords, 24.7
Lord of lords of universe, 22.5
Lord of people, 6.27
Lord of ceremonies, 14.6
Lord of world, 2.18; 6.27
Lord of universe, 1.6; 6.27; 14.8; 17.1; 24.3
lotus bud, 11.30
lotus feet, 1.10-13; 14.9
lotus navel, 19.10
lotus-eyed, 15.1; 17.27; 22.5; 24.2-3
luck as, 11.40
lunar month, 11.27
maintainer of beings, 11.2
maintenance, 11.35
majestic personality, 14.10
manifestation partial, 11.40
Manu as, 11.14, 25

Krishna, Lord, continued,
Master of masters of yoga, 7.16
material nature as, 7.19
material nature resistance, 20.12
material nature impregnated by, 1.16
attainment of, 14.2
meditated on, 1.11
memory of, 1.49
mento-emotions for, 7.10
mercy of, 7.15
Meru, 11.21
metals, 11.18
mind as, 11.11
modesty as, 11.40
modification as, 11.37
moon as, 11.16, 34
motivation as, 11.36
mountain stability, 11.33
movement as, 7.16
Mukunda, 18.58
musicians, 1.1-3
mystic skills, 10.36
Nārada as, 11.14
Nārāyaṇa, 2.18; 22.42
Nāra-Nārāyaṇa, 11.25
narrations effective, 9.27
natural modification, 11.37
nature, 10.18
Nīlalohita as, 11.13
non-violence as, 11.23
November, 11.27
objective as, 11.10
objective, 6.48; 14.2
occupation, 11.19, 20
Om as, 11.12
omniscient, 17.27
Govinda, 17.35
omniscient, 2.18
opinion as, 11.24
forgiveness, 11.31
origin of yoga, 2.14
originator, 11.4, 35, 45; 12.5; 13.45; 19.15
paradise hereafter, 14.2
partner, 2.2
passionate energy as, 7.19
pastimes, 1.49, 6.20, 14.20
perception energy, 6.3
Person of glorification, 6.26
Person of forms, 11.5
Person with fine hair, 1.43
personality as, 11.37
pilgrimage, 1.36-38
planetary attainment, 19.14
policy as, 11.24
popularity as, 11.40
potency as, 11.11
potency endless, 16.37

Krishna, Lord, continued,
Prahlāda as, 11.16
primal male being, 1.16
primal energy, 11.37
Primal Person, 6.28
Primeval God, 6.24
prosperity, 11.31, 40
protector of all beings, 11.2
protector of great souls, 14.32
protector of duty, 12.5
prowess as, 11.41
psychology details, 20.16
Pūrvacitti, 11.33
Reality Ultimate, 19.19
realization as, 11.40
receptacles of worship, 6.42
recognition of, 6.25
recommendations, 5.1
religious principles protector, 1.22
remnants effective, 1.46
renunciation as, 11.26, 40
renunciation for, 7.14-15
renunciation recommended, 2.14
residence, 2.18; 20.25
retardative energy, 7.19; 11.37
righteous lifestyle, 12.8
ruby, 11.30
salvation, 2.19
Śatarūpā, 11.25
Sātvata activities, 11.32
seeing as, 7.19
self in self, 14.6
self of beings, 7.15; 11.4, 9
self reliant on, 2.9
self restraint as, 11.24
self-salvation, 2.19
senses, master, 1.17
serpents, 1.1-3; 11.18
sexual arousal, 1.18
sexually potency, 7.19; 11.11
Shiva as, 11.13, 20
shrines, 11.5
silence as, 11.26
situated, core of being, 16.28
Skanda, 11.22
sky as, 11.37
slayer of Madhu, 12.6
smell as, 11.33
smelling as, 7.16
snakes, 11.19
Soul of all beings, 2.15; 11.38; 22.48
Soul of universe, 17.60
soul's partner, 6.4
sound as, 11.34

Krishna, Lord, continued,
source of Procreator, 24.37
sovereignty as, 11.40
speaking as, 7.16
spectacular, 1.5
speech as, 11.23, 26
speech, 7.16
spirit as, 11.11, 23, 38
spiritual existence, 13.45
spiritual form, 9.38-43
spiritual master, 14.43
spring, 11.27
stars as, 11.34
status known, 14.3
strength as, 11.40
strong person, 11.32
subject, 14.2
Sudarśan as, 11.29
Śukrācarya, 11.28
sun as, 11.17, 23, 34
superior, 1.14
supernatural rulers, 1.8-19, 21
Supreme Master of Yoga, 2.14
Supreme Mystic consultant, 24.6
Supreme Person, 1.15; 19.27
Supreme Reality, 11.37
Supreme Spirit, 6.28; 11.1
Supreme, 24.21
Svāyambhuva, 11.25
taste of water, 11.34
tasting as, 7.16
thinking cessation, 13.27
time, 1.14; 11.10; 19.15
tolerance as, 11.40
touching as, 7.19
transfer, 2.1
treasure of yoga, 2.14
Ucchaihshrava, 11.18
Uddhava compared, 9.15
Uddhava instructed by, 2.6
unaffected, 1.8, 17; 24.1, 4
unconfined, 10.36
universe controller, 19.21
universe owned by, 2.12
universe producer, 11.39; 19.10
unknown, 16.28
unlimited, 11.1
Vaikuṇṭha, 2.18
Varuṇa, 11.17
Vasiṣṭha as, 11.22
Vāsudeva, 11.29
Vāsuki, 11.18
Vedas proclaim, 16.43
Vedic teaching, 11.23
Vishnu as, 11.13
Viśvāvasu, 11.33
water as, 11.20,.23, 37

Krishna, Lord, continued,
water's taste, 11.34
wife of, 1.12,18
wind as, 11.23
wondrous, 11.5
work, faultless, 24.21
work-absolute, 24.21
worship duty, 13.43
worship exclusive, 6.33
worship, 14.3; 15.23; 20.33
Yadus, destroyer, 1.29-30
Yama, 11.18
year as, 11.27
Yoga in person, 2.14
yoga master, 1.42; 2.14
yogi philosopher dear, 14.3
yogis meditate on, 1.7
yogis visit, 1.1-3
Krita Age, 11.28
kriya succession, 22.3
kriya yoga,
effective, 22.49
highest well being, 22.1-2
Om sound, 9.35
universal application, 22.4
Kṛta yuga, 19.2
ksatriya, 12.17, 48
Kumaras, 8.21, 42; 11.25
Kumuda, 22.28
kundalini, 10.24
kusha grass, 11.30; 12.23; 22.37
Kuvera, 11.16

L

lack of independence, 5.17
lack of vitality, 20.4
Lakṣmi, Goddess, 1.12; 3.35; 9.15, 39
lamp, Deity, 6.40
land, 5.7; 22.51
language, 16.40
leaf garment, 13.2
learning,
from all, 3.10
insufficient, 9.22
self of self, 2.20
lecturer, 12.5
legs, organ, 17.15
leprosy, 18.16
lessons, 3.10
lethargy, 20.18
letter sound, 7.17
libations of water, 1.37
liberated soul, 6.8
liberation,
method requested, 9.31
qualifications, 1.47
questioned, 6.1
righteous duty of, 14.12
sensual control, 13.22
life energy control, 11.43
life force, 23.31

life span, 1,25; 15.16
lifestyles, 12.14, 15, 38
light joined into light, 9.45
light, 11.37; 17.14
light combustion, 17.21
linkage of attention,
cleansed mind, 10.17
cosmic power, 10.14
Deity Form, 6.46
effective, 23.40
tendency producing, 8.4
types, 10.3
lion, 4.14; 11.19
liquid,
factor, 17.14, 21
gas produces, 19.23
sky transcends, 2.43
status, 16.12
liquor, 8.36
listening,
Deity, related, 22.44
effective, 9.26
Krishna stories, 6.23
text, 24.28
living condition, 11.9
loafer, 2.28
location,
achievements of, 15.12
tendency producing, 8.4
types, 16.8
lock, anus, 10.24
logical analysis, 14.17
loneliness of spouse, 2.69
long life span, 2.27
Lord of universe, 24.3
Lord of White Island, 10.18
Lord, Krishna, 11.9
lordship, 14.40
loss of objectivity, 20.18
lotus bud, 11.30
lotus feet, 11.5
lotus flower, 6.46
lotus stalk, 9.34; 16.37
lotus, universe, 19.10
lotus-eyed Lord, 24.2-3
lovers, 2.54
loving expression, 16.1
luck, 5.24; 11.40
lunar month, 11.27
lung disease, 1.36
lust,
hell, 5.27
inexhaustible, 21.14
scorches, 2.29
tendency, 18.18-19
lyric, 18.42

M

mace, 22.27
Mādhava, 12.3
maggots, 21.21
magnanimity, 14.3

Mahabala, 22.28
Mahāpuruṣa, 22.31
Mahar zone, 19.14
maiden, 4.5, 4.10
maintenance, 11.35
majesty, 14.27
male donkey, 12.13
manifestation, 4.20; 11.41
manipulation, 10.4
mantra, 10.34; 22.10
Manu,
Brahmā instructed, 9.4
Krishna as, 11.14, 25
manual skill, 17.16
marriage life, 2.55; 12.14, 29
marriage suitors, 4.5, 4.10
marrow, 21.21
Marut, Krishna visited by, 1.1
master, 14.44
material existence,
bewilderment, 17.55
cessation, 9.46
details, 7.21-22; 23.22
hallucination, 8.34
imaged-self, 2.9
memory trivial, 8.35
mind formulated, 2.7
ocean, 22.46
unreal, 6.2
material mature,
attractive, 5.32
causal energy, 17.17
cause of, 7.20
conquer strategy, 8.1
diversity, 14.17
factors, 14.15
God motivates, 4.19
impregnated, 1.16
inconsequential, 5.3
intellect direct, 8.1
Krishna as, 11.38
Krishna transcends, 1.8; 20.12
mind promotes, 18.44
personality distinct, 17.29
reality aspect, 19.4
sexually charged, 4.19
spirit characterized, 17.26
spirit indirect, 8.1
material world,
explained, 4.20
perpetual? 5.14
worthwhile? 23.12
Mathura, 7.10
matted hair, 12.23
matter, 19.8
Maya, 7.6
means of attainment, 14.2
medicine, 16.23; 23.39
meditation,
alternatives, 6.22
assertion energy, 10.13
bhakti yoga, 6.47
brahmins, 12.26
Deity, 6.46; 22.37
details, 15.18-22
ineffective? 8.18
Krishna focus, 8.13
mystic skills, 10.9
nose focus, 9.32
samādhi, 9.42, 45
spiritual form, 6.47
student's, 12.26
worship, 6.44
memory, 17.37
men, 11.25
menial servant, 12.29
mental calmness, 20.2, 9
mental darkness, 5.28; 12.58
mental exhaustion, 20.18
mental knowledge, 17.19
mental vigor, 11.32
mentality affected, 20.30
mento-emotional energy,
cessation, 13.27; 17.56
feelings for Krishna, 7.10
interest of, 8.26
Krishna focus, 9.27
lower influences, 14.26
mundane focus, 14.26
pacified, 14.25
purity, 15.36
restraint, 2.9
mercantile class, 12.18
merchant, brahmin as, 12.47
mercy,
disposition, 12.16
insufficient, 9.22
Krishna's, 7.15
spiritual body's, 9.41
merit,
defined, 16.2
depletion of, 18.10
elaboration, 11.45
exhausted, 5.26
Meru, 11.21
metal, 22.12
methods,
three, 15.6
types, 9.9
yogis, 23.39-40
middle-aged body, 17.46
military commanders, 11.22
milk, 6.18
mind,
attracted to objects, 8.17
categorized, 17.15
cause, 18.43
clarifying? 8.9
connection hazard, 21.23
mind, continue,
control, 11.42, 43; 12.35
creation's source, 2.7
details, 15.18-22
factor, 17.22-23
focus, 4.11
influences, 18.44
Krishna as, 11.11
mastery special, 18.48
material nature affects. 20.12
preserved, 2.39
projection, 13.27
self-image? 18.45
senses, 19.25
spirit as, 17.23
steadiness process, 15.18
theatric, 8.34
transmigrates, 17.36
travel, 10.21
mind Deity Form, 22.12
mine, 12.56
minuteness, 16.10
mirage, 23.5
mirror, offerings, 22.35
misconception, 5.13
miser, 14.44
misery,
defined, 14.41
depressive energy, 20.4
examples, 6.19
God-sent type, 3.38
impulsion produces, 20.14
types, 10.18
misidentification, 2.12
mistake, 16.16
mix, spirit-matter, 19.16
modes of material nature,
agitation, 19.5
identifying, 8.5
personalization, 20.19
transmigration, 17.51
modesty,
defined, 14.40
Krishna as, 11.40
moral restraint, 14.33
modification,
3-part, 14.7
Krishna as, 11.37
material nature, 17.30, 32
money,
acquirement, 18.18
bothersome, 18.14
desperation, 3.24
focus on, 12.56
indifference, 5.7
root of bad tendencies, 18.19
wasted, 18.25
money-hungry nature, 12.18
monkey-faced humans, 11.29

months, 11.27
mood of devotion, 14.5
moon,
compared, 2.48
Krishna as, 11.16, 34
meditation, 9.37
ruler, 1.35, 36
Supersoul compared, 13.32
teacher, 2.33
moral restraint,
aim of life? 9.10
listing, 14.33
mind control, 18.46
required, 15.23
morality, 7.2
moth, 2.33; 3.7
motivational force, 17.32; 19.7; 20.3
motivations, 6.16
motivator, 7.20
mountain, 2.38; 11.33
mouth wash, 22.22, 25, 33, 35
movement, 11.36; 17.16
moving water, 17.53
Mukunda, 18.1
multiplicity,
detachment, 6.13
explained, 19.1-29
removal of, 14.40
mundane energy, 4.19
mundane influences, 20.32
mundane reality, 23.12
muscles, 21.21
music, 3.17
musicians, 5.24; 7.3
mutual interpenetration, 17.7-8
mystic connotations, 8.4
mystic experience, 17.10
mystic movement, 10.21
mystic perception, 13.44; 14.15
mystic poets, 11.28
mystic practice, 22.1
mystic ruler, 18.48
mystic skill (technique),
controlling others, 10.15
described, 10.1
desire fulfillment, 10.26
hearing, 10.19
itemized, 10.4-5
Krishna causes, 10.35
majesty, 14.27
meditation for, 10.9
obstacles, 10.33
omniscience, 10.28
quantity, 10.3
regulations, 10.31
required, 7.24
seeing, 10.20
sense control, 10.32
undesirable, 23.41-42
mystic vision, 23.9; 24.17
mystic yoga, 9.38-46

N

naad sound, 9.34; 10.19; 22.23
Nahusa, 2.36
nails, 3.33; 12.24; 13.3
Nanda, 22.28
Nārada, 11.14; 22.2
Nārāyaṇa,Lord,
Godhead, 4.16
Krishna as, 2.18
Nara-Nārāyaṇa, 11.25
Reality Personified, 22.42
yogi focus, 3.6; 10.16
natural modification, 11.37
nature, 5.34
neophyte, 24.17
nest, 7.22
net, 2.63
Nīlalohita, 11.13
nine factors, 17.14, 24
niyama, 12.34, 35
non-accumulation of wealth, 14.33
non-anger, 12.21
non-attachment,
moral restraint, 14.33
mystic skill, 10.5
perceptive influence, 20.2
purity, 14.38
non-craving, 12.21
non-greed, 12.21
non-injury,
moral restraint, 14.33
renunciant's duty, 13.42
required, 12.21
non-stealing, 12.21; 14.33
non-violence, 11.23
nose, 9.32
November, 11.27

O

obeisances, 13.43
object, 20.30
objective,
Krishna, 11.10; 14.2
mundane influence, 20.30
mystic attainment, 10.26
types, 9.10
unique, 10.34
objective world, 23.13
objectivity, 8.6
objects,
attracted to mind, 8.17
bewildering, 3.8
consciousness pursue, 8.25
oblation,
behavior, 14.3
carrier, 11.13
choice type, 22.16
ghee, 11.30
oblation, continued
householder's, 13.43
speech restraint, 12.24
obligations, 15.30
observances,
devotional 24.11
retiree's, 13.8
obstacles,
desires produce, 5.21
mystic skills, 10.33
ocean,
Krishna, 1.29; 7.12
Krishna as, 11.20
Vedas compared, 16.36
yogi compared, 3.5
odor, 17.16
offerings, 6.37, 41
ointment, 9.26; 22.32
old age, 17.46; 18.27
Om,
alphabet, 16.39
blended, 9.34
described, 9.34
Krishna as, 11.12
meditation, 10.19
sound kriya, 9.35
Veda, 12.11
omniscience, 10.28
one principle, 14.15
oneness, 15.34
opinion,
basis, 2.8; 17.4
cause of, 9.7
Krishna as, 11.24
opportunities, 2.14
options,
old age, 18.27
questioned, 9.1
orchard, temple, 6.38
organ of perception, 23.20
organs listed, 17.15
origination, 11.35; 14.15
originator, 12.5; 13.45; 19.15
ornaments,
bewildering, 3.8
Krishna's, 1.46
offering, 22.32, 35
osprey, 2.34
outer space, factor, 17.14, 19

P

paddy, 4.6
pain, 14.41
paint, 22.12
Pancajanya, 22.27
Paṅkti, 16.41
paradise; 2.1, 14.2
paramparā, 12.4
parents, child care, 2.59, 60
parks, 10.25
partial manifestation, 11.41
partner, 2.2

passion,
compelling, 8.11
intellect facilitates, 8.9
six hazards, 21.24
past life recall, 17.38, 40-41
pastimes,
effective, 1.49
householder's, 13.43
path of snake, 16.27
path,
defined, 14.42
independent type, 9.2
patience, 14.33
perceptive influence, 20.2
patron deity-earth, 11.16
pauper, 14.44
Paurṇamāsa, 13.8
peace of mind, 9.10
peaceful person, 9.16
pedigree bride, 12.39
peepul, 6.6-7
penance,
Krishna's regard for, 7.1
limited, 15.32
purpose preferred, 13.10
perceptible nature, 17.14
perception,
material existence, 13.26
nature causes, 17.30
potency, 6.3
primordial, 6.3
yogi's adjustments, 13.37
perceptive influence, 20.2
perceptive interest, 8.35
perceptive energy, 19.7
perfection,
physical body useful, 15.14
three methods, 15.6
performers, 5.14
pericarp, 9.36; 22.26
perpetrator, 22.55
personal initiative, 17.30
personality,
collective one, 19.5
Krishna as, 11.37
nature distinct, 17.29
reality aspect, 19.4
petals, 9.36
phases of moon, 2.48
philosophical inquiry, 5.11
physical actions, 13.43
physical body, 15.13-14
physical experience, 15.6
physical states, 17.20
pigeon,
love play, 2.55
nest building, 2.53
suffering, 2.52
teacher, 2.33
pilgrim sessions, 24.11
pilgrimage,
approved, 14.3
experience compared, 14.4
Krishna's view, 7.2
recommended, 24.10
Yadus, 1.36-38
piṇḍa, 1.37
Piṅgalā,
enjoying with God, 3.35
introduced, 3.22
relieved, 3.44
self critique, 3.30, 34
teacher, 2.34
pioneers, 11.22
pit, 14.10
place, 16.11; 20.30
place of execution, 5.20
planets, 18.43, 54
plant, 17.49
playground, 6.38
pleasure,
abandoning, 23.23
aim of life? 9.10
full fulfillment, 10.17
transcended, 14.41
plow, 22.27
poetic geniuses, 24.6
poison, 10.8
polarity, 2.73
policeman, 12.47
policy, 11.24
political control, 22.52
political influence, 9.10
political leadership, 12.17
politician, 12.45, 48
polygamy, 12.39
popularity,
aim of life? 9.10
impulsion, 20.14
Krishna as, 11.40
motivation, 20.3
pornography, 3.13; 12.34
possession, 3.29; 10.4
pot, 11.43
potency, 11,11; 17.18
power of appropriation, 10.13
Prabhāsa, 1.35
Prachaṇḍa, 22.28
Prahlāda, 11.16
praising, 22.44
prāṇa,
lifestyle derived, 12.12
Om mix, 9.35
technique, 12.12
Praṇavah, 12.11
prāṇāyāma, 8.13; 9.33; 13.17;18.32
celibacy restored by, 12.25
pranic energies, 10.1
prayers,
Deity Worship, 22.17
householder's, 13.43
motivation, 20.3
predestination, 18.41
predominance of modes, 20.13-15
pregnancy, 2.57
prejudice, 20.3, 14
pressure, 24.21
pride,
motivation, 20.3
tendency, 18.18-19
useless, 5.18
priest,
defined, 14.41
perception of, 6.18
Vasiṣṭha, 11.22
primal cause, 23.20-21
primal cosmic energy, 19.6
Primal Existence, 19.3
Primal Mundane Energy, 11.37; 19.25; 23.16
Primal Nature, 17.12; 19.19
Primal Person, 17.18
primal personality, 17.24
primal quiescent energy, 17.32
primal spirit, 17.17
primitive sounds, 2.59
prints, 22.32
private association, 2.52
procedures - righteous duty, 13.47
processions, 6.37
productive sector, 7.4
profit, 14.40
profound yogi, 3.5
progenitors, 1.1-2
programs, 6.36
prohibited activities, 2.11
prohibition, 7.14; 12.34
projection - desires, 4.22
promiscuity, 5.27
proof, 14.17
property, 22.54
prosperity,
impulsion, 20.14
Krishna as, 11.31, 40
objective, 2.27
prostitution, 3.23, 32
protection, 13.42
protector of duty, 12.5
providence,
inconveniences, 18.41
thief of wealth, 18.11
prowess, 11.40

psyche,
conquest, 14.37
lesson, 4.24
misunderstanding, 14.42
purified, 5.2; 16 14
restraint, 11.24
worship within, 6.45
psychic equipments, 5.11
psychosis, 20.14
pubic area, 12.24
pujāri, mystic, 22.19, 26
punya, 5.26; 21.33
purification,
air type, 22.23
association, 9.16
Deity worship, 22.21
emotional type, 9.23
fire type, 22.23
niyama rule, 12.34
righteous duty, 13.46
ritual type, 22.11
purificatory rites, 16.14
purificatory rituals, 8.4
purifier, 16.13
purity,
attainment, 10.18
conditional, 16.10
defined, 14.38
explained, 16.3
householder's, 13.43
Krishna's, 10.18
process of, 1.9
purpose of life? 2.70
Purūravā, 21.4, 25, 35
Puruṣa Sūkta, 22.31, 41
Pūrvacitti, 11.33
pus, 21.21
python, 2.33; 3.2

Q, R

quarrel,
basis, 4.10
depressive energy, 20.4
mind based, 18.49
questions, 8.22-23
radiant yogi, 2.46
rain, 13.4; 14.9
Raksha, 11.16
Rāma, Balarām journey, 7.10
Rānjana, 22.31
raw material, 19.18
reactions, 2.46
reading text, 24.27
realism,
aim of life? 9.10
defined, 14.37
disposition, 12.16
insufficient, 9.22
moral restraint, 14.33
perceptive influence, 20.2
Reality,
continuous, 19.17
described, 4.31; 19.3, 19
interpretation of, 6.4
residual energy, 14.16
reality-perceiving devotees, 6.25
realization, 11.40
reason, 23.18
rebels, 1.13
rebirth,
mind created, 18.50
passage, 17.51
reception, 6.44
recitation,
effective, 1.24; 9.26
Krishna as, 11.23
Krishna's glories, 6.34
purity of, 16.14
recollection, 20.2
refuge, 14.9
regulation,
Deity worship, 22.8-52
Vedic, 16.7
reincarnation, 17. 38-41
rejection of diversity, 14.17
relationship, 14.37
relatives,
indifference, 5.7
money affects, 18.20-21
shareholder, 18.24
temporary, 12.53
thief of wealth, 18.11
relativity, 17.9
religions, 9.8; 16.25-26
religious activities, 7.1
religious ceremony, 9.10; 14.39; 22.7
religious duty, 7.1
religious principles, 1.22
remembering Krishna, 1.49; 6.23, 47; 16.14
renunciant, 13.36
renunciation,
aim of life? 9.10
defined, 14.38
Krishna as, 11.26, 40
Krishna focus, 7.14
Krishna resists, 7.9
Krishna's view, 7.1
livelihood motive, 13.40
objective, 2.14
option, 12.38
origin, 12.14
result ultimate, 19.14
spirited devotion, 9.20
repeated birth/death, 3.41
reptiles, 4.28
reputation,
greed destroys, 18.16
protection of, 12.41
reservoirs, 11.20; 13.32
residences, 20.25
resignation, 15.34
respect, 13.39
restlessness, 6.21; 20.17
restraint, 16.18
results, 6.22
retarded person, 6.17
retardative influence,
hellish, 14.43
Krishna as, 11.37
products, 18.60
transmigration, 20.21-22
retiree,
begging rules, 13.18
ceremonies, 13.8
clothing, 13.15
diet, 13.2
food, 13.5-7
hereafter, 13.10
impediments, 13.14
isolation, 13.19, 21
non-violence, 13.16
option, 12.55; 13.1
origin, 12.14
possessions, 13.15
sannyās stage, 13.12-13
suicide, 13.11
retrogression,
element's, 14.16
existential, 2.9
meditation, 15.22
reverence, 13.43
reverses, 5.2
rewards, 14.38
Ribhus, 1.1
rice-flour cakes, 24.34
riches, 18.15
ridicule, 20.3
righteous duty,
--see also duty
aim of life? 9.10
antiseptic, 15.10
asset, 21.33
clarity enriches, 14.25
conducts, 24.8
consequence, 15.10
details, 12.1, 2, 6, 7, 8, 21
devotion, 13.44, 14.24; 15.11
devotional definition, 14.27
functional, 13.47
God as, 5.34
guarantee, 15.10
infallible, 24.20
insufficient, 9.22
Krishna controls, 10.35
liberation, 14.12
lifestyle, 13.42
limited, 15.32
merit, 16.2
mind control, 18.46

righteous duty, continue,
mundane? 20.7,8
purifying, 13.46
recommended, 6.24
risks, 15.10
sex factors, 16.14
spirited devotion, 9.20
waiver, 6.32
wealth, 14.39
well performed, 5.22
righteous lifestyle,
origination, 12.12
research into, 13.38
techniques, 12.12
righteous nature, 8.2-3
Ṛṣyaśringa, 3.18
risks, 15.10
ritual actions, 22.16
ritual worship,
householder, 13.42
Krishna resists, 7.9
ritual,
compared, 1.9
Deity, 6.37
Krishna's view, 7.2
tendency, 8.4
time, 22.4
unlimited, 22.6
rivalry,
effects, 5.21
eliminated, 24.15
tendency, 18.18-19
rivals, 3.14
rivers, 7.12
ṛkṣa, 7.6
roaming, 4.9
romance, 1,18; 2.54
roots, 7.22; 13.2
ruby, 11.30
Rudra, 1.1; 11.13
rulers, 1.1-2
ruling class, 12.12-13, 17
ruling over others, 10.4

S

sacred belt, 22.36
sacred thread, 12.22; 22.32
sacred words, 8.4
sacrificial ceremony,
animal, 5.28; 16.29
brahmin duty, 12.40
householder's, 13.43
Krishna's view, 7.2
sacrificial offering, 12.50
Sādhyā, 1.2
saint, 18.2
salvation, 2.19
Sāma Veda, 22.31
samādhi,
cleansed mind, 10.17
details, 9.42, 45; 15.18-22
discipline, 18.46
effective, 23.40
Krishna compared, 7.12
Sāṅkhya analysis,
discussed, 19.1-29
doubt, 19.26
Krishna Lord of, 10.35
Sāṅkhya analysis, continue,
Krishna resists, 7.9
Krishna's view, 7.1
practicality, 15.22
proficiency, 2.21
spirited devotion, 9.20
Swan taught, 8.38
sannyāsi,
childlike, 13.29
indifferent, 13.30-31
insignia, 13.17, 28
motivation, 13.40, 41
non-sectarian, 13.28, 30-31
option, 12.55
retiree's, 13.12-13
Sanaka, 8.14-15
sanctification,
food, daily, 12.50
purity, 16.10
water, 22.20
sand, 22.12
sandalwood paste, 22.30
sandalwood prints, 22.32
Saṅkarṣaṇ Balarāma, 9.15
sap, material existence, 7.22
Śatarūpā, 11.25
Sātvata clan,
1.10; 11.32; 22.1; 24.39
Satya zone, 19.14
schizophrenia, 20.14, 18
scientific research, 17.25
scriptural evidence, 23.9
scriptural history, 23.18
scriptural injunction, 5.4
scripture, incentives, 16.23
scriptures, influences, 8.4
sea, 2.33
seasons, 11.27
seat, 12.23
seclusion, 9.29
second birth, 12.22
secret sounds, 6.45
secret, 6.48; 11.26
sects, basis for, 9.8
security, 13.42
seed,
compared, 7.20
material existence, 7.21
oblations, 22.16
production, 19.22
witness, 17.49
seeing, mystic skill, 10.6, 20
self critique,
Pingalā's, 3.30, 34
Pururavā's, 21.16
self discipline, 12.16
self endeavor, 17.58
self happiness, 20.2
self protection, 3.42
self restraint, 11.24
self,
body unification, 5.16
conquest, 14.37
factor, 17.19, 21
independent? 5.17
Krishna as, 11.9
lessons, 2.33-35
purification, 16.14
similarity, 2.10
teacher of itself, 2.20
self-control,
defined, 14.36
near-absolute, 10.16
selflessness, 2.38
self-realization, 2.27
self-sacrifice, 2.38
self-salvation, 2.19
semen, 12.25
semi-vowels, 16.39
sense experience, 17.54
sense of assertion,
19.7; 17.14, 32
sense of initiative, 6.10; 20.6
sense organs,
factor, 17.19, 22-23
Krishna controls, 1.17
resisted, 6.9
sense pleasure, 23.23
motivational influence, 20.3
senses
control, 2.9; 11.42; 20.2
Krishna activates, 11.36
mastery, 10.1; 14.36
origin, 19.8
self pulled by, 4.27
submission, 14.44
sensory experience, 14.17
sensory powers, 17.24
sensual energy,
control, 9.33
creative, 5.31
hazard, 21.23
psyche part, 20.6
reversion, 19.24
sensual excitation, 20.16
sensual pursuit, 17.16
sensual resistance, 6.9
sensuous fulfillment, 20.7
separation of intellect, 8.28
separation of gopis, 7.10
serenity, 20.16
series existences, 5.15

serpent of time, 3.41
servant, 6.39
service to gurus, 7.7
service to teacher,
  approved behavior, 14.3
  celibate's duty, 13.42
servile tendency, 12.19
serving at shrines, 12.34
seven factors, 17.19
seventeen factors, 17.22
sex control, 14.36
sex desire,
  dangers, 21.6-7
  knowledge destroyed, 12.12
  self pulled by, 4.27
sexual arousal, 1.18; 17.16
sexual exposure, 3.23
sexual intercourse, 12.34
sexual life, 13.43
sexual organ, 17.15
sexual partners, 11.26
sexual saleswoman, 3.23
sexually-charged force, 4.19; 10.14; 17.13, 19.
shadow, 23.5
shame,
  perceptive influence, 20.2
  Pingalā's, 3.32
Shankara Shiva, 9.15
shape,
  production, 19.23
  sensual pursuit, 17.16
shareholders,
  householder's, 18.9
  listed, 18.24
shares, 18.24
sharing text, 24.30
she-ass, 21.11
shells, 4.8
Shiva,
  compared, 9.15
  Krishna as, 11.20
  Krishna requested by, 2.1
  Krishna visited by, 1.1
  Lordship, 1.1
  Nīlohita, 11.13
  succession, 22.3
shop, 22.51
shore, 1.29
shrines, 7,2; 11.5, 20
Shuka, 1.1, 31; 2.13; 12.8; 24.2
sibilants, 16.39
siddhi,
  controlling others, 10.15
  described, 10.1
  itemized, 10.4-5
  majesty, 14.27
  quantity, 10.3
sight ointment, 9.26
silence, 11.26; 14.33
similarity, 2.10; 14.37
sincerity, 12.18
singers, 7.3; 17.52
singing,
  about Krishna, 6.23
  Deity related, 22.44
  householder's, 13.43
situation, 20.16
six factors, 17.20
sixteen factors, 17.23
Skanda, 11.22
skill, 17.16
skin, 3.33; 16.12; 21.21
sky,
  detachment compared, 6.12
  Krishna as, 11.37
  Krishna compared, 24.12
  teacher, 2.33
  untouched, 2.43
  worship facility, 6.42-6.44
sky of consciousness, 9.44
slaughter house, 5.20
sleep,
  depression causes, 20.15
  deprivation, 3.25
  material existence, 23.14
  retardative influence, 20.20
smell,
  detecting potency, 17.15
  Krishna motivates, 11.36
  removal, 16.13
  self pulled by, 4.27
smelt objects, 16.12
smoke, 16.27
snake of time, 14.10
snake, prospers, 4.15
snake,
  association, 7.8
  rated, 4.28
  subtle type, 19.13
  teacher, 2.34
social life,
  basis, 20.6
  renounced, 7.14
soil, 19.22
soldier, 12.47
solids, 2.43; 17.14, 21
solitude, 4.14; 21.3; 23.9
song, 21.4, 35
songsters, 5.24
sons, 12.53
soul,
  factor, 17.22-24
  self-killer, 15.17
  secret type, 6.45
  sensual pursuit, 17.16
  subtle, 7.17
Soul of all, 11.38
sound
  infants', 2.59
  Krishna as, 11.34
  mind construction, 2.7
  original, 12.11
  production, 19.24
  retrogression, 19.25
sovereignty, 11.40; 22.52
space, 19.24
space travel, 10.25
spark, 7.18
species,
  celestial types, 1.1-3
  incidental, 18.43, 51
  living quarters, 4.28
  preference, 2.22
  shareholder, 18.24
  spirit furnished, 2.42; 16.5
  study, 2.33-35
Specific Spirit, 19.27
speech
  control, 11.42, 43; 12.35
  futile type, 6.20
  Krishna as, 7.18; 11.23, 26
  Krishna motivates, 11.36
  mind construction, 2.7
  preserved, 2.39
  projection, 13.27
  references, 6.19
  restraint rules, 12.24, 26; 13.17
  truthfulness, 14.38
  working organ, 17.16
spider,
  compared, 4.21; 16.38
  teacher, 2.34
spine, 3.33
spirit self,
  absorbent? 5.9
  assertive of body/mind, 23.16
  assumes body's nature, 5.9
  body different, 17.50
  body-supported, 1.14
  bound/freed, 5.37, 6.1
  compared, 5.7
  deathless, 17.45
  defined, 23.24
  dependency, 5.32
  disgust of, 8.29
  distinct, 5.8; 17.31, 33; 17.35
  diversification attracts, 5.32
  elimination of all else, 23.24
  entrapped? 5.35
  factor, 17.14, 22-24
  focus, 13.21
  God as, 5.34
  individualized, 2.51
  influenced, 5.31
  intellect imitated by, 17.52
  involved, 23.5

spirit self, continued
Krishna as, 11.11, 23, 38
Krishna's partner, 6.4
material nature indicated, 17.26
memory deficient, 17.37
mind as, 17.23
mind leads, 17.36
mind self-image, 18.45
mixed with moods, 5.35
neti neti, 23.24
non-partitioned, 2.42
not-this-process, 23.24
observes, 8.27, 32
operation of, 5.35
prevalent, 20.31
psyche unraveling, 18.31
purification, 16.14
realization, 14.5
required, 23.9
self endeavor, 17.58
self happiness, 20.29; 23.23
self protection, 3.42
sun compared, 2.51
superior factor, 5.9
Supreme Being in, 12.32
transcendent, 23.25
types, 6.5
unaffected, 2.49
witness, 8.32
worship facility, 6.42-6.44
spirited devotion, 9.18, 20, 21
spirit worship, 5.28
spiritual body, 10.30
spiritual cultivation, 13.43
spiritual form,
described, 9.38-43
meditation, 6.47
spiritual happiness, 2.30; 20.2
spiritual lineage, 12.26
spiritual majesty, 14.25
spiritual master,
defined, 14.41
fee, 12.37
Krishna as, 12.27, 14.43
served, 5.5; 7.24; 13.39
superior, 12.27
Supreme Being in, 12.32
worshipped, 12.26; 22.29
spiritual perspective, 8.32
spiritual plane, 9.4
spiritual power, 6.6
Spiritual Reality, 4.31; 24.23
sportive incarnations, 6.20
spring, 11.27
Śrīvatsa, 9.39; 10.31; 22.39
staff, 12.23
stamens, 22.26
stars, 11.16, 27, 34
state of mind, 20.30
steadiness,
defined, 14.36
disposition, 12.17
stomach,
self pulled by, 4.27
yogi's, 2.45
stone, 22.12
stool, 3.33; 21.21
storm creators, 1.2
straightforwardness, 12.16, 34
straw garment, 13.2
streams, 11.20
strength,
disposition, 12.17
energy control, 14.39
Krishna as, 11.40
wasted, 18.25
stress, 18.12
strong persons, 11.32
stubbornness, 20.3
student,
origin, 12.14
requirements, 12.22-32
text listed, 24.31
stupidity, 20.15
subject, 14.2
subtle body,
achievement, 15.12
mind produced, 7.17
Supersoul penetrates, 7.17
subtle elements, 17.22
subtle matter, 20.6
subtle perception, 13.42
subtle world, 10.7
Sudarśana, 11.29; 22.27
sugar candy, 24.34
Sugrīva, 7.6
suitors, 4.5, 4.10
Śukrācarya, 11.28
sun,
counteracting, 10.8
Deity worship, 22.17
detachment, 6.12
enlightenment, 19.28
Krishna as, 11.17, 34
material existence, 7.23
meditation, 9.37
spirit compared, 2.51
student worships, 12.26
teacher, 2.33
worship facility, 6.42-43
yogi compared, 2.50
Sunanda, 22.28
sunlight, 17.31
sunshine, 17.31
supernatural authorities, 22.29
supernatural influence, 17.30
supernatural power, 10.8
food controlled, 13.33-35
supernatural rebels, 1.13
supernatural ruler,
clarifying influence, 20.19
hereafter, 17.51
incidental, 18.43, 52
Krishna glorified by, 1.7
Krishna visited by, 1.1-2
mind rules, 18.48
origin, 19.8
retiree suppressed by, 13.14
shareholder, 18.24
student worships, 12.26
worship, 12.50; 16.30
Supersoul,
described, 7.17-21
lotus flower cause, 7.20
motivator, 7.20
primeval, 7.20
situation of, 13.32
Supreme Being, 12.32
supreme happiness, 21.1
Supreme Lord,
apprehension about, 5.33
described, 4.18
spider compared, 4.21
Supreme Mystic Consultant, 24.6
Supreme Person,
factor, 17.20
reality, 19.19
Supreme Reality,
Krishna as, 11.37
perception of, 6.18
transference to, 4.5
supreme secret, 6.48
Supreme Spirit,
attainment, 21.1
retrogression, 19.27
surface, 17.16
surrender, 6.35
svadhā, 12.50
svāhā, 12.50
Śvālphaka, 7.10
svar, 19.11-12
svarṇa-sharma, 22.31
Svāyambhuva, 11.25
Sviṣṭi-kṛta, 22.41
Swan, 8.20-21, 38-39; 12.3
sweet cakes, 24.34
sweet rice, 24.34
sweet dumplings, 22.34
sword, 22.27
sword of disgust, 3.28
syllable, 7.17

T

tantra, rules, 6.37; 22.7, 26, 49
tapa zone, , 19.14
tapah, 24.47
taste control, 3.21
taste, 11.36; 17.15

teacher,
defined, 14.41
disciple, 5.12
kindling compared, 5.12
Krishna Lord of, 10.35
twenty-four, 2.35
Uddhava Gītā, 24.26
variation, 4.31
teaching, 12.40
tears, 9.23
technical information, 2.13
technique,
bhakti yoga, 22.53
defined, 14.40
teeth, 13.3; 22.10
temple construction, 6.38; 22.50, 52
temple functions, 6.36
temple grounds, 22.50
temple services, 6.39; 12.34
temporary relativity, 17.43
tendency,
causes, 8.4
devotion purifies, 9.21
money affects, 18.19
opinions rely on, 9.7
sexual production, 17.13
undesirable, 12.20; 18.18-19
territories, 16.8
text, 24.32, 48
textiles, 16.12
theatrical play, 6.23; 22.44
theatrical mind, 8.34
theft, tendency, 12.20; 18.18-19
theism,
disposition, 12.18
moral restraint, 14.33
theory, limited, 14.1; 15.32
theory of Samkhya, 15.22
thesis, 24.23
thief, 3.15
thinking experience, 15.6
thinking expression, 16.1
thinking achievement, 15.12
third eye focus, 9.32
thirst, 4.27
thirteen factors, 17.23
thread, 7.21
tiger, 4.14
time,
agitator, 17.13
categories, 16.9
controls forms, 5.16
effects, 16.12
energy, 19.26-27
God as, 5.34
God's energy, 4.17
incidental, 18.43
knowing skill, 10.8
Krishna as, 11.10; 19.15
mundane influence, 20.30
time, continued,
object status, 16.10
perpetual? 5.14
pressure force, 17.42
reality, 19.19
sequential, 5.16
serpent, 3.41
sex desire distorts, 21.7-8
subtle type, 10.12
Supersoul potency, 7.20
tendency producing, 8.4
thief of wealth, 18.11
unseen, 17.42
Vishnu's form, 10.15
tolerance, 11.40; 14.36
tolerant person, 11.31
tone, 7.17
tongue
control, 14.36
demanding, 3.19-21
self pulled by, 4.27
touch impulse, 4.27
touch sensation, 11.36; 17.15
town, 20.25; 22.51
toy animal, 21.9
trader, 7.6; 16.31
tradition, 14.17
trance, 7.12
tranquility,
defined, 14.36
disposition, 12.16
renunciant's duty, 13.42
transcendence, 1.48
transcendental world, 23.26
transformation, 4.23
transit of life styles, 12.38
transmigration,
bewitching, 15.13
cause explained, 6.2
cultural activity, 20.32
details, 4.26; 20.21-22
false, 17.54
forgetfulness, 17.38-41
mind promotes, 18.44
passage, 17.51
tree-like system7.21
travelers, 12.53
tree,
bird detachment, 15.15
ignorance compared, 16.22
rated, 4.28
selfless, 2.38
liberated, 7.8
spirit compared, 17.53
tree-like system, 7.21
trend cycles, 11.28
Treta time cycle, 12.12
Triṣṭup, 16.41
troupe of dancers, 17.52
true, 19.26
trunk, 7.22
truthfulness,
defined, 14.38
disposition, 12.16
required, 12.21
tubers, 13.2
turīyam, 20.20
tvaṣṭri, 7.5
twigs, 7.22

U

Ucchaihshrava, 11.18
Uddhava,
advanced, 2.13
approach Krishna, 1.41-42
best person, 17.7, 29; 20.31
best realistic person, 24.21
Brahmā assessed by, 2.17
dear friend, 16.28
dearness compared, 9.15
devotees' predicament, 1.45
disciple of Bṛhaspati, 18.2
doubts, 7.16
easy process, 24.1
factors inquiry, 17.1
friend, 18.33
generous one, 17.39
great effulgent one, 24.13
inquiry expertise, 11.6
inquiry righteous, 12.9
instructed, 2.5
leader of devotees, 18.1
obeisances of, 24.36, 45
opinion/renunciation, 2.15
pilgrimage, 2.6
qualifications, 6.48
question on soul, 5.35
relationship, 6.48
renunciation, 2.14
request of, 1.43
rescue requested, 14.10
saint, 13.48, 16.21
Sanaka inquiry, 8.15
self critique, 14.10
sinless one, 11.19; 14.19
supernatural beings criticized by, 2.17
supreme secret given, 6.48
Ultimate Reality, 16.36-37
umbrella, 10.30
unadulterated spiritual plane, 9.4
Unaffected Reality, 23.26
unbaked pot, 11.43
unbroken grains, 22.33
uncertainties, 5.21
uncertainty, 6.13
unchangeable energy, 19.26
uncleanliness, 12.20
unconsciousness, 20.15
uncontrollable enjoyment, 23.15
understanding, 23.18

undesirable ethnic groups, 7.4
unified existence, 19.3
unity of spirits, 14.27
Universal Form, 12.13-15
universe,
contained, 19.21
Krishna created, 11.39
Krishna owns, 2.12
lotus, 19.10
unknown Krishna, 16.28
unmanifest potency, 19.26
unmixed energies, 20.1
unstable focus, 20.14
untruth, 20.4
urine, 3.33; 21.21
Urvaśī, 21.4
uśīra root, 22.30
Uṣṇik, 16.41

V

vagabonds, 18.36
Vaikuṇṭha, 2.18
valor, 12.17
vanaprastha,
begging rules, 13.18
details, 13.5-7
diet, 13.2
option, 12.55; 13.1
origin, 12.14
vapor, 2.43
variety,
cessation, 8.30-31
illusion, 23.4-7
Vasiṣṭha, 11.22
vastness, 16.10
Vāsudeva, 11.29
Vāsuki, 11.18
Vasus, 1.1; 11.13
Vedas,
authoritative, 16.36
Brahmā's reception of, 9.3
confusing, 16.42
daily recitation, 12.50
described, 9.3
details, 15.1-5
fanaticism, 16.34
God as, 5.34
incentives, 16.23
indirect, 16.35
Krishna proclaimed? 16.43
names/forms, 16.6
Om, 12.11
personified, 12.5
profound, 16.36
proof, 14.17
refutation, 15.5
revealer, 24.49
sound standard, 16.37
study required, 12.37
transcendental, 16.36
Uddhava defended, 15.1-5
unfathomable, 16.36
Vedas, continued,
unlimited, 16.36
worship rules, 1.11; 22.26
Vedic poetic meter, 16.39, 41
Vedic rites,
fanatics of, 16.27
ineffective? 7.9
recommended, 6.37
Vedic scriptures, 5.14
Vedic study,
compared, 1.9; 9.20
Krishna's view, 7.1
required, 23.18
unnecessary, 7.7
Vedic teaching, 7.9; 11.23
Vedic worship, 22.7, 49
vegetable sauce, 22.34
vermillion, 22.30
Vibhiṣaṇa, 7.6
vices, 18.18-19
Videha, 3.22, 34
vigilance, 7.24
vigor, 11.32
village, 22.51
Vinayaka, 22.29
violent tendency, 18.18-19
undesirable, 5.27; 16.38
Viriñci, 14.18
virtue,
basis, 2.8
beauty, 14.41
clarifying energy, 20.13
human objective, 2.27
transcended, 15.36
Viśālā, 24.47
Vishnu,
Aditi's son, 11.13
meditation upon, 10.15
Pingalā blessed, 3.37
vision,
detecting potency, 17.15
interactive, 17.31
Krishna motivates, 11.36
mind construction, 2.7
senses rob, 3.41
visual energy, 9.32
visualization, 17.37
Viśvadeva, 1.1
Viśvakṣena, 22.29, 43
Viśvāvasu, 11.33
vital air energy,
control, 11.42; 14.39; 18.32
factor, 17.19
lifting, 10.24
projection, 13.27
psyche part, 20.6
vitality, 7.17; 9.33; 18.25
vocal cords, 17.15
vowels, 16.39
vow,
aim of life? 9.10
approved, 6.37
dissipation, 11.43
householder's, 13.43
Krishna resists, 7.9
Krishna's view, 7.2
mind control, 18.46
unnecessary? 7.7
Vṛṣaparvā, 7.6
Vṛṣṇi, 24.39
vulture, 7.6; 21.19
Vyāsa, 22.2, 29

W

wakefulness, 8.27
wandering, 4.14; 23.9
warrior, 12.47
wasp, 2.34; 4.23
wastage, affects of, 5.21
waste of human body, 15.17
water place, 13.19, 21
water pot, 12.23; 22.20
water,
aquatics, 10.29
causal type, 19.10
compared, 2.44
counteracting, 10.8
effects, 16.12
filtered, 13.16
Krishna as, 11.20, 23, 37
offering, 1.37; 22.18
sanctification, 22.20
taste, 11.34
teacher, 2.33
tendency producing, 8.4
worship, 6.42-6.44; 22.17
wealth,
acquirement, 18.18
defined, 14.43
endeavor for, 4.26
financial gain, 20.7
happiness rare, 18.15
hell hereafter, 18.15
human objective, 2.27
non-accumulation, 14.33
renunciation, 13.43
righteous duty as, 14.39
thieves listed, 18.11
wasted, 18.25
weapons, 11.20
web, 16.38
weightlessness, 10.4, 12
welcome presentation, 22.22, 25
well being,
bird's, 15.15
highest, 15.35
means, 9.1
sources, 11.26
White Island Paradise, 10.18
white leprosy, 18.16

wife,
compared, 4.27
disloyal type, 6.19
husband, 2.56
indifference towards, 5.7
retiree, 13.1
temporary, 12.53
wild grain, 13.7
wind,
compared, 2.40, 2,41
detachment, 6.12
Krishna as, 11.23
wise man,
happiness? 5.18
passion resistant, 8.12
witness,
separate, 17.49
spirit, 8.32
wives of brahmins, 7.6
wives, Krishna's, 1.18
woman,
angelic type, 5.24; 10.25
association, 9.30; 21.22
bewildering, 3.8
familiarity prohibited, 12.33
figure of, 3.13
focus on, 12.56
foremost one, 11.25
God's bewilderment, 3.7
hazards, 9.30
liberated association, 7.3
womanizer, 3.32
wondrous manifestations, 11.5
wood, 16.12; 22.12
words, 8.4
work tendencies, 12.14, 15
worker, 12.49
working class,
disposition, 12.19
liberated association, 7.4
origin, 12.12-13
working organs
factor, 17.22
listed, 17.15
skills of, 17.16
working tendency, 4.27
world, 18.26
worries, 4.4
worship of devotees, 13.43
worship of gods, 16.32
worship of Krishna,
all-inclusive, 22.7
approved behavior, 14.3
articles, 22.27
contrary, 16.16
daily procedure, 12.50
devotion developed, 13.44
devotion mood, 14.5
exclusive, 6.33
facilities, 6.42-47
worship of Krishna, cont'
householder's, 13.43
Krishna resists, 7.9
Kumāras', 8.42
methods, 6.43-45
mode, 20.10-11
perfection, 14.6
procedure, 12.26
recommended, 20.33
regulations, 22.8-52
wrist, 4.6, 4.7

Y

Yādavās, 1.39
Yadu, King,
ascetic departs, 4.32
brahmins honored by, 2.31
freed, 4.33
matchless valor, 2.24
Nahusa's son, 2.36
questions ascetic, 2.25
Yadus, 1.23, 26, 29, 30
Yajna Vishnu, 8.38
Yaksha, 11.16
Yama, 11.18
year, 11.27
yearning,
gopi's, 7.13
misery, 14.41
yoga practice,
affection applied, 9.2
applications, 15.6; 16.1
bhakti type, 9.2
correction process, 15.25
death technique, 5.19
devotion applied, 14.8, 19; 15.33; 20.32
devotional result, 19.14
emotions applied, 15.8, 29
gist, 18.61
Krishna as, 11.24
Krishna Lord of, 10.35
Krishna resists, 7.9
Krishna's view, 7.1
limited, 15.32
meditation, 9.32
motivates search, 2.23
mystic application, 22.1
objective, 10.34
physical experience applied, 15.7
proficiency, 2.21; 10.1
required, 15.23
result, 2.45; 19.14; 23.43
samādhi, 18.46
Sanaka taught, 8.14-15
spirited devotion, 9.20
Swan taught, 8.38
systematic, 4.11
thinking experience applied, 15.7
yogi,
advanced details, 21.27
advanced type, 24.14; 27.18-19
attachment/non-attachment, 2.50
austerity, 1.47
begging, 3.12
benefactor, 6.29
body indestructible,? 10.29
culture transcended, 23.20
destination, 1.47; 13.10
determined, 23.29
devotional activities, 24.11
diet, 3.9
difficulties of, 23.38-39
disciplined, 6.29
elephant compared, 3.13
expert, 6.31
fame-resistant, 6.31
faultless, 6.29
food, 2.45
forbearing, 6.29
friendly, 6.31
gentle, 2.44
God focus, 3.6
gopis compared, 7.12
hereafter, 17.51
honey thief compared, 3.16
hygienic, 6.29
impartial, 6.29
indifference, 3.6; 6.17
Kapila, 11.15
knowing capacity, 10.28
Krishna as goal, 14.2
Krishna dear, 14.2
Krishna seen by, 2.21
Krishna's lotus feet, 1.10
Krishna's nature assimilated, 10.27
learned, 6.31
liberated association, 7.3
lifestyle, 18.32
merciful, 6.29
money, 18.19
most advanced, 11.28
music prohibited, 3.17
mystic skills, 10.1
non-enthusiasm, 3.4
non-possessive, 6.29
non-proficient, 11.43
pacified, 6.29
penetrating, 6.31
perception, 13.37
perfect stage, 24.43-44
philosophers, 11.25
pure natured, 2.44
purifies others, 2.44
qualifications, 1.7
qualities, 3.5; 6.29
relaxation of, 3.4

yogi, continued,
requirements, 13.17
resistant type, 24.3
satisfaction of, 2.39
self control, 10.16
sense control, 23.28
sense of values, 10.16
separated from moods, 2.40
shareholder, 18.24

yogi, continued,
spiritual master, 13.38
steady, 6.29
sun compared, 2.50
sweet, 2.44
transcendental, 2.41
turns away, 14.17
unaffected, 2.43; 6.29
worship daily, 12.50

yogurt, 22.34
youth, 17.46
Yudhisthira, 14.11

Z

zeal for worship, 13.43
zone/perfected beings, 19.12

Index to Commentary

A

Abhijit, 324
Absolute Truth, 65
absolute yogi? 283
abstinence, 471
accountability, 310
Acharya, 352
achievement, hereafter, 445
activity,
  basis, 55
  liability, 327
adbhuta-darśana, 13
adhyātma yoga, details, 20
Ādi Śaṅkara, 216
Adityas, 11
advaita, 559, 639
affection,
  components, 691
  development, 211
  purified, 625
  sexual force, 374
  yoga, 249
affection-needing stage, 113
Agastya, 154
agent, 683
Āghāra, 629
Agni, 351
Agnīdhra, 329
agonies, 293
ahankāra, 216
aims of life, 96
ākāśa, 292
akiñcana, 257
ākṛṣya, 230
Akrūra, 208
akṣa, 350, 532
akṣara dhāma, 292
akṣaram brahma, 653
Akṣardhām, 192
Almighty God, 78
alphabet, 482
alteration, 421
amalāśayah, 676
Americans, 283
ancestors, 406, 520, 521, 527, 594
Andhaka, 607
aṅga, 119
Angad, 251
angelic beings, 385
angelic body, 326
anguish, gopi, 208
aniha, 388, 500
anilāyāmāh, 388
animal, 205
animal sacrifice, 477
Aniruddha, 19
Annakūta, 627
ant, 370, 421, 660
anti-gravity, 283
antyeṣṭi, 329
Anu Gītā, 366
anumatena, 550
āpana mastery, 285
appearance days, 202
Araṇyaka Upanishad, 140
archeological evidence, 342
aristocratic status, 115
Arjuna,
  austerity, 273
  detachment, 96
  disagreed, 212
  eunuch, 286
  insight, 63
  instructed differently, 51
  Krishna's cremation, 10
  loss of vision, 400
  Nara Rishi, 323
  path involvement, 98
  questions, 312
  reversal, 366
  yoga practice, 694
arrogance, duty, 568
arrows, 517
artha,
  defined, 687
  spiritual substance, 246
artha-kāmukī, 116
Arundhati, 608
Aryamā, 11, 317
āsana,
  development, 134
  required, 222
asaty, 639
āśayam, 216
ascetic,
  detachment, 67
  donations, 365
  harassed, 512, 532
  isolated, 389
  king, 71
aśesa, 28
assertive force, 553
assertive sense, 562, 646-647
association,
  crucial, 394
  details, 185
  discarding, 583-584
  effective, 205-206
  hazards, 221
  imperative, 603
  Krishna attracted, 199, 203
  necessary, 588
  questioned? 133
  ruinous type, 136
  technical, 206
  women's, 266
assurance, 378
aṣṭanga yoga,
  avoidance, 569
  Krishna resists, 199
  Sanaka, 230
astral projections, 327, 390
astrology, 542
aśubha, 61
aśudhāśaya, 19
atheism, 419
atheist, 420
ātma, purity, 18
ātma dṛk, 73
ātma yoga, 20
ātma-samrodho, 321, 323
atmatayā sarva-bhāvena, 504
ātmatvam, 290
ātmavān, 403
atmaviśuddhaye, 199
attachment,
  elimination, 133
  Supreme Being, 209
  responsibility, 83
attention energy, 296
attitude, 70
attraction, 588
aum, 620
aura, 13
austerities,
  consistence, 154
  necessary, 696
  validated, 114

author,
Balarāma inspired, 634
Bhaktivedānta Swāmī, 368
books, 520
Brahma's planet, 358
brahmin, 368
commentaries lost, 634
Deity, 46
disciples, 397
disciplic succession, 431
exemption, 397
guru, 354
menial task, 368
mission, 397
subtle body, 283
woman hunter, 397
avadhūta, 65
Avanti brahmin,
advanced, 542
disguised, 531
kriyā yogi, 436
avatār, 479
avyavacchedan, 75
āyāmāh, 388
Ayu, 607

B

Bābāji, 139, 519
bachelor, 136
back side, 348
back to Godhead, 694
bacteria, 387
Badarāyaṇa, 27, 516
Badarinatha, 601, 693
Balarāma,
-208, 257, 577, 595, 634-635, 657, 669, 688
Krishna's partner, 49
yoga practice, 694
Bali, 22
bamboo root, 388
bandhas, 301
basis ultimate, 141
battle of psyche, 63
beads, 396
bear-men, 670
bears, 109
beauty, 435, 524
begetting, will power, 231
behavior,
details, 431
modes categorized, 579
yogi's, 78
belief,
Krishna, 310
mechanism, 63
modern, 275
salvation, 327
Bengali devotee, 265
betel nut, 631
bewildering energy, 88
Bhaga, 11
Bhagavad Gītā,
crash course, 222
summary, 314
targeted, 10
unbiased, 420
Bhagavān
Indian usage, 325
Nārāyaṇa, 292
reserved, 11
Bhāgavata Purāṇa,
Bhāgavatam, Śrīmad, 398, 595, 605, 620, 625, 665, 691
Bhagavati, 20
bhakti,
bhakti yoga? 196
control 457
defined, 442
problematic, 450
purity
redefined, 454
required, 425
spiritual type, 259
bhakti yoga
bhakti? 196
combination, 585
control, 457
details, 264, 442, 545, 656
independent, 249
kriyā yoga, 607
special, 458
Bhaktisiddhānta, 665
Bhaktivedānta Swāmī, Śrī,
-368, 388, 391, 431, 609, 616, 620, 633, 665, 673, 675, 690
head of lineage, 355
Bharat, King, 657
bhastrika, 295, 620
Bhima, 577
Bhishma,
death, 285
questioned, 417-418
Bhoja, 607
Bhṛgu, 317
bhūr, 555
bhūta-bhāvanah, 232
bhūva, 555
big joke, 696
bindu, 620
bird catcher, 90
birds, 174
birth
identity, 503
status, 345
stigma, 347
bleach out yoga, 273
blessing, 350
boar form, 372
boat compared, 38
body,
advantage of, 39
animalistic, 111
basis for next, 145
composition, 91
creator of, 86
genetic changes, 301
home, 436
lessons of, 144
light body, 215
owner, 144, 597
production, 539
protected, 400
reincarnation basis, 145
sexually matched, 82
special feature, 147
status, 508
types, 326, 652, 695
body-borne, 59
body-subsidized, 22
body-supported, 59
book publishing, 370
brahma, 559
brahma yoga, 359
Brahmā,
compared, 257
cultural activities, 421
God? 88
Mahādevah, 232
parent of, 10
planet attainment, 358
Procreator, 317, 482
reliance on, 232
respected, 33
self tantric, 324
soul of universe, 554
stipulation, 87
worries, 28
brahmacārī, 350
brahmān, 419
brahma-randra, 351
brahma-vādinām, 307
brahmin
caste, rigid, 364
disposition, 344
duties, 364
employment, 368
exalted type, 366
initiation, 612
suppressive, 347
tradition, 363
breast, 353
breath control, 656
Bṛhaspati, 59-60, 320
British authorities, 307
brow chakra protrusion, 283
brutality, 477
Buddha, 172, 174, 380, 387, 459

buddhi organ,
defective, 231
disabled, 176
orbs retracted, 280
sensing light, 212
spiritual sight, 391
buddhi yoga,
course, 649
necessary, 510
purpose, 158, 179, 216
bull, 341, 370
bullets, 517

C

cakṣu divyam, 678
cakṣuh, 295
calculator, 143
camel, 519
cannibalistic mystics, 252
canons, 619
carburetor, 228
casino, categorized, 579
caste
abuse, 465
system, 347
rule variation, 364
cat, 520
causal body,
cavity, 212
depressionless, 293
desire, 286
details, 21, 435
foundation, 216
penetration, 456
priority, 665
causal energy, 493
cause, 541
cave men, 342, 670
celibacy,
diet control, 589
essential, 351
life energy control, 449
required, 322, 362
risky, 523
rules, 363
Shiva's, 608
subtle body, 358
celibate ascetic, 107
celibate student, 343
ceremonial worship, 201
ceremony, 611, 613
cetasam, 388
Chaitanya Mahāprabhu, 19, 189, 195, 262-263, 327, 388, 414, 675
chakra, heart, 271-272
chance, 162, 174
chandāmsi, 202
Chandra, 37
change, 506
chanting,
confidence, 354
freedom from, 270
limited, 301
meditation, 390
nāda, 620
results, 451
reverential type, 602
stressed, 351
chaplain, 59
character, 436, 491
charity,
analyzed, 538
details, 346
Krishna resists, 201
child, 55, 131
children, 590
chit ākāśa, 176, 192, 270, 292, 694
Christ, Jesus, 88, 172
citta, 292
city, 579
clairaudience, 285, 295
clairvoyance, 285, 295
clarifying influence, 328
clay, 613
cleanliness,
association, 77
Krishna, 321
required, 366
yogic type, 352
cleansing agents, 321
cleansing power, 261
cleric, 108
clothing, 104
collateral, 371
Collective Person, 550
coma, 238
commentators, 665
companionship, 136
comparative similarity, 56, 194, 246, 495
compartmental space, 435
compartmentalized self, 419
compassion, 227
compatibility, 83
competition, 23, 98
components of psyche, 435
concentration energy, 303
concentration force, 281
conflict with destiny, 36
conglomeration, 159
congregation, 627
conjunction, 644
consciousness,
fourth stage, 576
inter-related, 237
conservation of energies, 77
constellations, 324
consultation, 669
consumption, 597
contact, 672
contaminant, 469
contention, 253
controversy, 487
convention, 467
conventional person, 659
converts, 206, 260
cosmic assertive sense, 551
cosmic awareness, 550
cosmic expansion, 283
cosmic force, 491
cosmic power, 290
cosmic subtle body, 342
cosmic vital energy, 482
cosmology, 487
couples hereafter, 164
cow, 317, 353, 370, 520
cowherd girls, 208
crash course, 222
craving, 174, 472
creation causes, 482
cremation, 10
critical energy, 119, 527, 596, 639
cruelty, 577
cruelty of life, 95
cultural activity,
abandoned? 187, 362
benefits, 177
body, 411
dead end, 153, 421
function, 373
limited, 409, 529
non-liberating, 384
obligations, 456
skills, 411
Universal Form, 470
yoga controls, 594
cultural personality, 498
curative repentance, 123
curse,
counteraction, 35
nullification, 40
spiritual master's, 350
customs officer, 505
cut-off point, 39

D

dairy animals, 520
Dakṣa, 10, 37, 317, 609
Dakṣiṇā, 201
daṅḍa, 388
Daśaratha, 52, 53, 111
Dattātreya, Lord, 149
dead end, 154
dear one, Yadu, 119
death,
details, 18, 163
forgetfulness, 503
mental condition, 143
preparations, 378, 390
regret, 528

death, continued,
rites, 617
salvation hoax, 390
singular experience, 390
subtle body experience, 293
time reliant, 39
decorating Deity, 220
deep sleep, 238
degradation, 471
Deity,
called, 614
cardinal points, 617
construction, 613
contact, 630
food, 618
limitation of, 293
mantra, 630
meditation, 303
movement, 614
turning away, 512
unnecessary? 390
visits, 366
Deity worship,
affection required, 616
audience, 615
complicated, 610
details, 615
deviations, 619
divine entry, 622
higher yoga, 195
kriyā yoga, 609
kriyās, 194
limited, 273-274
meals, 626
motive, 616, 635
mystic actions, 194
mystic type, 190
non-yogi, 633
play-house, 618
procedural basis, 625
samādhi, 629
secret procedure, 619
show type, 616
demerit, 454
depression,
causal body exempt, 293
cause, 118
energy, 567
hole, 40
nullification, 46
desire,
causal, 286
conquered, 120
desperation, 98
destiny,
bird catcher, 90
conflict with, 36
operations, 534
utility, 84
victimizes, 327
yogi adapts, 106, 517
detachment
devotional service, 99
elderly person, 380
possible, 55
required, 295
valuable, 96
determination, 513
detour, 203
deva,
duty, 60
Universal Form, 386
Devahūti, 59-61, 200
deva-kārya, 49
Devakī, 49, 53, 213, 325, 597
devatas, 353, 385
Devavrata, 418
Devī,
Goddess, 324
Urvaśī 591
Shiva's wife, 608
Devī Purāṇa, 136
Devil Kali, 50
devotee,
abusive? 344
best type, 188
deviant type, 423
endearing type, 257
greatest type, 258
helper assisted, 367
offering to Krishna, 189
reality-perceptive type, 186
yoga necessary? 259
yogi type, 44, 189
devotion,
compelling, 604
counterfeit, 413
crazy energy? 590
defined, 454
development, 211, 407, 428
difficult? 423
effective, 362
emotional energy, 691
faulty type, 260
gopi, 208
highlight, 408
impulsive energy, 572
limitations, 570-571
passionate type, 224, 260
profit as, 434
pulling force, 407
pure spiritual, 195
purity, 426, 427, 602
rapid method, 668
sentimental type, 570-571
spirited type, 259, 261
symptoms, 263
troublesome, 212
types, 570-571
devotional beliefs, 275
devotional meditation, 189
devotional process, 265, 266
devotional relationship,196
devotional service,
cultural disguise? 688
detachment as, 99
Krishna resists, 201
level of activity, 574
lifestyle, 184, 188
modes affect, 577
motive, 635
status affects, 368
types, 264
unpalatable? 151, 210
devotional yoga, 249
dhāranā,
clarified, 281, 303
described, 653-654
details, 176-177, 280, 287-289, 451
recommended, 182
technique, 296
dharma,
abandoned? 187
defined, 348, 687
deity, 622
details, 163
devotion? 426, 673
easy path, 443
king of law, 657
Krishna resists, 200
limited, 200
respected, 397
served not mastered, 568
social life only, 569
worrisome, 130
dharma yoga, , 568
Dhātā, 11
dhīra, details, 458
dhīrah, 216
dhoti, 396
Dhṛtaraṣṭra, 374, 378, 528
Dhruva, 261, 286
dhyāna,
clarified, 281
Deity worship, 195
described, 653-654
details, 280, 289
devotional, 189
misused, 583
diabetes, 55
diet, 114, 301, 589
difference of opinion, 488
Dilīpa, 530
dimension,
4th, 554
parallel type, 289
perception, 650
switching, 327
yogi transfer, 289
dinosaurs, 561
diplomacy, 322
discernment, 322, 506

disciple,
abuse, 370
advice, 356
rules, 363
disciplic succession,
Brahmā's family, 250
modern type, 251
yoga hostility, 191
disclaiming consequences, 200
disgust,
analyzed, 123
essential, 118
gained, 421
dishonor, worrisome, 130
disinterest, practice, 388
disparities, 343-344
dispassion, 435, 457
disposition,
clarity, 17
gauged, 570
important, 345
Diti, 11
diversity, 596
diversity of opinion, 322
divine beings, 300
divine emotions, 267
divine good luck, 445
divine grace, 71
divine vision, 678
divyam cakṣu, 685
dog, 369, 520
domestic animals, 520
donations, 365, 637
doubts, removed, 497, 686
Draupadī, 378, 694
dream,
affect dreamer, 645
comparison, 171
transmigration? 511
dṛṣṭim pratinivartya, 244
dry method, 98
durāśayanam, 21
Durgā, 179, 605, 608, 639
Duryodhana, 324, 349, 577
duty, 130, 409
dvādaśī, 202
Dvaipāyaṇa, 27, 516
Dvārakā, 10, 35
dvijah, 518
dvijottamah, 363
dying as desired, 285

E

earth, 445
earth Deity, 353
easy path, 267, 443, 474, 587, 655, 668, 673,
effects, 489
ekādaśī, 202
ekāntinam, 46
ekātmakam, 639
eko nārāyaṇo devah, 137
elastic, 493
elderly persons,
advancement, 528
austerity, 380, 381
respected, 353
wanderer, 385
electric current, 124
elephant, 68, 154
elevation, 576
embryo, details, 140
emotion,
components, 691
desire, 526
insensible, 94
life force, 690
low type, 443
match, 83
money, 526
motivation, 458
pleas, 385
purity, 450, 602
sorting, 695
struggle, 674
employee theft, 86
employment, 85, 369
endeavor, 100
endless happiness, 129
enemy within, 393, 433
energy, 297
England, 36
enjoyment, 597
entering another's body, 297
entwining manifestation, 140
environment, 436
evolution,
-22, 96, 215, 465-466
descent, 368
details, 576
pressure, 346
servants, 85
exemption, 396
exertion, 100
experiencer, 549
exploitation, 23, 38, 597
eye, 216

F

factors, details, 418
faith, 261, 399, 580
false guru, 403
fame, 370, 589
family,
abuse, 370
central issue, 82
diet, 522
individual fate, 371
pious asset, 522
spiritual type, 203
fanaticism, 310
fantasy, 107
farm land, 214
fasts, 202
fate, 534
favors, 365
fear, 697
female form, 91, 103
fifth class, 347
fifth Veda, 179
fire, 78-79
fire-god, 351
firewood, 78
fish, 112, 608
flag-pole insignia, 326
flames, 79
flirtation, 107
flower, 14
focus,
energy, 79
gopi, 208
immediate, 425
foes, 393
foliage, 277
food restriction, 656
force of bewilderment, 421
forest life, 379
forest, 393, 579
forgetfulness, 503
forgiveness, 328
form divine, 402
fortune, 521
four-handed form, 195, 197, 628
Four-handed Krishna, 200
fourth dimension, 292, 650-651
fourth stage, 576
fraud, 327
funds, 370
fusion, 641

G

gambling, 579
gandha, 561
Gāndhārī, 378
Gandhi, 307
Gaṇesh, 353
Ganga, 591
Gangotri, 295
garland, 14
Garuḍa, 317
Gautama Rishi, 364, 612
Gāyatrī, 20, 202, 608
genetic tendencies, 301
geography, 555
ghoṣa, 294, 329, 649
glories of Krishna, 29
glorification, 40
God,
appearances, 78
contact, 292
cooperation, 324
energy, 88
Goddess Ganga, 358
goddess Urvaśī, 591

Godhead, 192
gold, 56, 104
good/bad, 55
good luck, 111, 445
goodness, 203
gopas, 188
gopi,
anguish, 208
imitation, 569
privileged, 189
reached Krishna, 195
unique, 209
Gopīparanadhana dās Adhikārī, 149, 391, 620
Goraknatha, 608
Gour-Nitai, 675
Govardhana Pūjā, 627
Govinda, 195
grace of God, 530, 595
grace, 71, 123
grāmya-gītam, 110
granite, 56
greed,
instinct, 105
religious institutions', 105
senses inhabited, 569
spiritual leaders', 105
green bird, 277
gṛha-medhīyair, 374
grief mechanism, 372
group effort, 63
guarantee, 635
guṇa virtues, 246
guru paramparā, 191
guru, see spiritual master

H

habit, 132, 454
hamsa yogi, 294, 670
Hamsa, Lord, 341
handcrafter, 369
Hanuman, 207, 251, 325-326, 353
happiness,
mundane type, 581
spirit self's, 129
supreme type, 130
yoga details, 435
hardship dimension, 385
Hari, 532
harsh words, 517
harsha, 393
haṭha yoga,
criticized, 269
frugal practice, 105
genetic changes, 301
required, 222
haṭha yogi, 665
head of lineage, 352
hearing,
distant sound, 295
effects, 42
insufficient, 158
limited, 645
heart chakra, 270, 628
heaven,
belief, 93
details, 163
hereafter, 112
impediment, 18
hell, 165, 436
hereafter, 98, 163
hiding place, 373
high octane, 228
high speed perception, 285
higher power, 529
Himalayas, 601
Hiraṇyagarbha, 482
Hiraṇyakaśipu, 206, 261, 372, 665
Hiraṇyakṣa, 372
history, 421
hoarding, 106-107, 109
hoax, 400
home body, 436
honey bee, 105, 106
honey thief, 109
honor sannyāsi, 404
hook, 112
hooker, 116
hope, 118
horse, 36
hostility,
anti-social acts, 388
warded off, 177
hotel, 372
householder life,
begetting limit, 520
bothersome, 522
celibacy, 366
cultivation, 362
dispensable, 371
exalted type, 366
hiding place, 373
insanity, 523
kundalini yoga, 374
management, 371
mission, 522
origin, 343
recommended, 519
righteous duty, 590
risky, 523
sexual pawn, 592
shareholders, 520
spiritual practice, 136
Supreme Being, 92-94
troublesome, 519
waiver, 528, 591
wife abandonment, 378
yogi lifestyle, 373
Hrdayānanda dās Gosvāmī, 149, 391, 620
human being, 475, 673
human sacrifice, 477
humanity, 146
humility, 69, 119
hunger, 293
hunter, 95, 205
hygiene, 366
hymns,
limited, 202
variations, 625

I

I and my, 59
I exist, 552
ideation, 289, 571
identity, 498
ignorance, 490
iha, 388
Ikṣvāku, 99
Ilā, 589
illusion, 411
imagination orb, 273
importance, 660
incentive,
belief in, 475
leaders peddle, 475
motivation, 474
independent path, 249
India, 252
Indian tradition, 364
indifference, 388
individual practice, 63
Indra, 27, 386
Indradyumna, 154
infallible radiance, 304
infamy, 130
infatuation, 591, 593
influences, 187, 575
inherent nature, 543
initiation, 222
initiative, 500
injury, 541
insanity, 523
insect, 70, 105, 521
insight, 649
insignia, 396, 404
instinct, 144, 505, 551
institutional achievement, 63
instructions, 183
insults, 534
intellect,
calculator, 143
control of, 228, 239
curbing process, 157
dhyāna misused, 583
energy preference, 226
flawed, 225
habits of, 176
inaccurate, 104
instinct, 176

intellect, continued,
liberation resistant, 232
mind, 495
quiet condition, 598-599
reward-seeking, 510
speed, 227
truth-bearing, 646
yoga curbs, 158
intention, 613
introversion, 295
intuition, 235, 403
investing hopes, 118
involvers, 493
īśah, 27
I-sense, 280
isolation,
location, 534
psychological, 221, 284
waiver, 221
iṣṭā-pūrtam, 201
Īśvara, 419

J

jackstay plank, 36
Jaḍa Bharata, 136, 368, 396, 398, 597
jagatām īśvareśvaram, 40
jai śrī mahādeva, 353
Jain, 387
Jāmbavān, 206, 251
Janaka, 136
Janak, Yajñavalka, 140
Japa, elementary, 432
Jayadratha, 568
Jehovah, 88
Jesus Christ, 88, 172, 324, 519
jewel Deity, 613
jijīviṣubhir, 36
jita-svāsasya, 280
jitendriyasya, 280
Jīva Goswāmī, 19
jīvam mukta, 179
jīvāśayam, 216
jīvatma, 419
jñāna, 549
jñāna dīpena, 649, 685
jñāna yoga, 100, 233, 656
jñānam kevalam, 677
jñāni, 102
jobber, 369
joke, 696
judges, 350
jungle animal, 71
jurors, 350
jyotir jyotiṣi, 277

K

Kacha, 357
kaivalyam, 239, 458-459, 578, 676
Kālī, 20
Kali devil, 50
Kali Yuga, 520
Kāliya, 206
kāma, 373-374, 393
Kāmadhenu, 317
Kansa, 607
Kapila, 59-61, 200, 317
Kardama, 200
karma,
defined, 687
function, 373
householder's, 374
status cause? 507
yoga controls, 594
karma yoga,
compliance limited, 409
course, 222
cultural skills, 411
details, 568, 656
higher duty, 233
insufficient, 408
necessary, 235
obstructed? 397
respected, 99
stages, 98
wiped out, 52
karmāśaya, 362
Karṇa, 357
kathā, 264
kauśala, 106
kāya, 662
Kayādhu, 205
Keśava, 41
kevalam, 76, 578, 676
kevalam nirvikalpitam, 549
Khaṭvānga, 530-531, 584
Kimpuruṣa, 251
kindevas, 252
king,
ascetic, 71
hereafter, 367-368
liberated, 205
options, 369
responsibilities, 367
king of law, 657
kīrtan, 675
knowledge,
insufficient, 419
sources, unnecessary? 457
Krishna,
assists anyone, 324
attractions, 199
boar form, 372
body physical? 46
body special, 186
cooperation, 674
cremation, 10
denied, 311
director of self, 122
gopi focus, 208
humility, 32
Krishna, continued,
Lord of lords, 40
Lord of teachers, 307
love, 407
Master of yoga, 41
matches forms, 29
names, 168
Nārāyana, 24
origin of yoga, 57
pastime effects, 45
Personality of Godhead, 53
physical presence, 46, 690
preferences, 199
prime master of yoga, 57
protector of great souls, 430
relationships, 43
reliance, 297
residence, 579
responsibility, 33
sannyāsa, 323
spiritual form, 272, 274-275
spiritual master, 436
supernatural, 13
treasure of yoga, 57
unaffected, 29, 171
unbiased, 323
whimsical? 36
yoga person, 57
yoga practice, 694
yoga supportive, 435
yoga-sambhava, 57
yogātam, 57
yogeśa, 57
Krishna-Balarāma, 634, 675
Krishna Conscious lifestyle, 184
Krishna Conscious Societies, 260
Krishna Conscious training, 322
Krishna Consciousness,
Bhaktivedānta, 675
Krishna's lessons, 327
solution, 417
unnatural? 265
Krishna Dvaipāyaṇa, 516
Krishna kathā, 264
Krishna kathā, 264
Krishna Mūrti, 220
kriyā mystic acts, 610
kriyā yoga
bhakti yoga, 607
clarity, 501
Deity worship? 633
householder, 373
practice, 268
specialized, 609
summary, 694
teacher, 374
kriyā yoginis, 608
krodha, 393

Kṛṣṇa-Balarāma, 634, 675
Kṛta Age, 325
Kṛtavarma, 607
kṣemāṇām, 323
kṣetra, 436
Kṣīrodakśāyī Vishnu, 10
Kubera, 318
Kukura, 607
Kumāras,
-136, 320, 322
devotion of, 247
greatest yogis, 247
proud, 235
kundalini,
celibacy, 351
control 374
death passage, 298
movements, 296
rise/fall, 269
sex usage, 351
kundalini yoga,
householder, 374
life energy control, 449
purpose, 179
required, 269, 352
Kuru civil war, 203
kusha grass, 327
ku-yogī, 656

L

Lahiri Mahāśaya, 139, 222, 280
Lakṣmanji, 207
Lakṣmī, 20, 257
lamentation, 372, 385
language, 548
last act, 39
last minute changes, 530
law and order, 151
law of psychology, 504
leading devotees, 191
learning methods, 62
leonine form, 318
liability, individual, 327
liberation,
cultural activity, 384
efforts, 509
everyone, 420
facility, 527
ignored, 93
objective, 551
obligation, 417
requirement, 240
subjective, 551
life force, 60
lifestyle, 184, 363-364
līlā avatāras, 179, 181
limited beings, 412
lingering resentments, 534
linkage of attention,
details, 281
locations, 287
misused, 583
linkage of yogi, 296
linking the will, 280
lion, 136
lithurgy, 349
livelihood,
brutal methods, 388
violence of, 613
living quarters, 146
loans, 371
lobha, 393
location, 221
logic, 421
Lomash Rishi, 345
lotus feet, 19
lotus flower universe, 214
lotus pose, 268
love,
purified, 625
strongest, 458
lover, 124
lower energies advantage, 229
luck, 163, 445

M

Mā Durgā, 179
mad-arcanam, 432
Madhavānanda, Swāmī, 187, 293, 370
Madhvācārya, Śrīmad, 355
Madhva-Gaudiya sampradāya, 665
magic of reincarnation, 505
magistrates, 350
mahā yogis, listed, 45
Mahābhārata, 205
Mahabhisha, 358, 591
Mahādevah Brahma, 232
Mahāmāyā, 291
mahān, 551
Mahāpuruṣa, 635
mahāt ttava, 290-291, 551
Mahatma Gandhi, 307
Mahāvīra, Lord, 387
Mahāviṣṇu, 24
Maitreyī, 193
mamāham, 59
mana, 393
Mandana Mishra, 510
Mandella, Nelson, 307
manipulation, 260
mantra,
Deity, 630
effect, 470
secrecy, 620
usage, 223
Manu Samhitā, 465
Manu, 10, 99, 317, 322
Māricha, 252
Martikavat, 607
Marut, 11
master of yoga, 41
mat padam, 573
mat-dharma, 673
material nature/energy,
alterations, 421
detachment, 76
difficult to transcend, 514
divested, 499
evolutionary pressure, 346
fatiguing, 60
influences, 575
mother, 398
predominant, 582
promising power, 421
spirit self, 497
vegetation, 113
material world,
intertwining, 361
purpose, 557
termination, 559
unalterable? 417
Mathurā, 208
matimān, 665
mat-parah, 665
Matsyendranath, 608
mauna, 388
māyā, 290-291, 421, 549
māyā-mano-maya, 51, 53
māyayeme, 61
mayy āveśitayā yukta, 545
meals, 389
medicinal foods, 662
meditation,
prāṇāyāma required, 354
procedure, 653-654
membership, 424
memorial days, 202
memory rebirth, 505
menial service, 368
mental energy, 613
mental fabrication, 52
mental vigor, 328
merchantile evolution, 369
mercy energy, 125-126
mergence, 76, 277, 559
merit, 454
metal Deity, 613
methods, 234, 572
microbes, 660
microscope, 283
microscopic creatures, 387
milk/water comparison, 294
mind,
chamber, 292
connection, 436
control, 571
creator, 51
hygiene, 366
intellect, 495
muscle, 281
new body attitude, 504
operational instincts, 231
psyche ruler, 539

mind, continued,
self? 495
supernatural, 540
mineral, 56
misapplication, 201
misidentification, 56
missionary, 99, 413
Mitra, 11
modern civilization, 145
modesty, 435
moha, 393
mokṣa, 417, 687
money,
acquirement, 38
danger, 523
desire, 526
elusive, 525
happiness
instinct, 38
monk hoarding, 109
monkey-men, 670
monogamy, 363-364
monopoly worship, 620
moon deity, 353
moon, 202, 318, 353
moral principles, 203, 430
morality, neglect of, 471
moth, 103
Mother Earth, 353
mother nature, 398
mothering energy, 103
motivational energy, 567
motive ceremony, 613
motive, disciples, 357
mudrā, 268
Muktānanda, 280, 297
mukti-dvāram, 96
mūla mantra, 202
mūlādhāra, 298, 351, 653
multiplicity, 435
mumukṣur, 267
muner, 301
muni, 73, 102
muscles, internal, 433
music, 110
mutation, 500, 506
mystery, reciprocation, 208
mystic perception, 223
mystic skills, 287, 306
mystic vision, 650
mystics, gifted, 101

N

nād/naad,
inner sound, 294
meditation details, 653
practice, 449
sound, 176, 574
spiritual, 329
yoga, 269-270
naḍi, 270
nairapekṣa, 435
nanny goat, 520
Nara Rishi, 323
Nārada Pañcaratra, 608, 625
Nārada, 136, 317
detachment, 317
exceptional, 258
grace of, 205
Nara-Nārāyaṇa, 693
Nārasiṅgha, 318
Nārāyaṇa,
chosen Deity, 102
coverage, 103
God in Person, 630
invited, 40
Krishna, 24
One God, 137
pujāri contacts, 630
Rishi, 323
Vāsudeva, 668
yogi reaches, 292
nasal bindu, 620
nature's schemes, 371
neck bags, 396
nectar, 106
needle, 519
need-repression, 113
Nelson Mandella, 307
nigṛhāna manodhiyā, 545
nirguṇah, 578
nirvāṇa, defined, 278
nirvedah, 118, 421
Nityānanda, Swāmī, 396
nivṛtti mārga, 388
niyama,
introspective, 219
listed, 431
purpose, 202
subtle body, 348
non-devotee yogi, 324
non-energetic assertion, 553
non-excitation, 102
non-interference, 179, 639, 643
non-profit organizations, 346
nonviolence,
extreme type, 387
full, 406
hardest vow, 321
nose meditation, 268
November-December, 324
Nṛsiṅghadeva, 206
nullification, 40
nutrient-craving stage, 113
nutrition,
female form, 104
patron deity, 353
senses, 112

O

objectification, 551, 557
objectivity imparted, 81
oblations, 351
obligation,
elimination, 456
endless, 521
ultimate type, 417
observances,
appearance days, 202
details, 431
observers, 493
ocean compared, 38
offering oneself, 122
offering to Krishna, 189
offering activity, 574
om indrāya namah, 353
om somāya namah, 353
Om/omkāra sound,
-270, 341
buddhi stabilized, 276
kriya, 270-271
unchanted, 620
om suryāya namah, 353
omnipotence, 50
one consciousness, 243
oneness,
-501, 560
approved type, 639
details, 578
Krishna as, 329
opinion, 322, 488
opportunity sexual, 90
option,
Krishna, 261
limited being, 284
opulences, 328
orbit, 283
ornaments, 104
outlaws, 328

P

padmāsana, 268
paint Deity, 613
Pandavas,
austerities, 409
yoga practice, 694
Paramātmā, 174, 212, 418-420
Paramāyanam, 603
Paramhansa Ramakrishna, 139
paramhansa, 680
paramparā, 191
Parāśar Muni, 27
Pāraśurāma, 357
parental pride, 374
parental-guiding energy, 590
parents, 84, 89, 90
Parīkṣit, 10, 27, 516
participation, 174
particular individual, 215
partyāhar, 146
passion,
details, 55
overpowering, 599
subtle aspects, 404

past life activities, 144
pastimes, 42, 45
Patañjali,
139, 230, 239, 307, 391, 676
path of involvement, 98
path of non-involvement, 388
patron deity,
Sātvatas, 631
yogis' 353
pedigree, 345
penance, 200
perception,
dimensions, 650
direct, 62
high speed, 285
potency, 553
permanence instinct, 421
person/personality,
details, 659
multiple, 549
quantity in body, 550
unification of, 559
pets, 520
phala, 549
philosophers, 23
physical Krishna, 690
piety management, 527
pigeon, 82-84
pilfering, 86
pilgrimage,
expectations, 202
Krishna resists, 202
service, 366
Piṅgalā,
-116, 421, 532
appreciation, 123
pious activities, 385
placenta, 539
planet, as cause, 541
pleasure, stolen, 87
policy, 322
politician,
hereafter, 367-368
options, 369
responsibilities, 367
status, , 592
politics in temples, 533
polygamy, 363-364
popularity, 592
possessiveness, 129
postures, 134
potential, 471
pottery, 549
poverty, 64, 132
Prabhāsa, 36, 41
pradhāna, 551
Pradyumna, 19
pragalbhayā, 259
Prahlāda,
98, 205, 206, 261, 317, 318
prakṛtaya, 345
prakṛtih, 209, 549
Pramukha Swāmī, Śrī, 355
prāṇa, 60
prāṇa citta, 696
prāṇa karma, 222
prāṇavāyu, 500, 620
prāṇa vision, 272
praṇaya, 690
prāṇāyāma,
effects, 146, 285
necessary, 228
purpose, 280
required, 73, 242, 351
prasīdeta, 574
pratipatnī, 20
pratyah, details, 110
pratyāhar,
ākṛṣya, 230
details, 219, 280, 448
proficiency, 391
purpose, 244
pratyakṣa, 62
prāyah, 259, 577
predestination, 343-344
predisposition, 505
preference, Krishna's, 212
prejudice, 364
prema, 625
pretense devotion, 179
pride,
details, 160
parent's, 374
priest,
assumptions, 622
daily routine, 618
mystic required, 616
qualifications, 611
primal creative cause, 484
primal male being, 24
primal mundane potency, 562
Primal Reality, 549
Prime Mover, 642
principle of objectivity, 216
privacy, 81
priyatama, 257
problems in psyche, 539
product, 549
productive power, 549
profile human, 673
profit devotion, 434
progression, 218
prominence, 689
promising power, 421
prostitution, 116, 121
Protector of great souls, 430
providence,
acceptance, 100
confidence in, 106
submission, 372
proximity, 497
psyche,
components, 216, 435, 646
cultural activities, 378
details, 15
dissected, 659
faults, 499
purification, 670
restraint, 321
separation, 239
sorting, 690
psychic equipment, 103
psychic insight, 62
psychics, 101
psychology, 504
pujārī,
advisory, 194
assumptions, 622
caste type, 618
daily routine, 618
Deity meals, 626
destination, 636
discrepancies, 619
faults of, 192
ideal type, 190-191
mystic perception, 628
necessary, 627
non-yogi, 633
pretense, 609
requirements, 192
samādhi, 628
silence, 192
tradition respected, 617
types, 618
yoga qualifications, 191
Pumān, 24
Purāṇas, 419, 474, 608
Purāṇi, 146
purification, 19, 267-269
purificatory kriyās, 326
purified souls, 109
purity yoga, 293
Purūravā, 589, 595-596
puruṣa, 290, 419-420, 493,
498, 549, 559, 639
Pūrvacitti, 328-329
Pūṣā, 11

Q,R

quarrel, course, 472
quiescent nature, 551
Rādhā- Kṛṣṇa,
195, 624-625, 675
Rahūgaṇa, 368
rain, Ṛṣyaśṛṅga, 111
rāja yoga, 230, 269
rāja yogi, 665
rājarṣis, 28
Rakshas, 318
Rāma, Śrī, 51-54, 136,
206-207, 320, 353, 670
Rāma, Balarāma, 208
Rāma, Swāmī, 373

Ramakrishna Paramhansa, 139
Ramana Maharishi, 388
Rāmānujācārya, Śrīmad, 355
Rāmāyaṇa, 111, 205, 251, 325
Rāvaṇa, 252
reality,
abstract, 558
discussed, 120
unfavorable? 344
rebels, 22
rebirth,
details, 93
evolutionary thrust, 96
influences, 577
memory, 505
new body, 504
sexual cause, 108
recitation, 470
red-blue light, 646
regret invoked, 385
reincarnation 107, 436, 505
relationship, 61, 122
relatives,
displeased, 528
extensive, 297
sporadic, 579
Supreme Being, 125
religion,
diversity, 252
hoax, 402
limited, 107, 413
salvation hoax, 390
validity, 325
value, 476
varied, 255
victims, 478
religious hoarding, 107
religious work, 577
remembering Krishna, 195
renunciant,
definition, 433
psyche resists, 395
radical ones, 106
repentance, 37
repossession, sannyāsis, 106
repression, 113
research, 65
resentments, 177
residence temple, 533
resources, 472
response, 284
responsibility,
attachment dulls, 83
defined, 348
piety management, 527
unhappiness derived, 131
wealth, 527
worrisome, 130
restriction, 109
result, 549
retiree, 382, 386
retirement, details, 379, 382
retrogression, 179, 560
reverberation nāda, 620
reversal, 360, 394
rich man, 64
Rig Veda, 342
righteous duty,
abandoned? 187
devotion developed, 407-408, 426, 428
devotional service? 151
easy path, 587, 681-682
execution, 527
factors, 470
faults, 568
insufficient, 262
Krishna resists, 200
limited, 200
necessary, 463
righteous life style, 443
risk, disciple's, 425
rites, lifelong, 349
ritual hymns, 202
roadside inn, 372
rod, 388
Rohinī, 49
romance, 600
Ṛṣabhi, 657
Ṛṣyaśṛṅga, 111
ṛtambharā buddhi, 649
ruby, 327
Rudra, 12
Rudrākṣa, 350, 532
rulers, 350
run for it, 378
ruse, 390

S

śabdi nabhasah parah, 329
sacred recitation, 470
sacred thread, 396
sacred word, 223
sacrifice, 477
sacrificial ceremony, 202
sacrificial fire, 627
ṣaḍ-guṇah, 187
ṣaḍ-vargam, 393
ṣaḍ-vikārah, 393
saintly devotee, 603
salesman, 369
salvation,
before death, 374
easy path, 474
fantasy, 107
farce, 475
hoax, 390
instant type, 584
questioned, 43
requirements, 697
Sāma Veda, 342
samādhi,
clarified, 281
Deity worship, 195
faked, 414
full restraint, 321
memory, 274
yoga unnecessary, 414
Sāmba, 37
Sāṁkhya/yoga, 317
sampradāya, 191
samsāra, 140
sāmya, 246
samyama, 303, 391
samyojya, 296
samyutam, 277
Sanaka, 322
Sanandana, 322
Sanat Kumār, 322
Sanātana, 322
sand Deity, 613
Sandīpani Muni, 350
Śaṅkarācārya, Ādi Śrīpad,
-216, 257, 297, 355, 373
detached bird, 510
Sañkarṣaṇa, 19, 257
Sāṅkhya,
Krishna resists, 200
realized, 548
required, 63
yoga, 200, 245, 317
sannikarṣaṇam, 645
sannyāsa,
Krishna as, 323
mantra, 374
tyāgi, 433
sannyāsi,
defined, 65, 693
deviant type, 423
failure, 220
frustrated, 589
honor motive, 404
impediments, 373
insignia, 396
jailed, 616
radical ones, 106
santam, 120
Śantanu, 368
Sarasvati, 20
śarīra karma, 222
sat saṅga, 199
sat saṅgī, 203
sat, 662
Śatarūpā devī, 322, 323
satellites, 283
sat-pate, 430
Śatru, 11
sat-saṅga, 203
Satvata, 607
Sātvatas, 328, 607, 691
Saubhari Muni, 598
saving others, 527

Savitā, 11
Savitrī, 608
science, 557
scripture limitations, 220
secretive hymns, 202
seeds compared, 214
seer, separation, 239
self critique, 596
self focus, 135
self realization, 147, 175, 652
self tantric sexist, 324
self worship, 194
self,
-see also spirit self
mind? 495
psyche resistance, 543
self-ambition, 471
self-critical, 527
self-death, 108
self-directive person, 403
self-inflicted injury, 541
selfishness, inate, 193
self-ness, 290
self-reform, 121
seminal spills, 352
seniority, Kumaras, 233
sense of "I", 552
sense of identity,
compelling, 119
flawed, 226
sense of initiative, 216, 500
sense of possessiveness, 129
sense of survival, 466
sense of taste, 113
senses,
nutrition affects, 112
orbits, 112
perverted needs, 220
sense objects, 500
wives compared, 146
sensual energy,
conservation, 77
reliance broken, 597
sensual equipment, 125
sensuality, dictatorial, 596
sensuous, music, 110
separate equipments, 401
separation/Krishna, 41
servants of evolution, 85
seśah, 27
sevā, 370, 454
sex desire, water, 221
sex energy, 590
sexual affairs, 595
sexual attraction, 592
sexual emission, 351
sexual indulgence, 82, 374
sexual intercourse, 322, 590
sexual opportunity, 90
sexual pleasure, 374
sexual potency, 499
sexual release, 351, 374
sexual reproduction, 10
sexuality, resistance, 108
sexuality transcended, 116
sexually-charged potency, 140, 290
Shaivite devotee, 532
shareholders, 520
Shiva,
-134, 350, 520, 532, 595, 657, 662, 669, 688
extraordinary, 27-28
God? 88, 324
Mahādevah, 232
patron deity, 353
Supreme God? 10
shrine service, 366
Shuka, 136, 516
Shukracharya, 357
Shurasena, 607
siddha,
defined, 297
Indra respected, 12
political type, 28
Siddhārtha, 95
siddhāsana, 268
siddhis,
manifestation, 287
methods, 306
problematic? 281
silence technique, 388
similarity, 194, 246
simpleton, 396
Sītā, 670
śivo-ham, 374
six agonies, 293
six enemies, 393
six influences, 187
six-legged insect, 105
skills, 411
skin disease, 524
sky of consciousness, 272, 573
sleep, 640, 649
sloth, 101
soil, 560
soul of universe, 554
soul,
-see also spirit self
22, 195
sound, subtle, 212, 630
sour dealings, 77
sources, 420
South Africa, 307
South America, 36
South, 617
space and time, 493
species rights, 387
specific self, 124
speech, 15
spirit self,
absolute, 75
background, 79
bird comparison, 174
body supported, 22
body supported, 59
bound / freed, 169
centralized in mind, 241
confused concepts, 661
contrasted, 174
controlled, 412
decisive power, 145
detached, 510
distinct, 155
dominance struggle, 113
escape of, 241
faulty equipment, 103
identity sorted, 498
influenced, 79
instinct carried, 505
intellectual dependence, 510
Krishna director, 122
limited, 139
limited, 493
linkage with matter, 645
material nature, 497
mimics psyche, 155
mind attached, 537
new body attitude, 504
non-partitioned, 75
observer, 216
observer, 508
potency controlled, 291
potency type, 139
psychic equipments, 102
purification, 61
relation with other selves, 126
reliance on Supreme Spirit, 537
resource, 113
satisfaction, 651
self-rescue, 513
sensually reliant, 597
similarities, 71
subjective consciousness, 493
spirited devotion, 259, 261
spiritual body, 274-275
spiritual emotion, 695
spiritual eyes, 273, 685
spiritual form,
abstract, 238
symptoms, 283-284
spiritual master,
advancement, 371
approach, 356
blessings, 373
ceremonial worship? 354
differences with, 356

spiritual master, continued,
disciple abuse, 370
fame crazy, 370
faults, 424-425
forestalled, 301
incarnation? 371
individualistic, 148
isolated, 225
Krishna as, 435
Krishna substitute, 424
limited, 223
misguided, 683
monopoly, 407
old age, 384
political type, 28-29
qualifications, 358
rejection of, 154
risk of, 681
selection, 354
types, 106, 355
Universal Form conflicts, 221
spiritual plane, 414
spiritual progress reversal, 394
spiritual sky focus, 277, 573
spiritual vision, 304
spiritual world transfer, 273
spring, 324
śraddhayā, 261
Śrī, 20
Śrīdhara Swāmī Mahārāja, Śrīla, 149, 620, 665
śrīvatsa, 304
staff, 396
stagnation in temples, 533
stainless steel, 104
state treasury, 345
status,
discarding, 396
origin, 507
providence controls, 369
stokam stokam, 105
stone Deity, 613
straight-forwardness, 366
student rules, 363
study of Vedas, 200
stupidity, 125
subconscious mind, 505
substitution spiritual master, 424-425
subtle body/form
antigravity, 283
components, 15, 239
control, 176
cosmic type, 342
cultural form, 411
death impression, 293
disintegration of, 293
effects of, 144
elimination, 402
subtle body/form, continued,
energization, 134
essential, 216
sensual perception, 329
skeleton, 15
subtle energy, 146
subtle light link, 295
subtle perception, 399, 501
subtle sound, 212
śucih, 352
Sudāma Vipra, 258
sudarśan, 326
sugar, benefit, 55
Sugriva, 251
suicide, 400
Śuka, -see Shuka
sukhāsana, 268
Śukrācārya, 325
sukṣma karma, 378
Sumtotal Reality, 549
sun,
compared, 80
deity, 353, 615
destination, 215
light offering, 615
recognized, 353
super-energy, 297
supernatural form, 13, 304
supernatural geography, 555
supernatural rulers,
origin, 553
respected, 353
rulers, trek, 13
supernatural vision, 13, 63
Supersoul, 212, 495
- see also Paramātmā
suppression, 471
Supreme Being,
concept of, 138
denied, 311
fabulous, 420
independent agent, 125
unique, 139
Supreme, 496
Supreme God, 10
Supreme Person, 23, 214
supreme principle, 88
supreme reality, 56
supreme refuge, 603
surcharging subtle body, 303
surrender, Uddhava, 210
survival, 36, 466
survival instinct, 98
su-samyojya, 296
suśumna naḍi, 270, 271
suśumnā naḍi, 620, 653
sūtram,
-140, 213, 290-291, 481-483, 491, 493, 550
dangerous, 359
divested, 499
svadhā, 370
svādhyāyas, 200
svāhā, 370
svānanda-tuṣṭa, 651
Śvaphalka, 208
svar vāsam, 48
svayam-bhūh, 34
svayambhūr, 232
Swāmī Rāma, 373
Swāmīnārāyaṇa, 327, 387
Swan form, 233, 341
swan, mythical, 294
swan-like yogi, 670
swaying back and forth, 402
swim, 77
Śyāmasundara, 195
symbol of farming, 341

T

tantric ceremony, 611
tanu, 22
tapah, 200, 696
taste, 112, 329
tattva, 152
tax laws, 346
teachers, 148
tears, 690
technique, 157
tejah, 365
temple,390
temple attendance, 366
temple construction, 370
temple devotee, 373
temple services, 627
temple, property, 637
tendency,
curbing, 471
eternity, 104
permanence, 104
predestined? 343-344
tension, brahmin eased, 534
texture of existence, 18
theft, , 86
thief, birds, 87
thighs, 343, 599
thread, 396
tiger, 71, 136
tilak application, 366
time,
barrier, 289
functional supervision, 559
Universal Form's, 591
time-bound, 107
time-regulated, 22
tiny red-blue light, 646
tīrthāni, 202
Tirthankaras, 387
titanium, 104
tīvra tapasā, 362
tolerance, 533, 349
tooth and nail, 479
towels, 372

town, 579
trader 205, 478
tradition,
details, 467
ignorance, 376
limited, 421
respected, 617
trance, 237
transmigration,
animal form, 64
bewildering, 509
details, 140, 326, 502-504, 576
impulsive, 359
meaningless? 511
sequence, 647
sponsorship, 446
travelers, 372
travelers, 372
traveling salesman, 369
trek, 13
trespassing, 365
treta time cycle, 342
tri-gunayātmani, 16
triple staff, 404
Trivikrama, 22
truth-bearing intellect, 646
tulasī, 532
turn away, 512
Tvaṣṭa, 11
tvaṣṭri, 205
two persons, 550
two-handed Form, 196
tyāga, 200, 433
tyāgi, 65

U

Uddhava,
affections pure, 423
anuvrata, 39
dear, 197, 257
deserving, 39
detachment, 96
disagreed, 212
focused, 46
great devotee, 325
intelligent, 59
life force influence, 690
offered himself, 189
paranoid, 41
progression, 696
purification, 690
surrender, 210
yoga necessary, 273, 632
Ugrasena, 607
Ultimate Cause, 140
Ultimate Motivator, 642
Ultimate Responsible Agent, 349
unity of personalities, 559
universal exploitation, 95
Universal Form,
approval, 221
/Arjuna, 64
body parts productions, 343
central figure, 151
consultation, 154
contact essential, 409
employment by, 428
Krishna, 24
neglected, 591
obeyed, 149
production of, 550
scary? 191
source situation, 343
supernatural, 304
supreme, 470
universe, edge, 554
unknown place, 534
Upabarhana, 608
Upamanyu, 350
Upanishad, Araṇyaka, 140
ūrdhva retā, 269, 351
Urukrama, 11, 22
Urvaśī, 589, 591, 593
utensils, 372
utility of destiny, 84

V

vagabonds, 533
vagina, 591
vagueness, 497
Vaikuṇṭha, 292
vairāgya, 388
Vaishnava commentators, 665
Vaitasena, 605
Vāk, 608, 694
Vālmīki, 251
Vamadeva, 22
Vāmanadeva, 21
vanaprastha, 379, 382, 383
Varuṇa, 11
Vasiṣṭha, 320, 608
Vasiṣṭha philosophy, 51-52
Vasudeva, 49, 213, 325
Vāsudeva, 19, 325, 676
Vāsudeva Deity, 328
Veda,
criticized, 153
details, 684
manuals, 342
Personified, 358
Vedānta, 683
Vedic/tantric method, 611
Vedic knowledge, 421
Vedic study, 200
vegetation, 113
Vibḥāndaka, 111
Vibhu, 78
Vibudheśvara, 32
Vicharavirya, 27
victims of religion, 478
Videha, 123, 140
Vidhātā, 11
Vidura, 375, 534
vidvān, 175
vidyā, 357
vidyādharas, 12
vīkṣayā, 402
vikṣepo, 391
violence, 348, 349
violent nature, 477
vipadyeta, 56
viprās, 235
Viriñci, 421
viruses, 387
Vishnu,
isolated, 59
Krishna as, 292
parallel forms, 11
tulasī beads, 532
vision divine, 678
visual power, 268, 295
Viṣvakṣena, 631
Viśvanātha Cakravartī, 149
Viśvāvasu, 328
vital energy, details, 15
vitalizing air, 73, 212, 353
vīta-nidrah, 101
Vivasvān, 11
vivikta, 266
vocation, 369
voice, 595
vow, 201, 321
vratāni, 201
Vṛndāvan, 208
Vṛndāvan devotee, 265
Vṛṣṇi, 607
vṛtra, 205
vyakta, 493
Vyāsadeva, 27, 136, 325, 374
vyomi, 277
Vyūha, 19

W

waiver, 396, 591
wasp, 70
water,
compared, 77
Krishna as, 329
sex desire, 221
worship, 615
wealth,
acquirement, 521
bedfellow, 518
bewildering, 525
character affected, 436, 524
dependents' attitude, 519
desire, 526
enemies created, 526
spiritual life, 518
weather controllers, 386
weather deity, 353

weight lifting, 352
well-being, 323
wet dreams, 352
whimsy, 36
white rule, 307
Whole Energy, 139
wife, 146, 378
will power, 281, 296
wishes of the Lord, 528
woman,
affection personified, 323
association risky, 266
austerity, 378
liberated, 205
motivational, 104
nutrition, 104
risks, 104
wooden Deity, 613
words, 497, 517
world, 53, 411
worship, 201
worthy people, 38
woven cloth, 141

Y,Z

Yadava dynasty, 607
yadṛcchayā, 174
Yadu, 149, 607
Yadu, tyāgi, 65-66
Yadus terminated, 39, 49
Yajña, Lord, 245
yajña, 202
Yajñavalka, 140, 193
Yajur Veda, 342
Yakshas, 318
yamah,
introspective, 219
Krishna resists, 203
listed, 430
subtle body, 348
Yamarāja, 617
Yamunā River, 206
yarn, 141
yathārbhakah, 55
yati, 388
Yogācārya, 301, 391
yoga-caryām, 665
yoga-mārgah, 689
yoga-mayam vapuh, 301
yoga practice,
absence of, 622
applications, 373
bhakti compliments, 585
cultural activities, 594
curative, 453
details, 450
essential, 694
expertise Krishna, 246
karma controlled by, 594
yoga practice, continued,
Krishna resist, 199
lessons, 146
limited, 199
mystic skill, 287
necessary? 101
Patañjali defined, 394
prerequisite, 375
psychological actions, 269
purpose, 666
recommended, 268, 675
ridiculed, 668
Sāṅkhya, 245
stages, 303, 430
summary, 359
teacher forestalled, 301
tested, 326
theistic type, 256
Uddhava taught, 689
Uddhava's practice, 693
unavoidable, 677
unique, 307
yoga-śānta-cittasya, 301
yoga vasiṣṭha, 52
yogeśa, 41
Yogeśwarānanda, 280, 295, 297
-Vedas personified, 358
yogi,
absolute? 283
accredited, 496
admired, 16
angelic sex, 326
association, 77
badly motivated, 656
brahmins respect, 353
buried alive, 285
chanting 270, 361
conclusions, 421
conservation, 77
death, 298
descent, 75
destinations, 556
destiny cooperative, 517
determination, 513
type, 189
devotee? 44, 189
devotees harass, 512
dharma resisted, 163
dharma respected, 397
diet, 285
disciple process, 406
divine objects, 402
donations, 365
entering another's body, 297
example, 366
yogi, continued,
gāyatrī, 270-271
genetics, 301
god status, 291
God? 670
great type, 45
hard dealings, 77
householder, 519, 520
imagining Deity, 303
time barrier, 289
impediments, 385
knowledge, 420
Krishna transcends, 300
lifestyle, 373
light control 295
limited, 657
linkage practice, 296
mystic, 421
mystic perfection, 288
non-devotee type, 324
non-interference, 179
patron deity, 353
planet of, 382
prayers, 353
progression, 262
psyche purity, 670
pujārī type, 191
python compared, 101
radiance, 304
reserved attitude, 101
resistance, 77
samadhi, 295
selective, 355
serious type, 583
sexual intercourse, 406, 591
sexual pawn, 592
siddha planet, 12
siddhis, 288
similarity with Krishna, 300
spiritual sky attained, 277
spiritual transfer, 272
student, 305, 406
supernatural influences, 657
third eye control, 295
transfer other world, 289
under water, 285
willing release, 80
Universal Form, 221
yogini, 326, 608
Yudhiṣṭhira,
austerities, 273
Bhishma questioned, 417
classic yogi, 608, 694
Nārada lectured, 98
yuktasya, 280
zones, 554, 558

LIST OF TEACHERS

Gaudiya Vaishnava teacher:
Śrīla Bhaktivedānta Swāmī Prabhupāda
Haṭha yoga teacher:
Swāmī Vishnudevananda
Kundalini yoga teacher:
Mahāyogī Śrī Harbhajan Singh
Celibacy yoga teachers:
Swāmī Shivananda,
Śrīla Yogīrāj Yogeśwarānanda

Purity-of-the-psyche yoga teacher:
Śrīla Yogīrāj Yogeśwarānanda
Kriyā yoga teachers:
Śrīla Bābāji Mahāśaya,
Siddha Swāmī Muktānanda
Brahma yoga teacher:
Siddha Swāmī Nityānanda

About the Author

Michael Beloved (Madhvācārya dās) took his current body in 1951 in Guyana. In 1965, while living in Trinidad, he instinctively began doing yoga postures and trying to make sense of the supernatural side of life.

Later on, in 1970, in the Philippines, he approached a Martial Arts Master named Mr. Arthur Beverford, explaining to the teacher that he was seeking a yoga instructor; Mr. Beverford identified himself as an advanced disciple of Śrī Rishi Singh Gherwal, an aṣṭangayoga master.

Mr. Beverford taught the traditional AṣṭangaYoga with stress on postures, attentive breathing and brow chakra centering meditation. In 1972, Madhvāchārya entered the Denver Colorado Ashram of Kundalini Yoga Master Śrī Harbhajan Singh. There he took instruction in Bhastrika Prāṇāyāma and its application to yoga postures. He was supervised mostly by Yogi Bhajan's disciple named Prem Kaur.

In 1979 Madhvācārya formally entered the disciplic succession of the Brahmā-Madhava Gaudiya Sampradāya through Swāmī Kirtanānanda, who was a prominent sannyāsi disciple of the Great Vaishnava Authority Śrī Swāmī Bhaktivedānta Prabhupāda, the exponent of devotion to Śrī Krishna.

*After carefully studying and practicing the devotional process introduced by Śrī Swāmī Bhaktivedānta Prabhupāda, Madhvācārya was inspired to do a translation and three commentaries to the Bhagavad Gītā. This led to his completion of this translation of the instructions to Uddhava, advisories which complete the course given to Arjuna. An ✓**easy-read** English translation is published as Uddhava Gītā English.*

This translation does not concern religious affiliation. It is designed to give readers insight to what Śrī Krishna discussed with Uddhava. There is no conversion pressure. This is free of missionary overtones.

Anyone studying and reading this discourse is blessed by Lord Krishna:

su-viviktaṁ tava praśnaṁ mayaitad api dhārayet
sanātanaṁ brahma-guhyaṁ
paraṁ brahmādhigacchati (24.25)

He who concentrates on your questions which were thoroughly analyzed by Me, attains the Eternal Supreme Spiritual Reality which is a secret in the Vedas. (24.25)

ya etat samadhīyīta pavitraṁ paramaṁ śuci
sa pūyetāhar ahar māṁ jñāna-dīpena darśayan (24.27)

He who reads this purifying and flawless discourse, is purified day after day by showing Me through the use of the illuminating intellect which gives knowledge. (24.27)

Publications

English Series

Bhagavad Gita English

Anu Gita English

Markandeya Samasya English

Yoga Sutras English

Uddhava Gita English

These are in 21st Century English, very precise and exacting. Many Sanskrit words which were considered untranslatable into a Western language are rendered in precise, expressive and modern English, due to the English language becoming the world's universal means of concept conveyance.

Three of these books are instructions from Krishna. **In Bhagavad Gita English** and **Anu Gita English**, the instructions were for Arjuna. In the **Uddhava Gita English,** it was for Uddhava. Bhagavad Gita and Anu Gita are extracted from the Mahabharata. Uddhava Gita was extracted from the 11th Canto of the Srimad Bhagavatam (Bhagavata Purana). One of these books, the **Markandeya Samasya English** is about Krishna, as described by Yogi Markandeya, who survived the cosmic collapse and reached a divine child in whose transcendental body, the collapsed world was existing. Another of these books, the **Yoga Sutras English,** is the detailed syllabus about yoga practice.

My suggestion is that you read **Bhagavad Gita English**, the **Anu Gita English, the Markandeya Samasya English,** the **Yoga Sutras English** and lastly the **Uddhava Gita English**, which is much more complicated and detailed.

For each of these books we have at least one commentary, which is published separately. Thus your particular interest can be researched further in the commentaries.

The smallest of these commentaries and perhaps the simplest is the one for the Anu Gita. We published its commentary as the Anu Gita Explained. The Bhagavad Gita explanations were published in three distinct targeted commentaries. The first is Bhagavad Gita Explained, which sheds lights on how people in the time of Krishna and Arjuna regarded the information and applied it. Bhagavad Gita is an exposition of the application of yoga practice to cultural activities, which is known in the Sanskrit language as karma yoga.

Interestingly, Bhagavad Gita was spoken on a battlefield just before one of the greatest battles in the ancient world. A warrior, Arjuna, lost his wits and had no idea that he could apply his training in yoga to political dealings. Krishna, his charioteer, lectured on the spur of the moment to give Arjuna the skill of using yoga proficiency in cultural dealings including how to deal with corrupt officials on a battlefield.

The second commentary is the Kriya Yoga Bhagavad Gita. This clears the air about Krishna's information on the science of kriya yoga, showing that its techniques are clearly described free of charge to anyone who takes the time to read Bhagavad Gita. Kriya yoga concerns the battlefield which is the psyche of the living being. The internal war and the mental and emotional forces which are hostile to self-realization are dealt with in the kriya yoga practice.

The third commentary is the Brahma Yoga Bhagavad Gita. This shows what Krishna had to say outright and what he hinted about which concerns the brahma yoga practice, a mystic process for those who mastered kriya yoga.

There is one commentary for the **Markandeya Samasya English**. The title of that publication is Krishna Cosmic Body.

There are two commentaries to the Yoga Sutras. One is the Yoga Sutras of Patanjali and the other is the Meditation Expertise. These give detailed explanations of the process of Yoga.

For the Uddhava Gita, we published the Uddhava Gita Explained. This is a large book and requires concentration and study for integration of the information. Of the books which deal with transcendental topics, my opinion is that the discourse between Krishna and Uddhava has the complete information about the realities in existence. This book is the one which removes massive existential ignorance.

Meditation Series

Meditation Pictorial

Meditation Expertise

Core-Self Discovery

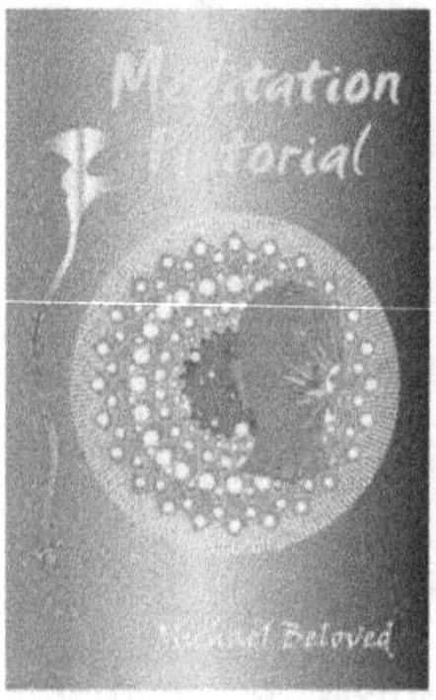
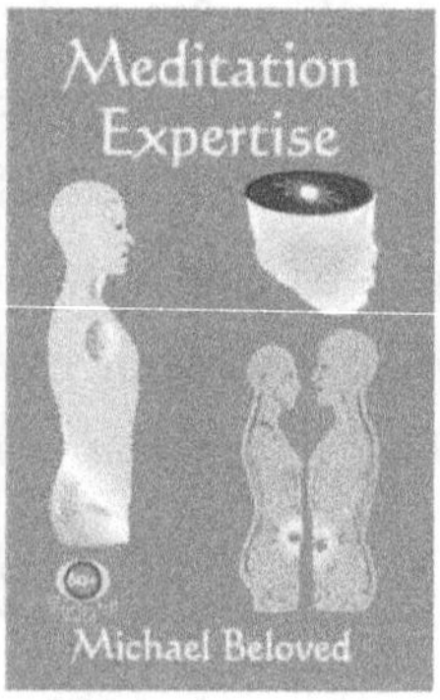

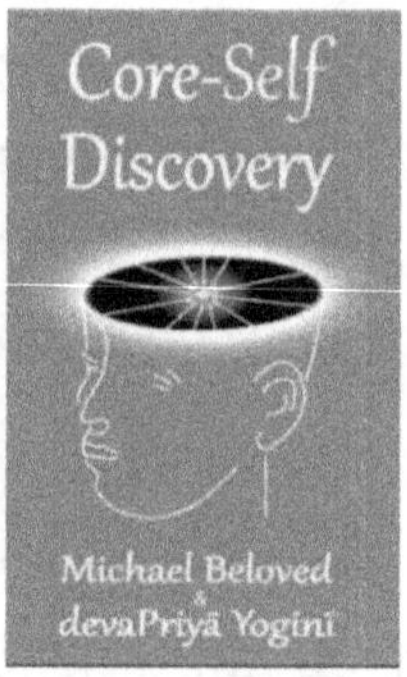

The specialty of these books is the mind diagrams which profusely illustrate what is written. This shows exactly what one has to do mentally to develop and then sustain a meditation practice.

In the **Meditation Pictorial**, one is shown how to develop psychic insight, a feature without which meditation is imagination and visualization, without any mystic experience per se.

In the **Meditation Expert**ise, one is shown how to corral one's practice to bring it in line with the classic syllabus of yoga which Patanjali lays out as the ashtanga yoga eight-staged practice.

In **Core-Self Discovery**, one is taken though the course of pratyahar sensual energy withdrawal which is the 5th stage of yoga in the Patanjali ashtanga eight-process complete system of yoga practice. These events lead to the discovery of a core-self which is surrounded by psychic organs in the head of the subtle body. This product has a DVD component for teachers and self-teaching students.

These books are profusely illustrated with mind diagrams showing the components of psychic consciousness and the inner design of the subtle body.

Explained Series

Bhagavad Gita Explained

Uddhava Gita Explained

Anu Gita Explained

The specialty of these books is that they are free of missionary intentions, cult tactics and philosophical distortion. Instead of using these books to add credence to a philosophy, meditation process, belief or plea for followers, I spread the information out so that a reader can look through this literature and freely take or leave anything as desired.

When Krishna stressed himself as God, I stated that. When Krishna laid no claims for supremacy, I showed that. The reader is left to form an independent opinion about the validity of the information and the credibility of Krishna.

There is a difference in the discourse with Arjuna in the Bhagavad Gita and the one with Uddhava in the Uddhava Gita. In fact these two books may appear to contradict each other. In the Bhagavad Gita, Krishna pressured Arjuna to complete social duties. In the Uddhava Gita, Krishna insisted that Uddhava should abandon the same.

The Anu Gita is not as popular as the Bhagavad Gita but it is the conclusion of that text. Anu means what is to follow, what proceeds. In this discourse, an anxious Arjuna request that Krishna should repeat the Bhagavad Gita and again show His supernatural and divine forms.

However Krishna refuses to do so and chastises Arjuna for being a disappointment in forgetting what was revealed. Krishna then cites a celestial yogi, a near-perfected being, who explained the process of transmigration in vivid detail.

Commentaries

Yoga Sutras of Patanjali

Meditation Expertise

Krishna Cosmic Body

Anu Gita Explained

Bhagavad Gita Explained

Kriya Yoga Bhagavad Gita

Brahma Yoga Bhagavad Gita

Uddhava Gita Explained

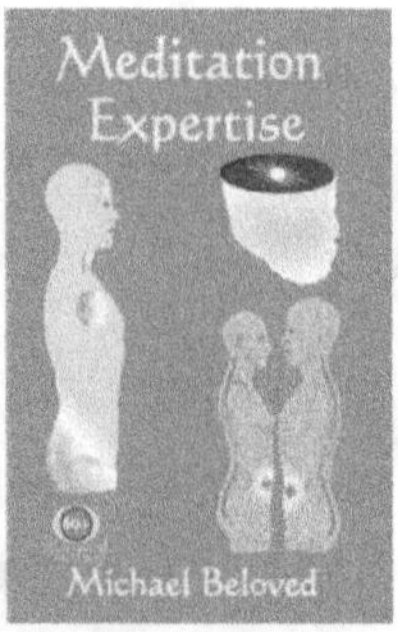

Yoga Sutras of Patanjali is the globally acclaimed text book of yoga. This has detailed expositions of yoga techniques. Many kriya techniques are vividly described in the commentary.

Meditation Expertise is an analysis and application of the Yoga Sutras. This book is loaded with illustrations and has detailed explanations of secretive advanced meditation techniques which are called kriyas in the Sanskrit language.

Krishna Cosmic Body is a narrative commentary on the Markandeya Samasya portion of the Aranyaka Parva of the Mahabharata. This is the detailed description of the dissolution of the world, as experienced by the great yogin Markandeya who transcended the cosmic deity, Brahma, and reached Brahma's source who is the divine infant, Krishna.

Anu Gita Explained is a detailed explanation of how we endure many material bodies in the course of transmigrating through various life-forms. This is a discourse between Krishna and Arjuna. Arjuna requested of Krishna a display of the Universal Form and a repeat narration of the Bhagavad Gita but Krishna declined and explained what a siddha perfected being told the Yadu family about the sequence of existences one endures and the systematic flow of those lives at the convenience of material nature.

Bhagavad Gita Explained shows what was said in the Gita without religious overtones and sectarian biases.

Kriya Yoga Bhagavad Gita shows the instructions for those who are doing kriya yoga.

Brahma Yoga Bhagavad Gita shows the instructions for those who are doing brahma yoga.

Uddhava Gita Explained shows the instructions to Uddhava which are more advanced than the ones given to Arjuna.

Bhagavad Gita is an instruction for applying the expertise of yoga in the cultural field. This is why the process taught to Arjuna is called karma yoga which means karma + yoga or cultural activities done with a yogic demeanor.

Uddhava Gita is an instruction for apply the expertise of yoga to attaining spiritual status. This is why it is explains jnana yoga and bhakti yoga in detail.

Jnana yoga is using mystic skill for knowing the spiritual part of existence. Bhakti yoga is for developing affectionate relationships with divine beings.

Karma yoga is for negotiating the social concerns in the material world and therefore it is inferior to bhakti yoga which concerns negotiating the social concerns in the spiritual world.

This world has a social environment and the spiritual world has one too.

Right now Uddhava Gita is the most advanced informative spiritual book on the planet. There is nothing anywhere which is superior to it or which goes into so much detail as it. It verified that historically Krishna is the most advanced human being to ever have left literary instructions on this planet. Even Patanjali Yoga Sutras which I translated and gave an application for in my book, **Meditation Expertise**, does not go as far as the Uddhava Gita.

Some of the information of these two books is identical but while the Yoga Sutras are concerned with the personal spiritual emancipation (kaivalyam) of the individual spirits, the Uddhava Gita explains that and also explains the situations in the spiritual universes.

Bhagavad Gita is from the Mahabharata which is the history of the Pandavas. Arjuna, the student of the Gita, is one of the Pandavas brothers. He was in a social hassle and did not know how to apply yoga expertise to solve it. Krishna gave him a crash-course on the battlefield about that.

Uddhava Gita is from the Srimad Bhagavatam (Bhagavata Purana), which is a history of the incarnations of Krishna. Uddhava was a relative of Krishna. He was concerned about the situation of the deaths of many of his relatives but Krishna diverted Uddhava's attention to the practice of yoga for the purpose of successfully migrating to the spiritual environment.

Specialty

These books are based on the author's experiences in meditation, yoga practice and participation in spiritual groups:

Spiritual Master

sex you!

Sleep **Paralysis**

Astral Projection

Masturbation Psychic Details

In **Spiritual Master**, Michael draws from experience with gurus or with their senior students. His contact with astral gurus is rated. He walks you through the avenue of gurus showing what you should do and what you should not do, so as to gain proficiency in whatever area of spirituality the guru has proficiency.

sex you! is a masterpiece about the adventures of an individual spirit's passage through the parents' psyches. The conversion of a departed soul into a sexual urge is described. The transit from the afterlife to residency in the emotions of the parents is detailed. This is about sex and you; learn about how much of you comprises the romantic energy of your would-be parents!

Sleep Paralysis clears misconceptions so that one can see what sleep paralysis is and what frightening astral experience occurs while the paralysis is being experienced. This disempowerment has great value in giving you confidence that you can and do exist even if you are unable to operate the physical body. The implication is that one can exist apart from and will survive the loss of the material body.

Astral Projection details experiences Michael had even in childhood, where he assumed incorrectly that everyone was astrally conversant. He discusses the life force psychic mechanism which operates the sleep-wake cycle of the physical form, and which budgets energy into the separated astral form which determines if the individual will have dream recall or no objective awareness during the projections. Astral travel happens on every occasion when the physical body sleeps. What is missing in awareness is the observer status while the astral body is separated.

Masturbation Psychic Details is a surprise presentation which relates what happens on the psychic plane during a masturbation event. This does not tackle moral issues or even addictions but shows the involvement of memory and the sure but hidden subconscious mind which operates many features of the psyche irrespective of the desire or approval of the self-conscious personality.

Online Resources

Visit The Website And Forum

Email:	michaelbelovedbooks@gmail.com axisnexus@gmail.com
Website	michaelbeloved.com
Forum:	inselfyoga.com

www.ingramcontent.com/pod-product-compliance
Lightning Source LLC
Chambersburg PA
CBHW080631230426
43663CB00016B/2833
* 9 7 8 0 9 8 1 9 3 3 2 1 4 *